DIDEROT

Diderot, bust by Jean-Antoine Houdon, 1771 (Louvre).

DIDEROT

by ARTHUR M. WILSON

NEW YORK OXFORD UNIVERSITY PRESS 1972

Preface to PART I: The Testing Years

A RECENT REVIEWER in *The Times Literary Supple-ment* remarked, regarding Diderot, that 'among the great minds of the eighteenth century Diderot has received less attention in this country than he deserves.'

Yet interest in Diderot has been increasing markedly of late. Partly this is because of an ever-widening persuasion that he has been too much neglected and too little understood. Partly it is because of the publicity attendant upon the celebration in 1951 of the bicentenary of the *Encyclopédie*. Most of all, it is because of the growing conviction of biographers, historians, and critics that Diderot was not only one of the most representative men of his age but also one of the most glowingly 'modern' figures of the eighteenth century. Certainly for Americans, who are children of the Enlightenment to a degree that is unique among twentieth-century peoples, the life and times of Diderot can have unusual interest and relevancy.

This book has therefore been written in the hope of meeting the needs of two audiences — the general reader and the specialist. The general reader, if he has no previous knowledge about Diderot, has a right to be shown why Diderot and Diderot's times and Diderot's vicissitudes should interest him. As for the specialist, it is hoped that the bibliographical information contained in this book will be useful; and that even for him a conspectus of the early career of Diderot will be of interest.

The reader will discover in the following chapters a good deal more information regarding the contents of the *Encyclopédie* than is usual in biographies of Diderot. By this analysis and description of the contents of such a great work of reference and instruction, it is hoped that the reader will gain a more vivid insight into the intellectual conditions of the Age of Enlightenment.

For every researcher it is a pleasure to record his obligations to the various libraries that have aided him in his work. In this instance, the author is under the greatest debt to the Dartmouth College Library and to the Bibliothèque Nationale. Also of very great assistance were the Library of Congress, the Mazarine and the Bibliothèque de l'Arsenal at Paris, the British Museum, the Bodleian Library, the New York Public Library, the Boston Public Library, and the university libraries of Harvard, Princeton, Yale, Iowa, Pennsylvania, Michigan, and Wisconsin. I also hold in grateful recollection all the numerous libraries, from Quebec to San Marino — I fear to list them lest the enumeration grow tedious — where, during vacation or sabbatical leave, we have sought out the manuscript source or the rare edition or the comparatively inaccessible book. To the administrations and staffs of all these institutions I here record my heartfelt thanks.

Research on Diderot has of course entailed the pleasant necessity of wandering about in Paris and Langres, seeking the sites and buildings associated with events in his life. In this connection I particularly desire to record my thanks to the Mayor and Deputy Mayor of Langres, M. Beligné and M. l'Abbé Rabin, for their courtesy and hospitality, as well as to express my appreciation of these qualities in the Librarian of the Municipal Library of Langres, the late M. Populus.

During the time when this book was in preparation, Dartmouth College granted me two years of sabbatical leave, as well as a reduction of teaching duties during one semester. I gratefully acknowledge this assistance, as also the fellowship granted by the John Simon Guggenheim Memorial Foundation.

Grateful acknowledgment is also made to the Éditions de Minuit, Paris, for permission to quote from M. Georges Roth's edition of Diderot's *Correspondance;* and to the Librairie Armand Colin, Paris, for permission to quote from the Dufour-Plan edition of Rousseau's *Correspondance générale.*

Several persons have had the kindness to read this book in manuscript. It has materially benefited from the judgment of Professor Thomas G. Bergin of Yale University, Professor W. M. Frohock of Harvard University, Professor Hayward Keniston of Duke University, Professor H. W. Victor Lange of Cornell University, and Professor Norman L. Torrey of Columbia University. To all of these scholars I desire to acknowledge gratefully my indebtedness. I have also been the beneficiary of the counsel of Professors Charles R. Bagley and François Denoeu, both of Dartmouth College, and Mr. Bradford Martin, of Thetford Hill, Vermont. Each has offered valuable suggestions from which I have greatly profited.

Two persons in particular have been of indispensable assistance in bringing this book into being. The first is Professor Ira O. Wade of Princeton University, whose helpful and encouraging suggestions are most gratefully acknowledged. The other is my wife. My debt to her, as research assistant and critic, simply defies description. So does my appreciation.

A.M.W.

Hanover, New Hampshire
March 1957

Preface to PART II: The Appeal to Posterity

SINCE the publication of *The Testing Years*, the ever-increasing interest in Diderot has been nourished by further discoveries of unpublished material, such as Diderot's 'Commentaire sur Hemsterhuis' (1773–4), as it has also by the completion of the indispensable Roth-Varloot edition of Diderot's *Correspondance*. At the same time there has been a constantly growing appreciation of the modernity of Diderot's outlook. It was with an awareness of these facts, and in the hope of attracting the general reader, that this account of Diderot and his concern for the good opinion of posterity was written. The specialist, a smaller segment of that posterity, will find the necessary bibliographical information tucked away in the notes.

Inasmuch as *The Testing Years* has been out of print for some time, it has been decided to reprint it here. A bibliographical essay, summarizing for the scholar recent publications concerning those early years, will be found at the end of this volume.

Any worker in the vineyard of the Enlightenment nowadays must recognize how greatly he is indebted to Peter Gay. But this volume owes a special debt to his generosity, for it has profited enormously from his having read it in manuscript. It has gained as much from Professor Gay's critical rigor as its author has, through the years, from his kindness and friendship.

The author acknowledges his gratitude to Dartmouth College for several sabbaticals, leaves of absence, and other favors accorded him in order to facilitate the researching and writing of this book; and also thanks the John Simon Guggenheim Memorial Foundation for Fellowships in 1939–40 and 1956–7, the latter one enabling him, among other things, to search for traces of Diderot in the USSR. The staff of the Saltykov-Shchedrin Library at Leningrad, as well as that of the Akademii Nauk USSR at Leningrad, is hereby thanked for their graciousness as well as their efficiency. Nor can one forget the kindnesses of the lamented Vladimir S. Liublinskiĭ, among them a tour of Leningrad during which he showed us the various buildings associated with Diderot's visit to the city in 1773–4.

Permission to use photographs of works of art owned by the National-museum, Stockholm, the Musée d'Art et d'Histoire, Geneva, and the Pierpont Morgan Library, New York, has been granted by these institutions and is gratefully acknowledged.

This book is greatly the better for having been read in manuscript also by my friend Professor Orest Ranum of Johns Hopkins University. His very helpful suggestions are most gratefully acknowledged.

As before and as always, the author is grateful for the kindnesses and co-operation he has received from the numerous libraries and archives visited in the course of his research. It would be tedious, alas, to list them all, but he holds each of them, from Helsinki and Stockholm to Madrid, Minneapolis, and San Marino, in grateful recollection.

My greatest obligation of all is to Mary Tolford Wilson. This book could not have been completed without her. Such close collaboration, as pleasurable for me as it was essential, has virtually reached the point of co-authorship. My only regret is that the necessities of my writing have kept her from her own.

A.M.W.

Norwich, Vermont
September 1971

Contents

List of Illustrations

xvii

PART I

THE TESTING YEARS, 1713–1759

The Announcement of an Important Event

I N NOVEMBER of 1750 there took place in Paris what might seem to be nothing more than an inconsiderable occurrence in the realm of letters. An editor of a forthcoming encyclopedia published a prospectus explaining to a hoped-for public what would be the content of his work and the principles of his editorial policy. Yet the work thus announced secured so many readers, the ideas it contained modified current thinking to such a degree, that now the publication of its prospectus is recognized as one of the most important events in the political as well as the intellectual history of the eighteenth century. To symbolize this importance, the French government published in 1950 a reprint in national commemoration of the bicentenary of the event.

The prospectus sought favor in a world familiar to us through the paintings of Nattier, Boucher, and Lancret — a world in which the charming gracefulness and frivolity of the rococo was succeeding to the stately majesty of the baroque. It was the world of wigs, smallclothes, and three-cornered hats; of panniers and beauty patches and pancakes of rouge laid on delicate cheeks. It was the world of the minuet, danced in rooms gleaming with gilt and shimmering with mirrors; of Meissen figurines and of ladies as fragile as the porcelain that portrayed them; the world of the harpsichord, the recorder, and the viola da gamba; of the musket, the frigate, and the balance of power. This was the time when Russia was becoming more important in European diplomacy, when Frederick II of Prussia was astonishing Europe by his temerity and dumbfounding it by his success. It was the time when immense French and British colonial empires were in the making and were providing stakes for great colonial wars. In the American context, it was the time that lay between King George's War and the French and Indian War, between the proud conquest of Louisbourg by the men of Massachusetts and the defeat of Braddock in the western forests. It was a time when the Church patently expected to continue confining men's thoughts within a narrow orthodoxy, and privileged classes patently expected to continue enjoying their privileges. Yet it was also a time when the merchant, banking, and professional elements of society were everywhere rising in esteem and wealth. In 1750 Johann Sebastian Bach had just breathed his last, Henry Fielding had published *Tom Jones,* Dr. Samuel Johnson was laboring upon his famous *Dictionary,* and George Washington was eighteen years old.

The prospectus was published in a country which was far from being benighted. Yet it was one which, in its acceptance of inequalities and in its denial of civil liberties, fell some distance short of Utopia. It was a society in which prisons and galleys existed for those confessing the Protestant faith, where one of the duties of the public executioner was the burning of books, where valor in the service of one's country could never quite make up for the lack of noble birth, where a peasantry dressed in rags, where a villager might find his taxes enormously and arbitrarily increased if the tax collector espied any chicken feathers on the doorstep, where decent burial could be refused to those who did not make their peace with the Church, where nothing could be legally published without undergoing censorship, and where a man could lawfully be arrested and indefinitely detained without cause being shown.

The prospectus announced a work so new in idea that even its name was unfamiliar and had to be explained, with learned reference to the Greek roots: 'The word "Encyclopedia" signifies the interrelationship of the sciences.' And in order to give a visual presentation of the interrelationships of the branches of learning, the author appended to his prospectus a much-admired chart of human knowledge. The visualized relationships in this 'genealogical tree of all the sciences and all the arts,' avowedly modeled upon a similar project by Lord Bacon, were to be emphasized constantly in the body of the work by means of cross reference.

Clearly the author of the prospectus coveted for people, as do present-day proponents of general education, the pleasure and excitement that comes from realization of how knowledge is interrelated and interlocked. This effort at integration was to be one of the proposed work's greatest enticements. It was to be accomplished, wrote the author, by 'indicating the connections, both remote and near, of the beings that compose Nature and which have occupied the attention of mankind; of showing, by the interlacing of the roots and branches, the impossibility of knowing well any parts of this whole without ascending or descending to many others; of forming a general picture of the efforts of the human mind in all fields and every century; of

presenting these objects with clarity; of giving to each one of them its appropriate length, and, if possible, of substantiating by our success our epigraph
[a quotation from Horace]:

> So great is the power of order and arrangement;
> So much grace may be imparted to a common theme.'

The French public had never before been offered just such an opportunity.
England had had a successful *Cyclopaedia,* edited by Ephraim Chambers
and published in two volumes in 1728. Indeed, it was this *Cyclopaedia* that
provided the stimulus for the great work of reference now to be published
in France. But the French work promised to outstrip its predecessor in size
and coverage. Moreover, it would possess the advantage of being published
in a language that, unlike the comparatively little-known English of that day,
was the circulating medium of ideas, the common coin, of all educated men.

The work thus announced was to be the result of the combined labor of a
considerable number of well-known men of letters, experts, and specialists.
It was to consist of ten volumes in folio, of which two were to contain engravings. This size would allow a range of subject matter vastly greater than
that of any existing work of reference. It was thus hoped to provide a book
'which one might consult on every subject.' 'The aim of the French Encyclopedia, as set forth in its prospectus,' wrote Frank Moore Colby, the
American encyclopedist and essayist, 'was to serve as a reference library for
every intelligent man on all subjects save his own. That has remained the
aim of general encyclopedias ever since.'

The lack of a comprehensive and extensive encyclopedia is hard for us,
who have such an abundance of excellent ones, to understand. But the author
of the prospectus was announcing his work at a time when the first edition
of the *Encyclopaedia Britannica* was twenty-one years in the future, and he
could say quite rightly that no existing work of reference did justice to the
great names and the great intellectual accomplishments of the seventeenth
century. 'What progress has not since been made in the sciences and the
arts?' asked the author of the prospectus, speaking of his puny and outworn
predecessors. 'How many truths known today, but only glimpsed then?
True philosophy was in its cradle [the author of the prospectus did not care
for scholastic philosophy]; the geometry of the infinite was not yet in being;
experimental physics was just beginning to show itself; the laws of sound
criticism were entirely ignored. Descartes, Boyle, Huyghens, Newton,
Leibniz, the Bernoullis, Locke, Bayle, Pascal, Corneille, Racine, Bourdaloue,
Bossuet, etc., either did not exist or had not written.'

The *Encyclopédie* was, in fact, very fortunate in its time of publication, for it fitted exactly into the intellectual and social needs of the time. We know now that the eighteenth century was moving more rapidly toward radical change, was more in need of it, than the age itself realized. It was not merely that new conceptions of truth, stemming from current hypotheses about physics and psychology, were having a profoundly unsettling effect upon conventional ideas of morality, religion, and even politics; it was also that the middle classes were daily becoming more qualified to exercise power while being denied their share of it; that a new technology was beginning, whether as cause or effect of the incipient Industrial Revolution; that new theories as to what constitutes the wealth of nations were in gestation; that new doctrines of agricultural husbandry were beginning to be canvassed; and that changing economic conditions were beginning to call attention to such matters as the legal status of peasants and town workers, the supply of labor, the incidence of taxation, and the conditions of occupancy of land.

No doubt the significance of these changes or of these emerging problems was hidden — save in glimpses to a few whom Carlyle would term 'Seers,' and of whom the author of the prospectus was one. But even though the ordinary citizen of the eighteenth century might not recognize the massiveness of the changes that were overtaking his world, he would probably have been aware, however obscurely, that a certain this-worldliness was beginning to overlie the emphasis of preceding generations on other-worldliness. Somehow he now seemed to need to know, or want to know, the names of more objects, the application of more theories, the purpose of more tools, and the geographical location of more places than ever before. The places and objects and relationships of a secular existence were increasingly obtruding themselves upon the attention of the most nonchalant, the most frivolous, the most devout.

The *Encyclopédie* was precisely the means for giving information about these myriads of external objects and relationships, especially as its principal editor, the author of its prospectus, was himself the son of a craftsman and had an extremely lively interest in the technology and craftsmanship of the day. Certainly no one preached the dignity of labor more adroitly than he, and to this purpose he went to great lengths to make his *Encyclopédie* a repository of knowledge concerning the mechanical arts:

. . . Everything accordingly impelled us to have recourse to the workers themselves. We went to the cleverest ones in Paris and in the kingdom. We took the pains of going into their workshops, of questioning them, of writing under their dictation, of developing their thoughts, of educing from them the terms peculiar to their profession, of drawing up tables of such terms, of defining them, of conversing with those persons from whom we had obtained memoranda and (an almost indispensable precaution) of rectifying, in long and frequent conversations with some, what others had imperfectly, obscurely, or unfaithfully explained.

Some crafts were so complicated, the prospectus remarked, that it was necessary to learn to operate the machines and even to construct them before the craft could be accurately described. And the author explained that draftsmen had been sent into the workshops to prepare drawings from which engravings for the *Encyclopédie* would be made.

The promises made by the prospectus were widely welcomed. The *Mercure de France,* remarking that the prospectus was much appreciated by the public, printed lengthy quotations from it. The magisterial and somewhat ponderous *Journal des Sçavans* spoke of the project as 'one of the most interesting and costly since the invention of printing . . .' and spoke with no less approbation of the drawings, 'of which we have seen a very considerable part, [and which] are of great beauty.' And the youthful Adam Smith, writing for the *Edinburgh Review* in 1755, declared that: 'The French work which I just now mentioned, promises to be the most compleat of the kind which has ever been published or attempted in any language.'

The need for the promised work was proved in the most convincing way of all: subscribers' names on the dotted line, subscribers' money in down payments. By the end of April 1751, a little less than six months after the prospectus had been published, there were 1,002 subscribers, each of them paying a deposit of 60 livres for a work scheduled to cost 280 livres in all. By the end of the year the number of subscribers had risen to 2,619, and the number finally rose to about 4000, to say nothing of the subscribers to several editions pirated in Italy and Switzerland. The demand, moreover, was general throughout the Western world. The publishers later asserted that nearly three-fourths of the 4000 subscriptions were taken up in the provinces or by foreigners.

The subscribers got the information they paid for — but conjoined with a special point of view. So distinctive was the particular outlook of the *Encyclopédie* (and of its editor, the author of the prospectus) that it infuriated many persons, while preparing many others for the reforms brought about by the Revolution of 1789. The contents of the *Encyclopédie* will be described in more detail later. Here it suffices to say that the *Encyclopédie* trusted much to the operation of common sense, and was not afraid of change. Essentially, what it advocated can be quite accurately described to American readers as Hamiltonianism plus the Bill of Rights. And because it gave currency to these ideas, it has often been called the Trojan Horse of the *ancien régime*.

There were many people and many vested interests in eighteenth-century France who did not want Hamiltonianism and the Bill of Rights. Their perfervid opposition made the expression of such ideas hazardous, especially since the *Encyclopédie* depended for publication upon an official license, a license which was twice taken away and only very grudgingly and qualifiedly restored. Therefore, to have the tact and energy and courage sufficient to keep the enterprise going, and to combine these with the intellectual breadth requisite in an editor of so vast a work, called for unusual qualities in unusual conjunction. These the author of the prospectus has always been acknowledged to have. 'At the distance of some centuries,' wrote Jean-Jacques Rousseau, '. . . [he] will seem a prodigious man. People will look from afar at that universal head with commingled admiration and astonishment as we look today at the heads of Plato and Aristotle.'

It is this 'prodigious man' who is the subject of this book.

Yet with all his prodigiousness, he still had much to learn — and much to endure — when he wrote his prospectus. Dedicated to the task he had accepted, he fortunately could not foresee the rigors of the years ahead, the enemies he was destined to arouse, the anxieties and frustrations he would have to experience before the mammoth work could be brought to a successful conclusion. In the decade between the publication of the prospectus and the suppression of the *Encyclopédie* in 1759, the Enlightenment in France was taking its characteristic 'set.' Ideas were being tested together with the men holding them. Of no one could this be said with greater aptness than of the young author of the prospectus, destined to become one of the great leaders of the Enlightenment — in some respects the greatest of them all. And because of this very process of testing, much of it painful, some of it unfelt and unseen, the author of the prospectus found himself equipped, ten years after it was written, to cope successfully with the greatest and longest crisis of his life.

This book is the story of that preparation.

CHAPTER I

Diderot's Family and Early Childhood

L ANGRES, the pleasant but somewhat austere old Roman town in which Denis Diderot was born, is situated imposingly and rather self-consciously on the northern extremity of the plateau of Langres, so that the land falls sharply away from it on three sides, and one of the principal modes of communication with the outside world is a cog railway connecting it with the nearby Paris-Basel railway line. The city is well remembered by many members of the AEF of 1917–18 as the site of numerous staff and training schools. No doubt many veterans (of both wars) will recall, as in their mind's eye they make the deliberate but exhilarating ascent, the bulk of the massive Charity Hospital, the old towers on the city walls, the second-century Gallo-Roman gate, and the delightful walk on the ramparts around the town, from which one overlooks the nearby plain where the River Marne has its source and can extend one's gaze in the direction of the Vosges and the Alps.

Perhaps they will remember, too, the rather severe-looking old houses, which frequently conceal a Louis XIV interior or screen a Renaissance garden front; the grimy children playing in the streets (Langres, because of its location, is short of playgrounds and water); the rather unusual number of priests and nuns, for Langres is still a conspicuously pious town; and a general air of quietude of which the inhabitants are very proud, speaking as they do of 'the calm of our provincial cities,' in transparent allusion to the bustle of iniquitous Paris.

It is easy for the visitor to Langres to feel a wistfulness for the long ago and far away. Even Diderot himself, never inclined to be unduly sentimental about the native town from which he had emancipated himself — although he was often a touch sentimental about other things — experienced on a visit to Langres in his middle age something of the spell exerted by tranquil and beautiful surroundings in a place where life has been flowing in the same channels for many generations. 'We have here,' he wrote to Sophie Volland, 'a charming promenade, consisting of a broad aisle of thickly verdured trees leading to a small grove . . . . 'tis there that I come afternoons at five. My eyes wander over the most beautiful landscape in the world. . . . I pass hours in this spot, reading, meditating, contemplating nature, and thinking of my love.'[1] The Park of the White Fountain, to the south and through the Gate of the Windmills, is now, as it was when Diderot described it in 1759, a place of beauty and of hushed delight.

Diderot later commemorated the history and antiquities of Langres in an article inserted in the *Encyclopédie*. This exercise in civic piety, couched in sentences uncharacteristically dry and antiquarian, recalled that Langres had been the ancient Andematunum, the capital city of the Lingones; that it was situated in Champagne, fourteen leagues from Dijon, forty from Reims, and sixty-three from Paris; and that it was the seat of a bishop.[2] Diderot might also have remarked that it lies in good wine country, that it had when he wrote a population of about ten thousand, and that it had long been celebrated for the quality of the cutlery that its craftsmen produced.

One of the characteristics for which Diderot became famous was a zest — not to say a weakness — for the divagatious. This intellectual volatility he ascribed, half-whimsically, half-seriously, to the climate of Langres. 'The inhabitants of this district have great wit, too much vivacity, and the inconstancy of weather-vanes,' he wrote. 'This comes, I believe, from the changes in their atmosphere, which passes in twenty-four hours from cold to hot, from calm to stormy, from clear to rainy. . . . Thus they accustom themselves from the most tender infancy to turn to every wind. The head of a man from Langres is set upon his shoulders the way a cock is set upon the top of a belfry. . . . Yet with such a surprising rapidity in their movements, desires, projects, fantasies, and ideas, they have a drawling speech . . . . As for me, I am of my district, except that residence in the capital and assiduous application have somewhat corrected me.'[3]

The appearance of the town reflected then, as it does today, the piety of a community traditionally devoted to Roman Catholicism. There were (and still are) standing in little niches in the housefronts charming madonnas carved in the hard and unweathering stone of the neighborhood. There was (and still is) the cathedral, dedicated to Saint-Mammès, a more than shadowy Cappadocian whose martyred head is said to have been brought to Langres soon after his death, which occurred about 274. There were the churches of Saint-Martin and Saint-Pierre, in the latter of which Diderot was baptized.[4] There was the church of Saint-Didier (now one of the local museums), dedicated to a sainted but somewhat misty bishop of Langres who was martyred about 264 and whose tomb may be seen in the apse of the museum. It is believed to have been the image of this local saint, cradling his mitred and martyred head in his arm, that occupied the Louis XIII niche in the façade of the house in which Diderot grew up.[5] Finally, there was the great crucifix standing in the Place Chambeau, the Place upon which the Diderot home faced. The square is still there, now appropriately named the Place Diderot. The crucifix is not. A statue of Diderot, done in 1884 by Frédéric-Auguste Bartholdi, the sculptor of the Statue of Liberty, has replaced it. There is little doubt that Diderot would have been vastly amused if he could have foreseen such a triumphant usurpation.

For Diderot came to be an earnest and devoted anticlerical. It is, therefore, all the more piquant to observe that his closest relatives were people who were either extremely pious laymen or else professional religious whose lives were spent in the service of the Church. For example, his mother's brother, Didier Vigneron, was a canon at the local cathedral until his death when Diderot was fifteen years old. Another uncle, Jean Vigneron, was curate at Chassigny, ten miles south of Langres, and died there the year of Diderot's birth. Two uncles of Diderot's mother and two of her cousins had also been country priests, and on the Diderot side of the family, an uncle, Antoine by name, was a Dominican friar.[6] Diderot sprang from a milieu that was not only intimately familiar with the tradition of the Church but also not in the least rebellious against it.

Such had been the way of his ancestors since the names of Diderot and Vigneron first began to appear in the records of the locality. The name Diderot crops up in Langres documents from the middle of the fifteenth century, that of Vigneron from 1558. Both families were of artisan stock, and predominantly devoted themselves through the generations to being either cutlers or tanners. Both families, moreover, displayed a talent for progenitiveness. The Encyclopedist's great-grandfather Vigneron had had nine children; grandfather Vigneron, eleven. Great-grandfather Diderot, for his part, had had fourteen children; grandfather Diderot, nine. Denis Diderot himself was one of a family to which seven children were born.[7]

Into this world, swarming with relatives, Diderot was born on 5 October 1713, the year haughty old Louis XIV had to accept the Treaties of Utrecht which put an end to the exhausting War of the Spanish Succession. But the abundance of Diderot's family connections seems to have left little impression upon him, if one may judge from the rarity of his subsequent allusions to them. He never mentioned his paternal grandfather, although

that Denis Diderot was also the boy's godfather and survived until young
Denis was in his thirteenth year. He never referred in his letters or writings
to his uncle, the Dominican friar, or by name to his aunt and godmother,
Claire Vigneron, though on one occasion, it is true, he included them in
family greetings sent through a friend.[8] And the retiring and no doubt well-
deserving lives of the Diderot collaterals, the cousins and the cousins-german
and the cousins twice removed, have remained, for aught of him, obscure.

Even Diderot's mother figures only infrequently in anything he ever
committed to paper. Angélique Vigneron, the daughter of a merchant
tanner, was born on 12 October 1677, and married Didier Diderot, a master
cutler, in 1711 or the beginning of 1712.[9] It was remarkable for the period
that she was not married before the age of thirty-four. Moreover, she was
eight years older than her husband. Her first child, a son, was born on
5 November 1712, and died soon thereafter.[10] Eleven months later the birth
of a second son, the subject of this biography, partially repaired the loss.
Diderot mentions his mother only four times, but perhaps the depth of
feeling revealed in the last two of these passages atones for the strange lack
of more references. The first two allusions come in letters to his friend,
Friedrich Melchior Grimm, in which Diderot simply remarks that he was
absent when his mother died.[11] The third allusion is in a letter to Sophie
Volland, written when he was forty-seven: 'There are two or three honest
men and two or three honest women in this world, and Providence has
sent them to me. . . . If Providence should speak and say to me, ". . . I have
given thee Didier for father and Angélique for mother; thou knowest what
they were and what they have done for thee. What is remaining for thee
to ask of me?," I don't know what I should say in reply.' [12]

The fourth allusion to his mother dates from 1770, when Diderot was at
Bourbonne-les-Bains and writing an account of the town and the medicinal
properties of its waters. 'When one is in a country, one should inform oneself
somewhat of what goes on there,' he began. Presently, in a characteristic
digression with characteristic dots: 'Now it is midnight. I am alone, and I
bring to mind these good folk, these good parents. . . . O thou, who used
to warm my cold feet in thy hands, O my mother! . . .' [13] Diderot's deep-
seated regard for his mother was displayed by the fact that both his daughters
— the first dying before the second was born — were christened Angélique.

Diderot was extremely fond of his father and often refers to him. Didier
Diderot (born 14 September 1685) was so good an artisan that his surgical
knives, scalpels, and lancets, stamped with his hallmark of a pearl, were

much in demand. A French doctor writing in 1913 spoke with respect of the elder Diderot and of his lancets, 'which he very greatly perfected: better in the hand, they cut more cleanly, and the lancets with the mark of the pearl were sought out by all the doctors teaching medicine. I possess one myself, bequeathed to me by an old physician of Langres, and I understand without difficulty the enthusiasm of contemporaries.'[14] The eminence of Diderot's father in his craft is attested also by the fact that in the Langres Museum at the Hôtel du Breuil there is a pair of small scissors of a design perfected, tradition says, by the elder Diderot.

Diderot's father was, moreover, a man of property who enjoyed a reputation for piety and integrity. During that same night in Bourbonne-les-Bains, his son wrote: '. . . one of the things that has occasioned me the greatest pleasure was the crabbed remark addressed to me by a local man some years after my father's death. I was crossing a street in my city when this man laid his hand on my arm and said, "Monsieur Diderot, you are a good man; but if you think you will ever be the equal of your father, you are mistaken." '[15]

How Diderot felt about his father is well illustrated by a statement that he made six years after the old man had died. Provoked by a dispute with a priest about the character of the Heavenly Father, Diderot made clear his sentiments concerning his earthly one: 'The first years I spent at Paris were considerably disordered; my conduct was more than sufficient to irritate my father, without there being any need to exaggerate it. Nevertheless, calumny had not been wanting. He had been told. . . . What *hadn't* he been told? The opportunity for going to see him presented itself. I did not hesitate. I set out full of confidence in his goodness. I thought that he would see me, that I should throw myself into his arms, that both of us would shed tears, and that all would be forgotten. I thought right.'[16]

Fifteen months after the birth of the future Encyclopedist, the eldest daughter, Denise, was born (27 January 1715). This sister, whom Denis Diderot greatly admired, sometimes referring to her, when they were both in middle age, as 'little sister' and sometimes as 'a female Socrates,' remained a spinster throughout her long life. Sometime in middle age she developed 'a pimple on her nose that became a cancer and entirely destroyed that part of her face.'[17] This affliction, necessitating the use of false noses (she even tried one made of glass), was evidently endured in a spirit of Christian cheerfulness.[18] Diderot's daughter spoke of her aunt as a woman who 'possessed the rare secret of finding heaven on earth,' and Diderot himself wrote in 1770, 'I love my sister to distraction, not so much because she is my sister as because of my taste for things excellent of their kind. How many fine characteristics I could mention of her if I chose!' [19]

Denise was followed in the Diderot family by three other sisters about whom very little is known. The first, Catherine, was born sometime in 1716 and buried 30 August 1718. The second, also named Catherine, was born and baptized on 18 April 1719. Then on 3 April 1720, Angélique Diderot was born. It was an eighteenth-century custom peculiar to Langres and its neighborhood, I have been told — though now quite general in France — to allow persons of extremely tender age to stand as godparents. Thus it was that Angélique's brother stood as godfather for this new sister and boldly signed the baptismal register with his own hand.[20]

It is evident, therefore, that Diderot grew up with considerable experience in being the elder brother of girls. When he left Langres for Paris in 1728 or 1729, his three living sisters were, respectively, about thirteen, nine, and eight years old, although the second Catherine may already have died. In the fullness of time — and, oddly, against the wishes of her family — Angélique became a nun, an Ursuline.[21] His daughter, in her memoirs of Diderot, declares that this sister became insane as a result of overwork in the convent and died at the age of twenty-eight.[22] This incident no doubt was one of the causes of Diderot's dislike of convents, which helped to provide the impetus many years later for his very effective novel, *The Nun*.

The Benjamin of the family was a boy born on 21 March 1722.[23] Didier-Pierre Diderot, as he was named in the baptismal ceremony in which his elder brother served as a proxy godfather, grew up to be a pious and evidently quite thorny Catholic priest, a canon in the cathedral at Langres who accounted his greatest shame to be his brother's impiety. The personal relations of the two brothers, although not hateful, were none too cordial. Each deplored the views of the other while entertaining a stubborn sort of reluctant affection entirely unmixed with respect. The Canon carried his disapprobation to the point of refusing to see his brother's daughter and her children, and when in 1780 he was invited by the mayor and aldermen of Langres to be present at a dinner where the Encyclopedist's bust, done by Houdon, was to be unveiled, he refused. Later, under pretext of some errand or other at the city hall, he went to see the bust by himself.[24]

There is no record of where or from whom Diderot received his elementary schooling. Indeed, there is almost no testimony extant concerning his earliest years, save that his daughter wrote after his death that 'from his tenderest years he gave evidence of extreme sensibility: when he was three years old he was taken to a public execution and came back from it so upset that he was attacked by a violent jaundice.'[25] There are in his works occasional allusions to his early days, as when, criticizing the figures in a landscape by Hubert Robert, he remarked that a Swiss guard in the picture was stiff and 'precisely like those given me one New Year's, when I was small';[26] or when he observed, perhaps in recollection of his childhood and of the ramparts of Langres, that it is characteristic of children to love to climb;[27] or when, writing in the *Encyclopédie* of the vagaries of orthography, he declared that we get accustomed to pronouncing one language and writing another, 'a bizarre state of affairs which has made so many tears flow in childhood.'[28] Perhaps much of his elementary education he received in his own home, for he wrote late in life that 'arithmetic was one of the first things my parents taught me.'[29] Regardless of how the young Diderot achieved his knowledge of the three R's, by the time he was ten he was qualified to begin his secondary education and in November 1723 (most probably) was enrolled in the lowest form of the Jesuit *collège* at Langres.[30]

The Jesuits exercised in Langres a monopoly of secondary education, just as they frequently did elsewhere in Catholic Christendom.[31] They achieved this pre-eminence as a result of the excellence of their teachers and their emphasis upon the more humane letters, the Latin and Greek which had stood so high in the estimation of cultivated men ever since the Humanists had revived the love of ancient letters. By this emphasis the Jesuits, who were the prime instruments of the Catholic Church in the Counter Reformation, once again showed their cleverness. For in their rigidly standardized curriculum — the *Ratio studiorum* that elaborately regulated Jesuit education everywhere had been promulgated in 1599 — excellent instruction in the ancient literatures was combined with considerable attention to Catholic devotions and thus, from the point of view of the Church, humanistic learning was prevented from becoming too secular.

From his home at Number 6, an edifice still standing and now adorned with a commemorative plaque, the schoolboy Diderot would walk the few steps across the Place Chambeau to the Jesuit *collège,* which stood just off the square at the head of a street since named for him.[32] The *collège* was destroyed by fire in 1746, but was quickly replaced by the present building which also bears his name. In 1770 Diderot referred to it as 'renowned.' It had quite a numerous clientele, perhaps 180 or 200 in the six forms, all of them day students, most of them (but by no means all) from Langres, and coming from diverse social backgrounds, astonishing if one considers what was usual in the tightly knit society of the *ancien régime.* There were noblemen as well as scions of the upper and lower middle classes, and there was also, in Diderot's own form, the son of a tinker.[33] Throughout his life Diderot showed an ability to esteem men for what they were by nature rather than what they were by rank, and it is not impossible that the relatively democratic conditions of his schooling habituated him to such a point of view.

Although Diderot was a sensitive child, he was also a robust one, and in later years he liked to recall the Spartan aspects of his early education, much as nineteenth-century Americans were prone to expatiate on the part played by the little red schoolhouse and the McGuffey readers in making a nation great and keeping its manners pure. Remembering the scars of ten slingshot hits on his forehead, he wrote: 'Such was provincial education in my time. Two hundred boys would divide themselves into two armies. It was not rare for children, seriously injured, to have to be carried off to their parents. . . . I remember that . . . my comrades and I got the idea of demolishing one of the bastions of my town and passing Holy Week in prison.' And then, carried away as he so often was by a sort of chain reaction of associations, and evidently remembering some childhood rival who had aroused his distaste, he apostrophized an imaginary 'Athenian' who did not approve of an education that was so Spartan and untrammeled: 'You recoil at the sight of their disheveled hair and torn clothes. Yet I was that way when I was young, and I was pleasing — pleasing to even the women and girls of my home town in the provinces. They preferred me, without a hat and with chest uncovered, sometimes without shoes, in a jacket and with feet bare, me, son of a worker at a forge, to that little well-dressed monsieur, all curled and powdered and dressed to the nines, the son of the presiding judge of the bailiwick court. . . . They could see in my buttonhole the token of my attainments in study, and a boy who revealed his soul by frank and open words and who knew better how to give a blow with his fist than how to make a bow, pleased them more than a foolish, cowardly, false, and effeminate little toady.' [34]

Diderot was never above showing off for the girls, and one of his reminiscences, inspired by this theme and referring to his youthful days in Paris, has the incidental merit of giving us some notion of his congenital endowments, at least so far as muscular co-ordination is concerned. 'I was young,' he wrote. 'I was in love, and very much in love. I was living with some fellows from Provence who danced from dusk to dawn, and from dusk to dawn took the hand of the girl I loved and embraced her right under my eyes. Add to this that I was jealous. I decide to learn to dance. From the

Rue de la Harpe to the far end of the Rue Montmartre I surreptitiously go for lessons. I keep going to the same dancing master for a long time. Then I leave him, out of vexation over having learned nothing. I take him up a second, a third time, and leave off with as much vexation and with just as little success. What was lacking in me to be a proficient dancer? An ear for it? I had an excellent one. Lightness? I wasn't heavy on my feet, far from it. Motive? One could scarcely be animated by one more violent. What didn't I have? Malleability, flexibility, gracefulness — qualities that cannot be had for the asking.

'But after having done everything to no purpose in order to learn how to dance, I learned without difficulty to fence very passably, and without any other motive than that of pleasing myself.' [35]

At his books Diderot was evidently an apt and quick pupil. Although in later years he became extremely critical of the value of this education, his youthful proficiency in it is attested by documents still extant.[36] In the museum at the Hôtel du Breuil in Langres is a parchment certificate, or *bene merenti,* signed by the prefect of studies and probably dating from August 1728, in which Diderot is called an *'ingeniosum adolescentem'* who in public exercises had explained and elucidated passages from Quintus Curtius and Horace, with the praise and applause of all (*'cum laude plausuque omnium'*). There are also in the same museum two quarto volumes of some six hundred pages each, a history of the Catholic Church in Japan by the Reverend Father Grasset, S. J., which Diderot won as prizes. These edifying volumes, suspiciously fresh and new, with the virginal appearance, even after two centuries, that books won as prizes are apt to have, bear inscriptions on their flyleaves indicating that Denis Diderot, 'a young man to be commended on many counts' (*'adolescens multiplici nomine commendandus'*), had received them on 3 August 1728 as a reward for securing the second prize in Latin verses and the second prize in translation. It is perhaps of this occasion that Diderot was thinking when he wrote to Sophie Volland: 'One of the sweetest moments of my life — it happened more than thirty years ago, though I remember it as though it were yesterday — was when my father saw me coming home from school with my arms laden with the prizes I had won and around my neck the academic crowns that I had been given and which, too large for my brow, had let my head pass through. From the farthest distance that he saw me, he left his work, came to the door, and began to weep.' [37]

It is always interesting to seek in a mature person the abiding traces of his early education. In the mature Diderot one can perceive, though in an

extremely contorted and inverted shape, the influence of the religious instruction imparted by his family and by the Jesuits. But much more easily
seen, quite pellucid in the continuity of its effect upon him, is his classical
education, reflected in the frequency of his allusions to ancient authors, in
his enjoyment of the fine points of Latinity and in his fondness for in-
dulging in exegetics, in the trust he reposes in the ancient languages as a
semantic guide, and, most important of all, in his conviction that in the
ancient authors is to be found the acme in genius, in good manners, and in
taste.

References to classic authors are abundant in Diderot's writings and frequently go beyond the casual quotation and passing allusion to be expected in an author whose range was encyclopedic. About 1775 Diderot
wrote for Catherine II a 'Plan for a University for the Government of Russia,' in the course of which he devoted several pages to comments about instruction in Greek and Latin, and incidentally showed how familiar he was
with the idiom and manner of various classic authors.[38] He wrote of his own
experience with the classics: 'Several years in succession I was as religious
about reading a book of Homer before going to bed as a conscientious priest
is about reciting his breviary. At an early age I sucked up the milk of
Homer, Virgil, Horace, Terence, Anacreon, Plato, and Euripides, diluted
with that of Moses and the prophets.'[39] And of Homer in particular he
wrote: 'Let me be pardoned for the little grain of incense I burn before the
statue of a master to whom I owe what I am worth, if I am worth anything.'[40] As a result of his love of the classics, Diderot wrote a long commentary on the works of Seneca; inspired and corrected a critical edition
of Lucretius;[41] elucidated difficult passages in Horace and Virgil;[42] ac-
claimed himself as the 'sacristan' in the 'church' of Pliny's Latinity;[43] wrote
an appreciative estimation (indeed, it is one of Diderot's best pieces) of
Terence;[44] annotated and commented upon the satires of the very difficult
Persius;[45] and composed in Latin numerous inscriptions for statues and
public buildings.

The abiding influence of an education founded on the classics and frequently demanding the use of spoken Latin in the classroom, with a corresponding outlawing of the vernacular, is also revealed in Diderot's interesting advice upon how to learn to read a foreign language. In his own
article 'Encyclopedia,' which he wrote for the fifth volume of the *Encyclopédie,* he declared, in speaking of linguistic and grammatical matters, that
'Nothing can be more poorly conceived for a Frenchman who knows Latin
than to learn English from an English-French dictionary instead of having

recourse to an English-Latin dictionary. . . . Furthermore, I speak according to my own experience. This method turned out very well for me.' [46]

Diderot's allusions to his childhood are few but full of flavor. In 1773 he was trying to puzzle out a difficult passage in Horace and using the evidence of some very unusual words and constructions. This recalled to him the days of his boyhood and the circumstances of his early education. 'When I used to study Latin under the iron rule of the public schools, a trap that I used to set for my teacher, and one that always worked, was to employ these strange turns of expression. He would cry out against them, he would storm at me, and when he had completely committed himself, what with storming and crying out, I would show by a little quotation that all his abusive remarks applied to Virgil, Cicero, or Tacitus.' [47]

The perversity of the gifted young has ever been the despair — and the secret pride — of the teacher.

CHAPTER 2

Diderot Becomes an Abbé and Goes to Paris

A s THE years went by and young Diderot flourished in learning, the question naturally arose as to what should be his career. There was a moment, but only a moment, in which it seemed possible that he might follow his father's trade. For Diderot, impatient of the remonstrances and corrections of his teachers, told his father one day that he didn't want to go to school any more.

'Well, then, do you want to be a cutler?'

'With all my heart.'

So he put on the workshop apron and started in by his father's side. As his daughter tells the story, he spoiled everything he touched, knives, penknives — everything. This ended in four or five days when he got up one morning, climbed upstairs to his room, took his books, and went back to school. 'I can stand impatience better than boredom,' he said.[1]

For persons who know only the Diderot of later life — a spirited and emphatic freethinker — it will come as a surprise to learn that at the age of thirteen he signified in a solemn ceremony his intention of becoming a priest. On 22 August 1726, the Bishop of Langres conferred the tonsure on Denis Diderot, a rite consisting of cutting off some locks of the candidate's hair in the form of a cross, the while the future ecclesiastic reads some verses from the Fifteenth Psalm.[2] As a result of this ceremony, Diderot was entitled to be addressed as '*Abbé*,' and was expected to wear an *abbé*'s characteristic attire, which consisted not of a soutane worn by priests, but black smallclothes, a short mantle, and an ecclesiastical collar with its white tabs. Thus he became for a time a member of a very numerous class of persons in eighteenth-century French life, for *abbés,* many of whom never proceeded to holy orders but all of whom were eligible for ecclesiastical benefices, were conspicuous features of the social landscape.

There is nothing to show that young Diderot went through this ceremony against his will. The timing of the ceremony, in all probability, was determined by the hope entertained by Diderot's relatives that he would be allowed to succeed to the lucrative prebend that his uncle, Canon Didier Vigneron, occupied at the local Cathedral of Saint-Mammès. Perhaps because of this consideration Diderot took the tonsure at so early an age, for it was extremely unusual and somewhat irregular, although not precisely uncanonical, to undergo this ceremony before the age of fourteen.

These hopes, however, presently foundered. Canon Vigneron found that his chapter objected to his being succeeded by his young nephew. To circumvent them the Canon went through the proper legal forms for handing over his prebend to the Pope in favor of 'Denis Diderot, tonsured cleric of the diocese of Langres, fourteen years and six months old, and no other.' But five hours after he had sent his representative off to Rome, the Canon died. Apparently his demission was not binding unless the Pope had accepted it while the Canon was still alive. The chapter immediately elected someone else, and the hopes of that career went glimmering.[3]

Soon afterwards, Diderot, influenced of course by his teachers in the Jesuit *collège* where he was becoming markedly successful, began to think of becoming a Jesuit himself. It may have been about this time, too, that he underwent the stress of a devout religious experience. His daughter states that for four or five months during the time that Diderot was desirous of becoming a Jesuit, he fasted, wore a hair shirt, and slept on straw.[4] The following passage from his novel *James the Fatalist,* written in 1773, may therefore be autobiographical in nature: 'There comes a moment during which almost every girl or boy falls into melancholy; they are tormented by a vague inquietude which rests on everything and finds nothing to calm it. They seek solitude; they weep; the silence to be found in cloisters attracts them; the image of peace that seems to reign in religious houses seduces them. They mistake the first manifestations of a developing sexual nature for the voice of God calling them to Himself; and it is precisely when nature is inciting them that they embrace a fashion of life contrary to nature's wish.'[5] It is piquant to learn that Diderot went through such a religious crisis, because in later life he is always assuming the pose, like Lucretius in the beginning pages of *De Rerum Natura,* of freeing men from fear of the gods. Yet even in these later years he now and again felt the tug of a previous persuasion. For instance, he wrote in 1765 of the necessity, in perpetuating a doctrine and an institution, for having concrete symbols that appeal to the imagination through the senses, and he gives as an example

the exaltation of the multitude at a Corpus Christi processional, 'an exaltation that sometimes lays hold of even me. I have never seen that long file of
priests in their sacerdotal robes, those young acolytes garbed in their white
albs, girt up with their wide blue sashes, and casting flowers before the
Holy Sacrament; the crowd that precedes and follows them in a religious
silence; so many men with their heads bowed down to earth; I have never
heard that solemn and affecting plain song of the priests, affectionately replied to by an infinity of voices of men, women, girls, and children, without
my feelings being deeply moved and without tears coming to my eyes.' [6]

Apparently it was young Diderot's desire to join the Jesuits that led to
his departure from Langres for the rest of his schooling. His daughter,
Mme de Vandeul, declares that Diderot intended to leave surreptitiously
in company with a Jesuit, but that his father, warned by one of Diderot's
cousins, waited up on the appointed night and made an unexpected appearance just as Diderot was creeping down the stairs. To the question as to
where he was going at this midnight hour, Diderot replied, 'To Paris, where
I am bound to enter the Jesuits.'

'It won't be tonight, though your desires will be accomplished. But first
let us get some sleep.' [7]

It is a little hard to believe that an order of the dignity of the Jesuits
would recruit its members quite so melodramatically. Mme de Vandeul's
extremely valuable account of her father, written in the year of his death,
can frequently be proved aberrant in details, although it is so accurate
in the main that she has become the ghost writer of many a later biography
of Diderot. Her source of information was of course her father, who was not
the sort of man to mar a tale in the telling. There may be some exaggeration
in this anecdote, just as there is in the statement that he gravely made in
an article written for the *Encyclopédie* claiming that his grandmother had
had twenty-two children, and by the time she was thirty-three years of age! [8]
A personal acquaintance named Taillefer published an account of Diderot
only one year after his death, and though this document, too, must be
taken with caution, the Taillefer and Vandeul accounts provide some opportunity for reciprocal control. With reference to Diderot's joining the
Jesuits, Taillefer says nothing of any attempted flight from Langres. [9]

There is something of a mystery here. Indeed, it may even be that Diderot
had fallen out with the Jesuits and that this caused him to go to Paris
for the balance of his education. Evidence for such a view is found in
something written by Jacques-André Naigeon, the familiar of Diderot
during the last twenty years of his life and his would-be Boswell. In the

year of Diderot's death, Naigeon asked Diderot's daughter and her husband for information about 'the quarrel with the Jesuits,' the context perhaps implying that this occurred before he went to Paris. 'M. Naigeon desires to write the life of M. Diderot,' wrote the son-in-law, '[and] persecutes me to give him an exact and very detailed memorandum of the precise date of his birth and the principal events of the philosopher's youth, of his early studies, of his leaving the *collège,* of the quarrel with the Jesuits, of his age when he was sent to Paris, how many years he stayed at the Collège d'Harcourt, how many at the Collège de Bourgogne, and with the lawyer M. Clément de Ris, his adventures with Mme Fréjacques, Mlle La Salette, etc. . . .' [10] We should like to know more about that quarrel with the Jesuits and when it occurred. As it stands, it is just another one of the little-known incidents in a career which was often and surprisingly inscrutable.

At all events and for whatever reason, Diderot left Langres for Paris, probably in the autumn of 1728, but possibly in 1729, his business being to finish his last year of study, his 'rhetoric,' in what would now be called a *lycée.* [11] Thus began the great adventure, the first going-away-from-home. There is no indication of his being reluctant to leave Langres, save perhaps for some sentimental thoughts about Mlle La Salette (a Langres girl born the same year as he and who, in the course of years, became the mother of the man who was to marry Diderot's daughter), or about another, but unidentified, girl of Langres who made a sufficiently lasting impression to cause him to mention her in a letter to Sophie Volland thirty years later. [12] His father accompanied him. Down the valley of the Marne they rode — 'my melancholy and tortuous compatriot, the Marne,' he later called it — [13] traveling, if they went by the slow coach, seven days to reach Paris. [14]

At Paris, Diderot's father made the necessary arrangements for his son's settling into school, took his leave as though he were going to depart from the city, and then stayed on in Paris a fortnight just to make certain that all was going well. Having then been reassured by young Diderot that he was happy and wanted to stay, and by his son's principal that the boy was an excellent student even though they had had to discipline him, the father went back to his knives and lancets at Langres. These incidents are completely in character, both for father and son. For young Diderot had thoughtlessly and big-heartedly undertaken to do someone else's work. He obliged a disconsolate fellow-student who was reluctant to address himself to the assignment of putting the serpent's seductive speech to Eve into Latin verse. Diderot's verses were good — too good to have been done by the lad who was supposed to do them. Both students were 'very roughly handled,' wrote Mme de Vandeul, 'and my father gave up others' business to occupy himself henceforth exclusively with his own.' [15]

A new phase of his career had begun — and a lasting one, for he was to be a Parisian to the end of his days.

*   *   *   *   *   *

From the time when he was about sixteen and went to Paris until the time when, at twenty-nine, he was already embarked on a career of letters and was desirous of getting married, little is precisely known of Diderot and of where and how he spent his time. This period of his life is a documentary desert, filled with shimmering mirages of assertion and whimsy, with widely spaced waterholes of verifiable fact upon which the panting searcher stumbles when just about to expire. By the year 1742 it becomes possible to follow his career with some certainty, but meanwhile some thirteen of the most important formative years of his life are shrouded and obscure. Diderot himself seldom spoke of them and, indeed, seems almost intentionally inscrutable about this period. It is amazing that no memoir writer contemporary with Diderot was able to recollect a youthful acquaintance with a man who was constantly resident in the nation's capital and who subsequently became so famous. Yet neither friend nor enemy has spoken from certain, personal knowledge of these years. The earliest notice of him recorded by a contemporary refers to the year 1742.

This account occurs in the memoirs of Johann Georg Wille, a German who lived most of his life in Paris and became one of the most celebrated engravers of the century. His likeness is preserved for us in a magnificent portrait by Greuze, which Diderot himself pronounced to be 'very beautiful' and very like.[16] In the year in which they met, Wille rented lodgings in the Rue de l'Observance, now called the Rue Antoine-Dubois, a very short street which at one end ascends by a stairway to the Rue Monsieur-le-Prince and on the other looked out on the Collège de Bourgogne, the site of which is now occupied by the Ecole de Médecine. 'I was curious to know who might be my neighbors in the house,' wrote Wille, 'and, in order to find out, I went downstairs to my landlord's rooms where by chance I found a very affable young man who in the ensuing conversation informed me that he was seeking to become a proficient man of letters and a still better philosopher, if that was possible; he added that he would be very happy to make my acquaintance, the more because he esteemed artists and loved the arts, because he thought we were of the same age, and because, moreover, he already knew that we were neighbors. I gave him a handclasp and from that moment we were friends. This young man was M. Diderot, since become famous. He occupied the entresol the floor beneath me, had a beautiful library there, and with pleasure lent me the books that might give pleasure to me.'[17]

This makes an engaging and attractive picture. A present-day reader, knowing that this is the picture of a young man about to enter a prodigious career of intellectual virtuosity, and realizing how little is known of the previous formative period, when this mind was broadening its range and deepening its mastery, is tantalized by this fleeting view into those misty years. What experiences had Diderot had to engender and confirm these tastes in philosophy and the arts? How much formal schooling had he had, and in what institutions of learning? How had he supported himself or been supported during all this time?

Even the school he entered on coming to Paris is a matter of conjecture. The evidence is conflicting and confused. A much younger contemporary says that Diderot entered the famous Collège Louis-le-Grand, the school where Voltaire was educated and whose imposing buildings still stand, just across the Rue Saint-Jacques from the Sorbonne.[18] Diderot's daughter and Naigeon declare that he entered the Collège d'Harcourt on the Boulevard Saint-Michel, just across from the Place de la Sorbonne, where the Lycée Saint-Louis now stands.[19] But his daughter also says that he was a school chum of the future Cardinal de Bernis, who indubitably was a student at Louis-le-Grand.[20] This conflicting testimony has touched off a controversy among scholars, nurtured by the fact that the Collèges' records for those years are no longer extant. One authority even argues for the Collège de Beauvais.[21] The recently published inquiry made by Naigeon of Diderot's daughter and son-in-law in 1784, previously alluded to, would seem to settle the matter in favor of the Collège d'Harcourt, but opens up an entirely new vista in suggesting that Diderot was also a student at the Collège de Bourgogne. The matter may be summarized by saying that it is extremely improbable that Diderot attended Louis-le-Grand *exclusively,* if he attended it at all. He probably went to the Collège d'Harcourt instead, but he could very possibly have attended both.

The point is more important than it may seem at first. If it were possible to know with certainty to what college in Paris Diderot belonged, then one could know whether in the important years when he was being introduced to formal philosophy, studied according to the scholastic method with its emphasis on metaphysics and categories and universals and with its strong tincture (at that time) of Cartesianism, he was being taught to see things from the Jesuit or the Jansenist point of view. For Louis-le-Grand was a

Jesuit college, whereas the Collège d'Harcourt was an active center of
Jansenism.[22] Those who dip into the study of seventeenth- and eighteenth-
century France quickly become aware that a chronic struggle went on within
the Catholic Church between these two factions. Moreover, in a society
where Church was as closely knit with State as it was during the *ancien
régime,* these theological disagreements had grave political repercussions.
In the early and middle eighteenth century it was scarcely possible for any
thinking Frenchman to avoid taking a position, even though publicly un-
avowed, in these disputes. Jansenist and Jesuit cordially hated each other,
and freethinkers scoffed at both.

The Jansenists took their name from Cornelis Jansen (1585–1638), Bishop
of Ypres. They constituted a puritanical and fundamentalist sect within
the Catholic Church, which by the time of the latter years of Louis XIV
seemed to be losing out to the Jesuits. The King, seeking uniformity and
orthodoxy, asked the Pope to settle the dispute once for all. The answer was
the papal bull *Unigenitus,* promulgated in 1713, which declared heretical
101 propositions set forth in a popular Jansenist book of devotions. But instead of settling the dispute, the bull only served to inflame it. The Pope's
action was resented by many as too great an interference in French domestic
affairs. Nevertheless, the energetic measures of the government to secure
acceptance of the bull forced the Jansenists undercover. They even published
an underground newspaper, *Les Nouvelles Ecclésiastiques,* which, in spite
of the determined efforts of the police, appeared with mocking and impish
regularity right up to its discontinuation in 1803. Ascetic and dour, stubborn
in adversity and embittered by it, the Jansenists were not the most broad-
minded people of their time. Both sides shocked the liberals of the century,
who feared the authoritarian proclivities of the one as much as those of
the other.

Which group, then, shaped Diderot's thinking during his college years?
Inasmuch as it is known that he was awarded the degree of master of arts in
the University of Paris on 2 September 1732, indicating a formal schooling
of some years' duration at Paris, it is possible to argue that Diderot transferred from the one college to the other following his 'rhetoric' and before
his 'philosophy.'[23] This conjecture has the advantage of reconciling conflicting accounts. It makes it possible for Diderot to have known the future
Cardinal Bernis at the Jesuit Louis-le-Grand, as Mme de Vandeul says he
did, and to have sat there under the famous teacher, Father Porée, as Diderot
claims in his *Letter on the Deaf and Dumb,* and still to have been a student
at the Jansenist Collège d'Harcourt, as his daughter and Naigeon declare

he was.[24] Yet another purpose can be served by this convenient conjecture. Diderot's general editorial policy, as well as the articles he himself wrote for the *Encyclopédie,* reveal a very considerable familiarity with exegetics, but without any special fondness or predilection for them. Therefore, could not the hypothesis that he attended both Jesuit and Jansenist colleges lead to the further one that, having become familiar with the point of view of each, he found himself repelled by both, so that instead of inclining him to the one or the other, each canceled the other out?

What he did immediately after receiving the master of arts degree is no less uncertain. Although it has generally been presumed that he thereupon discontinued his formal schooling, there is nothing in the evidence that demands that this be so. The account his daughter gives of his adventures implies that by this time Diderot, if he ever had the intention of studying for the priesthood, had given it up. This, too, tallies with Naigeon's testimony that while Diderot was a student at the Collège d'Harcourt he stopped wearing his ecclesiastical attire.[25] Documents show that twice during this crepuscular period of Diderot's life he considered entering the law, one document referring to the year 1736 and the other to about 1741.[26] Mme de Vandeul's account is probably accurate as far as it goes, although the biographer might well wish, with a sigh, for greater precision in dates: 'His studies completed, his father wrote to M. Clément de Ris, a solicitor at Paris and a fellow townsman, to take him into the household and have him study law. He stayed there two years; but the searching of deeds and the listing of inventories had few attractions for him. All the time he could steal from his employer was used in studying Latin and Greek, which he thought he did not sufficiently know; mathematics, which he always passionately loved; Italian, English, etc. Finally he gave himself up to his taste for letters to such a point that M. Clément felt he ought to inform his friend of the poor use his son was making of his time. Thereupon my grandfather expressly charged M. Clément to propose a profession to his son, to induce him to make his choice promptly, and to engage him to be a doctor, a solicitor, or a barrister. My father asked for time to think it over, and was granted it. After some months, the propositions were renewed. Then he said that the profession of doctor did not please him, he did not want to kill any one; that the profession of solicitor was too difficult to perform scrupulously; that he would gladly choose the profession of barrister, save that he had an unconquerable aversion to busying himself all his life with other people's affairs.

'"But," said M. Clément to him, "what do you want to be, then?"

'"*Ma foi,* nothing, nothing at all. I like study; I am very well off, very happy; I don't ask anything else."' Thereupon Diderot's father cut off his allowance and demanded that he either choose a profession or come home within the week. Diderot left the house of the solicitor, so as not to put him to any expense, and, says Mme de Vandeul, lived the next ten years on his own.[27]

At some time during this decade Diderot was a tutor in the household of a wealthy financier named Randon. But Diderot was not of the temperament to enjoy such confining work: '"Monsieur, look at me. A lemon is less yellow than my complexion. I am making men of your children, but each day I become a child with them. I am a thousand times *too* rich and *too* well off in your house, but I must leave it. The object of my desires is not to live better, but just not to die."'[28]

All this is completely in character and entirely credible. It shows Diderot's love of independence, his hatred of constraint. And it shows, too, a sort of lack of fondness for children which is also to be seen or sensed in his writings, even though he once asserted in middle life that he was very fond of old men and children. Diderot was constantly letting his feelings pour forth in jets of enthusiasm, but one can look long and far — that one instance excepted — for him to express any great enthusiasm for children and childhood, except, of course, his own.[29] And not even his own daughter seems to have interested him much until she began to make precocious remarks which gave him hope that she possessed an interesting and original mind. He seems to have pitied the state of childhood — its helplessness, its limited outlook, its wrong conclusions logically derived from false premises — but he did not admire it.

Aside from two years accounted for at the solicitor's and three months being a tutor at the financier's, Diderot, according to his daughter's account, was on the town. 'He passed ten whole years . . . having no other resource than those very sciences that were earning him the disapprobation of his father. He gave lessons in mathematics; if the pupil was quick . . . he would teach him the whole day long; but if he found a stupid pupil, he would not go back. He was paid in books, in furniture, in linen, in money, or not at all; it was all the same to him. He wrote sermons. A missionary ordered six from him for the Portuguese colonies and paid fifty *écus* apiece for them. My father thought this affair one of the best he ever brought off.'[30]

This testimony bespeaks a precarious existence. Now and again he was able in other ways to supplement the income he derived from giving lessons. For example, he tells us that he prepared the general formula and mathematical tables for a treatise published in 1741 on gnomonics, the science of sundials.[31] This task presupposes considerable mathematical competence and accuracy, and it is to be presumed, although not certainly so, that he was paid for it. Moreover, the censor's approbation of Diderot's translation of Temple Stanyan's *Grecian History,* dated 25 May 1742, proves that he had prepared the manuscript before that time, and for this translation he probably received something in advance.[32] Still, his was evidently a Bohemian, hand-to-mouth existence, provided that, as will be discussed later, he did not spend some of these ten years in formal theological studies. Diderot's daughter is emphatic that her grandfather sent no money to his recalcitrant son, although 'his mother, more tender and more compliant, sent him some louis, not by the post nor by friends, but by a maid servant who did the sixty leagues on foot, delivered to him the small sum from his mother, adding to it, without mentioning it, all her own savings, and then walked back the sixty leagues in return. This woman carried out this commission on three occasions.' [33]

With an income so uncertain and evidently operating in geyserlike intervals of fast and feast, it is not surprising to learn that sometimes his cupboard was bare. One Shrove Tuesday, a day when, like Christmas in America, absent youths were particulary likely to be homesick, Diderot arose to find that he had absolutely no money with which to buy dinner. Not wanting to disturb his friends upon such a day, he tried unsuccessfully to work, and then went out for a long walk. 'He came back to his tavern; upon entering, he sat down and felt ill. The landlady gave him a little toast soaked in wine, and he went to bed. "That day," he told me, "I swore that if ever I possessed anything, never in my life would I refuse something to an indigent person, in order not to condemn any fellow man of mine to put in a day as distressing as that." ' [34]

Diderot was not averse to receiving aid from fellow townsmen, knowing that his father would pay up. There is documentary evidence of this having occurred in 1736. On 20 August of that year, a man formerly from Langres named Foucou — fifteen years later Diderot acknowledged in his *Encyclopédie* article on 'Steel' the helpful information contributed by 'M. Foucou, previously a cutler' — signed a receipt for thirty-eight livres received from Diderot's father by the hands of Brother Angel, a Barefooted Carmelite friar. On the same receipt Didier Diderot wrote: 'This is the final receipt of the amount agreed upon with M. Foucou of Paris. I wrote him on 23 May 1736 not to advance anything to Diderot nor to take him into his house; *that he ought to remain with the solicitor.* . . . Therefore there will be no making it up to him [Foucou] if he [Diderot] stays with him at all, for it is against my wishes.'[35]

Need sometimes brought Diderot close to roguishness. Mme de Vandeul tells a long story of how Diderot convinced Brother Angel, the Carmelite friar mentioned above, a man who also came originally from Langres and was a distant relative of the Diderots, that he intended to become a friar in Brother Angel's monastery. On that understanding Diderot received payments amounting to some two thousand livres. When at last Brother Angel showed that he would advance no more, Diderot said to him, ' "Brother Angel, then you don't want to give me any more money?"

' "Assuredly not."

' "Well, then, I don't want to be a Carmelite any more. Write to my father and get yourself paid." '[36] Both Diderot and his daughter thought this sort of panhandling clever.

During the nine or ten years between the time of receiving a master of arts degree at the University of Paris and his writing the earliest of his letters now extant, Diderot existed in what to posterity has seemed a penumbra of obscurity. But the person whom Wille found so attractive has left scattered in his works various allusions to his tastes and to his doings in those early years, which help in some measure to answer the question of what manner of man he was on the eve of his public career. In the first place, it is probable that his greatest single intellectual competence lay at that time in the field of mathematics. When he published in 1748 his highly respected *Mémoires sur différens sujets de mathématiques,* he wrote in the Fifth Memoir, in which he made some corrections in Newton's calculations of the effect on pendulums of the resistance of air: 'It is true that I studied Newton with the intention of elucidating him; I shall even confess to you that this work was pushed on, if not with great success, at least with adequate vivacity; but that I no longer gave it a thought from the time that the Reverend Fathers Le Seur and Jacquier published their *Commentary* [1739], and I have not been tempted to take it up again.'[37]

In the second place, his random recollections show that during these early years he haunted the theater and was much enamored of acting—and actresses. Evidently, too, he deemed it possible that he could have made his living on the stage: 'I myself, when I was young, hesitated between the Sorbonne and the Comédie. In winter, in the worst sort of weather, I used to recite roles from Molière and Corneille out loud in the solitary walks of the Luxembourg. What did I have in mind? To be applauded? Perhaps. To live on familiar terms with women of the theater, whom I found infinitely lovable and whom I knew to be of very easy virtue? Assuredly. I don't know what I wouldn't have done to be pleasing to la Gaussin, who made her debut about that time and who was beauty personified; or to la Dangeville, who had so many attractive qualities on the stage.' [38]

The excitement that young Diderot found in going to the theater is well depicted in a passage that he wrote in 1758: 'Fifteen years ago our theaters were places of tumult. The coolest heads began to get heated upon entering them, and grave men shared there, more or less, the transports of giddy ones. . . . People moved about, fidgeted, jostled one another, one's soul was quite beside itself. . . . The piece began with difficulty and was often interrupted, but let a fine passage come along and there was an incredible tumult, encores were demanded endlessly, and people enthused over the actor and the actress. The enthusiasm passed from the pit to the dress circle, and from the dress circle to the boxes. People had come with ardor, they left in a state of intoxication: some went to visit the girls, others scattered themselves in society; it was like a thunderstorm which passes over, spending itself afar, but the mutterings of which last a long while after it has passed by. That is what pleasure is like.' [39]

Sometimes, as Diderot recalls in his *Letter on the Deaf and Dumb,* his interest in the stage was a little more philosophical and — shall we say — unconventional: 'Formerly I used to visit the theater very often, and I knew most of our good plays by heart. On the days when I proposed to study movements and gestures, I went to the third-class boxes, for the farther I was from the actors the better I was placed. As soon as the curtain went up . . . I would put my fingers into my ears, not without some astonishment on the part of those round about me . . . and stubbornly kept my ears stopped up as long as the action of the actor appeared to me to be in harmony with the lines that I was remembering. I listened only when I was thrown off the track by the gestures on stage, or thought I was.' And Diderot recalled with amusement the redoubled surprise of the people round him 'when they saw me shed tears in the pathetic parts, and that with my ears continuously stopped.' [40]

As a footnote to his love for the theater and his love of ideas, it may fairly be conjectured that Diderot often visited the Café Procope, for until 1770 the old Comédie-Française was located just across the street. The Procope, then a famous center for actors, playwrights, academicians, and other men of letters, is now reopened and operating at the old stand, 13, Rue de l'Ancienne Comédie. In its eighteenth-century heyday it was fully as famous as the Dôme and the Rotonde in the youthful days of Hemingway and Ezra Pound or the Café de Flore when Sartre was frequenting it, and it seems hardly possible that Diderot was not among the Procope's patrons.[41]

From scattered allusions in his later works, we can get some impression of Diderot's manner and appearance at this time. He was a young man of large frame — a friend later said of him that he was built like a chair-man or porter [42] — and well set up. He wore his own hair, which was blond, heavy, and thick, and he was, then as always, careless of dress, for he recalls in his *Rameau's Nephew* the days when he gave lessons in mathematics and wore 'an overcoat of gray shag, all played out on one side, with one of the sleeves torn; and black woolen stockings mended at the back with white thread.' [43] Moreover, he evidently liked to tease the girls: as he looked at Greuze's portrait of Mme Greuze, exhibited in the Salon of 1765, Diderot remembered when she was a girl in her father's bookshop on the Quai des Grands-Augustins, bordering the Seine. Diderot entered the shop one day, 'with that lively, ardent, and daft manner I used to have.

' "Mademoiselle, La Fontaine's *Fables,* and a Petronius, if you please."

' "Here they are, Monsieur. Are there any other books you'd like?"

' "I beg your pardon, Mademoiselle, but . . ."

' "Don't be hesitant."

' *"The Nun in a Shift."*

' "Fie! Monsieur; do you suppose that one keeps in stock, that one reads, nasty things like that?"

' "Why! why! is that a nasty book, Mademoiselle? I didn't realize that!" ' [44]

Finally, it may be conjectured with some assurance that Diderot took love where he could find it, a conclusion that might be drawn from his account, written in 1758, of an incident that would seem to have occurred in these early years: 'Oh! my dear friend, where is the time when I had long hair floating in the breeze? In the mornings, when my nightshirt collar was open and I took off my nightcap, my hair fell in great, disordered locks over well-knit and very white shoulders; and my neighbor would get up early in the morning from her husband's side, half-open the curtains of her window, intoxicate herself with the sight, and I would readily perceive what was going on. 'Twas thus that I seduced her from one side of the street to the other. When I was with her, for we came together at last, I acted with candor and innocence, with a manner gentle, simple, modest, and true. All has passed away, the blond hair, and the candor, and the innocence.' [45]

Diderot, it may be remarked, was always quite adequately appreciative of female charms. He was not, however, an unbridled libertine, even if the principal bridle was nothing more virtuous than a horror of venereal disease. He recalls, in a letter to Sophie Volland, how he escaped providentially from running the risk of it on two occasions that must date from these early times. 'I never think of it without having goose flesh,' he wrote.[46]

Now, what about the possibility, preposterous though it seems, that Diderot spent some time as a graduate student of theology? By his own statement, he was balancing 'between the Sorbonne and the Comédie' not long after Mlle Gaussin made her debut at the Comédie-Française, an event which took place on 28 April 1731. Diderot's reference to the Sorbonne was, of course, to the faculty of theology of the University of Paris, and it certainly is true that his degree of master of arts qualified him to take up advanced theological studies if he chose. Diderot says he wavered between a theologian's career and an actor's, and since the context of the passage shows that he did not go on the stage, it follows that it is *possible* that for a time he became instead a graduate student in theology. If only the register books of the faculty of theology were extant — but unfortunately they have disappeared.[47]

It should be recalled that Diderot was only nineteen years old when he received his master of arts degree, and it therefore seems unlikely that his father would have allowed him to go completely on his own. Of course, two of these years were spent, according to the family tradition, as apprentice to a solicitor. But were they the two years immediately following the conferral of his degree in September 1732? Probably not, for Diderot's father, writing in May 1736, says that Diderot ought to remain with the solicitor. Now, even if two of those intervening years had already been spent at the solicitor's, there is still a hiatus of some twenty months to be accounted for.

A statement in his father's will also gives color to the supposition that young Diderot spent more years living off money sent him by his parents than Mme de Vandeul's story credits, for in that document, drawn up in 1750, Didier Diderot remarks: 'You well know, you, Diderot the elder [son], the great expense I have been to for you these twenty years that you have been at Paris. If I added up nothing but what is of my certain knowledge, I have sent you more than ten thousand livres, not including what your mother and your sisters sent you and the interest on this sum. . . .'[48] Now, when it is recalled that board, room, and tuition at a place like Louis-le-Grand was only four hundred livres a year, it is easy to see that the purchasing power of ten thousand livres could account for quite a few years in a student's life.[49] Considering Diderot's relative youth, it seems not unlikely, therefore, that he continued his schooling after 1732, possibly in theology; that per-haps, if he did, he became disgusted with theological studies; and that then he and his father turned to the possibility of his becoming a solicitor.

Far more startling and sensational, however, is the probability that as late as about 1741 Diderot was seriously intending to become a doctor of theology. He himself alluded to it in a passage he wrote in the *Salon* of 1767. 'I arrive in Paris,' he wrote. 'I was going to take the fur and install myself among the doctors of the Sorbonne. I meet a woman beautiful as an angel. I want to sleep with her. I do so. I have four children by her and there I am, forced to give up Homer and Virgil, whom I always used to carry with me in my pocket; the theater, for which I had a fondness; very lucky to under-take the *Encyclopédie,* for which I shall have sacrificed twenty-five years of my life.' [50]

This passage needs explanation. In the first place, naming the Sorbonne was the usual way of referring not to the whole University of Paris, but only to its faculty of theology. In the second place, 'to take the fur' was a locution that signified taking a university degree more advanced than the master of arts.[51] In the third place, to become a doctor of theology at the Sorbonne, one had to be a priest and have completed five years of theological studies after receiving the master of arts degree.[52] In the fourth place, Diderot did not meet his future wife before 1740 at the earliest. The nub of the problem, then, is this: is it possible to lend credence to the astonishing view that Diderot was engaged in, or at least intended to embark upon, advanced theological studies at as late an age as twenty-eight or twenty-nine? If so, it is a fact his daughter either did not know or took pains to conceal.

Diderot's writings, especially his articles in the *Encyclopédie,* reflect great familiarity with theological sources and concepts, and this fact has been claimed as clear proof that he had engaged in advanced theological studies.[53] But although it is evident that Diderot could quote the Church Fathers with as much appositeness and skill as Anatole France and certainly knew his theology well enough not to blunder unwittingly into the innumerable pitfalls and booby traps of the thickly mined areas of theological contention, still the more we examine his writings, the less we feel justified in accepting this as incontrovertible proof of advanced study. A person hostile to Diderot might say of him, as Gibbon said of Saint Augustine, that his learning is too often borrowed and his arguments are too often his own. Therefore, the indirect argument, that internal evidence attests the advanced state of Diderot's theological studies, has some plausibility but is not incontestable.

More material evidence is found in letters sent from Paris by Pierre La Salette of Langres. After writing on 10 August 1741 that the shirts Diderot had received from Langres were quite unsuitable, La Salette wrote again eight days later: 'He needs linen, the dear son! As for the rest, he is well fitted out for from now to 1 January, the time that he has reiterated to me for the execution of his promises.' [54] La Salette's next letter, dated 4 September 1741, once more harps on linen, but it also reveals the nature of Diderot's promises: 'He has let me come to the conclusion that it would be better to send him the cloth for making shirts and collars instead of sending him the shirts and collars ready-made. I have examined his linen. He simply must have some: he was obliged to have the shirts that his dear mother sent him remade. . . . For the rest, he is very well and perseveres in his promises. Saint-Sulpice will be his residence on 1 January next. May God grant him the grace to carry it out for the satisfaction of his family, since it is the profession that he chooses and which no one has urged him to take in preference to all others.' [55]

These references to 'promises' suggest that Diderot really was thinking of an ecclesiastical career when he met his future wife. The celebrated Paris seminary of the order of Saint-Sulpice, founded in 1641 and situated just opposite the famous Parisian church of that name, was at that time the best known and most popular seminary in France for the training of priests. Not organized as a monastery, its object was to prepare young clerics for holy orders and concomitant ecclesiastical functions. So prominent was it that, according to the *Catholic Encyclopedia*, 'When the Revolution broke out the seminary of Paris alone had trained more than five thousand priests, and more than half the bishops who faced that dreadful tempest (about fifty) had been in Sulpician seminaries.'

In the passage from the *Salon* of 1767, Diderot spoke of being a doctor at the Sorbonne and did not mention the Seminary of Saint-Sulpice, of which Pierre La Salette wrote in 1741. Are these two bits of testimony therefore irreconcilable? Almost assuredly not; for, as we have already seen, one had to be an ordained priest to qualify for the doctorate of theology, and there was a close connection between the Sorbonne and the Seminary of Saint-Sulpice. This is demonstrated by a pertinent passage from one of the classics of French literature, published in 1731. In the *History of Manon Lescaut,* written by a man who was himself an *abbé,* the faithless Manon watches the young seminary student from Saint-Sulpice undergo his public examination in the school of theology at the Sorbonne. [56]

It may be concluded, then, that Diderot really intended about the year

1741 to take up an ecclesiastical career. There is no evidence, however, that
he ever actually did enter the Seminary of Saint-Sulpice, only evidence that
he *said* he intended to. Nor is there any evidence whatever that he was
eager to enter this profession. On the contrary, he tells us in an autobiographical passage written in 1773 or 1774 that in 'the classes of the University
my masters could never conquer my disdain for the frivolities of Scholasticism.' He devoured books of arithmetic, algebra, and geometry, he tells us,
and took pleasure in Homer, Virgil, Tasso, and Milton, 'but always coming
back to mathematics, as an unfaithful husband, tired of his mistress, returns
from time to time to his wife!'[57]

This analogy, as characteristic of eighteenth-century manners as it was
of Diderot himself, seems to show that if Diderot intended to become a
priest, it was not precisely because he had what the Methodists term a
'call.' On the other hand, there is no evidence that at this early time in his
life he was yet in flaming rebellion against the Church. It was not until
years later that the necessities of philosophical consistency turned him against
Christian belief. And it is quite possible that he contemplated the priesthood without either eagerness or reluctance. After all, the *abbé,* supported
by some benefice or commendam which provided for an untrammeled life
in secular society, was a very prominent element in the eighteenth-century
French scene. Perhaps, then, Diderot hoped to secure a benefice or sinecure
that would allow him to enjoy both security and the pleasures of scholarship; perhaps he was impressed by the fact that after all two priests were at
that very moment publishing their monumental commentary on Newton;
perhaps he was ready at last to give up his precarious and necessitous independence. At all events, meeting the girl whom he wanted to marry caused
him to lay aside any plans he may have had for a career in which celibacy
was a prerequisite, and presently Diderot was once again being urged by
his family to enter the law office of a solicitor.

CHAPTER 3

Clandestine Marriage

'IT WAS about this time, in 1741,' wrote Mme de Vandeul in her memoir of her father, 'that he made the acquaintance of my mother.' [1]

At this period Anne-Toinette Champion, who was born at La Ferté-Bernard on 22 February 1710, and was in consequence three and a half years older than her future husband, was living with her widowed mother in very modest and straitened circumstances.[2] The family was a respectable one, even though stricken by indigence. 'Mme Champion, a widow with no property,' continued Mme de Vandeul, 'came to Paris with her daughter, then three years of age. A childhood friend of my grandmother gave her a place to stay, and my mother was put into the convent of the Miramiones in order to learn to work with sufficient skill to have no need of the assistance of anyone.' [3] At sixteen, she settled with her mother 'in a small apartment, and both of them carried on the business of dealing in lace and linen. . . . My mother was tall, beautiful, pious, and modest. Various traders had wished to marry her; but she preferred her work and her liberty to marrying a husband whom she could not love.

'My father . . . saw her and wanted to see her again. . . . As he could not pay his attentions so assiduously to my mother without some reason, he told the ladies that he was destined to become an ecclesiastic; that soon he would enter the Seminary of Saint-Nicolas; that he had need of a certain provision of linen, and he besought them to take charge of the matter.' [4]

It does not require a professional detective to deduce some close connection between the collars and shirts that Diderot persuaded Pierre La Salette had to be done over and the fact that the Champion ladies were in that sort of business. Diderot's courtship, as a matter of fact, was an anticipation of the Hollywood boy-meets-girl formula, as he himself, in his later play-wright days, seemed to realize. In his *Father of a Family,* Diderot turned a fond and Narcissan gaze upon recollections of his earlier self. The reckless and impetuous Saint-Albin was modeled, Diderot told his daughter, on the young man who had courted Anne-Toinette.[5]

It is a matter of interest, almost astonishment, that Diderot was able to convince so many people on so many occasions that he intended to become a priest or a monk. In Langres, while still a lad, he intended to become a Jesuit; in Paris, he convinced Brother Angel of his intention to join the Barefooted Carmelites; in 1731 or 1732, according to Diderot's recollections recorded in a letter to Sophie Volland in 1765, he was willing to become a Carthusian monk, although on this occasion, it is true, the prior did not take him at his word;[6] in 1741 he persuaded La Salette that he intended to enter Saint-Sulpice, while at nearly the same time he was leading the Champions to believe that he was about to enter the Seminary of Saint-Nicolas-du-Chardonnet, a nearby and highly regarded training school for priests where Ernest Renan was to be a student a century later. From all these incidents we must conclude that Diderot not only had a convincing way about him but was also so familiar with seminary ways and various religious orders as to sound completely plausible.

Their married years were to prove, abundantly and regrettably, that Denis Diderot and Anne-Toinette Champion were far from temperamentally congenial. What was it about her, then, that so appealed to Diderot in the days of his courtship? The question is, it must be confessed, a silly one. What appeals to any young man in a girl 'beautiful as an angel'? But it is also possible that Diderot, already thirteen or fourteen years away from home and perhaps tired of an existence more than a little Bohemian, was feeling domestically inclined. Anne-Toinette Champion — her name sometimes appears as Anne-Antoinette — did much more for Diderot than she is usually given credit for. Not least of these benefits was the fact that her being hard to win drew Diderot away from that inclination toward dissoluteness and debauchery that was quite evidently a part of his bachelor existence.[7] Those shirts played a great role; how great may be detected in the implications of a remark that Diderot happened to toss off in casual conversation many years later. 'I have heard Diderot say,' wrote Nicolas de Chamfort, an anecdotist of some repute in his century, 'that a sensible man of letters might be the lover of a woman who writes a book, but he ought to be the husband of her only who knows how to sew a shirt.'[8] This remark of Diderot has in it unpremeditated sadness and poignancy because it sums up so accurately the history of his own marriage.

'Nevertheless, they [the Champions] unceasingly referred to his entry into the Seminary,' continues Mme de Vandeul, 'but, having perceived more than once that he was pleasing to my mother, he confessed to her that he had hit upon this fib only for the purpose of being allowed in her home, and assured her with all the violence of his passion and of his character that he was determined not to take orders but, on the contrary, to marry her. My mother made only such objections as reason might suggest; in view of their mutual affection, these objections had little weight. My grandmother declared it to be most contrary to reason to marry oneself to such a hot-head, to a man who did nothing, and whose whole merit, she said, was in having a *golden tongue* with which he turned her daughter's head; but this mother, who preached so sensibly, was herself fond of my father to the point of distraction. . . . Finally they all decided that my father should visit Langres and that he should come back fortified with his family papers and the consent of his parents.' [9]

Meanwhile, even before Diderot left for Langres, the idea of his becoming a lawyer had been revived. This we learn from an undated letter he wrote to Anne-Toinette: 'I have just received a letter from the papa. After a sermon two ells longer than usual, plenary liberty to do anything I want, provided I do something. Do I persist in the resolution of going into a solicitor's office? Order given to seek out a good one and pay down the first quarter right off. . . .' [10] It is interesting that this project of becoming a solicitor crops up a second time in Diderot's life. Perhaps we may conclude that not long previously Diderot had informed his family that he had decided not to enter Saint-Sulpice on 1 January 1742. But did Diderot actually again start work in a solicitor's office? Other letters to his fiancée give absolutely no indication one way or the other. Naigeon implies that he did, by saying that Diderot fell in love 'sometime before entering the solicitor's office,' and Naigeon, though tiresome, is an authority who may not with impunity be ignored.[11]

From these letters to his fiancée it can be deduced that Diderot left Paris for Langres on 7 December 1742.[12] He found his parents much concerned about his future, but also much impressed when galley proofs arrived of the translation he was doing from the English of Temple Stanyan's *Grecian History*: 'My dear sweetheart, these proofs of my book, sent to me thrice a week, are doing wonders. My father and mother, who didn't seem too much inclined to let me go back, are going presently to be the first to hasten my return, so convinced are they that I am occupied up there with something useful. . . .' [13] Moreover, Diderot found that 'the decision that my younger brother has just taken has put the finishing touch to deciding my father to

leave me my freedom.'[14] This 'freedom' may refer to Diderot's previously
stated intentions of becoming an ecclesiastic. Just at this time his younger
brother had entered the seminary to become a priest, and it may be that
the Diderot parents did not desire both their sons to adopt a calling that
precluded their having legitimate children.[15] This did not mean, however,
as Diderot soon found out, that the family was willing to accept any daughter-
in-law he might propose for them.

At first the Langres visit went well: no doubt Diderot's tactful gift of
a book of piety for his father, an Office of the Dead, was well received.[16] It
was probably during this visit, too, that Diderot went to see his sister who
had become a nun, a visit mentioned by Mme de Vandeul, but in a context
that is very vague.[17] It may be that during this comparatively lengthy visit
Diderot let slip some views on religion that made his mother fear for his
orthodoxy, for Diderot's father, writing some years later, makes an allusion
to 'the remonstrances that she made to you by word of mouth.'[18] Since this
visit to Langres is the only one known to have been made by Diderot between his first going to Paris and his mother's death in 1748, this testimony
provides useful evidence in dating the progression of his heterodox ideas,
although it should be admitted that it probably took very little to alarm the
simple faith of his unsophisticated and pious mother.

Diderot's strategy was to persuade his parents to fix an annuity upon him.
Following that, he intended to broach the subject of his intended marriage.
But by this time Anne-Toinette's letters, addressed to him in care of one
of his cousins named Humblot, were reaching him, and one of these epistles,
'full of injustices and cutting words' and evidently accusing him of being
too dilatory, caused him to force the pace.[19] A later letter from Diderot
mentioned that 'thy impatience, which I can only praise, since it is a proof
of thy love, has just hastened my declaration.'[20] This declaration was so
poorly received that Diderot appears to have demanded, in a fit of passion,
that he receive his share of the family inheritance out of hand, failing which
he actually threatened to have his father arrested. It must have been a
tempestuous scene. The fine plans of Diderot the son were quite undone and
Diderot the father took steps of his own. On 1 February 1743, he wrote to
Mme Champion: 'If your daughter is as well born — and loves him as much
as he believes — she will exhort him to renounce her hand. It is only at this
price that he will recover his liberty, because, with the aid of friends of mine
who have been made indignant by his impudence, I have had him put in
a safe place, and we have, I am sure, more than enough backing to keep
him there until he changes his mind.'[21]

Parental authority went rather far in the *ancien régime,* and it was not at all uncommon for heads of families to call to their assistance the supreme authority of the king in cases of particularly stubborn resistance. If passions were too hot, they were cooled off by the simple device of arrest and indefinite detention in some monastery, castle, or prison. Thus the power of the state operated to moderate the passions of junior members of a family while abetting those of the head of it. Unfaithful wives, daughters eager to elope, sons desirous of marrying beneath them could be made unwilling guests of the king for prolonged periods during which it was hoped that leisured meditation would temper the promptings of impetuous desire. The most famous example in the eighteenth century of arbitrary arrests and imprisonments used to enforce family discipline was that of the turbulent Mirabeau family. At one time the Marquis de Mirabeau had every single member of his family, save himself and one other, under lock and key.[22] This was operating on a grand scale, and the Diderots, of course, were not so magnificent. But it is quite evident that Diderot's father intended to utilize the power of the state indefinitely until his son should change his mind.

It is extremely interesting to learn that Diderot was put under coercive detention. It is no less so to know that he escaped it. 'After having experienced unheard-of torments [he wrote to Anne-Toinette], here I am at liberty. Shall I tell you? my father carried his harshness to the point of having me shut up with some monks who have employed against me all that the most determined maliciousness could imagine. I flung myself from the window the night of Sunday going on to Monday. . . . I have come thirty leagues on foot in detestable weather. . . . If you resent the lack of success of my journey and if you should show that you do, I am so overwhelmed with afflictions, I have suffered so much, so many trials still await me, that my decision is taken, I shall finish everything at one stroke; my life or death depends upon the welcome you give me. My father is in such a fury that I do not doubt at all that he will disinherit me, as he has threatened. If I lose you, too, what remains to me that can keep me in this world?

'I shall not be in safety at all in my former apartment, for I have no doubt that Brother Angel has already received orders to have me arrested, orders which he would be only too glad to carry out. Do me the favor then of finding me a furnished room near you or somewhere else. . . .

'[P. S.] I forgot to mention that to prevent my running away, they took the useless precaution of cutting off half my hair.

'In the whole family, I had on my side nobody but one aunt. I went to stay with her during our quarrels.'[23]

On his return to Paris Diderot apparently went underground for a considerable period. Perhaps the only wonder is that the police made no determined effort to catch up with him, for, after all, he had flouted the royal authority. This was an example, one is tempted to think, of how a revolution could incubate in France, for the authority of the state repeatedly showed itself arbitrary and irritating without being resolutely and effectively repressive. During this year of lying low, Diderot occupied lodgings in the Rue des Deux-Ponts on the old Île Saint-Louis, that islet in the Seine which even today preserves an air of detachment, as though living untouched by time in an age gone by.[24]

The family tradition, as reported by Mme de Vandeul, was that Anne-Toinette Champion intended to see no more of her lover: 'She assured my father very explicitly that she would never enter a family where she was not regarded favorably; she asked him to go away, and in spite of his importunities ceased to receive him.' But Diderot became ill, according to this family story: 'My mother could not remain at peace and know that he was suffering. She sent a friend to get news of him. She was told that his room was a regular kennel, that he was without hot food or any care, and was emaciated and melancholy. She thereupon made up her mind, went to see him, promised to marry him, and both mother and daughter became his nurses.' As soon as he could go out, writes Mme de Vandeul, they were married.[25]

It is noteworthy that the marriage, which occurred on 6 November 1743, was not solemnized until the groom had passed his thirtieth birthday. This was probably intentional, for by a royal ordinance of 1697 it had been established that a son who married without his father's consent before the age of thirty could be disinherited.[26] As for the customary marriage settlement, Diderot later wrote: 'My wife's relatives had our contract drawn up and I signed it without reading it. The reason was that I loved her.'[27] Concerning this marriage, the most copious source of information is provided by Jal, an indefatigable and reliable antiquarian: 'Diderot . . . had one ban published at the church of Saint-Louis [-en-l'Île, his parish church], and at the church of Saint-Séverin [Anne-Toinette's parish church], paid for dispensing with the two others, and presented himself before the parish priest of Saint-Séverin for permission to be betrothed and married on the same day in the church of Saint-Pierre-aux-Boeufs. Saint-Pierre shared with the Cardinal Le Moine and some of the small parishes of the city the privilege of solemnizing marriages that were quasi-clandestine. People went there to have marriages consecrated against which there were family repugnances or some scandal or other. Without display, without carriages, without guests, the people to be married presented themselves at an early hour at the sacristy, asked for a low mass, signed the marriage certificate witnessed by four persons, and left the church without bustle or pomp, just as they had arrived there. "Denis Diderot, a burgher of Paris, a son of full age of Didier Diderot, master cutler, and Angélique Vigneron," and "Anne-Toinette Champion, residing at Rue Poupée, in the parish of Saint-Séverin," presented themselves on 6 November, 1743 — the cold favoring the *incognito* that they wished to preserve — at Saint-Pierre-aux-Boeufs, and were united in the presence of "Marie Maleville, residing at Rue Saint-Séverin," of "Jacques Bosson, vicar of Saint-Pierre-aux-Boeufs, of Jean-Baptiste Guillot, former canon of Dôle, and of a neighbor of the bride." ' [28] Saint-Pierre-aux-Boeufs was located on the Île de la Cité, just a stone's throw from Notre-Dame, on a site now occupied by the Hôtel-Dieu. Mme de Vandeul says that the marriage took place at midnight.[29]

Diderot's letters from this period of courtship and engagement trace the familiar progress of a lover from the formal *vous* to the intimate *tu,* and then — when lovers quarreled — the regress back to *vous* again. Here are the endearing nicknames, with a special tinge of Diderot's exuberance on them: 'Ninot' writing to his 'Nanette,' his 'Tonton.' And the letters reveal, too, much of the character and temperament of the bride and groom. They allow us to perceive Anne-Toinette's hardheadedness, her evident ability to be coolly skeptical and disconcertingly realistic. These were congenital qualities, no doubt, but also ones confirmed by the narrowness of a necessitous existence and reinforced by the conviction that life is hard. They were qualities that always grated on that exuberance of his, on his easy enthusiasms, on that half of him that loved to gamble, to buy expensive prints, to be late to appointments, to forget what day of the week it was, and to ignore the fact that a cab he had ordered was standing outside running up a bill. So Diderot expostulates with her, as on 2 January 1743: 'You know my sensitivity. Judge, then, of the state you have put me into. You will be my cruelest enemy if you do not hasten to redress the wrong you have done to him who in the whole world merits it the least and loves you the most.' [30] And in the last letter extant from the period before their marriage, a letter which shows that Anne-Toinette came very close to breaking off the marriage entirely, Diderot complains of the 'hardheartedness of your way of doing things.' [31]

These letters also show us in the early Diderot a Diderot already striking some of his most characteristic poses — the plausible and persuasive Diderot of the golden tongue, facilely making assurances of eternal devotion; the disarmingly candid Diderot, blandly confessing the extent of his previous vagaries in order to show how greatly he had reformed: 'The fire that consumes a young libertine (for I have truly merited the name) for his neighbor's wife is a fire of straw which soon dies down forever; but that which consumes a virtuous man (for I merit this name since you have made me well-behaved) for his own wife never goes out.' Alas! this was not only an erroneous prophecy; it was fustian. Anne-Toinette, however, married him in spite of it, perhaps because of it. And finally, there is revealed in these letters the complacent Diderot, naïvely complimenting himself, as he so frequently did, concerning his own virtue: '. . . my gratitude, my probity, for I pride myself upon having as much of it as any one alive; the tears that I shed when I was on the point of losing you, my oaths of fidelity, thy love, thy qualities of body, heart, and mind, all ought to assure you of an eternal reciprocation on my part.' [32]

For the next year and more, documentary evidence concerning the newly married couple is exceedingly meager. On 13 August 1744 — those who like to count will notice that it was a few days more than nine months after their marriage — their daughter Angélique was born, and was baptized the next day at the church of their parish, Saint-Nicolas-du-Chardonnet.[33] At this time the Diderots were living in the Rue Saint-Victor, a twelfth-century street, part of which is still in existence and in which was located the Seminary of Saint-Nicolas, that seminary which Diderot had once told the Champions that he intended to enter. But between the birth and the death of little Angélique, the Diderots evidently moved. When their six-weeks-old daughter was buried on 29 September at the parish church of Sainte-Marguerite-de-Paris, their address was given as Rue Traversière, then a street in the suburbs, almost in the open fields, out beyond the Bastille.[34] It is astonishing, too, that the parish burial register describes Diderot as a day-laborer. Perhaps to conceal himself from his relatives or the police, Diderot had moved to this out-of-the-way suburb. There must have been some powerful motive operating to induce him to move from the Left Bank, for almost all his long career in Paris was spent in that part of the city. Diderot did indeed possess the Latin Quarter sort of temperament, and the *rive gauche* should be proud of so representative a son.

Diderot's wife lived an extremely retired life, partly because they were impecunious, partly because her husband was jealous, partly because they kept their marriage a secret from the relatives at Langres. So well, indeed, was the secret kept that it was not before 1749, six years after the marriage, that old Didier Diderot heard a rumor that his son was married and the father of children.[35] Moreover, during at least the first four years of their marriage, the Diderots attempted to conceal the fact of that ceremony by having Mme Diderot live under her maiden name.[36] From her point of view, convent-nurtured as she was, it must have been a real sacrifice to have people suppose her children illegitimate. For Diderot, the inevitable result was that he spent a good deal of his time acting like a bachelor, with the unfortunate consequence that he became entirely habituated to that situation. When conditions changed later, he did not change with them, but continued to go his own way, never dreaming of allowing his wife to share any part of his social or intellectual life. Unconsciously he took advantage of her willing self-sacrifice: 'My father was of too jealous a disposition to allow my mother to continue a business that would require her to receive and deal with strangers,' wrote his daughter. 'He exhorted her to give up this business. She experienced great difficulty in consenting to do so: destitution did not frighten her as far as she herself was concerned; but her mother was aged, she was faced with the possibility of losing her, and the thought of not being in a position to provide for all her mother's needs tortured her. Nevertheless, as she persuaded herself that this sacrifice would make her husband happy, she made it. A charwoman came each day to sweep the small apartment and bring the day's provisions. My mother provided for all the rest. Often, when my father was eating out, she dined or supped on bread, and took great pleasure in thinking how on the morrow she would be able to make her customary meal for him twice as good. Coffee was too considerable a luxury for this sort of household; but she did not want him to be deprived of it, and every day she gave him six sous that he might go take his cup at the Café de la Régence and watch them play chess.' [37]

These days of courtship and early marriage saw also the cementing of one of the famous friendships of the eighteenth century, that between Diderot and Jean-Jacques Rousseau. Rousseau's early life is so well known, and is so well told in his *Confessions,* that no mention of it needs to be made here, save to say that in August 1742 he had arrived in Paris with a new scheme of musical notation that he had devised. A Swiss named Daniel Roguin introduced him to Diderot, and there immediately grew up an intimate friendship, based initially on the interest they shared in matters musical.[38]

Temperamentally these two young men were very different, congenial though they were in the first ten years of their friendship. The fact that in their frequent games of chess Rousseau invariably won is itself an indication of their differing personalities and temperaments.[39] Diderot was big-hearted, well meaning, rather grandly negligent, brash, and tactless. Although he deemed himself shy, he was in reality endowed with an over-brimming measure of self-confidence, which Rousseau, to an unusual degree, both lacked and admired. Rousseau, shy, tortured by feelings of inferiority, now and then convulsively assertive, desirous of being led while living in jealous dread that he might be, was just as brooding and paradoxical a person then as he was in the later years when he became famous.

In July 1743, Rousseau left Paris for Venice, where he had an appointment as secretary to the French embassy. Fifteen months later he was back in Paris, having quarreled with his ambassador, and it was there, in March of 1745, that he became interested in Thérèse Levasseur, a servant girl at the hotel at which he was staying, and presently began to live with her.[40] He of course knew of Diderot's attachment and speaks of Anne-Toinette in unflattering terms: 'He had a Nanette just as I had a Thérèse; that constituted between us one conformity the more. But the difference was that my Thérèse, as good-looking as his Nanette, had a gentle disposition and an amiable character, suitable for attracting a virtuous man; while his [Nanette], a shrew and a fishwife, showed nothing to other people that could make up for her bad education.'[41]

In 1812, Anne-Toinette's daughter, herself fifty-nine years old in that year, commented explosively upon these lines, in a spectacular display of filial spirit. Yet she made admissions regarding her mother's difficult temper. 'Where my father was in error was in not forming her for the world, because, born jealous, he did not wish that she should see it. . . . Solitude, domestic cares arising from a very restricted income, the chagrin caused by the love affairs of my father, her ignorance of the manners of polite society, had soured her temper; and to scold became a habit. . . .'[42]

Diderot's marital difficulties were to a large degree his own fault and arose from the fact that he got into the habit of treating his wife as though she were a concubine.

CHAPTER 4

First Fruits

D IDEROT at the age of thirty was a necessitous young man without either reputation or livelihood. His recent quarrel with his family had cut him off from any paternal support, yet he was too independent in spirit to tie himself to a profession or undergo the constraint of being a tutor or take up the daily routine of some occupation in trade or commerce. He had described himself truly to his friend Wille as a person striving to become a philosopher and a man of letters; he was as yet a complete unknown. Certainly his career was not going to be distinguished by traits of unusual precocity, that was already evident; yet he yearned to find glory as well as truth, if we may take as being partly autobiographical his picture of the ambitious child whom the sensible father tries to restrain from leaving home: 'Wretched child, what are you going to do? You are not sure to attain glory, and you rush headlong into poverty.' [1]

The tenor of his life during these difficult years suggests that his principal objectives were intellectual freedom, the 'attainment of glory,' the maintenance of personal independence, and — survival! But to achieve all these things, in proper and desired combination, was not easy. Moreover, Diderot had compounded the risks of his precarious existence by assuming the added responsibilities of a wife and, presently, a child. Had Diderot been less jealous, he might have allowed his wife to continue meeting the public in the small lace and linen trade in which she had earned her livelihood before marriage. Had he been less proud, he might have sought the patronage of the great. It was like Diderot to do neither.

The price paid for this independence was insecurity and impecuniosity. The easy and traditional way would have been to find a rich man to whom to inscribe flowery letters of dedication. But just in these very years literary men of spirit were discovering that it was possible to live a life of independence, even though its cost was high. This is the purport of D'Alembert's

'Essay on the Intercourse of Men of Letters with the Great' (1753) and Dr. Johnson's famous letter to Lord Chesterfield (1755). Yet it was hazardous and far from easy, even for men of talent and courage, to be independent and still avoid hunger. Even the proud and sensitive Jean-Jacques Rousseau was fain to be a secretary to the condescending Mme Dupin. Diderot refused to be patronized. He sought contractual relations, not feudal ones. No doubt his publishers exploited him, as he and his friends were wont to complain, but at least he avoided dependence upon the haughty and uncertain largess of a patron.

Such an attitude led him into an existence of what would now be called free-lancing — and free-lancing at its hazardous and vicissitudinous worst. Probably he received some payment for writing several reviews in a periodical entitled *Observations sur les Ecrits Modernes*. This journalistic enterprise, which was published for eight and a half years beginning 1 March 1735, was edited by the Abbé Pierre-François-Guyot Desfontaines, a man of some literary ability who is remembered for little save that he had the misfortune or bad judgment to fall foul of Voltaire. In a statement made to the Lieutenant-General of Police in 1749, Diderot declared that several of the articles in the *Observations* 'were of my making.' [2] These contributions were published anonymously, however, and it is impossible now to identify Diderot's work in these superannuated pages.

Desfontaines, a competent critic, encouraged Diderot in another branch of letters, although the advice bore no immediate fruit. It is the Abbé de La Porte, writing for his newspaper, *L'Observateur Littéraire,* in 1758, who tells us of the incident. 'I recall what was said to me one day by the celebrated Abbé Desfontaines to whom M. Diderot, then still very young, had presented a dialogue in verse. "This young man," he said to me, "is studying mathematics, and I have no doubt that he is making great progress, for he has a great deal of ability; but from the reading of a play done in verse that he brought to me some time ago, I counseled him to give up these serious studies, and devote himself to the theater, for which I believe him to have a real talent." ' [3] This advice would have had to be given before 1745, since Desfontaines died in that year.

In 1742 Diderot had for the first time the satisfaction of seeing his name in print. His satisfaction may have been alloyed with some vexation, however, for the printer had garbled his name. Over the name of P. D. Diderot there appeared an epistle in verse to a Monsieur B * * *, probably Baculard d'Arnaud (1718–1805), a very second-rate man of letters. This bit of verse appeared in *Le Perroquet,* a collection now as rare as it was then obscure, published at Frankfurt am Main.[4] A flavorsome touch of the archaic is all that distinguishes these competent but rather commonplace lines, which bespeak an author rather more practiced than inspired. Throughout his life Diderot was to turn now and then to this form of expression, being able to produce well-polished occasional verse almost on demand. Some reflections caused by a cold sore, lines written on the back of a letter to Anne-Toinette, and the epistle in *Le Perroquet* are the earliest known examples of his occasional impulses to versify.[5]

It was not as an author, however, but as a translator from the English that Diderot managed to support himself for a number of years. When and why he learned the language is a matter of conjecture; certainly he had done so by 1742, for he was then translating the work on Greece. Perhaps his reason for learning it was the curiosity excited by a book like Voltaire's *Letters concerning the English Nation,* the French edition of which (1734) had introduced into France the ideas of Locke and Newton, as well as British notions of liberty and religious toleration. How he learned the language he tells us himself, by recalling that he passed it through the Latin.[6] This suggests that he taught himself, a supposition the more likely since he appears to have been unable to write English or to speak it, the draft of a letter composed in English late in his life being the sole evidence to the contrary.[7] Still, his ability to read English was an unusual accomplishment in eighteenth-century France, enabling him to go to the fountainheads of English science, literature, and philosophy, and to read English authors who, unlike Bacon and Newton, wrote only in the vernacular.

This was an inestimable advantage for an eighteenth-century Continental thinker. English influences — the writings of a host of deistic authors like Toland and Clarke and Wollaston, arguing for natural religion; the scientific ideas of Bacon, Boyle, and, most important, Newton; the psychological ideas of Locke, emphasizing that all we can ever really know is transmitted to us by one of our five senses — had an exciting and unsettling effect upon conventional ideas, especially upon conventional ideas in France. No doubt it all started innocently enough in the hope that by using the scientific method preached by Bacon and the rational methods used by Newton, men would be vouchsafed the privilege of peering a little deeper into the nature of things. But what happened was that the scientific and rational implications of English ideas greatly affected the metaphysical and theological thinking of the time. Moreover, the doctrines of the English writers and scientists, when transplanted to France, took on an exaggerated and revolutionary character that they did not have at home. Probably the reason was that

Catholic orthodoxy was more absolutist and had less 'give' than the orthodoxy of a Protestant country. At all events, English ideas were the most exciting ones of the eighteenth century, and English thoughts in French heads produced in the long run some astonishing and explosive consequences. Diderot, with his mind and temperament, would naturally have played a leading part in this exciting and dangerous decanting of ideas. But add to this the fact that he was able, unlike many others of his coterie, to grapple with these ideas in the original, and had done so in a number of his early literary chores, and a solid basis is established for his ability to assert and make good his intellectual leadership.

The earliest of Diderot's translations from the English was Temple Stanyan's *Grecian History,* the first complete edition of which had appeared in 1739. The *Dictionary of National Biography* speaks of Stanyan as an excellent scholar and of his history as 'a compilation which held the field until the appearance of the much larger history by William Mitford' almost fifty years later. As we have already seen, the galley proofs of Diderot's translation created a sensation upon their arrival in Langres. The work, entitled *Histoire de Grèce,* appeared in three volumes in 1743.[8] The fortnightly *Journal des Sçavans,* the blue-ribbon periodical of that era, did the history the honor of quoting it copiously in three installments, but of the translator's work it finally remarked, disappointingly, that 'it was written rather negligently.'[9] A Berlin review of Diderot's translation, written in 1773 and no doubt inspired by the malevolence of Frederick the Great, spoke of it superciliously as 'a long task during which the creative spirit of M. Diderot took a rest.'[10] Maybe so; but if one be content to ask no more of a translation than that it be accurate and faithful, a comparison of the original and of the French version shows that Diderot was a quite skillful translator. For the Stanyan work Diderot received the sum of three hundred francs.[11]

Diderot's next exercise in rendering from the English was more a paraphrase than a translation. Yet it is a very important work, indeed, for understanding the growth and development of his thought. The book in question was Lord Shaftesbury's *An Inquiry concerning Virtue and Merit,* which appeared in its French dress in 1745, purportedly published in Amsterdam under the title *Principes de la philosophie morale; ou Essai de M. S * * * sur le mérite et la vertu. Avec réflexions.* It was Diderot who furnished the 'reflections' in a preliminary discourse and lengthy footnotes to which students of Diderot now turn for precious indications of the unfolding of his ideas.[12] Since this book was published in 1745 — Diderot's presentation copy to Rousseau is dated 16 March 1745 — it is to be presumed that Diderot was engaged upon the work in the months following his marriage.[13]

It will be noticed that the French version is anonymous: neither Shaftesbury's name nor that of his translator was mentioned. The reason was that there was some danger involved in presenting to the French public a work that declared so boldly for the existence of a natural morality independent of the sanctions of any particular religion or church. Shaftesbury very much believed in God, but his religion and morality were such as are revealed more by reason than by Scripture. Happily, the French press reviewed the book quite favorably and without too much emotion. The Jesuit *Journal de Trévoux,* a very influential magazine edited at Paris and (since 1734) printed there, ran its review of the book as its leading article for the issue of February 1746. 'Imagine Locke's discoursing on morality,' it said. 'Thus the author appears to us, and, if one wishes, so does the Translator or Compiler of this volume.'[14] But the *Journal des Sçavans,* while favorable, had some mental reservations: 'If he [the author] conducts the human creature, as he says, to the doors of our temples, he seems at the same time to be wishing to excuse him from entering them.'[15]

A comparison of the translation with the original shows that Diderot was quite successful in wrestling with the convolutions of Lord Shaftesbury's syntax, which still remained seventeenth-century even though he wrote in the Age of Addison.[16] Whatever Diderot gained in clarity, however, he probably lost in savor.[17] This was, of course, the fate of almost all English authors in eighteenth-century French translations, Shakespeare most of all. Nevertheless, Diderot was quite faithful to his task — more, even, than he claims to be, for he wrote in his preliminary discourse, 'I have read and reread him; I have filled myself with his thoughts; and then I closed his book, so to speak, when I took up my pen.'[18] Still, there is a great deal of the characteristic Diderot in this little treatise: the mischievous and pointed placing of footnotes where Shaftesbury's implicit heterodoxy was most apparent; the lengthy quotation from skeptical authors like Montaigne or extremely pagan ancients like Petronius; the use of concepts, that, like leitmotives, occur in Diderot's later writings, such as the notion that human beings are like musical instruments of which our passions are the strings;[19] the extremely personal approach to the reader, even in works of philosophy, as in his remark, 'I have passions, and I would be sorry not to have them: I love very passionately my God, my king, my country, my parents, my mistress, and myself.'[20] Moreover, in these notes he indulged his inveterate fondness for flushing more ideas than he could bag, a failing that was alluded to by the reviewer in Desfontaine's *Jugemens sur Quelques Ouvrages Nouveaux,* who named Diderot right out and evidently knew him. 'Let me be permitted to say to him, following Doctor Swift, in whom he frequently takes refuge, that digressions in a book are like foreign troops in a state, making one suspect that the natives lack vigor and courage. . . .'[21]

Most characteristic of all in the *Essai sur le mérite et la vertu* is Diderot's appeal for religious tolerance, which was quite in the spirit of Shaftesbury, too. In the dedicatory epistle 'To my Brother,' Diderot wrote, 'But if you will recall the history of our civil troubles, you will see half the nation bathe itself, out of piety, in the blood of the other half, and violate the fundamental feelings of humanity in order to sustain the cause of God; as though it were necessary to cease to be a man in order to prove oneself religious!'[22]

There is much in Shaftesbury's thought that made a profound and permanent impression on Diderot, who shows in his footnotes to this essay his familiarity with all of Shaftesbury's works.[23] He liked Shaftesbury's doctrine that man is endowed by nature with a moral sense; that man's emotions and passions can work for good and not exclusively for evil, as the older generation of philosophers and Christian moralists had held;[24] that it is possible to build a morality based on reason; and that there is an extremely close relationship, practically an identity, among the good, the beautiful, and the true.[25] Many, moreover, of the anticlerical or anti-Christian facets of Shaftesbury's thought are directly reflected in Diderot's later work, for example, his influential *Philosophical Thoughts.*[26]

Diderot's dedication of his work on Shaftesbury, 'To my Brother,' was perhaps only figurative. Didier Diderot, then studying theology in Paris and approaching his ordination to the priesthood, can scarcely have welcomed the dedication of such a volume even though published anonymously. There is no record of his protesting against the dedication, nor indeed of any intercourse between the two brothers during their joint residence in the capital.[27] For some reason, however, the second edition found 'aunt' substituted for 'brother' in the dedicatory passage.

Diderot's next adventure in translation was a considerable one, but accomplished without 'reflections.' Briasson, the same bookseller who had brought out the Stanyan *Histoire de Grèce,* undertook to publish Robert James's medical dictionary, a work which had appeared in three folio volumes in London between 1743 and 1745. The scope of the work, which may very well have given Diderot ideas of how to lay out an undertaking of encyclopedic character, is worth indicating by quoting its title in all its eighteenth-century lengthiness: *A Medicinal Dictionary; including Physic, Surgery, Anatomy, Chymistry, and Botany, in all their Branches relative to Medicine. Together with a History of Drugs; and an introductory Preface, tracing the Progress of Physic, and explaining the Theories which have principally prevail'd in all Ages of the World. By R. James, M. D.* These ponderous folios (Volume I weighs eleven pounds, fourteen ounces), called by Mark Twain 'A Majestic Literary Fossil,' were illustrated by sixty-three quite good copper plates of surgical instruments and operations, so that the whole work with its broad approach, its sense of the interrelationship of the sciences, its engravings, and its cross references was of a nature to kindle in a person as imaginative as Diderot a lively conception of what a similar work could do for the whole sweep of human knowledge.[28] That there is so close a connection between the *Medicinal Dictionary* and the *Encyclopédie* is conjectural but nevertheless chronologically possible. And inasmuch as Diderot, by his own account, worked almost three years on the project, he must have learned a great deal about putting a work of considerable magnitude through the press.[29] Moreover, it is highly probable that Diderot's deep and abiding interest in physiology, anatomy, and medicine was established as a result of the extensive task of translating Dr. James. Briasson brought the work out in six folio volumes between 1746 and 1748 under the title *Dictionnaire universel de médecine,* etc., 'translated from the English of Mr. James by Messrs. Diderot, Eidous and Toussaint.'[30] It is of interest to learn that Samuel Johnson, a close personal friend of Dr. James, contributed to the *Medicinal Dictionary* its dedication, its prospectus, and some of its articles, so that Diderot probably translated some of Dr. Johnson's august prose.[31]

Diderot was an extremely generous man — though distinctly more generous of his time than of his money — and the work of translating the *Medicinal Dictionary* became the occasion for a remarkable display of this quality. 'He had just undertaken this business when chance brought him two men — the one Toussaint, author of a little work called *Les Moeurs,* the other an unknown — but both of them without bread and seeking work,' wrote his daughter. 'My father, having nothing, deprived himself of two-thirds of the money that he could count upon from this translation, and engaged them to share with him this little undertaking.'[32]

Mme de Vandeul speaks here with a note of unjustified condescension about François-Vincent Toussaint and his famous book *Les Moeurs,* published in 1748 and condemned on 6 May of that year by the Parlement of Paris.[33] *Les Moeurs* was one of the first (and therefore one of the boldest) works in the eighteenth century to set forth the arguments for a natural morality unbolstered by any religious belief or public cult. No doubt Toussaint was inspired and abetted in this daring enterprise, both as to the intellectual content of the essay and the publication of it, by the example of Diderot, whose *Pensées philosophiques* had appeared two years previously. A police report on Toussaint, under date of 1 April 1749, spoke of him as being closely associated with Diderot and D'Alembert and working with them on the *Encyclopédie*.[34] It is true that he contributed some articles on jurisprudence to Volumes I and II of the *Encyclopédie*, but thereafter he had no connection with it; we do not know why.

The 'unknown' mentioned by Mme de Vandeul was the Eidous (Marc-Antoine by given name) who appears on the title page of James's *Dictionnaire*. Eidous had been an engineer in the Spanish army before coming to Paris, where he eked out a long life by doing translations from the English 'by the yard,' as Grimm contemptuously described it.[35] Thus in the fullness of time Eidous became the translator (1767) of Horace Walpole's *The Castle of Otranto*.[36] Eidous existed on the periphery of literature, never translating very well — Grimm said he rendered the English into a language all his own: the Eidoussian language — [37] never venturing to embark by himself on the deep waters of original composition. It was he who was to contribute to chapter XLVII of Diderot's novel *Les Bijoux indiscrets,* a chapter describing the adventures of what Ernest Hemingway would call 'a big, international whore.' Some of Eidous' passages in English and Italian certainly do rival Aretino, as a secret police report of the time said of them,[38] and probably come close to surpassing in pornography anything else that has appeared in print. Diderot's association with this elevating companion appears not to have extended beyond these early years. Eidous did a few unimportant articles for the *Encyclopédie* and thereafter fades out of focus in the Diderotian kaleidoscope.

During this early period — certainly before 1749 — Diderot wrote some notes and comments on a French translation of Pope's *Essay on Man*.[39] This may have been intended to be nothing more than an exercise to improve his powers of rendering from the English, but it may also have had some lasting effect upon his thought. Certainly 'Virtue alone is happiness below,' comes close to expressing Diderot's whole philosophy of living.

Sometime between September of 1744, when they had buried their first-born child in the churchyard of Sainte-Marguerite-de-Paris, and May of 1746, when their second baby was baptized, the Diderots changed their residence back to the Left Bank. The baptism of François-Jacques-Denis Diderot accordingly took place in Saint-Médard, the parish church of the street in which they then resided. The churchyard of Saint-Médard had been from 1728 to 1732 the scene of some healings, alleged to be miraculous, that took place over the tomb of a Deacon Pâris. This man had been a Jansenist, and his fellow sectaries, delighted to discover among themselves a saint (for the Jansenists did not have many), lost no opportunity to publicize his thaumaturgical powers. The result was that enormous crowds visited the place, creating a frightening crescendo of religious frenzy and hysteria. This was the period of the *convulsionnaires*. The government, as unsympathetic to Jansenist miracles as to Jansenists, closed the cemetery, causing some unknown wit to place a placard on the gates: 'By order of the King, God is forbidden to work miracles here.' The excitement slowly subsided, but it left the 'philosophers' of the century shuddering, for to them it seemed to prove the ugliness of religious fanaticism, as well as to reveal that the Jansenists were quite as far gone in obscurantism as any of their antagonists.[40]

Saint-Médard, then, of unsavory memory to a person like Diderot, who alludes to the *convulsionnaires* in several of his *Philosophical Thoughts*, had now become the church of his parish. In the baptismal certificate the Diderots were mentioned as living in the Rue Mouffetard. This street, long, populous, odorous, and poverty stricken, probably looks very much now as it did then, and still offers to the tourist or photographer some of the oldest roofs, the oddest angles, and the most captivating juxtaposition of planes in all of Paris.

While the *Medicinal Dictionary* was still in the process of being translated, Diderot wrote a little book that ought to be considered, in view of the reverberations it caused and the polemics it aroused, one of the most important of the eighteenth century. This was the *Pensées philosophiques*, bought by the book publisher Durand, who was to be one of the partners in publishing the *Encyclopédie;* printed surreptitiously in 1746 by a man named L'Epine; and then sold clandestinely by various bootlegging techniques in which the eighteenth century was becoming remarkably proficient.[41] So incisive and effective was this little book that it came under the disapproving scrutiny of the Parlement of Paris. That court, the highest in the land, in an 'Arrest' of 7 July 1746 condemned the book to be 'torn up and burned . . . by the High Executioner as scandalous, and contrary to Religion and Morals.' In amplification of this decree the Parlement declared that the *Pensées philosophiques* 'presents to restless and reckless spirits the venom of the most criminal and absurd opinions that the depravity of human reason is capable of; and by an affected uncertainty places all religions on almost the same level, in order to finish up by not accepting any.' [42]

The Parlement might have been better advised to spare itself such tremendous ejaculations, for they simply served to draw attention to skeptical ideas and to the author who expressed them. People quickly learned — so many in French society were leisured and unoccupied — who the putative author was, and the ideas set forth immediately took on some of the delicious savor of forbidden fruit. Ideas, especially radical ideas, had an unusually broad and quick currency in eighteenth-century France, which is perhaps the principal explanation why a revolution occurred there rather than in some other country where misery, poverty, and inequality were even greater.

Diderot's work, bold and revolutionary though it was, was by no means the first eighteenth-century expression of skepticism about Christianity. During the first half of the century there circulated in France a very large number of manuscript works, the precursors of the flood of printed attacks that the presses presently began to pour forth. The circulation of these surreptitious manuscripts goes far to explain the rapid gain of new ideas, and the equally rapid collapse of the old, in the years after 1750.[43] And the number of these manuscripts still extant in French public libraries — Professor Wade of Princeton found some 102 separate titles, many of them in multiple copies — is testimony of their pervasion and influence. We can be pretty sure that Diderot was familiar with many of these writings, especially as manuscripts of two of them, now in the library at Fécamp, were copied out in his own hand.[44]

Diderot's book, then, has a close relationship with this underground literature; [45] but it also had characteristics of its own that made it a landmark in the chronic debate between skepticism and faith. The first of these characteristics was boldness, the very boldness of Diderot's allowing it to be printed. In eighteenth-century France it was taken for granted that a function and duty of the state was to punish the expression of opinions against 'Religion.' Therefore the police kept a close watch on authors, printers, and booksellers. Inasmuch as a larger number of persons had unavoidably to be let into the secret, the risks of printing a book were altogether different from the risks involved in the production and circulation of a manuscript. If these dangerous writings were printed in Paris, as they frequently were, they had to be clandestinely printed, often by unlicensed printers who set up their fly-by-night presses in out-of-the-way places and moved them frequently in order to escape the police. Yet some of these clandestine and peripatetic printers were themselves secret agents of the police.[46] By printing a work, one certainly ran a great risk of betrayal. But on the other hand, the very act of printing increased the circulation of one's work and extended its influence.

The *Pensées philosophiques* evidently found a considerable number of readers. In spite of the attempt of the Parlement of Paris to suppress the book, at least ten editions were published in the eighteenth century, plus five books that quoted it in entirety for the purpose of refuting it (a signally obtuse way of spreading the flames while trying to extinguish them), plus five printings in collected editions of Diderot's works, plus a translation into German.[47] Moreover, in contrast to practically all of the clandestinely circulated manuscripts, which had a decided tendency to be tedious and humorless, Diderot's was written with an epigrammatic concision and a sort of grave yet gracious persuasiveness that made his book very effective.* The tradition in his family was that he dashed off the *Pensées philosophiques* between Good Friday and Easter of 1746.[48] This is not impossible, considering that the sixty-two sections of the work comprise about ten thousand words; but it is not very likely, in view of the polish and literary elegance of the aphorisms. They have a gloss and quotability that indicate deliberation and care.

In skill of composition, as well as in boldness of publication, Diderot's *Pensées philosophiques* quickly achieved a position of pre-eminence in its genre. In the form of aphorisms it covered a good deal of ground, much of it no doubt suggested by the writings of Shaftesbury.[49] The tenor of the whole book is deistic, which is equivalent to saying that it suggests that what man can discover about God is made known by reason rather than by revelation. Some examples of the aphorisms will speak for themselves, and give some notion of the impact they must have had:

To judge from the portrait people paint me of the Supreme Being, from His inclination to anger, from the rigor of His vengeance, from certain comparisons that express the ratio between those whom He allows to perish and those to whom He condescends to stretch out a hand, the soul the most upright would be tempted to wish that He did not exist. . . . The thought that there is no God has never frightened anyone, but rather the thought that there *is* one, such as the one that has been described to me (Pensée IX).

Superstition is more injurious to God than atheism (Pensée XII).

What is God? A question which is asked of children, and which philosophers have a great deal of trouble in answering (Pensée XXV).

* An English translation is contained in Margaret Jourdain, *Diderot's Early Philosophical Works* (Chicago, 1916), 27–67.

People have a right to demand of me that I seek the truth, but not that I find it
(Pensée XXIX).

Skepticism is the first step toward truth (Pensée XXXI).

In this little work Diderot defends the passions (Pensée I), a very significant position to take against the prevailing ascetic view held by orthodox
Christian doctrine; he shows himself very anti-Jansenist (Pensées XIII,
XIV) and therefore very opposed to the views expressed by Pascal in his
famous *Pensées;* [50] he quotes Julian the Apostate with complacency, which
was enough, of course, to infuriate the orthodox; if he is not an atheist —
and he claims in this work that he is not, saying, 'I was born in the apostolic
Roman Catholic Church; and I submit myself with all my strength to its
decisions' (Pensée LVIII) — he certainly defends those who are (Pensées
XV, XXI); he casts doubts on miracles (Pensées XLVI, LI, LIII, LIV), an
attack regarded by some critics as the most aggressive and the most telling,
as well as the hardest to answer, in the whole book; [51] by arguing from the
evidence of current studies in natural history and biology, he throws new
light on metaphysical and theological problems, thus making his book a
remarkably original contribution to the literature of deism (Pensées XVIII,
XX, XLV); and in Pensée XIX he gives a sort of preview of his philosophy
of the origin of things, which he was to develop at greater length in later
works.[52]

Diderot became very skillful in the art of writing dialogue, and there
are some critics who feel that the *Pensées philosophiques* is a conversation
among an atheist, an orthodox Christian, and a deist. Both the atheist and
the Christian are confounded by the deist, and the book, in spite of its apparent looseness of construction, thus has an underlying unity.[53]

Diderot's book was important enough to draw considerable enemy fire,
but this counter-bombardment gives the impression of having been more
effective in betraying its own positions than in damaging its assailant.[54] The
defenders of orthodoxy probably realized that their antagonist was redoubtable: some of them acknowledged his book to be 'passably well written' in
'a spirited, energetic, and sprightly style.' [55] Nor was this the last time that
they would have occasion to make such a rueful admission.

CHAPTER 5

The Emerging Philosophe

As Diderot tried to discover for himself a satisfactory philosophy of life, his mind encountered trammels imposed by orthodox, revealed religion. His early works are more concerned with an examination of the truths of religion than his later ones, and there is a consistent directional trend in these first writings. From the theistic belief in a providential God, which we can see in his notes to the translation of Shaftesbury's *Inquiry concerning Virtue,* Diderot proceeds to a somewhat militant deism in the *Pensées philosophiques,* ending that little treatise with the suggestion that natural religion, revealed to us by our reason, is the best. From this point, as we shall see, he proceeds until he arrives finally at a position of outright atheism.

Anyone not well acquainted with a mind like Diderot's might suppose that he adopted skepticism and, later, atheism simply out of a desire to shock, to irritate, or to amuse. In reality, he went through this process of emancipation not to be impudent but to satisfy a sort of intellectual necessity. From first to last Diderot sought to understand the universe in which he lived, and in so doing he always seemed impelled to follow a principle that one might call the principle of greatest possible economy. Diderot was ever reluctant to make greater metaphysical assumptions than were necessary to provide a rational explanation of the world. Thus he found himself giving up Christian tenets simply because he did not find them indispensable and essential: 'If there were a reason for preferring the Christian religion to natural religion,' he wrote, 'it would be because the former offers us, on the nature of God and man, enlightenment that the latter lacks. Now, this is not at all the case; for Christianity, instead of clarifying, gives rise to an infinite multitude of obscurities and difficulties.'[1] Thus he passed from orthodox Christianity through phases of theism and deism to end in a basic physiological, psychological, and neurological materialism that left God out simply because the existence of God was unnecessary, according to this view, to explain the universe.

In the *Pensées philosophiques* Diderot purported to regard himself as still a Roman Catholic (Pensée LVIII). The last 'thought' of all, however, showed him developing the deistic argument that 'natural religion' was best. This theme he amplified in a short work entitled *De la Suffisance de la religion naturelle* ('On the Sufficiency of Natural Religion'), which was not published until 1770.[2] Assézat and Tourneux, editors of Diderot's works, assert that this brief essay was written in 1747, following his *Skeptic's Walk,* although they adduce no evidence to substantiate their assertion. On the other hand, the title and argument of the 'Sufficiency of Natural Religion' are so organically connected with the *Pensées philosophiques* that it seems likely that the little treatise was written in 1746 or early 1747, thus preceding the *Skeptic's Walk,* which in several respects is the more radical of the two.[3]

It is interesting to speculate why Diderot made no attempt to publish this little series of apothegms on natural religion. Perhaps he felt that they represented only a dialectical moment in the development of his thought. In this brief work Diderot speaks frequently of natural law, 'graven in the hearts of all men,' much as Saint Paul spoke of it in the Epistle to the Romans; he declares that religion best that best accords with the goodness and the justice of God; and he ends by saying that 'the truth of natural religion is to the truth of other religions as the testimony that I discover within me is to the testimony that I receive from someone else; as what I feel to what I am told; as what I find written within me by the finger of God, to what vain, superstitious and lying men have written on paper or chiseled in marble. . . .'[4] This sort of argument was common among English deists, not at all unknown among French seventeenth-century freethinkers, and became quite commonplace in the eighteenth century. Here we see 'Reason,' unaided by any reference to the outside world of phenomena, constructing by itself a sort of intellectual fabric. This type of ratiocination, so characteristic of one aspect of the Age of Reason, was nevertheless not at all characteristic of Diderot: his efforts to understand reality were guided not by turning the reason in upon itself, but by relating his mind and understanding to the physical, biological, and psychological phenomena of the outside world. Thus the eleven pages of the 'Sufficiency of Natural Religion,' although interesting, are scarcely a characteristic work. And it may be that this was why Diderot did not seek to publish it. At all events a more dangerous work was soon to come.

In 1747 Diderot was living with Anne-Toinette and their infant son in lodgings in the Rue Mouffetard, only too glad if the police did not know who he was or his family at Langres did not know where. No doubt it was exciting to be the author of a book that had been burned by the public executioner, but it was dangerous, too. A less daring man might have deemed it prudent to wait a while before committing to paper doctrines that were even more inflammable. But Diderot had that itch for writing that is the blessing, and sometimes the curse, of a prolific man of letters, so that an incendiary successor to the *Pensées philosophiques* and the *De la Suffisance de la religion naturelle* presently began to flow from his quill. This was an allegory, almost certainly written in 1747, which he called *La Promenade du sceptique* ('The Skeptic's Walk'), with a sub-title describing it as a 'conversation concerning religion, philosophy, and the world.' [5]

In the preliminary discourse to his allegory, Diderot shows his awareness of the risks run by any author who does not limit himself to the banal. Aristes, the supposed author, examines all the disadvantages of attempting to publish so controversial an item. One of his imagined interlocutors was of the opinion that it was better to be a bad author left unmolested than a good author persecuted. But Aristes, a Diderot-like figure, was reluctant to accept that choice. There was a solution to the dilemma, though rather a drastic one, inasmuch as it involved self-exile and putting oneself into the formidable hands of Frederick the Great: 'Appeal to . . . the philosopher-prince whom you . . . recently heard scolding Machiavelli with such eloquence and good sense.* Pass into his States with your work and let the bigots rage.' [6]

This advice to an author who is a sort of mirror-image of himself may reveal uneasiness on Diderot's part as to his own tranquillity. Police records show that he would have been completely justified in being apprehensive. On 20 June 1747, a man named Perrault wrote to Berryer, the Lieutenant-General of Police, denouncing 'this miserable Didrot' as 'a very dangerous man who speaks of the holy mysteries of our religion with contempt.' [7] Two days later more ample information came in, this time from the priest of the parish in which Diderot lived, a man who stated that he had previously written to Berryer's predecessor in complaint of Diderot. 'M. Diderot is a young man who passed his early life in debauchery. At length he attached himself to a girl without money, but of social position, it seems, equal to his, and he married her without the knowledge of his father. The better to hide his so-called marriage, he has rented lodgings in my parish at the house of M. Guillotte [Guillotte and his wife were the godparents of the

* Frederick's *Anti-Machiavel* was published in 1740.

second Diderot child]; [8] his wife goes by her maiden name. . . . The remarks that Diderot sometimes makes in this household amply prove that he is at least a deist. He utters blasphemies against Jesus Christ and the Holy Virgin that I would not venture to put in writing. . . . It is true that I have never spoken to this young man, that I do not know him personally, but I am told that he has a great deal of wit and that his conversation is most amusing. In one of his conversations he confessed to being the author of one of the two works condemned by the Parlement and burned about two years ago. I have been assured that for more than a year he has been working on another work still more dangerous to religion.' [9]

This 'still more dangerous' work, *La Promenade du sceptique,* described three separate paths and what took place on each. These were the paths of thorns, of chestnut trees, and of flowers, referring respectively to orthodox Christianity, philosophy, and life's more carnal enjoyments. The allegory about Christianity is particularly searching and savage, giving in very thin disguise a critical account of Biblical history and Christian institutions. The residents of this path of thorns are described as soldiers each equipped with a blindfold — that is to say, the symbol of faith — and a white robe, the symbol of innocence. They anxiously grope their way through life. 'The soldier's duties are limited to keeping his blindfold on right and keeping his robe from getting spots.' [10]

'The path of the chestnut trees provides a tranquil abode, and resembles very much the ancient Academy.' Here the mirror-image of Diderot heard representatives of the principal philosophical schools — the Pyrrhonians, the skeptics, the Spinozists, the Berkeleyan idealists or solipsists, the atheists, and the deists — engage in a discussion that critics regard as the solidest part of Diderot's allegory. Not infrequently the path of the chestnuts was invaded by the truculent soldiery of the path of thorns. 'Under our chestnut trees, the chiefs of the path of thorns are tranquilly listened to; their thrusts are expected and are parried, they themselves are brought to earth, they are confounded, they are enlightened, if possible; or at least their blindness is lamented. Gentleness and peacefulness regulate our proceedings; theirs are dictated by fury. We employ reason, they accumulate fagots. They preach nothing but love, and breathe nothing but blood. Their words are humane, but their hearts are cruel.' [11]

The description of the path of chestnut trees incidentally reveals that it was a place of men without women. This is quite enough to explain why Diderot's mirror-image found himself spending some time in the path of flowers. In this rather conventional and final part of the allegory, the burden of the argument is that all is not entirely well in the flower-strewn path. Proof of this contention rests in three little stories, written almost in dialogue form, about a man who swears eternal love to his mistress and then forgets her, about another who steals his friend's mistress, and about a third who by intrigue secures an appointment that he had learned about from a friend who had supposed he was going to get it himself. It is evident that Diderot recommended, if one had the resolution to do it, staying in the shade of the chestnuts.

Diderot's aptitudes were not best suited to the allegory, a literary form that he himself later described as 'the ordinary recourse of sterile minds.' [12] It may be that in experimenting with this form he was following the example of Swift in *The Tale of a Tub,* especially since we know that he was familiar with some of Swift's works.[13] It is interesting and significant that in *La Promenade du sceptique* he frequently seems on the point of breaking forth into the dialogue form, which later became his most effective and personal mode of expression. Indeed, another allegorical satire of Christianity that he is believed to have written about this time, a short tale called *Qu'en pensez-vous?* ('What Do *You* Think?'), is almost all in conversational form.[14] Although *La Promenade du sceptique* is not regarded as one of Diderot's major works, still it is by no means without interest: it shows the vigor and variety of his imagery; [15] it reveals the breadth of his reading, with references to Milton, Montaigne, Rabelais, and many others, besides, of course, a considerable familiarity with the history of philosophy; it reveals his usual dislike of the Jansenists; [16] it shows him already interested in the intellectual problems raised by a person's being deprived of one or more of his senses, problems which were presently to provide the central consideration of his *Letter on the Blind;* [17] and, finally, it again reveals his awareness of the impact of biological fact upon metaphysical speculations, a characteristic destined to make him perhaps the outstanding thinker of his century in the philosophy of science. Because of this emphasis on biological nature he eventually came to be a philosophical materialist, as we shall presently see. But for the moment it caused him to rest at a halfway station between the idea of a deistic universe with Voltaire's watchmaker God, on the one hand, and an atheistic one with no God at all, on the other.[18] This halfway station was a universe that makes God and nature the same thing, the position known as pantheism.

Presumably Diderot hoped to publish *La Promenade du sceptique.* But the police, one way or another, prevented it. According to one version, Diderot, without having to surrender the manuscript, was nevertheless forced to promise the Inspector of Publications, one Joseph d'Hémery, that it would not be published.[19] This story would seem to be confirmed by Diderot's deposition, when he got into trouble in 1749, that although he had written *La Promenade du sceptique,* he had subsequently destroyed the manuscript.[20] But another version of the story, this one told by Mme de Vandeul, is that D'Hémery searched Diderot's house, found the manuscript, and carried it away.[21] This version is confirmed by the fact that Diderot is known to have tried to get the manuscript back some thirty years later, when he was considering the publication of a collected edition of his works.[22] The result of his failure to repossess the work was that the world had to wait until 1830 before the allegory was published. And Diderot's fond recollection began to play him tricks, so that he came to believe that this was one of his best works, which is very far from being true.[23]

In writing about the path of flowers, Diderot described Aristes as meeting a beautiful woman, of whom he speaks in the somewhat rueful and wise-after-the-fact tone of a man looking back upon some untoward experience begun in a night club or bar. 'She was a blonde,' he wrote, 'but one of those blondes that a philosopher ought to avoid.'[24] We wonder if Madeleine d'Arsant de Puisieux was a blonde or if, at least, Diderot did not eventually come to think that she fitted the specification. For a time, however, Diderot was quite under the spell of this rather demanding young Parisienne, a woman seven years his junior. She was the wife of Philippe Florent de Puisieux, a non-practising lawyer who did a great deal of translating, especially from English.[25] It is impossible to say just when the relationship between her and Diderot began. His reference to loving a number of objects 'very passionately,' including 'my mistress,' had appeared by March 1745.[26] But this may not betoken more than Diderot's Gallic feeling that if a mistress did not exist, it would be necessary to invent one. Perhaps the approximate chronology can be established indirectly: in 1751, Mme de Puisieux published a book in which she speaks quite transparently of Diderot and mentions 'five years of familiarity.'[27] If the liaison lasted five years, then it must have begun not later than 1746. This would agree with the story as told by Mme de Vandeul, who says that Diderot wrote his *Pensées philosophiques* at Eastertime in 1746 in order to procure money for his mistress.[28] Probably this is substantially correct, although it must be confessed that Mme de Vandeul's account of the Puisieux affair is demonstrably incorrect in another particular, and consequently may be so in this one. For she claims that Diderot took Mme de Puisieux for his mistress during the absence of Mme Diderot at Langres, whither her husband had sent her in the hope of being able to reconcile his family to the marriage.[29] The fact is that there is documentary evidence that as late as September 1749, Diderot's father did not know that his son was married, and therefore the visit that Mme Diderot made to Langres in 1752 seems to have been her first.[30] Evidently someone in Diderot's family, whether his daughter or himself, was ashamed of his taking a mistress and consequently fabricated this tale, thinking that the plea of connubial privation would palliate the offense.

The little that is known of Mme de Puisieux has about it a disagreeable and distasteful flavor. Of her it has been said 'with too patent humour,' wrote Lord Morely, 'that she was without either the virtue or the merit on which her admirer had just been declaiming.' [31] Mme de Puisieux became a writer of books, no doubt encouraged by Diderot. She was an ambitious authoress, full of vanity and intellectual presumption, as her various prefaces and introductions show, and it galled her very much to be thought to have relied on Diderot for any literary assistance. Thus she is at very special pains in her preliminary discourse to her first book, *Conseils à une amie,* to assert that 'M. D * * *' had nothing to do with the writing or revision of her work.[32] Nobody believed her: the entry under her name in the police records of the office of censorship declared that 'it is Diderot, her very good friend, who did all the body of this book.' [33] The Abbé Raynal, author of a fortnightly news letter, wrote to his subscribers, 'I do not know whose book this is, but I am sure that it has been corrected by M. Diderot . . . .' [34] When the world proceeded to say the same thing about her second book, *Les Caractères,* the lady became shrill: 'When [the first part of] the *Characters* appeared last year, people were disposed . . . to attribute it to a savant who, removed from the world, glories in ignoring its maxims. . . . If the Editor of the *Encyclopédie* is capable of worthily completing so great a work, it would perhaps be impossible for him to compose any as futile as mine. . . .' [35] (These words were published in 1751, and betokened quite evidently that the love affair had ended in bitterness and despite.) As for her protestations of originality, critics observed that her later works, with such unremembered titles as *Alzarac, Histoire de Mlle Terville, Mémoires de la comtesse de Zurlac,* and *Zamor et Almanzine,* did not have the sparkle, nor fulfill the promise, of the early ones. 'The works on morals, by which Mme de Puisieux signalized her first steps in the career of letters,' wrote a mild and not unsympathetic critic, 'acquired for her a glory that she has not been able to dissipate by her novels.' [36] Mme de Puisieux survived until 1795, consumed by vanity to the end. A person who met her when she was sixty years old spoke of her 'ridiculousness,' and her deficiency in judgment and intellectual power, although she was evidently convinced of possessing both to a superlative degree. By that time Mme de Puisieux was stooped and becoming toothless, but 'she kept up all the little airs and affectations that are scarcely tolerable even in a young girl.'[37]

Diderot's love for Mme de Puisieux was consuming, as he himself confessed in a letter to Voltaire in 1749, saying that he was governed 'by a violent passion that has me at its almost complete disposition.'[38] Such an attachment naturally had an upsetting effect in his own home. 'My grandmother died,' wrote Mme de Vandeul, 'my mother remained alone, without companionship. The alienation of her husband doubled the grief of her loss; her character became melancholy, her disposition less gentle. . . . Had her tenderness for my father been able to weaken, her life would have been more happy; but nothing was able to distract it for a moment. . . .'[39]

*   *   *   *   *   *

The recollections of Rousseau in his *Confessions* allow us to see the Diderot of this period in close association with a little knot of friends: 'I spoke to Diderot about Condillac and his work; I made them acquainted with each other. They were made to get along together, and so they did. Diderot undertook to get the bookseller Durand to take the Abbé's manuscript. . . . As we lived in districts very far from one another, we used to meet, all three of us, once a week at the Palais-Royal, and then go to dine together at the Hôtel du Panier Fleuri. It must have been that these little weekly dinners were extremely pleasing to Diderot, for he, who used to miss almost all his appointments, never missed one of these. I was then forming the project of a periodical paper, to be called *Le Persifleur,* which Diderot and I were to do by turns. I sketched out the first number, and that made me become acquainted with D'Alembert, to whom Diderot had spoken about it. But unforeseen events blocked us, and the project remained where it was.'[40]

The power of Paris to draw to itself the talents of France is exemplified by the association around the table of the Panier Fleuri of these four young men — D'Alembert, the Parisian foundling; Condillac, the nobleman from Lyon; Rousseau, the plebeian from Geneva and Annecy; and Diderot, the bourgeois from Langres. Thus it had been for centuries — in university and intellectual affairs since the time of Peter Abelard, in political and social life at least since Francis I and the Age of the Renaissance and the time of Montaigne. A present-day map of the railways of France, all converging on Paris, is a chart, so to speak, of the intellectual history of France for the past few centuries. In Paris was to be found the stimulating and fructifying company of the first-rate, such as the D'Alemberts, the Condillacs, the Rousseaus, and the Diderots, teaching one another, exciting one another, profiting from the intellectual facilities and reveling in the history and monuments of so great and so venerable a city. Of all of this Diderot was now a part. He was a 'bourgeois de Paris,' as the birth certificates of his children described him. As he walked (if he took the closest route) from the Rue Mouffetard to his weekly rendezvous at the Palais-Royal, he would pass, as a tourist might do today, the great old church of Saint-Etienne-du-Mont, where Pascal and Racine are buried; the Pont-Neuf, where Henri IV was assassinated; and Saint-Germain-l'Auxerrois, where the tocsin sounded for the Massacre of Saint Bartholomew's Day. As he walked the streets of Paris, he may often have recalled Montaigne's words about the city, words he probably knew, for Montaigne was one of his favorite authors:

Paris has possessed my heart since my infancy. I am French solely because of this great city, especially great and incomparable in its variety; the glory of France and one of the noblest ornaments of earth.*

The little circle of friends mentioned by Rousseau was composed of men all destined to be eminent. Condillac, although handicapped by eyesight so poor that it is said he did not learn to read until he was twelve, became the leading psychologist of his generation. His specialty was interpreting to his countrymen the psychological doctrines of John Locke (although he was unable to read him in the original), and carrying these on to further conclusions. This sort of speculation placed him on the frontiers of knowledge, in the shadow ground between psychology and metaphysics, as may readily be seen in his works, for example *Essai sur l'origine des connaissances humaines* ('Essay on the Origin of Human Understanding,' the book Diderot helped get published in 1746). One year younger than Diderot, Condillac had taken holy orders in 1740 and, even though it is said of him that he celebrated mass only once in his life, he evidently was very careful not to write anything that could be proved hostile to the Church. Eventually Diderot and he drifted apart, perhaps on this issue. Remarkably enough, Condillac, though often quoted in the *Encyclopédie,* is not listed as having contributed any articles. It is hard to believe, considering Condillac's reputation, that Diderot did not desire him as a contributor, and accordingly it may be presumed that Condillac deemed his association with Diderot too compromising. Nevertheless, their close association, while it lasted, was of

* Paris a mon coeur dès mon enfance. Je ne suis Français que par cette grande cité, grande surtout et incomparable en variété, la gloire de la France et l'un des plus nobles ornements du monde. (These words are on the plinth of Landowski's statue of Montaigne, erected in 1937 on the Rue des Ecoles facing the Sorbonne.)

great value to both. On Diderot's side this can be seen in his *Letter on the Blind* (1749), a work much more basic in its psychological and metaphysical concepts than any previous one. As for the influence of Diderot on Condillac, the latter's *Traité des sensations* (1754) was the result of Diderot's pointing out in his *Letter on the Blind* the apparent congruence of Condillac's presuppositions with those of the British philosopher, Bishop Berkeley.[41] 'Diderot merely pointed out some troublesome affinities between two works that, in all other respects, had no relationship,' writes the leading authority on Condillac. 'With an astonishing critical sense, he had foreseen the problem which Condillac's attempt involved.' [42]

Jean Le Rond d'Alembert, of whom we shall hear much, was four years younger than Diderot. He was the illegitimate child of one of the most celebrated, not to say notorious, women of the eighteenth century, and of the Chevalier Destouches, a lieutenant general in the French army. He was left a foundling on the steps of the church of Saint-Jean-le-Rond (the baptistry of Notre-Dame de Paris), and from this circumstance took his name. The wife of a glazier, one Mme Rousseau, took care of him in infancy and mothered him into middle age. He remained with her, occupying a modest little room in her humble home, until he was forty-seven years of age and one of the most famous men in Europe, but without her ever realizing, it is said, how celebrated her adopted chick had become. Unlike Diderot, D'Alembert was unusually precocious. When only twenty-five years of age, he had become an associate member of the Academy of Sciences. At twenty-six he published his *Treatise on Dynamics,* which, according to the principal French biographical dictionary, was 'an event in the history of the sciences.' [43] D'Alembert was slight and small in stature, with a marvelously intelligent and attractive face, as we see it in La Tour's pastel of him, with a clear and piercing falsetto voice which permitted his enemies to hint that he was not quite a man, and with a skill at mimicry which was the hilarious delight of his companions.

In this small circle of friends, vis-à-vis the psychologist, the mathematician, and the musician (for Rousseau about this time undertook to write the articles on musical theory for the projected *Encyclopédie*), Diderot proved his versatility by being profoundly interested and instructed in the specialty of each. One earnest of this breadth and competence was an article he published anonymously in the October 1747 number of the *Mercure de France*. Entitled 'Project for a New Organ,' [44] it was later republished, under Diderot's own name, in his *Mémoires sur différens sujets de mathématiques* (1748), and excited a good deal of interest on the part of the editor of the *Gentle-*

man's Magazine, the leading London review of the day. What Diderot had in mind were improvements in the simple hurdy-gurdy bird organs or mechanical organs of the time. These instruments — for an excellent description of the bird organ, see Diderot's own article *'Serinette'* in the *Encyclopédie* and the corresponding engraving — had a range of only one octave and a repertory of only a few tunes.[45] Diderot's principal innovation, simple but effective, was designed to increase greatly both the acoustical range and the repertory of such an instrument. A barrel organ constructed according to his description would permit people, even those unable to play an instrument, to 'set up' quite complicated pieces of music, and thus make music more readily accessible to all. Apparently, too, Diderot had in mind the construction of instruments large enough to be played in churches. He also suggested a chronometer for accurately indicating tempi, in this respect anticipating Maelzel's metronome. Observing this early interest, it is not surprising to learn that, when the *Encyclopédie* was to be done, Diderot assigned to himself the articles on musical instruments, their construction, their acoustical characteristics, and the method of playing them.

Diderot's 'Project for a New Organ' was a very characteristic performance. In the first place, it shows him being alertly curious, original, and inventive and also reveals a constant fascination in the relation of pure theory to applied knowledge and to gadgets. Thus, as he discusses how to place the pins on the organ cylinder in order to increase its range, he shows an equal awareness of both theoretical and technological problems. Another of Diderot's hallmarks was his ability to introduce into a discussion of any subject a marked quality of subjectiveness, an intimate revelation of personality — even in an anonymous article on a technical subject. This quality delighted the editor of the London *Gentleman's Magazine* as much as the proposed invention itself. 'What suggested the notion to the author, who appears very well versed in physics and geometry,' wrote the editor in the leading article of the August 1749 issue, 'may be seen by the following extract from his work: "For my part, who am hardly more bashful, or less curious than a child, I had no rest nor ease, till I had examined the first German organ I heard; and, as I have no skill as a musician, but am a great lover of music . . . it came into my mind . . . that it would be very convenient . . . to have such an organ, or some other instrument, which might require neither more natural fitness, nor less acquired knowledge, and on which one might perform all sorts of musical compositions." ' [46]

Later in the eighteenth century there was a marked improvement, both in France and England, in instruments using the barrel-and-pin mechanism, but perhaps to attribute this to Diderot would be no more than argument on the level of *post hoc, ergo propter hoc*.[47] In the *Gentleman's Magazine* for September 1749, a reader from Lancashire inquired 'whether your account of M. Diderot's organ has yet set the musico-mechanical artists of London at work, or is likely to do so. The design in all probability must take. It has many recommendations, one especially, which will weigh both with those that are performers in music, and those who are not; I mean by having the barrel-pins moveable.'[48] It is therefore tempting to believe that Diderot's influence was at work during the late eighteenth and early nineteenth centuries, when the application of the barrel-and-pin mechanism to the organ became very common in England. Indeed, Dr. Scholes, the well-known British musicologist, found one of these organs still in weekly use in a Suffolk church in 1934.[49]

Diderot always delighted in being called a philosopher, or, better yet, *the* philosopher. In many respects he had been qualifying himself for the appellation in the usual sense of the term. For in 1746-7 he was already proficient, as his writings show, in the history of philosophy; he was already concerned with problems of ethics, of the nature of God and man's relation to Him, and with the problem of being. Already we see him rummaging about in the philosophy of science, trying to use mathematical, biological, and physiological insights as aids in the investigation of ultimate things.

But more than this, Diderot wanted to be a *philosophe* in that special sense of the French word which the English does not quite convey. What, then, is a *philosophe?* The answer is not easy, partly because in the eighteenth century the word was dynamic and fast-moving. At the beginning of the century, according to Muralt, a Swiss who wrote extensively on the manners of the French, the term *'philosophe'* was one of reproach and almost of insult, betokening a person who desired to live in moody and invidious solitude.[50] But fifty years had been changing all that; *'philosophes'* declared themselves to be as sociable as any other Frenchmen, and the word began to take on pleasing connotations. Moreover, it became a party name, with all the blood-quickening and adrenalin-stirring attributes that party names generate. It is easy to see in part what the *philosophes* meant by 'philosophy' if we turn to the article *'Philosophe,'* long regarded as one of Diderot's best, in the *Encyclopédie*. In reality this article was a shortened version of one written by some unknown person and first printed in 1743, possibly circulated in manuscript form before that.[51] It may be fairly assumed that Diderot was likely to have known the piece by this time (1746-7) when he was just moving into his responsibilities with the *Encyclopédie*. His enthusiasm for the article may be inferred from the fact that he published the scissors-and-paste version in the *Encyclopédie,* whether he 'wrote' it himself or accepted it from another hand. And the following excerpts from the 1743 edition, copied almost verbatim in the *Encyclopédie,* will give some idea of what an eighteenth-century *philosophe* thought himself to be:

Reason is to a philosopher what grace is to a Christian in the system of Saint Augustine. . . .

. . . .

The philosophical spirit is, then, a spirit of observation and exactness, relating everything to its true principles; but it is not the mind alone that the philosopher cultivates . . . Man is not a monster who should live only in the deeps of the sea or the depths of a forest . . . his needs and well-being engage him to live in society. Thus reason demands of him that he know, study, and labor to acquire sociable qualities.

. . . .

. . . our philosopher, who knows how to divide his time between withdrawal from men and intercourse with them, is full of humanity. He is the Chremes of Terence, who feels himself a man and who interests himself in the good or bad fortune of his neighbor out of humanity alone. *Homo sum, humani a me nihil alienum puto.*
. . . Civil society is, as it were, the only divinity that he recognizes on earth; * he worships it, and honors it by probity, by an exact attention to his duties, and by a sincere desire not to be a useless or troublesome member of it. . . .

. . . .

The philosopher, then, is an honest man who acts in all things according to reason, and who combines good morals [*moeurs*] and sociable qualities with a mind disposed toward reflection and preciseness.[52]

From these quotations it is possible to see some of the reasons why the term '*philosophe*' became a pleasant word in the eighteenth century, resonant with such happy overtones. On the affirmative side, it betokened a sense of social awareness and responsibility which appealed to the sympathies and large-mindedness of many well-intentioned persons. Moreover, the *philosophe* was inherently a man of probity and virtue, par excellence the virtuous man. On the negative side, it turned out that to be a *philosophe* was easy. No one need fret over such painful prerequisites as that of knowing the difference between ontology and epistemology. The ticket of admission to the chestnut path bore no pedantic stipulations having to do with a tech-

* The *Encyclopédie,* more circumspect, reads at this point, 'For him, civil society is, as it were, a divinity on earth . . .'

nical knowledge of the subject. As Professor Dieckmann points out, the author of this treatise (and, following him, the party of the Encyclopedists in general) 'does not conceive of the philosopher as the author of a system of ideas or the creator of a comprehensive interpretation of the world. . . . The philosopher thus conceived appears as a model, an ideal norm after which one strives, as one strove during the Renaissance to be an *uomo universale,* or *cortigiano,* and in the nineteenth century a *gentleman.*' [53]

Diderot was a philosopher. He was also a *philosophe.* His early writings, skilled in the technicalities of the philosophical method, using the word in its usual sense, were also beginning quite unmistakably to show the characteristic approach described by the author of the treatise on 'The Philosopher.' The *philosophe* was beginning to emerge.

CHAPTER 6

The Early History of the *Encyclopédie*

THE French *Encyclopédie,* as it stands today on the shelves of library treasure rooms in the select company of the very old, the very rare, and the very naughty, is an enormous work consisting of seventeen folio volumes of letterpress and eleven of engravings, to say nothing of four volumes of supplement, two of index, and one of supplementary plates. Yet at its inception the *Encyclopédie* was a modest venture, planned to be no more than a translation in four volumes (plus one of engravings) of Ephraim Chambers' *Cyclopaedia, or Universal Dictionary of the Arts and Sciences,* a very successful work first published in 1728 in two folio volumes embellished by twenty-one large plates. It was Diderot who in all probability was principally responsible for the expansion from the smaller project to the larger one. At the very least, it was he who became responsible for seeing it through. And thus was produced, as a modern French critic has remarked, 'not the finest, but surely the most characteristic, work of the French eighteenth century.' [1]

Previous to that time there were in existence various technical dictionaries or dictionaries of classical literature and learning.[2] There had even been a Latin *Encyclopaedia* published in 1630 by Johann Heinrich Alsted, a work which treated of philosophy, philology, theology, jurisprudence, medicine, history, and the mechanical arts. But by the end of the seventeenth century this estimable work was outmoded, and no less a person than the great Leibniz expressed the hope that a new encyclopedia would soon be forthcoming.[3] In view of the continuing spread of knowledge and education in Western Europe, a comprehensive reference work was needed that would inform its readers of the numerous discoveries in basic science made during the seventeenth century and also attempt to guide their understanding of the whole by means of some scheme or conspectus of the interrelationships of the several branches of knowledge. As we look back on the intellectual preparation of Western

European society two hundred years ago, we are not surprised that a considerable market existed for such works as Chambers' or the more ambitious one of Diderot.

Chambers' *Cyclopaedia* was prefaced by an elaborate scheme of the divisions and subdivisions of knowledge. It was 'the first attempt that had yet been made at once to arrange Knowledge by the Alphabet, and to exhibit a view of its relations and dependencies,' [4] features which the French *Encyclopédie* also adopted. Chambers' *Cyclopaedia* was very like a present-day dictionary, especially in its emphasis on the definition of common words. There was a particular abundance of medical and pharmaceutical terms, but no attempt was made to include geographical, historical, or biographical information. Moreover, it was severely limited in the number and scope of its engravings, which were devoted to such subjects as heraldry, surveying, sun dials, algebra, geometry, trigonometry, and navigation.

The plan and intent of Chambers' work was acknowledged by everyone, including Diderot, to be excellent. The execution, he contended, left something to be desired. Though more inclusive than any other existing work, it was still not comprehensive enough, and its treatment was frequently too brief. 'The entire translation of Chambers has passed under our eyes,' wrote Diderot in the prospectus of 1750, 'and we have found a prodigious multitude of things needing improvement in the sciences; in the liberal arts, a word where there ought to be pages; and everything to be supplied in the mechanical arts.' [5] So important a subject as 'Agriculture,' for example, was allotted in Chambers thirty-two rather jejune lines. In contrast, the article that Diderot wrote on that subject for the *Encyclopédie* fills fourteen columns and, among a host of other topics, gives publicity to Jethro Tull's discoveries in new methods of husbandry. This instance shows the breadth of Diderot's interests, and reveals also how the *Encyclopédie* became a forum for new ideas.[6] Diderot had a right to say that 'the articles of Chambers are laid out regularly enough, but they are empty; ours, though irregular, are full.' [7]

In France, during the very years when Chambers was preparing his *Cyclopaedia* for the press, there was formed an ephemeral Société des Arts (1726), which cherished the hope of publishing a sort of encyclopedia in which related arts, sciences, and mechanical arts would be described.[8] Though revealing the ferment of ideas, this project had no concrete result, nor any connection with the later *Encyclopédie*. Another project that might have resulted in an *encyclopédie* was of Masonic origin. A prominent Freemason named Ramsay declared in Paris in 1737 that 'all the Grand Masters in Germany, England, in Italy and throughout Europe exhort every savant and

artist in the brotherhood to unite for furnishing materials for a universal
dictionary of liberal arts and useful sciences, theology and statecraft excepted.' [9] Moreover, the Duc d'Antin, Grand Master of the Freemasons in
France, repeated and endorsed Ramsay's ideas in a discourse pronounced in
the Masonic Grand Lodge in 1740.[10] Statements such as these naturally have
caused historians to wonder whether there was not some direct connection
between Freemasonry and the *Encyclopédie,* and this supposition has been
heightened by the discovery that André-François Le Breton, one of the publishers of the *Encyclopédie,* was made a Master Mason in a lodge at Paris
in 1729.[11] No evidence, however, has yet been turned up to suggest that
Diderot was at any time a Mason.[12] In sum it seems safe to follow the judgment of a leading modern authority on the subject that Masonry and the
Encyclopédie, however similar in attitude, were born in two different and
distinct moments as a result of two different and distinct needs in the France
of the eighteenth century.[13]

   Actually, the project for translating Chambers was the result not so much
of an ideological enterprise as it was a search for profit. In June 1744 Le
Breton had signed a contract with one Godefroy Sellius, a German from
Danzig, for a translation of the works of a German metaphysician, at that
time of great repute, named Wolff.[14] This project appears not to have
achieved publication, but in January of 1745 Sellius suggested to Le Breton
the translation of Chambers' *Cyclopaedia.* Sellius claimed to have found a
'rich and opulent' partner, an Englishman named John Mills. In February
1745, Mills and Sellius entered into a contract, and just a few weeks later the
two of them contracted with Le Breton to provide a translation, corrected
and enlarged, of Chambers' *Cyclopaedia,* to consist of four volumes of letterpress and one of 120 plates.[15] During this time Le Breton was evidently in
negotiation with the authorities for a license, for there was issued in blank
on 25 February 1745 a license good for twenty years, which, in the further
processes of being sealed and spread on the records of the corporation of
booksellers, on 26 March and 13 April respectively, lost its anonymity and
appeared in Le Breton's name.[16]

   On the strength of these preparations, a prospectus was printed in the
spring of 1745, antedating by five years the more famous one that Diderot
launched in 1750. This comparatively unknown prospectus of 1745, announcing an *Encyclopédie, ou Dictionnaire universel des arts & des sciences,*
is a great rarity among book collectors.[17] Besides stating the terms of subscription, the prospectus emphasized its intention of providing a polyglot
cross-reference system for the titles of articles, and included some sample

articles, translated from Chambers, such as 'Atmosphere,' 'Fable,' 'Blood,' and 'Dyeing.' Several would-be subscribers presented themselves at once,[18] and the *Journal de Trévoux,* in its number for May 1745, quite outdid itself in the warmth of its remarks. 'To judge by the Prospectus,' it wrote, '. . . there is nothing more useful, more abundant, better analyzed, better related, in a word more perfect and finer than this *Dictionary;* and such is the gift that M. Mills is making France, his adopted country, while doing honor to England, his true one.' [19]

John Mills lived to become an appreciated writer on agricultural affairs in England, and the *Dictionary of National Biography* speaks of him with approbation. His relations with Le Breton, however, were exceedingly stormy, and ended in an exchange of blows on 7 August 1745. Mills, apparently, had misrepresented both his financial situation and his command of the French language. Moreover, Le Breton had supposed that his own relation with the enterprise would be merely as printer and agent rather than entrepreneur. It was necessary, for instance, that some French citizen be the intermediary for Mills and Sellius, both of them foreigners, in negotiations with the authorities for a license. Le Breton declared, when he printed his side of the story, that the translations by Sellius were so poor that they could not be used, that Mills was remiss and tardy in the revision of these articles, and that meanwhile he, Le Breton, was so frequently asked for advances in money that he became convinced that Mills and Sellius were making him their dupe.[20] Mills's urgent demand in August for a very large sum of money, coupled with Le Breton's discovery that far from being an heir to a large estate, Mills was only a sort of clerk in the Paris branch of a British bank, led to that kind of mutual explanation that is likely to end in an explosion.

Suit and countersuit were filed after the quarrel. Mills asserted that Le Breton had not only hit him in the stomach and struck him twice over the head with a cane, but had also cheated him of subscription money and was intriguing to get sole possession of the copyright.[21] Le Breton said, among a number of things, that he 'taught this arrogant Englishman that a Frenchman, if insulted, even though his weapons be inferior, avenges himself at once, as much as in him lies.' [22] The case did not come to trial. Instead, the Chancellor of France, the highly respected D'Aguesseau, one of the most famous magistrates in the history of the *ancien régime,* took direct cognizance of it. Such action was ordinary enough, for the chancellor of France was ex officio responsible for censorship and other matters pertaining to the policing of the book trade. Le Breton asserted many years later that

D'Aguesseau, upon examining Mills and Sellius, 'quite easily detected their incompetence and their swindling.' [23] No damages were assessed against Le Breton, and soon afterward Mills left France.[24]

The Chancellor allowed Le Breton to hope that after a short time he would be allowed to take up the project again. For the moment, however, the Council of State, on D'Aguesseau's recommendation, revoked the license that had been granted the preceding February, and declared Le Breton's contract with Mills and Sellius to be void. The 'Arrest' of the Council of State alluded to various infractions of the regulations regarding subscriptions committed by Le Breton but specifically mentioned the possibility of securing a privilege anew.[25]

Although the project was now in abeyance, sufficient public interest had been aroused by the prospectus of 1745 to encourage Le Breton to resume his plans as soon as possible. An earnest of public curiosity is to be seen in the remarks of an anonymous author, writing in the *Jugemens sur Quelques Ouvrages Nouveaux*: 'What an astonishing, an admirable dictionary is that of M. Chambers, entitled the *Cyclopaedia, or the Circle of Sciences,* which ought to be translated from the English into French, and for which subscriptions were even beginning to be taken at Le Breton's, bookseller of Paris, but for which the license has been revoked because the enterprise has appeared to be poorly planned. It is very much to be hoped that this project will be undertaken again without delay, under better auspices, and that our French printing industry, which, suffering grievously from the hardness of the times, has need of being encouraged and favored, may profit from so lucrative an undertaking, for it would be regrettable to see foreign countries, protected by the formalities of our regulations, enrich themselves, to the great shame of our own industry.' [26]

Unable to count upon the 'rich and opulent' Mills but now intent on publishing a translation of Chambers himself, Le Breton evidently felt that he needed more capital. In October 1745 he took into partnership for this particular venture three of his fellow-publishers, Briasson, the elder David, and Laurent Durand.[27] This partnership agreement was supplemented by another in which it was stipulated that Le Breton was to do the printing job for the whole venture, and a total edition of 1,625 sets was planned.[28] In December 1745, the government renewed the license that had been annulled the previous 28 August and this renewal was officially sealed and promulgated on 21 January 1746.[29] The translation of Chambers' *Cyclopaedia* was once more under way.

It is hard to say when or how Diderot first became associated with the project. It may have been as early as the summer of 1745, for Le Breton spoke in his memoir of that year of some unnamed 'intelligent person' who was to have corrected the whole Sellius-Mills translation, 'and without whom the Prospectus would not have been welcomed as favorably as it has.' [30] This 'intelligent person' may have been Diderot. Or perhaps it was through his publishers, Briasson, David, and Durand, that he became associated with the project. Briasson had been the publisher of Diderot's translation of the *Grecian History;* all three of them had collaborated in publishing James's *Dictionnaire universel de médecine;* [31] and one of them, Durand, was the publisher of Diderot's edition of Shaftesbury, off the press that very year.[32] The entries in the publishers' account book of the *Encyclopédie* show payments to Diderot beginning in 1746 — 60 livres in February, 30 livres on 4 March and 15 on 31 March, 90 livres on 30 April, 120 on 1 June.[33] At this time he was certainly on the pay roll, but still a goodly distance from being entrusted with the principal direction of the enterprise.

It has also been asserted that Diderot was introduced to the project of the *Encyclopédie* by the Abbé Jean-Paul de Gua de Malves, a brilliant but eccentric and unstable mathematician. According to the famous Condorcet, who wrote a eulogy of Gua de Malves at the time of his death (1786), it was the Abbé who recruited Diderot, among others, to assist in the work.[34] Gua de Malves, who was described in a secret police report in 1749 as having the manner and countenance of a crazy man, first appears in the account book of the publishers at the same time that D'Alembert makes his appearance there — December 1745 — and a few weeks before Diderot.[35] On 27 June 1746, the Abbé became the principal editor of the project that became the *Encyclopédie,* by virtue of signing a contract of which Diderot and D'Alembert were the witnesses. In accordance with this agreement, he was to 'extend the part having to do with the arts, preferably, as much as it will be possible for him to complete.' [36] Whether or not he had recruited them, Gua de Malves retained both Diderot and D'Alembert to work on the project, assigning to each of them twelve hundred livres, to be paid from the total of eighteen thousand livres that he himself was to receive. Moreover, Diderot and D'Alembert were to enjoy a sort of veto power in judgment of the accuracy of translation of the English articles.[37]

The new chief editor was a learned man, described in the contract as 'member of the Royal Academy of Sciences, of the Royal Society of London, Reader and Royal Professor of Philosophy at the Royal College of France.' He was also extraordinarily headstrong and stubborn, and, as Condorcet says, 'it would have been difficult for there not to arise frequent disputes between a savant who saw in the undertaking only an enterprise useful for the perfecting of human knowledge or public instruction, and booksellers who saw in it only a business matter. M. l'Abbé de Gua, whom misfortune had made more easily wounded and more inflexible, soon grew disgusted and abandoned this work on the *Encyclopédie.'* [38]

In the light of this documentary proof of their association with Gua de Malves, it is more than a little odd that neither Diderot nor D'Alembert ever alluded in their writings to the connection of Gua de Malves with the *Encyclopédie,* leaving us to wonder how much this taciturnity was inspired by a deliberate intent to mislead. Just what the relations between him and Diderot were can only be inferred, the sole evidence being a single remark about him made by Diderot in his later works, an allusion rather ungenerous in tone and one which made no reference to the *Encyclopédie.* Wanting an example of the tendency of some persons to run to extremes, Diderot found it in 'that old *abbé* one sees on one's walks. . . . the Abbé de Gua de Malves. He is a profound geometrician. . . . but in the street he does not have common sense. In one year he straitened his income by assignments upon it; he lost his professorship at the Royal College; he got himself excluded from the Academy, and consummated his ruin by the construction of a sand-screening machine that never separated out a single particle of gold; returning poor and dishonored, he fell on the way back while walking a narrow plank and broke a leg.' [39]

The lack of satisfactory evidence for determining to whom should belong the credit of first having proposed a much expanded project, Diderot or Gua de Malves, has occasioned something of a who-killed-Cock-Robin dispute among authorities. [40] Condorcet, who was personally acquainted with all the men involved, uncompromisingly declared that Gua de Malves had the idea first. 'He had had time to change the form of it; it was no longer a mere augmented translation — it was a new work, undertaken on a vaster plan.' [41] However, Condorcet adduces no documentation. Moreover, he was writing after the death of all the persons involved, so that any misstatements he may have made were not subject to contradiction. Condorcet says that Gua de Malves recruited Diderot and D'Alembert, but he also claims that Gua de Malves recruited other persons, such as Condillac, Mably, and Fouchy, who in fact did *not* co-operate. There does, then, exist a possibility that Condorcet was partially misinformed; and over against his testimony can be set that, equally unsupported, of Naigeon, who declared, to bolster his insinuation that Gua de Malves's association with the project did not amount to much, that 'the first project . . . was limited to the translation of Chambers' English *Encyclopedia,* with some corrections and additions that the Abbé de Gua, at that time the sole editor, took upon himself to do in order to make up for the important omissions of the English author and to finish the table of human knowledge of that epoch.' [42] In short, so conflicting and defective is the evidence that we are reduced to speculation and the weighing of probabilities. Therefore we might say, with great diffidence, that it seems more probable that Diderot was recruited by the publishers rather than by Gua de Malves; that the latter might very well have recruited D'Alembert, both of them being mathematicians, and that this may have provided the occasion for Diderot and D'Alembert to become acquainted; that both Gua de Malves and Diderot, being persons of learning and imagination, were capable of conceiving the idea, whether independently or in association, of expanding the project; and that Diderot, whether or not he got the idea first, unquestionably displayed the large-mindedness necessary for success in carrying it out.

The agreement between the publishers and Gua de Malves lasted some thirteen months and then was canceled by mutual consent on 3 August 1747.[43] There soon followed one of the biggest moments in Diderot's life. On 16 October the publishers entered into a contract with him and D'Alembert to replace Gua de Malves in the direction of the enterprise. Diderot was to get 7200 livres in all: 1200 of it to be paid in a lump sum upon publication of the first volume; and the remaining 6000 to be paid at the rate of 144 livres per month. D'Alembert was also to be paid at the rate of 144 livres per month, but the total was to be only 2400 livres. Thus the publishers contemplated a situation in which D'Alembert would continue on the project only another sixteen months, while Diderot, at this rate of payment, would be on the job another three and a half years.[44]

For Diderot the contract of October 1747 represented both independence and security. Although a sum of 144 livres per month was modest, he could now count on a constant income for the next forty-one months, with two-thirds of a year's salary extra and in a lump sum when the first volume was published. To know that he could keep the wolf from the door for at least four or five years — this was indeed something for a person who had lived as precariously as he. Actually, in return for this advantage he undertook responsibilities that lasted twenty-five years, for not until 1772 did he bring out the last volume of plates. In retrospect, Diderot was inclined to think that he had been grievously underpaid for his work on the *Encyclopédie,* and that the time it took robbed him of the opportunity for more substantial literary accomplishment. Maybe so, though this is far from certain. Without the *Encyclopédie* he might have become more undisciplined and *less* productive.[45] It must be admitted, however, that the necessity for writing a large number of articles in haste developed in Diderot, for better and for worse, a flair for a type of writing that may well be called journalistic. At its best his writing has a sublime impetuosity and, at its worst, it possesses characteristics of the impromptu and the improvised.

In the six months following the publishers' contract with Diderot, so great an expansion of plans occurred that it became necessary to ask for a new license. There had been no intimation of this during the thirteen months that Gua de Malves had been the chief editor of the project — at least so far as existing documents show — and consequently it is tempting to suppose that this expansion came as a result of Diderot's breadth of views and persuasive tongue, that 'gilded tongue' of which his mother-in-law had spoken more in admiration than anger. On some occasion during the early history of the *Encyclopédie* Diderot had a decisive interview with the learned and pious Chancellor d'Aguesseau. It is evident that the point of discussion had to do with plans for expanding the *Encyclopédie,* and that the freethinking Diderot impressed the Chancellor very favorably. This was the more extraordinary in that the Chancellor, whom Voltaire described as a tyrant desiring to prevent the nation from thinking, was customarily very stern and very conservative in his administration of the censorship.[46] But when could this interview have taken place? Probably not when the privilege of January 1746 was being mooted, for this month was the first in which Diderot's name appeared on the pay roll, and it is clear that he was not yet entrusted with any great responsibility in the enterprise. But by April 1748, when the new privilege was granted, he was one of the co-editors. Therefore it was probably at this time that he astonished D'Aguesseau by his intellectual powers and readiness of wit. At all events the new license was registered at the Royal Corporation of Booksellers on 30 April 1748, thus superseding the previous one of January 1746.[47] A comparison of the texts of the two documents shows very little difference between them, but evidently what difference there was, was considered very significant. Whereas the 1746 license set forth that Le Breton intended to publish a text 'translated from the English Dictionary of Chambers and of Harris, with some additions,' the 1748 privilege calls for a translation 'of the English Dictionary of Chambers, of Harris, of Dyche, and others, with augmentations. . . .'[48]

Lamoignon de Malesherbes, who between 1750 and 1763 was himself the magistrate in charge of regulating the book trade, is the source of two accounts of Diderot's interview with D'Aguesseau. The later account, written in 1790, is the better known, and is contained in Malesherbes' *Memoir on the Liberty of the Press*. Malesherbes recalls that 'the plan [of the *Encyclopédie*] was concerted with the most virtuous and enlightened of magistrates, the Chancellor d'Aguesseau. M. Diderot was presented to him as that one of the authors who would have the greatest share in the work.

'This author was already marked, by many of the pious, for his freedom of thought.

'However, the pious M. d'Aguesseau wished to confer with him, and I know that he was enchanted by certain marks of genius that shone forth in the conversation. . . .' [49]

The other account by Malesherbes of Diderot's interview with the Chancellor was written at a date much nearer to the event. In an unsigned and undated memorandum, written in Malesherbes' unmistakable and almost illegible hand, and which internal evidence shows to date from 1758 or early 1759, Malesherbes wrote that 'The late Chancellor had cognizance of this project [the *Encyclopédie*]. Not only did he approve it, but he corrected it, reformed it, and chose M. Diderot to be the principal editor of it.' [50]

Many years later Diderot wrote a cryptic declaration that might possibly refer to his relations with D'Aguesseau. 'I protest,' he wrote, 'that undertaking the *Encyclopédie* was not of my choosing; that a word of honor, very adroitly exacted and very unwisely granted, bound me over, hand and foot, to this enormous task and to all the afflictions that have accompanied it . . . .' [51] Whether or not this remark by Diderot refers to D'Aguesseau, one observation should be made concerning Malesherbes' statements. If Malesherbes' memory was more accurate in the account he wrote while still in office — while he still could refresh his memory from the office records about an event that had happened only ten years previously — than it was in the account written thirty years later, then it appears that the Chancellor did more than simply accept Diderot as an editor. Rather, D'Aguesseau *chose* him, thus investing him with some of the Chancellor's great prestige and authority, and making it more difficult to attack the *Encyclopédie* on ideological grounds. If so, this interpretation of events would go far to explain why Diderot, at that time a person still quite obscure, seems to have been so quickly accepted by both friend and foe as the leader of the great new enterprise.

CHAPTER 7

Two Very Different Books

As his thirty-fifth birthday approached, Diderot's time was filled by a variety of activities. Three rather cryptic entries in the publishers' account book for June, July, and August 1748 suggest that he may have been concluding his translating work on the James *Medicinal Dictionary*.[1] In addition, his new job as one of the chief editors of the *Encyclopédie* involved not only the translation and adaptation of a host of articles from Chambers' *Cyclopaedia,* combined with much planning for a greatly extended project, but carried with it concomitant necessities of looking about for collaborators and directing them in their assignments.[2] Documentary evidence of the minutiae of this important and time-consuming work has practically all disappeared. No doubt discarded in wastebaskets and trash fires as useless, the concrete evidence of the process of editing — the notes exchanged between editor and contributor, the manuscripts of proffered articles with perhaps Diderotian bluepencilings upon them, the galley proofs, the page proofs — has almost completely vanished. Nevertheless, there must have been an exhausting amount to do, especially as the *Encyclopédie* was planned to be the result of the labor of 'a company of men of letters.' And in addition to these tasks Diderot found time, or at least some time, for his domestic life with Anne-Toinette and baby François-Jacques-Denis back at the lodgings in the Rue Mouffetard; probably a good deal more time for Mme de Puisieux, and for his expanding circle of friends; and, finally, time snatched somewhere or other for the composition of one more in his series of risky and — as regards this particular work — risqué manuscripts.

This was the novel called *Les Bijoux indiscrets* ('The Indiscreet Jewels'). According to Mme de Vandeul, the book was written in a fortnight on a sort of wager with his mistress to show how easy it was to do this sort of thing.[3] The novel, having been bought by the publisher Durand for twelve hundred livres, was on sale, under the mantle or under the counter, in the early days of 1748.[4] This is about the time negotiations were under way with the Chancellor of France for a license for an expanded *Encyclopédie*. It was lucky for Diderot that D'Aguesseau, whose official duties were in some respects like those of a censor in old Roman times and whose temperament somewhat resembled that of Cato the Elder, was unaware of this excursion into the field of salacious literature.

Part of the interest — and the daring — of the book lay in its transparent allusions to living figures. The action is supposed to take place in the Congo at the capital city of Monomotapa (a name made familiar by the opening line of one of La Fontaine's fables), and the principal personages are the Sultan Mangogul and his charming favorite, Mirzoza. One did not have to be a medium to understand that the author had in mind Louis XV and Mme de Pompadour, who had become the King's acknowledged mistress three years earlier. The book is also filled with thinly disguised references to Paris, the Opéra, France and England, and to such personages as the Duc de Richelieu, Cardinal Fleury, the composers Lully and Rameau, Descartes, Newton, and Louis XIV. This in itself was sufficient to make the book audacious. Over and above this was the plot. The Sultan, to fend off boredom, to which he was unusually subject, was given a magic ring. This ring had the property, when turned toward any woman, of making that part of her anatomy talk which, if it ordinarily had the power of speech, would be most qualified to answer a Kinsey questionnaire. To a novelist perhaps unsure of his ability to write a tightly constructed novel, this plot was admirably calculated to keep up suspense. If interest flags, just bring in another trial of the magic ring. Diderot did so. There were thirty trials in two volumes, all of them attended by what might be called success.

There is a tradition that Diderot got the idea for his novel from a novelette entitled *Nocrion, conte allobroge*. This item, now exceedingly rare, was published in 1747 and written, perhaps by the Count de Caylus, perhaps by the Abbé (later Cardinal) Bernis, in the naïve manner and archaic language of a medieval fabliau.[5] Certainly Diderot could very well have taken from *Nocrion* the principal device of *Les Bijoux indiscrets*. But whether or not this was the source of *Les Bijoux*, Diderot, of course, did not invent the genre of licentious novels. Indeed, a very successful practitioner in this field, or perhaps swamp, of letters was living in Diderot's day — Crébillon the Younger, whose most famous novel, *Le Sopha*, had been published in 1740. Obviously there is a great similarity of device in the plots of Crébillon's and Diderot's novels. And there is a similarity of cynicism, too, in their common assumption that every woman, however demure and virtuous she may seem, is really morally corrupt.

Diderot would not have been Diderot if he had not strewn this work with a large number of thoughtful observations and lively criticisms of the social and intellectual life of his time. In consequence, no serious student of Diderot's ideas and their development can afford to overlook *Les Bijoux indiscrets*.[6] For example, the book contains a very good comparison and contrast of the music of Lully and Rameau (chapter xiii); there is also a critical animadversion to Louis XIV concerning his domination by Mme de Maintenon, and a disapproving reference to his Revocation of the Edict of Nantes (chapter i); there is a parody of a sermon which quite makes us believe Mme de Vandeul when she states that in the early years of vagabondage at Paris her father got fifty crowns apiece for six sermons written for the missionary who was going to the Portuguese colonies (chapter xv); there is much interesting speculation about the nature of dreams and the real character of the soul (chapters xlii and xxix);[7] the scientific and metaphysical views of the Newtonians are contrasted with those of the followers of Descartes (chapter ix); there is a good deal of criticism of the theater, views praised by Lessing, the great German playwright and critic, and which are the blood brothers of Diderot's later writings on the theater (chapters xxxvii and xxxviii);[8] and a chapter of literary criticism, rather redolent of Swift's *Battle of the Books,* in which Homer, Virgil, Horace, Pindar, Socrates, Plato, and Voltaire are admiringly mentioned and the Quarrel of the Ancients against the Moderns warmed up again (chapter xl).

Critics speak with great interest and respect of a chapter set forth as a dream, which really deals with the triumph of the scientific method over ignorance posing as knowledge.[9] It was like Diderot to include so serious a subject in a frivolous and licentious novel, telling it in the form of a dream or myth as Plato might have done. This was chapter xxxii, called by Diderot 'The best, perhaps, and the least read, of this History.' The Sultan Mangogul dreamed he had been carried into the Realm of Hypotheses. While there, he saw a child, Experiment, approaching and maturing and growing ever bigger as he advanced. At length, 'I saw Experiment draw nigh and the columns of the portico of the Temple of Hypotheses tremble, its roof cave in, and its floor yawn open beneath our feet. . . . it collapsed with a frightful roar, and I woke up.' The Sultan's sole comment about this dream, as Louis XV's might well have been, was that it had given him a headache.

People fond of Diderot are inclined to say that passages like these go far to redeem the work, and it is well to remember that André Gide noted in his *Journal* that he read *Les Bijoux indiscrets* 'with rapture.' [10] Moreover, many people argue, there is something of the scientific in Diderot's treatment of the sexual (and the sexually abnormal) in this novel. As one modern critic suggests, 'even the rather heavy-handed facetiousness of *Les Bijoux indiscrets* indicates an attention, an analyst's and psychologist's interest in the scabrous details of sexual life.' [11] Still, *Les Bijoux* has had quite enough editions, and enough illustrated editions, to prove that it is a dirty book. Within a few months of publication, six editions in French were printed in Holland alone.[12] In France, the book was highly contraband as well as popular: in 1754, for example, the police descended upon a bookseller and discovered a stock of sixty-four copies.[13] An English translation appeared in 1749, and German ones in 1776 and 1792.[14] The book is still of interest to collectors — and others: there have been ten editions in France since 1920. *Les Bijoux,* in short, is Diderot's most published work.

There is a school of critics that, when faced with the necessity of saying something about an obscene work, tends to take the it's-not-amusing-it's-just-dull line. Thus Carlyle, in his essay on 'Diderot,' spoke of Diderot's writing 'the beastliest of all past, present or future dull Novels; a difficult feat, unhappily not an impossible one'; and the late George Saintsbury agreed, in his *History of the French Novel,* that 'it really would require a most unpleasant apprenticeship to scavenging in order to discover a dirtier and duller.' [15] Actually, Diderot's work was far from dull. Quite to the contrary, it was lively — lively with ideas, lively with dialogue, lively with sallies. It was smutty — perhaps, as a French critic believes, the circumstances of Diderot's disordered youth had served to dirty his imagination — [16] but it wasn't dull. And the most honest criticism of it would be something like that which appeared in a recent history of French literature: 'Its verve and keenness do not excuse its obscenity.' [17]

Diderot was a little out of his element in writing about a king and his mistress, and this evidently was palpable to people of the time who were sensitive to social nuances. The Abbé Raynal, reviewing *Les Bijoux,* called the book 'obscure, poorly written, in a coarse and vulgar tone, and by a man ill-acquainted with the milieu he has desired to depict. The author is M. Diderot, who has very extensive knowledge and a great deal of wit, but who is not suited for the genre in which he has just written.' [18] Other contemporary criticisms were also adverse, although one of the most hostile of all admitted the verve of the work. 'One cannot deny,' wrote this critic, 'that his *Bijoux* frequently say some very sensible things; but they are wrapped up in so many dirty and cynical images and expressions, that their utility can never be comparable to the danger to which the most dispassionate mind would be exposed in reading them.' [19]

Years after the publication of *Les Bijoux indiscrets,* Diderot professed to Naigeon that he regretted having written it. 'He often assured me that if he could make good this error by the loss of a finger, he would not hesitate to sacrifice it for the sake of suppressing entirely this delirium of his imagination.' [20] Even so, some years after its publication he added two chapters to the original edition — internal evidence shows that it could not have been before 1757 — [21] and we can believe, along with Diderot's later editor, Maurice Tourneux, that if Diderot was willing to sacrifice a finger, it would have been the little one, and that on his left hand.[22]

Diderot was, as usual, running risks. It was dangerous to have written such a work, yet it was soon an open secret in Paris as to who the author was. Nor were the police the last to learn of it. An informer named Bonin, a most interesting character who operated a supposedly clandestine press, wrote to the Lieutenant-General of Police not later than 29 January 1748 that 'Dridot' had just given to the public *Les Bijoux indiscrets;* and on 14 February of that year the same informant wrote that 'it is Mr. Durand, Rue St. Jacques, who had *Les Bijoux indiscrets* printed and who sells them. He bought the copy from Dridot for 1200 livres. This publisher is very worried, as are also Messrs. David and Briasson, who fear that something might happen to Dridrot that would suspend the Dictionary of Medicine of which Dridrot is editor.' [23]

Diderot, moreover, increased the risks he was already running by having a hand in the preparation of a fairy story called *L'Oiseau blanc, conte bleu* ('The White Bird'), a *conte bleu* signifying a sort of unbelievable, fabulous tale.[24] *The White Bird* was patently inspired by the *Arabian Nights:* a sultana, finding it difficult to go to sleep, has this story told to her during a succession of seven nights, with infallible soporific effect. It is likely to have that effect on the reader too, for *The White Bird,* which recounts the adventures of Génistan, the son of the Emperor of Japan, whom a wizard had metamorphosed into a pigeon and who regained his pristine state only after being touched by the wand of the fairy Truth, is a mawkish and insipid tale even though it did receive the honor of a German translation in 1907. Presumably it was written as a sequel to *Les Bijoux indiscrets,* for it reintroduces some of the characters from that book, but it has none of the bite and none of the social comment that distinguished *Les Bijoux.* There are some commonplaces about truth and how truth does not customarily reside at courts, but these mild platitudes are far from the questing fierceness with which the mind of Diderot usually pursued truth, seeking her in the scientific and methodological developments of his time. Indeed, the contrast between this tale and anything else Diderot ever wrote is enough to raise the question of whether he really did write it. He himself emphatically disowned it. Then, under pressure, he added, 'It is by a lady whom I might name, since she herself doesn't conceal it. If I have any part in this work, it is rather in having corrected its orthography, against which ladies with the greatest intelligence are always somewhat at fault.' [25] Yet Naigeon, in spite of this testimony, published *L'Oiseau blanc* in his edition of Diderot's works appearing in 1798, the first publication of the tale. Naigeon, whom Diderot had appointed as his literary executor, was certainly in a position to know. Consequently, critics have accepted *L'Oiseau blanc* as being from the hand of Diderot, or at least greatly affected by him. [26]

The White Bird is really composed of very uninflammable stuff. But evidently rumors were rife about it at the time, for the police, under the impression that it contained derisive allusions to the King and Mme de Pompadour, tried hard to track it down. Considering its literary merits, all that can be said is that this official perturbation complimented the work a good deal more than it deserved.

Les Bijoux indiscrets was the sort of book that might seriously impair a man's scholarly reputation. What was even worse, Diderot did not yet have much of one to destroy. By his own confession, he hoped that his *Mémoires sur différens sujets de mathématiques,* on which he was working in early 1748, would 'prove to the public that I was not entirely unworthy of the choice of the associated publishers [of the *Encyclopédie*].' [27] At the same time he had undertaken a translation of Joseph Bingham's monumental *Origines ecclesiasticae, or the Antiquities of the Christian Church,* a translation which certainly was never published and possibly never completed. [28] It is probable, however, that Diderot put his knowledge of Bingham to good account in the *Encyclopédie,* especially in view of the fact that both works are well-informed about the multitudinous heresies of the Christian Church. Also in 1748 Diderot was persistently reported to be working on a 'History of the Expeditions of England,' but this rumor was evidently erroneous, for the French edition of Thomas Lediard's *Naval History of England,* published eventually at Lyon in 1751, was the translation, by all accounts, not of Diderot, but of De Puisieux, the husband of Diderot's mistress. [29]

Of greater importance in this year of varied intellectual activity was the fact, asserted by Diderot in his 1749 statement to the police, that 'I have done the *Exposition du système de musique de M. Rameau.*[30] This interesting remark — for Rameau was the most significant French composer of the eighteenth century, the 'discoverer' of thorough-bass, and a musician whose music still has both freshness and body — has set bibliographers wondering as to just which work was meant. Raynal, reviewing Diderot's *Memoirs on Mathematics,* remarked that Diderot was 'an intimate friend of M. Rameau, whose discoveries he is presently going to publish. This sublime and profound musician published formerly some works in which he did not include sufficient clarity and elegance. M. Diderot will rework these ideas, and he is most capable of setting them forth to excellent advantage.' Sometime later the same journalist remarked: 'Our very illustrious and celebrated musician, M. Rameau, claims to have discovered the principle of harmony. M. Diderot has lent him his pen in order to set forth this important discovery to its best advantage.'[31] Perhaps this work was Rameau's *Démonstration du principe de l'harmonie* (Paris, 1750), and indeed the evidence seems to suggest that it was. D'Hémery, the police inspector who confiscated *La Promenade du sceptique,* entered in his journal for 17 February 1752 that the *Elémens de musique théorique et pratique suivant les principes de M. Rameau* was done by Diderot.[32] This work, however, was always claimed by D'Alembert, and it is probable that in this instance D'Hémery was mistaken. It is certain, however, that the versatile Diderot was, in some ghost-writing way, associated with the greatest French musician of the century, an association which incidentally had a great cooling-off when Rameau began to attack Rousseau's articles on music in the *Encyclopédie.*[33]

Diderot's *Mémoires sur différens sujets de mathématiques* was published by Pissot and Durand, the latter being the Durand of the publishers of the *Encyclopédie,* and was brought out in a format de luxe, with six delightful engravings, as, for example, cupids tracing x's on a sheet of paper, or fixing pegs in the cylinder of a mechanical organ, so that, as Tourneux remarked, 'the volume is one of the most coquettish that was ever published on such arid subjects.'[34] Diderot wrote in his signed dedication to a Mme de P * * * — probably Mme de Prémontval, a mathematician and the wife of a mathematician, and not Mme de Puisieux — [35] 'I am giving up the cap and bells, never to take them up again.'

The five mathematical papers were summarized by Diderot as follows: I. The general principles of the science of sound, with a special method of fixing the pitch, in such a manner that one may play a piece of music on exactly the same pitch at whatsoever time or place; II. A new compass made of the circle and its involute, with some of its uses; III. Examination of a principle of mechanics concerning the tension of cords . . . ; IV. Project for a new organ . . . [this was the article that had been published anonymously in the *Mercure de France* the preceding year]; V. A letter on the resistance of the atmosphere to the movement of pendulums, with an examination of the theory of Newton on this subject.

The *Mémoires sur différens sujets de mathématiques* received a very good press. The censor to whom the manuscript had been submitted set the tone, for he remarked that these papers were treated 'with great sagacity.' [36] Diderot was beginning to make his mark. 'M. Diderot (to judge by this essay),' wrote the *Journal des Sçavans,* 'is very much in a position to give learned solutions to difficulties that require nice and intricate calculation.' [37] The Jesuit *Journal de Trévoux* invited the continuation of such researches 'on the part of a man as clever and able as M. Diderot appears to us to be, of whom we should also observe that his style is as elegant, trenchant, and unaffected as it is lively and ingenious.' [38] And the *Mercure de France* remarked: 'Here is quite a number of new views in a volume that with its table of contents includes not more than 250 pages. The author was already known to be a man of a great deal of wit. Upon reading these memoirs, one will discover that he adds to this advantage that of also being a learned musician, an ingenious mechanician, a profound geometrician.' [39] It is no wonder that the Abbé Raynal thought it time to modify his opinion of this rising star. In introducing his review of the *Mémoires sur . . . mathématiques,* he began: 'I don't know whether you have heard of a M. Diderot, who has a good deal of wit and very extensive knowledge. He has made himself known by his writings, most of them imperfect, yet filled with erudition and genius.' [40]

A recent and authoritative article on Diderot as a mathematician concludes that by this series of papers he proved himself competent and original. Moreover, he also demonstrated himself to be conversant with the current developments in the field, especially the works of Euler and D'Alembert. 'He was well grounded in the earlier mathematical literature, judging from his acquaintance with the ideas of Pythagoras, Aristoxenes, Gassendi, Halley and Flamsteed, Newton and others referred to in his *Mémoires.*' [41] And Julian Coolidge remarked, 'I cannot leave Diderot without expressing my admiration for his really stimulating mathematical work, when his other interests were so large and so varied.' [42]

We might well suppose that by this volume Diderot had proved once for all his mathematical competence. Yet by a strange twist of fortune he has become known to a large part of the English-reading public as a mathematical dunce. Some twenty-five years after Diderot had published these mathematical papers, a story circulated around Berlin about a practical joke that may (or may not) have been played upon him during his visit to Saint Petersburg. According to this story, a Russian philosopher offered to prove to Diderot algebraically the existence of God. So, in the presence of the Court and with the secret acquiescence of the Empress, the story goes, the Russian philosopher gravely approached Diderot and said in a tone ringing with conviction, 'Sir, $\dfrac{a + b^n}{z} = x$. Therefore God exists. Reply.' The point of this story, as originally told, was that Diderot, momentarily casting about for the most effective reply to the ineptitude of this alleged proof, sensed from the attitude of the courtiers that a joke was being played upon him and that all those present were in on it. The Berlin source did not include Diderot's reply, but it did state that this misadventure caused Diderot to apprehend that others might be in store and convinced him that the intellectual climate of Russia was not congenial, so that he soon signified his desire to return to France.[43]

In the course of time the point of this story became twisted, so that it is often told by authors of books on popular mathematics as an illustration of the horrible fate that awaits a person ignorant of mathematics. The anecdote was published in 1867 and 1872 by an English author, De Morgan, with gratuitous additions; first, that the Russian philosopher involved was Euler, and second, that algebra was Hebrew to Diderot.[44] Bell, in his *Men of Mathematics,* tells the story as it was twisted by De Morgan, his only variation being in the remark that 'all mathematics was Chinese to Diderot.' [45] And Lancelot Hogben begins his *Mathematics for the Million* with this same dramatic tale, *his* variant being that 'algebra was Arabic to Diderot.' [46] How the story has been contorted and has grown to this misshapen state has been remarked on by three contemporary scholars, one of whom says, in allusion to the De Morgan-Bell-Hogben fabrication, 'That is the story, and it is a very good story, except that it isn't true.' [47]

As Diderot went through life, he lost faith in Christian immortality, and instead fixed his hopes on the sort that comes from having one's deeds live in the memory of posterity. Could he be aware that the rank and file of posterity, at least in English-speaking countries, are now likely to remember him more for being mathematically illiterate than perhaps for any other thing, he might be tempted to hedge his bet.

CHAPTER 8

Letter on the Blind

THE French Enlightenment not merely originated new ideas: it applied them to existing institutions. And eventually, of course, the process burst a good many old bottles. This attitude made the *philosophes,* with Diderot a leader among them, the radicals and the unconscious revolutionaries of their day. Indeed, their pronounced interest in practical affairs has justly earned for the *philosophes* the reputation of being reformers but at the cost of their reputation as philosophers. Diderot's own progressive outlook and concern with practical matters were evidenced at this time by a pamphlet advocating a reform that finally was brought about in 1793. This anonymous work, dated 16 December 1748, was entitled *First Letter from a Zealous Citizen Who is neither a Surgeon nor a Physician, To Monsieur D. M. . . . . In which is Proposed a Means for Settling the Troubles that for a long Time have Divided Medicine and Surgery.*[1] The condition that had aroused Diderot's interest was a preposterous though long-standing division of labor in French medicine. This practice decreed that in the treatment of patients, physicians might not operate and surgeons working on the case might not express an opinion that in any way had to do with general or internal medicine. Moreover, the physicians considered themselves infinitely superior, socially and intellectually, to the surgeons. The origin of this irrational distinction, or what the sociologist is fond of calling the pecking-order, goes back to medieval times, when all physicians were clerics. This had the not unnatural tendency, incidentally, of causing them to neglect gynecology and obstetrics, a field which was left to the midwives; but what was more to the point, their status as clerics forbade their shedding blood. Since they could not perform operations, this was done by the barber-chirurgeons. Moreover, physicians, coming from the class of 'bourgeois notables,' were forbidden under pain of losing their status to exercise for gain any skill requiring the use of hands.[2] The social results of this sort of snobbery were painfully evident and, as is so often the case in jurisdictional disputes, it was the public who suffered the most. Against this Diderot inveighed. 'What are we about?' he cried. 'Where is our shame? Where is our humanity?'

Diderot's solution was for both physicians and surgeons to be united in the same body under the same name. Aesculapius, Hippocrates, and Galen practiced both medicine and surgery, he remarked. Therefore, 'what disadvantage is there today in the same person's ordering and executing a bloodletting? Let . . . doctors and surgeons form a single corps; let them be assembled in the same college, where students may learn the operations of surgery and where the speculative principles of the art of healing may be explained to them. . . .'[3]

The Letter from a Zealous Citizen bespeaks an interest in medicine which is not at all surprising in one who had spent so much time and energy in translating James's Medicinal Dictionary. This interest remained constant with Diderot throughout the years, so that one finds him a close friend of the Genevese, Théodore Tronchin, the most famous doctor of his generation in all of Europe, and of Théophile de Bordeu (1722-76), a pioneer in the study of glands and mucous membrane. Diderot also delighted in the study of anatomy, and lost no opportunity, for example, to praise the anatomical models devised by a Mlle Biheron.[4] Diderot's profoundly thoughtful and speculative D'Alembert's Dream is based upon a great variety of medical and physiological knowledge, and one of his last books was Eléments de physiologie (1774-80). 'The fact is,' he wrote late in life, 'it is very difficult to think cogently in metaphysics or ethics without being an anatomist, a naturalist, a physiologist, and a physician.'[5]

Even in the wording of its title, the Letter from a Zealous Citizen betokens the changing social values of an age beginning to be on the march. The eighteenth century was commencing to emphasize the concept of 'belonging,' of citizenship. Diderot was among the leaders of this movement, and the term 'citoyen' appears very frequently in the pages of the Encyclopédie. Destined by the time of '93 to bear pungent and sometimes bitter fruit, 'citizen' was one of the pleasant and slightly radical words of the eighteenth century. Thus we have Diderot ending his letter with a fine humanistic flourish: 'I am a good citizen, and everything that concerns the welfare of society and the life of my fellow men is very interesting to me.'[6]

Problems of citizenship, it so happened, were being canvassed rather generally in France in 1749, for this was a year of hunger and distress, accompanied by a considerable ferment of opposition to the government.[7] In part the unrest was caused by discontent with the Treaty of Aix-la-Chapelle, which had recently brought to an end the War of the Austrian Succession and which, said the captious, was the peace that passeth all understanding. There was also disquiet owing to the opposition of the privileged classes, especially the clergy, to the imposition of a tax called the vingtième, promulgated in May of 1749, which would have had the effect of introducing into the French governmental system the principle of the obligation of everyone to pay proportionate taxes.[8] The attempt to enforce this simplest sort of elementary fairness in the incidence of taxation was bitterly resisted and obstructed by the privileged classes, whose previous connections with public finance had been more on the receiving than the paying end.

In retrospect, 1749 seems a crucial year in the history of the eighteenth century and the annals of the French monarchy, in part because of what happened to Diderot and Rousseau within that twelvemonth. No doubt to a person taking the auspices at that particular moment, only the faintest hint of thunder could be heard on the left. Yet the intellectual climate of opinion experienced a new pressure front that very year. A nineteenth-century editor of Barbier's *Journal,* a major source for the history of France in the eighteenth century, remarked that 'the year 1749 is a remarkable date in the literary history of the eighteenth century. It is at this date that writings hostile to religion appear and multiply. . . . Henceforth war breaks out between skepticism and faith. Barbier, who up to this point has spoken only of ballad writers and poets, now speaks of the *philosophes*. It is at this point that the real eighteenth century begins.' [9]

Seventeen hundred forty-nine was a year of transition in France. It marked the epoch when intellectual prestige was transferring its headquarters to a new field, while subjects hitherto regarded as almost untouchable mysteries began to be matters for critical comment. The crucial nature of this year was observed by a French historian, Rulhière, even before the Revolution. Being welcomed into the French Academy in 1787, Rulhière mentioned in his formal discourse that the year 1749 was the one in which a general revolution in manners and in letters began. 'In that very year in which were produced all these great philosophical works, we saw beginning a succession of unfortunate events that little by little and from day to day stripped from the government that public approbation and esteem that up to that time it had enjoyed; and while we passed from the love of belles-lettres to the love of philosophy, the nation, owing to a change explained by causes quite different, passed over from acclamations to complaints, from songs of triumph to the clamor of perpetual remonstrances, from prosperity to fears of a general ruin, and from a respectful silence regarding religion to importunate and deplorable quarrels. . . . The capital [Paris], which for so long a time had been the prompt and docile imitator of the sentiments, taste, and opinions of the Court, at the same time ceased to have for the latter its old-time deference. Then it was that there arose among us what we have come to call *the empire of public opinion.* Men of letters immediately had the ambition to be its organs, and almost its arbiters. A more serious purpose diffused itself in intellectual works: the desire to instruct manifested itself in them more than the desire to please. *The dignity of men of letters,* a novel but an accurate expression, quickly became an approved expression and one in common use.' [10]

Manifestations of the growing malaise in the French body politic, first identifiable in 1749, were even then interpreted by some as the beginning of a revolution. The Marquis d'Argenson recorded in his famous journal on 1 May 1751 that 'people are talking of nothing but the necessity of an early revolution because of the bad condition in which the government finds itself internally.' [11] It is very much worth remembering that the *Encyclopédie* was being prepared and its first volumes published against this background of confused and muted discontent.

In contrast, Diderot's personal affairs seemed prosperous. In 1748 and 1749 he continued to receive regularly his monthly stipend of 144 livres. To this could be added the 1200 livres he is known to have received for *Les Bijoux indiscrets,* and he may have received something for *Mémoires sur différens sujets de mathématiques,* though of this there is no record. The added security of his financial position was reflected in his moving his family from the Rue Mouffetard to a third-floor apartment in a building, built in 1681 and still standing, at 3 Rue de l'Estrapade.[12] Perhaps, one thinks as one ascends the stairs, Diderot walked up and down these steps and slid his hand along this very stair rail. Perhaps it was at this very landing that Mme Diderot assaulted the neighbor's servant girl. Or, observing the house from across the street, one gazes at the very window from which Diderot's wife, perhaps with her three-year-old son at her side, looked down to see her husband carried away by the police.[13]

Diderot, although he was not now living quite so surreptitiously, was still keeping his marriage a secret from his relatives at Langres, and that may have been the reason why he seems to have made no effort to go home at the time of his mother's death in October 1748. He inherited some property from her estate, but just how much or when it became available is not known.[14]

During these months the *Encyclopédie,* of course, continued to be in active preparation, and Diderot, besides writing manuscripts to enhance his reputation as a savant (such, for example, as the forthcoming *Letter on the Blind*), was occupied with all the organizing, directing, persuading, and exhorting that his position entailed. Probably he made it a point to pay somewhat ceremonious visits to important contributors, if we may judge from an incident in 1751 when the Chevalier de Jaucourt proposed to call upon Diderot in order to volunteer his services. 'I shall be charmed indeed to have the honor of seeing you at my house,' wrote Diderot, 'but allow me to pay *you* a visit.'[15] No doubt Diderot went the rounds on errands like this in 1748, if his being reimbursed on several occasions for cab fare is any indication.[16] In addition he made extensive use of the Royal Library, now called the Bibliothèque Nationale, and on occasion was granted the unusual privilege of borrowing books from it. In his prospectus for the *Encyclopédie,* Diderot acknowledged the invaluable assistance of the Royal Librarian, and the registers in which are recorded his numerous withdrawals still exist.[17] The work on the *Encyclopédie* was going on apace, but, as the publishers of the venture were soon to learn, all came to a stop if Diderot was not there.

Seventeen hundred forty-nine was a memorable year in the life of Diderot. And so it was to many others. To the let-'em-eat-cake segments of society it was noteworthy for the first appearance of a live rhinoceros in Paris. 'To transport him on land, a covered wagon, drawn sometimes by twenty horses, has been used. He eats up to sixty pounds of hay and twenty pounds of bread a day, and drinks fourteen pails of water. He eats everything but meat and fish,' reported Raynal in his news letter. And then he added, 'It appears that so far rhinoceroses have not been very useful.'[18] To other elements of society, especially authors, 1749 came to mean a year selected by the government to attempt by confiscations, arrests, and imprisonments to discourage the expression of radical ideas.[19] D'Argenson remarked in August that because of the great number of such arrests the Paris prisons were so full that some of the culprits had to be sent to Vincennes and other outlying prisons.[20] And it was just this year that Diderot chose for the publication of an extremely original, controversial, and dangerous book.

This work, *Lettre sur les aveugles à l'usage de ceux qui voient* ('Letter on the Blind for the Use of Those Who See'), combined a great deal of scientific observation with some very upsetting metaphysical speculation. It was printed clandestinely by a printer named Simon; was sold — under the counter, of course — by Durand, one of the four publishers of the *Encyclopédie;* and was published — or, at least, was ready for bootlegging — on 9 June 1749.[21] The book greatly enhanced Diderot's reputation as a man of letters and a learned person, as the very fact of Voltaire's letter to him in acknowledgment of a presentation copy amply signifies; but its publication was also the occasion for a frightening experience which evidently chastened him a good deal. The appearance of the *Letter on the Blind,* therefore, ushered in a period of major crisis in the life of a man who could not keep himself from continually meditating on new ideas.

The particular occasion for the book, which had to do with the psychology of blind people and with what must be the ethical ideas of a person deprived of one of his senses, was an operation performed in Paris to restore sight. News had gotten about that a Prussian oculist, sponsored by the well-known French scientist Réaumur — he of the thermometer, and the man who first worked out the technique of the artificial incubation of eggs — was going to couch the cataracts of a girl born blind. Diderot claimed that he and many others with scientific interest in the case had asked to be present when the bandage was taken off the girl's eyes so that they might observe her at the moment when she was first able to see objects. But Réaumur had refused such requests: 'In a word,' wrote Diderot, 'he has not wished to let the veil fall except in the presence of some eyes of no importance.'[22] The eyes of no importance, according to Mme de Vandeul, were those belonging to Mme Dupré de Saint-Maur, the wife of an obscure writer who owed his seat in the French Academy either to his translation of *Paradise Lost* (1729) or to certain connections formed by his wife — no one seemed to be quite sure which. This lady was on very friendly terms not only with Réaumur but also with Count d'Argenson, the Secretary of State for War who, since 1737, had been the Director of Publications. It may have been, therefore, that personal reasons, as well as reasons of state, accounted for Diderot's arrest.[23] It is certain that Diderot's relations with Réaumur from then on were unsettled and at length became antagonistic.

The *Letter on the Blind* is a disarming book, written with the seeming artlessness of someone idly improvising on a musical instrument.* One subject suggests another, so that the reader, led on and on through a sort of steeplechase over most of the various metaphysical jumps, finally gets himself soaked in the water hole called 'Does God Exist?' The work begins with a number of acute firsthand observations of the behavior of a man

* An English translation is in Margaret Jourdain, *Diderot's Early Philosophical Works* (Chicago, 1916), 68–142.

born blind, a man of considerable intelligence whom Diderot knew personally. In addition, Diderot used supplementary information about the behavior of the blind, and especially about the acuteness of their senses of hearing and touch, which he found in the introduction to Nicholas Saunderson's *Elements of Algebra*. Saunderson, blind from birth, had been a famous Cambridge professor of mathematics, his particular specialty being, of all things, optics. To help himself in imagining geometrical problems and in making computations, he had devised a sort of arithmetical and geometrical abacus, 'a palpable arithmetic,' as the title of his book described it. After explaining the operation of this device, Diderot began to speculate upon the kind of concepts of God and of right and wrong that a person must have who has less than the normal number of senses. This was an original way of thinking about such matters, for it clearly suggested that our ideas about God and morality are not absolute but relative to our physical make-up and endowment. No wonder that some people sniffed materialism in this point of view, especially as Diderot invented what purported to be a veridical account of Saunderson's death-bed conversation in which the professor was made to declare that 'if you want me to believe in God, you must make me touch Him.' [24]

By this method of thinking, Diderot was experimenting with a type of investigation that has since been very successfully developed in medicine, biology, and psychology. It is the method of trying to find out about the nature of the normal by studying the abnormal, of learning about the nature of the well through studying the diseased. It was always characteristic of Diderot to study the pathology and teratology of a subject in order the better to understand its normalities. And because this line of thought led him to meditate on monsters and how their malformations make them unfitted to survive, he began to speculate about the emergence and modification of biological species in a way that clearly foreshadows Darwinism.[25]

The last third of the *Letter on the Blind* speculates on the famous question propounded by William Molyneux (1656–98): suppose a blind man, in the instant of recovering his sight, to see a cube and a sphere resting on a table. Would he be able to distinguish the cube from the sphere by sight, without touching them? This brain-cracker, fundamentally similar to problems in perception that are still puzzling psychologists, deeply concerned the philosophers of the eighteenth century because the answer to it would throw light upon such fundamental topics as how human beings think and how they know what they know.[26] It was in the hope of securing some light on the Molyneux problem that Diderot had wished to be present when Réaumur had the bandage taken off the girl with the cataracts.

The *Letter on the Blind,* which was addressed to a lady, perhaps Mme de Puisieux, reveals some interesting characteristics of its author. First, of course, there was that nimbus of the personal and intimate that characterizes so much of Diderot's writing, even the most scientific, and which frequently invades the columns of the *Encyclopédie,* where one might suppose all to be impersonal and austere. In the *Letter,* too, Diderot's notorious fondness for straying from the highroad of his theme and picking sweetly scented but somewhat irrelevant nosegays is strongly marked: 'There we are, a long way from our blind people, you'll say; but you must have the goodness, Madame, to forgive me all these digressions: I have promised you a conversation, and I cannot keep my word without this indulgence.' [27]

More importantly, the *Letter on the Blind* shows Diderot to be a considerable scientist: in his knowledge of the previous 'literature' of the subject, in the accuracy of his observations, as well as in the wealth of his hypotheses concerning what these observations might mean. His work shows, for example, that he was familiar with Descartes' *Dioptrics,* the writings of Bishop Berkeley and of Condillac, Voltaire's *Elements of Newton's Philosophy,* and Saunderson's *Elements of Algebra,* a book not translated into French until 1756.

It is impressive, too, to observe how seriously Diderot's observations on the psychology of the blind have been taken by scientists and professional workers in that field. One of the curiosities in the Boston Public Library is a translation of Diderot's work, made by Samuel Gridley Howe and 'printed' in raised letters at the Perkins Institution for the Blind in 1857. The preface remarks that the work 'abounds with beauties which they [the blind] can keenly relish, & with valuable suggestions by which they may profit.' In particular, as Dr. Gabriel Farrell, the present director of the Perkins Institution, has said: 'Diderot seems to have been first to call the attention of the scientific world to the superior sensory capacities of the blind.' [28] And the late Pierre Villey, a blind professor of literature at the University of Caen, although he contested Diderot's principal thesis, namely that a blind man's intellect, personality, and ethical notions are different from those of a man with sight, nevertheless acknowledged that Diderot had foreseen the proper treatment for a Helen Keller, had evinced a remarkable taste for psychological observation, and was completely a pioneer in his speculations upon the psychology of the blind.[29]

No doubt one of Diderot's intentions in publishing the *Letter on the Blind* was to display his qualifications for being editor of the forthcoming *Encyclopédie*. By this time it was generally known that he was to have an important connection with the publication, even though the formal prospectus was not to be circulated for over a year. The *Journal de Trévoux* of April 1749, for instance, alluded to his 'preparing' the 'Universal Dictionary of the Arts and Sciences.'[30] Certainly the *Letter on the Blind* disclosed to the public what he could do and on what platform he stood. It revealed as the cornerstone of Diderot's manner of thought his assumption, based on the writings of John Locke, that the only thing the mind has to work with is the evidence conveyed to it by the senses. Put the other way around, this doctrine asserted that the mind does not have born within it any notions of morality or religion, but simply builds up these concepts upon the evidence communicated to it by the senses. This constant and exclusive reference to the teachings of experience became the foundation stone for the psychological doctrine known as sensationalism. These views of Locke had first gained circulation in France through Voltaire, who cited them approvingly in his controversial and widely read *Lettres philosophiques* (1734). By mid-century they had become the official epistemology, so to speak, of the emerging school of *philosophes*. From the very first page of the *Encyclopédie,* from the very first words of D'Alembert's 'Preliminary Discourse,' which is rightly regarded as one of the monuments of the intellectual history of man, this point of view is taken for granted. This was the basis of the scientific and critical spirit that characterized the *Encyclopédie* and made it the engine for transmuting the values of a whole society. For this doctrine, as we explore its implications in problems like the nature of being, the nature of reality, the nature of knowing, and the nature of God, is extremely corrosive and dissolvent to any religious authority based simply upon revelation and to any political authority based simply upon prescription. To those writers who wanted to rally around such a battle standard, Diderot's *Letter on the Blind* served as a recruiting placard: Sign up with me! And it is perhaps this quality that accounts for the three editions of *Letter on the Blind* appearing in 1749, and for its receiving the flattering attention of Voltaire.[31]

Besides seeking to persuade people to have faith in his intellectual competence, the *Letter on the Blind* was a personal document constituting a further step in the development of Diderot's philosophical thought. Starting from the mildly theistic footnotes to his translation of Shaftesbury, written most probably in 1744, Diderot had come, in the course of five years, through the way stations of deism (the *Philosophical Thoughts* and *On the Sufficiency of Natural Religion*), and then of skepticism (*La Promenade du sceptique*), until by 1749 he had reached a pretty thoroughly materialistic position: 'If you want me to believe in God, you must make me touch Him!' All this had been accomplished at a fairly mature age, between thirty-one and thirty-six, and it was done in a spirit that could be described as more proscientific than antireligious. There was nothing hysterical or frenetic in Diderot's casting off his belief in orthodox Christianity and then his belief in any God at all. On the contrary, his attitude had been rather like that of a man who, without alacrity and without regret, simply discards tools that he no longer regards as capable of doing the job.

The *Letter on the Blind* was the occasion for putting Diderot into touch for the first time with Voltaire. The latter, evidently having received an advance copy of the book, replied at length in a letter dated simply 'June.' [32] Voltaire, who by conviction was a deist and who, moreover, thought that he would have his throat cut if his servants ever came to believe that there is no God, expostulated with Diderot on the tendency of his argument toward atheism. It was a skillful letter, written by the master whose flattery was so exquisite and so appetizing that, as Lord Macaulay said, 'It was only from his hand that so much sugar could be swallowed without making the swallower sick.' And he ended by inviting Diderot to come to see him and partake of a 'philosophical repast.'

It was a heady invitation, and Diderot replied that the moment of receiving Voltaire's letter was one of the sweetest of his life. Still, he did not go. There is in his reply a certain standoffishness which his relations with Voltaire constantly exhibited until the latter's death in 1778. Through the years it was usually Voltaire who accepted the burden of initiating a correspondence, infrequent as that was, and Diderot who delayed in replying or did not reply at all. Probably a stubborn desire to remain completely independent, added to the fact that the two men did not see eye to eye on matters of philosophical belief, explains why Diderot treated somewhat distantly the century's most famous man of letters.[33]

To Voltaire's arguments about a deistic universe, Diderot replied in this letter, 'I believe in God, although I live very happily with atheists. . . . It is . . . very important not to mistake hemlock for parsley; but not at all so to believe or not in God.' [34] And having disposed of the matter so summarily, Diderot went on to ask Voltaire to accept copies of the *Memoirs on Different Subjects of Mathematics,* one for himself and one for Mme du Châtelet, Voltaire's mistress and an excellent mathematician and physicist.

Diderot referred to this lady with deference and was evidently overawed by her mathematical accomplishments. Thus the lives of these two persons briefly touched in a year that was to be crucial for both. In six weeks Diderot saw closing upon him the gates of a royal prison of which a kinsman of Mme du Châtelet happened to be in charge; within three months of Diderot's sending her his book, the lady herself was dead, in tragic and grotesque childbirth. 'What shall we do about the child?' Voltaire had been asked when it was first realized that Mme du Châtelet, through a liaison with the poet Saint-Lambert, was pregnant. 'Don't let that trouble you,' said Voltaire airily. 'We shall give the child a place among Madame du Châtelet's miscellaneous works.' [35]

The portion of Diderot's letter referring to Mme du Châtelet has only recently been discovered. In this same overlooked portion Diderot excuses himself from meeting with Voltaire because of exhaustion and because of tensions in his private life. 'O Philosophy, Philosophy! what good are you if you do not blunt either the pricks of grief and of vexations or the sting of the passions?' [36] No doubt he was somewhat exaggerating, in order to make his excuses more plausible; but nevertheless his allusions to overwork, family dissension, and enslavement to Mme de Puisieux throw interesting light on Diderot's condition and state of mind in early June of 1749.

CHAPTER 9

Diderot in Prison

A T SEVEN-THIRTY in the morning of Thursday, 24 July 1749, two police officers climbed the stairs of the house in the Rue de l'Estrapade. One of them was D'Hémery, the man who had previously searched for the manuscript of *La Promenade du sceptique*. He and his companion, a man named Rochebrune, were admitted by Diderot to his apartment and began to search for any manuscripts 'contrary to Religion, the State, or morals.' It is possible, some authorities think, that Diderot may have expected such a visitation, for the police found nothing but twenty-one pasteboard cases containing manuscripts that they thought pertained to Chambers' *Cyclopaedia*. On a large table serving as a desk were found more manuscripts concerning the same work, and two copies of the *Letter on the Blind*. 'In the presence of the said Diderot,' reported the police, 'we continued our search in the other rooms, and having opened the wardrobes and chests of drawers, found no papers therein.' [1] This testimony of Commissioner Rochebrune incidentally affords some insight into the conditions of Diderot's daily work, suggesting that he did much of his writing at home, 'on a large table serving as a desk.' This routine, however, was about to be suddenly and completely altered, for D'Hémery told Diderot that he was under arrest.

It was by virtue of one of the notorious writs known as *lettres de cachet* that Diderot was arrested and imprisoned. *Lettres de cachet* have become one of the most odious symbols of the *ancien régime,* as every reader of *A Tale of Two Cities* can gauge by consulting his own feelings. Though numerous — the leading modern historian of Jansenism asserts that forty thousand were issued in the seventeen years of Cardinal Fleury's administration alone [2] — perhaps the *lettres de cachet* were not in reality so abusive as they came to seem. Apologists for the good old days point out that for the most part they were used to straighten out family tangles, just as Father

Diderot had secured one in 1742 in order to cool off his hot-headed son, or to enforce with contempt-of-court penalties what might be called injunctions in cases of private morality. Such apologists also emphasize that there is no evidence that these arrest warrants were issued in blank except under very carefully controlled conditions, so that the writs never became, as is often darkly suspected, the legal instruments of unjust vengefulness. There is no record of active maltreatment of persons detained by *lettres de cachet:* no evidence, for example, of torture or starvation, though there is of forget-fulness. Indeed, orders were given that people should be granted food and treatment in approximate accordance with their social rank. Diderot, for example, was to receive the equivalent of four livres a day for *'nourriture et attentions.'* [3] Finally, a *lettre de cachet* had to bear the countersignature of one of the king's principal ministers, and in this respect unquestionably satisfied the forms as much as could be expected of a warrant for arrest in any country at any time.[4]

But *lettres de cachet* were much less satisfactory in that they did not have to state the cause for arrest. Furthermore, persons thus arrested were held incommunicado, and it was entirely legal to detain them indefinitely, which was of course a frightening and demoralizing prospect. There came to be a rather widespread feeling in France while Sartine was Lieutenant-General of Police (1759-74) that the practice of issuing *lettres de cachet* was be-coming too extensive; [5] by the time of the Revolution, they had aroused a great sense of injustice. Perhaps *lettres de cachet* would not have come to seem so great an abuse had they not been the government's favorite method of attempting to discipline men of letters.[6] At first this policy was able to enforce an apparent conformity; but eventually it boomeranged, winning for the monarchy the persistent ill-will of the most articulate element of French society.

Two days before Diderot's arrest, Count d'Argenson, acting in his capacity of director of publications, wrote to the Lieutenant-General of Police, 'to give orders for putting Mr. Didrot, author of the book on the Blind Man, in Vincennes.' Berryer made the order the occasion for instructing his men to find out from Diderot all they could about *Letter on the Blind, Pensées philosophiques, Les Bijoux indiscrets,* a work called *L'Allée des idées* (prob-ably *La Promenade du sceptique*), and *L'Oiseau blanc, conte bleu.*[7] On 23 July the *lettre de cachet,* countersigned by D'Argenson, was made out at Compiègne.[8] And on 24 July Diderot and D'Hémery made the cab journey, at the king's expense, to Vincennes, an imposing medieval fortress and former royal residence six miles east of the heart of Paris.

Having been turned over to the governor of the place, François-Bernard du Châtelet, the relative of Voltaire's mistress and a man whose correspondence gives the impression that he was well-intentioned but bumbling, Diderot was immediately placed in the central keep.[9] This lofty tower was one of the most conspicuous symbols of the grimmer side of the *ancien régime,* 'the very sight of which,' wrote the author of an eighteenth-century guide book, 'causes fear.'[10] The edifice has had its most famous and its most gracious depiction in one of Fouquet's beautiful miniatures for the Duc de Berry's Book of Hours. It remains today just as it evidently looked to Fouquet in the fifteenth century, when he made his calendar-pictures. Diderot's place of confinement, according to tradition, was in the north-west *tournelle* of the third floor, the floor directly above the room where Prince Hal is said to have died in 1422. Diderot's room was octagonal in shape, approximately thirteen feet square and twenty-eight feet high, with graceful vaultings, a brick floor, a window looking out toward the château's entrance gate, and an enormous fireplace, its mantel jutting out about six feet above the floor. The room (at least as seen in 1939; it was later closed to the public), is light and airy and would not have been too unpleasant in the summer season, the time when Diderot was there. It was, in short, a suitable place for meditation; but there was always the very great risk that he would be left to meditate infinitely longer than he desired. Every day, Mme de Vandeul states, the jailer brought Diderot two candles. But he, who got up and went to bed with the sun, had no use for them, and after a fortnight's accumulation tried to return them. 'Keep them, keep them, Monsieur!' cried the jailer; 'You have too many of them now but they'll come in very handy in the winter'![11]

In her distress, Mme Diderot sought an interview with Berryer, who adopted the rough and tough approach. 'Well, Madam, we've got your husband and he'd better talk. You might spare him a lot of trouble and hasten his release if you would tell us where his manuscripts are. . . .' But his wife disclaimed knowing anything at all about Diderot's works, claiming never to have read any of them.[12] As for the publishers, they were much given in this emergency to bustling about in carriages, as their account books show.[13] The very day of the arrest the publishers addressed a petition to D'Argenson in which they stated that the *Encyclopédie* was on the point of being announced to the public and in which they declared that 'the detention of M. Diderot, the only man of letters we know of capable of so vast an enterprise and who alone possesses the key of this whole operation, can bring about our ruin.'[14]

The agitation of the publishers to secure Diderot's release was unremitting all through the time of his imprisonment. Four days after the arrest they had presented their case to the Chancellor and had come to the conclusion that nothing would be done until the Lieutenant-General of Police had interviewed Diderot and reported thereon. Consequently they besought Berryer to interrogate the prisoner: 'he [Diderot] is the center where all the parts of the *Encyclopédie* have to converge; his detention suspends all operations on it and will inevitably bring about our ruin if it should be at all long.' [15]

The interrogation, which took place in the tower, occurred on 31 July, exactly a week after the arrest. Apparently Diderot was still hoping that he could brazen things out. Already he had persuaded one of the prison officers — that golden tongue again — to present directly to Berryer a request to be allowed to use the large central room of the storey in which he was confined, a request evidently annoying to the Marquis du Châtelet, who did not care to have his authority thus short-circuited.[16] During the interview with Berryer, Diderot admitted nothing. Moreover, he declared under oath that he had not written the *Letter on the Blind* nor caused it to be printed nor had he sold or given the manuscript of it to anyone; that he did not know the identity of the author, that he had not had the manuscript in his possession either before it was printed or afterward, and that he had not distributed or given copies of the book to anyone. As for *Les Bijoux indiscrets* and *Pensées philosophiques,* he swore that he had not written them, and he specifically stated that he did not know who was the author of the *Pensées.* He further claimed not to have written or corrected *L'Oiseau blanc,* but admitted to having written *La Promenade du sceptique,* saying that the manuscript had been burned.[17] Inasmuch as Berryer learned the very next day from the publisher Durand that Diderot *was* the author of the *Pensées,* the *Bijoux,* and the *Lettre sur les aveugles,* the magistrate evidently adopted the policy of simply waiting until Diderot saw fit to volunteer more information.[18]

Under this sort of duress Diderot began to suffer very much. This was natural enough, for the extreme sociability of his nature and his talkativeness made him less fitted than most people for the rigors of solitary confinement. Though Diderot had been given much more freedom by the time Rousseau was allowed to see him, the visitor found Diderot 'greatly affected by his imprisonment. The keep had made a terrible impression upon him and, although he was [now] comfortable at the castle and allowed to walk where he pleased in a park that was not even surrounded by walls, he needed the society of his friends to avoid giving way to melancholy.' [19] Condorcet, a much younger contemporary of Diderot, is reported to have said that Diderot almost went crazy while he was in solitary confinement.[20] This is quite possible, especially in view of Diderot's unusually powerful and vivid imagination and sensitivity. His emotional response to situations — to music, to a generous action, to plays, to pictures, to an act of injustice, to anything either aesthetic or ethical that was beautiful or hideous — was extreme. It is therefore quite possible that there was little exaggeration in the long letter that he wrote to Berryer in which he darkly hinted that he might do violence to himself.

This letter of 10 August 1749, in which he states incidentally that 'my father is still ignorant of my marriage,' is as characteristic of Diderot as anything he ever wrote. It contains the sensibility for which he is famous — 'I feel that despair will soon finish what my bodily infirmities have greatly advanced'; the bouquets naïvely thrown at himself by his own willing hand; the torrential and expostulatory style that he made very plausible and convincing whenever he wrote in passionate defense of his own innocence and virtue; and a certain deliberate obtuseness in failing to conceive what he could possibly have done wrong. And in all this lengthy letter he does not say a word about the *Pensées*, the *Bijoux*, or the *Letter on the Blind!* [21]

Writing to D'Argenson the same day, Diderot made the same assertions, although more briefly and in a more reserved style. But in this emergency he had bait to dangle in front of the Secretary of War. 'Alas! Monseigneur, when he [Diderot is here talking of himself] was brought to this prison, he was on the point of publishing the prospectus [of the *Encyclopédie*] and of soliciting from Your Highness the permission to publish under your auspices this work that has been undertaken for the glory of France and the shame of England, and which is perhaps worthy, at least in this respect, of being offered to a minister who protects the arts and those who cultivate them.' [22] This proffer was obviously a bribe, a *quid pro quo*. It is very interesting to see that Diderot evidently regarded himself as so exclusively the director of the *Encyclopédie* that he felt free to offer the dedication without first consulting D'Alembert or the publishers. It may of course be true that he really had been intending all along to broach the subject to D'Argenson and had previously cleared the matter with his associates. But probably he had not, for if he had, the publishers would surely have alluded to it in their petition to D'Argenson. Whether D'Alembert knew of it or not there is no telling. At all events, when the first volume of the *Encyclopédie* appeared, there was the dedication to D'Argenson, the shabby reality making the high-flown phrases sound rather brassy and cracked.

Three days went by and Diderot wrote to Berryer again, on 13 August. This time he confessed. After an elaborate beginning, in which he tried to ensnare Berryer in the toils of his own generous impulses, Diderot wrote, 'I therefore avow to you, as my worthy protector, what the tediousness of a prison and all imaginable penalties would never have made me say to my judge: that the *Pensées,* the *Bijoux,* and the *Lettre sur les aveugles* are excesses that slipped out of me; but that I can on the other hand pledge my honor (and I have some) that they will be the last, and that they are the only ones.' Diderot was evidently in a state of panic, for he even offered to reveal the names of the printers and publishers of his illicit works. He made this offer, however, contingent upon Berryer's giving his word of honor not to use this information in any way whatever to their disadvantage unless they were guilty of recidivism. And Diderot, characteristically, offered to tell them himself what he had done, if Berryer demanded it.[23]

This confession got results. Sometime before 21 August, Berryer informed the Marquis du Châtelet that Diderot was to leave the keep and be allowed the freedom of the grounds: 'His Majesty also saw fit, in view of the editing work with which he is charged, to allow him freely to communicate by writing or orally in the château, with the customary precautions, with persons from the outside who come there either for that purpose or for his domestic affairs. . . . You will have the goodness to have assigned to him in the château one or two commodious rooms for sleeping and working, with a bed and such other furniture as you customarily furnish to prisoners in the keep, and nothing more, reserving for him to procure greater conveniences at his own expense if he desires them.'[24]

Berryer wrote out with his own hand the statement that Diderot had to sign in order to enjoy these new conditions: 'I promise the Lieutenant-General of Police that I will not go beyond the château nor its courts nor the enclosure of the royal garden nor the bridges [over the moat] during the time it shall please His Majesty to have me kept a prisoner, submitting myself in case of disobedience on my part regarding the foregoing to be shut up all my life in the keep whence it has pleased the clemency of the King to have me brought forth.'[25]

One of the traditions concerning Diderot's imprisonment in the tower is that he had to improvise writing materials. An account of this was first published in an obscure and rare magazine called *La Bigarure,* printed at

The Hague. In its number dated 30 October 1749, Diderot being still in prison, *La Bigarure* told how he used a toothpick for a pen, a mixture of wine and pulverized slate for ink, and for paper a copy of Plato, which the ignorant jailer had allowed him to keep on the theory that no one could get any meaning out of such stuff.[26] Differing versions of the story are told by Mme de Vandeul, Naigeon, and Eusèbe Salverte, each of whom presumably got his 'facts' from Diderot himself.[27] Their accounts are fairly well reconciled by a document found among the Diderot papers. This is entitled 'Copy of the Notes written on the Margins of a Volume of Milton's *Works* by M. Diderot during his Detention in the Château of Vincennes,' these notes being 'The Apology of Socrates, translated from memory.'[28] *Some* writing he assuredly did in the tower, whether authorized or unauthorized, for he wrote the Marquis du Châtelet in late September to ask whether the notebooks that he had filled up there, mostly with notes on Buffon's *Natural History,* might be returned to him.[29]

Because of his demonstrativeness, which always made him very conspicuous in whatever situation he found himself, Diderot's release from the tower was very likely just the sort of tableau that he admired in the pictures of Greuze, genre pictures such as 'The Village Bride' or 'The Paternal Curse,' which endeavored to 'freeze' on canvas a sentimental or violently emotional scene. For here is the situation, as recounted by Mme de Vandeul: 'At the end of twenty-eight days, my mother was told to go to Vincennes. The associated publishers accompanied her [the publishers' account book actually shows an entry for carriage expenses for this very day, 22 August 1749].[30] Upon her arrival, he was brought out of the tower. . . .' The imagination kindles at the scene: Diderot, very much the center of the picture and gesticulating, quite as in real life; his wife, with her back to the beholder and in a bad light, as always; the turnkey, with his keys in his hand; perhaps the Marquis du Châtelet himself, very elegant in courtly attire; at one side the publishers, dressed in sober, bourgeois colors; and, to give variety to the scene, no doubt a barking dog or two, come from the Lord knows where.

Mme de Vandeul went on to describe Diderot's life for the next ten weeks. 'The Marquis du Châtelet heaped kindnesses upon him, invited him to his table, and took the greatest care to make this stay as little disagreeable and as convenient as possible to my mother. They stayed there three months, then they were permitted to go home.'[31] Inasmuch as Rousseau says in the *Confessions* that he sometimes accompanied Mme Diderot from Paris to Vincennes to visit Diderot, it may be that Mme Diderot did not stay there continuously, in spite of Mme de Vandeul's statement that she did. A picture of Diderot's routine while in the château is also reflected in the Marquis du Châtelet's notes to Berryer. One on 30 August required correction and amplification, for Berryer replied to it the very next day, evidently in alarm lest Diderot was not being held strictly to his word. So Châtelet wrote again on 3 September that Diderot had profited only once from the permission to move freely in the courts of the château. 'He has gone out three times evenings for an hour with his wife in the park. He is well. Many people come to work with him, but I believe he is unable to get much done here.' [32]

Into this Eden Lilith came. Mme de Puisieux paid a visit. But Diderot had become suspicious of her and finally 'he slipped out over the walls, went to Champigny, saw his mistress there with her new lover, came back, and slept in the park. The next morning he went to inform M. du Châtelet of his escapade, and this little adventure accelerated his rupture with Mme de Puisieux.' [33]

It is very hard to know how much of this story to believe. On the one hand, a cooling-off in the relations between Diderot and Mme de Puisieux did occur at approximately this time. And although it may seem odd that Mme de Puisieux should visit Diderot at Vincennes while Mme Diderot was there, still Diderot could conceivably have arranged interviews without his wife's knowledge. But it seems unbelievable, considering the penalty he might incur, that Diderot would take the fearful risk of breaking his parole. Joseph Delort, writing in 1829 with a profusion of underlinings, claimed that Diderot 'afterward asserted (according to the note that lies before us) that he went out several times at night to go to see in Paris a woman he loved.' [34] M. Delort vouches for this. But who, as Gibbon might ask, will vouch for M. Delort? And Funck-Brentano, also without documentation, declares that the Marquis du Châtelet made these escapades possible by conniving at them.[35] Yet, considering the nervousness of Berryer's response to what he thought was an indication of laxity in Du Châtelet's dealing with Diderot, it does not seem likely that the governor of the prison would have been very eager to be accessory to such goings-on. This is the sum of the evidence, vague and uncertain as it is.

Diderot's arrest had caused some public stir and aided a great deal in making his name well known. As early as 26 July, an Abbé Trublet wrote to a lady of his acquaintance about Diderot's imprisonment: 'It is this last drop of water [*Letter on the Blind*] that has made the vase overflow, and this has come about, it is said, through the complaints lodged by M. de Réaumur. You know that he is not well treated in the first few pages.' [36]

Voltaire, writing from Lunéville, almost two hundred miles from Paris, knew of Diderot's imprisonment by 29 July, only five days after it had taken place.[37] The entries, not all of them accurate, in the journal of the Marquis d'Argenson, brother of the Secretary for War, show that the case was talked about in ministerial and court circles, just as a similar entry in the equally famous journal of the bourgeois, Barbier, proves that Diderot's name was becoming known among lawyers at Paris.[38]

Diderot's misfortune had the indirect effect of allowing posterity to know who were the persons, and presumably the most influential persons, with whom he had any connection in 1749. For in his letters to Berryer and D'Argenson he mentions as people who could vouch for him, a M. de Bombarde (of whom nothing is now known), Voltaire, Mme du Châtelet (who had acknowledged his gift of a copy of his book on mathematics),[39] Fontenelle, Mme du Deffand, Buffon, Daubenton, Clairaut, Duclos, the Abbé Sallier, Helvétius, and D'Alembert. Many of these came to be great names in the eighteenth century, and some were already so. This was true of Voltaire and Mme du Châtelet, and especially of Fontenelle, then ninety-two years old, the author of the *History of Oracles* and *On the Plurality of Worlds,* a wonderfully live nonagenarian whom an American sports-writer would inevitably have called 'the grand old man of French letters.' Mme du Deffand (1697–1780) was the celebrated hostess of one of the eighteenth century's most celebrated *salons,* a lady who maintained her commanding intellectual and social position in spite of the blindness that came upon her, and who is known to English literature primarily because of her interesting and informative correspondence with Horace Walpole. Buffon was the famous naturalist, author of the interminable *Histoire naturelle,* the first volume of which appeared in that year, a person much like Samuel Johnson in respect to the massiveness and authority of his literary style. His colleague Daubenton (1716–99) was also a naturalist, who later contributed many articles to the *Encyclopédie.* Clairaut (1713–65) was an astronomer and geometrician whose particular specialty was the movements of the moon. Duclos (1704–72) had written a history of Louis XI and had recently been elected to the French Academy. The Abbé Sallier (1685–1761) was a well-known philologist and custodian of the Royal Library, and Helvétius, then the least known of the lot but eventually destined to unenviable notoriety as the author of a book entitled *De l'Esprit,* was then a farmer-general with an income of some 300,000 livres a year. But if Diderot knew these people no better than it can be demonstrated that he knew Voltaire, Mme du Châtelet, and Fontenelle, then his acquaintance with them was slight indeed.[40] Nevertheless, it is known that Mme du Châtelet wrote to her kinsman, the governor of Vincennes, asking him to make Diderot's imprisonment as mild as possible, and therefore it is possible that others of these persons did what they could in his behalf.[41]

Of one thing Diderot was confident, if we may judge from the prediction contained in his letter to Berryer on 10 August: his father would hasten to Paris as soon as he learned of his son's arrest. How disconcerting it must have been to Diderot, therefore, to find that his father stayed right at Langres and would not budge. Diderot's first letter was not even answered. His second was replied to on 3 September in a missive of which the spelling was frequently phonetic but the meaning unmistakable. Diderot found that he was not the prodigal son. The elder Diderot, his letter shows, had other sources of information about affairs at Paris than just his son's letters. When he wrote, therefore, he wrote with a decidedly detached and astringent air, filling his letter with more sense than comfort. He reminded the son of his mother, 'In the remonstrances that she made to you by her own lips, she told you several times that you were blind.' Didier Diderot's best advice, at least in his estimation, was that Denis should straightway write a book of Christian edification! 'This will bring down upon you the bene-dictions of Heaven and will keep you in my good graces.' The father then asked whether it was true that his son was married and had two children. 'I expect that you will not refuse to your sister the pleasure of rearing them, nor to me the pleasure of seeing them under my eyes.' About money the crusty old man became quite sardonic but sent a hundred and fifty livres just the same.[42] And probably it was greatly needed in the household in the Rue de l'Estrapade, for the publishers' account book shows that Diderot's salary was discontinued by them during his imprisonment, there being no payment entered between 14 July and late November.[43]

The letters that Diderot had written to his father are not extant. Nor is it possible to know what effect the harshness of the letter just quoted had upon him. Probably it convinced him that he would have to make his own peace with the authorities, and that his liberation was not going to be brought about by sentimental arguments or the intercession of relatives. At all events, in this same month of September Diderot volunteered in an undated note a far-reaching promise as to his future conduct: '[he] promises to do nothing in the future that might be contrary in the slightest respect to religion and good morals.' Under this promise, Berryer wrote, 'If Count d'Argenson deems that he [Diderot] has done sufficient penance for his intellectual excesses, he is entreated to have the King's order sent for his release.'[44] Berryer's note suggests that Diderot's release depended upon his making a solemn promise. If so, it may explain why so many of Diderot's subsequent writings were carefully tucked away in a drawer and never published during his lifetime.

None of Diderot's friends was more alarmed or more solicitous in his behalf than Rousseau. 'Nothing can ever describe the anguish that my friend's misfortune made me feel. My somber imagination, which always expects the worst, took alarm. I thought he would be there the rest of his life. I almost lost my mind.' When he was first able to see Diderot after the release from the tower, Rousseau greeted his friend with embraces, sobs, and tears. D'Alembert and a stranger were present, and Diderot said to the latter, perhaps conceitedly but more likely appreciatively, after the strain of three weeks of solitary confinement, 'You see, Monsieur, how my friends love me.'[45]

Because of Diderot's imprisonment in Vincennes, the road thither became the scene of the most dramatic event of the Enlightenment. 'The summer of 1749 was excessively hot,' wrote Rousseau in his *Confessions*. 'It is two leagues from Paris to Vincennes. Scarcely able to afford cabs, at two o'clock in the afternoon I would set out on foot when I was alone, and I walked fast in order to get there the sooner. . . . often, quite spent by the heat and by fatigue, I would stretch out on the ground able to do no more. In order to go more slowly, I decided to take a book. One day I took the *Mercure de France* [the October issue] and as I walked and read, I lit upon the question proposed by the Academy of Dijon for its prize for the following year: *Whether the progress of the sciences and the arts has contributed to corrupting the morals or purifying them*. At the instant of reading this I saw another universe and I became another man. . . . Upon arriving at Vincennes I was in an agitation bordering upon delirium. Diderot perceived it: I told him the cause. . . . He exhorted me to give rein to my ideas and to compete for the prize.'[46]

Carlyle in his essay on 'Diderot' suggests the Biblical self-dedication of the Encyclopedists when he speaks of 'the *Acts* of the *French Philosophes*,' a phrase anticipatory of Carl Becker's *The Heavenly City of the Eighteenth-Century Philosophers*. Using such Scriptural comparisons, it may be said of Rousseau's revelation that in its suddenness and thoroughness it was similar to what happened to Saint Paul on the road to Damascus. Rousseau, in a sudden flash of mystical insight, discovered the state of nature, the pristine condition of virtue and purity. He saw with blinding certainty that the arts and sciences, contrary to usual opinion, had made us worse, not better. From then on he was to write books beginning with sentences such

as 'Everything is good as it leaves the hands of the Author of things; everything degenerates in the hands of man' (*Emile*), or 'Man is born free and
everywhere he is in chains' (*The Social Contract*). Rousseau threw himself
into this persuasion of the corruption of society with all the passion of a
pathologically sensitive person — Edmund Burke remarked that Rousseau
had no skin — a person of enormous although unsuspected talents, who
envies at the same time that he despises a highly sophisticated and polished
society in which he has not been quite successful. It is the boy from Geneva
not quite making good in Paris; the African from Tagaste, Augustine by
name, not quite successful in Rome or Milan. And because Rousseau was
one of the most eloquent writers who ever lived, his doctrines took on
enormous political importance in the eighteenth-century movement of ideas.
For he was dedicated, in brief, to the conviction that whatever is, is wrong.

As the years went by, Rousseau and Diderot quarreled in a spectacular
fashion, and Diderot subsequently fell victim to the temptation of asserting
that it was he who suggested the famous paradox to Rousseau.[47] For example, he once told Marmontel — at that time a very prominent man of
letters, though his laurel leaves are now much withered — that he had
asked Rousseau which side of the question he proposed to take.

'"The affirmative," said Rousseau.

'"That's the *pons asinorum*," I said to him. "All the mediocre talents
will take that path . . ."

'"You're right," he said to me, after having reflected upon it for a
moment, "and I'll follow your advice." '[48]

Exactly the same story is told by other contemporaries — by La Harpe,
by Collé, by Meister, and by the Abbé Morellet, who adds that this version
was accepted as established by all Baron d'Holbach's circle.[49] And Mme
de Vandeul states quite flatly that 'my father gave to Rousseau the idea of
his Discourse on the Arts.'[50] Rousseau, on the other hand, solemnly assured
a friend that he had made his choice without Diderot and solely by himself.[51]
Consequently, as might readily be expected, the question of whether Rousseau is to be denied any originality whatsoever has become a favorite battle-
ground for his partisans and his detractors, as well as a focal point for some
skillful exercises in impartial scholarship.[52]

In his *writings,* Diderot was much more cautious in his allegations about
Rousseau and the prize essay. Twice he alluded to the incident, in passages
one of which was published during his lifetime, the other posthumously. In
each instance he stops short of declaring that he gave Rousseau the idea;
he merely takes credit for knowing his Rousseau:

'When the program of the Academy of Dijon appeared, he came to consult me on the side that he should take.

' "The side you'll take," I said to him, "is the one no one else will."

' "You're right," he replied.' [53]

Although Diderot was now permitted to work on the *Encyclopédie,* his enforced residence at Vincennes was a handicap. As Du Châtelet had remarked, he was unable to get much done. The associated publishers, in support of what they called 'the finest and most useful enterprise yet undertaken by the book trade,' petitioned D'Argenson on this subject:

the enterprise on which Your Highness has deigned to cast some favorable regards cannot be finished so long as M. Diderot is at Vincennes. He is obliged to consult a considerable number of craftsmen, who do not like to be shifted about; to confer with a number of men of letters, who do not have the leisure to go to Vincennes; and finally, to have access constantly to the Royal Library, the books of which cannot and ought not to be carried so far away. Besides, My Lord, to supervise the drawings and engravings, one must have the workers' tools before one's eyes, an essential which M. Diderot can make use of only on the spot.[54]

Another and much more elaborate petition dated 7 September covered the same ground.[55]

Perhaps the publishers would not have been so importunate had D'Alembert filled in for the absent editor. But evidently he either could not or would not; the publishers declared that without Diderot it was impossible to instruct the printers how to set up mathematical material correctly.[56] From this it may be inferred that D'Alembert did not concern himself with correcting proof, even on material he himself had written, and he seems to have taken great care not to contract any guilt by association. At least such would seem to be a reasonable interpretation to put upon his letter of 19 September to Formey, the secretary of the Berlin Academy: 'The detention of M. Diderot has become much less severe; nevertheless it still lasts, and the *Encyclopédie* is suspended. I never intended to have a hand in it except for what has to do with mathematics and physical astronomy. I am in a position to do only that, and besides I do not intend to condemn myself for ten years to the tedium of seven or eight folios.' [57]

In a folder marked 'Diderot,' constituting part of the archives of the Bastille that long ago were transferred to the Bibliothèque de l'Arsenal at Paris, there is a little slip of paper addressed to the Marquis du Châtelet and written in the hand of Berryer. Dated 29 October 1749, it stated that the *lettre de cachet* ordering Diderot's release had been made out on 21

October, and that Du Châtelet was to release Diderot as soon as he received Berryer's note. Another hand, not Berryer's, scratched out the date 29 October and inserted instead '3 9bre'; and indeed it was on 3 November that Diderot was released.[58]

Now he was free to return to the Rue de l'Estrapade and to the enormous backlog of work that had been accumulating since his arrest 102 days previously. What were the ideas, the conclusions, that this unwelcome interlude caused to revolve in his mind? Many, no doubt, and deep-seated, for the atrabilious moods of his solitary imprisonment seem to have darkened his thought for several years. Rousseau speaks in his *Confessions* of the melancholy that Diderot acquired during his confinement and asserts that it is apparent in *Le Fils naturel,* written seven years later.[59] But of one thought in Diderot's mind we may be sure. Many years later he proposed to Catherine II of Russia that he edit, at her expense, a new and better *Encyclopédie:* one of the advantages would be 'to substitute the name of a great and worthy sovereign for that of a second-rate minister who deprived me of my liberty in order to wring from me a tribute to which he could not lay claim by merit.' [60]

CHAPTER 10

The Prospectus of the *Encyclopédie,*
and *Letter on the Deaf and Dumb*

I T IS more than likely that Diderot spent the last weeks of 1749 and the first months of 1750 in seeking to make up for lost time. As the publishers' second petition to D'Argenson had gone to great lengths to establish, Diderot was indispensable.[1] The preparation for publishing the *Encyclopédie* could not be carried on satisfactorily without him. Their statement conveys to us a precise notion of how complex a job it was to be chief editor of the *Encyclopédie,* entailing as it did duties requiring not only the conventional blue-penciling and proofreading, but also a great deal of what is now called 'leg-work' and technological 'know-how.' For over twenty years Diderot spent the greater part of his time and energy in just this sort of daily editorial work. His was a task demanding the combined qualities of the genius and the drudge.

In the year following his detention in Vincennes there continued to be reverberations of the publication of *Letter on the Blind.* Speaking to the quinquennial Assembly of the Clergy, the Archbishop of Sens denounced the current manifestations of irreligion, as a result of which that body requested the Sorbonne to make a report on impious books, among them *Philosophical Thoughts* and *Letter on the Blind.*[2] The fictitious deathbed conversation of Saunderson, invented by Diderot, called into being an equally fictitious one in reply.[3] Though the principal French periodicals, such as the *Journal des Sçavans* and the *Journal de Trévoux,* did not deign to notice a volume that was, after all, highly contraband, the *Letter on the Blind* received a flattering amount of attention in news letters and periodicals published outside the boundaries of France. 'This book,' wrote one editor, 'has caused too much stir not to devote an article to it here.'[4] The stir was, indeed, so great that demand far outran supply. D'Alembert, writing to a friend in Switzerland who had asked for a copy, declared in February 1750 that it was very hard to procure one.[5]

The year 1750 witnessed a number of important events in the private life of Diderot. Not least remarkable among them was a complaint against his wife lodged with the police on 2 April. This document is still in existence in the National Archives of France, a single quarto sheet rather hard to find as it lies unbound and higgledy-piggledy with scores of similar depositions in a cardboard box.[6] In this complaint the servant of one of Mme Diderot's neighbors testified that on that very afternoon Mme Diderot, after picking a quarrel, had kicked the servant several times and knocked her head violently against the wall. Nevertheless, the record bears no evidence that the authorities did more than simply file the deposition. Apparently Mme Diderot was not admonished or even interrogated. Yet the existence of this document may surely be cited as proof that Mme Diderot was indeed a formidable woman, and that there may have been some basis in fact for a report of a similar and equally violent incident involving Mme Diderot a year and a half later.

This story appeared in the news magazine *La Bigarure,* which, as has been noted, was printed at The Hague and had published the account of Diderot's improvising ink when he was in solitary confinement at Vincennes. Even previous to this, the anonymous editor of *La Bigarure* had shown himself to be well informed about Diderot, accurately attributing to him the authorship of his various unacknowledged works.[7] When, therefore, under date of 3 December 1751, *La Bigarure* gleefully chronicled a fight between Mme Diderot and Mme de Puisieux, the account should not *necessarily* be regarded as a canard without any basis in fact. On balance, it seems to be testimony, however suspect and unconfirmed, that ought not to be totally disregarded. According to this account, which, incidentally, declared that Mme de Puisieux was 'frightfully ugly' and Mme Diderot, although 'a second Xantippe,' was 'as pretty as her rival is frightful,' Mme de Puisieux one day insulted Mme Diderot in the street, calling out among other things, 'Here, Mistress She-monkey, look at these two children; they are your husband's, who never did you the honor of doing as much for you.' This provocation led to a very spirited brawl, which the anonymous author describes in some lines of very indifferent verse, as though he felt, as had Homer, Virgil, Dante, and Milton, that prose could not do justice to such a sublime situation. In conclusion we learn that cold water had to be poured upon the combatants in order to separate them, and that Diderot, meanwhile, stayed inside, afraid to show his face.[8] Whether or not the anecdote was a fact, at least the publicity about it was, and Diderot probably had to face many people who had read the story.

If Mme de Puisieux actually made any such derisive remark about the lack of children in the Diderot household, she uttered a taunt the more calculatedly wounding because it was cruelly true. On 30 June 1750, little François-Jacques-Denis, only shortly past his fourth birthday, had died of a violent fever and been buried the next day at the Diderot's parish church of Saint-Etienne-du-Mont.[9] Several months later a third child was born to the grieving parents and duly carried to Saint-Etienne for baptism. Laurent Durand, the book publisher, stood godfather for the new boy, Denis-Laurent. According to Mme de Vandeul, a careless woman allowed the infant to fall on the steps of the church on the day of his baptism. Whether this be true or not, certainly the baby did not live long, Mme Diderot herself recording that he died toward the end of the year.[10] Thus the Diderots had been parents three times, and were now childless. Nor was there to be another baby until more than three years later.

It was probably also in 1750 that Diderot made the acquaintance of a man who was to be his closest and dearest friend the rest of his life. This was a young German named Friedrich Melchior Grimm, son of a Lutheran pastor at Regensburg. Grimm, following some years of study at the University of Leipzig, had come to Paris as the tutor-companion of a highly placed young German nobleman.[11] Rousseau had made Grimm's acquaintance in August of 1749,[12] and found him an extremely attractive person, then twenty-six years of age — Grimm was ten years younger than Diderot — greatly interested in music, and already endowed with that coolly ironical but accurate judgment of matters artistic that he was later to display to such advantage in his now famous news letter, the *Correspondance littéraire*.

In some ways Grimm was an adventurer, and certainly a careerist. His correspondence with the great furnishes rather elaborate proof that he knew which side his bread was buttered on. With all his elegance of manner, he could be ruthless, and through the years he could calmly exploit the time and energy of a friend like Diderot while constantly deploring that others desired to do so too. Because of this domineering manner with his friends, added to a reputed fondness for wearing face powder, Grimm's intimates called him 'The White Tyrant,' a punning reference to Tirant lo Blanch, the principal character of a Catalonian epic poem of the fifteenth century which had recently been translated into French.[13] Probably both particulars of the indictment were true. Certainly there is plenty of documentary evidence about the face powder. Grimm's papers, sequestered during the

French Revolution, are now in the National Archives, and there, among a vast collection of bills and receipts, may be found numerous ones from Dulac, Merchant Glover-Perfumer, at the Sign of the Golden Cradle, Rue Neuve-des-Petits-Champs, billing Grimm for 'fine powder purged with spirits of wine and perfumed *à la maréchalle.*' [14] In 1750 Grimm was far from being the successful and much-decorated man of affairs who impressed Ambassador Thomas Jefferson as being 'the pleasantest and most conversable member of the diplomatic corps.' [15] He had yet to establish himself: it was to be some decades before Catherine the Great would be calling him in her letters her *gobe-mouche* — it was a joke between them — her 'fag.'

Rousseau, who brought Grimm and Diderot together — their first meeting was in Rousseau's rooms — [16] was saddened to discover that each presently became fonder of the other than either was of him. Nevertheless, the year was not without its triumphs for Jean-Jacques, for on 9 July it was announced that his essay, which he had discussed with Diderot at Vincennes, had won the prize offered by the Academy of Dijon.[17] Diderot, with his usual generosity — and his usual impetuousness — arranged to see it through the press, but he gave the manuscript to the publisher instead of trying to make some money out of it for Rousseau.[18] In the last fortnight of November 1750, Rousseau's startling and paradoxical contention that the development of the arts and sciences had been noxious to mankind was ready for public perusal.[19] 'It's catching on like wildfire,' wrote Diderot to Rousseau; 'there is no example of success like it.' [20]

While Diderot was seeing Rousseau's discourse through the press, he was also busy putting the finishing touches on the prospectus of the *Encyclopédie*. Much depended, in fame and fortune, upon presenting the proposed work in an attractive way. Several times in 1749 the publishers had alleged that they were on the point of launching the prospectus, but, probably because of Diderot's imprisonment, this was much delayed. According to an unpublished document written in 1771 or 1772 by Joly de Fleury, the *procureur général* of France, Chancellor d'Aguesseau had personally approved and initialed a copy of the prospectus, satisfying by this approbation the regulations governing the previous submission of manuscript; and according to the same authority, the Lieutenant-General of Police had written on the prospectus, 'Permission for printing and posting, 11 November 1750. Signed Berryer.' [21] On 21 November 1750, the publishers drew up an agreement upon the procedure for accepting subscriptions.[22] It seems quite certain, then, as is stated in the *Encyclopédie* itself, that the prospectus was first circulated in November 1750.[23] Eight thousand copies of it were stitched (and presumably disseminated).[24] Eight thousand copies! — and they are now rarer than the whooping crane, almost as rare as the dodo. Indeed, the director of the French National Archives had considerable difficulty in 1950 in locating a copy.[25]

The salient features of the prospectus have already been described in the prologue to this book. In one of the closing paragraphs of his address to the public, Diderot spoke with humbleness of the importance and significance of this venture, and then, in abrupt transition, he saluted the future in what was a sort of dedication —

TO POSTERITY, AND TO THE BEING WHO DOES NOT DIE.

* * * * * *

Along with the editing of the *Encyclopédie* and the preparation of the prospectus, Diderot found time in 1750 to put down his speculations in a new field of thought. This *Lettre sur les sourds et muets à l'usage de ceux qui entendent et qui parlent* ('Letter on the Deaf and Dumb, for the Benefit of Those Who Hear and Speak') started out with some firsthand observations on the behavior of deaf-mutes and went on to canvass a number of interesting and original theories on linguistics and aesthetics. The work revealed an astonishing number of ingenious insights into the metaphysics of beauty and into the psychology of communication, discussing both gestures and word symbols. Just as a famous twentieth-century work entitled *The Meaning of Meaning* 'attempted to restate the problem of knowledge by means of a rigorous analysis of the functions of language,' so Diderot in his century attempted to do the same thing, breaking new ground in the study of semantics and word symbolism.[26]

This time, Vincennes having made him cautious, Diderot submitted his manuscript to the proper authorities. But although the censor passed the manuscript on 12 January 1751, there evidently was something about it that caused Malesherbes, the new director of publications, to feel that he could not authorize its publication with Diderot's name on the title page and with the accolade of '*Avec Approbation & Privilège du Roi.*'[27] Instead he gave it a 'tacit permission.' This curious and very common practice constitutes an excellent example of the sort of paradoxical and illogical procedure that the anomalies of the *ancien régime* brought into being. A tacit permission was an official connivance at an infringement of the regulations.[28] The practice was so general and so regularized that a register of most tacit permissions was kept on file by the syndics of the corporation of booksellers. Other tacit permissions, however, were accorded orally and without registration, the author and printer merely being given private and non-documentary assurances that they might publish a particular manuscript without molestation from the police. In every case, however, the censors previously read the manuscripts in the usual way and the director of publications knew perfectly what was going on. Yet all these numerous books were printed anonymously, with misleading places of publication printed on their title pages, the point being that they should bear every mark of being illicit and clandestine in order to save the government from being officially embarrassed by any statements they might contain. The advantage to the monarchy of this practice was that it increased the employment of French printers and helped keep French money inside French boundaries.[29]

Any work that received even tacit permission was not likely to contain incendiary doctrine against Church or State. In comparison with the *Letter on the Blind,* therefore, the *Letter on the Deaf and Dumb* may have seemed a little dull. Although the work had three editions in 1751 and another in 1772, and although Mme Necker, Diderot's friend and the famous wife of the famous statesman, thought it Diderot's best work — she claimed that he wrote it in a single night, which seems incredible for a book of some seventeen thousand words [30] — in general Diderot received less applause for it from his own generation than he does from the present one.

Diderot did not, however, compromise in this little book any of his convictions regarding psychology or metaphysics. He consistently assumed that knowledge is completely dependent upon the senses and that therefore a man's 'answers,' even his views on metaphysical questions, will be relative to his senses and, indeed, to the number of them. 'A society made up of five persons, each having only one of the five senses, would be, in my opinion, an amusing one': each would have a view of the world relative to his own sensory equipment, each would treat all the others as being senseless.[31] Thus Diderot was striking at and undermining various absolutist modes of thought. He did not get into trouble because this time he avoided the expression of inflammatory sentiment that in his previous treatise he had put into the mouth of the dying Saunderson. Nevertheless the *Letter on the Deaf and Dumb* incorporated and carried forward the new psychology and the new methodology which was so corrosive to older and more absolutist ways of thinking.[32]

In the course of the twentieth century the *Letter on the Deaf and Dumb* has come to be regarded more and more highly, not only as a document for establishing Diderot's extraordinary versatility and sensitivity but also as a book intrinsically valuable because of the light it throws on fundamental problems of poetics. Professors Torrey and Fellows call it 'one of the out-standing examples of literary criticism in the eighteenth century,' and continue: 'In this first essentially scientific study of the deaf and dumb, Diderot was interested in the art of communication by gesture and of the relationship between gesture and language. From the great actor who projects in gestures what he expresses in words, we are led to the deaf mute who, standing before a color-organ, at last surmises what music is — like language, a means of communication. This was deduced from the fact that, often before as in conversation, he had watched people's faces and expressions while music was being played outside his world of silence. There follows a discussion of the theory that the painter is capable of portraying but a single moment within which the past and future should be suggested, whereas the poet is able to depict a succession of moments. The conclusion is drawn from this that some subjects are best described in one medium, some in the other. (The debt of Lessing's *Laokoön* to Diderot need hardly be insisted upon.) [33] But, we are told, the poet should realize that he is dealing with words, and words have both meaning and sound. The superior poet will then paint in sounds what he is expressing in meaning. Furthermore, poetry is the interweaving of hieroglyphs, that is, a series of pictures representing ideas. In this sense, Diderot adds, all poetry is "emblématique" or symbolical, but only the poet of genius succeeds in saying the inexpressible. Thus the reader, who has almost forgotten that he started out by reading a brief essay on the deaf and dumb, finds he has arrived at an esthetic theory which leads directly to Baudelaire and the Symbolists by means of certain fundamental principles which, quite possibly, have not yet been fully explored.' [34]

Diderot's doctrine that the words the poet uses are fraught with elusive and magical overtones has caught the imagination of contemporary critics, especially since he referred to such words as hieroglyphs, thus calling particular attention to their symbolic nature.[35] This theory seems a little startling in contrast to the formal verse — much of it exceedingly earth-bound — that the age composed; and it is the enunciation of a doctrine such as this that makes Diderot seem so 'modern' to the aestheticians and the creative experimenters of the nineteenth and twentieth centuries.[36] It was partly because Diderot was so proficient a classicist that this theory occurred to him. For the examples he cites are taken not simply from Corneille, Racine, Voltaire, and Boileau, but from the Greek of Epictetus and the Latin of Cicero and the Italian of Tasso. Rhythms and the quantities and stresses of syllables, with their subtle and elusive intertwining of sense impression and meaning, fascinated him. Can we not, as a French critic has recently suggested, can we not hear Diderot in these passages, declaiming with that accompaniment of gesture that was habitual with him and of which he was so fond? [37] He analyzes, much as Ruskin analyzed a passage of Milton in *Sesame and Lilies,* some of the haunting passages from the *Iliad* and the *Aeneid,* from Ovid and from Lucretius. 'All this inevitably disappears in translation,' he wrote, 'even in the best.' [38]

Modern critics, speaking of the *Letter on the Deaf and Dumb,* are likely to concur with a scholar who recently spoke of Diderot's mind as being 'like one of those complicated modern rockets which startle by the unsuspectedness and apparent inexhaustibility, as well as by the brilliance of their evolutions.' [39] The same point was made by the Abbé Raynal at the time, but in a much less complimentary vein: 'M. Diderot speaks on this occasion of a thousand things, on metaphysics, poetry, eloquence, music, etc., which have only a very tenuous connection with the principal subject. This letter is not pleasing, but it is instructive. . . . Everything that comes from M. Diderot's pen is full of new viewpoints and of well-grounded metaphysics; but his works are never finished: they are sketches; I doubt whether his vivacity and his precipitation will ever permit him to finish anything.' [40] This is one of the earliest examples of what came to be in the eighteenth and nineteenth centuries a commonplace of criticism of the works of Diderot.

The *Letter on the Deaf and Dumb* was by way of being a criticism, and by no means a gentle one, of a work published not long before that had sought to discover a single unifying principle of beauty applicable to all the fine arts. This book was the Abbé Charles Batteux's *Les Beaux-Arts réduits à un même principe* (1746), and Diderot, in his allusions to it, could be conceived to have gone considerably beyond the call of duty.[41] All these personalia are forgotten now, and only Diderot's interesting insights into the problems of aesthetics remain, but it need not be overlooked that Diderot had a taste for polemics and that his personality generated heat, causing both him and the people with whom he was in contact to glow, whether with a gratified sense of fellow feeling or with a consciousness of exasperated antagonism.

A few weeks later Diderot published what amounted to the second edition of the *Letter on the Deaf and Dumb,* with additions. His introductory remarks were dated 3 March 1751, and D'Hémery noted in his journal for 20 May that the *Additions to Serve as Clarification for some of the Passages in the Letter on the Deaf and Dumb* was already published, with Malesherbes' tacit permission.[42] Diderot says that these additions were written in reply to the comments and criticisms of a very intelligent young woman of his acquaintance, Mlle de La Chaux, whose pathetic love story he tells in one of his highly regarded short stories, *Ceci n'est pas un conte* ('This Is No Yarn').[43] In the same edition was also printed Diderot's lengthy observations in rebuttal of criticisms his book had received in the April issue of the *Journal de Trévoux*.[44]

Meanwhile, the publication of the prospectus had brought about a short but sharp passage at arms between Diderot and the Jesuit editors of that same periodical, the first skirmish in what was to become a bitter and protracted war. Diderot was a formidable antagonist, but so were his opponents. They were led by the chief editor, Father Berthier, an able person who carried on the *Journal de Trévoux,* it was said, 'to the satisfaction of all, as much for his skill in digesting works as for his prudent moderation in criticisms and eulogies. . . .'[45] He was certainly moderate in his eulogy of the prospectus: in his first number for 1751 he quite patently implied that the celebrated chart or scheme of human knowledge that the prospectus contained was nothing but a barefaced plagiarism of Bacon: 'The editors, MM. Diderot and d'Alembert, make known with reference to this system that they have principally followed Chancellor Bacon, author of the book *On the Dignity and Increase of the Sciences.* And this is so true that we intend to fall in with their views, while giving pleasure to the public, by printing an extract that will compare the work of the Chancellor with the Prospectus of the *Encyclopédie,* especially in regard to the tree of human knowledge.' In this extract, which appeared in the next issue, the editors found that 'the system of this learned Englishman was followed point by point and word for word by our Authors.'[46]

At this juncture Diderot took fire, and not without cause. He had expressly stated in the prospectus his obligations to Lord Bacon, so that the imputations of the *Journal de Trévoux* seemed all the more unfair, unnecessary, and aggressive. Perhaps the antagonism of the *Journal de Trévoux* in this connection can be explained, as was propounded at the time, by the Jesuits' previous expectations of being asked to take an important share in contributing to the *Encyclopédie* — D'Alembert later stated that their fury was caused by the refusal to confide to them the theological part of the *Encyclopédie* — [47] and their subsequent vexation at finding themselves ignored.

Diderot's response to this attack was in the form of a pamphlet containing, by way of sample, his forthcoming *Encyclopédie* article on 'Art,' and also, more to the point, an open *Letter from M. Diderot to the Reverend Father Berthier, Jesuit.*[48] This was a vigorous exercise in polemics, but contained nothing of interest beyond the dispute itself, although the contemporary journalist Clément spoke of it as being 'full of fire, wit, and charm.'[49] The *Journal de Trévoux* in turn replied, 'Diderot is a man of intelligence, and there is pleasure in receiving his letters when they concern literature. Other matters are too dangerous, he knows very well.' This exordium, sounding very ominous and menacing, was followed by a sneer: 'Several of these gentlemen of the *Encyclopédie* are known to us; we hold them in high esteem; they have competence, politeness, morals, and religion. M. Diderot has given a singular proof of his modesty by not naming them after him in the frontispiece of the Prospectus. Their names would have shed a great luster upon his.'[50]

The *Second Letter of M. Diderot to the Reverend Father Berthier* was written at nine o'clock in the evening of 2 February 1751, when Diderot was still red-hot from having just read the offensive article in the *Journal de Trévoux*.[51] D'Hémery, when noting in his journal that Malesherbes had granted permission to publish this reply, described it as 'a very judicious work.'[52] This may be so; but its arguments were simply *ad hominem,* and there is nothing in the letter that has survived in interest the storm and stress of the occasion that produced it.

It is a matter of doubt whether Diderot was wise to engage in such a dispute. Evidently the publishers of the *Encyclopédie* had misgivings on this point, for Diderot mentions in an undated letter that clearly seems to refer to this time and probably to this incident that 'Messieurs the associates . . . were not in favor of printing it.'[53] But whether wise or not, the exchange of salvos served to engage the public interest, as was evidenced by the publication of a number of pamphlets, all of them now very rare, regarding the dispute. One of these, a four-page *Lettre à M. * * *, de la Société Royale de Londres,* was thought by D'Hémery to emanate from Diderot's circle or even to have been written by Diderot himself.[54] While appearing to blame Diderot, it awarded him all the honors of the combat: 'M. Diderot, who is known to be a man of genius, gifted with a very brilliant imagination, and who enjoys a merited reputation, has had the weakness to write to Father Berthier with a vivacity which even his greatest partisans have disapproved of. His letter is in truth full of ingenious sallies, its style is firm and concise, but one might almost say that each sentence is a poignard wrapped up in a bolt of lightning.' Poor Father Berthier!

A Jesuit whom Diderot greatly admired evidently wrote to him at this juncture, endeavoring to moderate the dispute. This was Father Castel, a benign and ingenious person who is remembered as the inventor of a color-organ, a harpsichord-like instrument the intent of which was to suggest sensations of melody and harmony by combining multi-colored ribbons rather than sounds. Diderot frequently mentions this machine — for example, in *Les Bijoux indiscrets,* in the *Letter on the Deaf and Dumb,* and in the *Encyclopédie* — as creating what he calls ocular music or sonatas in color.[55] Father Castel's color-organ was of scientific interest because, as Diderot himself realized, it raised a number of interesting and complicated psychological problems, in particular the phenomenon of inter-sensory association now called by the name of synesthesia.[56] Father Castel's organ was, indeed, one of the most 'philosophical' inventions of the eighteenth century.

Diderot received Father Castel's letter with great respect, although it did not modify his sense of grievance. 'But in the name of God, reverend Father,' he replied, 'what is Father Berthier thinking about to persecute an honest man who has no enemies in society other than those he has made for himself by his attachment to the Society of Jesus and who, displeased as he ought to be, has nevertheless just refused with utter contempt the weapons he has been offered against it?' This virtuous feeling arose from the fact that just after the publication of his second letter to Berthier, Diderot had received a note proffering information and money if he would use them against the Jesuits.[57] It is clear that Diderot's letters to Berthier caused something of a sensation, for although the Jesuits were used to being opposed by Jansenists, this was one of the very first occasions when their position was openly challenged by a *philosophe.*[58]

Spring of this year brought a scholarly and academic honor to Diderot, and one of which he could make very profitable display. The Prussian Royal Academy of Sciences and Belles-Lettres made him a member, just in time to allow him to mention it on the title page of Volume I of the *Encyclopédie.* Diderot's letter of thanks to Formey, the secretary, was dated 5 March 1751.[59] It was Diderot's first academy and, even in a century pullulating with academies of various kinds, almost his last. It is preposterous, but still true, that the man with one of the most seminal minds of the century should have gained admittance to no more academies than the Prussian, two Russian ones, and the Society of the Antiquaries of Scotland. It was not because he spurned invitations, for the evidence is pretty clear that he joined every academy or learned society that ever asked him. The fact was that Diderot's thought was too radical and came too close to being openly atheistic to qualify him for membership in the most respectable and sedate circles. It might be supposed that the Royal Society of London, not being so committed to an official orthodoxy as were the French academies, might have extended him a bid, especially since they invited not only D'Alembert but also the indefatigable and rather limited Encyclopedist, the Chevalier de Jaucourt. But apparently, as D'Hémery noted in his journal in 1753, the Royal Society resented Diderot's insinuation in his *Letter on the Blind* that one of their former members, the blind Saunderson, had died an atheist — resented it to the point of blackballing him permanently.[60]

Even the membership in the Prussian Academy was evidently something of a *quid pro quo*. Beginning in 1742, Formey had been collecting materials for an encyclopedic compilation, and these he offered to the editors of the *Encyclopédie* after the prospectus of 1745 had appeared.[61] The account book of the publishers shows that in 1747 they contributed three hundred livres toward the acquisition of these manuscripts and promised to send Formey a set of the *Encyclopédie* free of charge and to name him in the preface.[62] Diderot acknowledged these manuscripts very handsomely in his prospectus but without mentioning that they had been paid for, and one can only put two and two together when three months later he was made one of Formey's academy colleagues.

Public anticipation of the appearance of Volume I was increasing, whetted not only by the controversy with the *Journal de Trévoux*, but also by the sample article on 'Art' which Diderot published.[63] 'It will be the best dictionary of things that there has been up to now,' wrote the anonymous author of the *Lettre à M. * * *, de la Société royale de Londres.* 'The prodigious multiplicity of its contents, its extensiveness, and the advantage of a large number of plates showing the work of various artisans, cannot but make it useful, interesting, and curious.' [64] No less a person than Buffon, writing in December 1750, had said that the authors had shown him several articles and that the work was going to be good; and again in April, he remarked of Volume I, 'I have gone through it; it is a very good work.' [65] The official censor, writing on 24 June, gave it a very resounding compliment indeed: 'By order of My Lord the Chancellor I have read in the first volume of the Encyclopedical Dictionary the articles concerning medicine, physics, surgery, chemistry, pharmacology, anatomy, natural history, and in general everything that does not appertain to theology, jurisprudence, or history.

'The various subjects have appeared to me to be well treated therein, conformable to the arrangement, extensiveness, and clarity that they demand: and I am of the opinion that the editors of this great work are beginning to carry out in a very satisfactory manner the vast plan that they sketched in the prospectus which the public received so warmly. I found nothing in this first volume that does not merit being printed.' [66]

As the reputation of the *Encyclopédie* grew, so did the list of subscribers, which stood at 1,002 in April of 1751 and 1,431 in July.[67] Meanwhile, on 28 June 1751, the much-heralded volume was published.[68] Its title page, simple as eighteenth-century titles go, ran as follows:

ENCYCLOPEDIE

or

ANALYTICAL DICTIONARY

OF THE SCIENCES,

ARTS AND CRAFTS,

By a Society of Men of Letters.

Placed in order and published by M. Diderot, of the Prussian Royal Academy of Sciences and Belles-Lettres; and, for the mathematical portion, by M. d'Alembert, of the Royal Academy of Sciences at Paris, of that of Prussia, and of the Royal Society of London.

PARIS

Published by Briasson, the elder David, Le Breton, and Durand

MDCCLI

With Approbation and License of the King.

CHAPTER 11

What Readers Found in Volume I
of the *Encyclopédie*

THE public that greeted the first volume of the *Encyclopédie* was neither impartial nor indifferent. Readers were in a mood to be particularly responsive to — or particularly repelled by — what they found therein. And what they found was a book that purported to be a book of reference but was in fact a sort of political tract. It was a work which, in the course of imparting information, helped to transform men's values. It was a work which helped to make men favorable to change. Historians are agreed that the *Encyclopédie* played an extremely important part as one of the disposing causes of the French Revolution. It was, in short, a publication with a profound political impact.

The *Encyclopédie* was like a great modern newspaper with a strongly defined editorial policy, one which is not always acknowledged but which, far from being confined to its editorial page, creeps into its reporting and even into its special features and comic strips. There was a great deal of skillful editorializing in the columns of the *Encyclopédie*. To use a term with unpleasant connotations, we must fairly admit that the authors of the *Encyclopédie* were propagandists. Yet in their behalf it can also be said that they were propagandists not in the too frequent sense of sophists industriously and knowingly attempting to make the worse seem the better cause, but in the more gracious sense of propagandists who recognize no higher authority than truth, who are convinced that they are in search of it, and who propagandize for what they are certain will enlighten and profit mankind. And because the *Encyclopédie* was pre-eminent in its field, its effectiveness as an instrument of propaganda was all the greater. Its audience was almost a captive one: the wariest and most sophisticated of its readers, as well as the most gullible and ingenuous, found it indispensable.

Not only was the *Encyclopédie* a work that hoped to persuade its readers to a certain point of view, but also a publication that, because of the conditions of censorship, had to pick its way with extraordinary care whenever it alluded to matters involving politics or theology. Any criticism of existing conditions had to be exceedingly oblique and indirect, for this was a publishing venture completely dependent upon official authorization. How else arrange for a subscription list, without which the enormous work would be financially too precarious? How else carry through successfully all the editorial complexities of so large an undertaking? Accordingly the sophisticated soon realized that it was necessary not only to read the lines of the *Encyclopédie* but also between them. The public soon learned to identify, whether with alarm or delight, the manifold contrivances of editorial guile. The *Encyclopédie* fascinated, quite as much because of what did not meet the eye as because of the new features and devices that did.

After the flowery dedication to D'Argenson which so bruised the spirit of Diderot, Volume I was introduced by a lengthy 'Preliminary Discourse' which set the tone for the ensuing work. This essay has been much admired by contemporaries and posterity alike, one modern editor placing it on a level with Descartes' *Discourse on Method* in scientific merit, and surpassing it in literary.[1] This much-praised piece was written by D'Alembert, not Diderot. Why is not known, unless perhaps it was on the theory that so conspicuous a part should be written by an editor who had not spent time in prison.

The 'Preliminary Discourse' was moving and persuasive because it conveyed and communicated the editors' spacious faith. It is patently a document written by a man who wishes well for mankind. And the conviction it imparts is not so much — to use one of Diderot's phrases — an eloquence that one hears as a persuasion one breathes in. From its lines shines the faith that knowledge will make men better, will make them more the masters of themselves as well as of their environment, will give them light. And there is pride in these pages, too — the pride that comes from feeling that the *Encyclopédie* will help to make this knowledge secure. 'May the *Encyclopédie* become a sanctuary where men's knowledge may be protected from revolutions and from time.'[2]

The 'Preliminary Discourse' is at once an exercise in epistemology and an intellectual history, albeit a somewhat episodic one, of Europe since the beginning of the Renaissance, 'done in the light of philosophy with the technical rigor of a mind profoundly mathematical.'[3] In the epistemological part, D'Alembert inquires whence human beings derive their ideas and answers this fundamental question as Locke had: 'All our direct knowledge is reduced to that which we receive by way of our senses; from which it follows that it is to our sensations that we owe all our ideas.' [4] The original statement of the dictum that nothing exists in the mind that has not been first in the senses (*Nihil est in intellectu quod non fuerit in sensu*) appears in Aristotle and had been quite readily accepted by the medieval scholastic philosophers. In the eighteenth century, however, the expression of this psychological concept, while not precisely heterodox, almost invariably made the devout exceedingly nervous, for it came close to denying the sovereign quiddity of the soul. The Lockean view proclaimed that human beings are not born with innate ideas of religion and morality, but simply derive them from their experience. Moreover, the Lockean psychology could be interpreted as coming very close to materialism, very close to the idea that sense impressions exist, that neurological impulses exist, but that the soul as an independent entity does not. Anybody who, like Diderot in his *Letter on the Blind* and now D'Alembert in the 'Preliminary Discourse,' emphasized the role of the senses in cognition could expect to earn the praise of people seeking positive knowledge without conventional metaphysical integuments, but at the same time to win the distrust or censure of persons who felt that this view had in it something inherently irreverent and dangerous.

After his analysis of the bases of psychological knowledge, D'Alembert lengthily discussed the various branches of learning, linking them together and grouping them under the three general components of the understanding, namely, memory, reason, and imagination. This was a scheme which he, like Jefferson in classifying his library, borrowed from Bacon. This part of the discourse corresponds to a visual scheme of human knowledge that was folded into Volume I following the 'Preliminary Discourse.' In this elaborate *'Système figuré des connoissances humaines,'* a diagrammatic depiction that aroused much admiration at the time, the editors arranged the various subjects in parallel columns. They gave the generic name of 'History' to all the branches of knowledge in the column allocated to the memory; of 'Philosophy' to all that they deemed to be principally dependent upon the reason; and of 'Poetry' to those dependent upon the imagination. Such a visual presentation of the relationships existing among the various branches of knowledge was plausible, and yet it betrays many of the prejudices and predilections of its contrivers. It is enlightening to notice how the editors have placed in visual and organic relationship two of the master words, the dynamic symbols of the age, 'Philosophy' and 'Reason,' each enhancing the prestige of the other. In contrast, 'History' is relegated to a very secondary position. It emanates from mere memory. This refusal to allow history to partake of the honors of philosophy or to consider itself as stemming from reason is one of the intellectual idiosyncrasies of the Encyclopedist school.

It was typical of the whole point of view of the *Encyclopédie,* and quite representative of the intentions of Diderot, that theology and religion were slyly relegated to a small, almost infinitesimal, area in comparison with the eye-filling space taken up by the subjects of positive knowledge. 'Divine Science' bulked just about as large spatially as 'The Manufacture and Uses of Iron.' Such were the *Encyclopédie's* unacknowledged ways of waging psychological warfare: for this was not the fashion in which the relative significance of things was understood by the faculty of theology of the University of Paris.

In the second half of his 'Preliminary Discourse,' D'Alembert briefly but masterfully indicated the contributions to knowledge made by many of the great names: principally Bacon, Descartes, Newton, Locke, and Leibniz. This was brilliantly done, and D'Alembert was highly complimented on his effort by such great persons as Buffon and Montesquieu, while Raynal wrote to his subscribers that 'I believe it to be one of the most philosophical, logical, luminous, exact, compact, and best written pieces that we have in our language.'[5]

Not that the 'Preliminary Discourse' was without its blind spot. It is worthy of remark that D'Alembert dates the history that he thinks really matters as beginning practically with the Renaissance. The reason for this was plain: both he and Diderot regarded medieval times as hopelessly obscurantist and priest-ridden, and the best thing that could be said of their own century, they thought, was that it resembled the Middle Ages so little. It was exceptionally difficult for men of the French Enlightenment to feel that medieval history had had any real significance save of a negative and deplorable sort. To them the history of the Middle Ages seemed an interruption instead of a continuum, and because of this belief, they never developed a philosophy of historical continuity or an attitude of historical-mindedness, relying upon knowledge of the past to illuminate the future, as did the nineteenth century.[6] Contrast for a moment their habit of mind with that of Edmund Burke, whose feeling for history was so profound that he declared that society is indeed a contract, binding the present generation to the ones that are dead. The Encyclopedists were apt to feel, as J. B. Bury remarked, a sort of resentment against history.[7] And because eighteenth-century men wanted their own age to be an Age of Reason, they had little praise for an Age of Faith. This astigmatism was common to a large part

of the Enlightenment, which felt none of the filial devotion of a Henry
Adams yearning for Mont Saint-Michel and Chartres.

As to the 'Preliminary Discourse' as a whole, it is fair to say that though
D'Alembert wrote it, Diderot heartily agreed with it. And if we should
ask how the 'Preliminary Discourse' would have differed had Diderot
written it, the correct answer would be 'very little,' save that Diderot would
probably have based his argumentation more on biological modes of thought,
whereas D'Alembert used the mathematical.

The *Encyclopédie* was novel in that it was a co-operative work written
by several hands, and more unusual still in that it identified its contributors.
According to the 'Preliminary Discourse,' articles marked with an asterisk
were written or revised by Diderot in his capacity as editor; but unsigned
articles without any identifying mark were also written by him; other
articles were initialed according to a scheme of symbols published in the
prefatory pages. The final pages of the 'Preliminary Discourse' were taken
up with identifying and thanking the contributors.

As a reader turned to the body of the work, his first impression might have
been of surprise that the *Encyclopédie* was organized alphabetically. It
might have been supposed that, having dilated so much upon his chart of
human knowledge, Diderot would have organized his presentation according
to this system rather than according to the alphabet. Evidently the editors
were uneasily self-conscious about this point, for they discuss at length why
they did what they did, the reasons appearing to be in part solid and intrinsic, in part (like Mr. Guppy's) owing to circumstances beyond their
control.[8] The *Encyclopédie* was criticized now and again for its arrangement,
yet subsequent experience seems to have proved that the alphabetical presentation in reference books, although less logical, is also less confusing.[9]

The *Encyclopédie* endeavored to compensate for this lack of the systematic
by freely using cross references to indicate close and organic connections.[10]
Chambers had done this and it has become, of course, a commonplace in
the construction of reference works; but for the *Encyclopédie* the apparatus
of cross references served a further purpose. It slyly suggested points of
view that, because of censorship, could not be openly canvassed.

Twentieth-century commentators naturally dwell on the most important,
usually the lengthiest, articles that the *Encyclopédie* contains. To the casual
contemporary reader, however, the work might have seemed most impressive because of the multiplicity of its brief entries; there were literally thousands. This is explained by the fact that the *Encyclopédie,* although it contained no maps, attempted to be a gazetteer. Moreover, it also served as a

dictionary, defining numerous words, some of them very common ones, and often giving elaborate examples of synonyms. The study of synonyms had become popular in France since the publication of a book of them by an Abbé Girard in 1718. The *Encyclopédie* frequently copied Girard, usually with acknowledgments, and often printed synonyms and illustrations of its own. Diderot was proficient in this department, as when, to give a very Gallic example, he distinguished between the figurative meanings of 'to bind' and 'to attach' by adding to the Girard examples: 'One is bound to one's wife, and attached to one's mistress.' [11]

The *Encyclopédie* also contained, besides these definitions and synonyms, a large number of highly regarded articles about grammar, some of them very lengthy, and most of them done by an amiable old freethinker named Dumarsais. 'We believe ourselves able to say,' Diderot had written in the prospectus, 'that no known work will be as rich or as instructive as ours concerning the rules and usage of the French language, or, indeed, on the nature, origin, and philosophy of languages in general.' Moreover, the editors of the *Encyclopédie* were extremely aware of what is now called the problem of semantics: 'How many questions and vexations would one spare oneself if one were finally to determine the meaning of words in a clear and precise manner,' wrote D'Alembert in his 'Preliminary Discourse,' thus capping his earlier remark that 'we owe many errors, as some philosophers have noticed, to the abuse of words. . . .' [12]

A modern reader interested in biographical information finds the *Encyclopédie* lacks an alphabetical listing of personages. Volumes following the second occasionally include some biographical information, but, oddly enough, listed under the name of the city in which the person was born. As much as the *Encyclopédie* was admired, it was distinctly deficient in articles of biography and systematic history. Their inclusion would have greatly increased its size, and the editors therefore referred their readers, not very satisfactorily, to a current historical and biographical dictionary, Moreri's *Grand dictionnaire historique,* first published in 1674 and followed by a number of editions and supplements.[13]

In other respects the *Encyclopédie* had very adequate coverage, with ample articles on the inescapable subjects of theology, philosophy, and belles-lettres. It made its special reputation, however, on both scientific articles and those describing the technology of the arts and crafts. In the first volume were found lengthy articles by Diderot on 'Steel' (*Acier*), 'Agriculture,' [14] 'Silver' (*Argent*), 'Needle' (*Aiguille*), and 'Accouchement,' as well as important articles by him on more conventional subjects, such as analyses of the

philosophy of the Arabs, the Hindus, and of Aristotelianism. Other contributors wrote important articles on such topics as 'Bee' (*Abeille*), 'Anatomy'
(twenty-eight pages where Chambers had had only one column), 'Trees'
(*Arbre*), 'Attraction,' 'Alsace' (mainly about the mines in that region), 'Atmosphere,' 'Slate' (*Ardoise*), 'Magnet' (*Aimant*), 'Alkali,' etc. These subjects were described with an attention to technical and technological detail
that was always one of the most conspicuous features of the *Encyclopédie*,
a feature that made it representative of a new social class and of a new
outlook on man. This attention to up-to-date technology is admirably displayed, for example, in Diderot's own article on 'Boring Machine' (*Alésoir*).
What he was describing, with information as to how it could be constructed,
was a machine for making cannon from solid castings. An anecdote, incidentally revealing the wide distribution of the *Encyclopédie,* will show
how useful this sort of information could be. About 1773 the Ottoman
Sultan commissioned a soldier of fortune, the Baron de Tott, to build up
the Turkish artillery and arm the forts on the Dardanelles. Tott had to
manufacture the cannon he needed, without having had previous experience in the work. 'A Greek, very expert in the Art of constructing Mills,'
Tott wrote in his *Memoirs,* 'was, however, of much service to me in making
my boring Machine. The Memoirs of Saint Remi and the Encyclopédie
were my constant guides and I wanted no other till I came to make the
Moulds. . . .'[15]

In short, the *Encyclopédie* was practical. It was useful. And since it contained much information unobtainable elsewhere, it was indispensable. The
Chevalier de Jaucourt pointed out these characteristics when he wrote of the
'Art of Heraldry' in an *Encyclopédie* volume published in 1765: 'There does
not exist a single pamphlet on the art of making shirts, stockings, shoes,
bread; the *Encyclopédie* is the first and unique work describing these arts
useful to men, while the book trade is inundated with books on the vain and
ridiculous science of armorial bearings.'[16]

Diderot's interest in technology, in the crafts, and in the mechanical arts
is very typical of him. There was nothing factitious about this interest in
the practical. On the contrary, it sprang directly from his social origins, from
the microcosm of the tanners and the cutlers of Langres, from the pride in
workmanship and the canniness in money matters of the self-respecting
craftsman who begot him. Diderot always respected craftsmanship, and
although he sometimes spoke disdainfully or despairingly of 'the people'
and employed the word in much the sense that we now give to 'the masses,'
he never spoke disparagingly of the artisan or his social usefulness. It was

this attitude, faithfully reflected in a thousand places in the *Encyclopédie,* that made the work so revolutionary. New *values* were here being set forth and admired, the dignity of just plain work was being extolled. 'Upon examining the products of the arts,' wrote Diderot in his 'Art' article, 'one has observed that some were more the work of the mind than of the hand, and that others, on the contrary, were more the work of the hand than of the mind. Such is in part the origin of the pre-eminence accorded to some arts over others, and of the classification of the arts into liberal arts and mechanical arts. This distinction, though well grounded, has had the unfortunate effect of degrading people who are very estimable and very useful, and of strengthening in us a certain sort of natural laziness which already was inclining us only too much to believe that to devote a constant and continuous attention to experiments and to individual, palpable, and material objects was to detract from the dignity of the human mind, and that to practice or even to study the mechnical arts was to lower oneself to things that are laborious to study, ignoble to meditate upon, difficult to expound, dishonoring to trade in, inexhaustible in number, and in value trifling. A prejudice tending to fill the cities with prideful praters and useless contemplators, and the countryside with petty tyrants, ignorant, idle, and disdainful. 'Twas not thus that Bacon thought, one of England's foremost geniuses; nor Colbert, one of France's greatest ministers; nor, indeed, the just minds and the wise men of any era. . . . How bizarre are our judgments! We demand that people should be usefully engaged, and we disdain useful men.' [17] These views are of great interest in themselves. Moreover, Diderot attached extraordinary importance to them, a fact proved by his publication of this article in advance, as a sample of the whole encyclopedia. It is evident that he intended to fix public attention upon this aspect of the new work.

In congruence with its interest in the crafts and technology, the *Encyclopédie* manifested an equal interest in the problem of dignifying or creating an adequate and accurate vocabulary for them; '. . . a science or an art commences to be a science or an art only when acquired knowledge gives rise to making a language for it,' wrote the author of the article 'Anatomy.' [18] Diderot himself had referred in his prospectus to the importance of nomenclature and returned to the subject, discussing it at some length in his article on 'Art.' In the opinion of the principal historian of the French language, the *Encyclopédie*'s interest in accurate and sufficient nomenclature is one of its most valuable characteristics. 'The *Encyclopédie* nonetheless remains the first and chief homage of the eighteenth century to the language of artisans

... a powerful effort not only to disseminate the knowledge of the arts and sciences but also to rehabilitate technical terms.' [19]

It would not have taken long for a reader of the first volume to discover that the *Encyclopédie* was interested in more than simply warming over old themes, reviving or inventing technical terms, or presenting subjects never before allotted space in a work of this kind. More than these, the *Encyclopédie* was interested in the scientific method. Indeed, it became an arsenal in which the weapons of critical thought were kept — polished, whetted, and instantly at hand. Perhaps the greatest function of the work in the estimation of its editors was that of making people more aware of the methodological problems that constantly beset the acquisition of knowledge and the pursuit of truth.

Obviously this was a campaign that had to be conducted on many fronts. One of them was the attack on words or names that in reality were devoid of meaning. Diderot's technique was to call attention to names, especially of plants and animals, about which little more was known than simply the empty name itself. For example, he wrote about *'Aguaxima'*: 'A plant of Brazil and of the islands of southern America. That is all that we are told of it; and I would willingly inquire for whom such descriptions are made. It cannot be for the natives, who very likely know more characteristics of the *aguaxima* than this description includes, and who have no need of being told that the *aguaxima* grows in their country; it is as if one said to a Frenchman that the pear tree is a tree that grows in France, in Germany, etc. Nor can it be for us; for what does it matter to us whether there be in Brazil a tree named *aguaxima,* if we know only its name? What purpose does the name serve? It leaves the ignorant in the condition they were; it teaches others nothing. If it happens, then, that I mention this plant, and several others equally poorly described, it is out of condescension for certain readers who prefer to find nothing in a dictionary article, or even to find nothing but silliness in it, than not to find the article at all.' [20] Similarly, of the word *'Aguapa'*: 'A tree that grows in the West Indies, the shadow of which is said to cause the death of those who sleep in it naked, while it causes all others to swell up in a prodigious fashion. If the natives of these countries do not know it better than it is identified for us by this description, they are in great danger.' [21] And in discussing the word *'Acalipse'* he remarked, 'Here is another one of these beings . . . of which one has only the name; as if one did not already have too many names empty of sense in the sciences, arts, etc.' [22]

Comments such as these would seem absurdly out of place in a present-day work of reference. But the seekers after positive knowledge who edited the *Encyclopédie* had a useful purpose in mind. Not only did they intend to make their readers more critical and sophisticated in the nomenclature of plants and animals, they also aimed, although somewhat furtively and indirectly, at various high-sounding metaphysical and religious abstractions. No doubt the 'et cetera' that concluded the preceding quotation referred to these, thus putting a cutting edge on what is usually a dulled and lazy abbreviation. 'True philosophy,' wrote the author of the article 'To Act' (*Agir*), 'would find itself considerably briefer if all philosophers would be willing, like me, to abstain from speaking of what is manifestly incomprehensible.' [23]

Another methodological front upon which the *Encyclopédie* conducted a campaign was that of the credibility of various kinds of evidence. Obviously this tactic was primarily to unsettle convictions concerning miracles and the truthfulness of Genesis, but it had a broader purpose, one applicable to all aspects of thought and not simply the religious and the theological. The skepticism of the *Encyclopédie* exercised itself overtly and entertainingly on old wives' tales and vulgar errors, with the charm of seeming to take the reader into partnership. But the very same methods that were used to expose ignorance and superstition and sham in regard to pagan gods, ancient oracles, and nonexistent animals and plants — *Agnus Scythicus,* for example — were also the ones that, by implication, led straight to the attack upon more portentous obscurantisms.

Of course the *Encyclopédie* had had predecessors in preaching the virtues of skepticism. The most important among them was Pierre Bayle (1647–1706), one of the great names in the history of free intellectual inquiry. Bayle was a French Huguenot refugee of awesome erudition, especially in the fields of theology, mythology, ancient history, and ancient geography, as well as the history of Europe in the sixteenth and seventeenth centuries. In 1697 he published his *Dictionnaire historique et critique,* a work which demonstrated the use to which crafty cross references could be put and a work, too, which bristled with such scholarship that it contains footnotes on footnotes. Bayle was a believer, though a critical one; and his skepticism, combined with his erudition, gave him the sort of dazzling intellectual authority over young people impatient of cant that H. L. Mencken enjoyed in the 1920's in America. But it was not an influence that could be safely acknowledged, especially if one happened to live in France. Bayle, then, should be remembered as perhaps the greatest exemplar and inspiration of the critical methodology preached by the *Encyclopédie*. If his influence was more negative than positive, if he showed none of Diderot's interest in the crafts and technology and other practical matters, still his work is incontestably the real ancestor of the *Encyclopédie,* from the point of view of ideas as well as form, and it has been well said that 'he cleared the ground for the steam-roller of the Encyclopedists.' [24] It is almost literally true that his was the great unmentioned and unmentionable name of the *Encyclopédie.*[25]

Bayle's skepticism was far from nihilistic. Quite to the contrary, it was of a fruitful sort, dedicated to the search for truth. Bayle, like his successors in the eighteenth century, thought of skepticism as a kind of detergent, the use of which would reveal truth. This was precisely Diderot's point of view. As early as the *Pensées philosophiques* he had declared that 'skepticism is therefore the first step toward truth,' and his daughter says that the last words she heard him say — it was the evening before he died — were: 'The first step toward philosophy is unbelief.' [26] This was the spirit in which the *Encyclopédie* was written. Its respect for truth, combined with a far-reaching skepticism about what conventionally passed for it, was one of the most exciting features of the new work.

Equally exciting, especially in the articles written by Diderot, was a certain quality of self-revelation, an air of making the reader a confidant and sharing with him literary and scientific judgments, an air both attractive and piquant which gave a suspenseful sense of the unexpected. These unconventional qualities stirred the wrath of the bigoted, the scorn of the pedantic, and the interest of the unprejudiced. The reader of the first volume might notice in the frequent articles devoted to cooking inferential evidence that Diderot was fond of the pleasures of the table.[27] There, too, he displayed his familiarity with the cutler's craft by writing a considerable article (*Affiler*) on the art of whetting knives and bringing lancets to a fine edge.[28] It was like Diderot to describe three or four methods for catching fish-worms (*Achées*), to use his columns for paying compliments to Réaumur and Frederick the Great, or to include rhetorical bits — though quite representative of his considered views — like those in the article on 'Alecto,' 'whose name corresponds to that of Envy. . . . what envious person would not be horrified at himself when he hears it said that Envy is one of the three Furies, and that she is the daughter of Hell and of Night . . . what could be likely to make virtue more attractive and vice odious . . . ?' [29] Such editorial policies generated some of the curiosity excited by a modern syndicated column. It cannot be denied that part of the interest inspired by the work arose from a desire to see what the authors would say next. The *Encyclopédie* was edited with a flair for showmanship.

It was also inspired by an eagerness for improvement and a passion for amelioration. About the last thing that could be said about the *Encyclopédie* was that it was content with things as they were. In the largest sense, it had a revolutionary attitude. But the expression of this desire for improvement was not limited to cautious verbalizations about religion and matters of state: it shone forth in the desire for all sorts of betterments and changes; in suggestions, for example, for reforming the alphabet as well as the orthography of the French language, or — these happen to be suggestions in articles written by Diderot himself — for more effective methods of agriculture, for better techniques of making steel, for the abolition of monopolies, and for closer supervision of midwives.[30] This sense of immersion in the circumstances of real life not unnaturally constituted for readers of the *Encyclopédie* one of its principal sources of interest. A sample of what Diderot wrote about monopolies in the very interesting article on the manufacture of needles is representative:

. . . but it seems to me that there is only one contingency as a result of which exclusive privileges may be accorded without injustice. This is when they are asked for by the inventor of a useful article. . . . to accord to a company the exclusive privilege of making a product that many people are able to manufacture is tantamount to willing that this product, instead of being perfected, should continuously become worse and always be sold more dear.[31]

And under the heading of '*Accoucheuse,*' Diderot called attention to current abuses practiced by midwives who gave instruction in their profession. '. . . I saw there examples of inhumanity [which he described] that would be almost unbelievable had they occurred among barbarians. . . . Therefore I invite those who are charged with taking care of the disorders that occur in society to keep their eyes on this one.'[32]

Remarks like these, well-intentioned though they were, were apt to be regarded as coming close to trenching upon the arcana of authority in general and the prerogative of the police power in particular. Diderot was of a temperament that could scarcely refrain from telling the political and religious authorities what their policies ought to be, nor could he have avoided, even had he desired, treating in some aspect or other of the *Encyclopédie* these two subjects that were the riskiest and touchiest of all. In the France of the eighteenth century, Church and State did not regard themselves as answerable in any way to the criticism of private persons, nor were they likely to consider the public discussion of public matters as even permissible.

Since the police power was of course all on their side, persons who felt inspired to say something on religion or government had to take either devious indirections or serious risks. Diderot took both.

It might be supposed that somewhere in the *Encyclopédie* would be found a plea for freedom in the expression of thought. And so there was, in an article written by Diderot about an obscure Roman divinity, Aius Locutius, the god of speech. In this unobtrusive corner Diderot wrote eloquently in favor of freedom of thought. But the caution that he had to exercise in daring to canvass such a view is demonstrated by the curious limitation that he voluntarily proposed. Let criticisms of the Church and the government be published in a learned language only. If they should happen to be translated into the vernacular, arrest and punish the translator. Thus freedom of thought could be reconciled 'with the respect due to a people's faith and to the national cult.' [33] To a twentieth-century reader this proposal seems shockingly undemocratic and illiberal, but to the eighteenth century, as many criticisms of the *Encyclopédie* show, it seemed shockingly radical.

In his article on 'Political Authority,' Diderot stated his opinions very plainly, thereby incurring so much criticism and coming, it is said, so close to having the work's license taken away, that for some time thereafter he refrained from expressing himself quite so unambiguously. This article did indeed sound like one by John Locke or Thomas Jefferson. 'No man,' he wrote, 'has received from nature the right of commanding others. Liberty is a present from Heaven, and every individual of the same species has the right to enjoy it as soon as he enjoys reason. . . .

'Power acquired by violence is only a usurpation, and lasts only as long as the force of him who commands prevails over that of those who obey, in such a fashion that if these latter become in their turn stronger and shake off their yoke, they do so with as much right and justice as did the former who had imposed it upon them. The same law that made the authority, unmakes it: it is the law of the stronger.

. . . .

'Therefore true and legitimate power necessarily has limits. . . . The prince holds from his subjects themselves the authority that he has over them; and this authority is limited by the laws of nature and of state. . . . Besides, the government, although hereditary in a family and placed in the hands of a single individual, is not a piece of private property, but is public property, which in consequence can never be wrested from the people, to whom alone it belongs essentially and in full ownership. . . . It is not the state which belongs to the prince, but rather the prince who belongs to the state; but it pertains to the prince to govern the state, because the state has chosen him for that, because he has engaged himself toward the people for the administration of affairs, and because these, for their part, have engaged themselves to obey him conformably to the laws.'[34]

This was stout doctrine, especially during a reign in which Louis XV was to tell a delegation of judges, 'I am your master, I intend to be obeyed. I am aware of all the rights that I hold from God. It belongs to none of my subjects to limit them or decide the extent of them.'[35] The *Encyclopédie* did not indulge very frequently in libertarian essays on the sources of political power, although this article on 'Authority,' another by Diderot on 'Natural Law' (*Droit naturel*), and a later one by Jean-Jacques Rousseau on '*Economie politique*' — in which there appears for the first time in his writings the famous concept of the general will — prove that it did so often enough to keep both friend and enemy on the alert.

Both friend and enemy eagerly turned to the first volume to learn what the *Encyclopédie* would say concerning the manifold matters relating to religious faith. The subject was quite inescapable. On the one hand, there existed an elaborate and established system of authoritarian faith, constantly manifesting an extreme sensitivity to anything that could be construed as inimical to it. And on the other hand there was the pressure of a growing scientific and positivistic movement, represented by the *Encyclopédie,* which sought the freedom to search for truth even at the cost of modifying or unsettling accepted articles of faith. What was occurring at that time was like the uproar and turmoil that took place in the nineteenth century over the 'higher criticism' and the concept of evolution. To translate the struggle into the idiom of a later time, the Encyclopedists were contending with fundamentalists. This aspect of the contest between them is admirably illustrated by a contemporary anecdote, even though the incident concerned Swedish Lutherans rather than Roman Catholic Frenchmen. 'One day in the eighteenth century, some Swedish scientists discovered a certain alteration in the shores of the Baltic. Immediately the theologians of Stockholm made representations to the government that "this remark of the Swedish scientists, not being consistent with Genesis, must be condemned." To whom reply was made that God had made both the Baltic and Genesis, and that, if there was any contradiction between the two works, the error must lie in the copies that we have of the book, rather than in the Baltic Sea, of which we have the original.'[36] In France there was no one with enough authority to speak to the clergy or their defenders in such terms, with the result that persons of the stripe of Diderot had to live under much the same apprehensions as that of a teacher in Tennessee attempting, about the time of the famous 'evolution trial,' to do what he could to impart scientific biological knowledge.

Since persons combating religious authoritarianism could never attack their adversary outright — and stay out of prison or continue to enjoy the right to publish — the contest became one of wits. The *Encyclopédie* is a subtle work, written, as Diderot himself declared, 'to discredit prejudices adroitly,' often concealing or almost concealing its real opinions, and prudentially conveying with a wink and a nudge what it did not dare to say aloud.[37] Diderot's attack on the illiberality of religious belief was set forth in the *Encyclopédie* under several guises, and to detect his various devices must have been as entertaining to his partisans as it was infuriating to his opponents. For example, the *Encyclopédie* contained frequent appeals to reason, though not without a certain air of smugness, implying that the writer already had all of it. Thus Diderot wrote, in an article defining 'to adore': 'The manner of adoring the true God ought never to deviate from reason, because God is the author of reason, and because He has desired it to be used even in the judgments of what is suitable to do or not to do in respect to Him.'[38]

A favorite contrivance of the Encyclopedists was to expose, in all their multitudinousness, the various heresies of the Christian Church. This was a trick they had learned from Bayle. Their descriptions, as Diderot's of the Agonyclytes — 'heretics of the seventh century, whose maxim it was never to pray on their knees, but standing up' —[39] were written impassively but not without a certain trace of unctuousness. Combined with the somewhat elaborate and ostentatious arrayal of the astonishing variety of belief that had occurred in the history of the Christian Church was a constant, undoubtedly sincere, and extremely characteristic appeal for toleration and broad-mindedness on theological subjects. This was the Enlightenment seeking to discredit scholastic discussion and religious dispute. Diderot wrote a typical example of this sort of appeal in an article on a Mohammedan sect:[40] 'Furthermore, I shall observe that the concurrence of God, His providence, His prescience, predestination, liberty, occasion disputes and heresies wherever they are discussed, and that Christians would do well in these difficult questions, says M. d'Herbelot in his *Bibliothèque orientale,* to seek to instruct one another peaceably, if that be possible, and to tolerate one another charitably on those occasions where they are of different sentiments. Indeed, what do we know of such matters? *Quis consiliarius ejus fuit?*' *

* Who was the authority for it?

Another device used by the *Encyclopédie* was the castigation of certain ancient pagan practices that, in reality, had close and obvious Christian analogues. Partly this technique bespoke an intellectual deficiency on the part of the *philosophes* in that they showed little understanding of the religious impulse in man's psychological nature, little realization that they were by way of building a kind of church of their own. Moreover, their scorn for all religious institutions, whether primitive or advanced, reveals to a twentieth-century reader that the sciences of anthropology, comparative religion, and sociology were then only embryonic. It cannot be denied, however, that the *philosophes* drew great advantage from what was essentially a propaganda device: no devout Christian could take them to task for heaping scorn on pagan customs. And so Diderot wrote, for example, of the eagle, in an article which was far from being ornithological: 'The eagle may be seen in the images of Jupiter, sometimes at his feet, sometimes at his side, and almost always carrying a thunderbolt in his talons. There is every appearance that this whole fable is founded simply upon observing the flight of the eagle, who loves to soar in the loftiest clouds and abide in the realm of the thunderbolts. That was all that was necessary to make it the bird of the god of heaven and the air, and give it a thunderbolt to carry. One had only to get the Pagans started when their gods were to be honored: rather than remain at rest, superstition conjures up the most gross and extravagant visions. Then these visions become consecrated by time and by the credulity of peoples; and woe to him who, without being bidden by God to the great and perilous calling of a missionary, loves his repose so little and knows mankind so ill as to take upon himself to instruct them. If you introduce a ray of light into a nest of owls, you will only injure their eyes and excite their cries. A hundred times happy are the people bidden by religion to believe only true, sublime, and holy things, and to imitate only virtuous actions. Such a religion is ours, wherein the Philosopher has only to follow his reason in order to arrive at the foot of our altars.' [41]

Thus Diderot ended this article with a pious flourish which the orthodox and the naïve found very edifying, but which the sophisticated presumed to be heavily ironical. This practice of saying, somewhat ostentatiously, the contrary of what he meant has raised through the years some contention as to Diderot's intellectual honesty. Even Voltaire, an expert if ever man was in covering his own tracks, was wont to complain that Diderot went to quite unnecessary lengths in his willingness to conform. The circumstances in which the two men wrote were quite different, however. Voltaire chose to live where he could nimbly skip across the border into Geneva when trouble threatened. Diderot lived in Paris, and also felt a heavy responsibility toward his Parisian publishers, whose fortunes were invested in the venture. This situation led to a number of complicated moral problems. Did not the stark necessity of bare survival justify an apparent acquiescence in orthodoxy? What were the moral rights and obligations of an editor under conditions so perilous and adverse? Could a man remain honest and still publish orthodox statements in which he had no belief? Were there any moral considerations conferring upon him the right to dissimulate his real opinions? These were problems Diderot lived with every day of the twenty-five years that the *Encyclopédie* was in preparation, and we find him now and again alluding in the *Encyclopédie* to the hazards of his exposed position. In the very first volume, he refers to criticisms of Pliny in a situation that is transparently also his own. In the article on 'Achor,' 'the fly-chasing god or god of the flies,' Diderot seems to be making a bid to his partisans for an understanding of the difficulties of his position. 'Pliny says,' he wrote, 'that the inhabitants of Cyrene sacrificed to him [Achor], in order to obtain deliverance from these insects, which sometimes occasioned contagious sicknesses in their country. This author adds that they [the flies] died as soon as the sacrifice had been made. A modern scholar remarks that Pliny could have contented himself with saying, for the honor of truthfulness, that this was the vulgar opinion. As for me, it seems to me that one ought not to demand a truth that might be dangerous to express, from an author accused of lying on so many occasions in which he would have been truthful had it not been for the consequences; and that Pliny, who, apparently, hardly believed in the divinity of the god of the flies, but who did undertake to instruct us of the prejudice of the inhabitants of Cyrene in that regard, could not express himself otherwise without jeopardizing his own tranquillity. This is, I believe, one of those occasions when one cannot draw from an author's testimony any conclusion either against himself or for the fact that he attests.' [42]

The *Encyclopédie*, far from seizing every possible opportunity to fly in the face of orthodoxy, frequently seemed to acquiesce in it. But often the reasons adduced for believing in a given matter were perfidious, arousing more doubts than they allayed. Sometimes a defense can be so extraordinarily nerveless and unconvincing that it leaves the reader, as Iago left Othello, with long and lingering doubts. Nowhere was this technique of the *Encyclopédie* more palpable than in articles in which the literal interpretation of the Old Testament was involved. It was not to be expected that the *Encyclopédie* would ever put itself into the position of flatly contradicting what was officially regarded as the revealed word of God, but by the proliferation of common-sense considerations or by the confusing juxtaposition of erudite, orthodox, and mutually contradictory authorities, it managed to stir up doubts. Nor was this sort of attack gratuitous or without justification. The battle over fundamentalism in the nineteenth century suggests that the leaders of the Enlightenment a century earlier were not mistaken in feeling that the infant biological and social sciences were fighting for breath and life against the suffocation that comes from a belief in the literal truth of the Book of Genesis. Had the Roman Catholic Church of two hundred years ago regarded scientific inquiry in the spirit of Pope Pius XII's address to the Pontifical Academy of Science in 1951, conditions would have been profoundly different. The scientists and social scientists of 1751 would not then have experienced the sense of intellectual strangulation that they did.

The *Encyclopédie,* of course, did not invent the technique of casting rationalistic doubts upon the Old Testament. That mine had been opened by Spinoza in his *Tractatus theologico-politicus* (1670) and had been industriously exploited by the English deists. Voltaire found many a nugget there, and the *Encyclopédie,* too, made many profitable trips to the pit head. One of the most interesting was the article in the first volume concerning 'Noah's Ark' (*Arche de Noé*), an article contributed by the Abbé Mallet.[43] With a very grave countenance and the mien of a person dancing a stately pavane, the Abbé set forth what the best authorities had conjectured concerning the time it had taken to build so large an edifice, especially considering that the Scriptures say that only four persons ever worked upon it; what must have been their strength, considering the size of the timbers needed; how many species of animals had to be provided for, making extrapolation for all those species not even yet known to Europeans; the dimensions and internal arrangement of the Ark, the probable number of decks, the amount of fodder needed, the disposition of weight to prevent tipping, storage space for fodder and fresh water, arrangements for cleaning and ventilating the animals' stalls, and the probable minimum number of the same; provisions for an extra number of lambs for food for the carnivorous animals; the possibility of a fish reservoir for the food supply of amphibious animals and birds, etc. By the time the Abbé laid down his pen it was evident that a considerable number of common-sense problems are presented by Noah's Ark. But, as Diderot remarked elsewhere in Volume I, 'the word of God, who explained Himself positively concerning these important matters, leaves no place for hypotheses.' [44]

* * * * * *

The several devices that Diderot and his collaborators employed to stimulate interest in the *Encyclopédie* were frequently combined in a single article. Many contributions that purport to be summaries of existing knowledge on certain subjects actually are vibrating and resonant with overtones of the Enlightenment. Let one very good sample suffice in illustration: the supplementary article, six columns in length, that Diderot wrote on *'Âme'* (Soul or Mind). The principal article on this tricky and touchy subject was treated by the Abbé Yvon in a conventional and innocuous manner. What Diderot did in addition was to speculate where in the body the *âme* resided; to show by his numerous references and citations that he was fully informed about current scientific investigations on the subject; to point out the close connection between soul and body, so that a disarrangement of a nerve fiber can bring on mental illness; to proffer some advice on child care; to give some interesting and specific case histories, one of which correlated religious hysteria with physical disease; and to end the whole by posing a problem bearing upon both aesthetics and psychopathology, namely whether painting has as much influence on the soul as music!

This was the sort of approach that opened windows and broadened horizons. Yet to the orthodox and conventional in matters of religion, any discussion of the soul that suggested any organic connection with the body was likely to seem vaguely impious and somehow impudent. Nevertheless the progress of knowledge indubitably required exploration of this very relationship. The problem was unfortunately and unnecessarily embittered by an accident of language: the French word *'âme'* means both 'soul' and 'mind.'[45] It is the portal word, the junction point, for both theology and science, for both metaphysics and psychology. Probably the intellectual crisis of the eighteenth century in France would not have engendered such bitterness had men been able to talk of the mind without theologians supposing that they were talking of the soul. Perhaps the growth of science in the eighteenth century, for which the *Encyclopédie* and Diderot fought so fiercely, would not have had to take a turn so aggressively anticlerical had the *philosophes* been able to talk of psychology, neurology, and psychopathology — in other words, of the mind — without being suspected of desiring to attack or demolish the concept of the soul. Perhaps the milder and less embittered form that the Enlightenment took in the English-speaking world was owing to nothing more than the fact that the English language has a word for each. No wonder Diderot often revealed an awareness of the problem of semantics.

The idea that the mind and the body, or the soul and the body, are bound together in close and reciprocal relationship would seem to be nothing but common sense. Yet in Diderot's day one had to be exceedingly careful what one said on this subject, lest one be traduced as a materialist and an atheist. Nevertheless this is a concept absolutely basic for the scientific understanding of mental disease, just as it is also the foundation of all neurological studies and of psychosomatic medicine. Diderot's most daring writings on this subject, such as *D'Alembert's Dream,* were much too dangerous to be published during his lifetime. But in the *Encyclopédie* he wrote what he could, never being one to fail to recognize an issue of importance or to avoid discussing it as much as was possible. 'Let us consider,' he wrote in his supplementary article on the *'Âme'* 'on what small things depend the functioning of the *âme:* a fiber out of order, a drop of extravasated blood, a slight inflammation, a fall, a contusion: and farewell to judgment, reason, and all that sagacity of which men are so vain. All this vanity depends upon a filament well or poorly placed, healthy or unhealthy.' [46]

* * * * * *

The *Encyclopédie* was a great reference book, a great repository of knowledge. But it was more than that, by far. The *Encyclopédie* conveyed to its readers a stimulus that was frequently as much emotional as it was intellectual. Consequently, the terms used to describe the *Encyclopédie*'s effect should not convey simply passive images. The words descriptive of it should be active. It was a detergent, a tool with a cutting edge, a window opener. It was something that one could learn to use for the performance of tasks one was insufficiently equipped to do before. And because this was so, it was unavoidable that the *Encyclopédie* and its principal editors were destined to figure conspicuously in the history and politics of the eighteenth century.

CHAPTER 12

'Up till Now, Hell Has Vomited Its Venom Drop by Drop'

BY THE time that Volume I of the *Encyclopédie* was finally published on 28 June 1751, public interest had been whetted to a sharp edge of expectation. There had been the two prospectuses, the one of 1745 as well as the more elaborate one in 1750; there had been the preliminary publication of sample articles, Diderot's on 'Art' and the naturalist Daubenton's on 'Bee' (*Abeille*) and 'Agate'[1] —that on the bee to show that the *Encyclopédie* would be an indispensable repository of information already acquired, the one on agate to show how it would include information entirely new and unavailable elsewhere; and gaining the most public attention of all, there had been the hot-tempered exchange between Diderot and Father Berthier of the *Journal de Trévoux*. In addition, Diderot's previous publications, both the salacious and the radical, had indicated that his editing would be anything but colorless, so that potential friends of the new work counted upon finding their best hopes, potential enemies their worst fears, fully confirmed.

The excellence of the *Encyclopédie* was attested by attempts of foreigners to pirate it. Only a few months after the publication of the first volume the publishers became aware that they were being paid this sincerest kind of flattery. A syndicate of English publishers, hoisting the Jolly Roger, prefixed to their translation of the 'Preliminary Discourse' and its accompanying documents the announcement that 'the Proprietors have engaged in a Design of reprinting the Whole at *London,* with a View to serve their Country, by encouraging Arts, Manufactures, and Trades; and keeping large Sums at Home, that would otherwise be sent Abroad. They offer their Work at Half the Price of the *Paris* Edition; and hereby promise, in case they meet with no Discouragement, to proceed regularly in printing the

subsequent Volumes.'[2] To head off this threat, the French publishers authorized Briasson and David to go to London to treat with the English booksellers and offer them copies of the French edition at very low cost. The
Frenchmen made this journey in November and entered into an agreement,
the details of which are obscure but which was ratified by their partners in
February 1752.[3] This is the last heard of this particular venture in piracy.
Still another English translation was proposed at about the same time, this
one by a Sir Joseph Ayloffe. Apparently the French publishers did nothing
about it, and Ayloffe's project, which appeared in weekly installments beginning on 11 January 1752 and costing six pence each, seems never to have
proceeded beyond the eighth installment.[4]

The publication of the first volume of the *Encyclopédie* made it the focus
of discussion in Paris. It had both censors and partisans, remarked Raynal,
who added that both were in the right, for the work was blameworthy for
the useless subjects included and praiseworthy because of its 'philosophic'
spirit.[5] The statement of the journalist Clément of Geneva, expressed in
his news letter of 15 August 1751, also reveals the volume's somewhat mixed
reception: 'You have remarked, Monsieur, that with his vagrant as well
as scientific imagination, M. Diderot would inundate us with words and
sentences. This is the complaint of the public against his first volume, which
appeared a little while ago. But an infinitely copious background of material
and a fine taste for sound philosophy, which gives value to it, compensate
for all these superfluities.'[6] Intellectual snobs complained that the *Encyclopédie* was a short-cut to culture,[7] a view rather frequently expressed as this
typical epigram shows:

> Well, here we have the *Encyclopédie*,
> What luck for the ignorant!
> How this learned rhapsody
> Will hatch out false savants! *

A little later Raynal remarked that one often finds in the *Encyclopédie* what
one is not looking for, and often searches fruitlessly for what one wants.
'Several of the authors write in a barbarous style, several in a precious manner,
and many possess nothing but prolixity.' Still later he wrote that 'the first
volume of the *Encyclopédie*, which at first succeeded very well, is quite generally scoffed at. One sees such revolutions only in France.'[8]

> * Voici donc l'*Encyclopédie*;
> Quel bonheur pour les ignorants!
> Que cette docte rapsodie
> Fera naître de faux savants!

The evidence of an increasing subscription list proves that Raynal was exaggerating. Le Breton was printing an edition of 2,075 in place of the 1,625 originally planned.[9] Yet criticism did exist, symbolized by a rather ominous epigram which D'Hémery picked up and recorded in his journal:[10]

Je suis bon encyclopédiste,
Je connais le mal et le bien.
Je suis Diderot à la piste;
Je connais tout, je ne crois rien.*

The first rumblings of the attack came in the September columns of the influential *Journal des Sçavans,* and greatly upset D'Alembert. The *Journal* praised the 'Preliminary Discourse,' but — 'we are obliged to warn that this work has its defects. . . . The author supposes that sensations alone constitute the origin of ideas. . . . The system of Locke is dangerous for religion, although one has no objections to make when those who adopt it do not draw noxious conclusions from it. M. d'Alembert is of this number; he recognizes rather eloquently the spirituality of the soul and the existence of God, but he is so brief on each of these subjects, concerning which there are so many things to say, and he is so copious on others that the reader has a right to demand the reason for the distinction. . . .

'One might suspect this Preface of an affected laconism in respect to religion.' [11]

Much more trouble was made by the *Journal de Trévoux.* The animadversions of these Jesuits proceeded in a crescendo. Their first review, sour and grudging, appeared in the issue for October 1751. D'Alembert had spoken in the 'Preliminary Discourse' of 'those pedantic puerilities honored by the name of Rhetoric,' and the Jesuits evidently felt that this shaft had been aimed directly at them, rhetoric being so important a part of the education they dispensed to Europe. (They also took some of Diderot's remarks in his article on 'Aristotelianism' as intended to disparage them.) [12] This made them captious. When D'Alembert remarked that Pope Zacharias had rebuked a bishop, they pointed out peevishly that it wasn't a bishop, it was a priest. When D'Alembert praised Voltaire for writing good prose, the *Journal* pettishly remarked that other poets were known to have written good prose, too. But the *Journal* was on firmer ground when it called attention

---

*I am a good Encyclopedist,
I know both good and evil.
I follow hot on Diderot's trail;
I know everything and believe in nothing.

to various editorial and typographical slips, especially to the frequent failure of the *Encyclopédie* to give adequate credit to its sources.[13]

Month after month, the *Journal de Trévoux* returned to the attack.[14] In November it complained of the *Encyclopédie*'s policy of excluding history and biography from its articles. 'The names of kings, savants, saints, etc., are excluded from the *Encyclopédie,* yet those of pagan divinities are admitted, and this occurs not only for gods of the first order, such, for example, as Amphitrite, Anubis, Apis, Apollo, Astraea, etc., but also for those of the second or third rank, such as Abellio, Achor, Acratus, Adephagie, Adramelech, Aius Locutius, and a multitude of others.' The last named article, in which Diderot had pleaded for the free expression of ideas provided they were written in 'a learned language,' presumably Latin, profoundly shocked the editors of the *Journal de Trévoux* as being contrary to the tranquillity of the state and religion. It was transparent that the editors felt that if ever there was an instance of liberty seeking to become license, this was it. The first volume of the *Encyclopédie,* they said ominously, showed no vestige of having been submitted to the customary censorship.[15] A remark such as this must have warned the editors of the *Encyclopédie* that their project was under ruthless and unscrupulous attack, for the volume *had* been submitted to the censors, as we have seen, and one of the most respected theologians of France, the Abbé Tamponnet, a former syndic of the Sorbonne, had certified on 15 March 1751 that 'by order of My Lord the Chancellor I have read the portion of the *Encyclopédie* concerning theology and ecclesiastical history, in which I have found nothing contrary to sound doctrine.' [16]

In attempting to undercut the prestige of the *Encyclopédie,* the *Journal de Trévoux* developed very effectively the technique of identifying and exposing plagiarisms. A little plagiarism goes a long way in discrediting a book's claim to originality, even though the vast mass of the work be new, and the editors of the *Journal de Trévoux,* with their talent for polemical in-fighting, naturally struck the *Encyclopédie* precisely where it hurt the most.[17] Unacknowledged borrowings were all too common in the *Encyclopédie*. It is true, although rather beside the point, that in spite of them the *Encyclopédie* was a work of great utility. This, in fact, the *Journal de Trévoux* cheerfully acknowledged, especially with regard to the arts and crafts. 'One may pillage the way the bees do,' wrote the *Journal de Trévoux,* carefully acknowledging *their* source, 'without doing anybody wrong, but the thievery of the ant, which walks off with the whole thing, ought never to be imitated.' [18] Indeed, these strictures were so devastating that Diderot and D'Alembert felt the necessity of inserting an explanation in the preface to their second volume.[19]

Besides dilating upon the matter of plagiarism, the *Journal de Trévoux* took very great exception to the article that Diderot wrote on 'Authority.'[20] It took equally great offense at a remark by the Abbé Yvon that 'most men honor letters as they do religion and virtue, that is to say, as a matter that they do not choose either to understand or practice or love.'[21] After three pages of comment set off by this fuse, the *Journal* concluded by saying, 'This is sufficient concerning this article which alarms (we happen to know) people of merit and which deserves the greatest attention on the part of the authors and editors of the *Encyclopédie* in order that henceforth nothing else of the sort creeps into it.'[22] In general, the attitude of the *Journal de Trévoux* might be described as touched with condescension: 'These reflections,' wrote the editor, 'are not intended to wound the authors of the great Dictionary. As the work advances, no doubt it will acquire a greater perfection; and we shall review it with an equal degree of care and impartiality.'[23]

Disagreeable as the *Journal de Trévoux* was making itself, its strictures were nevertheless scarcely influential enough by themselves to be catastrophic. Serious trouble did supervene, however, when, in addition to having to weather the attacks of the *Journal de Trévoux,* the *Encyclopédie* found itself involved in the celebrated scandal of the thesis of the Abbé de Prades, an episode that has been called 'the culminating point of the religious history of the eighteenth century.'[24]

On 18 November 1751 the Abbé Jean-Martin de Prades triumphantly defended during a ten-hour public examination — '*ab octavâ matutinâ ad sextem vespertinam,*' ran the posted thesis announcing the event — a theological thesis qualifying him for the licentiate in the theological faculty of the University of Paris. This was an advanced degree for which he had been several years in preparation, and for which he had satisfied all the usual requirements, such as securing the necessary approval of various Sorbonne doctors and officials before printing his thesis. Entitled *Jerusalem coelesti,* it was published in an edition of 450 copies and had been publicly posted for the statutory length of time before the public examination in the usual form of such theses, printed on extremely heavy paper, elephant folio size, on a single sheet. A considerable collection of these theses, De Prades's among them, may be seen today at the Bibliothèque Nationale in Paris.[25] Usually decorated with an engraving of a scene depicting a religious subject or suggesting religious awe, the theses, most of which were quite short, usually fitted readily into the single-page format. De Prades's thesis was considerably longer than the ordinary, approximately eight thousand words, so it was printed in extremely small type.

Indeed, the type was so small that apparently no one took the trouble to read it, including the reverend professor of theology, an Irishman named Luke Joseph Hooke, whose special and particular responsibility it was. The Abbè de Prades sailed through his examination triumphantly, and not until some days afterward did rumors begin to fly that the Sorbonne had solemnly placed its seal of approval upon a thesis that was later characterized by formal censure of the Sorbonne itself as 'blasphemous, heretical, erroneous, favorable to materialism, contrary to the authority and integrality of the laws of Moses, subversive of the foundations of the Christian religion, and impiously calling into question the veridity and divinity of the miracles of Jesus Christ.' [26]

Thereupon everyone began to read the small print. What everyone found in this dissertation, which purported to summarize all the arguments in proof of Christian revelation, was something that closely followed the psychological doctrines, and even their manner of presentation, in D'Alembert's 'Preliminary Discourse.' [27] De Prades further argued that any faith that preserves the natural law in all its purity is preferable to any revealed religion except, of course, the only true one. This was an argument practically identical with Diderot's in his manuscript work 'On the Sufficiency of Natural Religion.' [28] In other portions of his thesis De Prades expounded the fact that three different systems of chronology are to be found in the Pentateuch, from which he concluded that Moses had had nothing to do with any of them; and then the candidate proceeded to examine the nature of the proof requisite for a belief in miracles. He ended by declaring that the healings performed by Jesus Christ were similar in a number of respects to those performed by Aesculapius! [29]

The only plausible reason explaining why De Prades was able to pass an examination in defense of such propositions is that there must have been in the Sorbonne a number of ecclesiastics who were not yet opposed to the new 'philosophy' and the intellectual methods it entailed.[30] It is precisely for this reason that the incident is important in the intellectual history of the eighteenth century, for after this the lines were sharply drawn. 'Nothing is better calculated,' wrote a pamphleteer just at this time, 'for making obvious the danger of the system that places the origin of our ideas in the impression of the senses than does the use that the enemies of Religion make of it. Doubtless because it has been regarded as merely a philosophical opinion, there has been no alarm over the favor gained by this system, even in the Schools of the University, during the past few years. But the impious thesis of Monsieur de Prades has finally opened people's eyes concerning the disturbing consequences that result from it.' [31]

The Sorbonne now found itself in an extremely embarrassing position, for if ever there was an institution in the *ancien régime* expected to be vigilant in the protection of orthodoxy, it was the faculty of theology of the University of Paris. Reproached by its friends and mocked by its enemies, it was in the mortifying position of an armed service that discovers that its most famous battleship has, in a moment of negligence, gone aground.

The result, usual in such circumstances, was a search for scapegoats. A Sorbonne committee proposed on 3 January 1752 that ten propositions set forth in the thesis be censured. There then followed eleven general assemblies of the Sorbonne, during which no less than 146 doctors — were present, according to one authority; delivered speeches, according to another.[32] It developed that the unfortunate Hooke had approved De Prades's thesis without reading it, being much preoccupied at that moment with correcting the proofs of a book of his own! [33] Hooke lost his chair. De Prades's thesis was condemned by the Sorbonne, as well as by the Archbishop of Paris and the Pope.[34] The comments of the Bishop of Montauban, to whose jurisdiction De Prades was responsible, were particularly comprehensive. 'Up till now,' he wrote in a pastoral charge, 'Hell has vomited its venom, so to speak, drop by drop. Today there are torrents of errors and impieties which tend toward nothing less than the submerging of Faith, Religion, Virtues, the Church, Subordination, the Laws, and Reason. Past centuries have witnessed the birth of sects that, while attacking some Dogmas, have respected a great number of them; it was reserved to ours to see impiety forming a system that overturns all of them at one and the same time.' [35] De Prades fled to Berlin, in order to escape the warrant for his arrest, and there became reader to Frederick the Great. Some years later, he recanted and made his peace with the Church.

Meanwhile it began to be alleged that the whole imbroglio was simply the result of a conspiracy on the part of the editors of the *Encyclopédie,* a plot to overturn religion. Even the Jansenists, who regarded both the *philosophes* and the Sorbonne with equal malevolence, remarked in their underground newspaper, *Les Nouvelles Ecclésiastiques,* that the stir caused by the thesis 'has occasioned the discovery through different circumstances and by certain facts that the thesis of M. de Prades was the result of a conspiracy formed by some would-be freethinkers in order to insinuate their monstrous errors into the Faculty of Theology and moreover to make more conspicuous,

if possible, the irreligion and impiety that they affect.'[36] The same allegation
was made in a pamphlet entitled *Réflexions d'un Franciscain,* which, though
it had a frontispiece representing Diderot being flogged by a Franciscan,
probably was not written by a Franciscan at all.[37] Diderot, in his article
on 'Aristotelianism,' had provocatively declared that Duns Scotus, the famous
Franciscan theologian, 'made his merit consist in contradicting Saint Thomas
Aquinas in every respect; one finds in him nothing but vain subtleties and
a system of metaphysics rejected by everyone with common sense.'[38] It is
not surprising that some sort of counterattack in answer to this should soon
appear in the name of the Franciscans. The *Réflexions d'un Franciscain,* if
we may believe D'Hémery, who referred to the pamphlet in his journal
entry for 20 January 1752, was really written by Father Geoffroy, a Jesuit
professor of rhetoric at the order's famed Collège Louis-le-Grand.[39] Here
we see once again how the Jesuits took the lead in attacking the *Encyclopédie.*
The pamphlet pointed out that De Prades lodged under the same roof with
two priests associated with the *Encyclopédie* [the Abbés Yvon and Mallet],
that he was a contributor to it himself, and that among his colleagues on the
Encyclopédie were several quite capable of writing such a thesis.[40] Moreover, the 'Franciscan' contended that earlier theses by De Prades could not
compare in Latinity or intellectual competence with the *Jerusalem coelesti.*[41]
It was regarded as a particularly suspicious circumstance that the 'Preliminary Discourse' of Volume I had spoken in high praise of a forthcoming
work by De Prades on religion, although in reality there is nothing to
show that it was De Prades's *thesis* that D'Alembert had had in mind.[42]
Moreover, the Abbé was the acknowledged author of the long and important
article in Volume II of the *Encyclopédie* on 'Certitude.' This article, probably written by De Prades in good faith, explored searchingly the logical and
historical grounds for believing testimony regarding miracles, especially that
of the Scriptures in general and of the Resurrection in particular. It was
a sober and ingenious piece of work, but it must be admitted that while it
claimed to deepen faith, it could scarcely have done so save in the case
of persons already determined to believe. Since Volume II saw the light in
late January 1752 (even though the title page bears the date 1751), just at
the time of the greatest uproar over De Prades's thesis, it was easy to portray
the whole concatenation of incidents as nothing but the ramifications of
an Encyclopedist plot.[43]

What is the evidence for this persistent and frequently stated suspicion?
All of it is circumstantial and inconclusive. In their most extreme form, the
allegations insinuate that De Prades was mentally incompetent and simply

allowed himself to be a sort of ventriloquist's dummy for D'Alembert and Diderot. This can hardly be, for De Prades sustained a long and searching oral examination upon his thesis, a feat that requires both previous preparation and mental adaptability. There is no evidence that D'Alembert or Diderot wrote all or any part of De Prades's thesis for him, although there is a good deal of testimony to the effect that the Abbé Yvon did.[44] According to Naigeon, Diderot 'played no part in it except for the counsel he gave the two authors to leave the usual highway a little to one side and to make the hardened ears of the doctors listen now and again to the language of reason.'[45] Nor should it be forgotten that in their preface to Volume III of the *Encyclopédie,* Diderot and D'Alembert asserted that 'we had not even read [the thesis] at the time when people were making use of it in the effort to ruin us.'[46]

Or, if it was not insinuated that Diderot and D'Alembert wrote or practically wrote the thesis, the allegations reduced themselves to accusation of guilt by association. Association there certainly was. After all, De Prades was the contributor of a very important article, and it would be entirely natural for a contributor, living in the same city as the editor, to be in personal touch with him.[47] This association with the eloquent and crepitating Diderot must have had a powerful effect on De Prades. If not, he was the first to escape such influence. But association is not the same as conspiracy, in spite of many eighteenth- and twentieth-century attempts to equate them.

This is not to contend that Diderot had no influence on the thesis, only that there is no proof that he did. It may even be that Diderot and D'Alembert encouraged De Prades to see how far it was possible to go, as a means of feeling out public opinion to guide them in their own editing of the *Encyclopédie.*[48] This could be, although to play such a game involved considerable risks, as subsequent events were soon to prove.

In retrospect this period reveals itself as one of struggle between Diderot and the Jesuits, the stakes being, as it frequently came to be said, the editing of the *Encyclopédie* itself. The Jesuits were profoundly suspicious of the venture and, indeed, have remained so, as is evidenced by the fact that as recently as 1952 a writer in the Jesuit periodical *Etudes* referred to the *Encyclopédie* as 'the most formidable machine that ever was set up against religion.'[49] In 1752 the Jesuits appear to have been determined either to capture the *Encyclopédie* or to destroy it. Such was the interpretation several contemporary observers put on the effort to discredit Diderot and the *Encyclopédie* by representing the De Prades affair to be the result of a conspiracy. This interpretation of the incident was subscribed to not merely by such a weekly news letter as *La Bigarure,* which might have published the charge just for effect, but also by Voltaire, to whom is usually attributed the pamphlet called *Le Tombeau de la Sorbonne.* His asseverations, however, could conceivably be regarded as counterpropaganda, just as could those of Grimm, who referred in his confidential news letter to 'odious conspiracies.'[50] But the frequent declarations of the diarist Barbier, who wrote that 'this whole storm against this fine Dictionary comes by the medium of the Jesuits,' and of D'Argenson, the former secretary of state for foreign affairs, who asserted that 'this storm comes from the Jesuits,' have all the weight due to the conclusions of well-placed persons who, in their confidential diaries, may be presumed to have had no motive for altering what they conceived to be the truth.[51] As early as mid-January 1752, D'Argenson was predicting that the *Encyclopédie* would be suppressed and that the Jesuits would take it over.[52]

Powerful elements at the Court also joined in the fight against the *Encyclopédie.* Their leader was the tutor of the Dauphin, Boyer, the former bishop of Mirepoix, a man said to be devoted to the Jesuits.[53] Boyer was entrusted with the ecclesiastical patronage of the kingdom and consequently was a powerful and influential personage. He took alarm at the De Prades incident and linked it with what he regarded as the subversiveness of the *Encyclopédie.* 'The most ardent enemy of the *Encyclopédie,*' wrote Malesherbes, who ought to know, because his position as director of the book trade made him the one official to whom complaints of this sort were addressed in the first instance, 'was the former bishop of Mirepoix. He carried his complaints to the King himself, and said to him with tears in his eyes that one could no longer conceal from him that religion was about to be ruined in his kingdom.'[54] It is not very surprising, then, that an *Arrêt du Conseil du Roy* (7 February 1752) suppressed the further publication, sale, and distribution of the *Encyclopédie:* 'His Majesty has found that in these two volumes a point has been made of inserting several maxims tending to destroy the royal authority, to establish a spirit of independence and revolt, and, under cover of obscure and ambiguous terminology, to build the foundations of error, of moral corruption, of irreligion, and of unbelief.'[55]

For the second time in his life, Diderot found himself involved in the public policy of the state. Both incidents, the one leading to Vincennes in 1749 and this one, ending in the catastrophe of the suppression of the *Encyclopédie,* were crises in the history of the freedom of thought, making Diderot an important figure in the political history of the eighteenth century. But it was most uncomfortable to exist in such an exposed position. The

Encyclopédie had been solemnly and officially described in the royal decree as being close to treasonous. By inference its editor had been pilloried in a state paper and singled out as a target for public indignation, assailed (to use the parlance of American journalism) as Public Enemy No. 1. 'This morning,' wrote D'Argenson, 'appeared an *arrêt du conseil* which had not been foreseen: it suppressed the *Dictionnaire encyclopédique,* with some appalling allegations, such as revolt against God and the royal authority, corruption of morals . . . etc. It is said on this score that the authors of this dictionary, of which only two volumes have appeared, consequently must shortly be put to death, that there is no way of preventing their being hunted down and informed against.' [56]

Diderot came to think, in his later years, that his own compatriots showed him less honor than did foreigners. The obloquy of the *arrêt du conseil* of February 1752 could very well have contributed to making this sentiment burgeon within him.

CHAPTER 13

The *Encyclopédie* Recontinued

DIDEROT's very person may have been in danger during the days following the suppression of the *Encyclopédie*. D'Argenson reported on 12 February that it was rumored that a *lettre de cachet* had been issued against him, and supplemented this hearsay by the further entry, 25 February, that Diderot had taken flight in order to forestall arrest; and Barbier wrote that 'Diderot was afraid of being put a second time into the Bastille.' [1] In reality, there is no evidence from a source close to Diderot that he ever left his house in the Rue de l'Estrapade. Nevertheless this was probably a period of great anxiety and alarm, especially as he was forced to surrender what manuscripts he had in preparation for succeeding volumes. 'There have been taken away from him all the authors' manuscripts, as well as from the publishers all remaining copies of the first two volumes and twenty-five sheets already printed of the third.' [2] Apparently Diderot delivered the manuscripts personally, sometime around 21 February, either to Malesherbes, the director of publications, or to his father, Lamoignon de Blancmesnil, who since 1750 had been D'Aguesseau's successor as Chancellor of France. [3]

The impounding of the manuscripts was preliminary to the Jesuits' attempting to carry on the work. D'Argenson had recorded, a week after the suppression, that 'it is not doubted that the Jesuits will take the enterprise over and continue it. . . .' Barbier spoke of the Jesuits as having a devoted supporter in the person of Chancellor Lamoignon, and, if Grimm may be believed, it seems likely that the Jesuits were given a chance to see what they could do. 'Everything had been well concerted,' wrote Grimm a year later. 'The papers had already been taken away from M. Diderot. Thus it was that the Jesuits counted upon making away with an encyclopedia already completely finished . . . by arranging and putting in order articles that they believed to be all prepared. But they had forgotten to take away from the philosopher his head and genius as well, and to ask him for the key to a large number of articles that, far from understanding, they strove in vain to make out.'[4]

But all was not lost for Diderot, for through this lengthy crisis he had on his side a very powerful friend. This was Chrétien-Guillaume de Lamoignon de Malesherbes, a member of a very prominent family of lawyers and magistrates belonging to that class of the nobility called in the *ancien régime* the *noblesse de robe*. Since late in 1750, Malesherbes had been serving under his father, the Chancellor, as director of publications. He was only twenty-nine when he took up this office, in which he continued until 1763. During his administration the great battles over the *Encyclopédie* were fought, which almost entirely changed the intellectual complexion of France. It was scarcely possible for a man to occupy more of a key position than did he as arbiter and umpire during this momentous struggle.

At the time he took office, Malesherbes was already the presiding judge of the *cour des aides,* one of the tax courts of the *ancien régime.* This was a purchasable office, and the Lamoignon family, in accordance with the practice of the time, had simply bought it. What was out of the ordinary was that the person for whom the post was purchased should happen to be a man of intelligence, adequate legal training, and merit. Malesherbes was a man of unusual integrity, without any semblance of personal ambition, and had a fine sense of the responsibilities of his office along with a transparent desire to carry out its duties with justice to all. When unpretentiousness of character was being discussed one day at the famous Mme Geoffrin's, Malesherbes' name came up. 'So many people pretend to have it,' said Mme Geoffrin, 'but M. de Malesherbes, there's a man who is unpretentiously unpretentious.'[5]

Malesherbes' policy as director of publications was as simple and straightforward as the rest of him. This policy was molded by the fact that he held the highest view of the social usefulness of the man of letters, and once wrote that 'in a century in which every citizen can speak to the entire nation by means of print, those who have the talent for instructing men or the gift of moving them — in a word, men of letters — are, in the midst of a dispersed people, what the orators of Rome and Athens were in the midst of a people assembled.'[6] He himself alluded to his motives and policy in a letter written to one of the *philosophes* in 1758: 'As for what concerns me, you know that during many years I occupied myself exclusively with literature and lived only in the company of men of letters. When I found myself led by unforeseen circumstances — and perhaps against my will —

into a different sphere, I desired nothing else so much as to be able to render services to those with whom I had passed my life. I thought I had found the occasion of doing so when I was put in charge of the book trade, since I found myself in a position to procure for them the liberty of writing that I had always seen them sigh for, and to free them from many of the constraints under which they appeared to groan and of which they continually complained. I also considered this to be doing a service to the State, for this liberty has always seemed to me to have many more advantages than drawbacks.'[7] Thus Malesherbes brought to the performance of his duties the convictions expressed by Milton in *Areopagitica*. 'It is unjust and impossible to domineer over opinions,' wrote Malesherbes, 'and consequently [unjust and impossible] to suppress, garble, or correct the books in which they are set forth.'[8] Believing as he did that the exchange of ideas was good for a society, Malesherbes constantly favored as little repression — instead of as much — as the pressures that played upon him would permit. For this reason he granted many tacit permissions to books that could not be given the official imprimatur of the *Approbation et Privilège du Roi*. Such a policy, he believed, was necessary in order to keep up with the world: 'A man,' he wrote, 'who had read only the books that, when published, appeared with the express consent of the government the way the law prescribes, would be behind his contemporaries almost a century.'[9]

With these convictions, it is obvious that Malesherbes often found himself in the position of defending radical works. 'The Encyclopedists were mistaken in not believing in Providence,' wrote a witty historian of their doings, 'for it was manifestly for their sake that Providence gave to Malesherbes the direction of the book trade.'[10] Yet it must not be supposed that he was a prejudiced and one-sided doctrinaire. Very often he revealed himself as being more in favor of freedom of the press — freedom for both sides — than the Encyclopedists were themselves. Not infrequently it seemed that what the *philosophes* wanted was not so much freedom as immunity. What they often demanded was apparently tantamount to the right to say what they pleased when they pleased, plus protection against the counterattacks of their enemies. In fact, Malesherbes seems to have been about the only person in eighteenth-century France who desired real freedom of the press. But real freedom of the press was a reform that had to wait upon the unfolding of portentous events. Meanwhile Malesherbes did his job with dignity and skill, respecting his office and making others respect it too, resisting undue encroachments on his functions by rival agencies in the government, and revealing an almost endless willingness to endure patiently the massive and capricious manifesta-

tions of temperament displayed so frequently and copiously by the selfsame
men of letters whom he was endeavoring to assist.

Much later, in 1775, Malesherbes became one of Louis XVI's ministers but,
too eager for economy and reform to suit the court opinion of his day, he
felt obliged to resign in the very next year. In 1792–3 he served his monarch
for the last time: he was Louis XVI's principal lawyer and brilliant defender
in the trial preceding the King's execution. The Terror had a rejoinder for
such conspicuous devotion and in 1794 Malesherbes was tried and guillo-
tined. One of the few monuments to be seen today in the enormous and
echoing Salle des Pas-Perdus in the Palace of Justice in Paris is a statue of
Malesherbes. It is a fitting recognition of a courageous and honorable man,
who cast over the declining days of the *ancien régime* the refulgence of a
noble soul.

This was the man of whom one of Diderot's friends wrote that 'without
him the *Encyclopédie* would most likely never have dared to appear.' [11]
In this particular crisis of 1752 Malesherbes had not favored the suppression
or even the suspension of the *Encyclopédie,* according to D'Argenson, who
got his information from one of Malesherbes' cousins. Instead he had felt
that it would be sufficient simply to insert some substitute pages for the most
offending passages.[12] But in this he had been overruled. It was probably
owing to his influence, however, that the action taken by the King's Council
only suppressed the first two volumes instead of revoking the license of
the whole.[13] He may have been maneuvering, thought Barbier, to forestall
action by the Parlement, which might have been more severe.[14] Considering
the action the Parlement had taken six years before in having Diderot's
Pensées philosophiques burned by the hangman, Barbier's hypothesis may
have been correct.

During 1752 a number of questions regarding the final disposition of the
Encyclopédie had to be settled. Were the Jesuits going to continue the
enterprise? (If not, what were the factors preventing them?) If they did not,
what terms would the government impose upon Diderot and D'Alembert
as a condition of allowing the work to be recontinued? And finally, would
the latter raise any difficulties in consenting to these terms?

It is impossible to say why the Jesuits did not take over the *Encyclopédie,*
and Grimm's statement that they were incapable is extremely unpersuasive.
Still, it is the only testimony that we have on this tantalizing subject, leaving
us in the realm of vague and dubious conjecture. Probably the fate of the
Encyclopédie was involved in the chronic struggle for power at the French
court, for Mme de Pompadour, since 1745 the King's mistress, was an enemy

of the Jesuits, so that by a sort of Euclidean corollary, she was well disposed toward the *Encyclopédie*.[15] This very politically minded woman, the mistress of a man who usually regarded the affairs of his kingdom as no concern of his, was sincerely interested in the arts and somewhat in the sciences. La Tour's dazzling pastel of her, first exhibited in the Salon of 1755 and now hanging in the Louvre, symbolizes these interests: a portfolio of engravings is at her feet, in the background is a guitar resting on a sofa, she holds a piece of music in her hands, and on the table by her side are a globe and a number of volumes, including a folio on the back of which can be plainly read: ENCYCLOPEDIE, TOME IV.[16] D'Argenson, evidently on the authority of D'Alembert, remarked in his entry of 7 May 1752 that 'Mme de Pompadour and some ministers [perhaps D'Argenson's brother, to whom the *Encyclopédie* had been dedicated] [17] have had D'Alembert and Diderot entreated to devote themselves again to the work of the *Encyclopédie,* while practicing the requisite resistance to any temptation to touch upon religion or authority.' [18] This suggests that the anti-Jesuit coterie at the court, having somehow or other frustrated the Jesuits, were now in a position to turn to the former editors. Apparently those in responsibility had always intended to have the project eventually carried on somehow, probably because of the fact that many citizens and foreigners already had a vested interest in the *Encyclopédie* by virtue of having subscribed to it.[19] The jurisprudence of the *ancien régime* was especially regardful of property rights, and this deference to the vested rights of subscribers goes far to explain why the *Encyclopédie* was never permanently discontinued.

As might be expected, considering the previous uproar, the agreement for recontinuing the *Encyclopédie* involved arrangements for new censors. This was the more necessary because the original censors appointed by D'Aguesseau were patently finding very little to criticize. As we have already seen, the Abbé Tamponnet had given Volume I a clean bill of health in respect to theology and ecclesiastical history. Moreover, the censor Lassone had liked the second volume even better than the first: 'As the materials are assembled, a great edifice is being formed, where one sees developing with equal methodicalness and utility the various treasures that the human race has acquired for itself by its researches.' [20] This was not the way Mirepoix and the Jesuits spoke about the work! The solution to the problem was worked out by Malesherbes, who offered Mirepoix 'to have all articles without exception censored by theologians whom he would choose himself.

'He accepted my proposition with joy, and nominated the Abbés Tamponnet, Millet, and Cotterel, who were the ones in whom he had the most confidence.

'Volumes II [Malesherbes' memory was at fault here; the new arrangement was for volumes following the second], III, IV, V, VI, and VII of the *Encyclopédie* were censored in entirety by these three doctors. There was not a single article the manuscript of which was not initialed by one of the three.' [21]

No direct evidence exists describing Diderot's attitude and policy during this crisis. One is therefore reduced to the indirect and speculative device of attempting to descry Diderot through the medium of D'Alembert. For what D'Alembert thought and said about it all was quite explicit. He took care to apprise Voltaire of his sentiments in a letter dated 24 August 1752, a letter whose main purposes were to bespeak Voltaire's protection of the Abbé de Prades and to thank him for the handsome remarks regarding the *Encyclopédie* that he had inserted in the closing lines of his great history of the age of Louis XIV (*Le Siècle de Louis XIV*). 'My colleague in the *Encyclopédie* joins me in thanking you,' wrote D'Alembert, and then, after alluding to the suspension of it, he continued, 'I suspected that after having maltreated us as they did, they would come around to begging us to continue, and this has not failed to come about. For six months I refused, I shouted like Homer's Mars, and I may say that I gave in only because of the public eagerness.' D'Alembert's giving in to the public eagerness sounds like a reluctant politician's being persuaded by his eager constituents to run. D'Alembert used this letter to suggest, perhaps not very seriously, that it might be possible to edit the *Encyclopédie* in Berlin 'under the eyes and with the protection and enlightenment of your philosopher prince.' [22] To this Voltaire, then resident at Potsdam, hastily replied that 'there is a prodigious number of bayonets here, but very few books.' [23] But the principal interest in D'Alembert's letter arises from his use of pronouns. By saying '*I* refused,' '*I* shouted,' '*I* gave in,' rather than using the collective 'we' which he employs elsewhere in these lines, he implies that Diderot's part was a subordinate one. This may be, for what evidence we have shows that D'Alembert made himself rather assertive that year. On 1 March he wrote to Formey at Berlin, 'Doubtless you have learned of the suppression of the *Encyclopédie*. I don't know whether the work will be continued, but I can assure you that it will not be by me.' [24] In May, he was grumbling, in another letter to Formey, about the rather unfavorable review that the 'Preliminary Discourse' had received at the hands of the *Journal des Sçavans* in its number of the previous September. He would not go on with the

Encyclopédie, he wrote, unless the *Journal des Sçavans* 'makes me an authenticated apology just as I shall dictate it.' Moreover, he went on, 'there shall be given to us enlightened and reasonable censors, and not brute beasts in fur, sold out to our enemies. . . . There shall be allowed to us the sustaining of all opinions not contrary to religion or government, such as the one that all ideas come from the senses, which our illustrious Sorbonne would like to make a heresy of, and an infinity of others. . . . It shall be forbidden to the Jesuits, our enemies, to write against this work, to say either good or ill of it, or else it shall be permissible for us to engage in reprisals.' [25] But D'Alembert was unable to secure any such stipulations. Perhaps because he could not obtain these guarantees, he informed some of his correspondents that he was henceforth limiting his role in the *Encyclopédie.* Thus he wrote to Formey on 10 July that in the future he would be responsible for 'the mathematical portion on condition that I shall not take part in the rest.' [26]

D'Alembert's assertions are a little self-contradictory and confusing, and they raise the problem as to the relative importance of the editorial roles of Diderot and himself. Was Diderot really the principal editor? Or was D'Alembert in fact a co-editor with, in spite of the title page — 'and for the mathematical portion, by M. d'Alembert' — equal authority and responsibilities? If not, D'Alembert certainly seemed inclined to preen himself a bit before Voltaire as if he were. Voltaire, for his part, supposed for some years that D'Alembert was in fact the work's principal editor, an impression which D'Alembert does not seem to have disturbed when he visited Voltaire in 1756. It was not until Mme d'Epinay visited Ferney in 1757 that Voltaire learned to his surprise how matters really stood.[27] At this moment in 1752 we see D'Alembert (whose name, unlike Diderot's, had not appeared on the publishers' pay roll since early 1749) writing to Voltaire in such a fashion as to imply, by the use of pronouns, that the two men were co-editors, with Diderot the rather less active. Moreover, in refusing Frederick II's proffer of the presidency of the Berlin Academy, D'Alembert wrote in explanation on 16 September 1752: 'Besides I am in charge of a great work, as you know, conjointly with M. Diderot . . . it is absolutely necessary that this work should be done and printed under our eyes, that we see each other often and work in concert upon it.' [28]

The truth, however, about the relative responsibilities of D'Alembert and Diderot in editing the *Encyclopédie* is symbolized throughout the several volumes of the work by the typographical devices used to identify the contributions of each. D'Alembert's identification was always the letter 'O,' and thus he figured symbolically with all the other contributors, to each of whom a similar identifying letter had been assigned. Diderot's articles, on the other hand, were identified either by an asterisk or by no mark whatever. In spite of this uniform and consistent symbolism, suggesting as it does that Diderot was always the principal editor, D'Alembert's description of his functions was subject to somewhat confusing changes. He evidently thought of himself, in times of prosperity, as a co-editor; in times of adversity, as a contributor.

For some time the government contemplated the issuance of a new decree reauthorizing the *Encyclopédie,* but eventually decided against it and merely allowed the work to reappear on tacit sufferance and without public and explicit approval.[29] 'The Government has appeared to desire that an enterprise of this nature should not be abandoned,' D'Alembert was permitted to write in his preface to Volume III. Grimm, writing a confidential news letter, could be more circumstantial. 'The government,' he wrote when Volume III was published, 'was obliged, not without more or less confusion, to take steps to engage M. Diderot and M. d'Alembert to undertake again a work that had been attempted in vain by some people who for a long while have occupied the least place in literature. I say with more or less confusion because the government entreated the authors to continue, but without revoking the decrees issued against the work three months before.'[30] And in fact the *Encyclopédie,* though now allowed to proceed, henceforth did so on a very tentative and provisional basis in point of law.

Painful though the episode had been, and abused as Diderot and D'Alembert considered themselves to be, their enterprise greatly profited in the long run from the temporary and evanescent triumph of the opposition. They survived, which is sometimes a very considerable feat in itself, as the Abbé Sieyès felt about his own part in the French Revolution. The enemies of Diderot and D'Alembert had been unable to eliminate or supplant them or essentially alter the character of their encyclopedia. They had not been forced to disown either their principles or their methodology. Moreover, the turmoil had given their work an invaluable amount of publicity, as Barbier, who remarked upon it in his diary, had the shrewdness to see.[31] Interest in the *Encyclopédie* kept constantly mounting. The publishers had begun with plans for an edition of 1,625, which they presently increased to 2000. When Volume III was published, in November 1753, interest had been so greatly stimulated that an edition of 3100 was necessary, with further reprintings planned to bring the first three volumes and all those thereafter to an edition of 4200.[32] The impact of the *Encyclopédie,* both numerically and in the nature of its ideas, was such that one of the great French critics, Ferdinand Brunetière, said — although he was consistently hostile to Diderot — that 'it is the great affair of the time, the goal toward which everything preceding it was tending, the origin of everything that has followed it, and consequently the true center for any history of ideas in the eighteenth century.'[33]

A minor circumstance during 1752 gave Diderot his opportunity for scoring a considerable victory in polemics, and for stating with great vigor the methodological premises upon which the Encyclopédie stood. A well-known Jansenist prelate, the Bishop of Auxerre, decided to publish a pastoral instruction condemning the thesis of the Abbé de Prades. This was piling Ossa on Pelion, for it might be supposed that the Sorbonne, the Bishop of Montauban, the Archbishop of Paris, and the Pope, all of whom had pronounced on the matter, were competent to dispose of it. None of these was a Jansenist, however, and doubtless the Bishop of Auxerre felt that it was incumbent upon some Jansenist to prove his zeal for Catholicity at this juncture. But this intervention was skillfully exploited by Diderot, whose reply took the opportunity of playing off Jesuits against Jansenists, pronouncing a plague on both their houses, and drawing a sharp contrast between matters of faith and matters of scientific fact. Diderot wrote this adroit exercise in polemics in the name of the Abbé de Prades, who was at that time in Berlin preparing his own apology, which was to appear in two parts. Accordingly Diderot entitled his little changeling, which was on sale in Paris even before the Abbé de Prades had published his, the Suite de l'Apologie de M. l'Abbé de Prades . . . Troisième partie ('Continuation of the Apology of the Abbé de Prades . . . Third Part'). The little book, which purported to be printed in Berlin, appeared about 12 October 1752, and was followed in 1753 by another edition, a pirated one published in Amsterdam.[34]

Problems of intellectual method were uppermost in Diderot's mind in writing this work, as is shown by the vigorous passage in which he defends reason against obscurantism: 'I know nothing so indecent and injurious to religion as these vague declamations against reason on the part of some theologians. One would say, to hear them, that men cannot enter into the bosom of Christianity except as a flock of beasts enters into a stable, and that one has to renounce common sense either to embrace our religion or to persist in it. To establish such principles, I repeat, is to reduce man to the level of the brute, and place falsehood and truth upon an equal footing.'[35]

In the preface Diderot said right out that 'this third part is as much the defense of the "Preliminary Discourse" of the *Encyclopédie,* from which I [he is writing in the name of De Prades] drew my first position, as it is the defense of my thesis.'[36] And he lengthily discussed the implications in science and theology of the old axiom, by this time very familiar to the readers of this book, *nihil est in intellectu quod non prius fuerit in sensu.*[37] Diderot once more expounded the sensistic psychology that Locke and Condillac had developed. But this antithesis of the notion that human beings are born with innate ideas of God and morality was particularly suspect among French churchmen, as we have seen, because these new ideas of psychology were likely to get confusingly mixed up with orthodox ideas about man's soul. The Bishop of Auxerre put his finger on the precise issue when he complained of De Prades's thesis that the type of man discussed therein 'is not at all the man whose creation is described for us in Genesis.'[38] This was quite true. While the Bishop wanted to talk about Genesis, Diderot wanted to talk about 'man in nature,' as he himself said, and then of the herd man (*les hommes en troupeau*) and societal man (*les hommes en société*).[39] Thus we see Diderot trying to devise and apply concepts that are recognizable to us today as those fundamental to the social sciences. As a leading French social scientist has remarked, 'the principal effort of the Encyclopedists consisted in secularizing the social sciences.'[40] That is exactly what Diderot was trying to do here. But it was a point of view most upsetting to people who, when they said 'man,' meant 'Adam.'

Diderot's life is an episode in the long history of the scientific attitude's struggle against the constrictions of authoritarianism. What he and people like him have always hoped and believed is that the methods of free inquiry can reveal more of ultimate reality than can an unbending orthodoxy. Diderot expressed this hope in the terminology of a liberal theologian when he has the pseudo-De Prades declare, 'I have believed that the wing of a butterfly, well described, would bring me closer to Divinity than a volume of metaphysics.'[41] In this sentence is the difference between fundamentalism and science, between W. J. Bryan and Clarence Darrow.

For persons of Diderot's cast of mind, the fate of Galileo was always the hobgoblin that haunted their imaginations and inhabited their fears. And consequently Diderot has De Prades distinguish between what was appropriate to theology and what to 'philosophy': 'Let us take care not to identify the truth of our religion and the divinity of our Scriptures with facts that have no relation to these subjects and which might be overturned by time and by experiments. . . . We damage both theology and philosophy if we take it into our heads to produce physicists in our [theological] schools and if philosophers begin to make theologians in their assemblies.' [42]

Thus Diderot took the opportunity inadvertently offered him by the maladroit Bishop of Auxerre to strike a blow for what the eighteenth century proudly and perhaps a little vaingloriously called enlightenment. In doing so, Diderot belabored the Bishop a little, as when he wrote that 'it seems to me that this prelate has pronounced very superficially about topics that, to tell the truth, he was not required to understand, but upon which he was much less required to speak, and infinitely less required to insult those who do understand them.' [43] This was a way of showing, as indeed was the purpose of the whole book, the pains and penalties awaiting those who attempted to overawe the partisans of the new learning. But this was, after all, a negative and defensive tactic. More important was the appeal to toleration, and the assertion that De Prades and people like him were being unjustly persecuted. Such was the burden of Diderot's peroration, which Buffon — himself a famous connoisseur of literary style — considered to be one of the most eloquent passages in the French language.[44] Similarly extravagant in its praise was the judgment of a journalist of the time who wrote that some of the passages in the *Apology,* especially the one at the end, would make one suppose that they had been written by 'a resuscitated Bossuet,' a remark which, for a generation dazzled by the literary glories of the century of Louis XIV, was the highest possible praise.[45]

Doubtless as he wrote the conclusion, Diderot was seeing himself in the figure he drew of the persecuted Abbé de Prades. There is a vein of theatricality in the *philosophes* (and in Diderot) which makes it a little difficult to take them quite so seriously as they took themselves. And a good deal of this sense of the dramatic and even of the self-righteous appears in Diderot's closing remarks. But there is persuasiveness and conviction in them, too, from an author who had had his share of perturbations and alarms:

. . . I have seen that the state of all these people [his critics] is beyond hope, and I have said, Therefore shall I forget them; such is the counsel both of my religion and of my self-interest. I shall devote myself without respite to the great work that I have undertaken; and I shall finish it, if the goodness of God allows me to do so, in a manner that some day will make all my persecutors ashamed. At the head of such a work my vindication will find its appropriate place; it is at the beginning of a treatise on the truthfulness of religion that it will be fitting to place the story of the crying injustices that I have suffered, of the atrocious calumnies with which I have been blackened, of the odious names lavished against me, of the impious conspiracies by which I have been defamed, of all the evils of which I have been accused, and of all those that have been done against me. There, then, will this story be found; and my enemies will be confounded; and the people of virtue will bless the Providence that took me by the hand, when my uncertain steps were faltering, and that brought me to this land where persecution shall not follow me.[46]

Thus he concluded, in a pleasant incandescence of self-approval.

CHAPTER 14

Italian Opera and French Taste

DIDEROT was an extremely sociable man. He liked to oblige people. And he loved to talk. He spent so much time pouring forth his ideas to friends and acquaintances that it is remarkable that he ever found the opportunity to accumulate new stock. With Diderot communication was almost a compulsion. If absent from his mistress, he wrote her long letters; if left to his own devices, his works show that his thought patterns were set in a subtle dialectic of communication with himself; and if with friends, even casual acquaintances, he lavished his ideas upon them in such profusion that Grimm, tidy German and shrewd entrepreneur that he was, would frequently deplore the nonchalant outpouring of such dazzling gifts, much as a man who is part owner of an oil well might deplore the wastefulness of a gusher that has blown its top.

Moreover, Diderot delighted in thinking of himself as the very type and pattern of the Good-natured Man.[1] Consequently, he did not mind expending his time and his energies in behalf of those who had no real claim upon him. Nor did he really object to being imposed on, up to a certain point, for it fitted into his picture of himself as an affable, approachable, and generous person. This is illustrated by an anecdote that he told of himself as occurring at about this time in his life. 'Once upon a time I rescued from extreme poverty a young man of letters who was not without talent. I fed him, lodged him, kept him warm and in clothes, for several years. The very first flight of this talent which I had cultivated was a satire against me and mine. The publisher . . . suggested suppressing the work. I took care not to accept this offer. The satire appeared. The author had the impudence to bring me the first copy of it himself. I contented myself with saying to him: "You are an ingrate. Anyone else than I would have thrown you out, but I am obliged to you for knowing me better than that. Take back your work and carry it to my enemies, to that old Duc d'Orléans who lives on the other side of the street." I was living at that time in the Estrapade. The end of all this was that I wrote for him, I against my own self, a petition to the Duc d'Orléans, that the old fanatic gave him fifty louis, that the thing became known, and that the protector remained pretty ridiculous and the protected pretty vile.' * [2]

Diderot's extraversion did indeed carry with it the constant risk that he would dissipate his energies and allow himself to be distracted from more substantial accomplishment. It may be doubted, however, whether the profusion of Diderot's personality and ideas was really as wasted as Grimm feared. Among all of the *philosophes* Diderot was chief. In the vocabulary of his friends, he was more than a *philosophe,* he was THE *philosophe.* He was the leader of a party or, as his enemies would put it, of a sect. And it was by conversation as much as it was by what he published that he spread his influence and made his leadership felt. Perhaps even more; for much of what he thought was too dangerous to publish and had to remain in his desk drawer to await the random honors of posthumous publication. But his ideas, orally expressed, emanated in pulsations from the social circles that he frequented out into that highly centralized society in which everything focused upon Versailles and Paris. Add to this that Diderot was extraordinarily gifted in the arts of oral persuasion (many of his friends thought that, given different political conditions in France, he would have been an orator of the very highest rank), and it can readily be seen that not all the time he spent in company was wasted.

The ideal milieu in which to gratify his social proclivities was provided Diderot by the Baron d'Holbach, a man with whom Diderot became intimate about this time and who, like Grimm, was destined to remain a lifelong friend. D'Holbach's house, with its fine library and its quite extraordinary collections of prints and natural history, and D'Holbach's dinners attracted some of the greatest wits and intellects of his century. David Hume took Horace Walpole there in 1765, and the latter, recording the visit in his journal, spoke of D'Holbach as 'a good-natured German settled in France, who keeps a table for strangers, the *beaux esprits* of the country etc.' [3] Horace Walpole's judgment of persons was apt to be a little reductive, so that Morellet's testimony is valuable in revealing what the opportunities at D'Holbach's meant to persons of the 'philosophical' persuasion:

* The time, the street Diderot was living in, and the fact that he spoke of the publication as being 'against me and mine' suggest that this may have been *La Bigarure*'s account of the brawl between Mme Diderot and Mme de Puisieux.

Baron d'Holbach served two dinners regularly each week, Sundays and Thursdays; there assembled then . . . ten, twelve and up to fifteen or twenty men of letters and men of the world or foreigners . . . a society truly engaging, as could be realized by this symptom alone, that, being arrived at two o'clock, as was the fashion at that time, we often were almost all of us still there at seven or eight in the evening.

Now, there was the place to hear the freest, most animated and most instructive conversation that ever was. . . . There was no moot point, political or religious, that was not advanced there and discussed pro and con, almost always with great subtlety and profundity.

. . . .

It is there that I heard . . . Diderot treat questions of philosophy, art, or literature, and by his wealth of expression, fluency, and inspired appearance, hold our attention for a long stretch of time.[4]

Paul Thiry, Baron d'Holbach, later became the secret author of a long series of works which have qualified him in the eyes of posterity to be considered one of the paladins of atheism. Born in 1723, he was just ten years younger than Diderot. He was reared at Paris and educated at the University of Leyden, where he made friends with John Wilkes, the tempestuous Englishman who in the 1760's became the hero of the resistance to 'general warrants' (a sort of British counterpart of the French *lettres de cachet*) and who, in other ways as well, fell foul, like the Americans, of George III's attempts at personal rule. It was through D'Holbach that Diderot twenty years later made the acquaintance of Wilkes, who had become by then one of the best-known, not to say most notorious, men in Europe.[5]

D'Holbach settled down in Paris following the War of the Austrian Succession, became naturalized in 1749, and married, in decorous succession, two sisters, his second cousins.[6] These matches gave every indication of being for love, but they also served to keep the considerable family fortune under one roof, so that D'Holbach never had to worry, nor did any of his philosophical friends, where the next meal was coming from. That roof, still standing at Number 8, Rue des Moulins, covers a substantial five-storey building (six, counting the entresol) with its own court and porte-cochere.[7] In Diderot's day it was located in an area of tortuous and tangled streets which has since been much simplified by building the Avenue de l'Opéra. Another acquaintance of Diderot, Helvétius, lived hard by. It is difficult to say when Diderot first knew D'Holbach but it must have been at least some months before 1752, to judge from the latter's numerous contributions to Volume II of the *Encyclopédie*.[8] There is direct evidence of their connection by October of that year, for a French writer returning from Berlin mentioned meeting Diderot at the home of Mme d'Aine, D'Holbach's mother-in-law.[9]

Diderot and D'Holbach had a great deal in common, not only intellectually but also in matters of preference and taste. For instance, they both liked to overeat, they liked a walk in the country, they liked to possess fine prints and beautiful paintings, and they liked comfort. Also, without being promiscuous, they were both heartily heterosexual. In matters of philosophy and religion, they were in substantial agreement, although Diderot's doctrine is much more elusive, ambiguous, and therefore closer to life than D'Holbach's. Diderot's philosophy, hard to be sure of, has a great deal of poetic insight, and should properly be called godless rather than atheistic (to use a distinction frequently employed to discuss one aspect of the existentialism of Sartre). But there never was any question that the D'Holbach whom posterity knows was solidly and ponderously atheistic.

Oddly enough, there is testimony, although not of impeccable quality, that Diderot converted D'Holbach to atheism. The evidence comes from a book by a politician and man of letters named Garat, who in his younger days knew both men and was especially friendly with a member of their circle named Suard. Suard knew Diderot and D'Holbach at this early time and is the source of the following story: 'Having long been an adorer of God, Whom he [D'Holbach] saw in the order and laws of the universe, he had a missionary's zeal in regard to those whom he liked and who did not have the same belief. He pursued the incredulity of Diderot even into those workshops where the editor of the encyclopedia, surrounded by machines and workers, was taking sketches of all the manual arts; and drawing his text from these very machines . . . he asked him if he could doubt that they had been conceived and built by an intelligence. The application was a striking one, but it did not, however, strike either the mind or heart of Diderot. Diderot's friend, bursting into tears, fell at his feet. It has been said of Saint Paul, thrown from the horse upon which he was pursuing the Christians: *Falls a persecutor, and gets up an apostle*. It was quite the contrary that occurred in this instance: he who fell on his knees a deist, got up an atheist.'[10] There may indeed be something to this story, for as late as 1756 the curé of Saint-Germain-l'Auxerrois in Paris enthusiastically vouched for D'Holbach as 'making profession of the Catholic, apostolic and Roman faith, the duties of which he fulfills with edification.'[11]

However this may be, it is incontestable that Diderot and D'Holbach had innumerable intellectual interests in common, interests which might quite literally be called encyclopedic. Marmontel wrote of D'Holbach that he 'had read everything and never forgotten anything of interest,' and Rousseau spoke of him as maintaining his position among men of letters very adequately, owing to his knowledge and learning.[12] This passion for knowledge, especially in the fields of mineralogy and metallurgy where a mastery of German was essential, was extremely useful to the *Encyclopédie* and was acknowledged lengthily in the foreword to Volume II.

The consonant tastes of Diderot and D'Holbach were particularly revealed in this period 1752-4 by their taking the same side in an embittered debate over the comparative merits of the French and the Italian opera. On 1 August 1752, a visiting Italian company came to the French Opéra, then holding forth where the Palais Royal is today, and made their debut by singing Pergolesi's *opéra bouffe, La Serva padrona*. This company continued to give their repertory at the Opéra, singing once, twice, or sometimes three times a week until their final performance on 7 March 1754.[13] All of their thirteen pieces were short and consequently given either as curtain raisers or as concluding pieces with another work. The other attraction was always a piece from the regular French repertory, given by the regular company, so Parisian audiences had an excellent opportunity to make comparisons.

During a year that had already been enlivened by the Abbé de Prades affair and the suspension of the *Encyclopédie,* and that also saw tension heightening between the King and the Parlement of Paris caused by a very grave quarrel as to whether dying Jansenists could be denied the last rites if they refused to subscribe to the bull *Unigenitus* — a disagreement which ended with the 'exiling' of the Parlement to a provincial town in 1753 and the temporary suspension of their functions — in addition to all this, there began 'the quarrel of the buffoons,' in which the Encyclopedists found common and exciting cause. The enthusiasts for the new Italian genre tended to congregate in that part of the pit at the Opéra that was near the royal box assigned to the Queen. Consequently 'Queen's Corner' came to be the name for the *aficionados* of the Italian opera, while 'King's Corner' denominated the partisans of the French.

In D'Holbach's circle Jean-Jacques Rousseau had extolled the beauties of the Italian opera, of which he had had firsthand experience at Venice. Rousseau's friends could now judge for themselves, and what they heard charmed them utterly and seemed infinitely superior to the formalism and intellectualism of the conventional French opera which Lully (1632-87) had created. They found the Italian opera richer and more varied in musical devices, more melodious, more capable of building emotional mood, more adroit in suiting the music to the phonetics and meaning of the words. In contrast, French operatic music seemed stiff and monotonous, with long, boresome recitatives, and too much emphasis on harmony at the expense of melody. This last, they thought, was an inherent difficulty of the French language, which caused singers to bawl rather than sing. Although the French opera was excellent as a spectacle, it left much to be desired from the point of view of music. As the great Italian playwright Goldoni said of it, it was 'heaven for the eyes, hell for the ears.' [14] The French partisans of such pieces as *La Serva padrona* and Pergolesi's other comic opera heard in Paris at that time, *Il Maestro di musica,* were quite in agreement with this sentiment, and Rousseau wound up his *Lettre sur la musique française* by declaring, after a good deal of hyperbole, that 'the French have no music and cannot have any, or . . . if ever they do have any, it will be so much the worse for them.' [15]

During the quarrel of the buffoons, tempers reached an unbelievable pitch. Rousseau and Grimm, for example, were convinced that the former narrowly escaped arrest by *lettre de cachet* because of his *Lettre sur la musique française.*[16] Practically all of the Encyclopedists participated in the pamphlet war — especially Rousseau, Grimm, D'Holbach, and Diderot — and, characteristically enough, they all espoused the Italian side. They were never afraid of novelty, although their attitude was regarded by many of their enemies as practically a national betrayal. On the whole, wit was on their side, apoplexy on that of their opponents. The most effective pamphlet, and one still very amusing to read, was written by Grimm. This was *Le Petit Prophète de Boehmischbroda,* done in Scriptural language in an earnest, solemn, and deliciously naïve style. Even the outlandish place name of Boehmischbroda was funny. The Little Prophet, a famished musician in a Prague garret, was magically transported to the Paris Opéra, and what he saw and heard there, although *he* accepted it at its face value, would not, in the language of eighteenth-century English pamphleteering, bear examination.[17] This pamphlet deservedly established Grimm's reputation as a wit, and in the years to follow, Diderot's favorite and familiar epithet for him was 'prophet.' Diderot himself, whom Romain Rolland credited with a very exact knowledge of music, also entered the lists.[18] In his *Memoirs on Different Subjects of Mathematics* he had already proved his competence in musical theory from the point of view of mathematics and physics, and it will be remembered that he probably assisted Rameau in preparing some of his works for publication. Now, in early 1753, Diderot contributed three anonymous pamphlets to the controversy. They were entitled *Arrêt rendu à l'amphithéâtre de l'Opéra* ('Judgment Rendered at the Opera Amphitheatre'), *Au Petit Prophète de Boehmischbroda* ('To the Little Prophet of Boehmischbroda'), and *Les Trois Chapitres, ou La Vision de la nuit du mardi-gras au mercredi des cendres* ('The Three Chapters, or, The Vision of the Night from Shrove Tuesday to Ash Wednesday').[19] These pamphlets, though entertaining enough, are topical and ephemeral, and need not greatly detain a twentieth-century reader. What is perhaps most noteworthy about them is their air of moderation and conciliation. 'If, from the center of the pit, whence I raise my voice, I were fortunate enough to be heard by both the "Corners" . . . ,' he wrote — a statement which gives the impression that perhaps he was seeking to avoid making irreconcilable enemies of Rameau, who was after all a great contemporary composer, and his partisans.[20]

Of course Diderot in reality favored the Queen's Corner. Already in *L'Oiseau blanc* (1748) he had spoken briefly, but in praise, of Italian music.[21] At about this time — Grimm reports it in August 1753 — Diderot amused himself by composing a Latin motto to be painted (naturally it was not) on the curtain of the Opéra. The inscription clearly shows what he thought of the French opera of his day, but it is so laconic and lapidary that an explanation dilutes its humor: *Hic Marsyas Apollinem.*[22] This refers to the myth that Apollo, the god of song, flayed alive a very presumptuous and un-immortal mortal named Marsyas for presuming to challenge him to a singing contest. The piquancy of Diderot's motto is that it has no verb and therefore the nominative and accusative cases of the proper names carry all the meaning, which runs something like this: 'Here Marsyas [takes the hide off] Apollo.'

From the point of view of the *Encyclopédie,* the quarrel of the buffoons, although it served to unite the brethren in a common cause, presented an awkward contingency: it could cause trouble with Rameau. D'Alembert, as well as Diderot, had been on very friendly terms with him in earlier years. Moreover, Rameau had been asked to do the articles on music for the *Encyclopédie* but had refused, although he offered to look over and criticize the articles when prepared by someone else.[23] In consequence, the assignment was given to Rousseau, whose pieces, according to a modern critic, 'offered a faithful if somewhat jumbled and at times inept picture of Rameau's discoveries.'[24] Rousseau himself acknowledged his poor workmanship, saying that Diderot had wanted him to get them done in three months, and that he did so, but 'very hastily and very badly.'[25] Parenthetically, we may very well wonder why Editor Diderot did not see to it that the articles were improved, either by insisting that Rousseau revise them or by submitting them to Rameau for criticism. Perhaps he did not because Rousseau was so touchy as to render either alternative impractical, a hypothesis suggested by Rameau's remark that 'your Foreword makes sufficiently evident the reason that prevented you: it is better not to give offense to one's colleagues than to the public.'[26] Perhaps, too, Diderot and D'Alembert, not subscribing to all of Rameau's ideas, did not want to make the *Encyclopédie* a vehicle for them.[27]

At all events, the stand taken by the Encyclopedists in the quarrel of the buffoons made the *Encyclopédie* vulnerable, for their decided preference for Italian music might irritate Rameau into publicly remarking about some of the insufficiencies of the *Encyclopédie* articles on music. Evidently it was not the intention of the Encyclopedists to stir him up. Most of them specifically excepted him from their strictures regarding Lully and the school of French opera in general, and Diderot praised Rameau in the *Arrêt rendu à l'amphithéâtre de l'Opéra.*[28] He was taken as the exception proving the rule. But how could the tradition of French operatic music be attacked without including in the censure the greatest living practitioner of it? So, at least, Rameau appears to have thought, and in a series of little books he presently began to show the deficiencies of Rousseau's unfortunate articles. In 1755 he published *Erreurs sur la musique dans l'Encyclopédie,* in 1756 *Suite des erreurs sur la musique dans l'Encyclopédie,* and in 1757 *Réponse de M. Rameau à MM. les éditeurs de l'Encyclopédie.* This sort of controversy did not help the *Encyclopédie.* It was probably no exaggeration when a journal hostile to the *Encyclopédie* remarked that Rameau's brochures 'made a great sensation among the public.'[29] Diderot's irritation is attested by his unflattering description of Rameau in *Rameau's Nephew,* a dialogue that was not intended for publication in Diderot's lifetime but that still served (perhaps all the more) as an outlet for emotional release.

Rousseau, not content to lecture the French public by precept, undertook at this time to teach it by example. The result was his extremely successful operetta, *Le Devin du Village* ('The Village Soothsayer'), for which he wrote both words and music. In October 1752 the operetta was given before the King at Fontainebleau, a circumstance which indirectly led to the first open disagreement between Diderot and Rousseau. Jean-Jacques had been invited to meet the King the day following the showing, an interview that would have been almost certainly followed by the granting of a much needed pension. But for a number of reasons Rousseau returned to Paris instead, a decision which Diderot disapproved of so heartily that he sought out Rousseau to tell him so. 'Although I was moved by his zeal,' wrote Rousseau, 'I could not subscribe to his maxims, and we had a very spirited dispute, the first that I had ever had with him; and we never have had any other save of this kind, he prescribing to me what he contended I ought to do, and I resisting because I believed I ought not to do it.'[30]

It is possible that Diderot came to feel subconsciously that in the quarrel of the buffoons Rousseau had carried them too far. This is, however, completely conjectural. It is true, though, that tensions were already beginning to develop between Rousseau and the other Encyclopedists. He was inclined to think that it was because they were jealous of the success of *Le Devin du Village,* but Rousseau was a suspicious and highly imaginative man, and it is by no means certain that his fellow Encyclopedists *were* jealous of him. As Mme de Staël, writing about Rousseau ten years after his death, said of him, 'Sometimes he would leave you still loving you; but if you had said a single word that could displease him, he recalled it, examined it, exaggerated it, thought about it for a week, and ended up by quarreling with you. . . .'[31] But even if the other Encyclopedists were jealous of him, the emotional and intellectual causes of the eventual disruption were much subtler and deeper. It is quite surprising that the *philosophes* had not already realized how little of a *philosophe* Rousseau was. He did not have the faith that they did in the march of knowledge, in progress, and in reason. For years, apparently, they regarded his diatribe against the arts and sciences as more of a paradox than a conviction, failing to understand how deeply committed he was to this outlook on life. Rousseau believed in progress, too, but it was a progress that consisted in getting back to the uncomplicated and the undifferentiated, to the spirit of the simplicity and primitivism of a state of nature. This was not the point of view of men who believed in progress, as the Encyclopedists did, in terms of ever increasing knowledge, ever increasing technology, ever increasing understanding and domination of nature.

In fact, the signs of eventual disagreement could plainly be read in the disobliging way in which Rousseau spoke of 'philosophy' in the preface that he wrote to his unsuccessful comedy, *Narcisse.* This preface was written in December 1752 and published sometime in the first half of the following year, and could hardly please people who prided themselves on being called philosophers, for it discredited the very name. 'The taste for philosophy,' wrote Rousseau, 'relaxes all the bonds of esteem and benevolence that attach men to society. . . . Soon the philosopher concentrates in his person all the interest that *virtuous* men share with their fellow men: his disdain for others turns to the profit of his own pride; his self-love increases in the same ratio as his indifference for the rest of the universe. Family, fatherland, become for him words empty of meaning; he is neither a parent, nor a citizen, nor a man; he is a *philosopher.*' [32] These are strong and, indeed, quarrelsome words. Yet the *philosophes* were content to ignore them.

An incident on Shrove Sunday, 3 February 1754, in which both Diderot and Rousseau figured, gives some measure of Rousseau's growing irritation and malaise in his Encyclopedist associations. Superficially, the incident would seem to be no more than a disagreement over whether or not a certain situation was funny. But frequently like and unlike can be measured by what seems amusing to the one and deplorable to the other. What happened was this. In the summer of 1753 while walking in the Luxembourg Gardens, Diderot was introduced to a young curé from a small parish in Normandy, the Abbé Petit. He expressed delight at meeting the *philosophe,* for the Abbé wanted Diderot's comments on an original madrigal, seven hundred verses long. Diderot paled and told the Abbé that he ought to write tragedies and not waste his time on madrigals. 'Permit me, then, to say to you that I won't listen to a single verse of yours before you bring us a tragedy.' Some months later the Abbé showed up with his tragedy, and Diderot arranged for him to read it at D'Holbach's.[33] The tragedy, D'Holbach later recalled, was preceded by a discourse on theatrical composition so absurd that his listeners could not take him seriously. 'I will confess that, half-laughingly, half-soberly, I myself strung the poor curé along. Jean-Jacques hadn't said a word, hadn't smiled an instant, hadn't moved from his armchair. Suddenly he rose up like a madman and, springing towards the curé, took his manuscript, threw it on the floor, and cried to the appalled author, "Your play is worthless, your dissertation an absurdity, all these gentlemen are making fun of you. Leave here, and go back to do curate's duty in your village. . . ." Then the curé got up, no less furious, spewed forth all imaginable insults against his too sincere adviser, and from insults would have passed to blows and to tragic murder if we had not separated them. Rousseau left in a rage, which I believed to be temporary, but which has never ceased and which has done nothing but increase since that time.' [34]

This lively picture of Diderot and Rousseau in the company of their peers is complemented by another recollection of about this time, this one by the Abbé Morellet. It shows Diderot in his dressing gown in the privacy of his own home talking to men much his junior. The Abbé Morellet was twenty-five years old at the time and a theological student. His recollections of Diderot agree with those of almost everyone else who knew him well —

easy of access, generous of his time, full of ideas, and vivacious in the expression of them, sociable perhaps to a fault, and eager to persuade others to his line of thought:

The conversation of Diderot, an extraordinary man whose talent can no more be in dispute than his faults, had great ability and great charm. His discourse was animated, carried on in perfect good faith, subtle without being obscure, varied in form, brilliantly imaginative, fecund in ideas, and awakening ideas in others. One allowed oneself to be carried away by it for hours on end, as upon a gentle and limpid stream flowing through a rich countryside ornamented with fine habitations.

I have experienced few pleasures of the mind to surpass it, and I shall always remember it.

. . . .

. . . there never was a man more easy to live with, more indulgent than Diderot. He lent, and even gave, wit to others. He had in mind the desire to gain proselytes, not precisely to atheism, but to philosophy and reason. It is true that if religion and God Himself chanced to be in his path, he would not have known how to stop or turn aside; but I have never observed that he put any heat into instilling opinions of this sort. He defended them without any acrimony, and without looking unfavorably upon those who did not share them.

. . . The recollection of my Sunday meetings with Diderot leads me to speak of an *abbé* whom I sometimes met at his house, the Abbé d'Argenteuil. . . . He took it into his head to convert Diderot, and, inspired by a fine zeal, came to preach to him at the Estrapade. . . .

I shall always remember our mutual embarrassment the first time we encountered each other, and the excellent scene we provided Diderot, who saw us in his study as two shamefaced libertines meeting face to face in a house of ill repute. But after the first peals of laughter, we began to dispute. And there were the Abbé d'Argenteuil and I, carried on by the march of the conversation and entering into questions regarding toleration, while the philosopher, seeing the wrangling begun, put his hands into the sleeves of his dressing gown and made himself judge of the thrusts.[35]

Other glimpses into Diderot's private life at this time are afforded us. For one thing, we know that the family income had become greater. Beginning with 1751 the publishers paid Diderot five hundred livres quarterly. This was still far from being princely. There can be no doubt that the publishers purchased the services of a man of Diderot's ability at a very modest rate, and that they really did exploit him. Still, money was easier than it had previously been in the Diderot household, and this rate of payment continued until the beginning of 1755.[36] Of more than a little interest is the fact that in 1752 Mme Diderot visited her relatives-in-law at Langres for the first time. To judge as best we can from a letter to Mme Caroillon La Salette, now almost illegible, Diderot had hopes that she could do something to soften the intractability of Mme Diderot's character.[37] At all events, the visit terminated in mutual liking and esteem. And in the early weeks of 1753 Diderot, with his usual eagerness to do a friend a favor, moved heaven and earth in behalf of a fellow-townsman of Langres. Nicolas Caroillon, son-in-law of Pierre La Salette, wanted to be designated as the successor of his father-in-law in the lucrative post of bonded tobacco warehouseman in Langres. The episode has more than one facet of biographical interest. In the first place, some faint stirrings of an old sentimental attachment may have inspired Diderot, for Caroillon's wife, *née* La Salette, may have been one of his first calf-loves.[38] Secondly, by his assistance in this instance, Diderot put into his debt a family that eventually was to be linked to his by marriage. Thirdly, and most of all, the incident shows his eagerness to be obliging. As his daughter wrote of him, 'three-fourths of his life was spent in aiding all those who had need of his purse, his talents, or his negotiations.'[39] And with this desire to be helpful was compounded a certain gratification at being able to show off his prominent and influential connections.

Getting the position for Caroillon was an animated and complicated intrigue, involving some methods that one would like to think disappeared with the *ancien régime*. The mistress of the Controller General was promised two hundred louis, but it took another fifty before the matter was pressed to a successful conclusion; the private secretaries of the Controller General were friendly to Diderot and willing to attempt to secure for him an appointment with the minister; Buffon, 'who is very fond of me,' wrote a supporting letter; and the Controller General himself, Machault d'Arnouville, unexpectedly consented to see him. 'I believe,' wrote Diderot complacently, 'I owed this favor somewhat to his curiosity to see a man who had made such a stir.'[40]

Having thus tried to accomplish his purpose through the Controller General, Diderot also undertook to secure the support of the King's mistress. This he attempted to do through a personal friend, one of the celebrated names of the eighteenth century, a man who was Mme de Pompadour's official physician. This was François Quesnay (1694–1774), the founder of the physiocratic school of economic theory. Diderot was greatly influenced during the 1750's and the early 1760's by Quesnay's views, and opened the columns of the *Encyclopédie* to Quesnay's lengthy and substantial articles on 'Farmers' (*Fermiers*) and 'Grain.'[41] These articles afforded an excellent means for the diffusion of physiocratic ideas. Quesnay was very critical of the existing French national economy and the laws regulating it, for he felt that they put a premium on the production of luxury goods and the growth of cities at the price of impoverishing and depopulating the country-side.[42] It is easy to see how much influence Quesnay's thought exerted upon Adam Smith, for both men were seeking to understand the causes of the wealth of nations, and both — the older man more by implication — preached the virtues of increasing the net national product by allowing matters to proceed not by mercantilistic regulation but by the grace of the invisible hand. It is therefore true to say, as has often been done, that Diderot's friend Quesnay was one of the fathers of the science of political economy.

Quesnay, according to Marmontel, was 'lodged in very cramped quarters in the entresol above Mme de Pompadour, [and] occupied himself from morning to night with nothing but rural economy.' In a passage that is intensely interesting but unfortunately uncorroborated by any other memoir writer of the day, Marmontel went on: 'Below us they were deliberating concerning war and peace, the choice of generals, the dismissal of ministers, while we, in the entresol, argued about agriculture, calculated the net product, or sometimes dined gaily with Diderot, D'Alembert, Duclos, Helvétius, Turgot, Buffon; and Mme de Pompadour, not being able to induce this troop of philosophers to come down to her *salon,* came up herself to see them at table and chat with them.' [43]

For the purpose of getting the Langres appointment for his friend Caroillon, Diderot presented a memorandum to Mme de Pompadour through the good offices of Quesnay, received word from her through the same channel, and then wrote to her directly. The upshot of it all was that Caroillon got his appointment and Diderot, who evidently was not quite as convinced of Caroillon's transcendent qualifications for the post as he said he was, wrote him a page of good advice upon the scrupulous fulfillment of his official duties.[44]

It is interesting, incidentally, that Diderot kept his wife informed of the vicissitudes of this solicitation, showing that he did not always exclude her from his affairs.[45] Meanwhile, Mme Diderot had news of her own during this year, for Diderot remarked to the Caroillons in February that his wife had been very ill with morning sickness.[46] Childless Mme Diderot was forty-three years old at the time of this latest pregnancy, for which she had prayed many years. 'My mother took a vow to dress in white the next child to be born to her and consecrate it to the Holy Virgin and Saint Francis [a custom which, though it has become comparatively uncommon in France, is not unheard of to this day]. Nothing could get it out of her head that I owe my existence to this vow.'[47] Marie-Angélique Diderot, Angélique after her paternal grandmother, was born in the house on the Rue de l'Estrapade on 2 September 1753, and baptized at the parish church of Saint-Etienne-du-Mont the next day. The child's godparents, persons not otherwise known to posterity, declared themselves unable to sign their own names.[48] Now, for the fourth time, there was a baby in the house. This one was destined to a long life.

CHAPTER 15

Diderot's Thoughts on the Interpretation of Nature

ONE OF the ways in which the *philosophe* Diderot proved himself a philosopher was in his contributions to the philosophy of science. Evidence of this is especially to be found in a booklet written while he was engaged in the preparation of Volume III of the *Encyclopédie*. This essay — one of his most important and least read — was the *Pensées sur l'interprétation de la nature* ('Thoughts on the Interpretation of Nature'). An extremely rare edition of the *Pensées*, almost a pilot copy, was printed in 1753.[1] The two editions published in 1754 are more ample and better known. The work, though anonymous, was authorized. D'Hémery noted in his journal that the *Pensées*, 'attributed to Diderot,' had been published with tacit permission, another interesting and representative example of Malesherbes' policy of keeping the press as free as he could.[2]

The *Pensées sur l'interprétation de la nature* is a short book devoted to taking stock of some of the current implications of the scientific method and was intended to be a handbook for the 'philosophy,' the new learning, of the day. The somewhat solemn exordium addressed 'To Young People Preparing Themselves for the Study of Natural Philosophy,' which set Diderot's enemies laughing scornfully, reflects the seriousness of the author's purpose. 'Young man, take and read,' it began. The pages that followed opened up new points of view, sometimes by positive statements, sometimes by asking questions, sometimes by stating what Diderot labeled 'conjectures.' It was a book that suggested many of the most important problems in the philosophy of science, a tentative book sending out patrols along the frontiers of knowledge. And to at least one modern critic, comparing it with Descartes, Diderot's little book seems to be 'the *Discourse on Method* of the eighteenth century.'[3]

It might, however, be more accurate to say that the book was the *Novum*

Organum of the eighteenth century. For the *Thoughts on the Interpretation of Nature* was more Baconian than any other of Diderot's writings. Both in structure and in approach Diderot modeled his book on Bacon, whom he had been carefully studying for ten years according to the testimony of one of his friends.[4] For instance, the titles of the two books were significantly similar; the *Novum Organum* is subtitled 'True Directions concerning the Interpretation of Nature.' Moreover, the arrangement of the two books in a series of disjunctive paragraphs or 'aphorisms,' as Bacon called them, is exactly alike. And Diderot possibly was influenced by other writings of Bacon. The prayer at the end of the *Thoughts* may have been inspired by Bacon's invocation of God in his Proemium in *The Great Instauration;* Diderot's adjuration to young men, 'take and read,' is like Bacon's appeal 'Ad Filios.'[5] Critics of Diderot's book, therefore, could have spared themselves a number of irrelevant remarks had they realized that Diderot was consciously making himself a transmitter of the form and content of the Baconian philosophy of science. Diderot, in turn, could have made it easier for everyone had he explicitly acknowledged this. But perhaps he was skittish after his recent experience with the *Journal de Trévoux,* which had referred maliciously to Bacon's influence on the prospectus of the *Encyclopédie.*

In a thoughtful commentary on his friend's work, Grimm noted the parallels between Diderot and Bacon: 'There is the same depth, the same breadth, the same abundance of ideas and points of view, the same luminosity and sublimity of imagination, the same penetration, the same sagacity, and sometimes, for their contemporaries, the same obscurity, especially for those with weak sight.'[6] And he might have added that they were similar, too, in the striking aptness, variety, and vigor of their imagery. A more modern and less prejudiced critic has confirmed Grimm's high opinion: both Diderot and Bacon, writes Professor Dieckmann, 'were endowed with prodigious scientific imagination, in which the gift of exact observation and of realistic vision, the scientific spirit and the spirit of speculation, are strangely blended.'[7]

The influence of Bacon is to be seen particularly in those portions of Diderot's book that deal with methodological problems, as well as with descriptions or analyses of what should be the attitude of the scientific mind. Bacon, not as interested as Diderot in zoology, had no direct influence on the part of *Interprétation de la nature* that speculates, for example, about the origin and differentiation of species, as well as other problems posed by the rapidly emerging biological sciences.[8] But as regards general scientific method, Bacon insisted upon certain attitudes and predispositions that Diderot in his generation also stood for, and that science has learned are indispensable prerequisites for progress. The spirit of Bacon was the spirit of observation and experimentation. What, it asked, are the facts? And this solicitude for the facts was accompanied by a correlative de-emphasis on the preconceived and the a priori. Thus Bacon inveighed against the kind of scholasticism that contents itself with reading books about nature and trying to discover all about her through the use of syllogisms. This scholasticism is easy for any age to fall into, so that Diderot in his century, like Bacon in his, wrote of the necessity of having knowledge of *things*. 'The abstract sciences,' wrote Diderot, 'have occupied our best minds too long and with too little fruit. Either that which is important to know has not been studied, or no discrimination, insight, or method has been put into one's studies. Words have been multiplied endlessly, and the knowledge of *things* has remained in arrears.' [9]

By this emphasis on the knowledge of things, Diderot was implying that objects existing outside the mind do partake of objective reality. Wisdom therefore lies in the direction of attempting to link human intelligence with objective reality. This is, of course, the typical answer given by modern science to the problem of reality, the problem of being, and the problem of knowledge, namely that external objects are real and that human intelligence can know reality, at least in adumbration, by the study of them. There are many other answers that can be made to these ancient philosophical problems — that the external world has no reality but is simply illusion, or that it has reality but the human mind cannot know it, or that the human mind can find reality in terms simply and merely of itself, without relating mental processes to external objects. As Diderot remarked, 'unfortunately it is easier and shorter to consult oneself than it is to consult nature. Thus the reason is inclined to dwell within itself.' Diderot believed it essential to link the understanding with outer reality, and he remarked in his *Interprétation de la nature*: 'As long as things are only in our understanding, they are our opinions; they are notions, which may be true or false, agreed upon or contradicted. They take on consistency only by being linked to externally existing things. This linking takes place either by means of an uninterrupted chain of experiments or by an uninterrupted chain of reasoning that is fastened at one end to observation and at the other to experiment; or by a chain of experiments, dispersed at intervals between the reasoning, like weights along the length of a thread suspended by its two ends. Without these weights the thread would become the plaything of the slightest agitation occurring in the air.' [10]

According to Diderot, the interpretation of nature can be accomplished only by the reciprocal interaction in the mind of the scientist of sense impression and reflection. He expressed this idea in a much-admired image of the bee leaving the hive and returning to it, an image probably derived from Bacon: 'Men have difficulty in realizing how rigorous are the laws for the investigation of truth and how limited is the number of our instrumentalities. It all reduces itself to going from the senses to reflection and back again from reflection to the senses: ceaselessly to turn inward upon one's self and to turn outward again. This is the work of the bee: she has covered a great deal of territory in vain if she does not come back to the hive laden with wax. But she has made a lot of useless piles of wax if she does not know how to make a honeycomb out of them.' [11]

Greatly as Diderot counted upon the benefits arising from the advancement of learning, he did not suppose that advancement to be easy. On the contrary, he knew it to be very difficult. It is held back, for one reason, by human fallibility; for another, by the rarity of great scientific minds. As to the first, he wrote that 'the understanding has its prejudices, the senses their incertitude, the memory its limits, the imagination its glimmerings, instruments their imperfections. Phenomena are infinite, causes are hidden, forms are perhaps transitory. Against so many obstacles, both those inside ourselves and those outside presented by nature, we have only slow experimentation, only circumscribed reflection. Such are the levers with which philosophy proposes to move the world.' [12] Diderot realized that men capable of manipulating these levers are rare. Being a man of great imagination himself, he knew how necessary imagination and creativeness are to the discovery of nature's ways. In a passage that describes a man like Louis Pasteur or Robert Koch to a tittle, a passage which has been hailed as one of the most interesting eighteenth-century attempts to state the problem of genius and define what genius is, Diderot wrote: 'We have three principal means: observation of nature, reflection, and experiment. Observation gathers the facts, reflection combines them, experiment verifies the result of the combination. It is essential that the observation of nature be assiduous, that reflection be profound, and that experimentation be exact. Rarely does one see these abilities in combination. And so, creative geniuses are not common.' [13] Such a passage makes it clear that Diderot, in thinking about nature, did not content himself with mere empiricism, that is to say with the endless accumulation of facts, but insisted on the fecundating nature of hypotheses, even incorrect ones. 'Never is the time spent in interrogating nature entirely lost,' he wrote. An important part of his little book arises from his understanding of the reciprocal character, of the organic relationship, in the mind of a scientist between his empirical tendencies and his non-empirical intuitions.[14]

Implicit in the *Interprétation de la nature* are two attitudes very characteristic of the point of view of the whole eighteenth century. One of these attitudes is the distrust of elaborate and comprehensive philosophical systems. It is quite true that Diderot's aphorisms, like Bacon's, were disjunctive and disconnected, but this was intentional.[15] The eighteenth century distrusted the great philosophical *summae* which, like that of Saint Thomas Aquinas in the age of scholasticism or like those of Descartes and Malebranche and even Leibniz in the seventeenth century, fitted facts into a pattern only too often preconceived. D'Alembert remarked in his 'Preliminary Discourse' that 'the taste for systems, a taste more appropriate for flattering the imagination than for enlightening the reason, is today almost completely banished from sound treatises,' and he gives the credit for it to Condillac who, by publishing his *Traité des systèmes* in 1749, had, said D'Alembert, dealt the taste for systems its decisive blows.[16] The eagerness for analysis rather than systematizing and the dislike of revealed authority (with the equal dislike of a priori assumptions that had a way of hardening into something closely resembling revealed authority) caused Diderot to distrust the symmetry and consistency of an elaborate intellectual system that more often than not ignored essential facts. As he wrote in the *Encyclopédie* article *'Philosophie,'* 'the systematic spirit is no less injurious to the progress of truth. By systematic spirit I do not mean that which links truths one to the other in order to form demonstrations, for this is nothing but the true philosophical spirit, but I have in mind that spirit that builds plans, and forms systems, of the universe to which it consequently desires to adjust phenomena willy-nilly.' [17]

The other respect in which Diderot partook of the general attitude of the eighteenth century — his influence was so considerable that by accepting the attitude he reinforced it — was to regard reason more as an instrumentality than a thing in itself. Since the eighteenth century plumed itself on being the Age of Reason, we may well inquire what that century meant by the word. The seventeenth century, with its rationalistic philosophies — such as Descartes', based on the proposition *Cogito, ergo sum* — could be called an age of reason, too — but in a very different sense. An important semantic change had occurred. Whereas in the seventeenth century reason had meant the possession of a number of innate and transcendent ideas, much like the highest category of knowledge or reason described by Plato in *The Republic,* the eighteenth century regarded reason as a sort of energy, a force, a means by which to do something. It was not so much an essence as it was a process. What the eighteenth century thought reason to be was admirably and authoritatively expressed by the late Ernst Cassirer: 'To it reason was no longer an essence of innate ideas, granted anterior to experience, by which the absolute being of things is disclosed to us. Reason is much less a *possession* than it is a mode of acquisition. Reason is not the area, not the treasury of the mind, in which truth, like a minted coin, lies protected. Reason is rather the principal and original force of the mind, which impels to the discovery of truth and to the defining and assuring of it.' [18] The whole eighteenth century, he said, conceived of reason in this sense.

In the *Interprétation de la nature* Diderot proved himself familiar with the scientific discoveries and investigations going on in his day. They, in turn, suggested to him the paragraphs of 'conjectures' which are an enumeration of many promising experiments that had occurred to him as remaining to be done.[19] For example, proceeding from his knowledge of Benjamin Franklin's discoveries, which had been published in 1751 and in French translation the following year, he conjectured that there was a close relation between electricity and magnetism.[20] Diderot, however, was more of a philosopher of science than a scientist, more given to suggesting with quite extraordinary flair and insight what could be done than to doing it himself. And so he only glimpsed the promised land, staying the while in the wilderness with the *Encyclopédie.* But he had the imagination to know what should be done and yet how difficult it was: 'Open Franklin's book; leaf through the books of the chemists, and you will see what the art of experiment demands in insight, imagination, sagacity, and resourcefulness'; and he speaks of the divination that skilled experimenters acquire by which they smell out — the word he uses is *'subodorer'* — unknown procedures, new experiments, and results previously neglected.[21]

Diderot had caught the scent of a great change that was coming over the sciences in his century — the change in subject matter from pure mathematics to the natural sciences and the altered intellectual outlook that this involved. 'We are verging upon a great revolution in the sciences,' he wrote. 'To judge from the bent that it seems to me minds are showing for ethics, belles-lettres, natural history, and experimental physics, I would almost venture to say that in less than a hundred years there will not be three great geometricians [this is the eighteenth-century word for what we now call a researcher in pure mathematics] in Europe. This science will come to a full stop at the point where the Bernoullis, the Eulers, Maupertuis,

Clairaut, Fontaine, D'Alembert, and La Grange will have left it. They will have set up the columns of Hercules: there will be no going beyond that.'[22] There is a dash of exaggeration in Diderot — he was always just a little larger than life — and there is exaggeration in this passage, for within Diderot's predicted hundred years the German mathematician Gauss had opened up new horizons in pure mathematics. Thus Diderot's remark can be taken as just another example of the apothegm that prophecy is the most gratuitous form of error. Nevertheless, as Cassirer remarked in discussing this passage, Diderot was the one among the thinkers of the eighteenth century who possessed perhaps the sharpest sense of smell (*Spürsinn*) for all the intellectual movements and changes of the epoch.[23] His words should be taken in the sense of a new and fuller realization of the role to be played by the natural sciences, a new and fuller realization that mathematicians proceed by logical concepts and axioms that, although they have a rigorous self-consistency, possess no direct access to the empirical and concrete actuality of things. As Diderot remarked, pure mathematics is 'a kind of general metaphysics in which bodies are stripped of their individual qualities.'[24] He, on the contrary, with his sense of the importance of research into organic life, wanted to enlarge scientific method sufficiently to allow for the study of these individual qualities. A new ideal of science was growing up calling for purely descriptive studies and *interpretations* of nature. And this ideal, wrote Cassirer, Diderot conceived and sketched out in its general characteristics long before it was elaborated in detail.[25] This was the revolution that Diderot detected.

In his early writings Diderot had shown an awareness of the importance of biological researches, especially for the new light that they threw upon old problems of theology and metaphysics. This interest had been reflected in 1746 in the *Pensées philosophiques* and three years later in the *Lettre sur les aveugles*. The supposititious deathbed speech of Saunderson in the *Lettre sur les aveugles* had posed the problem of evolution and the necessity of studying process and change in life forms. Therefore, it is not surprising that Diderot carries these speculations one step forward in his *Interprétation de la nature*. The recent scientific writings of La Mettrie, of Buffon, and of Maupertuis, the president of the Prussian Academy, had provided a springboard, for they trenched on the very delicate question — delicate, considering that Genesis was thought to have decided the issue once for all — of the origin of life and the origin of species. Diderot took these speculations, especially those of Maupertuis, and, as Grimm remarked, 'adroitly adopted the policy of refuting the supposed Dr. Baumann [Maupertuis], under the pretext of the dangerous consequences inhering in this opinion, but in reality in order to push it as far as it could go.' [26] The results may be seen in some astonishing passages which read like a preview of the theory of evolution.[27]

These passages, like the one about to be quoted, reveal Diderot as a natural scientist who was a leader in introducing ideas of 'transformism' into modern scientific thought. Here we have the thinker who was aware of time and change, who had an intimation of the role of *process* in the elaboration of organic life, and who grappled with the concepts of the dynamic and the genetic. In his attempt to understand and interpret nature, Diderot surpassed the merely taxonomic, that part of science that classifies and arranges, and showed himself quite scornful of scientists like Linnaeus, whom he called a 'methodist.' [28] In contrast, Diderot sought to understand the functional and investigate the process of change itself. Diderot, wrote Cassirer, was one of the first to surmount the static eighteenth-century picture of the world and substitute for it a clear-cut dynamic one.[29] But whenever one begins to think, as Diderot did, in terms of concepts in which time and the changes brought about by time make all the difference — process, adaptation, development — one needs a new kind of logic to supplement the old logic of the Aristotelian syllogism, which takes no account of time. Diderot was a precursor of the nineteenth-century philosophers and scientists who, following Hegel, adopted the mode of logic represented by the dialectic of thesis, antithesis, and synthesis. Marxist writers in particular are appreciative of the dialectical character of Diderot's thought. Karl Marx himself once referred to Diderot as his favorite prose writer, and Henri Lefebvre, one of the most influential Marxist intellectuals in France today, declares that 'the importance of the *Pensées sur l'interprétation de la nature* in the history of the philosophy of sciences, of science itself, and of human thought, cannot be overestimated.' [30] The following passage is described by Lefebvre as one 'of real genius and truly revolutionary.' It was also one in which Diderot, somewhat masking the boldness of his thought, deemed it prudent to pretend to doff his hat to Genesis:

May it not be that, just as an individual organism in the animal or vegetable kingdom comes into being, grows, reaches maturity, perishes and disappears from view, so whole species may pass through similar stages? If the faith had not taught us that the animals came from the hands of the Creator just such as they are now, and if it were permissible to have the least uncertainty about their beginning and their end, might not the philosopher, left to his own conjectures, suspect that the animal world has from eternity had its separate elements confusedly scattered through the mass of matter; that it finally came about that these elements united — simply because it was possible for them to unite; that the embryo thus formed has passed through an infinite number of successive organizations and developments; that it has acquired in turn movement, sensation, ideas, thought, reflection, conscience, sentiments, passions — signs, gestures, sounds, articulate speech, language — laws, science and arts; that millions of years have elapsed between each of these developments; that there are perhaps still new developments to take place which are as yet unknown to us; that there has been or is to be a stationary condition of things; that the being thus developed is passing out of, or will pass out of, that condition by a continual process of decline, in which his faculties will gradually leave him just as they originally came to him; and that he will finally disappear from nature forever, or rather, will continue to exist, but in a form and with faculties wholly unlike those which characterize him in this moment of time? — But religion spares us many wanderings and much labor. If it had not enlightened us on the origin of the world and the universal system of beings, how many different hypotheses would we not have been tempted to take for nature's secret? [31]

Of this passage it has been remarked that there is contained within it 'not only the transformation of species, but also the sketch of a complete system of materialistic and ateleological evolutional philosophy, after the Spencerian fashion.' [32]

On the face of it, Diderot's *Interprétation de la nature* does not appear very antireligious. Nor should one expect it to appear so, for, after all, it had been published by tacit permission and had been approved by a censor, even though published without the king's license. Upon examination, however, it can be seen that Diderot was, as usual, trying to open up channels for freer thought, and was consequently challenging established attitudes and modes of thinking as much as he dared. No doubt he intended that the very epigraph of the book — an apt quotation from Lucretius' poem *De rerum natura,* 'Those things that are in the light we behold from the darkness' * — should by association remind his readers that Lucretius' avowed purpose was to free mankind, crushed, as he said, beneath the weight of religion. Moreover, Diderot's popularizing of Bacon, though intelligent and necessary, was also provocative, as can be demonstrated by the fact that years later the able and distinguished Catholic conservative, Joseph de Maistre (1753–1821), in books like *Les Soirées de Saint-Pétersbourg,* devoted much attention to singling out and attacking Bacon as the prime originator of what De Maistre regarded as the going-wrong of the eighteenth century. Finally, Diderot's 'transformist' views, such as those quoted above,

* *Quae sunt in luce tuemur e tenebris.*

in combination with his theory that all atoms, even in non-organic matter, have some sort of sensitivity — a view already apparent in the *Interprétation de la nature* and destined to bulk ever greater in his thought — moved him very close to a materialistic view of the universe.[33]

Although the *Mercure de France* and the *Journal Encyclopédique* spoke favorably of the *Interprétation de la nature,* on the whole it did not meet with a very enthusiastic reception.[34] Reviewers usually complained that it was obscure. The Abbé Raynal referred in his news letter to the fact that there were only four metaphysicians left in France — Buffon, Diderot, Maupertuis, and Condillac. 'The second has strewn about in two or three brochures, some quite acute ideas, but he has only insights without having any system and without developing their relationships.'[35] The journalist Clément remarked of Diderot, 'What a pity that . . . [he] should be so marvelously, so bristlingly, so desperately, metaphysical! You are about to see his *Pensées sur l'interprétation de la nature;* at one time it is a murky verbiage as frivolous as it is learned, at another an erroneous sequence of desultory reflections, the last of which proceeds to get itself lost a hundred leagues off to the left of the first. Only when he gets trivial does he become almost intelligible. But if you have the courage to follow him gropingly into his cavern, from time to time it may light up with some illuminating gleams. . . .'[36] Frederick the Great, who disliked Diderot, remarked apropos of the adjuration 'Young man, take and read,' 'There is a book that I shall not read. It's not written for me, for I'm an old fogy.' His continuing ill will can probably be detected in the fact that a Berlin newspaper, in a 1773 review of a collected edition of Diderot's works, said of the *Interprétation de la nature* that it was 'a sublime rigmarole in which the author, always in the clouds, contemplates phantoms which he takes for nature.'[37] And La Harpe, a one-time *philosophe* who later turned against them, wrote about 1799, having had some forty-five years in which to think up the epigram, that 'never has nature been more hidden than when Diderot made himself her interpreter.'[38]

The most painful contemporary review appeared as the leading article in the first number of the new Parisian periodical *Année Littéraire.* The position given to the review symbolized the editorial policy of the *Année Littéraire* for the next thirty years: it was always ready to focus its critical attention upon the ideas of the *philosophes.* The editor, a former Jesuit named Fréron (1719–76), proved himself a doughty and formidable adversary of the *philosophes,* and they retaliated by speaking of him as if he were the vilest of men. Voltaire, particularly, made him the butt of numerous jibes, a famous one being:

> They say a snake the other day
> Bit Fréron as in sleep he lay.
> What think you did thereon betide?
> Not Fréron, but the serpent, died.[39] *

In reality Fréron conducted his magazine with both skill and urbanity, a stalwart and hard-hitting conservative but an independent one.[40] Moreover, his journal was prodigiously successful — as widely read as the *Journal des Sçavans* and more widely read than the Jesuit *Journal de Trévoux*.[41] In March 1754, Fréron presented the *Année Littéraire* to the public, and his remarks about Diderot's little book provided the basis for a long and hearty mutual disesteem. After criticizing the 'prideful presumption' of the *philosophes* in general, he turned to Diderot. 'The author is perhaps a great genius; but this astral body is always covered with the clouds of an impenetrable metaphysics. . . . Although I do not at all understand what he was trying to say, I feel that there must be a way of expressing himself more clearly, and that the confusion of his words comes merely from that of his mind.' Fréron went on with his animadversions, not forgetting to envenom the quarrel between Diderot and Réaumur by meticulously quoting some unfair and ungracious remarks that Diderot had made concerning the great entomologist.[42] Most of all, Fréron objected to the praise that Diderot lavished on his friends and the epithets he showered upon his enemies. 'They [Diderot and his friends] render one another these little services. They are associated with certain others for this traffic in incense. These Philosophical Powers have concluded among themselves an offensive and defensive alliance.' [43]

Fréron was confident that the author of the *Interprétation de la nature* would not be esteemed by posterity. In this prediction Fréron was too sure of himself, for posterity finds in Diderot's views on science a greater penetration and spaciousness than many of his contemporaries could appreciate. And with it all is a marked desire on Diderot's part to make science useful and to make it understood by the people. First and last, Diderot was a man who sought the popularization and application of knowledge, and it was

---

* L'autre jour, au fond d'un vallon,
Un serpent mordit Jean Fréron.
Que pensez-vous qu'il arriva?
Ce fut le serpent qui creva.

this desire within him that made him a man of potent action as well as a man of potent thought. 'Let us hasten,' he wrote, 'to make philosophy popular. If we want the philosophers to march on, let us bring the people up to the point where the philosophers are now.' [44] And along with his desire to make science useful — 'Besides, the useful circumscribes all' [45] — Diderot breathed into his little book a Baconian humbleness toward nature, a feeling, as Bacon had put it, that we cannot command nature except by obeying her.

Diderot was sometimes humble but not often meek. In the face of the criticism that he evidently anticipated, he descanted in the *Interprétation de la nature* upon the obstacles besetting a researcher. Like many of Diderot's most eloquent pages, it is somewhat tinged with a trace of self-pity and self-praise. Still, it is a moving passage: [46]

. . . he who resolves to apply himself to the study of philosophy may expect not only the physical obstacles that are in the nature of his subject, but also the multitude of moral obstacles that will present themselves, as they have done to all the philosophers preceding him. When, then, it shall come about that he is frustrated, misunderstood, calumniated, compromised, and torn into pieces, let him learn to say to himself, 'Is it in my century only, am I the only one against whom there are men filled with ignorance and rancour, souls eaten by envy, heads troubled by superstition?' . . . I am, then, certain to obtain, some day, the only applause by which I set any store, if I have been fortunate enough to merit it.

CHAPTER 16

'Man Is Born To Think for Himself'

THE suspension of the *Encyclopédie* in February 1752 occurred only a few days after the publication of its second volume, not unnaturally causing people to be more concerned with the decision regarding the future of the venture than with the contents of the book. A close examination of Volume II, however, evidently convinced readers, as it had convinced the censor Lassone, that the work was carrying out its initial promise, and no doubt this impression contributed affirmatively to the decision to allow continuation of the work. Representative of some of the more important articles in its 871 double-columned folio pages were those on 'Ballet' by Cahusac, soon to publish his authoritative *Danse ancienne et moderne;* 'Barometer' by D'Alembert; 'Sundials' (*Cadran*) by D'Alembert and Diderot, a throwback to the latter's mathematical days; and, by Diderot, 'Stockings' (*Bas*), 'Bronze,' 'Cacao,' 'Wood' (*Bois*, showing his interest in forestry), 'Brewing' (*Brasserie*), 'Printing Characters' (*Caractères d'imprimerie*), and 'Playing Cards' (*Cartes*), to give a sampling of his many and varied articles. Something of the self-respect of the middle class is to be seen in the editors' remark concerning the article on 'Brewing': '"Brewing" is based upon a memorandum by M. Longchamp, whom a considerable fortune and much aptitude for letters has not detached from the occupation of his ancestors.'[1] And it is of interest to find Diderot saying in the article on 'Stockings,' 'I worked in M. Barrat's shop, the foremost craftsman of his kind and perhaps the last whom one will find of equal skill.'[2] Indeed, as Diderot had claimed in his prospectus and D'Alembert had reiterated in the 'Preliminary Discourse,' Diderot went to a great deal of trouble to familiarize himself with the construction and operation of machines.[3] Naigeon says that Diderot had scale models of the machine for knitting stockings and the machine for making cut velvet. 'Several times I have discovered him in his study intentionally dismantling the one or the other, in order to put it together again in a working condition, an operation which he executed with an ease betokening a pretty lengthy study of the art, its means of achieving its ends, and its results.' [4]

Throughout Volume II, as in Volume I, there continued to be an impatience with vulgar errors, as in the article 'Boa' for instance. Diderot recounts, 'in order to show how far exaggeration can go,' that some authors had set forth that a boa can swallow an ox: 'Historians are ordinarily the opposite of the mountain in labor. If it's a matter of a mouse, their pen gives birth to an elephant.' [5] There was the same eagerness for innovation and improvement, as when in the article 'Canvas' (*Canevas*) Diderot wrote, 'We are here going to propose a sort of canvas that will make embroidery, whether done in wool or in silk, infinitely more beautiful, less lengthy, and less costly.' [6] There was the same provocation of enemies, as when Diderot again twitted the Franciscans, in *'Capuchon,'* on the scholastic subtleties of their Duns Scotus; the same disconcerting juxtaposition of actual facts with Scriptural fantasies, as when Diderot contrasted the positive exploits of the Basque whalers with the defeatist quotation from Job, 'And are you able to pull up Leviathan with a hook?' [7] There was the same nagging at articles of Christian faith, as when, in the article 'Caucasus,' Diderot quoted the ancient geographer Strabo to the effect that the Caucasians put on mourning when children were born and rejoiced at their funerals. 'There is no Christian thoroughly penetrated with the verities of his religion who ought not to imitate the inhabitant of the Caucasus and congratulate himself upon the death of his children. Death assures the newborn child of an eternal felicity, while the fate of the man who appears to have lived the most holy life still remains uncertain. How our religion is at once both terrible and consoling!' [8] And there is Diderot's usual interest in matters having to do with anatomy, physiology, and medicine. 'The conservation of men and progress in the art of healing them,' he wrote in the article 'Cadaver,' 'are objects so important that in a well-ordered state the priests would receive cadavers only from the hands of the anatomist and there would be a law forbidding the inhumation of a body before it was opened. How many phenomena are unsuspected and will always be unknown because it is only by frequent dissection of cadavers that they can be learned.' Diderot was consistent in this view, for before his death he left instructions that an autopsy be performed upon him. And the last sentence of his article 'Cadaver' could be interpreted as making him one of the early proponents of a program of public health and preventive medicine: 'The conservation of life is an object that individuals adequately concern themselves with, but that it seems to me society neglects too much.' [9]

Though it waited until the appearance of Volume III, the *Journal des Sçavans* finally praised Volume II. This periodical, it will be remembered, had enraged D'Alembert by alleging that his 'Preliminary Discourse' had an antireligious tendentiousness. The editors had meanwhile made amends by praising his *Mélanges de littérature, d'histoire et de philosophie,* a move thought by some to be an attempt, although an unsuccessful one, to split D'Alembert and Diderot.[10] Now, belatedly, the *Journal* paid both volumes some very flattering attention.[11]

In addition to acknowledging the anonymous help of D'Holbach, the editors of the *Encyclopédie* were also able to announce in their Foreword to Volume II that Buffon had consented to contribute the article 'Nature.' This was a feather in their cap: the *Encyclopédie* was beginning to obtain the services of 'great names.' It is true that by the time the volume including 'N' was published, conditions had changed and so had Buffon, but for the nonce it was something to boast about.

The Chevalier Louis de Jaucourt was also announced as a new contributor. This man, who belonged to one of the oldest families in France, came to be of truly inestimable value to the enterprise. Unlike most members of the upper nobility, he had been carefully and broadly educated. While still a child, he was sent to Geneva and emerged from his training there a Protestant, a very latitudinarian and undogmatic one. It is, incidentally, a phenomenon of more than trivial interest that in Diderot's milieu there were so many Protestants or men of Protestant origin, like Grimm or De Jaucourt or, later, Meister — just as it is interesting to see how receptive he was to foreign influences, especially English, German, and Italian. This catholic and cosmopolitan urbanity has often been made a matter of reproach to Diderot on the part of nationalistically minded French critics, but these Protestant and foreign associations kept the windows open and prevented him from feeling stifled in the French society of his day, with all its unyielding and absolutistic tendencies.

Following his years in Geneva, De Jaucourt spent three years at Cambridge and then at Leyden, where he studied under the celebrated Boerhaave, was a fellow-student of Dr. Théodore Tronchin, and became a doctor of medicine. In 1736, at the age of thirty-two — De Jaucourt was nine years older than Diderot — he returned to Paris. The breadth of this training, combined with his unusual knowledge of languages, made him one of the most highly respected polygraphs of the century, and it was appropriate that he became a member of a number of foreign academies. Besides all these qualifications, he was a man of singular purity and uprightness, qualities of the greatest value to the *Encyclopédie,* especially as many were only too inclined to think that the work was edited by sinister and immoral men.[12]

As volume succeeded volume, De Jaucourt tended to take over the multitude of short articles on every conceivable subject that Diderot himself had done in the early days of the work; especially following the Great Desertion in 1759, De Jaucourt's symbol 'D. J.' was seen on almost every page of the last ten volumes. De Jaucourt was a great scissors-and-paste man and, because he frequently failed to mention his sources, can legitimately be regarded as the *Encyclopédie's* champion magpie. His intellect was not creative, but it was retentive, dogged, and quite accurate. His was a truly encyclopedic mind, in the quiz-program sense of the word, and while it is easy to scorn such talents, as Diderot himself was inclined to do, it ought never to be forgotten that it was the modest and unpretentious De Jaucourt who was as responsible as anyone for making the *Encyclopédie* the great focal point and gathering place of factual information.

It has become a truism that the *Encyclopédie* was of transcendent importance in transmuting values and changing the outlook of the eighteenth century. According to a present-day French critic, the *Encyclopédie* was — the metaphor is interesting and suggestive — the turntable of the epoch.[13] The new conception of the world and man that it propounded came as a result not only of following out the scientific and metaphysical implications of the sensistic psychology, but also from making new assumptions about the origins of man and society. There could be pieced together from the *Encyclopédie* — it was not safe to be too explicit upon subjects so delicate — an explanation of the nature of man and the beginnings of society that did not depend upon Genesis, an explanation of history and its meaning differing from that described in the Old and New Testaments and Saint Augustine's *City of God.* The new sociology and the new social science — if they can be dignified at this early period with such positive names, so tentative and groping were their beginnings — depended upon a view of man and society that of course differed from the traditional and authoritarian one. It can be bluntly described as the difference between conceiving of man and society as an act of creation and conceiving of them as the consequence of growth. The Encyclopedic view was the naturalistic view. The intimations and affirmations of it, traceable in numerous articles in the *Encyclopédie,* would amply repay the further researches of historians of the social sciences.[14]

This new and positivistic approach, which was to command the whole-hearted admiration of Auguste Comte, the founder of sociology, was in conflict, potentially or overtly, with established views, and continuously in danger of encountering some form of attempted suppression. On the principle, then, of always keeping one's opponent a little off balance, the *Encyclopédie* seldom overlooked an opportunity to sow doubt concerning Christian evidences, and Volume II followed this rule. Diderot's article on 'The Bible' outlined a complete scheme of exegetics, according to one critic. Another has remarked of this article that, by posing a whole host of exegetical questions, Diderot undermined the principle of the verbal inspiration of the Bible once for all.[15] He continued to make a display of these exegetical principles in his article on 'Old Testament Canon' (*Canon, en théologie*), an article of such erudition that it is one of the sources for supposing his theological studies had been carried to an advanced stage. He also suggested, rather gingerly, some telling criticisms of the institution of celibacy in '*Célibat,*' and the long article on 'Certitude,' contributed by the Abbé de Prades and no doubt written in good faith, manages in its examination of the credibility of miracles to be more unsettling than reassuring. Little can be found in the *Encyclopédie* that directly challenges prevailing and official doctrine, but there is much that raises doubt while professing to allay it.

A chance remark hidden away in a very long article in Volume II stirred up a storm of antagonistic derision against the *Encyclopédie*. The offending phrase was in the article devoted to 'Deer' (*Cerf*). Diderot probably did not write it — the author was probably Charles-Georges Le Roy, Superintendent of the Chase in the Royal Park at Versailles — but he made himself doubly responsible by printing it with an asterisk, and the incident shows, if nothing else, how closely the *Encyclopédie* was scrutinized by its enemies. Although the subject would appeal primarily to sportsmen, an important part of the article — and this is characteristic of the *Encyclopédie* — was devoted to a discussion of embryology, with references to Maupertuis' book *Vénus physique* and to the observations on the embryos of deer made by William Harvey, the discoverer of the circulation of the blood. But what excited the scorn and indignation of Diderot's enemies was the statement that many marvelous things are told about deer, '*especially when they have attained the age of reason.*'[16] One might suppose that this faintly ludicrous statement, the lucubration no doubt of a deer lover, was harmless enough. But actually it touched one of the exposed nerves of the eighteenth century, for the view that animals are automata and consequently without reason had become a matter of dogmatic religious belief in France. Descartes had asserted this in his *Discourse on Method,* arguing that all that animals display in their response to situations is a mechanical reaction set up by the vibration of fibers. This makes the brute soul a materialistic one; churchmen insisted upon making an absolute distinction between man and animals, the former, of course, having a soul untouched by materialism.[17] Here was still another impediment to free inquiry, for it thus became impious to make any conclusions about human psychology based upon animal analogies. Pavlov's dogs are an example of the fact that much can be learned about human psychology from animal behavior, but in the eighteenth century this channel of inquiry was almost wholly blocked. Diderot, as usual, was willing to dare for the sake of intellectual freedom by letting the remark pass about deer's attaining the age of reason and, more importantly, by presenting the pros and cons in the article entitled 'Bête, animal, brute.' Here he remarked that 'to assert that they have no soul and that they do not think is to reduce them to the status of machines, which one seems scarcely more authorized to do than to declare that a man whose language we do not understand is an automaton.' [18]

Included in this same volume was an article by Diderot that was an original contribution to aesthetics, and which has received a great deal of serious attention from specialists in that branch of philosophy.[19] This was the article on 'The Beautiful' (Beau). An unobtrusive essay, it summed up and criticized previous attempts to analyze the nature of beauty and then went on to break new ground by stating Diderot's conceptions. Here, therefore, is an excellent example of the function served by the Encyclopédie in the intellectual life of the eighteenth century. Not only did it assemble the accumulated facts of a couple of millennia, not only did it describe the mechanical arts and crafts as had never been done before, not only did it earnestly advocate new modes of thought in psychology and social philosophy, but it also had a contribution to make in matters involving art. Thus the universality of the Encyclopédie is further exemplified, as also the versatility and creative vigor of Diderot, who could strike off so substantial a piece just to satisfy the routine requirements of the Encyclopédie.

Diderot began by summarizing and discussing recent analyses of the nature of beauty, especially those of the Englishman Francis Hutcheson. Then, having criticized these views, he began to state his own. He disagreed with Hutcheson, who thought that we have an 'internal sense' of beauty, which, operating somewhat like an innate idea of God or morality, informs us of what is beautiful and what is not. Diderot's own theory is so simple that at first it seems slight. He declared that the perception of relationships is the basis of the beautiful.[20] In another article, on 'Beauty' (Beauté), he wrote, 'But I think that, philosophically speaking, everything that excites in us the perception of relationships is beautiful.' [21]

At first blush the definition of the beautiful as a perception of relationships may seem intolerably superficial. But as a matter of fact it allows ample latitude for the development of connoisseurship and taste. The more sensitive and perceptive the artist or the contemplator of art, the more relationships he perceives and the finer and more reliable will be his criteria of beauty. The artist or the connoisseur becomes like the skillful experimenter Diderot alluded to in his *Interprétation de la nature* — he develops a feel for his subject, he 'smells it out.'

Diderot's doctrine that our sense of the beautiful depends upon our perception of relationships is characteristic of his thought, which always demonstrated flexibility, relativism, and a sense of the importance of context. Diderot rebelled against authoritarianism as much in matters of artistic appreciation as in matters of religious belief. He was, in terms of the dispute that convulsed French letters in the closing years of the seventeenth century, more a Modern than an Ancient. Although he did not specifically allude to this famous quarrel in his *Encyclopédie* article, by denying that there is such a thing as Absolute Beauty he quite clearly attacked the traditionalist position of Boileau, the Ancients' principal defender. In accord with this line of reasoning, Diderot pointed out that a line in a play might be tragic in one context, deliciously comic in another.[22] Conditions, circumstances, and contexts determine our appreciation of beauty, he wrote, thus emphasizing, as modern aestheticians have noted, 'the infinitely conditional character of the esthetic experience.'[23]

Any theory of the beautiful rests upon a psychological doctrine of how the mind works in perceiving beauty. Diderot again applied the sensistic doctrine of John Locke: 'Whatever the sublime expressions used to designate the abstract notions of order, proportion, relationships, harmony — called, if one likes, the *eternal, original, sovereign, essential rules of beauty* — they have passed by way of our senses in order to reach our understanding. . . .' These remarks are a positive way of restating Diderot's denial of an internal and absolute sense of beauty. And they show how his conception of the understanding of beauty resembles his understanding of nature in *Interprétation de la nature*. Both the artist and the scientist must seek for reality in the external world. The scientist cannot discover truth by simply following 'reason' within the recesses of his mind, just as the artist or connoisseur cannot find beauty by that process. 'Therefore,' wrote Diderot, 'I call beautiful everything outside me containing in itself the material for awakening in my understanding the idea of relationships; and [I call] beautiful in regard to myself everything that awakens this idea. . . . Whence it follows that, although there is no *absolute beauty,* there are two sorts of the beautiful in relation to us, a *real beauty* and a *perceived beauty.'* [24]

Diderot believed human beings so constituted that the appreciation of relationships — and therefore, by his definition, the appreciation of beauty — was natural to them. The nature of man makes him conscious of the relationships upon which beauty depends. It is as fundamental as that. Man's mind by its nature seeks symmetry, order, proportion, harmony, which is tantamount to saying that it seeks the evidence of relationships and is pleased by them. Moreover, in Diderot's view, beauty is a reality. 'Whatever may result from all these causes of diversity in our judgments, this is by no means a reason for thinking that real beauty, that which consists in the perceiving of relationships, is a chimera. The application of this principle may vary to infinity, and its accidental modifications occasion dissertations and literary wars; but the principle remains none the less constant.' [25]

Diderot's theory of the beautiful allows for an infinity of nuances and gradations, and this was like him, too. Diderot was always aware of the shadings and paradoxes and ambiguities with which all of human experience is interwoven.[26] Therefore he responded unfavorably to absolutist definitions, to descriptions of experience in terms of black and white. It is this disposition of mind that entitles his thought to be called dialectical — always qualifying itself, always in a dialogue with itself. This mental disposition makes him a thinker, an artist, a critic, very hard to pigeonhole.

By his emphasis on the relative in the appreciation of the beautiful, Diderot inevitably raised the question of taste. For taste is inherently subjective, necessarily depending upon the judgment and appreciation of the person contemplating the art object, and thus varies widely, as Diderot realized. 'Everyone agrees,' he wrote, 'that there is a beautiful, that it is the result of perceived relationships; but according as one has more or less knowledge, experience, practice in judging, meditating, *seeing,* plus natural reach of the mind, one says that a certain object is poor or rich, confused or sustained, paltry or overcharged.' [27] It is the difference between the appreciation of a painting by Rouault and of a calendar picturing a girl with her skirt caught in a wringer.

The problem of taste brings us back to the problem of standards in judgment. If there is no absolute beauty, are there then *no* criteria to go by? Must the appreciation of beauty become, after all, purely anarchical, with everybody complacently belonging to the I-don't-know-art-but-I-know-what-I-like school? Diderot was well aware of this problem, as we have seen, and in later works, when he discussed what is meant by the imitation of nature and spoke of 'the line of beauty, the ideal line,' he made trenchant attempts to deal with it.[28] Those who are critical of his article on 'The Beautiful' usually argue that his doctrine is vague and inconclusive in the matter of exploring the relationship of beauty and taste. Perhaps Diderot was attempting to deal with the problem rather too much in terms of mere logic. At all events, we later find him learning to judge art more in terms of techniques than in relationships. Still, his analysis in the article concerning the beautiful was a vigorous statement. And it is not to be forgotten that he insisted that there is such a thing as objective beauty. Not absolute beauty, or beauty to be apperceived by absolute rules. Rather, Diderot's is the attitude of a man who, by an understanding of the relative, hopes to approach the absolute, yet knowing all the while that the absolute cannot be reached and knowing, too, that we should not want to reach it if we could. Perhaps this defines a liberal, whatever the object of his meditations and wherever and whenever he may be found.

* * * * * *

When Volume III of the *Encyclopédie* finally appeared in November 1753 after a year and a half of suspension, it contained an important preliminary notice written by D'Alembert in the name of the editors. 'The eagerness that has been shown for the continuation of this Dictionary,' he began, 'is the sole motive that could have induced us to take it up again.' In this moment of triumph, D'Alembert tended to allow his self-love to prevail, and the foreword is replete with a strange combination of apologetics, vainglory, and that irritating self-righteousness that the antagonists of the *philosophes* found so exasperating.[29]

D'Alembert not unnaturally used the occasion for a restatement of the *Encyclopédie*'s editorial doctrines. As has previously been remarked, Diderot and D'Alembert apparently were permitted to recontinue their work without having to compromise their principles. It is interesting to observe, as Grimm pointed out, that they had not even been required to tip any revised pages into the preceding volumes.[30] Their independence would seem to be confirmed by D'Alembert's statement in the foreword that 'it is principally by the philosophical spirit that we seek to distinguish this Dictionary.' Thus the *Encyclopédie* would not contain, he wrote, the lives of the saints nor the genealogical trees of ruling houses nor the detailed description of every village; 'nor the conquerors who have devastated the earth, but the immortal geniuses who have enlightened it; nor, finally, a crowd of sovereigns whom history should have proscribed. Not even the names of princes and grandees have a right to be in the *Encyclopédie*, except by the good they have done the sciences. For the *Encyclopédie* owes everything to talents, nothing to titles, and is the history of the human spirit and not of the vanity of men.' And then, with that yearning for a secular immortality so characteristic of men who deny heaven and hell, he wrote, 'May posterity love us as men of virtue, if it does not esteem us as men of letters!' [31]

Volume III, which ran to nine hundred pages and yet covered the alphabet only from CHA to CONSECRATION, began to develop some new departments or areas of interest. One was that devoted to business and business practices. Excellent articles, such as 'Exchange' (*Change*), 'Commerce,' and 'Competition' (*Concurrence*), were contributed anonymously by an economist named Forbonnais. His articles reflect the middle class, businessman's point of view characteristic of the whole *Encyclopédie*.[32] Another new development was the description of legal and administrative institutions (for example, various courts, councils, codes, and officers, such as 'Chancellor' and 'Commissioners'). These numerous articles were the work of the lawyer and legal antiquarian Boucher d'Argis (1708–91), the recipient of special editorial thanks in the forewords to Volumes III and IV. These multitudinous articles, which greatly increased the bulk of the work, were informative, authoritative, and dispassionate; and they gave the *Encyclopédie* a less contentious complexion than it had had in the first two volumes. Unquestionably they contributed greatly to the value of Volume III and its successors. 'It is already acknowledged,' wrote Clément six weeks after the publication of the third volume, 'that it is superior to the second, which in turn surpassed the first.' [33]

Diderot made fewer contributions to Volume III than to previous volumes, but the articles were substantial. There were the usual ones concerning the crafts, such as 'Post Chaise' (*Chaise de poste*), 'Hemp' (*Chanvre*), and 'Hat' (*Chapeau*). There was the usual call for reforms, as when, in the article on 'Hunting' (*Chasse*), he wrote of the damage done to crops and the savage punishments dealt out to poachers. 'If the life of a man is worth more than that of all stags, why punish a man with death for having made an attempt upon the life of a stag?' [34] Similarly, Diderot's remarks on the importance of actors (*Comédiens*) are interesting as testimony to his faith in the social value of the theater and to his desire to secure to actors their civil rights. 'If one considers,' he wrote, 'the purpose of our theater and the talents necessary to a person for successfully playing a role in it, the position of an actor will necessarily assume in every right mind the degree of consideration that is its due. It is now a matter, especially on our French stage, of inciting to virtue, inspiring horror of vice, and exposing that which is ridiculous. . . . In spite of which, they [actors] have been severely treated by some of our laws. . . .'[35] Diderot's own plays, written a few years later, exemplified this conviction that the theater could incite to virtue. Correspondingly, he always esteemed actors highly as the archpriests of what may be termed a secular church.

Particularly interesting, because it exemplified Diderot's versatility and adaptability, is the article on 'Composition in Painting.' As Diderot later told the story, 'we had hoped to have from one of our most vaunted amateurs the article "Composition in Painting." We received from him a couple of lines of definition, without exactness, without style, and without ideas, with the humiliating confession that he knew no more about it; and I was obliged to write the article, I who am neither a connoisseur nor a painter.'[36] In this article (which dealt with such subjects as the unity of time, place, and action in painting; the treatment of draperies; the subordination of figures; etc.), the reader will find many of the ideas that Diderot set forth years later in his *Salons*. His article was full of fresh and striking suggestions, and one great French critic, usually austere in his praise, wrote, 'This article is delicious. . . . Lessing's whole *Laocoön* [1766] is in it in substance.'[37]

The usual campaign of sowing doubts in regard to revealed religion was waged in Volume III. The delicate and tricky but inescapable subject of religion posed a truly Hamlet-like dilemma. Diderot solved the problem, sometimes at the price of his intellectual honesty, by never refusing lip service to the claims of revealed religion. But his treatment of such subjects as 'Christianity,' 'The Chaldeans,' 'Chaos,' and 'Sacred Chronology' (all of them lengthy and important articles appearing in Volume III), while superficially unexceptionable, was apt to raise doubts and lead to ambiguous conclusions. It became a favorite tactic of the *Encyclopédie* to indulge in chronological calculations affecting the Old Testament, for the Scriptures were demonstrably confusing and inconsistent, so that the thin wedge of higher criticism could most easily enter at this point. The article on 'The Chaldeans,' considering their proficiency in astronomy, gave Diderot an obvious opportunity; and in his article on sacred chronology, he discussed and compared various chronological systems, threw doubt on the accuracy of Old Testament manuscripts, referred learnedly to Samaritan texts and to the Septuagint, and inclined toward the conclusion reached by the Abbé de Prades — 'except that it would be impermissible to adopt it, now that the censures of several bishops of France and the Faculty of Theology have declared it prejudicial to the authority of the sacred books.' Diderot concluded this article abruptly, perhaps for the very purpose of leaving the reader uncertain and in the air. The article on 'Chaos,' too, was singularly — and probably intentionally — as chaotic as the subject it dealt with. It posed all sorts of difficult logical questions regarding the Creation, summarized with loving care the objections of Spinozists and materialists (while purporting, of course, to refute them), and concluded by leaving the question in a perplexing and confused condition.[38] The article on 'Christianity' was similarly tendentious. Instead of analyzing Christianity as a spiritual religion, it somehow managed to discuss it as if its principal importance had been as an instrument of government. Diderot plainly implied, to use Gibbon's famous phrase, that all forms of religion are regarded as equally true by the people, equally false by philosophers, and equally useful by magistrates. Accordingly he had the audacity, in eighteenth-century France, to suggest that Mohammedanism and Christianity had many points of resemblance; he quoted Montesquieu copiously; and altogether was not far short of adumbrating the sociology of religion.

What the *philosophes* meant by 'philosophy' is admirably exemplified by two quotations from articles that Diderot wrote for Volume III. The first one reveals their characteristic hatred of priestcraft and their high, humanistic views of the nature of man. Discussing the Chaldeans, Diderot wrote, in transparent allusion to authoritarian beliefs anywhere, that 'one must be oneself very little of a philosopher not to feel that the finest privilege of our reason consists in not believing anything by the impulsion of a blind and mechanical instinct, and that it is to dishonor reason to put it in bonds as the Chaldeans did. Man is born to think for himself.'[39] *

The second quotation is more Rabelaisian but equally 'philosophical.' In the article on 'Heat' (*Chaleur*) Diderot discussed the periodicity of the sex impulse in animals, and then compared it with that of a human being. 'It appears that the frequency of its accesses [in man], which begin with his adolescence and last as long and longer than his capabilities, is one of the consequences of his ability to think and of his suddenly recalling to himself certain agreeable sensations . . . . If this is so, the lady who said that if animals made love only at intervals, it was because they were beasts [this is a pun: *'bêtes'* means both 'beasts' and 'stupid'], made a more philosophical remark than she realized.'[40]

The most controversial article in Volume III turned out to be one by D'Alembert on the quality of education in the secondary schools (*collèges*) of the day. In these schools the child spent about six years in 'humanities,'

* L'homme est né pour penser de lui-même.

learning mostly Latin and some Greek; one or two years in 'rhetoric,' where he learned to write discourses called amplifications (a very suitable name, thought D'Alembert, 'since they ordinarily consist of drowning in two sheets of verbiage what one could and should say in two lines'); and two years in 'philosophy,' which smacked strongly of the content and methods of medieval scholasticism. This was the education that he himself had had, and in retrospect it seemed execrable. He wanted in the course of study more history, more modern languages, and more study of a child's native tongue. He thought that the study of English and Italian would be particularly useful, perhaps also German and Spanish. And then, knowing that his far-sweeping criticisms and suggestions for reform would engender against him a great deal of counter-criticism, he concluded by remarking that 'this is what the love for the common weal has inspired me to say on education, whether public or private. . . . I cannot think without regret of the time that I lost in my childhood: I impute this irreparable loss to the established custom and not to my masters; and I should like my experience to be useful to my country.' [41]

It was fully characteristic of the Encyclopedists in their general desire for reform not to overlook so important a matter as education. But it is also likely that in writing this article D'Alembert was satisfying his grudge against the Jesuits fully as much as gratifying his zeal for the public good. D'Alembert, a man who thought it bad policy ever to forget a slight, made a number of rather spiteful and quite unmistakable allusions, in his foreword to Volume III and in the list of errata, to certain persons who had been the sources of the *Encyclopédie*'s recent woes. In particular, he pointed out the plagiarisms in the *Dictionnaire de Trévoux,* while brazenly and impenitently defending his own.[42] And the proof that he was aiming at the Jesuits in his article on *'Collège'* lies in his severe criticism of the dramatic productions staged there, which, as everyone knew, were employed by the Jesuits as an educational device much more than by anyone else.[43]

D'Alembert's article provoked a pamphlet, probably written by a Jesuit with a keen eye for an *ad hominem* argument, for he was at great pains to show that Lord Bacon had highly praised Jesuit *collèges*.[44] Still another anonymous pamphlet, this one almost certainly written by a Jesuit, complained of Volume III generally. The pamphleteer disliked in particular the choice of subject matter. Articles such as 'Hat,' 'Collar,' 'Cat,' 'Dog,' 'Candle,' 'Post Chaise,' 'Mushroom,' 'Hemp,' and 'Coal' he thought too long. 'They have preferred to teach us how to plant cabbages, steep quinces, sow hemp, cook lemons and pumpkins, and other bagatelles of the sort;

but as for the Colosseum, they have said in a dozen lines all that one needs to know about it, or, rather, all that *they* know about it. . . . A work like the *Encyclopédie* . . . should contain only such knowledge as makes true savants.'[45]

Neither Diderot nor the *Journal de Trévoux* took any part, at least openly, in these bickerings. But the Jesuits in Lyon, the second city of France, took up the cudgels. Several times during the Lenten season of 1754 they preached against the *Encyclopédie,* and in November of that year they posted folio broadsides — there is a copy in the Bibliothèque Nationale signed by the principal orator's own hand — inviting the public to a meeting in behalf of the public schools against the Encyclopedists (*Pro Scholis publicis, adversus Encyclopaedistas*). According to a letter written to Malesherbes about this occasion, the orator inveighed for an hour and a quarter — in Latin, of course — accusing the *Encyclopédie* of disloyalty to the monarchy, pointing out its plagiarisms, and particularly attacking the article on '*Collège.*' D'Alembert was insulted by a sneering reference to his illegitimate birth allegedly made during the harangue, although this was subsequently denied and could not be substantiated. D'Alembert made as much trouble as he could for the orator, Father Tolomas, and the Royal Society of Lyon to which the priest belonged, but without obtaining much satisfaction, and thus the incident sputtered out inconclusively.[46]

His quarrel with the Jesuits at Lyon was not the only incident occurring at about this time in which D'Alembert made it a matter of policy to make people think twice before they lampooned an Encyclopedist. A budding provincial playwright named Palissot caricatured Rousseau in a play produced at Nancy in 1755. Palissot made his offense even worse in D'Alembert's eyes by having his play printed and published at Paris. D'Alembert leaped to Rousseau's defense, and caused as much difficulty for Palissot as he was able, his principal handicap being that the forgiving Rousseau wanted no trouble made at all.[47] This incident, occurring in 1755–6, made even more conspicuous the break between Rousseau and his former friends which came three years later.

* * * * * *

Volume IV of the *Encyclopédie,* published in October 1754, proceeded from CONSEIL to DIZ in eleven hundred pages, its dignity somewhat impaired by its own admissions that it was something less than perfect.[48] Thus the list of errata plaintively entreated its contributors 'to take care that their manuscripts be legible, especially in regard to proper names, and that punctuation be exact in the places where the sense is necessarily ambiguous.' This was in addition to a note that had already been published in the errata in Volume II: 'The work of the editors, as editors, consists solely in collecting and publishing the work of others together with their own; but they have never purported to undertake either recasting articles done by others or going back to the sources whence they might have been taken,' so that the editorial disclaimers, one implicit and one explicit, added up to a rather damaging admission of shortcomings.

Volume IV, of all the volumes that had yet appeared, gave the impression of being the most objective and the least controversial. Accordingly, criticisms of it were comparatively rare. The Abbé Raynal, writing in his confidential news letter, was an exception, but perhaps he was offended (being a historian who had published books on English, Dutch, and general European history) at not being asked to be a contributor.[49] That he was not is a fact that highlights the *Encyclopédie*'s lack of interest in political and military history.

A notable omission in this volume was the absence of any article on 'Constitution,' that is to say the papal bull *Unigenitus,* which had caused so much political and religious strife in France since its promulgation in 1713. This was a delicate topic indeed, especially as the Parlement of Paris had been 'exiled' to Pontoise over this very issue the preceding year, and passions were still running high. Drafts of a projected article are still in existence, but Malesherbes finally decided that the subject was too hot to handle and ordered Diderot not to publish anything concerning it.[50] Included, however, were all the usual features and some new ones: the usual abundance of articles of the type now grown familiar to us — long descriptions by Diderot, such as those on 'Ropemaking' (*Corderie*), and 'Lace' (*Dentelle*), and 'Cotton,' this last based on a memorandum furnished by Turgot, soon to become famous as a gifted public administrator. This was the type of article complained of by some as being too long, but which Diderot defended by saying that there was more to fear from their being too brief, everything in handiwork being almost equally essential and equally difficult to describe.[51] There were numerous articles once more by Boucher d'Argis on laws and legal and political institutions, as also articles by Forbonnais on business, besides contributions by interesting new authors. Dr. Théophile de Bordeu, who had recently published some important pioneering research on glands and who came to exert a considerable influence upon the thinking of Diderot, wrote an article, 'Crisis,' which was a description and discussion of the art of healing. Claude Bourgelat, who later founded the schools of veterinary medicine in France, began in Volume IV to contribute articles on horse-training and farriery so original and extraordinary that it has been said they were the first to give to the veterinary art a scientific direction. Another valuable acquisition was Duclos, historiographer of France and permanent secretary of the French Academy. But the shining jewel in the Encyclopedic diadem was the name of Voltaire, announced as the author of articles to appear in Volume V.

That Voltaire consented to contribute articles, or offered to do so — it is uncertain which is the fact — constitutes proof by itself of the success and prestige that the *Encyclopédie* had attained. For France's most famous man of letters, living at Geneva since he had worn his welcome thin at Potsdam, had a shrewd and foxy sense for keeping in the public view, and was unlikely to contribute to the prestige of an enterprise unless it offered a strong probability of enhancing his own. For the remaining twenty-five years of his life, until the apotheosis in Paris in 1778, Voltaire continued to live in or near Geneva, sometimes at Les Délices in Genevan territory or at Ferney in French, reluctant to live all the time in the one because playacting was forbidden, and poised in the other so that he could move agilely over the border if danger threatened. During this long period he managed to keep himself the cynosure of Parisian eyes, the dictator in many respects of Parisian tastes. This was, in reality, a very great accomplishment. It meant that he must miss no opportunity of feeling the pulse of Parisian opinion. It meant that to keep in the public eye he must have something to say on almost every subject and a piquant rejoinder to almost every pamphleteer. People who regret that Voltaire wasted his talents replying to every wretched hack who took it into his head to attack him miss the point: these replies kept him alive in the public recollection. Living practically in exile, two hundred and fifty miles from Paris in space and a fortnight in time, his problem was to manage by some feat of intellectual prestidigitation to seem to be leading Parisian public opinion while in reality following it. For twenty-five years he performed this sort of Indian rope trick. Voltaire, the cunning Voltaire, needed all his cunning not to be forgotten, and it is a testimony to the real success of the *Encyclopédie* that he saw self-advantage in being associated with it.

Although Volume IV gives the impression of settling down to a somewhat less controversial tone, it must not be supposed that fire and color were lacking. As always, the editors used the columns to flog their enemies, as in the anti-Jansenist article by D'Alembert on 'Convulsionnaires,' or the article on 'Controversy' in which Diderot ironically and solemnly cites the

authority of the *Dictionnaire de Trévoux*.[52] As always, there was the desire
for economic and social improvement, as in Diderot's wondering whether
there could not be found in the French dominions a plant with an under-
bark fiber suitable for weaving, or in the long article on forced labor on the
public highways (*Corvée*), in which the author suggested ways for increasing efficiency while reducing the hardships caused the peasants.[53] As
always, there were the admonitory articles on correct scientific method,
such as Diderot's on 'Credulity' and 'Belief' (*Croire*), articles which were
likely to bemuse their readers concerning the basis for faith in the evidences
of the Christian religion. As always, there were long and solemn articles
on subjects dealing with the Old Testament, as, for example, the article
'Deluge,' which raised about as many common-sense questions about the
Flood as the article in Volume I had done about Noah's Ark. And, as
always, there were Diderot's own contributions, colorful, volatile, impudent,
sometimes profound.

Diderot's use of irony and of what Americans call the 'dead pan' is
well shown in his article on 'Damnation.' Damnation, he wrote, signifies
'eternal punishment in Hell. The dogma of damnation or of eternal punishment is clearly revealed by Scripture. Therefore it is no longer a question of
seeking to determine by reason whether or not it is possible for a finite
being to do God an infinite injury; or whether or not the eternalness of
punishment is not more contrary to His goodness than conformable to His
justice; or whether, because it has pleased Him to ordain an infinite reward
for good, He has or has not been able to ordain an infinite punishment for
evil. In place of becoming entangled in a web of captious reasonings, likely
to shake a faith not well established, one should submit to the authority of
the Holy Books and the decisions of the Church, and, trembling, effect
one's salvation, ceaselessly considering that the enormity of the offense is
in direct proportion to the dignity of the offended, and in inverse proportion
to the offender, and [ceaselessly considering] what must be the enormity of
our disobedience, if that of the first man could be effaced by nothing less
than the blood of the Son of God.'[54]

Intentionally challenging as was this kind of article, deceptively planting
doubt while saying the unexceptionable, Diderot seems to have felt that
its apparent conformity needed justification. In this volume, he himself
wrote that 'one should not suppose that sages like Socrates, Plato, and
Cicero, and others, always spoke according to the ideas of the people:
nevertheless they were sometimes obliged to conform to them in order not

to be accused of atheism.' [55] Surely for contemporary readers of the *Encyclopédie* the application of this remark to certain living 'sages' must have been unavoidable.

Among Diderot's contributions were his customary articles of preponderantly literary interest, the articles on word definition and analysis of synonyms, the import of which was primarily psychological or belletristic rather than informative. Often Diderot fitted the rhythm of his prose to the mood of what he was describing, so that he not only explained his subject but represented it, as has been strikingly brought out in regard to the article 'Enjoyment' (*Jouissance*).[56] In Volume IV Diderot wrote an article of this sort, sensitively analyzing the various meanings of the word 'delicious' and especially describing the deliciousness of sinking into repose. Grimm called it 'one of the most precious things written in French,' and a modern critic, who specializes in the study of Diderot and of Baudelaire, speaks of it as a completely modern analysis of the consciousness of the fleeting and the evanescent.[57]

Two of Diderot's articles that Grimm particularly commended were long ones devoted to the philosophical schools of the Cynics and Cyrenaics.[58] These exercises by Diderot in the history of philosophy were not without precedent, for he had written the long article on 'Aristotelianism' in Volume I. In Volumes II and III, however, he had tended to delegate these tasks to the Abbé Pestré, a shadowy figure who, after the De Prades affair, fades out of the *Encyclopédie* in the unobtrusive way that Alice observed in the Cheshire cat. From that point on, Diderot took over this assignment. His articles were so highly regarded that Naigeon, thirty-five years later, collected and republished seventy-three of them in a successor of Diderot's *Encyclopédie*, the *Encyclopédie méthodique*, which first appeared in 1781 and ran to 229 volumes before it desisted in 1832. In practically every case the information in these articles by Diderot was freely borrowed from a recent history of philosophy written in Latin by a German named Brucker, a fact which Diderot did not attempt to conceal.[59] Naigeon says that Diderot regretted that the pressure of time necessitated his following Brucker, even to the point of adopting his arrangement and organization of subject matter.[60] But it is still true that Diderot put enough of himself into these articles to make them more than a mere transcription, and a French student of the *Encyclopédie* has declared, even after making allowance for Brucker and another source named Deslandes, that Diderot is practically the creator of the history of philosophy in France.[61] Moreover, his personal additions not infrequently have a biographical interest. In the articles on 'Cynics' and

'Cyrenaics,' for example, written as they were not later than mid-1754, Diderot betrays sentiments that probably betoken a growing antagonism to the austere views of his friend Rousseau.[62]

The *Encyclopédie* was a growing success. What is more, Diderot knew it. At least it is tempting to infer so from the fact that about this time he demanded greater remuneration from his publishers, as we shall see, and also from the fact that about this period he refused in an amusingly high-and-mighty way a contribution from one of the century's greatest names. The Abbé Trublet, who was a sort of literary representative of the famous Fontenelle, tells the story: 'MM. d'Alembert and Diderot appearing to desire to have something of M. de Fontenelle's for the *Encyclopédie*, I had delivery made to the second [i.e. Diderot] of the fragments on the Greek dramatic poets, the only manuscript of M. de Fontenelle that I then had, he being still alive [he died a centenarian in 1757]. Some time afterwards I asked M. Diderot whether he would use them. He replied to me with vivacity that he would take good care *not* to insert in the *Encyclopédie* a writing in which Aeschylus was treated as being crazy; and it is true that M. de Fontenelle said that approximately, although less crudely.'[63] It was like Diderot to respond emphatically and 'with vivacity.' Thus did its editor, in his reverence for the classics, defend Aeschylus at the cost of rejecting for the *Encyclopédie* a contribution from one of the most famous men of letters in France.

CHAPTER 17

Business and Pleasure: A New Contract, Mme Geoffrin's Salon, Sophie Volland

IN LATE 1754, with four volumes of the *Encyclopédie* off the press, Diderot could look back with gratification upon a number of arduous, eventful, and productive years. Not only had he borne the principal burden of editing a work of formidable size, but he had also found time in the years just preceding to write some influential books. Now he took time off for a visit to Langres, the first he is known to have made for twelve years and the last, it turned out, while his father was living. Having left his wife and year-old daughter in the apartment on the Rue de l'Estrapade, he spent at least ten days in Langres, where, among other things, he lent five hundred livres to a local husbandman and stood godfather to a Caroillon child, destined one day to be brother-in-law to Diderot's own daughter.[1] It is apparent that the Langres folk still thought of Diderot as being conscientiously able to accept the duties of a Christian godfather. It would be interesting, and more to the point, to know why Diderot, too, thought so.

It is quite evident that Diderot had an enjoyable time at Langres. His letter of thanks, a very long one addressed to all his relatives and friends, was that of a man writing to people he likes. It was written with a touch of robustiousness and vulgarity by no means foreign to the Diderot style, but in this instance specially tailored to please the taste of unfastidious provincial folk. It is a little as though Diderot thought of himself as writing to the people in a painting by Jan Steen. And a succeeding letter shows how thoroughly he had renewed old friendships. In it he describes to the Caroillon family how, upon his return to Paris, he shamelessly ingratiated himself, in their behalf, with a wealthy old Parisian aunt of theirs, and goes on exuberantly to speak of his hopes for the future marriage of his daughter (aged one and a half!) with a Caroillon son (aged nine), a marriage which, in fact, eventually came to pass.[2]

Diderot has left a vivid picture of the family circle at Langres in a dialogue entitled 'Conversation of a Father with his Children, or Concerning the Danger of Putting Oneself above the Law' (*Entretien d'un père avec ses enfants, ou du danger de se mettre au-dessus des lois*).[3] The discussion gave the author an opportunity to describe the compassionate but evenhanded justice of his father, the generous and tender impulses of his sister, the harsh and unbending qualities of his *abbé* brother, and his own magnanimous and somewhat quixotic impulses. Although written much later, it must surely describe the family group of this very time. Moreover, this lively and endearing dialogue probably reports a conversation much as it really occurred, for Diderot, while very imaginative and creative in matters of imagery and scientific thought, was remarkably uninventive in regard to plots and characters. He could observe meticulously, he could report with great verve, and once he had begun to take flight, he could soar. But it has been remarked that he frequently needed the memory of a real event or a real person to inspire him, so that it very often turns out that the stories he tells actually happened.[4] In this dialogue he mentions some of the persons by their real names, such as the family notary Jean-Louis Dubois, not bothering to conceal their identity even when he knew that the piece was going to be published. Therefore the presumption is all the greater that this conversation, which concerned difficult cases of conscience — Diderot loved to discuss difficult cases of conscience — really took place.

While at Langres Diderot consulted his relatives concerning his relations with the publishers of the *Encyclopédie,* even to the point of receiving elaborate legal advice from the notary Dubois. Thus he writes to his family, 'Scarcely had I returned to Paris when my publishers were informed of it and a day appointed for discussing our interests. We all put so much heat and so little reason into our first interview that I thought we would not be seeing one another again. There wasn't a single one of the articles of the contract drawn up by M. Dubois that was not attacked.' In this letter Diderot wrote as if he was determined to retire to Langres if he did not secure what he demanded.[5] But after an elaborate negotiation, involving many intermediaries and numerous compromises, a new contract was signed on 20 December 1754.

The preamble of this document recounts that Diderot had pointed out that the amount of work in the *Encyclopédie* had increased since the previous contract had been signed. Therefore the publishers agreed that beginning with the fifth volume they would pay Diderot 2500 livres a volume, 1500 livres payable when the first copy for a volume, the other 1000 when the last, was handed in. Moreover, within three months of the publication of the last volume of letterpress, Diderot was to receive a lump sum of 20,000 livres. All books hitherto supplied him as sources or for reference in editing the *Encyclopédie* were henceforth to be regarded as his property — these books were the backbone of the library he later sold to Catherine II of Russia — and the publishers put in writing that 'the said M. Diderot will be in the future, as he has been in the past, editor of all the parts of the *Encyclopédie.*' [6] It might be remarked that no previous document had so precisely defined Diderot's position.

About this time, probably because the new contract made it financially feasible, the Diderot family moved to more spacious quarters. For the remaining thirty years of Diderot's life the family lived on the fourth floor (fifth, American style) of a building in which Diderot also rented space for his study on the floor above, directly beneath the roof. The building stood on the corner of the Rue Taranne, which no longer exists, and the Rue Saint-Benoît, which still does. Were the building in which Diderot lived still standing — it was pulled down in 1866 — it would be on the Boulevard Saint-Germain directly across the street from the Café de Flore, in the heart of the domain of the existentialists. A fine statue of Diderot, done in bronze by Jean Gautherin in 1885, stands near the site.[7]

A phrase in his thank-you letter to Langres suggests that Diderot had come to distrust D'Alembert. 'I don't know how it was,' he wrote, 'that during this interval impatience did not seize me and I did not send them packing to all the devils, them, the *Encyclopédie,* their papers, and their contract; *a little more confidence in the probity of my colleague,* and that would have done it.' [8] This must mean that Diderot suspected D'Alembert of being willing to supplant him as principal editor. The lack of cordiality between the two men ultimately became marked enough to be noted by Marmontel. 'The house of Baron d'Holbach and, since some little time, that of Helvétius, were the rendezvous for this society, composed partly of the cream of Mme Geoffrin's guests and partly of some individuals whom Mme Geoffrin deemed too bold and too venturesome to be admitted to her dinners. . . .

'I have never known very well why D'Alembert held himself aloof from the society of which I speak. He and Diderot, associates in exertion and in glory in the enterprise of the *Encyclopédie,* had at first been cordially united, but they were no longer. They spoke of each other with much esteem, but they were not intimate and they scarcely saw each other any more. I never dared to ask them the reason for it.' [9]

The year 1754 was a particularly auspicious one for D'Alembert, for in the course of it he received the greatest honor his writings could earn in France, election to the French Academy. This institution, which had been founded by the great Cardinal Richelieu, existed under the direct patronage of the king of France, and inclusion among its forty members conferred such prestige that even princes of the royal blood, such as the Comte de Clermont in this very year, sought election to it. One of the Academy's most endearing and most pathetic conceits has ever been that its membership confers immortality. In the buildings of the Institut de France, on the eighteenth-century doors to the charming room in which the Academy does its work, there is wrought in intricate and garlanded design the phrase *A l'Immortalité*. It is scarcely necessary to remark, however, that laurel leaves also, like the men who wore them, can turn to dust.

D'Alembert fully deserved his election. He was more than a man of science, France's greatest living mathematician; he was also a talented and influential man of letters, as witness his 'Preliminary Discourse' to the *Encyclopédie,* as well as other writings collected and published in 1753 under the title of *Mélanges de littérature, d'histoire, et de philosophie.* Yet his election could not help but be widely interpreted as more than simply a personal recognition. It was also a victory for the *Encyclopédie* and for the new 'philosophy.' The prestige of the new outlook increased in step with his, and the fact that he had gained admittance to the citadel of French letters not unnaturally caused the *philosophes* to hope, and their enemies to dread, that this was to be only their first entry into the Academy. D'Alembert's election increased — if anything was still able to increase — the self-confidence and self-esteem of a group that was rapidly becoming a kind of party or sect.

This tendency of the *philosophes* to coalesce into a coterie became a subject of frequent and exasperated remark during the 1750's. Fréron in his *Année Littéraire* rarely let the opportunity pass to complain of it, and even the Abbé Raynal, who was more a friend than an enemy of the *philosophes,* remarked in his private news letter during 1754 upon 'the harsh tone and bad temper that some men of letters of today mistake for philosophy. . . . If the tone of criticism is abandoned [he went on], it is for the purpose of elevating to the third heaven the authors of the *Encyclopédie* and the author of the *Histoire naturelle* [Buffon]; aside from them there is nothing praiseworthy any more. They it is who have taught us to think and to write, who have re-established good taste and philosophy, and who preserve them. Nevertheless, one asks all the time, what have they done? These gentlemen, no doubt esteemworthy by virtue of their knowledge, wit, and manners, degrade their philosophy by a domineering and lawmaking tone, by an affectation of arrogating to themselves a despotism over literary matters, and by their propensity to burn incense to one another everywhere and endlessly. . . .' [10]

This flattering sense of being one of an elite was nurtured by the *salon*, a social institution of peculiar efficacy in generating a spirit of group cohesiveness. Given the centralization of French social and intellectual life, at least since the beginning of the seventeenth century, the Parisian *salon* has always been, like a gambling house, a place in which fortunes are made or lost. Often a *salon* has been of incalculable assistance in launching an author or, inversely, in wrecking another; and in no epoch was this more evidently true than in the eighteenth century. For that was a sociable age, and the ideas that were transforming society and predisposing it for change were ideas freely canvassed and exchanged in the agreeable leisure of these social hours. The connotation of the word '*salon*,' used in this special sense, was of an open house the purpose of which was intellectual discussion. Usually the word implied, too, that the hospitality was extended by a lady, acting as 'ringmistress,' or, as Henry James put it, directing 'through a smiling land, between suggestive shores, a sinuous stream of talk.' Although of course D'Holbach's was a *salon,* too, the more typical eighteenth-century *salons* were those of Mme du Deffand, Mme Geoffrin, Mlle de Lespinasse, and Mme Necker.

It took a great deal of skill and tact to run a *salon* successfully, to gain the respect of temperamental authors and intellectuals, to make them want to come again, to be able to steer a conversation without being obvious, to govern discussions so adroitly that they became neither anarchical nor contentious, to draw out the timid and circumvent the bores. No one was more proficient, more gentle but firm, in the exercise of these skills than Mme Geoffrin, so that her house came to be nicknamed, in deference both to her prestige and to her authority, 'The Kingdom of Rue Saint-Honoré.' [11] It is still standing, hard by the Place Vendôme and the Place de la Concorde, this house which became a rallying point for 'philosophy,' especially by virtue of the famous dinners she gave for men of letters every Wednesday. Artists were fed on Mondays.

This is not to say that discussions at Mme Geoffrin's were ever so bold and fearless as they were at D'Holbach's. Mme Geoffrin was rather timorous and very cautious, so that, as Marmontel remarked, she held Diderot, the most original and prolific thinker of them all, at arm's length. At Mme Geoffrin's, wrote Marmontel, the *philosophes* were 'led about and held in leading strings.' [12] But this very prudence and timidity worked to the profit of the Encyclopedists. 'At the moment when her *salon* was being opened,' wrote a distinguished editor of the *Revue des Deux Mondes,* 'those who were going to form the army of the Encyclopedists were still isolated, strangers, or hostile to one another, and little known or little appreciated by the public. They grouped themselves at Mme Geoffrin's: at her house they found a center of reunion where they learned to get together, to support one another, and to make common cause. There they submitted to discipline. A lover of propriety and moderation, the mistress of the house prevented them from colliding too violently with public opinion or governmental power, and she saved them from the danger of ruining themselves by their own impatience.' [13] This is well said. It may be supplemented by a police report of 1751 about Mme Geoffrin, giving some of the down-to-earth aspects of operating a *salon:*

There assembles every afternoon at this lady's house a circle of wits, among whom are especially M. de Fontenelle and Helvétius, Farmer General, who are her friends.

She often provides meals.

Also she sells the rarest new books; that is to say, the authors send her a dozen copies and she takes pleasure in making her friends buy them.[14]

The functioning of a literary circle resembling that of Mme Geoffrin is reflected in the 'Memoirs of M. de Voltaire' by Oliver Goldsmith, who claimed to have been an eyewitness of a spirited dispute involving Fontenelle, Diderot, and Voltaire. This must have occurred, if anything like it really did take place, during 1755, when Goldsmith was in France. It would be pleasant to think that Diderot and Goldsmith were acquainted, but the latter's story is demonstrably inaccurate in part (for Voltaire was not in Paris in 1755 and never met Diderot until 1778), leaving one to fear that perhaps it is false *in toto.*[15]

For Diderot the importance of Mme Geoffrin's *salon* was chiefly indirect. It existed. It was valuable. It provided a powerful support for the new outlook represented by the *Encyclopédie*. But it functioned almost exclusively without his presence, whether he voluntarily abstained because he disliked the constraint that Mme Geoffrin put upon her guests, or whether he was made to feel that she liked him better absent. Certainly there is no evidence of antagonism between them, and she was exceedingly generous with him in respect to money. Yet she distrusted him, for both his manners and ideas made him difficult to manage. As Marmontel remarked, Diderot was not admitted to her dinners. 'Diderot did not go to Mme Geoffrin's,' wrote another of his contemporaries. 'She feared his impetuosity, the rashness of his opinions, supported, when he was aroused, by a fiery and stirring eloquence.' [16] And she herself, writing in 1774 to her protégé, the King of Poland, spoke of Diderot in cool and measured terms. 'He is an upright man,' she wrote, 'but he is wrongheaded. And he is so wrongly constituted that he neither sees nor hears anything as it really is. He is always like a man in a dream, and who believes everything that he has dreamed.' [17]

At about this period Diderot made the acquaintance of a man whose recollection of their meeting imparts precious information as to what kind of first impression Diderot was likely to make. The new acquaintance was Charles de Brosses, a magistrate from Dijon, who had asked his former schoolmate, Buffon, for an introduction to Diderot, 'that extraordinary metaphysical head.' 'He is an agreeable fellow,' reported De Brosses, 'very charming, very likable, a great philosopher, a great arguer, but dealing in perpetual digressions. He made a good twenty-five of them in my room yesterday, from nine o'clock to one.' [18]

De Brosses was a man of broad intellectual attainments, and he and Diderot quickly became very friendly. Diderot almost importunately solicited from him for publication in the *Encyclopédie* the manuscript of a long article on 'Etymology.' [19] As De Brosses later described the episode, Diderot kept the manuscript for two or three years in spite of De Brosses's reiterated requests that it be returned for revision. The article that finally came out on this subject in the *Encyclopédie,* however, was written not by De Brosses but by Turgot, who evidently had used the De Brosses manuscript as a starting point. De Brosses was rather startled at this outcome, although he did not question that Turgot had acted in the best of faith. He was inclined, however, to accuse Diderot of 'negligence' and thoughtlessness.[20] Here we have a glimpse of the careless and nonchalant side of Diderot, whose possession of such disconcerting although sometimes endearing qualities made dealing with him an experience not infrequently frustrating.

At the time that Diderot made the acquaintance of De Brosses, the Academy of Dijon had just announced a prize contest on the subject, 'What

is the origin of inequality among men, and is it authorized by natural law?'
Since De Brosses was a member of the Academy of Dijon, Diderot's conversations with him naturally came around to this topic. The subject appealed strongly to Diderot, and yet he did not compete for the prize. De
Brosses reveals why: 'Diderot talks to me a great deal about the subject
of this prize. He finds it very fine but impossible to deal with under a
monarchy. He is a daring philosopher, with a vengeance.'[21]

Diderot's friend Jean-Jacques felt no such restrictions. He submitted an
essay which, though it did not win the prize, nevertheless became one
of his most famous works. In view of the foregoing evidence of Diderot's
preoccupation with the subject, it is interesting to speculate upon just how
much he may have influenced this essay. Rousseau declared in his *Confessions* that the *Discourse on Inequality* was the 'work that was more to
Diderot's taste than any other of my writings, and for which his counsel
was the most useful to me.' Somewhat later Rousseau even identified a
passage in the *Discourse on Inequality* that Diderot had written, but by this
time Jean-Jacques was no longer of the persuasion that Diderot had been
really helpful. 'It is certain,' he wrote, 'that M. Diderot always abused my
confidence and my compliance in order to impart to my writings a harsh
tone and a gloomy air that they no longer had as soon as he ceased to direct
me and I was left completely to myself.'[22] Recent scholarship is inclined
to the view that there may indeed have been in Diderot a vein of primitivism
fiercer and more stubborn than in Rousseau himself.[23] Building upon Rousseau's own admission, it is generally supposed that Diderot's share in the
ideas incorporated into Rousseau's *Discourse on the Origin of Inequality*
is considerable.[24]

As the *Encyclopédie* went into the letter 'E,' one of Diderot's contributions
was an article intended to be published under the title of 'Encaustic.'[25] For
some reason he decided to publish it separately, and accordingly there appeared anonymously in a very small edition in 1755, *L'Histoire et le secret
de la peinture en cire* ('The History and Secret of Painting in Wax').[26] The
article 'Encaustic' as it appeared in Volume V was done by another hand.[27]

This rather recondite subject was nevertheless topical because of the
considerable discussion in Paris just at this time as to precisely what had
been the method used by the ancients for painting in wax and for fixing
the colors by the application of heat. The technique is very difficult, but
gives special effects and is of extraordinary durability. It has been practiced
today in this country with remarkable technical and aesthetic success by

Karl Zerbe of the Boston Museum School of Fine Arts. One of Diderot's acquaintances, an artist named Bachelier, thought he had rediscovered the ancient technique in 1749, but had done nothing about publicizing it. In 1753 the Comte de Caylus published the first of a series of papers in which he claimed to have deciphered the cryptic passages in Pliny the Elder regarding this ancient technique and therefore to be the first to recover the long-lost method.[28]

Caylus, however, made a mystery of the actual technique employed in duplicating the ancient method. This sort of obscurantism in matters relating to the sciences or the arts, indeed any sort of obscurantism, always infuriated Diderot, and in consequence his pamphlet was as much aimed against Caylus as the *Letter on the Blind* had been a rebuke of Réaumur. The first words of the new work were: 'Nothing is more contrary to the progress of knowledge than mystery.'[29] Then he attempted to prove that neither Bachelier, in 1749, nor Caylus had really come upon the true ancient encaustic, but that Bachelier had since discovered it in further experiments. Since Bachelier was trying to keep the discovery secret, Diderot nonchalantly put himself into the invidious position of revealing a secret that was not his property. 'I do not doubt,' he wrote, 'but what M. Bachelier bears me a grudge for publishing his secret. . . . But I have my own character and my own fashion of thinking, which I find satisfactory and from which I shall not withdraw for the sake of M. Bachelier. What I know of his methods of painting I owe solely to the pains I took to teach myself regarding it. I promised no one to keep the secret.'[30] Diderot's attitude was consistent with his freely bestowing upon the public his own ideas for the improvement of barrel organs. Nevertheless, with a characteristic impetuosity and lack of second thought and with even a certain officiousness, he deeply disobliged both Caylus and Bachelier by what he claimed to be his zeal for the public good.

The Comte was a wealthy amateur and expert who was a sort of dictator, apparently a crotchety and crabbed one, in the world of art.[31] One can well imagine what he thought of Diderot. When an Italian correspondent innocently happened to inquire in 1761 how Diderot was, Caylus replied, 'I know Diderot very little because I do not esteem him, but I believe he is well. There are certain *bougres* who don't die, while, to the misfortune of letters in Europe, honest folk like Melot [Anicet Melot (1697–1759), a French antiquarian] die in their prime.'[32] And what Diderot thought about Caylus was expressed in an epitaph Diderot wrote in 1765. Caylus had expressed the desire to be buried in an Etruscan urn that was in his garden, and Diderot wrote, in a very well-turned couplet: [33]

> Ci-gît un antiquaire acariâtre et brusque;
> Ah! qu'il est bien logé dans cette cruche étrusque! *

The pamphlet on 'Encaustic' is characteristic of Diderot's point of view and redolent of his personality. Time and again he emphasizes the importance of disseminating knowledge.[34] 'If it happens,' he writes, 'that an invention favorable to the progress of the arts and sciences comes to my knowledge, I burn to divulge it: that is my mania. Born communicative as much as it is possible to be, it is too bad that I was not born more inventive: I would have told my ideas to the first comer. Had I but one secret for all my stock in trade, it seems to me that if the general good should require the publication of it, I should prefer to die honestly on a street corner, my back against a post, than to let my fellow men suffer. . . .'[35] And he wishes that there might be established a royal academy of the mechanical arts.[36] Moreover, Diderot's interest in the applied, the factual, and the practical (as well as in the generalized and the purely theoretical) is abundantly shown in this booklet. Here is a man who knows as much as any man in his day about the chemistry of paints. Here is an author fully aware of the technical procedures of artists, as well as of their problems of composition and aesthetic intent. The *History and Secret of Painting in Wax* reveals also the classicist, able to translate and analyze Pliny's elliptic and obscure remarks. Finally, in this pamphlet — which Grimm described as 'written with much fire, a rapid pace, and much gaiety,' and which Fréron declared to be 'diffuse and overburdened with notes, some of which try to be scientific and the others amusing' — we find the subjective and the personal starting out at one, especially in the notes.[37] 'There's a sentence,' Diderot comments concerning a paragraph composed of one single sentence of eighteen lines, 'very long and tortuous, which is going to be found displeasing. Were it the only one, I would correct it.'[38] At another place he notes that 'All that follows now seems to me to be out of place; but I have not the courage to delete it.' Then in the next note, 'If I continue in this vein, I shall not finish in a hundred pages what could be said in ten, and I shall be reproached for having been obscure and diffuse, two faults that usually go together.'[39]

---

* Here lies a crabbed and brusque antiquarian.
Oh, how appropriately lodged is he in this Etruscan jug!

And what could be more personal and more revelatory of Diderot's sensitiveness than the following?

'. . . we take as great pains to destroy [our masterpieces in painting and sculpture] as they [the Ancients] did to preserve theirs. They had a varnish that they applied to their pictures, their bronzes, and their marbles . . . . Regularly every year we rub the skin off ours with sponges full of a hard and gritty fluid. . . . On the days of this cruel operation I flee from the Tuileries as one flees from a public place on a day of execution.' [40]

The controversy over encaustic painting created some stir and inspired a pamphlet ridiculing Diderot's. Its translated title is *The New Art of Painting in Cheese, Invented for Carrying Out the Laudable Project of Gradually Finding Ways of Painting Inferior to Those Now in Existence*.[41] This effusion was by an anonymous author whom Fréron found diverting and Grimm thought to be 'in the worst taste since Attila, King of the Huns.' [42] Irony upon so lordly a scale apparently discouraged other champions from entering the contest. It was all very well for Grimm to grumble, but he and his brothers of kindred spirit did not choose to reply.

It was about this time that Diderot again fell in love, suddenly and violently and enduringly. Little is known of the lady, but evidently she possessed a character very different from and much finer than that of Mme de Puisieux. None of Sophie Volland's letters to Diderot is extant, so that the impression we have of her is very like overhearing one end of a protracted telephone conversation. Incomplete and distorted as this way of knowing her personality inevitably is, it is quite apparent that she was modest where Mme de Puisieux was conceited, and self-effacing where Mme de Puisieux was self-assertive. Certainly Diderot found in Sophie Volland the qualities necessary for a lasting attachment, an attachment — attenuated perhaps, but never broken off in bitterness — enduring the rest of their lives. Sophie Volland died five months before Diderot, and in her will she left him the keepsakes of a long devotion. 'I give and bequeath to M. Diderot seven little volumes of Montaigne's *Essays* bound in red morocco, together with a ring that I call my Pauline.' [43]

'Sophie' was a special name. Not the Louise-Henriette of her baptism, but the name given to her by Diderot himself in allusion, by means of the French form of the Greek word, to the wisdom which seemed to him the quintessence of her qualities.[44] It is as Sophie Volland that she has become posthumously famous, the inspirer and recipient of letters unexcelled in their revelation both of a particularly interesting social milieu and of an infinitely rich, complex, and humane personality. 'Grudge not the elderly spinster her existence, then,' wrote Carlyle in his essay on 'Diderot.' 'Say not she lived in vain.'

Sophie Volland came from a family, perhaps a wealthy one, of the middle class. Her father, Jean-Robert Volland, who died before the lovers met, had been an important functionary in the administration of the government monopoly of salt, and was closely associated, both in business and by marriage, with the class of financiers and tax farmers whose enormous incomes tended to make them the freest spenders of the *ancien régime*. The Volland family was not dedicated to this gospel of conspicuous waste, but the father had bought an estate and built a country house at Isle-sur-Marne, near the small city of Vitry-le-François — to which Sophie's mother spirited her away for half of each year in order to separate her from Diderot — and it is also evident that the family lived comfortably in their town house on the Rue des Vieux-Augustins. This was in a quarter now much run down but at that time conservatively fashionable, close by the Place des Victoires and the grandiose and imposing church of Sainte-Eustache.[45] There is some indication in Diderot's letters that the family when he knew it was less prosperous than it had been.

Sophie had two married sisters, and it is remarkable, considering her family's affluence, that she was not married too. Perhaps, as one biographer of Diderot has surmised, some obscure but unforgotten scandal had impaired her matrimonial chances.[46] When Diderot met her, probably in 1755, perhaps in 1756, she was about forty years of age, three years younger than Diderot, having been born on 27 November 1716.[47] What little is known of her mainly concerns the state of her health, which evidently was exceedingly precarious, so much so that Diderot was constantly fussing over her. 'Very warm days are succeeded by very cool evenings,' he wrote her. 'Watch your health. Don't expose yourself to the evening damp. You know what a weak little cat's chest you have and what terrible colds you are subject to.' Two weeks later he wrote, 'Adieu, my dear. I kiss your forehead, your eyes, your mouth, and your dry little hand, which pleases me quite as much as a plump one.'[48] Biographers, having so little to go on, make much of the dry little hand (*menotte*). And they are inclined to speak of Sophie's spectacles in the spirit of Dorothy Parker's remark about girls who wear glasses. 'It is from my workshop at Le Breton's that I have been writing to you for the past two hours this long, boring letter that you will have a good deal of trouble in deciphering. Just omit, pass over, whatever makes you rub your glasses on your sleeve,' Diderot wrote upon one occasion. And upon another, imagining them gathered together at the country house:

'I hear you all chattering, I see you all in your favorite attitudes, I would paint you if I had the time. My dear one would be standing erect behind her mother's armchair, facing her sister, and with her spectacles on her nose.' [49]

Had more of Diderot's letters to Sophie Volland remained in existence, we would not now be so desperately deficient in information regarding her. They are known to have numbered more than five hundred and fifty, but Mlle Volland herself destroyed all but one hundred and eighty-seven.[50] Moreover, the first one hundred and thirty-four, which might very well have been the most interesting of all, have disappeared, and the earliest one we can consult is dated May 1759. We are thus reduced to approximations when attempting to fix the date when the acquaintance began. Mme de Vandeul asserts that her father developed this passion in 1757, when Mme Diderot and little Angélique were on a visit to Langres.[51] But Diderot's own letters suggest 1755 as the date of meeting. In 1767 he writes somewhat vaguely in terms of 'ten to twelve years,'[52] though a year later we find him still talking of a dozen years.[53] There is the same indefiniteness in this passage from a letter of 1765, regarding a carriage trip on the morrow: 'I shall have the pleasure of passing the whole day with her whom I love (which is not surprising, for who would not love her?) but whom I love, after eight or nine years, with the same passion with which she inspired me on the first day that I saw her. We were alone that day, both of us leaning on the little green table. I remember what I said to you, what you replied to me. Oh, the happy time it was, the time of that green table!'[54] Earlier references are more precise. One of September 1760 remarks that it will soon be five years since they met; and in October of 1759 he writes, 'It was four years ago that you appeared beautiful in my eyes. Today I find you more beautiful than ever. This is the magic of constancy, the most difficult and the rarest of our virtues.'[55]

A good deal of ink has been spilled, perhaps rather needlessly, in speculation as to whether Diderot and Sophie Volland were really lovers or just good friends. Were Diderot's affections 'platonic'? This is certainly a problem of appropriate biographical interest, but one concerning which a non-French biographer might well defer to French *expertise*. It may be reported, therefore, that persons deserving to be regarded as connoisseurs in such matters, as, for example, a member of the Académie Goncourt or, for another, the author of a book entitled *La Vie amoureuse de Diderot*, have weightily considered the evidence. The majority conclude — as most people would have assumed from the start — that Sophie allowed Diderot what is delicately termed 'the ultimate liberties.' [56]

Much of what is known about Diderot, the most revealing and the most precious information, comes from his correspondence with Sophie Volland. It is posterity's loss that, in contrast, so little is known of Sophie herself. Was the quality of her mind what Diderot thought it to be, or did he mistake the echoing of his own ideas as the evidence of a powerful intelligence in her? It would not have been the first or last time that Diderot admired himself by seeing in a person or a book something that was not there but was simply a projection of his own personality. Besides, Diderot was given to some exaggeration in these matters, as when he wrote in his 'Essay on Women,' 'When one writes of women, one must dip one's pen in the rainbow and dry the line with the dust of butterflies' wings.' [57] A reader of the letters may easily sentimentalize with Diderot about Sophie Volland and perhaps invest her with a character and characteristics that she is not positively known to have possessed. But at the very least it can be said with certainty that Diderot's second mistress was better than the first. And it can also be said, in view of the contents of these letters, that she can scarcely be thought a prude.

CHAPTER 18

'Changing the General Way of Thinking'

D IDEROT was far from well during the closing
months of 1755. In late September he alluded
to his illness in a letter to Caroillon at Langres: 'I have been and still am
pretty badly off in my own affairs. I have had my whole chest affected. A
dry cough. Terrible sweats, difficulty in speaking and breathing. But things
are going much better, at the price of a drastic remedy: bread, water, and
milk for my whole diet. Milk in the morning, milk at noon, milk at "tea-
time," milk at supper. That's a lot of milk.' [1] In circumstances so adverse
—and for most Frenchmen (save perhaps M. Mendès-France), to have to
cope with that much milk is real adversity—Diderot continued his task of
editing the *Encyclopédie* and writing articles for it. In particular, he composed his article 'Encyclopedia' for Volume V during this difficult time.
Rousseau mentioned the article as being 'the admiration of all Paris,' and
then went on to say, 'what will increase your astonishment when you read
it is the fact that he wrote it while ill.' [2]

Despite this sickness, Volume V was delivered to subscribers during the
first days of November.[3] Like its sisters, it was a portly folio volume, a thousand pages and more, and carried the alphabet to ESY. Its title page took
cognizance of D'Alembert's new honors, mentioning that he was a member
of the French Academy, the Royal Academy of Belles-Lettres of Sweden,
and the Institute of Bologna. As usual, new contributors were welcomed to
the fold, especially Voltaire, whose articles on 'Elegance,' 'Eloquence,' and
'Esprit' were not only elegant but also concise, a virtue not always characterizing the *Encyclopédie*'s contents.

Once again a lengthy memoir by D'Alembert formed the introduction.
This one concerned Montesquieu, who had died in February 1755—Diderot,
incidentally, happening to be the only man of letters present at the funeral.[4]
Montesquieu had never engaged very deeply in the cause of the *Encyclopédie*,

232

but with the French proclivity for making political capital out of funerals, the editors appropriated him. Their excuse was that he was a contributor, having written the article on 'Taste' (*Goût*), a rather mediocre fragment as it turned out. Posterity is accustomed to regard the author of *L'Esprit des lois* with a good deal of veneration, as did, for example, the authors of the *Federalist Papers,* but in his own lifetime and in his own country conservatives looked upon Montesquieu with great disapprobation because he seemed to be too fond of talking about the nature of liberty and too pointed in implying that France had very little of it. Moreover, his positive and factual rather than theological approach to the study of history and politics offended many. To reactionaries Montesquieu seemed radical, and it was characteristic of the editors of the *Encyclopédie* to desire to make him their own. This they did not only in their introductory memoir but also in the course of an article by Diderot on 'Eclecticism,' written like many others of his with a sudden flashing swoop from the objective to the personal which seems so out of place in a work of reference but which is probably one of the major causes of this one's success. Having commented morosely upon society's neglect and abuse of genius, he remarked, 'I wrote these reflections on 11 February 1755, upon returning from the funeral of one of our greatest men, overcome by the loss that the nation and the world of letters had sustained in his person, and profoundly shocked by the persecutions that he had undergone.' [5]

One of the principal articles in Volume V was written by Diderot on 'Natural Right' (*Droit naturel*). This was a subject in the vein of the great natural lawyers of the preceding century, men like Grotius and Pufendorf, so that a highly competent political philosopher has been able to say with some justification of Diderot's article that it was 'a rhetorical flourish with conventional ideas.' [6] Still, this was a topic difficult to discuss with frankness in the France of the eighteenth century. Diderot did discuss it. His article, being in the tradition of the natural law school, contributed to keeping concepts current that later provided the inspiration for documents like the Declaration of Independence and the Declaration of the Rights of Man and of the Citizen. Diderot wrote of man's dignity and — in 1755 — of his 'inalienable rights,' [7] and frequently referred to 'the general will.' This phrase has become so deeply associated with Jean-Jacques Rousseau and his idea of the social contract that Montesquieu's earlier use of the term in *L'Esprit des lois* seems to have become generally forgotten. [8] In Volume V of the *Encyclopédie* both Diderot, in his article on *'Droit naturel,'* and Rousseau, in his on 'Economy,' used the term with some of the identical overtones of meaning that are found in the *Social Contract* seven years later.[9] Thus Diderot wrote that 'Individual wills are under suspicion: they might be good or bad, but the general will is always good. It has never deceived, it never will . . . the general will never errs.'[10] It is therefore possible that one of the two borrowed the term from the other, but, if so, very unclear who from whom.[11] At all events, when one begins to use the phrase, 'the general will,' the concept of popular sovereignty commences to stir. As De Jaucourt had the courage to write, and Diderot to publish, in the article on 'Government,' 'all *legitimate* sovereign power must emanate from the free consent of the people.'[12]

Articles like these were prophetic. And it is worthy of notice that Volume V dared to begin publishing again the liberal political articles for which Diderot had been so severely criticized when he wrote and published the essay on 'Authority' in Volume I. His article on 'Natural Right,' Rousseau's on 'Economy,' and De Jaucourt's on 'Natural Equality' (*Egalité naturelle*) expound ideas that already have the smell of 1776 and 1789. Nor did the significance of their publication in the *Encyclopédie* escape the observation of contemporaries. If one is ever tempted to suppose that the political views expressed in the *Encyclopédie* were so hesitant and timid as to be innocuous, let him recall the words of a British reviewer writing in 1768, words wherein a generous-minded liberalism may be seen contending with an English jealousy of French progress: 'We must observe likewise, to the honour of the authors who have had the conduct of the Encyclopedie, that the same manly freedom of sentiment which is observable in the philosophical and other departments of this work, is eminently conspicuous in the political. In short, whoever takes the trouble of combining the several political articles, will find that they form a noble system of civil liberty; and however, as Englishmen, we may have no reason to rejoice at the prospect of a gradual establishment of such a system among our rivals, yet as friends to the rights of mankind, we are delighted to see such a generous system every where expanding its influence.'[13]

As for the economic philosophy of the *Encyclopédie,* it is nowhere better depicted than in the long article on 'Thrift' (*Epargne*) contributed by an obscure boarding school director named Faiguet. Reminiscent of, say, Benjamin Franklin, it was an extraordinary piece to appear in 1755 in the midst of a monarchical and aristocratic society. For its values were middle-class values, very far indeed from those of the nobility. There is something symbolic in M. Faiguet's personal insignificance. He is faceless, which makes him the better representative of a class, the class that made the French

Revolution. This was the class that, like M. Faiguet, regarded thrift as a cardinal virtue and, like M. Faiguet too, wanted the medieval guild restrictions on production abolished; desired the abolition of apprenticeships and journeymen's associations; wanted the abolition of Colbertism 'by removing the obstacles on every hand regarding the transport and sale of merchandise and foodstuffs'; and further desired the suppression 'of three-fourths of our religious holidays.' M. Faiguet had a keen eye for the labor supply: he wanted the state to limit the number of persons admitted to religious orders. He thought that thrift would be encouraged by placing much more severe limitations on drinking places: 'The cabarets, being always open, disorder our workers so thoroughly that one cannot ordinarily count upon them nor see the end of a job once commenced.' He favored the institution of state-owned pawn shops which could also serve as banks of deposit. 'By this means there would circulate an infinity of sums great and small that remain today in inactivity.' M. Faiguet was much opposed to luxury, the taste for which he imputed to the mistaken education of the day. 'Nothing is more to be recommended to young folk than this virtuous habit [of thrift], which would become for them a preservative against vice. . . . Prizes in eloquence and poetry have been founded in a thousand places. Who will found among us prizes for thrift and frugality?' [14] M. Faiguet deserves immortality: he is the disembodied voice of an upthrusting bourgeoisie.

Among the articles descriptive of manufacturing or artistic processes that Diderot wrote for Volume V were those on distillation of brandy (*Eau-de-vie*) and on 'Enamel' (*Email*). In the latter he introduced the personal note by mentioning a certain artist and saying, 'I do myself the honor of being a friend of the last named.' [15] D'Alembert, too, permitted himself the luxury of personal remarks now and again in this volume, as when he praised Diderot's *Thoughts on the Interpretation of Nature* or launched forth in castigation of the clandestine Jansenist newspaper, *Les Nouvelles Ecclésiastiques.* 'The anonymous author of this work,' wrote D'Alembert, '. . . could probably name himself without being better known.' [16] Also in Volume V, to take some samples, were an interesting article on 'Copyright' (*Droit de copie*), contributed by David, one of the publishers of the *Encyclopédie,* and an article on 'Duels' written by Boucher d'Argis. Of very special interest to economists is the article on how pins are made (*Epingle*), contributed by a young friend of Diderot and Rousseau named Deleyre. Following the usual *Encyclopédie* pattern of meticulously describing manufacturing processes, Deleyre mentioned eighteen separate stages in the manufacture of a pin. This article gives us some means of judging how diffused the influence of the *Encyclopédie* could be, even though not always acknowledged. Surely it is not simply a coincidence that in the first chapter of the *Wealth of Nations,* Adam Smith illustrates his doctrine regarding the division of labor by choosing the now famous example of the lowly pin. 'One man draws out the wire, another straights it, a third cuts it, a fourth points it, a fifth grinds it at the top for receiving the head; to make the head requires two or three distinct operations; to put it on is a peculiar business, to whiten the pins is another; it is even a trade by itself to put them into the paper; and the important business of making a pin is, in this manner, divided into about *eighteen* distinct operations . . .' [17]

In Volume V Diderot continued his practice of writing long and important articles on the history of philosophy, such as his account of the Eleatics. No doubt Diderot devoted this liberal amount of space to the leaders of this school because their teachings were materialistic.[18] Similarly, the article on 'Epicureanism' was long, detailed, and full of loving fondness, although it purported to do no more than allow Epicurus to speak for himself.[19] The article 'Egyptians' gave Diderot the opportunity to declare that Moses was a disciple of the Egyptian priests, thereby undercutting the orthodox Christian contention that the Mosaic books portrayed original man and the earliest societies. Also he could speak disparagingly of priests in general while ostensibly discussing the priesthood of pagan Egypt.[20]

Writers of the Enlightenment rather commonly emphasized the antiquity of the Egyptians, a point they seem to have learned from Lord Shaftesbury.[21] This appealed particularly to the *philosophes* because it permitted them to indulge their distaste for revealed religion by insinuating that the laws of Moses were simply cultural borrowings.[22] The necessities of polemics therefore gave the views of the *philosophes,* rather fortuitously, an anti-Jewish cast. This was a field in which the playful Voltaire loved to caper. The *Encyclopédie,* too, did what it could to attack the fundamentalist assertion that the Pentateuch provided the only acceptable and allowable view of historical origins. Diderot and his colleagues, because of this dialectical necessity, were unfair to the Jews, unfair in the first place because they were insufficiently informed. Diderot, who wrote his article on 'Jews' in 1754, would have been more accurate, says Herr Sänger in his monograph on this subject, had he consulted rabbis.[23] And the *philosophes* were unfair in the second place because of their inability to appreciate religious genius and religious insights in any group. This was an area of human experience in which the Enlightenment was likely to be astigmatic. Consequently Diderot could interpose in his account of the Jews the following extremely unsympathetic notice: 'It will not be useless to warn the reader that one ought not to expect to find among the Jews either accuracy in their ideas, or exactitude in their reasoning, or precision in their style — in a word, anything that ought to characterize a sound doctrine of philosophy. On the contrary, there is to be found among them only a confused mixture of the principles of reason and of revelation, an affected and often impenetrable obscurity, principles that lead to fanaticism, a blind respect for the authority of the doctors and of antiquity — in a word, all the defects indicative of an ignorant and superstitious nation.' [24]

The article 'Eclecticism' is precious to a biographer because in it Diderot allows the reader insight into what he thought of himself. A long and quite diffuse article, it is frequently illuminated by flashes of value judgment or by remarks of a very subjective character. Diderot not only defines what it is to be an eclectic, he patently thinks himself to be one. For surely he does not want to exclude himself from the company that he describes in his opening words: 'The eclectic is a philosopher who, trampling under foot prejudice, tradition, venerability, universal assent, authority — in a word, everything that overawes the crowd — dares to think for himself, to ascend to the clearest general principles, to examine them, to discuss them, to admit nothing save on the testimony of his own reason and experience; and from all the philosophies he has analyzed without favor and without partiality, to make one for himself, individual and personal, belonging to him.' Diderot next asserts what all eclectics emphasize, namely that they are not syncretists, a term of opprobrium that an eclectic uses for any eclecticism not his own. 'Nothing is so common as syncretists, nothing so rare as eclectics.' He then discusses the eclectics of the ancient world at great length, finding the greatest exemplar to be, of all people, Julian the Apostate. (It is a wonder that the censors allowed so much as the mention of the Emperor Julian in any context that might be construed as favorable.) Modern eclectics, according to Diderot (and with his emphasis), were those *cultivating experimental philosophy:* 'Eclecticism, this philosophy so reasonable, which had been practiced by geniuses of the first order long before it had a name, remained forgotten until the end of the sixteenth century. Then Nature . . . produced at last certain men covetous of humanity's finest prerogative, the liberty of thinking for oneself, and the eclectic philosophy was seen to be reborn under Giordano Bruno, Jerome Cardan, Francis Bacon, Thomas Campanella, René Descartes, Thomas Hobbes . . . William Leibniz. . . .' [25] Obviously Diderot was calling the roll of names among which he hoped posterity would place his own as of a peer.

Probably the most important single article in the whole seventeen volumes of the *Encyclopédie* was the one written by Diderot on 'Encyclopedia.' By its richly textured consideration, first of what an encyclopedia is for, and then of an encyclopedia's relationship to language, science, and knowledge in general, Diderot's article was comparable in significance and scope to D'Alembert's 'Preliminary Discourse.' And the two were alike in their faith in progress, a faith which was one of the principal tenets in the gospel of the *philosophes*. 'In fact,' wrote Diderot in the first paragraph, 'the aim of an *Encyclopedia* is to gather together the knowledge scattered over the face of the earth . . . that our descendants, being better instructed, may become at the same time more virtuous and more happy; and that we may not die without having deserved well of the human race.'

There is a printer's mystery regarding this article, for it was published with page numbers on the eye-catching right-hand page, but with no pagination on the left-hand pages. Thus there are actually thirty-one pages between those numbered 633 and 649, a circumstance which naturally makes the reader wonder. Could it be that an article half the length was submitted to the censors, then one double the length inserted instead? Or was it that Diderot's illness delayed him in writing the article? The volume may have had to be put in page proof before his article was ready; but the article may have turned out to be twice as long as planned for, thus necessitating this unusual procedure.[26]

The article 'Encyclopedia' is a little book in itself, some 34,000 words in length — 'Such are the first ideas that offered themselves to my mind,' wrote Diderot in closing — 'on the project of a universal and systematic dictionary of human knowledge: on the possibility of it, its object, the arrangement of its materials both general and detailed, its style, method, cross references, nomenclature, its manuscript, authors, censors, editors, and typography.' It can well be imagined that when Diderot spread his net so wide, he caught a lot of fish. For instance, he descanted at length in the early part of the article on problems of linguistics. Profoundly impressed with how difficult it is to achieve accurate definitions, he wrote more like the scientist than like the creative artist who knows that words are symbols or hieroglyphs and therefore cannot be completely fixed. For he knew that the increase of knowledge necessitates an accurate and expanding vocabulary to implement it and he hoped that the *Encyclopédie* or a similar venture could assist in the fixation of language. This would be extensive, including not only all aspects of definition but even an analysis of sounds and a drastic orthographic reform by which spelling would become completely phonetic. In illustration he compared the current French and English phonetic rendering of a line of Greek verse, and in so doing conceived of something closely resembling the alphabet of the International Phonetic Association. Diderot may therefore be considered one of the pioneers in the emergent science of linguistics, although a modern expert has remarked, 'as a linguistic theorist his mind was of too meteoric a nature to submit to that patient discipline, that laborious exploration of linguistic facts which alone were capable of laying the foundations of a science of language.' [27]

Diderot disarmed critics of the *Encyclopédie* by candidly acknowledging defects. First he invited his reader to visualize the problems involved in securing a proper balance and proportion among the multitudinous articles in the work. Even if one man could write every entry, the problem would still be formidable. 'And he who supposes that he has taken precautions with his colleagues so that the contributed material will square approximately with his plan is a man who has no idea of his object or of his colleagues.' Some contributions will be too laconic, some too prolix. 'The proof of it is evident in a hundred places in this work. . . . In one place we are like skeletons; in another, we have a dropsical appearance. We are alternatively dwarfs and giants, colossi and pygmies; erect, well-made, and well-proportioned, humpbacked, limping, and deformed.' As for the prolixity of some of the articles, emulation among the contributors had the effect of producing dissertations instead of articles. Time and subsequent editions would take care of this. Besides, 'new inventions and new ideas necessarily introducing a disproportion; and the first edition being, of all, the one containing the greatest number of subjects that, if not newly invented, are at least as little known as if they had this characteristic, it is evident . . . that this is the edition in which will reign the most disorder, but which, on the other hand, will exhibit, through all its irregularities, an original air that only with difficulty will pass over into subsequent editions.' [28]

Diderot was not so fatuous as to suppose that the *Encyclopédie* would not be superseded: 'If our dictionary is good, how many works will it produce that are better!' [29] Repeatedly he wrote of the necessity of succeeding editions, as when he said explicitly that 'the first edition of an encyclopedia can be only a very incomplete and formless compilation.' [30] These admissions, as also the one about being either skeletal or dropsical, were promptly seized upon by his enemies, though this self-criticism has enhanced rather than decreased the estimation of the work by impartial critics. Diderot was never in doubt about the project itself, however, and constantly spoke of it in the ringing tones of a man who believes that the spread of knowledge will make mankind happier and better.

Occasionally in this long article Diderot allowed his reader to glimpse some of the editorial problems that had to be contended with: 'I examine our work without partiality; I see that there is perhaps not a single sort of error that we have not committed; and I am forced to admit that of an *Encyclopédie* like ours, scarcely two-thirds of it would be included in a true Encyclopedia. That is a great deal, especially if one acknowledges that in laying the first foundations of such a work, one was forced to take for a basis some inferior author or other, whether Chambers, Alsted, or some other. There is almost no one of our colleagues who could have been persuaded to work, if it had been proposed to him to compose all his assignment from the beginning; each would have been intimidated, and the *Encyclopédie* would not have been done. But by presenting to each one a roll of paper that had only to be re-examined, corrected, expanded, the work of creating, which is always what one dreads, disappeared and each, from a presumption that could not have been more chimerical, allowed himself to engage to do the work; for these disconnected fragments were so incomplete, so badly written, so poorly translated, so full of omissions, errors, and inaccuracies, so contrary to the ideas of our colleagues, that most of them threw them aside. Would that they had all had the same courage! . . . How much time lost in translating inferior things! What expenditures in order to obtain a continual plagiarism!' [31] Elsewhere Diderot remarked on his colleagues' propensity to quote verse, an inclination he discouraged save in articles on literary subjects; on the prolixity of contributors, encouraged, if not justified, by the editors' own; on the difficulty, and yet the importance, of keeping a proper balance; on the impracticability of insisting that the entire manuscript be turned in before the printing was begun, with consequent blunders and omissions in regard to cross references; and on the very particular difficulty of getting accurate information about the arts and crafts.[32] Regarding this last difficulty, he wrote: 'But as the arts have been the principal object of my work, I am going to explain myself candidly, both concerning the mistakes I have made and the precautions that would need to be taken to correct them.

'He who would take upon himself the subject matter of the arts will not acquit himself of his labors in a satisfactory manner either for others or for himself, if he has not profoundly studied natural history, especially mineralogy; if he is not an excellent mechanic; if he is not well versed in theoretical and experimental physics; and if he has not taken several courses in chemistry.'[33]

These rigorous requirements of an editor were more than hypothetical to Diderot for at this very time he was attending the lectures and demonstrations given at the Jardin du Roy by Rouelle, the leading French chemist of his day. For three consecutive years Diderot attended these lectures, and copies of the notes he took are still in existence.[34] In addition, he wrote a very engaging and informative character sketch of this eccentric and single-minded scientist.[35]

Having launched on a discussion of all the qualifications necessary to one hopeful of describing the arts and crafts, Diderot particularly mentions the problem of securing information from craftsmen: 'He [who would correct the articles on the arts] will not be long in perceiving that, in spite of all the care we have taken, there have slipped into the work some gross blunders (see the article *"Brique"*), and that there are whole articles that do not have a shadow of common sense (see the article *"Blanchisserie de toiles"*); but he will learn by his own experience to thank us for the things done well and pardon us for those done ill. Especially will he learn, after having for some time gone from workshop to workshop with cash in his hand and after having paid dearly for the most preposterous misinformation, what sort of people craftsmen are, especially those at Paris, where the fear of taxes makes them perpetually suspicious, and where they look upon any person who interrogates them with any curiosity as an emissary of the tax farmers, or as a worker who wants to open shop.'[36]

It was in this article that subscribers were first told about the engravings that were to illustrate the work, none having yet been published. Diderot announced that 'we have about a thousand plates.' The account book of the publishers shows that there had indeed been much activity in this department, with disbursements beginning in 1748. In 1751, very frequent and substantial payments began, especially to a man named Goussier, who ultimately did the drawings for more than nine hundred of the finished plates.[37] Moreover, they were superior ones. 'In spite of the prodigious number of figures that fill them, we have paid attention to admitting scarcely any that do not represent a machine now in existence and working. Let our volumes be compared with the collection of Ramelli [1588] which is praised so highly, the *Theatrum machinarum* [1724-7] of Leupold, or even the volumes of machines approved by the Académie des Sciences, and then one can judge whether, of all these volumes put together, it would be possible to take twenty plates from them worthy of inclusion in such a collection as we have had the courage to conceive and the good fortune to execute. There is nothing here that is superfluous or superannuated or imaginary: everything in it is in action and alive.'[38]

This was the first occasion — but not the last — when the engravings done for the *Encyclopédie* and those for the Royal Academy of Sciences were contrasted and compared. In 1675 Colbert, the great minister of Louis XIV, had requested the Royal Academy to publish a series of illustrations and explanations concerning the machines used in the arts and crafts.[39] The preparation of these drawings and engravings continued sporadically and dilatorily for decades, with Réaumur more responsible for them than anyone else; and the result was that the *Encyclopédie* was announced and its publication far advanced before the Academy of Sciences, under the spur of competition, finally published its first fascicle, that on 'Charcoal Burning,' in 1761.

Meanwhile Diderot and the publishers of the *Encyclopédie* had procured for their examination and comparison copies of a good many of the various Academy prints that had been engraved but not yet published. Diderot says as much in the passage just quoted, and it is unlikely that he would have called attention to this proceeding, and in so public a way, if he had supposed that there was anything dishonest about it.[40] Réaumur, however, evidently regarded it so and said as much to Formey who, about this time, was toying with the idea of editing an encyclopedia himself.[41] Apparently he had written to Réaumur inquiring about engravings, for the latter replied on 23 February 1756, 'I have had more than a hundred and fifty plates engraved in folio size, they being very pleasing pictures, and I have many others that are only drawings. I could have made the whole literary world resound with my cries over the theft that has been done me of the first-named and taken steps to have justice done. The infidelity and negligence of my engravers, of whom several are dead, have made it easy for people with little delicacy regarding their methods to collect proofs of these plates, and they have been engraved anew in order to insert them in the encyclo-pedical Dictionary. I have learned somewhat tardily that the fruits of so many years of labor have been taken away from me. I have preferred to appear to be ignorant of it than to trouble my repose by reclaiming my property.' The only other time he had ever discussed the matter, Réaumur went on to say, was in a letter to his friend the German metaphysician Christian Wolff, now dead two years.[42]

It is hard to pronounce upon the amount of moral turpitude involved in this incident. If Réaumur was convinced that a serious theft had occurred, how does it happen that he regarded it as a matter that concerned only himself and not the Academy of Sciences? Moreover, he writes to foreign scholars about it, but evidently takes care not to say anything about it in France, alleging a desire to keep his peace of mind. But if a theft had really occurred, it would certainly seem that an investigation was in order. Indeed, this was precisely what the publishers of the *Encyclopédie* demanded at once when the allegation of theft and plagiarism was made public in 1759, two years after Réaumur's death. As a result, the official commission of the Academy of Sciences testified that 'we have recognized nothing' in the *Encyclopédie* prints 'that was copied after the plates of M. de Réaumur.'[43] There is no question that Diderot and his publishers had had in their possession some of the Academy of Science proofs, depriving Diderot of the right to claim credit for originating plans for the attractive drawings in perspective illustrating the processes in each art or craft. Both works used this device, and the Academy of Sciences can clearly claim priority. But unless there was intent to defraud, there could be no moral turpitude in possessing some of the proofs of a languishing enterprise that had been begun seventy-five years previously and had not even yet made any announcement of intending publication.[44]

Diderot's discussion of the *Encyclopédie*'s cross-reference system in his article 'Encyclopedia' is amazingly frank. He explained at great length the organic relationship of subjects that the editors hoped to accomplish by the skillful use of cross references and, surprisingly enough, he described with complete candor the ideological purpose of the *Encyclopédie*'s system. For cross references can be used, he wrote, to contrast conflicting principles and to overthrow ridiculous opinions that cannot be frontally attacked. 'The entire work would receive [from such cross references] an internal force and secret utility, the noiseless effects of which would necessarily become perceptible with time. For example, every time a national prejudice requires respect, it should respectfully be set forth, at the appropriate place, with all its accompaniments of verisimilitude and seduction; but the edifice of mud ought to be overthrown, the useless accumulation of dust be dissipated, by referring to articles where solid principles serve as a basis for opposing truths. This manner of disabusing men operates very quickly upon good understandings; and it operates infallibly on every mind and without disagreeable consequences, secretly and without creating a sensation. It is the art of tacitly deducing the most radical conclusions. If these cross references of confirmation or refutation are foreseen far ahead of time and prepared with skill, they will give to an encyclopedia the character that a good dictionary ought to have, namely the character of changing the general way of thinking.' [45]

It seems clear that Diderot had France's established religion in mind when he referred to 'a national prejudice.' His revelation of the uses to which his cross references were put not unnaturally had repercussions. It was made the subject of a considerable amount of animadversion, as was also an incidental remark of his that caused the Archbishop of Paris to write in protest to Malesherbes. 'I join to my letter,' wrote Christophe de Beaumont, 'a note of what is to be read in the fifth volume of the encyclopedic dictionary, page 635 at the word "Encyclopedia." You will see that the Sorbonne is therein spoken of in a very indecent manner by asserting that it could furnish to the *Encyclopédie* only theology, sacred history, and *superstitions*. To regard the science of religion as a source of superstition is to attack religion itself. It is very regrettable that the censors did not notice an error like this, and I hope that you will have no objection to giving the necessary orders so that it may be corrected or at least amends be made.' [46] Amends of a sort *were* made. The list of errata in Volume VI declared that the passage, which 'contrary to our intention some persons have found ambiguous,' should read 'theology, sacred history, and the history of superstitions.' Diderot's explanation, which in reality rendered his original motives more inscrutable than ever, did not reveal a high degree of penitence.

Of course when Diderot allowed himself to speak this way about the Sorbonne, he was thinking of the troubles involving the Abbé de Prades. This is but one instance of his using the article 'Encyclopedia' as a vehicle for the expression of his animosities, his likes, and his personal ambitions. He begins and ends his long article by sneering at the Jesuits and their *Dictionnaire de Trévoux;* he asserts aggressively that 'among those who have set themselves up for censors of the *Encyclopédie,* there is scarcely one with the talent necessary for enriching it with one good article'; he scolds the French Academy for not finishing its dictionary and then broadly hints that he would be capable of doing so himself if he were a member; he breaks forth in praise of a personal friend — 'O Rousseau! my dear and worthy friend'; he boasts of having taught his fellow citizens to esteem and read Francis Bacon; he apologizes for himself, managing to praise himself at the same time, and betrays his true opinion of himself, one feels quite sure, as he defines his conception of the ideal editor for a work of this sort. 'A man endowed with great good sense, celebrated by the breadth of his knowledge, the elevation of his feelings and conceptions, and his love for work; a man loved and respected both for his private and his public character; never a frenzied enthusiast, save for truth, virtue, and humanity.'[47]

Truth, virtue, and humanity! Shining words. In their names Diderot led the assault upon minds apprehensive of change and defended himself from the allegations that he was subversive and unvirtuous. Diderot's enemies, and the enemies of the *philosophes* in general, constantly maintained that religious orthodoxy and right conduct were inseparable, and that one could not truly have the one without the other. This Diderot, believing as he did, emphatically denied, and he was always at pains to insist that to be a *philosophe* was necessarily to be virtuous. He never tired of asserting his probity and proclaiming his virtue, or of calling himself a good man, an *homme de bien*. Partly, perhaps mostly, it was because he was convinced of it; partly it was to combat the narrow-mindedness of those who would like everyone to believe that an unorthodox man must necessarily be a vicious one.

The moral note is struck more than once in Diderot's article 'Encyclopedia.' He speaks of 'inspiring the taste for knowledge, the horror of lying and of vice, and the love of virtue; for whatever has not happiness and virtue for its ultimate end is nothing,' and later on he remarks that 'it is at least as important to make men better as to make them less ignorant.'[48] There is in Diderot's manner of thinking a constant relating of truth to man and the ends of man. Truth not only exists of itself: it becomes usable only when humanly apperceived. This pronounced humanism in Diderot's thought — so pronounced that it has appropriately given the title *L'Humanisme de Diderot* to one of the best critical works concerning him — is well expressed by a passage in the article 'Encyclopedia': 'A consideration that above all must not be lost from view is that if man, or the thinking and contemplative being, is banished from the surface of the earth, this pathetic and sublime spectacle of nature becomes nothing but a mute and melancholy scene. . . . Why not [therefore] introduce man in our work as he is placed in the universe? Why not make of him a common center? . . . Man is the sole and only limit whence one must start and back to whom everything must return, if one wishes to please, interest, touch, even in the most arid considerations and the driest details. Setting aside my own existence and the happiness of my fellow beings, what does the rest of nature matter to me?'[49]

This insistence that knowledge to be meaningful must be related to man made of Diderot something more than a scientist — some people might say it made him less than one. But Diderot's humanism explains why he is so interested in ethics, why the search for the bases of moral sanction has for him so great a fascination. The ideal of the *philosophe*, as Diderot accepted it for his *Encyclopédie* article 'Philosopher,' was humanistic and social, the ideal of a thinker interested in his fellow man. Now, because this ideal was so humanistic and social — and so little religious or theological — Diderot time and again appealed for his ultimate justification to the unprejudiced judgment of his peers. And since contemporaries are likely to be prejudiced, Diderot turned to posterity for the comforting sense of ultimate justification. Thus, after describing all the difficulties attendant upon completing an encyclopedia, he writes: 'We have seen that the *Encyclopédie* could be the effort of only a philosophical century; that this century has arrived; that renown, while carrying to immortality the names of those who will finish it, will perhaps not disdain to take care of ours; and we have felt ourselves reanimated by an idea so consoling and so sweet, that we too shall be spoken of when we shall no longer exist; [reanimated] by this captivating murmur which gives us to understand, from the lips of some of our contemporaries, what shall be said about us by men to whose instruction and happiness we have sacrificed ourselves, whom we have esteemed and loved although they are not yet born.' [50]

Posterity shall judge, wrote Diderot.[51] For posterity, in Diderot's eyes, was the supreme court.

CHAPTER 19

Growing Tension with Rousseau:
'Only the Bad Man Lives Alone'

D IDEROT was a man expansive in temperament and rich in the outpourings of his imagination, sympathy, and sensitivity. Yet he also had a vein of cool and unemotional scientific objectivity which almost always came into play when his metaphysical views were at stake. An example of this capacity to remain detached when others are suffering is shown by his neutral attitude toward the greatest public disaster of the eighteenth century. Many of his contemporaries were saddened, their fondest convictions · undermined, by the earthquake at Lisbon on 1 November 1755 which wiped out the lives of many thousands within a few minutes. The earthquake not only shook Lisbon, it shook Voltaire, who had been living in a rather happy deistic faith. The impassive inscrutability and indiscriminacy of the event caused Voltaire to question shudderingly God's ways to man. To this questioning we owe *Candide*. But it is characteristic of Diderot, with his strictly naturalistic conception of a universe that he thought could be explained without having to predicate God, that the Lisbon earthquake presented him with no intellectual problem whatever.[1]

In the following year Frederick the Great precipitated the Seven Years' War by his incursion into Saxony. This was the war that saw the exploits of Montcalm and Wolfe in Canada and of Clive in India, a war which permanently affected the political destinies of a considerable fraction of mankind. This was the year of the Diplomatic Revolution, when France, since the days of Cardinal Richelieu the archenemy of the Hapsburgs, reversed her alliance system and became the ally of Maria-Theresa. It was the beginning of a war in which the luster of French arms at first was brightened by the capture of Port Mahon, only to be tarnished by the humiliation of Rossbach; a war in which the monarchy of Louis XV and Madame de Pompadour frittered away the substance of colonial and maritime power in exchange for some vague dream of Continental hegemony. The prestige and the finances of France suffered grievously in the Seven Years' War, and it may be accounted one of the predisposing causes for the later alliance with the infant United States, for instance, as well as for the Revolution of 1789 itself. Militarily and intellectually, the decade of the 'fifties was the decisive one in the history of France in the eighteenth century.

It is surprising to find Diderot scarcely aware of the Seven Years' War or its implications. He, a leader in one of the two great changes occurring in the life of his time, was oddly insensitive to the other. Save for the incident in his *Fils naturel* of the capture and imprisonment of Rosalie's father by the British plus a reference in his *Père de famille* to an episode in the Port Mahon campaign, neither Diderot's writings nor his letters refer to the war. It seems to have affected him only in regard to Grimm, who was attached to the staff of a French marshal for a few months in 1757 on campaign in Westphalia.[2] During these years of 1756-63 we shall hear much of Diderot's tribulations, for this was the time of his greatest trials and, in view of his spirited conduct in the face of great adversity, his nearest approach to heroism. And as if his personal life had absorbed all his energies, he lived through these years as though buffeted by everything except the war itself.

Diderot's correspondence in 1756 shows him now and again in that mood of heated and self-righteous expostulation that he easily fell into, and there is a note of distinct acerbity and irritability in his relations with people at this time that may be a symptom of overwork or a consequence of lingering ill health. One of these occasions had to do with a lawsuit over the appointment to a priory in which his younger brother, the Abbé, had become involved. Mme de Vandeul says that her father put himself to incredible trouble in accommodating this matter, and we see Diderot working on it in a couple of letters written to his litigious and unconciliatory brother. Of the Abbé's opponent Diderot wrote, 'I believe M. le Chevalier a very honest man, even though he be a good Christian'! And a few days later, washing his hands of the affair, Diderot wrote, 'You have written me the letter of a litigant and a fanatic. If these are the two qualities that are conferred upon you by your religion, I am very content with mine, and I hope not to change it.'[3] No doubt the Abbé Diderot was a very difficult person, but letters like this were scarcely calculated to sweeten the temper.

Another of these expostulatory outbursts occurred in a long letter written by Diderot in the summer of 1756 to a contributor to the *Encyclopédie*, probably Paul Landois.[4] Landois was an obscure writer of whom very little is known save that he wrote a one-act tragedy in 1742, *Sylvie* by name, which was in prose and dealt with the affairs of run-of-the-mill humanity, not personages of exalted rank. This tragedy, with its one act, its ordinary people, its prose, and its explicit stage directions, flouted so many of the established traditions of the French theater that it deserves remembering as an early exemplar of the reforms that Diderot expounded fifteen years later. In 1756 Landois, who contributed a few unimportant articles concerning painting for the *Encyclopédie*, was evidently seven to eight days' post-time away from Paris and fuming at not being paid so promptly as he wished. It is clear from the nature of Diderot's letter that Landois was an extremely temperamental man much given to supposing that he was greatly put upon. In order to correct this impression, Diderot wrote him at great length, attacking the problem on three successive levels. The first was Diderot's personal disclaimer of guilt; the second was a discussion of Landois' way of comporting himself, viewed in the light of conventional morality; the third was a discussion of Landois' behavior from the point of view of philosophy. Inasmuch as this letter provides what appears to be a clear-cut statement of Diderot's views on ethics, it is frequently and extensively quoted.

On the first level Diderot proceeds upon the theory that the best defense is a strong offense. 'Now, let's come to the business of your manuscript. It is a work capable of ruining me. After having charged me twice with the most atrocious and most deliberate outrages, you propose to me the revision and printing of it. . . . You take me for an imbecile or you are one yourself. . . .'

Having generated a sufficient amount of heat, Diderot passes to the second level of the argument by reproaching Landois for his 'detestable morality,' and then, describing his own code of ethics: 'I find in myself an equal repugnance to wrong reasoning and wrong doing. I am between two forces, one of which shows me the good and the other inclines me toward evil. One must choose. At the beginning the moment of struggle is grievous, but the intensity of it weakens with time. There comes a time when the sacrifice of one's passion no longer costs a pang. I can even certify from experience that it is pleasant: one takes on in one's own eyes so much stature and dignity! Virtue is a mistress to whom one is attached as much by what one does for her as by the charms one believes her to possess. Woe to you if the practice of doing good is not sufficiently familiar to you, and if you have not accumulated a sufficient stock of good actions to be vain of them, to compliment yourself about them ceaselessly, to intoxicate yourself with this heady vapor and be fanatical about it.

'"We take virtue," you say, "the way a sick man takes medicine," to which, if he were well, he would prefer any other thing that would please his appetite. That is true of a sick man out of his senses: but in spite of that, if this sick man had had the merit of diagnosing his malady himself, of having discovered and prepared the medicine for it, do you think he would hesitate in taking it, however bitter it was, or that he would not compliment himself for his acumen and courage? What is a virtuous man? It is a man vain with this sort of vanity, and nothing more. . . .' This is an unusual definition of a virtuous man, and might be considered an extraordinarily 'debunking' one. But Diderot suggests that nevertheless Landois weigh the advantages such people gain for themselves, and especially what disadvantages they avoid. Thus Diderot argues that virtue is the pursuit of happiness, a kind of utilitarianism in which pleasure is strongly compounded of the esteem that others express for one as well as the esteem of oneself: 'But if ever you undertake [this calculation], do not forget to estimate for all that they are worth the esteem of others and that of oneself. Moreover, do not forget that a bad action never goes unpunished. I say never, because the first one that one commits inclines one to a second, that one to a third, and thus one advances step by step toward being held in contempt by one's fellow men, the greatest of all evils.'

Diderot now comes to the third level of his argument. His object is to cure Landois of supposing 'that the whole of nature conspires against you, that chance has heaped up all the kinds of misfortune in order to pour them on your head. Where the devil did you get such pride? My dear fellow, you prize yourself too highly, you grant yourself too much importance in the universe.' In order to disabuse Landois of so much pride, Diderot says of himself that he must 'leave off the tone of the preacher to take up, if I can, that of the philosopher.' For now comes a discussion of the relationship between morality and determinism. Diderot believed that effect follows cause so inexorably in the training and experience of the human being that 'liberty' is a meaningless word. The context would seem to indicate that he uses the word 'liberty' in the sense of 'unpredictability' or 'caprice.' At all events, this important passage is as follows: 'Look at the matter closely and you will see that the word "liberty" is a word devoid of sense; that there are not, and cannot be, free beings; that we are only what is in consonance with the general order, with our organization, education, and the chain of events. That is what disposes of us invincibly. One can no more conceive of a being acting without motive than one can of the arm of a scales acting without the action of a weight, and the motive is always external to us, foreign to us, brought on by some nature or some cause that is not we ourselves. What misleads us is the prodigious variety of our actions, joined with the habit we contracted as soon as we were born of confusing the voluntary with the free. . . .'

It will be noticed that Diderot is expressing a theory of ethics that includes both heredity and environment: in his words, organization and education. Moreover, he recognizes that human beings have wills and exercise them, but he denies that human beings can exercise their wills capriciously and without relation to the totality of cause and effect in their previous experience. This is a conception of man's moral nature as full of 'horse sense' as of philosophy. Diderot conceives of ethics as a scientific matter, effect inexorably related to cause. By such determinism he conceives of human conduct in a fashion that avoids the uncertainty and the insecurity of a theory of moral indeterminism in which anything can happen, even the most chaotic, the most unlikely, or the most unpredictable.[5] 'A wholly free will in a finite world is a fair definition of insanity,' writes a modern author.[6] The point was, according to Diderot, that Landois could not suddenly 'cease at will to be evil. After having made oneself bad, is being good merely a matter of removing oneself a hundred leagues, or of saying to oneself, I want to be? The crease is set, and the cloth has to keep it.'

Far from feeling that nothing can be done in the moral training of human beings, Diderot emphasizes that 'although the beneficent or the maleficent man is not free, man is none the less a modifiable being. It is for this reason that the maleficent man should be destroyed at a place of public execution. From this fact [of his being modifiable, derive] the good effects of example, precepts, education, pleasure, pain, grandeur, poverty, etc.; from this fact, a sort of philosophy full of commiseration, attaching one strongly to good persons, but irritating one against a bad one no more than against a hurricane that fills our eyes with dust.'

Diderot is here describing a system of morality that operates independently of the hope for reward or the fear of punishment in another world. Perhaps it is the positive and this-worldly aspect of his doctrine that causes him to avoid relying upon the ordinary criteria of 'virtue' and 'vice': 'But if there is no liberty, there is no action meriting praise or blame, no vice nor virtue, nothing that must be recompensed or chastised. What then distinguishes men? Doing good and doing evil. The evildoer is a man to be destroyed, not punished. Beneficence is a good fortune, not a virtue.'

This way of stating moral doctrine seems harsh and forbidding, and in consequence the letter to Landois is very often cited as proving that Diderot's ethics had a hard, machinelike character, divesting human life of choice. But if one judges moral conduct from the point of view of *results* instead of from the point of view of *intention,* then Diderot's doctrine does not seem nearly so strange. His emphasis is then seen as one of social utility.[7] Good conduct, according to such a view, depends upon doing, upon the concrete and positive results of moral action. But man still remains a modifiable being capable of exercising choice. Diderot proves that he believes this by saying in the next few lines of the letter, 'Adopt these principles if you find them good, or show me that they are defective. If you adopt them, they will reconcile you with others and with yourself.'

While Diderot was engaged in this troublesome quarrel with Landois, his relations with other friends were also suffering deterioration. Probably there was some sort of quarrel with Condillac, to judge by Grimm's sudden and venomous attack after having praised Diderot's former friend only a little previously. Diderot and Condillac had not been intimate for some years and were now far removed from the days of the dinners at the Panier Fleuri. Their relations were further chilled, about this time, because Diderot felt that Condillac had pilfered from the *Letter on the Deaf and Dumb* (1751) one of the main ideas for his *Treatise on Sensations,* which appeared three years later.[8]

Coincident with this turbulence in Diderot's relations with his friends was, it seems, a delay in the publication of the sixth volume of the *Encyclopédie.* For although Grimm remarked in his news letter of 1 May 1756 that the volume had just been published, a friend wrote to Rousseau from Paris on 23 September that it had not yet appeared.[9] Diderot himself speaks of being in the country seeking rest and health after having completed the sixth volume, and the same correspondent of Rousseau dates this *villeggiatura* exactly by writing on 16 September that Diderot had just returned to Paris from a three-weeks' visit at the country house of Le Breton, his publisher.[10] This delay in publication, if delay there was, may have contributed to Diderot's apparent irritability of that year, although the tardiness may have been caused by Diderot's lingering ill health. Le Breton carried him away from Paris for a vacation; yet even after that Diderot suffered a very bad attack of 'colic,' which he attributed to his injudiciously discontinuing his diet of milk.[11]

When Volume VI finally appeared it was the least controversial of all the early volumes of the *Encyclopédie* and seems to have pleased everyone but Voltaire. The volume contained important articles by Turgot on 'Etymology,' 'Expansibility,' and 'Existence,' the latter a masterly exposition of the intellectual presuppositions shared by most of the Encyclopedists. Then there were articles on 'Evidence,' 'Fêtes,' 'Fireworks,' 'Fiefs,' 'Fevers,' 'Finances,' 'Fluid,' 'Flute,' and so on, the usual sort of intake of a work that called itself a methodical dictionary of the sciences, arts, and crafts. Especially noteworthy was Quesnay's long article on 'Farmers' (*Fermiers*), an article that has recently been called by a Marxist writer 'the origin of the whole physiocratic doctrine' because it analyzes 'the role of capital in production.' [12] Diderot's share as a contributor of articles was distinctly less in this than in the other volumes, a circumstance which may have been owing to his ill health. Voltaire contributed fifteen articles and, in direct proportion to his becoming more closely identified with the work, grew correspondingly concerned about its all too patent unevenness.

Voltaire had not originally been a subscriber to the *Encyclopédie*, so that he praised it, to begin with, more on hearsay than on firsthand knowledge.[13] He liked to refer to Diderot and D'Alembert as 'Atlas and Hercules, carrying the world on your shoulders.' [14] The *Encyclopédie* was 'the greatest and finest monument of the nation and of literature'; he adjured D'Alembert to hasten to 'finish the greatest work in the world.' [15] Symbolic of their growing association was D'Alembert's visit to Voltaire during the summer of the year in which Volume VI was published. It was during this very successful stay that Voltaire suggested D'Alembert write an article on 'Geneva,' an article which was to cause much trouble when it was published in Volume VII.[16] After D'Alembert's return to Paris, Voltaire's letters became much more frank than they had previously been. 'What I am told about the articles on theology and metaphysics wrings my heart. It is grievous to print the contrary of what one thinks.

'I am also sorry that people write dissertations and give private opinions for established truths. I should like definition and the origin of the word, with examples, everywhere.' [17]

A month later Voltaire professed himself unable to believe that in so serious a work the following sentence had appeared in an article on '*Femme*': 'Chloe presses her knee against one beau while rumpling the lace of another.' What the writer, a man named Desmahis, had really said about Chloe was not much better: 'she presses her knee against one, squeezes the hand of another while praising his lace, and at the same time tosses off some suitable words to a third.' Voltaire remarked of this article that it must have been written by the lackey of Gil Blas.[18] To this D'Alembert replied by a personal exculpation — 'these articles are not in my bailiwick' — and added, 'Besides, I owe my colleague the justice of saying that he is not always in a position to reject or condense the articles presented to him.'[19] This particular aspect of the correspondence was then brought to an end by Voltaire's very sensibly inquiring, 'Why have you not recommended a sort of instruction sheet for those who serve you, etymologies, definitions, examples, reason, clarity, and brevity?'[20]

During 1756 the friendship of Diderot and Rousseau moved into a penumbra that was close to eclipse. Even the play that Diderot was writing that autumn, his *Fils naturel* ('The Natural Son'), was destined to figure in this melancholy tale. The story of their friendship's end is tangled and complicated, hot with the passion of their clashing certainties of being in the right, mournful in the slow and inexorable ruin of their delight in each other. There is something epic and something symbolic in the confused, nightmarish deliquescence of their friendship, epic because of the intensity and vividness of the personalities of these two men, and epic, too, because of their articulateness. Symbolic it was in that the differences dividing them, although they did not realize it, were ideological. Rousseau was the precursor of Robespierre, Diderot of Danton, and a generation later one sent the other to the guillotine. The personal and temperamental irritations occurring during 1756–8 were exacerbated by profound and little-understood discrepancies in their outlook on life. These twisted their judgments and are likely to twist the judgments of their biographers, too, for it is almost impossible to watch the wavering scales of justice and refrain from jumping into one of the pans. Temperament and circumstance combine so momentously that detached judgment becomes difficult. We tend to be Rousseau-men or Diderot-men, just as we tend to be Hamilton-men or Jefferson-men, Erasmus-men or Luther-men, Caesar-men or Cicero-men.

Rousseau always claimed that the revelation that came to him on the road to Vincennes in 1749 marked the turning point of his life. This was the revelation, glowing within him with the incandescence of a truth believed self-evident, that man's fate had become worse as his life had grown more sophisticated and more complex. It was a revelation such as might conceivably come to a young man reared in puritanical simplicity on the shores, say, of Lake Tahoe, who comes to the metropolis to make his mark and lives precariously there, never quite at home and a success, never quite beaten and a failure, never quite sure enough of himself to be openly censorious of the life about him. The revelation of 1749 gave Rousseau the courage of his previously unasserted convictions. He still was sensitive, over-serious, and humorless. But these temperamental qualities now focused on what seemed to him the artificiality and conventionality of Parisian life. His friends could scarcely fail to notice his discontent. Their mistake was to suppose it merely superficial or even insincere.

It was not just with Paris that Rousseau was discontented. His friends, or most of them, galled him. He resented Diderot's unsolicited advice about accepting the King's pension; he suspected D'Holbach of trying to make people believe that Rousseau had plagiarized the music for the *Village Soothsayer;* he disliked the *philosophes'* baiting of the Abbé Petit, the man who had the theory of how to write a play in five acts; and he particularly abominated, as his preface to his play *Narcisse* shows so well, the anti-religious 'philosophy' of his own circle of friends. When, therefore, the wealthy Mme d'Epinay, a lady whom he had known since 1747, offered him the occupancy of the Hermitage, a spacious and specially remodeled cottage on her estate near Montmorency, ten miles to the north of Paris, Rousseau allowed himself to be persuaded to get away from it all.[21] His friends, regarding his decision as a ludicrous whim, loudly predicted that he could not endure it a fortnight. 'Sarcasms fell on me like hail,' Rousseau later recalled in his *Confessions.* On 9 April 1756, he began living at the Hermitage, vowing never to live in cities again.

There is no doubt that Rousseau's friends were disconcerted by his leaving Paris, and even more so by his remaining away. Life away from Paris hardly seemed worth living to that intensely sociable age, especially if compounded by solitude. Paris and, for courtiers, Versailles seemed to most persons who had lived in them the only really habitable places in France. This feeling is reflected in the word the eighteenth century used when the king deprived a minister of his office and commanded him to live upon his country estate until further orders. The eighteenth century always said that a minister in such circumstances was 'exiled,' as if living in a country house or château were equivalent to being banished to the ends of the earth. Rousseau's self-exile, as the D'Holbach circle thought of it, might be construed as a standing reproach to them, and was therefore a constant and subtle irritation. If he was wise, they were foolish. Moreover, if his exile was virtue, then it cast doubt on their mode of life. This they found intolerable, so that Diderot put into the mouth of one of the characters in his *Fils naturel* this extremely barbed and personal allusion: 'I appeal to your heart: ask it, and it will tell you that the good man lives in society, and only the bad man lives alone.'[22]

Rousseau, for his part, discovered more disillusionments in his new phase

of life than he had anticipated. In the first place, he expected Diderot to come
to the Hermitage regularly, a necessarily one-sided arrangement since Rousseau had renounced Paris.[23] In this expectation he was frequently disappointed. In the second place, he found that whenever his benefactress was in
residence at the big house, La Chevrette, his time was not his own. But
worse than that was the fact that he had no domestic tranquillity. He had
brought from Paris not only Thérèse Levasseur but also her aged mother.
The old woman played off her daughter against Rousseau, and poor Thérèse,
who had too little mind to be able to call what she had her own, was
completely under her mother's domination. Rousseau discovered, with exasperation and bepuzzlement, that nothing he did won Mme Levasseur's
loyalty or even her good will. She treated Rousseau with the cunning and
craftiness of a peasant outwitting the lord of the manor, and Rousseau
must often have felt like the well-intentioned Nekhlyudov in Tolstoy's *A
Landlord's Morning*. Added to this was the fact that Mme Levasseur, during
the days back in Paris, had negotiated mysteriously with Grimm and Diderot.
Rousseau now discovered this from Thérèse, but he could not fathom the
purpose of this secretive conduct.

After Rousseau's lively imagination had mulled over the information that
Grimm and Diderot had been in secret communication with Mme Levasseur,
he was quite ready to believe that a sinister conspiracy was afoot against
him. This conclusion probably strengthened his determination to remain
at the Hermitage through the winter. The grave illness of an old friend,
Gauffecourt, called him to Paris on two separate occasions, the first in late
December 1756 and the second for a two-week period the following January,
during which time he dined at Mme d'Epinay's and lodged at Diderot's.[24]
Indeed it was at this sickbed that Diderot first met Mme d'Epinay, a woman
whose acquaintance he had always refused to make in spite of her close
friendship with Rousseau and of her having become Grimm's mistress.[25]
In fact, Diderot had attempted to prevent the liaison. Having received a very
prejudicial view of the lady's character from a former suitor, Diderot had a
protracted interview with Grimm, during the course of which he claimed
to have asked his friend impatiently, 'That is to say that you sincerely believe that Mme d'Epinay is neither false nor a coquette nor a whore?' He
left the interview convinced that his informant was a rascal but still un-
persuaded that Mme d'Epinay was as virtuous as Grimm thought.[26] This
conversation had taken place about two years before the illness that brought
all Gauffecourt's friends, including the hermit from the Hermitage, to his
bedside. Mme d'Epinay had meanwhile become Grimm's mistress, but

Diderot remained distant. Now, however, a train of circumstances had begun that, as Rousseau saw it, ended by arraying all his friends, Diderot and Mme d'Epinay no less than Grimm, in a sort of conspiracy against him.

Rousseau left Gauffecourt and returned to the Hermitage just before the publication of Diderot's *Fils naturel*. It was not long before he came across the line 'only the bad man lives alone,' and accordingly he wrote Diderot — this particular letter is not extant — what in his succeeding letter he described as 'the tenderest and most candid letter I ever wrote in my life, complaining, with all the gentleness of friendship, of a very ambiguous maxim from which a most injurious application could be made to me.'[27] Diderot's answer was very nonchalant. Moreover, it was bantering in tone. But Rousseau was never of the temperament to bear either banter or nonchalance gladly, and least of all was he in the mood to do so now. The emotional crisis into which he was thrown by Diderot's letters at this juncture may be seen clearly in his letters to Mme d'Epinay, as well as in her efforts to soothe him in reply.[28]

Rousseau, who had made it a matter of principle not to go to Paris and who repeatedly declared to Mme d'Epinay at this time that he would never in his life go there again,[29] suggested that Diderot come to Montmorency to see him in order to clear up the point about the solitary man's being evil. Diderot wrote: 'You can very well see, my dear fellow, that because of the weather it is not possible to go to find you, whatever the desire and even the need that I have of doing so. . . . Do you know what you ought to do? Come here and stay a couple of days incognito. I would go Saturday to pick you up at Saint-Denis and from there we would go to Paris in the same cab that brought me.' Diderot finally gets around to discussing the line in the *Fils naturel* that had wounded Rousseau, but his reference to it is very airy, and compounded with chaffing remarks, especially in regard to Mme Levasseur: 'I am glad that my work pleased you and touched you [it certainly did, and on a very sore spot]. You are not of my opinion regarding hermits. Say as much good of them as you please, you yourself will be the only one in the world of whom I shall think such good things, and even then there would be something to say on that point if one could speak to you without angering you. A woman eighty years old! . . . Adieu, citizen! And yet, a hermit is a very singular citizen.'[30] It will be noticed that Diderot by no means claims that the offending line to which Rousseau took exception had been unintentional or inadvertent.

Rousseau said of this letter that it had pierced his soul.[31] His reply is not extant, but one can be sure that it made no attempt to disguise his feelings, and it very evidently was successful in annoying its recipient. 'What-soever pain my letter gave you,' wrote Diderot, 'I do not repent of having written it: you were too pleased with your reply.' Rousseau having refused to come to Paris, Diderot announced, not very good-humoredly, his in-tention of going to Montmorency. 'Very well, then, Saturday morning I leave for the Hermitage, whatever the weather. I shall go on foot. My engagements have not permitted me to go sooner, my fortune does not permit me to go there any other way. . . .' This letter, too, made much ado about Mme Levasseur, ending, 'Live, my friend, live, and do not fear lest she die of hunger.' [32]

The letter so infuriated Rousseau — he told Diderot that it was abominable — that he wrote to Mme d'Epinay that he now devoutly hoped that Diderot would not come. 'But I ought to be reassured [that he won't]. He has promised that he will.' [33] This remark is in allusion to the many times, according to Rousseau, that Diderot made appointments and then failed to keep them. This time, however, it was Mme d'Epinay who kept the friends from meeting by sending word that Rousseau would come to Paris instead. When he did not appear, Diderot wrote a third letter which is bright with his usual conviction of having done no wrong:

Once for all, ask yourself: Who took part in looking after my health when I was sick? Who supported me when I was attacked? Who was it who took an eager interest in my glory? Who rejoiced over my successes? Reply sincerely, and recog-nize those who love you. . . . Oh, Rousseau! you are becoming spiteful, unjust, cruel, ferocious, and I weep with sorrow. A nasty quarrel with a man whom I never esteemed and loved as I have you, has caused me affliction and insomnia [evi-dently a reference to Landois]. Guess, then, what pain *you* are causing me. . . . Indicate when you wish it, and I shall hasten to you; but I shall wait until you do.[34]

Rousseau's reply, a few days later, showed how far the mutual misunder-standing had carried. 'Had you intended to irritate me in all this business,' he wrote, 'what could you have done more?' He admitted that he had got Mme d'Epinay to prevent Diderot's coming to the Hermitage: they would only have quarreled. 'Besides, you wanted to come on foot; you risked making yourself sick, and perhaps you would not have been too sorry had you done so. I did not have the courage to incur all the perils of such an interview.' Each accused the other of self-righteousness. 'You constantly appear to be so proud of your conduct in this affair,' wrote Rousseau, and then he cried out, 'Diderot! Diderot! I see it with bitter grief: living unin-terruptedly in the company of spiteful men, you are learning to resemble them. Your good heart is being corrupted by their society, and you are forcing mine, by insensible degrees, to detach itself from you.' [35]

It was a pity that Montmorency was not a good deal farther from Paris. Distance made communication difficult but not impossible, just when mutual distrust was doing the same. As it was, Rousseau was near enough Paris for him to expect to see his friends constantly at the Hermitage. By his reluctance to set foot in the city he forced his friends into a one-sided intercourse whereby they paid the charges both in transportation and time.[36] And this resulted, in the case of a man like Diderot, never one to be very punctilious about his appointments, in broken promises and unfulfilled engagements. In Diderot's defense it might be said that he was an unusually busy man, occupied not only with his editorial duties but also with Rouelle's chemistry lectures and, just at this time, with his play and the complications that it brought in its train. Personal contact was difficult, correspondence generated as much misunderstanding as it did understanding — indeed, where mutual confidence was lacking, it generated more — and, to crown all, Diderot acted, although probably with the very best of intentions, with a singular lack of tact. One has the right to ask Diderot, as Rousseau did, what precisely were his motives in harping upon the fate of Mme Levasseur, and what precisely did he mean by so publicly and so gratuitously remarking that only the evil man lives alone. Candor must reply that, at least so far as documents now extant reveal, Diderot never quite justified himself satisfactorily upon either count.

CHAPTER 20

How To Write a Play: Example and Precept

THE impulse to write plays had come rather suddenly upon Diderot in his early forties. He wrote
two during this period and accompanied each of them with elaborate essays
upon all aspects of the theater, so that, taken together, his views could
scarcely be ignored, however much they might be disparaged. The first
to be published was the *Fils naturel* ('The Natural Son, or Virtue Put to
the Test. A Comedy in Five Acts and in Prose. With the True History of
the Piece'). The 'True History of the Piece,' to use Diderot's fiction, is
better known as the *Entretiens sur le Fils naturel* ('Conversations regarding
the *Fils naturel*') and consists of three dialogues with Dorval, the hero of
the play, in which numerous aspects of acting and dramatic composition
were discussed. Four editions of the *Fils naturel* appeared in the year of its
publication (1757),[1] and in 1758 there followed the *Père de famille* ('The
Father of the Family'), to which was attached the substantial *Discours sur
la poésie dramatique* ('Discourse on Dramatic Poetry'). Though neither
play was produced by the Comédie-Française before it was published — the
Père de famille had its *première* there in 1761 and the *Fils naturel* its
première (which was also its *dernière*) in 1771 — the public nevertheless
became very aware of Diderot as a playwright, whether because of the
intrinsic merit of his ideas or the unflagging efforts of his cabal.

Inasmuch as everyone in Paris who was interested in the theater knew
that Diderot was the author of the *Fils naturel,* it might at first seem odd that
his name did not appear on the title page. No doubt it was some rather
dour remarks, especially those in Act III, regarding heaven and the ways of
its providence, that prevented the work from being published under public
license. Indeed, the fashion in which the play was received by his relatives
at Langres shows that it had a tendentiousness that Malesherbes could not
have dared to endorse by allowing it approbation. On 29 November 1757,

Diderot wrote to his father, 'I am very sorry to have done something that displeases you . . . I beg you to believe that it is impossible for me to be pleased with myself when you are not.' [2] On the very same day he wrote to his brother, 'I learn, my dear brother, that my most recent work has greatly afflicted you. If that is the case, I'd wish I had not written it. . . . Tell me frankly what displeased you.' [3] But the Abbé refused to be drawn into an argument. It was not suitable between brothers, he wrote. Besides, he would just bring down on himself what had happened the last time, 'because the same thing is to be found in your book, and, doubtless being unshaken and constant in your principles, you would give me the same reply, that I am a fanatic, that it is so much the worse for me if I have need of my religion in order to be an honest man, that you do not feel this need, that you are contented with your own, and that you will never change it.' [4]

The *Fils naturel* was probably offered to the Comédie-Française.[5] If so, it must have been a severe disappointment to Diderot that it was rejected. He had to content himself with printing in the list of the dramatis personae the names of the Comédie-Française actors whom he deemed suitable for the various roles. This was an unusual procedure, a little ridiculous, a little pathetic.

The publication of the *Fils naturel* occasioned an uproar. In part, this was simply the result of the collision between people who like experimentation in the arts and people who detest it. The *Fils naturel* was sufficiently novel — in techniques of staging and acting as well as new emphases in character analysis and intellectual content — to make it controversial. This was not because the *Fils naturel* was the first of its kind to exemplify these new ideas in the theater.[6] It was 'tearful comedy,' but so was the theater of Nivelle de la Chaussée, whose plays, scornfully dubbed *'comédie larmoyante,'* had preceded Diderot's by a good fifteen years. Similarly, it was not the first to be written in prose; Landois' *Sylvie* (1742) was not in verse. Moreover, *Sylvie* and Mme de Graffigny's *Cénie* (1750) had both presented seriously and respectfully the virtues and vicissitudes of persons of ordinary social rank, thus deviating from the conventions of the classic French theater. Diderot was, therefore, not so much the first practitioner of what he called the *genre sérieux* as its greatest theoretician.[7] And as such he was cried up and cried down by those who welcome, and those who abominate, the sacrosanct old's being jostled by the irreverent new.

The plays of Diderot were in sober fact revolutionary, not merely in an aesthetic sense but also in a political one. The motivations, the values, the morality, the self-evident truths set forth in the *Fils naturel* and the *Père*

de famille were those of a new social class just beginning to feel its own
power and to respect its own intuitions. There was nothing, to be sure, so
revolutionary in Diderot's plays as there was in *The Marriage of Figaro*,
where Beaumarchais has Figaro say of his master, 'What did you do to
obtain all these benefits?' and then has him answer his own question by
replying, 'You gave yourself the trouble to be born.' The political and social
implications of the new outlook on playwriting, as revealed in Diderot's
pieces, were as yet more obscure than plain, but they were there; and it is
impossible to say anything more cogent about Diderot's plays than to repeat
what Alexis de Tocqueville wrote in *Democracy in America*. 'If you would
judge beforehand,' he remarked, 'of the literature of a people which is
lapsing into democracy, study its dramatic productions. . . . The tastes and
propensities natural to democratic nations, in respect to literature, will therefore first be discernible in the drama, and it may be foreseen that they will
break out there with vehemence.' [8]

In France they did break out with vehemence there. Diderot's notions
regarding the theater would no doubt have aroused controversy in any
event because of the technical innovations they propounded, but the political implications of the plays — as yet dim and obscure — were strangely
disturbing or exhilarating to readers. Moreover, Diderot's views became the
official dogma of an energetic and assertive coterie, resolved to make its
judgments prevail. Mme d'Epinay, probably motivated by the desire to
put Diderot under obligation to her, claimed to have disposed of more than
three hundred copies of the *Fils naturel* within two days of its publication,
a rather large number, which a later editor prudently divided by three.[9]
Grimm told the subscribers to his news letter what to think of the new work
in an ecstatic fashion that suggests his judgment was somewhat biased. The
Fils naturel was a 'work of genius. . . . [a] beautiful and sublime work':
Diderot, if he kept on in this way, was destined to become the absolute
master of the French theater. 'However unfamiliar may be the sort of comedy
in the *Fils naturel, ou les Epreuves de la vertu;* however new may be the
poetics contained in the three *Conversations* that accompany this play,
the enthusiasm of the first few days has been general. All the wits admired
this work, all the tenderhearted and sensitive souls honored it with their
tears. Envy and stupidity have not dared to raise their voices, and the public
has emerged from this bit of reading better and more enlightened than it
was.' [10] Even the hostile *Année Littéraire*, still edited by the formidable
Fréron, cheerfully though belatedly admitted — with the usual adversative
'but,' the usual sting in its tail — that the *Fils naturel* had caused a stir. 'I

cannot express with what warmth the public received this comedy . . . Let it suffice for you to know that this drama was for some time the subject of all the reading, of all the conversations, and of almost all the praise of Paris. Nothing is said of it today.' [11]

Critics of Diderot contended that the success of the *Fils naturel* was achieved by the art of puffery. This was the claim of the Encyclopedists' most dangerous antagonist, Charles Palissot. In a pamphlet entitled *Little Letters on Great Philosophers,* he focused his attention for some forty pages on the *Fils naturel.* 'Hitch yourselves to the chariot of the new Philosophy,' he advised obscure authors, '. . . make passers-by confess that the *Fils naturel* is a masterpiece, a marvel, a discovery more precious to the world of letters than that of America to Europe; and there you are, celebrated, immortal, and perhaps some day members of the Academy.' [12] Privately many must have felt what the poet and dramatist Collé confided to his journal: that the Encyclopedists 'ought to let themselves be praised by others, and not give themselves the trouble of taking care of it themselves, as they do every minute.' [13]

Just at the time that pamphleteers and editors were preparing to attack the *Fils naturel,* Malesherbes used his authority to protect it. So titanic was the struggle against the dead weight of all the elements of society opposed to change and hostile to reform that Malesherbes often tended to throw the weight of his authority on the side of the *philosophes* in order to equalize the contest. For instance, in 1756 he had written to the man appointed to be censor of Fréron's *Année Littéraire* and, after remarking that the authors of the *Encyclopédie* were quite justified in their annoyance at one of Fréron's quotations in which the *Encyclopédie* was referred to as 'scandalous' and the author of one of its articles as 'seditious,' he inquired how it was that the censor had let it pass.[14] The censor, Trublet, replied with some animation: 'It is true that Fréron has frequently desired to attack the *Encyclopédie* and its editors in his pages, because, he says, they have often attacked him in theirs. I have never allowed these attacks to pass. One day I gave the proof of this to M. d'Alembert, by letting him read what I had blue-penciled in some of the proofs. He appeared to be grateful for this consideration. Since then Fréron has often returned to the charge, and I to my blue-pencilings. Never have I allowed any extract from any work expressly written against the *Encyclopédie.*' [15]

Malesherbes' policy regarding the *Fils naturel* is revealed in the censor's report about the manuscript of a mild little pamphlet published in 1757. Its title, translated, was *The Legitimatized Bastard, or the Triumph of Tear-*

ful Comedy, with an Examination of the Fils naturel.[16] The author was a
dull dog, and appears to have used up all his wit in the title. But perhaps
his pamphlet, which was principally interested in showing that the techniques of 'tearful comedy' had been used by the ancients, was no sharper
than it was because censorship had toned it down. 'In truth,' wrote its
censor, a man named Gaillard, in his report to Malesherbes, 'there is nothing
bitter in this criticism. It is even tempered by strong praise, and M. Diderot
cannot complain of it without being unjust; but as you have had the kindness to inform me of the reasons that make you desire that his work not be
discredited, I thought that I should inform you of this part of the manuscript
before approving it. . . .'[17]

As far as hostile reviews of the *Fils naturel* were concerned, Diderot had
most to fear from Fréron. At this juncture Malesherbes let it be known that
he hoped that Fréron and Diderot would become reconciled. Upon receiving
this intelligence, Fréron stopped the presses — sixteen pages of an article on
the *Fils naturel* had already been printed — and wrote Malesherbes a letter.[18]
He suspected a trap and was full of distrust, not least because he knew that
about 1754 Diderot and D'Alembert, learning that Frederick II had authorized
the election of Fréron to the Prussian Academy, had written to the president of the Academy that they would resign their membership if Fréron
was elected.[19] Fréron now explained to Malesherbes the reasons for his
reluctance to agree to a reconciliation: 'He is at the head of a numerous
society that spreads and multiplies day by day by reason of its intrigues.
He would ceaselessly beseech me to deal gently with his friends, his associates, his admirers. I would be able to speak neither of the *Encyclopédie*
nor of any Encyclopedist. . . .

'Permit me to observe to you further, Monsieur, that it is rather peculiar
that the moment chosen for reconciling us, M. Diderot and me, is that in
which he has just given a work to the public. One does not need to be very
farsighted to see that M. Diderot is aiming at the French Academy, and
that those who wish him well apprehend, quite rightly, that I will demonstrate (as I believe I have done) that his *Fils naturel,* the only work he
has written in the Academy's line, is a detestable play.'[20]

It is not surprising that Diderot should, at some time, experiment with
writing plays. As mentioned earlier, he thought for some time, when he
was a youngster, of being an actor; he closely studied plays and acting; he
devoted several of the best pages of *Les Bijoux indiscrets* to a searching
criticism of the theater;[21] and he wrote some sort of play, now lost, on the
basis of which the Abbé Desfontaines is reported to have declared that Diderot

had a great talent for dramatic composition. There can therefore be no doubt that potentially Diderot was deeply interested in playwriting. If the question is posed why Diderot chose this particular and very busy moment in which to make lengthy and weighty experiments in a field of letters comparatively new to him, Fréron's theory that Diderot was aiming at the French Academy seems altogether likely. Why not? Diderot was short on memberships in academies. Moreover, D'Alembert was now a member, making the imbalance of official honors possessed by him as compared with Diderot more apparent than ever, while at the same time putting him into a favorable position to work among his new colleagues for Diderot's acceptance. Both enemy and friend hinted at the time that Diderot's object was to make himself eligible for membership in the Academy.[22] We may even conjecture that the publishers of the *Encyclopédie* hoped that their chief editor would be able to achieve such signal recognition. At all events, Diderot seems to have taken time from the *Encyclopédie* to work on the *Fils naturel* and the *Père de famille,* if the very scanty number of his contributions to Volume VII (published in October 1757) is evidence.

Diderot made his first play more difficult to criticize by pretending that the events of its plot had actually occurred.[23] Moreover, from the point of view of the theory of playwriting, this suggested that the function of the theater is to hold a mirror up to nature. But it was also a prime device for evading criticism, getting around awkward objections, and, in short, of trying to eat one's cake and have it too. These are the events that were supposed to have occurred:

It is daybreak, and the austere and virtuous Dorval is revealed ordering horses for the purpose of leaving at once, his reason being that he has fallen in love with Rosalie, the fiancée of his friend and host, Clairville. Rosalie is a motherless girl whose father has long been in the Indies and is now on his way back to France to bless Rosalie's nuptials with Clairville. Meanwhile, Rosalie is living in Clairville's house, under the care of his widowed sister, Constance. Constance is much upset by the news that Dorval is leaving, and makes to him a very thinly veiled declaration of love. 'That which follows must be hard to say for a woman like Constance,' say the stage directions parenthetically. At this point Clairville enters and begs Dorval to intercede with Rosalie in her fiancé's behalf. Something seems to have happened to her affections for him and Clairville believes that the juxtaposition of Dorval's virtue will easily put everything to rights: 'Such,' says Clairville, 'is the august prerogative of virtue: it impresses everyone who comes near it.'

In the John Alden-Priscilla Mullens interview that follows, Dorval, without acknowledging his love, learns that Rosalie loves him. This redoubles
his resolve to leave the house at once, but as he is writing some farewell
lines to Rosalie he is called out of the room to fly to the defense of Clairville,
who is being attacked by armed assailants. Constance enters the room and
reads the half-written letter, which she takes to be addressed to herself. At
one point in this second act Dorval's servant ejaculates, 'No! it seems as if
good sense had fled from this house. . . . God grant that we catch up with
it on the road.' Several contemporary critics regarded this as the best line
in the play.

From the conversation between Clairville and Dorval that begins Act III,
it is clear that Dorval has just saved Clairville's life. Constance enters,
shows the tormented Dorval that she has seen his letter and taken it to
be meant for her, and then, not seeming able to strike much fire from so
backward a lover, leaves. Clairville accepts Constance's interpretation of
the letter and speculates on why Dorval had not confided in his friend.
'Did you fear that my sister, learning the circumstances of your birth . . . ?'
'Clairville,' replies Dorval, 'you offend me. I possess a soul too exalted to
conceive such fears. If Constance were capable of entertaining such a
prejudice, I dare to say that she would not be worthy of me.' Rosalie enters,
learns from Clairville that Dorval is to marry Constance, swoons, and an-
nounces to Clairville upon reviving that she hates him. There then appears
a servant of Rosalie's father, who explains that master and man had been
within sight of the French coast when their vessel was captured by the
British and Rosalie's father despoiled of his fortune and thrown into prison.
A former business correspondent secured their release, and Rosalie's father,
now penniless, is in Paris and about to rejoin his daughter. Dorval receives
the news of the loss of Rosalie's fortune 'motionless, his head bowed, with
a pensive attitude, and his arms crossed (such is usually his ordinary attitude).' He secretly resolves to take from his own fortune in order to
restore hers, and as the curtain falls on Act III he is seen writing to his
banker.

In Act IV Dorval attempts to persuade the tenacious Constance that
he is not good enough for her, and that he is leaving in order to exist far
from men. This is the point in the play where Constance says that 'only
the bad man lives alone,' the remark that Rousseau took personally. There
follows a very edifying conversation, full of eighteenth-century 'philosophy'
regarding virtue. What, for example, would be the chances of their children's being virtuous? 'Dorval, your daughters will be virtuous and decent,

your sons noble and proud. All your children will be charming . . . and I do not fear that a cruel soul might ever be formed in my womb and of your blood!' When the virtuous but reluctant Dorval reveals the handicap of his illegitimate albeit almost guiltless birth, Constance replies, 'Birth is bestowed upon us, but our virtues we acquire.'

In the last act Dorval demonstrates his virtue and his forcefulness by persuading Rosalie in a long harangue that they could never be happy together and that she must accept Clairville. At that moment the father of Rosalie arrives, and Dorval recognizes him as *his* father! This remarkable coincidence provides a dénouement with a vengeance: Dorval and Rosalie suddenly finding themselves half-brother and half-sister, there is scarcely any use of their engaging in speculation as to whether *their* children would be virtuous, so Rosalie resolves to live happily ever after with Clairville, and Dorval with Constance. The curtain goes down with everyone on stage bathed in happy tears, according to eighteenth-century prints of the final scene.

Most of the attention paid to the *Fils naturel* has appropriately enough been devoted to its place in the history of the French drama. But it should also be pointed out that the play has great biographical significance, not only in respect to what Diderot wrote and when and why, but also in regard to its revelation of what Diderot valued and admired. Diderot delights in Dorval. To him the hero of his play is a hero indeed. And what a hero! A man whose charms are so irresistible that he receives two declarations of love in a single day, whose courage and prowess are so great that he saves the life of his friend, whose generosity is so ample that he divides his own fortune for the sake of his friends, whose virtue and eloquence are so overpowering that he can recall one of the ladies to her duty, and whose self-abnegation and self-control are so triumphant that he can marry the other whom he does not love. Surely Dorval was the Super-Man of the *salons*. His creator wrote of him in the spirit of a boy dreaming preposterous and fantastic dreams of glory. It may even be that Diderot saw himself in this creation of his imagination. Evidence for this identification may be found in the fact that Diderot has Dorval's servant saying to him, 'Monsieur, you are good, but don't go imagining that you are as good as your father.' [24] Now, these are almost the identical words that a neighbor at Langres used in speaking to Diderot about his real-life father, so that to many readers the psychological transference will seem apparent.

Dorval is one of the first in a long line of somber heroes whose souls are touched by *Weltschmerz* and whose hearts are swollen by feelings almost too delicate and subtle for ordinary mortals to feel. The unquestionable similarity between Dorval and Goethe's Werther and the presumable influence of the former in the shaping of the latter was noticed very early.[25] Such a hero, although usually divested of his preoccupation with virtue, became standard in the course of the Romantic Movement. And from Diderot's description of Dorval in the following passage, connoisseurs will have no difficulty in recognizing the type. 'He was melancholy in his conversation and bearing, unless he spoke of virtue or experienced the transports it causes to those who are strongly enamored of it. Then you would have said that he was transfigured. His face became serene. His eyes sparkled and became gentle. His voice had an inexpressible charm. His discourse became affecting and moving, an interlinking of austere ideas and touching images that held the attention in suspense and the soul in raptures. But as in autumn evenings, during cloudy and overcast weather one sometimes sees a shaft of light escape from a cloud, shine for a moment, and then vanish away in an overcast sky, so, too, his animation died away, and he suddenly relapsed into silence and melancholy.'[26]

The impact on public opinion of the *Fils naturel* was greatly fortified by Diderot's doctrines as expounded in the three supplementary dialogues. Within the framework of these imaginary interviews, Diderot propounded many new conceptions of the drama, conceptions that he was not the first to feel but that he was the first to express, at least in so comprehensive a way.[27] And because Diderot was an author singularly endowed with the gifts of plausibility and persuasion, his precepts as stated in these conversations were fully as influential as the example of the play itself.

Many readers will be surprised to learn that Diderot did not attack the unities of time, place, and plot which had become an iron rule of the French classic stage. Quite to the contrary, he wrote that 'The laws of the three unities are difficult to observe, but they make sense,' and both *Le Fils naturel* and *Le Père de famille* conformed to them.[28] The reforms he demanded were other. One of them was greater realism. He was emphatic in the 'Conversations' that stage settings are extremely important and really part of the action. As a corollary, he wanted the stage cleared of spectators.[29] Moreover, he interspersed his dialogue with explicit stage directions — had Dorval drink a cup of tea — and peppered his pages with exclamation points and broken-off sentences, in order to give some idea of the emphatic style of speech and the semi-inarticulateness of persons who labor under strong emotions.[30] This led him, incidentally, to discuss the problem of fitting prosody to music, a technical problem of the opera that always fascinated him. Thus he called for a reform in operatic composition that anticipated the opera of Gluck.[31] And he had much to say of the importance of pantomime and gesture. 'We talk too much in our dramas; and consequently our actors do not sufficiently act.' [32] And to enhance the illusion of reality, Diderot made his play contemporaneous. The scene was laid at Saint-Germain-en-Laye, twelve miles west of Paris, and the time was 1757. All this was new.

The purpose of this greater realism was to clear the way for the second of Diderot's desired reforms, the creation of what he called domestic and bourgeois tragedy.[33] This showed the very great influence that the contemporaneous English theater had upon him, especially George Lillo's melodramatic *The London Merchant, or the History of George Barnwell* (1731), and Edward Moore's almost equally melodramatic *The Gamester* (1753). In the conversations with Dorval, Diderot twice mentioned *The London Merchant* and once *The Gamester* as models of what he had in mind, and the abiding influence of Moore's play on him is symbolized by the fact that in 1760 he translated it for the edification of some of his friends.[34] As for the matter of 'domestic and bourgeois tragedy,' Diderot did not regard himself as having written in that mode. His plays, he thought, belonged rather to what he called in 1757 the serious kind of play (*le genre sérieux*), neither the old tragedy nor the old comedy but something new and in between, something as new as the *Fils naturel* and at the same time as old as the plays of Terence.[35] By the time he had published his *Père de famille* a year later, he was calling this sort of play a drama (*drame*). The word 'drama' in French has therefore come to have a much more specific and less generic meaning than in English. It connotes the particular sort of play written along the lines recommended by Diderot.[36]

Obviously bourgeois tragedy is tragedy mirroring the vicissitudes, conflicts, and values of the middle class. The temptations to which its characters are subject are peculiarly middle-class temptations, such as the peculations of the apprentice, George Barnwell. The virtues portrayed in such plays are those of an emergent and potentially powerful social class, thus illustrating De Tocqueville's remark concerning the drama in nations tending toward democracy. To people of the seventeenth century nothing could be more deliciously funny than the bare title *Le Bourgeois Gentilhomme,* for it incongruously associated what they deemed inherently incompatible, the *bourgeois* and the *gentilhomme*. For devotees of the *drame,* however, this attitude was beginning to seem out-of-date and contrary to 'philosophy.' In the *drame* the middle class is portrayed as having dignity and being worthy of respect. Commerce, for example, is no longer considered degrading. Clairville, upon being asked what he was going to do in view of his reduced fortune, says in the *Fils naturel,* 'I shall go into commerce. . . . [It] is almost the only occupation in which great fortunes are proportionate to the effort, the industry, and the dangers that make them respectable.'[37]

Along with the creation of domestic and bourgeois tragedy, Diderot hoped to aid in creating a whole new repertoire of plays to represent the various occupations and the various family relationships: 'The occupation ought now to become the principal object, and the character should be only the accessory.'[38] Thus there should be portrayed the man of letters, the philosopher, the businessman, the judge, the lawyer, the politician, the citizen, the magistrate, the financier, the nobleman, the public administrator. 'Add to that, all the [family] relationships: the family father, the husband, the sister, the brothers.'[39] Thus Diderot raised to a new level of artistic importance both the lives of persons whose family ties were strongly knit, as in the traditional manner of middle-class families, and the lives of those who worked for their living.

The third and principal object of Diderot in writing *Le Fils naturel* and in expounding his doctrines was to make the theater an institution for teaching morality. The *philosophes,* in almost everything they thought and wrote about, were strongly utilitarian. Things should have a use, a function. Carrying this axiom over into the theater, it was not enough for Diderot and the *philosophes* that plays should entertain, they must also impel to virtuous action. The usual consensus is that this is asking the theater to carry a very heavy extra burden, but Diderot demanded it. He has Constance say, 'Doubtless there are still barbarians; and when will there not be? But the time of barbarism is past. The century has become enlightened. Reason has become refined, and the books of the nation are filled with its precepts. The books that inspire benevolence in men are almost the only ones that are read. Such are the lessons with which our theaters resound, and with which they cannot resound too often. . . .'[40] Diderot also referred jocularly to an ideal republic to be set up in the island of Lampedusa. In that ideal society, actors would fulfill the function of preachers, so useful should the theater be.[41] What, asked Dorval, is the aim of dramatic composition? And Diderot replied, 'I believe it is to inspire among men a love of virtue and a horror of vice.'[42]

Such were Diderot's ideas on how a play should be written, ideas that aroused as much scoffing and scorn as they did enthusiasm and admiration.

The short-range opposition to these notions should not, however, be allowed to obscure the long-range importance of Diderot's ideas. 'No other part of Diderot's writings has given rise to a larger mass of studies and criticisms than his plays and his essays concerning dramatic literature,' writes a recent American critic.[43] And the scholar who is generally regarded as the best authority on the history of the *drame* began his work with these words: 'French literature in the eighteenth century saw a new dramatic form being born . . . Foreshadowed and prepared by the school of tearful comedy, the *drame* acquired with Diderot a very distinct and clear-cut personality. Thus it is from the publication of the *Fils naturel* (1757) that its real existence dates.'[44]

Although the play was not produced at Paris until 1771, there were at least two performances of it 'in the provinces' in the year of its publication. These occurred, probably in a private theater, at Saint-Germain-en-Laye, the very locale in which the action of Diderot's play was supposed to have taken place. Deleyre wrote to Rousseau that he had gone 'to the first performance, where I wept copiously, although not intending to.'[45] But Fréron declared that there was nobody at the second performance![46] Whether that be true or not, the interest aroused by Diderot's drama is attested by the number of editions it had. Between 1757 and 1800 it was published in twenty-five French editions, four German and three Russian, twice in Italian and in Dutch, and in Danish and English once each.[47]

Much of what Diderot wrote in the *Fils naturel* and its subsequent dialogues lent itself to sarcastic comment. In the 'Conversations' he talked a great deal about the forthcoming *Père de famille*, praised it in advance, and, contrary to his usual custom, brazenly sought a patron for it and that in cold print. The person he had in mind was a prince of the blood royal, the Duke of Orléans, whose chief passion was his love for the theater.[48] Moreover, Diderot's enemies did not fail to notice that the fiction he used of Dorval's having written the *Fils naturel* gave him the opportunity, while seeming to compliment Dorval, really to praise his own work fulsomely.[49] And if, in his dialogue with Dorval, he made some objections to this innovation or that, it was transparently done to allow Dorval to make a triumphant and unanswerable reply. 'The author makes some objections against his play,' wrote Palissot, 'and the Lord knows how much he "pulls his punches" (*il fait patte de velours*). The so-called Dorval replies in so satisfactory a manner that M. Diderot is always obliged to agree with him.'[50] Both Palissot and Fréron thought it a weakness in Diderot's play that he had to rely upon an extraordinary coincidence, a *deus ex machina,* in order to bring his piece

to an end, and Palissot spoke cuttingly of 'this old man tumbled down from
the clouds.' [51] Both critics objected to the 'philosophical and glacial jargon,'
and complained that there was no contrast between the personages of the
play, so that all of them seemed to have been cast in the same mold. 'It
is always M. Diderot, a philosopher, a metaphysician, who is speaking
. . . .' [52] There was a disposition among critics, too, to claim that even if
these new ideas were any good, it was not Diderot who invented them; and
one pamphleteer gave himself the satisfaction of calling Diderot the Amerigo
Vespucci of the new kind of play, other persons having been its Columbus. [53]

Diderot's enemies presently began to exult in a discovery they made —
that the *Fils naturel* was very closely modeled on a comedy entitled *Il Vero
Amico,* written by the celebrated Venetian playwright Carlo Goldoni,
and first produced in 1750 at Venice. Fréron wanted to publish the news
of this discovery by printing a letter purportedly written by Goldoni in
complaint of the *Fils naturel*. This Malesherbes refused to allow. He evidently accepted the proof of plagiarism, for Fréron had sent him a copy
of Goldoni's works, but his reason for refusing to allow Fréron to publish
the supposititious letter was that 'it would be a falsehood worse than all the
acts of plagiarism in the world, to give to the public under Goldoni's name
such a letter if it were not really from him.' [54] Fréron had to content himself with a very indirect although effective approach. In one issue he published a full synopsis of the *Fils naturel;* then in his next issue, under
pretense of reviewing Goldoni's comedies generally, he published an equally
detailed synopsis of *Il Vero Amico,* and in doing so he used, where relevant,
the identical words of his previous summary, thus creating a haunting echo
effect that would naturally cause readers to look back to try to find out
where they had read the same thing before. [55] By this device Fréron suggested
to his readers what Malesherbes did not allow him to say outright. [56]

A collation of Goldoni's *Il Vero Amico* and Diderot's *Fils naturel* shows
that the situations, the personages (save for an old miser who appears in
Goldoni's play and is left out of Diderot's), and a good deal of the dialogue
are extremely similar up through almost half the play. [57] This might be
called cultural borrowing on the grand scale. But thereafter the plots diverge.
Moreover, the spirit of the two plays is different throughout. Goldoni's is
more a farce than a play 'of the serious kind': it attempts to impart no
morality or 'philosophy,' and it has no special middle-class point of view.
That Diderot's sins had therefore been much exaggerated by his enemies
was the comforting conclusion pointed out by the contemporary *Journal
Encyclopédique:*

Finally, from a three-act farce (half of which was itself borrowed from Molière's 'The Miser') there has emerged a symmetrical piece in five acts, written in a vigorous, grave, elevated, and energetic style, and capable of expressing feeling, without which no style can speak to the heart. Let those who desire to despoil M. Diderot of his glory, in order to give it to Goldoni, attempt a similar metamorphosis with any one of the sixty plays that the fertile Italian has written. Far from reproaching them for their theft, we will congratulate them very sincerely for having had the skill to do it.[58]

It is difficult for people in the twentieth century to be quite sure how heinously Diderot had transgressed against the ethical code of his contemporaries in regard to plagiarism. 'Even in the seventeenth and eighteenth centuries,' a scholar in the problems of literary history reminds us, 'public opinion was still indulgent in this regard; it was not until the last century that plagiarism was condemned as out-and-out dishonesty.'[59] Malesherbes seems to have partaken of this attitude when he sharply distinguished between Diderot's plagiarism and Fréron's wanting to print a letter purportedly, but not really, written by Goldoni. In Malesherbes' eyes, there was patently no comparison in the relative guilt of the two offenses. On the other hand, it is obvious that Collé took a very severe view of the matter, and it is also clear that Diderot's enemies felt that they now had him at a considerable disadvantage, from which one may conclude that plagiarism was not entirely overlooked by contemporary opinion nor completely condoned.[60] Besides, Diderot himself felt constrained to justify his procedure, and in 1758, in his *Discours sur la poésie dramatique,* he made the best of admitting what could not be denied: 'I took possession of it as if it were a piece of property belonging to me. Goldoni had not been more scrupulous. He laid hold of the *Avare* without anyone's taking it into his head to find that bad; and no one among us has imagined accusing Molière or Corneille of plagiarism for having tacitly borrowed the idea of some play either from an Italian author or from the Spanish theater.' Diderot denied that his play and Goldoni's were similar in kind, that his characters and those of Goldoni had the slightest resemblance, that there was a single important word in the *Fils naturel* that had been taken from *Il Vero Amico*. And then, becoming quite heated, he asserted that 'I really wish that there were a dozen such larcenies to reproach me with. I do not know whether the *Père de famille* has gained anything by belonging entirely to me.'[61]

Public opinion eventually began to rally somewhat to Diderot's support, as the foregoing quotation from the *Journal Encyclopédique* shows. The *Mercure de France* for February 1759, in reviewing Diderot's *Discours sur*

la poésie dramatique, spoke very sympathetically regarding his explanation.
'I would never end,' wrote the reviewer, 'were I to cite all unacknowledged
translations made from one language to another without anyone's believing
himself obliged to announce them. This is the first time that the name of
plagiarism has been given to the use of a foreign idea that has been enriched,
ennobled, and, above all, applied to a genre that is not that of the original.' [62]

Nevertheless, Diderot's conduct when he later came unexpectedly face
to face with Goldoni betrayed a bad conscience. Goldoni's feelings had been
hurt, he tells us in his *Memoirs,* not so much by the possibility of plagiarism
— after all, plagiarism is a form of very sincere compliment — but by Diderot's
calling Goldoni's comedies farces! Besides, he thought that Diderot's public
references to him as Charles Goldoni, instead of M. Goldoni, betrayed both
irritation and contempt. 'I was sorry to see a man of the greatest merit pre-
disposed against me. I did everything possible to draw near to him . . .
to convince him that I did not deserve his indignation.' Finally, Goldoni
asked a common friend, an Italian musician named Duni, to take him to
call upon Diderot. Though obviously embarrassed, 'M. Diderot had the
honesty to say that some of my plays had caused him much vexation. I
had the courage to reply that I had noticed it.' [63] The interview seems to
have ended politely but inconclusively, and although Goldoni was in Paris
off and on for many years thereafter, their paths apparently did not cross
again.

The *Fils naturel* greatly enhanced Diderot's reputation, but it was a
source of mortification too. A few days after its publication he had written
to Jean-Jacques, 'Whatsoever success my work has had . . . I have received
scarcely anything but embarrassment from it and I expect nothing but
vexation.' [64] In this he was prophetic. For some years he had lived in comparative tranquillity, he and the more recent volumes of his *Encyclopédie*
having given little leverage to his enemies. But the *Fils naturel* had given
them a purchase. Presently other untoward events, directly or indirectly connected with Diderot, were responsible for bringing about the supreme crisis
in the history of the *Encyclopédie.*

CHAPTER 21

Rising Opposition;
D'Alembert's Blunder in Volume VII

D URING all the time that Diderot and Rousseau were inexorably proceeding from misunderstanding to misunderstanding, during the time that Diderot was publishing the *Fils naturel* and was being crowned with laurel leaves by his friends and contumely by his foes, France was locked in a struggle with England and Prussia that should rightly be regarded as one of the first world wars. It was in 1757, the year of the *Fils naturel,* that the British court-martialed their admiral Byng for letting the French capture Port Mahon and had him shot on his own quarterdeck — 'to encourage the others,' wrote Voltaire grimly; it was in 1757 that Pitt formed his second ministry and out of disorganization fashioned order, and victory out of defeat; and, finally, it was in 1757 that the French won a battle at Hastenbeck and suffered a national humiliation at Rossbach.

Little as Diderot concerned himself with the vicissitudes of the war, he and his *Encyclopédie* nevertheless came under some suspicion because of it. Principally this was because Frederick the Great, now a national enemy, had singled out Diderot and D'Alembert for honors. They were members of his Academy, as the title pages of the successive volumes of the *Encyclopédie* testified, and D'Alembert in particular seldom overlooked an opportunity in articles he wrote for the *Encyclopédie* to praise the 'philosopher King.' During the Seven Years' War anyone who could be called an Encyclopedist or a *philosophe* was by that very token imputed to be a bad citizen, recalled Condorcet, 'because France at that time was the enemy of a philosopher king who, justly appreciating merit, had given public testimonials of esteem to some of the authors of the *Encyclopédie.*' [1] In addition, the Encyclopedists, especially Diderot, were hospitable to ideas from abroad, most of all to

British ones, and in a time of national emergency this could be represented, even in that milder age, as faintly smacking of the subversive.

The year 1757 began on a somber note in the political history of France, for on 5 January Louis XV was attacked in the palace at Versailles by a man who, mingling freely and unchallenged among the courtiers, got close enough to the King to wound him slightly with a double-bladed knife.[2] French opinion was appalled. So was the King, who feared that the knife, since the wound it inflicted was so trifling, must be poisoned. Damiens, the attacker, was easily disarmed, and in due time impressively and horribly executed. The King, of course, recovered, but the net result of the incident was to suggest that the current freedom of canvassing ideas, limited as it was, had somehow unsettled Damiens' mind and was in general a threat to national security. An alarmed public opinion was ready to accept strong measures. In February the syndic of the press and his deputies warned the members of their guild neither to print nor to sell anything regarding 'present affairs.'[3] On 16 April there was promulgated a Royal Declaration, a stupendous pronunciamento that stipulated that 'All those who shall be convicted of writing or of having had written or of printing any writing tending to attack religion, to rouse opinion, to impair Our authority, and to trouble the order and tranquillity of Our States shall be punished by death. With reference to all other writings of whatsoever kind, not falling under the description of Article I, it is Our pleasure that, for not having observed the formalities prescribed by Our ordinances, authors, printers, booksellers, peddlers, and all other persons disseminating such writings among the public shall be condemned to the galleys for life, or for a term suiting the gravity of the case.'[4]

This was scarcely a favorable climate for the dissemination of new ideas. Nevertheless, from D'Alembert's point of view, the seventh volume of the *Encyclopédie* might be the best yet, if we may believe his letters to Voltaire. 'Without doubt,' he added, in a letter written in July, 'we have some bad articles on theology and metaphysics, but, with censors who are theologians, and with a license, I defy you to make them better. There are other articles, less in the open daylight, where everything is made up for. Time will make the distinction between what we have thought and what we have said.'[5]

Just as the seventh volume was about to be published, there appeared in the October issue of the *Mercure de France* a formidable attack upon the *philosophes*. For some time there had been a lull in the hail of pamphlets that had pelted the Encyclopedists, but this persiflage in the *Mercure* gave the signal and set the style for a new onslaught that was destined to end in catastrophe for the *Encyclopédie*. The article was written by a certain Jacob-Nicolas Moreau, a publicist who had currently been writing (in a little magazine called the *Observateur Hollandais*) a series of comments upon foreign affairs favorable to the policy of the French government and, in fact, subsidized by it.[6] Moreau was by no means a prominent man of letters, and never became one, but his invention of the word 'Cacouac' to ridicule the *philosophes* was one of the palpable hits of the eighteenth century. He published his attack in the form of a 'Due Warning' printed in the *Mercure*. These Cacouacs, recently discovered and hitherto unsuspected enemies of the public, were strange and loathsome creatures, 'Savages fiercer and more redoubtable than the Caribs ever were. . . . Their weapons consist solely of a poison hidden under their tongues. As they are no less cowardly than malevolent, they make a frontal attack only upon those from whom they believe they have nothing to fear. Most frequently they cast their poison from behind. . . . Their whole substance is nothing but venom and corruption. The source of it is inexhaustible and is always flowing.'[7]

Just as the public was becoming Cacouac-conscious in this autumn of 1757, Volume VII was published.[8] Many of its important articles were unexceptionable. Among these were 'Geometry' by D'Alembert, and 'Geography' by the King's Geographer (Robert de Vaugondy), and those presenting the most recent developments in technology, such as the long and detailed articles on 'Iron-works' (*Forges, Grosses-*) or 'Stoves' (*Fourneau*). But, as always with the *Encyclopédie,* its articles reflected a desire for improvement and a willingness to experiment with change. Quesnay, in his article on 'Grain,' wanted free trade in that commodity. Turgot, who was already enjoying a high reputation as a magistrate, wrote the article 'Fair' (*Foire*), and concluded that the great merchant fairs 'are never as useful as the restraint of trade that they entail is harmful; and that far from their constituting the proof of the flourishing state of commerce, they can exist, on the contrary, only in those states where commerce is hindered, overburdened with taxes, and consequently indifferently great.'[9] And, as always, the *Encyclopédie* sighed for a state of affairs wherein thought would be freer, tolerance more broad. Thus the Abbé Morellet dared to praise religious freedom in the United Provinces. 'The Dutch magistrates have finally learned,' he was allowed to write, in an article that he tells us was heavily censored, 'that for the sake of peace they should abstain from participating in such disputes; allow theologians to speak and write as they please; let them confer if they want to, and come to decisions, if that pleases them; and especially persecute no one.'[10]

In a very important and influential article on 'Endowments' (*Fondation*), Turgot examined, as he said, 'the utility of [perpetual] endowments in general in regard to the public welfare, or, rather . . . the disadvantages of them.' Even endowments made for the best of motives — to say nothing of those set up out of vanity — tend to outlive their usefulness, or to encourage mendicancy instead of discouraging it, or to be abusively administered. Salutary change could be brought about, he wrote, either by improved laws applying to all of society or by temporary endowments subject to discontinuation when the need was past, such as was then being done by associations of citizens in various places in England, Scotland, and Ireland for the purpose of increasing employment. 'What has occurred in England can take place in France: for, whatsoever one may say, the English do not have the exclusive right of being citizens' — a daring thing to publish in an absolute monarchy in the midst of a war with England. In this article Turgot used time and again the stirring word 'citizen,' and said that employments and offices of all kinds should become the recompense of merit. 'What the state owes to each of its members is the destruction of obstacles that would hinder them in their industry, or that would disturb them in the enjoyment of the products that are the recompense of it.' It was not for nothing that Turgot was a close friend of Gournay, the man who invented the formula of *laissez-faire et laissez-passer*. Noteworthy in this article is the sober but earnest appeal to public opinion, and the reference to public utility as the criterion of decision. 'Public utility is the supreme law,' wrote Turgot in this article — a principal tenet of faith of the Encyclopedists in regard to all social, economic, and political policy, and one capable of cutting through all the political obscurantisms of the *ancien régime*.[11]

This article was published without attribution to Turgot, so that Diderot, as editor, accepted the further responsibility of seeming to be its author. If to praise the English was to be unpatriotic, Diderot took the burden of it. If it was subversive to assume that the state owes something to its members, if it was disloyal to speak of the state rather than the king, Diderot shouldered that onus, too.

The *Encyclopédie*'s lack of interest in political and diplomatic history of the conventional sort is exemplified by the brevity of the article devoted to 'France.' This article, written by De Jaucourt, disposes of the subject in only nine hundred words, and many of these are taken up, not by an account of French history, but by deploring France's uneven distribution of wealth (comparing it to 'Rome at the time of the fall of the Republic'), the depopulation of the provinces, the overimportance of Paris, and the poverty of the cultivators of the soil. And De Jaucourt, using the technique of cross reference, declares that causes and remedies of these evils are not hard to find: *'See the articles "Tax," "Tolerance," &c.'* [12] But if the *Encyclopédie* was not interested in political history, nevertheless it had a political point of view, and in the article on 'Government' De Jaucourt wrote, 'The people's greatest good is its liberty. Liberty is to the corporate body of the state what health is to each individual. Without health, man cannot savor pleasure. Without liberty, happiness is banished from states.' [13]

In theological and religious matters, the *Encyclopédie* continued its policy of pinpricks and knowing winks. The article on 'Grace,' for example, which may have been written by Diderot, commented somewhat obtrusively upon the futility of a subject that had not seemed so to Saint Augustine. 'Besides,' wrote this unknown author, 'so much has been written upon this subject without in any way illuminating it that we apprehend laboring quite as uselessly. The principal works of the theologians of the several parties may be read concerning these matters. The discussions, very frequently minute and futile, to which they have given rise, do not deserve a place in a philosophical work, however encyclopedic it may be.' [14] Nor did the Encyclopedists forget to twit the Jesuits, as when Voltaire began his brief but ostentatiously learned article on 'Fornication': 'The *Dictionnaire de Trévoux* says that it [fornication] is a term in theology'! [15]

Regarding the history of religions, the *Encyclopédie* sought as usual to find a rational explanation for the origin of what it regarded as irrational practices. Thus Diderot wrote of the Roman sacrifice of milch cows heavy with calf (in *'Fordicides'*), his explanation of this pagan phenomenon being that Numa had instituted the practice to alleviate some calamity, such as a lack of forage, and that the sacrifice had continued long after the condition necessitating it had passed away. 'From which I conclude,' he wrote gravely, 'that one cannot be too circumspect when commanding something in the name of the gods.' [16] This method of studying primitive religious practices, not unlike Sir James Frazer's in *The Golden Bough,* was best displayed in Volume VII in a remarkable article on the 'Parsees' (*Guèbres*). Starting with the tenets of Parsee faith, the author, Nicolas-Antoine Boulanger, broadened out to give a theory of the origin of myths and of their role in all religions.[17] It was a way of suggesting, of course, the genesis of Genesis.

Diderot's contributions to Volume VII were not numerous, but a reader finds the now familiar touches: the graceful image — 'I regard these fragments of philosophy that time has allowed to come down to us as though they were planks that the wind casts up on our shores after a shipwreck, allowing us sometimes to judge of the size of the vessel'; the subjective — 'O sweet illusion of poetry! You are no less charming to me than truth itself. May you touch me and please me until my last moments'; [18] and the personal, this time a portrait of himself in reverse in his article on 'Formalists.' In his distaste for the pettifoggers of good form, Diderot showed himself par excellence the man who always hated to wear a wig.[19]

Famous among the articles of the *Encyclopédie,* and perhaps the most fateful of them all, was D'Alembert's ill-starred contribution on 'Geneva.' Usually the *Encyclopédie* had almost nothing to say under the heading of sovereign states — three-fifths of a column allotted to England, a column to Genoa, a little over a column to Spain, seventeen lines to Denmark — but to Geneva D'Alembert devoted four double-columned pages. His knowledge was firsthand, acquired during his visit to Voltaire in the summer of 1756. Gossip had it, after the storm broke, that Voltaire had put D'Alembert up to writing the article and that Voltaire might even have written part of it himself, as Rousseau believed, the purpose being to insert in it proposals for allowing the production of plays in Geneva.[20] In that Calvinist city-state the theater was looked upon with as much favor as it was at about the same time by, say, Cotton Mather, Jonathan Edwards, or the divines of Salem, Providence, and New Haven. To this subject D'Alembert devoted a whole column: 'Plays are not allowed at Geneva, not because stage spectacles are there disapproved of in themselves, but because, it is said, of the fear of the taste for display, dissipation, and libertinage that companies of actors communicate to the youth. Nevertheless, would it not be possible to remedy this drawback by having severe and strictly executed laws governing the conduct of actors?' [21]

On the whole, D'Alembert had evidently intended to be very complimentary to Geneva, especially because, like Tacitus writing about the Germans, he wished to improve his own countrymen by calling their attention to more virtuous foreigners. Thus he pointed out that the Genevese did not allow prisoners to be put on the rack, save in very special circumstances, and he spoke with great approval — perhaps he had imbibed this doctrine, too, from Voltaire, who had long believed in it — of their practice of burying the dead in a cemetery outside the city.[22] He also approved of the rigorous examination of the theology and morals of a minister before he was ordained and evidently before he was assigned to a pastorate, remarking that 'it is to be wished that most of our Catholic churches would follow their example.' But D'Alembert was a prim and schoolmasterish man, and he could not forbear remarking on matters that the Genevese could scarcely be blamed for thinking were none of his business. Thus he reproved them for retaining a certain part of their heraldic coat of arms. He told them that they should obliterate a certain inscription upon their city hall. Speaking of their divine services, he remarked that 'the singing is in rather bad taste and the French verses that are sung are worse yet. It is to be hoped that Geneva will reform itself upon these two points.' He observed that 'Calvin was as enlightened a theologian as a heretic can be,' a remark which probably displeased the Calvinists as being too grudging and the Sorbonne as being too generous.[23] In short, it is likely that a Genevese would have read D'Alembert's article with more irritation than gratification, and it is hard not to look upon it as a monument of tactlessness. From whatever point of view this article is regarded, one is tempted to say, in the vernacular of American sports, that D'Alembert led with his chin.

Nor was this the sum total of its offenses. The article 'Geneva' almost occasioned an official protest from the Genevese government to the French government because of the remarks D'Alembert made about the condition of religious belief in that sovereign city-state: 'Several [of the clergy] no longer believe in the divinity of Jesus Christ. . . . several of the pastors of Geneva have no other religion than a perfect Socinianism, rejecting everything having to do with mysteries, and conceiving that the fundamental principle of a true religion is to propose for belief nothing shocking to reason.'[24]

Soon after the publication of Volume VII, Grimm was calling this article a blunder, and reporting that it was creating a great stir at Paris.[25] It created an even greater one at Geneva, where the corps of Calvinist ministers were highly embarrassed by this public allegation that they were deists or, at the least, a variety of eighteenth-century Unitarian. To call a person a Socinian when he was officially committed to a belief in the Trinity and in revelation was to use fighting words, and it is not surprising that the ministers sought public amends. The Council of Geneva meeting on 9 December tried to find 'whether there be not some measures to take in order to have this article changed or suppressed.'[26] It hesitated to make a formal complaint to the French government only for fear that the French would make some disagreeable demand in return. As late as 15 January 1758, the possibility that an official complaint would be lodged with the French government was not entirely past.[27] Meanwhile, the Company of Pastors appointed a Committee of Nine to draw up a reply. The 'Declaration' they formulated was sent to all the editors of Europe and Fréron printed it in his *Année Littéraire* in February of that year.[28]

The secretary of this committee was a Genevese layman, Dr. Théodore Tronchin, the famous physician who in 1756 had made himself one of the best-known men in France by his successful inoculation against smallpox of the two children of the Duke of Orléans.[29] At that time he had become acquainted with Diderot, and in due course he became a contributor to the *Encyclopédie,* his article being, appropriately enough, the one on 'Inoculation.'[30] One of his first duties as secretary of the Committee of Nine was to write to D'Alembert and Diderot to secure a retraction. D'Alembert's reply gave him no satisfaction at all.[31] From Diderot he received a letter that illumines the relations between the two editors and implies that Diderot had disapproved of his colleague's action.[32]

This letter, evidently composed with great care, if we may judge from the profusion of conditional tenses, suggests a divergence in editorial policy between the two men. Although Diderot did not explicitly claim that he tried to prevent the publication of the article, he did say he had had 'no share' in it and he certainly implied that he would not have published it had the decision depended upon him. Did he really advise against its publication, or was he trying to deceive Tronchin into believing that he had? The latter alternative seems the less likely, for Diderot was not a pusillanimous man. An attempt on his part to cultivate Tronchin's good will at D'Alembert's expense is not in character. Besides, Diderot must have realized how much it was to the interest of the *Encyclopédie* to preserve a united front in this crisis. Indeed, one may well ask why he did not assume equal responsibility as far as Tronchin was concerned, whether or not this corresponded to the reality of the case, and try to brave it out. On the contrary, he steadfastly claimed not to be responsible, although offering to take the blame publicly on himself. Finally, if it be remembered that D'Alembert never alleged, either in his letter to Tronchin or in his correspondence with Voltaire, that Diderot had approved of the article on 'Geneva' before or after its publication, the inference that Diderot disapproved of publishing the article seems strong. Had D'Alembert been able to divide responsibility with Diderot, it would have been manifestly to his advantage to do so.

It is evident that Tronchin interpreted the situation as meaning that Diderot had not favored publication. Writing to a Swiss colleague a few days after receiving Diderot's letter, Tronchin remarked that 'His co-editor, Diderot, who is, of all the men I know, the most humane,' would never have done what D'Alembert did. And Tronchin continued (but unfortunately without citing sources), 'Opinion was unanimous against the article, before it was printed. Therefore M. d'Alembert cannot say that he did not foresee its effect. He alone held out against them all. Whatsoever reasons were used to combat his obstinacy, he did not wish to give in, [and] the article was printed.'[33]

What, after all, can explain Diderot's willingness to allow Tronchin to infer that he had not approved of D'Alembert's article? Could Diderot have been motivated by the desire to prevent Voltaire from ever again using the *Encyclopédie* to serve his own private purposes? As Grimm remarked in the *Correspondance littéraire* — and his and Diderot's ideas did not usually diverge very far — 'I cannot express how out of place this whole article was in the *Encyclopédie,* in which the city of Geneva ought to occupy the space of three or four lines, and not entire columns for the purpose of telling us what it should or should not do — a subject absolutely foreign to the arts and sciences that constitute the subject of this dictionary.' [34] Diderot's usual policy of holding Voltaire at arm's length made itself very conspicuous at this juncture. Voltaire repeatedly sent regards to Diderot in letters to D'Alembert and even in a letter to the publisher Briasson.[35] Diderot did not reciprocate. Then Voltaire, in this crisis, wrote directly several times, but to his extreme annoyance, Diderot neglected to reply.[36] Perhaps Diderot thought it outrageous of Voltaire — and D'Alembert, too — to jeopardize the fate of the whole *Encyclopédie* so that Voltaire might see a play in Geneva. It is therefore conceivable that Diderot welcomed the opportunity of a showdown with D'Alembert, once the latter had precipitated the issue of Voltaire's influence in so clean-cut a fashion. The distrust of D'Alembert that Diderot had already evinced in the letter written in 1755 makes this explanation even more likely.[37]

Unquestionably the *Encyclopédie* was made vulnerable by the article on 'Geneva.' It seemed presumptuous and arrogant in its cocksureness regarding matters both temporal and spiritual. It tended to reflect on the judgment of the editors. And just as it came close to involving the Ministry of Foreign Affairs, so, too, it almost precipitated an investigation by the Parlement of Paris. 'It is asserted,' wrote D'Alembert to Voltaire, reporting this new danger, 'that I praise the ministers of Geneva in a fashion prejudicial to the Catholic Church.' [38] The enemies of the *Encyclopédie* were becoming bolder, and scarcely anyone missed the significance of the fact that a Jesuit dared to preach a sermon at Versailles, in the presence of the King, attacking the *Encyclopédie*.[39] The article on 'Geneva' was not the sole cause of the increasing complaints against the work, but it undoubtedly encouraged the accelerating tempo of the attack.

Furthermore, it is probable that D'Alembert's ill-favored article on 'Geneva' precipitated the crisis regarding censorship that overtook the *Encyclopédie* following the publication of the seventh volume. If the Parlement of Paris should investigate the *Encyclopédie,* as it threatened, then it was inevitable that a number of searching questions would be asked as to how offending passages had happened to secure approval. Evidently Malesherbes deemed it prudent, for his own protection, to ask the questions first. An undated note in his almost illegible hand stated that 'I learned with the greatest surprise' that articles had been printed that had not been reviewed by any one of the three theologian censors.[40] In another notation Malesherbes revealed how this had happened. Undated and unsigned but unquestionably in his highly individual writing, it stated that the agreement of 1752 'was observed for the third volume and, at most, for the fourth. Since that time the editors and publishers have fallen again into the habit of arbitrarily sending each article to the censor in whose province they deemed it to belong. This is what has given rise to the complaints occasioned by the seventh volume.'[41] Nor did the publishers deny that this was what had occurred. Le Breton wrote to Malesherbes on 24 December to say that 'there have not been printed any sheets, particularly of the last five volumes of the *Encyclopédie,* without their being initialed by one of the censors whom you have assigned to us,' but he could not claim that everything had been reviewed and passed by one of the theologian censors.[42] From this Malesherbes evidently concluded that these censors had been negligent, for he drafted a very stiff rebuke to the chief of them, commenting on the publication of some articles 'which it is impossible that any one of you three had approved. . . . You ought to have complained that the present rule was being evaded, and because you have not done so, you have shared in the transgression of the authors and printers.'[43] Henceforth, every single sheet was to be initialed by one of the three theologian censors. Malesherbes was fortunate that the breakdown of his previous orders did not become public knowledge, and he was quite justified in insisting that the rules agreed upon in 1752 should be carried out punctiliously. Nevertheless D'Alembert, particularly, chose to regard Malesherbes' orders as a new encroachment and another grievance.

Hostile pamphlets also plagued D'Alembert at this time. One of them was *Little Letters on Great Philosophers* by Palissot whose enmity D'Alembert had earned in 1755 when he protested in Rousseau's behalf against *Le Cercle.* Now Palissot, young in years but old in enmity, returned to the attack, an attack which D'Alembert believed to have the protection of patrons in very high places. In just a few pages Palissot managed to touch a great many sore spots. He twitted Diderot and D'Alembert for having copied Bacon 'servilely'; ridiculed Diderot's opening words in his *Pensées sur l'interprétation de la nature,* 'Young man, take and read'; laughed at the statement that deer attain the age of reason; sneered at Diderot's pamphlet on 'Encaustic'; remarked that the editors *formerly* praised Rameau; and chided them for being so morbidly sensitive to criticism. Palissot accused his enemies of monopolizing the term 'philosopher'—'All these gentlemen call themselves Philosophers. Some of them are.' He took care to remind the public that D'Alembert was the beneficiary of a Prussian pension, and he also criticized the D'Alembert eulogy of Montesquieu which had appeared as a foreword to Volume V: 'There reigns in it a tone that is revolting. It is not so much the expression of public admiration as it is an order to the Nation to believe in the merit of this illustrious writer.' Most of all, Palissot complained of the *philosophes'* forming a party, of their pronouncing upon reputations, 'of the ostentatious praise that these gentlemen mete out to one another,' of 'this tone of inspiration on the part of some, of emphasis on the part of others,' of their intolerance, of their setting up for themselves a literary throne, of their saying in effect that 'No one shall have wit save us and our friends.' And Palissot hinted that the *philosophes* were by way of becoming a church: 'At the front of certain philosophical productions one may observe a tone of authority and assurance that until now only the pulpit has exercised.' [44]

This was quite bad enough, especially after Fréron lovingly reviewed it in his *Année Littéraire*.[45] But Moreau's 'New Memoir to Serve toward the History of the Cacouacs' was even worse. In this more extensive account of the habits and manners of those formidable creatures, the author informed the public that the only weapon that the Cacouacs feared was a whistle. Whistling put them into disarray and sent them headlong into flight, a remark disclosing that in the eighteenth century as in the twentieth, whistling is to a Frenchman what booing is to an American today. The author of the 'Memoir' had forgotten his whistle and was consequently captured by the Cacouacs. He was disarmed to the strains of Italian music, and then an old man came into the room with a book, and said, 'Young man, take and read.' The Cacouacs, according to their prisoner, were anarchists; they denied the existence of the gods; the only thievery they permitted themselves was that of the thoughts of others; 'they particularly coveted the glory of destroying'; they were absolutely indifferent to patriotism, no longer recognizing any other fatherland than that of the entire universe; and by common consent they accepted lying as a general practice. The captive discovered that the Cacouacs were great talkers: 'their language has something sublime and unintelligible in it that inspires respect and arouses admiration.' He himself became proficient in their idiom: 'I continued to shine. Ideas came to me. But if sometimes they failed me, I had some big words to put in their place, and I noticed that then it was that I was applauded the most vigorously.' He was initiated into their mysteries by being permitted to peep into their seven sacred coffers (the seven volumes of the *Encyclopédie*). 'With surprise I observed a confused mass of the most heterogeneous materials — gold dust mixed with iron filings and lead slag, diamonds half-concealed in piles of ashes, and the salts of the most salubrious plants mixed up with the most noxious poisons.' The prisoner was given a valet, who robbed him while virtuously quoting to him his own philosophical principles. This valet, moreover, had written a book entitled 'New Discoveries about Tragedy, or the Art of Composing Very Fine Scenes out of Grimaces.' After a number of adventures, the captive was able to return to his own country. There he discovered that it was later than he thought: the Cacouacs were already there! 'These dangerous and ridiculous Cacouacs . . . had been given the name of *Philosophes*, and their works were being printed!' [46]

Americans have a phrase to describe this kind of persiflage — a rock in every snowball. Diderot seems to have borne it without a flutter of nerves, but D'Alembert was overawed because he believed it to be officially inspired and because he claimed to know that Malesherbes, although desirous of preventing publication, had received orders from higher up to see that it was not suppressed. [47]

At this singularly unpropitious time, D'Alembert chose to draw a large draft on Malesherbes' fund of good will. Fréron, as may readily be imagined, had unctuously and gleefully digested the 'New Memoir' for his readers, forgetting none of the most painful parts. [48] But whereas Moreau had not alluded to D'Alembert by name, Fréron inserted in a footnote a reference to one of D'Alembert's works, thus making the connection unmistakable. It was, in fact, as Malesherbes called it, nothing but a subtlety, but nevertheless D'Alembert took great umbrage. [49] Malesherbes was sufficiently moved by D'Alembert's protest to inquire of Fréron by what right he used personalities in attacking his enemies, to which Fréron made sturdy and independent reply. [50] Yet it is evident that Malesherbes, although he wrote to Fréron, was nevertheless exasperated by D'Alembert's protest. Moreover, Malesherbes was very aware of his own delicate position at this particular time, for he wrote to the Abbé Morellet, who became the intermediary in the affair, 'I am even more sorry to see how the chagrin caused by the pamphlets has blinded him to the point of not sensing how indiscreet it is and, I venture to say, unreasonable, coolly to demand redress from Fréron at the moment when the seventh volume of the *Encyclopédie* and especially the article "Geneva" have excited the most powerful outcries, and when one cannot defend the work nor take the side of the authors without exposing oneself personally to very grave reproaches.'[51] In this letter and in one to D'Alembert, Malesherbes outlined the guiding principles of his administration.[52] These were liberal and inspiring documents, even though, as Malesherbes predicted and as Morellet tells us in his *Mémoires,* D'Alembert was very discontented with them.[53] The incident shows clearly enough that of the two men, the magistrate and the writer, it was not the writer who desired freedom of the press. Malesherbes implied that what D'Alembert wanted was the right to say what he pleased and the refusal of the same right to his enemies — an analysis very close to the truth. His protest to Malesherbes against Fréron was so poorly justified and so plainly ill-timed that Malesherbes began to suspect an ulterior motive. In the draft of his letter to Morellet, Malesherbes wrote (and then scratched out) the following sentences: 'If I knew M. d'Alembert less well, I might suspect him of seeking to prepare, relative to the public, a pretext for quitting the *Encyclopédie.* But I do not believe him capable of it.'[54]

As early as 1 January 1758 D'Alembert claimed to have informed Malesherbes and the publishers of his decision to give up the *Encyclopédie;* and in his reply of 6 January 1758 to Tronchin, he added a postscript: 'I ought to add, Monsieur, that reasons of an essential character, having no relation to the article "Geneva," oblige me to give up my work on the *Encyclopédie* absolutely and once for all. Thus it seems to me that this work, brought to a stop in the middle of its course, no longer merits becoming the subject of the complaints of your clergy.'[55] It is of great interest to notice that at this writing D'Alembert evidently took it for granted that his quitting would mean the end of the *Encyclopédie.* Five days later he wrote to Voltaire that he did not know whether the *Encyclopédie* would be continued or not. 'What is certain is that it won't be by me. I have just notified M. de Malesherbes and the publishers that they may search for my successor. I am worn out by the insults and vexations of all kinds that this work brings down upon us.'[56]

Before receiving the foregoing letter Voltaire heard a rumor that D'Alembert was intending to quit and hastened to urge him to stick it out.[57] Then, in answering D'Alembert's letter, Voltaire again urged him not to resign. 'Do not abandon it. Do not do what your ridiculous enemies want. Do not give them this insolent triumph. . . . I know that it is shameful that a society of superior intelligences, working for the good of the human race, should be subject to censors not worthy of reading you; but can you not choose reasonable revisers? Cannot M. de Malesherbes aid you in this choice?'[58] But D'Alembert, replying to the first adjuration, wrote that 'In regard to the *Encyclopédie,* when you press me to take it up again, you are ignorant of the position we are in and of the fury of the authorities against us. . . .

I don't know what course Diderot will take. I doubt that he will continue without me. But I know that if he does, he is preparing for himself trials and tribulations for ten years.' [59]

Quite suddenly Voltaire had an abrupt change of heart. Instead of beseeching D'Alembert to stay on, he now began to insist that everyone connected with the *Encyclopédie* should quit with him.[60] As long as Voltaire had supposed that the author of the memoir about the Cacouacs was a Jesuit or inspired by the Jesuits, he was brave. But when he learned from D'Alembert that these attacks were protected and perhaps inspired by the Court, he began to be very cautious and, while still lustily blowing the trumpet for a charge, hastily beat a retreat.[61] Reversing his earlier and braver sentiments, he now wrote that 'it is absolutely necessary that all those who have worked with you should quit with you. Will they be so unworthy of the name of philosopher, so cowardly as to abandon you?' [62] Frightened himself, Voltaire found it a good time for calling other people cowards. 'I have already told you,' he wrote to D'Alembert on 13 February, 'that I wrote Diderot more than six weeks ago, first to beg him to give you courage regarding the article "Geneva" in case they tried to intimidate you, secondly to say to him that he must join himself to you, quit with you, and not take up the work again except with you. I repeat to you, it is infamous not to be united as brothers in such a situation. I have also written to Diderot to return my letters [and my] articles. . . . Henceforth I do not wish to furnish a line to the *Encyclopédie*. Those who will not act like me are cowards, unworthy of the name of men of letters. . . .' [63]

'D'Alembert does well to quit,' wrote Voltaire to a friend in Paris, 'and the others, by continuing, are acting like cowards.' [64]

Throughout this flurry of volubly explaining why one should give up, there was one of the protagonists who said nothing. In all this scurry of letting go, one man held fast. Diderot simply kept on. No doubt the perplexities of the situation were increased by his friends' pressure on him. Even Rousseau, 'frightened by the rumors that are going about regarding the *Encyclopédie*' and fearing for Diderot's safety, wrote a letter urging him to quit if D'Alembert did, although it is not known (the letter not being extant) whether he too called Diderot a coward! [65] In mid-February Diderot at last wrote to Voltaire, excusing himself for not having replied earlier, and describing his motives for not giving up or finishing in a foreign country, as Voltaire had suggested. They were motives which Voltaire grumbled at and which D'Alembert obviously did not regard as decisive, but nevertheless the letter shows a willingness to accept moral responsibilities and honor them in the face of adversity that ought to be acknowledged as commendable and courageous:

. . . To abandon the work is to turn one's back on the breach and do what the rascals who persecute us desire. If you but knew with what joy they learned of D'Alembert's desertion and what maneuvers they undertake to prevent him from returning!

What Diderot really thought of D'Alembert's action is revealed by that word 'desertion.' His own attitude, Diderot wrote later in his letter, was not inspired by an overwhelming fondness for the *Encyclopédie:*

My dear master, I have passed my fortieth year. I am weary of bickering. From morning to night I cry 'Rest! Rest!' and there is scarcely a day when I am not tempted to go to live obscurely and die tranquilly in the remotest part of my province.

But this was the second movement, written in a minor key, of a battle symphony. What was it, then, that Diderot thought should be done?

That which is suitable for men of courage: Despise our enemies, pursue them, and profit, as we have already done, from the imbecility of our censors. . . . Is it honest to disappoint the expectations of four thousand subscribers, and do we have no obligations in respect to the publishers? If D'Alembert starts over again and we complete the work, won't we be avenged? . . . Someone else might rejoice over his desertion, seeing gain in it of honor, money, repose. As for me, I am disconsolate over it, and I shall neglect nothing to bring him back. Now is the moment for me to show him how much I am attached to him, and I shall not fail either him or myself. But for God's sake, do not counteract me. I know how great is the influence you have over him, and it will be useless for me to prove to him that he is wrong if you tell him that he is right.

. . . .

Don't be angry any longer, and especially do not ask me any more for [the return of] your letters; for I would send them back to you and never forget such an injury. Your articles I do not have, they are in D'Alembert's hands and you well know it.[66]

Voltaire did not receive Diderot's letter with very good grace. 'The trouble all arises from M. Diderot's not making from the first the same declaration as M. d'Alembert.'[67] 'It is a pitiful thing,' he wrote a month later, 'that associates of such high merit should be masters neither of their own work nor of their thoughts. Accordingly the edifice is built half of marble and half of mud.'[68]

Diderot's decision to carry on with the *Encyclopédie* was probably as much a disappointment to D'Alembert as it was to Voltaire, if we may judge from what D'Alembert wrote five years later regarding his own decision to quit. For in justifying himself he could scarcely avoid implying his disapproval of those who did not follow his example, especially as he was, according to the journal of D'Hémery, a man 'with a great deal of vanity and presumption.' [69] When his collected works were published in 1763, D'Alembert grasped the opportunity to tell how right he had been. But perhaps all that he proved was that Malesherbes had been correct in suspecting him of seeking a pretext to quit: 'In libels publicly distributed (and openly protected) the Authors of the *Encyclopédie* were represented as men without probity or morals, although not a single line in seven volumes was cited to support such atrocious accusations. The Author of this Preface deemed it incumbent upon him to ask for justice, less for himself (for he was not personally attacked in these libels) than for the good of a work that appeared to merit some little consideration and some support. The justice he asked for being refused him, he realized, perhaps too late, that henceforth nothing could make the *Encyclopédie* secure from the gravest and most unjust imputations, and from the sort of inquisition being prepared to be used against it. Therefore he adopted the wise policy of henceforth limiting himself exclusively in this Dictionary to the mathematical part, which cannot be subjected either to the clamors of false zealots or to the chicanery of a censor, and which, besides, is the only part for which he contracted solemn engagements with the public.' [70]

The article 'Geneva' had the disconcerting effect of putting D'Alembert at odds with people whom he assuredly did not want to antagonize — with the clergy of Geneva, with the Court at Versailles, with the Parlement of Paris, with Diderot, with Malesherbes, and even, most unexpectedly, with Rousseau. For Jean-Jacques, nostalgically remembering his childhood in the puritan city of his birth, took exception to D'Alembert's arguments for allowing theatrical productions in Geneva. The result was a spirited little book attacking the theater as an immoral and enervating institution and defending republican simplicity. Rousseau's *Lettre à D'Alembert sur les spectacles* was written just at the time of greatest strain and anguish in the relations of Rousseau and Diderot, and its publication revealed with dramatic emphasis to the jubilant enemies of the *Encyclopédie* that their foes' camp was divided, their united front broken. Thus was added still another to the catalogue of woes that the article 'Geneva' brought in its train.

CHAPTER 22

'I Used To Have an Aristarchus . . .
I Wish To Have Him No Longer'

PRECISELY at the time that his friendship with Rousseau was slowly going to pieces, Diderot was continually beset by other distractions and anxieties. As always, there was the routine of editing the *Encyclopédie,* the chronic and Spartan necessity of earning a livelihood, of paying the rent at the Rue Taranne. Added to this was the time spent in creating — and defending — his controversial experiments in playwriting. This was the year in which he had the exhilaration of being hailed as a dramatist of genius and the bitterness of being called a plagiarist of the very first rank. This was the time when he seems to have cherished the intoxicating hope of election to the French Academy. Perhaps it was the time, too, when he came to the grim realization that his hopes would never be fulfilled. This was the year in which he was held up to scorn as a Cacouac, when the article 'Geneva' put the *Encyclopédie* in jeopardy, when his relations with D'Alembert and Voltaire were under almost as great stress as were his relations with Rousseau. The strain of such events no doubt made it more difficult to maintain his balanced judgment in regard to Rousseau, just as his worsening relations with Rousseau probably affected adversely the other crises through which he was living. Reciprocally, one magnified the other.

Rousseau was meanwhile living on at the Hermitage, to all outward appearances calm, nevertheless seething within. His agitation was partly caused by an extremely sensitive and imaginative nature, which impelled him to be suspicious of the motives of his friends and created an appalling conviction of ever-threatening menace and ever-darkling doom. Partly his excitement came from meditating upon what was to become his great love story, *La Nouvelle Héloïse.* Rousseau was in the grip of a tumultuous and irresistible passion. He was in love with love. And, as usually happens to men in that condition, it was not long before his affections lit on a person who seemed to him to be the very incarnation of his dreams.

This lady, whom he had known slightly for several years, was Sophie, Countess d'Houdetot, the sister-in-law of his benefactress, Mme d'Epinay. In her person the Countess connects the French Enlightenment with the early days of the Republic of the United States, for Ambassador Thomas Jefferson frequented her social circle and found her charming. Now twenty-seven, she had married at the age of seventeen, had separated from her husband, and, when Rousseau fell in love with her, was living at Eaubonne, not far from the Hermitage. Mme d'Houdetot was a young woman full of high spirits, far from overserious, capable of witty badinage, and endowed with a fair share of coquetry. She could, moreover, turn a pretty piece of verse, and encouraged the supposition that she was the authoress of a much esteemed 'Hymn to Breasts,' written, it was suspected, for the purpose of stimulating curiosity regarding her own.[1]

The course of true love was troubled by some rather fundamental drawbacks. In the first place, the lady was not very much in love with Rousseau, if at all, although she seems to have been flattered by his attentions. In addition, she was already the mistress of another man, a man to whom she was to remain faithful for fifty-one years. Her lover was the Marquis de Saint-Lambert, a soldier and poet who some years earlier, because of his capacity for begetting, had been the indirect cause of the death of Mme du Châtelet. His liaison with Mme d'Houdetot had begun in 1752.[2] Now, in this crucial spring and summer of 1757, he was on active duty with the French army in Westphalia, where he now and again saw Grimm, and from whom he seems to have learned that Mme d'Houdetot was seeing more of Jean-Jacques than could be regarded as discreet. This was the end of the idyllic phase of Jean-Jacques's love affair. Saint-Lambert evidently rebuked Mme d'Houdetot. She in turn told Jean-Jacques, who hotly accused Mme d'Epinay of informing Saint-Lambert. This was an accusation that Mme d'Epinay found hard to forgive, and it is difficult to say whether much friendship was left between her and Rousseau after 'the day of the five notes,' occurring in late August of 1757.[3]

Throughout this prolonged crisis the much bedeviled Rousseau tried to conceal two pieces of material information, as a result of which all the other protagonists in the imbroglio, particularly Diderot, felt as though they were groping in the dark. In the first place, Rousseau was very reluctant to admit that he was in love with Mme d'Houdetot. It was transparent enough to anyone who lived in his society, yet he never admitted it to Mme d'Epinay nor to Grimm nor to Saint-Lambert, and he clearly implies that he did not confess to Diderot that he was in love until the last interview that they ever had, which took place at the Hermitage on 5 December 1757. But even then he concealed from Diderot a second bit of material information. As he himself wrote in his *Confessions* regarding this conversation, 'I never admitted that Mme d'Houdetot knew of it or at least that I had declared it to her.' [4]

Rousseau had of course declared his love. But his situation was perplexing and delicate, for Mme d'Houdetot was not supposed to be fancy-free. Rousseau, moreover, was under moral obligation not to take advantage of a man's absence to alienate the affections of his mistress. In these circumstances, Rousseau's high reputation for virtue being what it was, he was subject to the subtle temptation of awakening her moral scruples with regard to her liaison with Saint-Lambert. Rousseau's passion for Mme d'Houdetot is a rewarding subject for study in the casebook of the psychology of love. Every man is a Saint Anthony, but the forms in which temptation appears are various. The almost infinite capacity for subconscious self-deception, for confusing virtue and desire, is nowhere better shown than in the paradoxical, hypocritical, and pathetic figure of the austere 'citizen,' the stern, republican man of virtue, overwhelmingly tempted to arousing conscientious scruples in another man's mistress in the hope of seducing her himself. Of course Rousseau never put it this way to himself, yet he came close in his *Confessions* and in his letters to Saint-Lambert to admitting that this was what he was about. 'I protest,' he wrote in the *Confessions,* 'I swear that if, sometimes carried away by my senses, I attempted to make her unfaithful, never did I truly desire it.' And in a letter to Saint-Lambert, he wrote, 'I deprecate your connection . . . but a love such as yours merits some consideration, and the good it produces renders it less culpable.' [5] Indeed, Saint-Lambert's principal uneasiness regarding the attentions Rousseau was paying to Mme d'Houdetot seems to have arisen from just this apprehension that the citizen would undermine her attachment for Saint-Lambert by playing upon her scruples: 'I reserve, however, your promise which you give me of never speaking to her against our connection. . . .' [6] And Saint-Lambert might well think that there was ground for worry when he read Rousseau's reply, in which the citizen remarked that 'I told her that her attachment for you was *henceforth a virtue*'! [7] When some time later the exasperated Diderot was drawing up a list of Rousseau's malfeasances — 'Citizen Rousseau committed seven rascalities simultaneously, which have alienated all his friends' — one of the 'rascalities' was listed as follows: 'M. Rousseau then fell in love with Madame d'Houdetot; and to prosper his affair, what did he do? He sowed scruples in the mind of this lady regarding her passion for M. de Saint-Lambert, his friend.'[8] Authorities are in pretty general agreement that here Diderot described the situation as it truly was.[9]

When this nightmare of tangled personalities began, Diderot's relationship to it was extremely peripheral. At this time in his life he had not even met Mme d'Houdetot, he had just barely made the acquaintance of Mme d'Epinay and was reluctant to know her better, and he rarely saw Rousseau, who was at the Hermitage, or Grimm and Saint-Lambert, who were on active duty in the field. Although a whole book about this quarrel has been written on the assumption that Diderot was in a plot against Rousseau and pursued him step by step, the record seems to show more casualness than calculation. It is nearer the truth to think of a bumbling Diderot than a conspiratorial Diderot, of the nonchalant Diderot who antagonized his friends by not writing an expected letter or by absent-mindedly failing an appointment, of the naïve Diderot who was maddening in proffering unsolicited advice and ingenuous in the admiration of his own virtue.

In the history of the friendship of Diderot and Rousseau, the year 1757 had begun with bickerings about Mme Levasseur and about the offensive remark made by Diderot in Le Fils naturel. Diderot, who had been promising for a long time to go to the Hermitage, finally arrived there in early April, and a very satisfactory reconciliation seems to have taken place.[10] Then, in July, Rousseau stayed two nights at the Rue Taranne. The initiative for this meeting was evidently Rousseau's, his object apparently being to make sure that Diderot would at last be brought to giving his opinion and suggestions concerning the manuscript of La Nouvelle Héloïse. In his Confessions Rousseau says that he had sent Diderot the first two parts of the novel about six months previously, but that Diderot had not yet read them. Besides this, Rousseau claims to have had the generous motive of desiring to help Diderot, the latter being involved just at this time in the crisis regarding the plagiarism of Goldoni, and to signify to the world by this visit that the two men had not quarreled.[11] In the anti-Rousseau camp the tradition regarding this visit was that Rousseau kept Diderot slaving at the revision until all hours, then discreditably refused to listen to something of Diderot's when the latter wanted Rousseau's advice in return.[12]

Years afterward, in recollections clustering around these events, Diderot and his friends asserted that he visited the Hermitage and Montmorency very frequently during all the time that Rousseau was resident there. Thus Mme de Vandeul wrote that 'all the time that he stayed at Montmorency, my father had the constancy to go there on foot once or twice a week to dine with him.'[13] Marmontel quotes a similar declaration by Diderot: '. . . and I [he says Diderot declared] going on foot two or three times a week from Paris to his hermitage.'[14] Moreover, Morellet claimed in his *Mémoires* to have participated in these expeditions himself. 'Often we went, Diderot and I, from Paris to his hermitage near Montmorency to pass whole days with him. There, under the great chestnut trees adjacent to his little house, I have heard long extracts from his *Héloïse,* which enraptured me as much as they did Diderot. . . .'[15]

The testimonies of Mme de Vandeul, Marmontel, and Morellet were written down many years after the events they purport to describe. Mme de Vandeul's and Marmontel's remarks indicate that their sole authority was the assertions made by Diderot. Morellet, on the other hand, claims to have been an eyewitness. Yet his testimony is very hard to reconcile with the tone of the letters that Rousseau was writing, not years later in his *Confessions,* but at the very time of these alleged events. These show that all through 1757 Rousseau was greatly distressed that Diderot came so seldom to the Hermitage. Indeed, Rousseau's letters allow us to trace only four times, and no more than four times *for certain,* when Diderot and Rousseau saw each other face to face in the year 1757. Perhaps the frequent visits Morellet spoke of occurred in 1756, but the difficulty regarding this possibility is that Rousseau could not then have read to them his *Nouvelle Héloïse* because he did not begin to write it before early 1757, when his relations with Diderot were already extremely strained. To speak bluntly, Morellet's story does not hold water.

Regarding the four meetings between Rousseau and Diderot in 1757, we have already spoken of three. These were: the occasion in January when Rousseau went to Paris to be at the bedside of Gauffecourt; the one in April, when a reconciliation occurred at the Hermitage; and that in July, when Rousseau spent several nights at the Rue Taranne. The fourth meeting — the last in their lives — was at the Hermitage in early December. Over and above these, there may have been and probably was a fifth occurring early in September at the Hermitage. If it did occur, it was because Rousseau was in urgent need of advice, his relations with Mme d'Epinay, Mme d'Houdetot, and Saint-Lambert having suddenly become extremely vexed and complicated as a result of the agitation caused by 'the day of the five notes' (probably 31 August). According to Diderot's Catalogue of the Seven Rascalities, Rousseau 'accused Mme d'Epinay of either informing M. de Saint-Lambert or having him informed of his passion for Mme d'Houdetot. Embarrassed by his conduct with Mme d'Houdetot, he called me to the Hermitage in order to learn what to do. I counseled him to write M. de Saint-Lambert everything, and to keep away from Mme d'Houdetot. This advice pleased him, and he promised me that he would follow it.'[16] Although many authorities make no allowance for this September interview, the fact that Rousseau did write a long letter to Saint-Lambert on 4 September makes it seem very possible that the letter was written pursuant to Diderot's advice.[17] Diderot further declared, in his enumeration of the seven rascalities, that 'Later I saw him again. He told me that he had done it and thanked me for the advice. . . .'[18] Rousseau's letter of 4 September is the only one that fills these specifications. But it is much less candid than Diderot claims to have advised.

If Jean-Jacques was driven to distraction by his love affair, it is well to remember that Diderot, too, had recently become involved in one of his own. And during September and October of 1757, when his wife and little Angélique were at Langres on a three-month visit, he had 'three or four bouts of fever,' which debilitated him precisely at the time when Rousseau's relations with Grimm were being stretched to the breaking point. Grimm returned from campaigning and was with Mme d'Epinay through those months. Being jealous of Rousseau's ascendancy over Mme d'Epinay, Grimm treated Jean-Jacques very haughtily, with that calculated hardness that was an unpleasant part of his character. The incidents in this process of disattachment may be followed at length in Book IX of Rousseau's *Confessions*.[19] At the same time the decision was shaping up that Mme d'Epinay, whose health had been poor for some time, should travel to Geneva to be under the care of Dr. Tronchin. She herself did not put much emphasis into her proposal that Rousseau, who knew Geneva well, should accompany her thither. But Diderot did, in a letter written about mid-October which threw Rousseau into a tantrum. 'I learn that Mme d'Epinay is going to Geneva, but I do not hear it said that you will accompany her. . . . Overburdened as you are with the weight of the obligations you owe her, here is an occasion for paying her back in part and for relieving yourself.' Then, after discounting in advance Rousseau's protestations of ill health, Diderot continued: 'Moreover, aren't you afraid that your conduct will be misinterpreted? You will be suspected of ingratitude or of some other secret motive. I know very well, whatever you do, that you will have in your behalf the testimony of your conscience; but does this testimony suffice by itself? And is it permissible to neglect the conscience of other men up to a certain point? . . . I salute you, love you, and embrace you.'[20]

The enraged Rousseau at once accused Diderot of a plot.[21] Once Rousseau's suspicions were aroused, his lively imagination always carried him very far. Sometimes he realized this himself. For instance, he once took it into his head that his publisher, being delayed in sending him the proofs for *Emile,* was betraying him by giving the manuscript to the Jesuits. When Malesherbes wrote to soothe him, Rousseau remorsefully replied, 'Oh! Monsieur, I have done an abominable thing. . . . Nothing has changed since the day before yesterday, yet everything now takes on in my sight a different complexion, and where I thought I saw the clearest proofs I now see only some very ambiguous indications. Oh! how cruel it is for a sick and melancholy man, living alone, to have an unregulated imagination and to be informed of nothing concerning himself.' [22]

In scarcely any circumstances could Rousseau endure being told what to do. Moreover, if two of his friends were in agreement as to any course he should pursue, he promptly concluded that a conspiracy was afoot against him. And to allege that he had obligations to some person drove him quite frantic. Much can be said in justification of this sturdy love of independence, although it can scarcely be denied that Rousseau put himself into an ambiguous light, to say the least, by accepting the occupancy of the Hermitage. Rousseau's awkward position is by no means an unusual one. Multitudinous are the men of letters and the artists of every generation whom ambitious hostesses and lionizing friends have sought to put under obligations by the very extent of their generosity. Perhaps the only defense against this constricting menace of being loved into sterility is to adopt the practice of accepting favors without incurring a sense of obligation for them. Rousseau made the mistake, however, as did James I and Charles I, at odds with their parliaments, of arguing about it. His long letter to Grimm, dated 19 October, in which he referred to his 'two years of slavery' at the Hermitage, gave Diderot ample reason for asserting that Rousseau 'wrote against Mme d'Epinay a letter that is a prodigy of ingratitude.' [23]

So Rousseau did not offer to accompany Mme d'Epinay to Geneva and Diderot wrote this down as one of the seven rascalities. Among Rousseau's secret and unacknowledged reasons for not desiring to be seen with Mme d'Epinay at Geneva was his suspicion that her motive for going was that she was with child by Grimm and that she intended to have the child in secret there. Actually this was not the case — Mme d'Epinay had some sort of bona fide abdominal ailment — but inasmuch as she had previously had an illegitimate child by M. de Francueil, a circumstance of which Rousseau might quite well have been aware, his suspicions, though he could scarcely acknowledge them in writing and though they happened to be unfounded, were nevertheless not preposterous.[24]

Mme d'Epinay left for Geneva on 30 October, and a few days later Grimm wrote Rousseau, castigating him for his 'horrible apology' and his 'monstrous system. . . . I shall never in my life see you again, and I shall deem myself fortunate if I can banish from my mind the recollection of your behavior. . . .'[25]

In view of the situation, Rousseau began to feel that he should leave the Hermitage. Mme d'Houdetot counseled against it, fearing that such a move, occurring just at the onset of the worst season of the year when most people avoided the unpleasantness of moving, would cause a great deal of gossip and perhaps make Rousseau's passion for her common knowledge. Thinking that Diderot would advise the same thing, she wrote to him, although they were not yet personally acquainted, offering to take him to the Hermitage and to be present at the interview. Diderot replied that if she was present he would find it impossible to speak frankly: 'I am of an extreme timidity,' he wrote. And in a second letter he promised to go to the Hermitage on his own initiative as soon as he could.[26] Whether because of timidity or from fear of further complications, it is quite clear that he had no desire to become acquainted with Mme d'Houdetot, and this feeling lasted at least into January, for Mme d'Houdetot wrote Rousseau that she happened to meet Diderot at Baron d'Holbach's — 'I was wearing panniers and had my diamonds on' — and 'he fled from me.'[27] Diderot wrote to Rousseau about mid-November, and did advise him not to leave. In the course of the letter he denied the existence of the plot that Rousseau was so sure his friends had organized.[28]

Early in December Diderot at last found the time to go to the Hermitage. Although Diderot says in his Catalogue of the Seven Rascalities that he went to the Hermitage to demand of Rousseau why he had not confessed to Saint-Lambert as he had told Diderot he had done, the tone and sequence of Rousseau's *Confessions* and of his correspondence at this period do not confirm this at all. In fact, the Saint-Lambert affair did not come to its climax until several months later. On the contrary, the conversation during the December meeting seems to have concerned itself with the Mme d'Epinay-Grimm crisis, with Rousseau's unsuccessfully trying to get old Mme Levasseur to confirm that Mme d'Epinay had attempted to suborn her and Thérèse. No doubt there was a good deal of discussion as to whether Rousseau should leave the Hermitage, now that midwinter was coming on, and Rousseau further claims that this was the occasion when he learned what was for him the very upsetting intelligence that D'Alembert, in his article on 'Geneva,' was undertaking to tell the citizens of Jean-Jacques's native city what they should do.[29]

One can well imagine that such an interview, between persons so articulate, demonstrative, and emotional, was very much like a scene from one of Diderot's dramas. Tempestuous as it must have been, it nevertheless was far from ending in a break. It was in fact the last time that the two men met, but this was not their expectation at the time. The proof lies in the fact that a few days later Mme d'Houdetot wrote to Rousseau proposing that instead of his moving to Montmorency from the Hermitage, he should go to live with Diderot for the winter. Rousseau's reply, while deeming the project unfeasible, shows that he did not suppose that he would be unwelcome. 'Do you know my situation well enough?' he asked. 'Do you know his, the temper of his wife, to be sure that that is practicable . . . ?'[30]

Rousseau moved from the Hermitage into the town of Montmorency on 15 December 1757. In February he wrote to Diderot what appears to have been a friendly letter urging him to give up the *Encyclopédie* if D'Alembert did, for this was just at the height of the turmoil caused by the article on 'Geneva.' 'He did not even deign to answer me,' wrote Rousseau to Mme d'Houdetot, 'and thus he leaves in adversity the friend who so eagerly shared his [at Vincennes]. That is all that is necessary on his part. This abandonment tells me more than all the rest. I cannot cease to love him, but I will never see him again in my life.'[31] Yet Diderot was really not unmindful of Rousseau's situation, for Deleyre, a friend they had in common, wrote on 28 February, 'He [Diderot] is as uneasy as I regarding the resources that remain to you for subsisting. He fears lest you be in need at the present moment.'[32] This month and even early in March, Deleyre as well as Mme d'Houdetot herself were writing to Rousseau of the likelihood of Diderot's paying a visit to Montmorency.[33] Then, on 2 March, Rousseau wrote a letter, apparently never answered — it was not just Voltaire who could not extract replies from Diderot — in which he stated that he had heard that Diderot was blackening his character and imputing 'horrible things' to him. 'I must, my dear Diderot, write you once more in my life. . . . I am a bad man, am I?' he asked, and then he wrote, clearly alluding to Grimm, 'I should like you to reflect a little about yourself. You trust your natural goodness. . . . What a fate for the best of men to be misled by his own candor and to become, in the hands of bad persons, the innocent instrument of their perfidy. I know that self-esteem is revolted by this idea, but it merits

the examination of reason. . . . You could have been seduced and misled.
. . . Diderot, think about this. I shall not speak to you about it again.' [34]

And now for the catastrophe. Saint-Lambert, having been invalided at
Aix-la-Chapelle for several months, returned to Paris in March 1758.[35] He
seems to have learned quite quickly that Rousseau's attentions to Mme
d'Houdetot had been altogether more determined and passionate than he
had ever supposed or had ever been led to believe. This being true, Rousseau's letter of 4 September took on an altogether different aspect. Although
at the time he had answered it in friendly fashion, it now seemed to him
to be a hypocritical document.[36] As Diderot said of Rousseau in his Catalogue of the Seven Rascalities, 'he wrote an atrocious letter, of which M. de
Saint-Lambert remarked that one could reply to it only with a stick.' [37]
Following upon this unpleasant discovery, Saint-Lambert used his influence
with Mme d'Houdetot to cause her to break off all relations with Rousseau,
which she did in a letter of 6 May, complaining that 'these rumors have
come to my lover for some little time. . . . [because of] your indiscretion
and that of your friends.' [38] For Rousseau this was a thunderclap. Feeling
certain that it was Diderot who had informed Saint-Lambert and that he
had perfidiously divulged confidential information, Rousseau not long after
gave public notice that the friendship between him and Diderot was ended.

Was there, really, any perfidy involved? Ah! don't we all wish that we
knew. Nor perhaps shall we ever, for the motivations are probably as deeply
concealed and the points of view as various as those portrayed in *The Ring
and the Book*. Diderot stoutly asserted that there was no perfidy. After
Saint-Lambert's return from the army, Diderot wrote in his Catalogue of
the Seven Rascalities: 'He came to see me. Persuaded that Rousseau had
written to him along the lines we had agreed upon, I spoke to him [Saint-
Lambert] regarding this adventure as of an episode that he must know about
better than I. Not at all, for it turned out that he knew things only by
halves and that, by Rousseau's falseness, I fell into an indiscretion.' [39]

Had Diderot desired to be perfidious, this was the precise point where
double-dealing would be most effective and least detectable. Diderot liked
to suggest, in defense of his innocence, that proof of Rousseau's badness was
that he had lost all his friends. 'Our friends that we had in common have
judged between him and me. I have kept them all, and none of them remains his,' Diderot wrote to a Swiss pastor early in 1759.[40] The statement
is not quite true, for Deleyre, the minor Encyclopedist who had written the
article 'Pin' and who for a time in 1756 and 1757 was editor of the *Journal
Etranger,* remained friendly to both. But even so, one must acknowledge the

possibility that the defection of Rousseau's friends is not of itself proof of his being in the wrong. It might have resulted from unscrupulous manipulation of the evidence.

An attempt to determine the merits and motives in this tortuous story of six lives is of intrinsic interest as a study in human nature. Furthermore, it throws light on the personalities and characters of persons who are important in the intellectual history of the Western world. It reveals Diderot as much as Rousseau, each claiming to be justified, each standing on the threshold of crisis. The enemies of both used the quarrel as evidence to the discredit of each. And the break between Diderot and Rousseau came just at the time of, indeed was a part of, the more important crisis in the fate of the *Encyclopédie*. Here Diderot walked in peril, walked almost alone. It was the greatest test he had been called upon to undergo — the greatest in his life. To survive it required resources of stoicism, self-confidence, endurance, and conviction that make him one of the heroes, or — if it be thought that his sense of self-righteousness is too great to allow him heroic stature — one of the near-heroes, as he was certainly one of the seminal figures, in the history of thought. The mind therefore returns again and again to the problem of the sincerity and honesty of the man who was presently to undergo such a searching test of his stamina and nerve. Was Diderot as virtuous as he thought he was?

Probably not. It is vouchsafed to few men to be *that* virtuous. But in his behalf it may safely be said that to establish that he was perfidious in his relations with Rousseau, one would need to prove a degree of forethought, of calculation, and of ruthlessness that, although they may have existed in this instance, are most contrary to the usual tenor of his ways. Through all the months of this crisis, Diderot had no consistent policy regarding Rousseau. Of course it is true that during this crucial time Diderot was in daily association with Grimm, the man who had become Rousseau's bitterest enemy, and it is altogether probable that by the attrition of constant innuendoes Grimm was able to wear away a great deal of Diderot's lingering sympathy for Rousseau. But this does not seem to have resulted in any calculated policy on Diderot's part. His attitude remained passive, not active. What he did seems to have been the result of sudden impulse. His was the attitude and conduct of a man who, as Voltaire said of him at just this moment, found it harder to write a letter than a book.[41] Moreover, the tension with Rousseau was by no means the only preoccupation of these anxious times. It is hard to believe, with so much going on, with trying to finish *Le Père de famille* and edit the eighth volume of the *Encyclopédie* and contend with a reinvigorated censorship and parry the attacks of pamphleteers and deal with Voltaire and persuade D'Alembert to stay with the *Encyclopédie,* that he could think of the Rousseau problem by much more than fits or starts, or spend his time in contriving a plot against his former friend.

Besides, Diderot probably did not lie when he stated in his Catalogue of the Seven Rascalities, a list that was drawn up not later than 1760, and asserted at about the same time to Marmontel that Rousseau had asked for advice about Saint-Lambert and had promised to follow it.[42] Even this cannot be established beyond a doubt, and of course it is always possible that Diderot, without in any way being involved in calculated perfidy against Rousseau, did thoughtlessly blurt out to Saint-Lambert confidential information that ought to have been withheld, a lapse that he thereupon undertook to justify instead of frankly acknowledging. Nevertheless the fact that Rousseau did write to Saint-Lambert the long letter on 4 September regarding Mme d'Houdetot suggests that Rousseau had accepted Diderot's advice and that Diderot could assume that Saint-Lambert was fully informed. If this be so, then Rousseau really misled Diderot about what he had said in that letter, thus being the real cause of Diderot's inadvertently committing an indiscretion. And then, to Diderot's indignation, Rousseau, the cause of this false step, turned on Diderot and by a public break exacted double indemnity for the offense. As Professor Torrey remarks, Diderot felt taken in.[43] One can sense Diderot's exasperation and feeling of outrage in the very language and style of the Catalogue of the Seven Rascalities. It breathes the sense of injury of a man who honestly feels much put upon, rather than the factitious indignation of a conspirator simulating wrath.[44]

Following the interview with Saint-Lambert in which, according to his own account, Diderot was inadvertently indiscreet, he did nothing. There was no more talk of his going to Montmorency, there were no letters exchanged, there were no upbraidings. It was Rousseau, not Diderot, who took the initiative in notifying the public that the friendship had come to an end. On 6 May, Mme d'Houdetot broke off relations with Rousseau, and this was followed by Saint-Lambert's going to Montmorency a couple of times, as a result of which Rousseau decided that it was Diderot who had treacherously betrayed him.[45] Consequently, in the preface to his forthcoming *Letter to D'Alembert,* he gave public notice of the break: 'Taste, discrimination, correctness, will not be found in this work. Living alone, I have been unable to show it to anyone. I used to have an Aristarchus, severe and judicious. I have him no longer, I wish to have him no longer; but I shall regret him ceaselessly, and he is missing a great deal more from my heart than he is from my writings.' To this was appended a footnote, a quotation in Latin from the Book of Ecclesiasticus: 'Hast thou drawn sword against thy friend? Be comforted; all may be as it was. Hast thou assailed him with angry words? Thou mayst yet be reconciled. But the taunt, the contemptuous reproach, the secret betrayed, the covert attack, all these mean a friend lost.'[46]

When Deleyre, still friendly to both men, saw the celebrated footnote, he wrote to Rousseau, 'What a passage from Scripture you proceed to quote! You don't want friends any more, then, since you renounce the best one that by your own admission you ever had.'[47] Marmontel's *Memoirs* reveal the way in which this footnote was regarded in the circle of Diderot's friends. 'Finding myself alone with Diderot for some minutes on one occasion, I expressed my indignation, apropos of the letter to D'Alembert on plays, concerning the note that Rousseau had placed in the preface of this letter. It was like a stiletto thrust. . . . Everyone knew that it was Diderot to whom this infamous note was addressed, and many people thought that he must have deserved it since he did not refute it.'

Diderot replied to Marmontel that he could not defend himself against Rousseau's imputations without involving others. 'It is cruel to be calumniated,' he said, 'and that basely and in the perfidious accents of friendship betrayed, and [it is cruel] not to be able to defend oneself. But such is my position. You shall see that my reputation is not the only one involved. Now, as long as one can defend one's honor only at the expense of some one else's, one must remain silent, and I do.'[48]

Saint-Lambert, like Deleyre and Marmontel, was strongly and unfavorably impressed by the famous footnote. Rousseau had presented him with a copy of the *Lettre à D'Alembert,* only to receive this reply: 'Truly, Monsieur, I cannot accept the present you have just made me. At the place in your preface where, regarding Diderot, you quote a passage from Ecclesiastes [Ecclesiasticus], the book fell from my hands. After the conversations of this summer, you appeared convinced that Diderot was innocent of the alleged indiscretions that you imputed to him. He may behave badly with you. That I would not know. But I do know that he does not give you the right to give him a public insult. You are not ignorant of the persecutions he is undergoing, and yet you are going to add the voice of an old friend to the cries of envy. I am unable to conceal from you, Monsieur, how much this atrocity revolts me. I am not intimate with Diderot; but I honor him, and I feel keenly the sorrow you cause to a man whom, at least in my presence, you never reproached with anything but a little weakness.'[49]

Rousseau's preface was an attack masquerading as a defense, and controversy has raged over the question of who did whom wrong, much as scholars winnow the evidence regarding a question of war guilt. Diderot was not only deeply upset by the footnote in the preface, but also by the tenor of the whole book. Rousseau, in taking issue with D'Alembert as to the desirability of having a theater at Geneva, used arguments or illustrations that Diderot regarded as slurs or attacks upon himself. Accordingly he burst forth in passionate resentment of what he conceived to be Rousseau's malfeasances: 'His note is a tissue of infamy. I have lived fifteen years with that man. Of all the marks of friendship that a man can receive, there is none he has not had from me, and he never gave me any in return. . . . this man is false, vain as Satan, ungrateful, cruel, hypocritical, and bad . . . . Truly this man is a monster.'[50]

For almost all the *philosophes,* and pre-eminently for Diderot, it was a very sore point to allege, as Rousseau had done in the *Lettre à D'Alembert,* that it is impossible to be virtuous without first being religious, impossible 'to have probity without religion.' To the contrary, Diderot insisted that the two are entirely separable. He had found Lord Shaftesbury's ideas very attractive because the noble earl had made precisely this distinction, it being an important implication in the *Inquiry concerning Virtue and Merit* which Diderot had translated in 1745. A man could be virtuous, according to this view, without being inspired by the fear of hell. Indeed, he could be more virtuous, because he was animated by a love of virtue for its own sake. It was this line of thought that involved Diderot in a great deal of moralizing, an activity that he confessed he greatly enjoyed. Everyone has his idiosyncrasy, he wrote about 1773–4, and mine is to moralize.[51] Diderot wanted to prove that *philosophes* were better men than Christians were. He wanted to believe that he himself was a more virtuous man than his brother, for example, who was a priest. Consequently he scarcely ever tired of talking about virtue.

This sort of compulsion is well illustrated at this very time by Diderot's long response to a pastor in Geneva, probably Rousseau's friend, Vernes. Apparently Diderot was replying not only to words of praise but also to some tactfully phrased inquiries regarding the merits of the break with Rousseau. Probably Vernes was trying to discover whether there was any possibility of reconciliation. At all events, Diderot launched into a discussion of morality. It is not Diderot at his best. It is wordy and a little illogical. Moreover, the ideas in it give rise to the uneasy feeling that they were designed more to match the receiver's cloth than the sender's deepest beliefs. But there the letter is, in the Bibliothèque Publique et Universitaire of Geneva, with Diderot's signature upon it, testifying to what he said were the views he held regarding virtue. Diderot referred to himself as a man 'esteeming virtue to such a point that I would gladly give what I possess in exchange for having been up to the present moment as innocent as I was when I was born, or in exchange for coming to the end forgetful of the errors I have committed but conscious of not having increased the number of them!' The more one scrutinizes the latter half of this statement the more oracular and turgid it seems to become. Diderot continued by remarking that 'Virtue is, then, the greatest wealth of him who enjoys life and the most substantial consolation of him who is about to die. There is nothing in the world, accordingly, to which virtue is not preferable; and if it does not appear to us to be so, that is because we are corrupted and not enough of it is left to us to make us aware of all its value.' Then, passing to Rousseau, Diderot wrote, 'It is an atrocious action to accuse publicly an old friend, even when he is guilty. But what name can be given to the action if it happens that the friend be innocent? And what name, furthermore, should be given if the accuser avows to himself at the bottom of his heart the innocence of him whom he dares to accuse?' And then Diderot made it clear that he was seeking no reconciliation: 'For twenty years he has taught me how to pardon private slights, but this one is public, and I do not know any remedy for it.' [52]

Diderot might have been more forgiving had not the *Lettre à D'Alembert* been published at a time peculiarly unpropitious for him and for the *Encyclopédie*. Rousseau's *Lettre,* having received from Malesherbes a tacit approbation, was on sale in Paris by 28 September 1758.[53] It was not simply that this blast against the social utility of plays appeared less than a month before *Le Père de famille,* which, with its accompanying treatise on dramatic aesthetics, was intended to herald a new day in the theater. Scarcely anything could be better calculated to blunt the impact of the play or make Diderot's remarks about the drama, intended to seem self-evident, highly controvertible. This seemed grievous enough to Diderot, as his remarks in his Catalogue of the Seven Rascalities show. But more than that, the public character of the quarrel was very injurious to the *philosophes,* whether they deserved it or not. Up until this moment the public had thought of Rousseau as one of the Encyclopedists. He had been their leader in the controversy over Italian music, he had written the articles on music in the *Encyclopédie,* he had been the author of the important article on 'Political Economy,' and Diderot had apostrophized him by name in the article 'Encyclopedia.' [54] 'Oh! Rousseau, my dear and worthy friend,' Diderot had written for everyone to read in 1755; and now the dear and worthy friend was advertising to the wide world that Diderot was unworthy of further friendship because of 'the covert attack' and because of 'the secret betrayed.'

What Rousseau probably did not realize, but what Diderot and his friends, living in the hurly-burly of Paris could not forget, is that this quarrel by becoming public took on political significance. Rousseau's action, or, at least, Diderot's interpretation of it, can be thoroughly understood only in terms of its political context. Rousseau's *Letter to D'Alembert* appeared in the course of, and greatly complicated, a prolonged crisis during which Diderot's fortunes seemed to proceed with inexorable step from portent to paroxysm to catastrophe. The writings about the Cacouacs were the portent, the consequences of the publication in July 1758 of Helvétius' unlucky book *De l'Esprit* was the paroxysm, the suppression of the *Encyclopédie* in March 1759 was the catastrophe. In the whole eighteenth century this was the time of the crucial struggle to gain for one side or the other the support of public opinion. Eventually the *Encyclopédie* rose from its ashes. Eventually it became manifest that the Encyclopedists had won public opinion to their side just when the course of events would seem to indicate the contrary. But the years of 1757, 1758, and 1759 were grim and anxious for Diderot, years in which public anxieties were compounded with private distress. And it was hard for him to forget that precisely at the time when his *Encyclopédie* was most beset by his enemies, precisely at a time when he most needed to prove that a *philosophe* was an upright man and pure in heart, Rousseau gratuitously informed the public that his old friend was a scoundrel.

Inevitably, therefore, Rousseau's public denunciation, whether he realized it or not, assumed political significance. In consequence, the quarrel became a matter of consuming interest both to the friends and foes of the new philosophy. Everyone talked about it. To do so was more than a frivolity fit to fill up an idle moment. The implications of the quarrel were really of substantial interest to all. That an incident in the private lives of two middle-class writers could absorb the interest of the aristocratic society of the *ancien régime* to such a degree is a symbol of the revolution occurring in the French outlook. The Marquis de Castries, a nobleman destined to be a marshal of France, impatiently remarked one day when the quarrel of Diderot and Rousseau had become public knowledge, 'It's incredible. People don't talk of anything but of those fellows. Persons without an establishment, who don't have a house, who are lodged in a garret. One just can't get used to all that.' [55]

CHAPTER 23

Signs and Portents
of Approaching Eclipse

D'ALEMBERT's decision in January 1758 to forsake the *Encyclopédie*, which he announced as being resolute and which on the contrary was succeeded by over a year of wavering and irresolution, ushered in a period of protracted crisis and confusion. Deleyre wrote to Rousseau on 25 January, during a spell of very cold weather, that 'There is the *Encyclopédie* — spiked. It is no longer going, any more than the water mills have been running these past few days.'[1] The *Journal Encyclopédique* for 1 February mentioned that 'vexations of all kinds have finally obliged M. d'Alembert to give up the work absolutely and irrevocably.'[2] Indeed, the publishers themselves announced to the public in an eight-page pamphlet that the work had been brought to a standstill. This communication, printed in Le Breton's shop and carrying the self-explanatory title of 'Memoir of the Publishers Associated in the *Encyclopédie* regarding the Reasons for the Present Suspension of this Work,' must have been issued early in the year, for it was quoted lengthily in the *Mercure de France* in April. A goodly portion of this pamphlet was devoted to wheedling D'Alembert to return and, to judge from Diderot's informing Voltaire in June that D'Alembert had consented to continue with the mathematical part of the work, it apparently wheedled with a measure of success.[3] As late as 26 February, D'Alembert had written to Voltaire, 'I persist in the resolution not to work any more on the *Encyclopédie*'; yet presently he is to be found doing the opposite of what he had previously announced and adopting a policy diametrically the contrary of what Voltaire had been counseling.[4] The fact is that D'Alembert vacillated a good deal, much to the confusion of biographers, many of whom, putting his desertion in 1759 instead of 1758, seem to be unaware of how protracted and muddled the editorial crisis was,

with D'Alembert loudly announcing that he was quitting, then half-return-
ing, then quitting again, and — even so late as February and April of 1759 —
still considering staying on.

The publishers' appeal to D'Alembert galled Diderot very much. We have
the proof of this in a letter that he wrote about a year later to Sophie Volland.
By this time D'Alembert, who now had given up even the mathematical
part of the *Encyclopédie*, saw Diderot for the first time in several months
and rather lamely proposed being put onto the pay roll again. The fact was
that he was hard up. He lived off pensions, though very modest ones, from
the Prussian and French governments, and these were not being paid because
of the fiscal stringencies induced by the Seven Years' War. The occasion gave
Diderot an opportunity to read D'Alembert quite a lecture. When D'Alembert declared that if he came back, he would write no more prefaces, Diderot
replied, 'You might wish to write some in the course of time, and you
wouldn't be free to.'

'And why not?'

'Because your previous ones have brought down upon us all the animosities
with which we are now laden. Who is there who was not insulted in them?'

Alluding to the publishers' public declaration in the pamphlet of the year
before, Diderot said, 'Nevertheless you quit an enterprise into which they
have put all their fortunes. An affair of two millions is a bagatelle not
worthy of the attention of a philosopher like you. You entice away their
contributors, you throw them into a complication of difficulties from which
they will not soon extricate themselves.[5] All that you see is the slight satisfaction of getting yourself talked about for a moment. They are under the
necessity of addressing the public. You should see how they have regard for
you and *sacrifice me.*'[6]

In addition to causing him to tighten up the censorship of the *Encyclopédie*,
D'Alembert's article on 'Geneva' prompted Malesherbes to re-examine the
whole problem of the relation of the *Encyclopédie* to the government. The
autograph draft of his memorandum, dated about April 1758 and now in
the Bibliothèque Nationale, reveals a startling suggestion. In this letter sent
to Bernis, who was then a member of the Royal Council and soon to become
France's minister for foreign affairs, Malesherbes recommended a policy of
complete autonomy and self-responsibility for the *Encyclopédie*. His letter is
equally revelatory in the information it gives regarding Diderot's status in the
eyes of the authorities: 'As for M. Diderot, he has made some mistakes and
he has been severely punished for them, but are these transgressions irreparable? The disgraces he has already met with and the disfavor that he is

still experiencing, since entry into the academies is forbidden to him for the present moment, are they not sufficient?'[7]

Bernis' reply was affable but noncommittal, and it is not known whether Malesherbes carried his project any further, or whether Diderot realized that the academies were closed to him.[8] When this decision, so adverse to Diderot, was made is not known, but it is clear that not only the French Academy but also the Academy of Sciences were closed to him, and it may perhaps be true that the provincial academies, which at that time were flourishing everywhere in France, were aware of the official disapprobation of Diderot. This might explain why Diderot was never a member of an academy in France, no matter how provincial and obscure.

D'Alembert's decision in early 1758 to retire as an editor of the *Encyclopédie* evidently brought about a new contract between Diderot and the publishers, to judge by one of Diderot's rare letters to Voltaire. Even the latter, who had called Diderot cowardly for wanting to continue the venture, had changed his mind by June 1758, and had inquired whether Diderot would like him to contribute any more articles.

'Do I want your articles, Monsieur and dear master? [wrote Diderot on June 14]. Can there be any doubt about that? Shouldn't one make the trip to Geneva and beg them from you on one's knees, if they could be obtained at no other price? Choose, write, send, send often. I was not able to accept your offers sooner. My arrangement with the publishers is scarcely settled. We have made a fine contract together, like that of the devil and the peasant in La Fontaine. The leaves are for me, the grain is for them. But at least these leaves will be assured me.'[9]

During the early summer of 1758 the preparations for publishing the eighth volume of the *Encyclopédie* were resumed. But the work was badly crippled by D'Alembert's retirement, to judge from the statement of the publishers years later that his quitting was the reason for not publishing a volume in 1758.[10] This time Grimm helped with the reading of proof, Diderot busied himself with his ordinary editorial tasks and with the preparations for the publication of his play, *Le Père de famille,* while the storm brought on by Rousseau's reference to the Book of Ecclesiasticus had not yet broken.[11] But whatever serenity Diderot may have been enjoying in the summer of 1758 was shattered in a twinkling by the publication in late July of the book by Helvétius, *De l'Esprit* ('Concerning the Mind'). This treatise, which in spite of its name dealt more with the springs of ethical action than it did with psychology, had at first seemed so harmless that an official censor had approved it and it was published with tacit permission. All the evidence

points to the fact that Helvétius himself did not dream that his book would
be controversial, which seems to prove that he did not have a very lively
sense of the grand strategy of politics, for De l'Esprit put into grave jeopardy
the cause it intended to serve. The orthodox regarded the book as the most
shocking and outrageous that the century had yet seen in print, and they
contended, moreover, that it was completely representative of the point of
view of the philosophes. Especially was this asserted of Diderot and the
Encyclopédie. The two works were sedulously intertwined by the critics of
both, although Helvétius never contributed any articles to the Encyclopédie.
Nevertheless the latter was made to share by association in the general repro-
bation. In consequence, Diderot found himself living in an atmosphere of
mounting tension and suspense. And before long, crisis was succeeded by
disaster.

De l'Esprit seems rather commonplace to a twentieth-century reader and
reminiscent of that deathless line in the American theater, 'What's all the
shootin' fer?' For Helvétius was simply attempting to found a science of
morality on a basis of behaviorism without the use of transcendental sanctions. As he remarked in his preface, 'I have felt that morality should be
treated like all the other sciences, and that one should make an ethics as one
makes an experimental physics.' His doctrine now seems very much oversimplified, but certainly familiar, indeed almost platitudinous. In fact, he
was a predecessor of Jeremy Bentham and the utilitarian ethics based upon
the pleasure-pain calculus.[12] A twentieth-century student of ethics is likely
to take the basic assumptions of Helvétius regarding the moral nature of
man as true as far as they go, but stated in a simplistic and rather perverse
fashion.

At the time of its publication, however, the orthodox, the conservative, and
the conventional were profoundly shocked by the doctrines of Helvétius
because he made his system of morality quite independent of the will of God
or the behests of religion. There were no other-worldly sanctions. Egotism,
so to speak, was to be its own reward. For Helvétius dressed up his ethics in
the paradox of an exaggerated egotism, claiming that man was virtuous,
when and if he was, only because in that fashion he best satisfied the demands of his own ego. The famous Mme du Deffand remarked of the book
that it upset everyone so much because Helvétius had revealed what was
everyone's secret.

Nor did Helvétius confine himself to views regarding psychology and
ethics. He unburdened himself of a variety of obiter dicta, particularly in
his footnotes, which were as inflammatory as they were extraneous. He dis-

approved of the burdensome forced labor on the highways, he declared that savages were happier than the French peasantry, he attacked the Catholic priesthood as 'not being attached to the general interest,' he wondered whether the Catholic practice of getting rid of daughters by forcing them to take the veil was not more barbarous than the infant exposure of the Chinese, he inveighed against luxury, he insisted (thinking of the belief in miracles) that evidence must be statistical and based on 'the calculation of probabilities,' he praised Julian the Apostate, he very clearly implied that there was no real metaphysical difference between men and animals, and he delivered himself of such humanitarian generalizations as 'not a hogshead of sugar arrives in Europe undyed by human blood.'[13]

Helvétius' book is by no means an unalloyed delight to read, even for those who enjoy collecting antiques. It tiresomely reflects his egotism and humorlessness. The view of human motivation is very narrow. Conduct is motivated almost exclusively by self-esteem, the thirst for fame, and the desire for women, thus mirroring its author more than man.[14] *De l'Esprit* is diffuse. It is repetitious. It shifts ground confusingly by taking advantage of the extraordinary semantic complexities of the word *'esprit.'* Some of the time the book is talking about 'mind,' some of the time about 'wit,' and some of the time in special senses of the word peculiar to Helvétius, as when he makes *'esprit'* equivalent to 'taste' and to 'expertness.' Although metaphors and similes are profuse, the effect is surprisingly uninteresting because his imagery is commonplace and unimaginative and his presentation pedestrian and dull. Diderot remarked of the book that 'A paradoxical author ought never to state his conclusion but always his proofs. He should enter into the mind of his reader slyly, and not by force. . . . If all that the author wrote had been heaped up pell-mell, so that there had been only in the mind of the author an unacknowledged principle of arrangement, his book would have been infinitely more agreeable and, without appearing so, infinitely more dangerous.'[15]

De l'Esprit was published on 27 July 1758. On 10 August the Council of State revoked the license for its publication, and this was followed in turn by fulminations from the Archbishop of Paris (22 November) and Pope Clement XIII (31 January 1759).[16] The unfortunate censor of the book, one of the chief clerks in the Ministry of Foreign Affairs, a man named Tercier, lost his job for having passed the manuscript, and Helvétius himself was deprived of the honorific position he had held of *maître d'hôtel* of the Queen of France.[17] He also had to make a series of solemn retractions.[18] Beyond this, upsetting enough for many men but apparently not very distressing to

Helvétius, nothing much happened to him. As the clearheaded Turgot remarked, what Helvétius had done was 'the most suitable for drawing down upon him the notoriety of being persecuted, which does not do much harm to a rich man, and to make the real weight of it fall upon a large number of honest men of letters who get the lash that Helvétius deserved. . . .'[19] Precisely the same point was made by Grimm, who was particularly alarmed because of Diderot's association with Helvétius in the public mind. 'Philosophy will feel the effects for a long time of the upheaval of opinion that this author caused almost universally by his book. . . . In order to ruin M. Diderot, it has been spread about everywhere that he was the author of all the passages in the book of M. Helvétius that revolted people, although this philosopher has no connection with the latter, and although they do not meet twice a year.' And indeed it is almost certain that Diderot, in spite of what his friend Meister later asserted, had nothing to do with the writing of Helvétius' famous book.[20]

The accusation that the Encyclopedists found most damaging was the allegation that they were closely united in a conscious conspiracy against government and religion. This was very frequently alleged, at no time more crushingly than when the Attorney General of France solemnly declared in 1759 before the highest court in the land that 'It is with grief that we are forced to say it, [but] can one conceal from oneself that there is a project formed, a Society organized, to propagate materialism, to destroy Religion, to inspire a spirit of independence, and to nourish the corruption of morals?'[21] This was but to repeat and summarize the allegations of Palissot in his *Little Letters on Great Philosophers;*[22] of Moreau in his description of the Cacouacs; of an Abraham de Chaumeix, whose multi-volumed *Legitimate Prejudices against the* Encyclopédie, *together with an Essay in Refutation of this Dictionary* began to appear in October 1758; of an *abbé* calling himself De Saint-Cyr in his 'Catechism and Determination of Cases of Conscience, for the Use of Cacouacs.'[23] This allegation of conspiracy became one of the standard myths of the party opposed to the *philosophes,* as may be seen in the Abbé de Barruel's *Mémoires pour servir à l'histoire du Jacobinisme* (1797-8).[24] And it was an allegation that the *philosophes* always insisted, and rightly insisted, was not so. Grimm denied it, D'Alembert denied it, although he evidently decided that it was imprudent to publish the manuscript in which the disclaimer was contained.[25] Even the publishers of the *Encyclopédie* denied it. In their 1758 pamphlet explaining the reasons for the suspension of work on the *Encyclopédie,* they wrote that 'It is the strictest truth [to say] that for the twelve years and more since the *Encyclopédie* was begun, those who co-operate in it have not assembled together one single time. Most of them do not know one another. Each one works individually on the topic that he has adopted, then he sends his work to one of the Editors, without being in communication with the Authors of the other parts.' [26] That it seemed necessary to make so categorical a statement gives some indication of how damaging the constant asseveration of conspiracy must have been. Yet it must be confessed that the *Encyclopédie* invited such suspicions, for it claimed on the title page of each successive volume to have been written by a *society* of men of letters.[27]

In this atmosphere of increasing tension and foreboding crisis, Diderot put the final touches on his play, *Le Père de famille*. It had been a long time in the writing. He had announced to the public in the *Entretiens sur le Fils naturel* that *Le Père de famille* was being planned. This announcement appeared early in February 1757.[28] But Deleyre's letters to Rousseau show that Diderot was hard at work on *Le Père de famille* over a year later.[29] Indeed, the play with its accompanying 'Discourse on Dramatic Poetry' was not actually published until around the beginning of November 1758.[30] One of the reasons for the long delay was the fact that for a while Diderot gave it up in disgust. This is revealed in a letter written on 29 November 1757 to a fellow playwright, Antoine Le Bret, who was worried because of rumors that the plot of his forthcoming play, *Le Faux Généreux,* was similar to Diderot's. In a hand that showed haste and was, in comparison with the firm yet delicate writing customary to him, comparatively illegible, Diderot wrote that the plot of his play, of which Le Bret had evidently been previously informed, remained unchanged. 'The first [play] involved me in so many vexations that I have been on the point twenty times of abandoning the second and throwing into the fire what I have done. My friends have prevented me. I have taken it up again. I have worked at it a little, but so little that it is scarcely worth mentioning. I do not foresee that it can be printed for two months; the printing will take up another one.' [31] Le Bret's play had its *première* on 18 January 1758, but ten months passed before Diderot's play was published.

Diderot dedicated his play to an Exalted Personage, a Sovereign. Not a very important sovereign, it is true, but still a sovereign. This was not his usual way of doing things. Perhaps he did so because he felt his position weakened and needed to boast the support of an august name. Perhaps it was no more than the influence upon him of Grimm, a man who, as someone has remarked, by dint of great efforts finally promoted himself from the rank of foremost critic in Europe to that of third-rate diplomat. Diderot's letter was addressed to Her Serene Highness the Princess of Nassau-Saar-bruck, and concerned the problem of how to educate her children.* Diderot did not meet the Princess until 1765.[32] He submitted his dedication to her through the good offices of Grimm sometime before mid-June 1758, and apparently without having previously broached the subject. The lady ac-cepted gratefully — after all, she was not a very *great* sovereign — in a some-what tremulous shimmer of graceful eighteenth-century rhetoric.[33]

Diderot's dedicatory letter is mainly an exhortation to virtue, and has about it the sooty smell of an academic showpiece, even though Voltaire said he regarded it as a masterpiece of eloquence.[34] Yet Diderot could not touch a subject without leaving the imprint of his personality. It is interesting to see that he does not truckle or fawn. Indeed, putting into the mouth of the Princess the sentiments that he holds and that he professes to believe that she, too, holds, he says, 'I desire that they [the Princess' children] see poverty, in order that they be sensitive to it and in order that they know from their own experience that they are surrounded by men like themselves, *perhaps more essential than they themselves,* who scarcely have straw to lie on and who have no bread.' In view of the fact that Rousseau thought that man was good in the state of nature, it is of importance in understanding Diderot's outlook upon politics that in this letter he spoke critically of man in the state of nature, calling him 'imbecile and savage.' Moreover, he declared that men would have no need of being governed if they were not bad. Remember, Diderot thinks the Princess should tell her children, 'power does not give peace of mind, and labor does not take it away. . . . Virtue is the only habit that you can contract without fear of the future. Sooner or later all the others become importunate.'[35]

The manuscript draft of the dedicatory epistle contained a passage that the Princess particularly and urgently desired suppressed. It is easy to see why. For Diderot had put into her mouth the following words, addressed to her children: 'I shall take very good care not to speak ill of sensual pleasure and not to decry its allure. Its purpose is too august and too universal. I shall speak to you about it as if nature herself were listening. Wouldn't she have the right to reply to whoever should speak ill of sensual delight, "Be silent, foolish one! Do you think that your father would have concerned himself with your birth, that your mother would have risked her life to give you yours, were it not for the unutterable charm that I have linked to their em-braces? It was pleasure that brought you forth out of nothing."' Even for the eighteenth century, this was a little strong.[36]

---

* There is an English translation, *Concerning the Education of a Prince,* ed. John M. S. Allison (New Haven, 1941).

In October of 1758 the *Père de famille* was in the process of being printed and Diderot was extremely impatient to get it off the press. Dr. Lavirotte, Regent of the Faculty of Medicine and a friend of Diderot as well as the author of the article *'Docteur en Médecine'* in the *Encyclopédie,* was the censor assigned by Malesherbes.[37] 'I wanted to send both one and the other [the play and the supplementary "Discourse on Dramatic Poetry"] to M. de Malesherbes,' Lavirotte reported, 'but M. Diderot hurried me so much and is so impatient to see his work printed that he carried it away right out of hand.'[38] Malesherbes evidently informed Lavirotte that some changes would have to be made in both the play and its accompanying essay before they would be allowed to appear. Somewhat plaintively he wrote to the censor that apparently Diderot could not write even an essay on dramatics without mentioning government and religion in two or three places.[39] Nor did Lavirotte think it would be easy to persuade Diderot to make changes: 'I merely wish to beg you to observe that no one will have enough authority over the mind of M. Diderot to persuade him regarding these suppressions and alterations. He will resign himself to them only as a result of the most categorical orders.'[40]

Diderot did make some changes, though very reluctantly. 'Here are the *cartons* [substitute pages, to be tipped into volumes already printed and bound] that you have required. The things that have offended you have been suppressed and those that appeared harsh to you, softened.'[41] But Diderot tried to save from the blue pencil a passage occurring in the second act, where the Father of the Family recalls the prayer he prayed when his son was born. Malesherbes objected to Diderot's reference to God, on the grounds that people would regard it as hypocritical. 'How can you make out that I shall be accused of hypocrisy? I am no more the Father of the Family than I am the Commander; and if one has me in mind when reading me, then the piece must be poor indeed.'[42] Apparently Diderot was able to persuade Malesherbes to let the passage stand. It reads as follows: 'My son, it will soon be twenty years since I bathed you with the first tears you caused me to shed. My heart leaped up as I saw in you a friend given me by nature. I received you into my arms from the bosom of your mother, and, raising you toward Heaven and mingling my voice with your cries, I said to God, "O God! who have granted me this child, if I fail in the cares You have laid upon me this day, or if he is not destined to respond to them, have no regard for the gladness of his mother, but take him back." '[43]

The altercation regarding the prayer caused in Diderot a considerable effusion of temperament. 'I saw the man last evening at the Marquis de Croismare's,' wrote Lavirotte to Malesherbes, probably about 19 October.

'He was in such a violent fit of despair that we feared lest he throw himself out of the window.' [44] And Diderot's letter to Malesherbes, dated 20 October, bears the marks of strong emotion:

This prayer rings true. It is simple. It is moving. It is well placed. This is the opinion of M. de Saint Lambert. It is that of M. d'Argental. The latter was moved by it and the former told me that one does not conceive of such effects unless one has genius. I admit, Monsieur, that friendship for me has made them excessive in their praise. But I have tested this passage on other persons. My wife is a good woman who lacks neither common sense nor taste, and it has given her pleasure. . . .

. . . deign to consider my situation. Observe that for ten years, for thirty, I drink bitterness in a cup never empty. You do not know, Monsieur, how unfortunate my life has been. I have suffered, I think, all that it pleases destiny to make us suffer, and I was born with a sensitivity out of the ordinary. The present misfortune brings to mind misfortune in the past. One's heart swells. One's character grows embittered, and one says and does foolish things. If that has happened to me, I ask a thousand pardons.[45]

As Diderot was finishing his letter, his publisher brought news that Malesherbes was assigning a new censor to the job. This was even worse, wrote Diderot, for the new man would inevitably demand new changes, which meant new *cartons,* all at Diderot's expense. 'Monsieur, have the goodness to revoke an order injurious to a censor whom you esteem and which will be ruinous for me. . . . Monsieur, do not ruin me . . . do not destroy me.' [46] Nevertheless, Malesherbes sent the book not to one new censor but to two.[47] Censors, however, were becoming exceedingly shy, very conscious of the calamities overtaking the unfortunate censor of the book by Helvétius, on the one hand, or the sort of browbeating they were likely to get from the *philosophes,* on the other. One of the censors appointed by Malesherbes begged off for the first reason.[48] The second censor, a man named Bonamy, wrote on 29 October, 'I shall inform the publisher that I have had the honor of sending the work back to you, as being beyond my strength and my enlightenment to pass judgment on, which I confess to being true. But as I ask only for peace and comfort, and as I do not wish to have a quarrel with people who imagine themselves the sole possessors of all human reason, I dare to flatter myself that you will keep the word that you had the kindness to give me that you would not compromise me with them, for I am apprehensive of them as much as I am of the theologians.' [49] Apparently, after all this turmoil, Malesherbes was fain to let *Le Père de famille* be published without further change. In spite of the censorship Diderot had had his own way.

Not long after this display of temperament, Diderot had another adventure with the office of the director of publications. This was a real mystery story, and still remains so to a large degree — the Affair of the Dedications. Malesherbes referred to it as the most annoying and displeasing of his whole administration, and clearly the culprit would have been severely punished had Malesherbes been sure who was guilty of the hoax.[50] The facts are these: There had been timed to appear just after the publication of *Le Père de famille* two of Goldoni's plays, anonymously translated by two of Diderot's friends. *Il Vero Amico,* the play that it was alleged Diderot had plagiarized, was translated by Forbonnais, the man who had contributed to the *Encyclopédie* the admired articles on business and commercial transactions. *Il Padre di famiglia* was translated by Deleyre, the young journalist who in this same year had tried so hard to reconcile Diderot and Rousseau. These translations — usually bound together in one volume, if they can be found at all, so rare have they become — bear up creditably in a collation with the original. They are faithful and idiomatic. Nothing in the originals is suppressed, although not infrequently lines are added, especially to serve as transitions between scenes. No effort at all, however, was made to tamper with *Il Vero Amico* in any way favorable to Diderot. As for *Il Padre di famiglia,* it is so far removed in everything but name from *Le Père de famille* that there could be no question of borrowing.

These plays, when they were published, purported to be printed at Avignon and to be on sale at Liége at Etienne Bleichnarr's. There was no Etienne Bleichnarr. The name means in German 'pale fool,' of which the equivalent in French is *'pâle sot.'* Thus the word 'Bleichnarr' turned out to be simply a pun on the name of Palissot, the bitter enemy of the Encyclopedists and the author of *'Little Letters on Great Philosophers.'* In addition, each play carried as epigraph a long and puzzling Latin quotation and a dedication, one to the Comtesse de * * * and the other to the Princesse de * * * * * *, in flowery, insinuating, ambiguous, and probably insulting language.[51] Almost as soon as the plays were published, complaints were lodged with Malesherbes by two ladies of high position who happened to be well known as enemies of the *philosophes*. The Comtesse de La Marck, who by birth was a Noailles, claimed to be the person designated by the dedication in *Le Véritable Ami;* the Princesse de Robecq (who was the daughter of the Marshal of Luxembourg and had recently been the mistress of the Duke of Choiseul) by the dedication of the translation of *Il Padre di famiglia.*

In the code of eighteenth-century French manners, unfavorable personal allusions in the press or on the stage were regarded as a grave affront, no

matter how veiled or slight. This was one of the indirect consequences of
censorship. For everyone supposed that such attacks, if allowed publication,
were tacitly approved by the government. Consequently all such situations
became a matter of 'face.' Someone lost it, and a struggle would develop to
see which party enjoyed the greater public credit in the effort to get it back.
This was the reason why D'Alembert consistently showed himself very
touchy about allusions in the press that one is tempted to think it would have
been wiser to ignore. And in this instance, in conformity with this social
code, Malesherbes took a grim view of the incident of the dedications and
started a determined investigation to discover who had written them and was
responsible for their publication.

Malesherbes quickly satisfied himself of the innocence of the translators,
Forbonnais and Deleyre. The trail next led to Diderot, who had had the
manuscripts of the translations for some days, but who insisted that there
were no dedications either when they came into his hands or when they
left them.[52] The Comtesse de La Marck had supposed Diderot to be the
guilty one — D'Hémery noted in his journal that she was in 'a frightful
rage' against Diderot.[53] Diderot called upon her, and managed somehow to
placate her. Perhaps it was that gifted tongue of his. Probably, though, it
required something more substantial, for according to Palissot's account of
the matter to Voltaire, Mme de La Marck secured a signed confession from
Diderot.[54] Then Mme de La Marck, in a letter to Malesherbes quite charming in its phonetic orthography, so revelatory of the well-bred illiteracy of
the upper classes, informed him that she was satisfied and that Mme de
Robecq and she desired him to carry the matter no further.[55]

Malesherbes' reply pointed out that a legal offense had been committed, as
well as some moral ones: a premeditated attempt had been made to deceive
him, the responsible magistrate, and to make innocent persons, namely
Deleyre and Forbonnais, seem guilty. 'So, Madame, I beg of you to have
these authors [of the dedications] informed, since they have made themselves known to you, that all they have to do is to make their confession
likewise to me, and I promise you that they shall suffer from me nothing
more than the disesteem that their manner of acting necessarily brings in its
train.' But if they did not confess to him, he would put the affair into the
hands of the Lieutenant-General of Police.[56]

At this juncture Forbonnais wrote Malesherbes insisting that someone
must make public and explicit acknowledgment of personal responsibility
for the translations in their entirety. Otherwise, he wrote, he and Deleyre
would be unjustly suspected of being responsible for the dedications. If this

was not done, he and Deleyre would resort to the law, and the affair would become a public scandal.[57] Forbonnais went on to say that witnesses had seen a lackey in Grimm's service leaving a copy of the published translations at the door of Forbonnais' lodgings.

The protest from Forbonnais caused Malesherbes to write to the Comtesse de La Marck again. 'It is you, Madame, who brought M. Diderot to his senses, first out of fear and then out of admiration and gratitude for the nobility of your way of acting.' Malesherbes explained the difficulty with Forbonnais, and strongly implied that the Comtesse was the only person in a position to assure that Forbonnais be satisfied.[58] Evidently Malesherbes was hinting that she should persuade Diderot to take the public responsibility. At all events, this is what Diderot did, whether Mme de La Marck persuaded him or Forbonnais did. It was the latter who forwarded to Malesherbes the copy of a letter that Forbonnais had drafted and Diderot had signed.[59] And in due time there appeared in the November issue of the *Observateur Littéraire* and the December issue of the *Mercure de France* the following notice:

Ill-informed persons, Monsieur, having spread about that the published translation of *Le Père de famille* of Goldoni was done by M. Deleyre and that of *Le Véritable Ami* by M. de Forbonnais, the knowledge that I have of these two plays obliges me to declare that [the translations] just published are very different, and it is established that neither the one nor the other had a part in the printing and publication of these works.

I have the honor, etc.,

Paris, 21 November 1758   Diderot [60]

It will be noticed that Diderot, although he absolves Deleyre and Forbonnais, does not hint as to who was guilty. The hostile Palissot assured Voltaire that it was Diderot himself, but Voltaire replied that he could not believe it.[61] Grimm, commenting on Voltaire's letter, told his correspondents that D'Argental, investigating the matter for Voltaire, had been informed by Mme de La Marck that she had had the signed confession in her hand, that she had immediately burned it, and that the secret of who it was would die with her.[62] Certainly the affair had an air of mystery about it to the end. Malesherbes wrote to the Lieutenant-General of Police over a year later, 'This affair remains unpunished for lack of proof,' and added that the guilty parties were under strong suspicion but yet were not known with certainty.[63]

In fact, however, Grimm was the guilty one. The German pun on the name of Palissot, the lackey delivering a copy of the translations at Forbonnais' lodgings, pointed toward him. And A. A. Barbier, an early nineteenth-century literary antiquarian, asserted that Grimm was the author, that Diderot took the guilt upon himself, that the offended ladies soon learned that this was what Diderot had done, and that the affair had had no other consequences.[64] But all this remained a little conjectural until the recent discovery and publication of a letter from Diderot to Grimm written over twenty years after the incident had occurred. Diderot's letter permits no doubt that Grimm was the real author of the dedications.[65]

Why, then, did Diderot take the guilt upon himself? It is possible that this was a really heroic decision. Yet, in what was obviously an extremely complex situation, one can only speculate as to what were his motives. Perhaps one of his reasons was that his friend Grimm was a foreigner and might have had extremely harsh treatment meted out to him, such as deportation, which in Grimm's case would have been calamitous both professionally and personally. We should like to suppose that Diderot's conduct was simply the result of courageous generosity, but in view of the innumerable and varied pressures that must have been playing upon him in this emergency, it is impossible to say with assurance just why he acted the way he did.

Still another question must be asked, a very grave one indeed. How guilty was Diderot, from the point of view of the probity he was always talking about? Unknowingly involved in this intrigue were two men whom Diderot knew to be innocent, two men who thought of themselves as Diderot's friends. Did Diderot connive at attempting to make them seem responsible for having written the dedications? Even though he was protecting his friend Grimm, Diderot incurred some moral guilt in this respect, because it is a matter of record that only under pressure did he exculpate Forbonnais and Deleyre. It may have been, therefore, to this incident that Deleyre was referring when in a letter to Rousseau he spoke of having discovered a knave among the philosophers and of having been made his dupe.[66] Diderot's conduct certainly seems to have been ambiguous — perhaps it was laudable, perhaps it was culpable. Perhaps — for he was a man given to subtle rationalizations when cases of conscience were involved — he here revealed that his early moral training had been in the hands of the Jesuits, men who had long been accused of flagrant sophistry in such matters.[67] Diderot often showed in his writings and letters his awareness of life's real and constant ambiguities, ambiguities of conduct as well as ambiguities of thought. In fact, he wrote his liveliest play upon this very theme. In this piece the hero, Hardouin, is a picture of Diderot as Diderot conceived of himself, an affable and obliging man who, from the best of motives, involves himself in the most dubious and ambiguous conduct. In the final scene the question is asked that gives the name to the play: 'Is he good? Is he bad?' And Diderot-Hardouin replies, 'Alternately.' Similarly, one can ask the same question regarding the part Diderot played in the affair of the dedications: *Est-il bon? Est-il méchant?*

Perhaps the answer is the same.

CHAPTER 24

Le Père de Famille and the
'Discourse on Dramatic Poetry'

Like his *Fils naturel,* Diderot's *Père de famille* did not immediately receive the honors of a production at the Comédie-Française. This had to wait until 1761, but meanwhile the play quickly became a widely read and influential book. Between 1758 and 1800 there were thirty-two editions of it published in French; ten in German; three in English, plus a play by Gentleman Johnny Burgoyne more strongly influenced by Diderot than the General wished to acknowledge; three in Dutch; two each in Russian, Danish, Polish, and Italian; and one in Spanish.[1] Many of these editions, especially the ones in French, also contained the accompanying 'Discourse on Dramatic Poetry,' so that Diderot's ideas on the theater, expressed in this book as well as in the preceding *Entretiens sur le Fils naturel,* may safely be said to have reached a wide audience.

To *ancien régime* society it seemed self-evident that one of the principal preoccupations of a father was to secure suitable matrimonial arrangements for his children, and the two main 'pivots' in this new play, as Diderot himself pointed out, were to be the establishment in marriage of the Father of the Family's two children.[2] Diderot had already stated, in his *Entretiens sur le Fils naturel,* his conviction that the theater should concern itself with the points of view and behaviorisms of people's professional and family relationships — the judge, the businessman, the man of letters, the father of a family. 'The father of a family! What a subject!' he cried.[3] *Le Père de famille,* therefore, was a play in which parental prudence came into violent conflict with the impetuosity of a young lover. Its plot greatly resembled the real-life circumstances of Diderot's courtship of Anne-Toinette Champion, even to the use of a *lettre de cachet.* Interesting as such a play was to the eighteenth-century public, it is even more interesting to a person studying Diderot's life, for it is evident that the Father of the Family is Diderot's own; that Saint-Albin, the spirited young lover, is Diderot's recollection of himself; that the peevish and hateful Commander, the brother-in-law of the Father of the Family and therefore the uncle of Saint-Albin and Cécile, is Diderot's conception of the character of his younger brother, the Abbé; [4] that Cécile, the daughter of the family, 'a composite of loftiness of character, vivacity, reserve, and sensitivity,' is Diderot's idea of the character of his sister; [5] and that the heroine (whose name is Sophie and not Anne-Toinette) is probably Diderot's picture of what he supposed Sophie Volland to have been like when she was young.[6] Certainly the characterization of the part suggests that Diderot had Sophie Volland rather than his wife in mind when he wrote it. If so, Diderot consciously or unconsciously gave Mme Diderot the slight of transferring his mistress' character and his mistress' name to a role that his wife had played with him in real life. It is not very surprising that Mme Diderot did not go to see the play until its revival in 1769, nor did she go very eagerly even then, to her husband's annoyance.[7]

Still another interesting aspect of this play about family life is that no living mother nor wife figures in it. The Father of the Family is a widower. Now and again Diderot's characters refer with affection to the mother, but her absence is by no means essential to the plot. Therefore it is evident that Diderot felt unwilling or unable to deal adequately with this character in his play. Surely a psychiatrist could speculate very interestingly upon the biographical significance of Diderot's leaving the mother out of a play, the whole concern of which is with family relationships.[8]

The action takes place within the duration of twenty-four hours in the house of M. d'Orbesson, the Father of the Family. Saint-Albin, the son, has taken of late to staying out at night, and the family is revealed, as the curtain goes up, awaiting his return. After these characters have got the play started, they retire for the night, leaving the Father of the Family alone. Saint-Albin presently enters, dressed as an artisan, and explains that he has fallen in love with a virtuous young woman who supposes him to be a workingman. Sophie, temporarily stranded in Paris, is attempting to earn enough money by spinning to enable her to return home. Entreated by Saint-Albin, the Father of the Family consents to see her.

The Father finds the young lady attractive, but not of a sufficient fortune or social standing to be suitable for his son. He therefore offers to provide for her return if she will give up Saint-Albin. A very stormy scene ensues between the son and the father (who ends by pronouncing his malediction), and between the son and the uncle. The son resolves to kidnap his beloved, while the disapproving old Commander decides to secure a *lettre de cachet* that will get her out of the way. Many alarms and excursions follow, through the rest of the five acts, and the reader is likely to agree more than once with Fréron, who wrote that 'At every instant one feels the quandary he [Diderot] is in to stretch his play out. He imitates those unscrupulous manufacturers who pull their cloth violently in order to give it greater length at the expense of its quality.' [9] The play might even yet be unsatisfactorily resolved had it not turned out, by the greatest of coincidences, that the Commander is also Sophie's uncle! This revelation, a *deus ex machina* almost identical with the one in *Le Fils naturel,* establishes the fact that Sophie is of good family — obviously! for she is her lover's first cousin — so that all ends happily, save that the gruff and cantankerous Commander remains unyielding, unrepentant, and in character to the very end.

In accordance with the principles of playwriting that Diderot had already enunciated in his *Entretiens sur le Fils naturel, Le Père de famille* contained elaborate tableaux, quite in the fashion of Greuze, such as the scene at the beginning of the second act that portrays the Father of the Family's philanthropy, and the scene ending the play. Also included in the script were detailed descriptions of scene decoration and indications of stage business, and the speeches of the actors were often written in disjointed prose and unfinished sentences in order to indicate the use of gestures or the effect of strong passions. Frequently these speeches have a telling effect. Saint-Albin, especially, speaks the authentic language of an impulsive and mercurial young man overwhelmingly in love. Moreover, he speaks the language of a man who is purified by the experience. This accent upon the virtuousness of romantic love, preceding Rousseau's *Nouvelle Héloïse* by two years, represented something new and compelling in the French theater and shows that a subtle change was at work in the mores of the age.[10] 'You don't know what I owe to Sophie, you don't know. . . . She has changed me, I am no longer what I was. . . .' And when the worldly Commander asks Saint-Albin what he thinks he is going to live on, the latter replies with bright confidence, as though it were all the wealth of the Indies, 'I have fifteen hundred livres a year!' [11] The eighteenth century liked that.

Like Lucifer in *Paradise Lost,* the most absorbing character in the whole play is one who was scarcely meant to be so. This is the Commander, and it is a good touch to leave him to the very end unconciliatory and unreconciled. The Father of the Family, on the other hand, does not fill the role intended for him. He is too passive. He follows the action instead of dominating it.

Although *Le Père de famille* was a quite interesting play regarding a complicated tale of love, it was far from demonstrating what Diderot thought it demonstrated: the peculiar point of view of paternal relationship. To show that, he would have had to make his father of the family a much more positive and dynamic character, and much more in conflict with himself.[12]

Diderot was, however, proud of his plot, and declared that he had written it straight through, the first scene first and the last scene last.[13] While he was constructing it, he wrote to an acquaintance who had hinted that the plan of the work could be recontrived if necessary, 'This plot is sewn in such a manner, this framework is assembled in such a fashion, that I would not be able to rip a stitch or misplace a peg without the whole thing's collapsing.'[14] The complications in the play are symbolized by the fact that the synopsis of it in a standard contemporary dictionary of the theater ran to three tightly packed pages.[15] But in spite of its involutions, Diderot was ingenuously pleased with his plot — he admired it through several pages of his accompanying 'Discourse on Dramatic Poetry' — especially because he regarded it as psychologically sound and as having the proper sort of inevitability and inexorability about it.[16] Not every critic has agreed with him.[17]

By a passing allusion to an incident in which Saint-Albin had figured during the siege of Port Mahon, Diderot increased the feeling of contemporaneity in *Le Père de famille*. This made his references to such matters as convents and *lettres de cachet* all the more topical and daring. When Cécile declares her intention of entering a convent, the Father of the Family refuses to allow her 'to descend into a living tomb': 'Nature, by according you social qualities, did not destine you to uselessness.' Even more bold was Diderot's making the *lettre de cachet* the villain of the piece. Perhaps he remembered the villainous role a *lettre de cachet* had played in his own courtship. At all events, this instrument of the king's will was not used in Diderot's play, as it had been in Molière's *Tartuffe,* to make the play come out happily; to the contrary, it was only by *not* using the *lettre de cachet* that a happy denouement was reached. To imply that an exercise of the king's will would be equivalent to calamity was daring indeed. Moreover, Diderot insinuated that *lettres de cachet* were purchasable, and for reasons of private vengeance. For he has the Commander say of Cécile's maid, a person whom the Commander heartily dislikes, 'But I have overlooked one thing. The name of this Clairet would have done very well on my *lettre de cachet,* and it wouldn't have cost any more.'[18] Could Dickens be more pointed? When the play was finally produced, these lines were not spoken. The censor Bonamy had remarked to Malesherbes that it was none of Diderot's business either to praise or to blame *lettres de cachet*.[19] Nevertheless the book was printed as Diderot had written it.

Diderot presented Voltaire with a copy of *Le Fils naturel* and, a year later, of *Le Père de famille*. In each case Voltaire was plainly embarrassed as to how to reply. The tactics he used in acknowledging the first evidently seemed to him successful enough to bear a second trial, for the letter of thanks for the second was extremely like its elder sister. Voltaire's formula was a simple one. It consisted of praising the author rather than the author's play. 'The work you sent me, Monsieur,' he wrote in regard to *Le Fils naturel*, 'resembles its author; it appears to me to be full of virtues, sensitivity, and philosophy. Like you, I think that there is much to be reformed in the theater at Paris. . . . I exhort you to diffuse in the *Encyclopédie*, as much as you are able, the noble freedom of your soul.' [20] Acknowledging in its turn *Le Père de famille*, Voltaire wrote that it contained 'tender and virtuous things, in a new style, as with everything you write.' Then he hurriedly changed the subject to the *Encyclopédie*. 'You deserved to be better seconded,' he wrote, which was a very significant thing to say only six months after D'Alembert's desertion.[21] That Voltaire had no high opinion of *Le Père de famille*, however, is proved by his letter to Mme du Deffand regarding it. 'Have you had *Le Père de famille* read to you? Isn't it ludicrous? In faith, our century is a poor one compared to that of Louis XIV.' [22]

It might seem odd, since *Le Père de famille* was written in prose, that Diderot should entitle the little book accompanying it a 'Discourse on Dramatic Poetry.' He used the word *'poésie,'* however, in the figurative sense of signifying 'all that is lofty and touching in a work of art.' [23] In his several chapters Diderot dealt with such subjects as plot, dialogue, incident, the different kinds of plays, characterization, division of a play into acts and scenes, stage decoration, costumes, pantomime and gestures, and, most important of all, the social function of the theater. In illustrating his points he exhibited a broad command of classic and modern authors. Of course he had much to say about Corneille, Racine, Molière, and Voltaire, and he punctuated his discourse with allusions to Boileau, Fénelon, La Rochefoucauld, the Abbé Prévost, Buffon, and even, in spite of the censor's warning, to Helvétius.[24] He also referred to Aristotle, Plato, Homer, Euripides, Sophocles, Aristophanes, Plautus, Anacreon, Catullus, Lucretius, Horace, Shakespeare, George Lillo (author of *The London Merchant, or The History of George Barnwell*), and Samuel Richardson of current *Pamela-Clarissa* fame. The author whom he relied upon most, however, as providing models for his own type of play, was Terence.[25] Diderot was again at pains to show that his *drame* was really as old as Terence and yet as new as *Le Père de famille*.

Diderot's proposals for reform in the theater were inspired by his out-spoken conviction that almost everything about current play production rang false. In reply to some criticisms of his 'Discourse on Dramatic Poetry' that a well-known actress and novelist of the day, Mme Riccoboni, had sent to him, Diderot remarked, 'Indeed, my friend, I have not been to the theater ten times in fifteen years. The falseness of everything done there is unendur-able to me.' [26]

Diderot had a point. Much in the acting and play production of the day was needlessly conventional and artificial. There was more emphasis upon declaiming than upon acting. Diderot accused the actors of his day of acting with the face only, not with the whole body, and cited Garrick as the example they should emulate.[27] To correct the mannerisms of actors, Diderot favored rehearsals in an arena before a critical audience, a suggestion which entitles him, some people think, to be considered as the inventor of theater-in-the-round. Then, too, actors dressed magnificently and irrelevantly, with no regard to the nature of their parts.[28] Diderot believed in a greater co-ordina-tion of the various theatrical arts than was customary. For example, he emphasized scenic effects, to be achieved in part by the skillful grouping and teamwork of the players; he called these effects tableaux, having in mind what a modern director would probably call dynamics.[29] Furthermore, he in-sisted that the painting of stage scenery required a greater rigor and fidelity to truth than any other kind of painting.[30] All this implied, as a great student of French literature has remarked, the complete reformation of theatrical production. 'Every improvement in the art of production for the past 150 years has sprung from Diderot, and the innovators of today still take their rise from him, even when they deny it.' [31]

When Diderot wrote, the performances of the Comédie-Française were still much impaired by the presence of spectators on the stage itself. Even the best actors were hampered by this practice, for scarcely anything could be conceived more apt to destroy the illusion of the theater. The custom was a source of income to the company of the Comédie-Française, however, al-though everyone suffered from having to make entrances and exits while dodging around some count or marquis engaged in his own distracting con-versation. Diderot remarked in his letter to Mme Riccoboni that no one should be allowed on the stage: then improvements could be brought about at once in scene decoration.[32] As it happened, this particular reform, which marked the end of an epoch in the French theater, was about to be accom-plished. Thanks to a substantial endowment given by a Comte de Lauraguais, the company of the Comédie-Française agreed thenceforth to forego the revenue accruing from selling places on the stage. Dating from the Easter vacation of 1759, spectators were banished from the stage of the Comédie-Française.[33]

The 'Discourse on Dramatic Poetry' was a flavorsome essay because Diderot injected a great deal of his own personality into it.* For example, not only was the whole work dedicated 'To my friend, Monsieur Grimm,' but Diderot also wrote in the body of the work, 'One should always have virtue and virtuous people in mind when one writes. It is you, my friend, whom I invoke when I take up my pen; it is you whom I have before my eyes when I do anything. It is Sophie whom I desire to please. If you have smiled upon me, if she has shed a tear, if both of you love me more than ever, I am recompensed.'[34] As one biographer of Diderot has remarked, it is only in the eighteenth century that a situation like this would be likely to occur: a married man's unmarried mistress and his friend, the bachelor lover of another man's wife, are invoked as the twin inspirations of a play, the purpose of which is to glorify the family.[35]

Diderot was led into making the 'Discourse on Dramatic Poetry' a very personal book by the nature of his argument. Because I am what I am, he said in effect, I write the kind of plays that I do. Naturally, this line of thought made it necessary for him to tell the reader what sort of person he was, and one finds in the essay a number of pen portraits of the author as he seemed to himself. Now, of course, Diderot not only thought that he was as he described himself, but he also thought, quite obviously, that it would be well for others if they resembled him as much as possible. Doubtless this is a method of literary criticism that egotists find congenial and yet, when used by a great temperament of Diderot's range and depth, it cannot be condemned as simply fatuous. Diderot's views, subjective as they are, were extremely influential, and he has been called, quite rightly, not merely an author but a legislator.[36] To give some idea of how seriously Diderot's ideas were taken, it is apposite to recall that Lessing, the anonymous translator into German of Diderot's plays and dramatic essays (1760), declared in his introduction that 'I might well say that no more philosophical mind than his has occupied itself with the theater since Aristotle.'[37]

Diderot conceived of himself as having an upright and straightforward character, perhaps a little simple but all the more respectable because of it. 'Born with a sensitive and upright disposition, I confess, my friend, that I have never been dismayed by any task from which I could hope to emerge

---

* The first five sections of Diderot's 'Discourse,' out of a total of twenty-two, are published in English translation by John Gaywood Linn in *Dramatic Essays of the Neo-Classic Age,* eds. Henry Hitch Adams and Baxter Hathaway (New York, 1950), 349–60.

successfully through the use of reason and integrity. These are the weapons that my parents early taught me to manage: I have so often used them against others and against myself!' [38]

Although he spoke with gratification of his use of reason, he was equally proud of his ability to respond to situations emotionally. This was the sensitivity, the *sensibilité,* that he and most of his biographers have regarded as the central and most important characteristic of his personality.[39] This extreme response to the emotional implications of a circumstance is not merely one of the most significant phenomena in the personality of Diderot. It is also one of the interesting crosscurrents in the Age of Reason, coloring much of the literature of the second half of the eighteenth century.[40] Diderot had always appreciated the role of emotions in psychological experience, and the first apothegm in his *Pensées philosophiques* had burst out: 'People are forever inveighing against the passions . . . yet it is only the passions, and grand passions, that can lift the soul to great things.' And when, in 1758, he analyzed his own personality, in reply to an assertion by Mme Riccoboni that he had a great deal of wit, he emphasized once again his *sensibilité* and surprisingly denied his wit: 'I? One cannot have less. But I have something better: simplicity; sincerity; warmth in the soul; a mind easily kindled; an inclination to be enthusiastic; a love for the good, the true, and the beautiful; a disposition ready to smile, to admire, to become indignant, to sympathize, to weep. Furthermore, I know how to be carried beyond myself, a talent without which one can do nothing worth while.' [41]

When he thought of himself as a philosopher, he liked to think he resembled the ancients. This is apparent in his description of the philosopher, Aristes, who is obviously Diderot's conception of himself: '. . . almost the only thing that he lacked of an ancient philosopher was the mantle.' [42] Particularly, he thought of himself as having a great deal of the massive simplicity, the ruggedness, and starkness of the ancients. 'Nature has given me,' he wrote, 'a taste for simplicity, and I seek to perfect it by reading the classics.' [43] Thus, by mentioning the ancients, he makes the transition from talking about simplicity in himself to talking about simplicity in plays.

This simplicity he finds in the manners and morals of the ancient peoples, against which he contrasts the conventionalities and fussiness of the manners (and the plays) of his day. Of course it is easy — and true — to say of his doctrine that his precepts were better than his example. The mountain labored and produced a melodrama. But his precepts were, nevertheless, very good. By his constant reference to the manners and to the drama of the ancients, Diderot hoped to reveal essential insights into the twin mysteries of artistic creation and the aesthetic appreciation of it. For he accepted as self-evident that the elemental and unsophisticated folkways of the ancients, the simple and profound insights of the classic dramatists, could reveal the components of genius and clarify for moderns the proper criteria of taste. Much of Diderot's 'Discourse on Dramatic Poetry,' therefore, goes beyond mere problems of stagecraft to the deepest and most mysterious sources of creativity and the appreciation of creativity. One complements the other. The artist produces what the spectator appreciates. As Diderot formulated it, one facet of the problem was genius, the other was taste; one creation, the other appreciation.

As for genius, Diderot had a theory that it exists at all times, 'but the men who possess it remain torpid unless extraordinary events excite the mass and cause men of genius to appear. Then feelings accumulate in the breast, ferment there, and those who have a voice, feeling impelled, unleash it and feel relieved. . . . Poetry demands a certain something of the enormous, the barbarous, and the wild. . . . When will poets be born? After a period of disasters and great misfortunes, when the harassed peoples commence to breathe once more.'[44] Diderot's was a theory of art not unlike that of the Romantics; in particular, Victor Hugo.[45]

The mystery of genius fascinated Diderot, and speculation about it often recurs in his writings.[46] But he was almost equally interested in discovering the proper criteria of taste. Both required the faculty of imagination, of that he was sure, for he wrote, 'Imagination! — there's the quality without which one cannot be a poet or a philosopher or a man of reason or a man of wit or, simply, a man.'[47] In the search for the canons of good taste, Diderot felt and hoped that there is a discoverable standard, 'a rule anterior to everything else.'[48] 'In morals as in the arts,' he added, in his letter to Mme Riccoboni, 'there is no good or bad as far as I am concerned save that which is good or bad at all times and everywhere. I desire that my morality and my taste be eternal. . . . It is only the true that is of all times and places.'[49]

Diderot's mention of morals and arts in the same sentence emphasizes once again his utilitarian approach to problems of taste and artistic creation. In the last analysis Diderot found the supreme purpose of the playwright to consist of combining the moral and the aesthetic. In this view the theater becomes a kind of temple for a secular cult, wherein the good man is confirmed in his goodness and the bad man given pause. 'The pit of the theater is the only place in which the tears of the virtuous man mingle with those of the vicious one. There, the evil man becomes irritated against the very injustices he has himself committed, sympathizes with the misfortunes that he himself has caused, and grows indignant at a man of his own character. But the impression has been made; it lingers in us, in spite of ourselves; and the evil man leaves his box less disposed to do evil than if he had been scolded by a severe and harsh orator.' [50]

Such views are, of course, anathema to those aestheticians who analyze art simply in terms of itself, a process described, sometimes with unkind intent, as 'art for art's sake.' They were also anathema to the orthodox Christians of Diderot's day, who were inclined to be scandalized, as was the censor of Le Père de famille, at the proposition that the stage could be a better vehicle for preaching than the pulpit.[51] Diderot's attitude can be explained in part by his opposition to Christian morality, in part by his conviction of the positive effect the drama had had in ancient times and the effect that it still might have in his own day.

Diderot expected great things from the theater, provided that it was organized in accordance with principles he deemed correct. Should this be done, the theater could offer, in morals as in the arts, standards that are 'eternal.' Thus his 'Discourse on Dramatic Poetry,' which might at first seem only about how to contrive a plot or decorate a scene, in reality embraced some of the greatest and the most abiding themes — of the nature of genius and the criteria of taste; of the function of the artist; and, most of all, of the good, the beautiful, and the true. Nor was this all — as if in a work on aesthetics this was not enough. For Diderot had, as usual, a passion for melioration. His desire for the improvement of conditions, combined with his faith in the useful and utilitarian, caused him to hope that the playwright could indeed be a sort of 'legislator,' a Lycurgus magnificently devoting his genius to the betterment of his fellow man. 'Oh! what good would redound to men,' he wrote, 'if all the imitative arts would adopt a common purpose and one day would co-operate with the laws in making us love virtue and hate vice.' Such an attitude explains why his book was important in the general ferment of eighteenth-century ideas, even though one may contend that it was often mistaken. 'Every people has prejudices to be destroyed, vices to be attacked, ridiculous customs to be decried, and every people has need of plays, but plays appropriate to it. What a means of preparing for the changing of a law or the abrogation of a custom, if the government knows how to use it!' [52]

Thus, at the end, Diderot arrived at the threshold of politics.

CHAPTER 25

The Death of the Phoenix

WHILE Diderot the playwright was enjoying in the winter of 1785-9 a very considerable success, Diderot the Encyclopedist was faring badly. Crisis had become chronic in the affairs of the *Encyclopédie*. D'Alembert's resignation had greatly retarded the printing of Volume VIII just as the publication of *De l'Esprit* had created a feeling that the *Encyclopédie* was an incubator of subversion, spawning works like this of Helvétius which in their doctrinaire and inelastic psychology implied views about the nature of man and the universe profoundly inimical to established religion. Both externally and internally, therefore, the well-being of the *Encyclopédie* had become decidedly precarious and, as events were soon to show, the venture was in fact beginning to topple over into catastrophe.

Although the affairs of the *Encyclopédie* were consequently being carried on in an atmosphere of strain and crisis, it does not appear that Diderot labored under a sense of impending doom. 'The *Encyclopédie* advances, in the midst of all sorts and kinds of contradictions,' wrote Grimm in his news letter for 15 December 1758, and Diderot himself wrote to Turgot in January, soliciting articles and announcing, with remarkable optimism, that a new volume was about to be published and that the *Encyclopédie* was being reborn.[1]

In reality, the *Encyclopédie* was at that very moment in the gravest peril. Fate now began to rain hammer blows upon Diderot as though he were the protagonist — overwhelmed, yet tenacious and enduring — in some Greek tragedy. And perhaps it was with some consciousness of the Hellenic starkness and grimness of the struggle that he wrote some months later to Grimm, 'Fate, my friend, can change in a moment from good to ill, but not from ill to good; and mine is that of being tormented to the very end. He who devotes himself to letters sacrifices himself to the Eumenides. They will leave him only at the threshold of the tomb.'[2]

One of the blackest days in the history of the *Encyclopédie* was 23 January 1759, only two days after Diderot's optimistic letter to Turgot. On that day the Attorney General, a man named Omer Joly de Fleury, harangued the united assembly of magistrates who made up the Parlement of Paris. The burden of his indictment was that the kingdom was being jeopardized by the poison of impious books, foremost among them the *Encyclopédie*. With the rhetoric, earnestness, and exaggeration customary in this sort of verbal exercise, the Attorney General declared that a conspiracy was afoot:

Society, Religion, and the State present themselves today at the tribunal of justice in order to submit their complaints. Their rights have been violated, their laws disregarded. Impiety walks with head held high. . . . Humanity shudders, the citizenry is alarmed. . . .

It is with grief that we are forced to say it: can one conceal from oneself that there is a project formed, a Society organized, to propagate materialism, to destroy Religion, to inspire a spirit of independence, and to nourish the corruption of morals? . . .

In the picture that we have just drawn of the principal maxims of this work [*De l'Esprit*] you are seeing in fact, Messieurs, simply the principles and detestable consequences of many other books published earlier, epecially the Encyclopedical Dictionary. The book *De l'Esprit* is, as it were, the abridgment of this too-famous work, which according to its true purpose should have been the book of all knowledge and has become instead the book of all error. . . .[3]

Inasmuch as Helvétius had already made a solemn retraction, a fact which Joly de Fleury announced in his harangue, the weight of the Attorney General's attack obviously rested upon the *Encyclopédie*. In addition, the unrepentant Diderot was a special target of the indictment, shown by the fact that Joly de Fleury had included in his original draft of offending books, to be mentioned by name, not only the *Pensées philosophiques* but also the *Letter on the Blind,* the *Letter on the Deaf and Dumb,* and the *Thoughts on the Interpretation of Nature.*[4] The Attorney General also expressed in his indictment indignation regarding one of the *Encyclopédie*'s most emphasized and self-professed characteristics: 'all the venom rife in this Dictionary is to be found in the cross references. . . .'[5] It is not surprising that he should say so, seeing that Diderot's own article on 'Encyclopedia' had ostentatiously advertised the ideological use to which the cross references were to be put.[6] Let it be said in passing, however, that cross references were actually less used, and less skillfully used, than they should have been.[7] Even Le Breton admitted this, when replying in 1768 to an upstart proposal that the *Ency-*

clopédie should be completely redone.[8] Whether as a result of the pressure
of time or of simple negligence, the system of cross references did not turn
out to be so elaborate or insidious as Diderot had said it would. But Joly de
Fleury is hardly to be blamed for taking Diderot at his word.

Responding to the Attorney General's indictment, the Parlement of Paris
decreed that the sale and distribution of the *Encyclopédie* should be suspended, pending an examination of the volumes already published.[9] And on
6 February the membership of the examining commission was announced.[10]
Three doctors of theology, three lawyers, two professors of philosophy, and
one academician: nine men, and good Jansenists all.[11]

Joly de Fleury's indictment and the resultant action of the Parlement
were a testimonial to the influence and effectiveness of the Jansenist De
Chaumeix's *Préjugés légitimes contre l'Encyclopédie,* a work which kept
dropping relentlessly from the press, volume after volume, in the years 1758
and 1759.[12] The author of this compilation was not the only tormentor of
the Encyclopedists — there were also Moreau, Palissot, and others more obscure [13] — but at just this juncture he was the most excruciating, and with
one voice the *philosophes* exclaimed that he misrepresented their writings or
grossly quoted them out of context.[14] As the publishers presently wrote to
Malesherbes, 'We take the liberty of imploring you not to sacrifice us, as a
result of impressions unfavorable to the *Encyclopédie* caused by a writer who,
in altering the passages he quotes or in presenting them in a false light, has
passed beyond the limits of judicious criticism.' [15]

There can be no doubt that there existed among the devout in 1759 a great
deal of alarm about the progress of freethinking in France. In so far as this
was true, the action of the Parlement may be interpreted as sincere. Even
so, it may have been too zealous for the good of its own cause, for, as Barbier
remarked, 'perhaps it would have been prudent not to set forth eloquently,
in the discourse of the Attorney General, the systems of deism, materialism,
and irreligion, and the poison that perhaps exists in some of the articles,
there being many more persons with the capacity of reading this 6 February
decree of thirty pages than of thumbing through seven folio volumes.' [16]

It should also be noticed that the action of the Parlement, sincere though
it no doubt was, was partly inspired by shrewd political calculation and had
a certain captiousness about it. As Tom Paine observed in *The Rights of
Man* regarding eighteenth-century France, 'Between the Monarchy, the
Parliament, and the Church, there was a *rivalship* of despotism.' In this
instance the action of the Parlement was tantamount to insinuating that the
regularly constituted offices of administration — Malesherbes and his censors,

operating under the authority of the chancellor, who, in turn, received his authority from the king — were remiss. Rivalry between Crown and Parlement was chronic during the eighteenth century, and this incident furnishes an excellent example of the Parlement's attempt to encroach upon the power of the throne. So, too, did Malesherbes and others interpret it at the time.[17]

From the standpoint of the *Encyclopédie,* the Parlement forced the issue at a particularly touchy moment, for the quinquennial representative assembly of the French clergy was being held in 1758-9. At each of these assemblies the clergy voted the government what they meticulously and emphatically described as a 'free gift' (*don gratuit*), thus symbolizing the clergy's fierce resistance to the idea that church property should be taxed as other property was, or, indeed, that it should be taxed at all. In such circumstances, the clergy were usually able to see to it that their free gift really bought something. Their temper being what it was in 1759 — for example, in the preceding year an *abbé* had actually published a justification of the Massacre of St. Bartholomew's Day, as well as a defense of the Revocation of the Edict of Nantes * — it is fairly safe to conclude that even had the Parlement not forced the issue, the government would still have been under pressure to do something about the *Encyclopédie.* The Assembly of the Clergy got what it wanted in 1759, and was so well satisfied that, before it dispersed, it voted the government an unprecedented sixteen million livres.[18]

The appointment by the Parlement of the nine examiners was not in itself a deathblow for the *Encyclopédie,* although it was very bad news and the harbinger of worse. It came just at the time when Volume VIII was in press.[19] In spite of this adversity, Diderot, with astonishing perseverance, pushed on with plans for continuing the work. A letter written on 12 February by Nicolas Caroillon of Langres, who was then visiting the Diderots in Paris, remarked that 'M. d'Alembert and M. Diderot are going to commence work upon the continuation of the *Encyclopédie.*' And on 24 February D'Alembert wrote, somewhat scornfully, to Voltaire, 'As for Diderot, he continues to be dead set upon wanting to do the *Encyclopédie;* but it is being asserted that the Chancellor does not agree with this way of thinking: he is going to suppress the work's license, and give Diderot peace and quiet in spite of himself.'[20]

The blow fell on 8 March. On that day a royal decree was issued condemning the *Encyclopédie* and suppressing it in its entirety. 'The advantages to be derived from a work of this sort, in respect to progress in the arts and

* Abbé Jean Novi de Caveirac, *Apologie de Louis XIV et de son Conseil, sur la révocation de l'édit de Nantes . . . avec une dissertation sur la journée de la S. Barthélemi* (n.p., 1758).

sciences,' the decree declared, 'can never compensate for the irreparable damage that results from it in regard to morality and religion.' Thus the King, sitting in his council at Versailles, and upon the advice of the Chancellor, revoked the license, claiming to do so for good and all: 'Besides, whatsoever new precautions might be taken to prevent there creeping into the last volumes features as reprehensible as those in the earlier ones, there would always be an inherent drawback in allowing the work to continue, namely that it would allow of the dissemination not only of the new volumes but also of those that have already appeared.' [21] It was scant comfort to Diderot and the publishers that the decree took the matter out of the hands of the Parlement and the Parlement's nine examiners.

Diderot's policy had been to transform the *Encyclopédie* from a mere work of reference to a conveyor of ideas — ideas that in the last analysis were profoundly political in their effect. He was now paying the price of this daring policy; his work had become inextricably entangled among political forces vying with one another for power. Nor were old religious animosities unstirred. The reference in the royal decree to the advice of the Chancellor made Barbier suspect that Lamoignon was aiding his friends the Jesuits to forestall the Jansenist Parlement.[22] In all of these rivalries and antipathies the *Encyclopédie* was in part agent, in part scapegoat. No doubt the struggle was made more bitter by the irritations and frustrations caused by the failures and the disgraces of the French arms in the great war then being waged. Diderot was caught in the buffetings of a great and bewildering political storm.

Still, Diderot and the publishers did not despair. Private property — and indeed a great deal of it — was at stake, and even if the venture could not be saved on its intellectual merits, perhaps it could be on its commercial ones. The publishers had accepted from their subscribers — and there were now some four thousand [23] — advances of money considerably greater than the value of the volumes that had so far been issued. Later in 1759 the government declared this difference to be the not inconsiderable sum of seventy-two livres on each subscription.[24] In view of all the capital outlays that the publishers had already made in anticipation of being allowed to finish the many volumed work, it followed, of course, that if they were required to make a refund they might very easily find themselves bankrupt. Just Volume VIII alone, the four thousand copies of which were ready to be distributed to subscribers but were now forbidden by the royal decree, represented a large investment. In present-day prices the total edition of this volume was worth some $400,000, if one follows the calculations of a leading French

economist and uses for the basis of price comparison the wages of the no-
toriously underpaid, unskilled labor of that day and the wages for unskilled
labor in ours.[25] In the *ancien régime* it was always an extremely grave matter
in the eyes of magistrates to touch private property, and this, of course, constitutes the reason why Diderot and his friends so often talked about the
immense sums ventured upon the *Encyclopédie*.[26] The very starkness of
their financial outlook may, paradoxically, have caused the publishers to hope
that the government would stop short of ruthlessly bankrupting them.

So the publishers and Diderot did not quite despair. Instead, they took two
important decisions. At a dinner meeting, held probably in late March
(Diderot described these events in a letter to Grimm on 1 May), 'we made
our arrangements; we encouraged one another; we swore to see the thing
through; we agreed to work up the following volumes with as much freedom of thought as the preceding ones, even at the risk of having to print
in Holland. . . . But as it was to be feared lest my enemies redouble their
fury if this arrangement should become known, and persecution, changing
the object of its attack, be transferred from the book to the authors of the
book, it was agreed that I should not show myself and that David should
see to gathering in the parts still lacking.' [27]

Thus Diderot went 'underground': 'the bolts on my door were shot each
day from six in the morning until two in the afternoon.' [28] The *Encyclopédie*
was to go on. But clearly it was to be a lonely business. D'Alembert could
at most be counted on for some articles on mathematics, and Diderot told
Grimm that there was no question of trying to persuade D'Alembert to take
on again any of the duties of an editor. D'Alembert had been at the dinner,
but, according to Diderot, had comported himself outrageously and left
early. 'It is certain that the *Encyclopédie* has no enemy more determined
than he.' [29] No person with any official connection wanted henceforth to be
associated with a condemned work, so there was no use of counting any more
on Turgot. Marmontel and Duclos were already gone. The Abbé Morellet
explained in his *Mémoires* that 'The *Encyclopédie* having been suppressed
by decree of council, I did not think that I should henceforth share the discredit that this suppression would cast upon a man of my profession who
should continue to co-operate, in spite of the government, with a work
proscribed on the grounds of attacking government and religion.' [30] Even
Voltaire, who was safe enough far off at the Genevan frontier, decided to
make no more contributions.[31] Few colleagues were left to Editor Diderot,
save the untiring compiler, De Jaucourt — and himself.

Diderot's sense of loneliness was increased during this prolonged nervous crisis by the fact that Grimm left Paris in early March to rejoin Mme d'Epinay in Geneva, stopping off at Langres on the way in order to see Diderot's old father, who was to live only a few weeks longer.[32] Diderot's letters to Grimm contain an abundance of information regarding the events of this unhappy year. They are documents, too, that vividly reveal Diderot's state of mind, his exhaustion, his irresoluteness, his dejection, his sorrow over the death of his father, and his loneliness, which caused him to write to his absent friend in terms of a devotion quite feminine and seek to draw strength from the superabundance of Grimm's bland and sometimes brutal egotism.

Suddenly Diderot found himself in very real jeopardy of arrest and punishment. His underground routine of writing articles behind bolted doors was cataclysmically interrupted by a scare that was anything but imaginary. 'All of a sudden it has been necessary to carry off the manuscripts during the night, escape from my own house, sleep elsewhere, seek out a refuge, and think of providing myself with a post chaise and of traveling as far as the earth would carry me.'[33] What had happened was that there was being surreptitiously circulated in Paris a pamphlet misleadingly entitled *Memorandum for Abraham Chaumeix against the Would-be Philosophers Diderot and D'Alembert,* and that its authorship was generally ascribed to Diderot.[34] He described the pamphlet to Grimm as 'a long, insipid, boring, and flat satire. No lightness, nor finesse, nor gaiety, nor taste, but, in compensation, insults, sarcasms, and impieties. Jesus and his mother, Abraham Chaumeix, the Court, the city, the Parlement, the Jesuits, the Jansenists, men of letters, the nation — in a word, all the respectable authorities and all the sacred names that there are, dragged in the mud. That's the work being attributed to me, and that almost with unanimity.'[35] No doubt the pamphlet was ascribed to Diderot because Abraham Chaumeix had been such a gadfly of the *Encyclopédie;* but Diderot, in a letter the tone of which seems to reflect his awareness of Malesherbes' exasperation about the recent Affair of the Dedications, swore to Malesherbes 'on all that men hold most sacred, that I had no part in it directly or indirectly.'[36] Besides this assurance, Diderot had had to visit the Lieutenant-General of Police, the Solicitor General, and the Attorney General, in each place protesting his innocence. 'I have been overwhelmed by so much anxiety and so much fatigue, both at once, that I shan't get over it for a couple of months.' Diderot's acquaintances — he mentioned specifically D'Holbach, Malesherbes, Turgot, D'Alembert, and Morellet — all urged him to take to flight, all of them arguing that in regard to a criminal case the safest thing to do was to enter one's plea from afar.

'Yes, the safest,' answered Diderot, 'but the most honest is not to accuse oneself when one is innocent.' [37] So he stayed.

A famous story regarding the relations of Diderot and Malesherbes is told by Mme de Vandeul, and almost certainly pertains to this period. 'Some time afterwards [Mme de Vandeul had just been describing Diderot's imprisonment at Vincennes], the *Encyclopédie* was stopped again. M. de Malesherbes warned my father the next day he would give the order to seize his manuscripts and boxes.

' "What you tell me upsets me horribly. I shall never find the time to move out all my manuscripts, and besides it is not easy to find in twenty-four hours people willing to take charge of them and with whom they will be in safety."

' "Send them all to me," replied M. de Malesherbes. "No one will come here to look for them."

'My father did indeed send half of his papers to the very man who was ordering the search for them.' [38] The usual presumption has been, following the context of Mme de Vandeul's account, that this event occurred in 1752, when the first two volumes were suspended. But the letter to Grimm, which first became known in 1931 and which mentioned Diderot's having to remove the manuscripts during the night, has given rise to the conclusion that this famous incident was a part of the crisis of 1759.[39]

During the ensuing weeks Diderot was in such a state that D'Holbach saw to it that a change of scene was provided. 'We are in the process of making journeys,' wrote Diderot to Grimm on 20 May. 'The Baron is taking me around, and he has no idea of the good he is doing. We have been to Versailles, to the Trianon, to Marly. One of these days we are going to Meudon.' [40] Diderot described the trip to Marly in a beautiful letter to Sophie Volland, a letter suffused with a muted and haunting lyricism in prose. *'Je portois tout à travers les objets des pas errans et une âme mélancolique.'* [41] There is no doubt about the wistfulness of his mood. The very sound and cadence of the syllables re-enforces the meaning of the words.

His melancholy was increased by apprehensions about his father's health, and this emotion was fortified by a sense of guilt at not being in Langres during his father's last days. 'He's very sick, isn't he? Very old, very worn out? . . . My father will die, without having me by his side. . . . Ah! my friend, what am I doing here? He wants me, he is touching upon his last moments, he calls me, and I do not go. . . . I beseech you: do not detest me.' [42] And in a letter to Dr. Théodore Tronchin, thanking him for his advice regarding the ailing parent, Diderot wrote, 'I would subtract from my own life to protract that of my father, and no one in the world has greater confidence in your knowledge than I. I have only one regret, and that is my being unable to go and settle down beside the old man, look after his health myself, and carry out everything you have prescribed for his conservation. . . .' And then, apologizing for his delay in acknowledging Tronchin's prescription, he added: 'I hope that you will find somewhat extenuating the lengthy broils into which I have been plunged, and the sort of stupid numbness that has followed upon them. Just imagine, Monsieur, that several times I have been on the point of exiling myself, that this was the advice of my friends, and that I had to muster all the courage of inno- cence to stand fast against these alarms and remain in the midst of the dangers round about me. Now tranquillity commences to be born again. I am about to regain obscurity and recover peace. Happy the man whom men have forgotten and who can escape from this world without being noticed. You think that happiness lies beyond the tomb and I think that it lies in it. That is all the difference that there is between our two systems.' [43]

Diderot's nervous exhaustion increased the tension of his relationships with others. D'Holbach displeased him. Grimm was the only friend that he had or wanted to have. Sophie Volland's mother was so inscrutable that the sphinxes he had seen at Marly reminded him of her. 'Your mother's soul is sealed with the seven seals of the Apocalypse,' he wrote her daughter. 'On her forehead is written: Mystery.' In spite of his misery he forgot himself long enough to relish this phrase, which he repeated in a letter to Grimm. But there was not just the mother to contend with: Sophie's sister was sus- picious of him, too. And even Sophie, the incomparable Sophie, had shown herself to be jealous. 'That annoys me. . . . I don't like to be under sus- picion.' And as for jealousy, Mme Diderot had her share of it, and precipi- tated a quarrel over Sophie Volland so appalling that Diderot went to com- plain of her to the monk who was her confessor. Diderot did not find people easy to live with in 1759.[44]

Accompanying his depression was poor physical health. 'Let's speak no more about milk,' he wrote to Grimm. 'Health will come back to me as soon as trouble leaves me. No more troubles, no milk will be needed.' Slowly he began to mend, from time to time he felt energy once more stirring within him, occasionally his mood of listlessness and lassitude lightened. 'Now and then I feel once more some spark of enthusiasm,' he wrote to Grimm on 20 May, and on 5 June he wrote, coining a word that seems as quaint in French as it does in English, 'I encyclopedize like a galley slave.' But the news of the death of his father, which occurred on 3 June, struck him hard. 'The final blow left for me to receive has fallen: my father is dead.' [45]

It has been shown by Freud that the death of the father is an exceptional moment in the life of any man. With Diderot it seems to have been especially so, and a Freudian would find complete substantiation of this generalization in Diderot's saying, as he did in a later letter to Grimm, 'Other sorrows do not prepare a man for this one.' [46] For the first time, Diderot began to speak of death as something that might happen to him.[47] And perhaps because he felt closer to death, he was, in a mysterious way that was of enormous importance in the evolution of his creativeness, closer to life. From the miseries of this year and from the grimness and drudgery of the bleak years that followed it, something was distilled, exquisite and precious, in the development of an artist.[48] In the bitterness of misfortunes, heaped upon him as upon some hero in Sophocles, there was forged the soul of the man who has been called by a great French scholar 'the mind and the heart of the eighteenth century.' [49]

But of all this Diderot could not be aware, nor that, after six more years of clandestine editing and toilsome writing, it would be vouchsafed to his *Encyclopédie* to be published in one release with almost no opposition. This he could not know. Instead he could only cry out, as he did to Grimm, 'How I have suffered for the past two years!' [50] 'I am so tired out that I would like to be heard without having to speak, have my letters get done without my having to write them, and arrive where I want to be without my having to move.' [51] Yet in spite of such lassitude, he turned again to his work for the *Encyclopédie,* with a stubbornness and a tenacity that is close to heroism. 'The circumstances,' wrote Lord Morley, 'under which these five-and-thirty volumes were given to the world mark Diderot for one of the true heroes of literature.' [52] Diderot was, in many respects, the 'sanguineous, vehement, volatile mortal' that Carlyle called him, but he was not volatile in this. 'We swore to see the thing through,' he had written to Grimm, and so, in blackness of mood and exhaustion of spirit, he turned once again to his great editorial task, to that *Encyclopédie* of which it has recently and well been said, in bicentennial appreciation of its worth, 'In its subject matter almost everything is superannuated, in its aspiration everything is still alive.' [53]

Years later, when all the remaining ten volumes of letterpress were ready to appear, he reiterated in his foreword his oft-repeated appeal to posterity. 'We shall have obtained the recompense we expected from our contemporaries and from posterity, if we cause them to say, some day, that we have not lived altogether in vain.'[54] No doubt this thought inspired him in 1759, too, as he turned, with unquenchable determination, to the drudgery of the seemingly endless work that lay before him. 'We swore to see the thing through.' Perhaps he might even yet see dawn.

The Nature of the Ultimate Triumph

THE distressing events of 1759 brought Diderot close to the end of his endurance. Ordinarily he was a man resilient enough not to be a prey to depression and discouragement for long. Nevertheless, that year's dispiriting and discouraging occurrences might well have unmanned him had he been unable to draw upon reserves which had been silently accumulating through the years. So much seemed against him as he drank deeply from the well of loneliness: the contumely showered upon the dishonored *Encyclopédie* by the most august authorities of the whole kingdom; the clear imputation that he himself was guilty of twenty years of treason; the defection of colleagues and collaborators; the alarms regarding his personal safety; his lassitude and lack of resolution, aggravated by the sadness and foreboding which he felt because of his father's death, all this might permanently have unnerved him had there not been going on for a long time a testing which prepared him for a crisis so momentous.

It might all have ended with a whimper. Instead, what seemed like a year of ending turned out to be a year of beginning. And the crisis, which might have ended in demoralization and despair, culminated in affirmation and success.

Eventually the complete *Encyclopédie* was written and published after all. Confronting its suppression in 1759, Diderot's spirit rose to challenge the finality of the act. 'We swore to see the thing through.' And in 1765-6 the work was published in all the plenitude of its remaining ten volumes of letterpress — a phoenix rising from the ashes. To complete the *Encyclopédie,* in view of the discouraging circumstances, required boldness, stamina, perseverance and self-confidence. And even to make the try, Diderot had to know inside himself that through the apprentice years he had been developing and tempering the qualities and characteristics requisite to cope with an emergency like this.

In the crisis of 1759, Diderot's past entitled him to believe that he had developed moral and intellectual qualities equal to doing the job. What would an inventory of these qualities include? The answer is spread on the record of the preceding chapters. He had abundantly tested the quality of his intellectual competence. He knew that he had disciplined himself to endure the drudgery of backbreaking work. And his devotion since 1746 to the idea of the *Encyclopédie,* his perseverance through the years, was another test that he had passed: he knew himself to be a man who would not quit. The years had proved his doggedness, as they were now to do again. His writings, of course, were the visible signs of his qualifications for seeing an encyclopedia through and even writing much of it, for his books had given solid evidence of encyclopedic range. He had proved his competence in areas as diverse as epistemology, psychology, aesthetics, literature, science, and technology. But most of all, he knew himself to be the master and exemplar of something that was in part an attitude toward the world and in part a method of thought. He was a *philosophe,* indeed THE *philosophe,* a standard-bearer to whom men might repair. He was a tested leader of the Enlightenment, the experienced champion of an intellectual approach toward science and knowledge that in effect was a political movement. The ten years that had passed since the days when he was writing the *Letter on the Blind* or mulling over the prospectus of the *Encyclopédie* or discussing with D'Alembert its 'Preliminary Discourse' had clarified the issues and confirmed in Diderot — if it is fair to judge by the books he wrote — the consistency and sturdiness of those attitudes of intellectual sincerity and integrity and open-minded search for truth that had characterized him from early years. All these elements of leadership had been measured in him; and now, consciously or unconsciously, he was evidently able to feel that in the present crisis he had the qualifications to carry out the task.

And indeed he had. The qualities requisite for doing so were the qualities, enlarged and intensified by the emergency, that we have seen developing in the Diderot of earlier days. The emergency brought forth the familiar Diderot — written large. To paraphrase Talleyrand, the more Diderot changed, the more he was the same. The crisis of 1759, in short, produced a Diderot who was truly the climax and end-product of his testing years.

So much for the public Diderot — the Diderot identified with the *Encyclopédie.* But there was another Diderot, one more hidden and withdrawn, whose response to the crisis of 1759 was more subtle and more difficult to define. In one sense, as we have seen, the crisis of 1759 served to intensify the qualities that had been ripening in him during the years of trial. He was still the old Diderot, only more so. But in a subtler and perhaps more significant sense, he eventually emerged from the crisis a different Diderot. Fortunately this elusive change in his personality can be closely followed, for it is just at this breaking point in his life that we begin to have the riches of his letters to Sophie Volland. Consequently, students of Diderot are now realizing that the supreme significance of the crises of 1759 lies in their having induced in him a process of maturation built solidly on the foundation of his past experience but utilizing and interpreting it in a different way. It is the difference between the young Diderot—and not so very young, at that, for he was forty-six when the crisis came upon him—and the mature Diderot. This process of maturation was essential for the production of those later works which have become the subjects of such close study and such wide admiration in the twentieth century.

Yet Diderot grew old and died without allowing more than the merest handful of people to inspect the abundant evidence of this maturation. Masterpieces flowed from his pen—and then were put away in a drawer. Whether from prudence, whether from soul-weariness at the perverseness of his own generation, Diderot laid all his bets on posterity. After 1759 he published almost nothing, save of course the *Encyclopédie*, which is scarcely to be compared with unpublished masterpieces like *The Nun, Rameau's Nephew, D'Alembert's Dream, James the Fatalist,* or *The Refutation of the Work by Helvétius Entitled 'Man.'* This very reticence denoted a Diderot greatly changed, for before 1759 there had been almost nothing that he wrote that he did *not* publish. Now he was content to publish almost nothing at all, with the result that posterity has the privilege of knowing his mind—and, by doing so, of gazing into the central vortex of eighteenth-century thought—much more intimately than his contemporaries were able to do. Indeed, to most of his contemporaries Diderot seemed in his later life to be a most unliterary literary man, satisfied to grow fat upon the largesse of Catherine the Great and exhibiting, as for example in the circumstances of his hard-headed negotiations regarding the marriage of his daughter, little but the solid and unexciting qualities of the typical bourgeois.

But the real Diderot, the Diderot that the present generation (more than any of its predecessors) has come to esteem and admire, revealed himself in just these unpublished masterpieces. They have in them, characteristic of Diderot's later period, a quality both of seeking and having found and still of seeking again. They have in them a subtle and powerful dialectic that comes from questioning life and answering life. In short, Diderot's later writings have an elusive but unmistakable quality of seeming to see far and deep into the mysteries of life, further and deeper than he had seen before, perhaps further and deeper than any other man of his century save Goethe. To use a term liked by Emerson and Carlyle, he became one who really sees, a seer. Forsaken by his friends, bereaved of his father, forced to work on the *Encyclopédie* behind locked doors and almost singlehandedly, he found resources within himself that might otherwise have lain dormant. The ultimate effect was to refine his thought, make his relations with others more subtle, and deepen his humanity.

PART II

THE APPEAL TO POSTERITY, 1759–1784

CHAPTER 26

Taking Stock

IN 1759 DENIS DIDEROT, for thirty years a resident of Paris, made one of his infrequent visits to the place where he was born. Since the age of sixteen he had returned to Langres only twice. Now, at forty-five, the native returned.

It was a time when neither France nor Diderot was at peace. Seventeen fifty-nine marked the decisive engagements of the great struggle between the French and the English in the course of the Seven Years' War. It was the year of the French withdrawal from Ticonderoga and Crown Point in the American wilderness, the year of Montcalm's defeat on the Plains of Abraham, the year when a French army lost the battle of Minden in Westphalia and a French fleet was decisively defeated in Quiberon Bay. To Pitt and to the English the year came to be known as the *annus mirabilis,* but for Louis XV and Mme de Pompadour and the Duc de Choiseul it was a year of frustration and distress.

For Diderot, too, the year was one of sorrows. The rescinding of the license to publish the *Encyclopédie* was still a fresh wound, and as he left Paris on 25 July it had been only seven weeks since the death of his father. He was going in order to assist in the settlement of his father's estate. Two long days of hard travel, with only four hours' rest out of thirty-six, brought him to Langres. He arrived looking 'so changed, so done up,' that the old family servant remarked that he must have come in order to be buried at his father's side.[1]

The mixed feelings of almost all homecomers who visit the scenes of their childhood no doubt were his: a nostalgia for days that will not come again, blended with a thankfulness that one does not have to live out the rest of one's life in an environment so narrow and confined. 'Since I left this city all the people I used to know are dead,' he wrote, suggesting the ache of a man who realizes that he cannot really go home again; and, in contrast, 'It's scarcely four days that I've been here, and it seems like four years.'[2]

To the people in Langres Diderot must have seemed a figure that was at one and the same time fascinating and yet a little sinister. On the one hand, he had the prestige of the local boy who has gone to the metropolis and made good. He was widely known as an original and creative author, the editor of the famous *Encyclopédie,* and the creator, by his plays *Le Fils naturel* and *Le Père de famille,* of a new genre in the French theater. Consequently, in the press of the day he was often referred to as 'celebrated.' Even the inhabitants of sleepy old Langres must have known that. But on the other hand, was it not an open secret that he was the author of the *Pensées philosophiques,* one of the shrewdest and most searching booklets of the century in its challenging of accepted and orthodox religious belief? The fact that the book had been burned by the public executioner was sufficient to make the pious and conventional inhabitants of Langres shudder. Moreover, was he not also the author of that pornographic novel, *Les Bijoux indiscrets?* Diderot was an unconventional man, and he must have seemed all the more so to the people living in his small provincial home city, whose greatest virtues, as well as greatest defects, came from a willing and cheerful acquiescence in conformity. Almost every inhabitant of a city as small as Langres — perhaps some 10,000 in 1759 — would have known that Diderot had long been considered a scapegrace son, marrying against his father's wishes and spending several months in a royal prison in punishment for the daring things he had written. There were many to tell the inhabitants of Langres that Diderot was one of the most dangerous, as there were also others to assure them that he was one of the most brilliant, men in France.

The Diderot the neighbors saw was a man in middle age, noticeably powerful in frame, vigorous in movement, and so open of countenance and easy of approach that people readily sensed that he loved companionship and liked to be obliging. His lively conversation was accompanied by copious gestures. The Van Loo portrait of him, now hanging in the Louvre, shows the color of his eyes to have been chestnut brown. His gaze was quick and intelligent. He had the look (which the sculptor Houdon caught) of a man trying hard to hear the strains of far-off music or seize the implications of some half-glimpsed but especially subtle and elusive idea. Perhaps, as his mind, with its quickness and originality, caught at new insights into truth and beauty, he might be said to be always seeming to be straining to hear the pipes of Pan. He dressed soberly in bourgeois black — a costume that caused him to be mistaken on the road for a churchman — and of course

wore a wig, though he always wore one impatiently and took it off when
social propriety allowed of it (and sometimes when it did not), revealing
a high-domed head. The neighbors noticed a striking family resemblance
in him: 'When I pass by in the street, I hear people say as they look at me,
"It's the father himself." '[3] His neighbors would have noticed, too, that
Diderot no longer spoke as they did, with the provincial accent, especially
the slow and drawling speech, characteristic of the region.[4] To his neighbors
he was a man from the outside world; perhaps they even thought of him as a
man *of* the world. Actually he was a little too incorrigibly shy and a little
too incorrigibly gauche ever to be quite that.

Perhaps even more conspicuous to the neighbors was the fact that he no
longer drank wine. In 1759 Diderot had had enough frustrations to affect
his health. 'Of all the afflictions that life allots to man, there is none I have
not borne.'[5] His letters show that he had some digestive malady, and the
fact that he had given up drinking wine suggests that he suffered from what
today would be diagnosed as stomach ulcers. 'What a silly part one plays
when one is a water-drinker in a crowd of people whose principal merit,
in their own consideration and in that of others, consists in heavy drinking.'
And, with that painful clarity of judgment regarding the quality of alcohol-
inspired wit that is vouchsafed to a teetotaler at a cocktail party, he wrote of
his former townsmen, 'They are gay, tumultuous and noisy. And jokes!
ah, God! what jokes!'[6]

Part of Diderot's frustrations had to do with his professional activities,
part with his private life. As for the first, the prime uncertainty concerned
the question whether the *Encyclopédie* could ever be finished. There was a
possibility that its preparation would be tacitly allowed to continue in a
few months, as it had been following the suspension of the enterprise in
1752. Or had the *Encyclopédie's* avowed purpose of changing 'the general
way of thinking' made its publication so clearly a political act that no additional volumes could ever be tolerated? This crisis, so much greater than
the one of 1752, was still far from being settled when Diderot visited
Langres. And even if the government should allow the eventual publication
of the *Encyclopédie,* even if the publishers could solve very grave problems
of financing, even so the editorial work would be much heavier and lonelier
than in the past. D'Alembert's contributions were now much curtailed;
Turgot, Marmontel, Quesnay, Voltaire were no longer to be counted on;
the whole enterprise, instead of being buoyed up by public interest and
acclaim, had had to go underground. The prospect, instead of exhilarating
Diderot, was enough to make him feel numb.

Because the government had interrupted the publishing plans so drastically, it had become necessary for Diderot and his publishers to review and renew their business arrangements. The uncertainty of publication was reflected in the new contract. 'They undertake to continue exactly the same terms for manuscript copy that they previously did for printed volumes. This is very honorable of them.' Part of his salary was to be paid in such a fashion that as he delivered the finished manuscript for each of the remaining sixteen letters of the alphabet, he was to receive one-sixteenth of 15,000 livres. In addition, there was a small income from annuities.[7] These arrangements were not unsatisfactory, provided the enterprise itself could survive. This was not certain when Diderot went to Langres; one of the publishers, David, was at that moment trying to negotiate credit in Holland, to be followed there by another of the syndicate, Laurent Durand.[8] And as for the government, Diderot received word on his way back to Paris of official action which would quickly have the effect of forcing the publishers into bankruptcy. 'What enemies we have! How persistent they are! And how savage!'[9]

Never had Diderot been so emotional, nor under such stress, as he was in 1759. Worry about the fate of the *Encyclopédie* was heightened by his anxieties about his own personal safety as its editor. Not having been with his father when he died, Diderot reproached himself exaggeratedly.[10] Relations with his wife were still stormy. Diderot felt quite virtuous about it all, yet it had started because Mme Diderot recognized the handwriting of her rival, Sophie Volland, on a card left for him at the Diderot apartment in the Rue Taranne. He, of course, probably did not think of the two women as rivals, so high did he rate the one and so low the other. Once upon a time he had indeed been in love with his wife, but he had never treated her as in any sense his intellectual equal, and they had drifted apart through the years. The domestic outburst earlier this year had been so tempestuous that finally Diderot went to his wife's confessor to complain. Not getting the satisfaction he expected to receive, and 'raising my voice vehemently, as sometimes happens to me,' he threatened to turn his wife out and 'return her inside of twenty-four hours to the destitution from which I drew her.' Destitution was scarcely a factual way of talking about a woman who had brought him a dowry reckoned to be worth 5000 livres.[11]

Matters had improved in the following weeks, though there was another tempest, brief but shattering, only a quarter of an hour before he left for Langres.[12] Once arrived there, in a carriage belonging to Sophie's mother, Diderot wrote his wife a conciliatory letter. He did not, however, admit that he was in any way in the wrong. 'I am not perfect; you are not perfect, either. We are together, not in order for each to reproach the other bitterly for his faults, but in order to endure them reciprocally. . . . Nanette, even should you drive me to the tomb, you would be no better off. . . . I wish you a happy saint's day. I embrace you tenderly.' [13] Many years later Diderot once said to Mme Necker, 'I was married sixteen years [that would make it 1759] before I realized that it is easier to reshape one's own character than to correct other people's.' [14] A very cryptic remark.

Diderot's little daughter made his home life more endurable for him. She was now almost six years old and beginning to do needlework.[15] 'I am crazy about my little girl . . . ,' the father wrote to Grimm. 'When you come back, she will recite some chapters from the Old Testament for you, such as the crossing of the Jordan or the history of Joseph, which she calls the best one of her tales. This is her word for them, and her mother does not like it.' [16]

The various events of 1759 made a great impact upon Diderot psychologically because they all tended to reinforce one another, creating in him a feeling of instability and insecurity. Even his relations with the Volland family, which caused so much discord in his home, were not tranquil enough to give him the sense of peace for which he was obviously yearning. Diderot had first met Sophie Volland some four years before. His letters to her, universally regarded as one of the most interesting, intimate, and subtlest of eighteenth-century correspondences — some enthusiasts even declare it to be the best ever, without limitation of century — show that he always held her judgment and her intelligence in the highest regard. 'Ah! Grimm, what a woman. How tender, gentle, honorable, perceptive, judicious!' [17] Since her letters to him have not survived, it is hard for posterity to judge whether Diderot's estimate of her was correct. Yet it is probably fair to say that Sophie Volland had a serenity of temperament and sense of balance which Diderot liked to feel he was nurturing and which, much more significantly, allowed him to gain a frequently much needed objectivity. Probably, had the laws allowed it, Diderot would have divorced his wife and married Sophie Volland. About this time he wrote for the *Encyclopédie* some examples of the use of the word *'Indissoluble.'*

Marriage is an *indissoluble* engagement. The man who is wise shudders at the very idea. Legislators who have prepared *indissoluble* bonds for man have scarcely understood his natural inconstancy. How many people have they made criminal and unhappy.[18]

But had he married Sophie Volland, posterity would be without these letters, and know much less than it does about Denis Diderot.

The earliest of these letters now extant date from this very year. They are ardent letters, with enough references to voluptuousness and eroticism in them, though delicately put, to make one conclude that he knew, by one way or another, that Sophie was not a virgin. Of his letters it can fairly be said that if seduction was still necessary, he was certainly trying to provide it. But the letters also show a man anxiously asserting time and time again the depth and lastingness of his love, as though he were afraid that she had deep-seated doubts about it.

The correspondence reveals too that Diderot was quite afraid of Mme Volland, who tolerated Diderot's connections with her daughter with what was obviously only the greatest reluctance.[19] Tension was caused too by the very fact that the relationship was not openly acknowledged. Neither was it admittedly adulterous. Much energy and emotion were expended through the years in arranging for the secret exchange of letters. During the visit at Langres, for example, Diderot worried a good deal when one of Sophie's letters to him was inadvertently opened by his brother the priest. 'Address me by my title of member of the Berlin Academy,' he wrote.[20]

Not least among his worries was Sophie's younger sister, Marie-Charlotte, who in 1749 had married Jean-Gabriel Le Gendre, an engineer in government service with headquarters at Châlons-sur-Marne.[21] In 1759 Mme Le Gendre was visiting at Paris, in her mother's house on the Rue des Vieux Augustins, near the Place des Victoires. Diderot was not only afraid of Mme Volland, he was also afraid of Mme Le Gendre. Accordingly his letters to Sophie are full of solemn expressions of respect for the sister, combined with warm (but very decorous) regards. Moreover, Diderot was inclined to be more than a little jealous of Mme Le Gendre. He was suspicious that she was too fond of Sophie. Or rather, more accurately, that the two sisters were too fond of each other. These strange suspicions add a whiff of Krafft-Ebing to Diderot's relationship with the Volland family.[22] His suspicions, we may conjecture, arose from Sophie's not having the temperament to respond to him as passionately as he desired. He therefore must have concluded, with ineffable male vanity, that if she did not, it could only be because she was somewhat homosexually inclined.

Diderot liked to think of himself, that summer of 1759, as animated by the most generous and non-mercenary motives in the settlement of his father's estate. 'We have just divided 100,000 francs as one would divide a hundred liards. . . . It didn't take a half of a quarter of an hour.'[23] The income from the estate, which, until 1762, the two brothers and the sister shared without dividing into exclusive thirds, amounted to about 1500 livres per annum for each of them. 'They will be rich. The Abbé has an income of 3000 livres, Seurette about 1500. What do you need more than that, in the provinces? They are better off than if they had twice that much in Paris.'[24] The legal document, written out by Diderot himself in nine large pages, was signed by all of them on 13 August. Diderot left Langres three days later, going by way of Mme Volland's estate at Isle-sur-Marne near Vitry-le-François, whence Mme Volland and he thereupon traveled to Paris together.[25]

Part of the settlement entailed a decision by Diderot's sister and brother to live under the same roof, in the family house on the Place Chambeau. Diderot, though encouraging this, had great misgivings about it. 'There is a sort of antipathy between brother and sister. . . . I delude myself as much as I can about the diversity of their characters. I have to do so, or carry away from here a soul full of bitterness.'[26] And sure enough, a misunderstanding between the two suddenly broke out the very evening before he left, taxing all his powers as a conciliator.[27]

The Abbé Diderot was a sincere, devout, and determined Christian, which was just exactly what his elder brother thought was wrong with him. 'The Abbé was born with a sensitive and serene nature. He would have been intelligent; but religion has made him pusillanimous and full of scruples. He is melancholy, taciturn, circumspect, and peevish. . . . He would have been a fine friend, a fine brother, if Christ had not commanded him to spurn all such trifles. He is a good Christian who demonstrates every instant that it would be better to be a good man, and that what they call evangelical perfection is merely the noxious art of stifling nature, which might have revealed itself in him perhaps as strongly as it did in me.'[28] One can readily see in this criticism of his brother and this naïve praise of himself that Diderot might find misunderstandings with his brother very easy to come by.

Diderot was as lavish in praise of his sister as he was grudging of it with his brother. 'Seurette is vivacious, active, gay, downright, quick to take offense, slow to get over it, without worry either about the present or the future, and not allowing either situations or people to impose on her; free in her actions and even freer in her remarks. . . .' Diderot thought of his sister as a character, as indeed she was, and called her 'a sort of female Diogenes. . . . One of her characteristics is to be funny when she is out of temper and to make you laugh when she gets annoyed. When she has spoken out and had her laugh, she assumes that she has won her point, and that satisfies her.' [29]

Diderot tried very hard to please his brother and sister while he was at Langres. He knew that they hated to see him go, and he protracted his visit longer than he otherwise would have done. He attended church with them, in the family pew at the Dominican church where his uncle had served as a friar, and listened to a sermon preached by one of his former schoolmates.[30] He found the results of his efforts gratifying. 'The terrible moment, that of good-byes,' successfully passed. 'I left them charmed with me. . . .' [31]

At the first stopover on his return journey, Diderot wrote to Sophie with a pen — the only one in the village — that had had to be borrowed from the local *curé*.[32] And at the Volland estate he particularly enjoyed inspecting the barns and the barnyards, the grape press, the sheepfolds, and the stables. He liked the smell of the animals and the dung. And he delighted especially in the rows of poplar trees bordering the Marne. 'These *vordes* charm me. That's where I would live . . . where I would sacrifice to Pan and to Venus-of-the-fields at the foot of every tree, if it were desired and I were granted time. Perhaps you'll say that there's a lot of trees there; but when I promise myself a happy life, I promise to make it last.' [33]

Diderot's letters of 1759 are unusually self-revelatory. For one thing, he frequently characterizes himself, and in far from forbidding terms. For although he was very critical of Diderot the artist, he was not nearly so critical of Diderot the moralist. For example, he informed his wife that she had 'no substantial reproach to make against a man thoroughly resolved to occupy himself with providing her with a happy future.' No substantial reproach, indeed. Posterity may well think that he was rather too ready to give himself the benefit of all doubts.[34]

What, one might ask, was the cause in 1759 of all this show of self-estimation — and self-esteem? It was because quite suddenly most of his personal relationships had become insecure. His wife was in a fury over Sophie Volland. Sophie herself, to judge from the tenor of the correspondence, needed the comfort of being reassured about his sincerity and about the sort of person he was. Then, too, the competition with Sophie's sister that he deemed himself to be in was bizarre. During this year he had good reason to feel that he did not know just where he stood with a large number of his nearest relatives and friends — with D'Alembert, his former close associate; even with D'Holbach, who was urging him to come to stay at Grandval, his country house, and whom Diderot frequently mentions this summer in a surprisingly distrustful way. Moreover, he had just gone through a searing quarrel with Jean-Jacques Rousseau. There was only his friend Grimm whom he felt that he could trust without doubt. One of the effects of this sudden deterioration in his personal relationships was, not unnaturally, the desire to show himself to his correspondents in what he considered the best possible light. Diderot needed to reassure others — and himself. As far as he was concerned, he succeeded. In comparison with his brother and sister — 'it is impossible to imagine three beings with characters more different than my sister, my brother, and I' — he thought of himself as 'gentle, easy to get along with, indulgent, perhaps too much so.'[35]

Much of what he wrote was obviously inspired by a desire to impress Sophie Volland. 'I am naturally inclined to neglect faults and wax enthusiastic over good qualities. I am more affected by the charm of virtue than by the deformity of vice. I softly turn aside from bad people and I fly to meet the good. If there is a beautiful part in a book or a person's character or a picture or a statue, there it is that my eyes come to rest. I see only that; I remember only that. The rest is almost forgotten.'[36]

The most vainglorious things that Diderot said in his own behalf were intended for Mme Volland, to overcome her resistances. He even promised that posterity would not forget him. 'Tell her that I am an upright man; that nothing will be able to change me in regard to you; tell her that the highest consideration is assured me in men's memories.'[37] Yet he was right about posterity. The regard that posterity has had for Diderot, climaxed by the fashion in which our generation treats his achievements and his art, suggests that his prediction, though preening, was not erroneous. It may have been presumptuous. But it was also prescient.

CHAPTER 27

Second Wind

FOR THE next several years Diderot was to lead a life full of incident, anxiety, and turmoil. The reason for it was, in part, the richness and variability of his own mercurial temperament. Diderot was easily stirred up. The very least that can be said of him is that he was a man who readily responded to stimuli. In addition he found himself partly by design but in part simply through the necessities of the situation, engaged in the political life of France in a very real way. This was very likely to happen to almost any man of letters in the French Enlightenment. For the editor of the *Encyclopédie* it was inevitable.

The trouble that Diderot faced on his return home from Langres concerned, as usual, the *Encyclopédie*. At first his publishers were more implicated than he, but it was not long before he himself became deeply involved, his reputation for integrity deeply impugned. While he was in Langres, a royal decree of 21 July 1759 had ordered the publishers of the *Encyclopédie* to refund seventy-two livres to each subscriber.[1] This was no more than logical or just: the *Encyclopédie* having been officially discontinued at the letter 'G,' it was only right that the publishers should refund money previously received for goods that could not now be delivered. Nor was the sum of seventy-two livres exorbitant. Grimm, who was certainly sympathetic with Diderot even if he was not nearly so much so with the publishers, had previously declared that in his opinion the publishers really owed 114 livres.[2] So, it was only just; yet there is evidence that the publishers would have been quite willing to pocket this unearned money had not Malesherbes, the Director of the Book Trade, seen to it that the decree of 21 July was passed.[3] This galvanized the none too scrupulous publishers into belated action. Appalled by the prospect of massive restitution — 'for we are faced with having to do it for all if we do it for one' — they asked the government to do them the favor of not immediately making the decree public. The favor was granted, giving them in consequence the time to make the proposal, which Malesherbes had evidently had in mind all the time, that the publication of the volumes of illustrations of the *Encyclopédie* should be permitted and that the previous subscribers to the *Encyclopédie* should receive automatically a credit of seventy-two livres against the cost of these volumes.[4] This was an excellent compromise and bade fair to please almost every one, especially as the subscribers from the very first had been promised these illustrations as an integral part of their purchase. A license to publish these volumes of plates was issued on 8 September 1759.[5] Subscribers to the first seven volumes were to be allowed to purchase the four volumes of plates (at that time a total of 1000 engravings was contemplated) for an eventual net payment of 112 livres; but all others would have eventually to pay 360. Little wonder that the publishers and Diderot later boasted that not a single subscriber applied for his refund.[6] Just the same, a Dominican monk later testified that he had tried his hardest in 1759 to get his seventy-two livres back and had been unable to do so.[7] Meanwhile, the decree of 21 July 1759 regarding the restitution of seventy-two livres remained unrescinded. No doubt this was fully intended, being a way by which Malesherbes could keep the publishers under control.

All of this was being decided just at the time when, on 3 September 1759, Pope Clement XIII issued a brief pointing out that the *Encyclopédie* had been placed on the Index in March of that year. 'All and each of the faithful . . . who have possession of the said work' were warned 'to carry it to the Local Ordinaries or to the Inquisitors of the Faith or their vicars, who shall take pains to have such sets immediately burnt. . . .' Under pain of excommunication for laymen and suspension for priests. It is probable — and this was also Diderot's impression — that the Pope was more apprehensive about the edition of the *Encyclopédie* then being published at Lucca by one Ottaviano Diodati than he was about the Paris original.[8] Still, this pronouncement, being read from pulpits throughout Catholic Christendom, was not intended to do either edition any good. The French Jansenist newspaper *Les Nouvelles Ecclésiastiques,* widely read even though it was clandestine, exulted that the Pope had expressed himself so vigorously 'on this abominable book.'[9]

The decision to publish the engravings increased every one's workload at once. For although Diderot had vaingloriously announced in his article 'Encyclopédie' (published in Volume V, four years previously) that 'we have about a thousand plates,' the fact seems to be that they had drawings, not engraved plates. Thus, the publishers said in 1759 that they had paid for more than two thousand drawings in order to have a thousand suitably done, which no doubt was true; but in the same year Malesherbes stated more than once, in confidential memoranda, that 'not a single drawing had been engraved.'[10]

The enemies of the *Encyclopédie* probably sorrowed at the recovery it seemed to be making. The plates were non-controversial, or so it was argued, though in fact nothing could disseminate more efficiently than they the subversive doctrine that the daily routine of socially useful labor has inherent dignity and worth. But non-controversial they were supposed to be: a proof of this may be seen to this day in the distinction made between letterpress and engravings in the fine set of the *Encyclopédie* that used to be the property of the Spanish Bourbon kings. In the library of the Royal Palace at Madrid the volumes of engravings bear no mark of being forbidden; but the volumes of text all bear the command inside the cover of each volume, written in India ink and in eye-catching script: 'All volumes prohibited, except those containing plates.' *

Consequently it was in the department of the engravings that the enemies of the enterprise hit next. Fréron, the editor of the *Année Littéraire* and the ancient and inveterate foe of the *philosophes,* published a letter from an employee of the publishers of the *Encyclopédie,* recently discharged. This was one Pierre Patte, an architect whose signed receipt for wages shows that he had been employed in tracing drawings, making verifications, and other such duties connected with the preparation of the plates. Patte asserted that for seventy-seven of the French trades and crafts (which he then listed by name) the publishers possessed no drawings that were the result of their independent labor. What they in fact had were simply prints taken from the engravings that had been prepared for the use of the Academy of Sciences.[11]

In 1675 Colbert had requested the Academy of Sciences to publish a series of illustrations and explanations concerning the machines used in the arts and crafts. For decades the preparation of these drawings and engravings continued dilatorily, with Réaumur more responsible for them than anyone else. By 1759 not even one fascicle had yet been published, though some had been engraved.[12] Meanwhile Diderot and the publishers of the *Encyclopédie* had procured proofs of a good many of these unpublished engravings. 'According to this plan,' wrote Patte, 'M. Diderot, the same M. Diderot who in his conversation and his writings runs down M. de Réaumur on every occasion, looked up M. Lucas, who had engraved the

* Prohibidos todos los tomos, menos los de láminas.

greatest part of the work of this industrious Academician, and at the price of ten louis and some fine promises in regard to the new enterprise of the plates for the *Encyclopédie* (it is from M. Lucas himself that I have this information), he [Lucas] pulled proofs of what he had done; the same thing was done in respect to some other engravers employed by M. de Réaumur, in such a way that soon all the engravings of our Academician were assembled.'[13]

Patte's letter naturally forced a response. The *Observateur Littéraire* for 15 December 1759 announced that nearly two hundred plates for the *Encyclopédie* were already engraved and invited the public to go to see them at the publishers' bookshops. It also referred darkly to Patte as a man who had been excluded from the enterprise for two reasons.[14] 'I asked M. Diderot,' wrote the same journalist in a later number, 'what these two reasons were. "It is because," he replied, "this Monsieur is too clever a man and too honest a man." "Those are scarcely reasons for exclusion," I said. "True," replied M. Diderot, "but we are bizarre folk."'[15] Evidently Diderot had a way of his own for meeting the press.

Meanwhile, the publishers of the *Encyclopédie* made an admission. In reply to an inquiry from the surgeon Morand, a member of the Academy of Sciences, they conceded that they had several proofs of Réaumur's plates, but they claimed that they had not copied them, nor would they. And they offered, rather understandably, to submit to an inspection.[16] On 12 December, Morand brought up the matter at a sitting of the Academy of Sciences. As a result six members of the Academy visited Briasson's shop on 14 December for three hours. Their report, dated 19 December 1759, testified that they had seen a large quantity of drawings and engravings, but that only a small number of drawings or engravings belonging to the mechanical arts was finished. They were also shown about forty proofs from Réaumur's plates, 'of which only two or three appear to us, by some points of resemblance, to have served for a model for such plates of the publishers as deal with the same subjects.' The commissioners declared further that they pointed out to the publishers 'that it could well be supposed that they possessed more' of Réaumur's proofs than they were showing. To this the publishers replied that the forty proofs were all that they had, 'that they had used these engravings in order to imitate the composition and design, but that they were ready to engage themselves, by word and by writing, not to copy anything from Réaumur and to submit their plates to the revision of whatever commissioners the Academy should nominate, in order to examine the plates before publication.'[17] This was essentially the procedure that was followed in the years thereafter. For example, the first volume of plates published the censor's certificate of approval, stating that all of the 269 plates were taken from original drawings which had been shown him. The censor was Deparcieux, who had been one of the Academy's commissioners in the visitation of 14 December 1759.[18] Similar certificates of approval were published in each successive volume of what eventually came to be the eleven volumes of plates.

As one sifts the evidence in this tangled and perplexing affair, one cannot help but conclude that the Academy of Sciences would have been justified in making more of an outcry, especially as they were the entrepreneurs of a rival enterprise. Instead, they contented themselves with issuing an official certificate on 16 January 1760, stating that their commissioners had examined '600 drawings or engravings on 130 Arts, among which we have not recognized anything copied from the plates of M. de Réaumur.'[19] There was still a very sharp debate in the Academy about the matter in February. 'Le Breton hauled me off to work at his place from eleven in the morning till eleven at night,' Diderot wrote to Sophie Volland. 'It continues to be the cursed business of our plates. These Academy commissioners have reversed their first judgment. In the Academy they gouged one another's eyes out. Yesterday they reviled one another like fishwives. I don't know what they'll do today.'[20] But this is the last that we hear of the matter. The Academy of Sciences, apparently, contented themselves with buckling down in earnest to the publication of their own work, the *Descriptions des Arts et Métiers*, the first fascicle of which appeared in 1761. 'Thus one sees,' cheerfully comments a twentieth-century expert, 'to what a degree the emulation between the *Encyclopédie* and the Academy of Sciences, far from being harmful, was finally fruitful for both enterprises, as well as for the progress of technology in general.'[21]

If one asks oneself why the Academy was content to let the matter drop, one might conjecture, in the first place, that they had worked out a way for preventing plagiarism in fact, whatever had been the original intent of Diderot and the publishers. Besides, the Academy may have been greatly embarrassed by the public revelation that they had been neglecting Colbert's official orders for eighty-five years. In addition, since the Academy of Sciences as recently as 23 December 1757 had nominated Diderot as one of their two candidates for a vacancy in their membership (the other was Vaucanson, whom Louis XV then named in preference to Diderot), it may be that the Academy did not want to humiliate a man distinguished enough to have been nominated one of themselves.[22] Finally, it is likely that Malesherbes used his influence to soothe the Academy, for otherwise the compromise arrangement of 8 September for publishing the plates might have been unworkable, thus embarrassing or bankrupting the publishers and making the eventual publication of the rest of the *Encyclopédie* impossible. In a memorandum written some months before Patte's revelation, Malesherbes showed that he knew quite well that the publishers were in possession of the Réaumur proofs: not much escaped so sharp-eyed and sharp-witted a magistrate as Malesherbes.[23] And though his name does not appear in any of the negotiations, it is unlikely that he had no policy, or that he exerted no influence to see that his policy prevailed, for all of this business of publishing the plates clearly lay within the jurisdiction of his office. Consider, for example, the fact that Fréron published in his magazine a reply to himself. This 'Reply to the *Année Littéraire*' printed verbatim the Academy's certificate of 16 January ('. . . we have not recognized anything copied from the plates of M. de Réaumur') and also Patte's acknowledgment of having been paid by the publishers in full — a way, of course, of insinuating that Patte's motives were not as high-minded as they ought to be. The 'Reply' also stated that Patte had accused the publishers of plagiarizing many Arts which the commissioners acknowledged that Réaumur had not even begun. One can scarcely imagine Fréron's publishing such a 'Reply' of his own initiative; indeed, Grimm, who rejoiced, reported that Fréron had been commanded to do it.[24] Who had as much power as that? Only Malesherbes, or his father, the Chancellor of France.

All this turbulence occurred before any plates had been published. Naturally, when they did see the light, no single plate of the *Encyclopédie* was a facsimile of Réaumur's. The unanswered question is whether they would have been if Patte's exposé had not occurred.[25] Of that there is no deciding. But one can decide about the other half of Patte's accusation, namely that the descriptions of crafts that had already been published in the early volumes of the *Encyclopédie* showed by their cross references that they might well have been referring to the Réaumur plates.[26] Therefore, argued Patte, Diderot's vaunted field work, his visits to workshops, did not in fact take place. 'It was henceforth simply something one does in an office.'[27] Now, this correspondence can be tested, as Jacques Proust has meticulously done. From his research it is evident that there are several instances of greater correspondence between Diderot's verbal descriptions in the early volumes of the *Encyclopédie* and the Réaumur plates finally published by the Academy of Sciences than there is between these Diderot descriptions and the plates finally published by his own *Encyclopédie*.[28] Surely such corner-cutting comes very close to intent to defraud.

Grimm admitted, in discussing the Patte accusation, that 'the whole public cried out against M. Diderot as soon as the accusation appeared.' D'Alembert, writing to Voltaire, called it 'a persecution' and said that it was a trumped-up quarrel.[29] Grimm went on to make out that the Academy certificate of 16 January proved Fréron a liar and Patte a rogue; neverthe-less everyone must have noticed that the Academy had been conspicuously reticent about saying that there was nothing to the allegation at all.[30] No doubt it was also galling to Diderot to discover that the Academy presently hired Patte to work on their edition of engravings, which they would scarcely have done if they had had no confidence at all in his integrity.[31] Years later Diderot showed that this was still a sore point. He inserted a testy and gratuitous criticism of the Academy's enterprise in his *Salon de 1767*.[32] And in 1771 he hotly declared that 'we did not employ one single figure of Réaumur's.' Then, evidently remembering Patte's sneer that 'it was simply something one does in an office,' he wrote: 'Another fact regarding which I defy contradiction from anyone whomsoever . . . is that I have myself visited the various workshops in Paris; that I have sent [for information] to the most important manufactories of the kingdom; that on occasion I have brought workers from there; that I have had machines constructed under my eyes and operated where I was. If [some-one] possesses the secret of how to describe and get drawn the processes and tools of the paper mills at Montargis, for example, or the manufactories at Lyons, and all without having seen them, I do not.'[33]

Grimm's exasperation at this time, and his conviction that Diderot was being put upon, was expressed by his resentment at the adulation being showered posthumously on Réaumur. Réaumur had been cosseted and pampered by royal patronage and pensions, wrote Grimm in his *Corres-pondance littéraire*: 'Réaumur the academician died rich, honored by royal benefits. Diderot the philosopher will be well honored too, but not in his lifetime nor by the government, but by foreigners who honor merit and genius, and by posterity. . . .'[34]

On 15 January 1762 Grimm announced to his readers that 'the first vol-ume of the plates of the *Encyclopédie* is now being delivered . . . to the subscribers.'[35] The censor had given his approval on 26 October 1761. The volume appeared without any reference to its being a part of the *Encyclo-pédie*, purporting only to be 'A Collection of Engravings on the Sciences and Liberal and Mechanical Arts, with Explanations of Them.' The title

Diderot, drawing by Jean-Baptiste Greuze (The Pierpont Morgan Library, New York). Drawn from life, not later than 1767.

Jean-Jacques Rousseau, pastel by Maurice Quentin de La Tour (Louvre). Photo
Archives Photographiques — Paris.

Jean Le Rond d'Alembert, pastel by Maurice Quentin de La Tour (Louvre). Photo
Archives Photographiques — Paris.

Baron d'Holbach, engraving after drawing by Charles-Nicolas Cochin. Photo Archives Photographiques — Paris.

Mme d'Epinay, portrait by Jean-Etienne Liotard (Musée d'Art et d'Histoire, Geneva).

Mlle de Lespinasse, aquarelle by Louis Carmontelle, 1760 (Musée Condé, Chantilly). Photo Lauros-Giraudon.

Grandval, D'Holbach's country house, garden front. The house was demolished c. 1948.

Grimm (left) and Diderot (right), aquarelle by Louis Carmontelle (Collection Baron J. Le Vavasseur). Photo Lauros-Giraudon.

Grandval, carriage approach (1939). Photograph by the author.

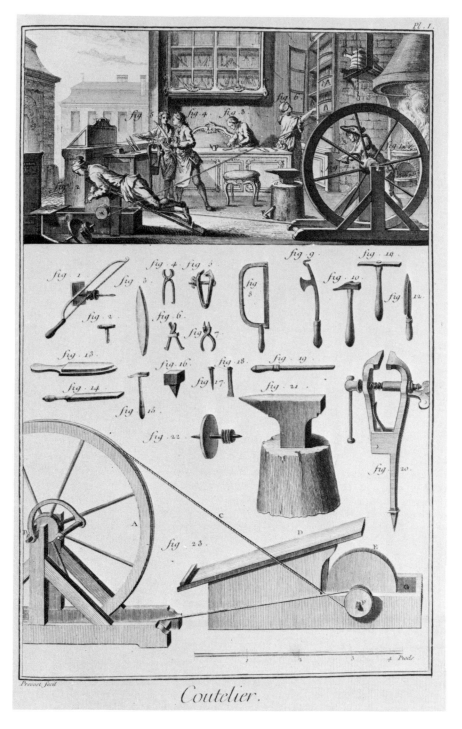

Coutelier.

Engraving from the *Encyclopédie*: 'Cutlery.' The shop shown is that of a Parisian cutler rather than that of Diderot's father at Langres. Diderot was the author of the article 'Coutelier' that appeared in the *Encyclopédie* (1754).

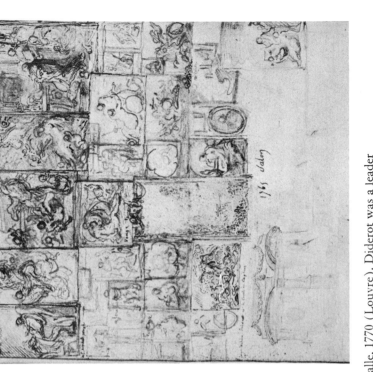

Left, Voltaire, statue by Jean-Baptiste Pigalle, 1770 (Louvre). Diderot was a leader in proposing this statue by public subscription; also it was he who insisted that the sculptor portray Voltaire in the nude. Photo Lauros-Giraudon.

Right, The Salon of 1765, from a drawing by Gabriel de Saint-Aubin (Louvre). This drawing shows how the paintings described by Diderot in his *Salons* were displayed at the biennial exhibitions.

Diderot, bust by Jean-Baptiste Pigalle, 1777 (Louvre). Photo Roger-Viollet.

Diderot, portrait by Dmitri Levifskiĭ (Musée d'Art et d'Histoire, Geneva). Painted while Diderot was in Russia, 1773-4.

Catherine II, mezzotint by Van Wilk.

Etienne-Maurice Falconet, bust by Anne-Marie Collot, 1773 (The Hermitage, Leningrad).

Elie-Catherine Fréron, engraving after drawing by Charles-Nicolas Cochin.

Statue of Peter the Great, by Etienne-Maurice Falconet (Leningrad).

Portrait believed to be of Diderot, by Jean-Simon Berthélemy (Musée Carnavelet, Paris). Photo Lauros-Giraudon.

Portrait believed to be of Diderot, by Michel Van Loo (Musée de l'Hôtel de Breuil, Langres). Photo Archives Photographiques — Paris.

Pastel believed to be of Diderot, by Louis-Marin Bonnet (Comédie-Française).

Portrait believed to be of Diderot, by Jean-Honoré Fragonard (Collection André Pastré). Photo Lauros-Giraudon.

Diderot, statue at Langres by Frédéric-Auguste Bartholdi, 1885, with Diderot's childhood home in the background at the left. Photo Roger-Viollet.

Diderot, bust by Anne-Marie Collot, probably done in 1766 (The Hermitage, Leningrad).

Diderot, portrait by Michel Van Loo, 1767 (Louvre). Diderot commented amusingly upon this portrait in his *Salon de 1767*. Photo Archives Photographiques-Paris.

Diderot, statue by L.-A.-J. Le Cointe, Place d'Anvers, Paris. Photograph taken in 1939. This statue disappeared during World War II.

House where Diderot died, 39, Rue de Richelieu, Paris. Photo Orest Ranum.

Saint-Roch, Paris, where Diderot was buried. Photo Archives Photographiques-Paris.

page, which gave the names of the publishers (Briasson, David, Le Breton, and Durand), also bore the important imprint, 'With the Approval and License of the King.' Of the 269 plates, eighty-three were devoted to agriculture, thirty-three to anatomy, eighty-one to architecture and building operations, thirteen to masonry and tiling, thirty-eight to military art, twelve to antiquities, and the others to needle making, the manufacture of starch, silver working, armor, the fabrication of muskets, and fire works manufacturing.

His work on the *Encyclopédie,* laborious as it was, did not pre-empt all of Diderot's energies. Though nervously overwrought and physically exhausted in the dark months of 1759, he nevertheless turned to blocking out the plots of new plays, called provisionally 'The Sheriff of Kent,' 'The Way of the World, or, Honest Manners as they Really Are,' 'Madame de Linan, or, The Honest Woman,' 'The Unfortunate Woman, or, The Consequences of a Grand Passion,' and 'The Death of Socrates.'[36] His principal reason for interesting himself in these projects was that it distracted him: '. . . work is the only way I have of numbing my misery.'[37] 'I hope,' he wrote to Grimm, 'that you will not be displeased by the use I am making of my melancholy hours.'[38] It was partly because of his friendship for Grimm that his interest in the theater was kept alive during this difficult time. To oblige Grimm, who was in Geneva in the late spring and summer of 1759, Diderot did some reporting for the *Correspondance littéraire* of what was going on in the Paris theater.[39] Thus he sent Grimm an account of a new piece, *La Suivante généreuse,* which the records of the Comédie-Française show he must have seen on 26 May 1759.[40] It was the first time that he had visited the Comédie-Française since the stage had been cleared of spectators, a happy state of affairs beginning with the performance of 23 April 1759, and he was extremely pleased with the change.[41] Moreover, his pleasure was increased by Sophie's being at that performance with her family. The day of the performance he had written to her, 'I shall be in the pit, towards the back and in the center, where I shall be looking for you,' but he was also quick to assure Grimm that her presence 'did not prevent me from seeing and hearing what I should have.'[42]

In addition to reporting on *La Suivante généreuse,* Diderot criticized for Grimm the manuscript of a play written by the Marquis de Ximénès. Diderot's synopsis of the plot, like almost all of his writings, is flavorsome and redolent of his personality, as when he exclaims, 'Oh! how that will teach me to be clear'; or, 'Here I am at the end of the second act, and nothing is getting forward!' 'What a scene to write. Racine, where art thou?'

'Here she is at last, this Princess of Eboli; it's pretty late, but better late than never.' And in general judgment of the plot: 'These people very much need before writing to be sent to a class in rhetoric in order to learn *quis, quid, ubi, quibus auxiliis, cur, quomodo, quando.*' [43] *

Diderot often wrote to Grimm that summer about his projects for plays, the most ambitious of which was 'The Sheriff of Kent.' The action was to take place in the England of James II, the villain was one of James II's minions, and the purpose of the play was to demonstrate the horrible nature of religious intolerance and religious persecution. This would have been, in short, a very political play, and even had he finished it, it is almost certain that he would not have been allowed to publish it in France, let alone produce it on a French stage. A play so implicitly anti-Catholic and so Whiggish, could scarcely have been authorized by a government which, only fourteen years before, had supported the invasion of Great Britain by Bonnie Prince Charlie for the purpose of restoring the Stuarts to the throne.

In Diderot's sketch for this play the noblest character is an old man whose identity is indicated simply by the station he had achieved in life: the Judge. This was in conformity with Diderot's celebrated theory, already dramatized in *Le Père de famille*, that the theater should portray the character development associated with people's functions and stations in life. Diderot lavished all his love on the character of the Judge, who was a father figure indeed. 'There is one inconvenience in this,' he wrote to Grimm. 'When I want to settle down to my work, my mind wanders and it is no longer the Judge of Kent but the cutler of Langres whom I see.' [44]

Diderot's play was never finished, and all that we know of it now consists of the barest bones of forty-nine scenes divided among five acts.[45] Had it been finished it would have been a monster of melodramatic violence — the old judge finally murdered in prison, his virtuous and beautiful daughter submitting to the lustful sheriff in purchase of her father's liberty, then being cynically betrayed and her eyes gouged out — surely no greater collection of horrors had been packed into one play since *The Duchess of Malfi* or *Titus Andronicus.*

In early June Diderot was writing Grimm about the play. 'Several scenes are blocked out in my head or on paper. It gets done without my thinking of it, in the street, out walking, in a cab. . . .' [46] By early July he was writing that other cares had driven it out of his head; and on 13 July he spoke of it as 'a task that frightens me. Imagine forty-six scenes to be written, all of them with enthusiasm and fire.' [47] By 18 July 'The Sheriff of Kent'

* Who, what, where, by what means, why, how, when.

seems to have been laid on the shelf, and Diderot was talking instead of his ideas for 'The Way of the World.' Just before he left for Langres he confessed to Grimm his feeling of impotence:

At the age of twenty, intoxicated with a desire for fame, increasing in vigor from day to day, and believing that I bore within me the germ of eternal existence, I would have fallen upon all these tasks and I would have taken no rest until they were finished. Today, when the wings of youth no longer support me, I lie heavy on the surface of the earth, I become numb, I feel that it is so, and every time that I want to launch forth, I say to myself *quid tibi prodest aerias tentasse domos, animoque rotundum percurisse polum morituro.*[48] *

The trouble was not exclusively that he was over-tired, or that he had lost his youth, or that for the first time he was realizing through and through that he was mortal. The trouble was also that with all his versatility and creativity Diderot was nevertheless not at his best in the department of writing plays. He was excellent in dramatic criticism and in appreciating the nature of the actor's art. This part of his writing seems to posterity to be still undimmed, yet *Le Fils naturel* and *Le Père de famille* seem to us to be turgid and lusterless.[49] It is a paradox that a man who was a supreme master of the dialogue as an art form should be so tedious in his plays. In his dialogues there is always a sparkle of intellect and even of wit, whereas in his plays he was so intent upon preaching virtue that he became dull. Overawed by the solemnity of his good intentions, he forgot that the theater also exists for entertainment. Moreover, there is a remarkable absence of imagery in Diderot's plays, though his dialogues throb with the most imaginative similes and metaphors.[50] It is significant that he does not often complain about the tedium and frustrations of the job of being a writer, but he does complain about the difficulty of constructing plays. And in this very summer he wrote to Grimm that 'the plot costs me nothing but the dialogue wears me out,' that if he has to go on to link up the scenes, he will do it, 'but the labor will be terrible.'[51]

While Diderot's zeal for writing plays was flagging in 1759, he began in that year to show what he could do in another department of writing for which he has become greatly and increasingly famous. This was in the criticism of art. Again to accommodate the absent Grimm, Diderot wrote an account of the exhibition of the work of the forty members of the Academy of Painting and Sculpture, which opened traditionally on Saint Louis' Day, August 25.[52] Beginning in 1748 the Salons had become bien-

---

* What advantage is it to you to have scaled the airy heights and by your intellect voyaged over the rounded pole, you who are about to die? (Horace, Odes, I, 28).

nial. They were held in the Salon Carré of the Louvre, with overflow into the adjoining Gallery of Apollo and the nearby staircases.[53] The Salons were one of the major events in Parisian life, so much so that comment upon them had for some years been appearing in pamphlets or in the periodicals of the day.[54] Grimm himself had discussed previous Salons, and it is only because of the accident of his being away from Paris that Diderot's gifts for art criticism came to be displayed.[55] Grimm knew a good thing when he saw it — he paid Diderot the compliment of exploiting him mercilessly — so that Diderot's *Salons,* growing in perceptiveness and subtlety as the years went by, became one of the special features of the *Correspondance littéraire.*

Because it was so searingly candid, Diderot's criticism of the Salons was carefully kept confidential. None of it became public knowledge until years after his death. When it did appear, it was by fragments, some in 1796 and 1798, some in 1819 and 1821, some in 1845 and 1857, so that it was not until 1876 that the whole succession of his *Salons,* from 1759 through 1781, some thousand tightly packed octavo pages, was published together.[56] Thus, by the time that modern critics had an opportunity to judge Diderot's work, the many other eighteenth-century writers on the Salons had been forgotten. The not unnatural result was that Diderot has often been given the credit for still another first, that of creating the practice of commenting upon exhibitions of art. This is a distinction Diderot himself never claimed. He could, however, have claimed to be the best. According to a recent authoritative evaluation of all the other contemporary criticism of the Salons,

There is indeed little to be gleaned in the multitude of these small pamphlets: a few jokes, here and there an accurate and sensible observation, a sincere impression — but at best, the reflections of a minor artist or a man of letters of the second rank. Their principal interest to us is that, taken all together, they reflect an average opinion: that is why they were worth looking through. Diderot as an art critic stands out in comparison in full relief and in his true stature.[57]

Diderot's *Salons* were naturally much affected by his knowledge that they would be read only by the subscribers to Grimm's *Correspondance littéraire.* This was a very select group indeed, never more than fifteen, none of them living in France, all of them crowned heads or German potentates.[58] Grimm's manuscript fortnightly news letter was usually sent out from Paris through diplomatic channels, making it all the more 'secure' and confidential. Thus the copy that went to Queen Louisa Ulrica of

Sweden, the sister of Frederick the Great — it may now be consulted in the Royal Library at Stockholm, its uncreased pages covered with neat handwriting from margin to margin — was almost certainly sent to her by way of the diplomatic pouch of the Swedish ambassador to France.

Since none of the recipients of Grimm's news letter was in a position to visit the Salon himself, it was always necessary to describe the paintings in detail, particularly their arrangement or composition. As Diderot himself had previously put it, in criticizing unseen pictures it was a question of 'awakening the imagination.'[59] For this he has often been harshly criticized by writers who forget that photographs did not then exist and who do not know that no drawings or engravings accompanied the news letter. Diderot's descriptions had to be explicit.[60] Not that he would ever have neglected to describe composition and disposition. He considered them absolutely basic in art.[61] On at least three previous occasions he had written suggestions for works of art, one a series of six subjects taken from Homer and suitable for tapestry, one a snuff box, and the third a memorial for the Marshal de Saxe. In each of these Diderot displayed a great preoccupation with arrangement and composition.[62] And inasmuch as the eighteenth-century French school was deficient in composition — 'composition is not the most brilliant aspect of our artists' accomplishments,' is the way Diderot put it — his absorption in matters of arrangement and of depicting the psychological moment in genre pieces and historical paintings was not inappropriate. 'Who, then, better than he,' asked a modern French connoisseur and critic, 'denounced the weakness of composition in our artists?'[63]

A little piece about Italian art that Diderot wrote in 1758 shows that he already knew, before he wrote his first *Salon*, the pitfalls besetting the man of letters who undertakes to write of painting. At the same time, by discussing how 'a continual observation of nature' is necessary to avoid becoming mannered in style, Diderot showed in this essay some of his own qualifications for speaking out. The years were to prove, *Salon* after *Salon*, that his association with artists continuously deepened his awareness of technique and made his critical touch more sure. Meanwhile he wrote in 1758,

I know scarcely any other book more calculated to make our simple-minded literary men circumspect when they speak of painting. The things they appreciate the worth of, and of which they are competent judges, like everybody else, are passions, movement, character, the subject, the general effect; but they do not understand either drawing or lighting or color or the harmonizing of the whole, or the technique of color application, etc. At every instant they run the risk of

praising some mediocre work to the skies and disdainfully passing by a masterpiece; of being struck by some obvious detail in a picture, good or bad, while
not noticing some surprising quality in it, in such a fashion that both their praise
and their blame would make even the man in a studio who grinds the colors
laugh out loud.[64]

The *Salon de 1759* was the shortest of them all. Interesting as it is, it
still does not display quite the dash, quite the sureness of touch, of his
later efforts.[65] Nevertheless, it is entertaining. 'Lots of pictures, my friend,'
he begins. 'Lots of bad pictures. I love to praise. I am happy when I can
admire. I do not ask for more than to be happy and admiring. . . .' Of one
quite academic artist Diderot remarks that he uses more oil in his lamp
than he does on his palette. And in discussing a 'Resurrection' by Jean-
Jacques Bachelier he shows why his readers found the *Salons* so entertaining
and why it was necessary to keep them confidential. 'Monsieur Bachelier,
my friend, believe me, go back to your tulips. Your picture has no color nor
composition nor expression nor draughtsmanship. This Christ suffers from
dislocations; he is a patient whose members have been incorrectly reset. Considering the way in which you have opened this tomb it is a miracle indeed
that he got out of it, and, were he to speak in accordance with his gesture,
he would be saying to the onlooker: "Adieu, messieurs. I am your humble
servant; things are not too good with you and I am leaving."' No wonder
that Diderot begged Grimm to 'take good care not to put my name to this
paper. Orpheus was not worse treated by the bacchantes than I would be
by our painters.' [66]

Diderot's criticism, one should be quick to add, is far from being made
up solely of gibes and wisecracks. It can be deeply moving, as when he,
anti-clerical and free-thinking though he was, criticized a painting showing
Carthusian monks at their meditations. It had, he said, 'no quietness, no
feeling of being withdrawn, nothing recalling divine justice, no [central]
idea, no profound adoration, no sense of inner concentration, no ecstasy,
no terror. This man never dreamed of any of that. If his genius said nothing
to him, why did he not go to Carthusian monasteries? There he would have
seen what he was unable to imagine. Yet do you think he would have seen
it? If there are few people who know how to look at a picture, are there
many painters who know how to look at nature?' [67]

Present-day art lovers rejoice to discover that Diderot thought highly of
Chardin. The eighteenth century did not praise Chardin so highly as he deserved, mainly because of the humble subjects he chose, but Diderot recognized him as a 'man of intellect, understanding the theory of his art; he

paints in a manner which is his own, and his pictures will some day be prized.' [68]

Diderot visited the Salon of 1759 at least on one occasion in the company of Sophie, her mother, her sister Mme Le Gendre, and a Mlle Boileau. It was then that Sophie remarked of a Christ by Vien, supposed to be depicted as suffering but actually looking very plump and hearty, that if he was ailing it must be that he had a corn.[69] Meanwhile the necessity of working hard and uninterruptedly upon his articles for the *Encyclopédie* was bearing down on Diderot. It was for this reason that he accepted D'Holbach's pressing invitation to stay at Grandval, the D'Holbach country house. Diderot went there on 3 September — we know this from a letter to Grimm which Diderot, who almost never knew what day of the month it was, had meticulously dated, thus surprising even himself. 'I know the day of the month, that's unusual,' he wrote in a postscript. 'Well, when I said that our letters were getting to have a business-like air, was I wrong?' [70] At Grandval he wrote the *Salon de 1759* just from recollection, for he had a prodigious pictorial memory. After a few restless days caused by worry over Sophie, who was not feeling well, he went back to Paris for a short time. Then he returned to Grandval equipped for a long stay. 'Madame Diderot was a little surprised at the quantity of books, togs, and linen I took.' [71] Diderot stayed in the country uninterruptedly the next six weeks, working hard. It was his way of getting second breath.

CHAPTER 28

Grandval

G RANDVAL became in the 1760's a sort of summer capital of the *philosophes*. It was a spacious dwelling, comfortable but not grandiose, about twelve miles east of the center of Paris, not far from a great loop in the Marne just before it empties into the Seine. The nearest village is Sucy-en-Brie. As Diderot traveled to and fro-between Grandval and Paris he would pass close by Vincennes. The sight of that lofty central keep where ten years previously he had been in solitary confinement for twenty-eight days was a nagging reminder of the difficulties besetting an author who would like to say what he thinks.

The chateau of Grandval, as a twentieth-century postcard called it, was a three-storied stucco structure of harmonious proportions. It was approached from the west by quite a lengthy and imposing driveway, and on that side there may have been smaller buildings as well, for we read of a separate chapel where the priest of nearby Sucy, scornfully called by the irreverent D'Holbach household a 'God-cruncher,' came to celebrate the mass. On the other side of the house was the garden front, with a graceful pilastered bay, surmounted by a stone balustrade, pleasingly projecting from the center of the façade. The garden was extensive, bordered by trees and confined by a moat.[1] Even in its wild and overgrown condition in 1939 it was an attractive place.

In 1759 Grandval had been recently acquired by the D'Holbachs and replantings and alterations were still going on. 'The weather has been charming this afternoon [Diderot wrote to Sophie]. Our gardens were alive with workers. I went to see the box being planted, the flower beds being laid out, and bowling greens being sown. I love to talk with peasants; I always learn something from it. The webs that in an instant cover a hundred *arpents* of newly cultivated land are spun by little spiders swarming in the soil. They are active only during this season and only on certain days.'[2]

It was a peaceful routine, but a busy one. 'I have been installed in a small separate apartment that is very quiet, cheerful, and warm. There, between Horace and Homer and the portrait of my loved one, I pass the hours reading, thinking, writing, and sighing. Such is my occupation from six in the morning until one. At one thirty I am dressed and I go down to the salon, where everyone has assembled. . . . We dine well and long. The meal is served here as it is done in town, and perhaps even more sumptuously. . . . It is impossible to be temperate here. One can't even think of it. I am rounding out like a ball. . . . Between three and four we take our sticks and go for a walk. . . . Nothing stops us, neither ridges nor woods nor bogs nor planted fields. The spectacle of nature pleases us both. . . . Sunset and the coolness of the evening bring us back to the house. . . . We rest a little while. Then we begin playing piquet. . . . Usually supper interrupts our play. . . . Upon leaving the table, we finish the game. It is ten thirty. We talk until eleven. At eleven thirty we are all asleep or we ought to be. The next day we do it all over again.'[3]

It sounds quiet and remote. One would not know from this that a world war was going on, that France was losing decisive battles in Canada and in Germany. Yet Diderot was not completely unscathed by the war. He knew that D'Holbach was deeply worried about the government's plans for forced loans and for a moratorium on the payment of public debts; he knew that D'Alembert was financially embarrassed because of the war, for his pensions were not being paid; and he knew that Mme d'Houdetot, visiting at Grandval, worried about her lover Saint-Lambert, who was in the French army that was poised at Brest for an invasion of England.[4]

It is surprising, considering the closeness of their association, to discover that Diderot found D'Holbach a very difficult companion. Though he felt morally compelled to do so, Diderot was reluctant to visit Grandval.[5] From time to time he complained. He found it hard to write to D'Holbach, though it was a pleasure to write to others. The only advantage of being at Paris at a particular moment was that the Baron was at Grandval. D'Holbach was being 'so despotic and so changeable.' He was not a person in whom one could confide.[6] Evidently D'Holbach was frequently bad-tempered, especially when he lost at cards. He was sometimes capable of an apology: 'The day after his outburst he came into my room in the morning and he said, "I have a bad trait, among many others which you already know I possess. It is this, that though I am not a miser, I am a bad loser. Yesterday I was ridiculously sharp with you. I am sorry."'[7] Diderot thought this was handsome enough. Yet he rarely praised D'Holbach.

On the contrary; he wrote during this time that D'Holbach took too little responsibility in arranging for the proper education of his children.[8] Diderot did not feel toward D'Holbach as he did toward that other German friend of his, Grimm.

Grimm had gone to Geneva some months before in order to be with his ailing mistress, Mme d'Epinay.[9] Diderot missed him sorely, as his frequent letters attest, and when the two met again, at Grandval, Diderot responded so melodramatically that, as one reads his account of it to Sophie, one begins to wonder. A final sentence suggests that perhaps he was only trying to hint to her that a man who was such a faithful friend would be no less a faithful lover. 'What pleasure I had in seeing him again. With what warmth did we embrace! My joy overflowed. I was unable to speak to him nor he to me. We kissed each other without speaking a word, and I wept. We weren't expecting him. We were eating dessert when he was announced: "It is Monsieur Grimm." — "It is Monsieur Grimm!" I repeated with a cry; and I arose and ran to him and fell on his neck. He sat down; he dined poorly, I think. As for me, I could not open my mouth either to eat or to speak. He was by my side. I held his hand and gazed at him. Conclude from that how happy I am soon going to be when I see you again.'[10]

The fortunes of Grimm seemed to be on the rise. For some years he had held quite an important position in the court of the Duke of Orléans. Now he added to it another appointment. The Imperial free city of Frankfort on Main found that as a result of being occupied by the French army — Goethe recalled in his autobiography many incidents of the French occupation, including the interesting fact that he saw Diderot's *Le Père de famille* played there during the war — it had a very special need for a diplomatic representative at Paris. Grimm was their choice, to be ranked as envoy.[11] This was auspicious. But presently he had a stroke of bad luck. A letter of his to a Swiss friend, criticizing the French conduct of the war, was intercepted and Choiseul, the French Secretary of State for Foreign Affairs, insisted that Grimm's diplomatic appointment be revoked. It took all the influence of the Duke of Orléans to keep Grimm from being deported.[12] This would have been a disagreeable mischance to happen to anyone, but for the careerist Grimm it must have been almost unbearable.

Around this time Grimm was the victim of a ludicrous practical joke which may be just worth mentioning because Grimm and Diderot never did. Someone concocted a series of love declarations sent to Grimm purporting to come from a dancer in the Opera, one Manon Leclerc (who really did exist). These letters, funny enough in their false innocence and phonetic spellings, were followed by one even funnier, purporting to be from the girl's mother and begging Grimm not to take advantage of the inexperience of her little girl. Last came a letter purporting to be from another dancer at the Opera, Magdeleine Miré (who also did exist), stating that poor Manon had perished as a result of unrequited love. Magdeleine, by the way, offered to console Grimm for his loss.[13] All very funny, but no doubt intended maliciously, for it was notorious that some years previously Grimm had made a spectacle of himself grieving over his infatuation, also unrequited, for a ballerina at the Opera, Mlle Fel.

Meanwhile, interesting people besides Grimm dropped in at Grandval. Mme Geoffrin, whose Paris salon was the most famous of all, came from time to time. Diderot wrote that he continued 'to get on marvelously' with her. 'I see her at the Baron's, and I see her nowhere else, which suits both of us.'[14] Then there was Marmontel, who read the company one of his 'Moral Tales' which to that age seemed so exquisite but seem so mawkish to ours;[15] and Charles-Georges Le Roy, Encyclopedist as well as Superintendent of the Royal Chase at Versailles, an old friend who used to see to it that Diderot received a brace of pheasants to send to his father: 'They are, in fact, from the King's park,' wrote Diderot in 1758, 'and I assure you that they don't eat better ones at Versailles.'[16] There was even a Scot at Grandval, one not completely identified to this day because he was known there only by the nickname that they gave him, Père Hoop. An eccentric, much afflicted by the spleen, he fascinated Diderot, who wrote Sophie at length about him. Perhaps the anecdote most revelatory to post-Freudian readers is the one concerning talk about a charlatan who claimed to have an elixir of youth. 'It was remarked that if this man has the secret of rejuvenating himself by one hour, he might, by increasing the dose, do so by a year, by ten, and thus eventually return to his mother's womb. "If I should ever get back there," said the Scot, "I do not think they would ever get me to come out." '[17]

The saltiest character at Grandval, if that is not too complimentary a word, was D'Holbach's mother-in-law. Mme d'Aine, then fifty-six, delighted in gross talk, much to the embarrassment of her chambermaid and much to the delight of Diderot. She loved to confuse words, calling the *Encyclopédie* 'Socoplie,' and managed to stultify pretty completely any conversation about intellectual matters. Nevertheless Diderot thought her 'the finest woman in the world.'[18] One evening the 'God-cruncher' from Sucy was at Grandval and, as he was leaning over a table, the finest woman in the world climbed on a chair and jumped on his back, 'one leg on one side, one leg on the other, and belabored him with her heels and excited him with her voice and fingers, while he whinnied and reared and kicked and his soutane climbed up towards his shoulders and the lady's petticoats crept up fore and aft, so that she was almost bare on her steed, and her steed down to the raw under her; and we laughing; and the lady laughing, and laughing harder, and laughing harder still, and holding her sides, and finally stretching out on the Abbé and crying out, "Mercy, mercy, I can't hold out any longer, something has to give; Abbé, don't move." And the Abbé, who did not yet understand what was up, did not move and let himself be inundated by a deluge of tepid water which ran into his shoes by the belt of his breeches, and he began to cry, "Help! Help! I'm drowning." And the rest of us falling on the sofas and choking with laughter. . . . The Abbé did not get annoyed and was wise not to. . . . Madame d'Aine is honorable. The little priest is poor. Next day he was ordered to buy a complete new outfit.' [19] Such were manners in the eighteenth century, or such, at least, they were at Grandval.

Diderot's letters to Sophie are universally admired for being practically a model for the delineation of sensitive perceptions, for the realistic description of milieu and character, and for the variety and skillful use of all the best devices and contrivances of rhetoric, to use a noble word that has now come down in the world. A notable instance of this is his long description of an evening's conversation with D'Holbach, Mme d'Aine, Mme d'Holbach, and Père Hoop. Diderot had been writing an article for the *Encyclopédie* on Mohammedanism, and much of what he included in his letter to Sophie were excerpts from that article. One might be tempted to suppose that quoting an article from the *Encyclopaedia Britannica,* say, even if one had written it oneself, is scarcely the most promising way of keeping one's mistress entertained. But Diderot orchestrated the dialogue with such skill, with such grotesque interruptions on the part of Mme d'Aine, with such 'philosophic' comments by the saturnine D'Holbach and the melancholy Père Hoop, and adorned the whole with such graceful interpolations of Persian tales taken from the books he had been reading that his letter shimmers with life and still smells unmistakably of the muskiness given off by strong and redolent personalities, even though they lived two centuries ago.[20]

Thus the days went by and the finished articles of the *Encyclopédie* accumulated. 'These [Saracens] are the ones, beloved, with whom I have been in conversation the past few days. Before then, it was with the Phoenicians; before that, with the inhabitants of Malabar; before that, with the

Indians.'[21] Thus Diderot refers to articles on the history of philosophy which, though now long since outdated, constituted in their time one of the most valuable and substantial — and also most 'philosophic' — parts of the *Encyclopédie*. Grandval, then, is indelibly associated with one of the most important departments of the last volumes of the *Encyclopédie*.

Diderot had not originally intended to make the history of philosophy his personal assignment. In the early volumes he had given this important task to others, especially to the Abbés Yvon, De Prades, Mallet, and Pestré. But these men became discouraged by the outcries of the conservative theologians of the time and faded out of the enterprise. Thus Diderot found himself shouldering the extra burden. He did it without compensation, too, as he tartly reminded his publisher, Le Breton, in 1769. 'I did it, this whole job. Did the company pay for it? No, monsieur. I gave, really gave to the company the history of ancient and modern philosophy, which is not an inconsiderable part of the work. Just look in our contracts and then tell me whether there has ever been any mention of this labor.'[22]

The very bulk of these articles was imposing. A three-volume collection of them was published at Bouillon in 1769, and Naigeon saw to it that seventy-three of them were republished in the volumes (1791-4) that the *Encyclopédie méthodique* devoted to philosophy. In composing them, Diderot did not pretend that he was not consulting earlier books of reference. In the early volumes of the *Encyclopédie* he had already acknowledged that he relied for much of his information on a Latin history of philosophy published a few years before by a German scholar, Johann Jacob Brucker.[23] This acknowledgment had not deterred Fréron, the tough and inveterate enemy, from raising once again the old cry that Diderot was a little too practised in borrowing:

. . . there is absolutely no new idea in this enormous Dictionary [Fréron wrote of the first seven volumes]; it is only a new edition, badly planned and poorly carried out, of an infinite number of books already in print; the philosophical views to be found in it are taken from every hand and especially drawn from the Philosophical Dictionary of Brucker, which is hardly ever cited, because people do not like to mention their creditors.[24]

If Fréron read Diderot's article *'Philosophie'* when it appeared some five years later, he could take satisfaction in observing that Diderot mentioned his creditors once more. There he again referred his readers to 'the excellent work that M. Brucker has published,' and went on to say, 'One can also read the *Histoire de la philosophie* by M. Deslandes.'[25] Anyone wanting to defend Diderot's reputation for originality and creativity might well wish that his lavish borrowing from Brucker had been on a somewhat less massive scale. Naigeon says that Diderot himself regretted that the pressure of time necessitated his following that author so closely.[26] Yet Diderot put much of himself into these articles and made them truly characteristic of the point of view of the *philosophes*.[27] Diderot's articles have more of a polemical edge than Brucker's. Where Brucker was bland and mildly deistic, Diderot subtly brings the articles out to be more materialistic in philosophical point of view. Where Brucker had contented himself with attacking myths in the ancient pagan religions, Diderot more boldly hints at the mythic element in Christian faith. Here we may observe a characteristic difference between the German Enlightenment and the French. The Enlightenment, which in numerous respects was common to all the countries of Western Europe and the English colonies in America, nevertheless exhibited subtle national and cultural differences between countries. The contrast in tone between Brucker's articles and Diderot's reworking of them measures to a nicety the differences between the *Aufklärung* in Germany and the *siècle des lumières* in France, the former more respectful of established religion, less critical of established institutions, the other sharper in comment, more dynamic and restless, more impatient and more acerb.

For example, neither Brucker nor Diderot liked scholasticism. But Diderot, though he used Brucker extensively in composing the article '*Scolastiques*,' expressed himself more explosively. Moreover, he brought his doctrine to a sharp focus by relating it to conditions in France at the time that he was writing:

. . . never was so much sharpwittedness so poorly employed, nor so many minds spoiled and ruined as there were during the reign of scholastic philosophy. . . . In a word, this philosophy has been one of the greatest plagues of the human mind. Who could believe that even today we are not thoroughly cured of it? What is the theology being dictated to our forms? What is the philosophy one learns in our colleges? Ethics, that part of philosophy to which all the ancient philosophers gave their principal attention, is absolutely neglected. Ask a young man who has finished his course, what is subtle matter? He will tell you. But do not ask him, what is virtue? He has not the least idea.[28]

His early schooling as a humanist well qualified Diderot to write or adapt such articles as '*Ionique*' (Anaximander and Anaxogoras), '*Platonisme*,' '*Scepticisme*,' or '*Pythagorisme*.' The article '*Pyrrhonienne*,' which dealt with scepticism both ancient and modern, was so daring that it devoted several columns to the discussion of Bayle, and so up-to-date that it contained, although veiled, a refutation of Berkeley and an attempt to answer Hume.[29] Finally, Diderot made the *Encyclopédie* the vehicle for disseminating what was then known of non-Western philosophies. In the light of twentieth-century resources of information these articles now seem pitifully inadequate but, for Diderot's contemporaries, horizons were widened by his long articles on *'Sarrasins,' 'Indiens,' 'Chinois,' 'Japonais,'* and *'Zend-Avesta.'* Here, as always, Diderot was a leader, doing his part in the broadening and universalizing of intellectual outlook that made the Age of Enlightenment cosmopolitan and exciting.

The article on the philosophy of the Japanese is typical. Diderot's ultimate source was the best authority available, a German named Kaempfer who had traveled extensively in Japan from 1690 to 1692 and whose *History of Japan,* first published in English, had appeared in 1727.[30] But Diderot made the article a vehicle for his own ideas on toleration, dogmatism, and intolerance, so that Kaempfer's neutrally phrased original became, in Diderot's hands, a means of aggressively challenging Christian orthodoxy while pretending to defend it. '. . . [this Japanese god's] statue promptly began to perform miracles; for peoples insist upon having them. . . . God has permitted this resemblance between the True Religion and false ones, in order that our faith might have merit; for it is only the True Religion that has true miracles.' In this article, too, we see the political thinker: 'Thus it is that despotism and superstition lend each other strength.' And here we see Diderot, as always, appealing to reason and progress, though betraying some wonderment, not untinged with self-pity, that reason is so much resisted and progress so much delayed. 'The fantasies of a Xekia spread throughout India, China, and Japan and became law for a hundred millions of men, while sometimes a man is born among us with the most sublime talents, writes the wisest things, yet does not change custom to the slightest degree, lives in obscurity, and dies ignored.'[31]

In respect to more modern philosophies, Diderot's lengthy and judicious article on Hobbes may be taken as an excellent example of his method, especially as this article won the praise of Voltaire, an exacting and discriminating critic.[32] Diderot was just beginning to get acquainted with Hobbes — his name had not appeared in D'Alembert's catalogue of the great in the 'Preliminary Discourse' of the *Encyclopédie* in 1751 — though even here Diderot appears to be quoting Hobbes at one remove, that is to say, through Brucker.[33] Diderot warmed to Hobbes, no doubt because of the materialism and atheism implicit in the latter's thought, and said of him, very wisely, 'No one marches ahead more boldly, nor is more logical.

Take care not to accept his first principles if you are not willing to follow him wherever he chooses to lead you.' The philosophy of 'M. Rousseau of Geneva,' wrote Diderot, 'is almost the inverse of that of Hobbes. The one believes man by nature good, the other believes him evil. According to the philosopher of Geneva, the state of nature is a state of peace; according to the philosopher from Malmesbury, it is a state of war. . . . Both of them exaggerate.'[34]

Diderot's articles were solid and substantial, as, for example, the twelve thousand words devoted to *'Leibnitzianisme'* somewhat oppressively prove. Though much of this article was derived from Brucker and some of it from Fontenelle, Diderot showed here (as he continued to do in various of his other writings) how much he was influenced by the philosopher of the Great Chain of Being.[35] In this Diderot differed from D'Alembert, who had condescendingly said of Leibniz in the 'Preliminary Discourse' that, '. . . less wise than Locke and Newton, he did not content himself with expressing doubts, he undertook to dissipate them.'[36] Now, writing about 1759 and perhaps at Grandval, Diderot enjoyed the delights of making amends to Leibniz and criticizing D'Alembert at one and the same time:

People have complained, and perhaps rightly, that we did not render to this philosopher all the justice he deserved. Here is the place to make amends for this mistake, if we have committed it, and to speak eulogistically and admiringly of this celebrated man, which we do with joy. We never intended to undervalue great men; we are too jealous for the honor of the human race. Besides, we would be speaking in vain, for their works, transmitted to posterity, would testify against us and in their favor; they would be seen to be no less great and we would be revealed to be pretty small.[37]

How gracefully Diderot paid his respects to the great, meanwhile striking a blow, with that ever-vigilant didacticism of the French Enlightenment, for the Moderns in comparison with the Ancients. Bayle, Descartes, Leibniz, and Newton, he wrote, may be contrasted favorably 'with the most astonishing geniuses of antiquity.'[38] This article, which to French critics has seemed 'a *tour de force*,' summarizes and paraphrases Liebniz' metaphysics and most skillfully insinuates that his famous monads can be interpreted materialistically.[39] Welling up in the article, too, was the irrelevant but fascinating revelation of Diderot's own self-awareness, a blend of modesty and self-pity: '. . . when one reflects upon one's self and compares the small talents one possesses with those of a Leibniz, one is tempted to throw one's books away and take oneself off to the farthest end of some out-of-the-way nook, quietly to end one's days.' Or again, speaking of Leibniz' unfinished plans for an encyclopedia, Diderot remarked that nothing came of the project, 'unfortunately for us who have succeeded him, and for whom this kind of work has been nothing but a source of persecutions, insults, and vexations, beginning more than fifteen years ago, springing up anew day after day, and perhaps not ending so long as we are alive.' [40] Outbursts like these, as we come across them in the now musty and dusty pages of the *Encyclopédie,* remind us of how incandescent was the resentment of Diderot and how deep his pessimism at this discouraging time of his life.

CHAPTER 29

The Nun's Story

(*La Religieuse*)

I<small>T ALL</small> began as a practical joke.

Marc-Antoine-Nicolas, Marquis de Croismare, was the delight of his friends. 'He was,' wrote Grimm, 'the archetype of the lovable Frenchman, all of whose good qualities he combined in the highest degree.'[1] No one had more wit or versatility or volatility than he. He was intelligent without being pedantic and witty without being malicious. 'Diderot compared his wit to the flame made by alcohol: "It runs over my skin," he used to say, "and envelops it without ever burning."' Croismare was a man of passionate enthusiasms, indeed a succession of them, including ideas on the best way to make chocolate or cook an omelette. 'No one knew Paris [including the slums] as he did. . . . He loved poetry, music, the arts, reading, and, above everything else, friendship, liberty, and independence.'[2] But he had left Paris to live on his family estate near Caen, and the question was how to entice him to return.

One of his impetuous enthusiasms had been his interest in an unusual law suit much talked about in Paris from 1755 to 1758. This involved the futile attempt of a nun to break her vows.[3] Croismare, though never becoming personally acquainted with the nun nor even knowing her name, had tried to help her but without success. In early 1760 Diderot, Grimm, and Mme d'Epinay remembered this case and decided to put it to their own use. They sent Croismare a letter, transcribed in a feminine hand, purporting to come from the very nun whom he had tried to assist some years before.[4] The letter announced that she had escaped from her convent and was living under cover in Paris, and asked Croismare's assistance in finding an asylum and any sort of respectable job, even though a humble one.

From the very beginning the affair took a turn unfavorable to the conspirators' schemes for getting Croismare back to Paris. He immediately sent instructions to the nun to hasten to Caen, where he had made arrangements for her safety. In order to temporize, the plotters quickly invented an illness which laid the nun low, and there followed, from February into May a considerable correspondence. Croismare's letters reveal him to have been a most admirable man. The letters to him were all concocted by Diderot save one — and that one, which Diderot feared might be so clumsy as to give the hoax away, does indeed show the difference between a duffer and a writer of consummate skill.[5] Diderot wrote either in the name of the supposititious nun, Suzanne Simonin, or of a woman named Madin. The latter, a real person living in Versailles, who was probably an acquaintance of Mme d'Epinay, simply acted as a letter-drop.

Sometime during the course of these months it occurred to Diderot to write a lengthier account of the nun's misfortunes. This eventually grew into the novel *La Religieuse*. Meanwhile Croismare had become so concerned about the nun that the conspirators evidently felt that something drastic must be done. Consequently they did the most drastic thing of all: they killed the poor girl off. This literary execution occurred early in May 1760. Croismare remained on his estate and did not return to Paris until 1768. It was only then, and then only because by coincidence he made the acquaintance of Mme Madin, that the truth came out and the hoax was confessed.

Grimm's account of this practical joke was written ten years after the event, in a document called the 'Préface-Annexe.' He included this account in one of the numbers of his *Correspondance littéraire,* and in almost all nineteenth- and twentieth-century editions and translations of *La Religieuse* this 'Préface-Annexe' is published as an appendix.* But even Grimm did not know all there was to know about the novel that Diderot wrote. For Grimm spoke of it in 1770 as never having existed other than in fragments; and, again, that it was a pity that the memoirs had not been written out, for they would have made very interesting reading.[6] Apparently Grimm's knowledge of the novel ended about the time that the conspirators brought Suzanne Simonin's career to an untimely end. Diderot, however, was still working on the account late in the summer of 1760. 'It's no longer a letter, it's a book,' he confided to Mme d'Epinay.[7] The lengthened manuscript appears to have then lain fallow for about twenty years, when Diderot offered it, in 1780, to Grimm's successor, Meister, to be used in the *Corres-*

---

* An English translation of *La Religieuse,* done by Francis Birrell, was published in 1928 in the 'Broadway Library of XVIII Century French Literature' under the title *Memoirs of a Nun* (republished in London: Elek Books, 1959). A paperback edition, *The Nun,* translated by Eileen B. Hennessy, was published in Los Angeles in 1968.

pondance littéraire.[8] At this time Diderot revised the manuscript slightly, perhaps in connection with his preparations for a collected edition of his works.[9] Thus the novel as we now have it, first published in 1796, is not just a first draft, struck off at white heat. The author carefully reviewed it and somewhat revised it, at least three different times.[10]

This matter of Diderot's revisions, important as it is from the point of view of literary criticism, is no less so from the point of view of biography. For Diderot also revised Grimm's account of the hoax, something unsuspected until recently.[11] One of the most famous of all anecdotes about Diderot appears in the 'Préface-Annexe.' It shows his susceptibility, his suggestibility, his enthusiasm, and the readiness of his emotional response. The story runs as follows: 'One day when he was completely immersed in his work [of writing the nun's story], M. d'Alainville, one of our friends in common, paid him a visit and found him plunged in grief and his face streaming with tears. "For goodness' sake, what ails you?" M. d'Alainville said to him. "What a state you are in." "What ails me?" replied M. Diderot. "I am in misery from a story I am writing." '[12] This anecdote is in character. No doubt it happened. Perhaps Diderot, with his streaming eyes, was overwhelmed by the memory of his younger sister, the nun who died insane in an Ursuline convent.[13] The anecdote certainly helps posterity to know Diderot and to see him. But more revealing biographically is the fact that it was not Grimm who included this anecdote in the account. The handwriting shows that the addition was made by Diderot himself.[14]

The story set forth by *La Religieuse* is swift.[15] Suzanne Simonin, who begins to realize that she will have no dowry and who ultimately discovers that she is the offspring of her mother's adultery, is coerced by her mother and by the man she supposes to be her father into entering a convent. There she becomes a postulant and then a novice. But feeling no vocation for such a life, she causes a scandal by refusing in the public ceremony to take the final vows. Withdrawn from that convent, she is visited with more coercion at home. As a result she reluctantly consents to enter the convent at Longchamps and eventually takes the vows there. At first her life is not unendurable because she deeply admires the Mother Superior. The latter's death causes matters to turn sharply for the worse, however, inasmuch as the succeeding Mother Superior is grim and vindictive. Sister Suzanne is so ill treated that she finally decides to bring suit to break her vows. She is able to establish the necessary contact with lawyers — not by any means an easy thing for a nun to do — because the Abbaye de Longchamps is so famous for its Easter music that a large audience from Paris is attracted there each year. This was a fact that Croismare would know and thus Diderot increased the verisimilitude of his narrative. He depicts Sister Suzanne as having one of the best voices in the convent, with the result that she is shown off a bit in the parlors, giving her an opportunity to become somewhat acquainted with the visiting public. However, she loses her suit and is so brutally treated by the spiteful Mother Superior and her subordinates that finally the Grand Vicar of the order interferes and Sister Suzanne is transferred to the convent of Arpajon.

At Arpajon she is treated kindly, though she still yearns for freedom and still feels no vocation for convent life. Although Sister Suzanne is too innocent to understand what is happening, the Mother Superior falls in love with her charge. This section of *La Religieuse,* therefore, is a realistic as well as detailed study in homosexual behavior, described concretely and almost clinically. Diderot's art is most impressive at this point, because he describes this relationship without prurience and as it would seem to an unsophisticated and uninitiated person who is quite bewildered by it all. The narrator understands nothing while the reader understands everything. For a man who was the author of *Les Bijoux indiscrets,* this is quite an advance in the art of writing a novel.

The Mother Superior falls into a state of religious mania. 'She passed successively from melancholy to piety, and from piety to delirium.' Finally she dies, in terrible despair. 'Father,' she says in confession, 'I am damned.'[16] This anguished cry is quite evidently the high spot of the book in Diderot's mind, and the rest trails off rapidly, much too rapidly. We learn only that Suzanne Simonin manages to escape from the convent without our being given any convincing information as to how so arduous a project was planned and carried out. Through her confessor, a Dominican who similarly feels no vocation for the religious life, Sister Suzanne is somehow able to escape and flee to Paris, though she hurts herself badly in a fall while making her escape. Eventually she dies from the ill effects of this accident. And this is the book.

It can well be imagined that *La Religieuse,* with such a plot, was boisterously welcomed by nineteenth-century anti-clericals as a stick with which to beat the Church. Many segments of Catholic opinion, too, have always assumed that Diderot's intentions were simply anti-religious. Thus, as late as 1966, the French government forbade the distribution both in France and abroad of the film *Suzanne Simonin, La Religieuse de Diderot,* in which Jacques Rivette, the director, had followed Diderot's plot and used verbatim a substantial part of Diderot's dialogue. This ban aroused a great outcry. 'Were it not prodigiously sinister,' wrote Jean-Luc Godard in an open letter to André Malraux, 'it would be prodigiously fine and moving to see a U.N.R. [i.e., Gaullist] minister in 1966 afraid of an encyclopedist spirit of 1789.' [17] The ban was lifted in 1967.

But to suppose that the book is merely anti-religious or even anti-clerical is to distort its meaning. The significance of the book lies not so much in its anti-clericalism as in its study of the cloistered life. Diderot portrayed Suzanne Simonin as devout, not at all a freethinker. The priests who figure in *La Religieuse* are depicted as humane and sagacious. [18] It is the deterioration of personality that occurs in convents, the pettymindedness, the vindictiveness, the frustration, the hysteria — these are Diderot's villains. In offering *La Religieuse* to Meister for the *Correspondance littéraire,* Diderot wrote that 'I do not think a more appalling indictment of convents has ever been written.' [19] And Suzanne Simonin remarks, in a passage that shows that Diderot was still smarting from his quarrel with Rousseau, 'Man is born to be in society; segregate him, isolate him, and his ideas become disjointed, his character changes, a thousand ridiculous affectations take root in his heart. Extravagant notions spring up in his mind, like brambles in untended land. Place a man in a forest and he will become ferocious; in a cloister, where the idea of necessity is combined with servitude, and it is even worse. One can leave a forest, one cannot leave a cloister. In a forest one is free, in a cloister one is a slave.' [20]

It is much nearer the truth to regard *La Religieuse* as a document consonant with the whole social program of the Enlightenment in France, as an argumentative book, using unobtrusively all the resources of forensic rhetoric. [21] 'Thus, by the pen of one of its best authors,' writes a contributor to a liberal-leftist French Catholic review, 'the social fabric of that century was revealed to be without pity, and, for certain people, almost without hope.' [22]

The *philosophes* were utilitarians; they wanted people and institutions to be useful; they were interested in population, in the sense that they equated national prosperity and national wealth with a high birthrate; and they were interested in extending the area of personal and civil rights, thus becoming the forefathers of the liberals of the nineteenth and twentieth centuries. The lesson of *La Religieuse* is that celibacy is unnatural, that the cloistered life is socially wasteful, that the warping of personality in the convent is inescapable. Exactly this point was made only a year after the work's first publication. In the excellent London edition of 1797 the anonymous translator, living in a country that had not had monasteries since 1535, wrote: 'It was the object of Diderot, to bring monastic institutions into detestation, by painting the extravagant shapes which the passions assume, when the intentions of nature are disregarded.'[23] Diderot has the nun's lawyer remark that, to his way of thinking, in a well-regulated state it would be difficult to be admitted to a religious community but easy to leave it. 'Are convents, then, so essential to a state's constitution? Did Jesus Christ institute monks and nuns? Is it impossible for the Church to get along without them? . . . Does God, who has created man to live in society, approve of his secluding himself? Does God, who created man so inconstant and so weak, authorize the rashness of the vows he takes? Can these vows, which go against the general inclination of nature, ever be thoroughly observed save by some poorly constituted creatures in whom the germs of the passions have withered?'[24]

Diderot simplified the issue — and sharpened it — by depicting Suzanne Simonin as being motivated solely by an unconquerable aversion to the conventual life in and of itself. It was not that she was in love, or wanted to marry, or was even interested in sex. She is presented as entirely innocent and sexually unawakened. Indeed, Diderot, like many another male novelist, delighted in his heroine's virginity. She simply had no calling for the religious life.

Was Diderot's highly charged picture of conventual existence true to life? Many people would like to think, and most people would suppose, that it was fanciful or at least exaggerated. But the files of the clandestine *Nouvelles Ecclésiastiques* challenge such assumptions. This journal, evading all efforts of the government to detect its authors and printers, reported from time to time incidents of the persecution of Jansenist nuns in convents. These reports, as a scholar has recently remarked, give 'the impression that the alleged fiction of Diderot falls considerably short of reality.'[25] He may even have used *Les Nouvelles Ecclésiastiques* as a source. Its recounting in 1745 and 1746 of irregularities in the convent of the Ursulines at Troyes shows that Diderot, in his account of the goings-on at Arpajon, did not go beyond the bounds of verisimilitude.

Posterity has taken a long time to think as highly of *La Religieuse* as Diderot did. The nineteenth century was inclined to be shocked by the novel, or at least to regard it as being in bad taste. Thus one of Diderot's most sympathetic nineteenth-century biographers bluntly said that Diderot was a lover of obscenities.[26] So enlightened an eminent Victorian as Lord Morley wrote of the Lesbian episode, 'It is appalling, it fills you with horror, it haunts you for days and nights, it leaves a kind of stain on the memory.' [27] Yet few have ever denied that *La Religieuse* has sweep and suspense and an ability to get inside walls and inside human skins. A German historian, writing in 1836, and who professed himself to be as shocked as anybody else, nevertheless remarked, 'The author of this history read the work many years ago in his youth, but he remembers that his attention was roused, fixed, and almost chained to the book. . . .' [28] Such testimony offsets, at least in part, that of Emile Faguet, a highly respected critic of the turn of the century, who thought he had disposed of the book by declaring that in it 'disgust vies with boredom.' [29]

These crushers of condemnation have never quite managed to obliterate the book, and now, in the opinion of mid-twentieth-century critics, it stands higher than ever. Marxists not unnaturally speak well of it. Henri Lefebvre, the foremost among French communist theoreticians of his generation, wrote in 1949 of *La Religieuse* as being 'a great psychological novel, very modern,' and he was followed in 1951 by a writer in *Pensée* who declared the book to be 'one of the great novels,' and 'one of the most calumniated, in our literature.' [30] But it is not just the Marxists: everyone is now engaged in rescuing *La Religieuse* from neglect. The present state of opinion is well represented by two British writers, one a student of French literature who speaks of the work as being 'now hailed as one of the five or six great works of fiction of the French eighteenth century.' [31] The other, an anonymous reviewer in *The Times Literary Supplement,* wrote that '*La Religieuse* is, by any standards, an amazing feat of imaginative creation. . . .' [32]

We have gotten far away from regarding Diderot's work as pornographic. The author of a monograph entitled *Sex Variant Women in Literature* wrote of *La Religieuse:*

Wherever Diderot gathered his material, his picture of fevered intrigue, jealousy, skilled seduction, and finally of the frustrated Superior's decline into acute neurosis, is unparalleled in fiction before the present century. Indeed, for clinical accuracy of detail it had no equal until Westphal's scientific case study of a homosexual woman was published in 1870. Thus it stands as a landmark in the literature of female sex variance.[33]

Diderot was too much aware of female homosexuality for his own peace of mind. Many critics have pointed out that the incident of the Mother Superior of Saint-Eutrope d'Arpajon was written just at the time when Diderot was most darkly suspicious of the relations between Sophie Volland and her sister. 'I am ashamed of what is going on inside me but I can't help it.'[34] And while the consensus of opinion now is that the book is not pornographic, the novel is nevertheless a troubled and troubling one, in which 'the atmosphere smells of incense and sulphur' both at once.[35] Diderot's own perturbation can be detected in this disturbing and deeply moving book.

The loud asseverations through the years that *La Religieuse* was either anti-religious or pornographic or both have had the effect of multiplying the editions prodigiously. Though Louis XVIII banned it in 1824 and Charles X did the same in 1826, seventy-three French editions of it as a separate work have appeared since its first publication in 1796.[36] There have been nineteen translations into German, ten into Italian, six into Spanish, seven into English, four into Russian, four into Serbo-Croat, two into Swedish, and one into Dutch.

What are the literary qualities that entitle *La Religieuse* to such high critical esteem? First, the novel has excellent structure; its theme is unified and it moves from incident to incident, from Mother Superior to Mother Superior, with economy and logic and inexorability. The speed of the narrative is enhanced by the use of dialogue. Diderot uses a great deal, more perhaps than novelists had ever attempted before, so that many of his pages look like early Hemingway. The trueness of this dialogue (for Diderot had a good ear) heightens the sense of verisimilitude. Particularly, he displays a remarkable ability to make his women speak in character, with a great deal of reserve and delicacy. He is skillful, too, in building up his effects. 'Like Richardson, he slowly accumulates apparently insignificant details, till the illusion of reality can finally no longer be denied.'[37] For example, 'One is aware that the third Mother Superior is unbalanced when she is first introduced, but it is only after Suzanne has copiously and innocently described her words and actions that the reader realizes the extent of her neurosis.'[38] Moreover, there is character change and character development in Diderot's delineations, so much so that a recent editor of Diderot's novels, exaggerating fondly, mentions him in the same breath with such august giants as Dostoevski and Proust.[39] Stylisticians have remarked how Diderot evokes the haunting memories of Plato or the Bible, how he moulds effects by clause structure and rhythmic patterns, how he can express harmonies or disharmonies by linguistic devices.[40] But most of all, there is in this book simply the magic with words that lies in the power of a writer of genius.

La Religieuse has had impact in the history of French literature and now in the history of the cinema. In addition, it has also become a subject of study in comparative literature. Scholars have shown that Richardson's technique was studied by Diderot and used in *La Religieuse,* just as in turn *La Religieuse* influenced later writings.[41] The Italians especially have shown a great deal of interest as to whether Diderot's nun influenced Manzoni, who likewise portrays, although with much less detail and incident, a nun-in-spite-of-herself in *I Promessi Sposi.*[42]

Much as it is now admired, *La Religieuse* is not without flaw. Now and then Diderot betrays by some illogicality the haste in which it was written, as, for example, describing in a letter something that happened the following day.[43] Nor are critics mistaken in complaining that Suzanne Simonin is too much of an abstraction. This is a price Diderot paid, intentionally or not, in order to heighten the effect of the whole book. By making Suzanne relatively neutral and passive in her relations with some very dynamic and aggressive women he was able to make the contours of the personalities of these Mothers Superior sharper and more memorable. This is what an English critic had in mind when he wrote that Suzanne 'is the least interesting, the least admirable, and the least pitiful of the four women whose destinies are here portrayed.'[44]

Diderot, though, would almost certainly have denied, and hotly denied, that Suzanne was the least interesting of the four. Like Pygmalion, he was in love with his creation and almost certainly had in mind, as he moulded her, persons whom he loved very much — perhaps his daughter (for a first draft of the manuscript shows that he then thought of calling his heroine Anne-Angélique) or perhaps Sophie Volland.[45] Diderot admired his heroine so much that he fell into the habit of having her constantly complimenting herself, a fact that he evidently noticed when he was revising the work twenty years later. At that time he tried, by an addendum at the very end of the novel, to have the nun explain as inadvertent what many readers might feel to be inordinate self-praise.[46]

Practical jokes are paid for out of the sensibilities of the people upon whom they are perpetrated. Croismare had been victimized by the appeal to one of the finest sides of his character, his compassion. In Grimm's account of the grand conspiracy he told of Croismare that 'After his return to Paris, we acknowledged this iniquitous plot; he laughed at it, as you might suppose; and the poor nun's misfortune served only to bind more tightly the ties of friendship among those who survived her.' But in a later copy of this manuscript the following sentence has been added, perhaps by Diderot himself, inasmuch as his handwriting proves that he altered the manuscript in other places: 'Nevertheless he [Croismare] never spoke of it to M. Diderot.'[47] Does this suggest that Diderot had enough of a bad conscience to have noticed Croismare's silence? Or that Croismare felt sufficiently bruised not to wish to discuss the incident? At all events, *La Religieuse* has its own life to live as a work of art, and is to be appreciated on its own merits.

CHAPTER 30

'That Tartuffe of a Diderot'

Diderot moved through the stresses and strains of his existence, as do so many of his middle-aged fellow men of the twentieth century, having stomach trouble. For some years previous he had been bothered by a malady that he called 'colic.' Much of the time he was on a bland diet, drinking large quantities of what to an eighteenth-century Frenchman seemed rather unnatural — milk. In March 1760 his trouble was especially acute. Writing to his friend, the famous Genevan physician Théodore Tronchin, he confessed, 'I am greedy. I bolt my food without chewing it. Then I get a stomach ache. But this is different.' Tronchin's response dwelt upon the fact that indigestion was, for men of letters, an occupational disease. Therefore Diderot was to take more exercise, write standing up, not stuff his stomach too full, and, 'if you have passions, moderate them.' [1]

Meanwhile the public uproar over the *philosophes* continued, to culminate in a lampooning of Diderot which he thenceforth regarded as the greatest grievance of his whole career. For Diderot acted under the conviction that what he did and what he stood for were identical with the public good. Whenever this congruence was impugned, he was inclined to turn away in disgust from his own generation and seek support from future ones. Never was he more personally assailed than in 1760.

The prelude to the main contest was a skirmish in the French Academy. A magistrate who was also a poet, though rather an obscure one, Le Franc by name and De Pompignan by vainglorious title recently assumed, had been elected to the Academy. In his speech, upon being formally received in March, he managed to antagonize everyone by his vanity and presumption. Most of all he incensed the *philosophes,* whom he accused of writing books 'bearing the mark of a depraved literature, a corrupted morality, and a haughty philosophy, undermining equally the throne and the altar.' [2]

It would have been hard to find a more public occasion on which to say such things. The French Academy being one of the citadels of public opinion, the *philosophes* found themselves practically forced to reply. Voltaire led the counterattack, in a shower of pamphlets that ended up by quite demolishing Pompignan.[3] But it had been a crisis. D'Alembert, who was himself a member of the Academy, wrote to Voltaire,

When one has the misfortune to live in a country of persecution and servitude, in the midst of a slavish and sheeplike people, it is very fortunate that there exist, in a *free* country, philosophers who can speak out.[4]

At the same time the knowledge spread that Palissot, the old enemy of the *philosophes,* the author of the bruising pamphlet entitled *Little Letters on Great Philosophers,* was at it again. He was writing a play:

The one thing lacking to Philosophy [D'Alembert reported to Voltaire] was to be kicked when down. A play is going to be produced at the Comédie-Française called 'The Modern Philosophers.' Préville is going to walk around on all fours to represent Rousseau. This play is heavily 'protected.' Versailles finds it admirable.[5]

The night of 2 May approached, and the partisans of both sides gathered for the *première.* 'Two furious cabals prepared themselves for the combat,' wrote a man who claimed to have been an eyewitness, 'and the most violent tumult was loudly predicted.' The guard of soldiers at the theater was doubled, with explicit orders to arrest anyone who made the slightest disturbance.[6] The registers of the Comédie-Française show that a crowd of 1439 spectators was present, the largest figure in twenty-six years and not surpassed for another eleven years. The parterre, open to men only, all of whom had to stand, was of course crowded to the point of suffocation. As a historian of the Paris theater remarks, '. . . this mass of men, packed together like sardines, were obviously in a position to express their reactions in a way which had considerable effect on the fate of the play.'[7] At the first night of *Les Philosophes,* 'The tumult was beyond description,' wrote the diarist Barbier. 'I was present, right up in front.'[8] The play was given to large audiences during the rest of May, a total of fourteen performances. Although it drew well, averaging an attendance of 937, it was not given after the end of the month. One suspects that the influence of the *philosophes* was somehow strong enough to prevent further performances.[9]

Les Philosophes is not much of a play. It was its wholesale dealing in personalities that made it exciting. It is written in the conventional Alexandrines of the age, and the plot is thickened by a couple of servants

masquerading as somebody else, as if servants masquerading as somebody
else had not been relied on to thicken plots since at least the time of
Plautus and Terence. Moreover, if the playwright had not introduced a
letter that need never have been written and had he not had it most conveniently intercepted, he might not have been able to bring his curtain down
even to this day.

Cydalise — so goes the play — had engaged her daughter Rosalie to
Damis, a young army officer away on campaign. Three months later,
when he returns, he finds that Cydalise has become enamored of philosophy,
has even written a book (quite a ridiculous one) in the genre. She now
insists upon marrying Rosalie to Valère, a rather mature suitor whom
Palissot portrays as being a confidence man under the guise of a *philosophe*. Valère discourses at length in speeches which show quite clearly
that he is meant to be Helvétius, the unlucky author of the notorious book
De l'Esprit. The grotesque Cydalise is just as obviously intended to represent Mme Geoffrin. Valère is aided and abetted by other 'philosophers,'
prominent among them one Theophrastus (meant to suggest Duclos) and
especially Dortidius, who of course is Diderot. The identification of Diderot
is made unmistakable by the explicit allusion to books said in the play to
have been written by Dortidius and which everyone in the audience knew
perfectly well had been written by Diderot. As Fréron admitted, 'to name
the works is to name the persons.'[10] He and Palissot tried to justify the
play by comparing it to the comedies of Aristophanes.[11] But when Dortidius is depicted as over-emphatic, much given to vehement utterance,
intellectually insincere, motivated simply by a calculated and 'frigid enthusiasm which imposes only on fools' (Act II, scene v); when he is
represented, what is more, as a rascal accessory to deceiving Cydalise and
bilking her of her daughter and her money, it could readily be said that
such lampooning came close to outstripping its ancient model. All the
philosophes are described as 'agreeable flatterers and adroit charlatans'
(Act I, scene i), whose philosophy hardened their hearts, and who, in
order to love the human race in general, excused themselves from loving
any one in particular (Act II, scene v). But Dortidius is singled out
specifically for odium and made to say, 'I care very little for the country
I live in; the truly wise man is a cosmopolitan' (Act III, scene ii). It is
very interesting to see how, with the disastrous Seven Years' War still
going on, the allegation that the *philosophes* were not '100% French' turns
up. And the plot? Well, by means of the intercepted letter the curtain is
lowered at last on the villains foiled and young love triumphant.

Concurrent with the production of *Les Philosophes* was the publication of a pamphlet also by Palissot which accused his enemies of 'a downright republican spirit,' and of being inspired in their talk and writings by 'the most detestable of the maxims of Hobbes and Spinoza.'[12] To prove his charges he misquoted flagrantly, so that one wonders, as one gazes today at Houdon's handsome bust of Palissot in the Mazarine Library, where he was director for many years, how a librarian could play so false with texts.

Even the greatest apologists for the play — the people who were the most vociferous in recalling Aristophanes — had to admit that the piece came close to character assassination. Following the *première,* Palissot did cut some of the most offensive lines, and changed the name Dortidius to Marphurius. Nevertheless, persons like Malesherbes, whose business it was to be as objective and impartial as possible, were made uneasy and melancholy by the play.[13] Personal allusions in the press or on the stage were universally regarded in eighteenth-century France as being in bad taste and quite unallowable. This play, accordingly, seemed to many to have gone far beyond bounds.[14] Moreover, there was a general feeling that it had official approval. 'It is the bitterest, most brutal and cruelest satire that could ever be authorized,' wrote Collé, who was himself a playwright. 'Not only is it certain that there were orders higher up to have it produced, but it is even more to be presumed that this is a commissioned work and that it could not even have entered the author's head that this play could be put on unless he had been told beforehand that it would be played by command.'[15] Palissot and his play were most conspicuously and energetically supported by the Princesse de Robecq, and since she was one of the mistresses of the Duc de Choiseul, everyone inferred that Choiseul himself was protecting the play.[16] Choiseul for his part was deceptively bland about it in writing to Voltaire, using the professional diplomat's most impenetrable manner:

Whatever people say, I am not protecting either the author or his play, unless having read it is protecting it. [It] appeared to me to be marvellously well written, and, as I am stupid, I was not able to recognize anyone in it.[17]

Like the others lampooned in the piece, Diderot was deeply offended. He wrote to Voltaire about it. The surviving fragment of that letter explodes with the high-speed muzzle velocity so characteristic of its energetic author: 'The only vengeance that one may take upon the absurd insolence. . . .'[18] Before the month was out Diderot was rumored to be the author of a violent anti-Palissot pamphlet. This he denied, but his letter to

Malesherbes was couched in terms that left no doubt about his sense of grievance:

I have not been to see the play of *Les Philosophes*. I have not read it. . . . I shall not be tempted to break the promise I made myself, and which I have kept up to date, not to write a word in reprisal. We do not have to be indignant for ourselves, when honest people are indignant for us.[19]

Among the indignant was Rousseau. Though he had quarreled with Diderot, he refused the proffer of a complimentary copy of the play. 'I do not accept this horrible present. . . .doubtless you do not know, or you have forgotten, that I have had the honor of being the friend of a respectable man who is infamously besmirched and calumniated in this libel.'[20] Dr. Tronchin too was sympathetic: 'I feel for our poor friend Diderot, who has been made to say and do a lot of things he never dreamed of.'[21] President de Brosses spoke of the play as being a very odious personal satire, and La Condamine, the old explorer and scientist, wrote to Formey in Berlin, 'A comedy is being played in which M. Diderot, Duclos, Rousseau of Geneva and Helvétius are very badly treated and cruelly torn to pieces.'[22]

Palissot was a disciple, almost a protégé, of Voltaire, so it is not surprising that Voltaire is not lampooned in the piece. More unexpectedly, D'Alembert too escaped. His relief at not being mentioned by name in Palissot's play is almost too evident in the letter he wrote Voltaire on 6 May. 'Neither you nor I is attacked *personally,* the only ones roughly treated being Helvétius, Diderot, Rousseau, Duclos, Mme Geoffrin and Mlle Clairon. . . .'[23] Farther along in this same letter D'Alembert wrote of 'the barbarism with which Helvétius is treated,' but made no comment on the treatment of Diderot. This omission seems to substantiate Diderot's suspicions that D'Alembert had become practically an enemy without acknowledging it. Later on, when D'Alembert thought that he himself was being attacked by Palissot, he responded by letters to the press. In them he took extreme care to prove that he had not said nor written the things Palissot attributed to him. But his care seems to have been no less extreme to dissociate himself from the persons lampooned in *Les Philosophes*.[24] Certainly no one can say that he publicly took up their defense.

Just as men of moderation feared they would, personalities called forth personalities in reprisal. 'If this pernicious school of satire once gets hold of the theater,' wrote the editor of the *Annonces, Affiches, et Avis Divers,* 'true comedy will be undone beyond retrieving.'[25] The most scurrilous retaliation against Palissot's play was an anonymous pamphlet, the *Vision de Charles Palissot,* written in mock-Scriptural style by the Abbé Morellet. Its most offensive passage referred to the dying Princesse de Robecq, Palissot's patroness:

And a Great Lady shall be seen, very ill, desiring before her death no other consolation than to be present at the first performance and to say: Now, O Lord, lettest thou thy servant depart in peace, for mine eyes have seen thy vengeance.[26]

The Princesse de Robecq did indeed die, of tuberculosis, early in July. It was frequently alleged that she did not know that her illness was mortal until she read the *Vision de Charles Palissot.*[27]

The authorities regarded this pamphlet as a very serious breach of public order. Malesherbes wrote to the Lieutenant-General of Police that the author, whoever he was, should be severely punished: '. . . one must make a sharp distinction between the misdemeanor of men of letters tearing one another to pieces and the insolence of those who attack persons of the highest consideration in the State.'[28] For a time Diderot was suspected of being the author. But on 10 June Morellet was arrested and imprisoned in the Bastille until 30 July.[29] 'All Paris has been ringing this month,' wrote the dramatist Collé in July, 'with nothing but the quarrel of the Encyclopedists and their adversaries. Nothing but pamphlets, and insults in print.'[30]

In this emergency, hard pressed as they were, the *philosophes* looked to Voltaire. He lived in safety in Geneva. He could publish what he pleased at almost no risk at all. Already in the crisis of 1759 Diderot had shown, in a letter to Grimm, how much he desired Voltaire's collaboration in the continuation of the *Encyclopédie.*[31] Now D'Alembert appealed to Voltaire:

It's all very well for the chief to recommend unity to the brethren, but the chief must stay at their head and not be prevented from speaking out for the good cause by the fear of humiliating rascals who are under protection. . . .[32]

Voltaire, who could be counted upon to play his own hand in his own way, never refused such appeals outright, yet he was apt to give the supplicator something else than what he had asked for. In 1759, for instance, Diderot received not the extra articles for the *Encyclopédie* that he wanted from Voltaire but instead the satisfaction, such as it was, of recognizing himself in the title role of a topical play by Voltaire called *Socrate.* It is arguable whether the satisfaction could have been very great. *Socrate* is a lamentable hodge-podge quite sufficient to wither the literary reputation of any lesser man than Voltaire.

Now, in 1760, what the *philosophes* wanted of Voltaire was a break with Palissot. What they got was a good deal less. The embarrassed Voltaire did write Palissot a letter which the *philosophes* duly handed around and made much of, for lack of anything more substantial. But the letter was an expostulation more than a rebuke. How much real comfort was there, for example, in remarks like this: 'Without ever having seen M. Diderot, without finding his *Père de famille* pleasing, I have always respected the profundity of his knowledge. . . . Twenty persons have assured me that he has a very fine character. I should be deeply distressed to be disabused, yet I wish to be informed.'[33]

Voltaire was in a dilemma, and he tried to solve it in a very characteristic way. Not being willing to fall upon the major culprit, Palissot, he fell instead upon an easier target. This was the ancient enemy, Fréron. Fréron had had the temerity to write in his *Année Littéraire* that he had found *Les Philosophes* 'infinitely pleasing.' He was also alleged to have been the one who had presented Palissot's play to the company of the Comédie-Française in the first place, to have insisted upon reading it to them, and to have told them that they had no choice but to accept it. Finally, he was said to have been assiduous in distributing free tickets for the opening performance.[34] Voltaire made him pay for all this by writing a play which the Comédie-Française produced, *L'Ecossaise* ('The Scottish Girl'). Its ogreish and repulsive villain was called 'Frelon.' Thus the French public, which had just seen Diderot unfavorably portrayed on the stage, now saw Fréron.

The personage of Frelon is not essential to the plot of *L'Ecossaise*, as Voltaire himself later admitted privately.[35] The part was hastily invented and then grafted on to the draft of a play that Voltaire no doubt had had lying in the bottom of a drawer. So odious is the character of Frelon, it is strange that the Comédie-Française undertook to produce the play. Critics were alarmed by the apparent new trend in the theater. 'What surprises us,' wrote the reviewer in *Annonces, Affiches, et Avis Divers*, 'is that permission was given to play it, even after *Les Philosophes*, which ought never to have shown itself on the stage of the foremost theater in Europe. May the Good Genius that still watches over the preservation of taste and good manners . . . put a stop to this odious license.'[36] And another journalist remarked, 'Two personal comedies on the same stage in three months. Citizens, of whatever rank you may be, watch out for yourselves.'[37]

L'Ecossaise was first produced (with the name of the character Frelon changed into its English equivalent, Wasp) on 26 July 1760, before an audience of 1150. Performed a total of twenty times during that year, the play remained in the repertory for some time.[38] It is fascinating to discover that Voltaire adopted in the structure and dialogue of *L'Ecossaise* some of the features of the *drame,* the new genre in the theater that Diderot had developed and which his *Le Fils naturel* (1757) and *Le Père de famille* (1758) exemplified.[39]

How would Fréron in the *Année Littéraire* review this satire of himself? Would his riposte be violent or subtle, sarcastic and ironical, or factual and restrained? The line he took was the mock heroic, undoubtedly the most effective in writing for a society as skilled in the appreciation of ridicule as was the leisured French public of the *ancien régime*. Yet before he was allowed to publish his 'Account of a Great Battle Waged at the Comédie-Française,' Fréron had trouble with his censor.[40] All of his frustration and sense of injustice thereupon came rushing to the surface in a letter that he wrote to Malesherbes:

What! that paltry Voltaire is allowed to vomit his calumnies, that infamous La Porte is allowed to tear me to pieces in his sheet [*L'Observateur Littéraire*], that Tartuffe of a Diderot, that base flatterer Grimm, are allowed to be in the pit at the *première* of *L'Ecossaise* in order to stimulate their cabal and give the signal for applause! And I am not to be allowed to cast some slight ridicule upon my vile enemies! [41]

In an earlier number of his journal, Fréron had commented upon the text of the play, remarking ironically that he was sure it could not have been written by Voltaire. 'Indeed, what likelihood is there that so mediocre a product could have flowed from so fine a pen?' [42] Later, in his 'Account of a Great Battle,' he cleverly drew attention away from the caricature of himself. He did this by ignoring Voltaire and making Diderot the butt of his sarcasms.

The redoubtable Dortidius was in the center; he had been unanimously elected general. His face was burning, his gaze was raging, his hair was dishevelled, all his senses were agitated, just as they are when, under the domination of his divine enthusiasm, he hands down his oracles from the philosophical tripod.

Fréron went on to depict 'the valiant Dortidius recounting the particularities of the action' to a group that had not been present. His style was 'sublime but unintelligible.' [43]

Meanwhile, Voltaire conceived of a surprising tactic. Perhaps he suspected that the Parisian *philosophes* were feeling that in the Palissot affair he had let them down. Now was the time, Voltaire wrote to his friends, to get Diderot elected to the French Academy. It is hard to believe that Voltaire had any faith in the success of this scheme, yet for the next few weeks his correspondence is full of it.[44] D'Alembert replied discouragingly on 18 July: 'I'd like more than you to see Diderot in the Academy. I know all the good that would come of it for the common cause; but it is more [nearly] impossible than you can imagine. The persons you speak of [Choiseul and Mme de Pompadour] would perhaps serve his cause, but very feebly so, and the devots would make an outcry and win out.'[45] Nevertheless, Voltaire continued his campaign. His letter of exhortation to Grimm and Mme d'Epinay, though worldly and cynical, was yet full of hope:

But let Diderot aid us, and don't let him just amuse himself by making scratches on paper when he ought to be acting. He has to do only one thing, but he must do it. This is to seduce some illustrious fool, male or female, some fanatic. . . . Let him be introduced to Mme . . . or Mme . . . or Mme . . . on Monday, let him pray to God with her on Tuesday, let him go to bed with her on Wednesday, and then he will enter into the Academy as much as he wants and when he wants.[46]

If Voltaire meant this seriously he had mistaken the character of Diderot. A letter of D'Alembert to Voltaire on 2 September revealed how impossible the situation was.

The difficulty is not one of finding votes for Diderot in the Academy, but (1) finding enough to elect him; (2) preventing his receiving twelve or fifteen blackballs, which would exclude him forever; (3) obtaining the King's consent. He would be only halfheartedly supported at Versailles; every one of the present candidates already has his supporters there. I know that this would cause a civil war; and though I agree with you that civil wars are amusing and worthwhile, nevertheless we don't want Pompey to lose his life in them.[47]

Diderot had been inert during Voltaire's frenzied campaign. Perhaps he thought of it as being embarrassingly inopportune. Or was it because of annoyance that Voltaire had not supported him against Palissot as much as he might have done? Did Diderot want to let it be known that he could not be so easily appeased? Perhaps so, if we may judge from Grimm's remarking to his subscribers at this time that 'if the first letter from Voltaire to Palissot was pardonable, the others are not.' No doubt it is significant of the state of feelings at this time, too, that Grimm's review of L'Ecossaise was very critical. Diderot himself, writing to Sophie Volland a few months later, spoke of Voltaire as 'that naughty and extraordinary child.' [48]

The events of 1760 disillusioned the Parisian *philosophes* about Voltaire. He had shown himself dismayingly unreliable, perhaps even a little insincere. With easy compliments they had always hailed him as their leader, and in their moment of need in 1760 he could have become their chief in very earnest. Being rebuffed, their relations with him were never quite the same again. They grew away from him and tended to become more radical than he in their political thought. As they were disenchanted with him, so was he with them. Or at least he was with the *Encyclopédie*, which he seems to have thought too bulky for the masses. He himself began to develop a sort of encyclopedia of his own, the *Dictionnaire philosophique:* it had the advantage of being portable. Henceforth the relations of Voltaire with the other *philosophes,* and theirs with him, were full of subtle reticences and inhibitions and nuances, relations that were far from being overtly antagonistic but which were covertly cankered by nagging sentiments of distrust. [49]

Diderot probably never got over his sense of outrage at being represented on the stage as a blackguard. In retaliation he published in the *Encyclopédie* an article the author of which, the Comte de Tressan, alluded transparently and cuttingly to Palissot. [50] Diderot himself set forth in his article *'Menace'* the following stout doctrine:

One may very well say, for example, that when the government of a people declares itself against philosophy, it is a bad government. . . . When honest folk are traduced upon the stage, they are *menaced* by a persecution more violent still. . . . [51]

This was pretty strong for official publication in the France of the *ancien régime,* and Diderot evidently feared that his publisher might be tempted to leave it out. Accordingly he wrote on the galley proof, 'I urge you very earnestly not to take it into your head to touch this article.' [52] And published untouched it was, allowing readers in 1765-6 and ever since to see how hotly Diderot resented what had happened in 1760.

This resentment was still burning in 1770. In that year the Lieutenant-General of Police asked Diderot to read the manuscript of still another play satirizing the *philosophes* and to say what he thought of it. Diderot made an effort to make his report seem balanced and unbiased, but what he really thought came out in a long and involved sentence in which his feelings almost got the better of his syntax. 'It is not for me, Monsieur, to tell you what to do; but if you could act in a way so that it could not be said that by your permission there twice were publicly insulted those of your fellow-citizens most honored in all parts of Europe; whose works are pored over near and far; whom foreigners revere, send for, and reward; who will be quoted and who will be contributing to the glory of the French name when you will no longer be living, nor they either; whom travelers make a point of visiting at the present time and whose acquaintance they glory in upon returning to their own country; — I think, Monsieur, that you would be wise.' [53]

How often Diderot sounds the note of being unappreciated by his own countrymen and his contemporaries. How often, then, does he remind himself — and others — that he will be contributing to the glory of the French name even when he is no more. 'The *philosophes* are nothing to-day,' he wrote the Lieutenant-General of Police in 1770, 'but their turn will come; they will be talked about, the history of the persecutions they underwent will be written, and of the infamous and vapid way in which they were treated on the public stage. . . .' For posterity, wrote Diderot in this same letter, 'posterity is always just.' [54]

Le Père de famille at the Comédie-Française

AFTER the anxieties and demoralizations of 1759, Diderot was in stride again. There was always the editing of the *Encyclopédie* to be done: by 29 May 1760 he had finished all the articles under 'L' and 'M' and was about to start on 'N.' In the article *'Natif,'* in a passage typically but oddly autobiographical in a work so public and supposedly impersonal, Diderot wrote, 'I am *natif* of Langres, a small city in Bassigny, devastated this year (1760) by an epidemic which has lasted four months and carried off thirty of my relatives.'[1] Then there was *La Religieuse,* which was growing to be a book. 'It stretches out under my pen and I don't know when I shall touch shore.'[2] Moreover, he was doing some book reviewing for Grimm's fortnightly *Correspondance littéraire.* He commented on a translation of Gessner's epic poem on the death of Abel.[3] And in a review of a small novel done in the manner of the ancient Greeks, Diderot made two characteristic comments. The one defines the limits of his admiration for the Ancients, humanist though he was; and the other shows his insistence that everything, even in art, should have utility: 'Let us then read the Ancients; let us write like them, if we are able to; but let us try to write on better subjects.' And again: 'It is not enough that a poem have a model in nature, it must also have a useful purpose.'[4]

In addition to all this, Diderot continued to be much concerned with writing for the theater, for he was translating Edward Moore's *The Gamester,* which Garrick had brought out at Drury Lane in 1753. Diderot's views regarding the theater had already been much influenced by this play: he especially mentions it in his 'Conversations regarding the *Fils naturel'* (1757).[5] The plot depicts the decline and fall of a compulsive gambler who, after losing his wife's and his sister-in-law's fortunes as well as his own, is thrown into a debtor's prison where he commits suicide. Diderot was perhaps drawn to the subject of the play by the fact that he himself had a weakness for gambling. 'He loved to gamble,' wrote his daughter, 'played badly, and always lost.'[6] Certainly it is true that Diderot wrote in the *Encyclopédie,* 'The passion for gambling is one of the most fatal that one can have. A man is so violently agitated by gaming that he can no longer endure any other occupation. After having lost his fortune, he is condemned to be bored the rest of his life.'[7] By translating Moore's play, Diderot was providing a concrete example of his conviction, expressed so emphatically in his 'Discourse on Dramatic Poetry' (1758), that the theater should serve as a means for 'making us love virtue and hate vice.'[8]

Diderot's command of English, quite sufficient for his earlier translations of expository works, such as Temple Stanyan's *Grecian History* (1743) or Lord Shaftesbury's *An Inquiry concerning Virtue and Merit* (1745) or Dr. Robert James's *A Medicinal Dictionary* (1746–8), was not always adequate for the colloquial turns of idiom in *The Gamester.*[9] *Le Joueur,* which Diderot called a *'tragédie'* rather than a *'drame,'*[10] followed the original plot very closely, but with some paraphrasing and with some lines added, especially in indicating transitions. Diderot did this, he tells us, in an effort to adapt the original to conform to the conventions of French taste. As a result, his translation was much diluted, containing more than twice the words of the original.[11]

Diderot was as melodramatic about *Le Joueur* as it was itself. Upon sending Mme d'Epinay his translation of the last act he cautioned her, 'I wouldn't want you to read it immediately after dinner. It would be quite likely to upset your digestion and cause a great deal of trouble.'[12] Diderot's friends — Grimm, Mme d'Epinay, the dramatist Saurin, and D'Argental, for sixty years the friend and adviser of Voltaire — liked the piece: 'They all want me to improve *Le Joueur* and give it to the French.'[13] Apparently the company of the Comédie-Française did give Diderot's translation serious consideration. He was formally invited to attend an official trial reading of his play, to which he replied by suggesting that either Grimm or D'Argental be accepted as his representative.[14] But the play evidently was turned down; and some years later Grimm passed off the effort as merely something Diderot once did 'to make the play known to some ladies who did not understand English.'[15]

In the letter replying to the representative of the Comédie-Française in its invitation to a trial reading of *Le Joueur,* Diderot brought up the subject of his *Le Père de famille.* Published two years earlier, it had made a great stir, but it had not yet been produced. 'I give Le Père de famille to them to dispose of as their own property. I set forth no claims to royalties from the performances. The only one of an author's privileges which I would ask to be allowed is that of choosing the actors.' [16] And the next day he wrote to Sophie, 'I have seen M^r d'Argental, who brought up once again the actors' project regarding Le Père de famille.' [17] By January 1761 the decision was made to produce Diderot's play and it was put into rehearsal.[18] Perhaps the company of the Comédie-Française decided to produce it as a solace to Diderot, particularly since they had disappointed him in respect to Le Joueur. More likely, though equally conjectural, the company, having produced Palissot's Les Philosophes, was under heavy pressure to demonstrate its equity and fairness. The Comédie-Française was, indeed, caught in what was essentially a political struggle, with each side trying to capture the media formative of public opinion.

Meanwhile, Le Père de famille had already caught on in the provinces and abroad. By April 1759 it had been produced at Toulouse and at Bordeaux; in November 1760 at Marseilles, in January 1761 at Hamburg, and twice in February 1761 at Lyon.[19] Diderot's other play, Le Fils naturel, was also being produced, though not in Paris. It was given at Baden in August 1759 and at Hamburg in November 1760, while the company at Marseilles was reported to be planning to produce it in January 1761.[20] Of course these performances did not have nearly the prestige that production at the Comédie-Française would have. Nevertheless, considering that Diderot was trying to reach a new audience, an audience responding to the realism and to the emotions of everyday, middle-class life, it is very significant that these performances were taking place. Moreover, these productions in the provinces of Le Père de famille 'mark an important date in the Third Estate's becoming aware of itself in eighteenth-century France: they inaugurate a new epoch in the history of the national theatre. . . .' [21]

For the latter part of 1760, while the negotiations culminating in the production of Le Père de famille were taking place, we have no fewer than twenty-eight letters, some of them as long as a novella, written by Diderot to Sophie Volland. They were written in the space of twelve weeks, and allow us to apply a sort of stethoscope to the heartbeat of his busy life. Sophie was at her family's country estate. Diderot was either at Paris, in his attic study on the Rue de Taranne or pestering his friend Damilaville, because it was at Damilaville's office that Sophie's letters were received; or if not at Paris, Diderot was staying at Grandval or at La Chevrette, Mme d'Epinay's house on her estate near Montmorency, some seven miles north of Paris. Much time and effort that autumn were spent in writing the letters, sending them, and wondering uselessly why the replies were so belated. In all of this, Damilaville, who was one of the principal administrators of the vingtième for all of France, made himself indispensable. Because of his position, letters bearing his frank went post-free. Damilaville used the privilege to facilitate the exchange of letters among all the *philosophes,* though perhaps Voltaire and Diderot profited from the arrangement most of all. Damilaville, sitting in his office in the handsome seventeenth-century Hôtel de Clermont-Tonnerre, could flatter himself that he was one of the most useful and most cosseted personages in the whole party of the *philosophes,* though whether he was loved for himself or for his frank he must often — and should often — have asked himself.[22]

Diderot had two accidents that autumn, one of them under circumstances he found rather compromising. In order to write up for the *Encyclopédie* the manufacture of tobacco, Diderot, taking with him the draughtsman who prepared the scale drawings for the engravings, called upon a young official named Destouches, who had promised to show them through the factory. When they arrived, Destouches was in conversation with a girl. Time passed, Diderot sent the draughtsman away, and finally the three others took a carriage to go to Le Breton's, Diderot's publisher. But right in the center of a very ill-famed street, the carriage axle broke. Diderot struck his head against the side of the carriage. 'Destouches got out at one side; the girl and I got out on the other, in full view of a company as numerous and as far from being choice as could be. Fortunately she had the appearance of being more virtuous than she probably was.'[23] Diderot's nose hurt for a few days (and his pride too, perhaps), but there were no permanent ill effects.

The other incident occurred at La Chevrette. 'I went to walk around a large pond on which there were swans. These birds are so jealous of their domain that as soon as you approach they come at you in full flight. I amused myself in keeping them busy, and when they had arrived at one of the bounds of their empire, I would suddenly appear to them at the other. To do this I had to run with all the speed I had [evidently behind concealing bushes]. This I was doing, when I struck one of my feet against an iron bar used to open the sluices built near dammed-up water. The shock was so violent that the edge of the bar almost cut my shoe buckle in two; my instep was gashed and became almost entirely black and blue. This has not prevented me from joking about my tumble, which keeps me in carpet slippers, my leg stretched out on a tabouret.'[24] How hard it is, most of the time, for posterity to find these eighteenth-century *philosophes* at play — or, at least, at non-intellectual play.

His letters to Sophie show Diderot in contact with a large number of vivid and interesting characters. There was the grievously wounded Baron Dieskau, the French commander at the Battle of Lake George in 1755. (Diderot's letters of November 1760 to Sophie Volland constituted a principal source for Parkman in the chapter he wrote about Dieskau in *Montcalm and Wolfe*).[25] There was Mme d'Epinay, the mistress of whom Grimm just then was beginning to show unmistakable signs of being tired.[26] Diderot had at length become very friendly with her, and it was at her house in Paris that he heard Count Oginski, the most celebrated harpist of his time.[27] In Mme d'Epinay's circle there was also the dramatist Saurin, the *première* of whose *Spartacus* Grimm and Diderot had seen together at the Comédie-Française and whose plans for a future 'Siege of Calais' Diderot, with the best intentions in the world, counseled altering from start to finish: 'I have turned it upside down from one end to the other.'[28] There were the poet Saint-Lambert and his mistress, Sophie d'Houdetot, a couple who had played so large a part, though innocently and indirectly, in the break between Diderot and Rousseau.[29] And then there was the diminutive and irrepressible Galiani, the Neapolitan diplomat, gay in disposition and witty and apt in anecdotes and mimicry, 'a treasure on rainy days.'[30] At Grandval there came now and again Mme Geoffrin, 'almost not bored, a very rare circumstance.' She played a game of piquet with Diderot and inquired about his wife and daughter. 'Madame Geoffrin never sleeps away from home. About six o'clock she embraced us and got back into her carriage with friend D'Alainville and off she went.'[31] And at Paris there was Thieriot, the friend and elderly errand-boy of Voltaire. 'He's a nice man, but with a cruel memory. He began to recite the verse of every poet in the world, and it was almost nine o'clock before he left.'[32] These, and many others, pass through the pages of Diderot's letters, as later a similar company of diverse and flavorful characters passed through the pages of his *Jacques le fataliste*.

Diderot's descriptions of some of these persons are done with a humor and a power of imagination worthy of Dickens. Of the corpulent *curé* at La Chevrette,

He is perhaps the only man who has an expressive nose. He praises with his nose, he blames with his nose, he decides with his nose, he prophesies with his nose. Grimm says that whoever understands the *curé*'s nose has read a great treatise of ethics.[33]

And of Mme Buffon, the wife of the naturalist: 'She has no neck any more. Her chin made half the journey, her breasts the other half, as a result of which her three chins repose upon two fine soft pillows.'[34] And after dining with a certain Colardeau, Diderot wrote:

He hasn't an ounce of flesh on his body. A little aquiline nose, an elongated head, a hatchet face; small, piercing eyes, a thin and lean body. Cover all that with feathers; affix long wings to his narrow shoulders, curve backwards the nails on his feet and hands, and you'd have a sparrow hawk.[35]

It will come as a surprise to many, who think of Diderot as a very sociable and gregarious man, to find him, nevertheless, seeking to avoid occasions or crowds that were simply indiscriminate. 'I hate a crowd,' he wrote. At one time he wanted to leave La Chevrette: 'We have too many people here for it to be pleasurable. In crowds, people are mixed up: outsiders interpose themselves between friends, who no longer feel in touch.' Diderot valued friendship highly, but thought of himself as being unqualified to be successful in casual social intercourse. 'Several times I have asked myself why, having a gentle and obliging character, with indulgence, gaiety, and a variety of knowledge, I should be so little fitted for society. It is because it is impossible that I should feel there as I do with my friends, and that I do not know the cold and empty language that one uses with casual acquaintances. In such situations I am either silent or indiscreet.'[36]

He felt himself to be a misfit in society, partly because he was timid — it is odd to think of Diderot as timid, but he earnestly believed it —, partly because he had no fund of small talk. 'I always stammer from timidity the first time I meet people. Besides, everything boils down at such a time to conventional phrases with which people pay each other off, and I don't have a sou of such money.' A fortnight later he was saying the same thing: 'I don't have a liard of such money. I can say anything except "good day." All my life I shall just be learning the abc's of all the tattle carried from house to house and which one hears in all quarters at the same time.'[37]

The extant letters to Sophie are abundant for eleven years. Thus, from the time that Diderot was forty-six on through his middle years, it is possible to use these letters for sounding his character in depth, which the more meager sources of the earlier years do not allow. One of the things quickly revealed is that Diderot was cheerfully ready to put himself out for his friends, even at the cost of his time and not infrequently of his feelings. This is a comparatively unusual quality in a man of genius. In 1760 Diderot had not really wanted to go to Grandval, because D'Holbach was in such a cross-grained temper. 'But there is no way of staying here. I would have the appearance of abandoning Mme d'Aine, who welcomed me so heartily on previous vacations. I feel right with myself only when I do what I ought to do.' And once at Grandval, he stayed, also for the sake of Mme d'Aine. 'Mme d'Aine is not a woman to leave in the lurch at a whim. One owes her too much.'[38] D'Holbach would end up, Diderot prophesied, by becoming 'ferocious'; Diderot had had 'to hold myself in with both hands'; 'I fear that at any moment everyone will avoid him and he will remain alone — save for me, of course. I have thought it over and I have made my choice. I would rather put up with it than expose myself to being suspected of ingratitude. Ruptures always make a bad impression in society; and besides, the inconvenience of accepting obligations is that if one has a naturally decent disposition, one never knows when one is quits.'[39]

Of course Diderot wanted to convince Sophie that he was capable of equal thoughtfulness and delicacy of feeling with her.[40] Some of his letters are perhaps not much better than banal. But often one comes across passages so sensitive in psychological analysis that they seem worthy of inclusion in an anthology of love:

It is for me and not for you that I tell you that I love you with all my soul; that you are in my mind ceaselessly; that I miss you every instant; that the realization of my not having you torments me, sometimes even without my knowing it; that if at first I don't know what I'm looking for, upon reflection I find that it is you; that if I want to go out without knowing where to go, upon reflection I find that it is to where you are; that if I am with agreeable people and yet, in spite of myself, feel boredom coming over me, upon reflection I find that it is because I no longer have hope of seeing you for a moment, and that apparently it is this hope that makes time endurable.[41]

Mme d'Aine would say of him, Diderot prophesied, 'If this keeps up, she'll have to drown me out of pity.'[42]

To Sophie he was explicit about his relations with his wife. 'The most sympathetic inquiries call forth from her such harsh replies that I never speak to her except under extreme necessity. . . . But I shall not have many domestic scenes. The time has passed since unreasonableness enraged me, when, in despair at not being able to lay my hands on her, I turned them against myself and struck myself or was about to butt my head against

the wall. I'm getting used to it.' Sometimes he was able to 'catechize myself a little on her account; one more walk with myself and I'll guarantee
that, whatever she does and says, she'll not wring out of me a single impatient word.' When Diderot returned from the country, his little daughter, seven years old, 'threw her little arms around my neck and kissed me,
crying "C'est mon papa, c'est mon petit papa." Her mother didn't say a
word. I went into my study, where I found a pile of letters. I read them.
Dinner was served, and we sat down to table without saying a word. And
there is more than that: we haven't spoken to each other yet.' [43]

By early November Diderot was back at the Rue Taranne, there to stay
throughout the winter.[44] The contributors to the *Encyclopédie,* who in September were 'enraging me by their dilatoriness,' were still causing him
trouble in November. 'What takes infinite time are the letters I am
forced to write to my lazy colleagues to hurry them up.' [45]

Voltaire's ambiguous conduct in respect to Palissot's *Les Philosophes*
also greatly tried Diderot's patience. Thus he wrote hotly to Sophie that
Voltaire 'complains to Grimm very bitterly of my silence. He says that it
would at least be polite to thank one's advocate. And who the devil asked
him to plead my cause? And who the devil told him that he pled it in
the way I wanted it?' [46] Still, the politics of 1760 being what they were,
it was no time to allow divergence of views to become the subject of
rumor. How awkward it was for Diderot, then, to find that Damilaville
and Thieriot had led Voltaire to expect he would hear from Diderot about
Tancrède. Voltaire's tragedy, which was of an altogether different stature
and dimension from his *L'Ecossaise,* produced only five weeks before, had
had its *première* on 3 September 1760, Diderot himself being in the audience.[47] *Tancrède,* having to do with chivalry at Syracuse in the year 1005,
appealed particularly to the patriotic feelings of a French audience, for
the French descent of the hero, Tancred, was often alluded to. Diderot had
not liked *L'Ecossaise,* finding its pathos 'slight and paltry' in comparison
with his own translation of *The Gamester.*[48] His impression of *Tancrède*
was much better. The first and second acts were cold, he wrote Sophie, but
'the third is one of the finest things I have ever seen . . . the fourth is lacking in action but is full of fine bits. One doesn't know what the fifth is.
It is long, long, long, cold, involved; insipid, upon the whole, except for
the last scene, which is again very beautiful.' But all this comment was
private. 'It was certainly not my intention to write to the naughty and
extraordinary child of the Délices [Voltaire's house at Geneva]. But how
am I now to get out of it? If it isn't Damilaville and Thieriot who have

put me under the necessity of sending him my observations on *Tancrède!* . . . There was nothing else for it but to write to the illustrious brigand of the lake.' [49]

Diderot's letter was tactful. It was also frank. He praised; but he also criticized. Still, he called Voltaire 'cher maître.' 'In fact, how many different wreaths heaped up on your head alone! You have gathered all the laurels; and we go gleaning in your footsteps, picking up here and there some miserable little leaves which you have overlooked and which we proudly pin over one ear like a cockade, sorry recruits that we are.' [50]

But the incident was not quite over, for a pamphlet was published in Paris attributing to Diderot a letter critical of *Tancrède.* Diderot hastened to disavow this, in a letter to the *Mercure de France* dated 15 January 1762. [51] The pamphleteer's allegations did not, so far as is known, poison Diderot's relations with Voltaire. On the contrary, he asked the Marquise de Fontaine to arrange a dinner party in Paris for Diderot, D'Alembert, Damilaville, and Mlle Clairon, the celebrated actress, at which Voltaire's play, *Cassandre,* still in manuscript, could be read. [52] Diderot, evidently appalled at the prospect, enumerated to Damilaville a whole host of reasons why he could not go, one of the most interesting being that 'I avoid people whom I have never met, and you know it. . . . Get me out of this without wounding anyone.' [53] Voltaire called off the party himself, his *Cassandre* needing in his estimation a good deal of revision. [54] Thereafter no similar dinner party seems to have been planned.

The *première* of *Le Père de famille* approached with all Paris aware of what was at stake. After the humiliation inflicted by Palissot's play, not only Diderot's standing as a playwright but also the prestige of the *philosophes* as a party were being put to the test. A resounding success of *Le Père de famille* would signalize a victory, perhaps even *the* victory, of the party of the Encyclopedists. 'Success is very necessary and very important,' wrote Voltaire. [55] Consequently, as one observer wrote to a correspondent in Brussels, 'It is easy to foresee that the *première* of this piece is going to be tumultuous.' [56]

The opening took place on 18 February 1761, with a very full house of 1178 spectators. But there was no riot. 'Everthing went off very quietly,' wrote the same observer to his correspondent in Brussels. The critic in *Annonces, Affiches, et Avis Divers,* a paper edited in Paris and with a large circulation in the provinces, did not himself care for the genre, but he reported that 'the play was very well received. . . .the piece was warmly welcomed. All the ladies in the first tier of boxes were seen to use their handkerchiefs copiously, and half the parterre was in tears.'[57] The dramatist Collé intensely disliked the play; but the *Mercure de France,* on the other hand, reported that 'the first performance was applauded and the succeeding ones have established its success. . . . The scene presents several tableaux of a domestic interior not previously seen in the theater.'[58]

But presently the *Annonces, Affiches, et Avis Divers* was remarking that 'As one quickly becomes bored with weeping, the crowd is daily diminishing at the play of *Le Père de famille,* and this piece will not go very far.' And Fréron, never one to over-praise Diderot, reported that 'As it was impossible to stage this play as printed, numerous alterations were made in it to make it bearable. To make it successful, it would have had to be entirely redone. It had only six or seven performances, just mildly applauded.'[59] In 1761 the play had six performances in all, the last one occurring on 4 March. The crowds were large for the time, but they were also declining, the attendance at the penultimate performance being only 616.[60]

Le Père de famille was not a failure outright, that was certain, yet its success was ambiguous and, most of all, inconclusive. The Comédie-Française had lent itself three times in 1760–1 to the staging of plays that were part of a political struggle — Palissot's *Les Philosophes,* Voltaire's *L'Ecossaise,* and now Diderot's *Le Père de famille.* It was clear, from the public reception of Diderot's play, that its success was not so resounding or impressive as to settle much of anything politically. As a weapon of propaganda this new genre in the theater was not irresistibly overwhelming. As a quite dispassionate and objective contemporary remarked, 'The success of this piece has not been very decisive.'[61]

What success it did achieve could not have been very inspiring for Diderot. It is plain from what he wrote to Voltaire about it that he would have liked to think that the fault lay with the production of the play, not with the play itself. Although he had asked the company for the privilege of assigning the roles, the only privilege he did ask for, he later wrote Voltaire that 'They distributed the roles among themselves, and acted the piece without my being mixed up in it.' Diderot was at the last two rehearsals, and is said by Grimm to have made some changes in the fourth and fifth acts. Diderot himself says nothing of this, and indeed no evidence now remains of the variants between the play as acted and the version of it as printed two years before. What Diderot did say was that the actors 'laid hold of the poor *Père de famille* and cut it, trimmed it, mutilated it, pruned it as the whim took them.' Moreover, the style of acting the new piece required 'was so foreign to them that most of them confessed to me that they trembled upon going on stage as if they had been making their début. . . . [It] succeeded at the première as much as is possible when almost none of the actors was in his role or suitable for it.'[62] Grimm's account was so explicit that it unintentionally trenched upon the hilarious:

If this piece had been played twenty years ago, it would have had the success and reputation of [Voltaire's] *Zaïre,* because the theater possessed at that time actors capable of filling their roles. Today the best actors are on the decline and ready to retire without being replaced and the roles of *Le Père de famille* could be distributed only to actors either miscast or mediocre. The greatest zeal and the best of good will which they brought to the execution of the piece could not remedy so essential a drawback, and the illusion suffered from this circumstance considerably. People could not visualize a child fifteen years old, such as Sophie, in the person of Mlle Gaussin, who is fifty, and whose figure and *embonpoint* managed to destroy the illusion. The role of Saint-Albin, full of petulance, movement, warmth, charm, liveliness, made to order for Grandval as he was twenty years ago, cannot be played by him today, now that youth, charm, and memory have left him. It was necessary to give the role to Belcour, who did his best, but his best is insupportably mediocre. Grandval took the role of Germeuil, not a very considerable one, though his failing memory nevertheless prevented him from making the most of it.[63]

Grimm went on to say that the role of the dour and sardonic Commander was taken by the most noted comic actor of the Comédie-Française, with the result that the audience was always laughing, and laughing in the wrong places. In contrast to the Paris production, Grimm spoke lamely of the prodigious effect made by the play in the provinces.

Although Diderot wrote to Voltaire, 'I do not know what opinion the public will gain of my dramatic talent, and I scarcely care,'[64] the evidence seems to point, on the contrary, to the conclusion that his lack of conspicuous success was very alarming and discouraging to Diderot, and caused him to raise some disquieting questions as to his own creative capacity. What if he did not in fact possess the creative ability he thought he had? Far from not caring, it is much more likely that he suffered not only bruising disappointment but also what has been termed the 'anguish of a setback.'[65]

CHAPTER 32

Frustration, Self-assertion, and Wistfulness

W HEN I wrote *Le Père de famille,* the police magistrate exhorted me to continue along that line,' Diderot recalled in his *Paradoxe sur le comédien.*

'Why didn't you?'

'It was because, not having obtained the success I had promised myself that I would receive, and not flattering myself that I would be able to do much better, I lost my taste for a career for which I did not believe I had enough talent.' [1]

The tranquillity with which he recorded it can scarcely have been Diderot's mood when he had come to this decision. If he must acknowledge to himself that he did not have enough talent to write successful plays, what other talents of a high creative order had he up to that time shown? He had, of course, brought off seven volumes of the *Encyclopédie,* a feat which assuredly demonstrated the possession of a rare combination of intellectual aptitudes and moral strength, but which did not of itself prove also that he possessed gifts of the highest creativity. What of his other books — the *Pensées philosophiques* (1746), the *Mémoires sur différens sujets de mathématiques* (1748), the *Bijoux indiscrets* (1748), the *Lettre sur les aveugles* (1749), the *Lettre sur les sourds et muets* (1751), the *Pensées sur l'interprétation de la nature* (1753)? Significant as they were for showing the variety of his interests and the originality of his mind, none of them had struck the reading public of that time as a masterpiece, a *chef-d'oeuvre,* and indeed none of these does to this day. It was his plays, *Le Fils naturel* and especially *Le Père de famille,* with their accompanying little treatises about the writing of plays and the staging of them, that Diderot intended to clinch the proof of his genius.

Genius was beginning to fascinate Diderot in these years, and the word is often found in his writings and letters.[2] Genius, he thought (as do we), is the highest gift of all. But what if, in spite of earlier promise, he did not really possess it? This sort of doubt, worrying and nagging a man when he is forty-eight years old, as Diderot was in 1761, can be excruciating and discouraging in the extreme. Nor could the spectacular success of Rousseau's *La Nouvelle Héloïse*, published in February of this year, have encouraged complacency in Diderot. A year earlier he himself had crushingly remarked of a fellow-playwright, 'The poet worked hard; but he did not have genius, without which effort is very laborious and produces nothing.' [3] What if the remark, written before the demi-success of *Le Père de famille*, applied to himself? Diderot's problem had rather suddenly become one of asking himself whether he was a *raté*, the man whose early promise has not been fulfilled.[4] Suddenly Diderot was in the position of having to ask himself: If I have genius, why does it not soar?

Certainly Fréron did not think that Diderot had genius. Five months after the ambiguous success of *Le Père de famille*, the *Année Littéraire* carried this estimate of the play's author:

It is too bad that the pompousness of his words, the lack of order in his ideas, and the obscurity of his style sometimes get in the way of what is really good in his writings. He is almost always abstruse or over-emphatic. He writes for the French, yet he assumes the air and tone of a legislator coming to enlighten savages. . . . he neither pleases nor persuades; but he dazzles, he astonishes, he benumbs, he overwhelms youthful minds, and perhaps this is all he wants. Nevertheless he was certainly born with a great deal of intelligence and imagination; he has a broad range of knowledge; he would produce some excellent things if he had more modesty, more composure, and greater taste. . . .' [5]

The period following the production of *Le Père de famille* happens to be one in which very few of Diderot's letters are extant. We do not have, in our conjectures regarding his state of mind, the corroboration of intimate letters. But we do have an important document, the more revealing because Diderot kept it so private that none of his acquaintances seems to have known of its existence. The fact that he wrote in 1761 the first draft of a piece that is in part concerned with the nature of genius and with this very problem of the *raté* allows it to be argued plausibly that anxiety with regard to himself was much on his mind. This piece was the now famous *Le Neveu de Rameau*.

Combined with disillusionment and anxiety was no doubt also frustration, along with humiliation and bitterness. Part of the role played by *Le Neveu de Rameau* in solacing Diderot was that he used the piece as a vent to pour out wrath on his enemies. Thus far, though he plainly felt that in recent years he had been much buffeted by an unkind fate and much maligned by his enemies, he had managed to contain himself. Now, in *Le Neveu,* he finds relief by exposing his enemies for what they were — or, at least, what he thought they were — immoral, hypocritical, parasitical, egotistical, and dull.[6] No wonder that Diderot left his masterpiece to lie waiting for posterity to stumble upon, as posterity eventually did; for it teemed with slander and with the potentialities of endless incarceration in the Bastille.

Diderot's exposure of his enemies, though indirect, was deadly. The literary device he hit upon was to portray Rameau's nephew, one of two interlocutors, as an impudent but articulate parasite. His associates turn out to be all of Diderot's enemies, and most of them parasites too. How scornfully did Rameau's nephew describe them. Fréron, Palissot, 'the heavy-going Abbé d'Olivet, the fat Abbé Le Blanc, the hypocritical Batteux'; Mlle Hus, the actress who had gained Diderot's dislike by playing the role of the heroine in Palissot's *Les Philosophes;* Bertin, one of the King's treasurers who kept up the establishment of toadies and spongers.[7] 'Our house, as you know, receives the largest and most select society. . . . All the fallen poets, we pick up . . . also the despised musicians, unread authors, hissed actresses, and hooted actors — in short, a band of shamefuls, of poor dull parasites at whose head I have the honor to be, myself the brave leader of a timorous band.' Nor were Diderot's enemies who were not parasites forgotten: the Comtesse de La Marck, a patroness of Palissot, a lady with whom Diderot had had a humiliating encounter in 1758;[8] and Jean-Philippe Rameau, the uncle, who had written such devastating booklets against the articles on music in the *Encyclopédie,*[9] they too came in for their share of barbs.

Diderot succeeded in giving *Le Neveu de Rameau* all the appearances of an actual conversation. After all, there really was a nephew of Rameau, a not very successful musician living spectrally in his uncle's shadow. In 1748 the nephew had been arrested for disorderly conduct at the Opera, for which he was imprisoned for three weeks. Grimm mentioned the younger Rameau in 1766 as being 'a sort of lunatic,' yet not incapable sometimes of 'new and singular ideas.' Several other contemporaries mention him, and it is known that about this time he held the official position of 'Inspector and Comptroller of Dancing Masters.' Diderot, as has been suggested, may have had just such a conversation with him in April 1761 as is depicted in *Le Neveu de Rameau.*[10]

The *mise en scène* of the dialogue was accurate, too: Diderot knew the Café de la Régence and its chess players very well. 'I shall be at the Café de la Régence at six,' he once wrote his friend Damilaville. 'You will surely find me there.' And he evidently enjoyed the privileges of an *ancien client:* one day in 1760 he was taken ill while on his way home in a cab from Mme d'Epinay's. 'I was no sooner on the Place du Palais Royal than I felt that I could never make the Rue Taranne. I got down. I went into the Café de la Régence, where they made a big fire for me. I practically got into it.' After a few hours he felt somewhat better and left.[11] By locating his dialogue in the Café de la Régence Diderot was exhibiting some of the realism that so impressed him in Richardson's novels. 'Fair weather or foul,' *Le Neveu de Rameau* begins, 'it is my habit to go for a walk about five o'clock in the Palais Royal. . . . If the weather is too cold or rainy, I take refuge in the Café de la Régence.'

Diderot's realism had the effect of greatly misleading nineteenth-century critics. An older generation than ours supposed that all of his writings were only effusions — the ebulliencies of a wonderfully facile temperament that never bothered to revise. Thus, to many older critics, *Le Neveu de Rameau* has seemed something more in the nature of a stenographic report than of an intricate and complex work of art. This is, of course, a misapprehension. Diderot's manuscripts, many of which have only recently come to light, show the evidence, in his own words, of 'the work of the file, the work that is the hardest and thorniest of all, exhausting, wearing one out, boring, and never ending. . . .'[12] It is now known that *Le Neveu,* though evidently composed 'in all its essentials' in the summer of 1761, was revised on several occasions, most notably in 1762, but also in 1766, 1767, and 1775.[13]

The figure of the nephew is one of the great creations of literature. The nephew lives. And because he is so real, Diderot's reader comes to accept him as a sort of oracle in his own right. It is as though the nephew, striking out in all directions and assassinating reputations, does so with an authority all his own. Posterity finds itself believing some scabrous tale or other about Bertin or Mlle Hus because the nephew said it was so, and almost forgets that the nephew says only what his creator makes him say. Thus Diderot, through the wizardry of art, finds a way of working off his own aggressions and counter-aggressions, and in the process gets his reader on his side. Well might he say of himself, as he has the nephew remark in the last line of the dialogue, 'He who laughs last laughs best.'

The Nephew of Rameau,* in form a dialogue of some one hundred pages, has a disarming air of casualness and off-handedness. It is just a running conversation, one thing seeming artlessly to lead to another, about how to get enough to live on, and about music and women and what is success. It is an exuberant and witty book that should be read, first and most of all, for the unusual entertainment it provides. It is enormously diverting, in its play of language, in the give and take of argument, in its vividly delineated descriptions of the nephew's miming, in its malice and its sensuality, and in its sudden turns, as when the nephew says, 'For no one feels so put out, not even a pretty woman who wakes up with a pimple on her nose, as does an author threatened with outliving his reputation — witness Marivaux and Crébillon the Younger.' [14]

And *Le Neveu de Rameau* is, of course, much more than a means for Diderot's unloading some of his frustrations, much more than just recreational reading. It is an examination, from points of view poles apart, of what is the good life, of what is the right way to live. It is, as Carl Becker remarked, 'a searching inquiry into the basis of morality.' [15] And here the reader is in for some repellent surprises. For the nephew not only cheerfully admits that he is a parasite, a liar, a procurer, a man who teaches his little son that money is everything, a bereaved husband who mourns the untimely death of his beautiful wife because he could have made so much money prostituting her — 'sooner or later she would have had a farmer general at least' — the nephew not only confesses all this but contends that this is the most moral way to live.

At this point we realize how significant it is that the piece is cast in the form of a dialogue. 'LUI,' that is to say the nephew, asserts this paradoxical morality against the struggles and strictures of 'MOI,' the narrator of the piece. It was always characteristic of Diderot's thinking to seek truth by the confrontation of opposites. One can see this dialectic in his writings even when he does not use the dialogue form — in the *Pensées philosophiques* or the *Promenade du sceptique,* for instance.[16] This struggle of opposites is the whole *raison d'être* of the dialogue. Paradoxically, the Diderot who only two years earlier was complaining to Grimm of the difficulty and labor involved in writing dialogue for plays became copious and spark-

---

* *Le Neveu de Rameau* is accessible in the following English translations: as an appendix to the second volume of any edition of John Morley, *Diderot and the Encyclopaedists;* Denis Diderot, *Diderot, Interpreter of Nature,* ed. Jonathan Kemp (London [1937]; 2nd ed., 1963); Diderot, *Rameau's Nephew and Other Works,* tr. Jacques Barzun, ed. R. H. Bowen (Library of Liberal Arts [Bobbs-Merrill]); Diderot, *Rameau's Nephew and D'Alembert's Dream,* tr. L. W. Tancock (Penguin Classics).

ling and seemingly inexhaustible when he turned explicitly to the dialogue form. And with what dazzling effect. *Le Neveu de Rameau* has been called 'probably the most lively and engrossing specimen of a conversation with an unforgettable character ever put on paper,' and a French scholar has remarked that 'it is the work, by the profundity of its thought and the boldness of its technique, showing the greatest genius in the literature of our eighteenth century.' [17]

Diderot's skill in managing the dialogue form adds immeasurably to the excitement of *Le Neveu de Rameau*. For this is a contest between athletes, and it is settled, with great confusion and disagreement among the judges — that is to say, among the readers — not by a knockout but on points.[18] There is wide disagreement among critics and scholars as well as among everyday readers as to who wins. This uncertainty lends to the dialogue that ambivalence and ambiguity in the face of life's greatest problems which so fascinates the twentieth century.[19] It is the fascination that accounts for the present high estate of all those masterpieces that Diderot wrote in his later life and kept locked up, to be enjoyed only by himself and by posterity. And because, in judging *Le Neveu de Rameau,* there is disagreement as to which athlete wins, as well as disagreement as to the meaning that Diderot himself found in his creation, the number of interpretations of Diderot's masterpiece has steadily increased. In the opinion of one scholar, they are 'already so numerous and various as to justify its comparison . . . with *Hamlet* and *Don Quixote.*' [20]

One of the contestants, the nephew, is hard and tough, and is regarded by many as having brilliantly won the day. The other, MOI, has let himself become a little flabby and his defense against the nephew's unorthodox jabs and punches seems merely conventional. But part of the consummate craftsmanship of the dialogue lies in the fact that the protagonists change in the course of their contest, each adjusting to the assaults of the other, so that MOI becomes somewhat less banal and more realistic, while LUI, though talking brassily and jauntily to the end, is brought close to admitting that his triumphs have been failures, that his peculiar way of pursuing happiness has brought him not pleasure but frustrations, and that his formula for the good life is only his contrivance for compensating for his lack of creativity.[21]

For *Le Neveu de Rameau* is not a discussion merely about ethics; it is also an exploration of the nature of genius and of the mystery of creativity, and of the relationship between genius and morality, of whether genius can be developed, of whether it can be forfeited.[22] All of this covers new ground, for the older view of genius had thought of it as simply talent carried to a higher exponential power, whereas Diderot defines genius as a gift of nature differing from talent not in degree but in kind.[23] Although the nephew inveighs against genius and pretends that he does not want it, it becomes evident that in reality there is nothing that he wants more. What the nephew has is talent, not genius. What he has is the capacity to perform, not the capacity to create.

Much of the variety of interpretations of *Le Neveu de Rameau* arises from the attempt to understand the biographical significance of the piece. What does it reveal or betray of the author and his previous experience? Obviously, at least part of the character of MOI is Diderot, as is proved by his references to his daughter and by the anecdotes regarding MOI's early life in Paris. This unquestionable resemblance to Diderot has made some interpreters assert that MOI is completely autobiographical. LUI is simply the nephew of Rameau and MOI is simply Diderot.[24] A more common view is that both LUI and MOI are aspects of Diderot and represent conflicting elements in his personality. One element represents Diderot the *philosophe;* the other represents Diderot the Bohemian, the Diderot that was (or the Diderot that came close to being) in those wild and disordered days of his early life in Paris.[25] According to this Faustian view — 'Two souls, alas! dwell in my breast' — the dialogue signifies a conflict of irreconcilable impulses in Diderot's own psyche.

There is, of course, an element of truth in this interpretation. Almost all critics continue to agree that one of the uses Diderot makes of his own creation is to submit one side of his character to a critique by the other. One critic has noticed the presence here of a pre-Freudian Freudian interpretation:

It would perhaps be pressing too far to find in Rameau Freud's *id* and in Diderot Freud's *ego;* yet the connection does suggest itself; and at least we have here the perception which is to be the common characteristic of both Freud and romanticism, of the hidden element of human nature and of the opposition between the hidden and the apparent.[26]

How interesting it is, then, that the Goncourt brothers spoke more than a hundred years ago of *Le Neveu de Rameau* as 'a descent by genius into the human consciousness.'[27] Another commentator has made the unusual suggestion that LUI serves for Diderot the function that the hideous picture served for Dorian Gray.[28]

For there are many levels of meaning in *Le Neveu de Rameau*. By internal evidence one may infer the variety and complexity of Diderot's problems that his writing of the dialogue was intended to solve. He was satirizing his enemies and relieving his feelings; he was, no doubt, using the dialogue to identify and attempt to integrate his own tensions and conflicts; [29] and he was also expressing in a very serious way his abiding interest in ethics, contemplated not solely as an individual and interior problem but also as a public and general one. Out of the particularity of a local situation, a casual conversation one eighteenth-century afternoon in a Paris café, Diderot raises his dialogue, by dazzling literary skill and also by moral earnestness, to the dimension of an argument transcending space and time. It is this moral earnestness — and this universality — that make *Le Neveu de Rameau* so much more than just a scintillating literary curiosity.

It has also been suggested that Diderot's purpose in composing *Le Neveu de Rameau* was predominantly a literary one. It may have been, as one scholar argues, a means of escape from the worries and discouragements he was living through.[30] Or it may have been inspired by the desire to experiment with a piece in the manner of Horace's Satires. Diderot himself entitled the dialogue 'Satire II.'[31] The epigraph of *Le Neveu de Rameau* — 'Born under the malignant influence of change' — is a quotation from Horace, and Diderot's other writings abundantly show that he was familiar with the poet, loved to explicate some of his difficult passages, and was awed by his creative accomplishments.

But *Le Neveu de Rameau* is also a very combative work, so that the motivations of escape and of belles-lettres seem inadequate in themselves alone to account for so dynamic and pugnacious a piece. In order to satirize his enemies, Diderot found himself being sarcastic also about the society in which people like these were able to prosper. Thus he was in effect writing social satire, in this respect like Lucian, as one critic has observed, or like Juvenal, or like Petronius, as a famous German historian observed over a century ago.[32] That Diderot was describing a decadent society in the last stages of deliquescence and corruption was a point made with great weight by Hegel. With stupefying jargon, but yet 'in pages astonishing for their profundity and intelligence,' Hegel interpreted the figure of the nephew as a person alienated from his society and, because of the corruption of that society, alienated from himself.[33] In this way, Diderot is visualized as having admirably described a pre-revolutionary state of mind.[34] It can easily be imagined that this interpretation of *Le Neveu de Rameau*, which Hegel made a part of his doctrine of the dialectical process in history, has been adopted by Marxist writers, beginning with Karl Marx himself.[35] But one does not have to be a Marxist to appreciate that *Le Neveu de Rameau* describes a social milieu that is corrupt and decadent and ripe for change. From this point of view the nephew is seen as accepting the role of the faithful servant of the existing Establishment, and Diderot's dialogue expresses the tension that a philosopher feels between himself and the out-of-jointness of his times.[36]

Inasmuch as Diderot never mentioned this dialogue in his other writings or even in his correspondence, posterity is reduced to conjecture as to his feelings about it. It is perhaps not unreasonable to suppose that he gained from writing *Le Neveu de Rameau* renewed faith in his own creative powers. For *Le Neveu* is an absorbingly intricate and complex work, in structure, in style, in characterization, even in the use of metaphor and simile.[37] So complex is it that a recent French critic has spoken of it as 'a Faulknerian inquiry.'[38] Combined with this complexity of structure is also an extraordinary concreteness of detail, as shown, for example, by Diderot's knowledge of music.[39] In fact, it has been argued that *Le Neveu de Rameau,* with its theme and variations like a passacaglia, *is* music. According to this view, *Le Neveu de Rameau* progresses, just as music does, by 'subtle associations [and] by oblique and affinitive communications.' Thus, when Diderot abandons a subject and later resumes it, 'he gives us a true musical illusion by multiplying our subconscious processes of association.'[40]

May one not infer, then, that Diderot took pleasure in *Le Neveu de Rameau* just in being able to bring it off? And such a pleasure would come not from having escaped from reality into a world of art for art's sake, but would come instead from a sense of self-vindication. Could he have escaped feeling that, unlike his creatures LUI and MOI, he could create? If so, this would be the answer to the setback that *Le Père de famille* had encountered and to the doubts that that ambiguous success had raised.

It is possible to see in *Le Neveu de Rameau* a very important stage in the development of Diderot as an artist, as an intelligent and self-knowing craftsman aware not only of his talents but also of his limitations. According to such an interpretation, one of the personal uses to which Diderot put the dialogue was to help him gain perspective on himself, to objectify himself, as Goethe might have said. There are elements of the character and proclivities of Diderot in both LUI and MOI. But he exaggerates the Diderotian characteristics in both LUI and MOI to the point of being self-defeating and inefficacious. It is as though he is warning himself of the danger in his own life of being too much like LUI and at the same time of being too much like MOI.

Thus MOI, though he prides himself as a moralist, is represented as courting inefficacy by being too abstract in his morality, too *a priori,* too conventional and therefore mediocre. Diderot is really critical of MOI: he represents MOI as a moralist whose views at the beginning of the dialogue are at one and the same time too dogmatic and too empty, too frigid, too unrealistic. Diderot's plays had been like that, too sentimental and unrealistic in a moral sense though very realistic in *mise en scène.* This taste for moralizing continued in Diderot's later years. As he subsequently wrote, when making the point that every man has his tic, 'Mine is to moralize.' [41] But his moralizing became more concrete, empirical, and self-questioning. Perhaps he learned from his own creature in *Le Neveu de Rameau* to rid himself in morals of the easy generalization and the dogmatic assumption.

LUI, on the other hand, is also represented by Diderot as being self-defeating. This came of LUI's being too impulsive, being out of control and not self-disciplined. His would-be creativity is more nearly automatism than creation, a reflex rather than a truly creative response to a situation. Diderot himself was much given to the exaggerated and automatic response that the French of that age called '*sensibilité*' and which has been aptly defined as 'exaltation in excess of the circumstances.' [42] Some writers interpret Diderot as being almost exclusively under the sway of *sensibilité.*[43] But in 1758 he had written, 'I also know how to alienate myself, a talent without which one can do nothing worth while,' [44] and now, in the figure of the nephew Diderot portrays a man whose uncontrolled impulses have wrought the greatest damage an artist can suffer — they have made him mediocre.[45]

Perhaps it was closer association with artists and sculptors, now that he was writing the *Salons,* that made Diderot slowly realize that art is the result not merely of quick emotional response but also of self-discipline and self-control. In *Le Neveu de Rameau* we find the intimation of his doctrine, expressed full-blown ten years later in the *Paradoxe sur le comédien,* that the greatest artist is the one who is most in command of himself. Finally, then, a reader comes away from *Le Neveu de Rameau* with the realization that it constitutes a discernible stage in Diderot's progress from *sensibilité* to self-conscious artistic control.

In the two years between his *Salon de 1759* and his *Salon de 1761,* Diderot had been contributing to Grimm occasional pieces of criticism, such as a caustic review of a poem entitled *Sur l'art de peindre* ('On the Art of

Painting') — 'The most insignificant among artists knows much more than this'[46] — and two pieces on architecture. The first was about Rheims and the extensive remodeling of the center of that town. Perhaps he was especially interested in this because Sophie Volland's brother-in-law was the architect in charge.[47] Intent as he always was upon the usefulness of things, Diderot here bespeaks in architecture and town planning what might fairly be called 'functionalism.' 'What is the principal object of [this] building? What will be taking place there? What are the occasions for assembling there? What occurs during these occasions?' And he made a generalization that all mankind at some time or other has to acknowledge ruefully is only too true: 'There are no foolish mistakes that last longer and are more conspicuous than those committed in stone and marble.'[48] Diderot's other piece on architecture was an appreciation, which included the interior decoration, of the newly-finished church of Saint-Roch, on the Rue Saint-Honoré.[49] This handsome building still contains several of the pieces of art Diderot commented upon. It is the church that was to become the backstop for Napoleon Bonaparte's famous 'whiff of grapeshot' in 1795, and which to this day bears upon its columns and façade the scars of that encounter. And this is the church, strangely enough, in which Diderot himself was destined one day to be buried, under the Lady Chapel.

Close to the time when he was composing his first draft of *Le Neveu de Rameau,* Diderot was writing two other important works, each of them revelatory of his mood at this period. One was his panegyric on Samuel Richardson, the author of *Pamela* and *Clarissa,* who had died on 14 July 1761. The other was the *Salon de 1761,* which shows Diderot being ever more aware of the necessity of having a thorough knowledge of the technique of painting if one wishes to be a judicious critic of it. This *Salon* is more sober than the others, although there is a touch of the salacious — or at least of the erotic — as in the discussion of Carle Van Loo's 'The Magdalen in the Desert.' Such observations, which no doubt came easily to the author of *Les Bijoux indiscrets,* served to maintain reader interest in the eighteenth century and certainly do not detract from it in the twentieth.[50] Yet it is quite remarkable how somber is the *Salon de 1761,* on the whole: thoughtful, comprehensive, but without the gaiety that had flashed here and there in the *Salon de 1759* and that was to distinguish so delightfully *Salons* yet to come. The sober tenor of his thoughts revealed Diderot's subdued mood in 1761.

Throughout the eighteenth century it was the so-called 'historical' pictures, large canvases the subjects of which were religious or taken from history or mythology, that conferred the greatest prestige on their creators. There was a hierarchy of painters in the Royal Academy of Art (and it was only members of the Academy who had the privilege of exhibiting in the biennial Salons at the Louvre). The great men of the day were those who told in paint some classic anecdote using an elaborate group of figures, and the Salons abounded in these outsize illustrations. One of Diderot's criteria in judging these pictures betrays the idiosyncrasy of the man of letters or the story teller. He believed that it was supremely important that the artist choose for depiction the right moment in the story, the instant that was most dramatic and therefore (he claimed) most pictorial. The painter's problem was to discover the right instant at which to arrest the action. Not unexpectedly, Diderot's choice of the right moment frequently disagreed with that of the artist. 'Were I a painter, here is the painting Homer would have inspired me to do. . . . I would have chosen, as you see, the moment just preceding the wounding of Venus; M. Doyen, on the contrary, has preferred the following one.' And of another artist, 'There are only two unsuitable moments in your subject, and it is just precisely one of the two that you take.'[51] Diderot thought, quite correctly, that it was easy to be tedious and insipid in such a genre. To combat this he insisted that 'One must have thrilled twenty times over one's subject before taking up one's brush, lost sleep, gotten up in the night and run in shirt and bare feet to get one's sketches down on paper by the glimmer of a night lamp.'[52]

The *Salon de 1761* shows Diderot becoming more proficient in the appreciation of technique, whether by virtue of talking with artists — 'Chardin is an intelligent man, and perhaps nobody talks about painting better than he does' — or by comparing their works with those of great predecessors, such as Rubens, Annibale Carracci, Correggio, Claude Lorrain, Van der Meulen, Le Brun, Salvator Rosa, Teniers, and Van Dyck. He thought of Boucher as being in art what Ariosto is in literature, which is a literary judgment but a perceptive one.[53] And in trying to explain to himself why the artists of his day were not more proficient in drawing the human body, he wrote: 'We never see the nude; our religion and our climate are against it.'[54]

Diderot might be somber, but he could still be trenchant. 'I should like to ask M. Parrocel how, when one has in one's recollection the composition of a subject by Rubens, one can have the courage to undertake the same subject.' 'Pierre, my friend, your Christ, with his livid and wasted head, is some drowned man trapped for at least a fortnight in the river nets at Saint-Cloud. How low he is! How ignoble!' And of 'Psyche Discovering Eros Asleep,' a picture by Vien, Diderot complained, 'And this lamp, ought she to be letting the light fall directly upon the eyes of Eros? Ought she not to be holding it away and be interposing her hand so as to diminish its brightness? . . . These people do not know that one's eyelids have a sort of transparency. They never have seen a mother come by night, a lamp in her hand, to look at her baby in the cradle, fearing lest she wake it.'[55]

Diderot's memory of the visual enabled him to write his criticisms from notes, in the leisure and tranquillity of his own study. And it provided him with the criteria for comparison that comes from the total recall of the Old Masters. 'Raphael's pictures come more vividly to me than Corneille's verse, than the fine passages of Racine. There are some figures that never leave me. I see them; they follow me, they obsess me. For example, this Saint Barnabas tearing the garments on his chest, and so many others, how could I get rid of specters like that?'[56] But when art communicated nothing to him, it left Diderot's memory unstirred. 'Perhaps,' he wrote to Grimm at the end of the *Salon de 1761*, 'there were some beautiful things among the paintings . . . [and] the sculptures that I do not mention: it is because they were mute and did not say anything to me.'[57]

The most famous of the pictures in the Salon of 1761 is still to be seen in the Louvre. This was Greuze's 'L'Accordée de village,' entitled in the catalogue of the exhibition 'A Betrothal, at the Moment when the Father of the Bride Hands over the Dowry to his Son-in-law.' In this composition a group of twelve persons are shown in the interior of a peasant's house. Everything is there, including the musket hanging on the wall and a hen with five chicks in the foreground. Diderot described each figure meticulously. He was especially pleased with the bride, whose modest dress, concealing her bosom, could not deceive so penetrating and observant an art critic as Diderot. 'I bet that there is nothing there lifting it up, it holds itself up by itself.' The picture is too sentimental for twentieth-century taste, but not so for the eighteenth: Diderot had trouble even seeing the canvas because of the crowds it attracted. Diderot liked it too; Grimm liked it even more than Diderot did.[58]

Working night and day in order to meet Grimm's deadline, Diderot finished the *Salon de 1761* in mid-September, at the same time, as it happened, that he was finding Mme Diderot especially hard to bear. 'But tell me what advantage this woman will get out of it if she makes me break a blood vessel in my chest or derange the fibers of my brain. Oh! how hard it seems to me to endure life. How many times I would accept the end of it with joy.' [59]

The remaining important literary work that he composed in 1761 was the *Eloge de Richardson*. It is a very characteristic piece, not least because of its copious emotional flow. 'Richardson is no more. What a loss for literature and mankind! This loss has affected me as though it were that of my brother.' [60] Diderot wrote impulsively and speedily. Grimm informed his readers that this *Eloge,* which is some 6500 words in length, was sketched out in twenty-four hours. Diderot himself referred to 'these lines that I have spelled out without connection, plan, or order, just as they were inspired in me by the tumult of my heart.' [61] Since posterity does not venerate Richardson so much as Diderot predicted it would, his eulogy seems to twentieth-century readers a little too florid and overripe. Moreover, he can frequently be detected in this essay in the unlovely posture of really complimenting himself while appearing to be complimenting Richardson. He often seems to insinuate that only a person of his sensitivity could appreciate Richardson adequately. What is more, Diderot's praise of Richardson may have had an unconscious and certainly unacknowledged purpose. It could have been a means of suggesting to French readers that Rousseau's *La Nouvelle Héloïse,* currently being compared with Richardson's works, was not really so original nor so great as the Richardson novels that preceded it. Certainly Jean-Jacques took exception to Diderot's praise of Richardson. [62]

The *Eloge,* even as it dropped a flood of tears on Richardson's grave, served also a solid critical purpose. It gave Diderot the opportunity to compose his 'first significant piece of critical writing on the novel.' [63] His panegyric, while sometimes causing an ironical smile, has nevertheless won the esteem of competent critics. A nineteenth-century essay on Diderot in the *Westminster Review* acknowledged that Diderot's admiration 'was extreme, but certainly not out of proportion to Richardson's historic importance.' And Herbert Dieckmann remarks that the *Eloge,* in spite of occasional faults, is 'one of the most important documents in the development of realism in the eighteenth century.' [64]

In this essay, and in his correspondence, Diderot reveals that he had read Richardson's works in the original, and had been familiar with them for some considerable time. [65] It is often noticed that *La Religieuse* shows the results of Diderot's having learned from Richardson. [66] Especially is this true in the technique of piling up details until the reader finally feels himself on the very spot. 'Realize,' wrote Diderot, 'that the illusion comes from this multitude of little things. . . .'[67] It was no small merit for Diderot to be able to identify in Richardson, and then to apply to his own novels, such as *Jacques le fataliste* as well as *La Religieuse,* the means of achieving a very great sense of accuracy and immediacy.[68]

Diderot also admired the moralist in Richardson. He sows germs of virtue in men's hearts: 'Who is there who would want to be Lovelace, with all his advantages? Who is there who would not want to be Clarissa in spite of all her misfortunes?'[69] Richardson was a moralist no doubt, but in the very special sense of portraying female virtue bedeviled by male lustfulness. Consequently there is in his novels, masking itself as a deep solicitude for the triumph of virtue over vice, a suspenseful sort of prurience and eroticism. Perhaps Diderot recognized this for what it was, though he does not say so; perhaps he was taken in by it. But at all events he did find in *Clarissa,* which he says was the Richardson novel he liked best of all, as well as in *Sir Charles Grandison* and *Pamela,* an anxiety as to how to live right, the identifying sign of the serious moralist. Moreover, Diderot was not only interested in ethics for its own sake, but was also deeply interested in the problem of the relationship of morals to art. In his 'Discourse on Dramatic Poetry' he had already asked whether the theater can teach morality, and he had answered that it can. In the *Salons* he often wrote of the relationship that he thought exists between art and morality. And here, with Richardson, he is thrilled by the awareness that the novel too can give insights into the problem of how to live not only wisely but right.

The *Eloge* reveals further that Diderot's knowledge of Richardson's books was precise. Thus he cites the hundred-and-twenty-eighth letter here and the hundred-and-seventy-fifth letter there, and remarks that 'I know the Harlowe house as I do my own; my father's home is not more familiar to me than that of Grandison.' Moreover, his frequent allusions in letters to Sophie show how deeply he was moved by Richardson's novels. This very September of 1761 he wrote:

What you tell me of the burial and will of Clarissa, I had felt too. . . . my eyes filled with tears; I could not read; I got up and began to grieve and to apostrophize the brother, the sister, the father, the mother and the uncles, and to talk out loud, to the great astonishment of Damilaville, who had no notion of either my discourse or my actions, and who asked me whom I had a grudge against.[70]

Just at this time, Diderot became extremely enthusiastic about the Ossianic poems, the first 'translations' of which had been published by James

Macpherson the year before.[71] Diderot's enthusiasm led him to translate some of the pieces into French, and in late 1761 and early 1762 these were published in the *Journal Etranger,* then being edited by two of Diderot's friends, Jean-Baptiste Suard and Abbé François Arnauld. The *Eloge de Richardson* also appeared in the *Journal Etranger,* in the number for January 1762, and thus became one of the very few works written by Diderot in the last quarter-century of his life that were published while he lived.[72] And because it was frequently reprinted, it may have had not inconsiderable influence in accustoming French taste to a greater appreciation of the novel as an art form, especially in that combination of moralism and realism so characteristic of Richardson.[73]

Diderot was a writer who sought contact with his readers to a most unusual degree. No one felt more than he the need to establish communication with them, and few have known better than he how to do it.[74] This eagerness to share experience makes Diderot's works, including the ones intended for immediate publication, intimate and self-revealing. The *Eloge de Richardson* ranks high in this regard, so that when he writes pityingly of Richardson, we sometimes feel that he is also feeling pity for himself.

He did not have the reputation he deserved. What a passion is envy! It is the cruelest of the Eumenides; it follows the man of merit to the edge of the grave; there it disappears, and the justice of the centuries sits down in its place.[75]

But most of all Diderot expresses a great wistfulness. In comparing his own achievement with that of Richardson, the one seems so great, the other so little. As he contemplates the passing of time, the approaching end of life with its promise unfulfilled, he writes in the language of a graceful mournfulness:[76]

Richardson's genius has suffocated mine. His phantoms roam ceaselessly in my imagination; if I try to write, I hear the plaint of Clementina; Clarissa's ghost appears before me; I see Grandison walking in front of me; Lovelace haunts me, and the pen drops from my fingers. And you, more gentle spirits, Emily, Charlotte, Pamela, dear Miss Howe, while I converse with you the years for accomplishment and for the gathering of laurels pass away; and I move forward toward the last boundary without having attempted anything that might recommend me too to the time to come.

CHAPTER 33

Concern for the Public Welfare

I AM A good citizen,' Diderot had written, 'and everything that concerns the welfare of society and the life of my fellow men is very interesting to me.' Thus he paraphrased the inspiring motto taken by the Renaissance humanists from Terence, expanding it to include a social consciousness which was to become, partly through his efforts, one of the trademarks of the Enlightenment. Beset though he might be with private vexations and professional problems, he was continuously engaged in trying to shape opinion and influence the course of public events. In this sense Diderot (like Montesquieu, Voltaire, and Rousseau) was involved in the political process. This was the fate, and also the glory, of the leaders of the Enlightenment in France.[1]

In 1761 this concern for the commonweal led Diderot, through his interest in preventing smallpox, back to mathematics. He wrote two papers on the theory of probability, that branch of mathematics that has had such an amazing development in the twentieth century and has proved itself such a valuable tool in the physical, biological, and social sciences. Diderot himself spoke of probability theory as being 'a calculation the application of which has so much importance and such great extent.'[2] His two papers, neither of which was published during his lifetime, were in response to D'Alembert's ineptitudes regarding the theory of probability.

D'Alembert had first exposed his views in the article *'Gageure'* (Wager) in Volume VII of the *Encyclopédie*. His calculations were challenged in Fréron's *Année Littéraire*:

The great number of letters I receive on every hand against the great Encyclopedical Dictionary is something astonishing. . . . Even chefs complain to me about certain ragouts and sauces recommended in this Reservoir of our knowledge. I had supposed that at least the part consecrated to Geometry, of which

M. d'Alembert is in charge, would be beyond any criticism. Yet here is a letter in which it is proved that he is mistaken in the easy calculation of the odds in so simple and common a game as Heads or Tails.[3]

D'Alembert returned to his heads or tails (though without alluding to the painful comments in the *Année Littéraire*) in an elaborate essay published in 1761.[4] The consensus of opinion, both at the time and since, is that he would have been better advised to let the matter drop. 'D'Alembert was completely mistaken on every point,' bluntly remarks one of his biographers, himself a famous mathematician and a pioneer in probability theory.[5] Diderot mentioned in September 1761 that he too had written a piece on probabilities, which he had sent to Grimm to use in the *Correspondance littéraire* if he chose, and though he later referred to it as 'jargon' that Sophie would not find amusing, modern critics speak well of it.[6] In the later volumes of the *Encyclopédie* it was Diderot (and not D'Alembert) who wrote the more important articles touching upon probability theory. The article *'Probabilité'* invites mathematical geniuses to develop 'so important a branch of our knowledge, so useful in the continuous routine of life';[7] and Diderot's article *'Jouer'* is a very competent essay in game theory.

As a corollary to his more abstract essay on probability, D'Alembert had read to the Académie des Sciences on 12 November 1760 a long and elaborate memoir against inoculation for smallpox. He argued that the method was not absolutely safe (as indeed it was not).[8] D'Alembert was, in fact, the sort of scientist constitutionally and temperamentally unable to appreciate what can be achieved by the application of probability theory. In spite of the previous work of Pascal, Huyghens, and Jacques Bernoulli, D'Alembert refused to acknowledge that the calculation of probabilities was really a legitimate branch of mathematics.[9] The contingent, the proximate, and the striking of averages made him very uneasy. In mathematics as in philosophy, he wanted to be absolutely certain, failing which he wanted to be absolutely sceptical. This attitude fully qualified him to be the father, or perhaps (considering Auguste Comte) the grandfather, of French positivism.[10] But by the same token it made it difficult for him to acknowledge the scientific character of methods incorporating probability or indeterminacy.

Diderot's reasons for writing a critique of D'Alembert's memoir on inoculation were mixed, an example of private pique serving the public weal, a phenomenon that is always of interest to biographers and of delight to cynics. In the first place, Diderot resented D'Alembert's desertion of the *Encyclopédie,* and still felt distrustful of him.[11] This disaffection showed itself in various ways. Thus, when D'Alembert read to the French Academy a discourse on poetry, Diderot wrote scornfully to Sophie,

This man doesn't know a word of the language of Homer; and even if he did, the heart of a young Arcadian does not beat there. Let him keep to his equations, then; that is his destiny.[12]

As for the memoir on inoculation, Diderot thought that D'Alembert had been guilty of egregiously bad manners:

You know that La Condamine is the apostle of inoculation in France. Well! at the public re-opening of the Académie des Sciences, D'Alembert, with no regard for what is due a colleague, has just read a memoir that every fool takes to be written against inoculation. . . .[13]

The mid-eighteenth-century debate in France over inoculation was contentious and intense. Diderot was an enthusiast for the cause of inoculation, and the *Encyclopédie,* in one of the volumes published in 1765-6, contained a lengthy article on that subject contributed by Europe's most famous practitioner of the new technique, Dr. Théodore Tronchin.[14] No doubt Diderot would have had himself and his family inoculated had it been necessary, but the fact was that they had all had smallpox.[15] D'Alembert was not really opposed to inoculation but, by increasing each individual's fears of the risks of immunization, he was jeopardizing, in Diderot's opinion, the best interests of society as a whole. 'M. d'Alembert says that public interest has been too much confused with private interest. *Maybe so, but he who teaches men to separate these two interests is a good mathematician, all right, but a very bad citizen.'* [16]

It was characteristic of Diderot to talk of citizenship, a word that the eighteenth century was coming to find very stimulating and exciting, and to take the high ground of a utilitarian point of view that accepts as its criterion the greatest good of the greatest number.

Is it believable [he asked, in concluding his critique] that this tissue of subtleties would be listened to patiently in Constantinople, in London, or Peking? Is there in those three great countries one single woman of the people who would not laugh at the efforts made by a mathematician to entangle himself in such spider webs? [17]

Diderot's continuing interest in mathematics (and in Newtonianism) is demonstrated by his authorship of a paper published in April 1761 in the *Mémoires de Trévoux*. This paper could not have been written before 1749 nor probably after 1758. Certainly it was not published under his name, and it may have been communicated to the Jesuit editors by a friend of Diderot without his permission and without the editors' being aware of who was the author.[18] Under the lengthy title of 'Reflections upon a Difficulty Advanced against the Way in which the Newtonians Explain the Cohesion of Bodies and Other Phenomena pertaining thereto,' Diderot, with his usual flair for lighting upon significant topics, was here addressing himself to a very important unsolved problem in Newtonian theory: was the law of attraction, which had been empirically verified in respect to celestial bodies, also valid with respect to terrestrial objects? Or were the equations for objects on earth something more than the inverse square of the distance — perhaps the inverse cube or even a higher power? Diderot, coming to Newton's defense, argued that the Newtonian theory of the inverse square of the distance held good for all types of phenomena. He stated his argument, which was based on logic and geometry rather than experimentation, quite modestly and diffidently. (It was not until 1798 that Cavendish verified experimentally that the Newtonian law of attraction holds true for terrestrial bodies as well as for celestial ones.) One of Diderot's remarks, confirmed by history, shows him struggling to free himself from Cartesian over-simplification. 'In vain,' he wrote, 'have some *philosophes* extolled the simplicity of the laws of nature, it being certain that several of these laws undergo considerable variations and modifications.'[19]

* * * * * *

Diderot had written airily in 1759 that the amicable disposition of their father's estate had not taken the three heirs 'a half of a quarter of an hour.' But during the next year there were now and again signs of family strain about money matters. Diderot was quick to suppose that the fault lay with his brother the priest rather than with his sister. 'Could this cursed saint have perverted her? Woe to the family that has a saint in it.' 'The holy priest has not yet done all the damage than can be, but I see that he has a good start.' Diderot went on to grumble about 'people who don't deserve a brother like me.' Perhaps he was irritated also by the fact that his sibling had recently been made Promoter General for the diocese of Langres, a conspicuous post partly judicial, partly administrative.[20] At all events, his exasperating brother had the unfortunate effect upon Diderot of bringing out his own self-righteousness like a rash and, like a rash, it was disfiguring.

By early 1760 Diderot had probably written the article *'Intolérance'* intended for the *Encyclopédie*. Late in 1760 he took this very rhetorical piece of fireworks about religious bigotry, eliminated a few of the introductory sentences, preserved everything else practically verbatim, and gratuitously addressed it as a personal letter to his brother, dated 29 December 1760. 'Here, dear brother, are some ideas I have gathered, and which I send to you as a gift of the season.'[21] Diderot was sufficiently pleased with this letter to let Grimm use it, for it appears in the Stockholm manuscript of the *Correspondance littéraire* for 1 January 1761, with the explicit assertion, which seems surprisingly personal, that 'This letter is addressed to the Abbé Diderot, canon of the cathedral church at Langres.'[22]

The Stockholm manuscript of the *Correspondance littéraire*, which until recently has been comparatively unknown and unconsulted, is the source for information regarding various short pieces associated with Diderot at this time of his life. Thus the number for 1 June 1762 contains a love poem by Diderot, 'Ils ont passé comme un moment,' intricately rhymed and neatly turned, reminiscent in its skillful play, of his earlier 'Chanson dans le goût de la romance.'[23] But the Stockholm manuscript giveth and the Stockholm manuscript taketh away. Notations in a hand different from that of the copyist state that three pieces that have customarily been attributed to Diderot, *Qu'en pensez-vous?*, *La Marquise de Claye et Saint-Alban,* and *Cinqmars et Deville,* were written 'by Madame***,' presumably Mme d'Epinay. And a fourth, *Mon Père et moi,* is by implication hers too.[24] If these must be expunged from the Diderot canon, Diderot admirers will be sorriest to lose *Cinqmars et Derville.* Though it does not have quite the bravura and zestfulness of Diderot's usual style, it is nevertheless a lively and realistic dialogue, and most suggestive of Diderot in the ideas it pursues and the questions it raises, in this case the nature and psychology of laughter.

Diderot may have been hard pressed for money in the early 1760's, perhaps another of the causes for his depressions and sense of frustration. Already in November of 1760 he was trying to sell his library. And in the *Eloge de Richardson* he speaks of the possibility of having to sell his books because 'of the mediocrity of my fortune.'[25] The root of all this stringency was no doubt the difficulty the publishers of the *Encyclopédie* were encountering in meeting their payroll. Although no money at all was coming in, the large number of printers and other crafstmen engaged in the surreptitious printing of the remaining volumes had to be paid. Even the impending publication of the first volume of the engravings would bring in no cash, since the volume was to go to subscribers in return for money already paid. Eventually, when the publishers collected for the last ten volumes of letterpress in 1765-6, the money poured in, but the years between 1759 and 1765 must have been stark.[26] We see evidence of this in the fact that on 2 October 1761 the publishers borrowed 12,000 livres from the Chevalier de Jaucourt.[27] Further, on 8 August 1761 they funded a debt of 30,000 livres that they already owed Diderot by agreeing to pay him five per cent of this sum as an annuity.[28]

The cares and vexations of his busy life were increased by Grimm's making Diderot feel that he must hasten to finish the *Salon de 1761*. Usually, Diderot accepted Grimm's ruthless exploitation of him as though he rather enjoyed it, but in 1761 he complained of Grimm's having sent him 'a tyrannical note.'[29] Moreover, Diderot continued to have trouble with his wife. 'Since the latest domestic storm we eat separately. I am served in my study. . . . I perceive, however, that all the consequences of this sort of divorce are being felt, and that there is great embarrassment as to how to get around them without being humiliated. The exhaustion of the exchequer, which is not far off, will put everything to rights.' Reconciliation did come about, and Diderot put himself on his best behavior, even making a special trip from Grandval to the Rue Taranne because he discovered that his wife had planned a birthday dinner for him and that little Angélique, aged eight, had prepared a speech for the occasion. The speech was a great success, made more piquant by her difficulty in pronouncing some of the words because she had lost two baby teeth. But the disdainful way in which Diderot wrote to Sophie of Mme Diderot's friends present at the dinner, and of how he turned on his charm, is not pleasant.[30]

Just at this time a young Alsatian, Ludwig Heinrich von Nicolay, bent upon lionizing, called on Diderot one morning under the false pretense of having an introduction to him. 'A thickset man in his dressing gown' answered the bell: it was Diderot himself. Never being one to stand on ceremony he swept Nicolay into his study and talked for an hour, almost entirely in monologue.[31] Later Nicolay introduced his friend, La Fermière. Diderot was delighted with his 'two little Germans,' as he called them. When presently they left Paris, he wrote them a note that shows something of the pressures under which he lived: 'Such is my unfortunate position that it does not leave me the leisure to be sick. Well or ill, I must be on the go. Therefore I shall be at Le Breton's all day long . . . . if your affairs allow you to come there to say good-bye, you will give me great pleasure.'[32] Meanwhile, Nicolay and La Fermière had entertained Diderot at their inn. Diderot, who was used to eating well, remembered of the occasion that 'the dinner was detestable; but that didn't prevent it from being gay.' Nicolay remembered the occasion too. In his memoirs, written as much as forty years later, he recalled the Diderot of that dinner party as 'wishing as always to show himself to be interesting and sublime.' [33]

Through his two little Germans Diderot came to know Lessing's *Miss Sara Sampson*. Grimm had been praising the tragedy, and now Nicolay and La Fermière translated it for Diderot 'in two or three days.' [34] Not long after this time, Diderot was considering publishing a volume of plays: his own translation of *The Gamester, Miss Sara Sampson* (presumably, though not certainly, the Nicolay-La Fermière version), a translation of Lillo's *The London Merchant,* 'and other pieces that I am arranging and which I shall publish with comments that will be worth the trouble of reading.' [35] The volume never appeared, but a draft of Diderot's intended preface has come down to us. It contains some striking and original thoughts, for in it Diderot traced the process by which old art forms become too confining and new art forms come to be created. Especially, of course, he was thinking of the *drame,* and perhaps also of himself: 'Finally there comes some man of genius who understands that there is no other way than to burst the narrow limits that habit and pusillanimity have imposed on art. . . . Why should not manners as represented on the stage more nearly resemble manners in private life?' [36]

It is likely, though not absolutely certain, that early in 1762 Diderot made the personal acquaintanceship of Laurence Sterne.[37] In April Sterne wrote to Garrick that he found *Le Fils naturel* too wordy, sentimental, and didactic, a common enough opinion.[38] In May Sterne noncommittally forwarded a translation of the work to his London bookseller, whom he also asked to send 'for Mon^r Diderot . . . the 6 Vols. of Shandy — NB. These place to my Acc^t for they are for a present to him — ' [39] Here we can witness the birth of an event in the history of comparative literature: the influence of *Tristram Shandy* upon *Jacques le fataliste* is obvious, even though subtle and suffused.

A book published in 1761 was the occasion for a ringing definition by the *philosophes* of what they meant by philosophy. This definition is thought to have been written by Diderot, and it allows us to see his social philosophy and his political philosophy in conjunction. His was a pragmatic philosophy which measured things in terms of their usefulness, and which yearned for social improvement, for ever widening enlightenment, and for a future that would prove itself better than the past. His philosophy was concerned as much with society as it was with epistemology or ontology. It is one of the paradoxes of the history of philosophy that philosophers treat this point of view so respectfully when dealing with Jeremy Bentham and especially John Stuart Mill, and yet treat it so negligently, not to say scornfully, when they put inverted commas around the *philosophes* of the eighteenth century.

The occasion for this striking pronouncement was the posthumous publication of a book by Nicolas-Antoine Boulanger (1722-59), one of the minor but by no means unimportant authors of the Age of Enlightenment. Boulanger, who by profession had been a road engineer employed by the government, was by avocation a scholar interested in mythology and in what has come to be called 'prehistory.' [40] Diderot published anonymously an admirable biographical sketch of Boulanger (1766), recalling that 'he read and studied wherever he was: I myself have encountered him on the open roads with a rabbinical author in his hand.' [41] The Boulanger book, published in 1761, was entitled *Recherches sur l'origine du despotisme oriental.* This was a most significant title. Following upon Montesquieu's writings, 'despotism' was becoming in the minds of the French a very nasty word. And a common one, too, as is revealed by Malesherbes' remark to Turgot in 1759 that despotism 'is the word *à la mode.*' [42] The fact that the concept of despotism was being bandied about, always with pejorative connotations, shows how political the thinking of Frenchmen was becoming, much more so than perhaps they realized.[43] But not more than Diderot and his circle knew. The open 'Letter of the author to M.***' that served as preface to Boulanger's work was a kind of political manifesto, specifically referring to itself as a 'Plan of Political Philosophy.' Nowhere can one find a more striking or more confident expression of the progress of enlightenment than in this pronouncement:

But I have much more confidence [than in ministers, good, bad, or indifferent] in the general state of mind, which is rising more and more in the scale of reason and humanity; I have much more confidence in the progress of knowledge, that immense river which grows larger every day and which no power (unless it be another Flood) can any longer presume to stop.

The 'Plan of Political Philosophy' coolly proposed that the state should disestablish the church. What is more, the government should ally itself with the *philosophes* and give them power. This modest proposal was made in the name of Reason, Philosophy, and Enlightenment, and the purpose of it all was to save society from anarchy:

Only Philosophy and Reason can today restore the police power to its original principles, and release it from the slavery into which it is bound. How strange it is to see the police power persecuting what will one day be its savior. . . . It is this Reason which therefore should be worshipped almost as a divinity, in place of enfeebling and humiliating it.

This daring letter, which in the name of reason and enlightenment blandly called for a revolution in the power structure of the state, is said to have been written by Diderot. In fact, we have Voltaire's word for it that it was, though much of the letter seems to betray the leaden style of D'Holbach rather than the mercurial one of Diderot. Certainly the letter does contain one of Diderot's favorite ideas: a healthy society should have its laws and its religious obligations in harmony with the law of nature and not in opposition to it. This idea is here expressed in conjunction with an attack upon Christianity,

. . . a religion both insufficient and false, that has founded the existence of natural duties upon a lie, in order to have the right to govern men by authority and not according to nature.[44]

The 'police power' was not a little scandalized by the brashness of the *Despotisme oriental*. Inspector d'Hémery reported to his superiors about the work, and Diderot later wrote that 'the police put all its instrumentalities to work, all its circumspection, all its authority, in order to stifle the *Despotisme oriental* of the late Boulanger. . . .'[45] In July of 1762 Diderot wrote that 'Boulanger's book is very rare here,' and inquired whether the copy the Vollands were reading included the dedicatory epistle.[46] The action of the police evidently convinced someone that the time was not ripe for a 'Plan of Political Philosophy,' for Voltaire reported to Damilaville that the Swiss publishers would take care to omit the dedicatory letter in the next edition.[47]

That the *philosophes* had the daring to publish the book at all is significant. As Franco Venturi has remarked, 'Boulanger's book served as an affirmation of the vitality of the *philosophes* after the greatest and latest of the crises of the *Encyclopédie*.'[48] Moreover, it was obviously a matter of choice on the part of Boulanger's friends when they would attempt to publish his posthumous work, so that the timing of its publication is almost certainly quite significant also. They were sounding out the political terrain, were becoming more consciously political in their calculations.

Boulanger's line of proof, arguing from the evidence of facts in early civilizations, brought to the attention of the Diderot-D'Holbach wing of the *philosophes,* more than they had encountered it before, the dimension of history. About this time, and perhaps as a result of the influence of Boulanger, we can see Diderot commencing to enlarge his categories of acceptable evidence by recognizing the validity of arguing from history. This constitutes a stage in the slow reaction of French thinkers of the Enlightenment against the intellectual authority of Descartes, whose thinking had been analytical enough, in all conscience, but scornful of history as a source of truth. In France the men of the Enlightenment were held more in thrall by Cartesian modes of thought than they realized. Here we see Diderot, in the van as usual, beginning to gain respect for the raw fact, the fundamental datum. As he wrote in 1766, while discussing Boulanger,

He used to say that if, with us, philosophy has encountered so many obstacles, it was because one had begun where one should have ended, by abstract maxims, by general reasonings, by subtle reflections which repelled people by their strangeness and audacity, and which would have been accepted without difficulty had they been preceded by the history of the facts.[49]

The dedicatory epistle not only expressed an invigorating faith in progress, it also implied a criticism of political conditions as they then existed in France. For this reason Voltaire disliked the whole book; it did not sufficiently respect the throne, he said.[50] The book was published at a time that was not one of the most lustrous in the annals of the French monarchy. The Seven Years' War was still in progress, and the strategy and generalship of the French armies were being disastrously hampered by court intrigues. 'I tremble and I am furious to be with so many cowards who are my superiors in rank and name,' wrote a brave officer while on campaign with the French army in Germany. His was the mettle of which the Revolutionary and Napoleonic armies were later made. And the *Despotisme oriental* was being published just at the time when 'The certainty of the fall of Pondicherry causes the greatest desolation.'[51] The parlous condition of French political affairs was not, it should be remembered, just a figment of lively *philosophe* imagination. In this very year an educated and well-informed Swiss wrote to a friend about the growth of agricultural societies in France and added the following observation:

To see such zeal in a country exhausted by war, suffering from bad administration, menaced by despotism, and left with only despair or a desperate courage to try and break its chains! It seems that they have chosen the only way open to them. Where other countries would revolt against such bad and despotic government, the French never cease to give good advice to their king — though with care and circumspection — and to concern themselves with reforms instead of complaining.[52]

The Government having been invited to co-operate with Philosophy and the *philosophes,* it remained to be seen whether it would do so. It became quite evident, as the months went by, that this was an invitation that was being tacitly declined. It may be that the Paris *philosophes* felt severely rebuffed and alienated as a result. Diderot's frustration may be gauged by a remark that he embedded in a solid article in the *Encyclopédie* about Leibniz: 'In Germany it is not supposed that a philosopher is incapable of public affairs.' [53]

Meanwhile, Diderot continued with the editing of the text of the last volumes of letterpress of the *Encyclopédie.* 'This terrible revision is finished [he wrote on 12 September 1761]. I put in twenty-five days in succession on it, at ten hours a day. My corsairs have all their manuscripts under their own eyes. It is an enormous mass that frightens them. They themselves overpraise my work. . . .' [54] He was also occupied with the engravings, the first volume of them being announced as available to the subscribers in January 1762. [55] 'Immured in a poorly lighted room,' he reported, 'I am wearing out my eyes over engravings bristling with symbols and references,' and a year later he spoke of having to keep on the job in order 'to exhort my printers and my engravers to their task.' [56] Three volumes (out of an eventual eleven), comprising a total of 703 engravings, were available to the public prior to the publication in 1765–6 of the main part of the *Encyclopédie.* [57] How exhausting Diderot thought this work is revealed by his thanks to a learned colleague, France's greatest orientalist of the day, for his explanations of the plates on Ancient Alphabets: '. . . he has even supervised the engraving of the plates; and those who have any idea of this toil will know how laborious it is.' [58] The very fact that the volumes of plates could enlist the services of a man like this, Michel Le Roux Deshauterayes (1724–95), who held the chair of Arabic in the Collège de France, goes far toward explaining why the volumes of plates had a warm public reception. They were vivid and authoritative, 'a monument precious to posterity,' as Grimm rather smugly pointed out. [59] Comparing these volumes of plates with the rival publication of the Académie des Sciences, an authority declares that the arrangement and explication of the plates supervised by Diderot are more logical, easier to follow, and technically superior to the other. [60]

As the *Encyclopédie* slowly came closer to its completion, three complicated public events, set in motion in 1761 and 1762 but taking years to unfold, greatly affected the complexion of political life in Europe and, in doing so, also affected Diderot and his circle of friends. One was the death on 13 October 1761 — was it suicide or was it murder? — of young Marc-

Antoine Calas of Toulouse. Another was the accession to the Russian throne of Peter III and then of Catherine II. The third was the lawsuit that ended eventually in the expulsion from France of the Jesuits, those stubborn enemies of the *Encyclopédie*. Each of these events had a close causal connection with the Seven Years' War, and serves to remind us how powerfully, even though indirectly, the life of the pacific and unmartial Diderot was nevertheless affected by the over-arching events of his time.

The Calas case, with which Voltaire's name is eternally and gloriously linked, was the most notorious law case in France in the eighteenth century, and ended up by permanently shaking faith in the justice and validity of French criminal law. For the trial of Calas had been carried out with a due regard for all the forms; and yet a monstrous miscarriage of justice had ensued. The upshot of the Calas case made it almost impossible for anyone, even conservatives who wanted to avoid change, to defend the status quo. As D'Alembert wrote years later, 'Truly, our criminal law is the very masterpiece of atrocity and stupidity.'[61]

Marc-Antoine Calas, a member of a devout Huguenot family in Toulouse, was a moody young man who met a violent death, almost certainly by his own hand. The authorities persisted in the attempt to prove that he had been a secret convert to Catholicism, for which, they alleged, he was murdered by his fanatical Calvinist family. As a result the father, Jean Calas, a man sixty-four years old, was adjudged guilty and on 9 March 1762 was broken on the wheel and then strangled by the public executioner. Research has now revealed that the outburst of fear and hysteria that led to the tragedy of Calas was really caused by apprehension in Toulouse lest the Calvinists take advantage of the Seven Years' War in order to revolt.[62] In a similar time of national weakness, during the War of the Spanish Succession, the Calvinists in the Cévennes had rebelled, holding out stubbornly from 1702 to 1710. Thus, whenever foreign wars, especially unsuccessful ones, weakened France, suspicion of the intentions of the Calvinists increased. Since the Revocation of the Edict of Nantes in 1685 these persecuted people had been deprived of all civil rights — legal marriage, legal inheritance, even church attendance at Calvinist services — and throughout the eighteenth century some of their men were sent for long terms to the galleys in Toulon and some of their women languished for years in the Tour de Constance at Aigues-Mortes for nothing more subversive than attending a Calvinist service. In time of peace the authorities were not especially rigorous, but in time of war they became more vigilant and suspicious.[63]

Though local conditions might explain hysteria at Toulouse, public opinion generally, goaded by Voltaire, was appalled by the Calas case. Mme de Pompadour herself wrote on 27 August 1762, 'You are right, Monsieur le Duc, the affair of this unfortunate Calas makes one shudder.'[64] For three years Voltaire kept hammering on the minds and consciences of the French. The result was that on 9 March 1765, three years to the day after the execution of Calas, the sentence of the Parlement of Toulouse was formally rescinded and ordered stricken from the record. Students of French letters of the 1760's need to remember that throughout this period the Calas case was nagging at the conscience of every Frenchman.

Diderot's share in the public agitation was surprisingly and disappointingly mute, although he did, after the case was settled, participate in a benefit subscription for the Calas family.[65] Perhaps his reason for disinvolvement was a desire not to implicate the *Encyclopédie*.[66] Whatever his motives, it is a fact that he assumed no position of public leadership. Privately, however, sensitive as he ever was to what was going on, whether in science, philosophy, literature, art, or politics, he enthusiastically appreciated Voltaire's interposition. 'Oh! my friend, what a fine employment of genius. This man must have soul, sensitivity, that injustice revolts him and that he feels the attractiveness of virtue. For what are the Calas to him? what can interest him in them? what reason has he for interrupting the work that he loves in order to occupy himself with their defense? If there were a Christ, I assure you that De Voltaire would be saved.'[67] A few weeks after this Diderot described the defense of Calas as he imagined 'the eloquence of Demosthenes and of Cicero would have taken hold of it,' a fact that suggests that he was identifying himself with the great masters of ancient oratory.[68] Diderot was often critical of Voltaire; but he was fairminded enough to put into *Le Neveu de Rameau* the remark that 'I know of certain deeds which I would give all I possess to have done. [Voltaire's] *Mahomet* is a sublime work, but I would rather have rehabilitated the Calas family.'[69]

A second series of events, beginning in 1762 and again intimately connected with the Seven Years' War, eventually concerned Diderot very closely, even though they took place a long way from the Rue Taranne. On 5 January 1762 the Czarina Elizabeth died, to be succeeded by her fatuous and poorly educated nephew, Peter III. Peter did not rule long, but still quite long enough to alienate the sympathies of many of his most powerful subjects and courtiers, so that his wife, who became Catherine II by the *coup d'état* of 6 July 1762, had little trouble in toppling him off the throne, thus exemplifying an eighteenth-century witticism to the effect that the throne of Russia was neither hereditary nor elective, it was occupative.

Catherine II was a sensible ruler, though none too squeamish a one. Contemporaries thought that they saw evidence of this callousness in the speedy and convenient demise of her husband. The dethroned Peter III, who was held in captivity following the *coup d'état,* died suddenly of what Catherine II's manifesto of 18 July 1762 (which incidentally contained no expression of regret) declared to be 'hemorrhoids and a colic.' What the eighteenth century really thought about that is well illustrated by D'Alembert's joking explanation to Voltaire as to why he had refused Catherine's invitation to be private tutor to the little Grand Duke Paul:

But I am too much subject to having hemorrhoids, they are too dangerous in that country, and I want to have pain in my backside with complete security.[70]

Catherine II's practicality was shown by the forthright way in which she sought to recruit influential friends. So far as European opinion was concerned, she was badly in need of good public relations. The influential friends whom she tried to win were, for the most part, the *philosophes.* Very likely Catherine made overtures to these famous men — Voltaire, D'Alembert, Diderot — not only because she knew that they had the ear of Europe but also because she was trading upon the fact that they were out of favor with the Establishment in their own country. They might be susceptible to the appreciation accorded them by foreign countries and denied them by their own.

Accordingly, Count Shuvalov, chamberlain to the Empress, was authorized to make Diderot a quite astonishing proposition. Dated 20 August 1762, only a few weeks following the *coup d'état,* it concerned the *Encyclopédie.* 'It is by her order . . . that I offer you all the assistance you deem necessary to hasten the printing . . . of the famous work. In the event that it meets obstacles elsewhere, it could be done at Riga or in some other city of this empire. If you need money to take care of the expenses, speak without hesitancy.'[71] On the same day Shuvalov described the proposal in a letter to Voltaire, who evidently sent the letter on to Diderot.[72] Diderot was perceptibly cool. He appears not to have replied directly to Shuvalov, and it is very interesting to observe that in his reply to Voltaire of 29 September 1762 he did not especially praise Catherine II. Apparently he felt, like D'Alembert, that Russia was a dangerous country. Besides, no one could yet tell whether Catherine had the strength and the skill to keep her throne, a point that Voltaire explicitly mentioned in his correspondence at this time.

No, my very dear and very illustrious brother [wrote Diderot to Voltaire], we shall not be going to Berlin nor to Petersburg to finish the *Encyclopédie;* and the reason is that at the moment I am speaking to you it is being printed here and I am reading the proofs. But hush!

. . . From the offers that are being made to us, I perceive that it is not known that the manuscript of the *Encyclopédie* does not belong to us, that it is the property of the publishers who acquired it at an exorbitant cost, and that we could not divert one page of it without being faithless.[73]

Thus ended the first attempt by Catherine II to capture the *philosophes.* Later they were to warm to her blandishments, especially as the passing years proved that she had staying power.

In November 1762 Diderot was working, among other things, on a small collection of aphorisms, not of transcendent importance, that has come to be known as the *Addition aux Pensées philosophiques.*[74] Since its publication in 1746, the original *Pensées philosophiques* had become a famous and influential book, in spite of (or perhaps because of) the pronouncement of the Parlement of Paris that it was 'scandalous and contrary to Religion and Morals.'[75] The *Addition* was much sharper in tone than the original *Pensées.* Where the *Pensées* had been an indirect defense of natural religion and had been deistic and sceptical, the *Addition* was savagely and specifically anti-Christian. It stopped short, however, of being overtly atheist. Naturally the *Addition* could not be published, although Diderot did allow it to be used in Grimm's *Correspondance littéraire.* In 1770 it was published anonymously in a collection of sceptical and anti-religious pieces. Three of the most cutting of the aphorisms run as follows:

Lost in an immense forest at night, I have only a little light to show me the way. Along comes a stranger who says to me: *Friend, blow out your candle the better to find your way.* This stranger is a theologian. (Pensée VIII).

The God of the Christians is a father who values his apples very much and his children very little. (Pensée XVI).

There is no good father who would want to resemble our Heavenly Father. (Pensée LI).[76]

Diderot's writing these aphorisms came about rather adventitiously — and very characteristically. To know Diderot well is to realize that he was a very responsive person — responsive to people, to situations, to ideas. It is this quality of responsiveness that makes the dialogue his most natural and most effective art form. He responded too, of course, to the books that he read, and it was precisely this that brought into being the *Addition aux*

Pensées philosophiques. 'This piece is not by me,' wrote Grimm in the Stockholm copy of the *Correspondance littéraire,* 'but by a Philosopher who declares that he drew it from a very rare little work entitled: *Observations* [*Objections,* Grimm should have written] *diverses contre les écrits de différents théologiens.'* In the Saltykov-Shchedrin Library at Leningrad there is a little manuscript book with precisely this title. Comparative study shows that Diderot read this work 'pen in hand,' as he loved to say. The *Addition aux Pensées philosophiques,* then, are restatements, more lively and literary and incisive than the pedestrian original, of some of the thoughts of this unknown author.[77]

Yet, adventitious though the writing of these aphorisms may have been, the savagery of them reflects a mood that was chronic with Diderot in these years. Vexations and frustrations in connection with the *Encyclopédie,* domestic sorrows and torments, self-doubting about his genius and creative capacity, resentment at being reviled on the stage and persecuted by his enemies, bitterness because his own country inadequately appreciated his accomplishments and his services made these years the ones of 'Diderot pessimiste.'[78]

Another savage 'Pensée philosophique,' perhaps written about this time, illustrates Diderot's feeling that it was misanthropy that accounted for the origin of religion:

A man had been betrayed by his children, his wife and his friends; perfidious associates had ruined his fortune and reduced him to penury. Inspired by a profound hatred and contempt for the human race, he left society and took refuge in a cave. There, . . . casting about how he could discover some revenge that would match his resentment, he said, '. . . Ah! would it were possible to imagine how to infatuate men with some great chimerical notion to which they would attach more importance than to their own lives and regarding which they could never come to any common agreement . . . ,' and suddenly he burst forth from his cave, shouting 'God! God!' . . . [Thus] the fatal wish of the misanthrope came to pass.[79]

Diderot's mood is revealed by a conversation reported by Grimm in August 1762. 'I was present the other day at the conversation of a wise man.' Destiny had granted him, wrote Grimm, 'the greatest of all gifts, an unalterable serenity of mind with a great passion for works of genius and for the north wind' — a description of Diderot which one authority on Diderot thinks is the best that has ever come to his attention,[80] The conversation was a mournful one, the men speaking with horror of what had happened to Calas and deploring the persecution of Rousseau. (Only a few weeks before, Jean-Jacques had fled from France to avoid arrest by the Parlement of Paris because of what he had written in 'The Confession of Faith of a Savoyard Vicar,' the essay on faith and morals that is embedded in his great work on education, *Emile*). Diderot's thoughts that day were of Socrates, and whether philosophers, just because of their very regard for mankind, must always suffer from intolerance, must always drink the hemlock.

Diderot identified himself with Socrates to a startling degree. References to Socrates are numerous in his writings, yet perhaps the surest proof of this identification is the fact that Diderot wore an intaglio ring bearing the portrait of Socrates, and used the ring as a seal to his letters. It was a symbol of Diderot's values, a trademark of his secret self. The flavor of this self-identification is strong in what Grimm quotes his 'wise man' as saying in 1762:

Socrates at the moment of his death was looked upon at Athens as we are looked upon at Paris. His morals were decried, his life calumniated, he was at the very least a turbulent and dangerous spirit who dared to speak freely of the gods. . . . My friends, may we resemble Socrates in all things, just as his reputation resembled ours at the moment of his execution.

And then Diderot sounded once again the appeal to posterity:

It is therefore to the justice of the centuries that the sage of Athens had to commit his memory and the apology of his life. Posterity has avenged Socrates oppressed.[81]

The third great public event that affected Diderot's life during these years in the 1760's, the disaster that overtook the Jesuits, came with dramatic unexpectedness. As Diderot wrote on 12 August 1762, 'Who would have guessed this event, a year and a half ago?'[82] Their troubles began when one of their number, Father La Valette, head of the order in Martinique, went bankrupt because of the British blockade. Exactly what the regulations and constitutions of the Society of Jesus were had always been a closely guarded secret, and there was nothing that the Parlement of Paris, always Jansenist in sympathies and always suspicious of the Jesuits, wanted to know more. Now, in the lawsuits that followed the bankruptcy, the Jesuits of their own free will submitted their constitutions as evidence to prove their nonliability, an action the shortsightedness of which brings to mind the classic observation that those whom the gods would destroy they first make mad. The Parlement fell upon these documents with the greatest delight. It soon became quite apparent, as had long been suspected, that the Jesuits took obligations of membership that made their loyalty to their French sovereign very precarious and unreliable. By judgment of 6 August 1761, the Parlement of Paris decreed that recruitment into the order should be suspended and the Jesuit schools should be closed.[83]

The Jesuits were then operating 111 secondary schools in France, and anything that shook them would also shake the structure of education in France. Perhaps this consideration governed the writing and publication in late 1762 of an anonymous essay entitled *De l'Education publique* with which it is now known Diderot had much to do. This work set forth in detail a curriculum for the primary and secondary years, with suggestions reaching into the universities and professional schools. It proposed what amounted to a truly national system of public education, for both boys and girls. The plan was practical enough to try to demonstrate how the innovation could be financed and staffed, and made the revolutionary declaration that 'the superintendence of schools belongs to the police power of the State.' [84]

At the time of its publication, *De l'Education publique* was persistently attributed to Diderot, and it was included in the unauthorized edition of his works that was published at Amsterdam in 1773.[85] Voltaire wrote of Diderot's being the editor of the essay, and even Grimm, though he evidently disliked the book, admitted that Diderot 'might have seen the manuscript and inserted a few phrases.' [86] But inasmuch as the book called for a good deal of religious instruction in the schools, it had seemed unlikely to most later authorities that Diderot could have had much of a hand in it. Then a letter of Diderot to Damilaville, first published in 1931, surprisingly put the matter beyond doubt:

I am very curious to know what will be thought of this work. People will recall that I worked on the manuscript, and that I reviewed the proofs. They will remember that I was invited to interest myself in this subject. They will read and they will find opinions so contrary to mine, mixed with details so strongly characteristic of me, that they won't know what to say.[87]

The style of *De l'Education publique* is not like Diderot's. It is slack rather than taut; it does not have the thrust, the eagerness, so characteristic of Diderot, nor his love of imagery and anecdote. Yet we must search the book for traces of him, since he has told us himself that he is there. Probably it is in the twenty pages of the preface that we should look hardest, and there we do find reflections of Diderot's concern for the public welfare. There, for example, it is declared that 'we need public education.' Diderot did indeed believe that education should be public, national, and secular, for such were his recommendations to Catherine II later on, in his *Plan d'une université pour le gouvernement de Russie*.[88] The preface of *De l'Education publique* also desires that 'The body be formed by a moderate diet and suitable exercise. . . . Men are too soft, because children are brought up too delicately. . . . Studies make education quite sedentary enough; they should be broken up by active recreations.' And the following remark is strongly characteristic of Diderot's most firmly held convictions:

The moral is inseparable from the physical; everything is linked in the sciences, just as everything is interconnected in the universe.[89]

It was some years, because of the rivalry of the Parlements and the Court, before the Society of Jesus was finally expelled from France. Diderot was anticipating a bit when he wrote in 1762, 'Here am I, delivered from a large number of powerful enemies.'[90] Still, it can be said that one of the reasons that the final volumes of the *Encyclopédie* were greeted with so little uproar when they appeared in 1765–6 is owing to the fact that the Jesuits were not around to draw attention to every suspected heresy and every alleged plagiarism.

CHAPTER 34

Diderot Sells His Library

SOPHIE VOLLAND was out of Paris for an unusually protracted period in 1762, with the result that between 14 July and 25 November Diderot wrote thirty-three letters to her that are still extant. Diderot missed her severely, a fortunate circumstance so far as posterity is concerned, for in his urge to communicate with her he has recorded vivid and indelible images of himself, of his life, and of his times. Sophie's mother, always distrustful of Diderot — 'I shall never be at my ease with Morphise, nor she with me'[1] — had taken her daughter to their country estate, and Diderot, moodily looking at the Seine in Paris, thought of Sophie, far upstream at her mother's house.

The long evenings . . . I now employ in reading, in taking the fresh air on the banks of the river, in seeing . . . the waters of the Marne flowing from you to me, and in asking them tidings of the white feet of her whom I love.[2]

A couple of family upsets contributed to protracting Sophie's stay in the country. One was a fire that burned many of the farm buildings. The news of this greatly concerned Diderot for Sophie's health. He also bestirred himself, with success, to arrange that Mme Volland be granted a tax reduction to compensate for the loss.[3] The other was the fraudulent bankruptcy of Pierre Vallet de Sallignac, the husband of Sophie's elder sister. Diderot's letters often allude to this event, with appropriate sympathy for the wife and the son and daughter, but with great disdain for the character of the husband.[4] The daughter, Mélanie, who was blind, was a very sensitive and perceptive girl. Her observations on her own blindness provided Diderot with valuable data which he used in his 'Additions à la Lettre sur les aveugles' that he wrote in 1782.[5] For the son, Vallet de Fayolle, Diderot exerted all the influence he could command to help the youth get a government position as a tax collector. Though failing in this, Diderot was successful in getting him a position at Cayenne, to which he proceeded in 1763.[6]

'. . . by writing to you I chat, as though I were standing beside you, my arm thrown over the back of your chair. . . .'[7] One can see the picture. It is like a drawing by Carmontelle. Added to this intimacy in Diderot's letters are his spontaneity, the piquancy of his expressions, the range of his perceptions, the variety of his moods. At one moment. he is describing the gaiety of an impromptu picnic at a farmer's house:

We had brought six bottles of wine, two of them champagne. They added two of their own. By the end of the meal we were all rather high. The farmer had become gallant and was making propositions to his wife. The good wife could see only one drawback, that they had no one in mind to be godfather and godmother. Mme Duclos and I removed this difficulty, and we were assured, point of honor, that we would not have crossed the ferry before we would have a godchild on the way.[8]

But contrasting with this ribaldry are passages of a very somber kind, reflecting the pessimism of these particular years in Diderot's career. What is life, he asks himself:

To be born in the state of imbecility and to the accompaniment of pains and cries; to be the plaything of ignorance, error, needs, sicknesses, malice, and passions; to return, step by step, to imbecility; to live, from the lisping of infancy to the mumbling of old age, among rascals and charlatans of all kinds; to sink away between one man who takes your pulse and another who troubles your head; to know not whence one comes, why one is here, where one is going, that is what is called the most important gift of our parents and of nature, our life.[9]

And when Sophie asks him, Why is it that the fuller life is, the less one is attached to it; his answer, for one who had so much vitality, is rather startling:

If that is true, it is because a busy life is usually an innocent one; because one thinks less of death and fears it less; because, without noticing it, one resigns oneself to the common lot of the beings one sees ceaselessly dying and being born around one; because, after having taken care for a certain number of years of the tasks that nature assigns year after year, one gets detached, one gets weary; energy fails, one gets weaker, one desires the end of life as, after having worked hard, one desires the end of the day . . . because life for certain persons is only a long fatiguing day, and death only a long sleep, and the coffin only a bed of rest, and the earth only a pillow upon which it is sweet to rest one's head at last without having to raise it again. I confess to you that death considered from this point of view and after the lengthy disappointments I have suffered, could not be more welcome. I want to accustom myself more and more to looking at it that way.[10]

In the course of 1762 Diderot was appalled to discover that he had been harboring a police spy, and that for four years! 'Isn't it the luckiest sort of chance that I have not written anything risky for a very long time? . . . When I think that he was on the point of working for Grimm as secretary for all his foreign correspondence, I shudder with fright.' The police had either planted this spy, a man named Glénat, or had suborned him after Diderot began to give him work copying manuscripts. Not only had Diderot employed Glénat and given him extra food and money, he had also solicited his friends to give Glénat work. One day Diderot had lent Glénat to one of Damilaville's friends to copy a manuscript. Diderot knew nothing about the manuscript, who its author was or what it was about. It was on 'religion and government,' as he later found out, and within a week it turned up on the desk of the Lieutenant-General of Police, Sartine. Glénat, when Diderot taxed him with this, more than half admitted it, and Diderot turned his back on him with contempt.

This incident greatly upset Diderot. For one thing, he was compassionate by nature and it deeply disturbed him to think that in the future he would have to appear hardhearted. 'A thing has just happened which is going to teach me a circumspection that will be disadvantageous to an infinitude of poor fellows of all kinds who stream here, whom I used to receive, and who are going to find my door closed.' Another dismaying implication of the incident was that Sartine, who had been Lieutenant-General of Police since 1 December 1759 and who was an old school friend of Diderot, had let this situation go on without warning him.[11] Diderot called on Sartine, ostensibly on other business, was received 'very cordially,' and then led the conversation around to Glénat. 'You have need of such people. You hire them. You pay for their services; but it is impossible that they are not as dirt in your eyes.'

'Sartine began to laugh,' wrote Diderot. 'At this point we broke off, and I came away thinking to myself that it was a very odious thing to abuse the benevolence of a man in order to insinuate a spy into his intimacy.'[12] It will be noticed that Sartine just laughed: he did not undertake not to do the same thing again.

The vein of compassion was very strong in Diderot. He goes on an outing to Marly and admires the palace and the magnificent gardens. But 'what would Henri IV have thought to find round about these immense and magnificent palaces, to find, I say, the peasants without a roof, without bread, and on the straw?' [13] He writes of a friend whose wife is pregnant, 'Before his marriage he used to detest pregnant women. That is a very unnatural feeling! What do you say? As for me, this condition always touches me. A pregnant woman concerns me. I do not even observe pregnant women of the common people [*du peuple*] without a tender commiseration' — a statement which establishes Diderot's empathy and his class consciousness at one and the same time.[14]

Grimm thought that Diderot's compassion was often quixotic. Sometimes, though rarely, Diderot agreed. 'Grimm must be right,' he admitted to Sophie at this juncture, 'time is not a thing of which we may dispose at our whim. We owe it first of all to our friends, our relatives, our obligations, so that there must be some vicious principle at work in prodigally spending time upon people who have no claim upon it.' [15] Here he was acknowledging what would now be called a 'compulsion.' Sometimes the good-natured Diderot was imposed upon so grossly that even he became indignant. His daughter tells of a man named Rivière, fair-seeming and poverty-stricken, to whom Diderot lent money and in whose behalf he solicited many favors. When Rivière had gotten all that he wanted out of Diderot, he said to him one day, 'Monsieur Diderot, do you know natural history? Do you know about the ant lion? It is a very industrious little insect; it digs a hole, . . . covers it over with a fine light sand, catches incautious insects in it, takes them, sucks them dry, and then says to them, "Monsieur Diderot, I have the honor of wishing you good-day." ' [16] Although his daughter says that Diderot laughed heartily over this adventure, nevertheless he did not want to re-experience it. In the little dialogue entitled *Lui et Moi,* written about this time, Diderot records the horror he felt when one day he encountered Rivière, as debonair, poverty-stricken, and impudent as ever.[17]

Characteristic of Diderot's good nature is the lengthy reply, precise and charming, he made to a stranger's request to distinguish between the words *'plaisir'* and *'allegresse'* (which in French has much the meaning of Milton's *L'Allegro*). Diderot's letter is a testimony to his skill in distinguishing among synonyms, as it is also to his willingness to let strangers use up his time.[18]

The dovecote of the *philosophes* was fluttered in 1762 by the approach of a cuckoo. It was a situation of drawing-room comedy, even including an anonymous letter. Mme d'Holbach had been coquettish well beyond the call of duty with several men, Grimm among them. Grimm's mistress,

Mme d'Epinay, was darkly suspicious, morose, furious. D'Holbach, always grumpy and saturnine, outdid himself. All was gloom and constraint. Diderot sat in the midst of this domestic confusion, appalled. To Grimm he said some very straight things about being too free with Mme d'Holbach. Diderot was apprehensive most of all lest the discord become public knowledge. And well it might have because of some indiscreet confidences Mme d'Epinay had shared with a Mme de Maux. 'If she begins to jabber, see what the ill-disposed people round about us and who spy on us will say . . . . what a crime they will make out of it against us, whom they rage against because they know that we are respectable people. Can't you hear them? "Well, now, these *philosophes,* is that the way they are?"' *Et coetera et coetera.'* [19]

Though he had spoken sharply to Grimm, Diderot still thought of him as 'my idol,' and when, in this same year, Grimm was threatened by the loss of his eyesight, Diderot was prepared to devote himself to his friend's needs: 'his cane and his dog are all ready' was the way Diderot put it.[20] Grimm's absence in Germany in the last weeks of 1762 necessitated Diderot's again providing some reviews of plays and books for the *Correspondance littéraire.* One of these books was by the chaplain of the royal Swedish church at Paris: 'I like this heretical almoner,' wrote Diderot, 'for he reads the *Timaeus* and the *Critias;* there is not one of our Catholic priests who knows what they are about.' Nevertheless, with his customary good sense and insistence upon rigorous intellectual method, Diderot thought the 'heretical almoner' had written a fanciful book: 'An excellent memorandum to read in order to learn to distrust the conjectures of the erudite.' [21]

The letters to Sophie repeatedly refer at this time to a case of conscience and to a private intellectual excitement. Each episode tellingly reveals aspects of his temperament and character. As for cases of conscience, Diderot loved to propound them, perhaps because of his early education by the Jesuits. The case in 1762 was this: an unattached and independent young woman desired to have a child, and, in the hope of its being a gifted one, had decided to ask a certain man, noted for his intelligence and talent, to be the father of it. It was not at all a question of love or passion, it was simply a question of eugenics. The man involved had other legal and emotional ties. Should he consent? Though Diderot said from the first that he was not the man, Sophie seems never to have been quite convinced that he was not. Numerous were the arguments that he set forth, all pro, none con; but Sophie, who called the woman 'bizarre,' evidently was unable to muster much interest in the case. At least, this was her tactic in dealing with it, and the subject finally fades out of the correspondence from inanition.[22]

The private intellectual excitement that Diderot came to feel in 1762 was a specific something that he often referred to in his letters but did not name outright, so that it bears a somewhat mysterious air. What it was, actually, was an attempt to solve the squaring of the circle! Through the years Diderot spent a good deal of time on this problem, to the dismay of his friends, especially because he became convinced that he had solved it and that it was one of the best things he had ever done.[23]

Another manifestation of Diderot's versatility was a 'Plan d'un opéra comique' written no later than 1763 and long unknown.[24] This libretto, with most of the dialogue but none of the lyrics worked out, is a very competent contribution to the genre of the popular theater. It is all about how Colette gets to marry her Colin in spite of the wishes of her guardian, who wants her for himself. The action takes place at a fair, and Diderot noted in his stage directions, with a characteristic regard for realism, that the scene would be like 'a fair in real life, such as the Saint-Germain fair' (which took place very close to the Rue Taranne). Critics are in agreement that the libretto is not likely to enhance Diderot's literary reputation very greatly. Nevertheless, as one of them says, 'It is a nothing, but a very agreeable nothing.'[25]

Diderot was much concerned in 1762 with problems of health, including his own. In November his attacks of colic and nausea returned, probably (he thought) because 'I have been bowed over my desk several days on end. . . . If I could find some logs to split, I would be all right.' Diderot thought, with Dr. Tronchin, that men of letters lead an unnatural life, and he clinched the argument with an eroticism, as was frequently his way: 'I would feel better had I bent over a woman part of the time I have spent bending over my books.'[26] Diderot was vomiting so alarmingly that he called in a famous Paris physician, François Thierry. Even in his extremity Diderot realized that the doctor was unconsciously comical, comical because he revealed his pedantry and betrayed that he was much more interested in the case than in the patient. 'You are a very happy man,' said the doctor delightedly, examining the basin into which Diderot had vomited. 'You have restored to us the *vitrified phlegm* of the Ancients, which we had lost!'[27]

The illness of Mme Diderot, who suffered from dysentery, turned out to be much more grave. At first Diderot supposed, as did the doctor, that she would not be dangerously ill. Accordingly Diderot was very aware of the peevishness and demandingness of the patient. 'In her bad temper she says things to her child that cannot be repeated and that annihilate me.'[28] But three weeks later Mme Diderot became silent and listless, convincing Diderot that she was really sick. 'The symptom that scares me more than anything else is her gentleness, her patience and silence, and, what is worse, a return of friendship and confidence towards me.'[29] After some six weeks she was out of danger. Meanwhile Diderot had worked hard helping to take care of her. With an unusual admission of guilt, he wrote to Sophie, 'The less one fulfills one's duties when one's wife is well, the more one should be attentive to her when she is sick.'[30] So sick had she been that it was thought that she would die, and Mme d'Epinay had offered to bring up little Angélique if this should occur.[31]

Angélique was all the dearer to her parents because of being their youngest and only surviving child. Diderot's letters are full of worries about her, for which he excuses himself by remarking that one is a father every day in the week.[32] Angélique's having been consecrated to the Virgin and Saint Francis by her mother and being always dressed in white gave the child a religious orientation which quite predictably led to friction between husband and wife. 'Angélique is reading fluently in the Old Testament,' her mother wrote when the child was only five.[33] Diderot repeatedly grumbled that his wife was ruining the child, and he greatly feared lest Angélique be sent, as her mother had been, to a convent.[34] 'She would be better off dead than abandoned to the mercy of such a mother,' he once wrote.[35] Yet he seems to have been powerless to interfere: in 1761 he wrote, '. . . her mother, who has taken her over, will never allow me to do anything.'[36] Conditions changed in 1762, what with Mme Diderot's illness, so that Diderot wrote on 19 September, '. . . I am going to busy myself a little with the education of my little girl. Her mother, who doesn't know what to do further, is permitting me at last to take a hand.' Thereafter Diderot frequently refers to his helping with the education of Angélique, references sometimes accompanied with his astonished recognition that his daughter was wilful and was 'stubbornness personified.'[37] No one seems to have thought of the anxieties and tensions that these years of discord developed in the child. 'Yesterday she was guilty of a slight indiscretion, though I cannot find it in me to take it ill. As we were talking together, she whispered to me, "Papa, why is it that Mama forbade me to remind you that tomorrow is her name-day?" That evening I gave her mother a bouquet.'[38]

Diderot greatly enjoyed Angélique's practicing on the harpsichord, and he predicted that she would become proficient, 'for she has the ear and fingers for it,' a prophecy which came to pass.[39] As Diderot looked into her future he began to worry about the size of the dowry he would be able to provide. For this reason he was glad to work as hard as he did on the *Encyclopédie:* 'My work is less displeasing to me because I am sustained by the hope of preparing my daughter's dowry.'[40] This solicitude probably fortified him in asking for a supplementary business arrangement with his publishers, to which they did indeed accede. Diderot found the settlement acceptable and just, but not generous.[41] This financial agreement probably convinced him that if he were to secure any substantial accretion to his daughter's dowry, it would not come from that source. It is in this year that we find him for a second time talking about selling his private library, which had been appraised by a Paris publisher as being worth 13,185 livres. The persons seeking to buy it thought it worth 3000 livres less, however, and consequently its sale remained dormant until it was finally revived, under very dramatic circumstances, in 1765.[42] Diderot also had hopes at this time of becoming a monthly contributor to the *Mercure de France.* This prospect, with a salary of 1500 livres a year, was held out to him by the historian, Abbé Raynal. But these negotiations, too, fell through, under circumstances not fully explained.[43]

Meanwhile, family financial affairs plagued Diderot, not so much because they affected his income, which they did very little, as because they further envenomed his relations with his brother. The cursed saint, as Diderot was fond of calling him, had decided to break up housekeeping with their sister and to renegotiate the settlement of their father's estate. All of this, which seemed to Diderot to be ungrateful to Denise, was done to the accompaniment of various allegations. These charges, which Diderot called calumnious and rendered him furious, asserted that the *philosophe* and his sister had received secret favors from their father while he was alive and from his estate after he was dead. This Diderot formally denied, in a document dated 8 January 1763.[44] The harmony of which Diderot boasted in 1759 had come to a lamentable end.

Denise Diderot, too, could be quick to assume that the *philosophe* brother was dishonest. In 1763 she seems to have taken for granted that Diderot was attempting to defraud a neighbor of hers who was having difficulty in getting delivery of some volumes of engravings of the *Encyclopédie.* Diderot explained to his sister what the difficulty was and then added: 'So, Seurette [and he wrote in the formal style, rather than in the familiar], try to moderate your vivacity, do not take sides mistakenly and at cross-purposes when you do not know what is involved. Nothing in my conduct and my way of thinking authorizes you to do so. If I had committed one vile and dishonest action in my life, perhaps the suspicion that I might commit a second would be allowable. But experience ought to have taught you that I never fail to do what is right.

'You always act towards me as though I were a stranger to whom you owe no mark of confidence or esteem.' [45]

New relationships brought relief from family tensions as Diderot's circle of acquaintances began to include more foreign visitors to Paris. When hostilities between the French and the English were brought to a close by the Treaty of Paris on 10 February 1763, a number of famous Britons came to France. Edward Gibbon, John Wilkes, David Garrick, and David Hume were among them.

Laurence Sterne was already there, for he had been allowed to cross the Channel in spite of the war because of his illness. In September Diderot wrote that he was gluttonously devouring 'the craziest, wisest, and gayest of all books. . . . This book that is so mad, so wise and so gay is the Rabelais of the English. It is entitled *La Vie, les Mémoires et les Opinions de Tristram Shandi.*' [46] Sterne was often at D'Holbach's: '— his house, is now, as yours was to me, my own,' he wrote to Garrick; and in letters in later years he sent 'respects' and 'compliments' to D'Holbach and Diderot.[47] The presumption is, then, that he and Diderot were personally acquainted. In May 1764 Sterne was the preacher at the first service ever held in the Anglican chapel at the British embassy: 'There was a concourse of all nations, and religions too.' [48] David Hume was among those present, and Diderot and D'Holbach are also said to have been there.[49]

Gibbon was in Paris midway between the time of his war service as a captain in the Hampshire Grenadiers and that memorable day when, 'as I sat musing amidst the ruins of the Capitol, while the barefooted fryars were singing Vespers in the Temple of Jupiter, the idea of writing the decline and fall of the City first started to my mind.' Gibbon was charmed with Paris. His reasons give us an appreciation of the intellectual climate in which Diderot lived every day: 'Indeed, Madam, we may say what we please of the frivolity of the French, but I do assure you that in a fortnight passed at Paris I have heard more conversation worth remembering, & seen more men of letters amongst the people of fashion, than I had done in two or three winters in London.' [50] Four days in the week Gibbon had a place at the hospitable tables of Mme Geoffrin, Mme du Bocage, Helvétius, and D'Holbach; among the men of letters whom he saw he wrote that 'd'Alembert and Diderot held the foremost rank, in merit, or, at least, in fame.' Gibbon listened 'to the oracles of d'Alembert and Diderot. . . . Yet I was often disgusted with the capricious tyranny of Madame Geoffrin, nor could I approve the intolerant zeal of the philosophers and Encyclopaedists the friends of d'Olbach and Helvetius: they laughed at the scepticism of Hume, preached the tenets of Atheism with the bigotry of dogmatists, and damned all believers with ridicule and contempt.' [51]

John Wilkes came to Paris in mid-March 1763, and was there off and on until the end of 1767. Wilkes had been a friend of D'Holbach when both were students at the University of Leyden, so that he naturally gravitated to what Diderot called 'the Synagogue of the Rue Royale.' The flamboyant and intemperate Wilkes, editor of the tempestuous *North Briton,* was regarded by the liberals of his day as a valiant fighter for the freedom of the press and, because of his being prosecuted for both seditious libel and obscenity, as a martyr to the cause of liberty. Diderot was especially fascinated by a tale of Wilkes's generosity, combined with sexual prowess, that occurred in Italy.[52] Years later Diderot, writing him jovial letters introducing French friends, addressed him as 'most honored Alderman' or 'Monsieur Gracchus' or 'Tribune of the People.' [53]

Garrick and his wife arrived in Paris in September 1763 and, after a brief trip to Italy, settled down at the luxurious Helvétius town house on the Rue Sainte-Anne, quite close to the D'Holbachs. Diderot called Garrick 'Roscius,' in allusion to the great Roman actor who was the friend of Cicero: 'Remember from time to time,' Diderot wrote him in 1767, 'the synagogue of the Rue Royale and the little sanctuary on the Rue Neuve des Petits Champs [where Mme d'Epinay lived]. There we often commemorate you, glass in hand, and drink to you in burgundy, in champagne, in malaga, in wines of every color and of every land.' [54]

David Hume, already famous as a philosopher and historian, came to Paris in October 1763 to act as Secretary of Embassy on the staff of Lord Hertford, the British ambassador. Within a few days Hume had met D'Holbach, and when, sometime thereafter, Hume dined for the first time at D'Holbach's, Diderot was one of the company.[55] By December Hume was writing back to England that among 'Those whose Persons & Conversation I like best are d'Alembert, Buffon, Marmontel, Diderot, Duclos, Helvetius; and old President Henaut.' [56] At their very first meeting Diderot is said to have told Hume that he would have taken him for a fat monk of the proverbially well-fed order of Cistercians.[57] This was the first but not the last time that Diderot, with an air of jocose intimacy, referred affectionately to the fact that 'le bon David' was well filled out. So Diderot writes of 'your round and smiling Bernardine appearance,' and again, 'If you ever return to these parts, I shall introduce you to Mme Diderot, who will add her thanks to mine and who will kiss you on both of your broad Bernardine cheeks.' [58]

While Diderot was making these agreeable friendships, he was also, at the request of his publishers, drawing up a memorandum on the book trade in France. The timing of this treatise was evidently determined by the fact that Sartine had just had his duties as Lieutenant-General of Police increased by those of Director of the Book Trade, thus replacing Malesherbes in October 1763. Presumably Le Breton, who at that time was the syndic of the corporation (or, as the Londoners say, of the 'livery') of booksellers in Paris, deemed the moment propitious for educating the new Director. Diderot, consequently, was entrusted with the congenial task of informing a minister of the Crown what his policy ought to be. With his usual zest, Diderot produced the *Lettre adressée à un magistrat sur le commerce de la librairie,* written probably between September and December of 1763.[59] The memorandum as presented to Sartine by the book publishers on 8 March 1764, however, was a considerably altered document. Partly, Diderot's style was too personal and too intimate for a sober memorandum; partly, his essay was much more critical of book publishers and much more aggressive in stating what should be the rights of authors than the Corporation of Booksellers felt suited their purpose. As the editor of the most recent edition of the *Lettre sur le commerce de la librairie* remarks, 'The book sellers had asked Diderot for a memorandum on the book trade and he gave them, willy-nilly, a memoir on the freedom of the press, which is an altogether different matter.' [60]

Diderot's purpose in the *Lettre sur le commerce de la librairie* was very serious, but his manner was, as usual, idiosyncratic and autobiographical. His arguments were couched in an *ad hominem,* very personal idiom, sometimes in the dialogue form of statement, objection, and counter-rejoinder. 'You desire, Monsieur, to know my ideas on a topic which appears to you to be important and is so.' Diderot promises to reply 'with the impartiality that you have a right to expect in a man of my character.' He recalls the joy and inspiration he felt the first time in his life he was paid for a manuscript. He refers to himself as a 'bibliomaniac.' And he loses himself in a typical digression and then suddenly extricates himself by saying, 'But I prefer to follow the history of the book seller's code and the institution of privileges than to give myself up to afflicting reflections upon the nature of man.' [61]

Nowhere has the case for what we now call copyright and freedom of the press been put more persuasively than it is by Diderot in this *Lettre sur le commerce de la librairie*. He himself, who was always opposed to legal monopolies, was aware that he might be thought to be inconsistent in seeking legal protection for the literary property of authors and publishers. 'It is not simply a question of the interests of a guild. Why, what difference does it make to me that there should be one guild more or less, to me who am one of the most zealous partisans of competition, taken in the widest possible sense? . . . [who] at all times has been convinced that the guilds are unjust and noxious and who would regard their complete and absolute abolition as a step toward a wiser government?' [62] Diderot was searching to express the now familiar distinction between copyright on the one hand and anti-trust action on the other. And he carries the debate to the high level upon which it should indeed rest, the level of the general interest, the interest of all of society, the commonweal. As he carries it to this high plane, Diderot's argument takes on many characteristics of the art of the orator which 'is already, in more than one respect, the direct and hot-blooded eloquence of the great orators of the Revolution.' [63]

Just at this time Diderot showed in another of his writings his awareness of the power of eloquence. It is a passage that reveals, too, how conscious of the great issues of politics he was coming to be. In the covering letter he wrote to Grimm accompanying the *Salon de 1763*, after commenting upon the excellence of the Ancients in various arts, Diderot declared that the Moderns could achieve comparable results if honors and recompenses were made big enough. With one notable exception, however, and that was in the art of oratory. Without freedom, honors and recompenses could produce only declaimers, not orators. Following the loss of liberty the declaimers appeared in Athens and in Rome at the same time as the tyrants. True eloquence reveals itself only in contests of great public interests. 'The orator must feel that the art of the word leads to the highest dignities in the State; without this expectation, the mind, occupied by imaginary and set subjects, will never be kindled by a real fire, by a profound ardor, and you will have only rhetoricians. To speak well, one must be a Tribune of the People or be eligible to become Consul.' [64] This is a passage eloquent in itself. Here we see the friend of John Wilkes. This is a passage filled with the potentialities of revolutionary discontents. It should not be surprising to find Diderot, a decade later, fiercely praising the revolution in America.

The Salon of 1763 opened at the Louvre on 25 August. Diderot was prompt in the reporting of it, for his account appeared in Grimm's *Correspondance littéraire* for 1 October. Diderot was amusingly forthright in saying what he thought of the works of art in the Salon, but he was also capable of surprising diffidence. 'I may have been mistaken in my judgments either from lack of knowledge or from lack of taste, but I protest that . . . there is not a word in these pages dictated by hatred or flattery. . . .' Diderot enjoyed writing criticism, but he did not rate it very high: 'What a dull and dreary trade is that of critic. It is so difficult to create a thing, even a mediocre thing; it is so easy to detect mediocrity.' [65]

The *Salon de 1763* is not the longest of Diderot's accounts of the biennial exhibitions — those for 1765 and 1767 are book length — but in freshness, spontaneity, and youthfulness it is one of the best. His *Salons* are memorable not only for their literary power but also for the instruction they provide 'in the art of looking at works of art,' [66] which as Diderot was coming to realize, is grounded in an appreciation of technique. This made Diderot humble: he realized that a painter might say to him, ' "What a eulogy I could make of all the beauties in this painting that you don't even see. . . ." This is because there are so many things concerning technique of which it is impossible to judge without one's having oneself spent time with one's thumb in the thumb-hole of a palette.' He knew perfectly well that Chardin's wizardry came from the perfection of his technique. 'Oh, Chardin! you do not mix white, red, black on your palette; it is the very substance of the objects, it is air and it is light that you take on the tip of your brush and put on the canvas.' [67] Diderot learned by talking with artists. He especially mentions Chardin as being able to converse luminously about the nature of his art.

In spite of Diderot's admiration for Chardin, he accepted the conventions of his age and continued to think of genre painting as being of lesser dignity than were the great historical 'machines.' The Salon of 1763 had its share of this type of painting by such artists as Pierre, Vien, Lagrenée, Restout, Deshays, Hallé, men who are all but forgotten now.[68] In point of fact, Diderot almost never saw a big historical 'machine' of which he completely approved, and he never saw a lowly Chardin canvas that he disliked.

Diderot thought that the history of the Christian church provided excellent subjects for historical painting, subjects fully as good — even better, on the average — than those afforded by ancient myth. But the reason for this was a curious and paradoxical one: historical painting flourishes on crime as its subject matter, and 'Never has any other religion been so fecund in crimes as Christianity; from the murder of Abel to the agony of Calas, there is not a line of its history that has not been bloodied. . . . The abominable Cross has caused blood to flow on every side.'[69] Though he was always very aware of Socrates' martyrdom, Diderot's anti-Christianism and anti-clericalism made him unsympathetic to martyrs who were Christians.

Diderot's art criticism is made lively and abiding by the fact that he constantly asked himself the philosophical questions that underlie all aesthetic judgments. These are easy to ask and devilishly hard to answer: what *is* art; and — a question that in 1763 concerned him as much as it had in 1751, when he wrote the *Lettre sur les sourds et muets* — what is the relationship of imitation to reality? He realized that art is more than just a copy of nature. Art is not reality; it is the illusion of reality (as Goethe subsequently thought also). 'It is no longer the real, true scene that one sees,' wrote Diderot, 'it is only, so to speak, the translation of it.' Art is the business of choosing, he wrote, which is why each artist has an individual palette, manner, and technique; and 'following upon this choice, however skillfully done, the best and most harmonious picture is only a tissue of falsehoods covering one another up.'[70]

Passages like these illustrate Diderot's concern with reaching toward the furthest limits of aesthetic appreciation and understanding. But the inclusion of such passages presented him with a very special literary problem, that of holding the interest of his reader. One of his devices was to present some of his deepest insights as though they were only digressions, and that he digressed for his own sake, not the reader's. 'Digression rests me,' he said in this very passage.[71]

Humor, personal allusions, and eroticisms enliven his pages. Pierre's painting of Mercury turning Aglaurus to stone leads Diderot to suggest that Mercury had also turned Pierre and his composition to stone. 'Tell me, M. Challe,' he asks of one of Pierre's peers, 'why are you a painter? There are so many other callings in society in which mediocrity is even useful.' He chides the coldness of a painting that depicted Esther fainting in the presence of King Ahasuerus: if Sophie should ever be in such a condition, 'how distraught I would be, what cries I would utter!' Addressing another artist, the painter of a large 'machine' about Abraham, Diderot wrote, 'You bore me, M. Hallé, you bore me.' But Diderot was not at all bored by Vien's painting depicting a Greek slave selling cupids to a Greek lady of quality. Diderot found an abundance of erotic symbols in this canvas. Likewise he found a tremendous amount of titillation in a canvas representing the temptation of Joseph. 'I do not know whether this painting is intended to be hung in a church, but if it is, it is enough to damnify the priest right in the middle of his mass and hand over all present to the devil. Have you ever seen anything more voluptuous?' The artist had depicted Joseph as being very sorely tempted: 'Everytime I go back to the Salon, I always have the hope of seeing him in her arms.' [72]

Diderot greatly approved of teaching morality by art, though quotations like these scarcely prove the point. In the *Salon de 1763* he praised Greuze for the sole reason that he was a moral artist. François Boucher, while pleasing, was a corrupting influence, Diderot thought, whereas of Greuze he wrote, 'First of all, the genre pleases me; it is moral painting. After all, has not the brush been consecrated to debauchery and vice long enough? Ought we not to be pleased to see it vie at last with dramatic poetry in moving us, teaching us, correcting us, and inviting us to virtue?' [73]

Sculpture, too, was included in the biennial Salons, and Diderot briefly describes the sculpture of the Salon of 1763, mentioning with particular delight Falconet's charming 'Pygmalion and Galatea.' Earlier in 1763 Diderot had contributed to the *Correspondance littéraire* a lengthy memoir about the eminent sculptor Bouchardon, whose Fountain of the Four Seasons, on the Rue de Grenelle, is still one of the sights of Paris. This essay, in the course of which Diderot remarked that 'were one only to make pins, one must be an enthusiast over one's trade in order to excel in it,' shows, in conjunction with his treatment of sculpture in the *Salon de 1763*, how careful a study he was making of sculpture and sculptors as well as of painting and painters. Indeed, he thought it harder for a layman to judge a statue than a painting. 'Who among us knows nature well enough to claim that a muscle has not been executed right?' [74]

About this time, Diderot wrote a brief philosophical catechism entitled 'The Proselyte Replying for Himself' [Le Prosélyte répondant par lui-même]. Short as it is, this piece is very useful in tracing the development and continuity of Diderot's ideas about philosophy, especially ethics. Naigeon is the authority for what knowledge we have of its origin. A devout acquaintance of Diderot, Naigeon says, showed him a dialogue in which the religious and philosophical ideas of the *philosophes* were attacked. Questions posed by 'A Wise Man' were answered by 'A Proselyte.' Diderot, with his usual quick responsiveness, took up the challenge he sensed in such a catechism. His reply, couched in the same literary form, assumes that a proselyte of truly independent mind would make answers of a very different sort and would confound the tendentious questions of 'The Wise Man.' [75] In an astonishingly brief compass Diderot poses here all the big questions: What is virtue? What is justice? What are the duties of man? He discusses the problem of miracles and the nature of historical evidence, revelation, the soul, immortality, and the origin of evil. Diderot's dialogue ends on a note characteristic of the Enlightenment: 'Let all men be enlightened; and Nature will speak to all of them the language of virtue.' [76]

In this catechism Diderot recognizes a world in which evil exists. 'I shall not say with Pope that all is good. Evil exists; and it is a necessary consequence of the laws of nature, and not the effect of a ridiculous apple. . . . Pope proved very well, following Leibniz, that the world cannot be other than it is; but when he concluded from that that all is well, he talked nonsense; he should have contented himself with saying that all is necessary.' [77] How different is this from the easy optimism that many people suppose to have been the trademark of the *philosophes,* depicted as they often are as philosophical optimists of a very naïve and superficial sort. The duty of man, Diderot then went on to say, is to make himself happy, whence is derived the necessity of contributing to the happiness of others, or, in other terms, of being virtuous.[78]

This doctrine of the pursuit of happiness emerges here with more emphasis than it had in Diderot's previous writings, and it continues to be the cornerstone of his ethical doctrine from now until the end of his career. The other main ideas of 'Le Prosélyte répondant par lui-même' are perfectly consistent Diderot: determinism, necessitarianism, and the view that historical proof of miracles is the weakest proof of all, being surpassed by proof through ethical analysis, though physical and scientific proof is much superior to either. There were also, familiar to readers of Diderot, his rejection of Providence and revelation, together with an abomination of monks and celibacy.[79] Diderot does not in this catechism deny the existence of God. In fact, the Proselyte often refers to God or to the Supreme Being. It is of course a very impersonal God. 'God can do everything, without doubt, although, nevertheless, it is not in his power to change essences. . . . God cannot make the part be greater than the whole, or make three one; because it is of the essence of a part to be smaller than the whole and of the essence of three to make three.' Aside from the anti-Trinitarian twist that the mischievous Diderot put on the argument, this is good straight Scholastic reasoning, right out of the mediaeval schools. It is also consistent with the view of God upon which Hugo Grotius founded his edifice of international law. It seems a little odd to find Diderot, who had moved far along on the road to disbelief in God, here using His name. But just as in his *Pensées philosophiques* (1746) Diderot had cried, 'Enlarge God,' so now, in this catechism, Diderot has his Proselyte warn the interrogator 'to take care lest you reduce the Eternal Being to the level of your own pettiness.' [80] Diderot may have used the name of God so frequently in this catechism simply because he was attempting to fit his replies, *ad hominem,* to the particular needs of the pious friend who had asked him for his opinion. Still, that he referred to deity at all, as late as 1764, makes one ponder.

Interesting and important as 'Le Prosélyte répondant par lui-même' is, it was only an *hors-d'oeuvre,* struck off at a busy time. The writing of it seems to be a little occasional and adventitious in the life of so busy and what might be supposed to be so preoccupied a man. But the energetic and restless Diderot was almost never too busy for a distraction or a digression. This is the many-faceted Diderot who found time to play piquet and checkers and go to cafés; [81] the Diderot who composed an unsolicited inscription for Pigalle's statue of Louis XV at Rheims; [82] the Diderot who, being asked by a young poet to criticize his play, overwhelmed him with lavish suggestions that would have required a complete substitution from beginning to end; [83] the Diderot whose volubility was spoken of at this very time as being 'notorious'; [84] the Diderot who one day informed Sophie Volland that he had had a nocturnal emission and described to her the dream that customarily accompanied these occasions; [85] the Diderot who habitually forgot to date his letters and who rarely knew the day of the month and week; [86] the Diderot who forgot a dinner invitation that he had accepted; [87] the Diderot who, looking for a book high on a shelf, imprudently stood on a chair placed on another chair and straightway came crashing down — 'I do not know why I did not kill myself'; [88] the Diderot who found time to compose a well-turned bit of erotic verse; [89] the Diderot who translated the difficult passage from Aelius Lampridius in the collection of the *Scriptores Historiae Augustae,* in which are recorded the furious imprecations of the Senate rejoicing over the death of Commodus;[90] the Diderot of whom Grimm wrote, 'Profound and vigorous in his writings, but much more astonishing in his conversation, he delivers oracles of all kinds on all sorts of subjects. . . . The force and impetuosity of his imagination would sometimes be excessive were they not

tempered by the child-like gentleness of his manners and by a good nature
that bestows a singular and rare distinction upon all his other qualities.'[91]

This is the Diderot of whom one could also find less flattering opinions.
A young Scottish gentleman wrote at this time:

Diderot is noisy and talkative, and somewhat fond of a Dispute; he is certainly
very learned, and very conscious of his own knowledge — he would be a better
philosopher and a more agreeable companion if he did not make philosophy a
matter of Party, and treat subjects of the gravest nature and which require a
cool examination too much like the head of an opposition.[92]

Fréron would have subscribed to that. And so would Palissot, the first
three cantos of whose mock-epic poem *La Dunciade* were published in
1764. It depicts Diderot and the *Encyclopédie* as the particular darlings, the
special protégés, of the Goddess of Stupidity. 'And Diderot thinks he is the
equal of Buffon,' ran the poem, which also described the *Encyclopédie* as an
'enormous, immense and impenetrable mass' and scornfully sang of it as
'Reason in alphabetical order.' Grimm was described as 'M. Diderot's sole
remaining admirer; it is true that he is a German.' The attack was rough
enough to cause Voltaire concern for Diderot.[93] Diderot's own correspondence, however, reveals no trace of his being aware of Palissot's attack.

Meanwhile, Diderot's library was still up for sale. The solution to his
problem came from a quarter that was quite unexpected. Not having been
able to sell the library to any of his compatriots, Diderot authorized Grimm
to propose to Catherine II that she buy it.[94] The proposal, asking 15,000
livres was made on 10 February 1765. It was conveyed in a letter from
Grimm to General I. I. Betzki, a bumbling and fussy old man who
was one of Catherine's chamberlains and who traded upon the spurious
reputation of being her father. The Empress acceded. What is more, she
did so with two generous and unexpected conditions. Diderot was to re-
tain the use of his library until further notice. In addition, he was to
receive each year an extra thousand livres. These were to recompense
him for 'the care and trouble to be taken by him in forming this collection.'[95]

These unforeseen and agreeable stipulations evidently took Diderot by
surprise. He had of course supposed that if he sold his books he would
have to surrender possession of them. As he put it, the father and husband had decided to despoil the man of letters.[96] But as it turned out, he
now had the use of them, and in fact they were not sent to Russia until
after his death. Moreover, the extra thousand livres each year put him on

the Russian payroll and in effect made him Librarian of Her Imperial Majesty Catherine II. This raised the transaction from a mere sale to a minor affair of state. Consequently Diderot wrote to the minister of the King's household and also to the Secretary of State for Foreign Affairs, asking the permission of Louis XV to accept this extra sum. 'I do not know whether this 100 pistoles should be called a pension or a simple honorarium; but I am not ignorant of the fact that a subject may not accept anything from a foreign power without being authorized thereto by the permission of the King.' The answer came: 'His Majesty allows you to accept the favor that the Empress of Russia wishes to do you.' [97]

Oddly enough, there is no trace of the letter of thanks that Diderot must have addressed to Catherine II. It is scarcely conceivable that he did not send one at all. A few months later D'Alembert, in the course of a letter to the Empress, thanked her on Diderot's behalf; to which she replied, engagingly, that she 'had not foreseen that buying M. Diderot's library would bring me so many compliments.' [98]

The news of Diderot's good fortune, spread assiduously by his friends, was warmly welcomed.[99] Even Fréron chronicled the event without sarcasm.[100] And rising young poets — Claude-Joseph Dorat, with an 'Epistle to Catherine II,' and Pierre Légier, with an 'Epistle to M. Diderot' — seized the occasion to draw attention to themselves in celebration of the event.[101] Diderot himself was so overwhelmed by the outcome, wrote Damilaville to Voltaire, that it practically put him in a state of stupor for twenty-four hours.[102]

CHAPTER 35

Perfidy Where Least Expected

Diderot was an effervescent man but he was also a surprisingly stable one. The proof of this is to be seen in the tenacity and perseverance with which he kept working at the *Encyclopédie* for twenty-five years. Such pertinacity and endurance is especially notable in the case of a man who was famous for the volatility of his temper and whose vivacity has often been mistaken for flightiness.

The years between 1759 and 1765-6 constituted the period of Diderot's greatest trial, preliminary — as we now can see — to the moments of his greatest triumphs. Stretching between the suppression of the *Encyclopédie* and its final publication, these were the years of Diderot's going 'underground,' carrying with him all the writing, editing, revising, and proofreading necessary to the eventual publication of ten folio volumes containing approximately eleven million words. The enormity of the drudgery that lay before him no doubt contributed to his mood of pessimism; and his letters, from time to time, reveal how much he was feeling the attrition of cumulative fatigue.

All of this surreptitious work, moreover, had to be done under circumstances that were not very stimulating or exhilarating. Even Voltaire did not know about the progress being made and had to be confidentially informed, with a precautionary 'Hush!'[1] Diderot, therefore, during these years had to find within himself, and without much outside encouragement, the energy and stamina to support the deadweight of the enterprise. It was deadweight that was not merely mechanical and physical, the deadweight of drudgery, but also psychological and moral, the deadweight of loneliness and discouragement. Nor were these years lightened by any great public triumph or endorsement. On the contrary, to the public and to his enemies Diderot appeared to be a man defeated, his life work in ruins. His enemies could say, as one of them did in 1760, 'The name of the

Encyclopédie and of the Encyclopedists has become odious, and what is worse, ridiculous.'[2] This was the time for Diderot's enemies to mock, for Palissot to impugn his morals and Fréron to condemn his style:

Perhaps I am mistaken [wrote the old enemy, with the air of a man who is quite sure that he is not mistaken at all], but it seems to me that M. Diderot does not write French too well. His style in general is obscure, ambiguous; overloaded with Latinisms, faulty constructions, intricacies; with vainglorious, out-of-the-way and labored expressions; with similes that he squeezes out to the point of surfeit.[3]

It was a time when Diderot's enemies could attack him without his being able to strike back. The accusation of plagiarism in regard to the plates, the very qualified success of *Le Père de famille,* the apparent ruin of the *Encyclopédie,* all put him on the defensive.

A great deal of Diderot's work for the final volumes of the *Encyclopédie* is concealed from us in the anonymity of supervising, editing, and revising. Because of D'Alembert's retirement from any participation in the editing of the *Encyclopédie* (though he continued to contribute some articles), Diderot's work as an editor became even more demanding after 1759. His work as an author was very extensive, too. After the suppression of the *Encyclopédie* several of the former contributors, such as Turgot and Marmontel, refrained from further contributions, while it understandably became more difficult to recruit new contributors for a work that was supposed to have been abolished officially and discontinued permanently.[4] The number of acknowledged contributors thus being drastically curtailed, it stands to reason that Diderot found himself under the necessity of filling in on a great variety of subjects. The articles that he himself wrote, however, became harder to identify, beginning with Volume X, when he discontinued using the asterisk at the beginning of an article to indicate his authorship. In the last ten volumes there is an abundance of articles of unidentifiable authorship which sound like Diderot and formerly were confidently attributed to him but that in fact ought to be regarded as truly anonymous.[5] It is nevertheless evident that Diderot's labors in these years were Herculean.

Much of Diderot's effort went into the simple task of seeing to it that the *Encyclopédie* was a consistent and usable work. In an early letter to Le Breton Diderot had outlined how to circumvent certain confusing procedures, 'failing which everything will be at cross-purposes and we will produce a badly constructed book, which is neither your intention nor mine.'[6]

Today almost no specific evidence, no manuscripts or proofs, remain of the techniques by which he accomplished his goal. All we now have are a few galley proofs and a few proofs of the engravings bearing in his hand the authorization for printing, 'bon à tirer.'

The *Encyclopédie* has always been regarded, and quite reasonably, as the supreme exemplar of the Enlightenment.[7] Emmanuel Kant's famous definition of *Aufklärung,* written the year Diderot died, announced in its first words that 'Enlightenment is man's release from his self-imposed tutelage.' This is a definition in which, almost certainly, Diderot would have concurred. It is consonant with his dictum that 'man is born to think for himself' and that an encyclopedia, such as the one he was editing, should have the property 'of changing the general way of thinking.'[8] It was with this continuing sense of mission that Diderot, from underground, shaped the final ten volumes of text that eventually were made accessible to the public in 1765–6.

Diderot was hailed as a leader by his friends and dubbed a ringleader by his enemies. He and his massive *Encyclopédie* were, after all, involved in politics. He was a leader of an intellectual movement that was something like a political party, although it also often acted as though it were a religious sect. At a time when official political theory was still committed to divine-right monarchy, when all of the governmental process right down to the minutiae of local administration was regarded as arcane and shrouded in mystery and secrecy, when the established church expected the state to use its full police power in enforcing a narrow conformity, Diderot's *Encyclopédie* was always preaching political liberalism and religious latitudinarianism. Even the friendly and sympathetic Dr. Charles Burney, who had known Paris and Diderot well, acknowledged this. Writing about 1800, he declared that the *Encyclopédie* 'was intended not only as a magazine of every species of human knowledge, but as an engine to subvert all established opinions.'[9] In the eyes of conservatives this was indeed being political.

From the beginning this policy had involved Diderot and the work in a cat-and-mouse game with the censors. As each of the first seven volumes had gone through the routine of satisfying official censors before publication, part of the fun had been to see how ingeniously one could outwit them. For the ten volumes now being prepared the editor and publishers would of course still be held responsible for what was said; yet, in a way, their problem of what to insert and what to leave out had become even more difficult. The reason for this was that the *Encyclopédie* had legally ceased to exist. As its license had been revoked in 1759, only by assiduously looking the other way were the authorities able not to observe that a considerable army of printers, engravers, and binders were busily engaged on some large undertaking in Le Breton's workshop. And since official censors can scarcely be assigned to a work that officially does not exist, Diderot and the publishers worked now under an added hazard. Previously, when furor arose, they had frequently been able to convince the authorities that the fault should not be ascribed to them but to the stupidity of the censors in passing censurable material. Now, there being no censors to use as scapegoats, the work itself would have to bear the full brunt of whatever displeasure was caused by its contents.

In a way, it was advantageous to Diderot and the publishers to publish all the last ten volumes at one time, consequently avoiding the successive spasms of crisis that had attended the publication of each volume in the fifties. Grimm later admitted that this was a policy, by which it was hoped 'to prevent new persecutions.'[10] Although this simplified matters, it did not resolve the very real awkwardness of having no official censors to authorize publication. Suppose these volumes were found upon publication to contain material regarded for one reason or another to be so subversive as to justify confiscation. For the publishers this would mean bankruptcy.

It is inconceivable that Diderot and the publishers had not discussed the problem. Ostensibly, the publishers had entrusted the whole responsibility to him, and such was his understanding of the situation until a day in late 1764, when the manufacture of the work was drawing to a close. Six years later, Grimm recounted the revelations of that day:

. . . M. Diderot, having occasion to consult one of his big articles on philosophy in the letter S, found it to be entirely mutilated. He was thunderstruck. . . . he began to go over the best articles he or his ablest assistants had done, and found almost everywhere the same disorder, the same traces of the preposterous destroyer who had ravaged everything. This discovery put him into a state of frenzy and despair that I shall never forget.[11]

Grimm did not exaggerate. This frenzy and despair are plain to see in the letter Diderot wrote to Le Breton soon after the discovery of the treachery. 'I wept with rage in your presence; I wept with grief at home, in front of your associate M. Briasson, in front of my wife, my child, and my servant. . . . I shall bear this wound until I die.'[12]

For it was Le Breton who was guilty, who had hoodwinked Diderot. Grimm described how Le Breton had done it:

. . . unknown to anybody, he promoted himself along with his principal foreman as sovereign arbiter and censor of all the articles of the *Encyclopédie*. They
were set up in print just as the authors had submitted them; but after M.
Diderot had read the last proof on each sheet and had written at the bottom
the order to print, M. Le Breton and his foreman laid hold of them, struck out
and cut up and suppressed everything they thought daring or likely to raise
an uproar and excite the clamor of the devout and of enemies. Thus, on their
own authority, they reduced the majority of the best articles to mutilated fragments despoiled of all that was precious in them; taking no account of liaison
among the bits of these mangled skeletons, or, if they did, linking them up by
the most irrelevant stitchery.[13]

It had been easy for Le Breton to commit his depredations without Diderot's immediately detecting them. Le Breton took advantage of the fact
that the whole work was being produced surreptitiously and at some personal risk. Evidently, therefore, manuscripts were destroyed as soon as
articles were set up in type, so as not to leave any evidence that could
compromise the authors. Moreover, Diderot's correspondence shows that
all the editing was done at Le Breton's, too. None of it was done at the
Rue Taranne, thus again avoiding compromising Diderot if there should
be a perquisition. 'The publication of this book,' wrote Diderot in the
Encyclopédie article *'Perquisition,'* 'occasioned the most rigorous *perquisitions*. With all these *perquisitions,* nothing was found.'[14] But these precautions gave Le Breton access to everything and custody of everything,
twenty-four hours a day. Perfidy was the consequence:

So that's the end of twenty-five years of labor, of anxiety, of expenditures, of
danger, of mortifications of all kinds! . . . you have failed me in every respect,
contrary to all decency and to every promise. . . . You have been deceiving me
in cowardly fashion for two years. You have massacred, or have had massacred
by a brute beast, the work of twenty upright people who employed their time,
their talents and their efforts without pay, out of love for truth and the good,
solely with the hope of seeing their ideas published and of reaping esteem as a
result. . . . It turns out in the end that the greatest damage of all that we have
suffered — contempt, shame, discredit, ruin, derision — comes upon us from the
principal investor in the whole venture! If one has no energy, no valor, no courage, one should know one's own limitations and leave perilous enterprises to
others.[15]

Diderot's first impulse was to renounce his editorship and expose Le
Breton publicly. Two considerations gave him pause. The first was, as
Grimm explained, that Le Breton's innocent partners, Briasson and David,

begged Diderot not to make the news public. They did not, apparently, try to excuse Le Breton; they simply appealed to Diderot not to punish the innocent with the guilty. 'I am giving in to M. Briasson's solicitations. I cannot help feeling a certain commiseration for your partners, who had no part in your betrayal of me.' The second consideration had to do with Diderot's own safety: 'M. Diderot could not inform the public of how he had been betrayed without putting into the hands of his enemies juridical proof of his having continued to carry forward the *Encyclopédie* in spite of the suppression that had been ordained against it. To publish such a confession was tantamount to condemning oneself to leave France.'[16] Diderot was trapped.

Even though he evidently did not find Le Breton wholly congenial (and certainly did find Mme Le Breton quite inscrutable), Diderot had previously been on quite friendly terms with them. In letters to Sophie, Diderot had chronicled visits to Le Breton's country place at Massy, just south of Paris, and dinners at Le Breton's Paris house, these 'plenty dull and plenty noisy.' Hitherto Diderot's problem with the Le Bretons had been merely one of safeguarding his independence. In 1762, for example, he explained why he avoided their inviting him to dinner: 'It comes down to this, that they are miserly and they set too much store on an inferior dinner for one to be able to accept it at such a price.' If relations, though a little uneasy and even contentious, had once been friendly, they were now inimical: 'You insist that I continue to visit your establishment as before, to mark proofs; M. Briasson asks it too. . . . I will go to your place without noticing you; do me the favor of not noticing me in return.'[17]

Few incidents in the history of publishing are more famous than this one of Le Breton's fall from a state of grace. Nothing substantiates more eloquently and emphatically the seriousness of Diderot's purpose and the moral earnestness he brought to the editing of the *Encyclopédie* than does the manifest agony he suffered when he realized his work had been mutilated. Just how great was the extent of the damage? There can be no doubt that Diderot thought that it was crippling. He wrote of the volumes as being 'surreptitiously mutilated, garbled, made hash of, dishonored. . . .' His daughter recalled after his death, 'Never have I heard him speak coolly on this subject; he was convinced that the public knew as well as he did what was missing in each article, and the impossibility of repairing the damage put him into a bad humor still, twenty years after.' And in 1769, writing once again to Le Breton, Diderot referred to the mutilation and declared, 'I suffered the cruellest woe that I have ever felt in my life.'[18]

Diderot himself was unable to make an accurate appraisal of the damage because he had no means of comparison. 'If only it were possible to get the proofs from you, in order to transcribe by hand the parts that you have suppressed.' When Diderot wrote this he evidently knew or assumed that the proofs were still in existence. 'The request is a just one, but I am not making it. When one is capable of abusing trust to the point that you have abused mine, one is capable of anything. Nevertheless this is my property, and the property of the authors whom you engaged. I am not giving it to you . . . [but] I do not insist upon this rightful restitution. From you I expect nothing that is just and upright.' [19]

The assumption until recently has been that all the proofs were destroyed. But in 1933 a unique set of the *Encyclopédie*, magnificently bound in red morocco, came on the market in Berlin. This set contains the bookplate of the Czarist Russian General Staff, raising the question whether it was part of Diderot's library which went to Russia in 1785. Internal evidence proves that the set was originally the property of Le Breton. What makes the set unique is that it contains an extra volume of blank pages, bound in red morocco like the others, where are pasted numerous documents concerning the history of the publishing of the *Encyclopédie*. Included are 284 pages of page proofs from the last ten volumes of the *Encyclopédie*. Here is exactly the sort of documentary evidence of alteration and suppression that everyone has been panting for.

These 284 pages of page proof contain forty-four articles altered surreptitiously by Le Breton. Many of these alterations were of only a few words or a sentence or two. For example, Diderot had written in the article *'Luxure'* (Lust), 'In the Christian religion, lust is one of the seven capital sins; *imagine how many damned there must be, since the slightest sin in this category is damning.'* Le Breton cut out the lines here italicized.[20] And he softened the article *'Paradis,'* the anonymous author of which had mischievously raised the question of where paradise is located now that the Copernican system has altered our understanding of the universe. Articles in which De Jaucourt revealed his Protestant proclivities were toned down by Le Breton (*'Puissance Papale'* [Papal Authority], *'Religion Protestante,'* *'Peines Purifiantes'* [a comment on the doctrine of purgatory]). As for Diderot, Le Breton evidently scented blasphemy in the sentence to illustrate the meaning of the word *'Périr'* (Perish): 'God allows an infinite number of souls to *perish* every day for want of an enlightenment which might save them, which He refuses them, and which only He can give.' [21] This was too much for Le Breton: he struck it out. Nor did he like better a sentence in Diderot's article '*Infidélité*,' a comment upon the permanency of marriage vows: 'The priest speaks in vain at the foot of the altar to two beings who are not made for each other, "I unite you and nothing shall separate you." Nature gives the priest the lie, takes the man or the woman by the hand and leads wherever she chooses.' [22]

Le Breton made more substantial deletions in Diderot's article '*Pyrrhon-ienne*' (or Philosophical Doubt). This was a long, rambling article, a kind of roundup of all the philosophers of skepticism that there ever were. It contains an analysis, still greatly admired, of the intellectual greatness of Montaigne.[23] This Le Breton let stand. But Diderot then embarked upon a discussion of an author who was still regarded by many of Diderot's contemporaries as an outlaw and a subversive influence, Pierre Bayle. Bayle's writings were still, in the 1760's, a source of scandal to the devout and of inspiration to the *philosophes*. 'The Encyclopedists were playing with fire when they dared to speak well of Bayle, and they realized it fully.' Nonetheless Diderot wrote of the Revocation of the Edict of Nantes (1685) which drove so many thousands of Huguenots into exile. 'At that time the most unheard-of vexations were carried out against members of the Reformed religion; France was made Catholic by ruining her; by violating the most sacred laws of humanity and by dishonoring religion, the extirpation of a heresy was carried forward. This is what Bayle demonstrated in a little booklet [*Ce que c'est que la France toute catholique sous le règne de Louis-le-Grand* (1686)].' Le Breton deleted this, as he did also a long passage in the same article about the need for tolerance, the nature of religious faith, and the proper relationship of church and state.[24]

In respect to tolerance, Diderot loved to contrast philosophers with theologians, of course very much to the disfavor of the latter. Surely it was pusillanimous of Le Breton not to let the following stand in the article '*Théologien*,' even though to twentieth-century taste it seems out of place in a work of reference. But perhaps he thought the memory of Calas to be too green:

It is shameful that philosophers should often be in a position to give theologians lessons in tolerance and humanity. It is shameful that these men [theologians], whose science is full of difficulties, mysteries, and incomprehensibilities, and who agree that people have no faith in their teachings save by God's special grace, should have employed fire and sword, and would be employing them today, if the sovereign would let them, . . .[25]

One of the articles abridged by Le Breton was that on Socratic philosophy ('*Socratique, philosophie*'). In all of the *Encyclopédie* no article was more characteristic of Diderot. Herein he displays his mastery of the history of philosophy; he also 'borrows from the rich,' as he was fond of saying in excusing the instances of his near-plagiarisms, by freely paraphrasing Brucker's long treatment of the subject; then he suddenly draws attention to himself by addressing Socrates — and in the familiar — 'Oh, Socrates! I resemble you very little; but at least you make me weep with admiration and joy'; he uses the article to make a thinly disguised attack on Rousseau by his hostile description of the misanthropic Timon, one of Socrates' disciples. Apparently Diderot was insinuating that he himself had been the Socrates-figure and Jean-Jacques was the savage and atrabiliar disciple. And in discussing Socrates' fate, Diderot included a provocative allusion to recent events:

The ignominy which has settled upon those who found him guilty should encourage every philosopher to speak the truth boldly, and should make those worldly people who so readily condemn the conduct of philosophers and who blame in us what they admire in Socrates, more logical and more circumspect.

Identifying himself with Socrates sustained Diderot in his time of troubles. But this passage was too much for Le Breton, and he surreptitiously struck it out.[26]

The fact that some of the proofs in the Extra Volume bear Diderot's marginal comments or his 'bon à tirer' proves that he saw at least some of the proofs after Le Breton's depredations were discovered. For instance, on the proof of the article 'Socratique,' in words which are hard to read because Le Breton thought he had effaced them by surcharging them with running spirals, Diderot wrote, 'I have read this proof after the Ostrogothic pruning-hook massacred the articles. You may print, and fling [them] out of the window for all I care.'[27]

In his passionate letter to Le Breton, Diderot predicted that when the volumes were published, the contributors 'will go to the articles they have written, and seeing with their own eyes the damage you have done them, will not hold themselves in, they will raise an outcry.' This prediction did not come true, as Grimm noted to his great surprise: 'A most singular thing! I never heard any one of the maltreated authors complain; the interval of years that had elapsed between the writing and the publication of their articles had no doubt made them keep less in mind what they had written, and so many obstacles had been raised to the publication of the ten volumes that the edition was sold to the subscribers in the provinces and abroad before the authors had been able to read a line.'[28]

What can account for this lack of outcry, the sensibilities of authors being what they are? Perhaps Le Breton took care to limit his depredations pretty much to the articles written by De Jaucourt and Diderot. Certainly this is true of the proofs contained in the Extra Volume: although one of the forty-four articles was by the Abbé Morellet (an appendant addition to the article *'Théologie, positive'* and completely deleted) and although two others (*'Mambré,'* probably by the Swiss, Polier de Bottens, and *'Tolérance,'* by the younger Romilly) were touched up, all the other forty-one, so far as they can be identified, were by De Jaucourt and Diderot.[29] Or it may be that Le Breton did tone down numerous articles by all the several authors, but so inconspicuously, with a word substituted here and a phrase deleted there, that no one, in the absence of the proofs, could be sure that it had happened.

Now that one has the evidence of the precious Extra Volume, one is perhaps disposed to think that the enormity of Le Breton's crime has been greatly exaggerated. Only forty-one articles altered, only three completely expunged (two of these, *'Théologie Scholastique'* and *'Tolérance,'* by De Jaucourt), only some 12,800 words substituted or deleted in ten folio volumes. As has been remarked, 'In comparison with the whole extent of ten folio volumes of text, the censored passages do not loom very large. They represent at best only the peaks lopped off the heights of Diderot's audacity.'[30]

This analysis is conclusive and definitive for the corpus of evidence that Le Breton (who collected these documents) has left to us. But suppose, as has been suggested, that 'these 284 pages were merely specimens of Le Breton's handiwork? . . . While no one could claim that it is impossible these 284 pages contain all or nearly all the alterations made by Le Breton, at the present moment we have absolutely no evidence to enable us to say what he did to getting on for 9,000 pages of these last ten volumes.'[31] Other scholars do not deny this possibility, although they somewhat discount it: 'It could hardly be maintained that these three hundred and eighteen pages constitute the total number of proofs altered or rejected in the publication of such an immense work. It is probable, on the other hand, that they give us the greater part of the material censored by Le Breton.'[32] It is not certain that Diderot would have subscribed to this opinion. In 1770 he told an acquaintance that Le Breton had 'carpentered' the last seven volumes, and in 1773-4 he told Catherine II that 'an infamous printer . . . cut up my work nighttimes without my knowledge, mangled ten volumes and burned the manuscripts that he did not deem fit to use.'[33]

In all of this mysterious business, so full of uncertainty and conjecture, it must not be forgotten that Le Breton held the whip hand. He had possession of the documents, and he could not be forced to produce more evidence than he chose. The internal evidence of the Extra Volume proves that it could not have been assembled without his providing the contents, and it therefore becomes most germane to speculate as to what his motives could have been for making such a collection. Aside from the possibility that he simply assembled them for their own sake, he could have had cogent reasons for hoping that these collected documents would serve one or more of the following purposes: 1) He may have thought that the Extra Volume would be useful as evidence in the unsuccessful lawsuit that was brought against the publishers of the *Encyclopédie* by one Luneau de Boisjermain. One of the plaintiff's claims was that the *Encyclopédie*, because it had been mutilated by Le Breton (a fact which Luneau had learned, incidentally, only because of Diderot's indiscretion) was not what its prospectus had promised. There is no evidence that the Extra Volume was in fact ever entered as evidence in the trial, but nevertheless Le Breton may have deemed it prudent to get the page proofs ready. 2) Le Breton may have intended to give the set to Diderot eventually. As we have already seen, Diderot said in 1764 that he regarded the proofs as his property. By adding to the page proofs in the Extra Volume all the papers concerning the trial, the whole constituting evidence in disproof of the allegation that the *Encyclopédie* failed to live up to its prospectus, Le Breton was at the same time undercutting Diderot's asseveration that the work had been grievously mutilated. Thus Le Breton's first and second motives could be combined and the Extra Volume serve a double purpose.

Diderot's daughter, writing not later than 1787, says that Diderot 'insisted that a copy be printed for him with columns in which everything was re-established; this copy went to Russia with his library.'[34] This testimony has greatly excited biographers of Diderot, who perennially have hoped to discover this precious copy.[35] Mme de Vandeul, inasmuch as she spoke of columns (and not volumes, nor signatures, nor even pages), may have been referring to this very Extra Volume in the Gordon set now at Baltimore. She could scarcely have been mistaken about *something* of the sort having been sent to Russia in Diderot's library, for she and her husband were the ones who assembled it for the journey. Certainly, it is possible that this set with the Extra Volume 'went to Russia with Diderot's library and that the page proofs it contained represented the restitution described somewhat vaguely by his daughter.'[36]

3) Le Breton, for a third motive, may have had in mind the possibility that these assembled documents would eventually plead his cause with posterity.[37] The sumptuous de luxe binding would itself tend to preserve the volume from being carelessly discarded until such time as someone — which in fact occurred a hundred and seventy-five years later — should realize the importance of its contents.

Each of these three purposes could be served very well by a cunning selection permitting the documents themselves to suggest that the Le Breton changes were not very numerous and were really quite minimal. Of course, if Le Breton was an undeceitful man, it is an injustice to him to make such an insinuation. But he had already tried to deceive Diderot once. Is it impossible, then, that he should try to deceive a court or deceive Diderot a second time or deceive posterity?

Diderot later on acknowledged to Naigeon that the letter to Le Breton, written in the white heat of recent discovery, had been intemperate: '. . . he never recalled this episode, one of the most critical of his life, without shuddering at the excesses to which resentment, even though completely justified, can sometimes carry the most upright man of the gentlest kind of character.'[38] Diderot's pride had been deeply hurt. 'You have made us insipid and flat. . . . Your subscribers will say that they subscribed to get my work and that what you give them is practically yours.' Diderot knew that 'what people looked for, and will be looking for, is the stout and bold philosophy' of some of the authors.[39] And since that was not there, then his own morale was sapped. On the proof of the article 'Souveraineté,' part of which Le Breton had deleted, Diderot wrote, 'He who laughs last, laughs best.'[40] It was a jaunty phrase, the very one the Nephew of Rameau ended with. It covered up, though with bravado that was only too vulnerable, the same sort of emptiness and despair. He had become apathetic. And indeed, after the perfidy of 1764 he almost never spoke of the *Encyclopédie* with any enthusiasm or any pride.

By 4 May 1765 the volumes had been manufactured up to the letter 'V.'[41] 'The task that for twenty years has been the torment of my life is drawing to a close,' Diderot wrote in June, and on 25 July he declared that there were only fourteen signatures left to be printed, a matter of eight or ten days. On 18 August, while ever lamenting Le Breton's 'massacre of our work,' Diderot thought that all would be finished within a week, 'after which I shall cry, Land! Land!' In mid-September he wrote to Damilaville that 'the great and cursed work is finished.'[42]

During the final month he wrote a preface to serve for the volumes about to be published, and which indeed figures at the beginning of Volume VIII. This was an important statement, for everyone from then to posterity would be reading it closely to see what the editor would have to say after so long an interruption. 'I don't know what to think of it,' wrote Diderot of his draft. 'Perhaps it is excellent, perhaps it is mediocre.' He did well to wonder, for the 'Avertissement' has a turgidity of style that betrays the fatigue of its author. While eloquent, it is also a little swollen and pretentious. And, as is not uncommon with Diderot, it strikes a note in which pride is mingled with self-pity.

Of all the persecutions, no matter in what time nor among what people, that persons have had to suffer who dedicate themselves to the seductive and perilous ambition of having their names inscribed in the list of benefactors of the human race, there is almost none that has not been practiced against us. . . . [How often, Diderot went on, have we been tempted] to seek tranquillity under a foreign sky. . . . But our native country was dear to us and we have always supposed that prejudice would give way to justice.[43]

When the subscribers finally received the last ten volumes, they must have been interested in identifying the authors of the articles, especially as the previous volumes had contained lists of contributors with their identifying marks. But now readers found that they had to scramble for such information. No more lists, though often individual articles were identified. Even the title pages, which formerly had named Diderot and D'Alembert, were now cloaked in the anonymity of 'by a society of men of letters.' Though Diderot was in fact everywhere, his sparing use of his identifying asterisk concealed the fact. D'Alembert was there, too, with his distinguishing mark of 'O' on about 450 articles in all.[44] None of these, however, since they were limited by his own choice to scientific subjects, was very redolent of 'philosophy,' nor did any of them reverberate so resoundingly as did articles such as *'Genève'* or *'Collège'* that he had written for the earlier volumes. Voltaire was there, but he, like the others, would have had to be looked for, and even so could be found in only two articles, *'Histoire'* and *'Idole, idolâtre, idolâtrie,'* though these were important ones.[45] D'Holbach also was a very significant and extensive contributor to the last ten volumes, much more so than met the eye. Many of the articles on chemistry and metallurgy, marked by a dash '——', have always been known to be his. Many others on political and religious issues, demurely anonymous, are almost certainly attributable to him. Even some of his technical articles were published without attribution. 'The only plausible explanation is that, in view of the much more dangerous content of certain other articles, it was felt desirable to make his total contribution to these last ten volumes as inconspicuous as possible.' Actually D'Holbach contributed more than eleven hundred articles to these last volumes.[46]

Very easy to identify in the last ten volumes were the articles by the Chevalier Louis de Jaucourt. There were thousands of them, each signed '(D.J.)'. Perhaps this was a mark of his vanity but those who have studied his career will believe that it was more likely a sign of his courage. De Jaucourt, because of his social standing and excellent reputation, was the figleaf of the *Encyclopédie*. He contributed as much to the work by his position and character as by his intellect. The stubborn faith of this ancient Huguenot family subjected them to legal disabilities in France without seriously impairing the esteem or the status in French society that they continued to enjoy. 'You are not unaware, . . . ,' wrote Voltaire to Palissot in 1760, 'that m^r le Chevalier de Jaucourt [comes] from a very great house, and [is] even more worthy of respect because of his morals than he is by his birth.' He and his family were universally respected for probity and integrity, and it is possible that he might have become a member of several French academies, as he already was of several foreign ones, had he not been legally disqualified as a Huguenot.[47]

De Jaucourt's Calvinism, his long residence at Geneva and Leyden, even his short stay at the University of Cambridge, whence he wrote that 'whoever is ignorant of the art of drinking a lot and smoking a lot is very unwelcome in this University,' made his frame of reference more spacious than merely that of Catholic and absolutist France. He was a highly civilized man and, moreover, a polymath, in all the splendor of that baroque and archaic word. And to the last ten volumes of the *Encyclopédie* he contributed some thirty-five per cent. His contribution to the whole seventeen volumes was a total of 4,700,000 words, constituting 17,050 articles.[48]

De Jaucourt's articles are agreeable though rarely sparkling, full of information and good sense. He was moderate in both political and religious beliefs, an advocate of political liberty and religious tolerance. He believed in God without being bigoted. In politics he advocated freedom of the press and the full panoply of civil rights. Examples taken almost at random show that he was full of sensible hypotheses and useful ideas. He suggested that the Louvre be made into a permanent art gallery housing the royal treasures in painting and sculpture;[49] he speculated that the Sermon on the Mount had been addressed to the Apostles alone, rather than to the whole body of believers;[50] he had a broad range of erudition and expert knowledge, as revealed, to take only one example, by the cluster of articles he wrote about medals;[51] and in a long article about his Leyden professor, Boerhaave, the originator of clinical teaching in medicine, he produced a charming biographical sketch, truly one for the anthologies.[52] One of De Jaucourt's idiosyncrasies was to make amends for previous omissions in the *Encyclopédie* by larding his own contributions with near-irrelevancies. His article on Paris is a good example. Making it mainly about the city's convents, monasteries, and churches — and commenting about a certain order of nuns that 'they strictly observe perpetual silence, for which the *beau sexe* is not by birth endowed' — he devotes almost eight columns to Athenian manners and morals, first, he says, because Parisians are said to be like the ancient Athenians and, secondly, because the *Encyclopédie* had failed to speak of Athenian manners before.[53]

The mind and the skills of De Jaucourt were those of a compiler rather than those of a creator. Diderot, always glad to use his aid, was sometimes scornful of De Jaucourt's talents. In 1760 Diderot wrote to Sophie, 'For six or seven years this man has been at the center of four or five secretaries, reading, dictating, working thirteen or fourteen hours a day, and this position has not bored him yet.' A month later, replying to some question she had asked, Diderot wrote, 'Le chevalier de Jaucourt? Don't fear lest he become bored with grinding out articles; God made him for that.'[54]

The public acknowledgment made by Diderot when the last ten volumes were published was much more generous: 'But since there is only one [of the contributors] that we have the liberty of naming, at least let us try to thank him as he deserves. This is M. le Chevalier de Jaucourt.' Even here, Diderot seems to think of De Jaucourt more as an indispensable research assistant than as a peer:

He was not disheartened by the most troublesome and thankless sort of research. He worked at it without surcease, satisfied with himself if he could spare others the trouble of doing it.

In fact, the more one analyzes Diderot's paeans of praise, the more one discovers that they sound more dithyrambic than they are:

But each sheet of this work will make up for whatever our eulogy lacks; there is not one that does not testify to the variety of his knowledge and the extensiveness of his assistance.[55]

Though De Jaucourt was the only contributor mentioned by name in the foreword to the last ten volumes, several score were identified at the end of their respective articles. The professions and social status of these persons is a matter of great interest. What manner of man was it who was invited to write for the *Encyclopédie* and consented to do so? There were of course the professional men of letters, striving to support themselves and lead independent lives untrammelled by the patronage of the great. Almost without exception the contributors were persons with the point of view of the bourgeoisie, frequently men whose talents and education had not yet achieved in that old and stratified society the status for which they felt themselves qualified. There were no writers in the *Encyclopédie* representing the point of view of the clergy or the nobility, even though some of the contributors were clerics and some of them were noble. Nor, on the other hand, was any major contributor a Freemason at the time of contributing. Moreover, though the contributors were without exception men of some property, or at least men who believed in private property even if they did not possess much of it, they were men of a special type within the bourgeoisie, the type interested not in being a *rentier* or in simply living on income, but those interested in production and in the increase of productivity.[56]

Accordingly, as a reader in 1765–6 turned to the newly published volumes, he would observe the same emphasis on the production of goods, on crafts, and on technological improvement as in the earlier ones. The same passion for the useful and for the widest possible dissemination of knowledge was apparent. 'If a discovery is essential to the welfare of society,' Diderot had written, 'depriving society of it is bad citizenship.'[57] Perhaps a quarter of the whole *Encyclopédie* was taken up by descriptions of the crafts. Many of the articles were virtually treatises. Such, for example, was the long one on *'Maçonnerie'* (Masonry), with its elaborate description of techniques of laying foundations on land or in water and with its detailed discussion of building materials.[58]

The concreteness and utility of *Encyclopédie* articles are well exemplified by the lengthy one on *'Laiton'* (Brass). This article, which was asterisked, implying that Diderot was unusually closely associated with its composition, was based upon observations made by some expert sent expressly to Namur in the Austrian Netherlands.[59] It was at Namur that calamine was mined in large quantities, and there too, in consequence, that large brass foundries and factories were located. It was characteristic of the *Encyclopédie,* in describing industrial processes, to get its data from the largest and most efficient establishments of the day, thus discussing brass at Namur, paper-making at Montargis, and salt-extraction in the Franche-Comté.[60] The article on brass was characteristic of the *Encyclopédie* in other ways as well. It was comprehensive. It was detailed. It had its touch of ideology, for in discussing the metallurgy of zinc, the article had its fling against the alchemists. It was up-to-date, for its account included the fact that 'it is not more than five or six years . . . since it was discovered that calamine is simply a combination of earth and zinc.' And, perhaps most characteristic of all, the article ventilated social issues associated with the industry: the problem, for instance, of technological unemployment, with suggestions as to what governments might do both in encouraging improvements and in preventing harmful monopolies.[61] This was the stuff out of which a revolution in social perceptions was gradually accomplished. This was the way in which, volume piled on volume, a work of reference made itself be perceived as a social and political program.*

The piquancy that Diderot had imparted to his early articles in the *Encyclopédie* by frequently inserting personal or subjective allusions is not lacking in the last ten volumes. The most gratuitous instance of this is to be found in the supplement that Diderot appended to the article *'Prusse'* written by De Jaucourt. It is evident that Diderot was not cut out to be a courtier. He remarked of Frederick the Great's French verse that 'It needs the merest breath of a man of taste in order to blow away some slight grains of dust from the sands of Berlin. . . .' Did Diderot suppose that he was complimenting Frederick II, who was more sensitive on this score than on almost anything else, when he wrote, 'This admirable flute needs merely a slightly clearer mouthpiece'?[62] The criticism could scarcely be more painful or more public, and no doubt goes far to explain why Diderot and His Prussian Majesty were not on very good terms.

There were numerous other instances of personal or subjective judgments, though none so egregious. In the article *'Partisan'* he wrote, anonymously, 'I am a great *partisan* of the Ancients; but that does not prevent me from rendering justice to the Moderns. I do not burn *Jérusalem délivrée* at the feet of the statue of Virgil, nor the *Henriade* at the feet of the statue of Homer.'[63] 'One loves one's native place,' he wrote in the article *'Natal,'* . . . one cannot take a step there without encountering things that are of interest to us because they recall our age of innocence. Here is my father's house; in that other one, I was born; here, I first went to school; there, I knew that man who was so dear to me; here, that woman who first awakened my desires. . . .' And in an article devoted to his birthplace: 'Modern *Langres* has produced several famous men of letters, not all of

---

* Some of the *Encyclopédie* plates on brass-making are excellently reproduced and easily accessible in Charles C. Gillispie, *A Diderot Pictorial Encyclopedia of Trades and Industry* (New York, 1959): see Plates 142–6, together with the descriptive note facing Plate 142.

whom, fortunately, are dead.' [64] The article *'Mâcher'* was evidently written after he had received medical advice from Dr. Tronchin: 'One cannot recommend too highly the mastication of one's food. It is a sure way of preventing several kinds of illnesses, but very difficult to practise. There is no habit more ingrained, perhaps, than that of eating fast.' [65]

Diderot made the *Encyclopédie,* which also promises on its title page to be a dictionary, a vehicle for illustrating synonyms and giving definitions. In the article *'Prostitution'* he thus was able to grind two axes at once: 'The acceptation of these words *prostitute* and *prostitution* has been extended to those critics, of whom we have so many today, and at the head of whom may be placed the odious personage whom M. de Voltaire put upon the stage under the name of Wasp in the play *L'Ecossaise. . . .'* [66] To illustrate the word *'Susciter'* (To stir up), Diderot wrote, 'This work [the *Encyclopédie*] has *stirred up* for us lots of enemies.' [67] And, somberly, for it seems to allude to his quarrel with Rousseau, he wrote in illustration of the verb *'Reconcilier,'* 'There are some offenses that one never forgets, and men with whom one is never reconciled.' [68]

How many of the eleven million words in the last ten volumes of the *Encyclopédie* were written by Diderot himself it is impossible to know. But as editor, if not as author, he knew them all, had passed upon them all, and included them in the work because he wanted them to be there. The *Encyclopédie* is as significant as it is in the history of culture and in the movement of ideas precisely because its editor, early and late, had a sharply defined editorial policy. The importance of the *Encyclopédie* had always lain in the fact that the editorial policy was bold and aggressive, that it consciously and pugnaciously fought for 'philosophy' and 'enlightenment.' 'Philosophy is advancing with giant steps,' Diderot had written in Volume II, 'and enlightenment is accompanying and following her.' [69] In view of its dynamic policy, the *Encyclopédie* was a supremely valuable instrument of civilization:

Were a revolution, the germ of which might perhaps be forming even now in some unknown corner of the earth or secretly be incubating at the very center of civilization [wrote Diderot in the foreword to the last ten volumes], . . . were a revolution to break out sometime, overthrowing cities, dispersing populations anew, and bringing back ignorance and darkness, if one single complete copy of this work should be saved, all would not be lost.[70]

Such sturdy self-confidence bespeaks a policy. The whole *Encyclopédie* was suffused both explicitly and implicitly with a sharply defined methodology. First of all, the *Encyclopédie* believed in the empire of facts. It stood also for a particular way of thinking about data. It stood for a belief in cause and effect; for a confidence in reason; for a disbelief in miracles; and for a belief in the efficacy of common sense, logic, and education. It disapproved of slovenly thinking, and aimed to teach people how to reason more critically. It was for scientific method, applied not merely to mathematics (a point carefully made in the article 'Méthode'), but also to the natural sciences and to what we now call the social sciences. It despised vulgar errors and obscurantism.[71] Such had been the teaching of the first seven volumes of the Encyclopédie, and such was the teaching of the last ten.*

The article 'Hypothèse' is an example of an essay in scientific method to be found in the last ten volumes of the Encyclopédie. If Diderot did not write this article — it cannot be proved that he did, but it also cannot be proved that he did not — its emphasis upon the fruitfulness of making hypotheses is entirely consonant with his own 'conjectures' published ten years before in his book on scientific method, Pensées sur l'interprétation de la nature:

Probabilities are not to be rejected in scientific work; one must make a start in any line of research, and this beginning almost always has to be a very imperfect attempt, often unsuccessful. There are truths that are unknown in the way that there are countries the best road to which can only be learned after having tried them all. Some persons have to take the risk of getting off the track in order to show the right road to others.

The article then develops the point that because the Cartesians had overworked hypotheses, the Newtonians in consequence had over-reacted against them. Nevertheless, 'Copernicus, Kepler, Huyghens, Descartes, Leibniz, Newton himself have all devised hypotheses useful for explaining complicated and difficult phenomena.'[72]

There is a large-mindedness about the Encyclopédie which strikes a reader even today and goes far towards explaining the stimulation and excitement that readers found in it two hundred years ago. Combined with spaciousness of outlook was a sense of humanity and of social conscience. This is to be seen in the outbursts against the slave trade.

This buying of Negroes for the purpose of reducing them to slavery is a trade that violates religion, morality, natural law, and all the rights of human nature

---

* Readily accessible and well-edited anthologies of Encyclopédie articles in English translation are Encyclopedia: Selections, edited by Nelly S. Hoyt and Thomas Cassirer (The Library of Liberal Arts, Bobbs-Merrill, 1965); and The Encyclopedia: Selections, edited by Stephen Gendzier (Harper Torchbooks, 1967).

[wrote De Jaucourt]. If this sort of commerce can be justified by moral principles, there is no crime, no matter how atrocious, that cannot be legitimized. . . . Let the European colonies be destroyed rather than make so many wretched.[73]

And in the article *'Humaine espèce'* (Human species), itself an early and noteworthy exercise in physical anthropology, the author, thought to be Diderot himself, wrote, 'We have reduced them [the Negroes], I do not say to the condition of slaves but to that of beasts of burden; and we are reasonable men! and we are Christians!'[74]

Compassion showed itself in Diderot's definition of *'Journalier'* (Day-laborer): 'This sort of man constitutes the largest part of any nation; it is the lot of this part that a good government ought to have principally in view. If the day-laborer is wretched, the nation is wretched.'[75] And in indignation against the nobility, flashing out unexpectedly from Diderot's article on a most obscure topic, *'Hondreous'*: 'This is the name given in the island of Ceylon to the nobles, who thus, as everywhere else, distinguish themselves from the common people by great haughtiness and arrogance.'[76] And there is compassion, and patriotism too, in Diderot's comment upon the Revocation of the Edict of Nantes:

There is no good Frenchman who has not long since bewailed the profound wound suffered by the kingdom by the loss of so many useful subjects. . . . The spirit of persecution should be curbed by any government that is enlightened. . . .[77]

This last quotation reminds us once again that the *Encyclopédie* was never far from commenting upon government and religion, even though its editor and contributors knew (as one of them wrote in illustrating the use of the word *'Précaution'*), 'One cannot use too many *precautions* when speaking of religion and of the government, especially in public.'[78] The temper of the *Encyclopédie* in the matter of religion was of course tolerant and broad-minded. It was almost exactly the temper of John Locke's *Letter concerning Toleration,* but what was printable in England in 1689 could scarcely be referred to out loud in France, even in the France of the 1760's. The last volumes of the *Encyclopédie* were being written just at the time that Jean Calas was being judicially murdered. They were published precisely when the young Chevalier de La Barre was being tried for impiety and blasphemy. These events deeply affected the consciences of Frenchmen, but one could never be confident, if one expressed oneself too candidly, that one might not get badly hurt by the police power of the state.

The *Encyclopédie* was always emphatic about moral conduct but always lukewarm about religious cults. 'Morality can exist without religion, and religion can exist, and often does, with immorality,' Diderot wrote in the article *'Irréligieux,'* thus repeating the point that Molière had tried so hard to make in *Tartuffe*. Religiousness, Diderot went on, is relative: no one at Paris is going to treat a Mahometan as a criminal if he manifests contempt for the law of Mahomet, nor will anyone at Constantinople treat a Christian as a criminal for forgetting Christianity — an argument for religious toleration that comes straight out of the pages of John Locke, though Diderot did not choose or did not dare to say so. 'It is not the same with moral principles. . . . Morality is the same everywhere. It is the universal law which the finger of God has written on all hearts. It is the eternal precept of common feeling [*sensibilité*] and of common need.' [79] And Diderot, who had already lectured his brother in the long letter that became the *Encyclopédie* article *'Intolérance,'* added this in the article *'Intolérant'*:

The intolerant man should be regarded everywhere in the world as a person who sacrifices the spirit and the precepts of his religion to his pride; he is the presumptuous one who believes that it is his hands that must hold up the Ark; he is almost always a man without religion, to whom it comes easier to display zeal than to be truly principled [*avoir des moeurs*].[80]

Although to the day of his death Diderot never forgave Le Breton's treacherous censoring of the *Encyclopédie,* charging him with frustrating the legitimate expectations of subscribers who had come to look in its pages for 'a stout and bold philosophy,' was this really so? Had Le Breton really 'emasculated, dismembered, mutilated it'? Had he made the contributors 'insipid and flat'? Fortunately, Diderot exaggerated. In spite of Le Breton's depredations, it is probably true that the *Encyclopédie* was more unaltered, more true to itself, than Le Breton wished it to be. 'The impartiality of many articles, the difficulty of locating and perceiving the unorthodoxy of others, the effort and expense of resetting type — all these circumstances preserved the *Encyclopédie* from being fundamentally transformed by its chief publisher.' [81]

What the *Encyclopédie* had to say was still venturesome and courageous. In philosophy, for example, there were here and there passages in which the most arrant and daring materialism came to the surface. The article *'Naître'* (To be born), which contains all the arguments later developed by Diderot in *Le Rêve de d'Alembert,* has been called 'one of the articles in which the materialistic ideas of the Encyclopedists were most boldly affirmed.' [82] And in the last paragraph of his article on Locke, Diderot wrote:

Even though sensitivity were the first beginnings of thought; even though it were a general property of matter; even though, unequally distributed among all the productions of nature, it were to manifest itself with less energy or greater according to how it was organized, what pernicious consequence would flow from that? Man would keep right on being what he is, judged by the good use and the bad he makes of his faculties.[83]

In many places the last ten volumes of the *Encyclopédie* strike the reader as being more tart and explicit than were the earlier ones. Take, for example, the tricky and touchy subjects of political theory and of social and political change. When Volume I was published there had been very severe criticism of Diderot's article on *'Autorité, politique.'* This article had contended that the legitimate power of a monarch ought to be subject to limitations, and had stirred up furious criticism on the part of numerous proponents of divine-right monarchy. Thereafter the *Encyclopédie* had had to walk more gingerly.[84] But in the last ten volumes there are numerous articles propounding the doctrine of limited monarchy: Diderot's own article *'Indépendance'* and his very important *'Souverains,'* and De Jaucourt's *'Monarchie limitée,' 'Monarchie absolue,' 'Loi fondamentale,'* and *'Liberté politique.'*[85] In articles ranging from theories of sovereignty to problems of civil rights, from questions involving representative bodies and constitutional limitations of authority to problems of public administration and tax reform, the last ten volumes of the *Encyclopédie* had an abundance of things to say, utterances that were both stout and bold.

Nor were these the only articles on statecraft. There were pugnacious articles on intolerance, especially *'Prêtres'* (Priests) and *'Théocratie,'* contributed by D'Holbach. There were articles on freedom of the press, notably *'Presse'* and *'Libelle':* 'In general, any country where it is not permissible to think and write one's thoughts must inevitably fall into stupidity, superstition, and barbarism.'[86] De Jaucourt's long article *'Impôt'* (Tax) inveighed against the arbitrariness of the existing tax structure and enumerated ten specific proposals for reform. He also devoted an eloquent article to the notorious salt tax *'Sel, impôt sur le,'* not forgetting to point out that farmers with pastures bordering seacoasts were forbidden under severe penalities to let their livestock drink sea water. 'In short, were not the arbitrary *taille* [the direct tax] already in effect, the tax on salt would be perhaps the most calamitous one possible to imagine.'[87] Diderot himself contributed to the very lengthy article by Damilaville on the *'Vingtième'* — 'what is good in it was stuffed into it by Diderot,' wrote Grimm.[88] In *'Vingtième'* the argument was set forth for a kind of single tax as over against the multiplicity of existing taxes on merchandise and food-stuffs, and the practice of house-searching used to enforce such existing taxes was denounced. 'If that is what it means to enjoy civil liberty, I would very much like to have some-one tell me what is servitude. If this is the way that person and property are guaranteed, then what must it be when they're not?' [89]

Diderot was always close to being critical of the existing régime — always close to exhibiting that feeling of alienation that Karl Mannheim has shown to be characteristic of the intellectual. Thus, in defining the word *'Mince'* (Slender), Diderot wrote, 'There are people of very *slender* merit to whom have been granted very important positions, whether in the judiciary, the Church, the government, or the army.' [90] Of course he was against privilege wherever he found it, which was almost everywhere one looked in the society of the *ancien régime.* 'The only legitimate privileges are those ac-corded by Nature. All others may be regarded as injustices perpetrated in favor of one man against all men.' [91] And as might be expected, he in-veighed against the power of the state's being used to enforce religious belief, an exercise of power which he baldly called 'tyranny.' *'Persecution* is the tyranny exercised by the sovereign, or permitted in his name, against such of his subjects as follow opinions different from his in matters of religion.' [92]

While these pronouncements are quite general and abstract, Diderot also proved that he had sharp opinions about the specific political and consti-tutional problems of the day. For example, he favored the constitutional contentions of the *parlements* of France, especially those of the Parlement of Paris. The *parlements* — there were thirteen of them in all of France in 1765 — were law courts and not legislative assemblies, but they had managed through the years to establish the principle that royal decrees were not enforceable until the *parlements* had officially registered them. This prin-ciple was of prime political importance, for while it did not go so far as to establish a veto on royal power — the king, visiting the Parlement of Paris in person in a ceremony called a *'lit de justice,'* could command the forced registration of a decree — it did have the effect of a slow-down. Resistance by the *parlements,* therefore, was almost the only institutionalized way in the eighteenth-century Bourbon monarchy by which absolutist royal power could be constitutionally opposed. Naturally, therefore, the *parle-ments,* in spite of the fact that they themselves were privileged bodies with vested interests of their own, were frequently able to make themselves ap-pear as the defenders of liberty against royal encroachment. Diderot was not blind to the fact that the *parlements* were often motivated by nothing more exalted than a desire to preserve their vested interests, but, realistically, he was glad to take what he could get. Already, in his *Apologie de M.*

l'Abbé de Prades (1752) Diderot had emphasized that the Parlement of Paris, constitutionally, was much more than just a judicial body. In his *Encyclopédie* articles on *'Obvier'* (Obviate) and on *'Parlementaire'* he continued to show in the last ten volumes that he was on the side of the *parlements* against the crown.[93]

In favoring the *parlements* Diderot was, in his own way, subscribing to the doctrine of the separation of powers. And his awareness of the constitutional issues at stake in the politics of France is further shown by his espousing the cause of the representative provincial assemblies which still existed in some of the French provinces. These provinces, among them Brittany, Burgundy, Dauphiné, and Languedoc, were known as *pays d'état* (in distinction from the other provinces of the kingdom, which were known as *pays d'élection*). 'The provincial estates are the best remedy for the drawbacks of a large monarchy,' the *Encyclopédie* stated in a passage that may have been written by Diderot himself. 'They even constitute the essence of the monarchy, which does not need powers so much as intermediary bodies between the prince and the people.'[94]

Diderot never gave up his fondness for intermediary representative bodies as an institutionalized way for tempering overmighty government. He was a constitutionalist. To the end of his life he continued to develop as a political theorist, so that his pronouncements in the *Encyclopédie* represent only one stage, and that not the most dramatic one, in his political theory. Nevertheless, whether as author or as editor, he introduced into the last ten volumes of the *Encyclopédie* political doctrines and proposals revolutionary enough to keep his readers turning the page. As an Englishman wrote of the *Encyclopédie* in 1768, 'In short, whoever takes the trouble of combining the several political articles, will find that they form a noble system of civil liberty.'[95] Thus, in spite of Le Breton's perfidy, the *Encyclopédie* broadcast a philosophy that was acknowledged by both friends and enemies, by both foreigners and Frenchmen, to be stout and bold.

What Diderot hoped for his *Encyclopédie* was that it would be useful, not only in being informative, but also in bringing about 'a revolution in men's minds.' It would be a revolution bringing more freedom, less oppression, more tolerance, less fanaticism.

This work will surely produce, in time, a revolution in men's minds, and I trust that tyrants, oppressors, fanatics, and intolerant people will not be the gainers for it. We shall have served mankind. . . .

We shall have served mankind; 'but before we're given much credit for that, we shall have long since returned to cold and insensible dust.'[96]

CHAPTER 36

Private Life and Public Alarms

I N FEBRUARY 1765 a close friend of Diderot, Didier
d'Arclais de Montamy, died and left a manuscript
for Diderot to see through the press.[1] Montamy was a physicist and chemist
and both Diderot and Grimm greatly admired him. 'No one is better informed than he. No one has better judgment, nor greater wisdom in his
conduct,' wrote Diderot; while Grimm said that he had 'never known
an experimenter less opinionated, less doctrinaire . . . more patient, more
indefatigable.'[2] Montamy prided himself upon being a Christian; Diderot
and Grimm, in turn, prided themselves upon being his friend in spite of it.
'Embrace me,' Montamy said on his deathbed to Diderot, 'we shall see each
other again. If you grieve, it will be because you don't believe.' Diderot had
been much struck by Montamy's trust in the face of death. ' "My friend,
you are going to be stopped short in the middle of your researches." "Oh!
what difference does that make?" he replied. "It will not be lost." '[3]

The sufficient reason why it was not lost was that Diderot edited the
manuscript, got a license to have it published, saw it through the press, and
then engaged the self-interest of a publisher by conveying the copyright
to him.[4] So far as is known, this was purely a labor of love, and Diderot
received no emolument. Nor was Diderot, as editor of this *Treatise on
Colors for Painting in Enamel and on Porcelain* . . . identified to the public in any way. Posterity can recognize from time to time the characteristic
marks of his editing. It can also admire a remarkable addendum that
Diderot wrote, a comprehensive essay on the latest techniques of producing
cobalt blue.[5]

Two other of Diderot's acquaintances died in 1765, the artist Carle Van
Loo and the mathematician Clairaut. Diderot wrote the notice on Van Loo
in the *Correspondance littéraire,* remarking that 'No one has better demonstrated than he how different genius is from intelligence. It cannot be

denied that he had great talent, yet he was also very stupid, and it was pitiful to hear him talk about painting.' Nevertheless Diderot admired Van
Loo, of whom he said '. . . the glory of a people and of an age is always
the work of a small number of great men, and disappears when they do.' [6]
In writing this Diderot may also have had in mind Rameau, who had died
the year before. Diderot probably also wrote part of the obituary of Clairaut
in the *Correspondance littéraire.* At least the explanation there of why
Clairaut had outlived his fame was consonant with Diderot's views: the
public taste 'has turned towards useful things, and what there is useful in
geometry can be learned in six months. . . .' The author described the striking change in intellectual interests which was characterizing the 1760's in
France: 'Geometry [has given way] to natural history and chemistry, which
have been in vogue most recently and which share the public interest with
governmental affairs, commerce, politics, and especially the mania for agriculture. . . .' [7]

During this year Horace Walpole met Diderot at D'Holbach's. Walpole
characterized the fifty-two-year-old Diderot as 'a very lively old man and
great talker. . . .' [8] Friends such as Morellet perceived Diderot with more
discrimination. To them he was a conversationalist with powers of dazzling,
even overwhelming eloquence. An indirect outcome of one of these sparkling improvisations was Diderot's essay 'On Terence,' published anonymously
in this very year. Jean-Baptiste Suard, one of the editors of the *Gazette
Littéraire de l'Europe,* had heard Diderot start talking one day about Terence and begged him to write it down. There is a tradition that Diderot
wrote this essay in one sitting, but Naigeon records that it took eight days.[9]

'Terence was the slave of the Roman senator Terentius Lucanus,' Diderot
began. 'Terence a slave! One of the greatest geniuses in the history of Rome!'
This leads Diderot to show his impressive knowledge of the nature of
slavery in ancient times, with philosophic reflections about the desirability of
creative freedom in his own. He then turns to an important literary and
critical distinction, that between verve and taste. Aristophanes and Molière
had verve; Terence had taste. There follow some thoughtful observations
on how hard it is to translate Terence — '. . . all that is delicate and subtle
in the Latin language is in this poet' — and this in turn conducts Diderot to
some stimulating speculations about the technics of poetry and the mysteries of style.[10]

The essay 'On Terence' is an example of Diderot at his best. Even a critic
usually hostile to him said of this work, 'One cannot be more simple, more
elegant, more clear. . . .' [11] Certainly there is a more contemplative, reflec-

tive quality in 'On Terence' than there had been in Diderot's *Eloge de Richardson*. Perhaps he was affected by his subject, for Terence is a playwright noted for the coolness and self-control by which he gets his effects. Diderot had a kindred feeling for Terence, believing that the eighteenth-century *drame*, exemplified most of all by his own *Le Fils naturel* and *Le Père de famille*, was trying to accomplish for itself what Terence had succeeded in doing so well. In consequence Terence is one of Diderot's heroes, whom he even defends against the criticism of one of his other heroes, Montaigne.[12] The fact that a writer whose work exhibits control rather than effusiveness, self-discipline rather than impulsiveness, was a hero to Diderot is significant. He was beginning to make his own transition from sensibility to self-control.

Self-control of physical appetites as well as of intellectual ones did not come easily to Diderot. His chronic stomach trouble was not helped by his eating habits. Now and again he victimized himself by a colossal display of intemperance. 'My father used to say to me,' wrote his daughter, 'that D'Holbach's house would kill him off very quickly if he dined there oftener than once a week.'[13] At no time did he describe this indulgence more amusingly than on an occasion in 1765:

I drank wines with all sorts of names; then a melon of an incredible perfidy was awaiting me; and do you suppose that it was possible to resist an enormous *fromage glacé?* And then liqueurs; and then coffee; and then an abominable indigestion that kept me up all night and has made me pass the morning between the teapot and another earthen vessel which it is not decent to name. But thanks be to God, here I am, purged to last ten years.

Moreover, he had gout, which he admitted he always called 'rheumatism': '. . . the thumb on my right hand is giving me a devil of a lot of trouble.'[14]

Mme Diderot, too, was ailing this year, complaining most of sciatica, which she treated by having her leg rubbed with a mixture of salt, brandy, and soap. 'I have been given the responsibility of this operation once or twice, and I have acquitted myself very well.'[15] And when the Diderots were not sick themselves, they called upon a sick friend, for such was D'Alembert during this summer. His recent triumphal visit to Prussia at Frederick II's invitation had not changed D'Alembert's style of life. He continued to live in the cramped quarters of his foster-mother's home in the Rue Michel-le-comte. It was there that he fell ill in 1765 and there that the Diderots came to see him. 'Ever since we learned he was sick, we have gone there regularly every day, Madame in the morning and I in the afternoon.' There were usually other friends in the room too, and Diderot met there for the first time — he misspelled her name — the passionate and perhaps more pathetic than tragic Julie de Lespinasse. Mlle de Lespinasse was destined presently to set up housekeeping with D'Alembert; and now, in Diderot's words, she 'established herself at his bedside by eight in the morning and did not leave it until twelve at night.'

Because of their solicitude for D'Alembert, the Diderots became involved in a social situation 'which is not pleasant,' as Diderot wrote, and in which he showed himself much more stern, and more regardful of his wife, than one might have expected. On her very first visit Mme Diderot found a circle of D'Alembert's friends already there, including the Abbé Morellet, a mimic and satirist with so caustic a tongue that Voltaire liked to pun on his name, calling him *'mords-les,'* 'Bite 'em.' When, on this occasion, D'Alembert inquired about Diderot's health, 'the good woman, who likes to chatter, did not let the opportunity slip.' The next day, at D'Holbach's, Morellet, who had been a friend of Diderot for fifteen years, began to ridicule her by mimicking her conversation and was 'beginning to excite the interest of his auditors.' Diderot stopped him short, 'pointing out in a tone both very serious and very firm that he was speaking of my wife. . . . Then, drawing an armchair up to his, I sat down and said to him: ". . . Abbé, it is your profession to make people laugh, but there are some rules that a jokester ought to know, that perhaps you do know, but that you always forget. The first is that, unless you have to do with the most contemptible of men, you should never expect that he will patiently tolerate a disparagement in his presence of his father, his mother, his wife, his son, his daughter, and his friends. . . . A fourth rule is that if one forgets the three previous ones, the jokester runs the risk of being thrown out of the fucking window." ' [16]

Several of Diderot's friends were missing from his circle in 1765. The vivacious Abbé Galiani was recalled to Naples in April for consultations and did not return to his post at Paris until December 1766.[17] Damilaville was chronically ill and went to Geneva to consult Dr. Tronchin. 'I greatly fear,' wrote Diderot, who had a horror of venereal disease, 'that he is going to have to pay with his life for a few casual and very undiscriminating pleasures. It's a very high price.' [18] Helvétius, who had been in England in 1764 and liked everything that he saw there, in 1765 was a visitor to Potsdam.[19] D'Holbach, too, visited England, in 1765, and was heartily welcomed there. Unlike Helvétius, however, D'Holbach returned with a most unflattering and disagreeable impression of the country. Nothing in six weeks pleased him except the system of post-chaises. He did not care for English manners; he criticized the inequality of wealth in England; and London displeased him, which recalled to Diderot 'a charming saying of our friend Garrick, that London is good for the English, but Paris is good for everybody.' [20]

A great change in French opinion about the government of England occurred in the 1760's. D'Holbach shared in this, in fact was one of the first to articulate it. For a generation the French, brought up on Voltaire's *Philosophical Letters,* had admired the British political system, and this admiration had been greatly fortified by Montesquieu's *Spirit of the Laws* (1748). But following the Seven Years' War and the accession of George III to the throne, the conviction began to grow that beneath the surface of cabinet government and parliamentary politics was widespread corruption. The Crown, according to this view, by buying its henchmen's way into Parliament, was in fact able to do what it pleased. D'Holbach and his circle could very readily have learned about this from John Wilkes, who regarded himself as a particular victim of the system. In England this interpretation of the realities of British politics was becoming a commonplace constantly harped upon by the Whigs. Edmund Burke came to be as convinced of it as John Wilkes. The root of D'Holbach's grumpiness about things British was his scenting this corruption. Diderot summarized his friend's impressions — and apparently adopted them for his own — in a long letter to Sophie Volland. 'The monarch . . . is as much the master of everything as any other sovereign, and even more so. Elsewhere the court commands and makes itself obeyed. There it corrupts and does what it pleases, and the corruption of its subjects is perhaps worse, in the long run, than tyranny.' [21]

With the tapering-off in 1765 of work on the *Encyclopédie,* Diderot evidently had time for making new friends. Mentioned for the first time in his letters are several persons with whom he henceforth became closely associated. There was Naigeon, a disciple so intent upon his self-appointed mission of discipleship that some people called him 'Diderot's ape.' Naigeon was a bore, long-winded, tiresome, and steeped in a particularly dull and monotonous form of atheism. Yet we owe a good deal of our knowledge about Diderot to Naigeon. When he edited the three volumes on philosophy that appeared in the *Encyclopédie méthodique,* he included several of Diderot's hitherto unpublished works, combined with a considerable amount of authoritative but previously unknown information about his life and writings. Moreover, in 1821 Naigeon published his own *Mémoires his-*

toriques et philosophiques sur la vie et les ouvrages de D. Diderot, which also is a mine of information. In addition, he published the fifteen-volume edition of Diderot's works that appeared in 1798. Thus we might say, to paraphrase Thomas Carlyle, 'Honor the tedious atheist! Say not he lived in vain!' [22]

In July, the same month in which he first mentioned Naigeon and became acquainted with Mlle de Lespinasse, Diderot also met the Princess of Nassau-Saarbruck. This was the lady to whom in 1758 he had addressed the letter on education which served as a dedication to *Le Père de famille.* Grimm and Diderot spent a morning with her. 'My hackles, which were up as never in my life, were smoothed down in an instant, and had I been seeing her for the hundredth time I couldn't have been more at my ease.' [23] Then, in August, Diderot made what he plainly regarded as a conquest. This was the young wife of the Swiss banker Jacques Necker, a girl who at one time had been Edward Gibbon's fiancée and who was presently to become the mother of a daughter marked for fame, the future Mme de Staël. 'By the way, do you realize that if I wanted to, I could be vain? There's a Mme Neckre here, beautiful and bright, who is crazy about me. It's a persecution the way she tries to have me at her house.' [24] The fact was that Mme Necker, imitating Mme du Deffand and Mme Geoffrin, was trying to form a *salon.*

This same year a neighbor of the Diderots, the widow of a Swiss watchmaker named Jodin, lost most of her possessions in a burglary. 'We asked her to come eat with us every day. . . .' Mme Jodin had an actress daughter, a violent young woman of more temperament than talent, who at this time was the leading lady of a French troupe in Warsaw. Diderot wrote to Mlle Jodin a series of very characteristic letters, advising her on how to improve her acting — 'Work especially hard to perfect your talent; the most wretched position in all of life, in my opinion, is that of a mediocre actress' — and showering her with unsolicited counsel on her private life.[25]

Several of Diderot's acquaintances, now mentioned in his correspondence for the first time, were associated with his growing expertness in art and his increasing acquaintanceship among artists. For example, he spends a morning in July at the studio of the sculptor Vassé, who had been commissioned to do an audience room for Catherine II. Young Prince Dmitri Galitzin, the Russian ambassador to France, had asked Diderot to give his opinion about it.[26] Or Diderot reports visiting the 1765 Salon before the opening, apparently admitted surreptitiously by his artist friend Choffard.[27] Or Diderot dines at the house of Louis-Michel Van Loo, the artist who was

soon to paint the portrait of Diderot that now hangs in the Louvre. At
Van Loo's Diderot met the Scottish portraitist Allan Ramsay, whose paintings of Rousseau and of Hume are so justly famous. In October Diderot and
Ramsay met again, this time at D'Holbach's, where the conversation turned
to Marivaux, Richardson, and the Ossianic poems, and where Horace
Walpole and the Abbé Raynal were among the other guests.[28] And it is in
1765 that we first read in Diderot's correspondence of Falconet, the gifted
sculptor of charming cupids and cool, svelte Venuses, a man who was
irascible, opinionated, and disputatious, and whom Diderot dubbed the
'Jean-Jacques Rousseau of his art.'

   It is also in this year that Diderot's correspondence first mentions Michel-
Jean Sedaine, a librettist and playwright whose drama *Le Philosophe sans
le savoir* ['A Philosopher without Knowing It'] had its *première* at the
Comédie-Française on 2 December. Eight months before, Diderot had read
it, and was so enthusiastic about it that he jumped up from his chair, embraced Sedaine, and cried, 'Ah, my friend, if you were not so old, I'd give
you my daughter!' (Sedaine was then a forty-six-year-old bachelor and
Angélique was twelve and a half.) [29] Diderot attended the *première:*
'Yesterday I sometimes had the vanity of feeling that I alone, in the midst
of two thousand people, was appreciating its merit, because people were not
beside themselves, drunk with it as I was, were not crying out. . . .' [30]
(Success was not certain until the third performance.) The next morning,
Diderot later recounted, using the short sentences and the present tense
which so often heightened the pace and dash of his style, 'I throw myself
into a cab, I rush to find Sedaine. It is winter and very cold. I go everywhere where I can hope to find him. I learn that he is way out in the Fau-
bourg Saint-Antoine. I have myself taken there. I find him. I throw my
arms around his neck. My voice fails me and the tears run down my
cheeks.' [31] And what did Sedaine, always the dispassionate observer, say in
response? 'Ah! Monsieur Diderot, how beautiful you are like that.' [32]

   What was it that aroused Diderot's enthusiasm to such a characteristic
pitch? The answer is that *Le Philosophe sans le savoir* is an almost perfect
exemplification of his own theories of what a play should be. It was about
non-noble people; it showed them endowed with heroic, even though
domestic, virtues; and it was presented with realism and without too much
coincidence, as something that had verisimilitude and could happen in
everyday life. Thus we see the admirable and beneficent *père de famille*
Vanderk, a wealthy merchant, who discovers one night just before dawn
that his mettlesome son is that moment departing to fight a duel. In fact,

the son was the challenger: he had called his opponent out because the latter had made some insulting remarks about merchants as a class. Sedaine presents Vanderk's suffering simply but convincingly: 'I went to bed with peace of mind, the happiest of fathers, and look at me now!' The father allows his son to go off to the duel and awaits the prearranged signal of the outcome. Presently it comes, three loud knocks on the door, announcing that the son is dead. This, however, turns out to be false, and the curtain comes down upon a reunited and happy family. Social historians might make more of this play, a monument as it is of eighteenth-century social stratification and bourgeois class consciousness.

Diderot plumed himself upon his enthusiasm for the play, because it proved, he said, that he was not an envious man.[33] He had a point (though perhaps it was a little vain of him to make it). For Sedaine's drama is much superior to *Le Fils naturel* or *Le Père de famille*. Diderot had laid down precepts and showed the way to the promised land. Sedaine entered it.

Sedaine's play naturally revived in Paris a great deal of talk about duelling. 'To Baron d'Holbach's,' wrote Horace Walpole in his entry of 8 December 1765. 'Baron de Gleichen, the Danish minister, Dr. Gem, and Diderot there. . . . Diderot said, the French were so changed, that it had been said lately, that Louis XV would find it as difficult to re-establish duels, as Louis XIV had to suppress them.'[34]

Our knowledge of this time in the life of Diderot is greatly enhanced by the fact that Sophie was out of town some nine months beginning in May 1765, during which time Diderot continued to follow 'the project that I set myself of not letting you be ignorant of any of the instants of my life.'[35] In his letters to her he often complains of overwork, especially in October and November when Grimm was driving him to complete the *Salon de 1765*. Diderot had hired a young artist named La Rue to help him, only to discover that La Rue's notes were scarcely decipherable. 'He writes as badly as a laundress or a bishop.'[36] Also increasing the daily burden upon Diderot was the beginning of the lively dispute that spontaneously but somewhat gratuitously arose between Falconet and himself concerning the relationship of an artist to posterity and which dragged on for many months.[37] Moreover, Diderot was prodigal, as always, in taking time to read the manuscripts of friends, so that he wrote on 20 December that

The day before yesterday I had on my desk a comedy [by Nicolas-Thomas Barthe], a tragedy [by Pierre de Belloy], a translation [of Terence, by the Abbé Le Monnier], a political work [by the Abbé Reynal] and a memorandum [concerning a famous law case], to say nothing of a comic opera [by Marmontel].[38]

The memorandum is of special interest, for Diderot had been retained to testify in the Douglas Cause, the most celebrated Scottish law suit of the century. As an expert witness, Diderot gave his opinion as to whether certain letters were written by a native Frenchman or a foreigner.[39]

Throughout these months and coming to a climax in 1766 were several series of events in which Diderot was intimately concerned. The first had to do with Rousseau and his ill-starred visit to England. The friendship between Diderot and Rousseau had been so close, and the breaking of it so rending, that in many ways the two men, aptly called 'enemy brothers,' never got over it and never left off affecting each other to the end of their lives.[40] Of the two Diderot felt the loss the more, or at least made more of an effort toward reconciliation. For a few years after 1758 there was no sign from either of any consciousness of the other's existence. With the publication in May of 1762 of *Emile,* containing as it did the deistic 'Confession of Faith of a Savoyard Vicar,' misfortune and persecution came upon Rousseau. He had to flee France and take refuge in the territory of Neuchâtel, thus becoming a guest of its sovereign, Frederick II of Prussia. Though Rousseau continued to be unbending in respect to Diderot, remarking about this time that Diderot had been born a better man than Voltaire but had become a worse one, his plight awoke Diderot's sympathy.[41] At first he had supposed that Rousseau would suffer no ill consequences for boldly publishing such a daring work under his own name: 'The devout are on his side. He owes the interest they take in him to the evil he has spoken of the *philosophes.*' In the same vein Diderot wrote to Sophie that Jean-Jacques was a man of excesses, and that his 'Confession of Faith of a Savoyard Vicar' was a kind of balderdash.[42] Nevertheless Diderot began to defend Rousseau. In June 1763 Lenieps, a Genevan banker at Paris, wrote Rousseau that 'M. Diderot takes the side of your writings in every respect and wherever he is.' A month later Lenieps again reported that 'Diderot . . . has taken your side against all comers.'[43] Nevertheless Rousseau said of Diderot, presumably in this same year, 'I have been his friend, I am no longer, I have said so to the public, therefore I can say nothing further to you regarding him.'[44]

Rousseau remained at Môtiers in the Val-de-Travers until September 1765, meanwhile becoming so embroiled in Swiss politics that in 1763 he renounced his Genevan citizenship. This was the period when he was writing his *Lettres écrites de la montagne,* a hammer blow against the Establishment in Geneva, and was also being consulted by Corsicans on what should be the constitution for their country, then trying to assert its independence from Genoa. (Rumor at that time had it that Diderot was also approached by the Corsicans, though this has never been confirmed.) [45] In September 1765 Rousseau fled from Môtiers, believing himself in danger of his life. After a few weeks of wandering, he was finally persuaded, through the good offices of a former benefactress, the Countess de Boufflers, to accept the protection of David Hume and settle down in England. Accordingly, in December 1765 Rousseau came to Paris, where he met Hume for the first time, and on 4 January 1766 the two left for England.

Diderot, meanwhile, was aware of Rousseau's whereabouts and his doings. The former is proved by Diderot's being able to give Rousseau's address to a Mme de Baugrand.[46] Moreover, Diderot was aware of a benevolent scheme hatched by Hume to raise a purse for the needy but touchy Rousseau under the guise of its being an unexpected payment owed to him by a publisher. Diderot wrote that he would have been glad to participate in this benevolent conspiracy, though apparently he went unasked.[47] As for knowing about Rousseau's doings, Diderot read the *Lettres écrites de la montagne* while they were still in page proof, and in a review of them written for the *Correspondance littéraire* spoke of them as being unnecessarily disruptive.[48]

In the winter of 1764-5 Diderot had sought, through François-Louis d'Escherny, a native of Neuchâtel then residing in Paris, to make peace with Rousseau. But only on condition that Rousseau should admit that it was he who had been in the greater wrong. Rousseau refused: 'I respect to the limit the obligations of friendship even when it has been extinguished, but I never rekindle it. Such is my most inviolable maxim.' [49] Now, as the news spread that Rousseau was going to pass through Paris on his way to England, Diderot had hopes of seeing him. On 20 December 1765, however, Diderot wrote to Sophie, 'Rousseau has been in Paris for three days. I do not expect he will come to see me; but I shan't hide from you that it would occasion me great pleasure and that I should be very glad to see how he would justify his conduct towards me.' Then he added something very similar to what Rousseau had written D'Escherny, showing how much both men, both 'enemy brothers,' suffered from the ruin of their friendship: 'I do well not to make easy the access to my heart. When once someone has entered it, he does not leave it without rending it; and it is a wound that never completely heals.' [50]

Rousseau passed through Paris without seeing Diderot. The evidence is quite confused as to which one refused to see the other. D'Holbach is the culprit as the greatest source of this confusion, for he wrote to David Garrick that it was Diderot who had refused to see Rousseau and to David Hume that it was reported that it was Rousseau who refused to see Diderot.[51] Rousseau himself told Hume that of all the men of letters formerly his friends, the only one who had not come to see him nor sent word to him when he was in Paris was D'Alembert.[52] Clearly this implies that Diderot did take some initiative and was refused, which would certainly be consistent with the policy Rousseau had previously explained to D'Escherny.

It was not long before the friendship of Rousseau and Hume exploded, causing extraordinary reverberations in France. Hume, egged on by D'Alembert, rushed into print with *A Concise and Genuine Account of the Dispute between Mr. Hume and Mr. Rousseau,* which, translated by Suard, a member of the D'Holbach group, became the *Exposé succinct de la contestation qui s'est élevée entre M. Hume et M. Rousseau.* It is most remarkable that the name of Diderot, who knew intimately all the members of the dispute, was never associated in any way with this controversy.[53] He conspicuously refrained from joining the hue and cry against Rousseau.

The second series of events looming large in the life of Diderot in 1765–6 concerned the very touchy business of securing permission to distribute the final volumes of the *Encyclopédie.* Under any circumstances the mere logistics of distribution would have been formidable, for each of the 4000 subscribers were entitled to ten folio volumes. Added to this was the fact that now once again the *Encyclopédie* became involved, even though indirectly, in the politics of eighteenth-century France.

Both the friends of Diderot and the government itself showed some trepidation as the time for distributing the volumes drew near, for no one could be sure how explosive the reaction would be to the appearance of a work that was not supposed to exist.[54] Diderot, for example, wrote a friend who was expecting Diderot to visit him at Châlons-sur-Marne that the visit would have to be given up: 'The announcement of the completion of the *Encyclopédie* will be made in the foreign newspapers at the beginning of next month and all my friends think it would be imprudent to be away, for a disappearance from Paris would infallibly be interpreted as a flight. . . .'[55] In order to disarm possibly hostile opinion, the elaborate fiction was maintained that all these volumes were manufactured at Neuchâtel, at the press of Samuel Fauche. His name does indeed appear on the title page of each of the last ten volumes, whereas Diderot's does not.[56] As for the government, the readiness of the *Encyclopédie* for distribution awkwardly coincided with the quinquennial meeting of the Assembly of the Clergy. These sessions occurred in 1765 from 25 May to 2 October and from 2 May to 6 July 1766. The clergy of France had been able to establish through the years the principle that their estate was not subject to taxation. In return for this privilege they condescended to make what they carefully called a 'free gift.' The amount was decided upon in these quinquennial assemblies, was probably only a fraction of what it should have been, and from 1750 on was never negotiated without being accompanied by new demands for sanctions against books critical of religion.[57] Thus this Assembly of 1765 on 22 August condemned both the *Encyclopédie* (i.e., the first seven volumes that had already been published) and, in Grimm's unsympathetic words, 'other works which few of our holy prelates are in a state of being able to comprehend.'[58] Moreover, they petitioned the King to be given the censorship of the booktrade, exercised by Malesherbes until 1763 and thereafter by Sartine.[59] Inasmuch as the King hoped to receive 12,000,000 livres from the clergy as a 'free gift,' it is no wonder that the government began to show some vacillation about authorizing the distribution of the new volumes.[60]

The government solved its problem by allowing the distribution abroad and in the provinces while strictly forbidding it at Paris and Versailles. By mid-January 1766 more than a thousand sets had been distributed under these restrictions. D'Holbach wrote Garrick on 9 February that a great number of copies had already been sent to England; not one, 'for prudent reasons,' had yet been delivered in Paris.[61] By 29 March the government was allowing subscribers to pick up sets at a warehouse near Paris, whence owners brought them into Paris at their own risk.[62] Very shortly even this was forbidden. Le Breton was arrested and sent to the Bastille on 23 April for 'having sold the last 10 volumes of the *Encyclopédie* contrary to the express orders of the King and for having sent a quantity to Versailles. This punishment,' the police notation continued, 'was indispensable in order to give satisfaction to the Clergy at their next assembly.'[63]

Le Breton was appalled by the misfortune that had so suddenly overtaken him. Diderot, in spite of his own deep-seated and legitimate grievances with Le Breton, did everything he could to help him out. 'Mr. Le Breton is taken to the Bastille. Then I forget the cruel injury he did me. I rush to his house. I rush to the police. I learn the time of his release and I have nothing more urgent to do than to carry this consolation to Mme Le Breton.'[64] Diderot was convinced that he had secured the release single-handedly. No doubt there was magnanimity in his acting so forcefully. But there was an element of self-protection in it too:

I extricated myself from a perilous situation at the time of Le Breton's imprisonment by intimidating the magistrate [Sartine]. I made him realize that he was as much involved as we were, and that he had either been the most negligent and maladroit watchman that ever was or else our accomplice. In consequence Le Breton was not put to interrogation and they were in almost as much of a hurry to send him back home as they had been to take him to the Bastille.[65]

As late as 4 December 1766 subscribers were still unable to get their volumes in Paris. Indeed, letters signed by Sartine show that the restrictions were still in force at the beginning of November 1767.[66] Most subscribers by that time had solved the problem by having their sets sent to them at their addresses in the country. It is not known precisely when the restrictions came to an end.

The third series of events in 1765-6 closely affecting Diderot was the appalling case of the young Chevalier de La Barre. At Abbeville, in the north of France, a crucifix standing on a bridge was mutilated during the night of 8–9 August 1765. In the inquisition of the whole community that followed, it developed that a luckless Chevalier de La Barre, then eighteen years of age, had once crossed the street in front of a religious procession carrying the Host (and within twenty-five paces of it, too) without doffing his hat or falling to his knees. Moreover, he was alleged to have committed various profanations and blasphemies, none of them ever proved, and it was brought out that on various occasions he had sung impious songs. There were five young men involved. Three were allowed to flee the country, and a fourth was eventually let off because he was only seventeen years old. La Barre alone was the one around whom the net tightened in a way that would take a Kafka to imagine or describe.

Meanwhile, none of this could be proved to have had anything to do with the mutilation of the crucifix, and as a matter of fact the perpetrators of that sacrilege were never discovered. Though the Church itself did not press the matter, and the Bishop of Amiens even tried to have the charges dismissed, local jealousies stoked the case against La Barre. On 28 February 1766 he was condemned to make public penance, have his tongue cut out, his head cut off, and his body burned. All this, as Diderot commented, for 'ineptitudes that merited no more than a slight paternal correction.'[67]

This was horrible enough. But up to this point the case might be discounted as having been exaggerated and ulcerated by small-town animosities and by the bigotry that still existed in the provinces. The case took on national significance, however, when it was appealed to the Parlement of Paris. At Paris one of the magistrates, Denis-Louis Pasquier, a well-known enemy of the *philosophes,* declared in his harangue that the profanations of Abbeville were the deplorable result of the spirit of philosophy spreading in France. He was alleged to have declared also that no progress could be made in setting things right so long as only books were burnt by the public executioner. On 4 June 1766 the Parlement of Paris confirmed the sentence of the lower court. On 1 July the Chevalier de La Barre was given a public execution, though without the preliminary tortures previously ordained, and his corpse was publicly burned.[68]

This 'monument of a horrible cruelty, occurring in a century that prides itself on its philosophy and enlightenment,' came just at the time when the gallant and unfortunate Lally-Tollendal had been executed (9 May 1766) for treason. During the Seven Years' War, Lally had been the French commander in India and had surrendered Pondicherry after a long siege. In his trial he, like La Barre, appeared to be charged not so much with what he had done as with what his accusers could think of, with the judges in a mood to encourage extremism.[69] Neither case was tried in a compassionate spirit. Each was enough to make persons liberally inclined fear that a spirit of vengefulness was taking hold of those at the center of power. Diderot showed very clearly his perception of the intolerance and bigotry of the Parlement of Paris in a letter he wrote to Voltaire:

I know well that once a ferocious beast has tasted human blood it can no longer get on without it. I know well that this beast lacks food and that, no longer having Jesuits to eat, it is going to throw itself upon the *philosophes.* I know well that it has its eyes upon me and that perhaps I will be the first it will devour. . . . I know well that they impute their failures to us because we alone are in a position to point out their stupid blunders. I know well that one among them has been atrocious enough to say that no headway can be made so long as they burn only books.[70]

Voltaire had become especially alarmist and fearful in this crisis. And well he might, for he had been alluded to by name in Pasquier's harangue to the Parlement. Moreover, Voltaire's *Dictionnaire philosophique* was alleged to have been found among the Chevalier de La Barre's books. Accordingly Voltaire feverishly exhorted Diderot and others of the Parisian *philosophes* to flee from France and set up shop in Cleves, in the Rhineland.[71] This proposal was quite similar to his trying in 1758 to get Diderot to give up the *Encyclopédie.*[72] And just as Diderot then had accepted the risks of staying on in Paris and continuing his work, so did he now. No doubt his decision was the easier to make because Cleves was a possession of Frederick the Great, a prince of whom Diderot was less than fond. Diderot himself acknowledged that 'inertia,' the inertia of not wanting to leave his relatives and friends, was keeping him in Paris. He admitted, nevertheless, '. . . my soul is full of alarms; I hear a voice at the bottom of my heart, joining itself to yours and saying, Flee, flee. . . . I know well that . . . when they want to destroy me, I shall be done for.'

The necessity of having to explain himself to Voltaire brought 'to the surface Diderot's feelings about the political regime under which he lived. His letter is surprising in the intensity and bitterness of his political awareness and of his distrust and defiance of the existing regime:

I know well that we are enveloped by the imperceptible threads of a network called the police, and that we are surrounded by informers. . . . I know well that an honest and upright man can in twenty-four hours lose his fortune here, for they are rascals; his honor, for there are no laws; his liberty, for tyrants are easily offended; his life, for they value the life of a citizen as though it were nothing. . . .[73]

Yet, 'though I were to have the fate of Socrates,' he stayed.[74]

CHAPTER 37

Diderot, Falconet, and Catherine II

EVER since her accession in 1762, when she had the suggestion made to Diderot that he transfer the publishing of the *Encyclopédie* to Riga, Catherine II of Russia had thrown her shadow across his path. And from the time that she purchased his library and made him the curator of it for life, Diderot became identified with her in the public mind and, subtly but surely, in his own mind as well. For better and for worse it was a shadow that henceforth went where he did. From now on Diderot had to wrestle with the subtle frustrations of a man caught in the toils of patronage.

This did not happen all at once. And like a love affair that ends ultimately in mutual distaste, its beginnings were sunny and pleasurable. The train of events leading to the sculptor Falconet's going to Russia illustrates this very well. Largely through Diderot's urging it was Falconet whom Catherine II commissioned to carry out her project of erecting a statue of Peter the Great, the giant monument that was to become Pushkin's 'Bronze Horseman.' This memorial turned out to be one of the successes of Catherine II's reign, an eloquent symbol of the pomp of Saint Petersburg and the circumstance of Russian power.

The influence of Falconet upon Diderot is already to be seen in the *Salon de 1765*. Each successive biennial *Salon* had revealed a Diderot more and more deeply involved in the theory of aesthetics, and more and more familiar with the techniques of artists such as Falconet. This increasing involvement manifested itself in the growing amplitude of his *Salons*, that of 1765 being some 85,000 words. Diderot wrote Sophie that Grimm had badgered him to get it finished, and when it was, '. . . he was astounded. He swore upon his soul . . . that no other man on earth had ever accomplished such a work or ever would, and frankly I had the unacknowledged vanity to agree with him. It is certainly the best thing I have done since I began to cultivate letters. . . .'[1]

The three previous *Salons* had devoted scanty attention to sculpture. But that of 1765 contained not only an essay comparing sculpture and painting, but also lengthy comments on the work of Falconet, Le Moyne, Pajou, Caffieri, and others less known. 'It seems to me that it is more difficult to judge sculpture well than it is painting,' Diderot wrote, saying that this should make him more circumspect. It also made him more dependent upon Falconet, to judge from his frequent references to him.[2]

In the *Salon de 1765*, which was written after the exhibition at the Louvre had closed, Diderot was aided as usual by his extraordinary visual memory. It failed him now and again, though rarely. 'I do not know, my friend, but what I am confusing two pictures here. In vain have I rubbed my forehead, painted and repainted in space, forced my imagination back to the Salon. It is useless.'[3] Combined with this almost total recall were the varied resources of a skillful writer who knows how, even by digressions and apparent irrelevancies, to prevent his remarks from falling into repetitiveness and monotony. Often he does it by inserting some personal and subjective observation: he calls Homer his god; he rebukes Boucher by saying, 'This man takes up his brush just to show me breasts and buttocks. I am very pleased to look at them but I cannot endure people pointing them out to me.' Of a picture of Saint Augustine ascending into Heaven, he writes scathingly, 'Will he make it or will he not? Upon my word, I do not know. I see merely that if he falls backward and breaks his neck it will not be his fault, but the fault of those two rascally angels who are looking at his strenuous efforts and making fun of them. Perhaps they are two *Pelagian* angels.' Or he makes a remark that suddenly dissects the social hierarchy of his time: 'Greuze would certainly have put a dog in here, for the lower classes all have one, so that they can have something to order around.'[4]

Diderot had no sooner finished the *Salon de 1765* than he found himself engaged in a spirited dispute with Falconet which ended in their writing letters at each other.[5] This exchange, indispensable for understanding Diderot's motivations and values, debated whether the hope of winning the applause of posterity was the chief incentive, or any incentive at all, for the artist. Diderot said yes: 'In truth, posterity would be very ungrateful if it entirely forgot me, me who have been so greatly aware of it.'[6] Falconet said no. 'He has told me a hundred times that he would not give an *écu* to assure eternal duration to the finest of his statues.'[7]

Falconet was a prickly person and full of paradox. It was hard to be his friend for long, as Diderot found out, who probably would have concurred in the judgment of Peter Gay that 'Falconet served the cause of the Enlightenment more disagreeably than anyone else.' A description of Falconet found among Diderot's papers emphasizes how difficult Falconet was:

. . . he was hard and tender, sophistical and argumentative; eager for praise and scornful of posterity; jealous of the kind of talent he lacked, and caring little for the one he possessed; loving passionately, and cruelly tyrannizing over those he loved; rich in talent, and a hundred, a thousand times more so in self-esteem; asking for advice and never following it; knowing everything, always questioning, and never learning anything; made up of all sorts of contradictions.[8]

Falconet, unjustifiably convinced of his own literary merit, was eager to publish the 'Letters on Posterity.' But Diderot, though not refusing, was reluctant to allow his to be published until he had revised them. This he never did, so that it was not until the nineteenth century that the posterity they argued over was able to consider this appeal to its judgment.[9]

The debate began on a very autobiographical, not to say narcissistic, level. Diderot was seeking in a posthumous and remote future the justification that he felt was being denied him in his lifetime. The intimation of one's reputation with posterity, he wrote, is like the music of flutes in the distant night, 'and my ear, more vain than philosophical, hears even at this moment some imperceptible sounds of that far-off concert.'[10] Thus he himself explains to us how he could write masterpieces and be content to tuck them away in a drawer:

Time was when a man of letters, anxious for the perfection of his work, would keep it twenty, thirty years in his portfolio. However, the possession of it in his imagination served as a substitute for the public enjoyment of which he deprived himself. He lived on the hope of leaving after him an immortal body of work and an immortal name. If this man is crazy, then all my ideas of wisdom are overturned.

'Posterity, to the philosopher,' wrote Diderot, 'is what the world beyond is to the religious man.'[11]

At this point Diderot evidently thought that a small personal disclaimer might be in order, lest he appear outrageously immodest:

The certainty that future centuries would be speaking also of me, that they would count me among the illustrious men of my nation, and that I should honor my century in the eyes of posterity, would be to me, I confess, infinitely sweeter than all present consideration, all present encomia. But I am a long way from having such certainty. If the history of letters accords me a line, it

will not be because of the merit of my works but because of the fury of my
enemies. Nothing will be said of what I have written but perhaps a word will
be mentioned of what I have suffered.[12]

The 'Letters on Posterity' were exchanged between December 1765 and
April 1767, at which latter date Falconet had already arrived in Saint
Petersburg. These are real letters, rather than formal and systematic developments of carefully prepared positions. The writers respond to each
other point by point and helter-skelter. And as they lift their voices to
reach posterity, they become a little forced and shrill. Moreover, the vanity of the two contestants comes to the surface in various ways. This is
especially true in a tedious discussion of the merits of Pliny and Pausanias
as authorities on art. Falconet, though he had taught himself Latin, repudi-
ates the authority of classical art and literature. He is particularly irritated
by what he feels is the presumptuousness of mere men of letters like
Diderot and Voltaire making judgments on the visual arts. So the dispute
drones on as to whether Polygnotus was indeed a great artist and whether
Pausanias is a valid authority in vouching for the greatness of Polygnotus'
art. It is, therefore, not surprising to find the Diderot-Falconet exchange
described as 'pedantic and tortuous' or 'very academic.'[13] A reader emerges
from an immersion in these letters more convinced that they are important
and significant than that they are entertaining.

A liberally and amply educated man, with careful training in Latin,
Greek, philosophy, and rhetoric, and a master of arts degree from the
University of Paris to show for it, Diderot was steeped in humanistic texts.
It shocked him to have Falconet call Pliny a 'dotard.'[14] 'I am the sacristan
of that church,' replied Diderot, and he proceeded to overwhelm Falconet
with references to Greek authors, whose language he knew Falconet did
not know, and to demonstrate that Falconet's latinity was often in error.
All this was rather petty. But on a higher and more spacious level the
debate was forcing Diderot to articulate some of his most tenaciously held
and deep-seated values.

The first article in Diderot's credo was a great respect for the taste and
artistic values of classical antiquity. In addition to all his faith in modernity, he also acknowledged the pulling power of a great and long-standing
tradition. What, therefore, seemed to Falconet an incubus seemed to Diderot an inspiration. When we talk about our posterity, Diderot wrote, we
must remember that 'We are posterity for those who have preceded us.'[15]
It is fundamental with him to feel himself part of a great tradition in arts
and letters that stretches across the ages.

This tradition reaches across time by establishing in cultivated men a kind of 'model' — Diderot's own word and concept, the very word and concept which in the twentieth century have become the cornerstone of systematic methodology in the social sciences. This model of good taste, Diderot thought, did not have to be created or conceived. It had always been in existence — a very striking instance of a Platonic idea in Diderot's thinking. 'Everyone says that taste came before rules, but few know why. Taste, good taste, is as old as the world, as man and virtue; the centuries have merely perfected it.'[16] Fortified by this sense of a great tradition, in which the past contributes to the present and the present contributes to 'posterity,' Diderot declared that 'good taste is an abstract being that does not die.'[17]

The implications of this remark are exceedingly important. First of all, it constitutes a kind of philosophy of history. 'In every nation, taste is the product of a long interval of time,' wrote Diderot later. One can see his presuppositions about history more clearly, perhaps, in the 'Letters on Posterity' than in any other of his writings.[18] Moreover, the strong sense of continuity, so important in Diderot's philosophical thought and especially important in his scientific speculations about the origins of life (as in *Le Rêve de d'Alembert*), is applied here to the course of human experience. In the second place, if good taste is an abstract being that does not die, it follows that each generation should try to transmit this heritage, not only unimpaired but improved. In short, it becomes a question of what you can do for posterity, not (as Diderot seems to have implied when the dispute began) of what posterity can do for you. Thus Diderot repeatedly speaks of a respect for posterity. 'It touches one's heart and elevates the soul.'[19]

Logically implied in this conception of the appreciation of art as a cumulative experience, in the third place, is the supposition that there is a goal, that of 'the perfection of the human spirit,' and that it can be achieved.[20] Diderot obviously believed that humanity could move along the road towards perfection. Frequently he speaks of the perfectibility of man. In these letters he wrote of his being convinced 'of the perfectibility of man and of his works,' and remarked that it was nature's wish 'that man be perfectible.'[21]

As usually happens with opinionated persons, the dispute had little personal effect beyond confirming the two men in their own prejudices. But it allows the posterity of whom Diderot spoke so fondly to perceive the convictions that he lived by. How characteristic they were of the Age of Enlightenment! Secular immortality, humanism and humanitarianism, a

willingness to adapt to change while still feeling the tug of the grand tradition, the perfectibility of man. In short, a belief in progress.[22]

It was while this dispute was going on that Catherine II instituted the
search for a sculptor who would come to Saint Petersburg to carry out her
wishes for the projected monument. In his capacity of Russian ambassador
to France and acting under instructions from General Betzki, Catherine
II's *major domo* in matters of the arts, Diderot's friend Galitzin received
a number of bids from leading Parisian sculptors. Their asking prices
ranged from 400,000 to 600,000 livres.[23] At first, apparently, Falconet was
not even considered, in spite of the fact that the pieces he had exhibited in
the Salon of 1765 had been very well received. Perhaps it was because his
pieces were small in scale and that previously he had worked only in
marble. It was Diderot who wrote to Betzki on 16 April 1766, evidently
urging the appointment of Falconet. In reply Catherine II demonstrated
her faith in Diderot's judgment: she authorized him to do all the necessary
negotiating. 'Orders have been sent to Prince Galitzin to ratify all that you
agree upon.'[24] By 16 July Falconet had made up his mind to go, and on
26 August he received the permission of the French government.[25] The following day he signed the contract. Its nineteen articles were quite elaborate, calling for traveling and moving expenses, maintenance at Saint
Petersburg, salaries for the assistant and three technicians, etc. The most
interesting aspect of the agreement was that in spite of Diderot's and
Galitzin's urging Falconet to stipulate a payment of 300,000 livres for the
commission, he insisted upon a sum of 200,000.[26] Falconet, accompanied
by his nineteen-year-old protegée and assistant, Marie-Anne Collot, a very
good sculptress in her own right, left Paris on 8 September and on 15 October 1766 arrived in Saint Petersburg.[27]

All of these preparations had been accompanied by a good deal of
bustle throughout the spring and summer, as may be seen in Diderot's
long letter to Betzki written just after the signing of the contract.[28] The
aim of the letter was to exhort Betzki to treat Falconet well, nor was it
unbecoming of Diderot to do so, for he had assumed a very considerable
load of moral responsibility in urging — indeed, almost browbeating —
Falconet to go.[29] Falconet was no mere adventurer or careerist. He was
already successful at Paris, with commissions earning him 10,000 livres a
year, a professorship at the Royal Academy of Painting and Sculpture,
and the directorship of the sculpture section of the royal porcelain works
at Sèvres, a post worth 2400 livres which he had held since 1757. Fortunately,
Falconet did fare well at Saint Petersburg, in spite of Betzki's fussiness

and petty jealousy, although after a few years the artist's own difficult personality began to antagonize his imperial patron. In 1766 Catherine II, still in a glow over acquiring Falconet's services, showed her awareness of what Diderot was able to do for her: '. . . he recommends his friends to us, he has brought about my acquiring a man who has, I believe, no equal.'[30]

Early in this year Diderot had received an unexpected recognition of his growing reputation as an authority on artistic matters. This testimonial came as a result of the death in the previous December of the Dauphin, a man whose reign had promised to be pious, orthodox, and uncongenial to *philosophes*.[31] In February the Vollands learned from an elated Diderot that he had been officially asked to submit ideas for the Dauphin's mausoleum to be erected at the cathedral at Sens. He submitted five, one of which was, in part, adapted and adopted.[32] By August he had finished writing an important work on art criticism, his *Essais sur la peinture*.[33] Meanwhile his private life went on much as ever, save that it became even more convenient for him to call upon the Vollands since they had moved to a quarter of Paris close to the Louvre.[34] At the Rue Taranne the widowed Mme Billard, Mme Diderot's older sister, moved in with the Diderots.[35]

Such was the posture of affairs on the eve of a dramatic event. When Catherine II had bought Diderot's library she volunteered to pay him an extra 1000 livres a year to keep it up. Then, whether intentionally or by forgetfulness, payment lapsed. 'The Empress forgot to have my pension paid. Prince Galitzin, who is friendly with me, complained to her about it.' The result was that Catherine II, saying that she did not want to run the risk of forgetting the matter again, ordered that Diderot be paid in a lump sum for fifty years in advance. 'At the turn of the century further arrangements will be made.' As Diderot remarked, there he was, committed to live another fifty years. That would make him one hundred and three.[36]

This sensational occurrence greatly contributed to making Diderot one of the most conspicuous and celebrated men of his time. His letter of thanks naturally tried to match in fervor the magnitude of the gift. 'Never were favors less merited nor more unexpected; and never has gratitude been more vividly felt or more difficult to express.' In the attempt to convey his thankfulness adequately he took to metaphor: 'A noble rapture steals over me; of themselves my fingers seek out an old lyre the strings of which had been cut by philosophy. I take it down from the wall where it hangs and, with head and chest bare as is usual with me, I feel myself inspired to sing.'[37] What he sang was not his own, however: the verses (which, as a

matter of fact, are far from having the rush and warmth of Diderot's headlong style) were probably written by his young friend Jean Devaines.[38]

Diderot was not a mercenary or grasping person. Following the purchase of his library, Catherine II instructed Galitzin to negotiate with
Diderot for the sale of his manuscripts too.

'I have already sold them,' Diderot told Galitzin.

'Sold them! How am I going to write that?'

'Nothing easier, Monsieur. I sold them with my books.' [39]

Still, even a non-mercenary person could not help but feel that his financial outlook had been revolutionized by a gift so princely. It came at a
most opportune time, too, for his salary from working on the *Encyclopédie*
was about to fall off sharply. His income from that source had been 3180
livres in 1763, 3400 livres in 1764, and 3548 in 1765; but it was only 700
livres in 1766, and in 1767 the sum dropped to 350.[40] Before long, because
of the completion of the engravings, it would vanish.

Diderot's income from investments was rather modest too. In 1759 he
calculated that he was inheriting from his father's estate the equivalent of
1500 livres a year, and that he could look forward eventually to an income
from all his savings of between three and four thousand. In 1766, before
the windfall, his income from investments was perhaps a little more than
four thousand. A large portion of this, however, the Diderots would be
able to enjoy for only a few years, for it would eventually have to go for
Angélique's dowry. Catherine II's gift invested at the prevailing rate of 5
per cent would bring in another 2500 livres. It would seem, therefore, that
after 1766 Diderot's income from investments was approximately 6500
livres.[41] Day-laborers in France earned on the average 255 livres per annum
in 1767–8, while, on the other hand, each of the twenty-three members of the
company of the Comédie-Française earned 11,132 livres.[42]

The impact of such good fortune was of course psychological as well as
financial. One of the ways in which it was felt was in giving Diderot the
luxurious assurance that he could afford to write what he wanted. Probably
this had much to do with the outpouring of his masterpieces in the late
sixties and early seventies, all of which he knew to be unpublishable in
his lifetime. Perhaps this sense of freedom is reflected in the staggering
length of the *Salon de 1767*. He could afford to write as he pleased.

In the autumn of 1766 the international prestige of the French *philosophes*
was demonstrated by Cesare Beccaria's visiting Paris. This young Milanese,
who had become famous almost overnight by his publication in 1764 of
Dei delitti e delle pene ('On Crimes and Punishment'), had been greatly

inspired by the *Encyclopédie.* 'D'Alembert, Diderot, Helvétius, Buffon, Hume . . . your immortal works . . . are the subject of my occupations during the day and my meditations in the silence of the night.' Particularly of Diderot he wrote, 'What an excellent man he must be! . . . Especially tell me the outcome of your conversations with M. Diderot about my book. I keenly wish to know what impression I have made on that sublime soul.' [43]

Diderot could read Italian, and had discussed *Dei delitti e delle pene* with Allan Ramsay and Suard at D'Holbach's one day, before the French translation by Morellet appeared.[44] In fact, when he did read the translation Diderot thought it spoiled the original.[45] Ramsay, in a long letter to Diderot, subjected Beccaria's book to some stringent criticisms. He made the point, most of all, that 'questions of politics are not to be treated abstractly, as questions of geometry and arithmetic are.' This sounds exactly like Edmund Burke. Diderot was sufficiently impressed by Ramsay's criticisms, Naigeon tells us, to translate the letter into French, intending to send it to Beccaria. Hearing of the latter's almost pathological sensitivity, he refrained from doing so.[46]

Meanwhile Beccaria, having been invited to Paris in the name of the leading *philosophes,* arrived on 18 October 1766, accompanied by his close friend Alessandro Verri. The next day they were taken to D'Holbach's. 'You would not believe,' wrote Beccaria to his wife, 'the welcome, the courtesy, the praise, the expressions of friendship and esteem with which we have been overwhelmed. Diderot, Baron d'Holbach and D'Alembert especially showed themselves enchanted with us.' And Verri wrote of Diderot, 'He declaims constantly, vehemently; he is in transports. He is ardent, ardent in everything, in conversation as in his books.' [47] Warmly as Beccaria was welcomed, he nevertheless came to feel very unhappy and alien in Paris. By 10 November he had already announced his intention of going home, which he did by the end of the month.[48] He never left Italy again, though Catherine II tried hard in 1767 to entice him to Russia.[49]

Morellet was less considerate than Diderot of Beccaria's feelings: he gave Beccaria Diderot's translation of Ramsay's criticisms, which to this day is to be found among Beccaria's papers, along with the criticisms by Diderot said to have been written by him on the margins of his copy of *Dei delitti e delle pene.*[50] The burden of Diderot's remarks, which were not very severe or cutting, was that in effect Beccaria was not realistic. 'I contest the reasons that he gives, but not his principles.' Diderot insisted that he revered Beccaria—'I admire the inexhaustible fount of humanity that has inspired him'—praising also his delicacy of feeling, 'the mark of a noble and generous soul.'[51] Diderot's final judgment is probably contained in lines written in 1771: 'I am neither hard-hearted nor perverse; nevertheless I am far from thinking that the work *Des Délits et des Peines* is as important, or its basic ideas as true, as is claimed for it.'[52]

As typical of Diderot as his exuberant behavior when he met Verri and Beccaria or when he claimed to be snatching an old harp down from the wall, was his effort at this very time, too, to be of assistance to his maid-servant. This woman, Louise Godenère, wished to have with her in Paris the personal belongings she had left on deposit with some neighbors in her native village in Burgundy. Moreover, 'Louison' claimed to have been bilked of her inheritance by her brothers, so that the air was heavy with mutterings of suit and countersuit. What was so typical of Diderot in all this? First, his willingness to spend a great deal of his time in behalf of others; secondly, the headlong and impetuous way in which he took sides and threw himself into the fray; third, his bearing down on his friends to take the trouble to help out in the good work — in this case the naturalist Philibert Guéneau de Montbeillard, whose sole connection with the case, unfortunate fellow, was that he happened to live nearby; and lastly, a certain gullibility, which made it possible for Diderot to be imposed upon, as in this case some of Guéneau de Montbeillard's letters evidently implied. At length Louison received what Diderot called her 'duds' (*nippes*). In value they were not quite worth what their carriage cost. Diderot gladly paid that out of his own pocket.[53]

Meanwhile, Diderot's relationships with Russia and the Russians continued to give him both pain and pleasure. On the debit side was an obscure imbroglio in which Diderot gave a man named Berard letters of introduction that would assist him in his schemes of settling some French families in Russia. The French government took this amiss: Diderot twice mentions that he was accused of trying to entice workers out of the country and that he was threatened with imprisonment in the Bastille.[54] On the credit side was Diderot's being named a Foreign Associate of the Academy of Beaux-Arts of Saint Petersburg. The diploma is dated 10 January 1767, but Diderot had not received it by July of that year. He had actually solicited membership in the Academy in a letter of 5 February 1767, but later discovered that membership had already been conferred upon him.[55] This Academy, evidently more a plaything of Betzki's than an organization of any real substance, seems to have been evanescent.

From the first instant of learning of Catherine II's bounty, Diderot had in mind an appropriate way of expressing his gratitude. He promised

Betzki, 'I swear that before I die I shall have raised to her glory a pyramid that will touch the sky . . . ,' and to Falconet he declared that 'If I ever get to Petersburg, I shall carry my pyramid in my arms.' Repeatedly he wrote of his eagerness to undertake work on his 'pyramid.'

. . . I offered to work on a general vocabulary in which all the terms of the language would be explained, bounded, defined. You understand that such a work can be done only when the arts and sciences have been carried to their furthest point of perfection. You understand that this would be a way of transmitting to an undeveloped nation [*une nation naissante*] all the results, all the enlightenment of three or four hundred years of a developed nation [*une nation policée*]. . . .

Diderot explained that his 'pyramid' would be translated into Russian and that when it was done he would go to Saint Petersburg to confer with his translators, which he would do in Latin. The work was to be entirely different from the *Encyclopédie,* yet based upon it; Diderot's own previous 'twenty to thirty years of work' would greatly shorten the time necessary for this new venture, he thought. It would be a dictionary, but it would do much more than simply record current usage: it was to be 'philosophical,' intended to rectify the inexact or empty use of words and, by doing so, improve the morals [*moeurs*] of a nation.[56]

All through his career, both as artist and as scientist, Diderot showed his fascination with language and his concern for its improvement. His discovery, made when a very young man, that he could achieve unusual accuracy in understanding a foreign language if he passed it through Latin, his remarks about the nature of language in his Prospectus for the *Encyclopédie* and in his article '*Encyclopédie*' in Volume V, his numerous articles on synonyms in the *Encyclopédie,* the whole editorial strategy of stressing preciseness and concreteness throughout the *Encyclopédie,* the linguistic and semantic problems he explored in his *Lettre sur les sourds et muets,* all show Diderot wrestling with problems of communication.[57] Questions of how to avoid using words inaccurately and, above all, how to eschew the use of words empty of meaning, 'words devoid of sense, all those words which in the last analysis cannot be related to some sensory representation.'[58] It is this concern for rendering language more precise and for linking words with things that stoked the outcry so common among the *philosophes* against what they called 'metaphysics.' Finding its source and its authority in the psychology and epistemology of John Locke, this aspect of eighteenth-century philosophy links up with Wittgenstein and the severely analytical school of philosophy in the twentieth century.

There is something both inspirational and presumptuous in Diderot's supposing that he could complete his 'pyramid' single-handed, 'although an Academy with numerous members has been occupied with it here for about a hundred and thirty years.' Presumptuous and inspiring, too, that he supposed he could be a sort of Lycurgus, moulding by correct intellectual methodology the character and the manners of a whole nation. But Diderot was not put to the test. To his disappointment he was made to feel in letters from both Betzki and Falconet that 'They want me and not my work.'[59] It was the beginning of his being made to understand that sometime soon he ought to make an appearance in Saint Petersburg.

Just as Diderot had helped to recruit a sculptor for Catherine II, now, though only in a minor way, he helped to recruit an economist for her. This was Le Mercier de La Rivière, a public administrator who had recently made a favorable name for himself as *intendant* of Martinique.[60] In 1767 he was trying to secure permission for the publication of his book, *L'Ordre naturel et essentiel des sociétés politiques,* which Adam Smith later described as 'the most distinct and best connected account' of the doctrine of the Physiocrats. Sartine, as director of the book trade, asked Diderot to make a confidential report on whether the book might be licensed to be published. Diderot recommended its publication enthusiastically.[61] He told his friend Damilaville that he had read the book with more pleasure and a hundred times more profit than he had Montesquieu's *L'Esprit des lois!*[62]

Catherine II, meanwhile, had come to learn through reports from her ministers at Madrid and Paris of Le Mercier de La Rivière's competence, and presently invited him to come to Russia. Her particular motive was thought to have been to secure his assistance in carrying out her *Nakaz,* or *Instructions to the Commissioners for Composing a New Code of Laws,* which she published in late 1767 and which became so famous.[63] Diderot's part in all this consisted in encouraging Le Mercier de La Rivière to go and in writing several strong letters of recommendation. Le Mercier de La Rivière left Paris in August and arrived in Saint Petersburg in October.[64]

The sojourn was an unlucky one. By the time he arrived in Saint Petersburg, Catherine II had gone to Moscow where she stayed all winter. The Frenchman never saw her at all, save for one formal interview of farewell just before he left Russia the following March.[65] Already in October, the month of his arrival, he was writing Diderot of his probable return.[66] Detractors claimed that he was intolerably overbearing and overweening, but the sensible and dignified tone of this letter would seem to belie them.

In part there was a misunderstanding, though it was one that seems to have been contrived by Catherine II: she intended him to join her service permanently, or so she said, whereas he contended — it was in the contract that he had signed with Galitzin — that he had promised to stay only two years. Closer to the real reason for Le Mercier de La Rivière's failure was the Czarina's fear that his reputation and celebrity would make people assume that the credit for her reforms more rightfully belonged to him than to her.[67] The envy and apprehensiveness of courtiers, combined with the jealousy of people like Grimm and Falconet, whose harsh sarcasms are unpleasant to read, did the rest.[68] Falconet tried hard to make Diderot feel guilty and foolish about having recommended Le Mercier de La Rivière, and he insinuated that Diderot's judgment had been so erratic and erroneous that he had lost face with the Empress. Diderot stoutly stood his ground.

I have received your statement against M. de La Rivière, and I could not be more scandalized. By presenting to the Russians an absolutely ridiculous scene you will have failed yourself and Mlle Collot and your nation. Two Frenchmen, both of them men of merit, cannot be together a month in Petersburg without scratching each other's eyes out. It seems to me that even from here I can hear the Russians saying, 'So that is what *franczouski* manners are.' [69]

Catherine II, by cultivating good relations with Voltaire, D'Alembert, Diderot, Beccaria, and others, was attempting to get on her side some of the most articulate and effective generators of public opinion in Europe. And there were many to say that, in the light of what had happened to her husband, she certainly needed it. In this very year the Duchess of Choiseul wrote to Mme du Deffand,

She [Catherine II] has had the wit to realize that she needs the protection of men of letters. She flatters herself that their base eulogies will impenetrably conceal from the eyes of her contemporaries and from posterity the heinous crimes by which she has astonished the universe and revolted humanity. . . . That obscure, vile, low mercenary writers lend to her their abject pens, I can understand; but Voltaire! [70]

And perhaps, if she had thought of it, the Duchess might have added, 'But Diderot!' Unless she thought she had already included him. The *philosophes* paid a heavy price in some quarters of French opinion for having any connection with Catherine II.

Quite soon there arose in Diderot's relationship with the Empress the question of his moral obligation to visit Russia in order to show his gratitude. This was a favorite theme with Falconet, whose drumbeat insistence makes one wonder whether he did not enjoy making Diderot feel guilty. By March 1767 Catherine II was writing Falconet that she would like to see Diderot in Russia, partly for his sake and especially for hers.[71] Diderot never disavowed his obligation, he merely tried to put it off: 'For the third time I say to you,' he wrote to Falconet, 'I shall do what you expect of me. I repeat my solemn oath.'[72] Falconet had mentioned the spring of 1768 as a suitable time. Diderot in reply enumerated the reasons that combined to hold him back. His wife was getting old and was in poor health. His daughter's education demanded his presence. Much more binding than these two ties — 'to my shame I confess it' — was his love for his mistress. He was not sure that either he or she would survive the separation:

I am attached by the strongest and sweetest of all feelings to a woman to whom I would sacrifice a hundred lives if I had them. Behold, Falconet, I could see my house go up in flames without being distraught; my freedom menaced, my life compromised, all sorts of misfortunes advancing upon me, without complaining, provided that I still had her. . . . It is at the end of ten years that I speak to you as I do now. I call Heaven to witness that she is as dear to me now as ever . . . that neither time nor habit nor any of what ordinarily diminishes passion has affected mine; and that since I have known her she has been the only woman in the world for me.

Incidental to Diderot's argument was his conviction, couched in self-flattering terms, that he did not have the temperament or character to be successful at a court:

I, whom you know to be uprightness, simplicity, and candor incarnate! I, . . . whose heart is always on his sleeve! I, who do not know how to lie or dissimulate! I, as incapable of disguising my affections as my aversions, of avoiding a trap as I am of setting one. Have you thought of all that?

'Communicate this to Her Imperial Majesty as you please. . . . If you believe that you cannot tell her that her philosopher is madly in love, then tell her, which is the truth, that I still have four volumes of engravings to publish.' Diderot went on to describe how it was that the enterprise still depended upon his presence. 'But within eighteen months I shall be free of my engagements.'[73]

Falconet showed the letter to the Empress, all twenty pages of it, in all its panoply of eighteenth-century sensibility. His reply to Diderot was characteristically gruff. 'Let us be clear. If Denis Diderot, imbued with gratitude and sensitive to true glory, were six weeks in making the trip from Paris to Petersburg, were to stay there two or three months, and were to take another six weeks in returning to his penates, that would make five or six months. Diderot would not be coming in order to settle down in Russia. He would be doing something much better: he would be coming solely to express his gratitude. . . .' If Denis Diderot did come, Falconet went on, he would not be chicken (*Denis Diderot ne seroit pas une poule*), and posterity would notice him in the annals of Catherine II.[74]

What a sly allusion to posterity. Diderot took six years to meditate upon it before he finally set out on the road to Russia.

CHAPTER 38

Diderot as Critic and Philosopher of Art

W E APPROACH the moment of the Salon,' wrote
Diderot to Falconet. 'Who will replace you
at my side? Who will point out to me the good parts, the weak places?'[1]
Nevertheless, Diderot managed, and managed triumphantly. The Salon
opened on 25 August 1767, and Diderot's letters to Sophie show that he
visited the exhibition not less than twelve times.[2]

Diderot approached this Salon with a vast panorama of ideas about the
appreciation of beauty and the philosophy of art. His self-education in art
had been proceeding for a long, long time. Between 1747 and 1751 he was
doing extensive reading in treatises on painting, as the register of books
borrowed from the Royal Library shows. Leonardo da Vinci's *Trattato
della pittura* especially influenced him, as did the seventeenth-century
French painter Le Brun's *Méthode pour apprendre à deviner les passions*
(1702). Le Brun's treatise described and illustrated the gestures and expressions accompanying emotional states. Diderot shows not only in his art
criticism but also in his dramas and novels an intense fascination with
the physical manifestations of the emotions. His study of gestures, pantomime, and tableaux, and his interest in physiognomy — the relation between character and physical appearance — either originated in or was
reinforced by his readings in Le Brun.[3]

Diderot also kept abreast of contemporary writings on art. His widely
known article *'Beau'* in the *Encyclopédie,* as well as his later writings, show
that he was familiar with the standard treatises though he often disagreed
with them. Thus he summarized and commented upon Francis Hutcheson's
Inquiry into the Origin of our Ideas of Beauty and Virtue (1725), the
Traité du beau (1715) of Jean-Pierre de Crousaz, the *Essai sur le beau*
(1741) by Père Yves-Marie André, *Les Beaux-Arts réduits à un même
principe* (1746) by Abbé Charles Batteux, and Daniel Webb's *An Inquiry*

into the Beauties of Painting (1760). Also influential, though Diderot mentioned it explicitly only once, was Abbé Jean-Baptiste Du Bos's *Réflexions critiques sur la poésie et sur la peinture* which had appeared in 1719. It furnishes many parallels to Diderot's ideas on allegory in painting and on the differences between poetry and painting, if indeed it is not the source. In the appreciation of art Du Bos was the schoolmaster of an age, a man whose influence in the long run was that of softening the rigidity of the rules of classicism. Du Bos was an empiricist much more than he was a traditionalist. His influence upon Diderot was considerable, so pervasive that perhaps it did not occur to Diderot that it required explicit acknowledgement. Diderot was also greatly influenced by the seventeenth-century painter and writer on painting, Roger de Piles.[4] Familiarity with such standard works grounded his training more solidly in understanding the principles of art.

Through the years Diderot also educated his taste by studying whatever works of the Old Masters were available to him.[5] Though his opportunities were restricted in comparison with those of the most casual tourist today, the collection of the Duke of Orléans at the Palais Royal and those of a few wealthy amateurs were accessible. He supplemented his knowledge by studying engravings; 'But what is a print,' he asked, 'in comparison with a painting?'[6] All of this gave him standards of comparison, however, and as one leafs through his *Salons* one finds his pages peppered with references to Annibale Carracci, Claude Lorrain, Correggio, Domenichino, Guido Reni, Le Brun, Le Sueur, Michelangelo, Poussin, Raphael, Rembrandt, Rubens, Teniers, Titian, Van Dyck, Veronese, Watteau, Wouwermans, and many others. Diderot was always hungry to see pictures. And when he did, his comparisons were quick. In this very year 1767 he wrote to Falconet, 'I never thoroughly realized how great is the decline in painting until the acquisitions Prince Galitzin has made for the Empress caused my eyes to rest upon [these Old Masters]. . . . The skill of Rubens, Rembrandt, Poelenburg, Teniers and Wouwermans is lost. What a beautiful collection you are about to receive.'[7]

Of all the painters of the past it was perhaps Poussin whom Diderot most admired. The references to Poussin, some forty of them scattered in Diderot's writings, show him seeking a model by which to inform his judgment and refine his taste. He mentions especially 'The Testament of Eudamidas.' This, he said, is 'the summit of painting.' What distinguishes this and all other Poussin paintings is great skill in grouping and composition, and deep concern for mood, gesture, and drapery. There

is a classicism and formalism in Poussin's genius that make his art austere and it is significant that Diderot constantly holds him up as an example and unceasingly tries to plumb the secrets of his art. That Diderot,
once the prophet of uncritical emotional response, could come to admire
Poussin's genius shows how forcefully having to write the *Salons* was changing Diderot's ideas about discipline and control.[8]

Although the exhibition of 1767 did not have the intrinsic interest of
that of 1765 — as Diderot himself wrote, 'There is nothing by Pierre nor
Boucher nor La Tour nor Bachelier nor Greuze' — it is memorable to all
students of Diderot for containing the Louis-Michel Van Loo portrait of
him. The artist subsequently gave this magnificent portrait to Diderot.[9]
It now hangs in the Louvre. Diderot's comments regarding it are almost
as revelatory as the portrait itself. He thought it a good likeness, 'But
what will my grandchildren say when they come to compare my sorry
works with this laughing, cute, effeminate, old male coquette? My children,
I assure you that this is not me. In any one day I had a hundred different
physiognomies, according to what was affecting me. . . . I have a mask
that eludes an artist, whether there are too many things blended in it or
because, the impressions of my soul painting themselves on my face in
very rapid succession, . . . his [the painter's] task becomes much more
difficult than he thought it was.'[10]

More necessary than ever in writing the *Salon de 1767*, because it was the
longest yet, was the inventiveness required to avoid monotony and keep
the reader turning the page. Diderot displays 'the most incredible literary
virtuosity in the art of incessantly varying the method of expression, tone
and style.'[11] His inveterate tendency to be divigatious, like an ill-trained
hunting dog (as he described himself) that indiscriminately pursues anything that jumps up, here stood him in good stead. His tendency toward free
association became an asset by awakening and keeping a reader's interest.
In addition, he always strove to be concrete, and if he had to be abstract,
at least not abstruse. Thus we see him criticizing a picture that he admires
of a hen, but pointing out nevertheless that a broody hen has her feathers
fluffed out. He interpolates a 'Satire against Luxury, in the Manner of
Persius,' posing numerous political and social questions as well as aesthetic
ones. When he comes to the seascapes of Joseph Vernet, he pretends that he
is on a trip to the seaside, where he describes seven sites. This 'promenade
de Vernet,' some fifty pages long and ranging over such subjects as the
nature of dreams and what is virtue and the impossibility of free will, is a
famous show piece, regarded as a model of Diderot's type of criticism.

He keeps his readers on the alert, too, so as not to miss any of the erotic patches. 'You see, my friend, that I am becoming dirty, like all old men.' [12]

Not least among the autobiographical bits that enlivened the *Salon de 1767* was Diderot's account of his misadventures in assisting a Polish-Prussian woman portraitist who was admitted to the Royal Academy of Painting in 1767 and who exhibited in the Salon of that year. This painter, Anna-Dorothea Therbusch, did not prosper in Paris at first and was in real necessity when Galitzin befriended her and put her up in the house he had rented from Falconet, on the Rue d'Anjou. Mme Therbouche (as she spelled her name in France) painted a portrait of Diderot that he and his daughter thought was superior to the one by Van Loo. This portrait depicted Diderot with only some loose covering thrown over one shoulder and in fact on his own initiative he had sat for this portrait in the nude. 'She painted me and we chatted together with a simplicity and an innocence worthy of the earliest times.' Nevertheless, Diderot confessed in the *Salon de 1767* that he had been apprehensively aware of the fact that 'Since the time of Adam's sin one cannot command all the parts of one's body as one does one's arm; and that there are parts which want to when the son of Adam does not, and which do not want to when the son of Adam would very much like to.'

Diderot — in retrospect he called himself 'the poor *philosophe*' — entered with his usual zest into the campaign of helping Mme Therbouche. 'The poor *philosophe,* who is sensitive to destitution because he has experienced it himself . . . put himself out for nine months peddling the work of the Prussienne,' so much so that people promptly concluded that she must be his mistress. 'The poor *philosophe* put both great and small, friends and strangers, under contribution and caused the spendthrift artist to earn five or six hundred louis, of which not a penny remained at the end of six months.' Eventually the lady left Paris, laden with debts.

What had not the poor *philosophe* done for her? And what reward did he get?

Why, the satisfaction of having done good.

No doubt, but nothing more than that except the marks of the blackest ingratitude. . . . The unworthy Prussienne ignores her creditors, who constantly come clamoring to my door. The unworthy Prussienne has already collected here her fees on pictures which she will not finish. The unworthy Prussienne insults her benefactors. . . . The unworthy Prussienne has given the poor *philosophe* a good lesson from which he will not profit; for he will remain goodhearted and foolish the way God made him.[13]

Sometimes even Diderot knew that he was an easy mark.

With the *Salon de 1767*, Diderot had reported on five of the biennial exhibitions over a period of eight years. Taking each by itself, it might readily be supposed that Diderot's criticism was merely and simply impressionistic. But taking them as a whole, it begins to be seen that Diderot was
consistently applying to them certain criteria and principles common to
them all. In the first place, though he had many ways of looking at pictures
and looked for many things in them, there was one method of seeing them
that he tells us in 1751 he always employed. He looked at pictures as a deaf
man (who already knows the topic of conversation) would observe the expressions and gestures of a group in conversation. This method, he claimed
in his *Letter on the Deaf and Dumb,* allowed him to detect what was fumbling and ambiguous in a picture, what was really false in it.[14] And long
after 1751, his abiding interest in gesture and expression suggests that through
the years this continued to be one of his criteria.

Diderot also trained himself to look for what he called 'the line of liaison.' In every composition, he claimed, there is a line that can be traced
from the summit of one mass or group to another, traversing planes, sometimes receding into the depth of the picture, sometimes advancing towards
the foreground. If this line is too tortuous and labyrinthine, the painting will be obscure. If the line comes to a full stop, then there will be a
'hole' in the picture. 'A well-composed picture will never have more than
one true, unique line of liaison.'[15] Here we see the basis of Diderot's consistent emphasis on the importance of composition.

With equal consistency Diderot combated the persistent notion that a
picture is just like a poem. This was what Horace had written in his *Ars
poetica,* line 361 — 'Ut pictura poesis' — or at least this was the conventional
way in which the Renaissance and its successors had interpreted the verse.[16]
Diderot was fond of pointing out that the attempt to follow 'Ut pictura
poesis' involved artists in trying to paint ideas that were more verbal than
pictorial. 'What goes well in painting will always go well in poetry, but
this is not reciprocal'; and Diderot, whose *Letter on the Deaf and Dumb*
had emphasized the difference between painting and poetry, returned to the
same point in his *Salon de 1767.*[17]

The distinction between painting and poetry was made even more emphatically by Lessing, whose *Laocoön* was published in 1766. Lessing had
admiringly reviewed Diderot's *Letter on the Deaf and Dumb* in 1751. In
all probability, therefore, his views as expressed in the *Laocoön* were influenced by Diderot. It is hard to say how much.[18]

One of the essential differences between painting and poetry, according to Diderot (and here he followed the Abbé Du Bos more than he chose to admit), is that poetry readily calls up to the imagination a whole series of successive moments. Painting, on the other hand, is limited to just one (or at least it was until twentieth-century artists began working out the implications of Marcel Duchamp's 'Nude Descending a Staircase'). Diderot demonstrated his contention by analyzing in the *Salon de 1767* some lines from Lucretius. This limitation of painting brings Diderot back to a point that he had made earlier: Whether inspired by poetry or his own imagination, it becomes very important for the painter to choose for depiction the most precisely appropriate moment. Thus Diderot scolds Le Prince: 'You have chosen the ambiguous moment and the insipid one.' He prided himself that he could plan a picture and designate the moment of greatest interest and greatest pictorial potential. 'Chardin, La Grenée, Greuze and others have assured me (and artists do not flatter literary men) that I am almost the only one among men of letters whose ideas can pass on to the canvas almost as they are arranged in my head.' [19]

Numerous are the other consistencies one may detect in Diderot's *Salons* through the years. He could always be counted on, again following the Abbé Du Bos, to dislike allegories in pictures; [20] he always deplored the fussiness and non-functionalism of modern dress, comparing it unfavorably to the dress of the Ancients; [21] he consistently valued 'historical' painting over genre painting or still lifes or portraits; [22] and he consistently asserted that technique alone, though he progressively valued it more and more highly, can never be an end in itself and can never be a complete substitute for the quality of the imagination of the artist. 'Painting,' he wrote in the *Salon de 1765,* 'is the art of reaching the soul through the eyes. If the effect stops at the eyes, the painter has gone only half way.' [23]

The *Salon de 1767* does not repudiate any of the critical insights Diderot had exhibited in the previous *Salons,* but it adds to them some striking new ones. Most significant of all is his new awareness of the sublime as a component in the impact made by art. Why is this a fact, he asks, and what constitutes the sublime? In asking these questions Diderot is clearly showing the influence of Edmund Burke, whose *Philosophical Inquiry into the Origin of our Ideas of the Sublime and Beautiful* had been published in 1757.[24] Diderot's answer is like Burke's. 'Whatever strikes the soul with wonder, whatever imparts a feeling of terror, leads to the sublime.' [25] Obscurity, dimness, shadows add to the sense of wonder and awe. 'Great noises heard from afar, waterfalls that one hears but does not see, silence, solitude, deserts, ruins, caverns, the sound of muffled drums . . . there is in all these things an undefinable something of the terrible, the grand, and the obscure.' [26]

Diderot, in pondering over what seems sublime, found that the consciousness of solitariness, of being alive when all about us has decayed or perished, the feeling of melancholy and nostalgia, are components of perceived sublimity. This led him to lay ever greater emphasis on the depiction of ruins, so that he has a great deal to say about the paintings of Hubert Robert, a young artist just back from Rome in 1767 and exhibiting in the Salon for the first time. 'The effect of these compositions, good or bad, is to let you sink into a gentle melancholy. . . . Majestic are the ideas awakened in me by ruins. All things come to nothing, everything perishes, all things pass away. Only the earth remains. Only time lasts. How old the world is! I walk between two eternities. Wherever I cast my eyes, the objects round about me announce their end and reconcile me to my own.' This, thought Diderot, was one of the ways in which Poussin was 'sublime': in a smiling, idyllic scene of shepherds in Arcadia, 'he lets my eyes fall on a tomb, where I read "Et in Arcadia ego." ' [27]

Another artistic interest of Diderot's accented more strongly in the *Salon de 1767* than in his previous ones was his speculation about sketches and their relation to the finished work of art. Why is it, Diderot asks himself, that sketches are so fascinating? The answer is Janus-faced: it concerns both the artist and the beholder. For each it signifies the overwhelming importance of the imagination. For the artist, the distinction between sketch and finished picture helps to define the relationship between genius and technique. 'A poor sketch will never give birth to anything but an inferior picture; a good sketch will not always give birth to a fine one. A good sketch can be the production of a young man full of verve and fire, whom nothing confines and who abandons himself to his impetuosity. A good picture can never be other than the work of a master who has deeply reflected, meditated, toiled. Genius it is that makes the good sketch, and genius cannot be had for the asking.' [28] With that fascination Diderot would have turned to that serendipity of the disastrous flood of 1967, the uncovered synopias on Florentine walls.

Similarly, for the beholder a sketch powerfully stimulates the imagination, not infrequently satisfying it to a greater degree than does the finished work of art. 'Movement, action, even the passions are indicated by a few characteristic strokes; and my imagination does the rest. I am inspired by the divine afflatus of the artist. . . . One stroke only, one main feature: leave the rest to my imagination.' [29] Diderot was here trying to analyze the secret of the elusive but indispensable communication between artist and viewer. It is not surprising that a man with an imagination as active and powerful as his would emphasize the role of the imagination not only in the creation of art but also in the appreciation of it.

Even before he began the series of the *Salons,* Diderot had declared that art — in this case he was discussing poetry — 'demands a certain something of the enormous, the barbarous and the wild.'[30] This conviction deepened because of his admiration of the poetic quality of the manners and customs of primitive peoples. Often he spoke of the Ancients in this regard, and the Ossianic poems, as we have already seen, were a revelation to him. In the *Salon de 1767* he continued to mention Ossian appreciatively, though the poem he paraphrased is in fact Thomas Gray's *The Bard.* 'The imitative arts,' wrote Diderot, 'need something savage, raw, striking, and enormous,' a conviction which had evidently been reinforced by Burke's ideas on the sublime.[31] Naturally such conceptions carried Diderot far from an admiration of the rococo and probably explain his dislike of Watteau.[32] 'By the late 1760's the creative impulse behind rococo art was virtually spent,' writes a British critic, 'and there are many signs in this *Salon [de 1765]* that Diderot is writing in the early stages of a period of transition.'[33]

Diderot's trajectory as a critic of art proceeded from the general to the specific and then, much enriched by the empiricism of the concrete, back to the general again. In his early career, as exemplified by his article *'Beau,'* his analysis of beauty was abstract and rather rigid and circumscribed.[34] But with the reporting of the Salons, Diderot's observations, focused on a continuing succession of actual paintings of all genres, became specific. Some years of this reporting made Diderot a humbler man. He became much more aware of the artist's point of view, of the way in which a painter or a sculptor perceives, and of the tremendous technique that a proficient artist must acquire. Had Diderot in the long run been satisfied only to comment on art picture by picture he would no doubt have ended up with a very impressionistic and disjunctive theory of aesthetics. Fortunately, as the years went by, his mind continued to work inductively on these problems, so that we see him trying to formulate general maxims as well as to express apt critiques on individual pictures. Such attempts at induction, at trying to state what might almost be called a 'field theory' of art, are visible in his *Essais sur la peinture,* completed in July 1766.[35]

He had announced his intention to write a small treatise on painting in the concluding paragraph of the *Salon de 1765:* 'After having described and judged four to five hundred pictures, let us finish by presenting our credentials.'[36] These credentials consisted of chapters whimsically entitled 'My Bizarre Thoughts on Draughtsmanship,' 'My Little Ideas on Color,' 'All that I have Ever Understood about Chiaroscuro,' 'What Everyone Knows about Expression, and Something that Everyone Does not Know,' 'Paragraph on Composition, in which I Hope that I Shall Speak of It.' This self-deprecatory way of presenting his credentials in fact raised some great issues. Diderot called for the scrupulous imitation of nature, the true imitation of nature, which of course he knew perfectly well was more difficult technically and philosophically than people commonly suppose. Incidentally, when Diderot used the word 'imitation,' as he did very frequently in his aesthetic writings, it was in the sense more readily conveyed to twentieth-century students by the word 'expression.' The scrupulous imitation of nature that he called for is accomplished by expressing her.[37] In the *Essais sur la peinture* Diderot deplored the mannerism that comes from studying models one step removed from observation of nature itself. 'Mannerism comes from the drawing master, the academy, the school, even from the antique.' He recommended students' studying carefully the changes brought about in the human body and countenance by the way people earn their livings, by their station in life, by the subtle and pervasive effects on their appearance of any crippling or maiming they may have sustained. As for the use of color, he said sententiously, 'It is draughtsmanship that gives form to beings, it is color that gives them life.'[38] And in regard to chiaroscuro he showed how minute and acute his own observations had been by mentioning the effect of gradations in light and 'the infinite reflections of bodies and shadows.' No wonder, then, that posterity has credited him with anticipating Monet and the impressionists, or, when he asks his reader to imagine a painting in which 'the depth of the canvas is cut up into an infinity of infinitely small planes,' with foreshadowing cubism.[39] The *Essais sur la peinture* also raised (but did not settle) the exceedingly controversial problem of the relationship of art to morality.[40]

The *Essais sur la peinture* is a transitional work, more experimental than satisfying.[41] It shows Diderot asking the big, universal questions, but not as yet articulating replies as satisfactory as, with further thought, his answers were later to become. Nevertheless, the *Essais sur la peinture* greatly stimulated Schiller and Goethe, and Goethe published in 1798 a translation and an extensive commentary upon it.[42]

In a letter to Grimm prefatory to the *Salon de 1767,* written perhaps a year later than the *Essais sur la peinture,* Diderot shows himself trying to find that eternal, immutable rule for the beautiful. And he has a name for it, 'the ideal model of beauty, the true line.'[43] To many people it seems strange that Diderot the empiricist, the skeptical Diderot, the nominalist Diderot, should be seen groping for what appears to be a universalist, Platonic solution to his question. But this is to misunderstand Diderot's method. He was still the experimentalist, the man looking for inductions. He was trying to apply to the understanding of art a kind of Baconianism, and when he assumes that it is possible for an artist to achieve the ideal model of beauty, he is talking as a Newtonian might do when seeking to descry a law of nature.

Finding the ideal model of beauty is in Diderot's mind very much like finding the good or searching for truth. To find them, he trusts the method that permeates his thinking and his writings, the dialectical method. In so unlikely a place as the *Essais sur la peinture* the presentation is essentially like a dialogue even though the second person is not present.[44] The method of seeking truth through the tension of opposites is as conspicuous a characteristic of Diderot in his aesthetic as it is in his scientific or ethical thought.

In the quest for the ideal model of beauty, Diderot no sooner assumes that the Ancients can reveal it to us than he acknowledges that the study of nature, on the contrary, must never be disregarded. Here is Diderot's habit of dialectical thought at work. What are the relative merits of the two positions, he asks himself. How far may they be combined? No sooner does he say to the artist 'Copy nature,' than he realizes that the imitation of nature is something very different from nature itself. No sooner does he say that we must find truth in nature than he admits to himself that perhaps we find the truth of nature paradoxically in illusion. No sooner does he declare that no man can be a genius without giving himself up to the onslaught of the emotions than he begins to explore the proposition that great artistic creation requires the exercise of perfect self-command and self-control.[45] This confrontation of opposing arguments, instead of rendering Diderot irresolute and inert, energizes and fructifies his thought.

By winnowing, it is possible to come to quite a firm conception of his aesthetics. But his method of articulating conflicting propositions makes it possible, indeed even unavoidable, to find numerous contradictory statements in his works. Perhaps the greatest virtue of this way of seeking truth is that it presupposes a tentative and non-dogmatic approach. There is little, if indeed there is any, of the *a priori* in Diderot's thought. Yet the forcefulness of his style often misleads a reader into supposing that his views are more dogmatic than they really are. And confusing and contradictory statements do abound, greatly comforting his critics and leaving his adherents not altogether undismayed. He himself put it best:

Look, my friend, if you consider the matter carefully, you will find that in everything our true opinion is not that from which we have never wavered, but that to which we have the most habitually returned.[46]

Just how, according to Diderot, is the 'true ideal model of beauty' to be found? Certainly not by any reliance upon innate ideas of beauty. By this time John Locke's theories of psychology, set forth in his *Essay Concerning Human Understanding* (1687), had pervaded the western world. Based on a principle as old as Aristotle and one that had been perfectly acceptable to the medieval schoolmen, *nihil est in intellectu quod non fuerit in sensu,* Locke taught that the mind at birth is a blank slate on which the evidence of the five senses begins to write. Considering the venerability of this doctrine, the impact with which Locke's restatement and expansion of it struck the learned world is surprising. But it was a world getting used to the scientific method, a world digesting the discoveries of a Galileo, a Harvey, a Torricelli, and, latterly, a Newton, and adjusting itself to the speculations of an empiricist like Lord Bacon. Locke's demolition of the doctrine of innate ideas had proved to be a powerful solvent of orthodox and traditionalist notions about religion and morality: the uproar in the eighteenth century over 'natural religion' and 'rational religion' testifies to that. But a doctrine corrosive to absolutist ideas in religion and ethics was equally so to absolutist ideas in art. God has not already placed inside us the criteria for judging art. What we know about the ideal model of beauty we have to learn.

This view of aesthetics fitted very comfortably into Diderot's accustomed patterns of thought. Even so, he still had the obligation of explaining who discovers 'the ideal model of beauty,' and how it is done. The discoverer, according to Diderot, is the genius. This is one of his functions, in fact his most important one. He is the one capable of new insights and fresh departures, and lesser men learn from him, distorting or attenuating his insights as they do so. 'The true line, ideal model of beauty, does not exist except in the head of the . . . Raphaels, the Poussins . . . the Pigalles, the Falconets.'[47] The genius is rare. He is perhaps the most precious thing on earth, and, incidentally, so valuable to mankind that it can be argued that in a sense he is above good and evil. Much of *Le Neveu de Rameau* had argued this point. Was it not more important for Racine to be a great genius than a good man, even at the cost of his remaining 'deceitful, disloyal, ambitious, envious, and mean. . . ? A thousand years from now he will be drawing tears, be admired all over the earth. . . .' In contrast, most other men are 'mediocre' — damning word — content to be 'servile and almost stupid imitators of those who have preceded them.'[48]

How does genius make the supreme discovery of the ideal model of beauty? One of Diderot's answers to this question is the common sense one that genius intuits the ideal model as a result of experience. Diderot was fond of telling how Michelangelo, seeking the most beautiful curve possible for the dome of Saint Peter's, hit upon exactly the one, as the calculations of the French geometrician Philippe de La Hire showed over a century later, that was the curve of greatest resistance.[49] This is functionalism with a vengeance. It is not surprising that Diderot, with his constant solicitude that things should have utility, should find functionalism aesthetically satisfying.

Where does genius go to get the experience requisite for discovering the ideal model of beauty? Obviously genius goes to nature. This is indispensable, says Diderot, though he makes some qualifications in regard to the study of nature and nothing but the study of nature. For, in addition, genius must learn from the Ancients.

Diderot's conclusions about the interplay between the study of nature and the study of the Ancients is an example of his dialectical thinking at what is perhaps its subtlest, its most ambivalent and confusing, and its best. On the one hand, he wanted it understood that he was not a slavish and undiscriminating admirer of the Ancients: 'I do not have anticomania,' he insisted to Falconet. Had he lived in the 1680's when the Quarrel between the Ancients and the Moderns was taking place, Diderot would of course have sided with Fontenelle in defense of the Moderns. This was a position from which Diderot never wavered; but at the same time he was convinced that 'It may be generally observed that one rarely becomes a great writer, a great man of letters, a man of great taste, without being intimately familiar with the Ancients.'[50] Falconet could insinuate that Diderot's knowledge of the Ancients was too much confined to their literature, and of course it is true that anyone in the eighteenth century trying to reach the spirit of ancient times had to rely in great part on literary remains. But Diderot not only attained a profound penetration of the Greek language, but was also well informed about Greek and Roman antiquities.[51] In fact, Diderot was quite severe about the deficiencies of others in this department of learning, leaving one to infer that he was quite confident of his own competency. As he contemptuously said of the author of a book on the discoveries at Herculaneum, '. . . you have written a pretty bad book; and how could you have done better, having no taste for the fine arts and no profound knowledge of antiquity?'[52] It is essential, if one is to understand Diderot the Modern, to know also Diderot the Classicist.

Diderot's knowledge of Greek sculpture was of necessity based on the Hellenistic and Roman period, rather than the classic Hellenic models. Even Johann Joachim Winckelmann, in his famous and influential *Geschichte der Kunst des Altertums* (1764) was 'restricted entirely to late Greek works and copies of them.'[53] And although Diderot poked fun at Winckelmann, saying that he was a fanatic who demanded that everyone acknowledge the superiority of the charms of his particular Dulcinea, it is nevertheless quite plain that Winckelmann's dwelling on the theme of ideal beauty had its influence upon Diderot's conception of the ideal model.[54]

The success of the Ancients, according to Diderot, came from their having closely studied all the differences and alterations and deformities of the human body, and in this they showed themselves as possessing infinite patience and the most prodigious skill in observing nature. But this was the lesser part of their accomplishment. Using this knowledge, and 'with an astonishing discrimination, constantly eliminating the alterations and deformities of a defective Nature . . . [they were able] to raise themselves to the true model of beauty, to the true line. . . .'[55] Diderot thought of this as the secret of the Ancients' tremendous achievement.

But the very success of the Ancients was a pitfall to their successors. A modern artist must learn from the Ancients, but he must do more than copy them. Merely to do so is no better than to copy a copy. The Modern artist must have the instinct, as they had had, of going to nature.[56]

At this point it might be argued that Diderot's high-minded musings on how to attain the ideal model of beauty land with a bump in bathos. To follow nature is a truism. All of the exponents of the theory that art is the imitation of nature have for centuries been pressing the point home. It is very important to realize that Diderot was not content with the ordinary banalities about imitating nature. According to his quite surprising view, nature herself may be defective. Diderot even thought that 'the rigorous imitation of nature will render art poor, small-scale, petty,' though he admitted that such imitation would never make art false or mannered.[57]

The ideal model of beauty, then, is not found merely by imitating the Ancients nor even by imitating what Diderot calls 'subsistent nature,' the nature that subsists about us.[58] The artist, while calling upon his knowledge of subsistent nature, must attain something that is more than *imitatio na-*

turae.[59] He does this by the creative act. Thus is achieved the true line, the ideal model.

This theory of art may seem to many to be too Platonic — Diderot refers to Plato in the letter introducing the *Salon de 1767.*[60] The merit of the theory, however, lies in the importance it allots to the artist. Implicit is a very exalted conception of his role. He is more than an imitator; he is a creator. Since the time of Plato and Aristotle the principle that art is an imitation of nature had been almost sacrosanct, and even in the eighteenth century the writings of Du Bos, Batteux, and even Burke and Hume had fitted in with it.[61] Diderot carries forward what is essentially a new aesthetic, formulated earlier in the century by Shaftesbury and involving revolutionary new conceptions of what the artist does.[62]

The novelty of Diderot's aesthetic lies in its analysis of the part played in the creative process by the imagination.[63] His ideal model of beauty is an interior model. It is related to outside reality and is shaped and formed by a knowledge of the realness of objective facts, but nevertheless it is something which exists in the mind of the artist and exists nowhere else. It is to be discovered by an act of the imagination, disciplined by observation of nature and by a knowledge of technique. 'Confess, then, that this model is purely ideal and that it is not borrowed directly from any individual image in nature.' Diderot believed this so deeply that he declared that Phidias 'had in his imagination something beyond nature.' This conviction was reinforced by the advice Garrick had given to a French amateur as to how to improve his acting: 'There is an imaginary being whom you must take for a model.' There is no sort of poet, cried Diderot — our idiom would say 'creative person' — to whom Garrick's lesson is not appropriate. Diderot of course recognized that less gifted persons, sensitive to nature and content with simply copying her, could also practise the arts, but such artists, he agreed with Garrick, will be mediocre.[64] The pace is set by the genius, whose knowledge of the ideal model is vouchsafed to him by the quality of his imagination.

Diderot's early conviction, a quite uncomplicated one, was that genius was little more than quickness of sensitive reaction added to copiousness of emotional response. Little by little he came to add to this formula the counterbalancing elements of self-discipline and self-control. Accordingly his aesthetic theory underwent a slow but extremely significant evolution which most of the nineteenth-century critics quite overlooked, deeming him simply an exponent of *sensibilité.* Today this evolution is being more

thoroughly explored.[65] Probably because Diderot was becoming familiar
with the professional hazards and difficulties of artists, he inclined more
and more to the view that the great artist, though his imagination must
be stimulated and fructified by emotional response, must not allow it to
overwhelm him and make him incoherent or, in Diderot's word, 'mediocre.' His theory, fully enunciated a few years later in his *Paradoxe sur le
comédien,* is strikingly similar to the Wordsworthean formula of emotion
recollected in tranquillity.

Diderot's theory of aesthetics was comprehensive enough to include not
only the artist but also the auditor and the viewer. Their paths cross at
the point on the aesthetic map marked 'Taste.' Like so many of his
generation, like Hume in his important essay 'Of the Standard of Taste,'
Diderot tried hard to answer satisfactorily the question, What is taste? The
eighteenth century wrestled mightily with this problem — which is one
of the reasons why the very word 'aesthetics' was invented at that time.[66]

The new Lockean epistemology and psychology, by undermining the doctrine that ideas of beauty are innate, inevitably raised the whole question
of how, then, does an artist or a public know when a thing is beautiful.
The very word 'taste' connotes standards and values against which a specific work of art can be measured. Therefore the concept of taste bulks large
in the consideration of any critic who is concerned, as Diderot was, lest the
artist become too exclusively subjective, too oblivious either of objective
reality or of artistic traditions. Correlatively, a critic such as Diderot is also
concerned with discovering the criteria by which the public can be educated, and educate itself, in the appreciation of beauty.

Writing in 1776, Diderot defined taste. His was a definition, it is to be
noticed, that includes both the artist and the public. Taste is acquired
through experience and study, both on the part of the one who creates
and of the one who appreciates.

[It is] a facility, acquired by repeated experimentation, of seizing hold of the
true or the good, with the attendant circumstances that make it beautiful, and
of being promptly and vividly touched by it.[67]

In the desire to understand the mystery of how an artist communicates
with the person who views his art — and probably in the desire to assist
in this process — Diderot became as fascinated with communication theory
in the domain of plastic art as he was in the area of linguistics. He believed, as one aesthetician has recently remarked, that works of art require
an active participation on the part of the beholder. And the artist, he further

believed, should communicate not only with his contemporaries but also with succeeding generations. By doing so the artist helps to shape both the present and the future. This is the artist's supreme function, this is his glory. And it is this conception, reached after a rather fumbling start, that explains why Diderot's letters to Falconet about posterity finally reach such a high plane.[68]

Surveying the artist's function from a height as lofty as this, Diderot is evidently thinking of a public — a posterity — that expands, rather than of one so specialized that it narrows to the point of vanishing. To Diderot art is socially important, so that in much of his art criticism he sounds like a sociologist quite as much as an aesthetician. He has in mind an art that speaks to a whole nation. Patently Diderot thought that art was too important to be left just to the patrons and collectors and 'amateurs,' a race that he emphatically cursed.[69] Probably he thought, though he never made such a claim explicitly, that people like himself performed the very important function of educating people's taste.[70]

Part of Diderot's problem, which he never solved satisfactorily, was to discover how to popularize art without vulgarizing it. It was highly characteristic of the Enlightenment to seek greater participation for an increasing number of human beings — participation in rational inquiry, in the benefits of technological improvement, in a broader range of decision-making: the logic of the whole orientation of the *philosophes* impelled them towards a greater democratization. Yet, with the exception of Rousseau, they were often hesitant and ambiguous about believing that *le peuple* was capable of making decisions without caprice. A comparable problem arose for Diderot in the realm of art. He was not satisfied to accept a greater democratization of art appreciation if its quality was threatened by the process. 'But what,' he had asked agonizingly, 'do all these principles signify, if taste is a matter of caprice, and if there is no eternal, immutable rule for the beautiful?'[71]

Diderot had identified an enormously important question. His difficulty lay in trying to define the term 'taste' in a way that anybody could readily follow and practise. How does one help a public to know what are the canons of good and bad taste? An insoluble problem perhaps. Diderot tried to be basic; he tried to trace aesthetic experience to its psychological fundamentals and to find in the nature of man the specifications for recognizing beauty. But his definition of taste becomes slippery and unsatisfactory because he links the abstract idea of beauty with those other abstract terms, the true and the good. Such a definition of taste, as Cassirer pointed out, though it tries to avoid dogmatism and preserve an empirical approach, despairs of defining beauty in itself and begins to speak of art in terms of ethics.[72]

The pitfall of making art a handmaiden of morals is an obvious one, but not easy to avoid when one entertains, as Diderot did, the very highest opinion of the function of art in a culture.[73] Had he thought of art as being a subordinate or insignificant aspect of culture, it would have been possible for him to adopt a top-lofty attitude of art-for-art's sake, thus escaping the confusions and ambiguities of the moral meaning of art. But this he did not do. Probably it was from Shaftesbury that he first derived the conviction that in some profound and unsentimental way art must serve a moral purpose.[74]

Some of Diderot's comments in the *Salons* are surprisingly puritanical. Speaking of lascivious works of art, he asked, 'What can strike the balance between a picture, a statue, no matter how perfect, and the corruption of an innocent heart?'[75] He admired Boucher's technique but thought that his subjects corrupted morals, and he was even harsher about Boucher's son-in-law, Pierre-Antoine Baudouin, whose subjects did rather tend towards the suggestive.[76] In the *Essais sur la peinture* Diderot wrote:

I am not over-strict. I read my Petronius sometimes. Horace's satire, *Ambubaiarum,* pleases me as much as it does the next man. The infamous little madrigals of Catullus, why, I know three-fourths of them by heart. . . . I pardon the poet, the painter, sculptor, even the philosopher, an instant of good spirits and folly. But I do not want a painter to dip his brush there all the time, and thus pervert the aim of the arts.

And a few years later he wrote,

I am not a Franciscan; nevertheless I confess that I would willingly sacrifice the pleasure of seeing beautiful nudes if I could hasten the moment when painting and sculpture become more decent and moral, would think of co-operating with the other fine arts in inspiring virtue and purifying *moeurs*.[77]

Diderot is here expressing the effect of the gradual disappearance of one style, the rococo, and the emergence of a new one, neo-classicism. He was in the spirit of the age, and he probably contributed considerably to its spread himself by his discussions of art with artists and connoisseurs, though of course his written *Salons* could have little direct effect on the substitution of the new style for the old.[78] The frivolity as well as the grace of the rococo, so admirably suited to the tastes of a leisured and aristocratic society, was giving way to a somewhat sterner art, more concerned with heroes, with Roman virtue, with grandness in simplicity, and with the family virtues that Diderot himself highly esteemed.[79] What, then, did Diderot think should be the aim of the arts?

To make virtue attractive, vice odious, and ridicule hard-hitting, such is the intention of every honest man who picks up the pen, the brush, or the chisel.

This statement excellently portrays Diderot's moral seriousness in relation to the arts, though it has often been criticized as laying too heavy a burden on them.[80]

Diderot's fondness for the paintings of Greuze has greatly contributed to the accusations that his taste was often 'dreadfully sentimental.'[81] Greuze nowadays is enjoying a revival of esteem, but it is for his portraits more than for the genre scenes that Diderot and his contemporaries admired him so much. Diderot was usually disdainful of portraiture, his reason being that the better the portrait as to likeness, the further it was from the ideal model of beauty. Although he admitted that 'there is no great painter who has not known how to do portraits' (he mentioned Raphael, Rubens, Le Sueur, and Van Dyck), what he found most to admire in Greuze were canvases like 'The Village Bride,' 'The Paralytic, or The Fruits of a Good Education,' 'Filial Piety,' and 'The Ungrateful Son.' 'This Greuze, truly he's my man. The genre pleases me; it is moral painting.' And of a picture entitled 'The Well-Loved Mother,' showing a large family of children romping with their mother — Mme Geoffrin called this picture 'une fricassée d'enfants' — Diderot wrote, 'It is excellent, both in respect to talent and to morals. It preaches population. . . .'[82]

Had Diderot confined himself to admiring Greuze's genre pictures, he would have saved himself from anything worse than seeming now to be slightly ridiculous. But he was also exceedingly fond of Greuze's sentimental pictures of young girls, canvases such as 'The Broken Pitcher,' 'The Little Laundress,' 'The Girl with a Broken Mirror,' and 'The Girl Weeping for her Dead Bird.' Of this last, hung in the Salon of 1765, Diderot wrote, 'Soon one surprises oneself conversing with this child and consoling her. This is what I remember having said to her on different occasions'; and there follow several pages of over-heated apostrophe.[83] It is dismaying to realize that Diderot mistook these feelings of his to be appreciation of art. The plain fact is that when he looked at these pictures he felt the way middle-aged men are likely to feel when they see a provocative young starlet in a movie. 'Such, alas, is the effect produced upon him,' Jean Seznec writes, 'by the false innocence of Greuze's girls, those little hypocrites who have always broken their pitchers, cracked their mirrors, or lost their pets.' [84]

Having reached the nadir of Diderot's art criticism, it is well to remind ourselves of his apogee. This is to be found in his admiration of Chardin. Of the some 120 contemporary artists with whose works he was familiar, Chardin is the one Diderot consistently praised the highest. This he did even though he thought Chardin's subjects, his still-lifes and domestic scenes, belonged to a subordinate and somewhat inferior category of art.[85] To explain why Chardin's paintings were nevertheless so excellent, Diderot repeatedly referred to Chardin's 'magic' and spoke of him as being 'the greatest magician that we have.' [86] Diderot sometimes wrote as though hard put to explain Chardin's greatness precisely. 'One pauses before a Chardin instinctively, just as a traveler, fatigued by the road, sits down almost without noticing in the spot that offers him a grassy seat, silence, flowing water, coolness and shade.' [87]

More specifically, Diderot speaks of the 'sublimity' of Chardin's technique, of the simplicity and lifelikeness of his pictures, of the 'largeness' of his execution. Largeness, he thought, is 'independent of the extent of the canvas and the size of the objects. Reduce a Holy Family by Raphael as much as you like, you will not destroy its largeness of execution,' a statement which shows Diderot thinking in terms of pictorial concepts.[88] Diderot spoke repeatedly of Chardin's being a consummate colorist, and also appreciated his skill in reproducing reflections. 'This is the man who understands the harmony of colors and reflections. . . . He it is who observes how the light and its reflections flow over the surface of objects, who inexpressibly seizes and reproduces them in their inconceivable confusion.' [89] In short, 'Nature,' wrote Diderot, speaking both of Buffon the naturalist and Chardin the painter, 'has admitted them into her confidence.' [90]

As the author of the *Salons,* Diderot has usually been favorably received by posterity, the precedent being set by Sainte-Beuve's influential essay 'Diderot' (1851) and continuing on to a recent judgment in the *Connoisseur* that the *Salons* are 'the best journalistic art-criticism that has ever been written. . . .' [91] Now and again a vociferous minority report has been filed, as in the fulgurous essay by Ferdinand Brunetière (1880), complaining that Diderot was too subject-bound and too literary in his judgments: 'There is nothing for us, or almost nothing, to take from the *Salons* of Diderot. It is even to be regretted that our century has taken as much as it has.' [92] And a twentieth-century Brunetière *redivivus* complains of Diderot's approach to art as being 'highly subjective, dogmatic, moralistic, and subject-oriented.' [93] The preponderance of critical opinion, however, is consonant with the recent judgment that it is 'his inimitable style, so living, so colorful, that makes the reading of him, even when one does not agree with him, an enchantment.' [94] The numerous reviews of Jean Seznec's definitive edition of the *Salons* testify by their consensus to the appeal of Diderot's criticism and to the impact that it has had.

As one surveys Diderot's aesthetic theory as a whole, including his criticism in the *Salons,* it is well to concede that his touch was surer in the discovery of unexplored relationships than it was in the neat and thoroughgoing disposition of them. This is because Diderot was, as has been well said, an uncompleting man, a finder and initiator, not a concluder and a finisher.[95] This is characteristic of almost everything he thought about, his views on science as well as on art, his theories of the origin of the universe and of life as well as his search for proper guidelines in ethics and in politics. But this characteristic, rather than being a reproach to him, is the reason for his importance in the life of his century and the source of his being so deeply interesting to ours.

CHAPTER 39

'It Is Really Bizarre the Variety of Roles I Play in This World'

S AVE for the two *Salons, de 1765* and *de 1767,* Diderot wrote no major works in the mid-sixties. Following the prolonged strain of editing the *Encyclopédie,* he allowed himself the luxury of an interlude of relative relaxation. Not that he was ever really idle. He merely wrote longer letters to his friends, and he was much about town. He enjoyed himself, much like a silkworm on a mulberry leaf, eating diligently and contentedly and with no intimation that the time for cocoon-spinning would presently be at hand. For Diderot this time was to come in 1769.

Meanwhile, much of his correspondence concerned his relations with the Volland family, especially in respect to Mme Le Gendre, of whom Diderot had once been jealous. This lady, whose character has been called 'enigmatic' in one language and 'demoniacal' in another, was now living (since 1765) in a fine house on the Rue Sainte-Anne, not too bothered by her husband (for he was usually away on inspection trips in connection with his service in the Ponts et Chaussées), and at liberty to indulge her coquettishness, which she did by teasing a couple of suitors named Perronet and Vialet. She was also at liberty to persuade herself that she was falling in love with her son's tutor. Diderot could see this coming better than she; his conversations with her, reproduced in his letters to Sophie, are masterpieces of realistic dialogue, of introspection, of Socratic midwifery forcing the coquette to recognize what she was doing.[1] Though often at her house, Diderot never learned to trust or respect Mme Le Gendre very much. She died suddenly in the summer of 1768, and left small echo or memory in Diderot's subsequent correspondence.[2]

Through the Le Gendres Diderot had known for some years Guillaume Vialet, an engineer in the service of the Ponts et Chaussées. He was a disputatious man — Diderot's fondness for dialogue impelled him towards characters like Vialet and Falconet, with results sometimes discomfiting — and Vialet scandalized Diderot in 1766 by writing a justification of monks and monasticism.[3] Nevertheless, a year later Diderot got himself into the most preposterous and humiliating situation imaginable with Vialet. Thinking to cheer him up for his lack of success with Mme Le Gendre, Diderot gratuitously offered his daughter to Vialet in marriage. When Vialet rejected the proposal with scorn, Diderot's outraged replies covered twenty-seven pages.[4]

Many of these twenty-seven pages were used in self-justification. Rarely, when Diderot gets into this kind of dispute, does he come close to admitting that maybe he too had been in the wrong. About this time, for example, he hotly justified himself against the allegations of Mme d'Epinay, D'Holbach, Grimm, and other of his friends that he was neglecting them. Their letters at this juncture have not survived, so it is hard to judge the merits of the dispute. Diderot may very well have been in the right, but there is no doubt of one fact — he was sure that he was.[5] Similarly, Diderot flared up in 1768 over the disposition of the family inheritance, causing his sister to write to him, 'It could only be some philosophical demon that could dictate to you the letter you wrote to me. I don't recognize you in it at all.'[6] It was this vein of sophistry in Diderot's self-justifications to Vialet that caused a great modern interpreter of Diderot to remark that one can understand why relations between Rousseau and Diderot inevitably reached the breaking point.[7]

Moreover, though Diderot was customarily long-suffering, he could become choleric if he supposed he was being ill-treated. As an eminent friend said of him, Diderot 'desired people to have for him the consideration that he deserved.' This comment was made apropos of an incident at the Opera, probably in the late 1760's. Diderot, 'thickset, with a build like a sedan-chair porter, and wearing a black suit and a bob-tail wig,' became involved in a dispute with a young man over a point of literature. Diderot began to think that his adversary was taking him 'for some lawyer dressed up for Sunday. He seized him by the collar and, strong as a Turk, jerked him up and threatened to throw him into the orchestra pit.' Peacemakers intervened and the young man escaped.[8]

Though Diderot's life in 1768 did not have quite the focus of other times, it had all the customary intensity. He argued for long pages with Falconet about Le Mercier de La Rivière, who had by this time returned to France.[9] He continued to advise the wayward Mlle Jodin.[10] He threw himself with his usual impetuosity into a lawsuit in which a Langres woman, long a friend of the family, was the defendant against her brothers. The outcome is unknown, but it is known that he wrote three eloquent letters to the judge in charge of the case, and that to Sophie Volland Diderot reported, 'Our good deeds are not turning out very well. We gave shelter to a fellow townswoman . . . who amused herself for three months, during which she shared my daughter's bed, in putting all my womenfolk into combustion with her cackle.' [11] And he continued to write letters of introduction, one to Garrick for a playwright named Fenouillot de Falbaire,[12] and two to Hume warmly endorsing a certain Neufville. Hume thereupon tried to interest one of his friends in Neufville:

. . . what I chiefly rely upon is the Recommendation of the Celebrated M. Diderot, whose Morals and Goodness, no less than his Genius and Learning, are known all over Europe.[13]

Diderot referred in this year to his own goodness of character (*bonté d'âme*), 'in which I take pride.' He took so much pride in it that he spent much time and energy in trying to affect decisions involving other persons, thus demonstrating his power in influencing people. He also boasted in 1768 that 'It is really bizarre the variety of roles I play in this world,' [14] fore-shadowing the autobiographical character he later created, Hardouin in *Est-il bon? Est-il méchant?* Never did he play a more bizarre role nor one in which he took greater pride than in being a ghost-writer of letters for a discarded and indigent mistress of one of the King's ministers. 'Oh! dear friends, a beautiful letter,' he exulted, 'truly sublime.' The minister sent an emissary who tactfully left some louis on the mantlepiece of the woman's apartment, with promises of further aid. 'Well, the sublime letter . . . was not without results. . . . Thus it is not completely useless to know how to write; and eloquence can break stones.' [15] Diderot thought of outcomes like this as proving his natural goodness of soul, and probably did not realize that they also served to gratify his sense of power.

From September 1767 until November 1768, Diderot worked off and on at the enormously lengthy *Salon de 1767*.[16] And during this time one hears the leitmotifs of health and finances in his letters. He suffered from gout — 'This cursed gout began to travel, in short stages, taking three whole months to make the tour of my machine.' And he was put on a milk diet again. 'Neither wine, nor liqueurs, nor coffee, nor women. Would you want good health at that price?' [17] As to finances, in addition to his agitations about his holdings at Langres, he invested 70,000 livres with a farmer-general — a very bourgeois thing to do when *philosophes* looked upon farmers-general as one of the curses of the country — and worried a great deal as to whether his farmer-general was going to remain solvent.[18]

In September 1767 Galitzin was relieved of his Paris post and in May 1768 left the city. His recall, the excuse for which was a dispute over protocol, reflected a chronic discontent on the part of Catherine II with the foreign policy of France, which supported the Poles and the Turks as much as it could against Russian pressure. After Galitzin's recall, and until 1778, Russia was represented at Paris and Versailles by only a *chargé d'affaires*.[19] Galitzin was sorry to go, which is scarcely to be wondered at, for in the eighteenth century Paris must have been the most attractive diplomatic post in the world. Moreover, he had a mistress, a Mlle Dornet, who for some unknown reason was a guest in 1767 of the Vollands at their country estate, presumably at Diderot's request.[20] Galitzin's feelings about Mlle Dornet changed, however. After leaving Paris he fell suddenly in love with a young Prussian countess and married her.[21] Thereupon he began to think that it would be desirable to recover from Mlle Dornet a couple of portraits of himself. The scorned lady was scarcely in a mood to accede to an outright request, so that Galitzin pressed Diderot into service to see what could be done.

Inasmuch as Mlle Dornet was in poor health and also very superstitious, Diderot got the idea of introducing to her an acquaintance of his named Desbrosses, who would pretend to be a Turkish physician educated at Tübingen.[22] As he began to win her confidence, Desbrosses suggested that the portraits were having a malign effect upon her health and that consequently she ought to get rid of them. Diderot obligingly offered to take them. All went well at first, but the scheme eventually collapsed.

Diderot was engaged in this deception during September and October of 1768. At the same time he wrote an account of it in his favorite dialogue form. This manuscript, which he entitled *Mystification,* embodies Diderot's customary skill of conversational play and economy of presentation, so that posterity, which discovered the item only a few years ago, immediately accepted it as an entertaining and significant addition to Diderot's works.[23] Diderot admirers find it somewhat disconcerting to discover their man engaged in a confidence trick, and it is noticeable that interpretations of Diderot's character since the publication of *Mystification* are beginning to reflect the knowledge that an impulse to mystify and play practical jokes was one of his traits. It is to be observed, however, that even had the scheme been successful it would not have done Mlle Dornet harm.

With Galitzin gone, Diderot took upon himself to perform some of the functions previously carried out by his friend. Thus Diderot mentioned a great opportunity for purchasing the Gaignat collection of art and books. 'Ah! if the prince were here,' he wrote to Falconet, 'how we would maneuver.'[24] Ultimately Catherine II commissioned Diderot to bid for the whole art collection and at the sale in December 1768 he acquired for her 'five of the finest pictures in France: a Murillo, three Gerard Dous, and a J.-B. Van Loo.'[25]

His activities as a purchasing agent of course made the public identify Diderot closely with Catherine II, and he himself in this year went out of his way to reinforce this image. In the foreword to the sixth volume of engravings (the editor of which was officially supposed to be anonymous), Diderot published these extravagant words:

Let it be allowed me to yield for a moment to the feelings of veneration and gratitude that I owe her for the extraordinary manifestations of her goodness that she has heaped upon me; let it be allowed me to say, Immortal Being, all-powerful, eternal, who dost make great destinies and watchest over them, save Catherine II for Russia.[26]

Diderot's devotion to Catherine II occasionally put him in some strange postures. In 1768, for instance, he tried to persuade a fellow man of letters to suppress a manuscript unflattering to her. This narrative recounted the events of the *coup d'état* of 1762 by which Catherine II seized the throne. Claude-Carloman de Rulhière had gone to Saint Petersburg in 1760 as an attaché of the French embassy. Thus he was in residence during the happenings there, which he claimed to have verified thoroughly by interviews with participants and with other diplomats. In 1768, at the request of the Countess of Egmont, a high-born lady who was the daughter of the Maréchal de Richelieu, Rulhière wrote his 'Anecdotes sur la révolution de Russie en l'année 1762.' It is an absorbingly interesting piece, an excellent example of contemporary history. The style is simple, urbane, without invective or sarcasm. The narrative reveals of course the incredible *maladresse* of Peter III, but it also shows that Catherine II, no doubt in self-defense, had been plotting against her husband for some time. Most interesting of all, the 'Anecdotes' reveals her cleverly utilizing two malcontent groups at one and the same time, without allowing the one to suspect the existence of the other. These were the careerist-adventurist group of the Orlov brothers, and what might be called the 'constitutionalist' group, of which the young Princess Dashkov was a leader. This second group hoped that the removal of Peter III would be followed by a regency and then by a limited monarchy, rather than by a continuation of the despotism. These hopes, of course, turned out to be vain. Rulhière's narrative finally recounts the death of the former Czar. 'It is not known with certainty what part the Empress played in this event.'[27]

The French friends of Catherine II were alarmed by the existence of this manuscript. Mme Geoffrin was the first to try to buy it up.[28] By May 1768 Rulhière had read it to many persons, among them Diderot, who endeavored to persuade Rulhière to suppress it. He replied that he had never intended to publish the manuscript, consequently he would not undertake to destroy it. 'It's a very delicate business, very delicate,' wrote Diderot to Falconet.[29] Catherine II gave orders to have Khotinski, the Russian *chargé d'affaires* at Paris, buy the manuscript from Rulhière, 'especially concealing from him that you have any instructions whatsoever from here on this subject.' [30]

Diderot was disagreeably surprised that Khotinski was charged with this mission rather than he, and he claimed not to know Rulhière's address, so that Khotinski had to discover it for himself. Diderot was present at Khotinski's second interview with Rulhière, where, Khotinski wrote, 'Diderot did everything he possibly could to persuade him to accede to my propositions.' Rulhière refused to be bought and there the matter rested. 'Everything was bungled,' Diderot wrote Falconet discontentedly. 'I suspected it would turn out so.' In fact, Rulhière continued to read his manuscript on occasion; Dr. Tronchin heard it at Mme Necker's on 8 April 1769.[31] Nevertheless, the manuscript remained unpublished until 1797, five years after Rulhière's death and the year after Catherine II's.

Other evidence of this year continues to show Diderot delighting in his Russian connections. In his introduction to the sixth volume of the plates he remarked that 'Our first volume of text has been translated in Russia, at the order of Her Imperial Majesty,' and hoped that '. . . a work which we intended for the use of our nation will also be useful to hers.' [32] He was pleased to discover that a Russian translation of *Le Père de famille* had been published.[33] And in response to the continued pressure upon him to visit Russia he promised Falconet that as soon as the *Encyclopédie* was finished — there were many engravings still to be prepared — 'I shall be off.' [34]

In these years Diderot found himself now and again hobnobbing with the great. This was usually because Grimm, wanting to provide entertainment for his German patrons when they came to Paris, expected to be able to show off Diderot at any moment, a circumstance which both amused Diderot and irritated him. In 1767 there had been the Prince of Brunswick-Wolfenbüttel, who wanted to meet Diderot incognito. Accordingly Grimm passed the Prince off at the Rue Taranne as a private citizen from Germany. The Prince had a lengthy and lively conversation with the *philosophe,* who was in nightcap and dressing gown.[35] Then there was the Landgravine Caroline of Hesse-Darmstadt, who came to Paris in May 1767 to consult Dr. Tronchin.[36] In 1768 Grimm tried to browbeat Diderot into calling upon the visiting Prince of Saxe-Gotha. Diderot hotly refused: 'I was out of all patience with this kind of forced labor.' The Prince, however, introduced himself at the Rue Taranne as a visiting Swiss, and a rollicking conversation ensued. Two days later Diderot met this 'M. Erlich' at D'Holbach's and pretended to have to be informed who this Swiss really was: '. . . the baron [d'Holbach] had tipped me off, and the betrayers were betrayed. I played my role like an angel.'[37] Later in 1768 the visit of King Christian VII of Denmark caused a stir in Paris, particularly among the *philosophes,* eighteen of whom, with Diderot among them, were presented to the King at a special reception on 20 November.[38]

During this latter half of 1768 Diderot's friend Damilaville was gravely and fatally ill. He succumbed on 13 December, at the age of forty-five.[39] Though Damilaville's self-esteem had profited from his close association with the *philosophes,* he had had to pay a price for it, for it appears that he missed being appointed director of the vingtième in the generality of Paris because the *intendant* of Paris denounced him as an atheist, a *philosophe,* and an Encyclopedist.[40] Damilaville seems not to have been a very amiable or admirable man. According to Grimm, Damilaville was 'dreary and heavy and the defects of his early education were always apparent . . . [he had] a kind of presumption that did not contribute to making him lovable.'[41] Diderot loved him, though. 'I sincerely rejoice that I found you,' he once wrote to Damilaville. 'It is one of the happy events of my life.' Always faithful and untiring in visiting sick friends, Diderot was very assiduous in these last months of Damilaville's illness. 'Those who do not feel,' he had written in that very year, 'that moral obligations are as strong as iron bands are much to be pitied.'[42]

It is remarkable how often this year Diderot complains of Sophie's neglecting or delaying to answer his letters, so often that it even suggests that her interest in him was waning.[43] As usual, his letters to her are full of details about his family. There was the chronic problem in respect to his daughter as to her religious upbringing. 'They say,' wrote Voltaire in 1767, 'that he lets his daughter be brought up in principles that he detests.'[44] This was true enough. Diderot mentions on an Assumption Day that mother and daughter had gone to Notre-Dame, and on another occasion he was unable to introduce Angélique to one of his friends because she had gone to confession.[45] Perhaps it was with such circumstances in mind that Diderot wrote,

I don't take a step without seeing children being led about in leading strings by women who ought to be in them themselves, beginning with the mother of my child.

One November Sunday in 1768, during a walk, Diderot suddenly made up his mind to tell his fifteen-year-old daughter about sex. 'I revealed to her everything that has to do with being a woman, starting with the question, Do you know the difference between the two sexes?' Diderot thought that the conversation came off satisfactorily, but he was not so sure of himself in this as he usually was. 'I have consulted several sensible people about this conversation. They all tell me I did well.' Even after this, perhaps all the more because of it, Diderot worried about Angélique's being exposed to licentious ideas, so that he fiercely rebuked one of his friends for sending to him unsealed a book with lascivious drawings which might have fallen into her hands.[46]

Diderot did not try to undermine Mme Diderot's authority. On the contrary, he strongly emphasized in this conversation how much Angélique owed her mother. Nor was Angélique a rebellious daughter. Yet her memory of their family life, as she looked back at it in 1816, is quite startling:

[My mother's] disposition, difficult to live with, eternally scolding, made our household a hell in which my father was the consoling angel. Had it not been for him, my mother would have deadened all my faculties and perhaps even destroyed my existence, for, at the age when this life became burdensome to me, my health became impaired.[47]

In her own way Mme Diderot was extremely generous and goodhearted. She was compassionate without, however, being tender. If a newly-installed servant — she was always hiring and firing them — fell sick, Mme Diderot regarded the girl as sent by Providence to be taken care of. The upstairs tenants at the Rue Taranne were usually destitute, and Angélique remembered being sent every day to take them soup, meat, or fruit. 'If these women became sick, my mother would climb up ten times a day to take care of them. If they had children, my mother would call them down to play with me, give them clothes, and send them back with their aprons full, after having made them eat.' Mme Diderot was abidingly concerned about the servant girl Jeanneton, and Mlle Jodin and her mother, and Mlle Collot, and about the litigious lady from Langres; and she kept at her husband to appeal to Catherine II to help an old sculptor named Simon who claimed payment for services performed for Russia in the time of Peter the Great.

Her sense of justice came into play this very year, when she tried to come
to the defense of an urchin being beaten by marketwomen. The police report
of this incident stated that the women turned on her and insulted and kicked
her.[48]

About this time Diderot redecorated his study, an event which became the
inspiration for one of his most delightful pieces, 'Regrets on my Old Dressing
Gown.' Grimm tells us that when he took Prince Adam Czartoryski to the
Rue Taranne to see Diderot, they found him wearing a brand-new and
magnificent dressing gown, while on the wall was a picture by Vernet,
painted according to Diderot's specifications. Grimm gave Diderot a mock
sermon on the dangers of luxury; and in a few days Diderot sent him the
'Regrets': 'Why did I not keep it? It was made for me, I for it. . . . My
friends, . . . fear the onset of riches. Let my example instruct you. Poverty
has its freedoms; opulence has its constraints.' * The new dressing gown,
Diderot went on, had seemed to call for other changes. Thus the Vernet
picture; thus a bronze and gold clock 'in the Geoffrin style'; thus a morocco
armchair; thus other items in an extensive catalogue of the changes he had
made. But there was a limit to the changes he was willing to bring about. 'I
have sworn and I swear again, the feet of Denis the *philosophe* will never
tread upon any masterpiece from La Savonnerie.' The 'Regrets' is a graceful
piece of writing, charming in its intimacy, and not quite so artless as it
seems.[49]

Much of this new finery may have been the gift of Mme Geoffrin, witness
the reference to the bronze and gold clock in the Geoffrin style. Mme Geoffrin is known to have called at the Rue Taranne now and again, for in September 1767 Diderot grumbled to Sophie Volland, 'I received a visit from
Mme Geoffrin, who treated me like a ninny and counseled my wife to do the
same.' One day in October 1768 she visited Diderot 'in my garret,' and she
may have got the idea at that very time that he needed a change in *décor*.[50]
Though Mme Geoffrin could be extremely critical of Diderot, she was a
woman who was very open-handed with her friends and protégés. She knew
how to give generously without humiliating the receiver; perhaps she had
been exercising this talent now.[51]

In his long letters to Falconet Diderot tried to keep his friend abreast of
occurrences in Paris. One of the things he reported in 1768 was that 'it is
raining infidel books. It is a running fire that is riddling the sanctuary from
all directions.' Most of all he was referring to *Le Christianisme dévoilé*. Pub-

---

* The *Regrets* is available in English translation in Denis Diderot, *Rameau's Nephew*, ed.
Ralph H. Bowen (Indianapolis: Bobbs-Merrill, Library of Liberal Arts, 1964), 309–17.

lished in 1766, it brought in Paris two years later the exceedingly high price of eighty livres. The author of this militant and bruising attack on all aspects of Christian faith was D'Holbach. Diderot had almost certainly seen the work in manuscript and made suggestions regarding it; if not this one, something by D'Holbach equally inflammatory. The government punished severely anyone it could find who had any connection with *Le Christianisme dévoilé*. For possessing one copy and selling another, an apprentice was sentenced to nine years in the galleys.[52] Yet D'Holbach's authorship was kept a close secret. He wrote blandly in 1769 to an Italian friend, 'We are inundated more than ever by impious books which evidently intend to undermine the foundations of religion.'[53]

During the course of 1769 Diderot adventitiously became the editor of what turned out to be an extremely influential book on political economy. This was Galiani's *Dialogues sur le commerce des blés* ('Dialogues on the Grain Trade'). The experience broadened and ripened Diderot's interest in politics and history, taught him the dangers of easy conclusions and abstract reasoning in making decisions about complex issues of public affairs, and thus reinforced in him the impulse toward empiricism, the compulsion to search for data, that he had already learned to apply in science, technology, and art.

Galiani's book was significant because it strenuously controverted the wisdom of that part of the decree of 19 July 1764 that had permitted the free export of grain stuffs from France without the numerous mercantilistic regulations or prohibitions that previously had trammeled the trade. Thus the commerce in grain became subject only to the play of supply and demand, making the decree a notable example of laissez-faire. The freedom of the grain trade was one of the shibboleths of the Physiocrats, of whom Quesnay, the elder Mirabeau, Le Mercier de La Rivière, and Dupont de Nemours were the leaders. They tended to identify the interests of the agricultural producers with those of the nation as a whole:

Despite their frequent assertion of the necessity of complete freedom of trade, the Physiocrats were primarily interested in achieving the *free exportation* of *grain,* and the bulk of their foreign-trade theorizing was oriented about this objective. . . .[54]

What inspired the Physiocrats was the search for the source of the wealth of nations. Colbert had supposed a century earlier that he knew the secret: according to Colbertism, it lay in elaborate governmental regulation of all industry and commerce, with a concomitant solicitude for manufacturing even, if necessary, to the neglect of agriculture. The Physiocrats reacted against this, root and branch. And they preached that a prosperous agricultural economy is the true source of the wealth of nations. Thus they argued, logically enough, that the freedom to export would prevent a depression of grain prices in France resulting from good harvests.

The Physiocrats, though they came to seem to be very abstract and doctrinaire in their reasoning, are nevertheless now regarded as important precursors of twentieth-century economic theory. '. . . our present-day concern with general equilibrium analysis, the development of under-developed countries, the economics of control, and input-output analysis, has in a certain sense made Physiocrats of us all,' wrote a prominent economic historian in 1963. And in 1768, according to the principal historian of the movement, the fortunes of the Physiocrats, or *économistes,* as they liked to call themselves, were at their height.[55]

Diderot had already demonstrated his openmindedness to the Physiocratic doctrine by publishing in the early volumes of the *Encyclopédie* two lengthy and important articles, 'Farmers' (*Fermiers*) and 'Grain' (*Grains*), both by Quesnay. In the mid-sixties Diderot practically became a convert. The *Encyclopédie* article *'Laboureur,'* which may have been written by Diderot himself, declared that 'It is the land, and only the land, that produces true riches,' and therefore argued for 'an entire freedom to export foodstuffs.' He was dazzled, as he showed in his correspondence with Damilaville and Falconet, by Le Mercier de La Rivière's book, *L'Ordre naturel et essentiel des sociétés politiques.*[56] Diderot even contributed two brief fables, one of them defending the Physiocratic principle of 'evidence,' to *Les Ephémérides du Citoyen,* the journalistic organ of the movement. This he did probably because he was on the friendliest of terms with the youthful Dupont de Nemours, who often visited the Rue Taranne and who had become the principal editor of *Les Ephémérides du Citoyen* in 1768.[57] When Diderot reviewed several volumes of the *Ephémérides* for the *Correspondance littéraire,* he applauded the sect for its contributions to public knowledge, though by this time he began to sound a note of scepticism regarding it:

What pleases me the most about this new school . . . is that, being highly protected, it says what it pleases, that it speaks with a freedom that we did not use to know, and that in the long run the police, the court, and the magistrates get used to hearing everything, and authors to saying it. Little by little the nation will familiarize itself with questions of finance, commerce, agriculture, legislation, and politics. By dint of agitation for or against issues, the most important ones for the happiness of society will be clarified. . . . Let us pray to

God that this school keeps going, though it be as ignorant and garrulous as our Neapolitan abbé [Galiani] thinks it is. These men are well-intentioned, head-strong, fired with enthusiasm, and vain; and even though they were mistaken in everything, they are to be blamed only by those who do not know that we are almost always condemned to experience error in order to arrive at truth.[58]

Galiani, whose youthful treatise 'On Money' is even today spoken of with admiration, was at first as Physiocratic about the grain trade as the Physio-crats. But he became progressively concerned as to the way the decree of 1764 was actually working out, regarding not simply cash income to land-owners but also the consequences of crop failures, high prices, and food shortages. He had a vivid recollection, moreover, of the horrible famine in the Kingdom of Naples in 1764.[59] The decisive event, at least in Galiani's and Diderot's relations to the subject of the grain trade, came in November 1768, when Galiani explained in detail his reasons for believing that the free exportation of grain was a mistake. 'I swear to you, my dear,' wrote Diderot to Sophie, 'no one else up to the present has said the first word on this question. I prostrated myself before him to get him to publish his ideas.'[60]

Presumably Galiani spent the winter planning and writing his *Dialogues.* But on 29 May 1769 he received the shattering news of his recall from Paris at the request of the French government. Galiani had incautiously written to a friend some prognostications about the Family Compact, a treaty system that allied the kingdoms of France, Spain (and Naples), and his letter had been intercepted.[61] Poor Galiani left Paris forever on 25 June 1769. He had written his last dialogue 'while sobbing,' he later recalled, and he entrusted the manuscript to Diderot and Mme d'Epinay to see through the press.[62]

For several reasons Diderot found the bringing out of Galiani's book quite troublesome. First, it needed very extensive copy-editing to make it French.[63] Second, Diderot himself had to find a publisher for it, who then did a printing job requiring a great deal of correction.[64] Third, Galiani was very impatient and touchy. 'Do you have the devil in your body,' asked Diderot hotly, 'to be overwhelming me with insults in all languages, living and dead, and addressed to me through all sorts of persons?'[65] And maybe Diderot was dilatory, as D'Holbach seems to have thought.[66] Then there was censor trouble, not perhaps unexpected, considering that the manuscript vigorously attacked government policy. Diderot and Mme d'Epinay used all the influence they had with Sartine to persuade him to relent, but without much success. However, the resignation in December 1769 of Maynon d'Invau, Controller-General of Finance, who had been steadily favorable to the decree of 1764 allowing the free exportation of grains, meant bad news for the Physiocrats and good news for Galiani. Sartine gave his consent, and the book appeared in the last days of 1769.[67]

Galiani's *Dialogues sur le commerce des blés* is most entertaining reading. His three interlocutors were modeled on persons from real life — our old friend the Marquis de Croismare, Galiani himself, and a young *maître des requêtes* of the Parlement of Paris named Baudoin.[68] Galiani was almost as skillful in the construction of dialogue as Diderot himself. The argument progresses swiftly, aided rather than impeded by the contrast of character between the intelligent but *frivole* Croismare-type, the sober and responsible magistrate-type, and the witty but serious Galiani-type. It was a controversial book not only because it attacked the decree of 1764 as being dangerous to the welfare of the nation but also because it undermined, though indirectly, one of the most cherished principles of Physiocratic methodology. This was the presumption — a very Cartesian way of going at things — that historical evidence, in comparison with abstract and logical reasoning, is irrelevant and immaterial.[69]

Galiani, however, perferred to argue from actual conditions rather than from syllogisms. Moreover, his constant deference to the validity of historical evidence, perhaps imbibed from his former teacher Vico, was highly instructive to Diderot.[70] And Galiani also taught Diderot that in politics everything affects everything else, a principle which Diderot had already discovered for himself in psychology, medicine, ethics, and art, and was now ready to extend to his political and social thought:

In this immense machine of the political state, everything hangs together, everything is linked, everything is connected, nothing must upset the equilibrium unless one wishes to see the whole machine overturned. . . . That is why political science is so difficult.[71]

Galiani's work had a somewhat divisive effect upon the *philosophes*. The Turgot-Condorcet-Dupont wing was inclined to look askance at the Galiani doctrine which the Diderot-Grimm-D'Holbach group had come to espouse. Turgot remarked that he found the book full of wit, but of wit infinitely ill-employed. 'He has the art of all those who want to make clear things muddled.'[72] Perhaps because of Diderot's close association with Galiani, one can detect in the following years a certain nuance of constraint in the cordiality of the relations between Diderot and Turgot.

Even before the publication of the *Dialogues* it was known that the Abbé Morellet, though not precisely a Physiocrat himself, was preparing a refutation of it. Sartine asked Diderot to be the censor of Morellet's manuscript, an adroit move because Diderot, with his deep-seated convictions about the freedom of the press, could scarcely recommend that the manuscript be refused publication. Nevertheless, his report to Sartine shows Diderot squirming. He told Sartine that he hoped that Morellet would choose not to have the manuscript printed.[73] It was not released to the public — though this was not Diderot's doing — until 1774, but meanwhile, as Diderot in November 1770 was annotating for his own use a copy of the Morellet refutation, the refutation engendered a refutation of its own. Diderot had become through all these months more and more committed to Galiani's point of view.[74] Consequently his *Apologie de l'Abbé Galiani,* a fragmentary and rough-hewn manuscript which remained in Diderot's desk during his lifetime, represents the climax of the whole episode.[75]

In the *Apologie de l'Abbé Galiani* Diderot responds to the abrasive Morellet quite abrasively himself. Most of all, Diderot was outraged by Morellet's preferring 'the sacred right of property' to human rights.

This principle [wrote Diderot] is the principle of a Tartar, of a cannibal, and not of a civilized man. Is not the sentiment of humanity more sacred than the right of property (which is infringed in an infinite number of occasions, in war and peace), respect for which is preached to us by M. the Abbé to the point of exposing us to killing one another, cutting one another's throats, and dying of hunger.

Diderot had seen bread riots in the provinces: '. . . only a drunk man would not be afraid of them.' It is easy to see, he wrote, that M. Morellet lives in Paris. Diderot, the provincial from Langres and the owner of some landed property there, wrote with knowledge and particularity about land-holding conditions and about agriculture. Besides, he had shown his concern about food supply as early as 1755, when he reviewed for the *Correspondance littéraire* a book about wheat smut; and his lengthy article on 'Agriculture' in the *Encyclopédie,* together with the numerous engravings on agriculture that appeared under his supervision in the first volume of the plates, testify to his interest and knowledge. Diderot objected to Morellet's theoretical and impractical approach: 'My dear Abbé, you utopianize [*vous utopisez*] as far as the eye can reach.' With the haughtiness — and pride — of a man who was himself the son of a craftsman and who as an encyclopedist had learned firsthand numerous processing techniques, Diderot wrote that '. . . to speak pertinently of the bakery business, you have to have had your hands in the dough.' 'You do not have the first idea,' wrote Diderot, 'of what really takes place in a time of famine.' He complained of 'most of the general principles which you advance with the finest intrepidity. There isn't one of them that is not subject to an infinitude of exceptions in practice.' [76]

His defense of Galiani shows how aware Diderot was becoming of the role of the specific exception and of the importance of a knowledge of history, if one is to come to sensible judgments about complicated current events. He objected to Morellet's method of beginning by formulating general principles out of one's head:

. . . it seems to me that in the sciences and in the crafts there is a method precisely the reverse of yours. One begins with individual cases . . . examined by themselves and compared to others; one perceives similarities and differences, one forms more or less general ideas, more or less less extensive theories. It is the facts, the existing phenomena which serve as rungs for climbing higher. . . .[77]

Diderot learned from Galiani, and inversely from Morellet, the need for minute observation in political affairs. His adventitious adventures as Galiani's editor prepared him for the meticulous efforts of information gathering which a few years later he achieved in Holland and tried to achieve in Russia.

CHAPTER 40

Le Rêve de d'Alembert
(1769)

THE RECORD of Diderot's activities in the first part of 1769 is arid and scant. Much of his time was taken up in writing the many book reviews for the *Correspondance littéraire* that date from this time. Moreover, he assumed charge of the enterprise from May until October, while Grimm was absent in Germany. Apparently the *Correspondance littéraire* was not sent out to its subscribers between 15 April and 1 October, which suggests that Diderot's responsibility may have been simply the accumulation of material for it.[1]

Diderot's attitude towards Grimm was usually submissive and self-deprecatory, though tempered now and again, as it was early in 1769, by his taking offense at Grimm's ruthless exploitation. This time Diderot referred to Grimm as having the soul of a Hyrcanian tiger: 'They are said to be the worst of all. . . .

Tell him also [continued Diderot to Mme d'Epinay] that he has certainly seen to it that I would not have a spark of the verve, warmth and gaiety required for the task that I have undertaken for his *Correspondance*.

'Grimm is taking up all my time,' he wrote in July, and, again, 'I would not continue this forced labor the rest of my life for my weight in gold.' Nevertheless, he continued to do a great deal of book reviewing, not only this year but also in 1770 and 1771.[2]

Diderot's most important review in 1769 was that of the much-heralded nature poem by Saint-Lambert entitled *Les Saisons*. Saint-Lambert is now remembered for his love affairs with Mme du Châtelet, Voltaire's mistress, and with Sophie d'Houdetot, Rousseau's inamorata, and not much else. In his lifetime he was celebrated for his poetry as well. Diderot knew Saint-Lambert intimately, though he declared that 'the tone he takes with me is rather more that of a patron than a friend.' At Naigeon's behest, Diderot prepared for judging *Les Saisons* by reading Virgil's *Georgics*. 'They gave me much pleasure and did Saint-Lambert a lot of damage.' Diderot complained that there was not enough familiarity with nature in Saint-Lambert's poem. 'His body was in the fields but his soul was in the city.' Diderot acknowledged, however, that it was very hard to write such a poem in French successfully, because 'we have never been a purely agricultural people; our customary idiom has emphatically not been of country life.' Accordingly Diderot spoke of *Les Saisons* with esteem and, with his fondness for the concrete, praised realistic passages when he could find them. Of a description of a partridge shot in flight he wrote, 'That is true; I too have shot partridges; and I vividly recall this somersaulting of the wounded bird.' [3]

These fugitive pieces that Diderot wrote for the *Correspondance littéraire* are not to be ignored. One reason is that he himself highly esteemed some of them, calling them 'delectable.' More important, their subjectivity — when one reads a review by Diderot one ends by knowing him more intimately, if not the book — leads us directly to some of his most cherished convictions most spontaneously expressed. Thus, in reviewing the *History of Russia* by Lomonosov, Diderot wrote, 'Whatever Jean-Jacques Rousseau and the fanatical enemies of the progress of the human spirit may say, it is difficult to read the history of the centuries of barbarism in the life of any people without congratulating oneself upon being born in an enlightened century and in a civilized nation.' Diderot's politics in 1769 may be inferred from the series of maledictions he called down upon some anonymous devotee of the good old days who could see about him nothing but deterioration and decay:

Cursed be he who does not see that the sciences and the arts have made incredible progress, bringing with them a gentleness of character that is the enemy of any barbarous action. Cursed be he who does not perceive that in no other time has enlightenment been so popular and that this popularity cannot help but lead us to something useful. . . . Cursed be he who does not see that the French have never breathed a more profound and considered spirit of liberty. Cursed be he so ignorant of present affairs as not to feel that never have humanity's two greatest scourges, despotism and superstition, been under such violent attack. . . .[4]

Liberal but not yet revolutionary, such were the political convictions of Diderot in 1769.

That summer was very hot and the sociable Diderot felt solitary in Paris. The Volland ladies were once again at their country estate, Galiani had gone to Italy, Grimm was in Germany, D'Holbach was in a temper at Grandval, and Damilaville was dead. Without the usual distractions there was little left to do save apply himself. 'I do not believe I have worked so hard in my life.' Out of it all, beyond his labor for Galiani and for Grimm, beyond his preparing two volumes of illustrations for the *Encyclopédie* at once, '. . . so that you see me surrounded by engravings from head to foot,' there came a great work.[5] This was *Le Rêve de d'Alembert* ('D'Alembert's Dream'), a view of the cosmos so bold, so much in advance of its time, and so personal that it naturally was kept secret in Diderot's lifetime and did not see publication until 1831.[6] In its philosophical sweep and imaginative power, *Le Rêve de d'Alembert* is Diderot's greatest work of all.

Le Rêve de d'Alembert addressed itself to the same range of problems that Diderot had begun to examine long before, when he wrote the article 'Animal' for the *Encyclopédie*.[7] Similarly, in his *Pensées sur l'interprétation de la nature* he had conjectured about the same type of scientific-philosophical questions that *Le Rêve de d'Alembert* grappled with, though his treatment in 1753 had been aphoristic whereas now, in the *Rêve,* it was dialectical. In 1765 he had prefigured in a letter to a friend the whole main argument of *Le Rêve de d'Alembert,* and his article *'Naître'* in the *Encyclopédie* had also foreshadowed much of it.[8] Clearly the ideas he set forth in the *Rêve* had been shaping in his mind for a considerable time.

Lucretius, whose *De rerum natura* answered the same questions as *Le Rêve de d'Alembert,* was much in Diderot's thoughts at this time. The tutor in D'Holbach's household, one La Grange, had translated and edited *De rerum natura,* and Diderot had gone over the translation before its publication in 1768. Numerous references to Lucretius appear in Diderot's review of Saint-Lambert's *Les Saisons* and in the *Salon de 1767* (which he wrote in 1768).[9] Moreover, the spell of ancient philosophy upon Diderot was so great that at first he intended to give ancient classic names to the interlocutors of the dialogue. 'Democritus, Hippocrates, and Leucippus would have been my personages; but keeping up verisimilitude would have restricted me within the narrow limits of ancient philosophy, and I would have lost too much.'[10]

Le Rêve de d'Alembert is organized as a kind of triptych. First there is a discussion between two philosophers, one of whom sets forth a thoroughgoing materialism to which the other objects. In the second and main panel of the triptych the demurring philosopher is disclosed as having had a very feverish night during which he talked a great deal in his sleep. His alarmed mistress wrote down his mumbled remarks and called a doctor, who pronounces the still-sleeping patient not in danger and then interprets the phi-

losopher's outpourings. The technique that Diderot uses here has been noticed as being thoroughly Freudian — observation of the phenomena, reporting of the phenomena, interpretation of the phenomena.[11] The philosopher's overheard remarks show that he has unconsciously accepted the
materialism he had rejected in the discussion the evening before, and is
carrying it even further. The third panel of the triptych is a conversation
later in the day between the doctor and the mistress concerning some scientific and moral problems involving sexuality.*

Making the dialogue depend upon a dream was an exceptionally effective
instrument for the presentation of the startling hypotheses in *Le Rêve de
d'Alembert,* many of them provisional and as yet unverified. Yet Diderot
knew that it would seem strange that the burden of the argument should
be expressed by a dreaming man. Accordingly he wrote of his dialogue as
being at one and the same time highly extravagant and profoundly philosophical. 'Often one must give wisdom the appearance of folly in order
to have it accepted.'[12] Throughout his career Diderot showed that he
was deeply interested in the phenomenology of dreams and often used
dreams as literary devices. The Dream of Mangogul in *Les Bijoux indiscrets*
is an early example. And in the *Salon de 1765,* Diderot uses a dream to
recount the events that precede Corésus' self-immolation to save Callirhoé,
'so that we gradually see Fragonard's picture come vividly into being, so to
speak, before our eyes — an extraordinary achievement in which the atmosphere of the painting is explored with great subtlety.'[13] Diderot's use of
the dream in *Le Rêve de d'Alembert* is essential to his purpose, for it allows
him to suggest heuristically what his readers would find unacceptable by
ordinary discourse.[14] In its scope and elevation *Le Rêve de d'Alembert* is
like another dream famous in literature, Scipio's dream as related by Cicero
in his *De republica.* Each is a vision of the universe.

The flavor and unique character of Diderot's dialogue depend in part upon
his *dramatis personae,* whose characters and idiosyncrasies are adroitly portrayed.[15] First, Diderot made himself the materialist philosopher. Then he
needed as a foil a scientist-philosopher who was brilliant and articulate and
not thoroughly persuaded of the validity of the materialist point of view.
There was just such a character in real life — D'Alembert.[16] Third, Diderot
needed for his dialogue a person to report what the invalid said in his sleep.

* The best English translation is that in the Penguin edition: Denis Diderot, *Rameau's
Nephew, and D'Alembert's Dream,* ed. L. W. Tancock (Harmondsworth, 1966). Other excellent translations: Diderot, *Rameau's Nephew, and Other Works,* ed. R. H. Bowen, 89–175;
and Diderot, *Diderot's Selected Writings,* ed. Lester G. Crocker (New York, [1966]), 179–
222.

Mlle de Lespinasse, with whom D'Alembert lived and who was his mistress in name if not in fact, filled this specification. And finally, Diderot needed a doctor who was also a scientist and a *philosophe,* capable of interpreting D'Alembert's fevered remarks. This was Dr. Théophile de Bordeu, not only one of the leading practitioners but also one of the leading medical researchers of the time. Bordeu is now remembered for having written an important treatise on the pulse, for having been the first to use the word 'tissue' as a medical term, and for being a pioneer in what has come to be called endocrinology. In addition to writing for the *Encyclopédie* the lengthy and important article *'Crise,'* Bordeu had been Mme Le Gendre's physician in 1766 and Damilaville's in 1768, so Diderot knew him well. Perhaps he was the Diderot family physician; at least, he was called in in the middle of the night when Mme Diderot was taken ill once in 1771, and she consulted him in 1773 about Angélique's health, when Diderot was in Russia.[17]

Le Rêve de d'Alembert is spirited, filled with intuitive insights worth pondering over and over again. To write it required a rare combination of literary skill, familiarity with the history of metaphysical speculation (for many of these topics go back to the pre-Socratics), and a thorough knowledge of current researches in physics, chemistry, biology, and medicine. Not many people besides Diderot could bend such a bow.

In *Le Rêve de d'Alembert* Diderot took on the formidable task of explaining how life began, and then how simple elementary forms could combine and differentiate into complex ones; how these forms appeared, developed, and disappeared in the flux of time; and how a sentient being could become a thinking one. Diderot begins with inert matter and, moving along the great chain of being, ends with man, his nature, and his morality. 'Serious subjects,' as Dr. Bordeu drily says. But they had been previously settled — in the Book of Genesis.

Anyone setting himself the task of explaining the origin of the cosmos has a choice of three philosophical stances from which to proceed. He can say that in the beginning was the idea; as the Christians say, in the beginning was the Word. Theories of Creation fall within this idealist position. Or he can predicate the dualist position, holding that both spirit and matter are primal. This was the position taken by Descartes.[18] Finally, there is the conception, the materialistic one, that only matter is primal, and that somehow or other the cosmos took shape, including Adam and Eve, without the interposition of a Creator. Just how this could happen is what *Le Rêve de d'Alembert* is all about.

Lucretius had gone over this ground and Diderot followed him in his uncompromising materialism. Yet Diderot's materialism differed considerably from that of the ancient Epicureans. In the first place, Diderot accepted the idea that motion is an inherent property of matter. This supposition had entered the mainstream of materialistic thought with the publication in 1704 of John Toland's *Letters to Serena*. The doctrine, a consequence of thinking about the motion of bodies in terms of kinetic and potential energy, was much in the minds of the D'Holbach group at the time when Diderot was writing *Le Rêve de d'Alembert,* for the D'Holbach coterie had translated and published the *Letters to Serena* in 1768.[19]

Diderot differed from Lucretius, in the second place, in that he conceived of the basic unit of the universe, the irreducible building block, as being not simply the mechanistic atom, but rather a special kind of atom capable of becoming something akin to what would now be called a cell. Here Diderot was probably influenced by Buffon, who had set forth a cosmogony in 1749, though he hastily retracted it when the mutterings of a theological thunderstorm began to be heard. Buffon's term was *'molécule organique.'* [20] Diderot needed a building block that could be vitalistic, compatible with the properties of life. In predicating something similar to the cell, Diderot was playing his hunches: no one had yet seen a cell, and its existence was not scientifically verified until the invention of the compound microscope in the early nineteenth century. It is this playing of hunches that makes *Le Rêve de d'Alembert* so exciting, carrying it to its 'dizzy speculative heights.' [21]

The difficult point in all materialistic cosmogonies is how to get from inorganic matter to organic matter without predicating some act of creation. Twentieth-century science has developed several very promising hypotheses, some of them under laboratory conditions, in the attempt to move this problem into the realm of scientific observation.[22] Diderot's way of managing the transition was bold. It was to deny that there is any difference between organic and inorganic matter. Sensitivity is a universal property. All matter is sentient. Stones feel. 'The statue, then, possesses only an inactive kind of sentience, whereas man, animals, perhaps even plants, are endowed with active sentience.' [23] By thus distinguishing between latent feeling and active feeling Diderot is able to assume that all matter, even the least particle, is inherently capable of animation. That is why his philosophy has sometimes been called a 'pan-vitalism.' [24]

Diderot affirmed that the transition from the inanimate (and back again), which seems so difficult a leap in logic, is readily demonstrable in everyday experience. In one direction, we can see living organisms dying and returning to dust (or, as Diderot put it, to a state of latent sentience). In the other direction, it can be said that marble becomes flesh. 'True or false,' Diderot has D'Alembert remark, 'I like this idea of marble changing into humus, humus into plant life, and plant life into animal life, in fact into flesh.' [25] Not quite in the way it happened to Galatea, but in a way that agronomists and physiologists understand. This idea was startling two hundred years ago.

Then Diderot, with his love of the concrete and specific, gives his reader a 'case history' to illustrate his doctrine; the 'case' is D'Alembert himself.

I would like to tell you the life story of one of the greatest mathematicians of Europe. Do you know what that marvelous being was in the beginning? Nothing.

D'ALEMBERT. How do you mean nothing? You can't make something out of nothing.

DIDEROT. You are using the word too literally. I mean only that before his mother, the beautiful and naughty canoness Tencin, had reached the age of puberty, and before the soldier La Touche had reached adolescence, the molecules that were to make up the first rudimentary beginnings of my mathematician were dispersed throughout the delicate young bodies of his future parents . . . were circulating in their blood streams, until the moment when the molecules were finally collected in certain reservoirs in preparation for their final meeting — I mean the sex glands of his mother and father.[26] Now we can observe the germination of this rare seed. . . . see how it grows and develops by stages into a foetus. At last the moment arrives when it is to leave its dark prison. Behold the newborn child, abandoned on the steps of the church of St.-Jean-le-Rond from which he will take his baptismal name; now he is placed in the orphanage and afterwards taken out of it again; now he is put to nurse at the breast of the good glazier's wife, Madame Rousseau. On her milk he grows strong both in body and in mind and becomes a man of letters, a physicist and a mathematician. And how did this all come about? As the result of eating and of other purely mechanical operations. I will give you the general receipt in a few words — eat, digest, distill in a closed vessel, and you have the whole art of making a man. If anyone wants to describe to the Academy the steps in the production of a man or animal, he will need to make use of nothing but physical agencies, for these can produce the successive effects required — an inert object, a conscious being, a thinking creature, a being who can solve the problem of the precession of the equinoxes — a sublime and marvelous being, but one that is still going to grow old, fall sick, die and finally return to humus.[27]

This passage contains the argument of the whole dialogue. It sums up Diderot's vision of the cosmos. Implicit in it are insights that modern science has now made familiar, insights into genetics, embryology, neurophysiology, and the variability of species. *Le Rêve de d'Alembert,* called one of the masterpieces of speculative literature of all time,[28] is still today an amazing work.

Starting out, then, by assuming that both motion and sentience are inherent properties of matter, Diderot now has to visualize how a sentient 'molecule' becomes combined with others in more complex and differentiated forms. How could these units ever become more than what they were to begin with, namely separate particles? How do aggregates become organs? How are animals formed? This was a formidable problem. As D'Alembert expostulated in his dream, 'I can readily see an aggregate, a tissue of little sensitive beings, but an animal! a whole! a unified system, itself having the consciousness of its own oneness! I do not see that!' Diderot's reply was, 'Friend D'Alembert, take care, you are supposing that there is only contiguity where there is in fact continuity.'

Contiguity becoming continuity is, to use Diderot's analogy, like two drops of mercury merging and becoming one. Current biology sees such unions taking place between ova and spermatozoa, but in all other instances looks to cell-division as the agent of continuity. Diderot, though he visualized something very much like the cell, did not happen to stumble on the conception of cell-division. He therefore had a harder task in surmounting this problem than a modern biologist would. His way of solving it was to think of analogies. The passage from contiguity to continuity is like our perception of a swarm of bees. When first one sees such a tightly compacted body, it is easy to think of it as a unit instead of an aggregate. And if one imagines the individual bees really united to the whole mass by some sort of mucilage cementing their feet, then one can visualize how in nature there can be cells and then whole organs that are units in themselves but are also integral and organic parts of a whole. Thus Diderot made the leap from mechanical contiguity to organic continuity.[29]

It is an important part of Diderot's cosmography that he greatly extends this analogy of the swarm of bees, so that he includes not only rudimentary forms but also the most highly organized and complex animals. In this he was following the Montpellier school, of which Bordeu was a member and which was famous for its vitalistic views. The article *'Sensibilité'* in the *Encyclopédie,* written by one of them, declared that '. . . each organ has its life, its tastes and its passions appropriate to it.'[30] If it seems strange to visualize an animal (or a man) as the sum of its component organs, each organ having developed in a way of its own, one needs only to recall that the technique of organ-transplants depends upon this conception.

By this means Diderot is able to conceptualize how, without an act of creation or the imposition of a supernal design, living structures come into being and become more complex. It is a visualization of the nature of the cosmos that carries with it a number of important corollaries. For one thing, it is predicated upon immense stretches of time. 'Why not? Time means nothing to nature.'[31] In the second place, it predicates an enormous proliferation and flux of forms: 'In this immense ocean of matter, not a molecule that resembles another molecule exactly, not a molecule that even resembles itself an instant. *A new order of things comes into being,* that is its eternal inscription.'[32] A third corollary is that in this eternal flux there will emerge and then pass away an incredible number of forms that are defective — defective in the sense that they do not happen to fulfill their function or adjust to environment in a way permitting them to survive. Monsters are as much a part of nature as any other form, and Diderot is equally interested in them. If a form exists, it can neither be contrary to nature nor outside nature.[33] Diderot's deep interest in teratology helps him to visualize the complexity and the consistency and the predictability of his cosmogony.

A fourth corollary is that there is no necessary fixity of species. 'If the question of which came first, the hen or the egg, bothers you, that is because you suppose that animals were in the beginning what they are now. What folly! We no more know what they were then than we do what they will become.' Thus Diderot continued to express, and to amplify, his belief in that pre-Darwinian 'transformism' that he had already revealed in his *Pensées sur l'interprétation de la nature.*[34]

Diderot's principle of continuity allowed him to ascend the scale of ever-increasing complexity of organic forms. In this respect he is like Leibniz and other philosophers of the Great Chain of Being. Leibniz had written in a letter that came to light in 1753:

All the different classes of beings which taken together make up the universe are, in the ideas of God who knows distinctly their essential gradations, only so many ordinates of a single curve so closely united that it would be impossible to place others between any two of them, since that would imply disorder and imperfection. Thus men are linked with the animals, these with the plants and these with the fossils, which in turn merge with those bodies which our senses and our imaginations represent to us as absolutely inanimate.[35]

This cosmological statement is admirably appropriate in Leibniz, a philosopher who was also a mathematician great enough to be one of the discoverers of the calculus, with its essential conception of the infinitesimal and almost infinite ordinates placed in order and perfection on a single curve. Diderot was sufficiently knowledgeable in mathematics to find such a mode of thought very congenial. It is quite certain that Diderot absorbed many of Leibniz' ideas, but it is quite uncertain how directly and consciously he was aware of this.[36] Profoundly influenced as he was by the Leibnizian philosophy, he modified it to accord with his own materialism. It is not altogether fanciful to say that to some degree Leibniz is to Diderot as Hegel is to Marx.

In *Le Rêve de d'Alembert,* D'Alembert presses Diderot to show how sentient matter can become thinking matter. It is here, in the philosophy of organism and in the philosophy of consciousness, that historians of philosophy see similarities between Diderot's thought and the ideas of Alfred North Whitehead.[37] Diderot suggests that if sentient beings are endowed with memory, they can think. Not all sentient beings are so endowed. But many are organized in such a way that sense impressions set up elaborate associations akin to the resonances of stringed instruments — we are musical instruments, Diderot says, endowed with sentience and memory [38] — and this kind of resonance is what we call memory. Such beings as are endowed with memory can have an active consciousness of selfhood that makes thought possible:

If then a sentient being has this organization requisite for remembering, if he combines the impressions that he receives, if he forms through this combination a historical sense of his own life and acquires the consciousness of himself, he denies, he affirms, he concludes, he thinks.[39]

Diderot uses the analogy of the spider's web to suggest how a sentient organism achieves consciousness. Just as a spider is conscious of everything happening to its web, so an animal is conscious of all events in the body. Thus memory and the consciousness of self that memory makes possible bring it about that judgment and reflection and all the components of thinking are not only feasible but inevitable. In this way sentient matter thinks.[40] And on this psycho-physical basis Diderot goes on to an examination of dreams, obsessions, illusions, and amnesia.[41] It is all a part of his contention that intelligence is a property depending solely upon how matter is organized.

Diderot's cosmogony could not be complete, he evidently thought, without his setting forth hypotheses to explain how new individuals are reproduced and how species might change in the course of time. This need led him to develop distinctive ideas on embryology, genetics, and transformism. In embryology, whether describing the development of the chick in the egg or the development of the human foetus, he speaks of 'points' becoming 'threads' and these in turn becoming 'bundles,' a clumsy terminology describing Diderot's intuitions about genes and chromosomes, though as accurate and suggestive as the knowledge of the day permitted.[42] In genetics, Diderot vigorously rejected the traditional theory called preformationism, according to which reproduction was thought of as being simply the mechanical enlargement of infinitely minute embryos encapsulated in an original ancestor.

Now, Mademoiselle, I'll bet that . . . you imagine that in the foetal stage you were a very tiny woman, and that in your mother's ovum you were a still tinier woman. . . . Yet that notion is as false as anything can be. In the beginning you were an imperceptibly small dot made up of still smaller molecules. These were dispersed throughout the blood and the lymph of your father and mother. The dot became a fine thread, then a bundle of threads. . . . But then each of the strands in the bundle of threads started to change — solely as the result of nutrition and in conformity with the special structure of each — into a particular organ.

Thus Diderot explained the complete generation of a human being, all in accordance with the doctrine of epigenesis.[43] As regards the eternal flux of changing forms, Diderot believed in the transmission of acquired characteristics. 'Organs produce needs and, reciprocally, needs produce organs.'[44] This is the doctrine later made famous by Lamarck. And in the concluding panel of the triptych comprising *Le Rêve de d'Alembert,* Dr. Bordeu and Mlle de Lespinasse hazard some theories regarding cross-matings and hybridizations.[45] From first to last, *Le Rêve de d'Alembert* is a demonstration of the impingement of biology on the scientific thought of the Enlightenment.

The total effect of *Le Rêve de d'Alembert* is curiously and impressively a humanistic one. Its ultimate impact is one of making the reader feel that he understands better the human condition. Late in *Le Rêve de d'Alembert* there are some pages treating of the question of the freedom of the will and of determinism and ethics. They relate *Le Rêve* to the social — which to Diderot meant also the biological — nature of man. (His doctrine has been called 'biological humanism.') [46] This turn of the dialogue, coming as a climax to it all, is a reminder of Diderot's perennial concern with humanistic problems. As he had written years before in the article *'Encyclopédie':*

A consideration that above all must not be lost from view is that if man, or the thinking and contemplative being, is banished from the surface of the earth, this pathetic and sublime spectacle of nature becomes nothing but a mute and melancholy scene. . . .[47]

One of the attractive features of *Le Rêve de d'Alembert* is that it is not polemical. It contains no tirades against religion or superstition, no attacks upon the idea of God. On the contrary, it is full of bold and bracing affirmations, affirmations perhaps erroneous but at least not merely wishful or inconsistent with the latest scientific knowledge of the time. In consequence, Diderot is able to convey to his readers a sense that he and they are treading new ground. *Le Rêve de d'Alembert* explains, it unites, it integrates, it conveys a sweeping vision of the cosmos which binds the universe together in a determinism breathtaking in its order and rigor. In doing so, it bypasses the assumptions of the Idealistic philosophers. Moreover, it tends to dissolve Cartesian dualism too. For it simply finds no substantive reality in the mind-body problem or in the sharp Cartesian distinction between human beings and animals.[48]

Le Rêve de d'Alembert is an important document in the life history of Diderot as well as in the intellectual history of the eighteenth century. It is safe to say that the very act of composing so elaborate and complex a work, especially one that could not be published during the author's lifetime, must have filled some deep personal need. An Encyclopedist of the range of Diderot, and one as much in tune as he with the growing importance of chemistry and biology, might very well feel, especially if he were a materialist, the need to work out a new synthesis, one that carries the mind along to an understanding of the totality of phenomena, their inner cohesion, their succession in space and time.

Of course, in this effort towards synthesis Diderot reflected the speculation and the discoveries of forerunners and peers. It would be grossly wrong to suppose that he had all these intuitions *de novo*. It was precisely because he was abreast of the scientific thought and discoveries of his time that his cosmology must be taken as something more than personal fantasy. It was because he was aware of the work of Hobbes and Toland, of Buffon and Trembley, of Bordeu and Robinet and Bonnet, of Needham and Réaumur and La Mettrie, of Haller and Maupertuis that he was able, by a great feat of synthesis, to work out his vision of nature, where 'everything is bound up with everything else.'[49]

Much of the persuasiveness of *Le Rêve de d'Alembert* comes from the literary deftness of its author. If one needs proof of that, one has only to compare *Le Rêve* with the contemporaneous *Système de la nature,* D'Holbach's dogged, dreary, indefatigable, pedantic, and merciless treatise on the same range of subjects. One of the ways in which Diderot shows his masterliness is in the nuances of expression. The dreaming D'Alembert expresses his ideas in a poetic language rich in images and metaphors, contrasting with the ensuing more analytical remarks of Dr. Bordeu and Mlle de Lespinasse, and contrasting also with the style of D'Alembert's remarks in those parts of the dialogue where he is shown awake.[50] Incidentally, in this dialogue, Diderot departs from his usual procedure and has all of his interlocutors contribute to the building up of the argument. The contrast of personalities brings out and heightens the points he makes, but in this dialogue they do not pose contradictions that are left standing. *Le Rêve de d'Alembert* is not written in such a fashion that it remains ambivalent and ambiguous.[51] Moreover, Diderot makes form follow function. The very disconnectedness of some of the conversation contributes to the ultimate persuasiveness of his discourse. Thus, in the lengthy passage developing the analogy of the swarm of bees, Diderot illustrates in style as well as in thought the transition, by means of contiguity, from the discontinuous to the continuous.[52]

Any reader of Diderot quickly becomes aware of the eroticism in his works. Nowhere is this more evident than in *Le Rêve de d'Alembert,* of which so large a part is by its subject matter necessarily devoted to questions of sex and sexuality. The erotic tone of *Le Rêve de d'Alembert* is much more restrained, however, than it was in *Les Bijoux indiscrets,* nor is it so overt and self-consciously Rabelaisian as one often finds it in Diderot's *Salons.* But though diffused, it is nonetheless pervasive. Diderot was striving for a literary device by which the impact of his philosophical ideas about generation and reproduction would be abetted and reinforced by the mode of their presentation. On such grounds, his having the sleeping D'Alembert masturbate is far from being an irrevelant and perhaps malicious invention.[53] It comes at a relevant point in the dialogue's exposition of the origin of life.

D'Alembert and Mlle de Lespinasse appear to have felt, when they discovered the existence of *Le Rêve de d'Alembert,* that they had been rather freely dealt with. One critic has charged Diderot with a kind of sadism: 'To place an interlocutor in an embarrassing situation and to take pleasure or make his reader take pleasure in the resulting embarrassment is in fact one of his constant attitudes.'[54] Regarding *Le Rêve de d'Alembert,* Mlle de Lespinasse wrote to Suard, probably the person who divulged the secret of its existence, that Diderot's conduct had been 'improper, because this lack of breeding and consideration might greatly inconvenience' her. 'In truth, in truth, one is not up to all the little vexations and great misfortunes that overwhelm one. M. Diderot, from his experience, ought, it seems to me, to prevent himself from speaking of, or making speak, women whom he does not know.'[55] Naigeon tells us that D'Alembert 'imperiously' demanded that Diderot destroy the manuscript and that the latter complied by throwing it into the fire.[56]   Diderot himself says, in a quite mysterious *'Lettre d'envoi,'* that

The pleasure of taking stock of one's own opinions produced them [the dialogues], the indiscretions of several persons drew them out of their obscurity, apprehensive love desired the sacrifice of them, tyrannical friendship insisted upon it, friendship that was too accommodating acquiesced in it, they were torn up [*lacérés*]. You have asked me to put the pieces together. I have done so.[57]

The manuscript of this reassembled version has never showed up in Diderot's literary remains. Perhaps the *'Lettre d'envoi'* was just a mystification.[58] What has shown up is a copy in Diderot's own hand of the version that was published in 1831.[59] In addition, a version of *Le Rêve de d'Alembert* as we have it today was circulated in the *Correspondance littéraire* in 1782, and the editor, who was very dependent upon Diderot's contributions, would not have included it without Diderot's consent.[60] It looks as though the preservation of the original text was either an accident as mysterious as it was fortunate or that Diderot deliberately deceived D'Alembert.[61]

Diderot, who loved to think of himself as *'le philosophe,'* loved also to think of himself as a man of letters. *Le Rêve de d'Alembert* is a remarkably successful example of this union of literature and philosophy. And the function of each was to afford insight into reality. 'For him, it has been said,

the aesthetic was an essential moment in the expansion of the conceptual categories through which men try to grasp the inner forms and processes of nature. (This effort of understanding appears to have been, in Diderot's mind, nothing less than nature's own striving for self-consciousness.) To Diderot, in sum, civilization is an on-going collective enterprise, which men who are themselves part of nature undertake in collaboration with nature. Nothing, for him, is absolutely separate from anything else. Everyone is at once an individual and a participant in other individuals. The self is inhabited by the other and the other inhabits the self.[62]

Such, then, was Diderot's vision, a vision which has been called 'materialistic mysticism.'[63] D'Alembert's Dream was Diderot's dream, a dream out of which 'a new order of things is born.'

CHAPTER 41

A Disturbing Involvement and
Its Literary Effects

READING through the letters of Diderot to Sophie Volland gives many people the impression that her emotional response to him was always rather measured and cool. Consistently through the years Diderot continues wooing her in his correspondence, as if, though sure of his own affections, he is much less certain of hers. If this impression of her moderate response is correct, it is perhaps explained by the fact that her health was not robust and her vitality evidently low. But in the late 1760's there is a new note in his letters. For one thing, he begins to include all the Volland ladies, addressing them as 'mes bonnes amies' and 'mesdames et bonnes amies.' What does this betoken? Is it a signal that his feeling for Sophie is cooling? Or does it signify his acceptance of the fact that hers is? Diderot appears to be under some apprehension that she is becoming indifferent to him. In 1768 he complains of her not answering his letters, and in 1769 he writes, not having heard from the Vollands since they had left Paris, 'If I were as malicious as I am candid, I would tell you, Mlle Volland, that this neglect surprises me less than it afflicts me.' [1]

So, when Diderot in the course of 1769 began to show interest in Damilaville's bereft mistress, Mme de Maux, it may have been occasioned in part by his feeling that Sophie was not so attached to him as once she had been. Whether he was ever deeply in love with Mme de Maux is a matter of controversy among biographers, but the evidence seems to indicate that by mid-1770 he was very hard smitten indeed. It was an experience that was very unsettling, happening as it did to him in his late fifties when he had long been under the impression that his affections were fixed once and for all. Perhaps it was his growing desire to be attractive to Mme de Maux that made him so upset to discover, by coming across his certificate of baptism, that he was much older than he thought he was. [2] Certainly the whole episode, in respect to his being a man of letters, had the effect of causing him to write some of his best stories and dialogues, all of them focused on problems of sexuality and the sociology of sex and the inscrutability of love.

Mme de Maux is a shadowy figure only recently become substantial. There are no complete letters to her in Diderot's handwriting, though some important fragments, at first supposed to be parts of letters to Sophie Volland, are now generally accepted as fragments of letters to Mme de Maux.[3] At this time forty-five, she was the natural daughter of a celebrated actor of the Comédie-Française, Quinault-Dufresne. In 1737, at the age of twelve, she had married a lawyer in the Parlement of Paris. Diderot's affection for her took about two years to develop into full flower. As early as July 1769 he was admitting to Grimm that 'to speak truly, I forget lots of things when I am in her company.'[4]

But he did not forget his usual program of trying to assist other people. He and Mme Diderot at this time taught Mlle Collot's younger brother to read and write, and Diderot then got him an apprenticeship in Le Breton's workshop; Diderot stood sponsor for Damilaville's nephew at the Collège Louis-le-Grand; he helped Mlle Jodin to keep her accounts straight and to invest her money; and he successfully secured permission for the return to Paris of a discharged and disgraced government employee named Chabert by offering also to become responsible for finding him employment.[5]

This year Diderot met a talented young North American, perhaps the only native of that continent whom he ever knew. Diderot refers to this man only as 'my young Pennsylvanian.' Actually this was Dr. Benjamin Rush of Philadelphia, destined to become a signer of the American Declaration of Independence and a great figure in the history of American medicine. In 1768 Rush completed his medical studies at the University of Edinburgh and on 16 February 1769 set out for Paris armed with letters of introduction from Benjamin Franklin. 'I . . . was introduced by means of my letters to . . . Nollet, lecturer upon natural philosophy, Jussieu, botanist to the king, Diderot, the philosopher and friend of Voltaire, and some others of less note.'[6]

This tantalizing information does not prove that Franklin and Diderot had a face-to-face acquaintanceship, nor does any other testimony do so, either.[7] 'Mr. Diderot entertained me in his library,' wrote Rush. 'He gave me a letter to Mr. Hume when I left him. I delivered this letter to Mr. Hume upon my return to London; it gave me an opportunity of spending a part of a forenoon in his company.' Diderot's letter is still extant:

Do you not find it very strange that a Frenchman should be introducing to you one of your compatriots? It is because everything is topsy-turvy at this moment. . . . We write against despotism; and there come to us from London pamphlets favoring tyranny. . . . At all events, receive my young Pennsylvanian graciously.[8]

Later that same year Diderot may have become acquainted with Johann Gottfried Herder, soon to become one of the great names in the *Sturm und Drang* movement, indeed one of the great names in all of German literature. Herder was very hostile to the French culture of his day, and one might well ask why he made the trip to France. In fact, that was what he asked himself. He was in Paris for some six weeks beginning in November. Though neither Diderot's correspondence nor Herder's *Journal meiner Reise im Jahre 1769* recounts any meeting, other passages in Herder's works, though they are not completely unambiguous, suggest that the two men did meet.[9]

Diderot's encounter in 1769 with a very radical thinker, Dom Léger-Marie Deschamps, reveals most interestingly what Diderot was attracted to politically and yet recoiled from. A Benedictine monk, Deschamps had come up from the country to make converts among the *philosophes*. He was promulgating what can only be described in terms of paradox. It was a kind of Christian atheism, atheistic enough to make him seem now to be one of the minor prophets in eighteenth-century materialism, but Christian enough in its general metaphysical approach to put off the *philosophes*.[10]

Deschamps saw Diderot several times, and wrote of him that he talked all the time and scarcely ever listened.[11] Nevertheless, Deschamps finally began to get through to Diderot. At first he had thought that Deschamps was merely naïve: 'This apostle maintains that his system, which attacks everything there is that is most revered, is harmless and does not expose him to any disagreeable consequences, whereas there is not a sentence that would not add a fagot to the fire.' Nevertheless, Diderot began to be quite impressed with Deschamps' 'True System.'

It is the notion of a social state . . . in which it is conceived that the human race will be wretched as long as there are kings, priests, magistrates, laws, a sense of mine and thine, the names of vices and virtues. Imagine how much this work, poorly written though it is, has given me pleasure, for suddenly I found myself back again in the world for which I was born.

Diderot claimed that there was not a line to be eliminated in the whole work, which he thought was full of bold assertions and new ideas.

Deschamps, for his part, was rather patronizing to Diderot. He alleged that Diderot had called him 'master,' but it is hard to believe that Diderot intended to be more than polite. Deschamps did declare that Diderot was capable of understanding him (though D'Alembert was not) and that Diderot had principles, whereas many other self-styled thinkers just had conclusions. Nevertheless, Deschamps claimed that Diderot was extremely plebeian [*extrêmement peuple*] in respect to morality, and actually conceived him to be still a man of faith who believed in the Devil.[12]

Deschamps' Utopianism attracted Diderot, though ultimately it repelled him. Diderot took pleasure in some Utopian speculation — his later *Supplément au Voyage de Bougainville* shows this — but even there he drew back from the logical extremes of it. Thus his contact with Dom Deschamps and the latter's 'True System' reveals one of the outer boundaries of Diderot's political thought. There was a distinct limit to the extent of his radicalism. The incident shows how far he was in thought and feeling from being able to write the *Code de la nature,* a work which, published anonymously by Morelly in 1755, came to be persistently and disingenuously attributed to Diderot in spite of his efforts to disclaim it.[13]

In the summer of 1769 the Comédie-Française successfully revived *Le Père de famille.* 'This work has enjoyed much greater success than when it was new,' commented the *Mercure de France.* It received twelve performances in 1769, six in 1770, and two in 1771, to very large houses averaging almost a thousand spectators.[14] Diderot wrote Sophie that he had not wanted 'to be dragged out in public.' (The play was the property of the company as a result of their producing it in 1761, and therefore he had no control over it.) He also wrote that it was being produced 'in spite of all the underhand maneuverings of my enemies.' With poignant memories of 1761, Diderot now felt quite puffed up. Admitting that this time the piece was helped by being well acted, nevertheless 'the work is so rapid, so violent, so strong, it is impossible to kill it. . . . It is, I assure you, a very great and beautiful work. I myself was surprised.' Diderot confessed all this to Sophie 'without partiality.' In fact, he was so invigorated by the play's success that for a time he thought of trying to finish *Le Shérif,* which he had laid on the shelf ten years before. *Le Père de famille* made a great impression within the Diderot family. Angélique went, and came back 'stupefied with astonishment and ectasy.' Even Mme Diderot went: 'She felt the indecency that there is in having to say she had not gone in reply to everyone's complimenting her. . . . Her daughter tells me that she [Mme Diderot] was as strongly moved as any other of the spectators.'[15]

This is the first summer that Diderot is known to have spent in villeggia-tura at Sèvres, on the banks of the Seine just west of Paris. His friend Belle, the jeweler, owned a large house there which became Diderot's customary summer residence until his death. In 1769 he was too busy in town to spare more than a few days at Sèvres, though his wife and daughter were sometimes there without him.[16]

As the year advanced, Diderot was aware that another 'Salon is about to fall on me.' Artistically this Salon, which opened on 25 August, was of less than usual interest, nor is Diderot's account of it so brilliant as were his *Salons* of 1765 and 1767. For Grimm's sake he was trying to be brief. 'You see, my friend, I am sparing you descriptions, the part that amuses me and stimulates my imagination.' Diderot wrote his *Salon de 1769* in the form of personal letters to Grimm, which the latter passed on to his subscribers without editing.[17] Thus the *Salon* contains allusions to An-gélique's illness of that autumn, as well as a gloomy and sorrowful account of the suicide of Desbrosses, who the previous year had shared in the 'Mystification' of Mlle Dornet. Various personal and autobiographical pas-sages in this *Salon* delight and inform posterity but perhaps seemed quite surprising to Grimm's royal patrons, their crowned heads nodding in German palaces:

Oh, the absurd condition of man! If you marry, you run the risk of an unhappy life. If you do not, you are sure to have a dissolute existence and a melancholy old age. If you have children, they are insipid, stupid, vicious, and you start out by being distressed and finish up by not caring any more. If you have lov-able ones, the least accident happening to them upsets you. You get up in the morning, you sit yourself down at your desk to work, nothing comes to you, and that is precisely the role that I am playing now.[18]

As always in reading a Diderot *Salon,* one learns a great deal about the art of the time — and about art in general — and one learns a great deal about Diderot, too. In the *Salon de 1769* he claimed that 'all poetry exaggerates,' and criticized artists unimaginative enough not to know that; he observed (with the usual sensitivity for expressiveness that one might expect of the student of acting he was) that hands belonging to a person feeling hatred or seeking vengeance are not the hands of compassion or surprise or admiration or grief or desire. He castigated an artist for being just 'a cold and monotonous copyist of nature'; he reported a long conversation with the pastelist La Tour about artistic technique. He recounted the history of Greuze's disastrous misadventures with a 'historical' painting that he had expected the Academy to accept as his reception piece; and for the first time, saying, 'I don't care for Greuze any more,' Diderot admitted that some people thought of Greuze's pictures as being lascivious. Diderot was critical, even of old favorites. He spoke of Vernet as repeating himself, incidentally showing us how aware Diderot was of needing to avoid monotony in his own writing. Evidently what seems so spontaneous had to be worked for:

It is well to be able to paint facilely, but one should disguise the routine that gives productions of any kind the appearance of having been manufactured. It is not to Vernet alone that I speak, it is also to Saint-Lambert, to Voltaire, to D'Alembert, to Rousseau, to Abbé Morellet, to myself.[19]

The name of Mme de Maux occurs with more and more frequency in Diderot's correspondence during the course of 1769.[20] The fragments of his letters thought to be addressed to her probably all date from this year. In them Diderot shows himself less gossipy and more contemplative and more didactic than was his habit in his letters to Sophie. This did not prevent him from saying some self-revelatory things: 'Do you think that men are ever made better? It is very certain that we are not so barbarous as our forefathers. We are more enlightened. Are we better? that is another thing.'[21] So much for those who suppose that Diderot believed in easy progress, inevitably and automatically achieved.

Beginning 20 September 1769 a comet was visible in Paris. When Sophie mentioned it, Diderot rather gruffly replied, 'But what fancy has taken you to observe this comet? Comets have not signified anything for more than a hundred years,' a reference to Bayle's *Pensées sur la Comète* of 1682. His response to Mme de Maux's question about the comet was much more indulgent. It was also very puzzling, for, unless it was intended merely in a spirit of playfulness, it throws a pall of uncertainty over the consistency and deep-seatedness of his doctrines:

Your question about the comet caused me to make a singular reflection: namely, that atheism is close to a kind of superstition almost as puerile as the other kind. Nothing is insignificant in an order of things linked and put into train by a general law; it seems that everything is equally important. There are no great phenomena — nor any little ones. The bull *Unigenitus* is as necessary as the rising and the setting of the sun. It is hard to abandon oneself blindly to the universal torrent, but it is impossible to resist it. Efforts, whether impotent or victorious, are also in the general order. If I think that I love you of my own free will, I am mistaken. It is nothing of the sort. Oh, what a fine system for the ungrateful! It makes me wild to be entangled in a devil of a philosophy that my mind cannot deny and my heart gives the lie to. I cannot abide that my feelings for you, yours for me, should be subject to anything in the world, and that Naigeon should make them depend upon the passage of a comet. I am almost inclined to become a Christian, in order to promise myself to love you in this world so long as I am here, and to find you again and love you in the other. It is so sweet a thought, I am not surprised that noble souls cling to it. If Mlle Olympe were on the point of dying, she would say to you, 'Dear cousin, do not weep, we shall see each other again.' And that is where your perfidious question on the comet has landed me.

The perfidious question or, rather, Diderot's answer to it, lands students of his philosophy in difficulty too. Is it possible that his philosophical convictions about necessitarianism were indeed so fragile? Had he been writing to Sophie, who had been hearing the other side from him for over ten years, a statement like this could only be interpreted as tergiversation. But he was writing to Mme de Maux, as the allusion to her cousin Olympe proves. Perhaps the passage smacks more of a lover's exaggeration than it does of philosophy.[22]

From Grandval that autumn Diderot wrote to Mme de Maux of the charms of nature in the country. 'I brought here a soul heavy with care, a mind oppressed by dark imaginings. . . . It seems as though everything soothes us in the fields. . . . Here, instinctively, one sits down, rests, gazes without seeing, abandons his heart and soul and mind and senses to their freedom. . . .' To such a one all of nature murmurs,

Stay at rest, stay at rest, remain where you are, like everything round about you; last, like everything round about you; live tranquilly, like everything round about you; let the hours, the days, the years go their way, like everything round about you; and pass away, like everything round about you. That is the continuous lesson of nature.

Mme de Maux wrote in appreciation that his letter was 'sublime'.[23]

Diderot worked very hard all through 1769. Even after Grimm's return from Germany, Diderot volunteered to continue to write for the *Correspondance littéraire* as a particular token of his friendship. So over-tired did he get that one night in November he nearly burned down the house: 'I work nights, as you know. . . . I was so weary with fatigue and worry that I fell asleep with my head on the desk. . . .' Half the books and papers on his desk were burned. His family suspected nothing, probably because his study was on the floor above his living quarters, and he took care not to tell them. He tidied up his desk himself so that no trace of the accident remained.[24]

During all this writing for the sake of another, Diderot was vexed by the publication of pirated editions of his writings. In one of his reviews intended for the *Correspondance littéraire* he complains of three instances: a book of synonyms, a collection of his moral writings, and his history of modern and ancient philosophy. Doubtless these latter were the three-volume *Histoire générale des dogmes et opinions philosophiques . . . Tirée du Dictionnaire encylopédique,* published in 1769, and perhaps the five-volume *L'Esprit de l'Encyclopédie,* published the year before.[25]

About this time another publishing venture began to occupy him. Already the *Encyclopédie* had become difficult to purchase and was selling at a premium. The Chevalier de Jaucourt wrote a friend on 28 October 1768 that he knew of a set that could be bought for 1150 livres (the price at publication having been 980 livres), and that 'the price of this work increases day by day.' In corroboration of this, one journal had reported in July 1768 that the *Encylopédie* was out of print, and in September 1769 the *Journal Encyclopédique* stated that the public was offering from 1300 to 1500 livres a set, '. . . for the first seven volumes especially have become very rare.'[26] Such conditions naturally induced entrepreneurs to think of a second edition. One was proposed to the government for approbation in 1768, but was not accepted.[27] Much more solid financially was the scheme of a rising young Paris publisher named Panckoucke, a scheme which finally developed into the project of reprinting the first edition enlarged by a multi-volumed supplement.[28] It was evidently very much a part of the plan that Diderot should play an important role in the editing of the supplement. But on 31 August 1769 he wrote, 'Here I am, at last, altogether disencumbered of this *Encyclopédie* edition, thanks to the impertinence of one of its entrepreneurs.'

This little Panckoucke [Diderot went on to Sophie], swollen with the arrogance of a newly-successful upstart . . . took it into his head to burst out at me, which did not turn out successfully at all. I let him go on as long as he wanted, then, rising abruptly, I took him by the hand and said, 'M. Panckoucke, wherever one is, on the street, in church, in a place of bad repute, to anyone whatever, one must always speak courteously. This is all the more necessary when one is talking to a man no more long-suffering than I am and when you speak to him in his own house. Go [here Diderot resorted to dots: *'Allez vous faire f . . .'*], you and your work. I do not want to work on it. You could give me twenty thousand louis and I could finish the task in the wink of an eye and still I would not do it. Have the goodness to get out of here and leave me alone.[29]

This incident is enough to explain why Diderot's name is not associated with the four volumes of *Supplément* to the *Encyclopédie* nor with Panckoucke's later *Encylopédie méthodique.*

Still another event in 1769 manifested Diderot's annoyance with publishers. A man of letters named Luneau de Boisjermain had edited and caused to be printed a de luxe edition of Racine, having properly sought and received the approbation of the censor and the royal license. But when he attempted to solicit subscriptions and distribute the sets from his own lodgings, the Paris guild of publishers and booksellers alleged that this contravened its legal rights and, with dubious legality, descended upon him in August 1768 and confiscated all his copies. The leading spirit in this foray was the syndic of the Paris guild, who at this time was none other than Le Breton, the principal publisher of the *Encyclopédie*. Luneau de Boisjermain brought suit. Men of letters quite generally sided with him in this dispute, and Diderot seems to have become acquainted with him because of it. In a letter to Sartine in whose competence the case lay, Diderot urged the minister to decide in Luneau's favor and hotly inveighed against publishers, '. . . these people whose fortunes we make and who condemn us to eat our laurel leaves.'[30] Diderot even volunteered, with Sartine's consent, to try to mediate the dispute. His interference infuriated Le Breton and Briasson. Diderot defended himself hotly.

My conduct has never been inconsistent, and I have always rendered M. Le Breton good for evil. M. Le Breton clandestinely massacred ten folio volumes. . . . An indiscreet word from me would have ruined him. I kept silent.[31]

Sartine settled the case in Luneau de Boisjermain's favor in early 1770.

Various other literary events in early 1770 concerned Diderot either directly or tangentially. A *Recueil philosophique* ('Philosophical Collection'), secretly edited by Naigeon, published for the first time Diderot's *De la Suffisance de la religion naturelle* (written in 1746 or 1747) and his *Addition* (written in 1762) to the *Pensées philosophiques*. Both of these appeared, of course, without being attributed to Diderot.[32] Of much greater significance was the appearance of D'Holbach's *Système de la nature,* his most important work, a complete and comprehensive explanation of the cosmos in terms of materialism and atheism. The *Système de la nature* occasioned a great stir. Ultimately, too, it caused a rift in the ranks of the *philosophes* and very effectively separated the deists from the atheists among them.[33] As late as the time of his death it was still being rumored that Diderot was the author of the whole book. A more substantial question, however, and one not even yet settled beyond doubt, is whether he contributed at all to the *Système de la nature,* and if so, how much. Although no less an authority than Diderot's friend Meister declared that some of its best pages were written by Diderot, this view has practically died away from lack of sustenance.[34]

Though Diderot did not contribute to the *Système de la nature,* its publication appears to have caused him to articulate his own thoughts on the ultimate forces of nature. This he did in a brief paper called *Principes philosophiques sur la matière et le mouvement,* written not earlier than 1770 and first published in 1792.[35] Just as he had recently done in *Le Rêve de d'Alembert,* so here, Diderot reveals himself to be anti-Cartesian in his thinking; here, too, he shows the influence of Toland's doctrine that motion is an inherent property of matter.[36] Yet the importance of Diderot's speculations in the *Principes philosophiques sur la matière et le mouvement* goes beyond the negative position of anti-Cartesianism, reaching instead new conceptualizations depending upon chemistry and biochemistry. Thus Diderot talks about the 'fermentation' of the universe. He specifically appeals to 'sound chemical principles,' and alludes to phenomena that can be observed 'in the laboratory every day.' Among the natural forces to be taken into account he specifically mentions chemical force.[37] This emphasis goes distinctly beyond his earlier speculations regarding matter in his *Pensées sur l'interprétation de la nature.* The difference could have been brought about by the fact that meanwhile Diderot had attended three years of Rouelle's lectures in chemistry. It may be that Rouelle's death in 1770, besides stimulating Diderot to write a biographical memoir full of the flavor of Rouelle's eccentricities, also created an urge in Diderot to put down on paper what he now thought about matter and movement and the principle of chemical force, 'the most internal one in our sublunar world.' [38]

The *Principes philosophiques sur la matière et le mouvement,* with its adumbrations of the electronic theory of matter and of the theory of the conservation and transformation of energy, is written with positiveness and self-assurance.

You can do your geometry and your metaphysics as much as you please; but I, who am a physicist and a chemist, who take bodies as they are in nature and not in my head, I see them existing, diverse, endowed with properties and actions, and in action in the universe as they are in the laboratory, where a spark cannot be found beside three molecules combined of saltpeter, carbon, and sulphur without an explosion necessarily following.

The appeal to facts, to observation, to the realities of the empirical method, are inherent in this quotation, just as they are in all of Diderot's natural philosophy.[39]

Another literary event of this year involved Sartine, who was in doubt about licensing a play that was under consideration at the Comédie-Française, and who solicited Diderot's advice. This play, Le Satirique, lampooned the *philosophes,* though not so savagely as Palissot's Les Philosophes had ten years before. Diderot, though he did not believe that this new piece was by the same author, nevertheless recommended against it, thinking it poor in quality as well as in bad taste. Whatever Sartine thought of this advice — and Palissot turned out to be the author after all — the play was not produced until 1782.[40]

Of greater significance, for it was a political as well as a literary event, was the decision taken enthusiastically by a group of seventeen *philosophes* gathered in Mme Necker's *salon.* This act initiated a plan to raise money by subscription for a statue of Voltaire to be presented to him. Diderot sat at Mme Necker's right hand on this occasion, a symbolically appropriate position, for he was the ringleader of the project and worked hard to secure subscriptions for it. Others present at Mme Necker's were D'Alembert, Marmontel, Saint-Lambert, Helvétius, Morellet, and Raynal, among others. The project took on a political tinge when the clerical party tried to ridicule the venture and cause its collapse, while the *philosophes,* thus challenged, labored to make it successful and awarded the commission to Pigalle. Convinced by the insistent Diderot, who considered modern apparel ridiculous, Pigalle persuaded Voltaire to pose in the antique manner. The result was a marvel of realistic modeling, but Voltaire was so nearly a skeleton that few have been able to gaze on the statue with much delight.[41]

In 1770 negotiations for Angélique's marriage began in earnest. As a kind of preliminary skirmish, Diderot talked of Grimm as a future son-in-law, but it is hard to know whether in complete seriousness.[42] In reality, the Diderots considered only one candidate, Abel-François-Nicolas Caroillon de Vandeul (born 29 January 1746), son of Diderot's childhood friends at Langres. The engagement was negotiated in the grand style, with Diderot contemplating elaborate family consultations and inviting his sister and even his *abbé* brother to come and discuss the match at the Rue Taranne. In March young Caroillon asked Diderot for Angélique's hand; in turn Diderot suggested that a formal engagement should be deferred for three years, until she was nineteen, and that meanwhile the Diderots would refuse to consider any other proposal.[43]

Simultaneously negotiations had been going on for a reconciliation between the two Diderot brothers. Diderot the *philosophe* had taken the initiative: 'I would have written direct to Monsieur l'Abbé had I been able to flatter myself that he would deign to open my letter and reply to it,' he wrote to his sister on 4 May 1770.

I am connected with, liked, esteemed, honored, by priests, *curés,* grand-vicars, monks, Sorbonne doctors, bishops. If the Abbé is right, then all these people must be wrong. However that may be, united or divided, I shall show him on every occasion that I am his brother and his friend.

The reconciliation hung fire, in spite of Diderot's quite patient and mild letter to his brother of 24 May. In August Diderot showed up at Langres and stayed there and in the vicinity for six weeks. When he arrived the reconciliation had not yet been arranged, although Canon Gabriel Gauchat, Abbé Diderot's colleague at the Cathedral of Saint-Mammès in Langres, was endeavoring to bring it about. Another letter to his brother, dated 20 August, shows Diderot surprisingly long-suffering and mollifying. But still there was no reconciliation: the Abbé refused to meet his brother. According to Mme de Vandeul,

The canon demanded a promise not to write any more against religion. My father agreed to this in writing. He [the Abbé] insisted that the letter be published, and that my father add to it a retraction of all that he had written previously. My father refused, and the negotiation went to the devil.[44]

Recollections of his parents, awakened by his visit, probably inspired Diderot to write at this time the dialogue entitled *Entretien d'un père avec ses enfants,* which he subtitled *ou du danger de se mettre au-dessus des lois* ('or the Danger of Putting Oneself above the Law'). In form, this was a fireside conversation in which Diderot's father plays the principal part — probably in remembrance of an actual discussion that may have occurred when Diderot visited Langres in 1754. In manner, the dialogue is a masterpiece of characterization; in substance, a discussion of natural justice as opposed to legal justice, of natural law as opposed to positive law. In this dialogue Diderot portrays himself as an impetuous and iconoclastic idealist who would overturn existing law in the name of a higher one. He represents his father, who tells how he once had to execute the codicil of a will disinheriting many needy people expecting to be the beneficiaries, as the compassionate but sagacious man of experience who believes that the greater good is served by following the law and not by taking it into one's own hands. The dialogue ends:

When it was my turn to bid him good night, I said to him as I embraced him, 'Father, when you come right down to it, there are no laws for the wise man.'

'Speak more softly.'

'Everything being subject to exceptions, it belongs to the wise man to judge which is the case where one submits and which the one where one breaks away.'

'I would not be too sorry,' he replied, 'if there were one or two citizens like you in a city; but if they all were, I would not live there.'

The *Entretien d'un père avec ses enfants* is a graceful and evocative piece, full of local color, tender memories, apt character delineation. Diderot allowed it to be published in 1772.[45] It seems rather strange that he did, for several persons figuring in the dialogue were still alive and his brother, the Abbé, is portrayed in quite an unfavorable light. Probably this was the bitter residue of Diderot's recent and unsuccessful attempt at reconciliation.

On his trip to Langres Diderot was accompanied by Grimm who stayed overnight at Langres and spent a week in nearby Bourbonne-les-Bains where Diderot joined him. Diderot's visits to Langres were so infrequent that the question arises as to what moved him to come this time. No doubt to confer with his relatives, since they were resisting coming to Paris; no doubt to confer with the widowed Mme Caroillon, mother of his future son-in-law. 'I did not come to the provinces for my amusement,' Diderot explicitly assured Sophie. 'I expected many disagreeable business matters there and I found more than I hoped for.'

He might more candidly have written, 'I did not come to the provinces solely for my amusement.' For the fact was that Mme de Maux and her daughter, Mme de Prunevaux, whose health was precarious following the birth of a child, were taking the waters at Bourbonne-les-Bains. Diderot wrote to Sophie about it in the exaggeratedly casual manner of a man with something to hide. 'I shall not tell you anything about the health of Mme de Maux and her daughter, whom you do not know and who cannot inspire in you very great interest.' To Grimm he expressed himself rather differently. 'One of the good deeds of our lives has been the visit of seventy leagues we paid these two poor unfortunates.' Clearly the timing of the trip to Langres was greatly influenced by the knowledge that Mme de Maux and her daughter were going to Bourbonne.[46]

Bourbonne was a lugubrious town, though its hot springs had been famous since the time of the Romans. 'Bourbonne is a place that is depressing daytimes because of the invalids you meet, nighttimes because of the noise of their arriving. Moreover, there is no promenade, the carriage road is detestable, and the environs are barren and displeasing.'[47] Diderot inquired about the water, its properties, the ways of using it, and the antiquities of the place. He then wrote his *Voyage à Bourbonne,* a casual and impromptu piece but also an instructive and sometimes delightful one, 'thanks to a pinch of philosophy thrown in here and there.' He wrote it for Grimm, should he want to use it, and also, with the usual Diderot instinct for utility, 'for the use of the unfortunate persons whose illnesses might bring them there.' 'Besides, it must not happen that I have no reply to the thousand and one questions which Dr. Roux and my friends will not fail to ask.' [48] Diderot began by reminiscing about his childhood and at last got to Bourbonne itself. He did not have much faith in hydrotherapy; journeying to the waters was more curative, he thought, than the waters themselves. 'The waters that are farthest off are the most healing, and the best doctor is he whom one follows but never catches up with.' Diderot then described many of the eccentric invalids at Bourbonne, recounted the history of the place, showed his Latin by reconstructing a Roman inscription, and ended with speculations showing that he was abreast of current knowledge regarding hot springs, volcanoes, and other violent geological phenomena.[49]

To while away the tedium at Bourbonne, Mme de Maux, Mme de Prunevaux, and Diderot made up stories to send to Naigeon who had sent them a copy of Saint-Lambert's recently published tale, *Les Deux amis, conte iroquois.* Saint-Lambert's North American story was mawkish, steeped in a false primitivism and with a plot full of incongruities. The work deserves to stand at the head of an anthology of the literary insipidities of the eighteenth century. Though it feebly attempted to achieve some local color by mentioning a war between the Iroquois and the Ottawas and by putting in a chance reference to Niagara Falls, the greatest of its failings was lack of verisimilitude. This was precisely the point of Diderot's rejoinder, *Les Deux amis de Bourbonne,* which demonstrated how, by its own seemingly artless simplicity of narrative and the unobstrusive accuracy of its detail, an author can imitate nature to the point of making his reader take illusion for reality.

Diderot liked mystifications, so the conspirators at Bourbonne led Naigeon to believe that the account he presently received of Felix and Olivier, the Two Friends from Bourbonne, had been written by Mme de Prunevaux and was simply an untutored account of a series of violent events recently occurring there. Eventually, however, Diderot acknowledged the tale as his own and, after making some revisions and adding an important postscript on the technique of achieving realism in such writings, allowed it to be published in 1772.[50]

Les Deux amis de Bourbonne struck the reading public as a decided novelty, excitingly fresh and vivid to some and bizarre and rebarbative to others.* The reason was that Felix and Olivier are uneducated, nonprivileged, poverty-stricken members of a submerged class, a class that numerically made up the great majority of the French nation. Moreover, though these are violent men and one of them is a smuggler, they are depicted as being instinctively and profoundly moral, as sterling human beings. 'Thus you see, little brother, that grandeur of soul and greatness of character occur in all conditions of life and in every country.' The crimes the two friends commit are the result of the repressions of a harsh and hierarchical society. This is a moral tale, in an unaccustomed sense. Felix and Olivier are heroes of a type new in French literature. The response of the public may be gauged by a remark made by Goethe: 'His children of nature . . . whom he elevated and ennobled with great rhetorical art, were very much to our liking; his brave poachers and smugglers delighted us. . . .'[51]

Les Deux amis de Bourbonne had a rather considerable influence on the development of French fiction.[52] In his postscript Diderot discussed the way in which the teller of a 'historical' tale, which would now be called a realistic tale, can compel belief:

He undertakes to deceive you; . . . rigorous truth is his object; he wants to be believed; he wants to interest, to touch, to carry away, to move, to make you shudder and shed tears. . . . How does a story-teller go about deceiving you? This is how: he will sprinkle his narrative with little details so closely related to the circumstances, touches so simple, so natural and yet so difficult just to imagine, that you will be forced to say to yourself, 'In faith, that is true; things like that are not made up.'

The proper technique in writing a story, Diderot went on, is like the technique of skillful portraiture in painting, by which a scar on the lip or a wart on a temple or a pockmark at the corner of an eye make all the difference between an idealized head and an individualized portrait. This was a technique, of course, that he quite obviously applied to his own writings. It is, therefore, an important part of his aesthetic theory. It is strange that Diderot scorns portraiture in painting as much as he does, while making it the cornerstone of literary art forms.[53]

Six weeks after leaving Paris, two separate weeks of which he had spent at Bourbonne, Diderot set out on his return journey. En route he visited the Volland ladies at their country estate for a week and also visited the

---

* For a translation in English, see Denis Diderot, *Rameau's Nephew and Other Works,* ed. R. H. Bowen (Indianapolis: Bobbs-Merrill, Library of Liberal Arts, 1964), 229–45. Here, too, may be found (246–75) the *Conversation between a Father and his Children*.

Duclos family, friends of Damilaville, at Châlons-sur-Marne. On a Sunday
night at Châlons all went to the theater, where Diderot was most unexpectedly welcomed from the stage. 'You know me. Just guess how embarrassed I was. I sank lower, lower, lower into the box; I very nearly concealed myself under the ladies' skirts, just out of modesty.'[54] At Bourbonne
Mme de Maux and Mme de Prunevaux had become acquainted with a
young sciatica patient named Foissy, a man whom Diderot greatly approved of so long as he supposed Foissy to be interested in the daughter
and not the mother. By prearrangement Diderot had expected to see both
women at Châlons-sur-Marne, but when they arrived he was quite startled
to discover Foissy accompanying them. By the time that everyone got back
to Paris, or very soon thereafter, Diderot realized that it was Mme de Maux
in whom Foissy was interested and that she was encouraging his attentions.
Diderot's letters to Grimm at this juncture — Grimm was a friend of Mme
de Maux and evidently tried hard to condone her conduct — are models of
what a disillusioned lover confides to a friend in such moments: Diderot
himself could not care less. Luckily he was too wise and experienced to be
leaving any of his fur in that trap. 'I have felt myself all over: I am not
suffering; I shall not suffer.' But he was sorry for Foissy. He hated to see
so worthy a young man led on and deluded. And he was greatly disappointed
in Mme de Maux. 'Does one permit oneself such pastimes at the age of
forty-five? . . . I prefer to believe her fickle rather than dishonest.'[55]

Much of this was only bravado. Before he is through, Diderot betrays
how much he is hurt.

And my happiness and tranquillity, what becomes of them in the course of these
maneuvers? . . . Admit, my friend, that I am treated very light-heartedly,
to say the least; admit that in her conduct there is not an iota of nicety. . . .
Even though she were sure of herself, has she no consideration for me?

'Does she not know that she is playing a game most dangerous to the
happiness of four persons? I include you, because if I go crazy, your head
will turn too.' Diderot referred to Mme de Maux as his mistress, and
wrote to Grimm that 'I was happy and tranquil. Her latest letter caused me
unbelievable distress.'[56]

This was about the end of it. There was no open break. Diderot continued to see Mme de Maux from time to time, and not infrequently,
through the years. But there was disillusionment there, and perhaps bitterness. 'One ought not to set oneself up as wonderful when one is not,' he
wrote of her to Grimm, 'so that, when one finds out that one is neither
better nor worse than other folk, one should gently bow one's head and

say, as some woman once said to her husband on her wedding night, "Well, monsieur, there you have it, that is the way it is." And spare oneself . . . all these useless efforts to persuade oneself and others that one's pattens are as high off the ground as one thought.' [57]

The evidence seems clear that his *affaire de coeur* with Mme de Maux, as Diderot himself called it, was an emotional experience with great impact. The documents do not permit us to determine in what way it hit him hardest, whether simply in sorrowing for having been unlucky in love, or in suffering from hurt vanity, or in feeling imperatively the need for retaining his self-respect and of not, therefore, being brought, like Hercules, to spin at Omphale's wheel. In a letter he wrote to the Volland ladies on 28 November there is a sense of desolation: 'Dear and good friends, You are choosing a very bad moment for growing cold, I assure you. I need, more than ever, to love someone and be loved in turn. I have been counting on you for as long as I live. If you leave me in the lurch, I shall be alone.' [58]

This Indian-summer episode exerted a strong influence upon Diderot's literary output in the next two years.[59] Previously he had not written about love relationships very searchingly or analytically. Even a sex-novel like *Les Bijoux indiscrets* had not been much concerned with the psychology of love. But now, in his *Ceci n'est pas un conte* ('This is no Yarn') and in his *Madame de La Carlière,* both of which were completed in 1772, Diderot reached into his recollection of two real-life case histories dealing with the inscrutabilities and irrationalities of the relation of man to woman.

Of the two tales, *Ceci n'est pas un conte* has more dash than *Madame de la Carlière.* Both use, very effectively, still another variation of the dialogue to secure realism, one in which the author or raconteur is in a constant conversation with the reader. In *Ceci n'est pas un conte* this reader-interlocutor is especially skeptical, critical, and rather comically irritable, thus giving contrast to the narrative and forcing the narrator to exert himself to induce belief. The story is that of a certain Tanié, exploited heartlessly by a Mme de Reymer; and of a Mlle de La Chaux, treated with equal harshness and coldheartedness by a man named Gardeil. Diderot exclaims at the hazards of the interplay of love and chance:

The wisest among us is very lucky never to have met the woman, be she beautiful or ugly, intelligent or stupid, who could drive him crazy enough to be fit to be put into an asylum.[60]

In the second story Mme de La Carlière is typical of the characters depicted in Diderot's tales, all of whom are endowed with very strong wills and very decided and sharply defined personalities. Her punishment of her

husband and her refusal ever to forgive him are pushed to the limit of the
bizarre — 'Yes, bizarre is the word.' *Madame de La Carlière,* like *Ceci
n'est pas un conte,* explores realistically and in depth a love relationship,
but it studies also the role of group judgments, of social expectations, of
public opinion. This is shown by what has long been taken to be the title
of the tale and probably was intended to be its subtitle: *Sur l'inconséquence
du jugement public de nos actions particulières* ('On the Inconsistency of
the Public Judgment of our Private Conduct'). This tale therefore provides
a transition to the sociological as well as the ethical concerns of Diderot's
Supplément au Voyage de Bougainville. In the concluding words of
Madame de La Carlière, Diderot leads us directly to the threshold of the
Supplément:

And then I have my own ideas, perhaps correct, certainly bizarre, about certain
actions which I regard not so much as the vices of men as I do the consequences of our absurd system of laws. . . .[61]

The French public in 1771 was greatly titillated by reading Bougainville's
Voyage autour du monde, with its news of the easy sex habits of the Tahitians. Bougainville, in fact, had named their island New Cythera. Diderot
wrote a review of the work, a preview of his later and more complex
Supplément au Voyage de Bougainville. 'This is the only book of travel,'
he reported solemnly, 'the reading of which has inspired in me a taste for a
country other than my own.' In his review Diderot displayed a marked
anti-colonialism, a result no doubt of his researches for the contributions
he was making to Raynal's *Histoire des deux Indes,* the first edition of
which was published in 1770.

Ah, monsieur de Bougainville, bear off from the shores of these innocent and
fortunate Tahitians. They are happy and you can only harm their happiness.
. . . This man whom you lay hold of as though he were a brute or a plant is
a child of nature like you. What right have you over him? Let him have his
morals; they are more decent and wiser than yours.[62]

Diderot's interest in the analysis of love and sexual relationships, indirectly
inspired by his love affair with Mme de Maux, was redoubled by the fantasies aroused by tales of the New Cythera. The result was a major work.
The strands of thought in the *Supplément au Voyage de Bougainville* are
complex and can best be suggested by Diderot's subtitle for it: *ou Dialogue
entre A et B sur l'inconvénient d'attacher des idées morales à certaines actions
physiques qui n'en comportent pas* ('or Dialogue between A and B on the
Disadvantages of Attaching Moral Considerations to certain Physical Actions

that do not Call for Them'). The work is something more and something less than just an exhortation to return to Nature, though many critics have declared that in this dialogue we see Diderot's Rousseauism coming out in him. It is a work which is more than just a satire on European corruption and decadence, though it has often been called an exercise in the manner of Tacitus; a work that is more than simply an adventure in Utopianism, for it is qualified by Diderot's conclusions on how the civilized man should live, conclusions regarded as sensible and liberal and progressive by some and as being unduly conformist by others. In the *Supplément au Voyage de Bougainville* Diderot produced an essay on the human condition—or, at least, the European one—that was characteristically searching, complex, and ambiguous. It is an essay on civilization and its discontents.

In structure the *Supplément au Voyage de Bougainville* falls into four sections.* First A, who has not read Bougainville, and B, who has, provide by their conversation a setting for the tale. Here, incidentally, Diderot briefly adumbrates what is now called the theory of the territorial imperative and the theory of continental drift. In the second section B goes on to recount the Old Man's Farewell. This highly rhetorical valedictory to Bougainville as he was leaving the island was invented by Diderot. No source of it can be found in Bougainville's book. Nor can there be found in Bougainville any trace of the third section of Diderot's dialogue, a long discussion on sex, eugenics, religion, morality, and law, between the expedition's chaplain and a native chief named Orou. These two middle sections thus constitute the so-called 'supplement' to Bougainville's *Voyage*. In the concluding section, A and B, going on from Orou's discussion with the chaplain, confront the problem of what sex practices and the laws regulating them in a civilized society should be.[63]

The fictitious incident which led to these discussions was one fully worthy of arresting anybody's attention. According to Diderot's account, the chaplain became the house guest of Orou for a stay of several days.

When he [the chaplain] was on the point of going to bed, Orou, who with his family had absented himself, reappeared, presented his wife and three daughters, all naked, and said: '. . . Here is my wife, here are my daughters; choose the one you like; but if you care to oblige me, give the preference to my youngest, who has not yet had a child.'

The chaplain replied that his religion, his holy orders, his morals and his sense of decency did not permit him to do so.

* For an unabridged translation in English, see Denis Diderot, *Rameau's Nephew and Other Works*, ed. R. H. Bowen (Indianapolis: Bobbs-Merrill, Library of Liberal Arts, 1964), 179–228.

Nevertheless he succumbed. He succumbed the next two nights, too, to the older daughters; on the fourth, 'out of fairness,' to the wife.

In consequence religion, holy orders, morals, and a sense of decency not unnaturally became the topics of a long discussion between Orou and the chaplain. It is not surprising that here Diderot tries to roll up a large score for his side. Of course Orou sounds very much like an eighteenth-century *philosophe* and of course the chaplain gets the worst of the argument. Orou was the mouthpiece for some of Diderot's favorite ideas, as in his inveighing against the indissolubility of marriage when everything else in life and in nature is in constant flux. Can anything seem more irrational, asks Orou, than demanding an oath of unchangeability from two beings of flesh and blood as they stand under a sky that is never an instant the same, in a den that will fall into ruins, under a tree that is splitting with age, at the foot of a cliff slowly decomposing into dust? [64]

Orou is of course asserting his views on sexual conduct in the name of Nature. But his argument is not merely that this is the way of the tribe or that this is the way of his fathers. Instead, this very rational savage reaches out to find a principle of conduct that is not culture-bound but on the contrary is applicable to all peoples and all situations.

. . . you cannot condemn the morals of Europe for not being those of Tahiti, nor our morals for not being those of Europe. You need a more dependable rule of judgment than that. And what shall it be?

Now we come to the crux of the whole question, and the reader trying to puzzle out Diderot's ethics approaches Orou's answer with a quickened sense that it is also Diderot's own. It is, of course, a secular answer, not depending upon any religious sanction in respect to sexual practices. It turns out to be a kind of natural law, not the old natural law of the theologians, but a newer kind, based on utility. It is the kind of natural law Jeremy Bentham appealed to when he said, 'Nature has placed mankind under the governance of two sovereign masters, *pain* and *pleasure*.'

Do you want to know [asks Orou] what is good and what is bad everywhere and always? Pay particular attention to the nature of things and of actions, to your relations with your fellowmen, to the effect your conduct has on your own individual utility and the general welfare.

Here we have Enlightenment utilitarianism, evolving out of the older natural law and basing itself on the emerging sciences of the nature and behavior of man.[65]

Too frequently the *Supplément au Voyage de Bougainville* has been interpreted simply as a call to promiscuous sexual pleasure for its own sake. But Orou's discourse as Diderot imagined it shows that sexual pleasure and the constant changing of sexual partners was not sanctioned simply for 'individual utility' but also for the general welfare. And the general welfare was served by the production of healthy children in large numbers. Diderot was concerned with eugenics and he was a populationist.[66] Far from advocating that there be no rules governing sexual practices, Orou asserts that sexual activity has a social purpose and that Tahitian society imposes sanctions if these purposes be wilfully frustrated. 'We do have some dissolute old women who go out at night without their black veils [the sign of sterility or of having passed the menopause] and take men when they know nothing can come of it. If they are discovered, they are punished by exile to the northern part of our island or by slavery.'[67] The severity of this punishment proves that Diderot, far from being amoral or nihilistic, was, within the terms of reference he himself set, positively puritanical.

When he has A and B begin to puzzle over 'what useful conclusions can be drawn from the bizarre morals and customs of a noncivilized people,' Diderot becomes irresolute. The *Supplément au Voyage de Bougainville* ends on a note much more timid than revolutionary. Granted that it makes many diagnoses of the condition of civilized man and that one of its 'striking and admirable characteristics' is that 'it raises so many insoluble questions,' perhaps we must be content with accepting it as 'a playful exploration of alternative moral positions, so typical of Diderot's experimental method.'[68]

One thing is abundantly clear. Diderot was convinced that the rules regulating sexual behavior in civilized societies had become irrational, greatly needing a re-examination of what are the proper limits. He believed especially that civilized man is subject to too many conflicting authorities, and that his unhappiness arises from trying to obey incompatible imperatives simultaneously.

Run through the history of both ancient and modern centuries and nations and you will find mankind subjected to three codes, the code of nature, the civil code, and the religious code, and condemned to breaking these codes one after another because they have never been in accord.

Diderot knew, in a general way, what he would like to have happen. Let morality be simplified by basing it on a humanistic conception of the nature of man. Let the civil code be a copy or pattern of the code of nature as much as possible. Let the religious code lose all its authority. It was a program, though in vague and abstract terms, of a secular and humanistic morality. As A says drily, 'This is not easy.' [69]

Had Diderot tried to elaborate on these remarks, he might have been carried afar, ending in a treatise on law and ethics as elaborate and as utilitarian as say, Bentham's *An Introduction to the Principles of Morals and Legislation*. Diderot does travel some distance down that road. For instance, he says that if the laws are good, morals will be good; that if the laws are bad, morals will be bad; and that if the laws, whether good or bad, are not obeyed, 'which is the worst possible condition in which a society can find itself,' then there is no morality at all. But he does not at this point open up the discussion to cover the whole of ethics and politics. Instead he carries the conversation back to marriage, gallantry, coquetry, jealousy, fidelity, modesty, even incest.[70]

The concluding pages between A and B clearly show that Diderot was uneasy about morals and civilization, already revealing in his century that sense of discontent with civilization that Sigmund Freud identified.[71] The *Supplément au Voyage de Bougainville* has been called 'a stage on love's way' in comparison with two other 'stages,' Rousseau's *La Nouvelle Héloïse* and Choderlos de Laclos' *Les Liaisons dangereuses*. It has also been called a fiction where the characters win by winning, unlike Choderlos de Laclos' work whose characters lose by winning, and unlike Rousseau's whose characters win by losing.[72] But if in Diderot's *Supplément* the natural man wins by winning, Diderot draws back from scooping in the gains.

What then shall we do? Shall we come back to nature? Shall we submit ourselves to the laws?

What Diderot would like—but what he evidently supposed was unattainable—is a society where the laws are based upon nature:

When we are born we bring nothing into the world with us except a constitution similar to that of other human beings — the same needs, an impulsion toward the same pleasures, a common dislike for the same pains: that is what constitutes man as he really is, and what should be the basis of a morality appropriate to him.[73]

What Diderot was willing to accept, and to some critics this has seemed rather shockingly conformist, is a very qualified hope for the future.

We shall speak out against irrational laws until they are reformed; while waiting, we shall submit ourselves to them. He who breaks a bad law on his own private authority, authorizes every one else to break good ones. There are fewer inconveniences attached to being mad among madmen than there are to being wise all by oneself.[74]

Writing the *Supplément au Voyage de Bougainville* was Diderot's response to a prolonged period of emotional crisis in his experience of dealing with women. It is a part, and an important part, of the whole panorama of moral obligation and ethical speculation that fascinated him all his life. But it is only a part. The *Supplément au Voyage de Bougainville* must itself be supplemented. It is a stage on the way to that humanistic ethic which in Diderot's thought comes to its climax in his refutation of Helvétius' book on man.

CHAPTER 42

'I No Longer Have a Child, I Am Alone, and My Solitude Is Unbearable'

AMONG the roles that Diderot loved to play, that of tender and considerate father ranked high. The events of the years just before he went to Russia gave him great scope in this regard, for this was the time of his negotiating Angélique's marriage contract and of his assiduous efforts to get his prospective son-in-law highly placed.

Angélique's marriage to Caroillon de Vandeul having been agreed upon in principle, 1771 was ushered in by a flurry of letters to Langres from the Rue Taranne. In his letter to the mother of his future son-in-law, Diderot hailed the approach 'of the moment when we shall be just one family.' To his future son-in-law Diderot's letter of wishes for the New Year was full of teasing recollections of their recent visit together at Châlons, where Vandeul had forgotten his smallclothes, left behind in a bedroom, and also had given the wrong advice on which road to take to Paris. Under the mask of jocosity one can feel Diderot's unconscious urge to put down any man with a claim to supplanting him in his daughter's affections.[1] A third letter, from Angélique to her Aunt Denise, revealed impeccable spelling, in contrast to the fourth, one from Mme Diderot to Denise, in which an elegant French was swathed in astonishing phonetic spelling. It is obvious that of the parents it must have been the father who was responsible for teaching Angélique orthography.[2]

Diderot was proud of his daughter's intellectual development, especially as it showed itself to be analytical, critical, and implicitly materialist.[3] He also continued to be concerned with her sex education, for which he summoned Marie-Catherine Biheron to his assistance. Mlle Biheron was famous for constructing wax anatomical models, which she displayed at a private museum at her house. The Academy of Sciences twice endorsed her work, and she sold collections of it to the King of Denmark and to the Empress of

Russia. In a letter to John Wilkes Diderot spoke of her pieces as being 'of a marvelous exactness and accuracy . . . . My daughter took a course in anatomy with her with ease and without disgust.'[4]

In writing to her future mother-in-law Diderot was explicit about his daughter's continuing her education: 'We make her foresee that the time is not far off when, preoccupied by domestic cares, she will have scarcely any time to give to her education.'[5] What Diderot particularly had in mind was the continuation of her musical training. For years he had been mentioning in his letters Angélique's progress on the harpsichord, which by this time had reached a very considerable level of proficiency. Grimm brought back from Germany a large amount of music for her, and she developed a special fondness for that school. In 1770 Philidor, a well-known composer (and even more famous chess player), called on Diderot. 'I was curious to know what he would think of her talent in harmony. He listened to her improvise for more than half an hour and told me that she had nothing more to learn on that score; all that remains is to feast herself on good music and ceaselessly regale herself to her heart's content.'[6] Dr. Charles Burney, the English musicologist and father of the future novelist Fanny Burney, also heard Angélique play at about this same time and reported that:

Mademoiselle Diderot . . . is one of the finest harpsichord-players in Paris, and, for a lady, possessed of an uncommon portion of knowledge in modulation. . . .[7]

Angélique's progress was especially gratifying to Diderot because of his own fondness for music. Just at this time he spoke of himself as being 'crazy about' music. In 1768 he had taken two visiting Englishmen to hear J. G. Eckhardt play, perhaps on the piano, for that instrument was just coming into use in Paris. 'For three hours on end he was divine, marvelous, sublime. . . . I no longer was aware that the world exists. The only thing existing for me were those marvelous sounds and I.'[8] It is not surprising, then, to hear that now and again there were impromptu concerts at the Rue Taranne. One of these occurred on Diderot's name-day in 1770. Young Mme Victor Louis, a friend of the Diderots and wife of the future architect of the famous theater at Bordeaux, sang and played 'like an angel.' Angélique's music master, a young Alsatian named Anton Bemetzrieder, played 'like an angel' too. The lutinist Cohault, who had come to scorn, went away with nothing to say. The party had been a great success.[9]

Bemetzrieder, whose name had first appeared in Diderot's correspondence in November 1769,[10] used a teaching method which appealed to Diderot's ever-alert sense of the practical and useful. 'The science of harmony is therefore no longer a matter of lengthy routine. It is a branch of knowledge that may be acquired in very little time, given an ordinary intelligence and a modicum of application. It could therefore be made a part of education, and every child who applied himself for a year or more could pride himself on knowing as much as any virtuoso, and more.'[11] Greatly impressed, Diderot suggested that Bemetzrieder's methods be published, and offered to put the book into literary form, carefully preserving the shape of Bemetzrieder's dialogues and making sure that 'the interlocutors maintain their character.' The result is a book of technique made up of lively and interesting dialogues.[12] The *Leçons de clavecin et principes d'harmonie* was published in 1771.[13]

Though Diderot studiously disclaimed having anything more to do with the manuscript than to correct its Teutonic French, posterity has stubbornly disbelieved him.[14] But, whether or not the *Leçons de clavecin* rightfully belongs in Diderot's *oeuvre,* it does bear his imprint. It contains numerous queries and suggestions which, though seeming to be random and casual, afford insights into the nature of music and into the philosophy of its appreciation. This is not characteristic of the real Bemetzrieder. His subsequent publications do not soar. They plod.[15]

When he came to Paris, Dr. Burney made a special point of calling on Diderot at the Rue Taranne. Unsuccessful then, he unexpectedly met Diderot at D'Holbach's a few hours later. They got on famously. Burney's estimate of Diderot's musical knowledge was very high.

With M. Diderot, I had the happiness of conversing several times; and I was pleased to find, that among all the sciences which his extensive genius and learning have investigated, there is no one that he interests himself more about, than music . . . he presented me with a number of his own MSS. sufficient for a volume in folio on the subject. . . . 'Here, take them, says he, I know not what they contain; if any materials for your purpose, use them in the course of your work, as your own property; if not, throw them into the fire.'[16]

Burney thought well enough of the Bemetzrieder book to have his daughters use it, though evidently not well enough to translate it and bring it out in England.[17] Diderot wrote Burney not infrequently. He introduced his acquaintance Philidor and—with the amazing comment that 'He is almost my only friend'—Grimm. In September 1771 Diderot requested a very substantial service: 'I have written about it to M. Grimm; I have written about it to Monsieur Jean Bach whom I knew when he stayed in Paris, and I take the liberty of writing about it to Doctor Burney. It is a question of getting for me a good, a very good pianoforte.'[18]

In November 1770 Princess Dashkov, who had played a leading role in the Russian *coup d'état* of 1762 but was now out of favor, visited Paris. Diderot saw her four times, and told her 'what I knew [about] the laws, customs, administration, finances, politics, morals, arts, sciences and literature' of France. He found her interesting, but he did not say that he found her charming or endearing. He saved her from herself on two occasions, first by persuading her not to be at home to Mme Necker and Mme Geoffrin, though both ladies presented their cards one evening. 'I felt that she had more to lose than gain from the opinion of these two women and of those around them, all of them people who would have insisted on her talking as though she were the chief of the conspiracy.' [19] His second interposition was to advise her not to see Rulhière, whom she remembered very pleasantly from the time when he was a diplomat at Saint Petersburg. 'One moment only, princess; let me ask you, when your travels are finished, whether you have an idea of returning to Russia?' Diderot made his point.[20]

An incident during Princess Dashkov's stay revealed that Diderot took pride to a surprising degree in being French. One of the Princess' callers was an Englishman whom Diderot spoke of as being secretary of embassy. 'This secretary Walpole having let himself go very inconsiderately with respect to my nation, I did not think that I ought to suffer it, and I brought M. Walpole around to making me an apology in which he assured me that he had not known he was speaking in the presence of a Frenchman. I pointed out to this gentleman that one ought not to have two ways of talking, one for those present, and another for those absent, assuring him that what I would have to say about him when he had departed I would certainly have the courage to tell him to his face. Walpole left.' [21]

At the time when Princess Dashkov visited Paris a chronic struggle between Crown and *parlements* in France was coming to a climax. This very complicated quarrel had begun in Brittany, which, like some other of the provinces (called *'pays d'état'*) on the perimeter of the kingdom, still had their medieval representative Estates. The Breton *Etats Provinciaux* vigorously objected to a network of military roads that was being built by forced labor. Their complaint was, in effect, that this was a kind of taxation without representation and violated their provincial rights. In the ensuing confrontation with D'Aiguillon, the royal governor of Brittany (who happened also to be one of the King's ministers at Versailles), the *Etats* were stoutly supported by the Parlement of Rennes, the vociferous and audacious leader of which was its Attorney General, La Chalotais. When the Crown attempted to punish La Chalotais all the *parlements* of France began to co-

operate in his defense. By doing so they discovered for the first time in their
history the strength that comes from union and they also, through exploring
their charters and asserting their powers, came close to denying the absolute
sovereignty of the king.[22]

In general, Diderot was no devotee of the *parlements*. Of the Parlement of
Paris he wrote in 1769, 'It is to be expected that the parlement which is
closest to the Court and the courtiers should be the most corrupt of all.'[23]
When Voltaire published his *Histoire du Parlement de Paris* (1769), a work
which argued that historically the Crown was right and the *parlements* were
wrong, Diderot eagerly secured the book from Geneva and, in his review
of it, remarked that Voltaire had not been critical enough. In an eloquent
passage Diderot heaped up an overwhelming series of accusations against
the Parlement, 'the irreconcilable enemy of philosophy and reason.'[24]

And yet, by the time of his letter to Princess Dashkov of April 1771,
Diderot had made a hard choice:

We are on the brink of a crisis which will end in slavery or liberty; and if it is
slavery, it will be slavery like that which exists at Morocco or Constantinople.[25]

His apprehensions over the policies of the newly-appointed Chancellor of
France, René-Nicolas Maupeou, had made the difference. Maupeou wanted
to make the censorship of books much more strict, and it was believed that
he intended to bring about the restoration of the Jesuits. The anti-Maupeou
views of *philosophes* like Diderot may have been reinforced, too, by their
observing how opposed to Maupeou was their old friend Malesherbes. He
was president of the important tax court called *Cour des aides,* and its resounding remonstrance of 14 August 1770, the work of Malesherbes, attacked the use of *lettres de cachet,* a subject on which men of letters vibrated
at a high pitch. On 9 April 1771 Malesherbes found his *Cour des aides*
abolished.[26] Diderot was afraid, as he wrote Princess Dashkov, that 'the
monarchy is degenerating into despotism.' Nor was he the only one with
such apprehensions: 'It seems to me,' wrote Turgot to Dupont, 'that we are
on the road towards legal despotism.'[27] In January 1771 Maupeou arrested
130 members of the Parlement of Paris and rusticated them to remote parts
of France. On 13 April Louis XV abolished that parlement. Voltaire favored
the new policy, which, according to one who knew Diderot and D'Holbach
intimately, made the *philosophes* at Paris so angry that they quivered. It
was at about this time that Diderot, wearing his customary black clothes, was
mockingly asked by the Comte de Broglie whether he was in mourning for

Russia. 'If I were to wear mourning for a nation, M. le Comte,' he replied, 'I would not have to look so far.'[28]

Diderot was a son of liberty. When he reviewed in 1769 John Dickinson's *Letters from a Farmer in Pennsylvania,* he wrote,

I have been somewhat surprised to see the translation of these *Letters* published here. I know of no other work more calculated to instruct peoples in their inalienable rights and inspire in them a violent love of liberty. Because M. Dickinson was speaking to Americans, they [evidently the authorities] did not realize that his discourses are addressed to all men. . . . fortunately tyrants are even more imbecilic than they are harmful. . . .

And now, even though full of foreboding, Diderot wrote to Princess Dashkov at the height of the Maupeou crisis, 'Each century has its characteristic spirit. Ours seems to be that of liberty.'[29]

Diderot's passion for liberty expressed itself at about this time in the most elaborate poem he ever wrote, one with the significant title of *Les Eleuthéromanes, ou les Furieux de la liberté* ('The Eleutheromaniacs, or Men Frenzied for Liberty').[30] One of Diderot's reasons for writing this was to see how well he could succeed with the dithyramb, the wild, vehement, and yet disciplined form of the Pindaric ode.[31] The occasion for his writing the poem was mock-heroic. At New Year's parties in 1770, 1771, and 1772, each time Diderot's piece of cake contained the bean designating him King of the Revels. He celebrated his accession to the throne in 1770 by 'Le Code Denis' in which he announced that 'J'aime la liberté' and signed himself

> DENIS, sans terre ni château,
> Roi par la grâce du gâteau.

The next year, when fate struck again, he wrote 'Verses upon Having Been King of the Revels Twice,' and also a graceful 'Rondeau of Denis, King of the Revels, Complaining of the Drawbacks of Royalty.'[32] In 1772 he abdicated, his declaration of abdication being *Les Eleuthéromanes.*

It has been noticed that the playfulness of all these four poems suddenly deepens into serious political reflections.[33] In *Les Eleuthéromanes,* though written to celebrate a private occasion with the prime intent mock-heroic, the undertone is graver. Unlike its three predecessors, which prattled about King Denis, this poem talks about all men and the liberty that is theirs by nature. A whole political philosophy is here, the political theory of the natural rights of man, of the institution of government among men, of a love cf liberty, of a hatred of tyrants.

Les Eleuthéromanes contained a fierce distich which Diderot very probably would have subscribed to on his own but which is also a close paraphrase of Jean Meslier, a deeply alienated and atheist Catholic priest of earlier in the century.

> For want of a string
> To strangle a king,
> Man with bare hands
> Will plait up the strands
> From the guts of a priest.[34] *

Les Eleuthéromanes was published in 1796, and this distich immediately earned for Diderot a foremost position in the demonology of those elements of French opinion who have always believed that the French Revolution was the result of a *philosophe* conspiracy.

Diderot's frenzy for liberty also expressed itself in 1771 in a letter written for publication but too incandescent for him to try to publish, one which has been named since its first appearance in 1937 'Unpublished Pages against a Tyrant.' [35] Diderot was angrily answering Frederick II of Prussia, who had let it be known to D'Alembert and Voltaire that he had written and published a small book entitled *Examination of the Essai sur les préjugés*. The *Essai sur les préjugés* was probably written by D'Holbach and certainly was published by him early in 1770, so that Frederick's reply cut the *philosophes* to the quick. Diderot pretended in the 'Unpublished Pages against a Tyrant' to be ignorant of the identity of the author to whom he is replying—'The author . . . is a *grand seigneur;* at least he pleads the case for ancestors as if he had some himself.' As he responded to the *grand seigneur* Diderot bristled with egalitarianism: 'I will not suffer being insulted by a titled snob any more patiently because he is the latest of his line. I am perhaps the first of mine.' Actually, Diderot knew perfectly well who his antagonist was. He was the leading warrior in Europe, and consequently the *Pages inédites contre un tyran* speak out vehemently against war. At issue in this spirited though indirect exchange was whether people should be told the truth, whether rulers can trust people, whether throne and altar can be defended only through obscurantism, deceit, and oppression. Frederick II, who for thirty years had been playing upon his reputation as a champion against intolerance, was beginning to show his true colors in the *Examination of the Essai sur les préjugés*. Diderot was showing his too, though to posterity

---

* Et ses mains ourdiraient les entrailles du prêtre
  Au défaut d'un cordon pour étrangler les rois.

rather than to his contemporaries. No wonder he did not want to go by way
of Berlin on his way to and from Russia.

What, then, have I learned from this little book? . . . That man is not made
for truth nor truth for man; that we are doomed to error; that superstition has
its good side; that wars are a fine thing, etc., etc., and that God preserve us
from a sovereign who resembles a philosopher like this.[36]

Despite his dedication to freedom, Diderot was still willing to do obliging things for the despot of All the Russias, so that in January 1771 he suggested to Galatzin that Catherine II purchase a celebrated art collection up
for sale. Her purchase of the Crozat-Thiers collection has been called 'one
of the most important [art] transactions since the break-up of the collection
of Charles I.'[37] Diderot engineered the whole affair, though he did not deal
directly with Saint Petersburg. He kept in touch with Galitzin, engaged
competent art appraisers, including François Tronchin of Geneva, whose
function was also to be, Diderot made clear, to supervise the packing and to
see that no frauds were perpetrated. In January 1772 Diderot signed the contract as the agent of Catherine II.[38] His correspondence abundantly reveals
how time-consuming and fraught with detail this transaction was. Oddly
enough, there is no indication whatever that Catherine II ever expressed any
satisfaction or gratitude for efforts that at one stroke had made her collections almost supreme in Europe. Considering the extraordinarily cheap
cost, 460,000 livres, of a magnificent collection of about 500 canvases, it might
well have come to her mind that Diderot had saved her several times over
the sums that she had given him. Later that year Diderot was able to get
two Poussins for her at a very cheap price, and also purchased in her behalf
a considerable part of the Choiseul collection. He claimed that his efforts
earned him the enmity of many Frenchmen who had hoped that these
works of art would not leave the country.[39]

Diderot was unusually busy in 1771. In addition to all the responsibility of
the negotiations for the Crozat collection, he was involved much more than
he wished in the lawsuit that Luneau de Boisjermain was pressing against
the publishers of the *Encyclopédie*. Moreover, from 1 September Diderot had
the task of getting out the *Correspondance littéraire,* Grimm having unexpectedly to accompany the Hereditary Prince of Hesse-Darmstadt on a trip
to England and then to Germany whence he did not return until late
January 1772.[40] During Grimm's absence the Salon of 1771 was exhibited,
and Diderot's *Salon de 1771* suffered grievously from his various preoccupations.[41] It is less original than his other *Salons,* for it paraphrases exten-

sively a current pamphlet entitled *Lettre de M. Raphael le jeune*.[42] Moreover, though the *Salon de 1771* is not brief, it is in a raw and unpolished state. Probably Diderot never found the time to whip his material into proper shape.[43]

Though the Salon of 1771 is not memorable for what Diderot wrote about it, it is memorable for having exhibited Houdon's splendid bust of Diderot. This was the first of Houdon's great portrait busts.* It is not known when Diderot sat for it; and his only comment upon it, in the *Salon de 1771*, is that it was a very good likeness.[44]

He may have scamped the *Salon de 1771*, but a letter to Dr. Antoine Petit, apparently written in midsummer 1771, shows Diderot still deeply interested in aesthetic theory. The problem he propounded was an aspect of how to achieve a correct representation of the human form through an accurate knowledge of anatomy and physiology. Diderot asked the doctor to imagine a well-formed young man of twenty-five, much like the ancient statue of Antinous. Suppose this young man desires to change himself into a Hercules. Describe what changes will have to occur in his body if he is to be successful in his desire: 'You will go from his wrists to his arms, to his shoulders, to his neck and head, to his back and chest, to his loins, his thighs, his legs, his feet. The more you go into detail, the better it will be. A word too about the action of his spirit on the parts of his face, and of the effect of the viscera on the appearance of the external parts.'

As a result, I shall have material for an academic discourse for Petersburg, in which I intend to demonstrate to artists that they are in need of a knowledge of anatomy that is much more than superficial, and that there is almost none of their figures that is not full of inaccuracies and errors from the point of view of physiology.[45]

In the *Salon de 1765* Diderot had already speculated on the differences between the bodies of Antinous 'who has never done anything,' and Hercules, 'a killer of men, a smasher of beasts,' ideas which appear to have been suggested to him by Hogarth's *The Analysis of Beauty* (1753).[46] So far as is known, Diderot never wrote this projected essay for Saint Petersburg. But his inquiry is all of a piece with his perennial interest in how occupation or profession, and also bodily defects, will affect the whole demeanor and aspect of a person, so that, for example, one can tell that a man is hunchbacked by looking only at his feet.

It is evident that Saint Petersburg was often in his thoughts. Besides his work for Catherine II, there was always his friend Falconet. In the course of

---

* A photograph of this bust serves as the frontispiece for the first part of this biography.

1771 Diderot misjudged Falconet and thought himself misjudged in turn. Ten years previously, a French scientist named Chappe d'Auteroche had gone to Tobolsk to measure the transit of Venus.[47] His elaborate account of his *Voyage en Sibérie,* published in 1768, contained an entertaining (but also appalling) description of the backwardness of the Russians. Although he held no brief for Chappe, having already described him in 1761 as 'a fool,' Diderot was very scornful of the reply to Chappe's work that presently came out of Russia, entitled *The Antidote.* Diderot incorrectly supposed Falconet to be the author of *The Antidote* and wrote of it to Grimm in scathing terms:

Here is the book, the worst book possible in respect to tone, the most paltry as to content, the most absurd as to pretentiousness. . . . He who has refuted Chappe is more contemptible by his toadyism than Chappe is by his errors and falsehoods.[48]

Though he thought Falconet the author of the book, Diderot did not up-braid him when acknowledging receipt of it. But he did not compliment it either, though Falconet wrote Catherine II that he had.[49] It is not known when Diderot discovered that the author of *The Antidote* was none other than Catherine II herself.[50] Meanwhile, in midsummer 1771, Diderot received a letter from Falconet that the *philosophe* described as 'outrageous' and as having offended him grievously. Upon what subject Diderot considered himself misjudged is not known, but it is evident that at last he began to be a little suspicious of his friend: 'Take care. The solitude of Petersburg and the favor of a great sovereign are corrupting you.'[51] The moment was scarcely auspicious for Falconet's trying to draw Diderot into another artistic debate. Nevertheless Falconet did, this time by his assertion that the equestrian statue of Marcus Aurelius in the Piazza del Campidoglio at Rome is a very bad work of art. His *Observations sur la statue de Marc-Aurèle* (1771) was dedicated 'A Monsieur Diderot,' but for the moment Diderot refused to be drawn.[52] It was only on 2 May 1773 that he wrote a searchingly critical, though mild and kindly, letter to Falconet, a letter which (since Falconet did not take criticism very gracefully) may go far to explain Falconet's chilly reception of Diderot when the *philosophe* arrived at Saint Petersburg later that year.[53]

In 1771 the Comédie-Française finally produced Diderot's *Le Fils naturel,* published fourteen years before.[54] According to Mme d'Epinay, Diderot consented to its being given, though without much eagerness. It was said that it was the actor Molé who insisted that the play be produced.[55] By July it was in rehearsal, and it received its *première* on 26 September before a large crowd of 1051 spectators. The play was so poorly received that the performance came close to breaking down several times.[56] Critics spoke of it as being insupportably frigid and of its reception as being humiliating to its author. Even Mme d'Epinay, who reviewed it for the *Correspondance littéraire* and who could be expected to be as indulgent as possible, admitted that there were several places where the play did not act so well as it read. Most of the time, however, she contented herself with deploring the decay of public taste in France. The play was advertised for a second performance but, either because of a quarrel that broke out between Molé and his fellow actors or because Diderot feared a downright fiasco, he withdrew the piece after its single performance.[57]

The lawsuit brought by Luneau de Boisjermain that Diderot found himself drawn into was linked with the earlier one in which Luneau had been awarded damages against the corporation of booksellers. The linkage was, however, 'only by resentment,' as Diderot quite rightly observed.[58] Now Luneau, as a subscriber to the *Encyclopédie,* claimed that he and every other subscriber had been overcharged 174 livres 8 sols. The case, brewing since late 1769, came to court in 1771. It was accompanied by a drum-fire of printed memoranda, of *Mémoires à consulter* and *Réponses* and *Précis,* which are tedious to read but have contributed greatly to knowledge about the manufacture and marketing of the *Encyclopédie.*[59] Luneau argued his case himself. '*Le sieur* Luneau pleaded with spirit, but not without getting off a large number of sarcasms against book publishers in general.' Inasmuch as Luneau had sent out invitations, a large audience heard him, on 21, 28, and 31 August.[60]

On 31 August Diderot fired off a letter to Le Breton and Briasson which he expected to be published and circulated, as it was. It was written hastily and heatedly, and Grimm always declared that it was a great mistake to have written it.[61] Diderot exonerated the publishers in a very peculiar way: he claimed that all the decisions and procedures that had increased the cost of the work and that Luneau was bringing suit about, had been his decisions not theirs. To a person reading the documents in the quiet of two centuries later Diderot's statement seems eloquent, torrential, and persuasive. Perhaps it was too successful, for patently it forced Luneau to lavish his sarcasms thenceforth not on the publishers but upon Diderot. By writing the letter Diderot afforded himself the delicious pleasure, while seeming to defend the publishers, of putting them in their place. Their role had been merely an entrepreneurial and humbly subordinate one, in which their function was simply to bring about what their betters had decided for them. But Diderot's peers evidently interpreted the letter as vaunting. A contemporary observer spoke of the ridicule Diderot had brought on himself in this affair and remarked that the failure of Le Fils naturel was partly ascribable to this cause.[62]

Apparently Diderot had already composed and was ready to publish a formal memorandum, Au public et aux magistrats, but was persuaded for his own sake not to publish it by Gerbier, the lawyer retained by Le Breton and Briasson. 'Your manuscripts got into the hands of Fauche [the publisher at Neuchâtel]. By whose act? Unless they were stolen from you or from the publishers, it will be concluded that you did it yourself, and there you are, culpable of breaking the Royal Decree of 1759. The tolérance tacite will not be an excuse. The Government will never admit it and we can never prove it.' [63] This advice is probably the cause of Diderot's speaking in his letter of 31 August only of the engravings and of the first seven volumes of text. These were legal. He avoided any mention of the last ten volumes published in 1765-6.

The fact that Diderot was humiliating his publishers while defending them, was lost upon most observers. All they could see was the ridiculousness of a man of letters defending his exploiters. Some of his fellow authors may even have thought of it as a kind of betrayal. The fact was, though, that Diderot had a bad conscience. He knew that at the time of the earlier trial, when he had come to be friendly with Luneau de Boisjermain, he had confided in him most indiscreetly. As early as the beginning of 1770 Diderot had taken alarm and appealed to Luneau de Boisjermain's sense of honor:

I have an altogether different favor to ask of you which you surely will not refuse me. Do not mention in your memoranda about the last seven volumes of the Encyclopédie's having been carpentered.[64]

For eighteen months the knowledge of his needless indiscretion hung over Diderot.

Luneau de Boisjermain replied in print to Diderot's letter of 31 August 1771 line by line and in parallel columns, for all the world to see. And the world, vastly entertained, snapped up the edition in a day. Luneau's reply was mocking and sarcastic, with broad hints about Le Breton's 'carpentering' and sneering references to Diderot's works and Diderot's foibles. 'It is to you that I owe the secret knowledge of everything that occurred between you and M. le Breton. I learned nothing save through you. You deny it. The public will easily guess why.' Luneau was vengeful, and he was merciless:

I write badly, Monsieur, I know very well. . . . To tell the truth, I do not yet have the good fortune of being obscure like you; but that will come if you are willing to keep up a little correspondence with me. . . . If nature had endowed me with a transcendent genius like yours, surely no one would be able to understand me even now.[65]

Luneau later published an even more sardonic amplification of this letter. He twitted Diderot for having 'in your works so much bad taste, mistaken ideas, absurd sentiments, ridiculous notions, convolutions, etc., etc., etc.' He also felt justified in publishing Diderot's appeal to him to keep confidential the fact of Le Breton's 'carpentering.' From this time on, then, it was public knowledge that Le Breton had altered the *Encyclopédie* without Diderot's knowledge or authorization.[66]

In order to reply, Diderot touched up his *Au public et aux magistrats,* had it printed, and was eager to distribute it, to judge by the efforts that Gerbier had to expend to persuade him not to. Gerbier hailed Diderot's pamphlet, which quite rightly has been described as 'written with superb force and logic,' as a masterpiece: he would use its arguments to excellent effect in his own pleading, he said, but he feared that if it was published 'People would forget the booksellers and think only of the author, and a quarrel over money would end by becoming a quarrel over religion.' Diderot let himself be persuaded, though very reluctantly. Luneau de Boisjermain added to the provocation by collecting the various papers referring to the lawsuit, including his own passages ridiculing Diderot's mannerisms and characteristics, and had them published. It can well be imagined with what unction Fréron quoted in the *Année Littéraire* those remarks about the man whom he called the 'infallible oracle of literature.' [67] The case was finally settled, years later, in favor of the publisher. Meanwhile Diderot had to allow the insolent Luneau de Boisjermain to have the last word.

Diderot's interposition of himself in this affair was one of his last official acts in connection with the *Encyclopédie*. Publication was almost finished, the censor's approval of the last volume of plates coming on 14 February 1772. Thus his relations with his publishers remained turbulent almost to the last. There had also been some very stormy moments in 1769; when the drawings of the animal kingdom were prepared for the sixth volume of plates, Diderot consulted Bernard de Jussieu, the well-known naturalist, as to their accuracy. Jussieu pronounced all of them hopelessly defective, so Diderot took it on himself to commission the naturalist Louis Daubenton to make new drawings and supervise the engraving and editing of them. This took three years. The incident illustrates that Diderot was forceful about maintaining high standards of excellence for the work. But the publishers reimbursed Diderot with great reluctance and at first refused downright to give Daubenton a set of the *Encyclopédie,* though this had been a part of his agreement with Diderot. Daubenton threatened Diderot with a lawsuit and the latter wrote two of his vehement expostulations to his publishers.[68] In the Luneau de Boisjermain affair, though Diderot came to the defense of his publishers, one does not get the impression that there was any resumption of cordial relations between them. And one may conjecture with a high degree of probability that Le Breton was delighted and Diderot annoyed that the public took with great equanimity the revelation that Le Breton had tampered with the articles.

Diderot was never too busy to concern himself with belles-lettres and with literary judgments. At this time or thereabouts he rebuked Grimm for not discerning the merits of the Le Tourneur translation of Young's *Night Thoughts;* he responded charmingly to a Dutch acquaintance who was positive that *'trace'* rhymes with *'grâce'* and was determined to make Diderot agree; he suggested to Grimm various fine points of French grammar and usage; and he complained of La Harpe, the author of a prize-winning oratorical set-piece, that 'He flows, but he does not surge. . . . nothing beats under his left nipple'; and of some poetry by La Harpe, 'It is a flavorless liquid that he distils drop by drop.' [69]

The inspiration of association with Diderot is well reflected in the composer Grétry's memories of that time. Diderot used frequently to visit Grétry, on condition that he keep on with his composing at the keyboard. Sometimes Diderot would strike a chord and then say of the piano, 'Lots of things in there.' Once Grétry had made several false starts with an aria. Diderot came in, observed what the words were, and began to declaim them in what he conceived to be the proper rhythm. Grétry wrote that 'I substituted sounds for the declaimed rhythms of this beginning, and the rest of the aria went right off.' [70]

* * * * * *

In the sixties it becomes noticeable that various writers, no doubt striving to become better known, address their productions to Diderot or dedicate them to him, an indirect but nevertheless certain proof of the prominence he had achieved. These were in a variety of literary forms and on very disparate subjects, as befits works addressed to an encyclopedist. Besides poems, there was an anthology of French readings published in Edinburgh in 1766, a pamphlet on how to make porcelain, and a proposal for reforming music by abolishing both measures and keys.[71] Now and again a false-Diderot appeared, such as the two-volume work published at Frankfort on Main in 1770 and calling itself the *Oeuvres morales de Mr Diderot*.[72] In 1772–3, moreover, there appeared, all of them published outside France, no fewer than four editions of his collected works. So far as is known, none of these appeared with his authorization. Their publication is striking evidence of the consolidation of his reputation.[73]

An unwelcome concomitant of two of these editions, however, was that they perpetuated the attribution to Diderot of some works that he had not written. These false attributions proved very hard to correct. Some of them may have done him harm, as in the case of Morelly's *Code de la nature,* which, as has been noted, even Diderot's brother supposed that the *philosophe* had written. At the least, these false attributions rendered distorted and inaccurate the impression any contemporary reader could gain of the whole of Diderot's writings and thought.[74]

During these years the shadow of Rousseau hung over Diderot, for Jean-Jacques was known to have written his memoirs. Diderot's apprehension of their publication may be seen in what he wrote in 1768 to David Hume:

I dread the moment when a man who so greatly loves to make a to-do, who has so little consideration and who has been connected so intimately with a great number of people, publishes such a work, especially considering the skill that he possesses of adroitly stigmatizing, of covering up, of garbling, of making a person suspect by praising him more than by blaming him.[75]

What, then, must have been Diderot's anxiety—and Grimm's and Mme d'Epinay's—when they learned that Rousseau, who had come to Paris to live in June 1770, was reading portions of his *Confessions* to various groups? On 10 May 1771 Mme d'Epinay wrote in complaint to the Lieutenant-General of Police, Sartine, as a result of which Rousseau was officially enjoined not to read to such groups any more.[76] This took care of the danger temporarily, as danger it evidently seemed to the Grimm-d'Epinay-Diderot group; but of course it did not and could not settle the question of what an eventual publication might do to their reputations.

What could they do, or what did they do, to blunt the effect of such an eventuality? The answer is obscure and ambiguous. Posterity does not know for certain that they intended to do anything to parry the blow. All posterity knows for certain is that at about this time Mme d'Epinay revised a very long novel which she may have begun as early as the mid-fifties and which she called the *Histoire de Madame de Montbrillant*.[77] This manuscript did not profess to be her memoirs, and she made no attempt to publish it, though it may be significant that in her will of 1782 she authorized Grimm to publish any of her manuscripts that he saw fit. Anyone who dips into this novel, so easy to mistake for serious and responsible memoirs, perceives at once that the narrative follows very closely her own life story; that the fictitious names she uses of 'Volx,' 'Desbarres,' 'Garnier,' and 'René' transparently fit Grimm, Duclos, Diderot, and Rousseau respectively; and that the novel incorporates numerous letters exchanged between René and Madame de Montbrillant which are identical with letters actually exchanged between Rousseau and Mme d'Epinay. When this novel was at last published, the unscrupulous editors substituted the real names for the fictitious ones and presented the work as Mme d'Epinay's memoirs. Naturally the public accepted it as a reliable historical source. Editions were published in 1818 and again in 1863, with the result that a whole century of biographers, led by Sainte-Beuve, fashioned their interpretations of the characters of Diderot and Rousseau on the basis of these 'memoirs.' [78]

By the time that Mme d'Epinay was revising this 'sketch of a long novel,' she and Diderot had long been accustomed to working in close collaboration. Together they brought out the *Correspondance littéraire* when Grimm was absent in England and Germany in 1771, and together they prepared for the press Galiani's *Dialogues sur le commerce des blés*. Though Diderot once in 1769 expressed extreme irritation with Mme d'Epinay because she got the Galiani publication all at sixes and sevens, nevertheless their literary association continued.[79] Consequently it should not have been really surprising when it was discovered early in the twentieth century that Diderot had made numerous suggestions concerning the plot and character development of her novel about Madame de Montbrillant.

These suggestions, in a series of numerous memo slips in Diderot's handwriting still attached to Mme d'Epinay's manuscript, are almost exclusively concerned with the presentation of the character of René — that is, of Jean-Jacques Rousseau. The first two-thirds of the manuscript remains as it was originally written, almost without change. But the last third, beginning with the appearance of René on the scene, is now known to have undergone massive alterations as a result of Diderot's suggestions. Mme d'Epinay's original depiction of René was rather neutral and bland; but this has been overlaid by

the picture of an altogether new René — 'Do this, do that; make René more
. . . [etc.]' is the burden of Diderot's memo slips. This new René is depicted
as consistently calculating and false, a man to whom insincerity, bad manners, and bad motives are uniformly imputed. Diderot painted with somber
colors. The image of René that emerges tallies exactly with the image of
Rousseau that Diderot had drawn in 1758, at the time of their break, in
the private bill of particulars that he entitled the Catalogue of the Seven
Rascalities.[80]

When Diderot's suggested alteration of the original manuscript was first
discovered, the discoverer assumed that this was irrefutable evidence that
Diderot was in a plot to calumniate Rousseau and assassinate his reputation.[81] A grave accusation, and one that may be true. It cannot be denied that
it is somewhat suspicious that Diderot waited until this particular time to
give Mme d'Epinay the benefit of his suggestions, although her manuscript
had already been in existence for some years. It is true, too, that Diderot
rather liked mystifications; it was not long previously that he had attempted
by devious means to retrieve Galitzin's portraits from Mlle Dornet. It is
probably true also that it was at this time that Diderot composed a letter
from 'Garnier' to 'Volx,' appearing in the *Histoire de Madame de Montbrillant* and purporting to have been written in 1758. This letter is very
prejudicial to René — 'This man is a madman,' it begins — and, although the
style seems certainly to be genuine Diderot, is spurious in the sense that it
appears to have been written after the event. Early editors of the memoirs
printed it as a bona fide letter from Diderot to Grimm.[82]

How damaging to Diderot's character is it, really, to learn that he made
suggestions to Mme d'Epinay for altering her manuscript? It is notorious
that he was always reading his friends' manuscripts and making copious
suggestions. Perhaps he was simply saying to Mme d'Epinay in effect, 'Evidently you do not know the sort of person Jean-Jacques is. This is what he
is really like.' Diderot's interpretation of Rousseau's character greatly soured
after their break in 1758, and the picture of Rousseau that he suggested for
the *Histoire de Madame de Montbrillant* is consistent with his other pronouncements about Rousseau's character. It is not a deceitful nor insincere
representation of Rousseau, so far as one can judge, even though it may very
well have been in error. Diderot appears to have believed that this was the
way Rousseau really was.

However, if Diderot conspired with Mme d'Epinay and Grimm to mislead
the public into mistaking her fiction for reliable, responsible memoirs, that is
indefensible. The 'memoirs' had the impact that they did because posterity

construed them as confirming the adverse view of Rousseau that Diderot was known to have held and to have stated publicly in the two editions of his work on Seneca in 1778 and 1782.[83] The public had no means of knowing that they were hearing, not two independent voices but only one, and the repetition of that one through a mask. If the publication of the 'memoirs' was a plot instead of a coincidence, it was certainly a diabolical one.

Was there a conspiracy? It is possible. A necessary precondition of it could readily be fulfilled by merely making sure that the 'sketch of a long novel' remained in existence. Thus it would become a kind of delayed bomb or booby trap waiting for someone to detonate it. This is the way Diderot treated his own manuscripts, trusting that posterity would eventually discover them. Grimm saw to it that the manuscript survived by giving a clear copy of it to a trusted friend in 1792.[84] This was the manuscript that eventually became the 'memoirs' of 1818. If this delayed bomb theory seems fanciful or over-elaborate, depending too much upon accident and coincidence, one has only to realize that after all this is really what did happen.

On the other hand, if there was a plot it does not seem likely that Grimm, who spent several final months in Paris in 1792 before becoming an émigré, would have left undestroyed the memo slips by Diderot that could subsequently be taken, and were in fact so taken when they were discovered, as proof of the existence of a conspiracy. Thus there is circumstantial but inconclusive evidence on both sides of the question. My own conclusions in this highly conjectural matter are that there probably was no plot; that Mme d'Epinay, Grimm, and Diderot, though they felt threatened, resorted to drift rather than to cunning; that Diderot's suggestions for changing Mme d'Epinay's manuscript were more self-therapeutic than conspiratorial; but that at present no one can positively say that there was no plot or no moral guilt.[85]

Diderot's was a busy life, with numerous interests, and posterity might very well wish that he had taken the time to write a diary. It would have made the chronology of his career much easier. Still, it is known that 1771 was the year when he received two Roman medallions discovered in a field at Langres;[86] visited an old friend, Simon de Bignicourt, whom he found cowering in a wretched room convinced that he was damned, and whom he persuaded that maybe he was not;[87] was present with a company of other prominent persons, including the young Lavoisier, at a chemical demonstration of the volatilization of diamonds;[88] wrote a series of gracious and playful notes to his friend, the poet and latinist Guillaume-Antoine Le Monnier, who just then was getting out a translation of Persius;[89] toiled over a translation of Persius himself — 'Upon my word, all this is pretty difficult'; [90] and demonstrated, or hoped he had, how a man of letters can have creative conceptions in the plastic arts as effective as those of any artist. His method was to hire a young sculptor to carry out literally and mechanically his instructions regarding composition and expression. No doubt he was urged to this by his running debate with Falconet and by the latter's sarcasms about men of letters who thought that they knew anything concerning artistic creation in the plastic arts. Diderot boasted to Falconet that his demonstration was triumphantly successful and that the finished terra cotta was standing on his mantle. Unfortunately it has not survived.[91]

Also in 1771 Diderot proposed to Salomon Gessner of Zurich that the *Entretien d'un père avec ses enfants* and *Les Deux amis de Bourbonne* be included in a forthcoming volume of Gessner's pastoral poems. It was a rather strange mixture of genres, especially considering the realism embodied argumentatively in *Les Deux amis de Bourbonne,* and the combination caused a critic to remark that Diderot's stories among Gessner's were like satyrs among nymphs. Diderot had long been familiar with Gessner's poetry, for he had reviewed *La Mort d'Abel* in 1760 and was well acquainted with Michael Huber, who translated Gessner into French. Diderot, though confessing that he did not understand a word of German, was sure that he could discern the line of poetic thought a poet was trying to express, whatever the language, so that he would often say to Huber about some poem the latter was translating, 'The poet did not say it like that; this is how he said it, this is the order of his ideas.' [92] Diderot had a profound admiration for Gessner, according to Jakob Heinrich Meister, a young Swiss acquainted with both Diderot and Grimm. It was largely because of Diderot, Meister wrote to Gessner, that France has 'the good fortune of knowing your works.' [93]

Gessner ecstatically accepted Diderot's proposal, transmitted by Meister, and was eager to pay Diderot liberally for his contributions. Meister, however, predicted that Diderot would refuse such payment and, so far as is known, he did.[94] Subscriptions were sold in France for a de luxe edition, and there was also to be a cheaper one published simultaneously. Meanwhile, however, Diderot procrastinated in sending the manuscripts. Gessner finally received them in early 1772, almost too late to be included in his book. A German edition, the Diderot items translated by Gessner himself, appeared in 1772, and the French edition in 1773.[95] The French censor was extremely reluctant to allow copies to be distributed in France. 'He has found very reprehensible things in it and especially very dangerous things for smugglers to read.' Accordingly Sartine gave permission to sell only copies of the de luxe edition.[96]

Ordinarily Diderot did not manifest much eagerness about the publication of his works, but his behavior with Gessner was an exception. The thought has been hazarded that perhaps he wanted to publish his novels — *La Religieuse* had been written long before and a version of *Jacques le fataliste* was in existence by September 1771 — and he used this means to test the temper of the authorities. The resistance he encountered, according to this speculation, convinced him of the inadvisability of trying to publish them during his lifetime.[97]

*   *   *   *   *   *

Diderot dreaded the oncoming of his daughter's marriage. He acted a little as though he were the first fond father in the history of fathers reluctant to be supplanted, the first to entertain doubts about the merits of a prospective son-in-law. But Diderot was not wholly wrong in his misgivings about Vandeul, whose later career showed him to have been ambitious, money-mad, and not overly scrupulous. As early as January 1771, while trying to use his personal influence to help Vandeul, Diderot discovered that the young man was strongly suspected of practices very close to fraudulent. 'I do not like fraud in any respect whatever,' wrote Diderot to Vandeul. 'It is a sort of theft. One should do business cleanly and openly. . . . This business chagrins all of us.' No wonder that Diderot wrote to Grimm later that year, 'I am not particularly crazy over her intended.' [98]

Moreover, Vandeul started to do some very hard bargaining about the terms of the marriage contract. His trying to skimp his future wife on her dower rights and rights of reversion should she be left a widow especially aroused Diderot. It enraged him to have his daughter haggled over. But, as he remarked to his sister, a marriage contract is the most important legal settlement in one's life, and it is impossible to remedy it if it is made wrong in the first place. Diderot asserted that he would not go back on his word, but he repeatedly gave Vandeul an opportunity to go back on his. After discussions over a period of about eighteen months the marriage contract was finally signed, on 8 September 1772, at the Rue Taranne.[99]

Meanwhile Diderot, too, showed that he was more than a little money-mad. He was indefatigable in his efforts to secure a place and fortune for Vandeul. Of course Diderot had strong incentives. Not only did he wish his daughter to be affluent. In addition, in order to keep Angélique in Paris, Diderot had to find something for Vandeul so lucrative that it would persuade him to live in the city, whereas he really preferred to remain in the provinces. 'I am moving heaven and earth to get the husband established.' He promised Vandeul's mother that he would either succeed in setting Vandeul up in Paris or he himself would retire to the provinces in order to be near the young couple, something he often talked about but quite transparently was unwilling to do. Vandeul did eventually promise to live in Paris, a promise he kept as long as Diderot lived.[100]

Diderot, accordingly, turned to all the influential persons that he knew. 'I have introduced him to all my protectors, great and small.' He solicited the Swiss banker, Jacques Necker. He solicited Trudaine de Montigny, *intendant général des finances*.[101] He solicited Devaines, a man whose own place-seeking Diderot had strenuously assisted and who was now an important financial officer in the government. And he solicited D'Aiguillon, Louis XV's minister, and was granted an interview. 'I saw the Duc d'Aiguillon Monday and was as much at ease as he was. Fathers have the courage of the devil when the welfare of their young ones is concerned.'[102]

But it was a slow and discouraging business, during which Diderot himself wrote some of the applications and petitions for Vandeul to sign. 'I could more easily find ten sons-in-law who are already placed,' he wrote his sister, 'than one place for a son-in-law.' All of those whom he solicited said to him, 'But, M. Diderot, are you then so very much attached to your provincial . . . ?' Though Diderot had confidently promised Mme Caroillon success in March 1771, by New Year's of 1772 he had to admit that he had not yet had any solid results, nor was Vandeul settled even by the time of the wedding, in September 1772. Two weeks after the marriage Diderot was still writing to Mme Caroillon of his hopes for placing Vandeul 'to my liking and to his.'[103]

This was not a very successful career of place-hunting. In fact, Vandeul never did receive an appointment in the bureaucracy. Instead, he began to solicit, with Diderot's aid, for leases of government lands and mineral rights, as a result of which he eventually became one of the wealthiest ironmasters of his time, a man who seems to spring right out of the pages of Balzac.

During the months just previous to her marriage, Angélique's knowledge of how the *haute bourgeoisie* lived profited from her father's friendship with Mme Necker. Several times Diderot mentions their having been at Saint-Ouen, the Neckers' luxurious country house just northwest of Paris, or of going places in the Necker carriage. The relations of Diderot and Mme Necker, two temperaments that at first blush might not seem to be completely congenial, were at that time very close. Diderot allowed Mme Necker

to read his *Salons,* an almost unprecedented favor because of their confidential nature, and in his dealings with her he tried hard to avoid shocking her
Calvinistic sensibilities. 'How many things will you find in them,' he wrote
as he sent her the *Salons,* 'that would never have been thought or written
had I had the honor of knowing you sooner. I dare say that the purity of
your soul would have entered into mine.' When Diderot was dead, Mme
Necker wrote harshly of him, but in these years of the early 1770's each
was tolerant of the other, a prerequisite of a successful and continuing
salon.[104]

Meanwhile Angélique's marriage approached apace. Mme Diderot cried
all the time before it and Diderot cried, or felt like crying, all the time
after it. The shock of adjusting to his daughter's marriage, which occurred
in the very year when he was composing or revising the pieces he wrote
following his love affair with Mme de Maux, also contributed to this side
of his literary production. His daughter's impending change of roles probably made especially vivid to his imagination the status of a woman, bio-
logically and socially. The concluding lines of his *Supplément au Voyage de
Bougainville* are about how men should treat women. They constitute, in
fact, almost the only firm conclusion of the whole dialogue:

And above all, be sincere and honest to the point of scrupulosity with these
fragile beings. . . .[105]

In the same vein, in the late spring of 1772 Diderot wrote an essay, *Sur les
femmes,* inspired by the publication of a book by one of his friends, Antoine-Léonard Thomas' *Essai sur le caractère, les moeurs et l'esprit des
femmes dans les différents siècles.* 'I like Thomas,' Diderot began. 'I like the
independence of his soul and the nobility of his character.' But then Diderot
began to complain. Thomas had thought a great deal, but he had not felt
enough. And Diderot was off on a demonstration of what Thomas should
have written. Diderot evidently thought of the book as he did of another he
was reviewing about this time: 'If I ever was tempted to re-do a book, it is
this one.' He begins to describe how women astonish us, 'beautiful as the
seraphim of Klopstock, terrible as the devils of Milton' (the only reference
to Klopstock in Diderot's works). Perhaps Diderot most revealed his mascu-
line point of view by saying, 'The symbol of woman in general is that of
the Apocalypse, on the forehead of which is written: Mystery.'

Thus far his essay is not especially new. But it becomes particularly
original as he begins to think on the legal status of wives — perhaps he was
thinking of Angélique, soon to be under the legal dominion of Vandeul —

and as he explores medical and sociological aspects of his subject. He discusses sexual hysteria and speaks of the effect upon women of menstruation, pregnancy, and the menopause. Although there is more than a trace of male condescension in his attitude — 'O women! what extraordinary children you are!' — nevertheless he is much more understanding of, and compassionate with, the physical and legal handicaps of women than most writers of his day.

In almost all countries the cruelty of the civil law has combined with the cruelty of nature, against women. They have been treated lilke imbecile children. There is no kind of vexation which among civilized nations may not be exercised with impunity by a man against a woman.[106]

As the wedding approached great efforts were made to conciliate the Abbé Diderot and to secure his blessing for the marriage. Angélique wrote him, most charmingly and most humbly, asking him to perform the marriage ceremony and saying that she preferred him to a bishop who had offered to do so. Diderot wrote too, but his letter was very prickly and self-righteous. The Abbé promptly interpreted all this as simply an effort to get him to bequeath his property to Angélique and her heirs. His reply to Angélique was harsh. Since he could not allege that she was irreligious, for he knew full well how strictly her mother had brought her up, he alleged instead that her bridegroom was. 'Entry to my house will be denied to you and to M. Caroillon, as it is to your father, for the same reason, religion.'[107]

On 9 September 1772 the young people were married in Saint-Sulpice, the parish church of the Rue Taranne. Save for the legal witnesses, persons otherwise unknown, only members of the two families were present. From Langres had come Angélique's mother-in-law and her three young brothers-in-law, as well as Aunt Denise, who had had written into the marriage contract her intention to bequeath to Angélique all her property. Also present was Angélique's aunt on her mother's side, Mme Billard. Diderot and Angélique had been unable to invite any of her father's friends. Mme Diderot would not allow it.[108]

Life was bleak and empty for the Diderots after the marriage. 'I no longer have a child, I am alone, and my solitude is unbearable.' Part of the time the emptiness of their lives made the parents bad-tempered. Mme Diderot took it out on Diderot, and he, in two long and bitter letters, took it out on his brother, whom he upbraided for having written so uncharitably to his niece and to whom he recommended reading the article *'Intolérance'* in the *Encyclopédie*. These letters in 1772 are the last the two brothers ever exchanged. Quite different was a letter Diderot gave Angélique soon after her wedding. It is a kind of farewell which, by its present condition, shows that it must have been carefully preserved and often reread. In it Diderot reaches a level of feeling and simple directness which make it a memorable and affecting document.[109]

Diderot took some comfort after the marriage in making gifts to the young people, and he showed his continuing interest in Angélique's education by paying for music lessons given her by Eckhardt three times a week. He described these activities to his various correspondents as 'bringing to the nest of these young birds a feather or a bit of straw that was lacking.' A sudden though temporary illness of both the young people in October was the occasion of a great deal of bustle and alarm. By December, when the lives of the couple were beginning to show an established routine, Diderot was gloomily convinced that Vandeul was making his bride a typically frivolous and clothes-conscious young woman. Yet he dared not interpose, lest they shut him out of their lives altogether. It was one of the few times in his career, no doubt, when he intentionally refrained from well-meaning interference in the lives of others, and his sense of frustration seems to have been correspondingly great. 'One must just . . . let everything go as it will. But one does not have to be a witness to it. Whence I conclude: Let us leave, let us leave quickly, and go far away to forget children who are not worth the trouble of being remembered.[110] Of course Diderot exaggerated. But it explains why the idea could come to him that the time was ripe to go to Russia.

All the more because the months following Angélique's marriage were sterile as far as literary productivity was concerned. Earlier in the year he had written or revised *Ceci n'est pas un conte, Madame de La Carlière, Sur les femmes,* the *Supplément au Voyage de Bougainville,* and some purple passages at the behest of the Abbé Raynal for use in a new edition of his *Histoire des Deux Indes.* But following this literary activity Diderot entered upon a fallow period during which his interest in problems like the complex one of how an actor acts — he had already dealt with it in a book review in 1769 — seemed to be latent and inert. He did write a piece at this time explicating a text by Horace, a feat of construing which was the result of a dispute between Naigeon and Diderot and was more erudite than creative.[111] This was all. He needed new environments to distract his mind and stimulate his creativity. The marrying-off of his daughter marked the end of an epoch in his life.

CHAPTER 43

First Visit to Holland and
the *Paradoxe sur le comédien*

WITH Angélique now married and set up in her own establishment, with the last volumes of the plates of the *Encyclopédie* in the hands of the subscribers, there was no good reason left why Diderot should not embark upon the journey to Russia which Falconet was always telling him he ought to take and which Catherine II plainly desired and expected. In late 1772, apparently, he made up his mind to go, and in early 1773 there were many rumors in Paris of his impending departure.[1] He finally got off on 11 June, going first to The Hague, where he visited his old friend Prince Dmitri Galitzin.[2]

Diderot was a reluctant traveler. Never in England, although he knew English books so well and had so many English friends; never in Italy, though sometimes he had talked, not very seriously, of going to see the pictures there.[3] He never in his life saw mountains, except for the rather gentle ones in Germany that he saw later this year; and he saw the ocean for the first time at Scheveningen, making a special trip '[to salute] Neptune and his vast empire' the very day of his arrival at The Hague.[4] His travels were customarily intellectual ones, journeys up and down his study, and it was only rarely — in 1741-2, 1754, 1759, 1770 — that he even made the trip to Langres. In fact, he spoke of travel as something slightly morbid, like an addiction. 'As for me, I do not approve of going far off from one's country except between the ages of eighteen and twenty-two.'[5] Yet here he was, going to Saint Petersburg when he was sixty years old.

His departure had evidently been accompanied by a good deal of hurly-burly, with Diderot at his most emotional. Still, he sensibly gave his wife power of attorney, by act of 28 April.[6] As the time of leaving approached, there were farewell visits to pay, such as calling on the scientist La Condamine.[7] There were also farewell calls to be received at the Rue Taranne, notably one by Devaines, who recounted later that Diderot told him that at their last family dinner, just over, his wife, his daughter, and he had been so upset that they could not eat. At that very moment Mme Diderot appeared before the two men — 'a priceless woman, with her little bonnet, her pleated dress, her bourgeois figure, her arms akimbo, her shrill voice' — and rebuked Diderot for having missed the meal at home in spite of his promises.[8]

Diderot certainly seems to have given the impression of being disorganized, for Mme d'Epinay wrote of him two days after he had gone,

He is a kind of peculiar child, this Philosopher. He was so astounded the day of his departure to be obliged to start out, so frightened at having to go farther than Grandval, so woebegone to be having to pack his bags.[9]

At The Hague Diderot was very comfortably installed (with a servant assigned all to himself) in the Russian embassy at 22 Kneuterdijk. This was a handsome house that had belonged in the previous century to the Grand Pensionary Oldenbarnevelt.[10] Diderot greatly enjoyed his stay in Holland. 'The more I get to know this country, the better I adapt myself to it. The soles, the fresh herrings, the turbots, the perch, and what they call *"water-fish"* are the finest folk in the world. Presently, though, he began to fear stomach trouble; this was averted by judicious internal applications of Rhine wine.[11] Of his hostess, Galitzin's bride, the Countess Amalie de Schmettau, Diderot wrote appreciatively, 'She has read; she knows several languages. . . . She plays the harpsichord, and sings like an angel. . . . As she is well informed and is logical, she argues like a little lion.'[12] He also mentioned the splendid walks to take and spoke especially of his fondness for the sea. 'Scheveningen was in all seasons my favorite promenade.' Life was quiet at The Hague, almost like life in the country, and he enjoyed it.[13]

But he had much writing he wanted to do, and many persons and places to see. While he was in the Netherlands he explored the possibility of having his collected works published by M.-M. Rey of Amsterdam.[14] He visited Haarlem, Amsterdam, Zaandam (where Peter the Great had learned the ship-building trade), and Utrecht. Two days after he arrived in The Hague, he went to Leyden. 'I have seen pictures, engravings, princes and savants.'[15] Among the princes were the brothers William and Charles Bentinck. Among the savants were the youthful Van Goens, professor of Eloquence, History, and Greek at the University of Utrecht; Isaac de Pinto, whom Diderot had previously known in Paris; and possibly François Hemsterhuis, the 'Dutch Plato.'[16]

During his stay at The Hague Diderot read Helvétius' posthumous

De l'Homme ['Concerning Man, his Intellectual Faculties, and his Education']. This work, which had just been published, was put through the press by Galitzin himself, and the French authorities suspected Diderot of having written the introduction to it. Diderot read the book 'pen in hand,' thus beginning the *Réfutation de l'ouvrage d'Helvétius intitulé L'Homme* which is one of Diderot's least known and most significant books.[17] Also during this summer he wrote what he called 'une petite satyre.' This is almost certainly the *Satire première,* the subtitle of which (though perhaps this is a would-be embellishment by Naigeon) is *On Characters and Words Connoting Character, Profession, &c.* The *Satire première* is an entertaining and masterly little piece of psychological analysis, full of precise observation. Cast mainly in a conversational form, it describes how professional training as well as deep-seated traits of character are amusingly and unconsciously revealed in a person's casual conversation. And in addition, during these months Diderot amplified an earlier essay, making it into the celebrated *Paradoxe sur le comédien.*[18]

Diderot had first set down the ideas embodied in the *Paradoxe sur le comédien* in 1769, when he was reviewing a pamphlet on Garrick for the *Correspondance littéraire.*[19] All these ideas were retained when, in the summer of 1773, he changed the form of the work to a dialogue. In the *Paradoxe* Diderot produced still another complex and controversial work, with layers of meaning intertwined.

On the face of it the dialogue is solely an examination of what constitutes great acting. The subject has been enough to make the *Paradoxe* one of Diderot's most frequently cited and quoted works, and several generations of actors, their vanity and their image of themselves involved, have cried the dialogue up and down. But there is more, much more, to the *Paradoxe sur le comédien.* From a consideration of acting, Diderot opens up his argument to include all the arts, so that the *Paradoxe* is an important supplement to the aesthetic theory he had arrived at in the *Salon de 1767.* Finally, the unusual anecdotal and autobiographical nature of the dialogue suggests that Diderot realized that there was an element of paradox also in himself. He seems to be analyzing himself, thus making it easier — or perhaps more difficult — for posterity to understand his personality.

What is the paradox of the actor? It is that the more a great actor appears to be overwhelmed by the emotion of his role, the cooler he is and the more in command of himself. And the converse is that a greatly talented actor or actress who really feels the emotion of the role is an actor who will give very uneven performances:

Do not expect any consistency on their part: their acting is alternately strong and weak, hot and cold, commonplace and sublime. Tomorrow they will fail in the passage where they excelled today, and on the other hand they will excel in that in which they failed the day before.

Diderot's doctrine has always been a shock to that rather numerous group of actors, both amateur and professional, who take pride in flinging themselves emotionally into their roles. They like to have it said that they do not play their roles, they live them. This implies, of course, that the more sensitive the emotional equipment of an actor, and the more he lets himself go, the better actor he is. This Diderot abrasively denied:

It is extreme sensibility which makes actors mediocre. It is middling sensibility which makes the multitude of bad actors. And it is the absolute lack of sensibility which qualifies actors to be sublime.[20]

Of course Diderot was not challenging the fact that an actor impersonates, or tries to.

> Tears in his eyes, distraction in his aspect,
> A broken voice. . . .
>   For Hecuba!
> What's Hecuba to him, or he to Hecuba
> That he should weep for her? [21]

Diderot was not asserting that this does not occur. His object was to inquire what happens to the actor psychologically to give the appearance of this emotional effect. Nor did he assume that actors would be pleased with his conclusions. 'These verities might be amply demonstrated, and yet actors would not admit it: that is their secret.' Nevertheless, he always claimed that he admired actors and deemed their profession essential to a civilized society. It must be confessed, however, that in the *Paradoxe sur le comédien* he described their art rather perversely and provokingly:

He [the actor] weeps as an unbelieving priest weeps, preaching the Passion; as a seducer weeps at the knees of a woman he does not love but whom he wants to betray; as a beggar in the street or at a church door, who insults you as soon as he despairs of moving you; or as a courtesan who feels nothing, yet swoons in your arms.[22]

It is not surprising, therefore, to find that many actors have been rather scandalized by the *Paradoxe*. They tend either to deny its truth or to regard it as a truism stretched to exaggeration. Naturally the *Paradoxe* has had its principal impact in France. Great names in the history of the French stage — Talma, Coquelin, Copeau, Mme Béatrix Dussane, Jouvet — have written about it.[23] And this interest on the part of French actors has extended into our own decades.[24] But abroad, also, actors and theoreticians everywhere have shown their interest in Diderot's paradox. An important book, *Masks or Faces?*, by William Archer, the man who brought Ibsen to the attention of the Anglo-Saxon public, is almost in its entirety an examination of Diderot's thesis.* A recent reprinting of *Masks or Faces?*, edited by a prominent American director, shows posterity's continuing recognition of the importance of Diderot's doctrine:

The *Paradox* is thus a challenge to the actor to recognize the high nature of his art, a plea that he discipline and control the flow of his imagination and feeling. . . . This demand for actors' discipline, for a technique of emotional experience, is an essential of any acting theory or practice. Here is the real historical significance of Diderot's contribution. With this demand Diderot becomes one of the pioneers of the modern concept of the theatre. This explains Stanislavski's recognition of Diderot's essay as one of the important contributions to acting theory.[25]

In 1766, when counseling Mlle Jodin on acting, Diderot had declared that an actor who possesses only good sense and judgment would be cold, one who has merely verve and *sensibilité* would be beside himself; he who combines the two would be sublime.[26] These are rather conventional ideas, very different from his categorical statement in the *Paradoxe sur le comédien* that sublimity is absolutely incompatible with sensibility. So downright a statement is much more absolutist than is customary with Diderot and encourages readers to search for the reasons why.

One reason was that Diderot was simply transferring to the realm of the actor the greatly expanded understanding the years of the *Salons* had been giving him of the conditions governing creativity in all the arts. In all of them, he now realized, self-control is the *sine qua non* for great achievement. Another reason was David Garrick. Diderot was so impressed by Garrick's mastery of technique that he began to assume, not quite justifiably, that Garrick was exclusively influenced in his acting by his intellect and never by his heart.

Garrick sticks his head between the two panels of a folding-door and in the interval of four to five seconds his face passes successively from wild joy to

---

* The *Paradoxe sur le comédien* is available in English translation in Diderot, *The Paradox of Acting* and William Archer, *Masks or Faces?*, ed. Eric Bentley (New York, 1957), 11–71. This edition reprints the translation by Walter Herries Pollock: Diderot, *The Paradox of Acting* (London, 1883).

moderate joy, from moderate joy to tranquillity, from tranquillity to surprise, from surprise to astonishment, from astonishment to sadness, from sadness to despondency, from despondency to fright, from fright to horror, from horror to despair, and then reascends from this level to that from which he began. Did his soul feel all these sensations and execute this sort of scale in unison with his face? I do not believe it, and neither do you. If you should ask this celebrated man . . . for the scene of the Little Pastry Boy, he would act it for you; if you should immediately ask for a scene from Hamlet, he would play it for you, equally ready to cry over spilling his pastries or to follow the path of a poignard in the air.[27]

'I wish you could have seen Garrick play the role of a father who has let his child fall into a well,' Diderot once wrote to Mlle Jodin.[28] He seems to have concluded from Garrick's mastery of technique that he allowed no warmth, no *sensibilité* whatever, in his acting. This conclusion was the easier to come to because Diderot always saw Garrick act in a drawing-room and never in a complete role on the stage. Garrick himself may have decided that Diderot somewhat misinterpreted the basis of his art, for he seems never to have responded to an invitation from Suard to comment upon what was probably a manuscript of the *Paradoxe sur le comédien*. It is possible that Garrick was embarrassed. Perhaps he deemed Diderot had misunderstood him, much as if a man observing a celebrated musician about to play Scarlatti and warming up to it by practising scales, had mistaken the scales for the sonata and gone away thinking that he had heard and seen all that there was to the musician's art.[29]

Diderot's high esteem for the acting technique of Mlle Clairon, the most celebrated French actress of her day, also confirmed him in the view that the sublime actor was one who acted with the head. Mlle Clairon was famous for the care with which she studied her roles and planned her effects, in this affording a great contrast with her principal rival, the tragedienne Dumesnil. 'What playing is more perfect than that of Clairon's?' asked Diderot, agreeing with Edward Gibbon, who recorded in an autobiographical sketch that

Two famous actresses then [1763] divided the public applause: for my own part I preferred the consummate art of the Clairon, to the intemperate sallies of the Dumesnil which were extolled by her admirers as the genuine voice of nature and passion.[30]

Diderot would have been amazed to learn that Garrick's private opinion of Mlle Clairon's acting was that it suffered from not having sensibility, an opinion that greatly undercuts the validity of the view that Diderot held so confidently and aggressively:

She has every thing [wrote Garrick to Peter Sturz on 3 January 1769] that Art and a good understanding, with great Natural Spirit can give her — But then I fear (and I only tell you my fears, and open my Soul to You) the Heart has none of those instantaneous feelings, that Life blood, that keen Sensibility, that bursts at once from Genius, and like Electrical fire shoots thro' the Veins, Marrow, Bones and all, of every Spectator.[31]

Though he may have been betrayed into exaggeration by his partisanship for Mlle Clairon and by his partial lack of understanding of Garrick's acting, Diderot nevertheless clarified issues and identified a subtle and important problem in acting which still excites psychologists and actors.[32] Moreover, he was attacking a weakness which at that time was endemic in the French theater. This was a time when French acting was too much under the spell of Du Bos's theory that only he who is moved himself can move others.[33] The practical effect of the *Paradoxe* was delayed, however, and has been felt only in the nineteenth and twentieth centuries, since the work was not published until 1831.[34]

One is tempted by Diderot's title, a temptation encouraged by the startled and discomfited cries of actors, to overlook the fact that this dialogue is an important part of Diderot's theories about all art. In the *Paradoxe* he bolstered his hypotheses by numerous references to the creative process in the sister arts. 'Why should the actor be different from the poet, the painter, the orator, the musician?'[35] Speaking of the 'great poets, great actors, and perhaps all the great imitators of nature in general, whoever they are,' Diderot characterized them as men endowed with a lively imagination, great discernment, delicate tact, and a sure taste, and then said of such great geniuses that they are, of all persons, the ones least overwhelmed by their emotions. 'They are too busy observing, exploring, imitating, to be keenly affected inside.'[36]

Thus the *Paradoxe sur le comédien* turns out to be a case study in aesthetic problems that are at least as old as Aristotle. Mainly through anecdotes, partly through assertion, sometimes through analysis, Diderot is trying to explain how the imagination gets channeled in art, so that it can be communicated and so that it can be effective. His explanation is that in all fields of creativity the great artist must be in as firm command of his sensibility as he is of his technique.

Hand in hand with this subtle and complex problem of expressiveness goes another one equally complex and subtle: how does one imitate nature?

Diderot's answer to this second problem is that the great artist discovers for himself 'ideal models.' This takes us back to the discussion of the 'modèle idéale' in the Salon de 1767, and it is noteworthy that in the Paradoxe sur le comédien Diderot specifically refers to 'my Salons' in confirmation of his argument.[37] It is by this means that he links his theory of the actor with his general aesthetic theory. In the Paradoxe sur le comédien he uses the phrase 'modèle idéale' twelve times. It is the 'ideal model' that a great actor has in mind while preparing his role. As a result of his visualization of the ideal model, he is able to achieve a precious and unique combination, an amalgam of his natural endowments with his technical education, with his observation of nature, and with his appreciation of what has gone on before in the tradition of his art. It is this amalgam that the great actor communicates; it is this that makes him sublime. But this, according to the Salon de 1767, is also what the painter or sculptor must do. For the layman this whole process, and therefore the concept of the ideal model itself, is probably easier to visualize in the case of the actor than in that of other artists. If this be so, then Diderot has provided in his Paradoxe a vehicle for the greater appreciation of all his aesthetic theory.[38]

By the time that he was beginning to think about the Paradoxe sur le comédien, Diderot's theory of artistic production had thus undergone a profound revolution, or, at the very least, a most remarkable evolutionary change. In 1758, though even this early he was talking about an ideal model, he had attributed creative productivity to sensibility:

The poets, actors, musicians, painters, the very best singers, the great dancers, tender lovers, the truly devout, all this enthusiastic and passionate troop feel vividly but think very little.

By 1769, however, when he was writing Le Rêve de d'Alembert, he had come to believe that sensibility is a kind of morbid condition of what would now be called the sympathetic nervous system. It is a condition of being 'abandoned to the discretion of the diaphragm.'

A great man, if by unlucky chance he has received such a disposition from nature, will concern himself ceaselessly with trying to weaken it, to dominate it, to make himself master of his own movements. . . . At the age of forty-five he will be a great king, a great minister, a great statesman, a great artist, especially a great actor, a great philosopher, a great poet, a great musician, a great physician. He will reign over himself and over his environment.

This is also the lesson of the Paradoxe sur le comédien, set forth fully in 1773. It had become a fixed part of Diderot's philosophy.[39]

How convinced was Diderot of his own doctrine? Was this paradox his considered judgment or was it a *jeu d'esprit?* The form of the *Paradoxe* itself would seem to show that he was thoroughly convinced of its truth. For in this dialogue, unlike most of his others, he does not query, he expounds. In this dialogue there is no clash of opinion between the two interlocutors. The first interlocutor has all the honors, makes all the points, and from beginning to end modifies his opinions not a bit. The second interlocutor suffers the fate of the subordinate interlocutors in the Platonic dialogues: he merely confirms or illustrates the master's argument. He does not challenge, or at least challenge effectively. He simply concurs. In the *Paradoxe* the ideas from Diderot's earlier book review are taken over verbatim and without dialectical sportiveness. In consequence, the *Paradoxe sur le comédien* has about it an air of dogmatism, unusual in Diderot.

Moreover, the exceptionally personal and autobiographical character of the *Paradoxe* in itself suggests that here Diderot is especially willing to identify himself with his doctrine. In the *Paradoxe,* besides referring to his *Salons,* he alludes to his plot for *Le Shérif,* speaks of the first time he met Mlle Clairon, recalls occasions when he played roles both in private life and on a stage, and reminisces about his early ambitions to be an actor. He speaks of looking up Sedaine after the success of *Le Philosophe sans le savoir* — Sedaine identifies him by name: 'Ah! Monsieur Diderot, que vous êtes beau!' — of being a guest at Necker's dinner table, of attempting to intercede for Rivière with his brother 'the theologal,' of a dispute with Marmontel, of the fact that Suard and Mme Necker had praised the *Salons,* of Sartine's urging him to write more plays, of seeing a naked model in Pigalle's studio, of an anecdote told him by Princess Galitzin and another by Galiani, and of how *Le Père de famille* had been signally successful at Naples.[40] Altogether, Diderot identified himself with the *Paradoxe sur le comédien* in a very marked way.

This identification of himself with his doctrine is, moreover, carried by Diderot into the domain of self-analysis. He insists that he has an exalted conception of the talent of a great actor. 'This man is rare; as rare as, and perhaps rarer than, a great poet.' Each was able to observe and imitate without being distracted by sensibility. This was what made them great. What, then, of himself? 'Shall I say it? Why not? Sensibility is scarcely the qualification of a great genius. . . . Sensibility is never without a defect of constitution.' And in a later passage he defines sensibility as a real constitutional weakness, 'inclining one to have no precise idea of the true, the good, and the beautiful, [and inclining one] to be unjust, to be mad.'[41] As a proof of his sincerity, Diderot calls attention to the fact that his doctrine about the great artist tended to prove that he was not one himself.

Moreover, when I declare that sensibility is the quality characterizing goodness of soul and mediocrity of genius, I am making a confession that is out of the ordinary, for if ever Nature moulded a soul characterized by sensibility, it is mine.

His admission has about it some of the wistfulness he had revealed when comparing himself with Samuel Richardson. But even here, in making such a melancholy confession, Diderot manages to compliment himself—few other men, he says, would be capable of such self-revelation.[42] Often in his life Diderot had shown himself complacent and self-gratulatory about his sensibility; yet here he is seriously saying that the impulsiveness of his feelings, the overmastering imperatives of his diaphragm, effectively preclude him from being numbered among the great. In the *Paradoxe sur le comédien* Diderot is in reaction against his own sensibility: he 'clearly chastised himself in the book. . . .'[43]

Thus Diderot's paradox is seen to be a double one — a paradox of the actor and a paradox of himself. He, the man of sensibility, the man of fervent responses and quick tears, is a man who has attained to a degree of self-knowledge that makes him speak of his own sensibility as a drawback. He reckons it a drawback even in his efforts to live wisely, for the vivacity of his sensibility makes his judgment waver and causes him to be sentimental and inconsistent. In a comment intended only for his Dutch acquaintance Hemsterhuis, Diderot at approximately this time described sensibility as a trait causing moral aberrations.

Sensibility carried to the extreme may well be the basis of the greatest suffering and the excuse for all sorts of injustices. How often has this characteristic in me caused me to grant to a visible need the assistance I ought to have given to a misfortune not so close at hand, [thus] causing remorse for what was actually a good action. . . . I would have committed many bad deeds, perhaps even heinous crimes, had my judgment not restrained my sensibility.[44]

This corroborative evidence has only recently come to light and, like other information now available from his comments on the book by Hemsterhuis, modifies our previous conception of Diderot. Formerly, thinking of his love of mystification and of his occasionally speaking of his role-playing, one had had to pose the possibility that Diderot may have utilized his knowledge of the actor's art to be an actor himself in real life.[45] But his testimony to Hemsterhuis, utterly private in intention and in a context that makes any desire to deceive highly improbable, would seem to prove that Diderot was convinced that his very sensibility might betray him. It is the testimony of a man who wants to be honest and sincere.

Meanwhile, he was spending the time pleasantly at The Hague, with the visit to Russia still to come. Through the summer interested persons in Paris and Saint Petersburg began to wonder whether he would get farther than The Hague after all.[46] He himself did not sound too sure.[47] Then a *deus ex machina* appeared on the stage and resolved all problems. This was a young Russian (born in 1742) from one of the great families, Alexis Vassilievich Narishkin, one of the chamberlains of Catherine II. Narishkin was a friend of Beccaria and had previously known Diderot in Paris. In May 1773 Narishkin was at Aix-la-Chapelle taking the waters. He 'has persuaded me that it would be a great pleasure for him and for me to travel and talk together some hundreds of leagues in the same coach.'[48] In August Narishkin showed up at The Hague and on 20 August the two travelers started out.

CHAPTER 44

Diderot in Russia

IT WAS generally supposed that on his journey to Russia, Diderot would stop off at Potsdam and Berlin on the way. Diderot's own correspondence shows that at first this was what he himself intended. Grimm's letters to his friend Count Nesselrode, at that time a chamberlain of Frederick the Great, show that it was also expected at Berlin and Potsdam that Diderot would spend a week there. Grimm, who trembled for Diderot's behavior at a court, begged Nesselrode to be the visitor's guardian:

I commend Denis to your charity. If you do not outdo yourself, he is capable of doing everything wrong. . . . Make him do what he ought to do and only what he ought. Ask him why he has not written me even once.[1]

In fact, however, Diderot and Narishkin took a more southerly route. Perhaps it was because, according to Grimm's theory, Princess Galitzin had made Diderot fear lest he be poorly received at Berlin.[2] Another explanation is that the travelers had to hurry, especially if they were to arrive in Saint Petersburg for a great state event on 9 October, the marriage of the heir apparent to a German princess. As a court chamberlain, Narishkin probably very much wanted, indeed needed, to be there.[3] When, therefore, they were delayed by Diderot's having a bad attack of colic at Duisburg, in the Ruhr, Narishkin evidently decided to avoid the additional delays attendant upon a visit to Berlin and Potsdam, and they went via Leipzig and Dresden instead.[4]

On his journey through Germany Diderot met the German man of letters Friedrich Heinrich Jacobi, who subsequently wrote of Diderot more in wonder than in admiration.[5] At Dresden he visited the art galleries, probably shown through by Christian Ludwig von Hagedorn, the author of the important *Betrachtungen über die Malerei* (1762) ['Observations on Painting']. At Dresden too Diderot had a conversation with the Spanish ambassador about the clergy in Spain.[6] Just previously, at Leipzig, Diderot's views on religion had displeased his auditors, according to the testimony of two dissenters:

His vivacity is extraordinarily great. . . . He speaks with a warmth and vehemence that almost benumbs us colder-blooded souls. Anyone who wants to make an objection or contribute something to the conversation must seize the moment quickly and at the same time speak with confidence. . . . He seizes all occasions to preach atheism, and sometimes he preaches it really with the passion of a fanatic.[7]

There is no doubt that he made a memorable impression.

The travelers pressed on, several times traveling night and day and going as much as forty-eight hours without stopping. The roads were abominable. Yet Diderot said he felt less tired than he would have been from a walk in the Bois de Boulogne. He concluded that the motion of the coach was a good counteraction to his too sedentary life. Indeed, he felt inspired to write eight occasional poems, about 'The Post from Königsberg to Memel,' about gnats in Poland, about Narishkin's toothache, and, in detail, about the purchasable but dangerous charms of 'The Servant Girl at the Sign of the Cloven Hoof, in Riga.'[8] But at Narva he was attacked by colic again. Not wanting Narishkin to be delayed, Diderot dissimulated his state, and they went on. They arrived, with Diderot 'more dead than alive,' on 8 October 1773, the day before the marriage of Grand Duke Paul to Wilhelmina of Hesse-Darmstadt.[9]

Diderot expected to stay at Falconet's, 'where I counted upon finding some herb tea, a syringe, and a bed.' For months he had been anticipating the delicious pleasure of a reunion: 'What a moment, for you and for me, when I shall be knocking at your door, when I shall enter and rush into your arms. . . .' Instead, sick as he was, he received a very brusque and chilling reception. Although a small chamber had previously been prepared for him, now there was none, for Falconet's artist son, a pupil of Sir Joshua Reynolds, had unexpectedly arrived from London and was now occupying it. Meanwhile, no alternative plans had been made for Diderot, so that when he arrived he had no choice save that of going to an inn or of asking the Narishkins to put him up. This they graciously did, and Diderot remained at the Narishkin town house throughout his stay at Saint Petersburg.[10]

Diderot's reception by Falconet must have been a very disagreeable experience for the newcomer. He was ill, in a strange country, the language of which he did not speak, and yet he was turned away by his old friend upon whom he had counted so implicitly. It is true that Falconet's son had arrived unexpectedly, but that was on 19 August, almost eight weeks before. Falconet subsequently attempted to explain his strange behavior by claiming that he had heard (though at second hand) that the Narishkins were preparing an apartment for Diderot and that consequently he had taken for granted that Diderot knew of this and had accepted the Narishkin offer. At the time Diderot, who was trying to calm down his wife, furious at the news of Falconet's reception, professed to find Falconet's explanation satisfactory. But in the long run Diderot evidently thought the excuses less than convincing, for his daughter, writing in 1787, declared that her father's 'soul was wounded forever.'[11]

Diderot had heard much of the royal marriage, especially as it was Grimm who had really engineered the match. Diderot could have been present at it, too, had it not been that his trunk was at the customs and the only clothes he had were those he was wearing; besides, he had forgotten his wig somewhere en route, 'three or four hundred leagues from here.' But perhaps he watched the wedding cortège from the Narishkin palace, for it is located on one side of the large square fronting on the great Cathedral of Saint Isaac, and the route of the procession passed that way. 'The Weather was remarkably fine,' reported Sir Robert Gunning to the Earl of Suffolk, 'which added much to the splendid appearance of the Equipages and Dresses, the Magnificence of which nothing could exceed.'[12]

Diderot's visit to Russia was a widely anticipated event. So much so that presently the British minister reported, 'Monsieur Diderot is at length arrived here.'[13] Even Diderot must sometimes have wondered just what experiences might be awaiting him. For Catherine II had recently dealt with D'Alembert very cuttingly, and Diderot must have known that she had. It proved how formidable a person — and a crowned head — Catherine II could be. D'Alembert, counting upon her good graces previously expressed at frequent intervals had asked her as a personal favor to release eight French volunteer officers who, while serving with the Poles, had been captured by the Russians. The Empress refused, but D'Alembert had the temerity to ask again. This time her refusal was peremptory and barely polite, indicating quite clearly that D'Alembert had more than used up his store of good will.[14] It is not surprising that Diderot wrote to his wife, who may have been suggesting that he ask Catherine II for some favor, 'Listen, my dear, the greater the sovereign's kindnesses towards me, the more I must use them with discretion.'[15]

Catherine II, being a politically minded woman to the point of obsession, was probably very grateful to Diderot for making the effort to come to thank her. There was great publicity value for her in his pilgrimage. People long remembered that Mme Geoffrin had traveled to Warsaw in 1766 to visit Stanislas Poniatowski, the King of Poland. Now an even more celebrated personage was traveling to Russia to see the Empress. It was good for public relations. Consequently she played up to the occasion, gave him a welcome that Grimm described as 'most *distingué*,' and certainly accorded Diderot a great share of her time. It is true, though, that she had an unusual amount of leisure just then: she had just dismissed Vasilchikov as her lover and had not yet designated Potemkin to that post.[16]

Soon after Diderot's arrival — probably no later than 15 October and certainly by the end of the month — he was seeing the Empress daily, with a standing appointment for a lengthy personal interview beginning at three in the afternoon. Diderot was profoundly impressed by Catherine II. He was especially moved by the sight of her visiting the School for Noble Girls that she had founded and of her letting the little things, 'no taller than cabbages,' gather around her, caress her, and throw their arms around her.[17] She, for her part, found Diderot astonishing but claimed that she was enchanted by him. In letters to Nesselrode, to Meister, and to Mme Necker, Grimm (who had been in Saint Petersburg since mid-September) spread the news of Diderot's success:

And with her he is just as odd, just as original, just as much Diderot, as when with you. He takes her hand as he takes yours, he shakes her arm as he shakes yours, he sits down by her side as he sits down by yours; but in this last point he obeys sovereign orders, and, as you may imagine, a man does not seat himself opposite to Her Majesty unless he is so obliged.[18]

A Carmontelle drawing of Diderot and Grimm in conversation shows the former with his hand on Grimm's shoulder in just one of these attention-demanding, sleeve-plucking gestures. 'Just as if he were in the synagogue of the Rue Royale,' wrote Grimm, meaning at D'Holbach's.[19] A letter from Catherine II to Mme Geoffrin, the original of which has never been found, is said to have been of the following tenor:

Your Diderot is a very extraordinary man. I cannot get out of my conversations with him without having my thighs bruised and black and blue. I have been obliged to put a table between him and me to shelter myself and my limbs from his gesticulation.

D'Escherny, the source for this anecdote, quite evidently accepted the story as being a fair description of Diderot's usual behavior. It was commonly said, remarked D'Escherny, that Diderot at table was in the habit of pinning the arms of his neighbors on both sides of him, talking ceaselessly, and still managing to eat with the heartiest of appetites.[20]

The courtiers must have found Diderot as difficult to deal with as he them, and for opposite reasons. He was not used to people who had trained themselves to be full of dissimulation; they were disconcerted by a person who was so naïve, so easy to mislead, but who had such august backing. One of Diderot's 'two little Germans,' who by this time had achieved an important post in Russia as secretary to Grand Duke Paul, put it this way:

He [Diderot] was at all the fêtes, all the galas, all the balls, always wearing a black suit. People's judgment about him is conditioned here by this singularity. Some look upon him with enthusiasm. Others say, 'Why, is that all it is?' . . . I perceive that it is terribly difficult to sustain a big reputation; and that it is very perilous to pass from one's study into a brilliant court. . . .[21]

On 25 October/5 November the Russian Academy of Sciences honored Diderot and Grimm by electing them foreign members.[22] The resident membership at that time seems to have been eleven, of whom by far the most distinguished were the Swiss Leonhard Euler and his son Jean-Albert Euler, both mathematicians. Diderot's letter of thanks to the Academy on 27 October/7 November contains an especially interesting statement: 'Had the Académie of Paris been free, long ago its choice would have justified yours.'[23] At the session of 1/12 November the new foreign members were inaugurated, and Diderot then read to his new confrères an elaborate questionnaire seeking information about Siberia.[24] This questionnaire revealed a great deal of knowledge of Siberia — at least to the extent of asking apposite questions about it — and of interest in it, and perhaps was inspired by Diderot's hope that he might soon be editing a new *Encyclopédie,* Russian style.[25] The answers to his questions were read to the Academy on 2/13 December but it was voted to submit these to the approval of the Director of the Academy, Count Vladimir Orlov, before sending them to Diderot.[26] It rather looks as though this consent was never given. If so, it shows how difficult it was for a person even with Diderot's backing to get any information on conditions in Russia. Strangely enough, the session in which he was inaugurated was the only meeting of the Academy of Sciences that Diderot attended, even though twenty-seven of them were held before he left the city in 1774.[27]

Meanwhile, what did Diderot and Catherine II find to talk about? The answer does not have to depend upon imaginings, for Diderot drew up a series of memoranda and left them with the Empress. These memoranda sometimes treat of literary matters but more often discuss political, economic, social, and legal questions, and are very reformist in tone. The 'Historical Essay on the Police Power in France' reaches from Clovis and Charlemagne and Charles VII to the current judicial changes of Maupeou, of which Diderot strongly disapproved. He had begun the preparation of this elaborate essay in response to Narishkin's suggestion, perhaps while still en route to Saint Petersburg, a pretty clear indication that Diderot took the initiative in these conversations of suggesting to Catherine II what the topic of discussion should be.[28] These memoranda, of which there were 65, with titles like 'The Action of the Sovereign and of a Third Estate,' 'Of Manufactures and Factories,' 'On Tolerance,' 'Concerning the Administration of Justice,' ranged from short notes to lengthy full-dress articles.[29] Their preparation required research as well as literary skill and in their detail and precise information strongly illustrate the fact that Diderot was becoming an empiricist in the social sciences as well as in the natural ones.

The title page of these memoranda, in Diderot's own hand, ran as follows: 'Philosophical and historical, etc. miscellany. . . . In the year 1773, from 15 October until 3 December.'[30] They were first published not too accurately, but a recent rigorously edited edition now allows it to be seen that Diderot's conversations with the Empress were at a level far above mere chit-chat. The serious purpose that these conversations had, in the minds of both the Empress and of Diderot, is attested by Diderot's recalling in a letter to Catherine II in 1781 that 'Your Majesty said to me that the press of daily affairs took up all her time and that, by placing me close to her, she would engage me to meditate upon various texts relative to legislation.' As Paul Vernière reconstructs what must have happened:

Before each meeting Diderot drew up some notes on subjects of his own determining or sometimes on those suggested to him by Narishkin. At the Winter Palace the reading of these would be followed by a discussion. After the interview, Diderot revised, sometimes corrected, and rearranged these memoranda before placing them in the hands of the Empress.[31]

Diderot's ambition was to convert Catherine II to the philosophy of the Enlightenment, or at least to reinforce what there were of her liberal convictions.[32] In order to accomplish this, he presented his views by tactful indirection or adroit analogy or skillful insinuation, rather than by open confrontation. One of his most serious and earnest chapters was entitled 'The Daydream of Denis the Philosopher.' After all, he was dealing with a sovereign whom Voltaire described at that very time as wielding 'the most despotic power on earth.' [33]

These notes and essays — on the desirability of free competition in commerce and in government jobs, on the importance of settling the succession to the Russian throne, on the legislative commission that Catherine II had convened in 1767, on public education, on luxury, usury, divorce, academies, 'On a Way of Drawing Benefit from Religion and Making it Good for Something,' etc., etc. — explain why Diderot could write to his wife, 'I worked a great deal while en route; I am working a great deal here.' [34]

Catherine II now and again asked him some very searching questions in return, and in answering them Diderot had to call on all his resources of tactfulness, a commodity which his friends thought he had in very slender supply. She pressed him to tell her what was in Rulhière's manuscript about the *coup d'état* of 1762. 'As for what concerns you in it, Madame,' Diderot replied, 'if you hold in high esteem the proprieties and the virtues, those outworn rags and tatters of your sex, this work is a satire against you; but if grand designs, if patriotic and manly ideas interest you more, the author depicts you as a great princess, and, taking everything together, does you more honor than harm.' To which she replied, 'You make me want to read it more than ever.' [35] Diderot praised the Empress fulsomely — 'the soul of Brutus with the charms of Cleopatra' — to her face, in conversations with others, and in his letters.[36] But he also had the courage to let her guess at his disapproval of the partition of Poland, an event which had occurred in 1772.[37] And he pertinaciously spoke out against despotic government:

A despot, be he the best of men, commits a crime by governing according to his own sweet will. He is a good shepherd who reduces his subjects to the level of animals. . . . One of the great misfortunes that could happen to a free nation would be two or three consecutive reigns of a just and enlightened despotism. Three sovereigns in a row like Elizabeth, and the English would have been imperceptibly led to a condition of servitude of which no one could predict the end.[38]

At Saint Petersburg Diderot suddenly found himself caught up in the diplomatic maneuverings of great powers, perhaps very much against his will. He had left Paris with no official responsibilities or commissions. On the contrary, the Duc d'Aiguillon wrote scornfully and resentfully about Diderot to the French ambassador at Saint Petersburg; and it was said around Paris that when Diderot inquired of the proper minister whether the government had any objection to his going to Russia, the reply was that far from there being any objection to his going, he could remain there if he liked.[39] But once arrived at Saint Petersburg, Diderot was made to feel differently by the French ambassador, François-Michel Durand de Distroff. 'I have told M. Diderot what I expect from a Frenchman. He has promised me he will efface, if it be possible, the prejudices that this princess has against us.'[40]

According to Sir Robert Gunning, the British minister at Saint Petersburg, who in this instance received his information from Count Panin, the Russian Minister of Foreign Affairs, Diderot vehemently resisted such a departure from his proper sphere.[41] Nevertheless, whether by flattery or by threats, he was persuaded to try to get Catherine II to change her foreign policy — this was the burden of the memorandum that he entitled 'The Daydream of Denis the Philosopher' — so that presently Sir Robert Gunning, reversing his earlier dispatch, was reporting that

Count Panin acquainted me in the utmost Confidence and under the seal of secrecy that Mo[r] Diderot had taken advantage of the constant Access he has had to the Empress to put into her hands a few days ago a paper given him by M[r] Durand containing proposals for a peace with the Turks; which the Court of France engage to obtain if its good offices were accepted by her. Mo[r] Diderot apologized for acting thus out of his sphere, by the fear he had of being thrown into the Bastille when he returned home, should he have refused complying with the French Minister's request. Her Majesty's answer, as Mo[r] Panin tells me, was that on that account she passed by the impropriety of his conduct, and on the condition that he faithfully reported to the Minister the use she made of the paper, which was throwing it into the fire.[42]

If this was the way it happened, it must have been discomfiting and humiliating to Diderot. Furthermore, he must also have greatly feared lest his standing with the Empress be disastrously undermined. Yet as late as 31 December 1773 the French ambassador was still under the impression that Diderot was continuing to try to influence her policy:

The conferences of Catherine and Diderot continue without interruption and get longer from day to day. He has told me, and I have reason to believe that he is not untrustworthy, that he has described the danger of the Russian alliance with the King of Prussia and the utility of one with us.[43]

Meanwhile, Diderot's success with the Empress did not preclude his being very homesick. Grimm reported on 25 November that Diderot had 'the Swiss sickness *in gradu heroico,* enough to make me anxious sometimes.'[44] The news from home, however, was reassuring. Angélique's first child, a daughter, was born in September: 'Well, my dear,' Diderot wrote to her, 'here you are, a mother. The Lord only knows what a grave and wise personage you are going to become.' Mme Diderot, who had spent the early weeks of Diderot's absence grumbling to her heart's content, constantly re-arranging the furniture, and discharging servants almost as soon as she hired them, was very helpful in her daughter's accouchement and earned Diderot's high praise for thinking to ask the sculptor Pigalle to be the child's god-father.[45]

How did Diderot spend his time when not in conference with the Empress? A good part of it was consumed in being ill. In November and into December he had a stubborn case of the colic and was unable to go with the Empress to Tsarskoe Selo, whither she had invited him. 'The cold and the waters of the Neva deranged his health prodigiously,' wrote his daughter later. 'I am convinced that the journey shortened his life.' His health was still uncertain in January, as Catherine II mentioned in a letter to Voltaire, and he was so ill in February that it delayed the start of his journey home.[46] Another considerable part of his time was spent in the literary work necessary for his preparation of memoranda of conversations with Catherine II, together with (most probably) his critique of the book by Hemsterhuis and, perhaps his *Réfutation de l'ouvrage d'Helvétius intitulé L'Homme*. 'I am working prodigiously, and with an ease that astonishes me.'[47] During his stay at Saint Petersburg he sat for the haunting portrait that Dmitri Levitskiĭ did of him.[48] And he spent part of his time, though perhaps not much of it, in studying Russian, as is proved by the interlineations and marginal notes he made on a Russian grammar and some other Russian books he brought back to Paris.[49]

Sometimes he visited Falconet, though there is no evidence that Falconet ever visited him. Diderot especially wanted to see the statue of Peter the Great. This sculpture was now far advanced in its modeling stage, and there had already been transported from a bog in Finland — one of the engineering feats of the century — an enormous granite boulder of 275 tons to serve as the statue's base. Diderot praised the sculpture to the skies. 'I always knew that you are a very able man; but may I die if I thought that you had anything like this in your head. How could I have guessed that this astonishing conception could exist in the same understanding by the side of the dainty image of the statue of Pygmalion?'[50]

A person as sociable as Diderot would want to spend much of his time in a congenial group. This, however, was not easy for him. He could not spend all his time with Catherine II; it was hard to recapture the feelings of intimacy he had once shared with Falconet; nor does he seem to have made the Narishkin palace the center of his social life, although he received the visits of Nolcken, the Swedish ambassador, there. Nicolay recalled in his memoirs that Diderot was often invited to the houses of highly placed courtiers, where he constantly played the role of a declared atheist and was abhorred by everybody. And Grimm admitted that Diderot had made 'no conquest here, save that of the Empress.'[51]

Diderot was fully aware of court factions at Saint Petersburg, for in 1768 he had reminded Falconet to remember, when he met Nicolay and La Fermière, Diderot's 'two little Germans' of some years before, that they belonged 'to M. Panin and the Grand Duke; while you belong to General Betzki and the Empress.' So perspicacious a comment may explain why Diderot had not been very eager to come to Russia in the first place.[52] But now, when Nicolay remonstrated with Diderot for being so disregardful of courtier opinion, he merely smiled and said, 'I court the favor of the lady of the house only, and scarcely care about the servants.'[53]

The circle at the court that Diderot found the most congenial and hospitable was that of which General Betzki was the bellwether. This included Nicolas-Gabriel Clerc, physician of the Corps of [noble] Cadets at Petersburg; Anastasia Sokolov, Betzki's natural daughter and a favorite maid-in-waiting of Catherine II; and Mme Sophie de La Font and her daughter Wilhelmine, both associated with the School for Noble Girls that Catherine II had established at the Smolny Convent in 1764.[54] This was the circle that was most concerned with Catherine II's art acquisitions and her educational reforms, precisely the areas of two of Diderot's enthusiasms. Diderot, in fact, having been greatly impressed by the amateur theatricals at the Smolny Convent but struck by the number of 'shocking utterances on these innocent lips,' had volunteered to clean up Molière and Racine and other classics of the French theater, 'sixteen or seventeen of them.' Thus would be eliminated anything inimical to the young girls' innocence. Voltaire had previously consented to adapt some of these works, but his zeal had flagged. 'What Voltaire has not done and what he could have done better than I, I shall do. I have promised it to Your Imperial Majesty and I shall keep my word.'[55] Over a year later Diderot was still promising 'the comedies for the young ladies.'[56] No actual examples of his bowdlerizing, however, have come to light.

In addition to this promise to the School for Noble Girls, Diderot also became connected with another of Catherine II's educational establishments, this time as honorary curator of the Asylum for Foundlings at Moscow. In gratitude the Council of the Imperial Household of Education, headed by

Betzki and with seven other signatories, awarded Diderot a diploma, though just what duties he undertook are not known.[57]

Diderot made serious efforts to secure information about conditions in Russia. 'I do not neglect any effort to inform myself here.' Though unsuccessful, so far as is known, in getting from the Academy of Sciences information about Siberia, he wrote on Catherine II's recommendation to Count Münich, the Imperial Director of Customs. 'Pardon this importunity on the part of a foreigner who would very much like not to return home entirely ignorant.' His questions were searching ones: what is the annual amount and value of the production of grain, of hemp and linen, of timber? How much of it is sold abroad? What is the approximate population of the Empire, of Moscow, of Petersburg, of other principal cities? What are the annual exports of pottery and leather goods, fish and caviar? What are the imports of horses, of oil? What is the ratio of a day laborer's wages to the cost of bread? What are maritime freight rates? Does the coastal trade employ many ships? The Empress begs you to try to find for me a tabulation as complete as possible of weights and measures. Also of monies. Are there any banks or insurance companies in the Empire? What is the total revenue of the Empire? What is the public debt? [58]

So far as is known, Münich never replied to this inquiry.

Diderot had asked the Empress these questions and many more. There are said to be 7,300 monks and 5,300 nuns in Russia. Is this number diminishing? What is the condition of the Jews in Russia? What are the laws regulating the grain trade? What is the annual distillation of grain alcohol? What are the regulations regarding tobacco? Are you increasing your mulberry culture and your silk farms? What are the legal rights of landowners in Russia? Does not the servitude of the rural workers adversely affect agriculture? To many of these questions Catherine II gave replies to her own satisfaction without referring to Münich. To Diderot's question about the serfs she replied, 'I know of no country where the worker loves his land and his home more than in Russia.' [59]

Catherine II always found Diderot's play of intellect brilliant and dazzling. But what was her considered opinion of him as the novelty wore off? She always praised him, but a cynic might say that that was to be expected as a part of the public relations game. Besides, the word that she repeatedly took refuge in when describing him to Voltaire, 'extraordinary,' can be ambiguous and not very discriminating. 'I find in Diderot an inexhaustible imagination, and I reckon him among the most extraordinary men who have ever existed.' In a letter some time later she wrote, 'Diderot's is a most extraordinary head.

. . . the hearts of all men should be of his stamp.' And again, 'It's a very extraordinary head. You do not often find any like it.' [60] The more one analyzes these judgments, the more ambiguously they can be interpreted. The Empress was reported by the French ambassador at the end of 1773 as saying that in certain respects Diderot was a hundred years old and in others he was not ten.[61]

It may be significant that Diderot's memorandum book of his discussions with Catherine II gives a terminal date of 5 December 1773, three whole months before he left Saint Petersburg. Does this not suggest that he himself was aware that after that date their conversations had not been of a nature that could change policy? [62] Perhaps so, for Diderot's questioning of the Empress and then of Count Münich, though occurring after 5 December, was merely for the purpose of Diderot's receiving information. Moreover, in spite of the French ambassador's reporting that the conferences got longer from day to day, Diderot himself wrote to his family on 30 December that, though he had the privilege of daily access to the Empress' study, he used the privilege only every three days, his reason being that he wanted to avoid exciting envy and enmity.[63] No doubt a good reason, but why had he not felt its cogency sooner? Perhaps sometime in November or December Catherine II had made him feel that she did not value his advice so highly as he had previously supposed. Such was her account of their relations when, years later, she talked about Diderot to the Comte de Ségur:

I frequently had long conversations with him, but with more curiosity than profit. Had I placed faith in him, every institution in my empire would have been overturned; legislation, administration, politics and finances, would all have been changed for the purpose of substituting some impracticable theories.

However, as I listened more than I talked, any one, on being present, would have supposed him to be the commanding pedagogue and myself the humble scholar. Probably he was of that opinion himself, for, after some time, finding that he had not wrought in my government any of those great innovations which he had advised, he exhibited his surprise by a sort of haughty discontent.

Then speaking to him freely, I said: 'Monsieur Diderot, I have listened with the greatest pleasure to all that your brilliant genius has inspired you with; but all your grand principles, which I understand very well, though they will make fine books, would make sad work in actual practice. You forget, in all your plans for reformation, the difference between our two positions: you work only upon paper, which submits to every thing; it is altogether obedient and supple, and opposes no obstacles, either to your imagination or to your pen; whereas I, a poor Empress, I work upon human nature, which is, on the contrary, irritable and easily offended.'

I am satisfied that, from that time, he pitied me, and looked on me as one possessed only of a narrow and ordinary mind. From that moment he spoke to me only on literary subjects, and politics disappeared from our conversations.[64]

It must be remembered that the moment of Diderot's visit became singularly inauspicious for liberal reforms in Russia. Not only was Catherine worried about bringing Russia's war with Turkey to a successful end but also this was precisely the time of the Pugachev revolt, perhaps the most serious and dangerous peasant uprising (from the point of view of the existing regime) in the history of the Czardom. Only some three weeks after Diderot's arrival in Saint Petersburg, the British minister reported that 'An extraordinary council was held the other day in consequence, it is said, of accounts being received of a fresh insurrection of the Don Cossacks, as well as of one in the Province of Oremburg. . . .'[65] In Saint Petersburg the revolt was treated as a non-event. 'Everything relative to the insurrection in the province of Oremburg is kept as secret as possible. . . .' On Christmas Day the government did issue a proclamation (in Russian) guardedly acknowledging the rebellion, but as late as February 1774, not long before Diderot left Saint Petersburg, the British minister remarked that the reports of the revolt were still 'kept very secret.'[66] So far as can be ascertained, Diderot may have had no intimation of the revolt at the time, though a year later, it is true, he claimed that Catherine II had told him about it.[67] The revolt intensified through December 1773 and January 1774, causing D'Alembert to wonder in a letter to Voltaire in February whether Catherine II could keep her throne.[68] Of course the worry of it nagged at her: 'The Empress is at present a good deal out of Order,' wrote Sir Robert Gunning on 24 January/4 February 1774. 'She has been frequently so of late; and it is possible that the disagreeable Turn affairs have taken has somewhat contributed to her indisposition. The Insurrection in Oremburg, and the Height it has been allowed to get to, has certainly given her great Uneasiness.' Eventually Pugachev was captured and executed and the revolt collapsed, but when Diderot left Saint Petersburg this was still months away. In February Gunning wrote,

It does not escape Observation that the Empress's Temper is much altered of late; that there does not appear the same Affability and Condescension about Her, that She has hitherto been remarked for. The embarrassed Situation of her Affairs has probably had an Effect upon her Disposition, as well as upon her Health. . . .[69]

This was scarcely a propitious time for a liberal *philosophe* to be suggesting change.

While at Saint Petersburg Diderot got a bitter taste of the malice of Frederick the Great. A review of the recent unauthorized edition of Diderot's collected works, published at Amsterdam in 1773, appeared in the *Nouvelles Littéraires* of Berlin on 21 December of that year. Within three weeks it was being sedulously circulated at the Russian court. Grimm thought that Samuel Formey, the Secretary of the Prussian Academy, was the author. Some 'charitable' person, said Grimm, had not only informed Diderot that this attack upon him was going the rounds in Saint Petersburg but also had said that it had been written 'by a most illustrious hand.' Heavy with sarcasm, the review was either written by Frederick II or inspired by him. It was up-to-date, thus conveying all the greater air of authenticity: the author mentioned that Diderot had become a member of the Russian Academy and even knew that he had asked it for information regarding Siberia. The reviewer remarked of Diderot's articles on philosophy reprinted from the *Encyclopédie* that they had not been hard to do; all that had been necessary was to translate them from Brucker, whose work, the reviewer stated, was far superior to what any Encyclopedist was capable of. He called Diderot's *Pensées sur l'interprétation de la nature* 'a sublime tissue of nonsense,' the *Bijoux indiscrets* 'a masterpiece of unreason and indecency,' and declared that Diderot's plays 'are not written so that they can be acted and are scarcely better suited to be read.' In short, the reviewer hoped that his comments would help potential buyers to decide 'whether to procure this treasure for themselves or to get along without it. It is probable that the majority of sensible folk will take the latter course.' At Saint Petersburg, according to Grimm, this review was being circulated by no less a personage than the Prussian ambassador.[70]

Frederick wanted Diderot to pass by Berlin, and even sent a special emissary, Count Goertz, to Saint Petersburg to talk Diderot into it.[71] No doubt it was a matter of general remark that Diderot had not traveled via Berlin on his way to Russia, and Frederick II wanted to be sure that this slight would not occur again. As late as 11 March 1774 he expected to be seeing Diderot in Berlin or Potsdam.[72] But at the same time the king was writing very critically of Diderot, as in a letter to D'Alembert:

Diderot is at St. Petersburg, where the Empress has heaped favors upon him. They say, however, that people find him argumentative, boring; he is forever harping on the same string. I do not know what there is about his works; I cannot abide reading them, intrepid reader though I am. There is a self-satisfied tone and an arrogance about them that revolts my instinct of liberty.[73]

And soon there began to circulate in Europe rumors coming from Berlin that Diderot had been subjected to derision by some of the courtiers in Saint Petersburg.[74]

Grimm wanted to return to Paris by way of Berlin for business reasons, with perhaps a call upon King Stanislas Poniatowski at Warsaw on the way, and at first it had been presumed that Diderot would go home in his friend's company, probably in February.[75] At this point, in spite of Grimm's efforts, Diderot absolutely refused to go near Berlin.[76] So resolutely did he refuse that the plans for their returning together had to be foregone, a decision made by mid-January.[77] As Diderot explained to Mme d'Epinay, how could he tell that Frederick II would not choose to insult or humiliate him, once the King had him there? 'I was thoroughly resolved . . . above all to avoid the King of Prussia, who does not like me, whom I heartily repay in kind, whose welcome would not have afforded me great pleasure and from whom a marked coolness would have mortified me exceedingly.'[78]

During the last few weeks of Diderot's stay in Saint Petersburg he seems to have passed into a strange stage of inactivity. He wrote only three letters between the first of the year and his departure on 5 March, one introducing the Comte de Crillon to Princess Dashkov, one of farewell to the Russian Academy of Sciences (in which he asked again for the reply to his questions on Siberia), and one of farewell to the Empress herself.[79] The only other specific event of record during those eight weeks was the presentation to Diderot by the Metropolitan of Saint Petersburg and Novgorod of a magnificent copy of the Bible in Cyrillic characters, published at Kiev in 1758. This treasure is now in the Bibliothèque Nationale at Paris, Diderot having sold it to the Bibliothèque du Roi as soon as he got home.[80] And that is the sum of his activities for two months as far as any evidence remains.

This meager record, especially the lack of letters to friends and relatives at home, what does it signify? Illness, certainly; but also, most likely, dispiritedness. 'M. Diderot has told me that he writes to nobody,' remarked Crillon to D'Alembert in late January. ' "I am too far off from my friends to talk with them. I have tried twenty times. After I have said, 'My relatives, my friends, I want to get away, I want to get away,' nothing else occurs to me." '[81]

Persons at Saint Petersburg friendly to Diderot acknowledged that he had been the victim of intrigues while he was there, so that perhaps the Berlin rumors of a mathematical prank having been played upon him were not made up of whole cloth.[82] Grimm wrote to Nesselrode in January, 'You would not be able to believe all the obscure and underhanded persecutions that Denis has experienced here.' Another of Nesselrode's Saint Petersburg correspondents spoke vaguely but unmistakably of the courtiers' dislike of Diderot, finally remarking that 'He had the fate that most men have who pay too little attention to envy and jealousy to answer calumnies.' And the Swedish ambassador (who tried hard to get Diderot to return by way of Stockholm) wrote of him at the time of his departure, '. . . during his stay at Petersburg he was exposed to the most envenomed jealousy and to the blackest calumny. Frankness and freedom from self-interest are virtues that slaves are unworthy of feeling and which they detest. The Russians were in despair that a man possessing these qualities should have free access to their sovereign . . . .'[83]

Since the two friends were not returning together, the Empress appointed a Greek named Athanasius Bala to accompany Diderot. Little is known of Bala, whom Grimm described as 'likable and reliable,' save that he was a minor official in the Russian diplomatic service, had been secretary of the Russian delegation at the Conference of Foksiany in Moldavia in 1772, and that Diderot came to like him very much.[84] By late January plans were settled for Diderot to return to The Hague, perhaps to stay there several months. And on 5 March 1774 he started out.[85]

During his stay in Saint Petersburg Diderot had refused gifts that he thought were too sumptuous. The Empress had wanted to give him an expensive muff, but he said he would only lose it; and an elegant pelisse, but he accepted only one of fox, 'such,' wrote Nolcken, 'as the lowest class of bourgeois wear in our country.'[86] He did accept 3000 rubles for his expenses, a sum which came to 12,600 livres when he exchanged it. In addition, he asked for an inexpensive memento of her, a 'bagatelle,' the value of which consisted only in her having used it: 'Your cup and saucer.' In response she gave him when he left a cameo ring, the stone of which was cut with her portrait. But the exchange was not all one-sided. Diderot made parting gifts too. He gave Catherine II an enamel plaque and two small pictures. These, added to the cost of gifts he felt he owed the Narishkins for their kindnesses to him, added up to a value of about six or seven thousand livres. The Parisian bourgeois, the boy from provident little Langres, was not exactly niggardly.[87] Of course, he could afford these gifts and still be ahead, for the Empress paid for his carriage and traveling expenses back to The Hague.

Diderot took great pains with his farewell letter to Catherine II, and asked the advice of Grimm and other trusted friends before submitting it. It is a courtier's document — no wonder Grimm approved of it. Diderot described the pain that he felt upon leaving and declared that his relatives and friends could not possibly receive a greater proof of his fondness and attachment than his tearing himself away from the Empress to return to them. Catherine II liked that, and quoted it to Voltaire. Diderot liked it too, and used large portions of his letter, unchanged, when he wrote to Sophie Volland.[88]

Later Diderot confessed that he had not really seen Russia. He had rejected the opportunity to go to Moscow, to his subsequent regret. As for Saint Petersburg, 'Petersburg is just the Court: a confused mass of palaces and hovels, of *grands seigneurs* surrounded by peasants and purveyors.'[89] But though he had not seen Russia, he made some shrewd observations about the Russians. Thus, in one of his memoranda to the Empress, he remarked that 'It seems to me that in general your subjects err on the side of one extreme or the other, either in believing their nation too advanced or in believing it too backward.' Here is the kernel of the century-old debate between the Slavophiles and the Westernizers.

Diderot thought that there was a furtiveness in Russian behavior which was the result of their political and social institutions.

. . . I seem to have observed quite generally a circumspection, a distrust which seems to me to be the opposite of that attractive and straightforward frankness which characterizes spirits that are lofty, free, and secure. . . .

A century later an eminent French intellectual who had lived in Russia and had once been the tutor of the Czarevitch who became Nicholas II expressed his recognition of the accuracy of this remark by Diderot. 'Whoever has observed that over there knows how to look.' His comment was inspired by Diderot's statement that in Russia 'there is a nuance of panic terror in the attitude of people. Apparently it is the result of a long series of revolutions and of a prolonged despotism. They always seem to be existing just before an earthquake or just after it, and they have the appearance of trying to find out if the ground is really firm under their feet.'[90]

The evidence regarding Diderot in Russia leaves one with the feeling that his visit turned out to be a not very joyous one. At some time — we do not know just when or where — Diderot burned the notes on Russia he had taken.[91] Why? No very cheerful reason suggests itself. Perhaps he himself provided the answer, indirectly, in what he wrote to Mme Necker in 1774:[92]

I will confess to you, very much under my breath, that we *philosophes,* who give the impression of best having known what despotism is, have seen it only through the neck of a bottle. What a difference there is between a tiger painted by Oudry and a tiger in the forest.

CHAPTER 45

Return to the West

DIDEROT left Saint Petersburg in a new carriage provided by Catherine II and so constructed that he could lie down in it.[1] On those wintry roads it lasted 635 versts (about 450 miles). His route lay through the Baltic Provinces and East Prussia — Narva, Riga, Mitau (where the carriage gave out), Königsberg, Danzig, Stettin — and by the time they arrived in Hamburg, Bala and he were in their fourth carriage.[2] As they had crossed the Dvina the ice began to give way under the carriage and the travelers very nearly drowned. This adventure inspired Diderot to verse, a graphic account in eight strophes, mock-heroic in form but serious enough in the sense of fright that it communicates.[3]

At Hamburg the unconventional traveler, seeking to buy some unpublished sonatas for his daughter, announced his presence to Karl Philipp Emmanuel Bach:

I am French. My name is Diderot. I enjoy some consideration in my country as a man of letters. I am the author of some plays, among which *Le Père de famille* is perhaps not unknown to you. I am also the editor of the *Encyclopédie*. I am a friend of Johann Bach, and my daughter, who plays your compositions, has long since taught me to admire you. . . . I come now from Petersburg, traveling by post, with a dressing gown under my greatcoat and without any other change of clothing; were it not for that, I would not fail to call upon a man as famous as Emmanuel.

Diderot had chosen this unusual traveling dress, Grimm explained to one of his correspondents, precisely in order not to have to make any ceremonial calls en route. Thus, though he left Hamburg with a promise of some sonatas from Bach, he did not pay a call upon the composer.[4]

Diderot and Bala arrived at The Hague on the morning of 5 April 1774. Comfortably reinstalled at the Galitzins', Diderot's first business was to announce to his correspondents his safe return to the West, taking care also to tell them what he wanted them to believe about his visit: it had been a triumph; the Russian courtiers had been very kind to him; he had completely maintained his independence and integrity by refusing to be mercenary; Catherine II 'is the soul of Caesar with all the seductions of Cleopatra.' [5]

Diderot's second item of business was to arrange for the publication of the edicts of Catherine II establishing her various charitable and educational foundations. Moreover, he stayed on at The Hague, despite his impatience, until he had seen the work through the press, incidentally forming a low opinion of Dutch printers and publishers. It was not until late October that he saw Paris; he had lingered all these months in Holland out of a sense of obligation to Catherine II. The edition of *Les Plans et les Statuts,* bearing here and there some slight indications of Diderot's pen, was published in 1775. [6]

While in Russia, Diderot had proposed to Catherine II the publication of a new *Encyclopédie* of which he would be the editor, undertaking to complete the manuscript within six years:

I seek no other honorarium than that of erecting a great literary monument in honor of Your Imperial Majesty; of leaving after me on earth some durable trace of my existence; of consecrating the last years of my life to raising a pyramid on which to inscribe the august and blessed name of my benefactress. [7]

During all the five months of his stay in Russia, he had negotiated with Betzki about the terms. When Diderot departed, his farewell letter to Catherine II clearly revealed that it was Betzki who was the impediment to an agreement. 'The *Encyclopédie* is not going to be redone, and my fine dedication is to remain in my head. . . . [But] My pyramid, which now is altogether set aside, will be re-erected at the least sign from Your Majesty,' a remark which suggests that Diderot was plainly trying to go over Betzki's head. When Diderot reached The Hague he learned from a letter sent by Dr. Nicolas-Gabriel Clerc that Betzki, save for three provisos all easy to carry out, was ready to proceed. Diderot wrote Mme Diderot that he would receive an advance of 200,000 francs for expenses, of which the Diderots would have all the interest until the fund was used up in six years, and he instructed his wife to get ready to move from the Rue Taranne to an apartment 'in some quarter in keeping with this undertaking.' But Mme Diderot was to say nothing about the project — 'first, because it is not a certainty, though it is likely'; and, secondly, because 'our children would torment us to get from us what ought to be regarded as a sacred trust.' [8]

A letter from Betzki, not now extant, would seem to have authorized the new *Encyclopédie,* and in anticipation Diderot left off preparing an edition of his own complete works. As late as mid-September he was writing to Catherine II as though he understood that it was still her will that the *Encyclopédie* be redone. But Betzki sent no money and this is the last that we ever hear of the project. Probably it is safe to conclude that Catherine II did not really want to commit herself to a work the editor of which was not under her dominion, and that it had been Betzki's role to temporize and frustrate and eventually to discourage.[9]

Still another item of Diderot's business at The Hague was to give François Hemsterhuis the criticisms he had solicited of his *Lettre sur l'homme et ses rapports,* published in 1772. Diderot's extensive comments, made in a copy of the book interfoliated with blank pages, along with internal evidence, make it seem probable that he took the volume with him to Russia and worked upon it there. Hemsterhuis' aim, in his own words, was to demonstrate 'that Reason alone . . . would never lead us to systems of materialism and libertinism.' Apparently, though he did not specifically say so, he was trying to refute D'Holbach's *Système de la nature.* The *Lettre sur l'homme et ses rapports* was a little book, but it was also a greatly ambitious one. It was a reactionary one, too, starting out as it does by complaining of the injury done to morality by the freedom of the press.[10] In short, in brief compass it challenged all of Diderot's most firmly held and deeply cherished beliefs, so that his response is of capital importance in coming to an understanding of his philosophy.

Starting with the assumptions of an Idealistic philosophy, Hemsterhuis quickly but clumsily raised all the metaphysical and ethical questions that had been besetting mankind since the time of Plato. In order to comment upon them, Diderot naturally had to reply upon a broad front, with the result that the 'Commentaire sur Hemsterhuis' presents an opportunity to glimpse the totality of Diderot's philosophy in one focus. During these years Diderot was writing some very important works on different aspects of philosophy — on cosmogeny and cosmology in *Le Rêve de d'Alembert,* on metaphysics in the *Principes philosophiques sur la matière et le mouvement,* on ethics in the *Réfutation de l'ouvrage d'Helvétius intitulé L'Homme,* on the philosophical implications of anatomy and physiology in the *Eléments de physiologie,* on the existence of God in the *Entretien d'un philosophe avec la maréchale de * * *.* Now, in the course of his comments — some 20,000 words that are in effect a dialogue, like so many other of his writings — he draws upon the arguments of all these works. Moreover, there is nothing in the 'Commentaire sur Hemsterhuis' that is inconsistent with

Diderot's other writings. Thus one is able to appreciate more readily the flexibility and complexity of his philosophical thought, and also to gain a clearer appreciation of its coherence, self-consistency, and substantiality.

Diderot's approach to the Hemsterhuis book was courteous, sober, and without expostulation. Even as he made constant objections to the vagueness and ambiguity of the words Hemsterhuis used, Diderot revealed once again, by his own clarity and precision, his abiding concern for accurate language as the indispensable tool for the expression of ideas. Diderot demanded of both Hemsterhuis and himself a high standard of logical thinking and consistency which imparts to his 'Commentaire' a sense of professional philosophic rigor.[11]

In concluding his comments, Diderot remarked to Hemsterhuis on the necessity experienced by several contemporary French authors — Buffon, Voltaire — to dress their philosophy in Harlequin's clothes in order to avert persecution. 'I myself have escaped by dint of using the subtlest tone of irony I could muster, by generalities, by being laconic, and by being obscure.' [12] This is a very interesting confession, for Diderot's contemporaries often complained that he was obscure, his enemies asserting that he was the Lycophron of the eighteenth century.

How characteristic it was of Diderot to take all the time that these elaborate comments cost him, and all for the exclusively private use of a somewhat casual acquaintance. It was generous, but it was also illustrative of that good-natured willingness on Diderot's part to use up his precious time, that characteristic of which Grimm complained so frequently and exploited so shamelessly. Diderot asked Hemsterhuis to copy out the comments and burn the interfoliated volume.[13] This Hemsterhuis, fortunately for posterity, did not do. Since 1964 Diderot's 'Commentaire sur Hemsterhuis' has been accessible for close study. It is having considerable impact upon the conception of Diderot as a philosopher.

Diderot arrived at The Hague fatigued, too tired to work, and looking very old. He slept a great deal and presently his literary interests began to stir again.[14] These took on a political complexion, partly because the death of Louis XV on 10 May raised hopes that significant changes would occur in France, partly because of Diderot's continuing dislike of Frederick II of Prussia, partly because of the effect upon Diderot of his Russian experiences with the tiger in the jungle.

The first manifestation of this reawakened interest was a series of some 225 aphorisms that he jotted down as he was reading Tacitus. Imagining himself a Machiavellian and despotic sovereign, Diderot distilled from the

Annals maxims of *Realpolitik,* giving them eventually the name of *Principes de politique des souverains.*[15] This compendium is aimed at Frederick II, who is unmistakably alluded to in some of the closing paragraphs; but Diderot may also have had Catherine II in mind, for many of the aphorisms could fit her as well.[16] Most of the remarks are unsurpassably cynical and grim, giving the work a flavor of bitterness under a satirical surface of heavy irony. The collection is, however, enigmatic and difficult to interpret. This is because Diderot frequently allows himself to forget the role he is playing and interjects his own sentiments and convictions. For instance, it would seem to be Diderot and not the supposititious sovereign who could write, 'There are no valid remonstrances save those made with a bayonet at the end of a gun.'[17] There can be no doubt that in this 'pamphlet,' as he called it, Diderot expresses his horror of despotism. But his mixing of personages makes the work baffling and ambiguous and gives the reader a feeling of having double vision.

During these six months and more that he spent at The Hague, Diderot also wrote his lengthy and substantial *Observations sur le Nakaz.*[18] This comprises his comments on a famous document written by Catherine II. In 1767 she had drawn up her *Instruction* (in Russian, *Nakaz*) for the guidance of the representatives from all over Russia whom she convened in Moscow. Her purpose had been to have them 'compose a new code of laws.' But the deputies, who after February 1768 met in Saint Petersburg, were sent home in December of that year, with nothing accomplished. Diderot had hopes as late as 1774 that she would recall them, but she never did.[19] Meanwhile, she had her *Nakaz* published, and dazzled Europe by the apparent liberality of her views.

The *Nakaz* touched upon all the standard topics of political theory, of jurisprudence, and of the causes of the wealth of nations. In the course of it Catherine II freely plundered the writings of Montesquieu and Beccaria. Diderot, rather oddly, shows no signs of having read the *Nakaz* before he visited Russia. But by September 1774 he had. Moreover, 'I have had the insolence,' he wrote the Empress, 'to reread it with my pen in hand.'[20]

Diderot plainly wanted Catherine to ask to see his *Observations sur le Nakaz,* for he alluded to it again in December 1774. She did not ask for it, however, nor did she read it until after his death, when his manuscripts arrived in Russia along with his books. The *Observations* made her furious. She declared that apparently his whole life long Diderot had had the sort of discretion that would have justified his being put under guardianship. 'This is a piece of genuine twaddle,' she wrote to Grimm, 'in which can be found neither knowledge of circumstances nor prudence nor perspicacity.'[21]

Of course Catherine II had had international public opinion in mind when she allowed the *Nakaz* to be published in Western languages. Insisting that 'Russia is a European State,' she cunningly implied throughout the work that Russia was not a despotism but a monarchy, thus making in her own favor a distinction that readers of Montesquieu would find both familiar and convincing.[22] As a corollary, she sedulously avoided using the ugly terms 'despot' and 'despotism.'

But if she was reluctant to use the word, Diderot was not. 'The Empress of Russia is certainly despotic. Is it her intention to maintain despotism and transmit it to her successors or to abdicate it?' Some of what he found, as he went through the *Nakaz*, had 'an odor of despotism displeasing to me.' And his conclusion was that 'I see in the Instruction of Her Imperial Majesty . . . the name of despot abdicated, but the thing itself preserved. . . .'[23] The fact was that Diderot's experience in Russia was most decidedly making his political theory more and more democratic.[24] 'There is no true sovereign except the nation,' he wrote, 'and there can be no true legislator save the people.' He refers to their having inalienable rights. When Catherine writes (*Nakaz,* #19), 'The Sovereign is the Source of all imperial and civil Power,' Diderot responds, 'I do not understand this. It seems to me that it is the consent of the nation, represented by deputies or assembled in a body, that is the source of all political and civil power.'[25]

Catherine was not the only one who could show the influence of Montesquieu. Diderot could, too, as when he speaks of the desirability of the separation of powers. 'If the legislative power and the executive power cannot be separated . . . then one of two things follows, either that one must submit oneself to despotism or that there is no good government save democratic government.' The danger, Diderot wrote, is not that the monarch will forget his prerogative but that his subjects will forget their rights. The very first line of a well-written code (when he said 'code' he meant what in more modern terminology would be termed 'constitution') ought to bind the sovereign.[26]

Diderot's manner in the *Observations sur le Nakaz* was mild, but it did not prevent him from alluding to a problem that Catherine II liked to pretend was not grave. He noticed that 'The Empress has said nothing about the emancipation of the serfs. Yet this is a very important point.' Little wonder that Catherine II, who ended her reign with Russia's laws more despotic than when she began, was annoyed. 'If in reading what I have just written and in listening to her conscience, her heart thrills with joy, she no longer wants slaves; but if she shudders, if her blood holds back, if she pales, she has believed herself better than she is.' [27]

Diderot's enthusiasm for liberty — one might say, remembering his ode, his eleutheromania — is observable in still another of his writings from the summer of 1774. This was his *Voyage de Hollande*. Diderot took notes of his travel in the Netherlands, thus following closely the suggestions made by Linnaeus in his *Instructio peregrinatoris* (1759) on the proper ways to travel instructively. The *Voyage de Hollande,* part of which was written in 1773, is a work with the true Diderot flavor, even though he depended for much of his factual material on two handbooks previously published.[28] He visited art collections, attended concerts and the theater, went aboard a man-o'-war, saw the windmills of Zaandam, and visited the synagogues in Amsterdam. He was, as always, aware of female presences: '[Dutch women] are beautiful, if one can be so with enormous breasts and buttocks . . . just as you see them in Rubens' pictures, so they are in their homes.' He noticed the habits of Dutch workmen; he watched the return of the fishermen to Scheveningen; he persuaded a housewife to write down the items of her annual and monthly budgets; he identified the existence of various occupational diseases. 'There is a fine treatise to be written on maladies in the arts and crafts.' Just as in his *Observations sur le Nakaz,* where he lengthily discussed commercial practices, so in the *Voyage de Hollande* Diderot looks around him with a sharp eye. This attention to the specific and concrete is something that he had perhaps learned from Galiani. At all events, Diderot liked the Dutch and felt comfortable in their country. 'Haarlem is a very pretty city; but of which city in Holland can this not be said?' It is true that he implied criticism of Dutch colonial practices.[29] But generally he found much to praise.

One of the things throughout all of Holland that continually and deliciously affects one is that one never encounters there either the sight of abject poverty or the spectacle of tyranny.

As he was leaving Holland he spoke of it in words that he did not use of Russia or of France. 'I have said my farewell to the country of liberty.' [30]

Still another of Diderot's writings this summer was his *Entretien d'un philosophe avec la maréchale de* * * *.[31] This graceful dialogue was modeled on a conversation that Diderot may really have had with the Maréchale de Broglie when he was negotiating the purchase of the Crozat collection for Catherine II. The work dealt with the familiar problem: Does God exist? It may seem surprising that Diderot would warm up this old subject, which he might be supposed to have settled in his own mind long since. It is probable, though, that his recent experiences in Germany, in Russia, and even in the Netherlands, had taught him that Christian faith and, therefore, resistance to materialistic thought were much more unshaken and tenacious than he had previously supposed. Moreover, the fact that a man as enlightened as Hemsterhuis could believe so rigidly and complacently in the whole array of presuppositions of the Idealistic philosophy may have given Diderot a jolt. The fact that he allowed the *Entretien d'un philosophe avec la maréchale de * *.** to be published, though under an assumed name, suggests that he had concluded that some further propaganda for the materialistic philosophy was both timely and necessary.[32]

In the *Entretien d'un philosophe avec la maréchale de * * **, we hear once again the arguments that had been reverberating in Diderot's works from the *Essai sur le mérite et la vertu* to *Le Rêve de d'Alembert*. The assertion that religion has no real effect on morals, the conviction that a man may be moral without being religious, the denial of immortality and therefore of moral sanctions other than those that are immanent, the assumption that no act of creation was necessary in order to get the universe going, all these old acquaintances march through the pages. But the tone of this dialogue is so gentle and gracious as to make it seem much less polemical than it is. 'I see that you do not have a mania for proselytizing,' says the Maréchale. 'None at all,' replies the *philosophe*.[33]

In addition to all these works, at The Hague Diderot revised and amplified his refutation of Helvétius, and he is thought to have worked also on his *Eléments de physiologie*.[34] All this literary activity kept him quite close to his headquarters at the Galitzins'. Diderot mentioned admiringly how scrupulously Princess Galitzin fulfilled her domestic obligations, and spoke too of how pleased he was to fit into their quiet routine. The French chargé d'affaires at The Hague reported to Paris in August that 'Thus far his [Diderot's] existence at The Hague is scarcely felt. He is not to be seen anywhere.' [35]

This was a marked change from the Diderot of the summer before. The Swedish orientalist Björnståhl remarked that 'Mr. Diderot is very reserved in social groups, carefully avoiding speaking of religion and other sacred subjects. This is precisely the contrary of what one observed in him at the time of his first visit to The Hague.' Hemsterhuis remembered Diderot as having a melancholy disposition, a description so contrary to Diderot's usual buoyancy as to make it doubtful that Hemsterhuis had in fact met him the previous year. Hemsterhuis downrightly asserted in 1784 that 'gaiety never resided in that somber spirit.' When he heard in 1780 that Diderot was happy and joyous, Hemsterhuis remarked, 'I would not have thought him capable of it.' [36]

Was Diderot dissembling or perhaps playing a role? A Dutch periodical, *De Denker,* announced on 6 June 1774 that 'A leading French Deist is in our country.' Without naming names, it spoke of the visitor as being on his way back from Russia, referred to him as a successor of La Mettrie (a comparison which Diderot detested), and called him an eloquent and brilliant propagandist for materialism.[37] This may have been enough to make Diderot take cover, for he himself remarked in the *Voyage de Hollande* that 'The nation is superstitious. . . . Materialism is held in horror.' [38] Or perhaps he was still feeling the effects of his illnesses in Russia and of his long journeys. Maybe there had indeed been some discomfiting experience at Saint Petersburg, the memory of which depressed him. Perhaps the growing antagonism of Princess Galitzin to him, for she remained a believer and indeed was quite pietistic, warned him against being his usual flamboyant and somewhat bumbling self.[39]

There were some flashes of spirit. To Prince Alexander Galitzin Diderot wrote a 'Pantagruelic' letter in which he captured the style and flavor of Rabelais very successfully; and he wrote a devastatingly severe critique of a statue that Falconet had done some years previously, a plaster cast of which Diderot examined in Hemsterhuis' collection. Here Diderot displayed a detailed knowledge of bones and muscles and anatomical nomenclature, and here he revealed too, understandably but not pleasingly, that his resentment of Falconet was a little venomous.[40] As for acquaintances, save those whom he met on a trip to Haarlem, Zaandam, Amsterdam, and Utrecht with his friend Gleichen, the people Diderot saw were predominantly those at Galitzin's dinner table.[41] Hemsterhuis, the French astronomer Lalande, a Briton named Gordon and a physician named Robert, and the 'good-hearted and celebrated' Camper.[42] Petrus Camper was the naturalist who first made a scientific study of the facial angle in human beings. Diderot, much taken with these investigations, offered to try to find a publisher for them in Paris. Diderot also received from Camper the answer to several questions he had asked about smallpox, reminding us how important this subject continued to be in a pre-Jenner Europe that was scourged by the disease.[43]

Though his trunks had been packed and sent off by 2 September, Diderot lingered on at The Hague until October, waiting for Grimm in order to accompany him to Paris. 'I expect Grimm from one moment to another,' he wrote on 3 September.[44] A very strange incident occurred about this time: apparently Galitzin surreptitiously went through Diderot's papers. It is hard to believe that Galitzin would treat an old friend and a guest in such a fashion, yet Naigeon wrote to the Vandeuls in 1786 (and he could scarcely have received his information from any other than Diderot) that 'Prince Galitzin stole the original [of the *Observations sur le Nakaz*] from Diderot by forcing his trunks like a highway robber.'[45] Presumably Diderot discovered the loss only later, in Paris. Some imbroglio certainly caused a rift between Diderot and the Galitzins, to judge from a letter Grimm wrote to the Princess in 1775. Evidently Grimm, who spoke with his usual condescension of 'this sixty-year-old child,' was trying hard to prevent Diderot from blurting out some accusations, and evidently, too, the Galitzins had been in great anxiety for four months lest he do so. At all events, the Galitzins are mentioned no more by Diderot after 1775, save for a chilly and aloof letter to the Prince in 1780.[46] A long-standing friendship thus came to a cheerless end.

During this summer of 1774 changes were occurring in the government at Versailles as a result of the accession of Louis XVI. Diderot's bugbear, Chancellor Maupeou, was dismissed on 24 August, and on the same day, among other changes, Turgot became *contrôleur-général* of finances. To anti-*philosophes* it seemed like the end of the world. The Duc de Croÿ wrote in his diary in 1775 that it was the greatest blow dealt to religion since perhaps the time of Clovis.[47] But to the *philosophes* it augured a new day.

The enthusiasm of the other *philosophes* for Turgot was shared by Diderot, though the situation was complicated by his personal and social relations with Mme Necker, whose husband was Turgot's rival and eventual successor. At this particular moment Diderot deemed the time propitious for getting something for his children out of the government. He mentioned to Catherine II that he would have been useful to them had he been back in Paris, but that he had remained firmly at The Hague in order to fulfill his obligations to her.[48] During this time Mme Necker too was trying to help the young couple. But most of all Diderot relied upon his friendship with Turgot. Even before the marriage Diderot had written Turgot, though he did not expressly ask for anything.[49] Now, when he wrote again, he evidently made his meaning quite clear. 'Go and see him, both of you together,' Diderot wrote his children, and predicted that Turgot 'will always be disposed to listen to me favorably.' Diderot was not so successful, though, as he hoped. As late as December 1775, when he wrote to his old friend Dupont de Nemours, at that time Turgot's closest assistant, Diderot was still trying to prime the pump, still trying to use his influence to get favors for Vandeul.[50]

The summer of 1774 marks the last of the extant letters Diderot wrote to Sophie Volland. Once he returned to Paris, no further exchange of lengthy letters was necessary, for the Volland estate at Isle-sur-Marne had been sold in 1773, and thereafter Sophie no longer spent extended periods outside Paris.[51] Mme Volland had died in 1772 and the next year Sophie and her sister, Mme de Blacy, moved from the Rue Saint-Thomas-du-Louvre to an apartment on the Rue Montmartre, back to the quarter of the Place des Victoires where they had lived when Diderot first knew them. Anyone who is an appreciative reader of Diderot's letters to Sophie Volland feels sad when he comes to the last of them. It is the end of an epoch. In his last letter, written at The Hague on 3 September, he remarked that he had perhaps ten years left 'at the bottom of my bag.'[52] It turned out that he was off by only thirty-six days.

Grimm finally arrived at The Hague, accompanied by two young Russians, Counts Nikolai and Sergei Rumiantzev. Though Diderot had lingered several weeks at The Hague, counting on traveling to Paris with Grimm, the two traveled together no farther than Brussels. There Diderot went on by public coach and arrived in Paris on 21 October 1774, having been gone a year, four months, and ten days.[53] His wife and daughter came to meet him, perhaps at Senlis. ' "Wife," he said to Mama, "count my duds, you will have no cause to scold me. I have not lost even a handkerchief." '[54]

It had been a celebrated trip, and its conclusion was accompanied by a kind of ritual, a ritual almost inevitable and predestined: Diderot's friends made it out a triumph, while his enemies tried to make his Russian visit seem small-scale and ridiculous. The *Année Littéraire* published an account from a correspondent in Stockholm who sneered at what he alleged to be Diderot's criticisms of the French government: 'You would not even agree that France has a fine climate if you thought the administration was responsible for it.' This correspondent averred, for all of Paris to snicker at, that Diderot's 'fanaticism got him into trouble more than once at Leipzig, where he tried to make proselytes of all the professors of the university. Moreover, stung by no one's even noticing him, he walked through parks, buildings, and picture galleries dressed in a most bizarre manner; now in dressing gown, again in yellow slippers, and everywhere in a night cap, and making it known in every city where he arrived that he had forgotten his wig in the city he had just left: all this to give himself a self-important air of philosophical absent-mindedness.'[55] (This charge of role-playing is striking.) And it was widely reported that he had returned from Russia declaring that it was a nation that was rotten before it was ripe. Diderot and his friends vehemently denied that he had made any such observation.[56] Indeed, it could scarcely be expected that he and his friends would describe his visit in any but the most glowing terms. La Harpe in his news letter, and Suard in his, reported that Diderot never tired of praising the marvels of Russia. 'He speaks of them to everyone he meets, before he even says *bon jour,'* wrote La Harpe, and Suard declared that Diderot was 'intoxicated with admiration for the Empress of Russia.' Suard asked him about Catherine II: 'She is the soul of Brutus in the body of Cleopatra.'[57]

Diderot was much more candid in writing to Mme Necker. In respect to Russian manners, laws, customs, and usages, he said,

> Of the Northern climate
> Neither my prose nor my verse will ever say a thing.
> I would be ungrateful if I spoke ill of it,
> I would be a liar if I spoke well of it.[58]

The first days at Paris were busy ones. There were numerous calls to make — Mlle de Lespinasse wrote eagerly on 25 October that he was going to call on her the next day — and objects to deliver, such as a collection of Siberian marbles that the Comte d'Angiviller had asked Diderot to gather, and a case of minerals for Dr. Jean Darcet, son-in-law of the chemist Rouelle.[59] But soon Diderot settled down, perhaps because of weakened health, for Mme de Vandeul says that at this time he began to suffer from difficulty in breathing. 'I found him thin and changed. . . . I am convinced that this journey shortened his life.' Perhaps, too, he was 'de-Russifying,' as Mme d'Epinay remarked of Grimm (or, perhaps, of Diderot himself).[60] During the winter Diderot lived so quietly that Meister wrote in April that 'M. Diderot has never lived in a more solitary fashion than he has since returning to Paris.' In his family life, according to one of Vandeul's brothers, Diderot and his son-in-law got along much better than they had before. As for Mme Diderot, 'she is an impenetrable being whose only good quality, in fact, is that most of the time she stays home.'[61]

While in Russia Diderot had promised to send Betzki a textbook of elementary mathematics that Clairaut had written. Apparently during this winter Diderot wrote just such a textbook himself.[62] His principal interest, though, was to continue his mental contortions over the problem of the squaring of the circle, that will-o'-the-wisp that had first begun to take up his time in 1762. In Holland he had explained his system to Hemsterhuis, who remarked later that 'for several weeks he made me sweat over his theorem concerning the squaring of the circle.' Now Diderot was at it again. He asked the youthful Condorcet for criticism, and tried as best he could to shore up some paralogisms in his demonstration in response to Condorcet's critique. Diderot spoke of the problem as being an excellent cure for insomnia or at least one of the best ways for abridging the lengthiness of the night.[63] Also during this time he was absorbed in devising two inventions, one a kind of portable mimeographing machine or perhaps typewriter which he described as 'performing the function of a printing press,' and the other a kind of coding and decoding machine so vaguely described that it is hard to conceive just what it would resemble. Neither of these inventions was much more, apparently, than an idea in Diderot's head, though Meister does speak of drawings of one of them as being in existence. No actual models of either is known to have been contrived. For a time Diderot thought of publishing a volume containing explanations of these machines, together with his proof of the 'cyclometry,' or squaring of the circle, but this project faded away.[64]

Diderot's absorption in mathematical puzzles and inventions signalized his gradual withdrawal from the busy social life of his middle years. Old age was indeed coming upon him and his vitality was running down. Never again does he seem to participate in such a round of dinners and of salon conversations as he did in the years before he went to Russia. More and more he is to be found at Sèvres, and the chronology of his daily affairs, for lack of information, becomes harder and harder to make out. The trip to Russia marked in his life the grand climacteric.

In a symbolic way, though no doubt unconsciously, Diderot put an end to his Russian trip by divesting himself of the books he had acquired there. These were some sixty volumes, most of them collections of ukases or military regulations or tables of regimental organization, and included the de luxe Bible he had been given.[65] Apparently these books, which could have been useful to him had he carried out the project of a new *Encyclopédie,* did not strike him as being part of his library and therefore already the property of Catherine II. The sale of these books symbolized his recognition of the end of his dream of a Russian *Encyclopédie.*

CHAPTER 46

Ethical Doctrine: Determinism and Humanism

A LL HIS life Diderot was interested in morals. His first book was an adaptation of an essay on merit and virtue. His last was about the ethics of Seneca. In between, his works are strewn with innumerable references to what is good conduct and bad, to customary morality (*moeurs*), to beneficence and maleficence, to vice and virtue. He said of himself with as much truth as drollery that his identifying idiosyncracy was to moralize.[1]

Since he spent his career in searching for certainty in ethical doctrine and in never quite finding it, it is not surprising that over a long life he made many false starts, groped around in numerous deadends, and said and wrote many inconsistent things. The Ariadne thread as we follow Diderot-Theseus in his search for an escape from the labyrinth is the principle he expressed in *Le Rêve de d'Alembert*: '. . . our true opinion is not that from which we have never wavered, but that to which we have most habitually returned.'[2]

Just as in all other aspects of his intellectual life Diderot gives the impression of wanting to avoid dogmatism while eagerly accepting empirical fact, so in his ethical doctrine he constantly conveys the feeling that he is searching, rather than making confident pronunciamentos. The matter is too important to bear of dogmatic assertions or over-hasty generalizations. 'I was quite young when it entered my head that all of morality consists in proving to men that, after all, to be happy one needs to do no more than be virtuous. Thereupon I began to meditate upon this question and I am still meditating upon it.'[3] Thus he wrote when he was fifty-six years old.

Although he was not a dogmatist in ethics, he was not a complete skeptic either. He was not, he knew, a Pyrrhonian, a man so skeptical that in the course of believing almost nothing he comes close to believing almost anything. Diderot sought, through the use of reason and the progress of knowledge, to come to something more positive and affirmative.

659

No matter how much Diderot's ethical doctrines shifted through the years, some points were fixed. Most important of all, and like a pole star around which his other convictions revolved, he believed that a human being could be moral without first having to be religious. It followed from this first premise that human beings can discover for themselves the basis for a sound morality. Access to this knowledge depends upon nothing more mysterious than the use of one's own reason. This is tantamount to saying that morality is immanent. It lies within man's nature and man can discover it there. Furthermore, a sound morality is not contingent upon knowledge of whether or not an after-life exists, of whether or not there is a Heaven and a Hell. Thus Diderot's ethical thought was grounded in secularism, in life here and now. The only after-life that he allowed for was that which a person might have by remaining in the memory of posterity.

The search for the basis of a sound morality in man's nature straightway led Diderot, as it had the ancient philosophers, to an attempt to discover what is the nature of man. Diderot's search for the nature of man was always predicated on the assumption that there are new insights still to be discovered. His quest continued to be an on-going and open-ended one, not something that stopped for the rest of time in the understanding of human nature achieved, say, by Cicero or Saint Thomas Aquinas. Thus the nascent social sciences, which in the eighteenth century encouraged the development of utilitarianism in ethical theory, increased Diderot's understanding of the nature of man. And he had the further merit of realizing that knowledge of medicine and biology is essential to him who wants to base his ethical theory on the conception of what is congruent with man's nature. 'It is very difficult to be a good metaphysician or a good moralist,' wrote Diderot in the *Réfutation d'Helvétius,* 'without being an anatomist, naturalist, physiologist, and doctor.'[4]

Diderot's moral theory was founded also on a belief that there is a fundamental nature common to all men in spite of the infinite variety of human behavior. Here Diderot was navigating in difficult waters, between the Scylla of moral absolutisms stated *a priori* and the Charybdis of complete relativism. Diderot tried to steer a middle course, avoiding the *a priori* by constantly taking into account the experiential and the observed, and avoiding complete relativism by seeking to discover trustworthy inductions about human nature among all the variants.

It is possible to find in our natural needs [Diderot wrote in his refutation of Helvétius], in our life, in our existence, in the way we are organized and in the sensitivity which exposes us to pain, an eternal basis for justice and injustice. . . .

What appears to have led our author into error is that he has limited himself to the data which show him justice and injustice under a hundred thousand opposing forms, and has closed his eyes to the nature of man, where he would have recognized the foundations and origin of them.[5]

Another fixed point in Diderot's ethical theory was his opposition to the notion of free will. In the ancient argument of determinism versus free will Diderot was a determined determinist. His 'Letter to Landois' in 1756 had succinctly stated his doctrine, a standpoint from which he never wavered. The intensity of his opposition to the notion of free will was so great as to make one speculate about the causes of it. Probably it was linked up emotionally with his disbelief in miracles and with his dislike of the various superstitions and other obstacles to critical thinking which numerous articles in the *Encyclopédie* made it a policy to combat. It was an aspect of his scientism, of his belief in the universality of cause and effect.[6]

Diderot also believed — and this was supremely important in his ethical doctrine — that man is modifiable. Man is not 'free,' but he is plastic. He is not free to act by mere caprice, for he must necessarily act within the limits of all the variable factors of his previous experience. But these variable factors can be modified and then, of course, man will be modified too. It can readily be understood why, with a hopeful and dynamic conviction like this, the most advanced thinkers of the Enlightenment believed in progress. Diderot's views on modification are well expressed in one of his articles for the *En-cyclopédie, 'Modification, Modifier, Modificatif, Modifiable,'* slyly placed as though he were merely discussing a point of grammar:

Man, free or not, is a being subject to modification. . . . There is no cause which does not have its effect; there is no effect which does not modify the thing on which the cause acts. . . . The modifications that have been imposed upon us change us ineluctably, both at the very moment and for all the rest of life. . . .

And in the article *'Malfaisant'* (Maleficent), which likewise appeared under the demure guise of being an article on grammar, Diderot wrote, 'But men are nonetheless modifiable for good or for evil. Good examples, good precepts, chastisements, recompenses, blame, praise, laws, always have their effect. . . .'[7]

If one takes these elements all together, it becomes clear that Diderot was shaping up a theory of ethics that was secular, immanent, absolutely deterministic, and, with its emphasis on the nature of man, an empirical version of natural law. His doctrine, which recognized that nature has placed mankind under the governance of two sovereign masters, pain and pleasure, was abreast of the nascent utilitarian thought of the time. In numerous aspects of his ethical and social thought, Diderot was as advanced and radical as any other thinker of the eighteenth century; however, his hankering after the sense of certainty that belief in any form of natural law affords might seem to some critics an unexpectedly conservative element in his thought.

But what if this modified kind of natural law, far from being conservative and traditionalist, could become the kernel of a new morality, the core of a new humanism, the source of energy for a new enlightenment? What if a deepened understanding of what man is by his nature, an understanding that was critical and rigorous and scientific, could be made the basis of a new ethics and a new politics? This is as exciting and enticing a vision as a man can come to.

Helvétius' *De l'Homme,* by its very weaknesses and deficiencies, helped Diderot to glimpse the possibility of a more humanistic morality. That this book (which Diderot often remarked would have caused Helvétius serious trouble had he published it in his lifetime) made a deep impression upon Diderot is proved by the extent of his comments, in length a good-sized volume.[8] He read *De l'Homme* three times in 1773 and again in 1774, and internal evidence shows that he reviewed it again as late as 1777 or 1778. As happened so frequently in his reading, Diderot used Helvétius' book dialectically, to develop his own thought. He mentioned in the *Réfutation* itself that he had no intention of publishing it.[9]

Diderot's running debate with Helvétius — often he slips into the dialogue form [10] — centered around only a few points, though these few were of great significance. In many respects the two men were in agreement. Both were materialists and many of their metaphysical assumptions were identical. Accordingly there are large sections of *De l'Homme* with which Diderot had no disagreement, such as the section in which Helvétius lengthily expounds his doctrine that man has no freedom of the will. What they disagree upon is fundamental to the search for what is the nature of man.

Helvétius' book made such a deep impression upon Diderot for the paradoxical reason that he found it superficial. With blissful cocksureness Helvétius composed a book made up of abstractions, of deductions (which Diderot often called 'sagacious,' but in the pejorative sense, evidently, of their being more astute than wise) that he did not verify and which Diderot claimed had no basis in experience. 'Only a superficial mind, seduced by clever antitheses, could be imposed upon by these pages,' complains Diderot; and at another point he remarks, 'There is not a professor in any of our colleges who would not shrug his shoulders in pity at these clever ideas.' And again,

'Everything that the author adds here would make one believe that he has never observed children.' [11]

Diderot's ideas on the nature of man — and therefore of the morality consonant with that nature — experienced a kind of violent confrontation when he read Helvétius' book. What were its assumptions that upset him to such a degree? The most fundamental was the notion that animal nature and human nature, because each has only the testimony of the five senses to go on, are indistinguishable. Though Diderot shared with Helvétius the belief that animals are not automata and that man is himself a species of animal, he sharply disagreed with the supposition that animal behavior can tell us anything significant about human morality. As has been dryly observed, 'The anthropology of the Enlightenment has its complications.' [12] Diderot had already made the distinction between man and animal in the *Salon de 1767*:

What is man? . . . An animal? . . . Without doubt. But the dog is an animal also; the wolf is an animal also. But man is neither a wolf nor a dog. . . . What precise notion can we have of good and evil, of beauty and ugliness, of good and bad, of true and false, without a preliminary knowledge of man? . . . How many philosophers, failing to make these simple observations, have prescribed for man the morality of wolves, as stupidly as though they had prescribed for wolves the morality of man.[13]

Of course man is an animal. But he is a certain species of animal, the species 'that combines ideas.' Helvétius was not being discriminating enough. 'What use shall I be able to make of a whole array of consequences equally characteristic of the dog, the weasel, the oyster, the dromedary?'

I am unable to put up with such generalizations: I am a man and I must have explanations appropriate to man.[14]

The effect of Helvétius' ideas upon Diderot was to strengthen and deepen Diderot's humanism.

Leaving congruence with animal nature aside, Helvétius made other assumptions about human nature that Diderot did not find any more palatable. Helvétius was a thinker who ascribed everything in a human being's development to environment. It was an easy thing to do in a century that had adopted Locke's critique of innate ideas and his doctrine that an infant is born with a mind that is a *tabula rasa* upon which experience writes. Helvétius interpreted this doctrine to mean that there are no hereditary or genetic differences between men. He was an environmentalist of the most extreme kind.

This interpretation of Locke by Helvétius had some amazing corollaries. For example, he explained differences of achievement in any two men as arising from one man's having more desire to enjoy, having more incentive, than the other. It was not a question of any difference in 'natural endowments.' Ah, then! how do you explain genius? The same way, Helvétius would reply. Genius is more a result than a cause, the result of any average man's determination to try harder. Besides, Helvétius laid enormous importance upon the role of chance in human accomplishment. The discoveries and achievements usually ascribed to genius were, according to Helvétius, just the result of hazard and luck. As Diderot said, trying to make the assertion seem even more preposterous, the discoveries of the calculus just happened to happen to a man named Newton and a man named Leibniz. They might have happened to anybody.[15]

Thus Helvétius had a theory of human nature that in effect made society just an aggregation of interchangeable parts. He was able to state this theory seriously because he was more proficient in abstract reasoning than he was in verification and in the methods of empirical research. Moreover, his psychology recognized sensation only, and did not recognize the reality of any spider at the center of the network. 'To sense is to judge,' wrote Helvétius, thus making sense impressions the same thing as ratiocination. Since it is easy to conceive of innumerable situations in life where the external sensory stimuli affecting X and Y are identical, Helvétius concluded that the responses of X and Y would be identical too.

Diderot, in contrast, asserted that it is 'important not to make *feeling* and *judging* two perfectly identical operations,'[16] and he internalized psychic phenomena. He was supremely interested in whatever it is that functions as the spider at the center of the web, and thought that in this process the brain must play an important part. It was only in the course of the eighteenth century that doctors and scientists came with some unanimity to think of the brain as the site of the thought processes. Diderot, as usual, was up to date about advances being made in the sciences. In the *Réfutation d'Helvétius* Diderot mentions the brain frequently and complains that Helvétius does not mention it at all. 'You have neglected to examine an organ without which the condition of the others [i.e., organs], more or less perfect, does not signify, an organ whence emanates the astonishing differences between men relative to intellectual operations.'[17]

Another source of the astonishing differences in men, which Helvétius with a strange myopia seemed unable to observe, caused differences in sensitivity. As Diderot ascribed the one source of these differences to the brain —

and wondered why Helvétius had nothing to say about insanity [18] — so Diderot attributed the other source of differences to the diaphragm, thus harking back to a subject which had been much in his thoughts when he was writing the *Paradoxe sur le comédien*. 'The head makes man wise; the diaphragm makes him compassionate and moral. You have said nothing about these two organs, nothing at all, and yet you fancy that you have made the circuit of man.' [19]

Whereas Helvétius emphasized the similarity of men, Diderot constantly appealed to experience in depicting their variety.[20] A large part of his *Réfutation d'Helvétius* is concerned with this point. His word for the quiddity that is the cause of these differences was 'organization'; ours would be 'constitution' and 'genetic inheritance.' Part of Diderot's argument is by analogy from the animal world: there is a difference by nature among breeds of dogs, why not such differences among men? 'You cannot give a bird dog's nose to a greyhound, you cannot give the speed of the greyhound to a setter.' And if you insist upon making them do what they are not fitted by nature to excel in, you will simply have mediocrity. Going on from this analogy, Diderot speaks of how many misfits there are in human society and of how the goal of education should be to help to discover children's aptitudes and not force them into doing what their parents insist upon their doing whether it fits their abilities or not.[21]

Nor did Diderot believe that human beings can achieve excellence simply by wanting it and applying themselves. 'Alas! the schools are full of children so desirous of glory, so studious, so diligent! In vain do they labor, torment themselves, sometimes weep over their lack of progress, they do not get any further along on account of that.' The art of changing lead to gold, he said, is less ridiculous an alchemy than that of making a Regulus of the first man who comes along. 'Monsieur Helvétius, a little question for you: Here are five hundred babies just born; they are going to be entrusted to you to be brought up at your discretion. Tell me, how many of them are you going to make men of genius? Why not five hundred?' [22]

The confrontation with the views of Helvétius did not impair Diderot's belief in determinism.[23] He continued to take for granted that the multitudinous factors of nature and nurture, if they could all be known, would reveal a being absolutely determined by the sum total of the previous influences bearing upon him. Such a being, however, was at the same time a human organism endowed with the potentiality of self-knowledge. Diderot's interpretation of human nature conceived of man as being energetic and activist within the framework of a rigorous determinism. Consequently, his determinism is more bracing than the somewhat flaccid environmentalism of Helvétius. The large role given by Helvétius to chance and accident leads to a passive conception of man, very unlike Diderot's. The happiness which Helvétius talks about seems to lie in enjoyment; that which Diderot talks about, while enjoyment is of course a large component of it, is a happiness which also lies in doing.[24]

Diderot was like Helvétius in acknowledging that 'Pleasure and pain are and always will be the sole principles of the actions of men.'[25] But whereas Helvétius confined his hedonism to a very crass calculus — mainly, Diderot complains, to the enjoyment of women: 'Always the author's portrait presented as the portrait of Man' — Diderot sensibly opens up the inquiry to the whole range of exquisite subtleties of moral satisfactions and dissatisfactions. Diderot claims that Helvétius' kind of reward is 'abject.'[26] Moreover, it is not comprehensive enough: 'When one sets up a general law, it must incorporate all the phenomena, both the actions inspired by wisdom and the aberrations caused by folly.'[27]

Thus did Diderot object to a utilitarianism that calculated pain and pleasure merely on a quantitative and non-qualitative basis. It was the same argument that John Stuart Mill made a century later in his essay on *Utilitarianism*. 'It is better,' wrote Mill, 'to be a human being dissatisfied than a pig satisfied; better to be Socrates dissatisfied than a fool satisfied.' Diderot, especially with his admiration of Socrates, would have agreed heartily with the humanistic and qualitative impetus of Mill's argument.[28] In these distinctions Diderot stood to Helvétius as Mill stood to Jeremy Bentham.

What Diderot would have liked to find, and probably what every moralist would like to find if he could, is a corpus of ethical doctrine so sure and so easily applied that virtue always triumphs and vice never prospers. Here he had the honesty to admit defeat. And this had the great advantage of preventing him from being dogmatic.

. . . if there are some apparently quite complicated questions which have seemed simple to me upon examination [Diderot wrote in the *Réfutation*], there are others very simple in appearance which I have found to be beyond me. For example, I am convinced that in a society even as badly regulated as ours, wherein successful vice is often applauded, and virtue is almost always ridiculed when it fails, I am convinced, I say, that, taking everything together, one could not do better for one's own happiness than to be an upright man. . . . This is a question that I have meditated upon a hundred times and with all the concentration of which I was capable. I had, I think, the necessary qualifications. Shall I confess to you, I have not even dared to take up my pen to write the first line of it? I said to myself, If I do not emerge victorious from this effort I become the apologist of wickedness: I shall have betrayed the cause of virtue, I shall have encouraged men to vice. No, I do not feel myself adequate for this sublime work.[29]

Diderot at one time did indeed have plans for writing a formal treatise on ethics, and had settled on a name for it. Evidence comes from the father of J. H. Meister (who became Grimm's successor as editor of the *Correspondance littéraire* in March 1773). Meister's father, writing from Paris in September 1771, mentioned that 'Diderot has not yet commenced his treatise *De vita bona et beata.*' The title makes it sound like something by Plutarch or Boethius.

Two years or more later, Diderot acknowledged in the *Réfutation d'Helvétius* that he had felt himself incapable of 'this sublime work.' If, then, he gave up his plans, perhaps sometime in the 1760's, for a full-dress presentation according to the canons of formal logic, it would seem likely that, with his taste for moralizing, he would cast about for an alternative literary form. In lieu of the logical approach he perhaps might convince by substituting the heuristic.

When logical proof fails, the recourse of a literary artist often is to tell a story. And this is what Diderot does with *Jacques le fataliste*. In its elaborate, disconnected, and disconcerting way, *Jacques le fataliste* expresses the epitome of Diderot's moral convictions. Meister's father must have felt this, for in the continuation of his letter to Bodmer the association of ideas can be seen at work: 'Diderot has not yet commenced his treatise *De vita bona et beata,* but he has written a charming story, *Jacques le fataliste.*' [30]

Like *Le Neveu de Rameau,* like *La Religieuse,* like Jacques himself, whose adventures it recounts, *Jacques le fataliste* has experienced many vicissitudes. Though much of it was written by 1771, by 1778 substantial additions had been made to it, so that the *Réfutation d'Helvétius* and *Jacques le fataliste* can be treated as contemporaneous works. Unpublished during Diderot's lifetime, *Jacques le fataliste* was known only to the small circle of select readers who had access to the *Correspondance littéraire.* This was how Goethe came to devour this enormous and delicate banquet, as he called it, which he gulped down at one sitting five and a half hours in duration.[31] In 1796 *Jacques le fataliste* was published in Paris and readers ever since have been ejaculating, '*Qu'est-ce que c'est que ça?*' For *Jacques le fataliste* is an odd book as well as a complex one. On first reading, as one critic has observed, it almost invariably irritates. Yet its experimental techniques, which to the nineteenth century seemed dazzling but chaotic, have raised it in the estimation of the twentieth century to a very high pinnacle of esteem.[32]

Jacques le fataliste, then, is a multiplex work of great significance in the history of the French novel and of equal or even greater significance in understanding Diderot's final position on ethics. Inasmuch as the meaning of the novel, including its ethical meaning, depends upon its form and structure, it will be necessary to examine *Jacques* first as a specimen of literary technique before proceeding to what may be its philosophical teachings.

Jacques le fataliste et son maître is a novel, or an anti-novel, in which the reader is almost all the time aware of the author, who frequently sticks his head in to interrupt the narrative, ask the reader questions, and frustrate his expectations.[33] It is a technique which poses all sorts of interesting problems about narrative form, which raises nagging but cogent questions about the proper relationship between the author and his reader, which highlights and puts into relief various levels of meaning, and which delights twentieth-century critics.[34] The novel begins:

How had they met? By chance, like everyone else. What were their names? What does that matter to you? Whence came they? From the place closest by. Where were they going? Does anyone know where he is going? *

Jacques le fataliste is influenced in many places by *Tristram Shandy.* In the first few lines of the book Jacques says, 'My captain added that every bullet shot had its billet,' similar to Corporal Trim's quoting King William that 'Every bullet had its billet.' Moreover, *Jacques le fataliste* begins and ends in the history of Jacques's love affair. This is again reminiscent of the structure of *Tristram Shandy.* 'So thou wast in love, Trim! . . . I have never heard a word of it before.' Both novels, too, are full of interruptions and divagations and, especially in *Jacques le fataliste,* of elaborate tales within a tale. Consequently the nineteenth-century reader was usually glad to put the novel down as an example of Diderot's alleged propensity to plagiarism. More recent critics have found nothing of the sort, though they have discovered it fascinating and fruitful to contrast meticulously Sterne's and Diderot's intentions and styles.[35]

Jacques is a character who wins the affection of most readers and the respect of all. He is a man-servant, he is of the people, he limps from a wound received at the battle of Fontenoy, and he has a monomania for explaining by one formula everything that happens — 'It was written up there.' He is likewise prudent, illogical (because he tries to change events though he

---

* *Jacques the Fatalist and his Master,* tr. J. Robert Loy, Dell Laurel Editions (New York, 1962).

claims that they are fore-ordained), loyal, brave, intelligent, resourceful, and self-respecting, and all of this without suspecting that he is. In contrast — and this is evidently an important part of Diderot's intention — the master is a two-dimensional man of whom we get to know little more than that he constantly takes snuff and constantly looks at his watch. This story of picaresque adventures on the road takes place over an eight-day period. It would seem that Diderot had *Don Quixote* in mind when he wrote it, for some of the episodes are identical, such as that of the smugglers pretending that they are a funeral cortège.[36] But the master is shallow in comparison with Don Quixote, which throws the spotlight all the more on Jacques, who is much more like Figaro than Sancho Panza. That two great artists were creating Jacques and Figaro at about the same time (and also creating the Maître and Count Almaviva) tells us much about the revolutionary potential of late eighteenth-century French society.

The structure of *Jacques le fataliste,* it has been observed, 'is like a set of Chinese boxes since it consists of narrative units within narrative units. The largest of these, containing all the others, is the dialogue between the hypothetical narrator and the hypothetical reader.' Diderot was experimenting in *Jacques le fataliste* with a technique now often called 'reader participation.' The next Chinese box is the journey of Jacques and his master, and the next contains the recital of Jacques's love affair. This in turn contains various anecdotes and stories.[37]

Two of these stories are exceptionally instructive in displaying Diderot's skill as a narrator, as well as his fascination with people of strong character and violent passions. The first depicts a Père Hudson, a masterful scoundrel of great energy and ability whom two other monks try to bring to book, and who turns the tables on them.[38] The other tale is a novella which recounts the revenge taken on her lover by a Mme de La Pommeraye. Finding that she is no longer loved by the Marquis des Arcis, Mme de La Pommeraye decides to get her revenge. She pays a mother and daughter (both prostitutes) to act the role of pious ladies living in genteel retirement, and, by allowing the Marquis to meet them, and by other wiles and subtleties, cunningly manages to inflame his interest in the daughter. The Marquis finally find himself so much in love that he marries the girl, whereupon Mme de La Pommeraye reveals what sort of woman he has married.

This story, told by the hostess of an inn where Jacques and his master sheltered, to the realistic accompaniment of all the hurly-burly of the daily routine of inn-keeping, has always been regarded as a fine example of Diderot's artistry. It is also an instance of his sense of life's ironies, for the

Marquis des Arcis soon forgives his wife and Mme de La Pommeraye's revenge comes to nothing.[39]

Twentieth-century students of narrative form have observed that many of Diderot's tales are close to being movie scripts, and in fact the story of Mme de La Pommeraye has been made into a well-known film. The other parts of *Jacques le fataliste* likewise show their affinity with cinematographic forms, as in the use of the flashbacks that delay Jacques so comically in recounting the simple story of his love affair. 'In *Jacques le fataliste* the selective method for building up the action is what is called in the cinema *montage*. . . . Diderot, like certain avant-garde directors of our own time, has broken away from the documentary to demonstrate the fuller possibilities of a new artistic form, better able to present realism.'[40]

Jacques le fataliste is a document about the human condition, and is unusually stimulating and humorous and provoking both in what it says and how it says it. By the novelty of his fictional forms and by the planned confusion resulting from his personal interpositions Diderot almost forces the reader to look in a new way at life's most common phenomena. While solemnly asserting that 'this is not a novel,' and declaring 'how easy it is to write stories,' Diderot's disarming manner disguises the fact that he is probing deeply into love relationships; into the role of sexuality; into the drive for domination, whether it expresses itself in love or in thirst for power; into the loneliness and the difficulties of communication between human beings. It is an existentialist novel, and a frank one. Take, for example, what the author says to his reader about prudery in literature:

And what has the genital act, so natural, so necessary, and so right, done to you that you exclude the name of it from your conversations and imagine that your mouth, eyes and ears would be soiled by it? It is good that the expressions which are least often spoken and written and most often suppressed should be the best known and the most generally recognized. That is the way it is. Thus the word *futuo* is no less familiar than the word bread; no era is ignorant of it, no language but has it; it has a thousand synonyms in every tongue. . . . I can hear you say, 'Fie! the cynic! Fie! the shameless person!'[41]

Like any other creative artist, Diderot found himself confronted by all the familiar and difficult problems of expression and communication. What is truth, and, if you can glimpse it at the bottom of its well, how can you communicate it? What is reality, and what feats of imagination are required to imitate it and pass the imitation off for reality itself? No one knew more than Diderot how hard it is to express the truth. 'Tell the thing as it is? . . . That does not happen, perhaps, twice a day in a whole big city.' The novelty of *Jacques le fataliste* is that the author, instead of wrestling with these problems in private, forces them on the attention of the reader by constantly interrupting his story as he goes along. The spectacle of a creative artist struggling with these difficulties in public is an appealing one to students of literature, who have responded to it with a host of articles and books. It is impressive to find *Jacques le fataliste* mentioned as one of 'perhaps the two outstanding "experimental" novels' in French, the other being André Gide's *Les Caves du Vatican*.[42]

Accordingly there is a growing critical literature of the devices Diderot employs. His dizzying changes of tenses and other manipulations of time relationships; [43] his devices for enhancing realism; [44] his practice of adapting actual incidents to a work of fiction; [45] his way of setting up a kind of dialogue between the old Diderot and the young and in general his use of autobiographical materials; [46] the economy of his effects — 'I mortally hate portraits. . . . Tell me the facts, reproduce faithfully the conversation, and I will soon find out the sort of man I have to deal with. A word, a gesture have sometimes taught me more than all the chatter of a whole city;' [47] the social criticism implicit in the contrast between the active servant and the passive master (who, in reality, is much more of a fatalist than Jacques); [48] all these devices win the admiration of critics. And students of the history of literature also perceive in the works of Stendhal and especially in those of Balzac the influence of Diderot's ideas on the novel and on how to tell a story.[49]

Readers also notice the symbolism of *Jacques le fataliste* — of being on the road, of not knowing exactly where one is going — and they appreciate in it a buoyancy and youthfulness that raises the spirits.[50] *Jacques le fataliste* is not a glum book. As for its philosophical ideas, students of philosophy observe that a good part of *Jacques le fataliste* (as well as *Le Rêve de d'Alembert*) is evidently the result of prolonged meditations on Spinoza, or at least that brand of Spinozism that was textually available to thinkers in the eighteenth century.[51]

The whole point of Diderot's novel lies in his ironical and humorous treatment of Jacques's faith in fatalism. An older and less discriminating generation of critics took Diderot with absolute literalism on this point. They assumed (from the title of the book, no doubt) that Diderot was a fatalist too, and thus overlooked the remarkable dialectical interplay of Diderot's ideas. Diderot was a believer in a necessitarianism so fundamental that it can be traced, if only one has knowledge enough, from antecedent to antecedent right back to atoms and genes. This Diderot had already done in

Le Rêve de d'Alembert, with constituent matter at one end of his spectrum and the moral world of human beings at the other. But there is quite a difference between being a necessitarian or a determinist and being a fatalist. The word 'determinism' is a nineteenth-century invention, and Diderot had to make do with the word 'fatalism,' which thus bore a double burden.[52] No doubt he would have expressed himself even more clearly had he had at hand this extra semantic tool. A man who believes that we are determined by all the multiple factors in our past can still believe that human nature is plastic and subject to modification. If he be a humanistic determinist, he even believes, as Diderot did, that human nature bears in itself some potentiality of self-modification and therefore, though it can never be free in the sense of being capricious or arbitrary, can be to some extent autonomous.

The irony with respect to Jacques is that Jacques acted autonomously while supposing that he was unable to. In every vicissitude, at every crisis, Jacques responds as a sensible, courageous, and morally responsible person, while constantly exclaiming, 'It was written up there. . . .' As has been well said, 'Through sheer monotony . . . Diderot forces upon the reader a realization that a formula which explains everything explains nothing.'[53]

Critics of Diderot's ethical theory find inconsistency or at least dualism in a doctrine which on the one hand insists that all is necessity but on the other hand teaches that a man can be morally autonomous. There is no doubt that Diderot was aware of the difficulty, for there are some pages in *Jacques le fataliste* where he seems to lower his mask and speak to his reader directly and without persiflage:

According to this system, one might suppose that Jacques was not rejoiced or afflicted by anything. However, that was not true. He conducted himself just about the way you and I do. He thanked his benefactor, and tried to do even better for him in return. He raged against injustice. . . . Often he was illogical, like you and me, and given to forgetting his principles, except in certain circumstances in which his philosophy clearly dominated him. Then it was that he said, 'It had to be, for it was written up there.'[54]

Looked at one way, it seems strange indeed to have a moralist pose his ethical doctrine on the cornerstone of illogicality. Looked at another way, however, it is realistic and empirical, true to human behavior. Faced with such dichotomies, Diderot resolves them in what Cassirer calls the whirl-pool of his dialectic:

Diderot saw and expressed clearly all the antinomies into which the system of fatalism finally leads. . . . He admits a vicious circle but he transforms this situation into a grand jest. . . . *Jack the Fatalist* endeavors to show that the concept of fate is the alpha and omega of all human thinking; but it also shows how thought time and again comes into conflict with this concept, how it is forced implicitly to deny and revoke the concept even while affirming it. There is no alternative but to recognize this situation as inevitable, and to extend our very idea of necessity so as to include that inconsistency. . . . According to Diderot it is this oscillation between the two poles of freedom and necessity which brings the circle of thought and existence to completion. By such oscillation, not by a simple assertion or denial, we can discover the all-inclusive concept of nature, that concept which in the last analysis is just as much beyond agreement and contradiction and beyond truth and falsehood as it is beyond good and evil because it includes both extremes without differentiation.[55]

The merit of Diderot's search for an ethic comes from his trying to understand the interrelatedness of all phenomena — physiological, psychological, moral, aesthetic.[56] 'Everything is tied together, linked, co-ordinated, in this world,' he wrote to Hemsterhuis, and at approximately this same time he also declared that 'The moral universe is so closely linked to the physical universe that it is scarcely likely that they are not one and the same machine.' This perception, a scientific intuition that is almost mystical, makes Diderot a materialist and a humanist in the same breath.[57] It also makes him a moralist who, quite seriously, is willing to put his trust in Jacques's illogicality. The message of *Jacques le fataliste,* the message for all us anxious moralists, is that the future of human values is safe in the hand of Jacques. He can be trusted to be a good steward of them, even though he thinks that everything is already written on the grand scroll up there.

Jacques le fataliste affirms the dignity of man and the paradox of moral autonomy in a deterministic universe. And since it especially affirms the dignity of human beings like Jacques, it takes on a distinctly egalitarian and pre-revolutionary air. Jacques, for example, casually suggests at one point that an apprentice boy may become a Cromwell. Perhaps Diderot intended to connote this by the very name he used, for Jacques is the traditional name of the French peasantry, and Frenchmen still remembered, of course, the outbreaks of the medieval *jacqueries*.[58] And though, as the title implies, *Jacques le fataliste et son maître* live in a close symbiosis, it is a symbiosis which the author lets us see is often reversed.[59] It reminds us somehow of Sieyès' remark in 1789 that the Third Estate is nothing and should be everything. Thus, according to one critic, *Jacques le fataliste* is a kind of hymn to the glory of the French people.[60] Yes, because of its being founded so firmly in the idiom and the *moeurs* of the French. But it is also a book for all of us. In its courage, in its refusal to take life tragically, in its absence of pretentiousness, *Jacques le fataliste* is a bracing tonic and a parable of man's fate.

CHAPTER 47

Indian Summer

THOUGH preoccupied during the decade of the seventies with such major works as *Jacques le fataliste* and the *Réfutation d'Helvétius,* Diderot was meanwhile fitting himself into the routine of life with the visit to Catherine of Russia behind him. In March 1775 she rather unexpectedly requested 'Messieurs les philosophes,' apparently meaning Grimm and Diderot, 'to draw up a plan of study for young people, from the ABC's to the university, inclusive.'[1] Diderot might have responded to this request as superficially as did Grimm, whose essay (long thought to be by Diderot) was only a few pages long. But Diderot felt complimented to be asked to undertake a work of such difficulty and magnitude: 'Sufficiently grounded in all the sciences to know the value of them, but not profound enough in any one to have a professional preference, I shall arrange them all without partiality.'[2] Thinking that she intended to make use of his suggestions immediately, he finished his *Plan d'une université pour le gouvernement de Russie* by late July, in spite of a chronic 'chest ailment' that afflicted him during the spring. By December his *Plan* had reached the Empress.[3]

The great merit of Diderot's plan is that he wanted education for all. Education gives man dignity, he said. 'A university is a school the door of which is open to all the nation's children without distinction and in which masters paid by the State initiate them into an elementary knowledge of all the the sciences.' Of course, not all needed the same education, as he pointed out. His suggestions show Diderot, as has been well said, groping for a principle: 'an aristocracy of education emerging from a democracy of opportunity.'[4]

The general burden of Diderot's advice was to adjure the Empress to keep education the monopoly of the state and to watch out for priests.[5] As for educational method, though he recommended rest periods and exercise, he showed himself a great believer in discipline and hard work. In his opinion

674

there could be no substitute for the laborious accumulation of knowledge. This was true for everyone, and not least for the greatest. 'What particularly distinguishes Voltaire from all our young literary men? Education. Voltaire knows a great deal and our young poets are ignorant. The work of Voltaire is full of things; their works are empty.' [6]

Diderot was very critical of education in the liberal arts in France. In consequence, he advised against the study of Greek and Latin for younger students. He advised this in spite of his own competence in both languages and in spite of the fact, too, that a large section of his *Plan* is devoted to characterizations of an astonishing number of the ancient authors.[7] Nor did he anywhere recommend the study of living foreign languages, which seems a strange omission. He recommended that throughout the system there be open competitions for teaching positions, frequent inspections, and liberal retirement policies in order to attract talent. The aim of any educational system has always been and ought always to be to produce virtuous and enlightened men.[8]

As might be expected, considering his interest in medicine, his proposals for that faculty were lengthier and less routine than was his treatment of either law or theology. In medicine he urged plenty of clinical instruction, and praised the Russian climate for being very favorable to the progress of anatomical studies. 'An anatomist can carry on his dissections on the same cadaver for fifteen to twenty days without interruption.' And he remarked amusingly that a bad doctor is a small-scale epidemic that rages as long as he lives.[9]

As Diderot treated subject after subject and fitted them into his curriculum, he mentioned also the leading books on each, thus displaying a broad knowledge regarding educational and technical treatises. His research in preparation of the *Plan d'une université* made him sharply aware of the lack of what he called 'classic books' (because they were for use in classes) in almost every subject. In a covering letter to Catherine II he strongly urged her to have these textbooks written. The ablest men in the world should be asked to do them — D'Alembert, for example, for mathematics. And it is with a similar recommendation that he concluded the report itself. The *Plan d'une université pour le gouvernement de Russie* is an estimable book, concrete, useful, and judicious, even though it is not one of Diderot's greatest. He would have liked to make it better and regretted that, thinking the Empress needed it at once, he had finished it so hastily. Though 'great persons, both French and foreign, have tormented me to do so,' he scrupulously refused to let others see it. Nevertheless, he set good store by the *Plan d'une université:* he repeatedly asked Grimm how the Empress liked it; and he was 'scandalized' to hear that she was giving the Jesuits so many teaching positions in Russia.[10]

First and last, Diderot's contributions to educational theory were extensive. In the fifties there had been the letter to the Princess of Nassau-Saarbruck on the education of her children; in the sixties he had participated in the preparation of *De l'Education publique;* and now, in the seventies, came the lengthiest of all, the *Plan d'une université pour le gouvernement de Russie.* Also most probably from the period of the seventies, though it is not possible to date it precisely, comes his 'Letter to the Countess of Forbach on the Education of Children.'[11] The Countess, who was the morganatic wife of Christian IV, Duke of Zweibrücken, often visited Paris, and Diderot knew her personally.[12] The exordium of his letter to her suggests that she had sent him her own educational scheme and expected him to comment upon it. 'Before casting my eyes upon your plan of education,' he wrote, 'I have asked myself what my own would be,' and in his last paragraph he observed that 'Among several ideas that we hold in common, there was not one where we completely differed.' It is conjecturable that this was a device adopted by Diderot in order to avoid having to comment too specifically on the lucubrations of the Countess. His essay is brief and quite general. He lays great emphasis on moral training and development, fully as much as on intellectual; and he points out the necessity for aesthetic and social training as well. The 'Letter' rather conspicuously takes the turn of suggesting numerous things that the Countess could do, as well as the children, to contribute to their education, much as though he felt privately that that was where the need lay. The *Lettre à Madame de Forbach sur l'éducation des enfants* is a respectworthy but rather grandfatherly work, and admirers of Diderot should be glad that his reputation does not depend upon it alone.[13]

In addition to asking Diderot to write the *Plan d'une université,* Catherine II also commissioned him to recruit for her an artillery specialist. Her first choice had been Gribeauval, the military engineer who modernized the French artillery in 1765 and made it the best in Europe. Diderot knew him personally and had recommended him to Catherine II in 1773–4. Gribeauval having refused, Diderot found for her two others in his stead. Also in 1775, because of his knowledge of Russia, Diderot was interviewed by a young French diplomat who was being posted there.[14] And during August and September, to complete the list of that year's connections with Russia, Diderot was in touch at Paris with Grigor Orlov, the former lover of Catherine II, a man whom Diderot heartily disliked because of his arrogance and ignorance.[15]

Political events in France in 1775 caught Diderot in a conflict of loyalties, to Turgot and to the Neckers, a conflict in which he is to be seen writing very tactfully, trying hard not to have to take sides. In general and on principle, he was in sympathy with the Turgot ministry.[16] But in 1774, in consonance with his liberal economic policy in general, Turgot had restored the freedom of trade in grain and flour inside France. Unluckily for him, a shortage ensued and caused riots, disturbances somewhat derisively called the 'Flour War' but severe enough to make Turgot's political position vulnerable.[17] In this instance Diderot presumably remained faithful to the ideas he had imbibed from Galiani and consequently thought Turgot's policy injudicious; but just as the riots were reaching their climax, Necker published his *Sur la législation et le commerce des grains,* a book which attacked Turgot's grain policy. Diderot's letter to Necker on this work evinced tact and circumspection. He did not choose to break with Necker, but he mentioned that there were some points on which they held differing views. Choosing his ground carefully and by-passing the grain trade, Diderot wrote instead of the important role of intellectuals in forming public opinion on any issue. Moreover, he audaciously suggested that '. . . if one has a delicate sense of smell, one seems to perceive that you do not have a very high esteem for philosophy and letters.' His comments could scarcely be taken as unalloyed praise. The total effect, though, so tactful was he trying to be, was probably one of increasing Necker's complacency.[18]

So long as the Turgot ministry lasted, Diderot did not give up asking for privileges for his children. During 1775 a second grandchild was born, Denis-Simon Caroillon de Vandeul, baptized at Saint-Sulpice the day of his birth, 27 June, his grandfather Diderot being the godfather. ('My daughter . . . has grandfatherized me,' he announced, and he often went to see the infant at the home of the wet-nurse.) [19] Now, in a letter of July to Sartine, recently become minister of the navy, Diderot asked in his family's behalf for the monopoly of supplying ship timbers to the Toulon naval base from the provinces of Lorraine, Franche-Comté, and Burgundy. 'Here, Monsieur, are grandchildren increasing around me and despite my long standing connections with the finance minister [Turgot] and my intimacy with his principal aide [Devaines], my poor little fortune remains the same. . . . Ambition, which I totally lack for myself, I have for my children. . . . I should like to see them rich; yes, Monsieur, very rich.' [20] Diderot also made a similar request of the Comte d'Angiviller, whom he

had long known in Mme Necker's circle and who now had the important position of Director of the King's Buildings, Arts, and Manufacturers.
This time it was a question of supplying drain pipes. D'Angiviller refused
in October 1775, but in terms so gracious as to make one suppose that this
incident occurred previously to another one which he describes with aversion in his memoirs. On this second occasion Diderot's daughter, he says,
demanded to see him in spite of his being ill and thereupon pressed upon
him a request to intercede with Turgot for the lease of a royal iron works
already assigned to a satisfactory lessee. D'Angiviller, 'revolted by the injustice of this affair,' asked Mme de Vandeul why Diderot had not gone directly to Turgot. 'Her response was, word for word, literally: "If the request
had been a just one, my father, Monsieur, would not have had recourse
to you." ' [21] D'Angiviller was a man of honor and his testimony cannot be
ignored. It is hard to believe, though, that Diderot, even if capable of
being so cynical and immoral, could also be so inept. Perhaps the French
Revolution, which intervened between this incident and D'Angiviller's
writing of his memoirs, soured his recollections.

Art criticism again claimed Diderot's attention in 1775. His *Salon* of that
year is, however, perfunctory and jejune. In form it is a dialogue between
Diderot and an embittered and caustic painter named Jacques-Philippe
Saint-Quentin, a former pupil of Boucher. In substance it is a harshly
negative piece of criticism, in which Saint-Quentin takes the initiative and
Diderot makes more or less feeble and laconic rejoinders.[22] More substantial and satisfactory is Diderot's *Pensées détachées sur la peinture, la
sculpture, l'architecture et la poésie* ('Random Thoughts on Painting,
Sculpture, Architecture, and Poetry'), which was composed sometime in
1775 and 1776, and which Diderot may have been revising up to the time
of his death.[23] The *Pensées détachées* is Diderot's last important contribution to art criticism, and is of particular interest, too, because it shows the
influence of his visits to the art galleries of Germany, Russia, and the Low
Countries. He mentions Rembrandt repeatedly, as well as Van Huysum
and Gerard Dou, and remarks that 'It was at Düsseldorf or at Dresden
that I saw "A Wild Boar" by Snyders.' [24]

The inspiration to set these thoughts on paper probably came from Diderot's reading the *Réflexions sur la peinture* (1775) by Christian Ludwig von
Hagedorn. The two men may have met at Dresden when Diderot passed
through on his way to Russia. In any event, he now had in his own
language Hagedorn's *Betrachtungen über die Malerei,* first published in
1762 and translated by Diderot's old acquaintance, Michel Huber. Diderot

followed the sequence and structure of the Hagedorn book closely, and authorities have noted the very large number of instances where Diderot adopts Hagedorn's ideas and often his very words. It therefore seems a little airy of Diderot to refer to Hagedorn by name in only one place. Nevertheless, there is much to be learned about Diderot's aesthetics from the *Pensées détachées,* so that one of his countrymen says of him, somewhat ruefully, 'If he does not emerge from the situation morally enhanced . . . he is not intellectually diminished.' [25]

Diderot's reading of Hagedorn did not transform his aesthetics; it simply reinforced in some areas of his thinking ideas he had already formed. In the *Pensées détachées* he advanced one step further in his criticism of the rococo art of the earlier part of the century, and one step nearer an aesthetic that insisted on greater moral earnestness.[26] There are multitudes of Hagedorn's observations that Diderot shows no interest in at all. He used Hagedorn as 'a foil or a springboard,' with the result that the *Pensées détachées* shows a man still maturing and deepening his understanding of art.[27]

An important part of the *Pensées détachées,* and one that does not seem to depend upon Hagedorn, is Diderot's exploration of the meaning of a word he had not much used before. This is the concept of the naïve. The naïve in art is the opposite of mannerism in art, according to Diderot's definitions. 'Mannerism is to the fine arts what hypocrisy is to morals,' a very evocative suggestion.

Not all that is true is naïve, but everything that is naïve is true, and of a trueness that is piquant, original, and rare. Almost all of Poussin's figures are naïve, that is to say perfectly and purely what they ought to be. Almost all of Raphael's old men, his women, his children, his angels, are naïve; that is to say, they have by nature a certain originality, a grace with which they were born.[28]

At this point, though, Diderot shows once again that he is aware of the great difficulties involved in an artist's imitating nature, difficulties disguised by the apparent simplicity of the effect which a successful imitation of nature achieves. 'Naïveté is a great resemblance of the imitation to the thing imitated, accompanied by a great skill in execution. It is water taken from the brook and thrown upon the canvas.' [29] Diderot, the man loving paradoxes, knew how paradoxical it is that the great artist finds himself interpreting or even profoundly modifying nature in order to achieve the illusion of successfully imitating her. Diderot was never a man to think that art is easy.

The *Pensées détachées* gives the impression of being more worked over and more polished than most of Diderot's other writings. The thoughts seem more abstract, too, and do not have the dash and bravura of much of the rest of his oeuvre. The expectant reader, hoping that Diderot would carry on from where he left off in the *Salon de 1767,* is accordingly likely to experience some sense of anti-climax. Perhaps it was just part of his getting old, similar to what can be observed in the quiet patience and resignation of his 'New Year's Lines of a Philosopher to His Old Friend,' a poem he wrote at the end of 1775, apparently, and presumably with Sophie Volland in mind.[30]

In comparison with the crowded and sociable years of the late 1760's and of the period before his journey to Russia, Diderot's life in the decade after the return from Saint Petersburg seems muted and crepuscular. He no longer had the vitality of earlier years, and in addition, his growing taste for life in the country made him less accessible and less visible. It is harder to feel that one is close to the throb of his day-to-day life.

Most of the year 1776 Diderot was at Sèvres, with a month from mid-October to mid-November spent at Grandval. There D'Holbach was agonizing with gout. 'An almost equally alarming symptom,' Diderot wrote to Grimm, 'is that he is thoroughly pleasant to his wife and children.'[31] Among the dozen letters written in 1776 was one to Voltaire, introducing the Marquis de Limon, 'a man of great merit'; one to Dr. Burney, thanking him for sending the first volume of his *A General History of Music;* and one to John Wilkes: 'I have read with great satisfaction the various orations you have delivered on the affair of the provincials [i.e., the American insurgents].' And then Diderot, knowing his man, gave Wilkes some congenial advice:

Be gay. Drink fine wines; and when the fancy takes you to be tender, address yourself to ladies who do not have to be sighed after for long.[32]

Five of the 1776 letters went to Grimm, who was in Saint Petersburg from September 1776 to August 1777:

Greetings, my friend, my old friend. We have lost Dr. Roux [who died 28 June 1776]; we thought we were going to lose the Baron; Mlle de Lespinasse is no longer here [she had died on 23 May 1776]; Mme Geoffrin might not be tomorrow [Mme Geoffrin had suffered a stroke on 28 August 1776]. Hurry up a little if you want to find anybody. Just think that October second I shall be sixty-three, four or five years old, which is it? It is an age when one counts the years, very close to the age when one counts the months and which is a close neighbor to the age when one lives from day to day.

Most of the time Diderot fell in with Grimm's constantly belittling him as a kind of immature child; and he fell in with it now. 'I shall die a child who never grew up. Some days ago I cracked my head against a block of marble in Pigalle's studio. After this fine adventure I went to see my daughter. My three-year-old grand-daughter saw me with an enormous bump on my head, and said, "Ah, grand-papa, do you bump your nose against doors too?" I laughed and I thought to myself that I have not been doing anything else since I was born.' [33]

To both Grimm and to Denise Diderot the *philosophe* spoke in similar terms of the onset of age. 'As for me, I am moving out little by little; I am sending the bulky baggage on ahead, such as teeth that are either falling out or loose, eyes that no longer see well at night, ears that have commenced to become hard of hearing, and legs that prefer rest to exercise.' But in itemizing this catalogue to Grimm Diderot added, with perhaps not unpardonable vainglory, that in spite of these depredations of age, 'I nonetheless carry up in the air the augur's wand.' [34]

The grimmest political happening in France in 1776 was the fall of Turgot, which occurred on 12 May. Galiani was about the only *philosophe* in Europe who was pleased by this event; the others now began to despair that any real reforms could ever be made to stick. Diderot, remembering the experiences of his sensible old craftsman father, had disagreed sharply with Galiani, who disapproved of Turgot's suppression of the guilds. Diderot did not comment much in his correspondence about Turgot's dismissal — after all, at about this time several letters that Diderot addressed to the publisher Rey in Amsterdam never arrived and presumably were intercepted by the police — but he did say to Grimm about Necker, who succeeded to Turgot's functions in October 1776, 'I hope that the impossibility of accomplishing good will not disgust him with the simple function of preventing evil.' [35]

In 1776 the literary scene was greatly enlivened in France by an assault on Shakespeare from no less a personage than Voltaire and in no less august a place than the Académie Française. Voltaire's letter to the Academy, which was read in its session of 25 August, attacked the Le Tourneur translation of Shakespeare, the first two volumes of which had been published in March. Even more, it inveighed against Shakespeare for what Voltaire alleged to be his bad taste and his barbarous mixing of genres.[36]

Diderot was not involved in the public dispute. Nevertheless his feeling about Shakespeare can be inferred from the fact that he had subscribed to no fewer than six sets of the Le Tourneur translation. Moreover, the sub-

ject of Shakespeare arose just at this time in connection with Diderot's
effort to help his friend François Tronchin, who in his youth had written
a tragedy entitled *Térentia* and now in his old age was trying to finish it.
Diderot did considerable work on this tragedy — 'It is the rapid scribbling
of five mornings' — and, besides blocking out a draft of the play, wrote
Tronchin a letter of suggestions in which the subject of Shakespeare suddenly came to the fore. To understand Diderot's vivid metaphor, it should
be recalled that in his time there was a colossal statue of Saint Christopher
at Notre-Dame de Paris, put up in the fifteenth century and between the
legs of which people passed to get into the cathedral.

Ah, Monsieur, this Shakespeare was a terrible mortal. He is not the Dying
Gladiator nor the Apollo Belvedere, but rather the misshapen and uncouth Saint
Christopher of Notre-Dame. A Gothic colossus, but between the legs of which
we all could pass without the tops of our heads touching his testicles.[37]

Voltaire, who often saw Tronchin at Geneva, may perhaps have discovered
Diderot's opinion from him. In any event, if Voltaire and Diderot did
meet face to face at Paris fifteen months later, the subject of Shakespeare could easily have arisen and easily caused mutual discontent.

Diderot ended the year by writing with great satisfaction of the prosperity of the Vandeul brothers, who had just received the lease of another
valuable iron-works. 'This is not at all bad for young people just starting
out.' His only worry at that moment was that they were trying to carry
on too many enterprises at once. But presently, since part of their fortune was menaced by a regulation of the new administration, Diderot
was worrying again. He wrote to Necker to ask him not to do his children
any harm. 'I cannot tell you how much your forgetting this would grieve
me.'[38]

For several months in the winter of 1776–7 Diderot was hard at work
in the country writing material for the Abbé Raynal to use in the
third edition of his *Histoire philosophique et politique des établissements
et du commerce des Européens dans les deux Indes* ('Philosophical and
Political History of the European Establishments and Trade in the Two
Indies').[39] This perennial best-seller, which was first published in 1770
and had gone into an enlarged edition in 1774, proceeded from edition to
edition in an exciting crescendo of humanitarianism and anticolonialism.
The dry and platitudinous Raynal furnished the statistics (and it should
be remembered that the *Histoire des deux Indes* is an impressively data-

laden work); he also had the commercial acumen to realize that his book needed passion and flair, and for this he turned to several unnamed collaborators, the most important of whom was Diderot.

According to Mme de Vandeul, who speaks of a task undertaken for one of his friends, he sometimes worked fourteen hours on end. His desire, wrote his daughter, was to make his friend's book 'a model of eloquence.' [40] Diderot contributed to all three of the Raynal editions: least of all to the first; considerably but hurriedly to the second; and substantially and passionately to the third.[41] The degree of his involvement can be gauged by the explosiveness and fury of his letter in 1781 to Grimm in defense of Raynal.

It is interesting to speculate as to why Diderot became so emotionally identified with the libertarianism and humanitarianism of Raynal's book. One of the reasons was the increasing political-mindedness of the last fifteen years of Diderot's life. During them he moved consistently, as would be said now, to the left. From 1771, when he wrote the *Apologie de l'Abbé Galiani,* right through 1782, when he published his *Essai sur les règnes de Claude et de Néron,* it is striking to observe how much of his writing is devoted to political questions, or to social and moral ones that have strong political overtones. His intense dislike of Maupeou's policies are often reflected in his writings from 1770 to 1774, such as in his letter to Princess Dashkov, his poem on eleutheromania, and his remarks to the Empress in his *Mémoires pour Catherine II.* Then there was his growing animosity against Frederick II of Prussia, as illustrated by the *Pages inédites contre un tyran* and the *Principes de politique des souverains.* The visit to Russia reinforced Diderot's love of freedom and detestation of despotism, as can be seen in his *Observations sur le Nakaz.* Meanwhile, there is much political theory, as well as ethical theory, in the *Réfutation d'Helvétius;* and his *Plan d'une université pour le gouvernement de Russie* has democratic overtones.

And yet this was a Diderot who published very little. The radicalization of his politics was an aspect of his thought completely unsuspected by most of his contemporaries. Scholars are still piecing together his political thought and putting it into perspective as the various Diderot manuscripts are rediscovered and assimilated. Actually, the seasoned old propagandist, the scarred but triumphant veteran of the *Encyclopédie,* must constantly have had the impulse to declare himself in print, however veiled and Aesopian his language might have had to be. In one instance during this period he did publish what was covertly a political work. This was the *Essai sur Sénèque* (1779) which, in 1782, became the enlarged *Essai sur les règnes de Claude et de Néron*. Why did he not publish more?

It has been suggested that Diderot suppressed his views on politics during this period because he did not want to prejudice the financial prospects of Angélique and her money-hungry husband. Diderot had hostages to fortune. They depended for favors upon the very persons most influential in the Establishment that Diderot was in his private thoughts coming more and more to deplore. This plausible hypothesis would explain why he entered with such passion and such a sense of engagement into contributing to Raynal's book. It was a means of expressing himself. It was a way, although an indirect one, of disseminating his views.[42] It was a medium by which he could attenuate his frustrations. Thus it is no wonder that his sense of identification with the *Histoire des deux Indes* can be demonstrated to have grown from edition to edition.

According to Mme de Vandeul, Diderot read numerous books in order to qualify himself appropriately for his contributions. This tallies with the impression that scholars now have that Diderot's writings show the result during these years of new enrichment. Not only a continuation of the deepening of his political thought but a great extension of his sense of history can be observed at this time. The ever-developing Diderot was becoming a man more aware of history and the philosophy of history.[43]

Sometimes Diderot questioned Raynal's confidence: 'But, my friend, who is going to be daring enough to publish and take responsibility [for these inflammatory statements]?'

'I! I! . . . I see that you think that I have much less courage than I do.'

Another time, 'Tired of working, and seeking a pretext that would curtail the length and fatigue of my task,' Diderot continued to Grimm in 1781, 'I wrote to the Abbé. "But, dear Abbé, are you not afraid that all these digressions, however eloquent you think them, may somewhat spoil your book?" "No, no," he replied, "keep right on with what I ask you. . . . I know the taste of the public a little better than you do. Your lines will compensate for the boredom of my everlasting calculations." '[44] So extensive were Diderot's contributions that Meister declared in 1786 that Diderot had been occupied with the *Histoire des deux Indes* to the exclusion of almost everything else for two whole years. 'Who does not know today that more than a third of this great work belongs to him?'[45]

Raynal revised Diderot's contributions, probably for the purpose of making the whole work as uniform in style as possible. He had every right to do this, inasmuch as he paid Diderot for his contributions.[46] The result, however, has been to raise many intricate questions of textual analysis when it becomes important, as it is, to identify precisely what belongs to Diderot. Manuscripts discovered in the mid-twentieth century have helped to make posterity realize how integrated and consistent is all of Diderot's political thought. His contributions to Raynal are suffused with reflections from his other political writings during this period.[47]

As an illustration of Diderot's democratic political theory, which he made available for Raynal, consider the following:

It has sometimes been said that the best government would be that of a just and enlightened despot. This is a very dubious proposition. It might easily happen that the will of this absolute master would be in contradiction to the will of his subjects. Then, in spite of his justice and his enlightenment, he would be wrong to despoil his subjects of their rights, even to their advantage. One can abuse one's power to do good as well as to do evil; and it is never allowable to any man, whoever he is, to treat persons committed to his charge as if they were a herd of beasts.

Here Diderot coined a new word and propounded a revolutionary idea. Even a good sovereign, he declared, if he goes against the general will, is guilty, as he expressed it, of 'lèse-société.' The legal concept of 'lèse-majesté' was old, hoary with antiquity and with abuse; the word 'lèse-société' was new and sounds like Robespierre.

Peoples, do not allow your self-styled masters to do good, even, against your volonté générale.[48]

Throughout these years and up to the time of his death Diderot worked off and on at collecting and arranging his own works in view of eventual publication, so that if we do not know precisely what was occupying him at a given moment, it is tempting — and probably quite accurate — to say that he was arranging and editing his works. In 1777 he twice wrote to Rey of Amsterdam about publication, declared that he did not want to die without having published his works, and promised to bring his books and manuscripts to Amsterdam in person whenever they were ready. In later years he ceased to speak of an edition to be published in his lifetime, perhaps because he had persuaded himself that even if it were published, the authorities would not allow it to be sold in France.[49] Nevertheless the actual collecting of his works seems to have occupied him to the end.

Much of 1777 was spent in the country, at Sèvres.[50] Diderot wrote of having 'escaped' from the city, as well as of his 'disgust with the city, where my time is not my own; where I am abandoned to a crowd of people whom my wife calls "the itchy ones who come to me to be scratched." '[51] This was the new Diderot, trying to hold his sensibility in check. In this year he withdrew himself so much from the affairs of Paris that he declined, though graciously and with many compliments, invitations from Beaumarchais and from a lesser-known dramatist, Sébastien Mercier, to participate in an 'insurgency' of the playwrights against the company of the Comédie-Française.[52]

Some idea of the extent of Diderot's celebrity can be gained from an incident in the Emperor Joseph II's visit to Paris in 1777. Traveling incognito as the Count of Falkenstein, the Emperor included in his visitations the French Academy, where he caused some embarrassment by asking D'Alembert why Diderot and Raynal were not members.[53] Also during that year the sculptor Pigalle finished a bronze bust of Diderot which is now in the Louvre. Diderot, who that year was continuing to give François Tronchin advice about how to revise his youthful plays, promised him one of the Pigalle busts. The Pigalle sculpture shows a Diderot without a wig and with his shirt open at the throat. It is a Diderot who is quite fleshy, with the contours of the cheeks beginning to sag, a Diderot who has been grandfatherized — an aging man but a still vigorous one.[54]

In 1777 Diderot wrote to Grimm that he had written a gay comedy, all between a Saturday evening and the following Monday morning. This was almost certainly *La Pièce et le prologue,* which is the intermediate stage of what, a year or two later, became Diderot's best play, *Est-il bon? Est-il méchant?* [55] As early as November 1775 he had blocked out the series of scenes for his idea, calling it merely a *Plan d'un divertissement domestique.*[56] It is thus possible to trace the development of an ingenious and witty dramatic idea through its several stages. Though the final version has long been known, *Est-il bon? Est-il méchant?* remained unstaged for over a hundred years, nor did it have its *première* at the Comédie-Française until 1955.[57]

Est-il bon? Est-il méchant? is a beguiling play, most of all because of its central character, Hardouin. Not only is Hardouin a personage strongly savorous of Diderot himself, but Diderot intended it to be so. And he intended it to be realized, for he has a character say to Hardouin at one point, 'That is a fine reward for a man of letters who has spent three-quarters of his life in an honorable and useful way, has not yet received the least sign of recognition from the government, and who, without the munificence of a foreign sovereign. . . . Adieu.'[58] The image of himself that

Diderot projects in Hardouin is that of an obliging and good-natured man who cannot restrain himself from trying to resolve other people's problems. He thus finds himself gratuitously and simultaneously involved in no fewer than six complicated human entanglements. Consequently, in his capacity as a playwright, Diderot finds himself faced with the task of co-ordinating a formidably intricate plot. He is very successful with it, and the dénouement of *Est-il bon? Est-il méchant?*, unlike those of Diderot's other plays, does not depend upon coincidence. This in itself, it must be acknowledged, is an improvement. The point of the play is that Hardouin resolves all of these problems happily but by means of deceit, so that everyone ends up by being angry with him. Is it good to act this way, or is it bad? The playwright leaves us with the distinct implication that it is more good than bad. Still, he does ask the question. And he leaves the spectator or the reader with a lively awareness of the ambiguities of the human condition.

Numerous circumstances and events in Diderot's life seem to be alluded to in *Est-il bon? Est-il méchant?* Hardouin's lodgings, as described by a footman, seem to resemble the Rue Taranne. The character named Surmont is pretty plainly the dramatist Sedaine. Diderot was well acquainted with highly placed secretaries in the ministries, such as a *premier commis* for the colonies named Dubucq, and a man named Rodier. In *Est-il bon? Est-il méchant?* the character Poultier becomes a kind of amalgam of these, with Rodier predominating.[59] And Diderot in real life did try to help out a rich friend beset by a litigious lawyer: this was Mme Geoffrin, and the incident can be followed in Diderot's letters to Sophie Volland.[60]

Est-il bon? Est-il méchant? was in germ intended merely for a private theatrical, perhaps at Mme de Maux's. Diderot himself played the part of Hardouin in a private performance.[61] Such being the modest intention of the play, it does not carry all the portentous freight of dramatic theory that Diderot loaded upon *Le Fils naturel* and *Le Père de famille*. Being less pretentious, it has turned out to be more entertaining. Also, it portrays with skill a variety of persons — lackeys, a lawyer, an irate mother, a government official, a widow of a ship's captain — and Diderot makes them speak like themselves. This, too, was different from his earlier plays, of which one of his friends told him, 'You have the opposite of a dramatist's talent. He must transform himself into his characters, and you transform them into you.'[62]

Est-il bon? Est-il méchant? is, then, an inventive and innovative play.[63] It may be, too, that Diderot intended the play to be a social satire. One cannot be certain of his intentions in this respect and, in any event, *Est-il bon? Est-il méchant?* is far less pointed and intense than *Le Neveu de Rameau*. But it is possible that part of his purpose was to depict a society in decay. According to this view, endorsed by several critics, the accepted procedures of society having become corrupted as they were, Hardouin had to be 'bad' in order to be good.[64]

Biographically, the form and the content of *Est-il bon? Est-il méchant?* tells us a great deal about the Diderot of the last ten years of his life.[65] It is a Diderot who has not lost his creative powers, for it is no small feat to be able to co-ordinate satisfactorily so complicated a machine; it is a Diderot who is still ebullient, still effervescent, still bubbling; it is a Diderot who continues to pose moral questions, and, under a surface of what appears to be a somewhat frivolous casuistry, explores serious moral predicaments; it is a Diderot still questing, a man who asks ethical questions not in a spirit of resignation or of hopelessness, but in the spirit of a self-examining man exploring the ambiguities of the moral world. It is not an especially triumphant Diderot, but it is an undefeated one.

In 1778 Voltaire dared to return to Paris, after an absence of almost thirty years. He arrived on 10 February, and spent the next few weeks in a fever of being lionized and hero-worshiped. He died on 30 May, of apotheosis and over-excitement. During this visit he certainly met Benjamin Franklin. But did he also meet Diderot? It would seem to be very natural that the two should meet. Voltaire had written to Diderot of his repugnance at having to die before their meeting face to face; Diderot had often expressed, to Naigeon and to others, his admiration of Voltaire, and had done so eloquently and magnanimously.[66] Now that an occasion for their conveniently meeting was at last at hand, it is astonishing that very little direct evidence exists to prove that such an encounter really took place. A journalist of the time, Métra, says that it did, and records the very witty and graceful remarks that each man made of the other after the interview. Diderot is alleged to have said, 'He resembles one of those ancient fairy castles that is falling to ruin on all sides; but you can easily see that it is inhabited by an old sorcerer.' And Voltaire, who is said to have had difficulty getting a word in edgewise, is alleged to have remarked, 'This man certainly has great wit; but one talent nature has refused him, and that is an essential one, that of dialogue.'[67]

Then there are two accounts, predicating a discussion face to face, in which it is said that a dispute arose over the merits of Shakespeare. Each account states that Diderot in his discussion with Voltaire compared Shake-

speare to the colossal statue of Saint Christopher at Notre-Dame.[68] Finally,
Diderot himself wrote in the *Essai sur les règnes de Claude et de Néron,*

I recall his complaining bitterly one day of the stigma that magistrates were
putting on books and persons. 'But,' I added, 'this stigma that afflicts you, do
you not realize that time takes it away and shifts it onto the unjust magistrate? The hemlock was as good as a temple for the philosopher of Athens. . . .'
Then the old man took me in his arms and pressing me tenderly to his breast,
added, 'You are right, and this is what I expected of you. . . .' [69]

None of this evidence is specific as to time and place, though all of it is
in character and rings true. It is odd, considering the celebrity of the two
men, that there is not a cloud of witnesses eager to tell their versions of
the encounter, if it really occurred. Even if the interview was an extremely
private one, why did not the participants frequently mention it as having
taken place? And how does it happen that Mme de Vandeul does not speak
of it in her biographical memoir of her father? To this it could be answered
that Diderot did speak of it, if only once; that Voltaire, in the short time
remaining to him to live, was too occupied to mention it to other persons;
and that Mme de Vandeul happened to be absent from Paris in early 1778.[70]
Some noted authorities believe that the interview never did occur.[71] A
possible conjecture, which at least has the merit of reconciling both the evidence and the lack of it, would be that the interview really did take place,
under circumstances so private that almost nobody knew of it, and that
in the course of it a dispute arose, very likely over Shakespeare, which
ruffled each of the protagonists and disposed each of them to avoid mentioning their meeting.
Meager though it is, information concerning Diderot during his last
years shows him in character. During these months in 1777–8 he aided
the dramatist Barthe in writing *L'Homme personnel.* For the New Year of
1778 he produced some occasional verse, and during these months he wrote
warm and earnest letters of recommendation, one to Mme Necker, and
another to Count Münich in Russia, entreating aid for protégées.[72] To his
sister Denise he wrote again of his getting old, but perhaps in terms not to
be taken too seriously, and scolded her for being too frugal, too self-de-
nying. 'Whatever harm that you do to your health is not guiltless. . . . Often it is a better action to remain warmly in bed than to go get numb
in church.' [73] During 1778 the Dutch scientist Camper, with whom Diderot
had been friendly at The Hague, saw him in Paris. Also, in June, Diderot
received a visit from the Swiss Moultou, a friend of the Neckers, and read

to him portions of *Jacques le fataliste* and the *Essai sur Sénèque*. In October we find Diderot goodnaturedly obliging the actor Desessarts, a fellow-townsman from Langres, who had asked for a letter supporting his request to the Comédie-Française to be assigned exclusively the role of the Commander in *Le Père de famille*.[74]

Diderot's principal writing effort in 1778 was his *Essai sur Sénèque*. He mentioned in the previous July having commenced reading for the project, and enough of the *Essai* was finished by June 1778 to allow him to read parts of it to a company that included Moultou. The approbation of the censor was received on 25 November and the book was published the next month, the title page bearing the date 1779.[75]

His essay constituted the seventh and last volume of a translation of Seneca's works which had been undertaken by La Grange. He died in 1775, but the edition was carried on in his memory, with most of the work, apparently, being done by Naigeon. Naigeon and D'Holbach invited Diderot to write this supplementary essay, which, as Diderot remarked, grew from a very small number of pages to be a volume (and, in the edition of 1782, further grew to almost twice the size). Once begun, Diderot's researches on Seneca became an obsession, and Mme de Vandeul avers that it sapped the remains of his strength.[76]

Diderot had previously not been fond of Seneca. In the *Essai sur le mérite et la vertu* there had appeared a very scornful note. 'It will be found that I treat this philosopher a little harshly; but it is not possible, by Tacitus' recounting, to think of him more favorably.' But by 1778 Diderot had turned quite around, as he explicitly admitted in the *Essai sur Sénèque*, quoting and criticizing himself at length. What had changed was that he had become profoundly impressed by 'the difficulty and the dignity of his [Seneca's] role.'[77] Diderot read widely in preparation for writing the *Essai*, so that he cites not only all of the works of Seneca (except the plays, which in the eighteenth century were thought to have been written by someone else) but also several scores of ancient and modern authors: 'Quintilian . . . Columella, Plutarch, Juvenal, Fronto, Martial, Sidonius Apollinaris, Aulus Gellius, Tertullian, Lactantius, Saint Augustine, Saint Jerome, Justus Lipsius, Erasmus, Montaigne and many others.'[78]

An English divine visiting in Paris wrote that 'Diderot has just published a very clever book, with which I am exceedingly pleased, *La Vie de Sénèque*; one volume, 519 pages; but I cannot find a page *de trop*.'[79] Other commentators were much more qualified. The *Correspondance littéraire*, now being edited by Meister, did say in praise that 'The task of avenging a great man calumniated was worthy of the philosopher who was himself so often exposed to the most envenomed arrows of calumny and persecution.' But even so sympathetic a critic had to admit that 'The reproach most generally addressed to M. Diderot is that he is disjointed; the complaint is made that he too frequently abandons his subject in order to give himself up to purely subsidiary reflections; that he passes too rapidly from one subject and sometimes even from one tone to another, from the historical style to the moral style, from a conversational tone to one of the most exalted eloquence. . . .'[80]

Fréron, meanwhile, had died. But the review of Diderot's *Essai sur Sénèque* in the *Année Littéraire* might well persuade some Rip Van Winkle reader that the old warrior was still alive. Two installments were required to do justice to the reviewer's feelings. The first disposed of Seneca: 'In a word, of all the crimes committed by Nero, was there a single one openly opposed by Seneca, a single one that he attempted to make the prince ashamed of after he had been defiled by it? I defy M. Diderot to cite it.' The second disposed of Diderot:

M. Diderot knows no other style than that of the ode or epic. His weightiest dissertations are always animated by some Pindaric outbursts. The enthusiasm that possesses him, the demon who agitates him, never quit him; he is the Pythian priestess, forever seated on the tripod. . . . Such is the motive and such are the means by which the prime architect of the *Encyclopédie,* past master of the art of inflating compilations, has been able to blow up to 520 pages an essay that would not contain a hundred if all that is irrelevant to the justification of Seneca were cut out.[81]

The severest criticisms, however, came from those who were scandalized by Diderot's having inserted a note which, without naming names, could have been aimed at no one but Rousseau. He had died that year, on 2 July, and it was generally expected that his *Confessions* would thereupon be published. Through the years Diderot had allowed himself to speak to third persons about the blackness of Rousseau's character: he did so at The Hague in 1773, and evidently continued to do so, for in 1778 Rousseau told the Lieutenant-General of Police, Le Noir, 'You have wished to do me a service. If it were possible for you to oblige me a second time, it would be to make Diderot keep quiet.' Bachaumont's *Mémoires secrets* recorded on 20 July 1778 that 'M. Diderot is one of those who most fears the publicity of the *Mémoires* of Rousseau. . . . One would judge from his [Diderot's] remarks that at bottom Rousseau was a bad man.'[82]

It was entirely gratuitous of Diderot to allude to Rousseau in the *Essai sur Sénèque,* and the fact that he did so proves what an obsession his *'frère ennemi'* had become. Probably it was Rousseau's impenetrability, his invulnerability, his inaccessibility that irritated Diderot through the years to the point of now impairing his judgment. For it could scarcely be called good judgment to admonish his readers darkly to 'detest the ingrate who speaks evil of his benefactors; detest the atrocious man who does not hesitate to blacken his former friends; detest the coward who leaves upon his tomb the revelation of secrets either confided to him or which he had surprised.' Meister wrote of this paragraph that 'the worshipers of the citizen of Geneva' were indignant, while 'the best friends of M. Diderot, who most have the right of sharing the just resentment that dictated the note, find it useless and out of place.' [83]

Diderot's *Essai sur les règnes de Claude et de Néron* is useful to an extraordinary degree in helping us to observe his tensions and frustrations in the latter years of his life.[84] The two editions, the *Essai* of 1779 and the *Essai* of 1782, show how concerned he was in his last years with problems of political theory and of public morality. These two editions, moreover, are extremely autobiographical in flavor.[85] They constitute a kind of *apologia pro vita sua.* It is an apologia, however, that he did not have to write and almost surely would have been wiser not to have written. That he could not desist from doing so bespeaks a condition of psychological turmoil that must greatly have affected his last years.

Diderot identified himself strongly and even intemperately with Seneca, the man of letters who found himself in a morally ambiguous relationship with a despotic and tyrannical ruler. This suggests that Diderot was aware, and even very uncomfortably aware, that public opinion was equating his relationship to Catherine II with Seneca's to Nero. In each instance the moral question was, What is the proper role (and what are the limits of the proper role) of the *philosophe,* the man of letters, the intellectual, in relation to a despot? It is very noticeable that Diderot does not make his book a paean of praise of Catherine II, as one might have expected him to do. In fact, he mentions her very rarely, though each time with praise.[86] Hers is the unseen presence in the *Essai sur les règnes de Claude et de Néron,* throwing her shadow over his life until the end.

Having embarked upon an essay on Seneca for the sake of his dead friend La Grange, Diderot was unable to avoid letting his obsessions come to light. He could not keep himself from revealing the sense of guilt of a freedom-loving man who has let himself be caught in the bonds of moral obligations to a despot. Nor could he prevent himself from betraying his deep-seated and permanent agitation over Rousseau. The *Essai sur Sénèque,* and its later amplification, the *Essai sur les règnes de Claude et de Néron,* are important books for studying points at which Diderot's unconscious comes surging to the threshold of conscious recognition.

CHAPTER 48

Last Writings, Ill Health, and Death

D URING the winter that the *Essai sur Sénèque* was published, Diderot was much concerned with journalists and their ways. His *Essai* was being mauled by reviewers; he permitted a young Alsatian friend, François-Michel Leuchsenring, to publish a few fugitive pieces in the latter's *Journal de Lecture;*[1] and in February the widely-read *Mercure de France* published a hilarious description of Diderot written by a young man of letters named Garat. His is the most graphic word-picture of Diderot's behavior that we have, as valuable of its kind as the drawing by Greuze or the bust by Marie Collot.

Some time ago the need came upon me, as it has to so many others, to put black on white, which is called writing a book. I sought solitude, the better to collect all my reveries and meditate upon them. A friend lent me an apartment in a charming house in a countryside that would make a poet or a philosopher of anyone capable of feeling its beauties. Scarcely am I there when I learn that M. Diderot lodges next to me, in an apartment of the same house. I am not exaggerating at all when I say that my heart beat violently and I forgot all my projects in prose and verse to think only of seeing the great man whose genius I had so many times admired. I enter his apartment with the break of day and he seems no more surprised to see me than to see day dawn again. He spares me the embarrassment of gauchely mumbling the reasons for my visit. Apparently he guesses it from that look of great admiration which I must have been wearing. He spared me, too, the lengthy detours of a conversation that I was absolutely determined to bring around to prose and verse. Scarcely does the subject come up, he rises, he fixes his eyes on me, and it is very evident that he no longer sees me at all. He begins to speak, but at first so low and so fast that, though I am close to him, though I touch him, I have difficulty in hearing and following him. I perceive instantly that my whole role in this scene is going to be limited to that of admiring him in silence: and this course is not hard for me to follow. Little by little his voice rises and becomes distinct and sonorous. At first he was almost immobile. His gestures become frequent and animated. He never saw me before this meeting; but when we stand, he puts his arms around me, when we sit he slaps me on the thigh as though it were his own. If the quick and nimble linkages of his talk bring forth the word 'laws,' he outlines to me a plan of legislation. If they bring up the word 'theater,' he offers me the choice among five or six plots of plays. Apropos of the tableaux that ought to be put on the stage, where one should see scenes and not hear dialogues, he recalls that Tacitus is the greatest painter in antiquity and he recites or translates the *Annals* and the *Histories*. But how deplorable it is that the barbarians buried under the ruins of architectural masterpieces such a large number of the masterpieces of Tacitus. Thereupon he is moved to tears over the loss of so many fine things, which he regrets and weeps for as if he had known them personally. If only the monuments disinterred in the excavations at Herculaneum might at least uncover some books of the *Histories* or the *Annals!* And this hope transports him with joy. Yet how often have ignorant hands destroyed the masterpieces preserved in tombs while uncovering them! And thereupon he descants like an Italian engineer on the way to proceed with excavations in a prudent and successful manner. Then letting his imagination wander over the ruins of ancient Italy, he recalls how the arts, taste, and politeness of Athens tempered the terrible virtues of the conquerors of the world. He carries himself back to those happy days of the Leliuses and the Scipios when even the conquered nations participated with pleasure in the triumphs for the victories gained over them. He plays for me an entire scene from Terence. He almost sings several carmina of Horace. He finishes by really singing a song full of grace and wit which he wrote himself impromptu during a supper, and recites to me a very agreeable comedy of which he has had one single specimen printed in order to spare himself the trouble of having to copy it. Several people then enter his apartment. The noise of carriages advancing and backing up causes him to emerge from his enthusiasm and his monologue. He discerns me among the company and comes up to me as one does to someone one meets again after having met him pleasurably somewhere before. He still remembers that we exchanged some very interesting views on the laws, on dramas, and on history. He knew that there was much to be gained from my conversation. He invites me to cultivate an intimacy the value of which he fully appreciates. As we separate he kisses me twice on the forehead and withdraws his hand from mine with real regret.[2]

Diderot himself laughingly agreed that the caricature was apt. 'One will be tempted to take me for some sort of character; but what difference does that make? Is it so great a fault to have been able to keep some remnants of nature while constantly moving in society, and to distinguish oneself by a few rough edges from the multitude of those uniform and smooth pebbles that abound on every beach?'[3] In fact, he was proud of being different. Grimm once wrote to Mme Necker about Diderot, 'He would rather invent the minuet than dance it the way others do.'[4]

Garat's account was evidently not much of an exaggeration. A very similar encounter had taken place about twenty years before, with the youthful La Harpe. 'The interview lasted about four hours; he stood almost all the time, moving about or walking; and if by chance he sat down, it was all a part of his pantomime.'[5] Contemporary observers often spoke of Diderot's conversation as being a pantomime. 'No one knows better than he the pantomime of an account,' Luneau de Boisjermain wrote of Diderot. He was a man of 'indescribable vivacity,' wrote Björnståhl.[6] His conversation was full of ejaculations and dramatic pauses. Speaking usually with great rapidity and vehemence, sometimes his voice fell to a whisper for effect.[7] Those who liked him and who liked to be borne along by the torrent of his discourse spoke of the charm of his conversation and its endearing qualities.[8] Others, like Mlle de Lespinasse, though not antagonistic to him, nevertheless complained that he forced himself upon one's attention. Moreover, she claimed, his *sensibilité* was only skin-deep.[9] And his enemies, of course, asserted that his eloquence and passion were factitious and contrived.

Diderot struck many observers, as he did Catherine II, as being an unusual combination of the wisdom of a venerable sage with the waywardness of a child. Grimm often referred to Diderot's being childish, though perhaps Grimm's motives in doing so were mixed.[10] Other of Diderot's friends, too, noticed this mixture of sagacity and childishness. When Catherine II remarked of him, 'Sometimes I see you a hundred years old and often, too, I see you as a child of twelve,' Mlle de Lespinasse commented, 'That portrays Diderot,' and Suard, 'This is to visualize him marvellously well.'[11]

In Paris it was difficult to be objective about Diderot's idiosyncrasies and behavior. They were too closely identified with what amounted to a political party. Perhaps more objective, therefore, was the judgment of a foreigner like Hemsterhuis, even though he had been criticized by Diderot and was critical of him in turn. Nevertheless, Hemsterhuis wrote, 'I do not know why it is, but I never think of this man without a lively desire to see him again.'[12]

Diderot's letters in 1779 show that he began his day's work at Sèvres (or at Mme de Maux's house in the nearby village of Boulogne) between four and five in the morning, thus confirming in that respect Garat's account of visiting him at the break of day. Presumably Diderot, who earlier had been a nocturnal worker, was now finding his sight too dim to work by candlelight. In May of 1779 he mentioned being hard at work on material for the Abbé Raynal (which evidently went into the 1780 edition of the *Histoire des deux Indes*).[13] In the latter months of the year Diderot assiduously and successfully tried to secure a desirable government appointment for Vallet de Fayolle, the nephew of Sophie Volland who had emigrated to Cayenne fifteen years before on Diderot's advice.[14] Why Diderot solicited and received a gift from Catherine II of 2000 rubles in the course of 1779 is not known.[15]

In the late 1770's Diderot's attention was attracted to events in Spain as never before. The reason was no doubt his need for information in view of what he was writing for Raynal's *Histoire des deux Indes*. It was during these years that Diderot became closely acquainted with a Spaniard named Miguel Gijón.[16] As a result of information derived from him, Diderot wrote for the *Correspondance littéraire* an interesting biographical essay on Don Pablo de Olavide. Born in Lima and growing up to be a very able public administrator, Olavide was among all the Spaniards of the eighteenth century (save perhaps Feyjóo) the one who came nearest to being a *philosophe*. Sources close to him said that he had had a complete set of the *Encyclopédie* smuggled into Spain and walled up in the altar of a new church being built in a region of which he was the administrator. Evidently Olavide believed in posterity too. It is not surprising that he became a hero to Diderot or an object of suspicion to the Inquisition.

We have written this abridged account of the misfortunes of Olavide in order to apprise men of how dangerous it is to do good contrary to the will of the Inquisition, and [to teach them] to watch themselves wherever this tribunal exists.[17]

At the same time, presumably also from information supplied by Gijón, Diderot wrote an account of 'The Jesuits Expelled from Spain.'[18]

Totally unexpected recognition of his celebrity and eminence came to Diderot in 1780–1 from his native city. One of the magistrates of Langres offered the city a complete set of the *Encyclopédie,* to be kept in the City Hall and to be available to any citizen. The Municipal Council of Langres not only accepted the gift but also voted by acclamation to have a portrait painted of Diderot, to be hung in one of the rooms of the Hôtel de Ville. Diderot, who never in his life scorned his native city nor his provincial origins, presumably was delighted. It is a pity that his letter has been lost, for one can readily imagine how richly redolent of him it must have been. His response was a generous one. Instead of merely sitting for his portrait, he gave to Langres a bronze bust of himself done by Houdon. It is perhaps the finest of all of Houdon's busts of Diderot. The city fathers, evidently following his suggestion, celebrated the donation and the donor by a dinner, the menu of which proves it to have been Gargantuan but which was described in the official minutes as being 'a frugal repast.' Diderot's brother, the Abbé, was invited to the frugal repast, but refused; soon thereafter, on some pretense of business, his curiosity took him to the Hôtel de Ville to see the bust.[19]

In October 1780, when Falconet once again wanted to publish the Diderot-Falconet letters on immortality, Diderot frostily refused. Some other important (but unspecified) task had priority, he said.[20] This could scarcely have been the work for Raynal, for by that time the third edition of the *Histoire des deux Indes* must already have been in press. Probably, then, it was the *Eléments de physiologie,* a great hulking carcass of a work which tells us worlds about the mentality of Diderot without nevertheless achieving much of a position in a catalogue of his works. This repository of information, a kind of compendium of medical knowledge, follows closely in structure and arrangement the monumental *Elementa physiologiae corporis humani* of Albrecht von Haller.[21] It is conjectured that Diderot began to gather this material in the 1760's and that the collection served as a source for his ideas in *Le Rêve de d'Alembert.*[22] He continued this compilation up to the time of his death. Accordingly the *Eléments de physiologie* is hard to date; its accumulation extends over fifteen years. But the fact that in August 1780 he was trying to acquire the tables of contents of the eight volumes of Haller's work — 'which tables are missing in my set' — suggests that the *Eléments de physiologie* was especially occupying him in that year.[23]

It was in 1780, too, in reviewing a treatise on the history of surgery, that Diderot emphasized once again his conviction that 'there is no sound philosophy without medicine':

Speculative philosophers would have walked at a quicker and surer pace in the search for truth had they derived through the study of medicine a knowledge of facts which cannot be guessed at and which alone are capable of confirming or destroying metaphysical reasonings. How many peculiarities of the nature of the mind will such philosophers be ignorant of unless they are informed of what doctors have said about the nature of the body.[24]

Diderot was always a strong believer in what would now be called 'psycho-somatic medicine.' It was congenial to him both scientifically and meta-physically, for it reinforced his philosophy of materialistic monism by un-dercutting the assumptions of dualism or idealism. And a conspicuous characteristic of the *Eléments de physiologie* is that Diderot neglected no opportunity for exploring the phenomenology of the mind-body relation-ship.

The difficulty experienced by critics in judging the *Eléments de physio-logie* arises from no one's being quite sure 'just what kind of book Diderot really intended to write.'[25] About 1778 he drew up a formidable list of authors and books on medicine and physiology that he evidently proposed to study. This suggests that he was contemplating a major work, and tallies with Naigeon's testimony that Diderot planned 'a natural and experi-mental history of man.'[26] Thus, according to a recent hypothesis, Diderot probably intended to compose a positivistic treatise which, while utilizing the same concepts as those in *Le Rêve de d'Alembert,* would transmute its poetic vision into scientific statements. But deteriorating health prevented the realization of so ambitious a project. Time and energy ran out. What remains, under the name of *Eléments de physiologie,* is a work which in part reflects Diderot's creative organization and arrangement of this accumu-lated material while in part it signifies merely his collection of it. Much of the contents of the *Eléments de physiologie* is derivative, and yet some of it is original and brilliant and uniquely (for his generation) prescient of the development of science in ours. It is impressive that great biologists, some of them men of genius like Claude Bernard, have found the ideas in the *Eléments de physiologie* stimulating and in key with the future develop-ments of science. 'It is in large part owing to biology,' remarks a historian of science, 'that Diderot was at one and the same time the most daring and the most humble of the great philosophes of the eighteenth century.'[27]

The *Eléments,* as one would expect from a general work in physiology, covers a great range of processes, functions, and parts — membranes, blood, lymph, bile, muscles, all the organs, maladies, etc., etc. Experts declare that the most original part of the *Eléments de physiologie* lies in the sections that deal with neurology and psychophysiology.[28] And there are interesting pages in which Diderot introspectively examines the nature of memory, con-scious and unconscious, voluntary and involuntary, in a manner that re-minds commentators of Proust.[29]

With Diderot physiology leads from the body to the mind, and biology blends into psychology, and psychology leads to ethics. This is not sentimental, it is inexorable — Diderot continued to go as deep as he could in search of the nature of man. There is much ethical thought in the *Eléments de physiologie,* and it is as utilitarian as something Bentham might have written:

There is only one passion, that to be happy. It takes different names, according to its objects: it is vice and virtue, according to its violence, the means it uses, and its effects.[30]

However difficult it is to use the *Eléments de physiologie,* nevertheless it is plain to see that the direction and momentum of the book fortify Diderot's humanistic materialism. This is of particular interest because he was evidently working on this manuscript, off and on, up to the time of his death, so that it can be said of his materialism (as it can of his political radicalism) that it was not attenuated by age. He was a man of convictions, but he was also surprisingly undogmatic, and this, too, came out repeatedly in the *Eléments de physiologie.* 'What we know least is ourselves,' he wrote. And in the conclusion to the work he showed himself completely questioning and with the Stoicism of a man who has recently been reading Seneca:

What do I perceive? Forms. And then what? More forms. I am ignorant of the thing itself. We walk between shades, shades ourselves for others and for us.

. . . .

There is only one virtue, justice; only one duty, to be happy; only one corollary, not to overvalue life and not to fear death.

Thus, with a reference to virtue, to happiness, and to justice, did Diderot end a work on physiology.[31]

The third edition of Raynal's *Histoire des deux Indes* was of such a nature that its author did not attempt to publish it in France. It was brought out in Geneva, with Raynal's name now on the title page, and smuggled copies of it began to appear in Paris in the early weeks of 1781.[32] Grimm, more of a courtier than ever, did not like the new edition. He prided himself upon devising a dilemma on one of the horns of which Raynal would have to impale himself: 'Either you believe that those whom you attack will not be able to retaliate, and [therefore] it is cowardice to attack them; or you believe that they can and will retaliate, and it is an act of madness to expose oneself to their resentment.' Grimm delivered himself of this either-or proposition in the salon of Mme de Vermenoux, a lady who was the godmother of the Neckers' only child (the future Mme de Staël) and who often spent her summers at Sèvres in the same house where Diderot spent his. Moreover, Grimm repeated it at Angélique de Vandeul's, Diderot being present. He went home furious — '. . . it [the dilemma] does not have common sense. Common sense is evidently not too common' — and wrote a letter to Grimm of molten but coherent and controlled rage.[33] It is a letter that may not have been sent, probably never was sent, for it is hard to believe that the two men could possibly have remained on speaking terms if it had.

Ah, my friend, I see clearly, your soul has been whittled down at Petersburg, at Potsdam, in the Bull's Eye Chamber, in the antechambers of the great. . . . I no longer recognize you. You have become, perhaps without your knowing it, one of the most concealed but one of the most dangerous anti-philosophes. You live with us but you hate us. . . .[34]

Is it possible that Grimm did not know that Diderot himself was the author of most of the impassioned pages that flung out against tyrants and despots? Did he not know that Diderot was probably the author of the apostrophe to Louis XVI? Did he not know that Diderot himself was the author of Eliza Draper's funeral oration, a fragment which Diderot described in his letter to Grimm as having 'the simplicity of the Ancients and the delicacy of the Moderns'?[35] Part of Diderot's perturbation over Grimm's criticism of Raynal's writings was because some of these writings were his own. Much of his hurt, too, came from the realization that Angélique was more on Grimm's side than on her father's. 'My daughter is extremely grateful for the evening that you gave up for her. It appears to me that your sophism has taken her in. I had supposed her to be more courageous and more logical.'[36]

But the issue between Grimm and Diderot was not merely private and personal. It was a conflict between two political theories, between two minds at one time in unison but now traveling in opposite directions. The discovery and publication of this letter from Diderot to Grimm, still comparatively recent, has greatly changed posterity's conception of Diderot's final political stance and of the fierceness and intensity of his convictions. These two men had once shared sentiments of liberalism and reformism. Now the one had become more and more conservative and traditionalist, while the other had come more and more to despair of reform and was becoming revolutionary. 'The book that I love and that kings and their courtiers detest,' wrote Diderot, 'is the book which causes Brutuses to be born.'[37]

On 25 May 1781 the Parlement of Paris condemned the *Histoire des deux Indes* to be burnt and its author (who had prudently gone abroad) to be imprisoned. Diderot added a postscript to his letter to Grimm:

May there fall upon the heads of these infamous men and on the old imbecile [the minister Maurepas] whom they serve the ignominy and the execrations which fell of old upon the heads of the Athenians who made Socrates drink the hemlock.[38]

This letter to Grimm about Raynal demonstrated that Diderot still could write with great power. It is, however, one of the last pieces of writing that he accomplished. It is true that the expanded edition of the *Essai sur Sénèque* was not published until 1782, but evidently Diderot had written his amplifications for it by as early as mid-July 1780, to judge from a letter by Naigeon vainly trying to dissuade him from publishing any of it at all.[39] There are two items in Diderot's writing career that come later than the letter to Grimm about Raynal. One is the *Salon de 1781,* a jaded and lackluster report with little power of imagination or much of any virtue save doggedness. None of his remarks was especially memorable, save for his recognizing the merit and skill of Jacques-Louis David, whose 'Belisarius' everyone admired. 'Every day I see it and always think I am seeing it for the first time.'[40]

The second item, probably Diderot's last creative writing, was his 'Additions à la Lettre sur les aveugles,' supplementing what he had written thirty-three years before. The 'Additions' was evidently part of his project of collecting and revising his works. It is an interesting account, scientific in intent, of the behavior of the blind, and especially of Mélanie de Sallignac, Sophie Volland's niece. It is also endearing, for it is unconsciously suffused with the radiance of the blind girl's personality. The 'Additions' also proves that Diderot was still closely in touch with the Volland sisters, for it was with the aid of Mme de Blacy, the girl's mother, that 'I have collected the details which might otherwise have escaped me.'[41]

Meister wrote that 'the *Salon de 1781* has been one of the last efforts of M. Diderot's pen. Since that time his poor health has scarcely allowed him to do any kind of work.' Nevertheless during these years Diderot continued his interest in letters and belles-lettres. He counseled Philidor on how to set Horace's *Carmen Saeculare* to music.[42] He became acquainted with Joseph Joubert, like Garat a rising man of letters, and may have employed Joubert for a time as a kind of secretary. He recommended to Catherine II a young historian named Chabrit, once again demonstrating by the warmth and generosity of his remarks that consistent and magnanimous eagerness to assist younger men which was one of his most attractive and praiseworthy traits.[43] He agreed, as much as his health would permit, to help Naigeon in adapting for the *Encyclopédie méthodique* the articles on philosophy Diderot had written for his own *Encyclopédie*.[44] In 1781 he was elected an honorary member of the Society of the Antiquaries of Scotland, an invitation which he answered in English:

Your letter came very seasonably to make me amends fort [*sic*] past sufferings, and to give me firmness against those to come. I cannot forget the persecutions I have suffered in my own country; but with that painfull remembrance, I shall place that of the marks of esteem I have receiv'd from foreign nations.[45]

In his letter to Edinburgh Diderot remarked that 'I am at present preparing a compleat edition of my works.' Several other of his letters in 1781-2 prove that he was at that time making a major effort to have his writings copied by professional copyists. For this purpose he hired no fewer than four, and to help in paying them he dunned his old friend Sedaine to repay a loan of 349 livres. The manuscripts copied at that time constitute the major part of the manuscript collection that went to Russia in 1785 along with the books of his library.[46]

Diderot did not go to Sèvres during the summer of 1781. It is possible, but only barely so, that he visited Langres that year.[47] From time to time at Paris he saw various Russian acquaintances. Prince Grigor Orlov called upon him. Princess Dashkov saw him again, and he sent her off to Geneva fortified with a letter of introduction to François Tronchin. Lexell, a member of the Russian Academy of Sciences, called on Diderot and reported that he was much changed. He was eager to know from Lexell whether the Falconet statue of Peter the Great was still standing, there being widespread doubt as to whether Falconet had been successful in designing the statue so that the hind feet of the rearing horse could sustain the full weight of horse and rider. 'He received me very politely, and not a word about atheism, for which I was very glad.'[48] A Russian of very high rank came to Paris in 1782, Grand Duke Paul, Catherine II's son, traveling under the incognito of the Comte du Nord. Paul had shown in Saint Petersburg ten years before his disapprobation of Diderot, and this had evidently not changed. The Grand Duke treated Diderot very coolly, conspicuously failing to invite him to his table. Once Diderot accosted the Grand Duke as he was leaving church after mass. 'Oh! it's you,' exclaimed the Grand Duke. 'You! At *mass*?' 'Yes, M. le Comte, one often saw Epicurus at the foot of altars.'[49] The sentiment of disapproval was mutual. When Diderot was in a company that was praising the Comte du Nord for his good manners, Diderot is reported, according to John Quincy Adams, who was told the anecdote by Joseph de Maistre, to have said, 'You are very credulous to believe all that. Just open his shirt and you will see fur.' The Grand Duke's wife granted Diderot an audience, but it did not go well. She had read Diderot's essay on Seneca, told him that he ought not to have written it, and dismissed him.[50]

One of Diderot's callers in 1781 was Samuel Romilly, a young man later to become celebrated as a legal reformer in England. His recollections show us Diderot's principal preoccupations in the period when the expanded edition of the essay on Seneca was moving through the press and help us to realize how completely representative that book was of the final phase of his ethical and political thought:

Diderot . . . was all warmth and eagerness, and talked to me with as little reserve as if I had been long and intimately acquainted with him. Rousseau, politics, and religion, were the principal topics of his conversation. The *Confessions* of Rousseau were, at that time, expected shortly to appear; and it was manifest, from the bitterness with which Diderot spoke of the work and of its author, that he dreaded its appearance. On the subject of religion he made no disguise; or rather he was ostentatious of a total disbelief in the existence of a God. He talked very eagerly upon politics, and inveighed with great warmth against the tyranny of the French government.[51]

Much of this warmth is to be read in the lines and between the lines of the greatly expanded second edition of Diderot's essay on Seneca, renamed *Essai sur les règnes de Claude et de Néron*. Diderot's first intention had been to have this printed in France under the authority of a tacit permission.[52] Because of many threatened mutilations, he had it printed unaltered in Bouillon (which was then an independent foreign principality). It was ready for distribution about February or March of 1782. Le Noir, the Lieutenant-General of Police at Paris, had authorized Diderot to import the books, addressed to Le Noir himself. Six hundred copies were sent, but these were impounded as they reached Paris, not by Le Noir's police but by the Corporation of Parisian booksellers.[53] And in this way, evidently, the contents of the book came to the attention of the highest authorities in France. According to Le Noir's recollection,

The Keeper of the Seals, in fact, asked the King for orders and His Majesty, without explaining himself more explicitly, said that this philosopher, the enemy of religion, must be punished. M. de Miromesnil [the Keeper of the Seals] wished to hear him first, out of consideration for his old age, and had him [Diderot] appear before him in my presence. He spoke to him with a firm dignity that appeared to confound Diderot.'

Diderot instantly acknowledged that he deserved chastisement and expressed his repentance. Thereafter he frequently called upon Le Noir, so frequently that one suspects he had been put on probation and had to report to his probationary officer. Diderot's repeated asseverations of his guilt and contrition, as Le Noir recalled them, seem almost too abject, and they caused Le Noir, as he looked back upon the episode, to wonder whether Diderot was 'sincere or hypocritical.'[54] It is quite startling to find Diderot in trouble with the authorities at the end of his career, just as he had been at the beginning of it.

As readers thumbed through the pages of the *Essai sur les règnes de Claude et de Néron,* probably what they were most curious about was to see what he would say in this expanded edition about Jean-Jacques Rousseau. This time he designated Rousseau by name, and defended and justified everything he had said about Rousseau in the earlier edition. 'It is an agglomeration,' wrote La Harpe, 'of the most virulent invectives.'[55] Public opinion was at that time definitely making up its mind about Rousseau, and in his favor. So much so that when Palissot's *Les Philosophes* was revived at the Comédie-Française on 20 June 1782 — on orders from high authority, it was rumored — at the point where Jean-Jacques is represented on all fours and eating a lettuce the curtain had to be lowered to prevent a riot.[56] In a climate thus unfavorable to Diderot's dark but unsubstantiated indictment of Rousseau, Diderot nevertheless continued to make it. 'For seventeen years on end I was the dupe of a crafty hypocrite.' Diderot seemed unable to realize that he was not convincing. On the contrary, more and more people apparently were saying to themselves, as a defender of Jean-Jacques had earlier said in print, 'It is clear that he [Diderot] so much dreads finding his portrait [in the *Confessions*] only because he is sure of having provided his painter with some odious features.'[57]

Nor did the second and expanded edition enhance Diderot's literary reputation, for, as even the friendly *Correspondance littéraire* had to admit, the book had become more disconnected than ever. Conceding that 'This disorder is no doubt a blemish,' the editor claimed, 'nonetheless this blemish does not make the work any less original or less piquant,'; and then drew attention to how masterfully Diderot had translated passages from Tacitus.[58]

The historian of French literature may find little in the two editions of the essay on Seneca to linger over, but the biographers of Diderot find it a mine of information, and one that is far from being yet exhausted. All the more like a mine, too, because, while some of its pay dirt may be scooped up by strip-mining, most of it lies beneath the surface.

Diderot realized that this was an autobiographical book. 'I am not composing, I am not being an author. I read or I talk, I interrogate or I reply.' Thus he described his method in his prefatory statement. 'One will not be long in perceiving that I paint my own soul as much as those of the different personages who figure in my account.' And as any autobiographer does, he mentioned aspects of character and personality that he thought true of him and that any person interested in him would like to know. 'I would prefer being the dupe of a hundred hypocrites to being the accuser of a single honest and upright man.' He acknowledged his willingness to spend time aiding all the people (whom Mme Diderot called the 'itchy ones') who came to him for help. ' "People do not steal my life from me . . . I give it." '

I have been forced all my life to follow occupations for which I was not fitted, and to leave to one side those to which I was attracted by my taste, my talent, and some hope of success. I believe myself a tolerable moralist, for this science presupposes merely a certain soundness of judgment, a heart in the right place, a turn for frequent soliloquy, and the most rigorous honesty with oneself, to know how to accuse oneself and not know the art of self-absolution.[59]

Quite unexpectedly, Diderot had discovered in himself a real affinity with Seneca, a realization that made him exclaim, 'Ah! if I had read Seneca's works sooner, if I had been imbued with his principles when I was thirty, how many pleasures would I have owed to this philosopher, or, rather, how many afflictions would he have spared me.' Reading Seneca, Diderot discovered the uses and the pleasures of biography:

A kind of tender gratefulness combines with a laudable curiosity to interest us in the private lives of those whose works we admire. The place of their birth, their education, their character, the date of their productions, the reception accorded them, their inclinations, their tastes honorable or dishonorable, their friendships, their whims, their faults, their exterior appearance, the features of their face, everything concerning them attracts the attention of posterity.[60]

Though earlier (and up to a quite recent date) Diderot had written of Seneca quite scornfully, evidently those biographical researches changed his mind. He identified with Seneca. 'After having read Seneca, am I the same as I was before reading him? This is not so. That cannot be.' In many respects Seneca was like Diderot, encyclopedic in his interests, given to writing impromptu — '. . . he does not compose; he pours his mind and soul onto the paper.'[61] Diderot's response to Seneca was a very personal one, and the *Essai sur les règnes de Claude et de Néron* is an extremely subjective book. It is evident that in writing it Diderot achieved a great sense of self-justification.

Of course this was a political book, both generally and specifically. 'It seems to me that if one had kept silence up to now regarding religion, peoples would still be submerged in the most grotesque and dangerous superstitions, . . . regarding government, we would still be groaning under the bonds of feudal government, . . . regarding morals, we would still be having to learn what is virtue and what is vice. To forbid all these discussions, the only ones worthy of occupying a good mind, is to perpetuate the reign of ignorance and barbarism.' As to specifics, Diderot referred glowingly to 'these brave Americans':

After some centuries of general oppression, may the revolution that has just taken place overseas, by offering to all the inhabitants of Europe an asylum from fanaticism and tyranny, instruct those who govern men on the legitimate use of their authority.

Diderot commented more on French politics in the *Essai sur les règnes de Claude et de Néron* than he had in the earlier *Essai sur Sénèque,* that edition having been subject to censorship. He praised Turgot, Malesherbes, and Necker, though by attribute rather than by name. The expanded edition also contained an elaborate and easily identifiable comparison of Louis XV with the Emperor Claudius, 'which,' wrote the *Mémoires secrets,* 'is stirring up a violent tempest against the modern Tacitus.' Diderot had ended this passage by saying, 'Weakness that is unable either to prevent evil nor promote good multiplies tyranny.'[62]

Long before this, Diderot had observed that politics and morals are closely related. It was this realization on the part of a man who thought of himself as a moralist that makes him also something of a political theorist. 'Politics and morals go hand in hand,' was the way he put it.[63] The morals of which he spoke are the values maintained by a society or, as we now would say, a culture. Such morals are, in Diderot's understanding of them, something like social reflexes. They are in the safekeeping of the people, *le peuple,* so that Diderot, who had a low opinion of the potential of the people as independent thinkers or decision makers, had the highest opinion of them as the preservers of what is most precious to a culture.[64] Diderot thought that the safeguarding of *moeurs* is absolutely essential for the well-being of a state, and thus he asserted, speaking of his brave Americans, that '. . . it is neither by gold nor even by the multitude of men that a state is sustained, but by morals.' [65] Yet Diderot also thought that the manners and customs of a country, which, if preserved, keep a society sound and strong, are nevertheless incessantly vulnerable to the attrition of corruption. It was precisely this corruption that Diderot thought had occurred, probably throughout Europe, certainly in France. 'Corruption' and 'moeurs' are words therefore frequently encountered in the *Essai sur les règnes de Claude et de Néron*. There is, however, a solution, one that Diderot mentioned more than once, though not, it is true, in this book published under his name. The solution is drastic and revolutionary:

I was asked one day how one could restore morals to a corrupted people. I replied, 'The way Medea restored youth to her father, by cutting him up and putting him on to boil.' [66]

The *Essai sur les règnes de Claude et de Néron* has a hero: Seneca. Maybe also, Diderot. It has a villain, too. This was La Mettrie, the French materialist who died in 1751 at the court of Frederick II of Prussia. Diderot included in his essay a savage attack on La Mettrie, and it was not merely because La Mettrie had dared to write a book he called *Anti-Sénèque*.[67] The point really was that the metaphysical assumptions of both La Mettrie and Diderot were practically identical, issuing in philosophical materialism. But in ethical theory they were worlds apart, and Diderot quite clearly feared that an undiscriminating public might think that his ethical views were the same as La Mettrie's just because his metaphysical ones were.[68] La Mettrie argued for a very narrow and individualistic hedonism. Diderot, in sharp contrast, though of course he too believed in the pursuit of happiness, sought happiness in a much more other-directed, outer-directed way than did La Mettrie, and with a very vivid sense of social obligation.[69] All this was a part of Diderot's utilitarianism. So ingrained was his sense of social consciousness that he developed an ethic of sacrifice.[70] La Mettrie's ethical doctrine stopped far short of a humanism like this. The contrast in ethical teaching of these two materialists may perhaps be described best by saying that for La Mettrie happiness was to be found in enjoyment, while for Diderot, with his activism as well as his sense of social obligation, happiness is to be found in activity. Diderot's final ethical position was one in which he did indeed equate virtue with happiness. It was a virtue, however, not cloistered or untried. Happiness, according to the evolutionary kind of morality developed in Diderot's humanistic materialism, depends upon a dialectical conflict, upon tension, and upon a mastery of self.[71]

Looking round about him at what he deemed general corruption and decay, Diderot did not really despair. What the *Essai sur les règnes de Claude et de Néron* is about, when Diderot himself does not get it off the track by his own digressions, is to inquire what is possible and what is proper for the philosopher who finds himself in an adverse political and social situation. The philosopher may have to wait. He may find that he can speak forcefully 'only from the depth of his tomb.' [72] Just the same, Diderot ended his career in a crescendo of ethical and social commitment and concern.

In the course of 1783 Diderot passed permanently into the penumbra of ill health, and the chronicle of his remaining life is melancholy and brief. In February or March he was very ill and was bled three times.[73] He never really recovered his strength thereafter, though he was somewhat better during the summer. Plainly, though, he was approaching the end, and Meister wrote in September that 'We are on the point of losing MM. d'Alembert and Diderot.' [74] D'Alembert did die, on 29 October. Diderot's generation was passing away. Voltaire was gone; Jean-Jacques was gone; David Hume had died in 1776 and David Garrick in 1779. Mme Geoffrin succumbed, after a long illness, in 1777. Two *Encyclopédie* associates died, Le Breton in 1779 and De Jaucourt a few months later, in February 1780. In 1781 Turgot died, and Dr. Tronchin. In 1783, when Diderot was dangerously ill, Mme d'Epinay died (in April) after a long and heroic struggle with cancer. And on 22 February 1784, Sophie Volland died in her sixty-eighth year.

Even during the last year of his life, when his energy was almost gone, Diderot attempted some work upon the arrangement of his papers, as three notes to his copyist Girbal attest.[75] His principal ailment was dropsy. His legs were swollen and he sometimes found it very difficult to walk, but the ministrations of the Alsatian doctor, Georges-Frédéric Bacher, a specialist in this disease, kept it in check.[76] Diderot also suffered from emphysema, and so grievously that his doctors constantly warned him against climbing the stairs at the Rue Taranne and finally disposed the Diderots to think of the possibility of moving to some ground-floor apartment.[77] The winter of 1783–4 was exceptionally severe. In the course of it, on 19 February, Diderot suffered what was then thought to be a stroke, though it is now argued that what he suffered was partial heart failure causing an insufficient flow of blood.[78] He recovered from this crisis to some extent, though slowly, and was able to go to Sèvres about the first fortnight in May.[79] The flow of his energy had come to almost a complete halt.

Family letters exchanged between Paris and Langres constantly refer to his condition, but he himself tells us nothing. It is not known whether he was informed of the death of Sophie (which occurred three days after what was thought to be his stroke), nor even whether he knew of the sudden death, about mid-March, of his eleven-year-old granddaughter, Marie-Anne de Vandeul. In a charming letter of 1779 to the mother, Diderot had spoken of how much he loved his grandchildren, 'even though they think me poorly educated because I was unable to tell them where Charlemagne died.' 'Minette' bore a strong physical resemblance to her grandfather Diderot, and had given every promise of being prodigiously intelligent.[80]

Grimm, meanwhile, suggested to Catherine II the renting of some ground-floor residence. She instructed him to proceed, with the result that a very fine apartment on the Rue de Richelieu (present number 39 and now marked with a plaque as being the *'maison mortuaire'* of Diderot) was rented for occupancy beginning in June. In mid-July, probably not later than the eighteenth, the Diderots moved into their new lodgings. Mme de Vandeul called them palatial and remarked that Diderot was delighted with them.[81]

Considerations in addition to those of health were most probably in the minds of Grimm and the Vandeuls in transferring Diderot's legal residence from the Rue Taranne to another part of Paris. In the months of Diderot's grave illness it became a matter of concern to his family (and to the public) as to whether he would be granted decent burial when he died. This was by no means certain, for the *curé* of the parish in which his death occurred could prevent burial there if he wished. Before the Revolution of 1789 there was really no dignified alternative to Christian burial in France. Cremation was illegal. The *curés* of parishes were in a commanding position as to whether a person suspected of being a freethinker could qualify for Christian burial. If the *curé* said no, it was very hard to get him overruled. In such cases the cadaver was interred in the equivalent of a potter's field, or, as the French idiom had it, the body was thrown on the garbage dump (*jeter un corps à la voirie*).

When Voltaire died, the *curé* of the parish in which Voltaire was living, Saint-Sulpice, refused to give him Christian burial. Thereupon Voltaire's nephew, the Abbé Mignot, had the body clothed, hastily smuggled it out of Paris by having it ride in Voltaire's own coach, and thus took it as swiftly as possible to the Abbey of Scellières, in Champagne, where Christian burial was given by the local clergy. The prohibition of such burial arrived from Paris after the ceremony. Now, five years later, Diderot was living in that same parish of Saint-Sulpice and the *curé* was still the same man, the Abbé de Tersac.

D'Alembert, whose lodgings were in the Louvre and whose parish church was consequently Saint-Germain-l'Auxerrois, was visited by that *curé* six times before his death. 'There was always someone close to the invalid to receive the pastor cordially but to turn the conversation aside when he tried to open up the subject.' D'Alembert died without receiving the sacraments, and he did receive Christian burial. But the *Mémoires secrets* of Bachaumont declared that '. . . it appears established that M. d'Alembert was buried only perforce, that the priests had decided to have his body thrown *à la voirie,* and that it was necessary to get an order from the King and send to Fontainebleau [because D'Alembert had been secretary of the French Academy when he died, and this was a royal establishment.]'[82]

Before recounting this information about D'Alembert, the *Mémoires secrets* had announced:

At present the death of M. Diderot, who is under censure by the faculty [of theology of the University of Paris] is being awaited with impatience. As this atheist, for such at least is the title given him by the priests and the devout, belongs to no academy, is not related to any great family, has no imposing public standing in his own person, and does not possess powerful associates and friends, the clergy intend to avenge themselves upon him and to make his dead body suffer every religious insult unless he satisfies the externals.[83]

In the course of 1783 the Abbé de Tersac called upon Diderot at the Rue Taranne. Mme de Vandeul says that he came two or three times a week, and that Diderot greeted him cordially, praised the institutions he had perfected for assisting the poor, and spoke to him constantly of the good deeds he had already done and those yet to be accomplished. It is interesting that Diderot did not avoid talking with the *curé* nor did he refuse him the house. 'My father did not initiate such topics of conversation, but neither did he refuse to engage in them. One day when they found themselves in complete agreement on several points of ethics relating to humaneness and good works, the *curé* let it be understood that if my father would publish these maxims, together with a small retraction of his other works, it would make a very fine effect in the world. "I am sure it would, Monsieur le curé, but you will agree that it would be telling an impudent lie." ' Mme de Vandeul insists that either she or her mother was present all the time at these conversations, in order to spare Diderot 'persecution.'[84]

There is no evidence whatever that at that time or later Diderot compromised his principles in any way. The impression one gets of him in these last two years is of a man growing dim before our very eyes, because the documentary evidence is becoming slight; but it is also of a man who is stoical in his sufferings and steadfast in his beliefs. Perhaps the Stoicism that he admired in Seneca was becoming a part of him, too. Perhaps his belated enthusiasm for Seneca became a real affinity and helped him to be stoical. The night before he died he said to some of his friends who were discussing the different ways of arriving at a knowledge of philosophy, 'The first step towards philosophy is incredulity.' This remark is very similar to one of his *Pensées philosophiques,* written thirty-eight years before: 'Skepticism is the first step towards truth.' According to Mme de Vandeul, visiting with him that night, these were the last words she ever heard him say. 'The first step towards philosophy is incredulity.'[85] Let us hope her memory was accurate. It is a great curtain line for a *philosophe.*

Diderot's steadfastness with the Abbé de Tersac must have made it seem unlikely to his family that he was going to qualify for burial in the parish of Saint-Sulpice. Therefore when he finally was moved from the Rue Taranne (where he was close to the house of the Vandeuls, who also lived in that parish), the residence chosen for him was in the parish of Saint-Roch, across the Seine. There is no evidence that Diderot, sick as he was, was conscious of this aspect of the move, but it seems unlikely that Vandeul and his wife and his mother-in-law were not.

Diderot died suddenly, instantaneously, about midday on 31 July 1784, while sitting at table.[86] Thus he was not hounded by anyone seeking a death-bed conversion. According to his express instructions that an autopsy be performed, Dr. Bacher and two colleagues carried out his wishes on 1 August.[87] The *curé* of Saint-Roch, according to Mme de Vandeul, permitted interment with very little demur. The fact that the Abbé de Tersac was known to have had a series of conversations with Diderot helped to allay objections.

So sudden an end [wrote Meister in the *Correspondance littéraire*], joined to the consideration with which he [Diderot] received the visits of the *curé* of Saint-Sulpice last year, . . . has not left the priests any pretence for troubling his last moments nor for refusing to carry out the last honors.

The scruples of the *curé* of Saint-Roch were overcome by the considerations set forth by the son-in-law, continued Meister, who added maliciously that the *curé* asked '1500 to 1800 livres' for the obsequies.[88]

Diderot's funeral, which occurred at Saint-Roch at seven in the evening of 1 August 1784, was accompanied by a good deal of pomp, as the itemized and receipted bills for the occasion prove. For instance, priests could be hired (at a livre apiece) to be present at funerals. M. de Vandeul paid for fifty of them.[89] Interment was in the Chapelle de la Vierge, the very Lady Chapel that Diderot had once described in detail, analyzing the artistic effect of the Gloire and the Annunciation that are part of its decoration.[90] Corneille was buried at Saint-Roch, and Duguay-Trouin, the naval hero. Maupertuis was buried there, and Mme Geoffrin; and D'Holbach was to be buried there, five years later. Diderot's body was placed in the vault of the Chapelle de la Vierge, but all traces of it have long since disappeared.[91] It seems odd to think of Diderot's remains resting within the four walls of a church. But that was a decision that did not depend upon him.

A decade later, in the time of the Revolution, many of the churches of Paris were secularized and renamed.[92] How appropriate (even though it was merely a coincidence) that the church where Diderot lay buried was renamed the Temple of Genius.

The Appeal to Posterity

THE WORD 'posterity' stands out in Diderot's writings with much more frequency than was usual among eighteenth-century men of letters. But Diderot was a quite uninhibited writer, not afraid to wear his heart on his sleeve. He admitted that 'I would ask for nothing better than to enjoy great consideration during my life and to leave an illustrious name after my death. . . .'[1] And whereas other writers might be restrained by modesty or by doubt as to whether posterity would show much concern over them, Diderot referred to posterity often, for he had great confidence in it.

It was part of the wishfulness and wistfulness of a man of talent who feels insufficiently appreciated by his own generation. Diderot thought of his taste as being surer than that of his contemporaries, requiring the lag of a generation or more to catch up with him. About his essay on Seneca he wrote that 'It is in fifty years, when I no longer exist, that people will do justice to Seneca, supposing that my apology survives.'[2] He once wrote to Grimm, 'I feel sensitively, I judge accurately; and time always ends up by accepting my taste and my opinion. Do not laugh: it is I who anticipate the future and who know its thought.'[3] And in the article *'Encyclopédie,'* after speaking of the class of authors who are popular in their lifetimes but whose reputations fade away, Diderot spoke in contrast of those others, who,

on the contrary, too advanced for the time in which they lived, were little read, little understood, not at all appreciated, and have long remained in obscurity, until the moment when the century that they were in advance of has elapsed and another century, to which they belonged before it had arrived, catches up with them and finally renders justice to their merit.[4]

This is the fate of gifted men. It is the lot of almost all men of genius, Diderot wrote, to be beyond the comprehension of their own century. 'They write for the following generation.'[5] It is their function to form the taste of the men of the future.

In what respect, then, and when, is the multitude right? In every respect: but only at the end of a very long period, because then it is an echo repeating the judgment of a small number of judicious men who form in advance the judgment of posterity.[6]

Diderot emphasized the idea of posterity all the more because this was the only immortality that his materialistic faith allowed him. In the *Encyclopédie* he had defined this sort of *immortalité:* 'It is that kind of life that we acquire in the memory of men. . . . We hear in ourselves the eulogy which they [our fellow men] will make of us some day, and we sacrifice ourselves. We sacrifice our lives; we really cease to exist in order to live in their memory. If immortality considered from this aspect is a chimera, it is the chimera of great souls.'[7] This, too, was of course the burden of his discussion on immortality with Falconet. There is no reason to suppose that Diderot was insincere in his belief, or that it did not count with him heavily.

These are philosophical reasons, or the reasons of a *philosophe,* for resting one's faith in the judgment of posterity. In addition, moreover, several realistic and practical considerations dictated why Diderot pinned his hopes on the good will and understanding of future generations. In the first place, he had never found it easy to publish what he wanted to say. As early as the *Pensées philosophiques* and the *Promenade du sceptique,* as late as the *Essai sur les règnes de Claude et de Néron,* he discovered that what he most felt and most wanted to express was forbidden or officially frowned upon. In the *Promenade du sceptique* he had the principal character remark, 'I see only two [subjects] that merit my attention, and those are precisely the ones you forbid me to speak about. Impose silence upon me regarding religion and government and I have nothing more to say.'[8] Patently it follows that Diderot believed that his true views on religion and politics could be known in their entirety only after he was dead.

This point of view was expressed with great impact in the *Essai sur les règnes de Claude et de Néron,* though it is possible that in this context he was thinking more of Seneca than of himself:

The constraint of despotic governments shrinks the mind without one's noticing it. Automatically one forbids oneself a certain class of daring ideas, as one avoids a physical obstacle that would hurt one; and once one has accustomed oneself to this circumspect and pusillanimous course, one comes back with difficulty to a frank and audacious one. One thinks, one speaks with forcefulness only from the depths of one's tomb. It is there that one must place oneself. It is from there that one must appeal to men.[9]

The fact that Diderot did not publish an authorized edition of his works in his lifetime is a second respect in which he appealed to posterity in a very pragmatic fashion. In the seventies there had been ample time and he had had ample energy to bring such an edition off the press, and, as has already been noted, he was in touch with the Amsterdam publisher, M.-M. Rey, regarding such a project. Yet, for some reason, Diderot gave it up. The effect of this outcome, whether by intentional decision or by default, was to leave the judgment of his complete oeuvre to those only who survived him.

When Diderot remarked to Hemsterhuis that he had had to be ironical and cryptical and ambiguous in what he had published during his career, as a means of averting persecution, then he was saying by implication that only a knowledge of his unpublished and posthumous works would present a fuller picture and be easier to understand.[10] This, then, is another respect in which Diderot discovered, or thought that he had discovered, that he had to appeal to the judgment of the future. It was as much as to say that he had no other recourse.

Besides, Diderot believed that only posterity could be fair to his works. Those he did publish had been subjected to attack and ridicule, and it is significant how frequently Diderot speaks of envy on the part of one's contemporaries:

What a passion is Envy! It is the cruelest of the Eumenides. It follows the man of merit right up to his tomb. Then it disappears; and the justice of the centuries sits down in its place.[11]

It has been suggested that Diderot did not publish in his lifetime the dialogues which now rank among his greatest writings because of 'an intense fear of seeing these difficult and subtle works misunderstood by his contemporaries. . . .'[12] Diderot himself specifically admitted as much in the last work he ever published. 'I had promised myself not to publish any more anything I might write,' he remarked in the *Essai sur les règnes de Claude et de Néron*. 'Not that I would hold in disdain the consideration that comes from literary success; but our critics are so bitter, the public is so hard to please. . . .'[13]

Diderot's policy of appealing to the judgment of his successors over that of his contemporaries can be traced through the last quarter-century of his life in many statements and in a sequence of consistent decisions. His reasons were hard-headed and realistic. And underlying them all was his confidence in the verdict of posterity.

List of Abbreviations

AHRF   *Annales historiques de la Révolution française.*

AIEF   *Cahiers de l'Association internationale des Études françaises.*

AJJR   *Annales de la Société Jean-Jacques Rousseau.*

Année Littéraire   *Année Littéraire,* ed. Elie-Catherine Fréron, 202 vols. (Paris, 1754–90).

D'Argenson   René-Louis de Paulmy, Marquis d'Argenson, *Journal et mémoires,* 9 vols. (Paris, 1859–67).

ASNSL   *Archiv für das Studium der neueren Sprachen und Literaturen.*

Asse   Eugène Asse, 'Diderot et Voltaire, d'après les papiers inédits de la censure,' *Cabinet Historique,* nouvelle série, 1 (1882), 3–38.

A.-T.   Denis Diderot, *Oeuvres complètes,* ed. Jules Assézat and Maurice Tourneux, 20 vols. (Paris, 1875–7).

AUMLA   *AUMLA* (Australasian Universities Modern Language Association).

AUP   'Conférences faites à la Sorbonne à l'occasion du 2ᵉ centenaire de l'*Encyclopédie,*' *Annales de l'Université de Paris,* xxii ([Oct.] 1952), numéro spécial.

Barbier, *Journal*   Edmond-Jean-François Barbier, *Journal historique et anecdotique du règne de Louis XV,* 4 vols. (Paris, 1847–56).

Besterman   Voltaire, *Correspondence,* ed. Theodore Besterman, 107 vols. (Geneva, 1953–65).

B.N., MSS, Fr.   Bibliothèque Nationale, Département des Manuscrits, Fonds Français.

B.N., MSS, Nouv. acq. fr.   Fonds Nouvelles Acquisitions Françaises.

B.N., MSS, Joly de Fleury   Fonds Joly de Fleury.

Bonnefon   Paul Bonnefon, 'Diderot prisonnier à Vincennes,' *RHLF,* vi (1899), 200–24.

BSHAL   *Bulletin de la Société Historique et Archéologique de Langres.*

CAIEF   *Cahiers de l'Association internationale des Études françaises.*

CI   Denis Diderot, *Correspondance inédite,* ed. André Babelon, 2 vols. (Paris, 1931).

Corr. litt.   Friedrich Melchior Grimm, *Correspondance littéraire, philosophique et critique par Grimm, Diderot, Raynal, etc.,* ed. Maurice Tourneux, 16 vols. (Paris, 1877–82).

Courtois, 'Chronologie'   Louis-J. Courtois, 'Chronologie critique de la vie et des oeuvres de Jean-Jacques Rousseau,' *AJJR,* xv (1923), 1–366.

Cru   R. Loyalty Cru, *Diderot as a Disciple of English Thought* (New York, 1913).

DNB   *Dictionary of National Biography.*

De Booy, 'Inventaire'   Jean Th. de Booy, 'Inventaire provisoire des contributions de Diderot
               à la *Correspondance littéraire,' Dix-huitième Siècle,* 1 (1969), 353–97.

DS   *Diderot Studies.*

Diderot, *Corr.*   Denis Diderot, *Correspondance,* ed. Georges Roth and Jean Varloot, 16 vols.
               (Paris, 1955–70).

Diderot, *Salons*   Denis Diderot, *Salons,* ed. Jean Seznec, 4 vols. (Oxford, 1957–67).

Encyc.   Denis Diderot, ed., *Encyclopédie, ou dictionnaire raisonné des sciences, des arts
               et des métiers, par une société de gens de lettres,* 17 vols. (Paris, 1751–65).

Encyc., Planches   Denis Diderot, ed., *Recueil de planches sur les sciences, les arts libéraux et
               les arts méchaniques, avec leur explication,* 11 vols. (Paris, 1762–72).

FR   *French Review.*

FS   *French Studies.*

Gordon and Torrey   Douglas H. Gordon and Norman L. Torrey, *The Censoring of Diderot's
               Encyclopédie and the Re-established Text* (New York, 1947).

Guillemin   Henri Guillemin, 'Les Affaires de l'Ermitage (1756–1757),' *AJJR,* xxix (1941–2),
               59–258.

Guyot   Charly Guyot, *Diderot par lui-même* (Paris, [1953]).

JAAC   *Journal of Aesthetics and Art Criticism.*

JHI   *Journal of the History of Ideas.*

JWCI   *Journal of the Warburg and Courtauld Institutes.*

Le Gras   Joseph Le Gras, *Diderot et l'Encyclopédie* (Amiens, 1928).

Leigh   Jean-Jacques Rousseau, *Correspondance complète,* ed. R. A. Leigh (Geneva,
               1965–).

Lough, 'Problem'   John Lough, 'The Problem of the Unsigned Articles in the *Encyclopédie,'*
               SVEC, xxxii (1965), 327–90.

Luneau de Boisjermain   *Mémoire pour Pierre-Joseph-François Luneau de Boisjermain, sou-
               scripteur de l'Encyclopédie . . .* (Paris, 1771).

May   Louis-Philippe May, 'L'Histoire et les sources de l'Encyclopédie, d'après le registre
               de délibérations et de comptes des éditeurs, et un mémoire inédit,' *Revue de
               Synthèse,* xv (1938), 5–110.

MLN   *Modern Language Notes.*

MLQ   *Modern Language Quarterly.*

MLR   *Modern Language Review.*

Naigeon   Jacques-André Naigeon, *Mémoires historiques et philosophiques sur la vie et les ouvrages de D. Diderot* (Paris, 1821).

Part I   Wilson, *Diderot: The Testing Years, 1713–1759.*

PMLA   *PMLA* [Publications of the Modern Language Association of America].

RDM   *Revue des Deux Mondes.*

RFor   *Romanische Forschungen.*

RGS   *Revue Générale des Sciences Pures et Appliquées.*

RHLF   *Revue d'Histoire Littéraire de la France.*

RHPHGC   *Revue d'Histoire de la Philosophie et d'Histoire Générale de la Civilisation.*

RHS   *Revue d'Histoire des Sciences et de leurs Applications.*

RLC   *Revue de Littérature Comparée.*

RQH   Louis-François Marcel, 'Une Lettre du père de Diderot à son fils, détenu à Vincennes (3 septembre 1749),' *Revue des Questions Historiques,* cix (1928), 100–13.

RR   *Romanic Review.*

RScH   *Revue des Sciences Humaines.*

Rousseau, ed. Hachette   Jean-Jacques Rousseau, *Oeuvres complètes,* ed. Hachette, 13 vols. (Paris, 1885–1905).

Rousseau, *Corr. gén.*   Jean-Jacques Rousseau, *Correspondance générale,* ed. Théophile Dufour and P.-P. Plan, 20 vols. (Paris, 1924–34).

Sbornik   Russkoe Istoricheskoe Obshchestvo, *Sbornik,* 148 vols. (St. Petersburg, 1867–1916).

SPTB   *The Age of the Enlightenment: Studies Presented to Theodore Besterman,* ed. W. H. Barber [and others] (Edinburgh, 1967).

SV   Denis Diderot, *Lettres à Sophie Volland,* ed. André Babelon, 3 vols. (Paris, 1930).

SVEC   Geneva. Institut et musée Voltaire. *Studies on Voltaire and the Eighteenth Century.*

Mme de Vandeul Marie-Angélique de Vandeul, *née* Diderot, 'Mémoires pour servir à l'histoire de la vie et des ouvrages de Diderot,' A.-T., i, pp. xxix–lxii.

Venturi, *Jeunesse*   Franco Venturi, *Jeunesse de Diderot (de 1713 à 1753)* (Paris, 1939).

Venturi, *Origini*   Franco Venturi, *Le Origini dell'Enciclopedia* (Florence, 1946; 2nd ed., Turin, 1963).

Voltaire, ed. Moland   Voltaire, *Oeuvres complètes,* ed. Moland, 52 vols. (Paris, 1877–85).

WZUB   Berlin. Universität. *Wissenschaftliche Zeitschrift. Gesellschafts- und sprachwissenschaftliche Reihe.*

WZUL   Leipzig. Universität. *Wissenschaftliche Zeitschrift. Gesellschafts- und sprachwissenschaftliche Reihe.*

ZFSL   *Zeitschrift für französische Sprache und Literatur.*

Notes

CHAPTER 1

1. Diderot, *Corr.*, ii, 194.
2. *Encyc.*, ix, 244–5.
3. Diderot, *Corr.*, ii, 207–8. For an attempt by Diderot to represent this speech phonetically, see Diderot, *Corr.*, i, 143.
4. Louis-François Marcel, 'Le Baptême de Diderot,' *Semaine religieuse du diocèse de Langres*, 18 Oct. 1913, 675–80; George R. Havens, 'The Dates of Diderot's Birth and Death,' *MLN*, lv (1940), 31–5.
5. Louis-François Marcel, *Le Frère de Diderot* (Paris, 1913), 3 and n.
6. Ibid. 22–3; Louis-François Marcel, *Un Oncle de Diderot: Antoine-Thomas Diderot de l'Ordre des Frères Prêcheurs (1682–1756)* (Ligugé [Vienne], 1930), 3.
7. Marcel, *Le Frère de Diderot*, 14–23, 191–7.
8. 4 Sept. 1741 (Louis-François Marcel, *Le Mariage de Diderot* [Largentière (Ardèche), 1928], 17 n.; Marcel, *Un Oncle de Diderot*, 10 n.).
9. *RQH*, 110 n.; Martin Löpelmann, *Der junge Diderot* (Berlin, 1934), 9–10.
10. Löpelmann, *Der junge Diderot*, 10.
11. Diderot, *Corr.*, ii, 119, 157.
12. *SV*, i, 198 (30 Sept. 1760).
13. A.-T., xvii, 333, 334, 335.
14. François Helme, 'Diderot dans notre art. A propos de son bi-centenaire,' *Presse Médicale*, vol. ii for 1913, 1247.
15. A.-T., xvii, 335.
16. *SV*, ii, 266 (1 Aug. 1765).
17. Memorandum *ca.* 1821 by Mme de Vandeul for her doctor (Jean Massiet du Biest, *La Fille de Diderot* [Tours, 1949], 218).
18. Massiet du Biest, 186; Louis-François Marcel, *La Soeur de Diderot: Denise Diderot (27 janvier 1715–26 mars 1797)* (Langres, 1925), 42 n.
19. Massiet du Biest, 175; A.-T., xvii, 335.
20. Facts in this paragraph are from a registry book in the Archives municipales at the Hôtel de Ville at Langres: 'Etat civil, 1699 à 1721, de la Paroisse de Saint-Martin.' Diderot's aunt, Catherine Diderot (d. 26 Dec. 1735 at the age of 46), is sometimes confused with his younger sister, the second Catherine (Diderot, *Corr.*, i, 23).
21. *RHLF*, lv (1955), 236.
22. Mme de Vandeul, lviii; Massiet du Biest, 207.
23. Marcel, *Le Frère de Diderot*, 1.
24. Mme de Vandeul, lviii–lx. The Houdon bronze is in the council room of the Hôtel de Ville at Langres.
25. Mme de Vandeul, xxix.
26. A.-T., xi, 250.
27. A.-T., xi, 253.
28. A.-T., xiv, 439.
29. Herbert Dieckmann, *Inventaire du Fonds Vandeul et Inédits de Diderot* (Geneva, 1951), 204.
30. Löpelmann, *Der junge Diderot*, 21–2; Louis-François Marcel, 'Diderot écolier,' *RHLF*, xxxiv (1927), 379.
31. Regarding the Jesuits and secondary education in France, see Pierre Clarac, 'L'*Encyclopédie* et les problèmes d'éducation,' *AUP*, xxii ([Oct.] 1952), numéro spécial, 215; also the excellent article by Marcel Bouchard, 'L'Enseignement des Jésuites sous l'Ancien Régime,' *Information Historique*, xvi (1954), 127–34.
32. Diderot was born at 9, Place Diderot (then called Place Chambeau). On 20 July 1714, his father bought the house across the square at 6, Place Diderot, occupied by the Diderot family for the rest of the eighteenth century. The marker upon it which claims that it is

Diderot's birthplace is incorrect: see Léon Guyot, 'La Maison natale de Diderot,' *BSHAL*, *Année* 1931, 34–40; Hubert Gautier, *Le Père de Diderot, 1685–1759.* . . . (Moulins, 1933), 8.

33. A.-T., xvii, 359; Marcel, 'Diderot écolier,' *RHLF*, xxxiv, 382–3.

34. Maurice Tourneux, *Diderot et Catherine II* (Paris, 1899), 349–50, 353.

35. A.-T., ii, 333.

36. A.-T., ii, 450–51.

37. *SV*, i, 243 (18 Oct. 1760). Mme de Vandeul, xxix–xxx, and Naigeon, 3, describe a similar incident, but with much more sensational details.

38. A.-T., iii, 421, 468–88. Diderot's familiarity with the classics is emphasized by Eric M. Steel, *Diderot's Imagery: A Study of a Literary Personality* (New York, 1941), 48–51.

39. A.-T., iii, 478.

40. A.-T., iii, 481.

41. *Corr. litt.*, viii, 151–3.

42. A.-T., vi, 289–302; *Corr. litt.*, viii, 153–4. Cf. Ernst Robert Curtius, 'Diderot und Horaz,' in his *Europäische Literatur und lateinisches Mittelalter* (Berne, 1948), 556–64.

43. A.-T., xviii, 167.

44. A.-T., v, 228–38.

45. Gustave Charlier and Léon Herrmann, 'Diderot, annotateur de Perse,' *RHLF*, xxxv (1928), 39–63.

46. A.-T., xiv, 438.

47. A.-T., vi, 298.

CHAPTER 2

1. Mme de Vandeul, xxx.

2. Marcel, *Le Frère de Diderot*, 25.

3. Ibid. 30–33. The Canon died on 28 April 1728. In the *Entretien d'un père avec ses enfants*, Diderot gives a rather different account of the succession to the prebend and the Canon's death (A.-T., v, 302). The circumstances as reconstructed by Canon Marcel seem to me to have more verisimilitude.

4. Mme de Vandeul, lx.

5. A.-T., vi, 182. Diderot may have been very gravely ill about 1729, for he is alleged to have declared in 1747 that at the age of sixteen, finding himself in danger of death, he had called a priest and received the sacraments (Bonnefon, 203).

6. A.-T., x, 391. See also Diderot's remark in a memorandum for Catherine II (Tourneux, *Diderot et Catherine II*, 159).

7. Mme de Vandeul, xxx.

8. A.-T., xvii, 231, s.v. 'Subvenir.'

9. Antoine Taillefer, *Tableau historique de l'esprit et du caractere des littérateurs françois, depuis la renaissance des lettres jusqu'en 1785*, 4 vols. (Paris, 1785), iv, 215 ff.

10. Jean Massiet du Biest, 'Lettres inédites de Naigeon à M^r et Mme de Vandeul (1786–1787), concernant un projet d'édition des oeuvres de Diderot et opinion de ceux-ci sur le même sujet, d'àpres leur correspondance inédite (1784–1812),' *BSHAL*, 1 Jan. 1948, 2. Nothing is otherwise known as to the identity of this Mme Fréjacques.

11. A convincing argument for the year 1728 is made by Marcel, 'Diderot écolier,' *RHLF*, xxxiv, 390–91; cf. Löpelmann, *Der junge Diderot*, 36 n.

12. The unidentified girl: Diderot, *Corr.*, ii, 195. Diderot's early feelings for Mlle La Salette: Diderot, *Corr.*, i, 145. She married Nicolas Caroillon on 16 April 1736 (Louis-François Marcel, 'Les Premiers Aérostats à Langres,' *BSHAL*, viii [1919], 8).

13. *SV*, i, 187 (25 Sept. 1760).

14. Canon [Louis-François] Marcel, 'La Jeunesse de Diderot, 1732–1743,' *Mercure de France*, ccxvi (1929), 68 n.

15. Mme de Vandeul, xxx–xxxi.

16. A.-T., x, 351.

17. Johann Georg Wille, *Mémoires et journal*, ed. Georges Duplessis, 2 vols. (Paris, 1857), i, 91. Wille dates this meeting in 1740, but Emilia Francis (Strong), Lady Dilke, *French En-*

gravers and Draughtsmen of the XVIIIth Century (London, 1902), 73, proves that it must have been after May 1742.

18. Taillefer, *Tableau historique,* IV, 217.

19. Mme de Vandeul, xxx; Naigeon, 5.

20. Mme de Vandeul, xxxi. Bernis, however, makes no mention of Diderot (François-Joachim de Pierre, Cardinal de Bernis, *Mémoires et lettres,* ed. Frédéric Masson, 2 vols. [Paris, 1903], I, 16–20).

21. Marcel, 'Diderot écolier,' *RHLF,* xxxiv, 396–9; R. Salesses, 'Diderot et l'Université, ou les conséquences d'une mystification,' *Revue Universitaire,* April 1935, 322–33; cf. Ralph Bowen, 'The Education of an Encyclopedist,' *Teachers of History: Essays in Honor of Laurence Bradford Packard* (Ithaca [N.Y.], 1954), 33–9. My friend, Professor François Denoeu, suggests the possibility that Diderot was a *pensionnaire* at one *collège* and went out to special lectures at the others.

22. Salesses, in *Revue Universitaire,* April 1935, 329. Cf. Aram Vartanian, *Diderot and Descartes* (Princeton, 1953), 40–43.

23. This ingenious supposition is set forth by Jean Pommier, *Diderot avant Vincennes* (Paris, 1939), 9. Yvon Belaval, *L'Esthétique sans paradoxe de Diderot* (Paris, 1950), 15, thinks that Diderot transferred from the Collège d'Harcourt to Louis-le-Grand. An anonymous polemical pamphlet of 1759 declared that Diderot did his 'philosophy' under a Dominican. If this was true, it is clear that even if Diderot was in the Jesuit Louis-le-Grand for his first year of studies in Paris, he did not remain there for his second (*Lettres sur le VIIe volume de l'Encyclopédie* [n.p., 1759], 37 n.: 'M. Diderot a fait son cours de Philosophie sous le P. Rozet, dominicain'). Evidence of Diderot's master of arts degree is on fol. 35 of a University register ('Index Magistrorum in Artibus,' B.N., MSS, Fonds latin 9158); reproduced in Guyot, 6.

24. A.-T., I, 383–4; but as M. Salesses, *Revue Universitaire,* April 1935, 325, points out, the *Lettre sur les sourds et muets* was published anonymously, and therefore Diderot's references to Louis-le-Grand and to Father Porée may have been intended merely to mystify.

25. Naigeon, 8; Salesses, 'Diderot et l'Université,' *Revue Universitaire,* April 1935, 325 n.

26. Diderot, *Corr.,* I, 23, 29.

27. Mme de Vandeul, xxxi–xxxii; she implies that Diderot read law with the *procureur* before he tried tutoring, but Naigeon, 15, says that it was the other way around. Regarding Clément, see Marcel, 'La Jeunesse de Diderot,' *Mercure de France,* ccxvi, 49–53.

28. Mme de Vandeul, xxxiii–xxxiv. There were several persons of the name of Randon contemporary with Diderot. Assézat declared (A.-T., I, xxxiv n.) that it was Randon de Boisset, and that he was the Randon to whom Diderot referred in his *Salon* of 1767 (A.-T., XI, 274). But he died a bachelor (Comte L. Clément de Ris, 'Paul Randon de Boisset, 1708–1776,' *Bulletin du Bibliophile et du Bibliothécaire,* 39e année [1872], 201). Canon Marcel, 'La Jeunesse de Diderot,' *Mercure de France,* ccxvi, 60–64, believes that Diderot's employer was an Elie Randon de Massanes d'Haneucourt; Naigeon, 13–15, stated that it was a M. Randon d'Hannecourt.

29. This characteristic of Diderot is commented upon by Steel, *Diderot's Imagery,* 175–7.

30. Mme de Vandeul, xxxiii.

31. A.-T., III, 460. This work was by Antoine Deparcieux (1703–68), *Nouveaux Traités de trigonométrie rectiligne et sphérique . . . avec un traité de gnomonique* (Paris, 1741). It contains no mention of the part played by Diderot in its preparation.

32. *Histoire de Grèce, traduite de l'Anglois de Temple Stanyan,* 3 vols. (Paris: Briasson, 1743), III, 349.

33. Mme de Vandeul, xxxii–xxxiii. Her name was Hélène Brûlé (Marcel, *La Soeur de Diderot,* 12).

34. Mme de Vandeul, xxxvii; the same story, almost verbatim, in Taillefer, *Tableau historique,* IV, 224–5. François Génin in *Nouvelle Biographie générale* (Hoefer), s.v. 'Diderot,' 82, dates this 1741, but adduces no proof.

35. Diderot, *Corr.,* I, 23; my italics. A.-T., XIII, 210, s.v. 'Acier.'

36. Mme de Vandeul, xxxiv–xxxvi.

37. A.-T., IX, 168. The work alluded to is Isaac Newton, *Philosophiae naturalis principia mathematica,* ed. Thomas Le Seur and François Jacquier, 4 vols. (Geneva, 1739–42).

38. A.-T., VIII, 398; cf. A.-T., VII, 108.
39. A.-T., VII, 400–401.
40. A.-T., I, 359.
41. For a description *ca.* 1726 of the discussions that went on at the Café Procope, see Charles Pineau Duclos, *Oeuvres complètes*, 10 vols. (Paris, 1806), x, 55–69. Cf. Jacques Hillairet, *Evocation du vieux Paris*, 2 vols. (Paris, [1952–3]), I, 619–20.
42. Jean-Nicolas Dufort de Cheverny, *Mémoires*, 2nd ed., 2 vols. (Paris, 1909), I, 459.
43. A.-T., V, 411–12.
44. A.-T., X, 349. The book in question was *Vénus dans le cloître, ou la Religieuse en chemise*, first published at Cologne in 1683.
45. A.-T., VII, 404.
46. *SV*, II, 101–2 (28 July 1762).
47. R. Salesses, 'Les Mystères de la jeunesse de Diderot, ou l'aventure théologique,' *Mercure de France*, CCLXXX (1937), 501 n.
48. Archives Départementales de la Haute-Marne, Fonds Vandeul E-4, quoted by Gautier, *Le Père de Diderot*, 17. Cf. the same document: 'Vous, mon fils l'aîné . . . vous savez ce que j'ai fait pour vous; j'ai dépensé tant pour vous que pour votre soeur la religieuse et pour Diderot le prêtre plus que le patrimoine que, moi et Angélique, nous avons eu, tant en mariage que de succession' (ibid.).
49. Marcel, 'Diderot écolier,' *RHLF*, XXXIV, 400.
50. A.-T., XI, 265–6.
51. *Encyc.*, VII, 262b, s.v. 'Fourrure.' See also ibid. IX, 893b, s.v. 'Maître ès arts.'
52. *Encyc.*, V, 5a.
53. Salesses, loc. cit., *Mercure de France*, CCLXXX, 503–11. M. Salesses thinks it probable that Diderot even knew Hebrew (ibid. 511–12); but cf. Joseph Edmund Barker, *Diderot's Treatment of the Christian Religion in* The Encyclopédie (New York, 1941), 24–6.
54. Diderot, *Corr.*, I, 25–6. In 1784 the grandson of Pierre La Salette, he being also the son-in-law of Diderot, wrote that La Salette had undertaken to try to get the elder Diderot to settle an annuity of 200 livres upon his older son but that his good offices were unsuccessful (Massiet du Biest, 'Lettres inédites . . . ,' [*supra*, ch. 2, note 10], 2–3).
55. Diderot, *Corr.*, I, 26.
56. L'Abbé Prévost, *Manon Lescaut* (Oxford: Blackwell's French Texts, 1943), I, 93–4; this edition is a facsimile of the authoritative 1753 edition.
57. A.-T., II, 399.

CHAPTER 3

1. Mme de Vandeul, xxxvii. Lester Gilbert Crocker, 'La Jeunesse de Diderot: Quelques précisions,' by L. G. Krakeur, *PMLA*, LVII (1942), 134–5, believes the couple became acquainted in 1742. For lively (though undocumented) articles regarding Mme Diderot, see Henriette Célarié, 'Le Philosophe mal marié: Diderot et son épouse,' *Monde Français*, XII (1948), 39–60, and Jules Bertaut, 'Madame Diderot,' *Revue de France*, 1 June 1924, 574–94, reprinted in his *Egéries du XVIIIᵉ siècle* (Paris, [1928]), 183–212.
2. For Anne-Toinette's baptismal certificate, see Marcel, *Le Mariage de Diderot*, 8.
3. The principal building of this convent is now the Musée de l'Assistance Publique. Regarding Mme Diderot's family and ancestry, see Massiet du Biest, *La Fille de Diderot*, 7 n.; also Diderot, *Corr.*, I, 24. Her elder sister, Marie-Antoinette Champion, married Michel Billard (or Billaud). In her declining years she lived with the Diderots (Marcel, *Le Mariage de Diderot*, 9–10; Louis Marcel, 'Un Petit Problème d'histoire religieuse et d'histoire littéraire: La Mort de Diderot,' *Revue d'Histoire de l'Eglise de France*, XI [1925], 40 n., 46 n., 211 n.). In the marriage contract of Diderot's daughter, as printed in *Cahiers Haut-Marnais*, No. 24 (1ᵉʳ trimestre 1951), 19, she is referred to as the widow of Michel Belliard.
4. Mme de Vandeul, xxxvii–xxxviii.
5. Ibid. xxxviii; also Massiet du Biest, *La Fille de Diderot*, 207.
6. *SV*, II, 324 (21 Nov. 1765).
7. See Pierre Mesnard, 'Le Caractère de Diderot,' *Revue de la Méditerranée*, VII (1949), 279; see also his *Le Cas Diderot: Etude de caractérologie littéraire* (Paris, 1952), 67.

8. Comte Pierre-Louis Roederer, 'Sur Diderot,' *Journal de Paris*, 17 Fructidor An vi [3 Sept. 1798]; reprinted in Roederer, *Opuscules mêlés de littérature et de philosophie* (Paris, An VIII [1800]), 53; and in Roederer, *Oeuvres*, 8 vols. (Paris, 1853–9), iv, 215.
9. Mme de Vandeul, xxxviii–xxxix.
10. Diderot, *Corr.*, i, 29.
11. Naigeon, 26.
12. Crocker, 'La Jeunesse de Diderot,' *PMLA*, lvii, 134.
13. Christmas Eve, 1742 (Diderot, *Corr.*, i, 37).
14. Diderot, *Corr.*, i, 36. 17 Dec. 1742, according to Lester G. Crocker, *La Correspondance de Diderot*, by L. G. Krakeur (New York, 1939), 109.
15. Diderot, *Corr.*, i, 35–6. Diderot's brother entered the seminary eight days before Diderot arrived in Langres in 1742 (ibid. 35); he received the tonsure on 29 June 1743, and entered holy orders sometime in 1746, probably in May (Marcel, *Le Frère de Diderot*, 42–4).
16. Diderot's father mentioned this book in his will (Gautier, *Le Père de Diderot*, 15); cf. Marcel, 'La Jeunesse de Diderot,' *Mercure de France*, ccxvi, 78 n.
17. Mme de Vandeul, lviii. Cf. Georges May, *Diderot et 'La Religieuse'* (New Haven, 1954), 146–52.
18. 3 Sept. 1749 (*RQH*, 110).
19. Diderot, *Corr.*, i, 38, 39.
20. Diderot, *Corr.*, i, 40.
21. Arch. départ., Haute-Marne, Fonds Vandeul, ii E 3; published in Diderot, *Corr.*, i, 41–2, and in Marcel, *Le Mariage de Diderot*, 21–2. This letter reproduced in facsimile in *Cahiers Haut-Marnais*, No. 24 (1er trimestre 1951), Supplément illustré.
22. Evelyn B. Hall (pseud. S. G. Tallentyre), *The Life of Mirabeau* (London, 1908), 90.
23. Diderot, *Corr.*, i, 43–4. This aunt was probably his godmother, Claire Vigneron (b. 17 Nov. 1665; date of death unknown). So far as is known, no other of Diderot's aunts was alive at this time (Marcel, *Le Frère de Diderot*, 193, 197).
24. A.-T., i, lxiii.
25. Mme de Vandeul, xxxix.
26. *CI*, ii, 17 n.
27. *CI*, ii, 122. The marriage contract was signed 26 Oct. 1743 (Dieckmann, *Inventaire*, 162).
28. Auguste Jal, *Dictionnaire critique de biographie et d'histoire . . . d'après des documents authentiques inédits*, 2nd ed. (Paris, 1872), 495.
29. Mme de Vandeul, xxxix. She states, however, that the marriage took place in 1744, an example of how her account of her father is not to be trusted implicitly. For Saint-Pierre-aux-Boeufs, see the Abbé Lebeuf, *Histoire de la ville et de tout le diocèse de Paris*, 5 vols. (Paris, 1883), i, 317–19; and also the same work, *Rectifications et additions*, by Fernand Bournon (Paris, 1890), 329–30. Cf. the Marquis de Rochegude and Maurice Dumolin, *Guide pratique à travers le vieux Paris*, nouv. ed. (Paris, 1923), 41.
30. Diderot, *Corr.*, i, 39.
31. Ibid. 46.
32. Ibid. 32.
33. Charles Nauroy, *Révolutionnaires* (Paris, 1891), 244; also in his *Le Curieux*, i (1883–5), 248.
34. Nauroy, *Révolutionnaires*, 246; Edmond Beaurepaire, 'Les Logis de Diderot,' *Revue des Français*, xvii (1913), 313.
35. *RQH*, 109.
36. Bonnefon, 203.
37. Mme de Vandeul, xl.
38. Courtois, 'Chronologie,' 36; Rousseau, ed. Hachette, viii, 199.
39. A.-T., xi, 127.
40. Courtois, 'Chronologie,' 41, 48, 40, and esp. 50 n.; Louis Ducros, *Jean-Jacques Rousseau: De Genève à l'Hermitage (1712–1757)* (Paris, 1908), 131 n., argues that the summer of 1746 is the correct date.
41. Rousseau, ed. Hachette, viii, 246.
42. *CI*, ii, 14 n.

CHAPTER 4

1. A.-T., II, 378.
2. Bonnefon, 212.
3. A.-T., VII, 17.
4. *Le Perroquet, ou mélange de diverses pièces intéressantes pour l'esprit et pour le coeur*, 2 vols. (Frankfurt am Main, 1742), I, 78–80; also A.-T., IX, 63–4. See Gustave L. Van Roosbroeck, 'Diderot's Earliest Publication,' *MLN*, XXXIX (1924), 504–5. The identification of Baculard d'Arnaud is made by Venturi, *Jeunesse*, 41–2, 340, 342.
5. Diderot, *Corr.*, I, 29–30.
6. A.-T., XIV, 438.
7. Herbert Dieckmann, 'Diderot, membre honoraire de la Société d'Antiquaires d'Ecosse,' *Cahiers Haut-Marnais*, No. 24 (1er trimestre 1951), 25. For a photograph of Diderot's draft, see ibid. Supplément illustré.
8. See above, chap. 2, note 32. The *privilèges* were dated, respectively, 14 July, 14 Dec. and 19 Dec. 1742 (B.N., MSS, Fr. 21958, foll. 30–31, 81–2, 84).
9. *Journal des Sçavans*, August 1743, 451–62; Sept. 1745, 547–55; April 1746, 231–8, this quotation, 238.
10. *Les Nouvelles Littéraires de Berlin*, 21 Dec. 1773, quoted by Tourneux, *Diderot et Catherine II*, 529. The translation comprised one volume of the five-volume (unauthorized) edition of Diderot's works published at London [Amsterdam] in 1773.
11. Mme de Vandeul, xl.
12. Cf. Venturi, *Jeunesse*, 46–71, 342–58; Pierre Hermand, *Les Idées morales de Diderot* (Paris, 1923), 50–63; Cru, 119–33; Pommier, *Diderot avant Vincennes*, 20–25.
13. Hippolyte Buffenoir, *Les Portraits de Jean-Jacques Rousseau* (Paris, 1913), I, 240, plate 48. Diderot also gave a copy, with the flattering inscription 'Totum muneris hoc tui est,' to a Mme de Sainte-Croix, of whom nothing else is known; for this facsimile, see *Pierre Berès: Catalogue 48: Beaux livres anciens* (Paris, [1951?]), item 118.
14. P. 200. On the *Journal de Trévoux*, see Gustave Dumas, *Histoire du Journal de Trévoux depuis 1701 jusqu'en 1762* (Paris, 1936), *passim*, esp. 137, and Albert Cazes, 'Un Adversaire de Diderot et des philosophes: Le P. Berthier,' in *Mélanges offerts . . . à M. Gustave Lanson* (Paris, 1922), 235–49, esp. 239–40.
15. *Journal des Sçavans*, April 1746, 219.
16. Löpelmann, *Der junge Diderot*, 84, 100–101, 121–2, esp. remarks on the skill of Diderot's translation.
17. Such, too, is the judgment, in a very perspicacious essay, of a former member of the French Academy (Charles de Rémusat, 'Shaftesbury,' *RDM*, 15 Nov. 1862, 475).
18. A.-T., I, 16.
19. A.-T., I, 75. The importance of this passage has been emphasized by Venturi, *Jeunesse*, 355; by Pommier, *Diderot avant Vincennes*, 25; and by Mesnard, 'Le Caractère de Diderot,' *Revue de la Méditerranée*, VII, 283, who calls it 'le modèle unique de la sensibilité.'
20. A.-T., I, 25 n.
21. *Jugemens sur Quelques Ouvrages Nouveaux*, VIII (Avignon, 1745), 86–7.
22. A.-T., I, 10.
23. Venturi, *Jeunesse*, 50; Hermand, *Les Idées morales de Diderot*, 56; John Morley, *Diderot and the Encyclopaedists*, 2 vols. (London, 1878), I, 59–61.
24. Venturi, *Jeunesse*, 59–61.
25. A.-T., I, 32–6.
26. Venturi, *Jeunesse*, 359–63; René P. Legros, 'Diderot et Shaftesbury,' *MLR*, XIX (1924), 192–4.
27. Marcel, *Le Frère de Diderot*, 43–4. The brother was a student in canon law at Paris from 1744 (probably) until early 1747 (ibid. 43, 47). Succeeding editions of the translation of Shaftesbury were (1) *Philosophie morale reduite à ses principes, ou Essai de M. S. * * * sur le mérite et la vertu* (Venice [Paris], 1751); (2) *Les Oeuvres de Mylord Comte de Shaftesbury*, 3 vols. (Geneva, 1769), II, 3–166, but with no intimation that Diderot was the translator. The Shaftesbury *Essai* was included in all five of the eighteenth-century collected editions of Diderot's works.

28. Mark Twain, 'A Majestic Literary Fossil,' *Writings (Author's National Edition)*, XXI, 524–38.

29. Bonnefon, 212. Cf. James Doolittle, 'Robert James, Diderot, and the *Encyclopédie,*' *MLN*, LXXI (1956), 431–4.

30. 'Registre des privilèges accordés aux auteurs et libraires, 1742–1748' (B.N., MSS, Fr. 21958, fol. 262). The title page is dated 1746, but the first volume was published shortly before October 1745 (*Journal des Sçavans*, Oct. 1745, 634); the second, promised for June 1746, was ready for distribution on 11 May of that year (*Journal de Trévoux*, July 1746, 1541). An Italian translation (*Dizionario universale di medicina . . . tradotto dall'originale inglese dai Signori Diderot, Eidous e Toussaint . . .*) was published at Venice in 1753.

31. *DNB*, s.v. 'James, Robert, M.D.' In 1771 Diderot reviewed admiringly (but without knowing the identity of the author) the *Histoire de Richard Savage*, just translated into French by Le Tourneur (A.-T., IX, 451–2), but aside from these slight instances, no relationship between Diderot and Johnson is known.

32. Mme de Vandeul, xl.

33. *Arrest de la cour du Parlement, qui ordonne qu'un livre intitulé, Les Moeurs . . . sera laceré & brûlé par l'Exécuteur de la Haute-Justice* (Paris: P.-G. Simon, 1748), mounted in B.N., MSS, Fr. 22176, foll. 258–9. Benedict XIV placed the book on the Index in 1757 (Franz Heinrich Reusch, *Der Index der verbotenen Bücher*, 2 vols. [Bonn, 1883–5], II, 873).

34. B.N., MSS, Nouv. acq. fr. 10783, fol. 124. See also Maurice Pellisson, 'Toussaint et le livre des "Moeurs",' *Révolution Française*, XXXIV (1898), 385–402; and Gustave Charlier, 'Un Encyclopédiste à Bruxelles: Fr.-V. Toussaint, l'auteur des "Moeurs",' *Annales Prince de Ligne*, XVIII (1937), 5–22.

35. *Encyc.*, I, xlij; *Corr. litt.*, VI, 391–2. See ibid. VI, 143–4, 285, 454 for notices of other translations by Eidous.

36. *Corr. litt.*, VII, 234.

37. Ibid. 308. For a similar judgment on Eidous, see l'Abbé Sabatier de Castres, *Les Trois Siècles de la littérature française*, 5th ed., 4 vols. (The Hague, 1778), II, 148.

38. Bibliothèque de l'Arsenal: Archives de la Bastille 10301 (14 Feb. 1748). In 1749, Eidous was reported to be thirty-six (B.N., MSS, Nouv. acq. fr. 10782, fol. 2).

39. Dieckmann, *Inventaire*, 3–4.

40. Baptism: Nauroy, *Révolutionnaires*, 244–5; cf. Diderot, *Corr.*, I, 53. For the *convulsionnaires*, see Albert Mousset, *L'Étrange histoire des convulsionnaires de Saint-Médard* (Paris, 1953).

41. Bonnefon, 210.

42. *Arrest de la cour du Parlement . . . Du 7. Juillet 1746* (Paris: P.-G. Simon, 1746), 2, mounted in B.N., MSS, Fr. 22176, foll. 210–11.

43. Gustave Lanson, 'Questions diverses sur l'histoire de l'esprit philosophique en France avant 1750,' *RHLF*, XIX (1912), 2–4.

44. Ira O. Wade, *The Clandestine Organization and Diffusion of Philosophic Ideas in France from 1700 to 1750* (Princeton, 1938), 10–18, 166, 294, *et passim*.

45. Venturi, *Jeunesse*, 73–4.

46. See the reports of Bonin and Mme de La Marche during 1748 and 1749 (Bibliothèque de l'Arsenal: Archives de la Bastille 10300–10302). Regarding the latter, see also Hugues de Montbas, 'La Littérature clandestine au XVIIIe siècle,' *RDM*, 15 July 1951, 326–7. For a comprehensive account of the administration of censorship, see David T. Pottinger, 'Censorship in France during the Ancien Régime,' *Boston Public Library Quarterly*, VI (1954), 23–42, 84–101.

47. For bibliographical information regarding the *Pensées philosophiques*, see the critical edition, ed. Robert Niklaus (Geneva, 1950), 47–63; also further information in Diderot, *Lettre sur les aveugles*, ed. Robert Niklaus (Geneva, 1951), lxvi. Regarding the German translation (Halle, 1748), see Joachim Abrahams, 'Diderot, französisch und deutsch,' *Romanische Forschungen*, LI (1937), 42–50, 387.

48. Mme de Vandeul, xlii. Taillefer, *Tableau historique*, IV, 263–4, says that Diderot wrote it in four days.

49. Shaftesbury's influence was alleged by [Georges-P.-G. Polier de Bottens], *Pensées chrétiennes mises en parallèle, ou en opposition, avec les Pensées philosophiques* (Rouen, 1747), 7; as

also by the reviewer of the *Pensées philosophiques* writing in the *Bibliothèque Raisonnée des Ouvrages des Savants de l'Europe*, XL (Jan.–March 1748), 112–23.

50. David Finch, *La Critique philosophique de Pascal au XVIIIe siècle* (Philadelphia, 1940), 39–46; Morley, *Diderot and the Encyclopaedists*, 1, 52.

51. Albert Monod, *De Pascal à Chateaubriand: Les Défenseurs français du Christianisme de 1670 à 1802* (Paris, 1916), 304, 509.

52. The importance and novelty of Diderot's biological approach is well brought out by Aram Vartanian, 'From Deist to Atheist: Diderot's Philosophical Orientation, 1746–1749,' *Diderot Studies*, I, 48–52. Cf. Lester G. Crocker, 'Pensée XIX of Diderot,' *MLN*, LXVII (1952), 433–9, and the ensuing controversy between Drs. Crocker, Vartanian, and James Doolittle, *MLN*, LXVIII (1953), 282–8.

53. Robert Niklaus, 'Les *Pensées Philosophiques* de Diderot,' *Bulletin of the John Rylands Library, Manchester*, XXVI (1941–2), 128; Guyot, 67.

54. For a bibliography of refutations of the *Pensées philosophiques*, see the Niklaus editions (*supra*, note 47), 58–63 and lxvi, resp.; also Robert Niklaus, 'Baron de Gaufridi's Refutation of Diderot's *Pensées Philosophiques*,' *RR*, XLIII (1952), 87–95. The young Turgot wrote a criticism of the *Pensées philosophiques* (Turgot, *Oeuvres*, ed. Gustave Schelle, 5 vols. [Paris, 1913–23], I, 87–97). This remained in manuscript, however, and it is not certain just when it was written. Mention might also be made of Pierre-Louis-Claude Gin, *De la Religion*, 4 vols. (Paris, 1778–9), I, 135; III, part iii, 103, 237–9, 253–4; III, part iv, 54–5, 162–4, 203–4, 215–16, 227–8, 277–8; IV, 238. For summaries of the refutations of the *Pensées*, see Venturi, *Jeunesse*, 91–104, 363–7, and Monod, *De Pascal à Chateaubriand*, 304–8.

55. David-Renaud Boullier, in Lettre XII (1 Feb. 1748), *Le Controlleur du Parnasse*, IV, 10; Polier de Bottens (*supra*, note 49), 8.

CHAPTER 5

1. A.-T., I, 269–70.

2. [Jacques-André Naigeon, ed.], *Recueil philosophique, ou Mélange de pièces sur la religion & la morale*, 2 vols. (London [Amsterdam], 1770), I, 105–29; in A.-T., I, 261–73. Naigeon attributed this falsely to Vauvenargues (*Recueil philosophique*, II, 253), because Diderot was still alive, while Vauvenargues had died in 1747. This piece 'was in part inspired by Wollaston's *The Religion of Nature Delineated*' (Lester G. Crocker, *The Embattled Philosopher: A Biography of Denis Diderot* [East Lansing (Mich.), 1954], 28).

3. So, too, thinks M. Pommier (*Diderot avant Vincennes*, 38 n.); but cf. Venturi, *Jeunesse*, 72–3, 106–7.

4. A.-T., I, 270, 264, 272.

5. Although Naigeon declared in 1786 that Diderot wrote the *Promenade du sceptique* in 1749 (Massiet du Biest, 'Lettres inédites. . . .' [*supra*, ch. 2, note 10], 4), all other authorities believe it to have been written in 1747. Wade, *Clandestine Organization*, 166, found a note in the library at Fécamp declaring that the *Promenade* was composed in 1747.

6. A.-T., I, 186–7.

7. Bonnefon, 202.

8. Nauroy, *Révolutionnaires*, 245.

9. Bonnefon, 203. Berryer was appointed Lieutenant-General of Police on 27 May 1747 (B.N., MSS, Fr. 22176, fol. 238).

10. A.-T., I, 192.

11. A.-T., I, 215, 220.

12. A.-T., VI, 30.

13. See *supra*, ch. 4, note 21; Pommier, *Diderot avant Vincennes*, 41–2. Cf. A.-T., I, 15, 185.

14. A.-T., IV, 443–8. Cf. A.-T., II, 524–6. Leif Nedergaard, 'Notes sur certains ouvrages de Diderot,' *Orbis Litterarum*, VIII (1950), 5.

15. Steel, *Diderot's Imagery*, 262–3; but cf. Venturi, *Jeunesse*, 108–10.

16. A.-T., I, 199.

17. A.-T., I, 212.
18. Vartanian, 'From Deist to Atheist,' *Diderot Studies*, I, 52–5, 60–61. See also the analysis of the *Promenade* in Venturi, *Jeunesse*, 108–19; and Paul Vernière, *Spinoza et la pensée française avant la Révolution* (Paris, 1954), 567–72; also Paul Vernière, ed., *Oeuvres philosophiques*, by Diderot (Paris, [1956]), x.
19. J. Delort, *Histoire de la détention des philosophes et des gens de lettres à la Bastille et à Vincennes*, 3 vols. (Paris, 1829), II, 213 n. Concerning D'Hémery, consult Ernest Coyecque, *Inventaire de la Collection Anisson sur l'histoire de l'imprimerie et de la librairie, principalement à Paris*, 2 vols. (Paris, 1900), x–li. See also Frederick Charles Green, *Eighteenth-Century France* (London, 1929), 205–8.
20. Bonnefon, 209.
21. Mme de Vandeul, xlvi. André Billy, ed., *Oeuvres*, by Diderot (Paris: 'Nouvelle Revue française,' 1951 [Bibliothèque de la Pléiade, No. 25]), 15, dates this in June 1747, but cites no authorities.
22. Naigeon, 142–3 nn. A manuscript copy of the *Promenade* was in Malesherbes' library in 1789 (Wade, *Clandestine Organization*, 166); perhaps this was the confiscated manuscript itself. Cf. Venturi, *Jeunesse*, 171–4.
23. Naigeon to Vandeul, August 1786 (Massiet du Biest, 'Lettres inédites . . .' [*supra*, ch. 2, note 10], 4).
24. A.-T., I, 248.
25. *Nouvelle Biographie générale* (*Hoefer*), s.v. 'Puisieux, Philippe-Florent de,' and 'Puisieux, Madeleine d'Arsant de'; see also J. de Boisjoslin and G. Mossé, 'Quelques meneuses d'hommes au XVIIIe siècle: Madame de Puysieux; Sophie Volland; Mesdames d'Epinay et d'Houdetot,' *Nouvelle Revue*, nouvelle série, XXXIV (1905), 519–21. De Puisieux is mentioned in the *Encyc.*, I, xlv, as having aided Diderot in the description of several of the arts.
26. A.-T., I, 25 n.
27. Madeleine d'Arsant de Puisieux, *Les Caractères*, Seconde Partie (London, 1751), ii; in print by 8 Feb. 1751 (*Corr. litt.*, II, 29).
28. Mme de Vandeul, xlii. A police report on Diderot, evidently written in 1749 because it gives his age as thirty-six, says, 'Il est marié et a eu cependant Made de Puyseux pour Maitresse pendant assez de tems' (B.N., MSS, Nouv. acq. fr. 10781, fol. 146).
29. Mme de Vandeul, xli.
30. *RQH*, 109; Diderot, *Corr.*, I, 145.
31. Morley, *Diderot and the Encyclopaedists*, I, 42.
32. Mme de Puisieux, *Conseils à une amie* (n.p., 1749), vii–x.
33. B.N., MSS, Nouv. acq. fr. 10783, fol. 51.
34. *Corr. litt.*, I, 281.
35. Mme de Puisieux, *Les Caractères*, Seconde Partie, iii, vi. Nevertheless, D'Argenson remarked that *Les Caractères* was attributed in part to Diderot (D'Argenson, VI, 182 n.). A letter from [J.-N.] Moreau, 19 April 1750, presumably to the Lieutenant-General of Police, said that the work was attributed to Diderot, although appearing under a lady's name (Bibliothèque de l'Arsenal: Archives de la Bastille, 10302). *Le Petit Reservoir* (Berlin [The Hague]), I (1750), 316–23, printed some 'Extraits du Livre intitulé; les Caracteres de Madame Puisieux, attribué à Mr. Diderot qui s'en deffend.'
36. Joseph de La Porte, *Histoire littéraire des dames françoises*, 5 vols. (Paris, 1769), V, 154. See also Sabatier de Castres, *Les Trois Siècles*, III, 385–6; and *Corr. litt.*, II, 29, III, 31, VIII, 17.
37. Marie-Jeanne Phlipon, Mme Roland, *Mémoires*, ed. Cl. Perroud, 2 vols. (Paris, 1905), II, 144.
38. Arthur M. Wilson, 'Une Partie inédite de la lettre de Diderot à Voltaire, le 11 juin 1749,' *RHLF*, LI (1951), 259.
39. Mme de Vandeul, xlii. Canon Marcel believed that Mme Diderot's mother died about 1745 (Marcel, *Le Mariage de Diderot*, 9 n.).
40. Rousseau, ed. Hachette, VIII, 246–7.
41. A.-T., I, 304–5; Georges Le Roy, *La Psychologie de Condillac* (Paris, 1937), 92–3.
42. Le Roy, 102; cf. E. Vacherot, in *Dictionnaire des sciences philosophiques*, ed. Ad. Franck, 3d printing (Paris, 1885), s.v. 'Diderot,' 388.

43. *Dictionnaire de biographie française,* ed. J. Balteau, M. Barroux, and M. Prevost (Paris, 1933–   ), I, col. 1398.
44. *Mercure de France,* Oct. 1747, 92–109; in A.-T., IX, 156–67. The standard work on this subject (M.-D.-J. Engramelle, *La Tonotechnie, ou l'art de noter les cylindres* [Paris, 1775]) bears no evidence, however, of any influence of Diderot's ideas.
45. *Encyc.,* XV, 96–7; ibid. *Planches,* V, s.v. 'Lutherie,' planche IV.
46. *Gentleman's Magazine,* XIX (1749), 339.
47. Cf. A.-T., IX, 77 n.
48. *Gentleman's Magazine,* XIX, 405.
49. Percy A. Scholes, *The Oxford Companion to Music,* 8th ed. (London, 1950), 553. Dr. Scholes does not, however, mention Diderot's project.
50. B.-L. de Muralt, *Lettres sur les Anglois et les François* (Bibliothèque de la Revue de Littérature Comparée, LXXXVI [Paris, 1933]), 168, 171. These remarks were written not long before 1700, but not published until 1725 (ibid. 45).
51. Herbert Dieckmann, ed., *Le Philosophe. Texts and Interpretation* (Washington University Studies, New Series, Language and Literature, No. 18 [St. Louis, 1948]), 2–3 *et passim.* Voltaire declared that this work was 'de l'année 1730' (Wade, *Clandestine Organization,* 15).
52. Dieckmann, *Le Philosophe,* 32, 42, 46, 58.
53. Ibid. 68.

CHAPTER 6

1. André Cresson, *Diderot: sa vie, son oeuvre* (Paris, 1949), 35.
2. For a good description of previous compendiums and works of reference, see Cru, 225–38.
3. *Supplement to the Fourth, Fifth, and Sixth Editions of the Encyclopaedia Britannica,* 6 vols. (Edinburgh, 1824), I, ii–iii. This work contains (i–ix) a good account of early encyclopedias, including the one edited by Diderot.
4. Ibid. iv.
5. A.-T., XIII, 132.
6. Diderot was commenting upon Duhamel de Monceau's *Traité de la culture des terres suivant les principes de M. Tull* (1750–61). Regarding this work, see T. H. Marshall, 'Jethro Tull and the "New Husbandry" of the Eighteenth Century,' *Economic History Review,* II (1929–30), 51–2.
7. A.-T., XIV, 456.
8. Venturi, *Origini,* 11–12.
9. Lanson, 'Questions diverses . . . ,' *RHLF,* XIX, 314. Regarding Ramsay, see Albert Chérel, *Un Aventurier religieux au XVIIIᵉ siècle: André-Michel Ramsay* (Paris, 1926), 182; and esp. concerning his Masonic activities, the note by Depping in *Biographie universelle* (Michaud), s.v. 'Ramsay, André-Michel de,' as also Gustave Bord, *La Franc-Maçonnerie en France des origines à 1815* (Paris, 1908), 62–8.
10. *Diderot et l'Encyclopédie: Exposition commémorative,* ed. Georges Huard (Paris: Bibliothèque nationale, 1951), 18.
11. Lanson, 'Questions diverses . . . ,' *RHLF,* XIX, 315–16; Albert Lantoine, *Histoire de la Franc-Maçonnerie française: La Franc-Maçonnerie chez elle* (Paris, 1925), 55; Albert Lantoine, *Le Rite écossais ancien et accepté* (Paris, 1930), 73; J. Emile Daruty, *Recherches sur le rite écossais ancien accepté* (Paris, 1879), 85, 84–6 nn.; Bord, *La Franc-Maçonnerie,* 121–3, 327–8. Le Gras, 31, argued that the Le Breton involved was not André-François; but Louis-Philippe May, 'Note sur les origines maçonniques de l'Encyclopédie,' *Revue de Synthèse,* XVII (1939), 182–4, was inclined to think that it was André-François Le Breton after all; and recent researches seem to have established the fact (Jean Gigot, 'Promenade encyclopédique,' *Cahiers Haut-Marnais,* No. 24 [1ᵉʳ trimestre 1951], 70 n.; and Jean Pommier, reviewing M. Gigot's article, *RHLF,* LI [1951], 378). Nevertheless, the question is not yet fully settled: see G.-H. Luquet, 'L'*Encyclopédie* fut-elle une entreprise maçonnique?' *RHLF,* LIV (1954), 29–31.
12. Bord, *La Franc-Maçonnerie,* xvii; also Le Gras, 21–2, 29–30; but cf. Pommier, *RHLF,* LI (1951), 378.

13. Venturi, *Origini*, 130. Cf. Pierre Grosclaude, *Un Audacieux Message: L'Encyclopédie* (Paris, 1951), 198–9; and Luquet, loc. cit., *RHLF*, LIV (1954), 23–31.
14. *Mémoire pour André-François Le Breton*, . . . *Contre le Sieur Jean Mills, se disant Gentilhomme Anglais* (Paris: Le Breton, 1745), 2.
15. 17 Feb. and 5 March 1745 (ibid. 2–3).
16. 25 Feb. 1745 (B.N., MSS, Fr. 21997, fol. 103: 'Registre des privilèges et permissions simples de la librairie'). Action of 26 March 1745: *Arrest du Conseil d'Etat du Roy, rendu au sujet du privilège ci-devant accordé pour l'impression de l'ouvrage intitulé, Dictionnaire universel des Arts & des Sciences. Du 28 Août 1745* (Paris: Imprimerie royale, 1745), 1, mounted in B.N., MSS, Fr. 22176, foll. 202–3. Action of 13 April 1745: 'Privilege de l'Encyclopédie de Chambers. Du 13 avril 1745,' printed in Luneau de Boisjermain, *Pièce justificative* No. III. The *privilège* of 13 April 1745 is listed in a manuscript 'Registre des privilèges accordés aux auteurs et libraires, 1742–1748' (B.N., MSS, Fr. 21958, fol. 374).
17. The title page is reproduced by Douglas H. Gordon and Norman L. Torrey, *The Censoring of Diderot's* Encyclopédie *and the Re-established Text* (New York, 1947), facing p. 10. The prospectus is printed in Luneau de Boisjermain, *Pièce justificative* No. VI.
18. *Arrest* . . . *du 28 Août 1745*, 2.
19. *Journal de Trévoux*, May 1745, 934–9; this quotation p. 937. See the equally warm remarks in *Jugemens sur Quelques Ouvrages Nouveaux*, VIII (Avignon, 1745), 70–72.
20. *Mémoire pour André-François Le Breton*, 6 ff. Even so, Le Breton signed a new contract with Mills on 7 July 1745, recognizing Mills's sole right in the enterprise; then, on 13 July, Mills retroceded to Le Breton one half of his rights (*Arrest* . . . *du 28 Août 1745*, 1–2).
21. *Sommaire pour le Sieur Jean Mills, Gentilhomme Anglois, contre le Sieur le Breton, libraire-imprimeur à Paris* (Paris: Prault, 1745), reprinted in Luneau de Boisjermain, *Pièce justificative* No. IV.
22. *Mémoire pour André-François Le Breton*, 13.
23. *Mémoire pour les libraires associés à l'Encyclopédie, contre le Sieur Luneau de Boisjermain* (Paris: Le Breton, 1771), 3–4.
24. *DNB*, s.v. 'Mills, John (*d.* 1784?),' which also says that Sellius died in 1787 in an insane asylum at Charenton, near Paris. Mills was a co-translator of the *Mémoires de Gaudence de Lucques* (Paris, 1746), a Utopian novel by Simon Berington, *The Memoirs of Signor Gaudentio di Lucca* (London, 1737). It was said of Mills in Fréron's publication, *Lettres sur quelques écrits de ce temps*, VIII (1753), 315, that 'il sçavoit médiocrement notre langue.' In the 'Avertissement' to the second French edition (Amsterdam, 1753), Dupuy-Demportes, the French translator, refers to 'Miltz' and says that he himself had to 'purger sa [Mills's] traduction des vices et des anglicismes qui lui échapperoient.'
25. *Arrest* . . . *du 28 Août 1745*, 3. A manuscript volume of 'Rapports et Decisions, Librairie,' constituting vol. 80 of the Anisson-Duperron collection, gives the minutes of discussions having to do with the revocation of the old license and the granting of a new one (B.N., MSS, Fr. 22140, foll. 102, 104, 105, 109, 112).
26. *Jugemens sur Quelques Ouvrages Nouveaux*, X, 106. This quotation was part of a lengthy article (ibid. X, 105–15) regarding the prospectus of the James *Dictionnaire universel de médecine*.
27. May, 15–16. The contract was signed 18 Oct. 1745. Le Breton kept a half-interest; each of the others had one-sixth. One of the signed copies of this contract is in B.N., MSS, Nouv. acq. fr. 3347, foll. 196–8.
28. 14 Nov. 1745 (May, 17).
29. Renewal of the *privilège*, 26 [or 28?] Dec. 1745: B.N., MSS, Fr. 21997, fol. 103. Document of 21 Jan. 1746, printed in Luneau de Boisjermain, *Pièce justificative* No. VII. The renewal was entered in the books of the corporation of book publishers on 8 Feb. 1746 (B.N., MSS, Fr. 21958, foll. 471–2).
30. *Mémoire pour André-François Le Breton*, 10.
31. B.N., MSS, Fr. 21958, fol. 262.
32. Diderot, *Pensées philosophiques*, ed. Niklaus, 48 n.
33. May, 32–3. In the second half of 1746 Diderot received a total of 1,323 livres (May, 33–5).

34. Antoine-Nicolas de Condorcet, 'Eloge de M. l'Abbé de Gua,' *Oeuvres de Condorcet*, 12 vols. (Paris, 1847–9), III, 248.
35. Venturi, *Origini*, 133. For another description, written about 1750, see *Corr. litt.*, I, 375.
36. May, 18.
37. May, 21, 19.
38. Condorcet, 'Eloge de M. l'Abbé de Gua,' *Oeuvres*, III, 247–8.
39. A.-T., XI, 125.
40. According to the 'Histoire de l'Académie Royale des Sciences et Belles-Lettres,' published (with separate pagination) in the *Nouveaux Mémoires de l'Académie Royale des Sciences et Belles-Lettres, Année MDCCLXX* (Berlin, 1772), 52, the Abbé de Gua 'forma le premier cette grande entreprise.' This 'Histoire' was probably written by Formey, the permanent secretary of the Academy. Subsequent authorities agreeing with this view are *Biographie universelle (Michaud)*, s.v. 'Gua de Malves'; Larousse, *Grand Dictionnaire universel du XIXe siècle*, s.v. 'Gua de Malves'; Maurice Tourneux in *La Grande Encyclopédie*, XV, 1009, s.v. 'Encyclopédie'; May, 9 n. Douglas and Torrey, 11–12, believe that Diderot should be given the credit.
41. Condorcet, 'Eloge de M. l'Abbé de Gua,' *Oeuvres*, III, 248.
42. Naigeon, 45.
43. May, 21.
44. Ibid. Sometime before April 1748, Le Breton paid out 46 livres for a dinner given by the publishers for Diderot and D'Alembert (ibid. 41).
45. George R. Havens, *The Age of Ideas: From Reaction to Revolution in Eighteenth-Century France* (New York, 1955), 303.
46. Charles-Augustin Sainte-Beuve, 'Daguesseau,' *Causeries du lundi*, III, 426–7.
47. B.N., MSS, Fr. 21958, foll. 828–9. The decision to grant a new license was taken on 14 March 1748 (B.N., MSS, Fr. 21997, fol. 103).
48. For the texts of the 1746 and 1748 licenses, see Luneau de Boisjermain, *Pièces justificatives* Nos. VII and VIII.
49. Chrétien-Guillaume Lamoignon de Malesherbes, *Mémoire sur la liberté de la presse* (Paris, 1814), 89. Malesherbes is believed to have written this *Mémoire* in 1790 (J.-P. Belin, *Le Mouvement philosophique de 1748 à 1789* [Paris, 1913], 7). The principal biographer of D'Aguesseau, Aimé-Auguste Boullée, *Histoire de la vie et des ouvrages du chancelier d'Aguesseau*, 2 vols. (Paris, 1835), II, 120–21, vaguely mentions the Chancellor's interest in Diderot, without substantiation.
50. B.N., MSS, Fr. 22191, fol. 22. This autograph note is reproduced in *AUP*, XXII ([Oct.] 1952), numéro spécial, facing p. 72.
51. Maurice Tourneux, *Un Factum inconnu de Diderot* (Paris, 1901), 40; cf. D'Alembert's foreword to Vol. III of the *Encyclopédie* (*Encyc.*, III, i).

CHAPTER 7

1. May, 44–5.
2. Early recruits, though there is no evidence that it was Diderot who recruited them, were the Abbés Mallet and Yvon, who contributed articles on theology and ecclesiastical history (Venturi, *Origini*, 40, 136; cf. May, 40, 55). See D'Alembert's obituary of Mallet (*Encyc.*, VI, iii–v).
3. Mme de Vandeul, xlii.
4. As reported by the informer Bonin, 14 Feb. 1748 (Bibliothèque de l'Arsenal: Archives de la Bastille 10301); also Durand's signed statement (Bonnefon, 210).
5. The Abbé de Voisenon, hostile to Diderot, remarks inaccurately that the *Bijoux* was Diderot's first work, and then says: '. . . c'est un vol qu'il fit au Comte de Caylus, qui lui montra un manuscrit tiré de la Bibliotheque du Roi . . .' (Claude Henri de Fusée de Voisenon, *Oeuvres complèttes*, 4 vols. [Paris, 1781], IV, 175). Cf. Guillaume Apollinaire, Fernand Fleuret, and Louis Perceau, *L'Enfer de la Bibliothèque nationale*, 2nd ed. (Paris, 1913), 23; and S. Paul Jones, *A List of French Prose Fiction from 1700 to 1750* (New York, 1939), 94, s.v. 'Bernis.'

6. Cf. e.g. Pierre Trahard, *Les Maîtres de la sensibilité française au XVIIIᵉ siecle* (*1715–1789*), 4 vols. (Paris, 1931–3), II, 161–3; Marie-Louise Dufrenoy, *L'Orient romanesque en France, 1704–1789*, 2 vols. (Montreal, 1946–7), I, 112–17.

7. Sermons: Mme de Vandeul, xxxiii; nature of the soul: see comment by Vartanian, *Diderot and Descartes*, 242–3.

8. A.-T., IV, 279–80 nn. See Belaval, *L'Esthétique sans paradoxe de Diderot*, 36, 39–40; and Havelock Ellis, 'Diderot,' *The New Spirit*, 4th ed. (Boston, 1926), 52.

9. Karl Rosenkranz, *Diderot's Leben und Werke*, 2 vols. (Leipzig, 1866), I, 67, speaks of it as 'ein Meisterstück'; see also Paul Hazard, *European Thought in the Eighteenth Century: From Montesquieu to Lessing* (New Haven, 1954), 28–9.

10. André Gide, *Journals*, tr. and annotated by Justin O'Brien, 4 vols. (New York, 1947–51), II, 349.

11. Henri Lefebvre, *Diderot* (Paris, 1949), 207.

12. A.-T., IV, 135.

13. B.N., MSS, Nouv. acq. fr. 1214, fol. 111.

14. For the German translations, see Abrahams, 'Diderot, französisch und deutsch,' *Romanische Forschungen*, LI, 61–2, 387.

15. George Saintsbury, *A History of the French Novel*, 2 vols. (London, 1917–19), I, 403. Saintsbury, in his *French Literature and its Masters* (New York, 1946), 249, refers to the *Bijoux* as 'Diderot's one hardly pardonable sin.' Cf. John Garber Palache, *Four Novelists of the Old Régime* (New York, 1926), 110–12. For good critical remarks by recent authors, see Pommier, *Diderot avant Vincennes*, 59–72, and Venturi, *Jeunesse*, 123–34.

16. Mesnard, 'Le Caractère de Diderot,' *Revue de la Méditerranée*, VII, 278.

17. René Jasinski, *Histoire de la littérature française*, 2 vols. (Paris, 1947), II, 208.

18. *Corr. litt.*, I, 139–40.

19. L. Charpentier, *Lettres critiques, sur divers écrits de nos jours contraires à la Religion & aux mœurs*, 2 vols. (London, 1751), II, 22. See also Pierre Clément, *Les Cinq Années Littéraires, ou Nouvelles littéraires, etc., des années 1748, 1749, 1750, 1751, et 1752*, 4 vols. (The Hague, 1754), I, 26–30.

20. Naigeon, 37.

21. Venturi, *Jeunesse*, 134, 370.

22. A.-T., IV, 135. Cf. Roland Mortier, 'Le *Journal de Lecture* de F.-M. Leuchsenring (1775–1779) et l'esprit "philosophique",' *RLC*, XXIX (1955), 216.

23. Bibliothèque de l'Arsenal, Archives de la Bastille 10301.

24. Pommier, *Diderot avant Vincennes*, 57–9, 72–7.

25. Bonnefon, 209, 216.

26. Printed in A.-T., IV, 381–441. See Venturi, *Jeunesse*, 138, and Dufrenoy, *L'Orient romanesque en France*, 118–19.

27. Bonnefon, 212. The license to publish was granted on 10 May 1748 (B.N., MSS, Fr. 21958, fol. 837).

28. Bonnefon, 212.

29. Bonin's report, 29 Jan. 1748 (Bibliothèque de l'Arsenal: Archives de la Bastille 10301). Regarding the Lediard translation, *Corr. litt.*, II, 106–7; attribution to De Puisieux is in *Catalogue générale des livres imprimés de la Bibliothèque nationale*, XCII (1928), col. 366.

30. Bonnefon, 212.

31. *Corr. litt.*, I, 202, 313.

32. B.N., MSS, Fr. 22157, fol. 31; published by David, Le Breton, and Durand.

33. See the cryptic allusion in the 'Avertissement des éditeurs' (*Encyc.*, VI, i).

34. A.-T., IX, 75.

35. A.-T., IX, 79–80, also 81 and n., and Diderot, *Corr.*, I, 55–6, 56–7 nn.; but Venturi, *Jeunesse*, 341, is inclined to think that it was Mme de Puisieux who was meant. Diderot refers in *Jacques le fataliste* (A.-T., VI, 70–71) to the love affair of M. and Mme Prémontval. It is probable that Diderot was well acquainted with them, and that he was present at some of the mathematical lectures given by Prémontval from *ca.* 1737 to 1745. Cf. André-Pierre Le Guay de Prémontval, *Mémoires* (The Hague, 1749), esp. 1–62.

36. A.-T., IX, 77. The *Mémoires* were mentioned favorably but superficially by Clément, *Cinq Années Littéraires*, I, 199–200 (20 April 1749).
37. *Journal des Sçavans*, Année 1749, 8.
38. *Journal de Trévoux*, April 1749, 620.
39. *Mercure de France*, Sept. 1748, 135.
40. *Corr. litt.*, I, 202.
41. Lester Gilbert Crocker [formerly Krakeur] and Raymond L. Krueger, 'The Mathematical Writings of Diderot,' *Isis*, XXXIII (1941), 228; cf. Gino Loria, *Curve piane speciali*, 2 vols. (Milan, 1930), II, 125 n.
42. Julian Lowell Coolidge, *The Mathematics of Great Amateurs* (Oxford, 1949), 185.
43. Dieudonné Thiébault, *Mes Souvenirs de vingt ans de séjour à Berlin*, 3d ed., 4 vols. (Paris, 1813), II, 305–6.
44. Augustus De Morgan, *A Budget of Paradoxes* (London, 1872), 250–51. De Morgan first published his version in a letter to the *Athenaeum*, 31 Dec. 1867 (ibid. 474).
45. E. T. Bell, *Men of Mathematics* (New York, 1937), 147.
46. Lancelot Hogben, *Mathematics for the Million* (New York, 1937), 13–14.
47. Bancroft H. Brown, 'The Euler-Diderot Anecdote,' *American Mathematical Monthly*, XLIX (1942), 302–3; see also Dirk J. Struik, 'A Story concerning Euler and Diderot,' *Isis*, XXXI (1939), 431–2; and R. J. Gillings, 'The So-called Euler-Diderot Incident,' *American Mathematical Monthly*, LXI (1954), 77–80.

CHAPTER 8

1. *Premiere Lettre d'un citoyen zélé, qui n'est ni chirurgien ni medecin, A M. D. M. . . . Où l'on propose un moyen d'appaiser les troubles qui divisent depuis si long-tems, la médecine & la chirurgie.* In the Bibliothèque Nationale copy of this exceedingly rare pamphlet, which is bound into a 'Recueil de pièces et mémoires pour les maîtres en l'art et science de chirurgie,' someone has written in on the title page that Monsieur D.M. is De Morand, i.e. Sauveur-François Morand (1697–1773), a famous surgeon. Diderot's pamphlet is dated (p. 33) 'A Paris, 16 Décembre 1748.' Reprinted in A.-T., IX, 213–23; cf. Dieckmann, *Inventaire*, 60, 129–30.
2. Dr. Raoul Baudet, 'La Société sous Louis XV: Médecins et philosophes,' *Conferencia*, vol. II for 1926–7, 136–41. Cf. Dr. A. Bigot, 'Diderot et la médecine,' *Cahiers Haut-Marnais*, No. 24 (1er trimestre 1951), 42–3.
3. A.-T., IX, 217.
4. E.g., A.-T., IX, 240.
5. A.-T., II, 322.
6. A.-T., IX, 223.
7. Félix Rocquain, *L'Esprit révolutionnaire avant la Révolution, 1715–1789* (Paris, 1878), 126–33; Venturi, *Jeunesse*, 177–86.
8. Marcel Marion, *Histoire financière de la France depuis 1715*, 6 vols. (Paris, 1914–31), I, 171–5.
9. Edmond-Jean-François Barbier, *Chronique de la Régence et du règne de Louis XV (1718–1763)*, 8 vols. (Paris, 1885), IV, 378 n.
10. Claude-Carloman de Rulhière, *Oeuvres de Rulhière, de l'Académie française*, 2 vols. (Paris, 1819), II, 15, 16, 24, 26.
11. D'Argenson, VI, 403.
12. Bonnefon, 204; Beaurepaire, 'Les Logis de Diderot,' *Revue des Français*, XVII, 314.
13. Mme de Vandeul, xliii.
14. Marcel, *La Soeur de Diderot*, 19; Marcel, *Le Frère de Diderot*, 70 n.
15. A.-T., XIX, 423; the date of this note was 20 Sept. 1751 (*Diderot et l'Encyclopédie: Exposition commémorative*, 52). Similarly, see Diderot's elaborate note of thanks, 8 Jan. 1755, to Dr. d'Aumont at Valence, who contributed 34 articles to the *Encyclopédie* (A.-T., XX, 87).
16. May, 44, 45.
17. A.-T., XIII, 139. For withdrawals by Diderot between 1747 and 1751, see *Diderot et l'Encyclopédie: Exposition commémorative*, 72–3; cf. A.-T., XIII, 114 n.
18. *Corr. litt.*, I, 273.

19. D'Argenson, vi, 10–11; Edmond-Jean-François Barbier, *Journal historique et anecdotique du règne de Louis XV*, 4 vols. (Paris, 1847–56), iii, 88–90 — this edition hereafter cited as 'Barbier, *Journal.*' See also Venturi, *Jeunesse,* 177–86, and Jean-Paul Belin, *Le Commerce des livres prohibés à Paris de 1750 à 1789* (Paris, 1913), 93, 100.

20. D'Argenson, vi, 15.

21. B.N., MSS, Nouv. acq. fr. 10781, fol. 146; Bonnefon, 210.

22. A.-T., i, 279. Ibid. mistakenly reads 'aveugle-né,' whereas the original edition clearly states 'Aveugle née.' The contemporary journalist, Pierre Clément, reported (*Cinq Années Littéraires,* I, 229) that Réaumur admitted only a very few persons for the lifting of the bandage. Mme de Vandeul, xlii–xliii, says that Diderot was among those present.

23. Mme de Vandeul, xliii. Regarding M. and Mme Dupré de Saint-Maur, see *Corr. litt., x,* 518. Concerning D'Argenson, see Albert Bachman, *Censorship in France from 1715 to 1750* (New York, 1934), 72–4.

24. A.-T., i, 307.

25. A.-T., i, 309–10; Lefebvre, *Diderot,* 104, 110. Regarding Diderot's interest in the abnormal, see Hermann Karl Weinert, 'Die Bedeutung des Abnormen in Diderots Wissenschaftslehre,' *Festgabe Ernst Gamillscheg* (Tübingen, 1952), 228–44, esp. 233, 237. The publication of Benoît de Maillet's *Telliamed* (1748), with its elements of a 'transformistic' theory, evidently influenced Diderot (Vartanian, 'From Deist to Atheist,' *Diderot Studies,* i, 59), as did also Buffon's *Théorie de la Terre* (1749) (Vartanian, *Diderot and Descartes,* 116).

26. Ernst Cassirer, *Die Philosophie der Aufklärung* (Tübingen, 1932), 144–56.

27. A.-T., i, 305.

28. Gabriel Farrell, 'How the Blind See: What Is This "Sixth Sense"?' *Forum,* xcvi (1936), 85.

29. Pierre Villey [-Desmeserets], 'A propos de la *Lettre sur les Aveugles,' Revue du Dix-huitième Siècle,* i (1913), 410–33, especially 412, 421–2; also Pierre Villey [-Desmeserets], *The World of the Blind* (New York, 1930), 101, 180–83.

30. *Journal de Trévoux,* April 1749, 610.

31. For complete bibliographical information, consult the critical edition of the *Lettre sur les aveugles,* ed. Niklaus, 103–11.

32. Voltaire, ed. Moland, xxxvii, 22–3.

33. Norman L. Torrey, 'Voltaire's Reaction to Diderot,' *PMLA, l* (1935), 1107–43, but especially 1107, 1109, 1115.

34. Wilson, 'Une Partie inédite . . . ,' *RHLF, li,* 259.

35. Georg Brandes, *Voltaire,* 2 vols. (New York, 1930), ii, 51. Mme du Châtelet died on 4 Sept. 1749.

36. Wilson, 'Une Partie inédite . . . ,' *RHLF, li,* 259.

CHAPTER 9

1. Bonnefon, 204–5.

2. Augustin Gazier, *Histoire générale du mouvement janséniste,* 2 vols. (Paris, 1922), ii, 2.

3. Bonnefon, 205, 216.

4. Frantz Funck-Brentano, *Les Lettres de cachet* (Paris, 1926), *passim;* and the same, *The Old Regime in France* (New York, 1929), 201–32: 'Lettres de cachet.'

5. Louis Ducros, *French Society in the Eighteenth Century* (London, 1926), 142–5; Jules Flammermont, ed., *Remontrances du Parlement de Paris au XVIIIe siècle,* 3 vols. (Paris, 1888–98), iii, 442–4.

6. Arthur M. Wilson, 'Men of Letters and *Lettres de cachet* in the Administration of Cardinal Fleury,' *American Historical Review, lx* (1954–5), 55.

7. Bonnefon, 207; reproduced by Guyot, 8.

8. Archives du Département de la Seine et de la Ville de Paris; printed in facsimile by Marius Barroux, *Soixante Fac-similés de documents de 1182 à 1871* (Paris, 1928), No. 17.

9. Bonnefon, 205.

10. Jacques–Antoine Dulaure, *Nouvelle Description des environs de Paris,* 2 vols. (Paris, 1786), ii, 327.

11. Mme de Vandeul, xliv.

12. Ibid. xliii–xliv.

13. May, 53–4.
14. Bonnefon, 206.
15. Ibid. 206.
16. Ibid. 208.
17. Ibid. 208–9.
18. Ibid. 210.
19. Rousseau, ed. Hachette, VIII, 248–9. See also D'Argenson, VI, 34.
20. Le Gras, 54; also Alphonse Séché and Jules Bertaut, *Diderot* (Paris, n.d.), 62. The same statement was made as a matter of general knowledge by G. Peignot, *Dictionnaire critique, littéraire et bibliographique des principaux livres condamnés au feu, supprimés ou censurés,* 2 vols. (Paris, 1806), I, 103; also by Charles-Yves Cousin d'Avallon, *Diderotiana* (Paris, 1810), 29.
21. Diderot, *Corr.*, I, 83–8. The concluding page of this letter, erroneously stated to be addressed to D'Argenson, is reproduced facing p. 12 of *AUP*, XXII ([Oct.] 1952).
22. Bonnefon, 214; also in Diderot, *Corr.*, I, 82–3.
23. Bonnefon, 215; a page from this letter reproduced in Guyot, 24.
24. Bonnefon, 216. In November 1749 Le Breton was reimbursed for paying 32 livres 8 sols to the treasurer of Vincennes (May, 54), perhaps for extras supplied to Diderot. The château in question was the governor's lodgings, just to the north of the Sainte-Chapelle in the Vincennes enclosure (André Billy, *Diderot* [Paris, 1932], 137). It no longer exists.
25. 21 Aug. 1749 (Bonnefon, 217).
26. *La Bigarure ou Meslange curieux, instructif et amusant de nouvelles . . .* , 20 vols. (The Hague, 1749–53), I, 61–2. This account is not, however, factually impeccable: it has Diderot imprisoned in the Bastille; it declares on 30 Oct. 1749, that he is already liberated; and it states that Toussaint, author of *Les Moeurs,* had for long been a prisoner in Vincennes. Delort, *Histoire de la détention des philosophes . . .* , II, 216, would appear to have used *La Bigarure* as his source for his account of Diderot's imprisonment.
27. Mme de Vandeul, XLIV; Naigeon, 131–3; Eusèbe Salverte, *Eloge philosophique de Denys Diderot* (Paris, An IX [1800–1801], 96).
28. Dieckmann, *Inventaire,* 56, 114–17, is dubious about their being translated from memory. Diderot recalled in 1762 that while he was in the tower at Vincennes 'J'avois un petit Platon dans ma poche . . .' (*SV*, II, 175 [23 Sept. 1762]).
29. 30 Sept. 1749 (A.-T., XIX, 422–3).
30. May, 53.
31. Mme de Vandeul, XLIV.
32. Bonnefon, 217–18.
33. Mme de Vandeul, XLV.
34. Delort, *Histoire de la détention des philosophes . . .* , II, 218.
35. Frantz Funck-Brentano, *Légendes et archives de la Bastille* (Paris, 1904), 153.
36. *La Correspondance de l'Abbé Trublet,* ed. J. Jacquart (Paris, 1926), 10. Canon Marcel mentioned having seen a manuscript news letter that devoted a page and a half to the event (*RQH*, 102 n.).
37. Voltaire, ed. Moland, XXXVII, 36.
38. D'Argenson, VI, 10–11, 26; Barbier, *Journal*, III, 89–90.
39. A.-T., XIX, 425.
40. For instance, Grimm wrote on 15 Feb. 1757 of Diderot seeing Fontenelle for the first time in his life *'il y a deux ou trois ans'* (*Corr. litt.,* III, 345; italics mine).
41. Voltaire, ed. Moland, XXXVII, 38.
42. *RQH*, 109, 110, 111. The money was to be paid by M. Foucou, who had befriended Diderot in 1736 (see *supra,* p. 29). For a meticulous transcription of this letter, together with a photograph of it, see J.-G. Gigot, 'Sur une lettre du père de Diderot à son fils,' *Cahiers Haut-Marnais,* No. 38 (3e trimestre 1954), 131–4, 138–40.
43. May, 52, 54.
44. Delort, *Histoire de la détention des philosophes . . .* , II, 227; Du Châtelet's covering letter is dated simply 'Septembre' (ibid. 226); Bonnefon, 222–3.
45. Rousseau, ed. Hachette, VIII, 247, 248.

46. Ibid. 249.

47. This version of the story seems to have been circulated sedulously in the late 'seventies, when the enemies of Rousseau were apprehensively anticipating the publication of the *Confessions* (Alexis François, 'La Correspondance de J. J. Rousseau dans la querelle littéraire du XVIIIe siècle: Diderot et les Lettres à Malesherbes,' *RHLF*, xxxiii [1926], 357–8).

48. Jean-François Marmontel, *Mémoires d'un père pour servir à l'instruction de ses enfants*, 4 vols. (Paris, 1804), ii, 240–41.

49. J.-F. La Harpe, *Lycée, ou cours de littérature ancienne et moderne*, 15 vols. (Paris, 1816), xv, 238; Charles Collé, *Correspondance inédite* (Paris, 1864), 66–7; *Corr. litt.*, xi, 285 (June 1776); André Morellet, *Mémoires inédits*, 2 vols. (Paris, 1822), i, 119–20.

50. Mme de Vandeul, lx.

51. François-Louis, Comte d'Escherny, *Mélanges de littérature, d'histoire, de morale et de philosophie*, 3 vols. (Paris, 1811), ii, 39 n.

52. This controversy is admirably analyzed and summarized by George R. Havens, ed., *Jean-Jacques Rousseau: Discours sur les sciences et les arts* (New York, 1946), 6–9, 21–3. See also his 'Diderot and the Composition of Rousseau's First Discourse,' *RR*, xxx (1939), 369–81; F. Vézinet, 'Rousseau ou Diderot?' *RHLF*, xxxi (1924), 306–14, and republished, with some additions, in his *Autour de Voltaire* (Paris, 1925), 121–41; Lester Gilbert Crocker, 'Diderot's Influence on Rousseau's First *Discours*,' by Lester Gilbert Krakeur, *PMLA*, lii (1937), 398–404; Eugène Ritter, 'Le Programme du concours ouvert en 1749 par l'Académie de Dijon,' *AJJR*, xi (1916–17), 64–71. Cf. Albert Schinz, *Etat présent des travaux sur J.-J. Rousseau* (New York, 1941), 171–2.

53. A.-T., iii, 98, and in identical words in A.-T., ii, 285. Diderot also gave exactly the same account in 1773 or 1774 during one of his visits at The Hague (Philippe Godet, *Madame de Charrière et ses amis . . . (1740–1805)*, 2 vols. [Geneva, 1906], i, 432).

54. Bonnefon, 219; also in A.-T., xiii, 111.

55. Bonnefon, 220–22; also A.-T., xiii, 111. Bonnefon states (p. 220) that the publishers got President Hénault, author of the famous *Abrégé chronologique de l'histoire de France*, to present their petition to D'Argenson. Perhaps this was what D'Alembert had in mind when he wrote to Hénault, *ca.* 1751: 'Diderot pense là-dessus comme moi, et nous n'oublierons jamais ni l'un ni l'autre ce que nous vous devons' (Albert Tornezy, *La Légende des 'philosophes'* [Paris, 1911], 172).

56. A.-T., xiii, 113.

57. Venturi, *Origini*, 55.

58. Bibliothèque de l'Arsenal: Archives de la Bastille 11671, fol. 20.

59. Rousseau, ed. Hachette, viii, 277 n.

60. Tourneux, *Diderot et Catherine II*, 442.

CHAPTER 10

1. A.-T., xiii, 111–13 (7 Sept. 1749).

2. *Corr. litt.*, i, 475.

3. *Lettre de M. Gervaise Holmes à l'auteur de la Lettre sur les aveugles, contenant le véritable récit des dernières heures de Saounderson* (Cambridge [Berlin], 1750). This was by Formey, the secretary of the Prussian Academy (Jean-Henri-Samuel Formey, *Conseils pour former une bibliothèque peu nombreuse, mais choisie*, 3rd. ed. [Berlin, 1755], 117–18).

4. *Bibliothèque Impartiale*, Jan.–Feb. 1750, 76; this periodical was edited by Formey and printed at Leyden (Formey, *Conseils pour former une bibliothèque*, 118). See also Clément, *Cinq Années Littéraires*, i, 229–31, and Charpentier, *Lettres Critiques*, ii, 101–28.

5. D'Alembert to Cramer, 12 Feb. 1750, quoted by Tamizey de Larroque in *Revue Critique d'Histoire et de Littérature*, vol. ii for 1882, 478.

6. Archives Nationales, Y 12594; published by Emile Campardon, *Les Prodigalités d'un fermier général* (Paris, 1882), 119–21.

7. *La Bigarure*, i, 20–22.

8. Ibid. xiii, 58–61.
9. Mme de Vandeul, xlvi; A.-T., i, lxiv; Jal, *Dictionnaire critique*, 495; Diderot, *Corr.*, i, 99.
10. Born 29 Oct. and baptized 30 Oct. 1750 (Diderot, *Corr.*, i, 100); but according to baptismal records copied by Nauroy, *Révolutionnaires*, 245, the dates were 29 and 30 Sept. 1750. Regarding the accident, Mme de Vandeul, xlvi; A.-T., i, lxiv; but cf. Jal, *Dictionnaire critique*, 496, and Diderot, *Corr.*, i, 100.
11. André Cazes, *Grimm et les Encyclopédistes* (Paris, 1933), 9; Joseph R. Smiley, *Diderot's Relations with Grimm* ('Illinois Studies in Language and Literature, xxxiv, No. 4' [Urbana, 1950]), 9–10.
12. Louis-J. Courtois, 'Notes critiques de chronologie rousseauiste,' *Mélanges d'histoire littéraire et de philologie offerts à M. Bernard Bouvier* (Geneva, 1920), 120.
13. Joseph A. Vaeth, *Tirant lo Blanch* (New York, 1918), 5.
14. Archives Nationales, T 319^5.
15. Jefferson to John Adams, Monticello, 8 April 1816 (*Memoir, Correspondence, and Miscellanies, from the Papers of Thomas Jefferson*, ed. T. J. Randolph, 4 vols. [Boston, 1830], iv, 272).
16. Diderot to Grimm, 25 March 1781 (Dieckmann, *Inventaire*, 252).
17. Courtois, 'Chronologie,' 59.
18. Rousseau, ed. Hachette, viii, 258, 260.
19. Courtois, 'Chronologie,' 60; also George R. Havens, 'Rousseau's First Discourse and the *Pensées philosophiques* of Diderot,' *RR*, xxxiii (1942), 356, and George R. Havens, ed., *Jean-Jacques Rousseau: Discours sur les sciences et les arts*, 30. The censors were opposed to letting the *Discours* be published, but Malesherbes overruled them (Belin, *Le Mouvement philosophique de 1748 à 1789*, 78).
20. Rousseau, ed. Hachette, viii, 258.
21. Douglas H. Gordon's Extra Volume, fol. 678: '. . . or en marge de la page 1ere du prospectus, il est ecrit de la main de l'illustre M. Daguesseau, *Bon D.G.*, Cette approbation est seule une preuve que les éditeurs avoient satisfait aux Reglements.
    'On trouve encore ecrit sur un autre titre du même ouvrage, de la main du Commissaire du Roy pour la librairie, *Permis d'imprimer et afficher: ce 11. 9bre 1750. Signé Berryer.*'
22. May, 24–5.
23. *Encyc.*, i, i n.; also *Corr. litt.*, i, 486. Buffon wrote to Formey on 6 Dec. 1750, 'Le projet du *Dictionnaire encyclopédique* paraît ici depuis quelques jours' (Georges-Louis Leclerc, Comte de Buffon, *Correspondance inédite*, ed. H. N. de Buffon, 2 vols. [Paris, 1860], i, 49–50).
24. May, 59.
25. Charles Braibant, 'Autour du Prospectus,' *Cahiers Haut-Marnais*, No. 24 (1er trimestre 1951), 5.
26. Herbert James Hunt, 'Logic and Linguistics. Diderot as "grammairien-philosophe",' *MLR*, xxxiii (1938), 217, alluding to C. K. Ogden and I. A. Richards, *The Meaning of Meaning*.
27. Approval by the censor (B.N., MSS, Fr. 22138, fol. 22). D'Hémery noted on 18 Feb. 1751 that the book was already published (B.N., MSS, Fr. 22156, fol. 33^v).
28. Malesherbes, *Mémoire sur la liberté de la presse*, 49–50, 53, 56. Regarding tacit permissions, see Comte de Montbas, 'La République des Lettres au XVIIIe siècle et l'avènement de la tolérance,' *Revue des Travaux de l'Académie des Sciences Morales et Politiques, Année 1950, premier semestre*, 50–51. For Diderot's opinion regarding them: A.-T., xviii, 66 *et passim*.
29. Cf. Ferdinand Brunetière, 'La Direction de la Librairie sous M. de Malesherbes,' *RDM*, 1 Feb. 1882, 580–81; and Bachman, *Censorship in France from 1715 to 1750*, 146–53. As an example of a censor's report regarding a tacit permission, see the letter from De Cahusac to [Malesherbes], 'Paris ce 22 xbre 1751. . . . Je pense en effet qu'avec les adoucissements que j'y ai fait mettre, il peut etre susceptible, non d'un privilege; Mais d'une permission tacite' (B.N., MSS, Fr. 22137, fol. 49).
30. [Suzanne Necker, née Curchod], *Nouveaux Mélanges extraits des manuscrits de Mme Necker*, 2 vols. (Paris, An x [1801]), i, 255.

31. A.-T., I, 353. Cf. Karl von Roretz, *Diderots Weltanschauung, ihre Voraussetzungen, ihre Leitmotive* (Vienna, 1914), 14, 16.
32. See George Sidney Brett, *A History of Psychology*, 3 vols. (London, 1921), II, 289.
33. Cf. Katharine Everett Gilbert and Helmut Kuhn, *A History of Esthetics* (New York, 1939), 307. Diderot also anticipated some of the conclusions of Edmund Burke in his treatise *On the Sublime and Beautiful* (Dixon Wecter, 'Burke's Theory concerning Words, Images, and Emotion,' *PMLA*, LV [1940], 177 n.). Cf. J.-J. Mayoux, 'Diderot and the Technique of Modern Literature,' *MLR*, XXXI (1936), 528.
34. Otis E. Fellows and Norman L. Torrey, eds., *Diderot Studies*, I, ix–x. Cf. ibid. 94–121: Anne-Marie de Commaille, 'Diderot et le symbole littéraire,' esp. 110–13; and particularly James Doolittle, 'Hieroglyph and Emblem in Diderot's *Lettre sur les sourds et muets*,' *Diderot Studies*, II, 148–67.
35. A.-T., I, 374.
36. Mayoux, 'Diderot and the Technique of Modern Literature,' *MLR*, XXXI, 525–6; Hunt, 'Diderot as "grammairien-philosophe",' *MLR*, XXXIII, 215–33; Margaret Gilman, 'The Poet according to Diderot,' *RR*, XXXVII (1946), 41; Margaret Gilman, 'Imagination and Creation in Diderot,' *Diderot Studies*, II, 214–15; and Marlou Switten, 'Diderot's Theory of Language as the Medium of Literature,' *RR*, XLIV (1953), 192, 196.
37. Jean Pommier, 'Diderot et le plaisir poétique,' *Education Nationale*, 23 June 1949, 2. Concerning prosody, Dupont de Nemours declared that Diderot 'la marquait, la déclamait peut-être un peu trop. . . . Chez Diderot, la prosodie était un chant . . .' (Turgot, *Oeuvres*, ed. Schelle, II, 704).
38. A.-T., I, 376.
39. Hunt, 'Diderot as "grammairien-philosophe",' *MLR*, XXXIII, 215.
40. *Corr. litt.*, II, 32, 67. For similar contemporary judgments, see Clément, *Cinq Années Littéraires*, III, 43–4, and Lessing, writing in *Das Neueste aus dem Reiche des Witzes*, June 1751 (Gotthold Ephraim Lessing, *Werke*, ed. Julius Petersen and Waldemar von Olshausen, 25 vols. [Berlin, (1925)], VIII, 49).
41. Jean Pommier, 'Autour de la *Lettre sur les sourds et muets*,' *RHLF*, LI (1951), 262–7, 270–71; Jean Pommier, 'Etudes sur Diderot,' *RHPHGC*, X (1942), 163. Batteux is said to have been much upset by Diderot's criticism (A.-T., XIV, 529 n.). Cf. *Corr. litt.*, XII, 439.
42. B.N., MSS, Fr. 22156, fol. 70.
43. A.-T., V, 328.
44. *Journal de Trévoux*, April 1751, 841–63. Diderot's rejoinder: A.-T., I, 411–28. The *Journal de Trévoux* amplified its remarks in its volume for July 1751, 1677–97. A very colorless review of the *Lettre sur les sourds et muets* appeared in Formey's *Bibliothèque Impartiale*, III (May–June 1751), 409–17.
45. Ignacio de Luzan, *Memorias literarias de Paris* (Madrid, 1751), 282–3.
46. *Journal de Trévoux*, Jan. 1751, 188–9, 317. Still another article on the parallel is in the issue for March 1751, 708–37.
47. Venturi, *Origini*, 113.
48. *Lettre de M. Diderot au R. P. Berthier, Jésuite* (n.p., 1751) [B.N., Imprimés, Z.11855]; and in A.-T., XIII, 165–8.
49. Clément, *Cinq Années Littéraires*, III, 45.
50. *Journal de Trévoux*, I Feb. 1751, 571–2, 577.
51. *Seconde Lettre de M. Diderot au R. P. Berthier, Jésuite* (n.p., 1751) [B.N., Imprimés, Z.11855 (2)]; and in A.-T., XIII, 168–70.
52. B.N., MSS, Fr. 22156, fol. 25ᵛ. According to the early nineteenth-century bibliographer, A.-A. Barbier, D'Alembert told an Abbé Goujet that it was he, using Diderot's name, who had written the two letters to Berthier (J.-M. Quérard, *Les Supercheries littéraires dévoilées*, 2nd ed., 3 vols. [Paris, 1869–70], I, 937).
53. Arthur M. Wilson, 'Un Billet inédit de Diderot, [1751],' *RHLF*, LV (1955), 56–7; but the editor, M. Pommier, cautions (p. 57 n.) that the letter Diderot refers to is quite likely the *Lettre sur les sourds et muets*.
54. N.p., n.d. [Mazarine, 24665.X, pp. 304–6]. D'Hémery's entry (B.N., MSS, Fr. 22156, fol. 42ᵛ). Other pamphlets published at this time were *Lettre de M. * * *, l'un des*

XXIV, à M. Diderot, Directeur de la Manufacture Encyclopédique (n.p., 1751) [Mazarine, 41774, pièce 2]; and *Lettre d'un souscripteur pour le Dictionnaire Encyclopédique, à Monsieur Diderot* (n.p., 1751) [Mazarine, 34481-A, pièce 8]; cf. D'Hémery's entry, 25 Feb. 1751 quoted in Venturi, *Origini*, 152.

55. A.-T., I, 356–8; A.-T., IV, 202–3, 305; *Encyc.*, III, 511–12, s.v. 'Clavecin oculaire'; see Shelby T. McCloy, *French Inventions of the Eighteenth Century* (Lexington [Ky.], 1952), 131–2; and esp. Donald S. Schier, *Louis Bertrand Castel, Anti-Newtonian Scientist* (Cedar Rapids [Iowa], 1941), 135–96, 202. Also E. Noulet, 'Le Père Castel et le "clavecin oculaire",' *Nouvelle NRF*, I (1953), 553–9.

56. Cf. Erika von Erhardt-Siebold, 'Harmony of the Senses in English, German, and French Romanticism,' *PMLA*, XLVII (1932), 577–92, esp. 578; Erika von Erhardt-Siebold, 'Some Inventions of the Pre-Romantic Period and their Influence upon Literature,' *Englische Studien*, LXVI (1931–2), 347–63, esp. 355; Erika von Erhardt-Siebold, 'Synästhesien in der englischen Dichtung des 19. Jahrhunderts,' *Englische Studien*, LIII (1919–20), 1–157, 196–334, esp. 43–5.

57. A.-T., XIX, 425–6. Diderot wrote again to Father Castel, 2 July 1751, in reply to his letter regarding the *Lettre sur les sourds et muets* (A.-T., XIX, 426–7; original in B.N., MSS, Fr. 12763, fol. 222).

58. Venturi, *Origini*, 107.

59. A.-T., XIX, 424. The diploma of membership was dated 4 March 1751 (Dieckmann, *Inventaire*, 162). *La Bigarure*, X (3 June 1751), 45, chronicled the fact of Diderot's membership and added, 'Quelques personnes ont paru étonnées que notre Academie des *Quarante* ne leur [Diderot and Toussaint] ait pas fait cet honneur . . .'

60. D'Hémery's entry, 30 March 1753 (B.N., MSS, Fr. 22158, fol. 129). This was Naigeon's opinion also (Naigeon, 138–9). D'Alembert became a Fellow of the Royal Society in 1748 and De Jaucourt in 1756.

61. Formey, *Conseils pour former une bibliothèque*, 112; 'Histoire de l'Académie Royale des Sciences et Belles-Lettres' (sep. pagination), *Nouveaux Mémoires de l'Académie Royale des Sciences et Belles-Lettres, Année MDCCLXX*, 52.

62. May, 21–2. For a list of the articles by Formey used in the *Encyclopédie*, see E. Marcu, 'Un Encyclopédiste oublié: Formey,' *RHLF*, LIII (1953), 302–5.

63. Formey praised it highly in his *Bibliothèque Impartiale*, III (Jan.–Feb. 1751), 306–7.

64. Cf. *supra*, n. 54.

65. Buffon to Formey, 6 Dec. 1750 (J. Matter, *Lettres et pièces rares ou inédites* [Paris, 1846], 372); Venturi, *Jeunesse*, 399.

66. B.N., MSS, Nouv. acq. fr. 3345, fol. 144; the censor was Joseph-Marie-François de Lassone.

67. *Réponse signifiée de M. Luneau de Boisjermain, au Précis des libraires associés à l'impression de l'Encyclopédie* (Paris, 1772), 2; May, 25.

68. *Corr. litt.*, II, 73.

CHAPTER 11

1. F. Picavet, ed., *Discours préliminaire de l'Encyclopédie*, by Jean Le Rond d'Alembert (Paris, 1929), lviii–lix.

2. *Encyc.*, I, xxxviij.

3. Ernesto Orrei, *L'Enciclopedia e la Rivoluzione francese* (Rome, 1946), 45.

4. *Encyc.*, I, ij.

5. Marcel Hervier, *Les Ecrivains français jugés par leurs contemporains*, II: *Le dix-huitième siècle* (Paris, n.d.), 249–50; *Corr. litt.*, II, 73.

6. See René Hubert, *Les Sciences sociales dans l'Encyclopédie* (Paris, 1923), 142. This view is in disagreement with that of Nelly Noémie Schargo, *History in the* Encyclopédie (New York, 1947), *passim*; cf. also Nelly Schargo Hoyt, 'Méthode et interprétation de l'histoire dans l'*Encyclopédie*,' *RHLF*, LI (1951), 359–72. Although the *Encyclopédie* undeniably contains a host of references to past events, my own feeling is that Dr. Hoyt tries to make a rope out of a mosaic. As a recent historiographer has remarked, 'It is possible to be interested in history without having real historical-mindedness, and it is beyond dispute that such was the case with the eighteenth-century historians' (R.N. Stromberg,

'History in the Eighteenth Century,' *JHI*, xii [1951], 297). In further defense of my point of view, see Lynn Thorndike, 'L'Encyclopédie and the History of Science,' *Isis*, vi (1924), 367–71; Emile Faguet, 'L'Encyclopédie,' *RDM*, 15 Feb. 1901, 803, 814; Benedetto Croce, *History as the Story of Liberty* (New York, 1941), 70; R. G. Collingwood, *The Idea of History* (Oxford, 1946), 77, 80; Herbert J. Muller, *The Uses of the Past* (New York, 1952), 280; and David Easton, *The Political System* (New York, 1953), 13.

7. J. B. Bury, *The Idea of Progress* (London, 1920), 171.

8. *Encyc.*, i, xxxvj.

9. *Année Littéraire*, vol. vi for 1757, 302–3.

10. *Encyc.*, i, xviij.

11. A.-T., xiii, 388. For instances of Diderot's debt to Girard, see Pierre Hermand, 'Sur le texte de Diderot et sur les sources de quelques passages de ses *Oeuvres*,' *RHLF*, xxii (1915), 363.

12. A.-T., xiii, 138; *Encyc.*, i, xij, viij.

13. *Encyc.*, i, xlj.

14. See David J. Brandenburg, 'Agriculture in the *Encyclopédie*: An Essay in French Intellectual History,' *Agricultural History*, xxiv (1950), 96–108. Though ostensibly conventional (Brandenburg, 99–100), Diderot's ideas on rotation of crops were in reality very revolutionary, for they necessitated a fundamental change in property holding (Lefebvre, *Diderot*, 14–19).

15. *Memoirs of Baron de Tott. Containing the State of the Turkish Empire and the Crimea, during the Late War with Russia*, 2 vols. (London, 1785), ii, 118. Pierre Surirey de Saint-Rémy, a French general, published his *Mémoires d'artillerie* in 1697. For further information regarding the influence of the *Encyclopédie* in foreign countries, see *AIEF*, No. 2 (May 1952): Gilbert Chinard, 'L'*Encyclopédie* et le rayonnement de l'esprit encyclopédique en Amérique,' 3–22; Jean Fabre, 'L'*Encyclopédie* en Pologne,' 31–45; Charly Guyot, 'Le Rayonnement de l'*Encyclopédie* en Suisse,' 47–60; D. M. Lang, 'L'*Encyclopédie* en Russie et au Caucase,' 61–5; and Jean Sarrailh, 'Note sur l'*Encyclopédie* en Espagne,' 77–83.

16. *Encyc.*, viii, 143a.

17. A.-T., xiii, 361, 362. Cf. Georges Friedmann, 'L'*Encyclopédie* et le travail humain,' *AUP*, xxii ([Oct.] 1952), numéro spécial, 123–35.

18. *Encyc.*, i, 412a.

19. A.-T., xiii, 368–9; Alexis François, in Ferdinand Brunot, *Histoire de la langue française des origines à 1900*, vi² (Paris, 1932), 1181, 1174.

20. A.-T., xiii, 265–6.

21. *Encyc.*, i, 191a.

22. A.-T., xiii, 183.

23. *Encyc.*, i, 175b.

24. William A. Nitze and E. Preston Dargan, *A History of French Literature* (New York, 1922), 378; see also E. A. Beller and M. du P. Lee, Jr., eds., *Selections from Bayle's Dictionary* (Princeton, 1952), xxvii–xxviii. Cf. *Diderot et l'Encyclopédie: Exposition commémorative*, xiv; Kingsley Martin, *French Liberal Thought in the Eighteenth Century* (London, 1929), 46; Louis Ducros, *Les Encyclopédistes* (Paris, 1900), 32–7; Victor Giraud, 'Les Etapes du XVIIIe siècle, i: Du Dictionnaire de Bayle à l'Encyclopédie,' *RDM*, 15 July 1924, 356; and Havens, *The Age of Ideas*, 22–37.

25. An eloquent passage regarding Bayle, written by Diderot, was expunged by Le Breton before publication (Gordon and Torrey, 48–53, 75–8). D'Alembert praised Bayle rather gingerly in the *Encyc.*, iv, 967a, s.v. 'Dictionnaire.'

26. A.-T., i, 140; Mme de Vandeul, lvii.

27. E.g., *Encyc.*, i, 38–9, 74b, 177b, 266–9, 721–2: s.v. 'Abricots,' 'Accomoder,' 'Agneau,' 'Aliments,' and 'Artichaut.' Cf. Georges May, *Quatre visages de Denis Diderot* (Paris, 1951), 13–33: 'Diderot gastronome.' Diderot's source for these culinary matters was chiefly Noël Chomel, *Dictionnaire œconomique*, 4th ed., 2 vols. (Paris, 1740).

28. *Encyc.*, i, 159.

29. *Encyc.*, i, 95–6, s.v. 'Achées'; regarding Réaumur, ibid. 102, 108a; regarding Frederick the Great, ibid. 55b; ibid. 252–3, s.v. 'Alecto.'

30. Agriculture (A.-T., xiii, 256–65); cf. Lefebvre, *Diderot*, 14–17. Steel (A.-T., xiii, 210).

Monopolies (*Encyc.*, I, 205). Midwives (A.-T., XIII, 186). For reforms in spelling, see Marcel Cohen, 'L'*Encyclopédie* et l'orthographe académique,' *Europe*, Dec. 1951, 25–6.
31. *Encyc.*, I, 205a; for attribution to Diderot, see ibid. xliij.
32. A.-T., XIII, 186.
33. A.-T., XIII, 268.
34. A.-T., XIII, 392–5.
35. Orrei, *L'Enciclopedia e la Rivoluzione francese*, 88.
36. Ducros, *Les Encyclopédistes*, 123.
37. A.-T., XIV, 461.
38. A.-T., XIII, 223–4.
39. *Encyc.*, I, 181.
40. A.-T., XIII, 374.
41. A.-T., XIII, 266, s.v. 'Aigle.'
42. A.-T., XIII, 186–7.
43. For the Abbé Mallet, see Venturi, *Origini*, 35–7, 136.
44. A.-T., XIII, 285, s.v. 'Amenthès.'
45. Robert R. Palmer, *Catholics & Unbelievers in Eighteenth Century France* (Princeton, 1939), 147.
46. *Encyc.*, I, 242b. Cf. La Mettrie's remark: '*Un rien, une petite fibre, quelque chose que la plus subtile Anatomie ne peut découvrir*, eut fait deux Sots, d'Erasme, & de Fontenelle, qui le remarque lui même dans un de ses meilleurs *Dialogues*' (Julien Offray de La Mettrie, *Oeuvres philosophiques*, 2 vols. [Amsterdam, 1753], I, [*L'Homme Machine*, sep. pagination, 24]).

CHAPTER 12

1. 'Abeille' (*Mercure de France*, April 1751, 41–73); 'Agate' (ibid. vol. II for June 1751, 105–12).
2. *The Plan of the French Encyclopaedia, or Universal Dictionary of Arts, Sciences, Trades, and Manufactures. Being an Account of the Origin, Design, Conduct, and Execution of that Work. Translated from the Preface of the French Editors, Mess. Diderot and Alembert* (London, 1752), 'Advertisement.' Printed for W. Innys, T. Longman, C. Hitch and L. Hawes, J. and P. Knapton, S. Birt, J. Ward, J. Hodges, R. Hett, J. and J. Rivington, T. Osborne, J. Shuckburgh, M. Senex, D. Browne, and A. Millar.
3. May, 25–7; D'Hémery's journal, 25 Nov. 1751, mentions the trip David and Briasson took to London (B.N., MSS, Fr. 22156, fol. 143). See J. Lough, 'The "Encyclopédie" in Eighteenth-Century England,' *French Studies*, VI (1952), 291–3.
4. *London Daily Advertizer*, 11 and 16 Jan., 29 Feb. 1752; *DNB*, s.v. 'Ayloffe, Sir Joseph'; Lough, 'The "Encyclopédie" in Eighteenth-Century England,' *French Studies*, VI, 293–4. Cf. *Gentleman's Magazine*, XXII (1752), 46–7, and John Nichols, *Literary Anecdotes of the Eighteenth Century*, 9 vols. (London, 1812–15), III, 184 n. A Dutch publisher claimed in 1751 to have had the idea of translating and enlarging Chambers before the Paris publishers did, but there is no evidence to bolster his assertion (G. L. Van Roosbroeck, 'Who Originated the Plan of the *Encyclopédie?*' *Modern Philology*, XXVII [1929–30], 382–4).
5. *Corr. litt.*, II, 85.
6. Clément, *Cinq Années Littéraires*, III, 164–5.
7. *Corr. litt.*, II, 85.
8. Ibid. 86, 101.
9. May, 25.
10. B.N., MSS, Fr. 22156, fol. 94; also *Corr. litt.*, II, 86.
11. *Journal des Sçavans*, Sept. 1751, 625–6.
12. Venturi, *Origini*, 109.
13. *Journal de Trévoux*, Oct. 1751, 2261–4, 2279–82, 2285–6, 2288–90.
14. Ibid. Oct. 1751, 2250–95; Nov. 1751, 2419–57; Dec. 1751, 2592–2623; Jan. 1752, 146–90; Feb. 1752, 296–322; March 1752, 424–69.
15. Ibid. Nov. 1751, 2425, 2439–48, esp. 2439 and 2447.

16. B.N., MSS, Fr. 22139, fol. 146.
17. *Journal de Trévoux*, Oct. 1751, 2290; Nov. 1751, 2428–38; Dec. 1751, 2594–2608; Jan. 1752, 148–51, 172–3; Feb. 1752, 301–3, 320, 380.
18. Ibid. March 1752, 468 n.
19. *Encyc.*, I, Avertissement, ii.
20. *Journal de Trévoux*, March 1752, 456–67.
21. *Encyc.*, I, 368b.
22. *Journal de Trévoux*, Feb. 1752, 314.
23. Ibid. 382.
24. Gazier, *Histoire générale du mouvement janséniste*, II, 42.
25. B.N., MSS, Fonds Joly de Fleury 292, fol. 354; other examples in Joly de Fleury 1687, foll. 225 ff., and 1708, foll. 298, 345. Cf. Gazier, op. cit., II, 43.
26. Camille Daux, 'Une Réhabilitation: l'Abbé Jean-Martin de Prades,' *Science Catholique*, XVI (1901–2), 1025–39, 1095–1109; this quotation, 1097. Cf. Barbier, *Journal*, III, 333. The De Prades affair is well summarized by Charles Jourdain, *Histoire de l'Université de Paris au XVIIᵉ et au XVIIIᵉ siècle* (Paris, 1862), 391–2; and by Pierre Grosclaude, 'Le Bi-Centenaire de l'Encyclopédie. La pittoresque affaire de l'Abbé de Prades,' *Acropole*, III (1951), 14–16.
27. For an interesting comparison of De Prades's thesis and D'Alembert's 'Preliminary Discourse,' done in parallel columns, see B.N., MSS, Joly de Fleury 292, foll. 327–30.
28. See *supra*, p. 60.
29. The thesis summarized: A.-T., I, 435–7; also Monod, *De Pascal à Chateaubriand*, 333–4.
30. Palmer, *Catholics & Unbelievers in Eighteenth Century France*, 122–4. For an excellent estimate of the whole controversy, see ibid. 117–28.
31. *Remarques sur une thèse soutenue en Sorbonne le samedi 30 octobre 1751, par M. l'Abbé Delomenie de Brienne* (n.p., n.d.), 1 (Mazarine 41191, pièce 7; also mounted in B.N., MSS, Joly de Fleury 292, fol. 291).
32. *Mercure de France*, April 1752, 197; M.-P.-J. Picot, *Mémoires pour servir à l'histoire ecclésiastique pendant le dix-huitième siècle*, 2nd ed., 4 vols. (Paris, 1815–16), II, 246.
33. *Lettre de M. l'Abbé Hooke, Docteur de la Maison & Société de Sorbonne, Professeur de Théologie, à Monseigneur l'Archevêque de Paris* (n.p., n.d.), 27–8 (Mazarine 41191, pièce 8).
34. Latin and French texts of the Sorbonne censure mounted in B.N., MSS, Joly de Fleury 292, fol. 293, and Fr. 22092, foll. 183–91, resp.; the *mandement* of the Archbishop of Paris mounted in Fr. 22092, foll. 191–9. Consult these volumes, *passim*, for other documents concerning the De Prades case, and also B.N., MSS, Fr. 22112, foll. 139–63. Among printed sources, see Barbier, *Journal*, III, 333 *et passim;* D'Argenson, VII, 30, 68, 71, 106; Reusch, *Der Index der verbotenen Bücher*, II, 874–5.
35. *Mandement de Monseigneur l'Evêque de Montauban, portant condamnation d'une these* . . . (Montauban, 1752), 3, mounted in B.N., MSS, Fr. 22092, foll. 526–9.
36. *Nouvelles Ecclésiastiques*, 27 Feb. 1752, 35. Three whole issues and part of a fourth, viz. 27 Feb. and 5, 12, and 19 March (pp. 33–47) were given over to a meticulous account of the affair.
37. Frontispiece reproduced in E. Abry, C. Audic, and P. Crouzet, *Histoire illustrée de la littérature française* (Paris, numerous editions), s.v. 'L'Encyclopédie.'
38. *Encyc.*, I, 663b. Doubt has been expressed whether this article was by Diderot (A.-T., XIII, 359 n.), but it is now regarded as being his (Raymond Naves, *Voltaire et l'Encyclopédie* [Paris, 1938], 106 n.; Lois Strong Gaudin, *Les Lettres anglaises dans l'Encyclopédie* [New York, 1942], 95).
39. B.N., MSS, Fr. 22157, fol. 12; cf. *Corr. litt.*, II, 198 and n. This pamphlet is, however, variously attributed. A Father Bonhomme, presumably a Franciscan, is sometimes mentioned as its author, while the *Catalogue général des livres imprimés de la Bibliothèque Nationale*, LV (1913), cols. 1042–3, mentions another Jesuit, F.-M. Hervé, together with a Father Fruchet, as the joint authors of the work. The *Réflexions* was published without going through the ordinary channels of censorship, in consequence of which 'M. de Malesherbes is making a good deal of fuss about it' (D'Hémery's journal, ibid.; cf. Belin, *Le Mouvement*

philosophique de 1748 à 1789, 107). An expanded edition, *Réflexions d'un Franciscain sur les trois premiers volumes de l'Encyclopédie*, was published in 'Berlin' (actually Paris) in 1754. This time D'Hémery noted that its authors were Hervé and Fruchet, a Franciscan (B.N., MSS, Fr. 22159, fol. 71). Still another edition, almost identical in content, was published at The Hague in 1759, under the title of *L'Eloge de l'Encyclopédie et des Encyclopédistes*. Jesuit susceptibilities are revealed in this pamphlet by the author's remarking that he was shocked because of the ostentatious silence of the *Encyclopédie* regarding the part played by the Jesuits in the renaissance of letters (ed. 1752, 45).

40. *Réflexions d'un Franciscain* (1752), 11.

41. Ibid. 9–10. The 1754 edition printed these several theses by De Prades, the *tentative*, the *Sorbonique*, the *mineure*, and the *majeure* (179–88; cf. Palmer, *Catholics & Unbelievers in Eighteenth Century France*, 121).

42. *Encyc.*, I, xlj; cf. *Encyc.*, II, 846b; *Réflexions d'un Franciscain* (1752), 7.

43. *Encyc.*, II, 845–62, s.v. 'Certitude.' Vol. II was published on 22 or 23 Jan. 1752 (Barbier, *Journal*, III, 337); Venturi, *Jeunesse*, 211, gives 25 Jan. D'Hémery noted on 27 Jan. 1752 that Vol. II had been published 'depuis quelques jours' (B.N., MSS, Fr. 22157, fol. 18). The allegation that the De Prades thesis was the result of a plot was also made by the Bishop of Auxerre in his Pastoral Instruction in 1752 (A.-T., I, 445) and by Joseph-Robert-Alexandre Duhamel, *Lettres flamandes*, deuxième partie (Mons, 1753), 139–47, and by the Protestant writer, David Renaud Boullier, *Court examen de la thèse de Mr. l'abbé de Prades et Observations sur son Apologie* (Amsterdam, 1753), esp. 29.

44. A police report dated 1 Jan. 1753 says of Yvon: 'Il a été obligé de s'expatrier et de passer en Hollande pour l'affaire de l'Abbé de Prades, avec lequel il étoit intimmement lié, et on pretend meme qu'il a eu bonne part à la composition de sa Theze' (B.N., MSS, Nouv. acq. fr. 10783, fol. 159). Cf. ibid. fol. 43: '. . . on le [Yvon] soupçonnoit d'avoir bonne part à la Theze.' Louis Petit de Bachaumont, *Mémoires secrets pour servir à l'histoire de la république des lettres en France*, 36 vols. (London, 1777–89), I, 41, states under date of 4 Feb. 1762 that Yvon '. . . passoit pour avoir contribué en grande partie à la these de l'abbé de Prades. . . .' Yvon is said to have stated in Paris, after De Prades's reconciliation with the Church, that he, Yvon, had written the thesis (Jean-Baptiste de Boyer, Marquis d'Argens, *Histoire de l'esprit humain*, 14 vols. [Berlin, 1765–8], x, 351 n.).

45. Naigeon, 160–61 nn.

46. *Encyc.*, III, Avertissement, i.

47. Morellet recalls meeting Diderot in De Prades's rooms, but *after* the storm broke, and in no way suggests that Diderot planned to exploit the thesis in any fashion (Morellet, *Mémoires*, I, 28). According to Charles-Philippe d'Albert, duc de Luynes, *Mémoires sur la cour de Louis XV*, 17 vols. (Paris, 1860–65), XI, 369, De Prades had set forth his ideas to Diderot merely to learn what arguments Diderot would use in refutation; but Diderot had overwhelmed him with his 'sophisms.' This is very interesting, but purely hearsay.

48. Emile Regnault, *Christophe de Beaumont, Archevêque de Paris (1703–1781)*, 2 vols. (Paris, 1882), I, 346.

49. Joseph Daoust, 'Encyclopédistes et Jésuites de Trévoux (1751–1752): Deuxième centenaire de l'*Encyclopédie*,' *Etudes*, CCLXXII (1952), 179.

50. *La Bigarure*, XV, 70, 72; Voltaire, ed. Moland, XXIV, 17–28, esp. 18; *Corr. litt.*, II, 298. Regarding Voltaire and *Le Tombeau de la Sorbonne*, see Naves, *Voltaire et l'Encyclopédie*, 11–12; Grosclaude, *Un Audacieux Message*, 64–5; J. Nivat, 'Quelques Enigmes de la Correspondance de Voltaire,' *RHLF*, LIII (1953), 442–3; and Donald Schier, 'The Abbé de Prades in Exile,' *RR*, XLV (1954), 182–90. A request from Diderot to La Condamine, 16 Dec. 1752, for the loan of a copy of *Le Tombeau de la Sorbonne* (Diderot, *Corr.*, I, 147) mentions that the pamphlet was rare.

51. Barbier, *Journal*, III, 344; cf. also ibid. 336–7, 339, 346. D'Argenson, VII, 56; cf. also ibid. 57, 63. See also Luynes, *Mémoires*, XI, 385–6 (5 Feb. 1752). For an excellent discussion of the whole affair, including evidence of a 'plot,' see Venturi, *Jeunesse*, esp. 201–4.

52. D'Argenson, VII, 71–2.

53. Barbier, *Journal*, III, 344, 355.

54. Malesherbes, *Mémoire sur la liberté de la presse*, 90. For other contemporary testimony of

Mirepoix's influence, see D'Argenson, VII, 93; Voltaire, *Le Tombeau de la Sorbonne, passim; Les Nouvelles Ecclésiastiques,* 19 March 1752, 45.

55. For the printed *arrêt,* see B.N., MSS, Fr. 22177, fol. 54.

56. D'Argenson, VII, 110. Apparently the *arrêt* was not published until 13 Feb. 1752 (ibid.); but on 7 Feb. Malesherbes on his own authority had forbidden the further distribution of the *Encyclopédie* (Barbier, *Journal,* III, 344).

CHAPTER 13

1. D'Argenson, VII, 106, 122; Barbier, *Journal,* III, 355.

2. Clément, *Cinq Années Littéraires,* IV, 21 (15 March 1752); cf. *Corr. litt.,* II, 298, and D'Argenson, VII, 122.

3. Barbier, *Journal,* III, 355; Lester Gilbert Crocker, 'The Problem of Malesherbes' Intervention,' by L. G. Krakeur, *MLQ,* II (1941), 556–7.

4. D'Argenson, VII, 112; Barbier, *Journal,* III, 355; *Corr. litt.,* II, 298 (15 Nov. 1753).

5. *Corr. litt.,* XI, 407. Sainte-Beuve, 'M. de Malesherbes,' *Causeries du lundi,* II, 512–39, though old, is far from antiquated.

6. *Corr. litt.,* XI, 36, from Malesherbes' discourse upon being admitted into the French Academy (1775).

7. Malesherbes to Morellet, *ca.* 23 Jan. 1758 (Coyecque, *Inventaire de la collection Anisson,* I, xcvii–xcviii).

8. Malesherbes, *Mémoire sur la liberté de la presse,* 70.

9. Ducros, *Les Encyclopédistes,* 223.

10. Ibid. 220.

11. *Corr. litt.,* XI, 36. See Pierre Grosclaude, 'Malesherbes et l'Encyclopédie,' *AUP,* XXII ([Oct.] 1952), numéro spécial, 57–79.

12. D'Argenson, VII, 112.

13. Brunetière, 'La Direction de la librairie sous M. de Malesherbes,' *RDM,* 1 Feb. 1882, 591.

14. Barbier, *Journal,* III, 346.

15. Ducros, *Les Encyclopédistes,* 57.

16. Mme de Pompadour owned a set of the *Encyclopédie* (*Catalogue des livres de la bibliothéque de feue Madame la marquise de Pompadour* [Paris, 1765], 39; also a copy of the *Bijoux indiscrets* and the *Histoire de Grèce* [ibid. 243, 278]).

17. Cf. Ducros, *Les Encyclopédistes,* 56–7.

18. D'Argenson, VII, 223–4; for his relations with D'Alembert, see ibid. 63, 68 n.

19. For proof of this, see an unsigned and undated minute in Malesherbes' hand, probably written in 1758 (B.N., MSS, Fr. 22191, fol. 22).

20. B.N., MSS, Nouv. acq. fr. 3345, fol. 145. See also the approbation of the censor who had read the articles concerning jurisprudence in Vols. I and II (B.N., MSS, Fr. 22139, fol. 121).

21. Malesherbes, *Mémoire sur la liberté de la presse,* 90; cf. his memorandum *ca.* 1758 (B.N., MSS, Fr. 22191, fol. 23).

22. 24 Aug. 1752 (Voltaire, ed. Moland, XXXVII, 471–2).

23. 5 Sept. 1752 (ibid. 481).

24. Matter, *Lettres et pièces rares ou inédites,* 386.

25. Venturi, *Origini,* 57, 59–60.

26. Ibid. 60.

27. Clara Adèle Luce Herpin (pseud. Lucien Perey) and Gaston Maugras, 'Madame d'Epinay à Genève (1757–1759),' *Bibliothèque Universelle et Revue Suisse,* 3ᵉ période, XXI (1884), 553, quoting a letter from Mme d'Epinay to Grimm; Torrey, 'Voltaire's Reaction to Diderot,' *PMLA,* L, 1111.

28. D'Alembert to D'Argens, 16 Sept. 1752 (Jean Le Rond d'Alembert, *Oeuvres,* 5 vols. [Paris, 1821–2], V, 19); regarding the publishers' pay roll, see May, 50 *et passim.*

29. Venturi, *Origini,* 124, 126.

30. *Corr. litt.,* II, 299.

31. Barbier, *Journal,* III, 339.

32. Agreement of 6 Feb. 1754 (May, 27).

33. Ferdinand Brunetière, *L'Evolution des genres dans l'histoire de la littérature* (Paris, 1890), 210.

34. D'Hémery's journal, entry of 12 Oct. 1752: '. . . imprimé sans permission. Il ne m'a pas encore été possible de découvrir l'imprimeur' (B.N., MSS, Fr. 22157, fol. 123). For speculation as to whether or not Diderot contributed to the first two parts of De Prades's *Apologie,* see the points set forth in Dieckmann, *Inventaire,* 56–7.

35. A.-T., I, 448.

36. A.-T., I, 440.

37. A.-T., I, 449–55, 470–71.

38. A.-T., I, 449.

39. A.-T., I, 450, 454–5, 466. See Antoine Adam, 'Rousseau et Diderot,' *Revue des Sciences Humaines,* Jan.–March 1949, 26–7, for favorable comment regarding this statement of social origins.

40. René Hubert, 'L'Esprit des sciences sociales dans l'*Encyclopédie*,' *RHPHGC,* IV (1936), 113. Cf. Lefebvre, *Diderot,* 114–24.

41. A.-T., I, 477.

42. A.-T., I, 457–8.

43. A.-T., I, 456.

44. A.-T., I, 482 n.

45. Clément, *Cinq Années Littéraires,* IV, 214.

46. A.-T., I, 483–4. On Diderot's adroit use of this Jansenist attack, consult Venturi, *Jeunesse,* 214–25.

CHAPTER 14

1. A.-T., VII, 168.

2. A.-T., XVIII, 271–2. This particular Duc d'Orléans died in 1752. Mme de Vandeul's version differs (Mme de Vandeul, xlvii–xlviii).

3. *Horace Walpole's Correspondence with Madame du Deffand and Wiart,* ed. W. S. Lewis and Warren H. Smith, V (New Haven, 1939), 262.

4. Morellet, *Mémoires,* I, 133–4.

5. B.M., Add. MSS 30867, foll. 14, 18–19, 20–21. D'Holbach was 'élevé presque dès son enfance à Paris,' acc. to *Biographie universelle (Michaud),* s.v. 'Holbach,' 532.

6. Complete genealogical information in W. H. Wickwar, *Baron d'Holbach* (London, 1935), 19–20, 233–5. D'Holbach's naturalization in August 1749 is recorded in the Archives nationales, P. 2593, fol. 80 (*Diderot et l'Encyclopédie: Exposition commémorative,* 49).

7. Billy, *Diderot,* 314–15, quotes the undated bill of sale.

8. Rousseau stated in the *Confessions,* in a context that suggests the year 1751, that Diderot and D'Holbach had been intimate 'for a long time since' (Rousseau, ed. Hachette, VIII, 263). Acc. to Vernière, *Spinoza et la pensée française avant la Révolution,* 632 n., they became acquainted in 1749.

9. S. Lenel, 'Un Ennemi de Voltaire: La Beaumelle,' *RHLF,* XX (1913), 115 n.

10. Dominique-Joseph Garat, *Mémoires historiques sur la vie de M. Suard, sur ses écrits, et sur le XVIIIe siècle,* 2 vols. (Paris, 1820), I, 208–9.

11. *Diderot et l'Encyclopédie: Exposition commémorative,* 49–50. Cf. Wickwar, *Baron d'Holbach,* 62–3.

12. Marmontel, *Mémoires,* II, 312; Rousseau, ed. Hachette, VIII, 263. Cf. Garat, *Mémoires . . . de M. Suard,* I, 207.

13. Louisette Reichenburg, *Contribution à l'histoire de la 'Querelle des Bouffons'* (Philadelphia, 1937), 30–37.

14. Carlo Goldoni, *Mémoires,* 2 vols. (Paris, 1822), II, 184. John Wilkes's views were similar (Frederick Charles Green, 'Autour de quatre lettres inédites de Diderot à John Wilkes,' *RLC,* XXV [1951], 459). For an excellent comparison and contrast of eighteenth-century French and Italian music, see Violet Paget (pseud. Vernon Lee), *Studies of the Eighteenth Century in Italy* (London, 1880), 71–9.

15. Rousseau, ed. Hachette, VI, 198.

16. Rousseau, ed. Hachette, VIII, 274; *Corr. litt.*, II, 313, 322; cf. D'Argenson, VIII, 180.
17. D'Hémery mentioned Grimm as being the author: entry of 21 Dec. 1752 (B.N., MSS, Fr. 22157, fol. 140). The *Petit Prophète* is printed in *Corr. litt.*, XVI, 313–36. Grimm was almost challenged to a duel by Chassé, one of the artists he satirized (Dieckmann, *Inventaire*, 245).
18. Romain Rolland, *Some Musicians of Former Days*, 4th ed. (London, n.d.), 257. For a much more critical view of Diderot's knowledge of music and capacity as a critic, see Adolphe Jullien, *La Ville et la cour au XVIIIe siècle* (Paris, 1881), 153–66, 193–204.
19. A.-T., XII, 143–51, 152–6, 157–70, resp.; for their dates, ibid. 139–40, and Reichenburg, 50 n. Their attribution to Diderot was challenged by Ernest Thoinan in his excellent bibliography of the 'Querelle des Bouffons' in the *Supplément* (2 vols. [Paris, 1878–80], II, 450–51, s.v. 'Rousseau') to F.-J. Fétis, *Biographie universelle des musiciens,* 8 vols. (Paris, 1860–65); cf. J.-G. Prod'homme, 'Diderot et la musique,' *Zeitschrift der internationalen Musikgesellschaft,* XV (1913–14), 157, and A.-T., XII, 141, 155 n. However, Rousseau's annotations on copies of these pamphlets are the basis for attributing them to Diderot (Diderot, 'Les Trois Chapitres,' *Revue Rétrospective,* 2e série, I [1835], 94, 94–5 nn.; Paul-Emmanuel-Auguste Poulet Malassis, *La Querelle des Bouffons* [Paris, 1876], 14–17). Rousseau's note regarding *Les Trois Chapitres* was published by Guillemin, 133.
20. A.-T., XII, 155.
21. A.-T., IV, 408.
22. *Corr. litt.*, II, 272. See Diderot's article for the *Encyclopédie,* s.v. 'Intermède' (A.-T., XV, 233–4), for an enthusiastic judgment of Italian opera, especially of Pergolesi.
23. *Réponse de M. Rameau à MM. les éditeurs de l'Encyclopédie sur leur dernier Avertissement* (London and Paris, 1757), 53. Cf. René de Récy, 'La Critique musicale au siècle dernier: Rameau et les Encyclopédistes,' *RDM,* 1 July 1886, 138–64, esp. 140.
24. Alfred Richard Oliver, *The Encyclopedists as Critics of Music* (New York, 1947), 112.
25. Rousseau, ed. Hachette, VIII, 247; he evidently wrote them in early 1749 (Rousseau, *Corr. gén.*, I, 287).
26. *Réponse de M. Rameau . . .* (1757), 53.
27. This point is developed by Oliver, 101–13, who thinks that the *Encyclopédie* was more sinned against than sinning in the Rameau controversy.
28. A.-T., XII, 147; see also D'Alembert's treatment of Rameau in his *De la Liberté de la musique* (1760), reprinted in his *Mélanges de littérature, d'histoire, et de philosophie,* 5 vols. (Amsterdam [Paris], 1763–7), IV, 387–9.
29. *Année Littéraire,* vol. 1 for 1757, 304. Cf. Bernard Champigneulle, *L'Age classique de la musique française* (Paris, [1946]), 283–90: 'Rameau et les Encyclopédistes.'
30. Rousseau, ed. Hachette, VIII, 271.
31. Anne-Louise-Germaine Necker, Baronne de Staël-Holstein, 'Lettre sur le caractère de Rousseau,' *Oeuvres complètes,* 17 vols. (Paris, 1820–21), I, 81.
32. Rousseau, ed. Hachette, V, 105 (my emphasis).
33. *Corr. litt.*, III, 60–61; regarding this incident, see Armand Gasté, *Diderot et le curé de Montchauvet: une mystification littéraire chez le baron d'Holbach, 1754* (Paris, 1898). Cf. A.-T., V, 496.
34. D'Holbach's account was first published in the *Journal de Paris,* Supplement to No. 336, 2 Dec. 1789, 1567–8; reprinted in Morellet, *Mémoires,* II, 336–7, and *Corr. litt.*, XV, 575–6. The Abbé Petit was mentioned earlier in the *Corr. litt.*, II, 503–4.
35. Morellet, *Mémoires,* I, 29–30, 34–5.
36. May, *passim.*
37. Diderot, *Corr.*, I, 145–6. Cf. Diderot's letter to Mme Caroillon La Salette, 25 Aug. 1752 in which he apparently alluded to his wife's intractability (ibid. 142).
38. *Supra,* 23.
39. Mme de Vandeul, xlvii. For other instances of Diderot's composing memoranda, one in 1741, the other in 1755, to oblige members of the La Salette family, see Diderot, *Corr.*, I, 26, 198–9.
40. Diderot, *Corr.*, I, 151.
41. Cf. Henri Denis, 'Deux collaborateurs économiques de l'Encyclopédie: Quesnay et Rous-

seau,' *Pensée*, Sept.–Oct. 1951, 44–54; also Anita Fage, 'Les Doctrines de population des Encyclopédistes,' *Population*, VI (1951), 609–24.

42. *Encyc.*, VII, 812a, s.v. 'Grains'; cf. ibid. 816a, 820a.

43. Marmontel, *Mémoires*, II, 28, 33–4.

44. Diderot, *Corr.*, I, 151–2, 155–8. In view of this evidence of Diderot's personal relationship with Mme de Pompadour, it is possible that an undated letter alleged to have been written by him to Mme de Pompadour and apparently referring to the crisis of 1752 is not apocryphal (*Lettres de Madame la Marquise de Pompadour . . .*, 2 vols. [Paris, 1811], II, 16–18; also in A.-T., XX, 100–101). Mme de Pompadour's alleged reply was published in *Lettres de madame la marquise de Pompadour . . .*, 2 vols. (London, 1771), I, 15–16; in idem, ed. 1811, II, 19–20; and in English translation, *Letters of the Marchioness of Pompadour . . .*, 2 vols. (London, 1771), I, 15–16. Her alleged letter was also published by E. Mignoneau, 'Une Lettre inédite de Madame de Pompadour à Diderot au sujet de l'Encyclopédie,' *Revue Occidentale*, XXI (1888), 70–75, who dated it 7 April 1754. Cf. Mignoneau, ibid. XXI, 222–3. Mme de Pompadour's letter is couched in friendly and anticlerical terms. It is hard to believe that she would confide such indiscretions to paper. Professor Dieckmann, however, found a copy of what appears to be precisely this letter, in Mme de Vandeul's hand. This fact, and also the fact that 'cette copie ne fut pas faite d'après le texte imprimé dont elle diverge en plusieurs endroits, lui donne un caractère d'authenticité' (Dieckmann, *Inventaire*, 110–11).

45. Diderot, *Corr.*, I, 152.

46. Ibid. 158.

47. Mme de Vandeul, xlvi–xlvii.

48. Nauroy, *Révolutionnaires*, 245.

CHAPTER 15

1. Léon Delamarche, 'Carnet d'un bibliophile,' *Eclair*, 14 May 1923, 3; Léon Delamarche, 'Les Bibliophiles et Diderot,' *Eclair*, 26 May 1924, 4; also identified by Avenir Tchemerzine, *Bibliographie d'éditions originales et rares d'auteurs français des XVe, XVIe, XVIIe, et XVIIIe siècles*, 10 vols. (Paris, 1927–33), IV, 442–4. A copy was exhibited at the Bibliothèque Nationale in 1951 (*Diderot et l'Encyclopédie: Exposition commémorative*, 26). See Herbert Dieckmann, 'The First Edition of Diderot's *Pensées sur l'interprétation de la nature*,' *Isis*, XLVI (1955), 253–66.

2. 6 Dec. 1753 (B.N., MSS, Fr. 22158, fol. 91).

3. Jean Luc, *Diderot* (Paris, 1938), 107.

4. [Alexandre Deleyre], *La Revue des Feuilles de M*r *Fréron* (London, 1756), 387; Vartanian, *Diderot and Descartes*, 136–7.

5. Cru, 202; cf. ibid. 193–206.

6. *Corr. litt.*, III, 116–17. Cf. ibid. II, 485–6.

7. Herbert Dieckmann, 'The Influence of Francis Bacon on Diderot's *Interprétation de la Nature*,' *RR*, XXXIV (1943), 329.

8. Ibid. 305.

9. A.-T., II, 18–19; my italics.

10. A.-T., II, 13–14.

11. A.-T., II, 14. On this passage, see Dieckmann, loc. cit. *RR*, XXXIV, 317; also Herbert Dieckmann, 'Goethe und Diderot,' *Deutsche Vierteljahrsschrift für Literaturwissenschaft und Geistesgeschichte*, X (1932), 497; and Fernand Papillon, 'Des Rapports philosophiques de Goethe et de Diderot,' *Séances et travaux de l'Académie des Sciences morales et politiques*, CI (1874), 259–60.

12. A.-T., II, 20.

13. A.-T., II, 18. Cf. Herbert Dieckmann, 'Diderot's Conception of Genius,' *JHI*, II (1941), 172. 'Claude Bernard, dans son *Introduction à la Médecine expérimentale*, ajoutera peu aux formules de Diderot' (Lefebvre, *Diderot*, 144).

14. A.-T., II, 40 *et passim*; Dieckmann, loc. cit. *RR*, XXXIV, 319–22, and Dieckmann, loc. cit. *JHI*, II, 174. See also Vartanian, *Diderot and Descartes*, 138, 161–71.

15. Cf. Bacon, *Novum Organum*, part I, § lxxxvi.

16. *Encyc.*, I, xxxj; see esp. Etienne Bonnot de Condillac, *Oeuvres philósophiques*, ed. Georges Le Roy, 3 vols. (Paris, 1947–51), I, 127 *et passim*.

17. A.-T., XVI, 291.

18. Cassirer, *Die Philosophie der Aufklärung*, 15–16. Cf. Walter L. Dorn, *Competition for Empire, 1740–1763* (New York, 1940), 195.

19. Cf. Herbert Dieckmann, 'Théophile Bordeu und Diderots "Rêve de d'Alembert",' *Romanische Forschungen*, LII (1938), 119.

20. A.-T., II, 27–8; see I. Bernard Cohen, 'A Note concerning Diderot and Franklin,' *Isis*, XLVI (1955), 268–72.

21. A.-T., II, 39, 34.

22. A.-T., II, 11.

23. Cassirer, *Die Philosophie der Aufklärung*, 98; see also Dieckmann, loc. cit. *Isis*, XLVI, 251–2.

24. A.-T., II, 10. Cf. Crocker and Krueger, 'The Mathematical Writings of Diderot,' *Isis*, XXXIII, 229.

25. Cassirer, *Die Philosophie der Aufklärung*, 99. Cf. A.-T., II, 10–12. See also Abraham Chaim Lerel, *Diderots Naturphilosophie* (Vienna, 1950), 49, 69. For a sharply differing view, see Vartanian, *Diderot and Descartes*, 181–9.

26. *Corr. litt.*, II, 352. So also thought Maupertuis himself (Pierre-Louis Moreau de Maupertuis, 'Reponse aux Objections de M. Diderot,' *Oeuvres*, 4 vols. [Lyon, 1768], II, 197); cf. Vartanian, *Diderot and Descartes*, 270–72, and Paul Ostoya, 'Maupertuis et la biologie,' *Revue d'Histoire des Sciences*, VII (1954), 73, 75–6. Regarding these 'terrible consequences,' see Max Wartofsky, 'Diderot and the Development of Materialist Monism,' *Diderot Studies*, II, 297–8. For the influence of Maupertuis' thought upon Diderot's, see Pierre Brunet, 'La Notion d'évolution dans la science moderne avant Lamarck,' *Archeion*, XIX (1937), 39–40. Regarding the probable relations, even though unacknowledged by Diderot, of Diderot's thought to that of La Mettrie, see Aram Vartanian, 'Trembley's Polyp, La Mettrie, and Eighteenth-Century French Materialism,' *JHI*, XI (1950), 270, 274.

27. A.-T., II, 15–16. Cf. Arthur O. Lovejoy, 'The Argument for Organic Evolution before "The Origin of Species",' *Popular Science Monthly*, LXXV (1909), 513; and Arthur O. Lovejoy, *The Great Chain of Being* (Cambridge [Mass.], 1936), 268.

28. A.-T., II, 44–5.

29. Cassirer, *Die Philosophie der Aufklärung*, 120.

30. Lefebvre, *Diderot*, 153. Marx's statement was a reply to a sort of questionnaire made up by one of his daughters (D. B. Goldenach [pseud. D. Ryazanoff], *Karl Marx, Man, Thinker, and Revolutionist* [London, 1927], 269).

31. A.-T., II, 57–8; translation by Professor Lovejoy (Arthur O. Lovejoy, 'Some Eighteenth Century Evolutionists,' *Popular Science Monthly*, LXV [1904], 326). Regarding this passage and its prophetic nature, see Oscar Schmidt, 'Die Anschauungen der Encyclopädisten über die organische Natur,' *Deutsche Rundschau*, VII (1876), 86; also the excellent article of J. Charpentier, 'Diderot et la science de son temps,' *Revue du Mois*, XVI (1913), 547.

32. Lovejoy, loc. cit. LXV, 326.

33. A.-T., II, 49–50. Cf. Dieckmann, 'The Influence of Francis Bacon on Diderot's *Interprétation de la Nature*,' *RR*, XXXIV, 329.

34. *Mercure de France*, Jan. 1754, 130–35; *Journal Encyclopédique*, vol. II for Jan. 1756, 3–18. Grimm, of course, praised it fulsomely (*Corr. litt.*, II, 308).

35. *Corr. litt.*, II, 203. Charles de Brosses declared the book 'un vray traité d'inintelligibilité' (Joseph-Théophile Foisset, *Le Président de Brosses* [Paris, 1842], 540); cf. Charles Collé, *Journal et mémoires*, 3 vols. (Paris, 1868), II, 77.

36. Clément, *Cinq Années Littéraires*, IV, 284–5.

37. A.-T., II, 4; *Nouvelles Littéraires de Berlin*, 21 Dec. 1773, quoted by Tourneux, *Diderot et Catherine II*, 527.

38. La Harpe, *Lycée*, XV, 1–2. Some modern scientists have likewise declared their inability to understand the book, e.g. the French astronomer Camille Flammarion, 'Diderot, à l'occasion de son bi-centenaire,' *Revue*, CIV (Sept.–Oct. 1913), 440.

39. Alan Conder, tr., *A Treasury of French Poetry* (New York, 1951), 138, by kind permission of Mr. Conder.

40. For a good biography of Fréron, see François Cornou, *Trente Années de luttes contre Voltaire et les philosophes du XVIIIe siècle: Elie Fréron (1718–1776)* (Paris, 1922); cf. also Paul Chauvin, 'Un Journaliste au XVIIIe siècle (L'*Année littéraire* et Fréron),' *Revue des Pyrénées*, XVII (1905), 46–74; also Jules Soury, 'Un Critique au XVIIIe siècle — Fréron,' *RDM*, 1 March 1877, 80–112; also Green, *Eighteenth-Century France*, 111–54: 'Voltaire's Greatest Enemy.' Cf. Francis W. Gravit, 'Notes on the Contents of Fréron's Periodicals,' *RR*, XXXIV (1943), 116–26.

41. Daniel Mornet, 'Les Enseignements des bibliothèques privées,' *RHLF*, XVII (1910), 479.

42. A.-T., II, 51; but see also Vartanian, *Diderot and Descartes*, 176–7.

43. *Année Littéraire*, vol. 1 for 1754, 1–14, esp. 1–2, 2, 3–4, 14.

44. A.-T., II, 38.

45. A.-T., II, 13.

46. A.-T., II, 51–2.

CHAPTER 16

1. *Encyc.*, I, xliv.

2. *Encyc.*, II, 105b. Professor Dieckmann attributes this remark to a workman (Herbert Dieckmann, 'L'*Encyclopédie* et le Fonds Vandeul,' *RHLF*, LI [1951], 325).

3. A.-T., XIII, 140–41; *Encyc.*, I, xliij; Naigeon, 49.

4. Naigeon, 50–51.

5. *Encyc.*, II, 289a.

6. *Encyc.*, II, 596b.

7. *Encyc.*, II, 35b.

8. A.-T., XIV, 39.

9. A.-T., XIV, 5.

10. *Journal des Sçavans*, March 1753, 169–75; Venturi, *Origini*, 58–9.

11. *Journal des Sçavans, combiné avec les Mémoires de Trévoux* (Amsterdam), vol. 1 for 1754, 305–22, esp. 307, 312–13, 321–2. The *Journal des Sçavans* was surprisingly forbearing, for meanwhile D'Alembert had grumbled for a whole folio half-page in the foreword to Vol. III about the *Journal*'s original attack upon him (*Encyc.*, III, xj–xij).

12. *La Biographie universelle (Michaud)*, s.v. 'Jaucourt,' and *La Nouvelle Biographie générale (Hoefer)*, s.v. 'Jaucourt.' Also Ducros, *Les Encyclopédistes*, 76–7.

13. Lefebvre, *Diderot*, 41.

14. See René Hubert, *Les Sciences sociales dans l'Encyclopédie* (Paris, 1923), *passim*; René Hubert, 'L'Esprit des sciences sociales dans l'*Encyclopédie*,' *RHPHGC*, IV, 107–33; René Hubert, 'Essai sur l'histoire des origines et des progrès de la sociologie en France,' ibid. VI (1938), 111–55, 281–310; René Hubert, 'Introduction bibliographique à l'étude des sources de la science ethnographique dans l'*Encyclopédie*,' ibid. I (1933), 160–72, 331–55; also, see Raymond Lenoir, 'Les Sciences sociales dans l'Encyclopédie, à propos d'un ouvrage récent,' *Revue de Synthèse Historique*, XXXIX (1925), 113–25.

15. Hubert, 'L'Esprit des sciences sociales dans l'*Encyclopédie*,' *RHPHGC*, IV, 114; Cassirer, *Die Philosophie der Aufklärung*, 251. See Barker, *Diderot's Treatment of the Christian Religion in* The Encyclopédie, 42–57, 125–9, esp. 43; also Hermann Sänger, *Juden und Altes Testament bei Diderot* (Wertheim am Main, 1933), 90–93; and Paul Vernière, 'La Critique biblique dans l'*Encyclopédie* et ses sources spinozistes,' *Revue de Synthèse*, LXIX (1951), 75–6; also Vernière, *Spinoza et la pensée française avant la Révolution*, 582–3.

16. *Encyc.*, II, 840a; my italics. 'Le mot *Cerf* est un des articles qu'on a relevés avec le plus d'aigreur' (*Mémoire des libraires associés à l'Encyclopédie, sur les motifs de la suspension actuelle de cet ouvrage* [Paris, 1758], 4).

17. For thorough discussions, see Hester Hastings, *Man and Beast in French Thought of the Eighteenth Century* (Baltimore, 1936), *passim*; and Leonora Cohen Rosenfield, *From Beast-Machine to Man-Machine: Animal Soul in French Letters from Descartes to La Mettrie* (New York, 1941), *passim* and esp. 46–50.

18. A.-T., XIII, 429. For an excellent discussion of this whole issue, see Vartanian, *Diderot and Descartes*, 207–15.

19. Gilbert and Kuhn, *A History of Esthetics*, 280–87; Władysław Folkierski, *Entre le classicisme et le romantisme: Etude sur l'esthétique et les esthéticiens du XVIIIe siècle* (Cracow and Paris, 1925), 375–91; K. Heinrich von Stein, *Die Entstehung der neueren Ästhetik* (Stuttgart, 1886), 245–50. Cf. André Fontaine, *Les Doctrines d'art en France de Poussin à Diderot* (Paris, 1909), 296–7, who finds Diderot's doctrine extremely deficient, as does also Mario Roques, 'L'Art et l'*Encyclopédie*,' AUP, XXII ([Oct.] 1952), numéro spécial, 99–100. For a comprehensive study of the importance of Diderot's article, see Lester G. Crocker, *Two Diderot Studies: Ethics and Esthetics* (Baltimore, 1952), 53–67, 96–7, *et passim*.

20. A.-T., x, 35; foreshadowed in A.-T., IX, 104; cf. ibid. 84. See Crocker, *Two Diderot Studies*, 61, 66, 113.

21. A.-T., XIII, 423.

22. A.-T., x, 30–31.

23. Gilbert and Kuhn, *A History of Esthetics*, 282.

24. A.-T., x, 25, 26, 27.

25. A.-T., x, 25, 41.

26. Jean Thomas, *L'Humanisme de Diderot*, 2nd ed. (Paris, 1938), 61–2.

27. A.-T., x, 36; my italics.

28. A.-T., XI, 10.

29. E.g. *Encyc.*, III, xiv. Professor Dieckmann inclines to the view that Diderot was co-author of this *Avertissement* (Dieckmann, *Inventaire*, 57).

30. *Corr. litt.*, II, 299. Diderot, however, felt constrained to insert this disclaimer in his list of errata (*Encyc.*, III, xvj): 'En un mot, nous n'avons prétendu dans notre article AUTORITÉ que commenter & développer ce passage, tiré d'un ouvrage imprimé par ordre de Louis XIV. & qui a pour titre, *Traité des droits de la Reine sur différens états de la monarchie d'Espagne . . .*'

31. *Encyc.*, III, iv, xiv.

32. *Encyc.*, III, 833a. François Véron de Forbonnais (1722–1800) collected his *Encyclopédie* articles in his *Elémens du commerce* (Paris, 1754; 2nd ed. [Amsterdam, 1755]; 3d ed. [Leyden, 1766]; 4th ed., 2 vols. [Paris, 1796]).

33. Clément, *Cinq Années Littéraires*, IV, 282 (31 Dec. 1753). Cf. his earlier and severer criticism of Vol. I (ibid. III, 113–15 [15 June 1751]).

34. *Encyc.*, III, 225b. Although asterisked, this article may not have been by Diderot.

35. *Encyc.*, III, 671b.

36. A.-T., XIV, 454–5.

37. Emile Faguet, 'Diderot et Naigeon,' *Revue Latine*, I (1902), 721; A.-T., XIV, 197–204, s.v. 'Composition (en peinture).'

38. 'The Chaldeans' (A.-T., XIV, 170–71); 'Chaos' (A.-T., XIV, 88–93; see Vartanian, *Diderot and Descartes*, 121–2).

39. A.-T., XIV, 79.

40. A.-T., XIV, 84.

41. *Encyc.*, III, 635–7. See also 'Etudes,' written by Faiguet (*Encyc.*, VI, 87–94).

42. *Encyc.*, III, vij, xvj.

43. *Encyc.*, III, 636a.

44. *Observation de M * * *, principal du College de * * *, sur un des articles du Dictionnaire Encyclopédique* (n.p., n.d.), 42–3 (Mazarine call number 34481-A, pièce 6).

45. *Avis au Public sur le Troisième Volume de l'Encyclopédie* (n.p., n.d.), 18–19, 21 (Mazarine call number 34481-A, pièce 7). For its Jesuit authorship, see Venturi, *Origini*, 143.

46. Relevant documents in B.N., MSS, Nouv. acq. fr. 3348, foll. 253–63. The harangue of Father Tolomas occurred on 30 Nov. 1754. See Voltaire to Dupont, Lyon, 6 Dec. 1754 (Voltaire, ed. Moland, XXXVIII, 296). For an account of the whole affair, see Joseph Bertrand, *D'Alembert* (Paris, 1889), 86–92.

47. Daniel Delafarge, *La vie et l'oeuvre de Palissot (1730–1814)* (Paris, 1912), 43–68; also Edouard Meaume, *Palissot et les philosophes* (Nancy, 1864), 13 ff.; and J.-A. Vier, 'L'Activité d'une académie provinciale au XVIIIe siècle: L'Académie de Stanislas de 1750

à 1766,' *RHLF*, xxxiii (1926), 350–52, who also points out that D'Alembert was striking at Fréron as well as at Palissot.

48. D'Hémery's journal, 17 Oct. 1754, mentioned that Vol. iv was published (B.N., MSS, Fr. 22159, fol. 71ᵛ). Rousseau wrote Vernes that it was published on 14 Oct. (Rousseau, *Corr. gén.*, ii, 103).

49. *Corr. litt.*, ii, 198–9.

50. Drafts of the proposed article (B.N., MSS, Nouv. acq. fr. 3345, foll. 157–64, 165–74). Malesherbes' letter to Diderot, 11 July 1754, was exhibited in 1932 at the Bibliothèque Nationale (*L'Encyclopédie et les Encyclopédistes* [Paris: Bibliothèque Nationale, 1932], 54); Malesherbes' draft of it (B.N., MSS, Nouv. acq. fr. 3345, fol. 150); published in Diderot, *Corr.*, i, 167–8; the same day Malesherbes stated his reasons to the Chancellor (ibid. ii, 331–3). Cf. D'Argenson, ix, 22, and Gazier, *Histoire générale du mouvement janséniste*, ii, 52 n.

51. *Encyc.*, iv, 238a–b, s.v. 'Corderie.'

52. *Encyc.*, iv, 171a; A.-T., xiv, 221.

53. A.-T., xiv, 236–7, s.v. 'Coupon'; *Encyc.*, iv, 283–8, s.v. 'Corvée.'

54. A.-T., xiv, 274; emphasis mine.

55. A.-T., xiv, 281; s.v. 'Dieux.'

56. Leo Spitzer, 'The Style of Diderot,' *Linguistics and Literary History* (Princeton, 1948), 137–46, 175.

57. A.-T., xiv, 277–78; *Corr. litt.*, vi, 115; Pommier, 'Etudes sur Diderot,' *RHPHGC*, x, 174. For the existentialist implications of this article, see Ian W. Alexander, 'Philosophy of Organism and Philosophy of Consciousness in Diderot's Speculative Thought,' *Studies in Romance Philology and French Literature Presented to John Orr* (Manchester, 1953), 18.

58. *Corr. litt.*, ii, 408.

59. Cf. *Encyc.*, iii, ix; A.-T., xiv, 267, 274. The full title of Johann Jacob Brucker's work was *Historia critica philosophiae a mundi incunabulis ad nostram usque aetatem deducta*, 5 vols. (Leipzig, 1742–4). Diderot also referred frequently to Thomas Stanley (1625–78), *The History of Philosophy*, a fourth edition of which was published at London in 1743. Occasionally Diderot referred (e.g. *Encyc.*, iii, ix) to André-François Boureau Deslandes, *Histoire critique de la philosophie*, 3 vols. (Amsterdam, 1737).

60. Jacques-André Naigeon, in the three-volume section of the *Encyclopédie méthodique* devoted to 'Philosophie ancienne et moderne' (Paris, 1791–4), i, vi–viii.

61. Hubert, *Les Sciences sociales dans l'Encyclopédie*, 327; cf. Cassirer, *Die Philosophie der Aufklärung*, 301–2.

62. Pommier, 'Etudes sur Diderot,' *RHPHGC*, x, 172. Cf. A.-T., xiv, 253, 255, 257.

63. *Mercure de France*, vol. i for Oct. 1757, 23; reprinted in Nicholas-Charles-Joseph Trublet, *Mémoires pour servir à l'histoire de la vie et des ouvrages de Mʳ. de Fontenelle*, 2nd ed. (Amsterdam, 1759), 172.

CHAPTER 17

1. Marcel, *Le Frère de Diderot*, 66 n.; *RQH*, 113 n. Rousseau mentioned to Vernes on 15 Oct. 1754 that 'Diderot est à Langres' (Rousseau, *Corr. gén.*, ii, 103).

2. Diderot, *Corr.*, i, 172–87 (6 Jan. 1755); ibid. 188–91.

3. A.-T., v, 279–308.

4. May, *Quatre visages de Diderot*, 162–8.

5. Diderot, *Corr.*, i, 178, 180. For Dubois, see Marcel, *Le Frère de Diderot*, 7 n.; for Diderot's annoyance with his publishers, see also Rousseau, *Corr. gén.*, ii, 150.

6. Diderot, *Corr.*, i, 185–6; also May, 27–8. The publishers' account book (May, *passim*) shows that these salary arrangements with Diderot were carried out for Vols. v, vi, vii, and viii; consult it also for the titles and cost of the various reference books thus provided.

7. The building on the site of Diderot's house is 149, Boulevard Saint-Germain (Beaurepaire, 'Les Logis de Diderot,' *Revue des Français*, xvii, 316 n.). Numbers 155–75, Boulevard Saint-Germain, are almost all of them survivors of the former Rue Taranne (*Guide bleu: Paris*, ed. 1937, 62). See also Auguste Vitu, *Paris* (Paris, [1889]), 271–2.

8. Diderot, *Corr.*, i, 178; my italics.

9. Marmontel, *Mémoires*, II, 306–7.
10. *Corr. litt.*, II, 144–5.
11. A commemorative plaque is affixed at No. 374; and see Hillairet, *Evocation du vieux Paris*, II, 63. But Roger Picard, *Les Salons littéraires et la société française, 1610–1789* (New York, 1943), 204, claims that No. 372 is correct.
12. Marmontel, *Mémoires*, II, 311–12.
13. René Doumic, 'La "Royauté" de Madame Geoffrin,' *RDM*, 15 June 1897, 918–19. For a recent essay on the *salon* of Mme Geoffrin, see G. P. Gooch, 'Four French Salons: I. Mme Geoffrin,' *Contemporary Review*, June 1951, 345–53.
14. B.N., MSS, Nouv. acq. fr. 10782, fol. 45.
15. Arthur L. Sells, *Les Sources françaises de Goldsmith* (Paris, 1924), 13, 14, 16; Cru, 81–4.
16. D'Escherny, *Mélanges*, III, 128.
17. Pierre de Ségur, *Le Royaume de la rue Saint-Honoré: Madame Geoffrin et sa fille* (Paris, 1897), 315.
18. Foisset, *Le Président de Brosses*, 540, 546: this letter probably written on 24 April 1754. Diderot tells an obscene story about De Brosses (A.-T., XI, 246), possibly heard from Buffon since Buffon and De Brosses had been schoolmates, and therefore it may be true. For De Brosses's proclivities in this regard, see Marcel Bouchard, *De l'Humanisme à l'Encyclopédie: L'Esprit public en Bourgogne sous l'Ancien Régime* (Paris, 1930), 654.
19. Foisset, 546; A.-T., XIX, 429–30, and XX, 106.
20. De Brosses to M. de Farges, 1761 (Foisset, 550–51).
21. Foisset, 545.
22. Rousseau, ed. Hachette, VIII, 277; Rousseau to Saint-Germain, 26 Feb. 1770 (Rousseau, *Corr. gén.*, XIX, 252 n.; cf. ibid. 245, 246). For the passage written by Diderot, as identified by Rousseau, see A.-T., IV, 101–4.
23. Gilbert Chinard, ed., *Supplément au Voyage de Bougainville*, by Diderot (Baltimore, 1935), 51–3, modifies the conclusions expressed earlier by Jean Morel, 'Recherches sur les sources du *Discours de l'Inégalité*,' *AJJR*, v (1909), 119–98, esp. 122–5. Cf. remarks by Norman L. Torrey, reviewing the Chinard edition, *MLN*, LI (1936), 470.
24. C. E. Vaughan, ed., *The Political Writings of Jean Jacques Rousseau*, 2 vols. (Cambridge [Eng.], 1915), I, 19 n., 120–21.
25. A.-T., X, 46.
26. A.-T., X, 47–83; Bibliothèque Nationale call numbers: V.24896 and V.36741. Although undated, the pamphlet mentions events in 1755 and was reviewed by Fréron, *Année Littéraire*, vol. III for 1755, 145–66, on 19 May. His hostility suggests that Fréron suspected Diderot was the author. Cf. also *Année Littéraire*, vol. VI for 1755, 87.
27. *Encyc.*, v, 607–15; by a M. Monnoye (*Encyc.*, VI, vi), otherwise unknown.
28. *Encyc.*, v, 614b; *Corr. litt.*, II, 427–8, 478.
29. A.-T., X, 47.
30. A.-T., X, 68. Regarding Bachelier, see McCloy, *French Inventions of the Eighteenth Century*, 77–8.
31. See *Corr. litt.*, VI, 364–7, for an interesting and not unsympathetic account of him; also Lady Dilke, *French Architects and Sculptors of the XVIIIth Century* (London, 1900), 66; and Eugène Muntz, 'Un Précurseur et un ennemi de Diderot: Le Comte de Caylus, d'après des documents nouveaux,' *Revue Bleue*, 29 May 1897, 674–8.
32. Caylus, Anne-Claude-Philippe, comte de, *Correspondance inédite du comte de Caylus avec le P. Paciaudi, théatin (1757–1765)*, 2 vols. (Paris, 1877), I, 237–8.
33. *Corr. litt.*, VI, 366 n.; A.-T., X, 45 n.; A.-T., XVIII, 251.
34. A.-T., X, 47, 69, 81–2.
35. A.-T., X, 69.
36. A.-T., X, 71.
37. *Corr. litt.*, III, 15; *Année Littéraire*, vol. III for 1755, 147.
38. A.-T., X, 57 n.
39. A.-T., X, 69 nn.
40. A.-T., X, 80.
41. *L'Art nouveau de la peinture en fromage, ou en ramequin, inventée pour suivre le louable*

projet de trouver graduellement des façons de peindre inférieures à celles qui existent (Marolles, 1755): B.N. call number 8°Vp 7724.

42. *Année Littéraire*, vol. III for 1755, 167–71; *Corr. litt.*, III, 25, 94–5.
43. Archives nationales, Y77, foll. 167–8; dated at Paris, 20 June 1772.
44. Michel Corday, *La Vie amoureuse de Diderot* (Paris, 1928), 49.
45. *SV*, 2 vols. (1938), I, 7–8 nn.; more informative than the 1930 edition. The *Annuaire de la Noblesse, 1884*, 138, referred to Sophie Volland's father as a Palatine count; see also Diderot, *Corr.*, II, 133–4.
46. Billy, *Diderot*, 272.
47. *SV* (1938), I, 7 n.
48. *SV*, II, 97 (25 July 1762); *SV*, II, 127 (15 Aug. 1762).
49. *SV*, II, 75–76 (14 July 1762); *SV*, I, 293 (3 Nov. 1760).
50. *SV* (1938), I, 12–13, according to a holograph note of Diderot's son-in-law.
51. Mme de Vandeul, xlvii. Rousseau, *Corr. gén.*, III, 114, and Diderot, *Corr.*, I, 255.
52. *SV*, III, 70 (8 Sept. 1767); *SV*, III, 105 (28 Sept. 1767).
53. *SV*, III, 126–7 (24 Aug. 1768).
54. *SV*, II, 240 (31 May 1765).
55. Diderot, *Corr.*, II, 277 (14? Oct. 1759); *SV*, I, 162 (2 Sept. 1760). The collection of letters to Sophie Volland in the Fonds Vandeul is headed by the notation, written at the time the letters were collected, 'Lettres . . . écrites par Mr Diderot à Mad^{elle} Voland depuis le 1er juillet 1755 . . . .' (Diderot, *Corr.*, II, 8).
56. Billy, *Diderot*, 265–70; André Billy, 'Diderot de pied en cap,' *Conferencia*, vol. I for 1939, 657; Corday, *La Vie amoureuse de Diderot*, 121–46. Cf. Pierre Mesnard, 'Sophie Volland et la maturité de Diderot,' *Revue des Sciences Humaines*, Jan.–March 1949, 12–13; Pierre Mesnard, *Le Cas Diderot*, 164–5; E. Caro, *La Fin du dix-huitième siècle: Etudes et portraits*, 2nd ed., 2 vols. (Paris, 1881), I, 307; Alyse Gregory, 'Denis Diderot,' *Horizon*, IX (1944), 37–38; Guyot, 38–39; and Crocker, *The Embattled Philosopher*, 149–50.
57. A.-T., II, 260.

CHAPTER 18

1. Diderot, *Corr.*, I, 197–8 (22 Sept. 1755). He was still on his milk diet in late December (ibid. 200); and on 24 Jan. 1756 (ibid. 204).
2. Rousseau to Vernes, 23 Nov. 1755 (Rousseau, *Corr. gén.*, II, 239).
3. D'Hémery's journal, 6 Nov. 1755 (B.N., MSS, Fr. 22159, fol. 145); *Corr. litt.*, III, 129; Rousseau, *Corr. gén.*, II, 239).
4. *Corr. litt.*, II, 491; Rousseau, *Corr. gén.*, II, 160.
5. A.-T., XIV, 349. Montesquieu, replying to D'Alembert on 16 Nov. 1753, had declined to write the articles 'Démocratie' and 'Despotisme,' but had volunteered to do 'Goût' (Charles de Sécondat, Baron de Montesquieu, *Correspondance*, ed. François Gebelin and André Morize, 2 vols. [Paris, 1914], II, 492).
6. George H. Sabine, *A History of Political Theory*, revised ed. (New York, 1950), 582. For Diderot's borrowing from Pufendorf, see René Hubert, *Rousseau et l'Encyclopédie* (Paris, 1928), 32–5. See also Robert Derathé, *Jean-Jacques Rousseau et la science politique de son temps* (Paris, 1950), 58, 81.
7. A.-T., XIV, 299, 300.
8. Montesquieu, *L'Esprit des Lois*, book XI, ch. vi.
9. Cf. *Encyc.*, V, 338b, 339b, 340a, 340b, 341b, 346b, s.v. 'Economie.' But regarding incipient divergencies of point of view, see Antoine Adam, 'Rousseau et Diderot,' *Revue des Sciences Humaines*, Jan.–March 1949, 30–32. Cf. Vaughan, *The Political Writings of Jean Jacques Rousseau*, I, 322–3, 426, 445 n., 447, 450–54; and Georges Beaulavon, 'La Question du Contrat social: une fausse solution,' *RHLF*, XX (1913), 594–5.
10. *Encyc.*, V, 116a, 116b; also in A.-T., XIV, 299, 301. As Hubert, *Rousseau et l'Encyclopédie*, 46–9, points out, however, Diderot appears to mean by *volonté générale* a general consensus, while Rousseau means a specific contract.
11. Vaughan, *The Political Writings of Jean Jacques Rousseau*, I, 424–6; Sabine, *A History of Political Theory*, 585.

12. *Encyc.*, VII, 789a; my italics.

13. Owen Ruffhead, writing in the *Monthly Review*, XXXIX (1768), 545 (Lough, 'The "Encyclopédie" in Eighteenth-Century England,' *French Studies*, VI, 296).

14. *Encyc.*, V, 745–50, esp. 747b, 748b, 749a, 750b. Other writings by Faiguet are analyzed by André Lichtenberger, *Le Socialisme au XVIIIe siècle* (Paris, 1895), 334-8.

15. *Encyc.*, V, 536b.

16. *Encyc.*, V, 445a, s.v. 'Elasticité'; ibid. 223a, s.v. 'Nouvelles ecclésiastiques.'

17. My italics. Cf. Franco Venturi, 'Deleyre e la società degli Enciclopedisti,' *Aretusa*, Jan.–Feb. 1946, 81–93; also John Lough, 'Le Rayonnement de l'*Encyclopédie* en Grande-Bretagne,' *AIEF*, No. 2 (May 1952), 71. The principle of division of labor had already been isolated and described by Diderot in 'Art' in Volume I (A.-T., XIII, 372), a passage of great interest to Marxist writers, who see in the *Encyclopédie* a powerful instrument in bringing about French industrialization: e.g. Marcel Prenant, 'L'Encyclopédie et les origines de la science moderne,' *Pensée*, Nov.–Dec. 1951, 32; also René Metz, 'Les Racines sociales et politiques d'une idéologie nationale: L'Encyclopédie,' *Pensée*, Jan.–Feb. 1952, 68–81.

18. A.-T., XIV, 400.

19. A.-T., XIV, 508.

20. A.-T., XIV, 386–7.

21. Sänger, *Juden und Altes Testament bei Diderot*, 67 n. For Shaftesbury's unacknowledged influence in Diderot's article on the 'Egyptians,' see Pierre Hermand, 'Sur le texte de Diderot et sur les sources de quelques passages de ses "Oeuvres",' *RHLF*, XXII (1915), 367; and the same, *Les Idées morales de Diderot*, 265 n.

22. Hubert, *Les Sciences sociales dans l'Encyclopédie*, 42, 48, 51, 79.

23. Sänger, 86; for date of 1754, ibid. 32 n.

24. A.-T., XV, 378.

25. A.-T., XIV, 304, 306, 334–7, 346, 345.

26. Similar vagaries of pagination occur in *Encyc.*, VII, 233 ff., 451 ff., 458–63, 575 ff.

27. Hunt, 'Diderot as "grammairien-philosophe",' *MLR*, XXXIII, 233; A.-T., XIV, 416–50.

28. A.-T., XIV, 454–6. Diderot also alluded to the problem of colleagues' contributions in his article 'Editeur' (A.-T., XIV, 379).

29. A.-T., XIV, 468.

30. A.-T., XIV, 479.

31. A.-T., XIV, 477.

32. A.-T., XIV, 462, 456, 473, 471, 490–91 resp.

33. A.-T., XIV, 489.

34. A.-T., VI, 407; cf. A.-T., XIX, 442, and *Encyc.*, VI, vj. A manuscript 'Cours de Chymie de M. Rouelle rédigé par M. Diderot et éclairci par plusieurs notes,' consisting of nine volumes with a total of 1,258 folios, is MS 564 in the Bibliothèque publique de la Ville de Bordeaux; the headings of this 'Cours de Chymie' are listed by Charles Henry, *Introduction à la chymie. Manuscrit inédit de Diderot, publié avec notice sur les cours de Rouelle* (Paris, 1887), 81–101. The introduction to this Bordeaux manuscript appears to be by Diderot, and was first published by Charles Henry, 'Introduction à la chymie. Manuscrit inédit de Diderot,' *Revue scientifique*, 3me série, XXXIV (1884), 97–108; later reprinted by M. Henry in 1887 (op. cit. *supra*, 17–78). M. Henry believes that this introduction was written after 1758 (ibid. 14). From the point of view of Diderot studies, the principal problem is to determine whether this introduction should be regarded as an original Diderot work. In response to M. Henry's article, Edouard Grimaux, 'Le Cours de chymie de Rouelle,' *Revue Scientifique*, 3me série, XXXIV (1884), 184–5, declared that he, too, possessed a manuscript notebook of Rouelle's lectures. Collation showed, he said (p. 185), that 'à mon avis, les pages que vous avez publiées renferment toutes les idées, et rien que les idées de Rouelle, avec le style de Diderot en plus.' The Bibliothèque Nationale also possesses a copy of these manuscript notes (Maurice Tourneux, 'Les Manuscrits de Diderot conservés en Russie,' *Archives des Missions Scientifiques et Littéraires*, 3me série, XII [1885], 463 and n.). In 1885 M. Henry published another portion of the Bordeaux manuscript which he thought was written by Diderot, but the evidence, both external and internal, is far from conclusive (Charles Henry, 'L'Utilité de la Chymie, par Denis Diderot,' *Revue Scientifique*, 3me série, XXXV [1885], 802–4).

35. A.-T., VI, 405–10. Cf. Charles Bedel, 'L'Avènement de la chimie moderne,' *L' 'Encyclopédie'* *et le progrès des sciences et des techniques* (Paris, 1952), 123–4.

36. *Encyc.*, V, 647aʳ; this passage not faithfully transcribed in A.-T., XIV, 491.

37. Louis-Jacques Goussier (1722–99). See *Encyc.*, I, xliv; also May, 42, 48, 58, 61, *et passim*.

38. A.-T., XIV, 479.

39. Arthur H. Cole and George B. Watts, *The Handicrafts of France as Recorded in the De-scriptions des Arts et Métiers, 1761–1788* (Boston, 1952), 5–6.

40. Such, too, is the opinion of Pommier, *Diderot avant Vincennes*, 92 n.

41. Georges Roth, 'Samuel Formey et son projet d' *"Encyclopédie reduite"*,' *RHLF*, LIV (1954), 371–4.

42. Jean-Henri-Samuel Formey, *Souvenirs d'un citoyen*, 2 vols. (Berlin, 1789), II, 169. Part of this letter is reproduced by Jean Torlais, *Réaumur, un esprit encyclopédique en dehors de 'l'Encyclopédie'* (Paris, 1936), facing 252, but with the erroneous information (pp. 254–5) that Albrecht von Haller, the Swiss physiologist, was the recipient: see Georges Huard, 'Les Planches de l'*Encyclopédie* et celles de la *Description des Arts et Métiers* de l'Académie des Sciences,' *L' 'Encyclopédie' et le progrès des sciences et des techniques*, 37.

43. *Encyc.*, *Planches*, I, 6.

44. See Bertrand Gille, 'L'*Encyclopédie*, dictionnaire technique,' *L' 'Encyclopédie' et le progrès des sciences et des techniques*, 188–9, 199. Intent to defraud is vigorously argued by Huard, 'Les Planches de l'*Encyclopédie* et celles de la *Description des Arts et Métiers* de l'Académie des Sciences,' ibid. 42–3. Cf. George B. Watts, 'The *Encyclopédie* and the *Descriptions des arts et métiers*,' *French Review*, XXV (1951–2), 447.

45. A.-T., XIV, 462–3.

46. 2 March 1756 (B.N., MSS, Nouv. acq. fr. 3345, fol. 175). For the offending passage, see *Encyc.*, V, 635ᵛ, or A.-T., XIV, 418.

47. The Jesuits (A.-T., XIV, 415, 502); 'one good article' (ibid. 494); the Académie Française (ibid. 415, 418–21, 481; cf. Pommier, 'Etudes sur Diderot,' *RHPHGC*, X, 163 n.); Rousseau (A.-T., XIV, 485); Bacon (ibid. 494); apology plus self-gratulation (ibid. 471); the ideal editor (ibid. 502).

48. A.-T., XIV, 461, 483.

49. A.-T., XIV, 453. This passage quoted in evidence of the humanism of the *Encyclopédie* by Bury, *The Idea of Progress*, 159; and by A. Wolf, *A History of Science, Technology, and Philosophy in the Eighteenth Century* (New York, 1939), 39. It is also emphasized by René de Messières, 'L'*Encyclopédie* et la crise de la société au milieu du XVIIIᵉ siècle,' *French Review*, XXIV (1950–51), 395. Cf. Jean Thomas, *L'Humanisme de Diderot*, 2nd. ed. (Paris, 1938), *passim*. Diderot's humanism, esp. as revealed in his article 'Encyclopédie,' is emphasized by Paul Vernière, 'L'Encyclopédie de Diderot et d'Alembert,' *Revue de Synthèse*, XXVI (1950), 142. See also Diderot's remark regarding *humanité* (A.-T., XIV, 493).

50. A.-T., XIV, 473.

51. A.-T., XIV, 474.

CHAPTER 19

1. His sole reference to the Lisbon earthquake seems to be the slight one in *Jacques le fataliste* (A.-T., VI, 51).

2. A.-T., VII, 53–6, 232.

3. Mme de Vandeul, lix; Diderot, *Corr.*, I, 220, 221. Cf. Marcel, *Le Frère de Diderot*, 53–63.

4. A.-T., XIX, 432–8; also printed in *Corr. litt.*, III, 249–55 (1 July 1756), and Diderot, *Corr.*, I, 209–17. Although Grimm specifically refers to Landois as the recipient of this letter (ibid. 255), it is argued by Frederika Macdonald, *Jean Jacques Rousseau*, 2 vols. (New York, 1906), II, 7–13, 249–51, that Grimm hoped his readers would conclude that it was really Rousseau to whom the letter was addressed. Mrs. Macdonald's is a rather speculative conclusion, especially as it does not take cognizance of a passage (A.-T., XIX, 442) of a letter written to Rousseau by Diderot in Jan. 1757. Nevertheless, her conclusion is also subscribed to by Hélène Pittard (pseud. Noëlle Roger), 'Jean-Jacques Rousseau et les drames de l'Ermitage,' *RDM*, 1 June 1925, 660–61; by Cazes, *Grimm et les Encyclopédistes*, 288–9; and by Georges Roth, ed., *Les Pseudo-Mémoires de Madame d'Epinay: Histoire de*

Madame de Montbrillant, by Louise de La Live d'Epinay, 3 vols. (Paris, [1951]), III, 576. The letter to Landois was printed by Babelon as having been addressed to Naigeon (*CI,* I, 308–12). But Naigeon was then only eighteen; moreover, he did not claim to have known Diderot before this year, and Diderot refers in this letter to having known his correspondent for four years at least (A.-T., XIX, 433, 437; Rudolf Brummer, *Studien zur französischen Aufklärungsliteratur im Anschluss an J.-A. Naigeon* [Breslau, 1932], 3–4). See also Dieckmann, *Inventaire,* pp. 148–9.

5. Otis E. Fellows and Alice G. Green, 'Diderot and the Abbé Dulaurens,' *Diderot Studies,* I, 78; Avédik Mesrobian, *Les Conceptions pédagogiques de Diderot* (Paris, [1913]), 45.

6. Edmond N. Cahn, *The Sense of Injustice* (New York, 1949), 10.

7. Hermand, *Les Idées morales de Diderot,* 85–7, 200; cf. Crocker, *Two Diderot Studies: Ethics and Esthetics,* 18–19; also Alice Green Fredman, *Diderot and Sterne* (New York, 1955), 29, 220.

8. *Corr. litt.,* III, 111–12 and 111 n.; cf. A.-T., I, 345–6, 352–3. It is significant that Naigeon (in the three-volume section of the *Encyclopédie méthodique* devoted to 'Philosophie ancienne et moderne,' II, 5–7) stressed Condillac's dependence upon Diderot regarding this very point. Condillac, on the other hand, declared that 'il y avoit déjà long-temps que mademoiselle Ferrand m'avoit communiqué cette idée. Plusieurs personnes savoient même que c'étoit là l'objet d'un Traité auquel je travaillois, et l'auteur de la Lettre sur les Sourds et Muets ne l'ignoroit pas' ('Réponse à un reproche qui m'a été fait sur le projet exécuté dans le Traité des Sensations,' *Oeuvres philosophiques,* I, 318).

9. *Corr. litt.,* III, 222; cf. Courtois, 'Chronologie,' 86. Rousseau, *Corr. gén.,* II, 338.

10. A.-T., VII, 19; Rousseau, *Corr. gén.,* II, 336. Cf. *Corr. litt.,* IV, 56–7. Le Breton's country house was at Massy, near Sceaux (Billy, *Diderot,* 209).

11. Rousseau, *Corr. gén.,* II, 349, 350.

12. Ronald Grimsley, 'Turgot's Article "Existence" in the *Encyclopédie,*' *The French Mind: Studies in Honour of Gustave Rudler* (Oxford, 1952), 126–51; also Georg Misch, 'Zur Entstehung des französischen Positivismus,' *Archiv für Geschichte der Philosophie,* XIV (1901), 24–6, 30, 36; Denis, 'Deux collaborateurs économiques de l'Encyclopédie: Quesnay et Rousseau,' *Pensée,* Sept.–Oct., 1951, 45.

13. Voltaire, ed. Moland, XXXIX, 117.

14. Ibid. XXXVIII, 125.

15. 9 Dec. 1755 (ibid. 519); 13 Nov. 1756 (ibid. XXXIX, 131).

16. Naves, *Voltaire et l'Encyclopédie,* 19–20.

17. 9 Oct. 1756 (Voltaire, ed. Moland, XXXIX, 117); cf. Voltaire to D'Alembert, 24 May 1757 (ibid. 211).

18. 13 Nov. 1756 (ibid. 130); *Encyc.,* VI, 474b. See also Voltaire to D'Alembert, 29 Nov. 1756 (Voltaire, ed. Moland, XXXIX, 135–6).

19. 13 Dec. 1756 (ibid. 139).

20. 22 Dec. 1756 (ibid. 144).

21. Date of Rousseau's first acquaintance with Mme d'Epinay (Eugène Ritter, 'J. J. Rousseau et Madame d'Houdetot,' *AJJR,* II [1906], 18).

22. Act IV, scene iii. For an excellent analysis of the difference of point of view of Diderot and Rousseau, see Ernst Cassirer, *Rousseau, Kant, Goethe* (Princeton, 1945), 7–9.

23. Rousseau, *Corr. gén.,* II, 279, 282, 338, 342, 349.

24. Courtois, 'Chronologie,' 89–90.

25. Mme d'Epinay to Rousseau [Dec. 1756] (Rousseau, *Corr. gén.,* II, 359).

26. Louise de La Live d'Epinay, *Mémoires,* ed. Paul Boiteau, 2 vols. (Paris, 1865), II, 101–11, esp. 106; also Mme d'Epinay, *Pseudo-Mémoires,* II, 601–8, esp. 604. Regarding this passage, see D. C. Cabeen, gen. ed., *A Critical Bibliography of French Literature,* IV: *The Eighteenth Century,* ed. George R. Havens and Donald F. Bond (Syracuse, 1951), 255, item 2237.

27. [26 March 1757] (Rousseau, *Corr. gén.,* III, 49). Cf. Rousseau to Saint-Germain, 26 Feb. 1770 (ibid. XIX, 244).

28. Rousseau, *Corr. gén.,* III, 20–49.

29. Ibid. 21, 36.

30. A.-T., xix, 438–9. Regarding Diderot's attitude, see the comments by F. C. Green, *Jean-Jacques Rousseau: A Critical Study of his Life and Writings* (Cambridge, 1955), 150–51.
31. Rousseau, *Corr. gén.*, iii, 21.
32. A.-T., xix, 440–41. I accept the date of 14 March 1757 for this letter, according to Rousseau, *Corr. gén.*, iii, 23–5.
33. Rousseau, *Corr. gén.*, iii, 32, 50.
34. A.-T., xix, 442; also Rousseau, *Corr. gén.*, iii, 40–41, which dates it either 22 or 23 March 1757.
35. [26 March 1757] (Rousseau, *Corr. gén.*, iii, 49–52).
36. Cf. Deleyre's difficulties in getting away from Paris in order to visit Rousseau (Rousseau, *Corr. gén.*, ii, 336, 338; ibid. iii, 38).

CHAPTER 20

1. Besides the three editions listed by Tchemerzine, *Bibliographie d'éditions originales et rares d'auteurs français*, iv, 447, there was also one in 1757 published in Amsterdam by Marc Michel Rey; a copy of this edition is in the Boston Public Library.
2. Diderot, *Corr.*, ii, 20.
3. Ibid. 21.
4. 10 Dec. 1757 (ibid. 23).
5. So asserted by Collé, *Journal et mémoires*, ii, 74; by the *Année Littéraire*, vol. ii for 1758, 29; and by Charles Palissot de Montenoy, *Oeuvres complettes*, 7 vols. (London, 1779), ii, 125 n.; cf. Thieriot to Voltaire, 10 April 1757 (*RHLF*, xv [1908], 150). On 23 April 1757, Diderot, writing to Marmontel, refused the pass to the Comédie-Française performances that the famous actress, Mlle Clairon, had offered him (Herbert Dieckmann, 'Three Diderot Letters, and *Les Eleuthéromanes*,' *Harvard Library Bulletin*, vi [1952], 71). Authors whose plays were produced were given permanent passes; therefore, it is possible that Mlle Clairon's offer just at this time was something in the nature of a consolation prize having some connection with a refusal by the Comédie-Française to produce the *Fils naturel*.
6. Corneille had set forth ideas in his *épître dédicatoire* to *Don Sanche* (1650) tantamount to the theory of a *tragédie bourgeoise* (Lester Gilbert Crocker, 'Aspects of Diderot's Esthetic Theory,' by L. G. Krakeur, *RR*, xxx [1939], 251; Cru, 301 n.). There is no evidence, however, that Corneille's notions, which seemed paradoxical even to himself, had any effect upon the French theater or influenced Diderot.
7. Edith Melcher, 'Trends in Recent Criticism of the Eighteenth-Century French Theatre,' *RR*, xxix (1938), 160–66. See Gustave Lanson, *Nivelle de la Chaussée et la comédie larmoyante*, 2nd ed. (Paris, 1903), i, 277. Diderot specifically mentions *Sylvie* as a concrete example of his ideas (A.-T., vii, 119), but it is noticeable that he hardly ever mentions Nivelle de la Chaussée (Lanson, 276, 277). Regarding *Sylvie*, see esp. Henry Carrington Lancaster, *French Tragedy in the Time of Louis XV and Voltaire, 1715–1774*, 2 vols. (Baltimore, 1950), i, 262–5; and also his critical edition of *Sylvie* (*Johns Hopkins Studies in Romance Literatures and Languages*, xlviii [1954]).
8. De Tocqueville, *Democracy in America*, ii, book i, ch. xix: 'Some Observations on the Drama amongst Democratic Nations.' For a discussion of the significance of Diderot's plays from the point of view of historical materialism, see P.-B. Marquet, 'Diderot et le théâtre au XVIIIe siècle,' *Europe*, Sept. 1951, 115–28.
9. Mme d'Epinay, *Pseudo-Mémoires*, iii, 61; Mme d'Epinay, *Mémoires* (1865), ii, 187. Publication occurred about mid-Feb. 1757 (Courtois, 'Chronologie,' 90).
10. *Corr. litt.*, iii, 354, 357 (1 March 1757).
11. *Année Littéraire*, vol. iv for 1757, 146.
12. Palissot, *Oeuvres complettes*, ii, 123–4.
13. Collé, *Journal et mémoires*, ii, 75.
14. B.N., MSS, Nouv. acq. fr. 3531, fol. 62; quoted by Le Gras, 101–2, but with faulty volume reference. Cf. *Année Littéraire*, vol. iii for 1756, 193. D'Alembert's letter of complaint to Malesherbes, 25 June [1756] (B.N., MSS, Fr. 22191, fol. 134; also in Le Gras, 101).
15. Paris, 28 June 1756 (B.N., MSS, Nouv. acq. fr. 3531, foll. 63–4).

16. [Jean-Jacques Garnier], *Le Bâtard légitimé, ou le triomphe du comique larmoyant, avec un examen du Fils naturel* (Amsterdam [Paris], 1757) [B.N., Imprimés, Y^f 9433].

17. B.N., MSS, Nouv. acq. fr. 3346, fol. 12.

18. Fréron to Malesherbes, 21 March 1757 (Etienne Charavay, 'Diderot & Fréron,' *Revue des Documents Historiques*, III [1875–6], 157).

19. Fréron to Malesherbes, 27 Jan. 1758 (Charavay, 166).

20. 21 March 1757 (Charavay, 160–61).

21. A.-T., IV, 283–9.

22. Palissot, *Oeuvres complettes*, II, 124; A.-T., VII, 17.

23. Cf. A.-T., VII, 19–21, 92, 93, 97.

24. A.-T., VII, 111; cf. *supra*, p. 13.

25. Garat, *Mémoires . . . de M. Suard*, II, 18–19. See also Hans Sckommodau, ' "Il n'y à que le méchant qui soit seul." ' (Zu den Anschauungen der französischen Aufklärung über Menschenhass und Weltflucht),' *Romanistisches Jahrbuch*, I (1947–8), 213–4.

26. A.-T., VII, 19.

27. E. B. O. Borgerhoff, *The Evolution of Liberal Theory and Practice in the French Theater, 1680–1757* (Princeton, 1936), 113 *et passim*.

28. A.-T., VII, 87.

29. A.-T., VII, 94–8, 114. Cf. Edith Melcher, *Stage Realism in France between Diderot and Antoine* (Bryn Mawr, 1928), pp. 31–2.

30. A.-T., VII, 105–6.

31. A.-T., VII, 162–5; cf. Romain Rolland, *Some Musicians of Former Days*, 255, 277; also Julien Tiersot, 'Gluck and the Encyclopædists,' *Musical Quarterly*, XVI (1930), 349. Diderot once wrote a sketch of the libretto of a comic opera (J. Robert Loy, 'Diderot's Unedited *Plan d'un opéra comique*,' *RR*, XLVI [1955], 3–24). This may have been written in the 1750's, but I am inclined to date it in the late 1760's.

32. A.-T., VII, 104; see also ibid. 100. According to A. Lombard, *L'Abbé du Bos, un initiateur de la pensée moderne (1670–1742)* (Paris, 1913), 335–6, this and a good many other of Diderot's ideas can be found in Du Bos's *Réflexions critiques sur la poésie et sur la peinture* (1719).

33. A.-T., VII, 120, 161.

34. A.-T., VII, 95, 120, 411–525. Cf. Cru, 304–16.

35. A.-T., VII, 135.

36. Just before this new development, 'drame' had been defined very broadly and loosely by Mallet in the *Encyclopédie* (*Encyc.*, V, 105b).

37. A.-T., VII, 71–2.

38. A.-T., VII, 150.

39. A.-T., VII, 150–51.

40. A.-T., VII, 68; also ibid. 128.

41. A.-T., VII, 108–9.

42. A.-T., VII, 149.

43. Cru, 288.

44. Félix Alexandre Gaiffe, *Le Drame en France au XVIIIe siècle* (Paris, 1910), 1.

45. 1 Oct. 1757 (Rousseau, *Corr. gén.*, III, 128). Cf. A.-T., VII, 17–18.

46. *Année Littéraire*, vol. II for 1758, 29–30.

47. Not infrequently these editions included the *Entretiens sur le Fils naturel*, thus increasing the dissemination of Diderot's ideas. According to A.-T., VII, 10, a Spanish edition, evidently of the *Entretiens*, was published in 1788. Interest in the concept of the *Fils naturel* is attested by the existence of a novel falsely attributed to Diderot: *The Natural Son . . . Translated from the French of M. Diderot*, 2 vols. (London: T. N. Longman, 1799).

48. A.-T., VII, 166–7; cf. Collé, *Journal et mémoires*, II, 74.

49. Cf. A.-T., VII, 110, 129, 151, *et passim*.

50. Palissot, *Oeuvres complettes*, II, 161.

51. Ibid. 131; *Année Littéraire*, vol. IV for 1757, 159.

52. Palissot, *Oeuvres complettes*, II, 139, 140; *Année Littéraire*, vol. IV for 1757, 170. Even the friendly Lessing made some very unfavorable judgments of the *Fils naturel*: see no. 85 (23 Feb. 1768) of Lessing's *Hamburgische Dramaturgie*.

53. *Supplément d'un important ouvrage. Scène dernière du Fils naturel, avec une lettre à Dorval* (Venise [Paris], 1758), 59.
54. These documents in Manlio D. Busnelli, *Diderot et l'Italie* (Paris, 1925), 273-4.
55. *Année Littéraire*, vol. IV for 1757, 145-73, 289-316.
56. Yet Palissot had been allowed to remark in his *Petites lettres sur de grands philosophes* 'que le *Fils Naturel* lui-même n'est qu'une copie défigurée du *Vero Amico*, de M. Goldoni' (Palissot, *Oeuvres complettes*, II, 162). The anonymous *Supplément d'un important ouvrage* (n. 53, *supra*) mischievously claimed to be printed at Venice, 'chez François Goldino, à l'Enseigne del Fido Amico.'
57. Through Act II, scene vi, of Goldoni; and Act III, scene iii. of Diderot. Cf. Pietro Toldo, 'Se il Diderot abbia imitato il Goldoni,' *Giornale Storico della Letteratura Italiana*, XXVI (1895), 350-76; and Susanna Gugenheim, 'Drammi e teorie drammatiche del Diderot e loro fortuna in Italia,' *Etudes Italiennes*, III (1921), 167-9.
58. *Journal Encyclopédique*, vol. VIII for 1758, 3me partie, 122-4 (15 Dec. 1758).
59. André Morize, *Problems and Methods of Literary History* (Boston, 1922), 83.
60. Collé, *Journal et mémoires*, II, 108-9.
61. A.-T., VII, 337, 339; cf. ibid. 317. Diderot was likewise defended by the Abbé de la Porte in *L'Observateur Littéraire* for 5 Nov. 1758 (Busnelli, *Diderot et l'Italie*, 108-10). A later version of the Abbé's remarks was published in the *Oeuvres de théâtre de M. Diderot, avec un Discours sur la poésie dramatique*, 2 vols. (Paris, 1771), I, 319-36; reprinted in A.-T., VII, 11-18.
62. *Mercure de France*, Feb. 1759, 91.
63. Goldoni, *Mémoires*, II, 177-8.
64. A.-T., XIX, 441.

CHAPTER 21

1. 'Eloge de M. d'Alembert,' *Histoire de l'Académie Royale des Sciences, Année MDCCLXXXIII* (Paris, 1786), 103. D'Alembert's allusions to Frederick the Great (*Encyc.*, I, 55b, s.v. 'Académie,' and *Encyc.*, IV, 969b, s.v. 'Dictionnaire'; cf. Venturi, *Origini*, 78).
2. Cheverny, *Mémoires*, I, 179-86. Cheverny was then official Introducer of Ambassadors.
3. B.N., MSS, Fr. 22177, fol. 197.
4. B.N., MSS, Fr. 22177, foll. 200-201. Cf. Belin, *Le Commerce des livres prohibés*, 114; Belin, *Le Mouvement philosophique de 1748 à 1789*, 110; and an undated letter from D'Alembert to Voltaire, probably in late March 1757 (Voltaire, ed. Moland, XXXIX, 199).
5. Voltaire, ed. Moland, XXXIX, 235; cf. D'Alembert to Voltaire, 11 Jan. 1758 (ibid. 363).
6. For Moreau's authorship of *L'Observateur Hollandais*, see D'Hémery's journal (B.N., MSS, Fr. 22159, fol. 87).
7. *Mercure de France*, vol. I for Oct. 1757, 15-19.
8. D'Hémery mentioned the publication of Vol. VII in his entry of 24 Nov. 1757 (B.N., MSS, Fr. 22160, fol. 63ᵛ); cf. *Corr. litt.*, III, 457. But some authorities declare that Vol. VII was published 10 Oct. 1757 (Courtois, 'Chronologie,' 95; Cazes, *Grimm et les Encyclopédistes*, 71 n.; and Clara Adèle Luce Herpin [pseud. Lucien Perey] and Gaston Maugras, *La Vie intime de Voltaire aux Délices et à Ferney, 1754-1778* [Paris, 1885], 168).
9. *Encyc.*, VII, 41b. The articles 'Foire' and 'Fondation' were published anonymously (ibid. xiv); A.-T., XV, 12-21, erroneously attributes the latter to Diderot. For attribution to Turgot, see Turgot, *Oeuvres*, ed. Schelle, I, 59, 577-93.
10. *Encyc.*, VII, 735b, s.v. 'Gomaristes'; Morellet, *Mémoires*, I, 42-3.
11. *Encyc.*, VII, 72b-75b. Regarding Turgot and Gournay, see W. Walker Stephens, *The Life and Writings of Turgot* (London, 1895), 20.
12. *Encyc.*, VII, 282a-b.
13. *Encyc.*, VII, 790b.
14. *Encyc.*, VII, 802b.
15. *Encyc.*, VII, 188b.
16. *Encyc.*, VII, 128b.
17. *Encyc.*, VII, 979a-81a. The best analysis of Boulanger's thought is by Franco Venturi,

L'Antichità svelata e l'idea del progresso in N. A. Boulanger (1722–1759) (Bari, 1947).

18. *Encyc.*, VII, 907a, 907b, s.v. 'Grecs (philosophie des)'; A.-T., xv, 53. An important article, 'Génie,' is attributed to Diderot by ibid. 35–41. Grimm, however, attributed it to Saint-Lambert (*Corr. litt.*, III, 458), and Saint-Lambert himself, writing to his publisher in 1798, claimed it as his (Pierre Marot, 'A propos du deuxième centenaire de l'*Encyclopédie*. Saint-Lambert au Musée lorrain,' *Pays lorrain*, XXXII [1951], 196); cf. Venturi, *Jeunesse*, 344–5. It is likely, however, that Diderot edited or re-worked the article (Barker, *Diderot's Treatment of the Christian Religion in* The Encyclopédie, 116 n.; and Dieckmann, 'Diderot's Conception of Genius,' *JHI*, II, 163 n.: 'I am still convinced that great parts of the article "Génie" must have been either inspired or revised by Diderot himself').

19. A.-T., xv, 23.

20. Naves, *Voltaire et l'Encyclopédie*, 38–49; René Pintard, 'Voltaire et l'*Encyclopédie*,' *AUP*, XXII ([Oct.] 1952), numéro spécial, 39–57, esp. 51; John Stephenson Spink, *Jean-Jacques Rousseau et Genève* (Paris, 1934), 153; Rousseau, *Corr. gén.*, IV, 91.

21. *Encyc.*, VII, 576b, s.v. 'Genève.'

22. *Encyc.*, VII, 576b, 577b, s.v. 'Genève'; Naves, *Voltaire et l'Encyclopédie*, 44.

23. *Encyc.*, VII, 577b, 575a–b, 578b, s.v. 'Genève.'

24. *Encyc.*, VII, 578a, s.v. 'Genève.'

25. *Corr. litt.*, III, 458.

26. Naves, *Voltaire et l'Encyclopédie*, 35.

27. Voltaire to Théodore Tronchin, 15 Jan. 1758 (Voltaire, *Correspondance avec les Tronchin*, ed. André Delattre [Paris, 1950], 309); cf. D'Alembert to Voltaire, 11 Jan. 1758 (Voltaire, ed. Moland, XXXIX, 362).

28. *Année Littéraire*, vol. II for 1758, 59–69. D'Alembert republished this protest, with comments, in his *Mélanges de littérature, d'histoire, et de philosophie*, v (1767), 571–600.

29. *Corr. litt.*, III, 205–7; Naves, *Voltaire et l'Encyclopédie*, 37.

30. *Encyc.*, VIII, 769–71. See Pierre Astruc, 'Les Sciences médicales et leurs représentants dans l'Encyclopédie,' *L' 'Encyclopédie' et le progrès des sciences et des techniques*, 177.

31. Tronchin to D'Alembert (Gustave Desnoiresterres, *Voltaire et la société au XVIIIᵉ siècle*, 2nd ed., 8 vols. [Paris, 1871–6], v, 175–6); D'Alembert to Tronchin, 6 Jan. 1758 (Voltaire, *Correspondance avec les Tronchin*, ed. Delattre, 299–300).

32. 30 Dec. 1757 (Diderot, *Corr.*, II, 26–8).

33. Tronchin to Pictet, 24 Jan. 1758 (Herpin [pseud. Perey] and Maugras, *La Vie intime de Voltaire aux Délices et à Ferney*, 179).

34. *Corr. litt.*, IV, 53.

35. See Voltaire to Briasson, 13 Feb. 1756 (Voltaire, ed. Moland, XXXVIII, 551); and to D'Alembert: [19?] Feb., 23 July, 29 Aug., 29 Dec. 1757; and 3 Jan. 1758 (ibid. XXXIX, 181, 236, 255, 341, and 343 resp.).

36. Ibid. 363–4, 375–6; Naves, *Voltaire et l'Encyclopédie*, 53–62. See Voltaire's indignant letters to D'Alembert: 5, 13, 19, and 25 Feb. 1758; and to D'Argental, 9 and 26 Feb. 1758 (ibid. 387–8, 396–7, 400, 406–7, 392, and 408–9 resp.).

37. *Supra*, p. 220.

38. 11 Jan. 1758 (Voltaire, ed. Moland, XXXIX, 362).

39. In Jan. 1758 (Le Gras, 112); cf. D'Alembert to Voltaire, 11 Jan. 1758, and Voltaire to D'Alembert, 13 Feb. 1758 (ibid. 362, 396).

40. B.N., MSS, Fr. 22191, fol. 24.

41. Ibid. fol. 23.

42. Ibid. foll. 25–6. Precisely the same claim was made publicly by the publishers (*Mémoire des libraires associés à l'Encyclopédie, sur les motifs de la suspension actuelle de cet ouvrage* [Paris, 1758], 4–5).

43. B.N., MSS, Fr. 22191, fol. 20ʳ–20ᵛ. Fol. 20ʳ is reproduced in *AUP*, XXII ([Oct.] 1952), numéro spécial, facing 62.

44. Palissot, *Oeuvres complettes*, II, 106, 107, 110, 111, 112, 114, 117–18, and 120, resp.

45. *Année Littéraire*, vol. VIII for 1757, 238–52.

46. [Jacob-Nicolas Moreau], *Nouveau Mémoire pour servir à l'histoire des Cacouacs* (Amsterdam [Paris], 1757), 4, 5, 16–17, 20–21, 23, 26, 38, 58–9, 71, 73, 82, 97–9, 102.

47. D'Alembert to Voltaire, 28 Jan. 1758 (Voltaire, ed. Moland, xxxix, 383–4); also the same to the same, 11 Jan., 20 Jan., and 8 Feb. 1758 (ibid. 362–3, 374–5, and 390–91, resp.).

48. *Année Littéraire*, vol. 1 for 1758, 3–22, esp. 8.

49. D'Alembert to Malesherbes, 23 Jan. 1758 (B.N., MSS, Fr. 22191, fol. 140; published by Sainte-Beuve, 'M. de Malesherbes,' *Causeries du lundi*, 11, 530–31).

50. Fréron to Malesherbes, 27 Jan. 1758 (B.N., MSS, Fr. 22191, fol. 141; published by Charavay, 'Diderot & Fréron,' *Revue des Documents Historiques*, III, 165–7, and [in part] by Sainte-Beuve, 'M. de Malesherbes,' *Causeries du lundi*, 11, 531).

51. B.N., MSS, Fr. 22191, fol. 138. For the letter in entirety (Morellet, *Mémoires*, 1, 46–50; also Coyecque, *Inventaire de la collection Anisson*, 1, xcvii–xcix).

52. B.N., MSS, Fr. 22191, foll. 136–7. Published, under date of 16 Feb. 1758 in Morellet, *Mémoires*, 1, 50–54, and in Coyecque, op. cit. 1, xcv–xcvii.

53. Morellet, *Mémoires*, 1, 46, 53. Cf. D'Alembert to Voltaire, Paris, 23 Jan. 1757 (Voltaire, ed. Moland, xxxix, 163).

54. Draft of the letter to Morellet (B.N., MSS, Fr. 22191, foll. 148–51; the quotation is from fol. 148ᵛ).

55. Yves Laissus, 'Une Lettre inédite de d'Alembert,' *Revue d'Histoire des Sciences*, VII (1954), 1–5; Voltaire, *Correspondance avec les Tronchin*, ed. Delattre, 300.

56. Voltaire, ed. Moland, xxxix, 362. Cf. D'Alembert's letter to the Genevese, J. Vernes, 15 Jan. 1758 (Eugène Ritter, *Revue Critique d'Histoire et de Littérature*, nouvelle série, XLVI [1898], 291–2). The *Journal Encyclopédique*, vol. 1 for 1758, 3ᵉ Partie (1 Feb. 1758), 116, referred to D'Alembert's retiring from the *Encyclopédie*, and added: 'Ainsi cette grande entreprise . . . va donc de nouveau être interrompue!'

57. 8 Jan. 1758 (Voltaire, ed. Moland, xxxix, 356).

58. 19 Jan. 1758 (ibid. 369, 370).

59. 20 Jan. 1758 (ibid. 374–5).

60. Voltaire to D'Alembert, 29 Jan. 1758 (ibid. 385).

61. Ibid. 352; cf. Naves, *Voltaire et l'Encyclopédie*, 55. At first Grimm also thought the author a Jesuit (*Corr. litt.*, III, 458).

62. 5 Feb. 1758 (Voltaire, ed. Moland, xxxix, 387).

63. Ibid. 396.

64. Voltaire to Tressan, 13 Feb. 1758 (ibid. 397–8).

65. Rousseau to Mme d'Houdetot, 13 Feb. 1758 (Rousseau, *Corr. gén.*, III, 279).

66. Diderot, *Corr.*, II, 37–40. A rather clumsy reply to Palissot, Moreau, and Fréron, coupled with a defense of Diderot, was contained in a pamphlet entitled *L'Aléthophile, ou l'Ami de la Vérité* (Amsterdam, 1758), esp. 13, 30–31; cf. *Corr. litt.*, III, 486. Fréron replied to it effectively (*Année Littéraire*, vol. II for 1758, 24–38).

67. Voltaire to D'Argental, 26 Feb. 1758 (Voltaire, ed. Moland, xxxix, 410).

68. Voltaire to D'Argental, 12 March 1758 (ibid. 422).

69. Venturi, *Origini*, 144.

70. D'Alembert, *Mélanges de littérature, d'histoire, et de philosophie*, 1 (1763), 320.

CHAPTER 22

1. *SV*, 1, 202 (30 Sept. 1760); the author was really Charles Bordes (Hippolyte Buffenoir, *La Comtesse d'Houdetot, une amie de Jean-Jacques Rousseau* [Paris, 1901], 331–8).

2. Ritter, 'J. J. Rousseau et Madame d'Houdetot,' *AJJR*, II, 18.

3. According to Guillemin, 70, 154–7, the 'day of the five notes' was probably 31 Aug. 1757; his reasoning appears to me to be conclusive. But other authorities argue for earlier dates: cf. Mme d'Epinay, *Pseudo-Mémoires*, III, 178 n.; and Ritter, loc. cit. *AJJR*, II, 42.

4. Rousseau, ed. Hachette, VIII, 349. According to Diderot, however, Rousseau confided in him at an earlier date: he told Marmontel that Rousseau came to Paris to ask his advice (Marmontel, *Mémoires*, III, 2–3). The only visit that Rousseau is known to have made to Paris during the time of his love affair with Mme d'Houdetot was in July 1757. In his catalogue of the 'sept scélératesses,' Diderot says that, having given Rousseau this advice,

'Je le revis dans la suite' (*Corr. litt.*, xvi, 220). Since they did not meet after 5 Dec. 1757, the original confession must then have occurred on an earlier occasion. Both these assertions by Diderot date from 1758 or thereabouts (Guillemin, 73).

5. Rousseau, ed. Hachette, viii, 318; Rousseau, *Corr. gén.*, iii, 120.
6. 11 Oct. 1757 (Rousseau, *Corr. gén.*, iii, 145; also ibid. 144).
7. 28 Oct. 1757 (ibid. 153; my italics).
8. *Corr. litt.*, xvi, 219, 220.
9. Ritter, 'J. J. Rousseau et Madame d'Houdetot,' *AJJR*, ii, 99. Cf. Schinz, *Etat présent des travaux sur J.-J. Rousseau*, 337.
10. Deleyre to Rousseau, 31 March 1757, announcing the forthcoming visit (Rousseau, *Corr. gén.*, iii, 52–3); Rousseau to Mme d'Epinay, 10 April 1757 (ibid. 67): 'Au reste, vous savez que le Philosophe m'est venu voir.'
11. Rousseau, ed. Hachette, viii, 330–31; Courtois, 'Chronologie,' 92–3. On Rousseau's motives for visiting Paris, see Guillemin, 69, 187.
12. Mme de Vandeul, lxi.
13. Ibid. lx–lxi.
14. Marmontel, *Mémoires*, iii, 8.
15. Morellet, *Mémoires*, i, 106.
16. *Corr. litt.*, xvi, 220.
17. Rousseau, *Corr. gén.*, iii, 118–21, under date of 5 Sept. 1757. The date should be 4 Sept., according to Guillemin, 221.
18. *Corr. litt.*, xvi, 220.
19. Mme Diderot at Langres: Rousseau, *Corr. gén.*, iii, 114; Diderot, *Corr.*, i, 255. Diderot's illness: Rousseau, *Corr. gén.*, iii, 146. For evidence independent of Rousseau's *Confessions* regarding Grimm's frosty treatment of Rousseau, see Henri Piguet, *Mélanges de littérature* (Lausanne, 1816), 255–8.
20. A.-T., xix, 443.
21. Rousseau to Diderot, ca. 19 Oct. 1757 (Rousseau, *Corr. gén.*, iii, 135).
22. Rousseau, *Corr. gén.*, vi, 325.
23. Ibid. iii, 136–43; *Corr. litt.*, xvi, 219.
24. Ritter, 'J. J. Rousseau et Madame d'Houdetot,' *AJJR*, ii, 60–61. The child by Francueil was born on 29 May 1753 (Guillemin, 67 n.).
25. P.-P. Plan inserts this letter in his edition of Rousseau, *Corr. gén.*, iii, 170–71, though he calls it 'fausse.' A convincing case, however, for its genuineness is made by Norman L. Torrey, 'Rousseau's Quarrel with Grimm and Diderot,' *Essays in Honor of Albert Feuillerat* (*Yale Romanic Studies*, xxii [New Haven, 1943]), 165–72; see also Guillemin, 215–16. Among articles discussing the Grimm-D'Epinay aspect of the quarrel with Rousseau should be mentioned Rodolphe-Louis Hébert, 'Grimm and Rousseau,' *French Review*, xxv (1951–2), 262–9; Gustave Charlier, 'Mme d'Epinay et J.-J. Rousseau,' in his *De Ronsard à Victor Hugo* (Brussels, 1931), 193–220; and Eugène Ritter, 'Nouvelles recherches sur les *Confessions* et la correspondance de Jean-Jacques Rousseau,' *Zeitschrift für neufranzösische Sprache und Literatur*, ii (1880), 326.
26. Undated (Hippolyte Buffenoir, *La Comtesse d'Houdetot, sa famille, ses amis* [Paris, 1905], 46–7; and in Rousseau, *Corr. gén.*, iii, 243–4). Guillemin, p. 205, dates Diderot's first letter about 10 Nov. 1757.
27. 28 Jan. 1758 (Rousseau, *Corr. gén.*, iii, 270).
28. A.-T., xix, 444–5. Cf. Rousseau's letters to Mme d'Epinay and to Mme d'Houdetot (Rousseau, *Corr. gén.*, iii, 157, 159–60, 161).
29. Rousseau, ed. Hachette, viii, 349–50, 355.
30. 17 Dec. 1757 (Rousseau, *Corr. gén.*, iii, 230), in reply to a letter of 14 Dec. (ibid. 225). See also Rousseau to Mme d'Houdetot, 28 Jan. 1758 (ibid. 268): 'A la bonne heure, pour moi, je ne changerai point pour lui, et j'attendrai paisiblement qu'il revienne.'
31. 13 Feb. 1758 (ibid. 279).
32. Ibid. 295.
33. Ibid. 289, 295, 299. Cf. Ritter, 'J. J. Rousseau et Madame d'Houdetot,' *AJJR*, ii, 83 n.

34. Rousseau, *Corr. gén.*, III, 296–8.
35. Ibid. 299, 308. See also Torrey, 'Rousseau's Quarrel with Grimm and Diderot,' *Essays in Honor of Albert Feuillerat*, 177.
36. This is the hypothesis of Torrey, 'Rousseau's Quarrel with Grimm and Diderot,' 180; also of Lucien Brunel, 'La Nouvelle Héloïse et Mme d'Houdetot,' *Annales de l'Est*, II (1888), 508. For other theories as to which was the 'lettre atroce,' see Ritter, 'J. J. Rousseau et Madame d'Houdetot,' *AJJR*, II, 100–101, 103.
37. *Corr. litt.*, XVI, 220.
38. Rousseau, *Corr. gén.*, III, 320.
39. *Corr. litt.*, XVI, 220.
40. 9 Jan. 1759 (Diderot, *Corr.*, II, 108).
41. Voltaire to D'Argental, 15 June 1758 (Voltaire, ed. Moland, XXXIX, 454).
42. *Corr. litt.*, XVI, 220. Cf. Guillemin, 70–71; Torrey, 'Rousseau's Quarrel with Grimm and Diderot,' *Essays in Honor of Albert Feuillerat*, 173. For dating the Catalogue, see Anatole Feugère, 'Pourquoi Rousseau a remanié la Préface de la *Lettre à D'Alembert*,' *AJJR*, XX (1931), 147–48.
43. Torrey, loc. cit. 181. See also Professor Torrey's remarks in the *Romanic Review*, XXIX (1938), 189 n. And Professor F. C. Green remarks (*Jean-Jacques Rousseau*, 169): 'I see no reason to doubt Diderot's story of what happened.'
44. Nevertheless, there are chronological difficulties about accepting Diderot's story (*Corr. litt.*, XVI, 220) that he made a trip to the Hermitage to upbraid Rousseau for not making the confession that he said he had and to find out whether he was 'fou ou méchant.' Diderot used the very same words, 'fou ou méchant,' in telling this story to Marmontel (Marmontel, *Mémoires*, III, 5), in a conversation that probably took place in 1758 (Guillemin, 73). Inasmuch as the Saint-Lambert crisis did not occur until March or April of 1758, when Diderot and Rousseau were no longer seeing each other, it seems unlikely that this alleged interview really occurred. Was it simply braggadocio that made Diderot boast to Marmontel — and set down in his private notes — that he had told Rousseau off? Or was he uneasy about having committed a real indiscretion, and wanted to imply, by claiming that he taxed Rousseau with it, that Rousseau was just as much to blame, or more, than he? Cf. Mme d'Epinay, *Pseudo-Mémoires*, III, 255 n., 258 n., 280 n.
45. Rousseau, ed. Hachette, VIII, 356–7.
46. The preface is dated 20 March 1758, but Rousseau added in June the paragraph alluding to Diderot (Feugère, 'Pourquoi Rousseau a remanié la Préface de la *Lettre à D'Alembert*,' *AJJR*, XX, 128). The quotation is Ecclesiasticus XXII: 26–7 (Vulgate, tr. Father Ronald Knox).
47. Liége, 28 Oct. 1758 (Rousseau, *Corr. gén.*, IV, 65).
48. Marmontel, *Mémoires*, II, 316–17; III, 1–2. Cf. the 'Sept Scélératesses': 'Sa note est d'autant plus vile qu'il savait que je n'y pouvais répondre sans compromettre cinq ou six personnes' (*Corr. litt.*, XVI, 221–2).
49. 10 Oct. 1758 (Rousseau, *Corr. gén.*, IV, 74–5).
50. *Corr. litt.*, XVI, 221.
51. A.-T., VI, 315.
52. 9 Jan. 1759 (Ville de Genève: Bibliothèque Publique et Universitaire: Collection Rilliet); for the attribution to Vernes as the recipient, see Guillemin, 112; published in Diderot, *Corr.*, II, 106–9.
53. According to D'Hémery's entry of that date (B.N., MSS, Fr. 22160, fol. 108). Malesherbes had appointed D'Alembert to be the censor (Rousseau, *Corr. gén.*, IV, 23, 35, 49), a clever move which tied D'Alembert's hands. Rousseau predicted to Rey, his Amsterdam publisher, that Durand, the Paris bookseller, would refuse to serve as the Paris agent for Rousseau's book, 'attendu qu'il est le libraire de M. Diderot . . .' (13 Sept. 1758: Rousseau, *Corr. gén.*, IV, 53). Durand did, however, handle the commission (*Année Littéraire*, vol. VI for 1758, 327).
54. A.-T., XIV, 485.
55. Sébastien-Roch-Nicolas Chamfort, *Maximes et pensées, caractères et anecdotes* (Porrentruy, [1946]), 194.

CHAPTER 23

1. Rousseau, *Corr. gén.*, III, 274.
2. Gustave Charlier and Roland Mortier, *Le Journal Encyclopédique (1756–1793)* (Paris, 1952), 85.
3. *Mémoire des libraires associés à l'Encyclopédie, sur les motifs de la suspension actuelle de cet ouvrage* (Paris, 1758), 5. *Mercure de France,* vol. II for April 1758, 97–104. Diderot to Voltaire, 14 June 1758 (A.-T., XIX, 454).
4. Voltaire, ed. Moland, XXXIX, 411.
5. According to André Billy, ed., *Oeuvres,* by Diderot (Paris: 'Nouvelle Revue française,' 1951 [Bibliothèque de la Pléiade, No. 25]), 17, Marmontel and Duclos quit the *Encyclopédie* in March 1758.
6. Diderot, *Corr.,* II, 272–5 (14? Oct. 1759; my italics).
7. B.N., MSS, Fr. 22191, fol. 9; quoted and paraphrased by Sainte-Beuve, 'M. de Malesherbes,' *Causeries du lundi,* II, 527–9. Thieriot wrote to Voltaire on 27 Dec. 1757 that the Jesuits were back of the agitation over the Cacouacs, their motive being to prevent Diderot from being elected to the Academy of Sciences (Fernand Caussy, 'Lettres inédites de Thieriot à Voltaire,' *RHLF,* XV [1908], 154).
8. Versailles, 8 April 1758 (B.N., MSS, Fr. 22191, fol. 10).
9. Diderot, *Corr.,* II, 61. Cf. Voltaire to Diderot, 26 June 1758 (Voltaire, ed. Moland, XXXIX, 462). The allusion is to La Fontaine's *conte,* 'Le Diable de Papefiguière.'
10. *Mémoire à consulter pour les libraires associés à l'Encyclopédie* (Paris: Le Breton, 1770), 4.
11. Cazes, *Grimm et les encyclopédistes,* 73; Smiley, *Diderot's Relations with Grimm,* 83, 84.
12. Claude-Adrien Helvétius, *De l'Esprit,* 2 vols. (Amsterdam and Leipzig, 1759), I, XX, 50–51 nn., 88, 89, 151, 198, 253, and esp. 262.
13. Helvétius, *De l'Esprit,* I, 22 n., 23 n., 171, 154 n., 26–8 and nn., 6–9 nn., 238, 3, 29 n., resp.
14. See the remarkable criticism of the book by Turgot, *Oeuvres,* ed. Schelle, III, 636–41.
15. A.-T., II, 272, 273.
16. *Arrest du Conseil d'Etat du Roi, rendu au sujet du privilége ci-devant accordé pour l'impression de l'Ouvrage intitulé, de l'Esprit* (Paris: Imprimerie royale, 1758); a copy is mounted in B.N., MSS, Fr. 22177, fol. 247. For the *mandement* of the Archbishop of Paris, see Hervier, *Les Ecrivains français jugés par leurs contemporains,* II, 259–60. For the condemnation issued by Pope Clement XIII: *Damnatio et prohibitio Operis, cui Titulus: De l'Esprit . . .* (Rome, 1759); a copy is mounted in B.N., MSS, Fr. 22094, pièce 6. For a very good account of Helvétius' difficulties and woes, see Belin, *Le Mouvement philosophique de 1748 à 1789,* 114–27.
17. Barbier, *Journal,* IV, 307–8.
18. E.g. *Lettre au révérend pere * * *, Jésuite* (n.p., n.d.), 6–7; mounted in B.N., MSS, Fr. 22191, foll. 73–6.
19. Turgot, *Oeuvres,* ed. Schelle, III, 639.
20. *Corr. litt.,* IV, 80. A.-T., I, xvii n.; Virgil W. Topazio, 'Diderot's Supposed Contribution to Helvétius' Works,' *Philological Quarterly,* XXXIII (1954), 319–22.
21. *Arrests de la Cour de Parlement, portant condamnation de plusieurs Livres & autres Ouvrages imprimés. Extrait des registres de Parlement. Du 23 Janvier 1759* (Paris: P. G. Simon, 1759), 2; mounted in B.N., MSS, Fr. 22177, foll. 257–72, and Fr. 22094, pièce 1.
22. See also Palissot's open letter to Fréron (*Année Littéraire,* vol. VIII for 1757, 121–31).
23. Abraham-Joseph de Chaumeix, *Préjugés légitimes contre l'Encyclopédie et essai de réfutation de ce dictionnaire,* 8 vols. (Paris and Brussels, 1758–9); vols. I and II were published in Oct. 1758 (Naves, *Voltaire et l'Encyclopédie,* 64). [Odet-Joseph de Vaux de Giry, Abbé de Saint-Cyr], *Catéchisme et décisions de cas de conscience, à l'usage des Cacouacs, avec un discours du patriarche des Cacouacs, pour la réception d'un nouveau disciple* (Cacopolis, 1758).
24. Augustin de Barruel, *Mémoires pour servir à l'histoire du Jacobinisme,* 4 vols. (London, 1797–8), I, 2, 61, 189–94, *et passim.*
25. *Corr. litt.,* III, 458 (15 Dec. 1757). D'Alembert's manuscript, written in 1760, was pub-

lished by Lucien Brunel, *Les Philosophes et l'Académie française au dix-huitième siècle* (Paris, 1884), 361–6; see esp. 364–5.

26. *Mémoire des libraires associés à l'Encyclopédie*, 4. Cf. Ducros, *Les Encyclopédistes*, 213 n.

27. Cf. H. de Montbas, 'A propos d'un bicentenaire. Les Encyclopédistes n'ont pas voulu la Révolution,' *Revue de Paris*, Nov. 1951, 122–3.

28. A.-T., VII, 167; cf. *Corr. litt.*, III, 357 (1 March 1757).

29. 3, 25 Jan., 28 Feb. 1758 (Rousseau, *Corr. gén.*, III, 252, 274, 294).

30. D'Hémery's entry for 2 Nov. 1758 noted that the *Père de famille* had been published by Lambert, with tacit permission (B.N., MSS, Fr. 22160, fol. 113). Grimm discussed the play in his number for 15 Nov. 1758 (*Corr. litt.*, IV, 47–9).

31. First published by Cru, 472–4, as also by him in 'Lettres inédites de Diderot,' *Revue du XVIIIᵉ Siècle*, III–IV (1915–17), 111–12. Cru read '1753' for '1757,' however. The original is in the B.M., Egerton MSS 19, fol. 46; now available in Diderot, *Corr.*, II, 18–19.

32. *SV*, II, 255–6 (25 July 1765).

33. To Grimm, 13 June 1758 (Sophia Christina Charlotte, Princess of Nassau-Saarbruck, *Concerning the Education of a Prince*, ed. John M. S. Allison [New Haven, 1941], 37–42). Also to Diderot, 15 Nov. 1758 (ibid. 42–3), and to her son, 15 Nov. 1758 (ibid. 44–8). See also Asse, 4–6, 9–10, 13–14, 15–17.

34. Voltaire, ed. Moland, XL, 410–11.

35. A.-T., VII, 182, 180, 182, 181, 184, resp. (my italics).

36. B.N., MSS, Nouv. acq. fr. 1182, fol. 7ᵛ; Diderot, *Concerning the Education of a Prince*, ed. Allison, 34–5.

37. Louis-Anne Lavirotte (1725–59) was also one of the editors of the *Journal des Sçavans* (*Biographie universelle* [*Michaud*], s.v. 'Lavirotte').

38. Asse, 18.

39. Brunetière, 'La Direction de la librairie sous M. de Malesherbes,' *RDM*, 1 Feb. 1882, 595.

40. Asse, 20–21.

41. Diderot to Malesherbes, 20 Oct. 1758 (B.N., MSS, Nouv. acq. fr. 1182, fol. 25ʳ); also Asse, 25.

42. B.N., MSS, Nouv. acq. fr. 1182, fol. 25ᵛ; also Asse, 26.

43. A.-T., VII, 221. One censor objected to the line (A.-T., VII, 244): 'Anges du ciel, prenez cette enfant sous vôtre garde, et conduisez-la' (Asse, 23–4).

44. Asse, 24.

45. B.N., MSS, Nouv. acq. fr. 1182, fol. 25ʳ and 25ᵛ; Asse, 25–6.

46. The ellipses are Diderot's (B.N., MSS, Nouv. acq. fr. 1182, fol. 26ᵛ); also Asse, 27; now available in Diderot, *Corr.*, II, 68–71.

47. Lambert to Malesherbes, 24 Oct. 1758 (Asse, 27–8).

48. Moncrif to Malesherbes, 25 Oct. 1758 (Asse, 28); republished by E. P. Shaw, 'An Unpublished Letter of Moncrif concerning Diderot's "Père de Famille",' *MLN*, LXVII (1952), 424–5.

49. Pierre-Nicolas Bonamy (1694–1770) to Malesherbes (Asse, 29).

50. Malesherbes to Mme de La Marck, 21 Nov. 1758 (B.N., MSS, Nouv. acq. fr. 3344, fol. 281); also in Busnelli, *Diderot et l'Italie*, 277–8.

51. Title pages and epigraphs printed in *Corr. litt.*, XVI, 258; also Delafarge, *La Vie et l'oeuvre de Palissot*, 104–6. The insulting nature of the epigraphs explained by Meaume, *Palissot et les philosophes*, 45–6 nn.

52. Diderot to Malesherbes, 16 Nov. 1758 (*Corr. litt.*, XVI, 258–9).

53. 23 Nov. 1758 (B.N., MSS, Fr. 22160, fol. 118ᵛ).

54. Delafarge, *La Vie et l'oeuvre de Palissot*, 107.

55. B.N., MSS, Nouv. acq. fr. 3344, fol. 274; in Busnelli, *Diderot et l'Italie*, 275.

56. 20 Nov. 1758 (B.N., MSS, Nouv. acq. fr. 3344, foll. 282–3); in Busnelli, 275–6.

57. 20 Nov. 1758 (B.N., MSS, Nouv. acq. fr. 3344, foll. 279–80); in Busnelli, 276–7.

58. 21 Nov. 1758 (B.N., MSS, Nouv. acq. fr. 3344, fol. 281); in Busnelli, 277–8.

59. 21 Nov. 1758 (A.-T., XIX, 454 n.). For an undated letter from Diderot to Suard, written about this period regarding presentation copies of the translated plays as well as a copy of the *Père de famille*, see *Corr. litt.*, XVI, 259–60.

60. Also in A.-T., XIX, 454, and Busnelli, 106-7.
61. Busnelli, 104 n. Cf. *Corr. litt.*, IV, 257-8, and Morellet, *Mémoires*, I, 92.
62. *Corr. litt.*, IV, 259.
63. Delafarge, *La Vie et l'oeuvre de Palissot*, 109.
64. Quérard, *Les Supercheries littéraires dévoilées*, III, col. 1129.
65. 25 March 1781 (Dieckmann, *Inventaire*, 245).
66. 24 May 1759 (Rousseau, *Corr. gén.*, IV, 255). Cf. Deleyre to Malesherbes, 23 Nov., and Malesherbes to Deleyre, 28 Nov. 1758 (Busnelli, 278-9).
67. See Morley, *Diderot and the Encyclopaedists*, I, 17.

CHAPTER 24

1. In English there appeared (1) *The Father, A Comedy. Translated from the French of Monsieur Diderot* (Lynn, 1770); (2) *The Family Picture. A Play Taken from the French of Mons. Diderot's Pere de famille* (London, 1781); (3) John Burgoyne, *The Heiress* (London, 1786); and (4) Charles Stearns, *Dramatic Dialogues for the Use of Schools* (Leominster [Mass.], 1798), 281-98: 'The Father of a Family' (follows Diderot's plot very closely but without any allusion to his having been the author). Regarding Burgoyne's play, the *Monthly Review*, LXXIV (Jan.-June 1786), 207-13, reviewed *The Heiress* and gave Diderot all the credit for the plot (209). The *Père de famille* also influenced Charles Jenner's *The Man of Family* (1771) and Sophia Lee's *The Chapter of Accidents* (1780). Cf. David Erskine Baker, *Biographia Dramatica*, 3 vols. in four parts (London, 1812), II, 289; John Genest, *Some Account of the English Stage, from the Restoration in 1660 to 1830*, 10 vols. (Bath, 1832), VI, 381; and Allardyce Nicoll, *A History of Late Eighteenth Century Drama, 1750-1800* (Cambridge [Eng.], 1927), 120.
2. A.-T., VII, 309.
3. A.-T., VII, 150-51.
4. Mme de Vandeul, xxxviii.
5. A.-T., VII, 325.
6. Cf. Louis Ducros, *Diderot: l'homme et l'écrivain* (Paris, 1894), 264.
7. *SV*, III, 202 (2 Sept. 1769).
8. Cf. Arthur Eloesser, *Das bürgerliche Drama: Seine Geschichte im 18. und 19. Jahrhundert* (Berlin, 1898), 73.
9. *Année Littéraire*, vol. III for 1761, 303.
10. Trahard, *Les Maîtres de la sensibilité française au XVIIIᵉ siècle*, II, 205; Gaiffe, *Le Drame en France au XVIIIᵉ siècle*, 260.
11. A.-T., VII, 199, 230. Diderot said he had once overheard this ejaculation in a similar situation in real life (Salverte, *Eloge philosophique de Denys Diderot*, 102-3).
12. Eloesser, *Das bürgerliche Drama*, 71.
13. A.-T., VII, 336.
14. Diderot to Le Bret, 29 Nov. 1757 (Diderot, *Corr.*, II, 19).
15. Joseph de La Porte and S.-R. Chamfort, *Dictionnaire dramatique . . .* , 3 vols. (Paris, 1776), II, 398-401.
16. A.-T., VII, 322-6. Cf. Edna C. Fredrick, *The Plot and Its Construction in Eighteenth Century Criticism of French Comedy* (Bryn Mawr, 1934), 69, 74.
17. Cf. La Harpe, *Lycée*, x, 401-4.
18. A.-T., VII, 232, 210, 284.
19. Asse, 35.
20. 28 Feb. 1757 (Voltaire, ed. Moland, XXXIX, 181-2).
21. 16 Nov. 1758 (ibid. 532-3).
22. 27 Dec. 1758 (ibid. 563).
23. Littré, *Dictionnaire de la langue française*, s.v. 'Poésie.'
24. See Bonamy to Malesherbes (Asse, 32). The passage Bonamy objected to, and which may indeed have been modified (Asse, 36), appears to be one regarding the imagination (A.-T., VII, 333). Diderot also quotes Helvétius by name (ibid. 353).

25. A.-T., VII, 311, 367; cf. *Journal Encyclopédique*, vol. VIII for 1758, 3e partie, 139 (15 Dec. 1758). Felix Vexler, *Studies in Diderot's Esthetic Naturalism* (New York, 1922), 71.

26. A.-T., VII, 400. Mme Riccoboni's letter was dated 18 Oct. 1758, and his reply 27 Nov. (Dieckmann, *Inventaire*, 107); they were first published in the Brière edition (1821).

27. A.-T., VII, 399, 402.

28. A.-T., VII, 400, 376. Cf. Max Aghion, *Le Théâtre à Paris au XVIIIe siècle* (Paris, [1926]), 418–23.

29. A.-T., VII, 361–2.

30. A.-T., VII, 374.

31. Gustave Lanson, *Esquisse d'une histoire de la tragédie française* (New York, 1920), 125–6.

32. A.-T., VII, 398. Cf. ibid. 374. Melcher, *Stage Realism in France between Diderot and Antoine*, 31–2, points out that in Diderot's view the setting is an integral part of the action.

33. Green, *Eighteenth-Century France*, 164–7; H. Carrington Lancaster, *The Comédie Française, 1701–1774: Plays, Actors, Spectators, Finances* (*Transactions of the American Philosophical Society*, New Series, XLI, Part 4 [1951]), 594, 797; *Corr. litt.*, IV, 111, 118. These last items were very likely written by Diderot himself, for Grimm was in Geneva at the time.

34. A.-T., VII, 310.

35. Ducros, *Diderot*, 265.

36. Aghion, *Le Théâtre à Paris au XVIIIe siècle*, 39. Cf. Gustave Larroumet, 'Diderot. — Sa théorie dramatique. — "Le Père de famille",' *Revue des Cours et Conférences*, VIII (1899–1900), 2e série, 837.

37. *Das Theater des Herrn Diderot*, 2 vols. (Berlin, 1760), II: '*Vorrede des Uebersetzers*' (separate pagination), 3ᵛ.

38. A.-T., VII, 320.

39. E.g. Trahard, *Les Maîtres de la sensibilité française au XVIIIe siècle*, II, 49–286, esp. ch. iii: 'La Sensibilité de Diderot' (49–70). But see the criticism of Trahard by Herbert Dieckmann, 'Zur Interpretation Diderots,' *Romanische Forschungen*, LIII (1939), 52–3 nn.

40. Cf. Arthur M. Wilson, 'Sensibility in France in the Eighteenth Century: A Study in Word History,' *French Quarterly*, XIII (1931), 35–46.

41. A.-T., VII, 404; cf. Venturi, *Jeunesse*, 80–82.

42. A.-T., VII, 390. An Aristes had also figured as the hero of *La Promenade du sceptique*.

43. A.-T., VII, 339.

44. A.-T., VII, 371, 372.

45. Cf. Hubert Gillot, *Denis Diderot* (Paris, 1937), 308–10.

46. See Dieckmann, 'Diderot's Conception of Genius,' *JHI*, 151–82, esp. 166.

47. A.-T., VII, 333.

48. A.-T., VII, 310.

49. A.-T., VII, 403.

50. A.-T., VII, 312.

51. Bonamy to Malesherbes (Asse, 31–2).

52. A.-T., VII, 313, 369.

CHAPTER 25

1. *Corr. litt.*, IV, 59. Turgot, *Oeuvres*, ed. Schelle, I, 594; also in Diderot, *Corr.*, II, 110.

2. Diderot, *Corr.*, II, 119.

3. *Arrests de la Cour de Parlement . . .* (1759), I, 2, 13. Joly de Fleury's *réquisitoire* is quoted in part in Hervier, *Les Ecrivains français jugés par leurs contemporains*, II, 261–2. The allegation of conspiracy was repeated (but without naming the *Encyclopédie*) in the *Censure de la faculté de théologie de Paris, contre le livre qui a pour titre, De l'Esprit* [11 May 1759] (Paris: J. B. Garnier, 1759), 8, mounted in B.N., MSS, Fr. 22094, pièce 10.

4. Belin, *Le Mouvement philosophique de 1748 à 1789*, 129. The edition of the *Pensées philosophiques* attacked was the *Etrennes des esprits forts* (London [Amsterdam], 1757): cf. Diderot, *Pensées philosophiques*, ed. Niklaus (1950), 50.

5. *Arrests de la Cour de Parlement . . .* (1759), 18.

6. A.-T., XIV, 462–3; cf. *Encyc.*, I, xviij.

7. Herbert Dieckmann, writing in *RR*, XXXIV (1943), 176; Gaudin, *Les Lettres anglaises dans*

l'Encyclopédie, 207. A contrary and more conventional view in Grosclaude, *Un Audacieux Message*, 152–6.

8. 'Réponse au Prospectus de M. Fromageot,' 2 March 1768 (Douglas H. Gordon's Extra Volume, foll. 64–5).

9. Barbier, *Journal*, IV, 302. A facsimile of the warrant served upon Le Breton on 25 Jan. 1759, in Gordon and Torrey, *The Censoring of Diderot's* Encyclopédie, facing 20.

10. *Arrests de la Cour de Parlement* . . . (1759), 30; Barbier, *Journal*, IV, 304–5. The text of the *arrêt* of 6 Feb. 1759 also in [Louis Chaudon], *Dictionnaire anti-philosophique* (Avignon, 1767), 415–18.

11. Malesherbes, *Mémoire sur la liberté de la presse*, 93.

12. The first two volumes were published in Oct. 1758; the other six in Nov. 1758 and Jan. 1759 (Naves, *Voltaire et l'Encyclopédie*, 64).

13. Also published in 1759 were [Père Bonhomme], *L'Eloge de l'Encyclopédie et des Encyclopédistes* (The Hague, 1759), a new edition, brought up to date by references to *De l'Esprit*, of the *Réflexions d'un Franciscain* (see *supra*, ch. 12, n. 39); David Renaud Boullier, *Pièces philosophiques et littéraires* (n.p., 1759), a collection of earlier papers critical of the Encyclopedists' tendency towards materialism, by a courteous but rather dull Protestant writer; and *Lettres sur le VIIᵉ volume de l'Encyclopédie* (n.p., 1759) (Mazarine 41774, pièce 6). This last took umbrage (p. 16) that the *Encyclopédie* (VII, 285b) had praised Julian the Apostate; was much upset (pp. 31–6) by D'Alembert's article on 'Frères de la Charité' (*Encyc.*, VII, 301) and De Jaucourt's on 'Franciscains' (ibid. 284); and asserted (pp. 17–18) that the article 'Franconie' praised the Free-Masons. This article, signed by De Jaucourt (ibid. 287) does not even mention the Masons, but a brief article of fourteen lines on 'Francs-Maçons' (ibid. 281b), in itself an avowed and indeed tolerably close translation (cf. Chambers, *Cyclopaedia*, s.v. 'Masons, *Free* or *Accepted*'), states that 'Tout ce qu'on peut pénétrer de leurs mysteres ne paroît que louable . . .'

14. *Corr. litt.*, IV, 59; Le Gras, 126.

15. 18 Feb. 1759 (B.N., MSS, Nouv. acq. fr. 3348, fol. 170).

16. Barbier, *Chronique* . . . (1885), VII, 129–30.

17. Barbier, *Journal*, IV, 303; Belin, *Le Mouvement philosophique de 1748 à 1789*, 130 n. See Malesherbes' five memoranda for the Dauphin (Chrétien-Guillaume Lamoignon de Malesherbes, *Mémoires sur la librairie et sur la liberté de la presse* [Paris, 1809], IV). Frequent allusions (ibid. 5, 7–9, 15–17, *et passim*) reveal how much Malesherbes disliked the Parlement's action.

18. Monod, *De Pascal à Chateaubriand*, 365; Belin, *Le Commerce des livres prohibés*, 113; Belin, *Le Mouvement philosophique de 1748 à 1789*, 128, 130.

19. *Corr. litt.*, IV, 81 (15 Feb. 1759).

20. Archives . . . Haute-Marne, Fonds II E 16; a photograph published in *Cahiers Haut-Marnais*, No. 24 (1ᵉʳ trimestre 1951), Supplément illustré. Voltaire, ed. Moland, XL, 45.

21. *Arrest du Conseil d'Etat du Roi* . . . *Du 8 Mars 1759* (Paris: Imprimerie royale, 1759), 2; mounted in B.N., MSS, Fr. 22177, foll. 273–4; complete text in A.-T., XIII, 118–19.

22. Barbier, *Journal*, IV, 310; A.-T., XIII, 118.

23. *Corr. litt.*, III, 457.

24. *Arrest du Conseil d'Etat du Roi* . . . *Du 21 Juillet 1759* (Paris: Imprimerie royale, 1759); mounted in B.N., MSS, Fr. 22177, fol. 324; text in A.-T., XIII, 119–20.

25. Jean Fourastié, 'L'*Encyclopédie* et la notion de progrès économique,' *AUP*, XXII ([Oct.] 1952), numéro spécial, 144.

26. Gustave Lanson, *RHLF*, IX (1902), 152.

27. Diderot, *Corr.*, II, 120, 121–2. For the new financial terms, see ibid. 121.

28. Ibid. 122.

29. Ibid. 120.

30. Morellet, *Mémoires*, I, 88. Diderot wrote Grimm that he suspected Turgot, D'Alembert, Bourgelat, and Morellet of being in a plot against the *Encyclopédie* (Diderot, *Corr.*, II, 130).

31. Voltaire to Bertrand, 22 March 1759 (Voltaire, ed. Moland, XL, 65).

32. *Corr. litt.*, IX, 253.

33. Diderot, *Corr.*, II, 122.

34. *Mémoire pour Abraham Chaumeix, contre les prétendus philosophes Diderot et d'Alembert* (Amsterdam, 1759).

35. Diderot, *Corr.*, II, 122–3. It was probably Diderot who, in Grimm's absence, described this pamphlet for the *Corr. litt.*, IV, 108–111; see Dieckmann, *Inventaire*, 16.

36. 7 April 1759 (Diderot, *Corr.*, II, 117). Antoine-Alexandre Barbier, the eminent bibliographer, declared in his 'Remarques sur la Correspondance de MM. Grimm et Diderot,' in Friedrich Melchior Grimm, *Supplément à la Correspondance littéraire de MM. Grimm et Diderot* (Paris, 1814), 323, that Diderot was the author.

37. Diderot, *Corr.*, II, 123.

38. Mme de Vandeul, xlv.

39. Lester Gilbert Crocker, 'The Problem of Malesherbes' Intervention,' by L. G. Krakeur, *MLQ*, II (1941), 551–8. Malesherbes remarked in his *Mémoire sur la liberté de la presse*, 53, that it was common to allow a publisher to publish a book 'secretly,' with the understanding that if a search and seizure had to be made, warning would be given in advance. The Diderot incident does not seem to be different in essence from such cases.

40. Diderot, *Corr.*, II, 140.

41. Ibid. 135 (10 May 1759). A critic writing in a review edited by T. S. Eliot called a paragraph of this letter 'almost a piece of music' (Francis Birrell, 'Things Diderot Could Do,' *Criterion*, XII [1932–3], 633).

42. Diderot, *Corr.*, II, 119.

43. Henry Tronchin, *Un Médecin du XVIIIᵉ siècle: Théodore Tronchin (1709–1781)* (Paris, 1906), 375–6; also Diderot, *Corr.*, II, 139.

44. Diderot, *Corr.*, II, 124–6, 138, 140, 146, 151. Diderot was so fond of the Apocalypse-mystery phrase that he used it again several years later in his essay *Sur les femmes* (1772): see A.-T., II, 260.

45. Diderot, *Corr.*, II, 150–51, 140, 150, 156 resp. Contrary to Babelon (*CI*, I, 42 n.), the correct date is 3 June (George R. Havens, 'The Chronology of Diderot's Journey to Langres in 1759,' *MLN*, LIX [1944], 33).

46. Diderot, *Corr.*, II, 157.

47. Ibid. 165.

48. Pierre Mesnard, 'Sophie Volland et la maturité de Diderot,' *Revue des Sciences Humaines*, Jan.–March 1949, 12, 20. Regarding the Freudian significance of the death of Diderot's father, see ibid. 13; also Pierre Mesnard, *Le Cas Diderot: Etude de caractérologie littéraire* (Paris, 1952), 163–76.

49. Paul Hazard, 'Les Origines philosophiques de l'homme de sentiment,' *RR*, XXVIII (1937), 336.

50. Diderot, *Corr.*, II, 167.

51. Ibid. 164.

52. Morley, *Diderot and the Encyclopaedists*, I, 112; similarly, Jean Thomas, 'Le Rôle de Diderot dans l'*Encyclopédie*,' *AUP*, XXII ([Oct.] 1952), numéro spécial, 14–15, 25; also Crocker, *La Correspondance de Diderot*, by L. G. Krakeur, 37.

53. Paul Vernière, 'L'Encyclopédie de Diderot et d'Alembert,' *Revue de Synthèse*, XXVI (1950), 148–9.

54. A.-T., XIII, 175.

CHAPTER 26

1. Diderot, *Corr.*, II, 186; cf. George R. Havens, 'The Chronology of Diderot's Journey to Langres in 1759,' *MLN*, LIX (1944), 34.
2. Diderot, *Corr.*, II, 195, 188.
3. Diderot, *Corr.*, II, 213. Black clothes (ibid., 225).
4. Diderot, *Corr.*, II, 207–8.
5. Diderot, *Corr.*, II, 164.
6. Diderot, *Corr.*, II, 201.
7. Diderot, *Corr.*, II, 121; for a record of payments to Diderot in accordance with these terms, see May, 71–6; also Jacques Proust, *Diderot et* l'Encyclopédie (Paris, 1962), 99–100. For the contract of 1754, see Part I, 219–20.
8. Le Gras, 132. David wrote to Malesherbes from Amsterdam on 9 Aug. 1759 that the loans (1500 livres at The Hague, 1000 livres at Leyden) were personal and not for the *Encyclopédie* (B.N., MSS, Nouv. acq. fr. 3348, foll. 120–1). But does one go clear to Leyden from Paris to establish credit for sums as small as this? Perhaps the publishers wanted the French authorities to fear that arrangements might be in the making for completing the *Encyclopédie* outside France (Proust, *Diderot et* l'Encyclopédie, 74–5; Jacques Proust, *L'Encyclopédie* [Paris, 1965], 65–6).
9. Diderot, *Corr.*, II, 234.
10. Diderot, *Corr.*, II, 119, 139, 157.
11. Diderot, Corr., II, 124; Arthur M. Wilson, 'The Dowry of Diderot's Wife,' *FR*, XXXIII (1959–60), 286–7.
12. Diderot, *Corr.*, II, 154, 183.
13. Diderot, *Corr.*, II, 186–7. Traveling in the Volland carriage (ibid., II, 198); inventory description of what may have been this very vehicle (ibid., II, 182).
14. Suzanne Curchod Necker, *Mélanges extraits des manuscrits de Mme Necker*, 3 vols. (Paris, An VI [1798]), II, 246.
15. Diderot, *Corr.*, II, 103.
16. Diderot, *Corr.*, II, 129, 154.
17. Diderot, *Corr.*, II, 178.
18. *Encyc.*, VIII, 684a, s.v. 'Indissoluble' (A.-T., XV, 205).
19. Diderot, *Corr.*, II, 125, 138, 140, 147, 149, 154.
20. Diderot, *Corr.*, II, 192.
21. Diderot, *Corr.*, II, 134.
22. Diderot, *Corr.*, II, 125, 147, 193, 196, 233; ibid., III, 63, 69, 74; cf. Georges May, *Diderot et "La Religieuse"* (Paris and New Haven, 1954), 142–4.
23. Diderot, *Corr.*, II, 200, 204, 210. Four liards made a sou, twenty sous made a livre.
24. Diderot, *Corr.*, II, 210. For an analysis of the value of Diderot's inheritance from his father, see Proust, *Diderot et* l'Encyclopédie, 101–4.
25. This document is in the Archives départementales de la Haute-Marne (Chaumont), série II-E-4, pièce 4 (Paris. Bibliothèque Nationale, *Diderot et l'Encyclopédie: Exposition commemorative*, ed. Georges Huard [Paris, 1951], item 86); it has been published by Hubert Gautier, *Le Père de Diderot, 1685–1759.* . . . (Moulins, 1933), 24 *et sqq.* For information regarding various properties owned by Didier Diderot, see Louis-François Marcel, *Le Frère de Diderot* (Paris, 1913), 70–1 nn.; cf. Diderot, *Corr.*, II, 186, 209. Return to Paris (Havens, 'The Chronology of Diderot's Journey to Langres in 1759,' *MLN*, LIX, 34–7).
26. Diderot, *Corr.*, II, 210, 196.
27. Diderot, *Corr.*, II, 219–20.
28. Diderot, *Corr.*, II, 188, 218; cf. ibid., 198.
29. Diderot, *Corr.*, II, 188, 204–5.

30. Diderot, *Corr.*, II, 202; cf. Marcel, *Le Frère de Diderot*, 19–20 and nn.; also Louis-François Marcel, *Un Oncle de Diderot: Antoine-Thomas Diderot de l'Ordre des Frères prêcheurs (1682–1756)* (Liguge [Vienne], 1930), 11.

31. Diderot, *Corr.*, II, 221, 222.

32. Diderot, *Corr.*, II, 217.

33. Diderot, *Corr.*, II, 228–9. Cf. R.-L. Wagner, ' "Ces vordes me charment" (Diderot),' *Revue de Linguistique Romane*, July–Dec. 1967, 239–45.

34. Diderot, *Corr.*, II, 187.

35. Diderot, *Corr.*, II, 188, 189.

36. Diderot, *Corr.*, II, 208.

37. Diderot, *Corr.*, II, 147.

CHAPTER 27

1. A.-T., XIII, 119–20. A copy of this *Arrest du Conseil d'Etat du Roi . . . Du 21 Juillet 1759* (Paris: Imprimerie royale, 1759) in B.N., MSS, Fr. 22177, fol. 324.

2. *Corr. litt.*, IV, 97 (1 April 1759).

3. Pierre Grosclaude, 'Malesherbes et l'Encyclopedie,' *RScH*, No. 91 (July–Sept. 1958), 372; also Pierre Grosclaude, *Malesherbes, témoin et interprète de son temps* (Paris, [1961]), 134. Malesherbes wrote to D'Hémery, Inspector of Publications, on 15 July 1759, asking what was the original price of subscription and how much the subscribers had already paid (Centre International de Synthèse, Paris, *L'Encyclopédie et les Encyclopédistes: Exposition organisée par le Centre international de synthèse* [Paris, 1932], 22).

4. Grosclaude, art. cit., 366–8, 370, 372; Grosclaude, *Malesherbes, témoin et interprète de son temps*, 131, 132, 133 n., 134–6. The subscribers (David to Malesherbes, Amsterdam, 6 Aug. 1759 [B.N., MSS, Nouv. acq. fr. 3345, fol. 116]). For text of Malesherbes' letter to Marc-Antoine Laugier, editor of the *Gazette de France*, 30 July 1759, ordering him not to publish the arrêt of 21 July regarding the 72 livres, see Wolfgang Herrmann, *Laugier and Eighteenth Century French Theory* (London, 1962), 206; Laugier's reply, 1 Aug. 1759 (ibid., 206–7). The arrêt of 21 July 1759 did appear, however, in the *Annonces, Affiches, et Avis Divers* for 2 Aug. 1759 (Proust, *L'Encyclopédie*, 66).

5. B.N., MSS, Fr. 22120, pièce 38, foll. 114–5; printed in *Encyc., Planches*, I, 6; and II, 10.

6. *Mémoire à consulter pour les libraires associés à l'Encyclopedie* (Paris: Le Breton, 1770), 5; cf. Le Gras, *Diderot et l'Encyclopédie*, 133; and Gordon and Torrey, 20. For the financial arrangements, see Proust, *Diderot et l'Encyclopédie*, 56–7; and Ralph H. Bowen, 'The *Encyclopédie* as a Business Venture,' in *From the Ancien Régime to the Popular Front: Essays in the History of Modern France in Honor of Shepard B. Clough*, ed. Charles K. Warner (New York, 1969), 17.

7. *Mémoire pour P. J. Fr. Luneau de Boisjermain, servant de réponse à un Mémoire du Sieur Le Breton & des Associés, intitulé: Dernier Etat des choses à juger, Pièces justificatives* (Paris: Knapen, s.d.), *Pièces justificatives*, 17. For further evidence of subscribers' attempts to secure the refund, see the conclusive remarks in John Lough, 'Luneau de Boisjermain v. the Publishers of the Encyclopédie,' *SVEC*, XXIII (1963), 142–4.

8. *Condamnation et prohibition d'un ouvrage divisé en plusieurs volumes, ayant pour titre: Encyclopédie, . . .* (Rome, 1759), 3, 8. [Mazarine Library, Paris, 41191, pièce 6]; a different edition in B.N., MSS, Fr. 22094, foll. 99–101, pièce 19: *Damnatio et prohibitio operis in plures tomos distributi, cujus est titulus: Encyclopédie* (Rome, 1759); for a photograph of the document issued by the Spanish Inquisition banning the *Encyclopédie* on 9 Oct. 1759, see the frontispiece of Marcelin Defourneaux, *L'Inquisition espagnole et les livres français au XVIIIᵉ siècle* (Paris, 1963).

Regarding the Lucca edition (Diderot, *Corr.*, III, 338; John Lough, *Essays on the Encyclopédie of Diderot and d'Alembert* [London, 1968], 21–9; Salvatore Bongi, 'L'Enciclopedia in Lucca,' *Archivio Storico Italiano*, 3rd series, XVIII [1873], 64–90; Giulio Natali, 'Enciclopedie italiane del Settecento,' *Nuova rivista storica*, III [1919], 97–103; Ettore Levi-Malvano, 'Les Editions toscanes de l' "Encyclopédie",' *RLC*, III [1923], 222–8; Hermann Karl Weinert, 'Frankreich in der Sicht italienischer Enzyklopädisten des 18. Jahrhunderts,'

ZFSL, LXVI [1956], 223–30; the same, 'La Repubblica di Lucca presentata nell'edizione lucchese dell'*Encyclopédie* di Diderot,' in *Studi in onore di Angelo Monteverdi* [Modena, 1959], 911–22). The Lucca edition and papal politics in 1759 are brilliantly analyzed by Robert Shackleton, *The 'Encyclopédie' and the Clerks* (Oxford, 1970), 12–20. See also his 'The *Encyclopédie* as an International Phenomenon' in American Philosophical Society, *Proceedings*, CXIV (1970), 392–3.

9. *Nouvelles Ecclésiastiques*, 23 Oct. 1759, 173–4. The *Journal Chrétien* published the text of the papal condemnation in its number for Jan. 1760 (Lough, *Essays on the* Encyclopédie *of Diderot and d'Alembert*, 387–8).

10. Part I, 241. As early as Dec. 1750 the *Journal des Sçavans* had mentioned that the drawings were beautiful, 'dont nous avons vu une partie très-considérable. . . .' (p. 2626). The 2000 drawings (undated memorandum from the publishers to Chancellor Lamoignon, evidently in 1759 [B.N., MSS, Nouv. acq. fr. 3348, fol. 172; cf. *Corr. litt.*, IV, 97]). 'Not a single engraving' (B.N., MSS, Nouv. acq. fr. 3348, fol. 144^v; also B.N., MSS, Nouv. acq. fr. 3345, fol. 183^v–4; the publishers' letter to Malesherbes, 28 July 1759 [B.N., MSS, Nouv. acq. fr. 3348, foll. 137–8] implicitly admits the allegation.

11. *Année Littéraire*, vol. VII for 1759, 341–51, esp. 346–9. Patte's receipt (ibid., vol. II for 1760, 48; *Observateur Littéraire*, vol. I for 1760, 284]). The publishers' account book shows a payment to Patte of 600 livres (May, 71).

12. Part I, 242.

13. *Année Littéraire*, vol. VII for 1759, 345–6.

14. *Observateur Littéraire*, vol. V for 1759, 216; a similar 'Avis aux souscripteurs de l'Encyclopédie & autres' appeared in the *Mercure de France*, vol. I for 1760, 176.

15. *Observateur Littéraire*, vol. I for 1760, 273–4.

16. Registre de l'Académie des Sciences, 1759, fol. 810 (séance du 12 déc. 1759).

17. Registre de l'Académie des Sciences, 1759, foll. 817–8 (séance du 19 déc. 1759). These facts published in *Année Littéraire*, vol. I for 1760, 250–3; and *Observateur Littéraire*, vol. I for 1760, 269–73.

18. *Encyc., Planches*, I (1762), 6.

19. Ibid., and in every other volume of the plates as they successively appeared; *Corr. litt.*, IV, 227 (1 April 1760). 'On sent bien que les réponses vagues . . . étaient des paroles diplomatiques, réponses que l'on sait faire à toutes les époques de scandale public' (Mae Mathieu, *Pierre Patte, sa vie, son oeuvre* [Paris, 1940], 38).

20. Diderot, *Corr.*, III, 22 (23 or 25 Feb. 1760); cf. ibid., 19, nn. 9, 10; also Jean Torlais, *Réaumur, un esprit encyclopédique en dehors de* "l'Encyclopédie" (Paris, 1936), 255–6 n.

21. Jacques Proust, 'La Documentation technique de Diderot dans l' "Encyclopédie",' *RHLF*, LVII (1957), 345. For an excellent description of the Academy's publication, see Arthur H. Cole and George B. Watts, *The Handicrafts of France as Recorded in the* Descriptions des Arts et Métiers, *1761–1788* (Boston, 1952); also Bertrand Gille, 'L'*Encyclopédie*, dictionnaire technique,' in *RHS, L' "Encyclopédie" et le progrès des sciences et des techniques*, ed. Suzanne Delorme and René Taton (Paris, 1952), 203–7; also Maurice Daumas and René Tresse, 'La *Description des Arts et Métiers* de l'Académie des Sciences et le sort de ses planches gravées en taille douce,' *RHS*, VII (1954), 163–71. Very useful is Jean-Pierre Seguin, 'Courte histoire des planches de l'*Encyclopédie*,' in *L'Univers de l'Encyclopédie*, ed. Roland Barthes, Robert Mauzi, and Jean-Pierre Seguin (Paris, 1964), 23–34.

22. Embarrassment of the Academy of Sciences (Seguin, art. cit., 28). For Diderot's nomination to the Academy of Sciences, the following is a transcription from the Registre de l'Académie des Sciences, 1757, fol. 647 (séance du 23 déc. 1757): 'L'academie ayant procedé suivant la forme ordinaire à l'election de deux sujets pour la place d'associé mechanicien vacante par la promotion de Monsieur l'Abbé Nollet, la pluralité des voix a été pour Messieurs de Vaucanson et Diderot.' Thieriot wrote to Voltaire on 27 Dec. 1757 about the Jesuits that 'On prétend, et il est très vraisemblable, que le fiel de ces gens de bien ne s'est fermenté si violemment que pour empêcher M. Diderot d'être reçeu à l'académie des Sciences' (Besterman, No. 6839). On 7 Jan. 1758 the Comte de Saint-Florentin wrote to the secretary of the Académie des Sciences, 'Je vous donne avis, Monsieur, que le Roi a

nommé M. de Vaucanson pour remplir la place d'associé mécanicien. . . .' (Registre de l'Académie des Sciences, 1758, foll. 1–2). Diderot's nomination reported, not quite accurately, in Jean Torlais, *Un Physicien au siècle des Lumières, l'Abbé Nollet, 1700–1770* (Paris, 1954), 203. On 8 Feb. 1749 the Académie des Sciences had voted on Diderot as a candidate for 'Adjoint Mécanicien' but had not chosen him (James Doolittle, 'A Would-be Philosophe: Jean Philippe Rameau,' *PMLA*, LXXIV [1959], 236 n.).

23. B.N., MSS, Nouv. acq. fr. 3345, fol. 184ʳ, in Malesherbes' own unmistakable and almost illegible hand.

24. *Année Littéraire*, vol. II for 1760, 45–8, esp. 46–8; *Corr. litt.*, IV, 222 (1 April 1760).

25. George B. Watts, 'The *Encyclopédie* and the *Descriptions des arts et métiers*,' *FR*, XXV (1951–2), 447; cf. Pierre Grosclaude, *Un Audacieux message: L'Encyclopédie* (Paris, 1951), 97 and n.

26. *Année Littéraire*, vol. I for 1760, 255–7. Later issues documented the point by dissecting the *Encyclopédie* articles 'Ardoise' (ibid., vol. I for 1762, 208–14, esp. 213–4); 'Charbon de bois' (ibid., vol. VIII for 1760, 51–60); and 'Ancre' (ibid., vol. VIII for 1760, 254–62).

27. *Année Littéraire*, vol. VII for 1759, 345. Regarding the Patte affair, see Proust, *Diderot et l'Encyclopédie*, 50–1, 54, 69; also Proust, *L'Encyclopédie*, 35–7, 67–9.

28. Proust, 'La Documentation technique de Diderot dans l' *"Encyclopédie"*,' *RHLF*, LVII, 341–6. See also Seguin, art. cit., 29–33, esp. 31: 'Donc, Diderot a menti.'

29. Besterman, No. 7942 (22 Dec. 1759).

30. *Corr. litt.*, IV, 222–3 (1 April 1760).

31. Georges Huard, 'Les Planches de l'*Encyclopédie* et celles de la *Description des Arts et Métiers* de l'Académie des Sciences,' in *RHS*, L' *"Encyclopédie" et le progrès des sciences et des techniques*, ed. Delorme and Taton, 43; cf. Mathieu, *Patte*, 353–5, for a list of the Academy plates drawn, engraved, or retouched by Patte.

32. Diderot, *Salons*, III, 279.

33. Diderot, *Corr.*, XI, 150, 151 (31 Aug. 1771). The plates illustrating the great Montargis paper mills are reproduced and easily available in the excellent edition edited by Charles Coulston Gillispie, *A Diderot Pictorial Encyclopedia of Trades and Industry, Manufacturing and the Technical Arts in Plates Selected from 'L'Encyclopédie, ou Dictionnaire Raisonné des Sciences, des Arts et des Métiers' of Denis Diderot*, 2 vols. (New York, 1959), II, plates 359–68.

34. *Corr. litt.*, IV, 223 (1 April 1760).

35. *Corr. litt.*, V, 22; also ibid., IV, 493 (1 Dec. 1761); cf. Louis Petit de Bachaumont, *Mémoires secrets pour servir à l'histoire de la république des lettres en France*, 36 vols. (London, 1777–89), I, 25 (19 Jan. 1762). Regarding this source, see Robert S. Tate, Jr., *Petit de Bachaumont: His Circle and the* Mémoires secrets (*SVEC*, LXV [1968], esp. 161–201); also Claude Bellanger, Jacques Godechot, Pierre Guiral, and Fernand Terrou, *Histoire générale de la presse française*, I (Paris, 1969), 183–5.

36. Published, respectively, in A.-T., VIII, 5–15 (*Le Shérif*); 245–56 (*Le Train du monde, ou Les Moeurs honnêtes comme elles le sont*); 261–3 (*Madame de Linan*); 337–8 (*L'Infortunée, ou Les Suites d'une grande passion*). Diderot mentions all except *Le Shérif* to Grimm, 20 or 21 July 1759 (Diderot, *Corr.*, II, 176), 'sans compter ce *Socrate* que vous me condamnez à refaire.' Cf. A.-T., VII, 381–5; and Jean Seznec, *Essais sur Diderot et l'antiquité* (Oxford, 1957), 15–7. Out of date because of subsequent discoveries of Diderot texts is Fritz Beck, *Die dramatischen Entwürfe Denis Diderots* (Kallmünz, 1932); cf. ibid., 61–5, 13–6, 53–8, 66–7.

37. Diderot, *Corr.*, II, 126.

38. Diderot, *Corr.*, II, 176.

39. Diderot, *Corr.*, II, 128.

40. *Corr. litt.*, IV, 113–4 (1 June 1759), 118–9 (15 June 1759); H. Carrington Lancaster, *The Comédie Française, 1701–1774: Plays, Actors, Spectators, Finances*, in American Philosophical Society, *Transactions*, New Series, XLI, part 4 (1951), 794. These pages in the *Corr. litt.* should be added to the list published by Joseph R. Smiley, 'A List of Diderot's Articles for Grimm's *Correspondance Littéraire*,' *RR*, XLII (1951), 189–97. On occasion Diderot had previously reviewed plays for Grimm, as, for instance, Guymond de la

Touche's *L'Iphigénie en Tauride* (*Corr. litt.*, III, 394–6 [1 Aug. 1757]; also published in A.-T., VIII, 427–9).

41. *Corr. litt.*, IV, 118; Lancaster, op. cit., 797.

42. Diderot, *Corr.*, II, 146. (Roth dates this letter 2 June 1759, but Paul Vernière suggests [*RHLF*, LIX (1959), 104], that the date should be 26 May; this is confirmed by Lancaster, op. cit., [*supra*, n. 40], 794.) The complete text of Diderot's report to Grimm published by Herbert Dieckmann, *Diderot und Goldoni* [*Schriften und Vorträge des Petrarca-Instituts Köln*, XVI] (Krefeld, 1961), 37–9.

43. A.-T., VIII, 430–8; quotations, respectively, 432, 433, 434, 437, 436. 'J'ai passé la nuit à lire sa tragédie . . .' (Diderot, *Corr.*, II, 146 [26 May 1759 (see preceding note for the dating)]). The autograph MS of this critique is in B.N., MSS, Nouv. acq. fr. 24932, foll. 51–6; cf. Herbert Dieckmann, *Inventaire du Fonds Vandeul et Inédits de Diderot* (Geneva, 1951), 14–5.

44. Diderot, *Corr.*, II, 172.

45. A.-T., VIII, 3–15. Regarding the manuscript, now accessible at B.N., MSS, Nouv. acq. fr. 13722, see Dieckmann, *Inventaire*, 9. See the valuable article by Jacques Proust, 'A propos du "Shérif",' *Cahiers Haut-Marnais*, No. 75 (4ᵉ trimestre 1963), 162–70; also Raymond Joly, *Deux Etudes sur la préhistoire de réalisme: Diderot, Rétif de la Bretonne* (Quebec, 1969), 42–3.

46. Diderot, *Corr.*, II, 150.

47. Diderot, *Corr.*, II, 167, 171.

48. Diderot, *Corr.*, II, 174–5, 176.

49. But see the enthusiastic article by Roger Lewinter, 'Diderot et son théâtre,' *Temps modernes*, XXIV 1 (1968), 698–721.

50. Eric M. Steel, *Diderot's Imagery: A Study of a Literary Personality* (New York, 1941), 37; cf. A. Brun, 'Aux origines de la prose dramatique. Le style haletant,' in *Mélanges de linguistique française offerts à M. Charles Bruneau* [Société de publications romanes et françaises, XLV] (Geneva, 1954), 41–7.

51. Diderot, *Corr.*, II, 200. Cf. ibid., II, 19; and Part I, 313, 325. On Diderot's difficulty in writing plays, see June Sigler Siegel, 'Grandeur-Intimacy: The Dramatist's Dilemma,' *DS IV* (1963), 247–60.

52. Diderot may have volunteered unsolicited (Diderot to Grimm, 2 Sept. 1759 [Diderot, *Corr.*, II, 241]), but it seems unlikely that Grimm would not have had plans before this late date for reporting the Salon of 1759, especially as he himself had reported the Salons of 1753, 1755, and 1757 (*Corr. litt.*, II, 279–85; III, 90–5, 427–35).

53. Diderot, *Salons*, I, 1–8; Grimm, *Corr. litt.*, V, 394–5 (1 Oct. 1763) gives an interesting account of the history of the Salons.

54. See, for example, the authors and writings listed by Jean Locquin, *La Peinture d'histoire en France de 1747 à 1785* (Paris, 1912), 138–40. For Raynal's account of the Salon of 1748 (*Corr. litt.*, I, 217–9); of the Salon of 1750 (ibid., 461–6). Grimm wrote in 1755, 'Le Salon n'était pas sitôt ouvert que les peintres se sont vus accablés de brochures' (*Corr. litt.*, III, 97). See also Roland Desné, 'L'Eveil du sentiment national et la critique d'art. La Font de Saint Yenne précurseur de Diderot,' *Pensée*, No. 73 (May–June 1957), 82–96. The definitive monograph is that by Hélène Zmijewska, 'La Critique des Salons en France avant Diderot,' *Gazette des Beaux-Arts*, LXXVI (1970), 1–144.

55. Salon of 1753 (*Corr. litt.*, II, 279–85); Salon of 1755 (*Corr. litt.*, III, 90–5); Salon of 1757 (*Corr. litt.*, III, 427–35). Yvon Belaval, *L'Esthétique sans paradoxe de Diderot* (Paris, 1950), 7, suggests that Diderot may have written an account, now lost, of the Salon of 1753. Some authorities believe that the *Salons* of 1755 and 1757 written by Grimm show Diderot's influence (Joseph R. Smiley, *Diderot's Relations with Grimm* [Illinois Studies in Language and Literature, XXXIV, No. 4 (Urbana, 1950)], 91–7; Florens Deuchler, 'Diderots Traktat über das Schöne,' *Jahrbuch für Aesthetik und allgemeine Kunstwissenschaft*, III [1955–7], 223 n.).

56. The *Salons* are published in A.-T., X, 91–454; XI, 3–547; XII, 3–71. Most of the information about previous publications of portions of the *Salons* (A.-T., X, 87–90).

57. Diderot, *Salons*, I, 8; for a digest of the pamphlet literature of 1759, see ibid., 31–3.

58. Joseph R. Smiley, 'The Subscribers of Grimm's *Correspondance littéraire*,' *MLN*, LXII (1947), 44–6. See also J. Schlobach, 'Die frühen Abonnenten und die erste Druckfassung der *Correspondance littéraire*,' *RFor*, LXXXII (1970–1), 8–9 and *passim*.

59. A.-T., XIII, 13.

60. Diderot, *Salons*, I, 12; Jean Seznec, 'Les *Salons* de Diderot,' *Harvard Library Bulletin*, V (1951), 280; Marie-Luise Roy, *Die Poetik Denis Diderots* (Munich, 1966), 106.

61. August Langen, 'Die Technik der Bildbeschreibung in Diderots "Salons",' *RFor*, LXI (1948), 324–87, esp. 338–9 *et sqq.*

62. (1) *Corr. litt.*, II, 486–8; also in A.-T., XIII, 10–1; (2) *Corr. litt.*, III, 95–7; (3) *Corr. litt.*, III, 298–300; also in A.-T., XIX, 430–2.

63. Diderot, *Salons*, I, 114. Samuel Rocheblave, *L'Art et le goût en France de 1600 à 1900* (Paris, 1923), 199; repeated by him in the chapter he wrote for *Histoire de la langue et de la littérature française des origines à 1900*, ed. Louis Petit de Julleville, 8 vols. (Paris, 1896–9), VI, 804.

64. 'Sur le Voyage en Italie, par Cochin' (A.T., XIII, 12–5, this quotation 13–4; also in *Corr. litt.*, IV, 15–8).

65. Herbert Dieckmann, *Cinq leçons sur Diderot* (Geneva, 1959), 137.

66. Diderot, *Salons*, I, 63, 63–4, 67, 69.

67. Diderot, *Salons*, I, 64.

68. Diderot, *Salons*, I, 66. Cf. Gita May, 'Chardin vu par Diderot et par Proust,' *PMLA*, LXXII (1957), 403–18.

69. Diderot, *Corr.*, II, 246; Diderot, *Salons*, I, 65.

70. Diderot, *Corr.*, II, 242.

71. Diderot, *Corr.*, II, 263.

CHAPTER 28

1. Diderot, *Corr.*, II, 306 (30 Oct. 1759). Grandval was demolished about 1948–9; a modern villa stands in its place.

2. Diderot, *Corr.*, II, 292 (20 Oct. 1759).

3. Diderot, Corr., II, 264–5, 291 (1 and 20 Oct. 1759).

4. Diderot, *Corr.*, II, 318, 273, 284–5 (3 Nov., 14 [?] and 15 [?] Oct. 1759).

5. Diderot, *Corr.*, II, 176 (to Grimm, 20 or 21 July 1759).

6. Diderot, *Corr.*, II, 202, 210–1, 235, 173, 129, 321, 287.

7. Diderot, *Corr.*, II, 269 (8 Oct. 1759); cf. ibid., 291.

8. Diderot, *Corr.*, II, 291 (20 Oct. 1759).

9. Auguste Rey, *Le Château de la Chevrette et Madame d'Epinay* (Paris, 1904), 79; André Cazes, *Grimm et les encyclopédistes* (Paris, 1933), 253 n.

10. Diderot, *Corr.*, II, 268 (8 Oct. 1759). 'Quel parti un psychanalyste tirerait-il de ces sentiments troubles éprouvés pour des soeurs par un homme chez lequel il décèlerait sans doute des tendances homosexuelles?' (Yvon Belaval, 'Les Protagonistes du "Rêve de d'Alembert",' *DS III* [1961], 45, also 45 n.).

11. Edmond Scherer, *Melchior Grimm: L'homme de lettres, le factotum, le diplomate* (Paris, 1887), 187; contrary to Scherer's assertion, Grimm's emoluments were not 24,000 livres a year from this appointment (Paul Wohlfeil, 'Das Testament eines Notleidenden,' *Deutsche Rundschau*, CLI [1912], 299–300). Grimm presented his first *aide-mémoire* to Choiseul under date of 4 Dec. 1759 (Diderot, *Corr.*, II, 144 n.).

12. *Corr. litt.*, I, 5; Scherer, *Melchior Grimm*, 188; Clara Adèle Luce Herpin [pseud. Lucien Perey] and Gaston Maugras, *Dernières années de Madame d'Epinay* (Paris, 1884), 208–12; Cazes, *Grimm et les encyclopédistes*, 366.

13. *Corr. litt.*, XVI, 507–10. Adolphe Jullien, 'Une Mystification amoureuse: Grimm et Mademoiselle Leclerc (1760),' in his *Amours d'opéra au XVIIIe siècle* (Paris, 1908), 151–77.

14. Diderot, *Corr.*, II, 155 (to Grimm, 5 June 1759); cf. ibid., 257 (Sept. 1759), and ibid., IV, 68 (25 July 1762).

15. Diderot, *Corr.*, II, 257.

16. Diderot, *Corr.*, II, 33.

17. Diderot, *Corr.*, II, 281–2. The Scot was probably a John Hope (b. Edinburgh, 10 March 1725), who became professor of botany at the University of Edinburgh in 1761 (R. L. Graeme Ritchie, 'Le "Père Hoop" de Diderot: Essai d'identification,' in *A Miscellany of Studies in Romance Languages and Literatures Presented to Leon E. Kastner*, ed. Mary Williams and James A. de Rothschild [Cambridge, 1932], 409–27).

18. Diderot, *Corr.*, II, 306; cf. ibid., 243. André Billy, *Diderot* (Paris, 1932), 317, says that she was born in 1706; also see Pierre Naville, *Paul Thiry d'Holbach et la philosophie scientifique au XVIIIe siècle* (Paris, [1943]), 19–21. Cf. Henriette Célarié, 'Une Amie de Diderot: La joyeuse Madame d'Aine,' *Revue de France*, May–June 1939, 344–54; also Wladimir d'Ormesson, 'Diderot au Grandval,' *Revue Universelle*, XIII (1923), 691–701.

19. Diderot, *Corr.*, II, 307–8 (30 Oct. 1759).

20. Diderot, *Corr.*, II, 295–306. Cf. *Encyc.*, XIV, 663–78, s.v. 'Sarrasins *ou* Arabes, *philosophie des*'; also in A.-T., XVII, 35–84. This was one of the articles surreptitiously changed in proof by Le Breton (Gordon and Torrey, 36, 54–6, 78–81). Diderot could have utilized French translations of Sadi's *Gulistan, ou l'Empire des roses, traité des moeurs des rois*, which had been published at Paris in 1634, 1704, and 1737. More likely, however, he made his own translations from a Latin version published at Amsterdam in 1651 (Jacques Proust, 'Diderot savait-il aussi le persan?' *RLC*, XXXII [1958], 94–6). Diderot published anonymously in the *Journal Etranger*, Nov. 1761, 167–8, a translation in verse of a fable taken from Sadi (also printed in *Corr. litt.*, IV, 489 and n.); and Grimm used another of Diderot's verse translations of a Sadi fable in his news letter of 15 Nov. 1761 (*Corr. litt.*, IV, 490).

21. Diderot, *Corr.*, II, 316 (1 Nov. 1759).

22. Diderot, *Corr.*, IX, 32 (4 March 1769).

23. *Encyc.*, III, ix; also A.-T., XIV, 267, 274, 344, 375, 378; and A.-T., XV, 56; cf. Part I, 216. The extent to which Diderot used André-François Boureau-Deslandes, *Histoire critique de la philosophie*, 3 vols. (Amsterdam, 1737) is discussed by John L. Carr, 'Deslandes and the *Encyclopédie*,' *FS*, XVI (1962), 154–60; see also Rolf Geissler, 'Die Entstehung einer kritischen Philosophiegeschichte in der französischen Aufklärung: Boureau-Deslandes' "Histoire critique de la philosophie",' in Werner Krauss, ed., *Neue Beiträge zur Literatur der Aufklärung* (Berlin, 1964), 59–75, esp. 70.

24. *Année Littéraire*, vol. III for 1760, 264–5.

25. A.-T., XVI, 280.

26. Jacques-André Naigeon, in the three-volume section of the *Encyclopédie méthodique* devoted to 'Philosophie ancienne et moderne' (Paris, 1791–4), I, vi–viii.

27. Diderot's use of Brucker has been thoroughly and admirably analyzed by Proust, *Diderot et l'Encyclopédie*, esp. 264–93; see also his *L'Encyclopédie*, 9, 149–51; and Jacques Proust, 'Diderot et l'"Encyclopédie",' *Information Historique*, Sept.–Oct. 1963, 166–7. Cf. Paolo Casini, *Diderot 'philosophe'* (Bari, 1962), 259–60. On Brucker, see the excellent comment by Peter Gay, *The Enlightenment: An Interpretation*, 2 vols. (New York, 1966–9), I, 364–8, 548. See also Louis Trenard, 'Le Rayonnement de l'Encyclopédie (1751–1789),' *Cahiers d'Histoire Mondiale*, IX (1965–6), 716.

28. A.-T., XVII, 108–10.

29. A.T., XVI, 471–92. Allusions to Berkeley and Hume (Laurence L. Bongie, 'Hume, "Philosophe" and Philosopher in Eighteenth-century France,' *FS*, XV [1961], 222).

30. A.-T., XV, 264–272; Yuko Yamamoto, 'Diderot et Kaempfer. Note sur l'article "Japonais" de l'*Encyclopédie*,' *Hikaku Bungaku*, II (1959), 60–79. Diderot's access to Kaempfer may have been exclusively through Brucker; cf. Proust, *Diderot et l'Encyclopédie*, 551.

31. A.-T., XV, 267, 268, 266.

32. A.-T., XV, 94–124; Voltaire to D'Alembert, 5 April 1766 (Besterman, No. 12362).

33. Proust, *Diderot et l'Encyclopédie*, 342–4; Cru, 277; Leland J. Thielemann, 'Thomas Hobbes dans l' "Encyclopédie",' *RHLF*, LI (1951), 341; see also Leland J. Thielemann, 'Diderot and Hobbes,' *DS II* [1952], 228–9.

34. A.-T., XV, 122; cf. Thielemann, art. cit., *RHLF*, LI, 346.

35. Derivation from Brucker (Proust, *Diderot et l'Encyclopédie*, 552); and from Fontenelle

(Proust, ibid.; Pierre Hermand, 'Sur le texte de Diderot et sur les sources de quelques passages de ses "Oeuvres," ' *RHLF*, xxii [1915], 365 and n.; Pierre Hermand, *Les Idées morales de Diderot* [Paris, 1923], 242; Cru, 280). The formidable difficulty of determining to what extent Diderot was familiar at first hand with Leibniz' writings is emphasized by Yvon Belaval, 'Note sur Diderot et Leibniz,' *RSch*, No. 112 (Oct.–Dec. 1963), 435–51. W. H. Barber, *Leibniz in France from Arnauld to Voltaire: A Study in French Reactions to Leibnizianism, 1670–1760* (Oxford, 1955), mentions Diderot only briefly (e.g., p. 174), no doubt because of his self-imposed chronological limitations.

36. *Encyc.*, i, xxviij. For D'Alembert's disagreement with the philosophy of Leibniz, see J. Morton Briggs, Jr., 'D'Alembert: Philosophy and Mechanics in the Eighteenth Century,' *University of Colorado Studies, Series in History*, No. 3 (Jan. 1964), esp. 39–41; cf. Ronald Grimsley, *Jean d'Alembert (1717–83)* (Oxford, 1963), 274–5.

37. A.-T., xv, 473.

38. A.-T., xv, 436. Cf. Paul Hazard, *Quatre études* (New York, 1940), 150.

39. 'Tour de force' (Louis Barthou, *Diderot* [Paris, 1914], 14–5; cf. Emile Faguet, *Dix-huitième siècle: Etudes littéraires* [Paris, n. d., (Nouvelle bibliothèque littéraire), 294]). For recent estimates of this article, see Proust, *Diderot et* l'Encyclopédie, 290; and Casini, *Diderot 'philosophe'*, 260. For an extremely interesting linking of the thought of Diderot with that of Leibniz, see Ian W. Alexander, 'Philosophy of Organism and Philosophy of Consciousness in Diderot's Speculative Thought,' in Victoria University of Manchester, *Studies in Romance Philology and French Literature Presented to John Orr* (Manchester, 1953), 3–4, 13–4; see also Maurice Got, 'Sur le matérialisme de Diderot,' *Revue de Synthèse*, lxxxiii (1962), 155–9.

40. A.-T., xv, 437, 440.

CHAPTER 29

1. *Corr. litt.*, x, 47.

2. *Corr. litt.*, x, 50, 48 (1 Sept. 1772). The whole passage (ibid., 47–50) is a remarkable character sketch of Croismare, who had died on 3 August 1772; see also ibid., ix, 497, 505–6 (15 May 1772). Mme d'Epinay wrote a pen portrait of Croismare under the fictitious title of M. le marquis de Saint-Abre in her *Histoire de Madame de Montbrillant* (Louise de La Live d'Epinay, *Les Pseudo-Mémoires de Mme d'Epinay*) ed. Georges Roth, 3 vols. (Paris, 1951), iii, 91–2. Croismare was born 5 May 1695; regarding him, see Fausto Nicolini, *Amici e correspondenti francesi dell'abate Galiani* (Naples, 1954), 125–50; Georges Huard, *Deux académiciens caennais des XVIIe et XVIIIe siècles: Les Croismare, seigneurs de Lasson* (Caen, 1921); Diderot, *Corr.*, ii, 113 n.; ibid., iii, 17. See also Constantin Photiadès, *La Reine des Lanturelus: Marie-Thérèse Geoffrin, marquise de la Ferté-Imbault (1715–1791)* (Paris, [1928]), 10–3.

3. Georges May, 'Le Modèle inconnu de "La Religieuse" de Diderot: Marguerite Delamarre,' *RHLF*, li (1951), 273–87; also May, *Diderot et "La Religieuse"*, 47–56.

4. Mme d'Epinay's complicity (Diderot, *Corr.*, iii, 18).

5. The offending letter (A.-T., v, 184–5).

6. A.-T., v, 179, 203.

7. Diderot, *Corr.*, iii, 221 (dated by Roth as the beginning of Nov. 1760, though this may be a little late in the year); see also ibid., 40 (1 Aug. 1760) and 63 (10 Sept. 1760); also ibid., 116.

8. Diderot to Meister, 27 Sept. (1780) (Dieckmann, *Inventaire*, 39; May, *Diderot et "La Religieuse,"* 44.

9. Cf. a note from Diderot to Girbal, Grimm's professional copyist, regarding an important addition to *La Religieuse*, probably *c*. 1780 (Arthur M. Wilson, 'Leningrad, 1957: Diderot and Voltaire Gleanings,' *FR*, xxxi [1958], 356–7).

10. Jean Parrish, 'Conception, évolution, et forme finale de la *Religieuse*,' *RFor*, lxxiv (1962), 361–84; Nola M. Leov, '*La Religieuse*, 1760–1780,' *AUMLA*, No. 14 (1960), 23–35.

11. See the very important article by Herbert Dieckmann, 'The Préface-Annexe of La Reli-

gieuse,' *DS II* [1952], 21–40, esp. 29–31. There are many unsolved problems in the 'Préface-Annexe' (Vivienne Mylne, 'Truth and Illusion in the "Préface-Annexe" to Diderot's "La Religieuse",' *MLR*, LVII (1962), 350–6.

12. A.-T., v, 179.

13. 'C'est le destin de cette soeur qui a donné à mon père l'idée du roman de la *Religieuse*. . . .' (Mme de Vandeul to Henri Meister, 7 July 1816 [*Lettres inédites de Mme de Staël à Henri Meister*, ed. Paul Ustéri and Eugène Ritter (Paris, 1903), 63]). See also Jean Massiet du Biest, *La Fille de Diderot* (Tours, 1949), 207; May, *Diderot et "La Religieuse*," 146–7; Part I, 14.

14. Dieckmann, 'The Préface-Annexe of La Religieuse,' *DS II*, 28–9; for a photograph of this document, see ibid., 77. See also the essay by Roland Desné in Denis Diderot, *La Religieuse*, ed. Roland Desné (Paris, 1968), esp. 31–2.

15. The English translator, Francis Birrell, especially mentioned 'the amazing pace of the original' (Denis Diderot, *Memoirs of a Nun* [London, 1928], 10).

16. A.-T., v, 162. Cf. Georges May, 'Diderot, Baudelaire et les femmes damnées,' *MLN*, LXV (1950), 395–9.

17. *Cahiers du Cinéma*, No. 177 (April 1966), 9. This number reports the whole incident, as does also *Le Monde*, 2 April 1966, 24, and 2 May 1966, 6. See also *L'Express*, No. 773, 11–17 April 1966, 22–5. The role of the religieuse was played by Anna Karina.

18. See Pierre Sage, *Le "Bon Prêtre" dans la littérature française d'*Amadis de Gaule *au Génie du Christianisme* (Geneva, 1951), 308 n. 4.

19. Dieckmann, *Inventaire*, 39.

20. A.-T. v, 119–20.

21. See Robert J. Ellrich, 'The Rhetoric of *La Religieuse* and Eighteenth-Century Forensic Rhetoric,' *DS III* (1961), 129–54; also Robert Mauzi in his excellent edition of *La Religieuse* (Paris, [1961]), xx–xxi.

22. Annette de Bergevin, 'Suzanne Simonin, la religieuse de Diderot,' *Esprit*, XXXIV (July–Aug. 1966), 120–1; see also Mireille Latil-Le Dantec, 'Diderot, Rivette und die Nonne,' *Dokumente*, XXII (1966), 239–42; and Georges Sadoul, 'La culture et le revolver. (A propos de "La Religieuse" interdite),' *Lettres Françaises*, 21–7 April 1966, 13. Diderot's artistic realism and social consciousness is characteristically emphasized by Soviet scholars: see, e.g., L. ÍA. Potemkina, 'Istoriia sozdaniia romana D. Didro "Monakhinia",' *Nauchnye doklady vysshei shkoly. Filologicheskie nauki*, 1959, No. 3, 118–29.

23. Diderot, *The Nun*, 2 vols. (London, 1797), II, 45 n.

24. A.-T., v, 87. Mauzi, in his edition of *La Religieuse*, xxx–xxxii, emphasizes Diderot's humanism and his conviction that sociability is the strongest drive in human nature.

25. Jacques Proust, 'Recherches nouvelles sur *La Religieuse*,' *DS VI* (1964), 197–214, esp. 202.

26. Louis Ducros, *Diderot: L'homme et l'écrivain* (Paris, 1894), 201.

27. John Morley, *Diderot and the Encyclopaedists*, 2 vols. (London, 1878), II, 53.

28. Friedrich Christoph Schlosser, *History of the Eighteenth Century and of the Nineteenth till the Overthrow of the French Empire*, 8 vols. (London, 1843–52), II, 115–6.

29. Faguet, *Dix-huitième siècle: études littéraires*, 310.

30. Henri Lefebvre, *Diderot* (Paris, 1949), 252; his whole discussion of *La Religieuse* (ibid., 249–55) is interesting and persuasive. Jean-Louis Lecercle, 'Diderot et le réalisme bourgeois dans la littérature du XVIIIᵉ siècle,' *Pensée*, No. 38 (Sept.–Oct. 1951), 67. Cf. Jean Luc, *Diderot: L'Artiste et le philosophe* (Paris, 1938), 65.

31. Robert Niklaus, in *FS*, IX (1955), 77; cf. Vivienne Mylne, *The Eighteenth-Century French Novel: Techniques of Illusion* (New York, [1965]), 198–214, 220. For a very hostile critical opinion, however, see Sergio C. Landucci, 'Diderot,' *Cenobio*, Nuova Serie, VI (1957–8), 608–19.

32. *Times Literary Supplement*, 18 March 1959, 150.

33. Jeannette H. Foster, *Sex Variant Women in Literature: A Historical and Quantitative Survey* (New York, 1956), 55. Cf. May, *Diderot et "La Religieuse*," 98–114.

34. Diderot, *Corr.*, III, 74 (17 Sept. 1760). May, *Diderot et "La Religieuse*," 142–6; Georges May, *Quatre visages de Denis Diderot* (Paris, [1951]), 80–3; Frederick C. Green, *Minuet:*

A Critical Survey of French and English Literary Ideas in the Eighteenth Century (New York, 1935), 453; Robert Niklaus, in *FS,* IX (1955), 78. But cf. Jacques Proust, in *RHLF,* LV (1955), 236.

35. Anonymous editorial comment in Diderot, *La Religieuse* (Paris: Alphonse Lemerre, n.d. [1927?], 13.

36. Seven editions appeared before 1800; two in the time of Napoleon; five, 1815–30; ten, 1830–48; three, 1848–70; twenty, 1870–1914; twenty, 1914–40; six since 1940. May, *Diderot et "La Religieuse,"* 183.

37. Frederick C. Green, *French Novelists, Manners & Ideas, from the Renaissance to the Revolution* (New York, 1929), 149.

38. Alice Green Fredman, *Diderot and Sterne* (New York, 1955), 127.

39. Dostoevski and Proust (Henri Bénac, in Diderot, *Oeuvres romanesques* [Paris, 1951], 870, 871).

40. See Georges May's excellent discussion of Diderot's novelistic technique and devices in May, *Diderot et "La Religieuse,"* 197–237; also Leo Spitzer, 'The Style of Diderot,' in his *Linguistics and Literary History* (Princeton, 1948), 146–51, 178–80.

41. Dieckmann, 'The Préface-Annexe of La Religieuse,' *DS II,* 32–5; René Taupin, 'Richardson, Diderot et l'art de conter,' *FR,* XII (1938–9), 181–94; Louis Reynaud, *Le Romantisme: Ses origines anglo-germaniques* (Paris, 1926), 92–3; Hermann Hettner, *Literaturgeschichte des XVIII Jahrhunderts,* 7th ed., 3 parts in 6 vols. (Braunschweig, 1913), II, 333. Mario Praz, *The Romantic Agony,* 2nd ed. (New York, 1951), 97, speaks of *La Religieuse* as being an anticipation of Sade's *Justine.* Diderot's novel also served as a model for C. R. Maturin, *Melmoth* (1820) (Mario Praz, 'An English Imitation of Diderot's *La Religieuse,*' *Review of English Studies,* VI [1930], 429–36; H. Ashton, 'Maturin and Diderot,' *Royal Society of Canada Proceedings and Transactions,* 3d series, XV, section ii [1921], 123–34). See also Alan J. Freer, 'Une Page de *"La Religieuse"* jugée par la génération romantique: Diderot et l' "Amende honorable" de Delacroix,' *Rivista di Letterature Moderne e Comparate,* XVI (1963), 180–208.

42. Luigi Russo, 'De Diderot à Manzoni: "La Religieuse" de Longchamps et la religieuse de Monza,' in *Mélanges de philologie, d'histoire et de littérature offerts à Henri Hauvette* (Paris, 1934), 635–47; Alessandro Luzio, *Manzoni e Diderot: La "Monaca di Monza" e la "Religieuse"* (Milan, 1884); reprinted in his *Studi e bozzetti di storia letteraria e politica,* 2 vols. (Milan, 1910), I, 213–71; Manlio D. Busnelli, 'Per la genesi della "Signora di Monza," nuovi raffronti fra le storie claustrali del Manzoni, del Diderot e del La Harpe,' *Atti del Reale Istituto Veneto di scienze, lettere ed arti,* XCII (1932–3), parte seconda, 850–74; Manlio D. Busnelli, *Diderot et l'Italie* (Paris, 1925), 262; Giovanni Getto, 'I capitoli "francesi" de *I Promessi Sposi,*' in *Studi in onore di Carlo Pellegrini* (Turin, 1963), 559–608, esp. 572–6; Jerrold Orne, 'The Sources of *I Promessi Sposi,*' *Modern Philology,* XXXVIII (1940–1), 405–20.

43. Paul Chaponnière, 'Une Bévue de Diderot dans la "Religieuse",' *RHLF,* XXII (1915), 573; the same mistake was later noticed by the *Mercure de France,* CCLXXIV (Feb.–March 1937), 221, 668; and by Yvette Louria, 'Slip or Mystification in Diderot's *La Religieuse?*' *Symposium,* VIII (1954), 158–9. But regarding this *bévue,* see May, *Diderot et "La Religieuse,"* 208. For still another slip, see J. Haas, 'Über Diderots Religieuse,' *ZFSL,* XXIV ¹ (1902), 75. See also Philip Stewart, 'A Note on Chronology in *La Religieuse,*' *Romance Notes,* XII (1970–1), 149–56.

44. Green, *Minuet,* 455. Susanne Simonin too much of an abstraction (Haas, art. cit., *ZFSL,* XXIV ¹ [1902], 82; Taupin, art. cit., *FR,* XII [1938–9], 193; Henri Blaze de Bury, 'A propos de la Religieuse de Schubert et de Diderot,' *RDM,* 3ᵉ période, L [March–April 1882], 437).

45. May, *Diderot et "La Religieuse,"* 146.

46. A.-T., V, 171. Diderot's instructions to the copyist Girbal (Wilson, 'Leningrad, 1957: Diderot and Voltaire Gleanings,' *FR,* XXXI, 356–7); see also Diderot, *Corr.,* XV, 290–1. For other corrections by Diderot, trying to obviate this weakness, see the editor's remarks in Diderot, *La Religieuse,* ed. Jean Parrish, *SVEC,* XXII (1963), 54–5.

47. Compare the photographs of the two manuscripts in Dieckmann, 'La Préface-Annexe of La Religieuse,' *DS II,* 44–5, 85–6.

CHAPTER 30

1. Diderot, *Corr.*, III, 26–8; probably written in March 1760, for Tronchin's reply is dated 31 March 1760 (Jean-Daniel Candaux, 'Consultations du docteur Tronchin pour Diderot, père et fils,' *DS VI* [1964], 53–4; cf. Dr. Jean Olivier, 'Les Registres de consultations du Docteur Tronchin,' *Revue Médicale de la Suisse Romande*, LXIX [1949], 666–7). 'Tronchin recommande à ses pratiques de scier du bois et aussi de frotter leurs chambres; les "bureaux à la Tronchin" étaient des pupitres sur lesquels on écrivait en se tenant debout' (Georges Snyders, *La Pédagogie en France aux XVIIe et XVIIIe siècles* [Paris, 1965], 377). My friend Dr. William N. Chambers of the Hitchcock Clinic, Hanover, N.H., remarks of Diderot's ailment, 'Aerophagia is certainly a possibility. But it seems to me even more likely that Diderot's symptoms were caused by a diaphragmatic hernia, and aggravated by a nervous disposition. Other possibilities such as gall bladder trouble should also be thought of.'

2. Jean-Jacques Le Franc de Pompignan, *Discours et mémoire de M. de Pompignan* (n.p., 1760), 5 (B.N. call-number: Z. Beuchot 896); liberally quoted in *Année littéraire*, vol. II for 1760, 264–78, this quotation 268. Cf. *Corr. litt.*, IV, 235–8.

3. Complete account in Lucien Brunel, *Les Philosophes et l'Académie française au dix-huitième siècle* (Paris, 1884), 73–81. See also Diana Guiragossian, *Voltaire's Facéties* (Geneva, 1963), 46–51. An excellent and hilarious account in Gay, *The Enlightenment*, II, 80–2.

4. 14 April 1760 (Besterman, No. 8114), emphasis mine. D'Alembert's first word, 'When,' alludes to the series of 'when' clauses used by Voltaire as a rhetorical device in his attack on Pompignan ([Voltaire], *Les Quand, notes utiles, sur un Discours prononcé devant l'Académie française, le 10 mars 1760* [Geneva, 1760]). This pamphlet was printed in red ink. Cf. Maurice Pellisson, *Les Hommes de lettres au XVIIIe siècle* (Paris, 1911), 275–86; and Pierre Grosclaude, 'Deux épisodes de l'histoire de la librairie d'après une lettre inédite de Malesherbes,' *RHLF*, LIX (1959), 496–500.

5. 14 April 1760 (Besterman, No. 8114).

6. [Jean-Louis-Marie Dugas de Bois Saint-Just], *Paris, Versailles et les provinces au dix-huitième siècle . . . par un ancien officier aux Gardes-françaises*, 2 vols. (Paris, 1809), II, 286–7. For a detailed account of the production of *Les Philosophes* and of its aftermath, see Hilde H. Freud, *Palissot and Les Philosophes* (*DS IX* [1967]), 133–78; a standard but much older account in Gustave Le Brisoys Desnoiresterres, *La Comédie satirique au XVIIIe siècle* (Paris, 1885), 124–36.

7. John Lough, *Paris Theatre Audiences in the Seventeenth & Eighteenth Centuries* (London, 1957), 102.

8. Edmond-Jean-François Barbier, *Chronique de la Régence et du règne de Louis XV (1718–1765)*, 8 vols. (Paris, 1885), VII, 249–50.

9. Lancaster, *The Comédie Française, 1701–1774 . . .*, 797 and *passim*. For accounts of the audience at the *première*, see *Année Littéraire*, vol. III for 1760, 214, and Barbier, *Chronique*, VII, 248–50. There was opposition within the Comédie-Française to the production of Palissot's play, especially on the part of Mlle Clairon (Charles Collé, *Journal et mémoires*, Nouvelle édition, 3 vols. [Paris, 1868], II, 236; also D'Alembert to Voltaire, 6 May and 22 Sept. 1760 [Besterman, Nos. 8155, 8496]). Palissot declared later that 'La secte représentée par Voltaire . . . traita avec le duc de Choiseul de puissance à puissance; et le principal article du traité fut que la comédie des Philosophes . . . ne serait pas représentée à la cour, qu'elle cesserait même de l'être à Paris. . . .' (Charles Palissot de Montenoy, *Mémoires pour servir à l'histoire de notre littérature, depuis François Ier jusqu'à nos jours*, 2 vols. [Paris, 1803], II, 233. In general, the company of the Comédie-Française tried to make the first run of a play as brief as possible, 'since, once the play had been taken off, it became their property and the author had no further claim on them' (John Lough, *An Introduction to Eighteenth Century France* [New York, 1960], 239).

10. *Année Littéraire*, vol. IV for 1760, 221; Daniel Delafarge, *La Vie et l'oeuvre de Palissot (1730–1814)* (Paris, 1912), 150–1.

11. For Palissot (Delafarge, op. cit., 137); for Fréron (*Année Littéraire*, vol. IV for 1760, 218–9,

222, 226-7, 238-9), passages in which Fréron very cleverly insinuates that Aristophanes did exactly what Palissot is accused of doing.

12. [Charles Palissot], *Lettre de l'auteur de la Comédie des Philosophes, au Public, pour servir de Préface à la Pièce* (n.p., 1760), 6. When Voltaire rebuked him for his inaccurate quotations (23 June 1760 [Besterman, No. 8257]), Palissot publicly corrected some of them in a letter to *L'Observateur Littéraire*, vol. III for 1760, 212–6; also in *Année Littéraire*, vol. v for 1760, 134–41. Cf. Delafarge, op. cit., 227–8; and Freud, *Palissot and Les Philosophes (DS IX)*, 186, 189–90.

13. Concerning Malesherbes (Delafarge, op. cit., 127); regarding cutting offensive lines (*Année Littéraire*, vol. III for 1760, 215–6; and D'Alembert to Voltaire, 6 May 1760 [Besterman, No. 8155]: '. . . à la seconde représentation on a été obligé de retrancher plus de 50 vers'; see also *Corr. litt.*, IV, 253 [1 July 1760]; and *Annonces, Affiches, et Avis Divers*, No. 20 [14 May 1760], 80). Changing of Dortidius to Marphurius (Freud, *Palissot and Les Philosophes (DS IX)*, 148.

14. Charles-Simon Favart, *Mémoires et correspondance littéraires, dramatiques et anecdotiques*, 3 vols. (Paris, 1808), I, 29, 36, 37–8; [Gabriel-François Coyer], *Discours sur la Satyre contre les Philosophes* . . . (Athènes [Paris], 1760), 13, 84, 90–1.

15. Collé, *Journal et Mémoires*, II, 235–6.

16. For the Princesse de Robecq, see Part I, 317–8. Turgot wrote to Condorcet, c. 1762 or later, that Choiseul had been 'protecteur de la pièce de Palissot' (Anne-Robert-Jacques Turgot, *Oeuvres*, ed. Eugène Daire, 2 vols. [Paris, 1844], II, 797). 'Elle a été jouée par l'ordre de la Cour' (Antoine-Léonard Thomas to Nicolas-Thomas Barthe, 8 May 1760 [Maurice Henriet, 'Correspondance inédite entre Thomas et Barthe (1759–1785),' *RHLF*, XXIV (1917), 489]. The fact is that Choiseul had commissioned Palissot to write a satirical poem against Frederick the Great, which was held in reserve to be used in reprisal should Frederick II publish a poem he had written satirizing Louis XV. The production of *Les Philosophes* at the Comédie-Française was Palissot's reward (Freud, *Palissot and Les Philosophes [DS IX]*, 127–33).

17. 12 May 1760 (Besterman, No. 8165).

18. Besterman, No. 8163.

19. 1 June 1760 (Diderot, *Corr.*, III, 34).

20. To Duchesne, 21 May 1760 (Leigh, No. 995). On 24 May Rousseau spoke of himself to Duchesne as a man 'qui déteste la satire particulière, et ne peut sans indignation voir outrager le mérite et diffamer son ancien ami' (Leigh, No. 998).

21. Tronchin to Jacob Vernes, 14 June 1760 (Edouard de Callatay, *Madame de Vermenoux: Une Enchanteresse au XVIIIe siècle* [Geneva, 1956], 24).

22. 1 June 1760: 'Vous aurez appris comme on a laissé indécemment mettre au théâtre une satire personnelle très odieuse contre les Diderot et compagnie, . . .' (Charles de Brosses, *Lettres du Président de Brosses à Ch.-C. Loppin de Gemeaux*, ed. Yvonne Bezard [Paris, 1929], 278).

La Condamine to Formey, 11 May 1760 (Jacques Matter, *Lettres et pièces rares ou inédites* [Paris, 1846], 424).

23. Besterman, No. 8155.

24. *Journal Encyclopédique*, vol. III for 1760, part ii (15 April 1760), 141; *Mercure de France*, 1 July 1760, 121–2; *Observateur Littéraire*, vol. II for 1760, 344–5 (2 June [1760]).

25. *Annonces, Affiches, et Avis Divers*, 30 July 1760, 124, à propos of a one-act play by Antoine-Alexandre Poinsinet called *Le Petit Philosophe* and produced by the Comédiens-italiens on 14 July 1760. There was also published in July 1760 an anti-*philosophe* play for marionettes, *Les Philosophes de bois, comédie en 1 acte en vers. Par M. Cadet de Beaupré* (pseud. for Louis Poinsinet de Sivry), the censor of which (as shown by the Approbation) was Crébillon. Cf. Frank W. Lindsay, *Dramatic Parody by Marionettes in Eighteenth Century Paris* (New York, 1946), 150–3.

26. [André Morellet], *Préface de la comédie des Philosophes, ou la Vision de Charles Palissot* (Paris, 1760), 12.

27. Choiseul himself said so, 16 June 1760 (Besterman, No. 8235); cf. Voltaire to Charles

de Brosses, 16 July 1760 (Besterman, No. 8317), and Voltaire to Thieriot, 18 July 1760 (Besterman, No. 8323).

28. M. Monmerqué, 'Détention à la Bastille de Marmontel et Morellet (1760),' Société de l'Histoire de France, *Bulletin*, 2e partie, II (1835), 354; see also Edward P. Shaw, *Problems and Policies of Malesherbes as Directeur de la librairie in France (1750–1763)* ([Albany], State University of N.Y., 1966), 59.

29. Diderot, *Corr.*, III, 33–4. Morellet's arrest had not been quite regular, judging from a report to Saint Florentin, Minister of the King's Household, the day after the arrest: 'Je vous prie, Monsieur, de vouloir bien m'envoyer les ordres du Roi nécessaires, de la date du 10, pour arrêter ces deux particuliers, et autoriser les perquisitions faites chez eux par un commissaire au Châtelet' (Monmerqué, loc. cit., 356). The standard monograph on the Morellet incident is the one by Daniel Delafarge, *L'Affaire de l'abbé Morellet en 1760* (Paris, 1912).

Another one of the *philosophes*, Marmontel, had been imprisoned in the Bastille a few months previously (27 Dec. 1759–7 Jan. 1760), but for reasons that were not ideological. A letter that he is alleged to have written to Diderot from the Bastille (Diderot, *Corr.*, IV, 21–5), seems to me, however, to contain anachronisms and to be almost certainly spurious. It was first published by E. Fialon, 'Lettre inédite de Marmontel à Diderot,' *Travaux de l'Académie Impériale de Reims*, XLIX (1868–1869), 98–109; no one has ever seen a holograph or manuscript of this letter.

30. Collé, *Journal et mémoires*, II, 248. Among the pamphlets at this time there should be mentioned, all of them very hostile to Diderot and the *Encyclopédie*, [Louis Coste], *Le Philosophe ami de tout le monde, ou Conseils désintéressés aux littérateurs* (Sophopolis [Paris], 1760), B.N. call-number: Z. Beuchot 911 (7); *Conseil de lanternes, ou la véritable vision de Charles Palissot, pour servir de post-scriptum à la comédie des Filosofes* ([Paris], 1760); *Le Coq-à-l'asne; ou, l'éloge de Martin Zèbre, prononcé dans l'assemblée générale tenue à Montmartre par MM. ses confrères* ([Paris], 1760). Favorable to Diderot was the *Lettre d'un original aux Auteurs très-originaux de la comédie très-originale des Philosophes* (Berlin [prob. Paris], 1760), dated May 1760.

31. 18 July 1759 (Diderot, *Corr.*, II, 172–3).

32. 16 June 1760 (Besterman, No. 8234); see also John Lough, 'The *Encyclopédie* in Voltaire's Correspondence,' in *SPTB*, 57–9.

33. 4 June 1760 (Besterman, No. 8214); see also Lough, *Essays on the* Encyclopédie *of Diderot and d'Alembert*, 309–11.

34. *Année Littéraire*, vol. III for 1760, 216; Collé, *Journal et mémoires*, II, 236; 'Fréron avoit pris et distribué plus de deux cents billets' (Thomas to Barthe, 8 May 1760 [Henriet, art. cit., *RHLF*, XXIV, 490]). Cf. D'Alembert to Voltaire, 6 May 1760 (Besterman, No. 8155).

35. Voltaire to D'Argental, 3 Aug. 1760 (Besterman, No. 8357, inc. editor's commentary, note 2).

36. *Annonces, Affiches, et Avis Divers*, 13 Aug. 1760, 132.

37. Coyer, *Discours sur la Satyre contre les Philosophes*, 90–1. Cf. Ira O. Wade, *The "Philosophe" in the French Drama of the Eighteenth Century* (Princeton, 1926), 52–3.

38. Lancaster, *The Comédie Française, 1701–1774* . . . , 798–9, 802–38. There was a grand total of 86 performances, the last occurring on 23 Jan. 1774.

39. The Stockholm manuscript of the *Correspondance littéraire* of the *livraison* for 15 June 1760 (Kungl. Biblioteket, Vu. 29: vol. 1) has a passage regarding the *Ecossaise* that does not appear in *Corr. litt.*, IV, 246–7: 'Au reste on voit aisément que c'est le pere de famille de M. Diderot qui a produit la comédie du Caffé [an alternative title for *L'Ecossaise*]. . . . Le plus celebre ecrivain de l'Europe s'est assujetti ici à la poetique du Philosophe; il a écrit la pantomime; il a cherché du spectacle de l'action, du mouvement, des discours simples et vrais; il a travaillé dans son genre et d'après ses idées. . . .' A similar observation was made by Jules Béraneck, 'Diderot et la réforme du théâtre au XVIIIe siècle,' *Bibliothèque Universelle et Revue Suisse*, LVII (1893), 548–9, and, more recently, by Henri L. Brugmans, 'Autour de Diderot en Hollande,' *DS III* (1961), 69.

40. Fréron to Malesherbes, 1 and 20 Aug. 1760 (B.N., MSS, Fr. 22191, foll. 274, 277–8).

41. 31 July 1760 (B.N., MSS, Fr. 22191, fol. 272; published in extenso by Pellisson, *Les*

Hommes de lettres au XVIIIe siècle, 291–2); cf. Fréron to Malesherbes, 21 Aug. 1760: 'Vous avez été témoin vous même, Monsieur, des applaudissements effrenés qu'on donna à ce role de Wasp le jour de la première représentation, applaudissements qui n'auroient pas eu lieu si je n'avais été l'objet de l'application' (B.N., MSS, Fr. 22191, fol. 279). Cf. John Lough, 'A Paris Theatre in the Eighteenth Century,' *University of Toronto Quarterly*, XXVII (1957–8), 294; also Lough, *Paris Theatre Audiences in the Seventeenth & Eighteenth Centuries*, 200–1.

42. *Année Littéraire*, vol. IV for 1760, 110; the whole review (ibid., 73–116).
43. *Année Littéraire*, vol. V for 1760, 209, 210, 214; the whole 'Account' (ibid., 209–16).
44. Voltaire to D'Alembert, 9 and 24 July and 13 Aug. 1760 (Besterman, Nos. 8296, 8333, 8381); to D'Argental, 9, 11, 19, and 25 July 1760 (Besterman, Nos. 8297, 8301, 8326, 8337); to Mme d'Epinay, 9, 24, and 28 July 1760 (Besterman, Nos. 8298, 8334, 8340); to Grimm, 11 July 1760 (Besterman, No. 8306); to Grimm and Mme d'Epinay, c. 10 Aug. 1760 (Besterman, No. 8375); and to Charles Pinot Duclos, 25 July and 11 Aug. 1760 (Besterman, Nos. 8336, 8378).
45. Besterman, No. 8324.
46. *C.* 10 Aug. 1760 (Besterman, No. 8375).
47. 2 Sept. 1760 (Besterman, No. 8428). Voltaire wrote to Diderot on 3 Sept. 1760 but this letter is not extant (Besterman, No. 8432). Voltaire and the Diderot candidacy have been carefully studied by Brunel, *Les Philosophes et l'Académie française au dix-huitième siècle*, 91–101 (he thinks Voltaire showed poor judgment), and by Raymond Naves, *Voltaire et l'Encyclopédie* (Paris, 1938), 79–86 (more favorable to Voltaire).
48. *Corr. litt.*, IV, 259 (1 July 1760); ibid., IV, 260–3 (15 July 1760); Diderot, *Corr.*, III, 264–5 (25 Nov. 1760).
49. Cf. Lucien Febvre, 'Deux esprits: Voltaire et Diderot,' *Revue de Synthèse*, XVIII (1939), 167–8; also John Pappas, 'Voltaire et la guerre civile philosophique,' *RHLF*, LXI (1961), 528–30, 531–2; and René Pomeau, *La Religion de Voltaire* (Paris, 1956), 332–3; John N. Pappas, *Voltaire & D'Alembert* (Bloomington [Ind.], 1962), 22–6, 88–9.
50. *Encyc.*, XI, 888a–9b, s.v. 'Parade': 'Cet article est de M. le comte de Tressan.' For documents concerning the ensuing Tressan-Palissot controversy, see Leigh, III, 298–9, 361–4.
51. *Encyc.*, X, 331b; also in A.-T., XVI, 115.
52. Gordon and Torrey, 37, 70.
53. Diderot to Sartine, June 1770 (Diderot, *Corr.*, X, 74–5); also in *Corr. litt.*, IX, 52–4 (15 June 1770).
54. Diderot, *Corr.*, X, 75.

CHAPTER 31

1. Letters 'L' and 'M' (May, 73). 'Natif' (*Encyc.*, XI, 36a). For the *maladie de Langres*, see also Diderot, *Corr.*, III, 196 (26 Oct. 1760).
2. To Damilaville, [1 Aug. 1760] (Diderot, *Corr.*, III, 40).
3. *La Mort d'Abel* (A.-T., VI, 324–31; the Stockholm manuscript of the *Corr. litt.* carried this in the *livraison* for 15 Feb. 1760 [De Booy, 'Inventaire,' 361–2]).
4. A.-T., V, 500; this appears in the Stockholm manuscript of the *Corr. litt.*, May 1, 1760 (De Booy, 'Inventaire,' 362).
5. A.-T., VII, 120; cf. Part I, 269.
6. Mme de Vandeul, li.
7. *Encyc.*, VIII, 888a, s.v. 'Jouer.' Cf. Robert Mauzi, 'Ecrivains et moralistes du XVIIIe siècle devant les jeux de hasard,' *RScH*, April–June 1958, 219–56; and Alan J. Freer, 'Isaac de Pinto e la sua *Lettre à Mr. D[iderot] sur le jeu des cartes*,' *Annali della Scuola Normale Superiore di Pisa*, série 2, XXXIII (1964), 107–10.
8. A.-T., VII, 313; cf. Part I, 330–1. Also, Robert Niklaus, 'La Propagande philosophique au théâtre au siècle des lumières,' *SVEC*, XXVI (1963), 1231. In working on *The Gamester*, Diderot was also influenced by *The Fatal Extravagance* (1721), 'tout à fait dans le goût du *Joueur*' (To Sophie, 30 Sept. 1760 [Diderot, *Corr.*, III, 111–2]); cf. Jacques Voisine, 'Traduttore, traditore: *L'Extravagance fatale*,' *DS X* (1968), 175–86.

9. Cru, 311–5; Charles Dédéyan, *L'Angleterre dans la pensée de Diderot* (Paris, 1959), 54–6. Cf. Władysław Folkierski, 'L'Anglais de Diderot,' *RLC*, xxxiv (1960), 226–44.

10. Dieckmann, *Inventaire*, 14, 128.

11. Diderot, *Corr.*, iii, 63 (10 Sept. 1760). E. Clavering, *Diderot et le théâtre* (Toulouse, 1939), 100–8, esp. 103.

12. Diderot, *Corr.*, iii, 39; cf. ibid., 37–8.

13. Diderot, *Corr.*, iii, 57 (5 Sept. 1760). Regarding D'Argental, see the *Dictionnaire de biographie française*, ed. J. Balteau, M. Barroux, and M. Prévost (Paris, 1933–), s.v. 'Argental.'

14. To Mme d'Epinay (Diderot, *Corr.*, iii, 48–9 [1 Sept. 1760]). Cf. ibid., iii, 78.

15. *Corr. litt.*, vii, 364 (1 July 1767). The Diderot translation first published in 1819 (*Supplément aux Oeuvres de Denis Diderot* [Paris: A. Belin, 1819], 88–182); also in A.-T., vii, 417–525. A rival translation, done by Bruté de Loirelle and published in 1762 (A.-T., vii, 414), was lengthily reviewed in the *Année Littéraire*, vol. v for 1762, 73–110.

16. Diderot, *Corr.*, iii, 48 (1 Sept. 1760). The representative was Pierre-Jean Blainville, who had made his début at the Comédie-Française on 3 Sept. 1757; it is possible that Blainville was speaking of a trial reading of *Le Père de famille*, rather than of *Le Joueur*.

17. Diderot, *Corr.*, iii, 51.

18. 'Ici les Comédiens François se disposent à mettre au Théâtre le *Père de Famille*' (*Annonces, Affiches, et Avis Divers*, No. 1 for 1761 [7 Jan. 1761], 4); cf. Godefroid van Swieten to Charles de Cobenzl, 24 Jan. 1761: '*Le Père de famille* de Diderot est à l'étude, et les rôles sont distribués' (Gustave Charlier, 'Une Correspondance littéraire inédite,' *RHLF*, xxvii [1920], 107).

19. *Mercure de France*, vol. ii for April 1759, 200; *Annonces, Affiches, et Avis Divers*, 10 Dec. 1760, 199; ibid., 25 Feb. 1761, 32. *Corr. litt.*, iv, 353 (1 March 1761). Clavering, *Diderot et le théâtre*, 49, 52; Roland Mortier, *Diderot en Allemagne, 1750–1850* (Paris, 1954), 61. On the production at Marseilles (Diderot, *Corr.*, iii, 280 [1 Dec. 1760]).

20. Mortier, *Diderot en Allemagne*, 60, 61; *Annonces, Affiches, et Avis Divers*, No. 1 for 1761, 4.

21. Clavering, *Diderot et le théâtre*, 179.

22. Hôtel de Clermont-Tonnerre is now 27, Quai de Tournelle. For an excellent description of Damilaville, see Pomeau, *La Religion de Voltaire*, 330–1; also Fernand Caussy, 'Damilaville ou le gobe-mouche de la philosophie,' *Mercure de France*, ciii (May–June 1913), 76–9.

23. Diderot, *Corr.*, iii, 118–9 (7 Oct. 1760); cf. ibid., 113. This occurrence formed the basis of two versions used by Diderot in his later writings: one in the *Salon de 1765* (Diderot, *Salons*, ii, 140), the other in *Jacques le fataliste* (A.-T., vi, 193–4). Cf. Paul Vernière, 'Diderot et l'invention littéraire: A propos de "Jacques le fataliste",' *RHLF*, lix (1959), 159; and Richard T. Arndt, 'Two States of a Diderot Text,' *RR*, li (1960), 93–102; also Jean-Louis Leutrat, 'Sur trois pages de Diderot,' *RHLF*, lxix (1969), 831–6. Of accidents like these Louis-Sébastien Mercier remarked in his *Tableau de Paris*, 4 vols. (Amsterdam, 1782–3), i, 90: 'Rien de si commun que la soudaine rupture des soupentes ou des roues: vous avez le nez cassé ou une contusion au bras; mais vous êtes dispensé de payer la course.'

24. Diderot, *Corr.*, iii, 72 (17 Sept. 1760).

25. Dieskau (Diderot, *Corr.*, iii, 220, 224–7, 230–1).

26. Diderot, *Corr.*, iii, 267 (25 Nov. 1760).

27. Diderot, *Corr.*, iii, 41 (2 Aug. 1760). Michael Casimir Oginski (1731–1803) wrote the article 'Harpe' for the *Encyclopédie*, viii, 56b–58a. He is said to be the one who invented the addition of pedals to the harp. Cf. Albert Sowiński, *Les Musiciens polonais et slaves anciens et modernes* (Paris, 1857), 439; Ewa Rzadkowska, *Encyklopedia i Diderot w polskim oświeceniu* (Warsaw, 1955), 22.

28. Diderot, *Corr.*, iii, 20 n.; *Corr. litt.*, iv, 194. The *première* of *Spartacus* was 20 Feb. 1760 (Lancaster, *The Comédie Française, 1701–1774 . . .* , 796). Diderot described it to Sophie (Diderot, *Corr.*, iii, 20–1 [23 or 25 Feb. 1760]) and wrote a review of it for the *Corr. litt.*, iv, 228–30 (15 April 1760). Diderot's advice to Saurin (Diderot, *Corr.*, iii,

105, 88–93); it was first published by Georges Roth, 'Diderot "renverse" *Le Siège de Calais* de Saurin,' *SVEC*, II (1956), 233–40.

29. Diderot, *Corr.*, III, 64, 67, 101, 106–7; cf. Part I, 292–303.

30. Diderot, *Corr.*, III, 75–6, 103–4, 164, 268. For excellent examples of his stories: the *porco sacro* (ibid., 104–5); the monks at the inn (ibid., 258–9); the cuckoo and the nightingale (ibid., 166–9). This last has been excellently translated in Norman L. Torrey, *Les Philosophes: The Philosophers of the Enlightenment and Modern Democracy* (New York, [1960]), 224–6. Later in 1760, probably on 27 Dec. (Clarence D. Brenner, *The Théâtre Italien, its Repertory, 1716–1793* [Berkeley, 1961], 248), Diderot went with Galiani, Mme d'Epinay, and D'Alainville to the Comédie-Italienne (Diderot, *Corr.*, IV, 168; date corrected, ibid., VII, 274; Georges May, 'L'Angoisse de l'échec et la genèse du *Neveu de Rameau*,' *DS III* [1961], 289–90).

31. Diderot, *Corr.*, III, 164, 165, 166.

32. Diderot, *Corr.*, III, 250; cf. ibid., 265.

33. Diderot, *Corr.*, III, 109.

34. Diderot, *Corr.*, III, 258.

35. Diderot, *Corr.*, III, 263.

36. Diderot, *Corr.*, III, 66, 101, 187–8; cf. his similar remarks to Mme d'Epinay (ibid., III, 221).

37. Diderot, *Corr.*, III, 121, 197.

38. Diderot, *Corr.*, III, 122, 209.

39. Diderot, *Corr.*, III, 235, 210, 208. For a subtle analysis of Diderot's relations with his friends, see Jack Undank's remarks in his edition of Diderot, *Est-il bon? Est-il méchant?* (*SVEC*, XVI [1961], 96–100).

40. Combined with passion and eroticism; e.g., 'Je te baise partout' (Diderot, *Corr.*, III, 52; cf. ibid., 70–1). An inverse manifestation of this eroticism is his jealousy of Mme Le Gendre at this time (ibid., 63, 69, 74–5).

41. Diderot, *Corr.*, III, 46–7.

42. Diderot, *Corr.*, III, 103.

43. Diderot, *Corr.*, III, 117, 119, 211, 247–8.

44. Diderot, *Corr.*, III, 237.

45. Diderot, *Corr.*, III, 52, 265.

46. Diderot, *Corr.*, III, 247; Diderot is referring to Voltaire's letter of 29 Oct. 1760 (Besterman, No. 8604).

47. Lancaster, *The Comédie Française, 1701–1774* . . . , 798; Diderot, *Corr.*, III, 54–5. Of *Tancrède*, Virgil W. Topazio, *Voltaire* (New York, 1967), 100, remarks that '. . . the play's vapid exposition and monotonous speeches scarcely seem to warrant the reception it received.'

48. To Mme d'Epinay (Diderot, *Corr.*, III, 39).

49. Diderot, *Corr.*, III, 55–6, 264–5, 280. Cf. Voltaire to Damilaville, 19 Nov. 1760, and to Thieriot, same day (Besterman, Nos. 8645, 8647).

50. Diderot, *Corr.*, III, 271–6, esp. 274–5; published also in Besterman, No. 8660. Voltaire's reply, 10 Dec. 1760 (Besterman, No. 8685). Cf. John S. Henderson, 'Voltaire's *Tancrède*: Author and Publisher,' *SVEC*, LXI (1968), 37–8.

51. *Mercure de France*, Feb. 1762, 92–3.

52. 8 Feb. 1762 (Besterman, No. 9520).

53. Diderot, *Corr.*, IV, 34.

54. 16 Feb. 1762 (Besterman, No. 9538).

55. To Mme d'Epinay, 19 Feb. 1761 (Besterman, No. 8863); cf. Voltaire to Damilaville, 3 March 1761 (Besterman, No. 8885).

56. Van Swieten to Cobenzl, 24 Jan. 1761 (Charlier, 'Une Correspondance littéraire inédite,' *RHLF*, XXVII, 107).

57. Van Swieten to Cobenzl, 19 Feb. 1761 (Charlier, art. cit., 107); *Annonces, Affiches, et Avis Divers*, 25 Feb. 1761, 32. For a modern and convincing defense of Diderot's stagecraft in *Le Père de famille*, see Ernst Howald, 'Die Exposition von Diderots "Père de famille",' in *Ueberlieferung und Gestaltung: Festgabe für Theophil Spoerri* (Zurich,

1950), 51–76; also Lewinter, 'Diderot et son théâtre,' *Temps Modernes*, xxiv¹, 698–721.
58. Charles Collé, *Journal historique inédit pour les années 1761 et 1762* (Paris, 1911), 36–48; *Mercure de France*, March 1761, 192–3; cf. ibid., April 1761, 161.
59. *Annonces, Affiches, et Avis Divers*, 4 March 1761, 36. *Année Littéraire*, vol. iii for 1761, 317–8. The whole review, dated 2 June 1761 (ibid., 289–319).
60. Number of performances and attendance at *Le Père de famille* (Lancaster, *The Comédie Française, 1701–1774* . . . , 800; Henry Carrington Lancaster, 'The Cast and the Reception of Diderot's *Père de Famille*,' *MLN*, lxix [1954], 416–8; cf. A. Joannidès, *La Comédie-Française de 1680 à 1920. Tableau des représentations par auteurs et par pièces* [Paris, 1921], 34). The dates of performances in 1761 and number of spectators were:

18 Feb.	1178
21	1013
23	818
25	745
28	860
2 March	616
4	767

61. [Augustin-Simon Irailh], *Querelles littéraires, ou Mémoires pour servir à l'histoire des révolutions de la république des lettres, depuis Homère jusqu'à nos jours*, 4 vols. (Paris, 1761), ii, 381.
62. 23 Feb. 1761 (Diderot, *Corr.*, iii, 291); cf. ibid., iii, 48. The *Annonces, Affiches, et Avis Divers*, 18 Feb. 1761, 28, likewise reported that 'l'Auteur a fait les changemens nécessaires pour l'accommoder au Théâtre.' For the regulations of the Comédie-Française in respect to authors' rights, see Max Aghion, *Le Théâtre à Paris au XVIIIᵉ siècle* (Paris, 1926), 400–1.
63. *Corr. litt.*, iv, 353–6, esp. 354 (1 March 1761). Cf. ibid., 358–60 (15 March 1761).
64. Diderot, *Corr.*, iii, 292.
65. May, 'L'Angoisse de l'échec et la genèse du *Neveu de Rameau*,' *DS III*, 295–300; cf. Robert Niklaus, 'La Portée des théories dramatiques de Diderot et de ses réalisations théâtrales,' *RR*, liv (1963), 13.

CHAPTER 32

1. In *Paradoxe sur le comédien* (1773) (A.-T., viii, 401).
2. Cf. Herbert Dieckmann, 'Diderot's Conception of Genius,' *JHI*, ii (1941), 151–82.
3. To Sophie Volland, 23 or 25 Feb. 1760 (Diderot, *Corr.*, iii, 21).
4. For this interpretation, see a number of excellent essays: Georges May, 'Diderot pessimiste,' in his *Quatre visages de Denis Diderot* (Paris, 1951), 34–99; May, 'L'Angoisse de l'échec et la genèse du *Neveu de Rameau*,' *DS III*, 285–307; Lester G. Crocker, ' "Le Neveu de Rameau," une expérience morale,' *CAIEF*, No. 13 (June 1961), 133–55, esp. 140; Herbert Dieckmann, *Diderot und Goldoni* [*Schriften und Vorträge des Petrarca-Instituts Köln, xvi*] (Krefeld, 1961), 27.
5. *Année Littéraire*, vol. v for 1761, 23–4 (18 July 1761).
6. May, 'L'Angoisse . . . ,' *DS III*, 301. That *Le Neveu de Rameau* was a vial for pouring out Diderot's hatred of Palissot is emphasized in Freud, *Palissot and Les Philosophes* (*DS IX*), 192–214.
7. Denis Diderot, *Le Neveu de Rameau*, ed. Jean Fabre (Geneva, 1950), 58. Regarding these persons, see ibid., 145–53, 155–6, 168–70, 201–2. See also Rudolf Schlösser, *Rameaus Neffe: Studien und Untersuchungen zur Einführung in Goethes Übersetzung des Diderotschen Dialogs* (Berlin, 1900), 65–6, 281; Milton F. Seiden, 'Jean-François Rameau and Diderot's *Neveu*,' *DS I* (1949), 168–9.
8. Diderot, *Le Neveu de Rameau*, ed. Fabre, 57, 21; also ibid., 158. Part I, 317–20.
9. Cuthbert Morton Girdlestone, *Jean-Philippe Rameau: His Life and Work* (London, [1957]), 492, 499; Doolittle, 'A Would-be *Philosophe*: Jean Philippe Rameau,' *PMLA*, lxxiv, 233–48. Cf. Part I, 89, 179–80.
10. Regarding Jean-François Rameau, the nephew of Jean-Philippe Rameau, see Schlösser,

Rameaus Neffe, 32–48; Diderot, *Le Neveu de Rameau,* ed. Fabre, xlvi–l, 243–54; Seiden, 'Jean-François Rameau and Diderot's *Neveu,*' *DS I,* 143–91; and Girdlestone, *Jean-Philippe Rameau,* 506–7; also *Corr. litt.,* VII, 61 (15 June 1766). His imprisonment (Frantz Funck-Brentano, *La Bastille des comédiens, le For l'Evêque* [Paris, 1903], 299–302). 'Inspector and Comptroller of Dancing Masters' (Yves Benot, 'Du nouveau sur *Le Neveu de Rameau,*' *Lettres Françaises,* 21–27 Sept. 1961, 1, 5). April 1761 (Diderot, *Le Neveu de Rameau,* ed. Fabre, xxxiv; Jean Fabre, 'Le Chemin de Diderot,' *Europe,* Nos. 405–6 [Jan.–Feb. 1963], 13; Diderot, *Corr.,* III, 293).

11. Diderot, *Corr.,* III, 357, 115–7; cf. ibid., IV, 204–5 (24 Oct. 1762). Regarding the Café de la Régence, see Jacques Hillairet, *Evocation du vieux Paris:* Tome II: *Les Faubourgs* (Paris, [1953]), 42–3.

12. Maurice Tourneux, *Diderot et Catherine II* (Paris, 1899), 450.

13. Summer of 1761 (Schlösser, *Rameaus Neffe,* 29; Dieckmann, *Inventaire,* 74; May, 'L'Angoisse . . . ,' *DS III,* 289–98, 307; Jean-Louis Leutrat, 'Autour de la genèse du "Neveu de Rameau",' *RHLF,* LXVIII [1968], 421–47, esp. 427; and esp. L. W. Tancock in his edition [Penguin Classics] of Denis Diderot, *Rameau's Nephew and D'Alembert's Dream* [Harmandsworth, 1966], 23). For detailed speculation regarding the date of composition, but with inconclusive results, see *Entretiens sur "Le Neveu de Rameau",* ed. Michèle Duchet and Michel Launay (Paris, 1967), 139–85. Yves Benot, 'Diderot épistolier, De ses lettres à ses livres,' *Pensée,* No. 99 (Sept.–Oct. 1961), 101–2, inclines towards 1762 instead of 1761 as the date of original composition. For the dates of successive revisions (Schlösser, *Rameaus Neffe,* 20–9; Dieckmann, *Inventaire,* 72).

14. *Le Neveu de Rameau,* ed. Fabre, 6. A stage version, starring Pierre Fresnay, was produced at the Théâtre Michodière in Paris in 1963. For the text, with photographs and much other information, see *L'Avant-Scène du Théâtre,* No. 303 (15 Jan. 1964).

15. Carl Becker, 'The Dilemma of Diderot,' *Philosophical Review,* XXIV (1915), 65. Cf. Lionel Trilling, 'On the Modern Element in Modern Literature,' in *Varieties of Literary Experience,* ed. Stanley Burnshaw (New York, 1962), 428.

16. Charly Guyot, 'L'Homme du dialogue,' *Europe,* Nos. 405–6 (Jan.–Feb. 1963), 153–63.

17. Paul H. Meyer, 'The Unity and Structure of Diderot's "Neveu de Rameau",' *Criticism,* II (1960), 386; Roger Laufer, 'Structure et signification du "Neveu de Rameau" de Diderot,' *RScH,* No. 100 (Oct.–Dec. 1960), 413.

18. Roland Mortier, 'Diderot et le problème de l'expressivité: De la pensée au dialogue heuristique,' *CAIEF,* No. 13 (June 1961), 294–6; Crocker, ' "Le Neveu de Rameau," une expérience morale,' *CAIEF,* No. 13 (June 1961), 138; Frederick Plotkin, 'Mime as Pander: Diderot's *Neveu de Rameau,*' *SVEC,* LXX (1970), 27–41.

19. Ronald Grimsley, 'L'Ambiguité dans l'oeuvre romanesque de Diderot,' *CAIEF,* No. 13 (June 1961), 233–4.

20. Norman L. Torrey, in *RR,* XLI (1950), 302. One of the most ingenious, erudite, and multi-faceted interpretations is that by Donal O'Gorman, *Diderot the Satirist* (Toronto, 1971). O'Gorman, who displays an admirable knowledge of ancient philosophy in general and the philosophy of Socrates and Plato in particular, believes (199) that '*Le Neveu de Rameau* owes its principal inspiration to ancient literature' (cf. ibid., 92–135, 192). Moreover, he believes that Diderot's purpose in writing the dialogue was to provide 'an idealized confrontation of himself with Jean-Jacques' (215). For the development of this theme, see ibid., 110–8, 121–2, 131–3, 136–84).

21. James Doolittle, *Rameau's Nephew: A Study of Diderot's "Second Satire"* (Geneva, 1960), 37; Jacques Ehrmann, in *MLN,* LXXVII (1962), 111; Jean-Yves Pouilloux, 'L'Esthétique dans le "Neveu de Rameau",' *Pensée,* No. 129 (Oct. 1966), 73–90, esp. 86, 90. Similar conclusions were reached by a team of researchers at the Sorbonne (Michel Launay, 'Etude du "Neveu de Rameau": Hypothèses pour une recherche collective,' *Pensée,* No. 118 [Dec. 1964], 85–92; see also Michel Launay, 'Sur les intentions de Diderot dans le *Neveu de Rameau,*' *DS VIII* [1966], 117). Lilo Ebel, 'Apologie des "Neveu de Rameau",' *Schweizer Monatshefte,* XXIV (1944–5), 530–7, composes an interesting imaginary monologue in which the Nephew is portrayed as being motivated by his 'Verzweiflung über sein Versagen als Künstler' (537). That MOI is the winner is suggested by W. D. Wilson,

'A Hidden Parable in the *Neveu de Rameau?*' *RFor*, LXXVIII (1966), 115–8. On the subtle relationship between LUI and MOI, see Sharon L. Kabelac, 'Irony as a Metaphysics in *Le Neveu de Rameau*,' *DS XIV* (1971), 97–112.

22. L. Natalie Sandomirsky, 'The Ethical Standard of the Genius in Diderot's *Neveu de Rameau*,' *Symposium*, XVIII (1964), 46–55; see also Klaus Heitmann, *Ethos des Künstlers und Ethos der Kunst. Eine problemgeschichtliche Skizze anlässlich Diderots* (Münster, [1962]), 8–9 and *passim*.

23. Eleanor M. Walker, 'Towards an Understanding of Diderot's Esthetic Theory,' *RR*, XXXV (1944), 277–87, esp. 284; Margaret Gilman, 'The Poet according to Diderot,' *RR*, XXXVII (1946), 37–54, esp. 49–50, 54. Of particular excellence is Dieckmann, 'Diderot's Conception of Genius,' *JHI*, II, 159, 181–2; for a contrary view, see F. C. Green, in *MLR*, LI (1956), 274. See also Otis Fellows, 'The Theme of Genius in Diderot's *Neveu de Rameau*,' *DS II* (1952), 196; and Amy L. Marsland, 'Identity and Theme in *Le Neveu de Rameau*,' *RR*, LX (1969), 34–46.

24. This view is adopted by Milton F. Seiden, 'The Protagonists in Diderot's *Neveu de Rameau*,' *Dissertation Abstracts*, XIV (1954), 1729–30; see the dissertation itself, same title (Ann Arbor: University Microfilms, 1954), 60, 172.

25. Daniel Mornet, 'La Véritable signification du *Neveu de Rameau*,' *RDM*, 15 Aug. 1927, 881–908, esp. 892; Daniel Mornet, *Le Neveu de Rameau* (Paris: Les Cours de lettres [mimeographed], 1948), 17 [a reprinting of this work, with an excellent bibliography compiled by Alexander Cioranescu, was published in 1965]); Louis Barthou, 'Quelques réflexions sur le "Neveu de Rameau",' *Revue de France*, 1 Dec. 1924, 544–51.

26. Lionel Trilling, 'The Legacy of Sigmund Freud: Literary and Aesthetic,' *Kenyon Review*, II (1940), 154; also Lionel Trilling, *The Liberal Imagination* (New York, 1950), 36.

27. Edmond and Jules de Goncourt, *Journal: Mémoires de la vie littéraire*, 22 vols. (Monaco, 1956–8), II, 218 (13 April 1858).

28. C. J. Greshoff, 'Diderot's *Neveu de Rameau*,' in his *Seven Studies in the French Novel* (Cape Town, 1964), 20.

29. Ronald Grimsley, 'Psychological Aspects of *Le Neveu de Rameau*,' *MLQ*, XVI (1955), 196; cf. Yvon Belaval, 'Nouvelles recherches sur Diderot,' *Critique*, XIV (1956), 402 n.

30. Diderot, *Le Neveu de Rameau*, ed. Fabre, lxiii–lxv, xciv–xcv.

31. Ernst Robert Curtius, 'Diderots *Neveu de Rameau*,' *RFor*, LVI (1942), 128–43; also G. Rohlfs, in *ASNSL*, CLXXXII (1943), 137–8. See also E. R. Curtius, 'Diderot und Horaz,' in his *Europäische Literatur und lateinisches Mittelalter* (Bern, 1948), 556–64; and Karl Maurer, 'Die Satire in der Weise des Horaz als Kunstform von Diderots "Neveu de Rameau",' *RFor*, LXIV (1952), 365–404. The epigraph is: 'Vertumnis, quotquot sunt, natus iniquis' (Horace, *Satires*, lib. II, Sat. VII, v. 14; translation by Gilbert Highet).

   'Satire II' (Dieckmann, *Inventaire*, 71–2). The 'Satyre Ière' is that entitled 'Sur les caractères et les mots de caractère, de profession, etc.' (A.-T., VI, 303–16; the best edition of this is in O'Gorman, *Diderot the Satirist*, 226–41. For historical and critical comment, see ibid., 3–17). See also Herbert Dieckmann, 'The Relationship between Diderot's *Satire I* and *Satire II*,' *RR*, XLIII (1952), 12–26. For an excellent discussion of what Diderot meant when he called his work a satire, see O'Gorman, *Diderot the Satirist*, 201–12.

32. Lucian (John Jay Chapman, *Lucian, Plato and Greek Morals* [Boston, 1931], 73–4). Juvenal (Gilbert Highet, *Juvenal the Satirist* [Oxford, 1954], 217–8, 331). Petronius (Barthold Georg Niebuhr, *Kleine historische und philologische Schriften*, 2 vols. [Bonn, 1828], I, 350–1). The comparison with Petronius was also made by Edmond de Goncourt, *Journal: Mémoires de la vie littéraire*, XVIII, 11 (12 April 1891); cf. Donald Schier, 'Voltaire and Diderot in the Goncourt *Journal*,' *FR*, XXXIX (1965–6), 258–64.

33. Mortier, *Diderot en Allemagne*, 281; cf. ibid., 281–8. The whole passage in Hegel is in his *The Phenomenology of Mind*, 2 vols. (London, 1910), II, 488–533, esp. 496, 527–8. Cf. Yvon Belaval, 'Le "Philosophe" Diderot,' *Critique*, VIII^{2} (1952), 234–5; also Gottfried Stiehler, ' "Rameaus Neffe" und die "Phänomenologie des Geistes" von Hegel,' in *WZUB*, XIII (1964), 163–7; and Henri Mougin, 'Hegel et le Neveu de Rameau,' *Europe*, Aug. 1946, 1–11. See also Hettner, *Literaturgeschichte des achtzehnten Jahrhunderts*, II, 333–4.

34. Jean Hyppolite, *Genèse et structure de la* Phénoménologie de l'Esprit *de Hegel* (Paris, [1946]), 387, 398–9, 401.
35. Marx to Engels, London, 15 April 1869 (various eds.: e.g., Karl Marx/Friedrich Engels, *Ausgewählte Briefe* [Moscow-Leningrad, 1934], 213–4); for the significance of this letter, see Roland Mortier, 'Diderot sous le prisme de la critique marxiste,' in International Comparative Literature Association, *Proceedings of the Second Congress* (Chapel Hill [N.C.], 1959), II, 680–2. Lefebvre, *Diderot*, 209–13; Mougin, art. cit., *Europe* (Aug. 1946), 1–11.
36. Roland Desné, '*Le Neveu de Rameau* dans l'ombre et la lumière du XVIIIe siècle,' *SVEC*, XXV (1963), 494–5, 503; the same, 'Monsieur le Philosophe et le fieffé truand,' *Europe*, Nos. 405–6 (Jan.–Feb. 1963), 193–6; Diderot, *Le Neveu de Rameau*, ed. Roland Desné (Paris, [1963]), LX–LXii. See also Roland Desné's excellent remarks in *Entretiens sur "Le Neveu de Rameau,"* ed. Duchet and Launay, 263–72.
37. For analyses of the structure of *Le Neveu de Rameau* (Patrick Brady, 'Structure and Substructure of *Le Neveu de Rameau,*' *Esprit Créateur*, VIII [1968], 34–41; Doolittle, *Rameau's Nephew, passim;* Laufer, art. cit., *RScH*, No. 100 [Oct.–Dec. 1960], 399–413; Meyer, art. cit., *Criticism*, II, 362–86). For stylistic analyses (Spitzer, 'The Style of Diderot,' in his *Linguistics and Literary History*, esp. 151–62; Stephen Ullmann, in *FS*, III (1949), 159; Richard A. Sayce, *Style in French Prose: A Method of Analysis* (Oxford, 1953), 15, 30, 93, 99–101, 119–20; Yves Le Hir, 'Diderot: Le Renégat d'Avignon,' in his *Analyses stylistiques* (Paris, 1965), 139–47). Regarding Diderot's use of metaphor and simile (Egon Huber, 'Bemerkungen zu Diderots Gebrauch von Vergleich und Metapher in "Le Neveu de Rameau",' in Günter Reichenkron, Mario Wandruszka and Julius Wilhelm, ed., *Syntactica und Stilistica. Festschrift für Ernst Gamillscheg* [Tübingen, 1957], 229–42). For detailed stylistic analysis, see *Entretiens sur "Le Neveu de Rameau,"* ed. Duchet and Launay, 53–87.
38. Laufer, art. cit., *RScH*, No. 100 (Oct.–Dec. 1960), 412.
39. Jean Thomas, 'Diderot, les Encyclopédistes et le grand Rameau,' *Revue de Synthèse*, LXIX (1951), 46–67.
40. Jean-Pierre Barricelli, 'Music and the Structure of Diderot's "Le Neveu de Rameau",' *Criticism*, V (1963), 98, 103, 105.
41. A.-T., VI, 315.
42. Fellows, 'The Theme of Genius in Diderot's *Neveu de Rameau,*' *DS II*, 195.
43. Pierre Trahard, *Les Maîtres de la sensibilité française au XVIIIe siècle (1715–1789)*, 4 vols. (Paris, [1931–3]), II, 49–286. Regarding Diderot's slow but firm change-over, see Arthur M. Wilson, 'The Biographical Implications of Diderot's *Paradoxe sur le comédien,*' *DS III* (1961), 374–6; and O'Gorman, *Diderot the Satirist*, 197–9.
44. A.-T., VII, 404.
45. Crocker, art. cit., *CAIEF*, No. 13 (June 1961), 148–9; Horst Baader, 'Diderots Theorie der Schauspielkunst und ihre Parallelen in Deutschland,' *RLC*, XXXIII (1959), 200–23, esp. 204, 206, 209; Pouilloux, 'L'Esthétique dans le "Neveu de Rameau",' *Pensée*, No. 129 (Oct. 1966), 85–6.
46. A.-T., XIII, 16–26 (15 March 1760), esp. 26.
47. A.-T., XIII, 27–31; also *Corr. litt.*, IV, 249–53 (1 July 1760). Diderot visited Jean-Gabriel Le Gendre at Châlons in 1759, en route from Langres to Paris (Diderot, *Corr.*, II, 245). In 1765 Le Gendre himself described the embellishment of Rheims in a magnificent elephant folio volume, *Description de la place de Louis XV que l'on construit à Reims, des ouvrages à continuer aux environs de cette place et de ceux à faire dans la suite pour l'utilité et l'embellissement de cette ville* (Paris, 1765). Diderot probably helped Le Gendre write this *Description* (Diderot, *Corr.*, VI, 54 [14 Feb. 1766]).
48. A.-T., XIII, 28, 27. Cf. Thomas Cassirer, 'Awareness of the City in the *Encyclopédie,*' *JHI*, XXIV (1963), 388.
49. *Corr. litt.*, IV, 328–33 (15 Dec. 1760); also in A.-T., XIII, 3–9, wrongly dated 1753.
50. Diderot, *Salons*, I, 110.
51. Diderot, *Salons*, I, 131, 117.
52. Diderot, *Salons*, I, 136.

53. Diderot, *Salons*, I, 125 (Chardin); 114, 133 (Rubens); 113 (Annibale Carracci); 110 (Correggio); 127 (Claude Lorrain); 126 (Van der Meulen); 120 (Le Brun); 140 (Salvator Rosa); 127, 143 (Teniers); 129 (Van Dyck); 112 (Boucher and Ariosto).
54. Diderot, *Salons*, I, 116.
55. Diderot, *Salons*, I, 133, 113, 119.
56. Diderot, *Salons*, I, 133–4; see also the editors' remarks on Diderot's retentive memory (ibid., I, 18: 'Diderot est un visuel'). See also Gita May, *Diderot et Baudelaire, critiques d'art* (Geneva, 1957), 62; Dieckmann, *Cinq leçons sur Diderot*, 135.
57. Diderot, *Salons*, I, 138.
58. Diderot, *Salons*, I, 141–4; Peter Gay remarks of Diderot's comment on 'Une gorge faite au tour qu'on ne voit point du tout' (*Salons*, I, 142), 'Diderot was by all odds the oddest modern Stoic I know' (Peter Gay, *The Bridge of Criticism* [New York, (1970)], 166). Grimm's comments (Diderot, *Salons*, I, 144–6). Greuze's picture was not ready to be hung until 19 Sept. 1761, almost a month after the opening of the Salon (ibid., I, 74, 99).
59. Diderot, *Corr.*, III, 307, 305 (17 Sept. 1761); cf. Diderot to Mme d'Epinay, 16 Sept. 1761 (ibid., III, 304).
60. A.-T., v, 222. *Journal Etranger*, Jan. 1762, 5–38.
61. *Corr. litt.*, v, 24 (15 Jan. 1762); A.-T., v, 227. In 1778 Diderot, writing to Naigeon, implied that he had written the *Eloge de Richardson* in a day (A.-T., III, 11).
62. In his *Confessions* Rousseau wrote, '. . . les romans de Richardson, quoique M. Diderot en ait pu dire, ne sauroient sur cet article, entrer en parallèle avec le mien' (Rousseau, *Oeuvres complètes*, 'Bibliothèque de la Pléïäde,' I, 547 and 1541). See Joseph Texte, *Jean-Jacques Rousseau et les origines du cosmopolitisme littéraire* (Paris, 1895), 266, 280–1.
63. Marlou Switten, 'L'Histoire and La Poésie in Diderot's Writings on the Novel,' *RR*, XLVII (1956), 260. See also Hans Robert Jauss, 'Nachahmungsprinzip und Wirklichkeitsbegriff in der Theorie des Romans von Diderot bis Stendhal,' in Hans R. Jauss, ed., *Nachahmung und Illusion* (Munich, 1964), 157–63, 237–46.
64. [Anon.], 'Diderot,' *Westminster Review*, CXXXII (1889), 231–46, this quotation 239; Dieckmann, 'The Préface-Annexe of La Religieuse,' *DS II*, 32. Cf. Philippe Van Tieghem, *Les Influences étrangères sur la littérature française, 1550–1880* (Paris, 1961), 96–8, 101. Joseph Wood Krutch refers to 'the famous "Eloge" in which, by reflection, we can perceive far better than we can by any effort at direct comprehension, what "Clarissa" meant to the Eighteenth Century' (Joseph Wood Krutch, *Five Masters* [London, 1931], 168).
65. A.-T., v, 214, 218; Diderot, *Corr.*, III, 173–4.
66. Taupin, 'Richardson, Diderot et l'art de conter,' *FR*, XII, 181–94; Cru, 357–69; Denis Diderot, *Oeuvres romanesques*, ed. Henri Bénac (Paris, 1951), xii; Texte, *Jean-Jacques Rousseau et les origines du cosmopolitisme littéraire*, 265.
67. A.-T., v, 218. Ducros, *Diderot: L'homme et l'écrivain*, 193. Cf. Hans Robert Jauss, 'Diderots Paradox über das Schauspiel (*Entretiens sur le "Fils Naturel"*),' *Germanisch-romanische Monatsschrift*, XI (1961), 399, 409.
68. Herbert Dieckmann, 'The Presentation of Reality in Diderot's Tales,' *DS III* (1961), 108–10; Frank Howard Wilcox, *Prévost's Translations of Richardson's Novels* (Berkeley, 1927), 408; Luc, *Diderot*, 63; Mylne, *The Eighteenth-Century French Novel: Techniques of Illusion*, 192–3.
69. A.-T., v, 214, 215.
70. A.-T., v, 224–6, 220. Diderot, *Corr.*, III, 306 (17 Sept. 1761); see also ibid., III, 173–4, 310–1, 317–8; ibid., IV, 151–2.
71. 'Ce qui me confond, c'est le goût qui règne là; avec une simplicité, une force, et un pathétique incroyable' (Diderot, *Corr.*, III, 337 [12 Oct. 1761]).
72. *Journal Etranger*, Jan. 1762, 5–38. Diderot's translation of 'Shilric et Vinvela' appeared in the *Journal Etranger* for Dec. 1761, 52–4, and was also included by Grimm in the *Corr. litt.*, IV, 495–6 (1 Dec. 1761). Diderot may also have translated the fragment 'Connal et Crimora' in the same issue of the *Journal Etranger*, 59–60 (Alfred C. Hunter, *J.-B.-A. Suard, un introducteur de la littérature anglaise en France* [Bibliothèque de la *RLC*, XXII] [Paris, 1925], 54); moreover, according to Hunter, op. cit., 54–5, Diderot was the translator of

'Lathmon,' *Journal Etranger*, Jan. 1762, 135–59, and 'Oithona,' *Journal Etranger*, Feb. 1762, 194–207. Cf. Paul Van Tieghem, *Ossian en France*, 2 vols. (Paris, 1917), I, 130–2.

73. Georges May, 'The Influence of English Fiction on the French Mid-Eighteenth-Century Novel,' in Earl R. Wasserman, ed., *Aspects of the Eighteenth Century* (Baltimore, 1965), 271–4, 278. By 1804 the *Eloge* had been reprinted, usually in editions either of Diderot's works or of Richardson's, eighteen times in French, once in German, and once in Italian. In half of these instances Diderot was not mentioned as the author.

74. Dieckmann, 'Diderot et son lecteur,' in his *Cinq leçons sur Diderot*, 15–39, esp. 36–8.

75. A.-T., v, 226.

76. A.-T., v, 227.

CHAPTER 33

1. 'Je suis un bon citoyen. . . .' (A.-T., IX, 223). For the author of *L'Esprit des lois* and the author of *Du Contrat social*, the point is obvious; regarding Voltaire, see the admirable study by Peter Gay, *Voltaire's Politics: The Poet as Realist* (Princeton, 1959); for Diderot, see Arthur M. Wilson, 'The Development and Scope of Diderot's Political Thought,' *SVEC*, XXVII (1963), 1871–1900.

2. A.-T., IX, 192–3. In the *Plan d'une université pour le gouvernement de Russie* Diderot again mentions the value of probability theory (A.-T., III, 456).

3. *Année Littéraire*, vol. II for 1758, 109.

4. Jean Le Rond d'Alembert, *Oeuvres*, 5 vols. (Paris, 1821–2), I, 451–62.

5. Joseph Bertrand, *D'Alembert* (Paris, 1889), 51; cf. Grimsley, *Jean d'Alembert*, 7; also Louis de Broglie, 'Un Mathématicien, homme de lettres: d'Alembert,' *AUP*, XXII (1952), 31.

6. Diderot, *Corr.*, III, 319, 349; for the memoir, see A.-T., IX, 192–206. The text is made more intelligible through the researches of Otis Fellows and Donal O'Gorman, 'A Note concerning Diderot's Mathematics,' *DS X* (1968), 47–50. Jean Mayer, 'D'Alembert et l'Académie des Sciences,' in International Federation for Modern Languages and Literatures, *Acta*, VI, *Literature and Science* (Oxford, 1955), 202–5; see also Jean Mayer, *Diderot homme de science* (Rennes, 1959), 80–3, and Lester G. Krakeur and Raymond L. Krueger, 'The Mathematical Writings of Diderot,' *Isis*, XXXIII (1941–2), 225.

7. *Encyc.*, XIII, 399b (cf. Mayer, *Diderot homme de science*, 68). I follow Mayer, op. cit., 85–6, in believing Diderot to be the author of the article 'Probabilité.'

8. D'Alembert, *Oeuvres*, I, 465–514. His reading the memoir to the Académie des Sciences was reported in the *Gazette de France*, 15 Nov. 1760, 184.

9. This point is made in the excellent study by Thomas L. Hankins, *Jean D'Alembert: Science and the Enlightenment* (New York, 1970), 146. See also Bertrand, *D'Alembert*, 49–50; cf. M.-J. Laboulle, 'La Mathématique sociale: Condorcet et ses prédécesseurs,' *RHLF*, XLVI (1939), 40; also Maurice Muller, *Essai sur la philosophie de Jean d'Alembert* (Paris, 1926), 42–4.

10. Georg Misch, 'Zur Entstehung des französischen Positivismus,' *Archiv für Geschichte der Philosophie*, XIV (1901), 1–39, 156–63. Especially thoughtful on this point is Robert E. Butts, 'Rationalism in Modern Science: D'Alembert and the *Esprit simpliste*,' *Bucknell Review*, VIII (1958–9), 127–39. See also Briggs, 'D'Alembert: Philosophy and Mechanics in the Eighteenth Century,' *University of Colorado Studies, Series in History*, No. 3, 38–56, esp. 41, 55.

11. May, *Quatre visages de Denis Diderot*, 66; John Pappas, 'Diderot, D'Alembert et l'*Encyclopédie*,' *DS IV* (1963), 204. Cf. Part I, 287–90, 307–8.

12. Diderot, *Corr.*, III, 46 (31 Aug. 1760).

13. Diderot, *Corr.*, III, 267 (25 Nov. 1760). On La Condamine, see the excellent biographical study by Pierre M. Conlon, 'La Condamine the Inquisitive,' *SVEC*, LV (1967), 361–93, esp. 384–91.

14. *Encyc.*, VIII, 755–71. Cf. Dr. Jean Olivier, 'Tronchin et l'inoculation,' *Progrès Médical*, LXXVII (1949), 321–2; also Arnold H. Rowbotham, 'The "Philosophes" and the Propaganda

for the Inoculation of Smallpox in Eighteenth-Century France' (Berkeley, 1935), 265–90; also Genevieve Miller, *The Adoption of Inoculation for Smallpox in England and France* (Philadelphia, 1957), esp. 216–20, 225; and Renée Waldinger, 'Voltaire and Medicine,' *SVEC*, LVIII (1967), 1800–5.

15. Diderot to Guénau de Montbeillard, 8 April 1767 (Diderot, *Corr.*, VII, 49); 'ma petite bonne en étoit quitte avant que sa mère fût relevée de ses couches' (ibid.).

16. A.-T., IX, 211; see Mayer, 'D'Alembert et l'Académie des Sciences,' [*supra*, n. 6], 203; and Mayer, *Diderot homme de science*, 379–80. Diderot's 'De l'inoculation' was first published in A.-T., IX, 207–12; Grimm sent it to Stockholm in the *Correspondance littéraire* for 1 Dec. 1761, quite freely edited and without attribution to Diderot.

17. A.-T., IX, 212.

18. *Mémoires de Trévoux*, vol. II for April 1761, 976–98; reprinted in *Journal des Sçavans, combiné avec les Mémoires de Trévoux*, LIX (May 1761), 121–35; A.-T., IX, 183–91. Regarding the history of this paper, see Jean Th. de Booy, 'A propos d'un texte de Diderot sur Newton,' *DS IV* (1963), 41–51.

19. A.-T., IX, 185–6, 184. See Krakeur and Krueger, art. cit., *Isis*, XXXIII (1941–2), 227; Mayer, *Diderot homme de science*, 196–200. I am unable to agree at this point with the excellent book by Colm Kiernan, *Science and the Enlightenment in Eighteenth-Century France* (*SVEC*, LIX [1968]), 139–40, who regards Diderot's paper as an attack on Newtonianism.

20. Diderot, *Corr.*, III, 64, 96–7, 256, 270. Marcel, *Le Frère de Diderot*, 76–7; cf. A. E. A. Naughton, 'Diderot and his Brother,' *RR*, XXVI (1935), 17–26.

21. Inasmuch as Diderot was paid on 29 May 1760 for the articles beginning with L and M (May, 73), I infer that an article beginning with I was written by that time. 'Dear brother' (Diderot, *Corr.*, III, 283–8, this quotation 288; also in A.-T., I, 485–90). A manuscript copy of this 'Lettre à mon frère' is in the Fonds Vandeul (Dieckmann, *Inventaire*, 85).

22. Kungl. Biblioteket (Stockholm), Vu. 29:2, foll. 9–12. See Vincent Eugene Bowen, *Contributions from Diderot and Grimm in the Stockholm Manuscript of the* Correspondance littéraire (*1760–1774*) (Ann Arbor: University Microfilms, 1957), 60–3. For the article 'Intolérance' as published, see *Encyc.*, VIII, 843–4; also in A.-T., XV, 235–40.

23. Vincent E. Bowen, 'Two Unpublished Poems by Diderot,' *MLN*, LXXIII (1958), 188–90; also published in *Europe*, Nos. 405–6 (Jan.–Feb. 1963), 210. For the 'Chanson dans le goût de la romance,' see *Corr. litt.*, IV, 12–5 and A.-T., IX, 60–2.

24. *Qu'en pensez-vous?*, in the Stockholm manuscript for 1 Feb. 1761, bears a note added to the text in another hand, stating that 'Le morceau suivant est de Madame *** . . .' (De Booy, 'Inventaire,' 362). *Qu'en pensez-vous?* was first attributed to Diderot in the Brière edition of his works (*Oeuvres de Denis Diderot*, 20 vols. [Paris, 1821], II, 554–60), but with no information concerning provenance; it was republished in A.-T., IV, 444–8. However, no copy of it appears among the Diderot manuscripts in Leningrad or in the Fonds Vandeul (Bowen, *Contributions from Diderot and Grimm in the Stockholm Manuscript. . .*, 131–44). In 1961 Herbert Dieckmann wrote that 'There exists only some probability that the latter conte [*Qu'en pensez-vous?*] is by Diderot' ('The Presentation of Reality in Diderot's Tales,' *DS III* [1961], 116 n.); his detailed analysis in 1963 of 'the complexity of the question' made him less sure that it was not by Diderot (Diderot, *Contes*, ed. H. Dieckmann [London, 1963], 27–8. See also the review by Jacques Proust, in *RHLF*, LXV [1965], 317). Although I attributed *Qu'en pensez-vous?* to Diderot in *The Testing Years* (Part I), 63, 730 n. 14, my subsequent examination of the Stockholm manuscript makes me now believe that the allegory is by Mme d'Epinay. It was published in the (so-called) *Mémoires et correspondance de Mme d'Epinay. . .*, 2nd edition, 3 vols. (Paris, 1818), II, 77–83, and in the (so-called) *Mémoires de Madame d'Epinay*, ed. Paul Boiteau, 2 vols. (Paris, 1863), I, 395–400, as well as in the authoritative *Les Pseudo-Mémoires de Madame d'Epinay*, ed. Roth, II, 426–30, the editor stating (II, 426 n.) that the conte is by Diderot. A shortened version of the allegory is used by Diderot in his *Entretien d'un philosophe avec la maréchale de ***** (Denis Diderot, *Oeuvres philosophiques*, ed. Paul Vernière [Paris, 1956], 548–51; cf. esp. ibid., 549 n.), which provides a strong argument, I confess, for concluding that the earlier version was by him also. Tangentially, some light is thrown on

the problem of authorship — at least, it is not by Rousseau — by Pierre-Maurice Masson, 'Mme d'Epinay, Jean-Jacques . . . et Diderot chez Mlle Quinault,' *AJJR*, IX (1913), 1–28, esp. 23–6.

In the Stockholm manuscript for 1 Aug. 1761 is the following notation: 'Le Dialogue suivant est de Madame *** dont vous avez lu le Qu'en pensez-vous? il y a quelques mois. . . .' There then follows: 'Premier Dialogue. La Marquise de Claye et le Comte de Saint-Alban.' (De Booy, 'Inventaire,' 363). This piece was first attributed to Diderot in *Oeuvres de Denis Diderot*, 7 vols. (Paris: Belin, 1818–9), VII, 294–304, and republished in A.-T., IV, 449–61. Trahard, *Les Maîtres de la sensibilité française au XVIIIe siècle*, II, 164 n., speaks of it as a 'chef-d'oeuvre' and attributes it to Diderot. However, no copy of this dialogue appears among the Diderot manuscripts at Leningrad or in the Fonds Vandeul (Bowen, op. cit., 145–6). This complex question is analyzed by Dieckmann in his edition of Diderot, *Contes*, 26–9; he claims a strong probability for Diderot's authorship, which is a slight attenuation of his opinion in 'The Presentation of Reality in Diderot's Tales,' *DS III*, 119. It must be remembered that a passage in *La Marquise de Claye et Saint-Alban* (A.-T., IV, 456) is paralleled in Diderot's *Sur les femmes* (A.-T., II, 251), thus suggesting Diderot's authorship of both (Leif Nedergaard, 'Notes sur certains ouvrages de Diderot: Sources, dates, parallèles,' *Orbis Litterarum*, VIII [1950], 18–9).

Cinqmars et Derville. A marginal notation in the Stockholm manuscript of 15 Aug. 1761 states: 'Le dialogue suivant est de la même main que le précédent.' In the Stockholm manuscript this piece is entitled 'Second Dialogue' (De Booy, 'Inventaire,' 363). *Cinqmars et Derville* was first attributed to Diderot in the Belin edition of the *Oeuvres de Denis Diderot*, VII (1819), 305–14, and was republished in the Brière edition of the *Oeuvres de Denis Diderot* (1821), II, 525–41; and in A.-T., IV, 463–74. No copy of it appears in the Diderot manuscripts at Leningrad or in the Fonds Vandeul (Bowen, op. cit., 155–6). Diderot's authorship is 'a strong probability,' according to Dieckmann (Diderot, *Contes*, 28–9; cf. his 'The Presentation of Reality in Diderot's Tales,' *DS III*, 113).

Mon père et moi appears in the Stockholm manuscript for 15 Dec. 1761 without specific attribution of authorship. However, it is entitled 'Troisième Dialogue,' thus evidently belonging in a series the first and second of which were *La Marquise de Claye et le Comte de Saint-Alban* and *Derville et Cinqmars*, both of which were specifically attributed to 'a Lady' and not to Diderot. No copy of this third dialogue has been found in the Diderot manuscripts at Leningrad or in the Fonds Vandeul (Bowen, op. cit., 162). *Mon père et moi* was first attributed to Diderot in the Belin edition of his works, VII (1819), 314–20, and was republished in the Brière edition, II (1821), 542–53; and in A.-T., IV, 475–82. De Booy is categorical in denying Diderot's authorship of these four pieces (De Booy, 'Inventaire,' 362–3, 364). For identical evidence in the Gotha manuscript, confirming the Stockholm manuscript regarding the authorship of these four dialogues, see Jean Varloot, 'La "Correspondance littéraire" de F.-M. Grimm à la lumière des manuscrits de Gotha: Contributions ignorées, collaborateurs mal connus,' in *Beiträge zur französischen Aufklärung und zur spanischen Literatur*, ed. Werner Bahner (Berlin, 1971), 438.

25. Diderot, *Corr.*, III, 212, 321; A.-T., V, 216. These facts mentioned by Tourneux, *Diderot et Catherine II*, 4; Antoine Sauro, *Diderot* (Bari, [1953]), 34.

26. Mme Geoffrin's daughter declared that her mother had pledged a sum of not less than 300,000 livres to the publishers, thus enabling the work to be continued (Pierre-Marie-Maurice-Henri, marquis de Ségur, *Le Royaume de la rue Saint-Honoré: Madame Geoffrin et sa fille* [Paris, 1897], 318–9). But the daughter did not say just when this occurred, nor does the publishers' account book bear any trace of it. Lough cautions that there is no evidence that Mme Geoffrin handed over any money to the publishers (John Lough, 'Mme Geoffrin and the "Encyclopédie",' *MLR*, LVIII [1963], 219–22).

27. May, 108; see also ibid., 91, 97. John Lough, 'Louis, Chevalier de Jaucourt (1704–1780), A Biographical Sketch,' in Durham, Eng., University, King's College, Newcastle upon Tyne, *Essays Presented to C. M. Girdlestone* (Newcastle upon Tyne, 1960), 210.

28. May, 77–8, 108; Proust, *Diderot et l'Encyclopédie*, 104–5. Beginning on 8 Aug. 1761, quarterly payments of 375 livres were accordingly made regularly on the 8 of August,

November, February, and May, for as long as the publishers' accounts are extant, i.e., through 8 November 1767 (May, 79–80, 82–94, 96–7).

29. Diderot, *Corr.*, III, 307, 313, 319.

30. Diderot, *Corr.*, III, 313, 316, 329, 333–4, 335–6, 343.

31. Edmund Heier, 'The Encyclopedists and L. H. Nicolay (1737–1820),' *RLC*, XXXVI (1962), 497; Ludwig Heinrich von Nicolay, *L. H. Nicolay (1737–1820) and his Contemporaries*, ed. Edmund Heier (The Hague, 1965), 76.

32. Diderot, *Corr.*, VII, 272; also ibid., III, 321 (28 Sept. 1761), 337 (12 Oct. 1761), and 347–9 (25 Oct. 1761); see also Roland Mortier, 'Diderot et ses "Deux Petits Allemands",' *RLC*, XXXIII (1959), 192–9; and Mortier, *Diderot en Allemagne*, 14–5.

33. Diderot, *Corr.*, III, 347; Nicolay, *L. H. Nicolay*, ed. Heier, 77.

34. Diderot, *Corr.*, III, 321 (28 Sept. 1761). Their translation is probably the one now in the Fonds Vandeul (B.N., MSS, Nouv. acq. fr. 13737; see Dieckmann, *Inventaire*, 34–6; also Robert Niklaus, 'La Portée des théories dramatiques de Diderot et de ses réalisations theâtrales,' *RR*, LIV [1963], 10 and n.).

35. Diderot, *Corr.*, IV, 106 (15 Aug. 1762); cf. Hermann Hettner, *Literaturgeschichte des achtzehnten Jahrhunderts*, II, 329–30.

36. A.-T., VIII, 441, 440. Cf. Robert R. Heitner, 'Diderot's Own *Miss Sara Sampson*,' *Comparative Literature*, V (1953), 40–9. Maurice Tourneux, 'Les Manuscrits de Diderot conservés en Russie,' *Archives des Missions Scientifiques et Littéraires*, 3ᵐᵉ série, XII (1885), 448, believed that this preface dated from 1755, but internal evidence as well as Diderot's correspondence both make 1762 seem more likely. A summary and critique of 'Miss Sara Sampson, Tragédie bourgeoise de M. Lessing,' *Journal Etranger*, Dec. 1761, 5–41, was attributed to Diderot by Karl Rosenkranz, 'Ueber Diderot's Theater,' *Jahrbuch für Litteraturgeschichte*, I (1865), 135; but see Fred O. Nolte, 'The Authorship of a Review of Lessing's *Miss Sara Sampson*,' *PMLA*, XLIII (1928), 220–36.

37. Fredman, *Diderot and Sterne*, 5–6; but cf. Rodney E. Harris, in *Comparative Literature*, VIII (1956), 268–9.

38. Laurence Sterne, *Letters*, ed. Lewis Perry Curtis (Oxford, 1935), 162.

39. Ibid., 166.

40. John Hampton, *Nicolas-Antoine Boulanger et la science de son temps* (Geneva, 1955); Franco Venturi, *L'Antichità svelata e l'idea del progresso in N.A. Boulanger (1722–1759)* (Bari, 1947); Frank E. Manuel, *The Eighteenth Century Confronts the Gods* (Cambridge [Mass.], 1959), 210–27; J. Chaix-Ruy, 'Un disciple hétérodoxe de Jean-Baptiste Vico: Nicolas Boulanger,' *RLC*, XXI (1947), 161–89.

41. A.-T., VI, 339–46, this quotation 344.

42. Grosclaude, *Malesherbes, témoin et interprète de son temps*, 152.

43. See the valuable article by Richard Koebner, 'Despot and Despotism: Vicissitudes of a Political Term,' *Journal of the Warburg and Courtauld Institutes*, XIV (1951), 275–302.

44. [Nicolas-Antoine Boulanger], *Recherches sur l'origine du despotisme oriental* ([Geneva], 1761), xx–xxi, xxii. See Venturi, *L'Antichità svelata*, 66–74: 'Un Manifesto illuminista del 1761.' Voltaire on Diderot's authorship (Franco Venturi, 'Postille inedite di Voltaire ad alcune opere di Nicolas-Antoine Boulanger e del barone d'Holbach,' *Studi Francesi*, II, [May–Aug. 1958], 233). Hampton, op. cit., 38–40, on the contrary, assumes that the letter was written by Boulanger. Grimm, in *Corr. litt.*, V, 366, says that the letter was written to Helvétius, and also remarks that 'Ce morceau est mieux écrit que l'ouvrage même de M. Boulanger' (ibid., 367). I incline to believe that Diderot was the author, for I believe that Voltaire would have been well informed. See also Wilson, 'The Development and Scope of Diderot's Political Thought,' *SVEC*, XXVII, 1880–2.

45. D'Hémery's report, 29 April 1762 (B.N., MSS, Nouv. acq. fr. 1214, foll. 370–1; cf. Venturi, 'Postille . . . ,' *Studi Francesi*, II, 231–2; Hampton, op. cit., 46–7); A.-T., XVIII, 62.

46. Diderot, *Corr.*, IV, 69 (25 July 1762).

47. Voltaire to Damilaville, 8 Feb. [1762] (Besterman, No. 9519).

48. Venturi, *L'Antichità svelata*, 68. See also the review of *L'Antichità svelata* by Eugenio Garin, in *Giornale Critico della Filosofia Italiana*, 3rd series, X (1956), 445.

49. A.-T., VI, 344.

50. Voltaire to Damilaville, 30 Jan. [1762] (Besterman, No. 9499). Cf. Pappas, *Voltaire & D'Alembert*, 92–3.

51. 'Sous Louis le bien-aimé,' ed. Jean Lemoine, *Revue de Paris*, vol. IV for 1905, 854 (4 Aug. 1762), 575 (30 July 1761). These articles comprise the exchange of letters between A.-R. de Mopinot and Mme de ***

52. Vincent Bernard de Tscharner to J. G. Zimmermann, 4 March 1761 (Enid Stoye, *Vincent Bernard de Tscharner, 1728–1778: A Study of Swiss Culture in the Eighteenth Century* [Fribourg, 1954], 127).

53. A.-T., XV, 449, s.v. 'Leibnitzianisme.'

54. Diderot, *Corr.*, III, 300; cf. ibid., III, 298 (To Mme d'Epinay, 19 Aug. 1761).

55. *Corr. litt.*, IV, 493; ibid., V, 22; *Annonces, Affiches, et Avis Divers*, 11 Nov. 1761, 181.

56. Diderot, *Corr.*, III, 310, 325; ibid., IV, 189 (7 Oct. 1762). Cf. ibid., III, 305, 321; ibid., IV, 171–2 (26 Sept. 1762); ibid., IV, 207 (24 Oct. 1762).

57. *Recueil de Planches, sur les Sciences, les Arts Libéraux, et les Arts Méchaniques, avec leur Explication*: vol. I (1762), 269 planches; approbation signed by De Parcieux, 26 Oct. 1761. Vol. II (1763), 233 planches, and vol. III (1763), 201 planches; approbation for both signed by De Parcieux, 18 March 1763, who also certified 'toutes gravées d'après des Desseins originaux qui m'ont aussi été représentés.'

58. *Recueil de Planches*, II, at the end of the 17 pp. of text explaining 'Alphabets anciens.'

59. *Corr. litt.*, V, 295 (15 May 1763). Scattered hither and yon in Diderot's correspondence are miscellaneous evidences of his work with the plates: plates on cheese from a M. Desmarets (Diderot, *Corr.*, III, 355); plates from Vialet on slate quarries (ibid., III, 333; IV, 35); plates that had to be redone because of Deferth, one of the engravers (ibid., IV, 250–1 [1 May 1763]); and especially an unpublished receipt, 19 May 1761, in the John Boyd Thacher Collection dossier 56, of the Library of Congress: 'J'ai reçu de Mr. Le Breton la somme de sept livres vin sols pour une planche et le port, la quelle planche represente un nouveau fourneau de la saline de Salins.'

60. Seguin, 'Courte histoire des planches de l'*Encyclopédie*,' in *L'Univers de l'Encyclopédie*, ed. Barthes, Mauzi, and Seguin, 31–4.

61. To Voltaire, 22 Feb. 1770 (Besterman, No. 15182).

62. David D. Bien, *The Calas Affair: Persecution, Toleration, and Heresy in Eighteenth-Century Toulouse* (Princeton, 1960), *passim*; see David D. Bien, 'The Background of the Calas Affair,' *History*, New Series, XLIII (1958), 192–206; also René Pomeau, 'Nouveau regard sur le dossier Calas,' *Europe*, No. 398 (June 1962), 57–72.

63. For instances of persecutions of the Calvinists during the administration of Cardinal Fleury and especially during the War of the Austrian Succession, see Jaques Serces, *Correspondance*, ed. Frédéric Gardy [*Publications of the Huguenot Society of London*, XLIII] (Frome, 1952), *passim*; and about the galleys and the Tour de Constance at Aigues-Mortes, ibid., 30–1, 56, 67, 131, 136, 167–70, 198, 208, 213.

64. Besterman, No. 9864; on the Calas case, see Edna Nixon, *Voltaire and the Calas Case* (New York, [1962]), esp. 139–40. For Voltaire's intervention, see the excellent discussion by Gay, *Voltaire's Politics*, 273–308.

65. Diderot's public passivity in the Calas case has been commented upon by Paolo Alatri, *Voltaire, Diderot e il "Partito Filosofico"* (Messina-Florence, [1965]), 287; see also Daniel Mornet, *Diderot, l'homme et l'oeuvre* (Paris, [1941]), 76. On 22 April 1765 Damilaville wrote to Voltaire of a scheme to engrave a drawing by Carmontelle, to be sold for the benefit of the Calas family. 'Nous sommes six honêtes gens,' he wrote, and it is quite likely though not absolutely certain that Diderot was one of the six (Besterman, No. 11717). The relative documents concerning the subscription are in B.N., MSS, Nouv. acq. fr. 1185; published, but without indication of provenance, in *Corr. litt.*, XVI, 352–63. Cf. Diderot, *Corr.*, V, 93–4 (18 Aug. 1765). An *exemplaire* of the Carmontelle engraving, done by Delafosse in 1765 (B.N., Département des Estampes, N 3).

66. This is hinted at by Mornet, *Diderot, l'homme et l'oeuvre*, 76.

67. Diderot, *Corr.*, IV, 97 (8 Aug. 1762). For other allusions to the Calas case, see ibid., 142–3, 143, 153–4, 179–81, 187.

68. Diderot, *Corr.*, IV, 179–81 (30 Sept. 1762).

69. Diderot, *Le Neveu de Rameau*, ed. Fabre, 42.

70. 25 Sept. 1762 (Besterman, No. 9917). For the text of the invitation to D'Alembert, see Bertrand, *D'Alembert*, 159–61; also *Corr. litt.*, v, 198–200 (1 Jan. 1763); cf. Grimsley, *Jean d'Alembert*, 172–3. For excellent bibliographical suggestions about Catherine II, see Gay, *The Enlightenment*, ii, 687–8.

71. The sole source for this letter is *Corr. litt.*, v, 199–200 (1 Jan. 1763); reprinted in Diderot, *Corr.*, iv, 173–4.

72. Besterman, No. 9852; Voltaire to Diderot, 25 Sept. 1762 (Besterman, No. 9914). Also on 25 Sept. 1762 Voltaire replied to Shuvalov: 'Je doute que les savant [*sic*] auteurs qui ont entrepris l'enciclopédie puissent profiter des bontez de Sa Majesté Impériale, attendu les engagements qu'ils ont pris en France' (Besterman, No. 9916).

73. Diderot, *Corr.*, iv, 175–6. Doubt as to whether Catherine II had staying power (Voltaire to the D'Argentals, 28 Sept. 1762 [Besterman, No. 9920]).

74. To Sophie Volland, 11 Nov. 1762 (Diderot, *Corr.*, iv, 220).

75. Part I, 55–8.

76. A.-T., i, 159, 160, 165; the whole *Addition* (ibid., 157–70). The *Addition* appeared in the Stockholm manuscript of the *Correspondance littéraire* for 1 Jan. 1763 (De Booy, 'Inventaire,' 365). The *Addition*, under the title of 'Pensées sur la Religion,' was published in the *Recueil philosophique ou Mélange de pieces sur la Religion & la Morale. Par différents Auteurs* [ed. Jacques-André Naigeon], 2 vols. (Londres [Amsterdam], 1770), ii, 113–24. The *Addition*, this time explicitly attributed to Diderot, was published by Naigeon in the three-volume section of the *Encyclopédie méthodique* devoted to 'Philosophie ancienne et moderne' (Paris, 1791–4), ii, 160–5. Cf. René Glotz, 'Conjecture sur un vers de Molière. Remarques et conjectures sur quelques passages de Diderot,' *RHLF*, xlii (1935), 554.

77. De Booy, 'Inventaire,' 365. Franco Venturi, 'Addition aux "Pensées philosophiques",' *RHLF*, xlv (1938), 23–42, 289–308; see also Venturi, *Jeunesse*, 72. Roland Mortier, 'A propos de la source de l' "Addition aux Pensées philosophiques" de Diderot,' *RHLF*, lxvii (1967), 609–12. See also the editorial comment in Diderot, *Oeuvres philosophiques*, ed. Vernière, 53–5.

78. May, *Quatre visages de Diderot*, 34–99: 'Diderot pessimiste: La Crise de mélancolie des années 1760–1762.'

79. A.-T., i, 169–70; cf. Leif Nedergaard, 'Notes sur certains ouvrages de Diderot,' *Orbis Litterarum*, viii (1950), 5–7.

80. *Corr. litt.*, v, 132–8 (1 Aug. 1762), this quotation 133; Paul Vernière, in *RHLF*, lv (1955), 77.

81. *Corr. litt.*, v, 134–6. Especially useful is Seznec, *Essais sur Diderot et l'antiquité*, 1–22: 'Le Socrate imaginaire.' See ibid., Planche 4, for the wax impression of Diderot's ring. Also valuable is Raymond Trousson, *Socrate devant Voltaire, Diderot et Rousseau: La conscience en face du mythe* (Paris, 1967), *passim*. In this connection, see also Jacques Chouillet, 'Le mythe d'Ariste ou Diderot en face de lui-même,' *RHLF*, lxiv (1964), 565–88.

82. Diderot, *Corr.*, iv, 98.

83. For this information I have relied heavily upon Jean Egret, 'Le Procès des Jésuites devant les Parlements de France (1761–1770),' *Revue Historique*, cciv (1950), 1–27; see also Paul Dudon, 'De la suppression de la Compagnie de Jésus (1758–1773),' *Revue des Questions Historiques*, cxxxii (May–Sept. 1938), 85–9. A comprehensive and reliable account in Furio Diaz, *Filosofia e politica nel Settecento francese* (Turin, 1962), 228–47.

84. [Jean-Baptiste-Louis Crevier], *De l'Education publique* (Amsterdam [Paris?], 1762), 187. For this attribution, see A.-T., xx, 99; but see *infra*, n. 87.

85. Denis Diderot, *Collection complette des oeuvres philosophiques, littéraires et dramatiques de M. Diderot*, 5 vols. (London [Amsterdam], 1773), i, 41–137. Attribution to Diderot (Bachaumont, *Mémoires secrets*, i, 185 [21 Jan. 1763]; *Catalogue des livres de la bibliothèque de feue Madame la marquise de Pompadour* [Paris, 1765], item 191; *La France littéraire*, 2 vols. [Paris, 1769], i, 242). Johann Georg Hamann wrote to F. H. Jacobi on 31 May 1788 that *De l'Education publique* was 'réellement de Diderot' (Roland Mortier, 'Le Prince de Ligne, imitateur de Diderot,' *Marche romane*, v [Aug.–Oct. 1955], 129 n.); his information came from Princess Galitzin, who had known Diderot well. The

attribution to Diderot was learnedly argued by Ed. Dreyfus-Brisac, 'Petits problèmes de bibliographie pédagogique,' *Revue Internationale de l'Enseignement*, xxiv (1892), 286–300, but his conclusions seem quite speculative, although Tourneux, *Diderot et Catherine II*, 328, thought them convincing. See Mayer, *Diderot homme de science*, 397–8 nn.; and Dieckmann, *Inventaire*, 139–40.

86. Voltaire to Damilaville, 13 Feb. 1763 (Besterman, No. 10187); *Corr. litt.*, v, 259 (15 April 1763). Thieriot to Voltaire, 2 Feb. 1763 (Besterman, No. 10165): '. . . M. Diderot a été l'Editeur. . . . On ne sait qui est cet auteur et Platon [Diderot] lui tient le secret qu'il lui a promis.'

87. First published in *CI*, i, 275; now more readily available in Diderot, *Corr.*, iv, 234 (Dec. 1762 or Jan. 1763). According to the persuasive argument by Roland Mortier, 'The "Philosophes" and Public Education,' *Yale French Studies*, No. 40 (1968), 68–70, the author (or, with Diderot, the co-author) was probably Dominique-François Rivard. For the French text of this article, see Roland Mortier, 'Les "Philosophes" français et l'éducation publique' in his *Clartés et ombres du siècle des lumières* (Geneva, 1969), 104–13.

88. *De l'Education publique*, iv. Cf. A.-T., iii, 515, 517.

89. *De l'Education publique*, xiii, xiv, xvi, 37; cf. ibid., 85. For examples of Diderot's holding similar views, see A.-T., iii, 524, and Part I, 16.

90. 12 Aug. 1762 (Diderot, *Corr.*, iv, 98).

CHAPTER 34

1. Diderot, *Corr.*, iv, 197.

2. Diderot, *Corr.*, iv, 74 (28 July 1762).

3. Diderot, *Corr.*, iv, 114–5, 116–8, 119, 131–2, 147, 150, 155–6, 179, 201, 207.

4. Diderot, *Corr.*, iv, 189–91, 193–4, 199–200, 208, 210–1, 219, 229–30.

5. The 'Addition à la Lettre sur les Aveugles' appeared in the Stockholm copy of the *Corr. litt.* for May 1782 (Vincent E. Bowen, 'Diderot's Contributions to the Stockholm and Zurich Copies of the *Correspondance littéraire*, 1773–1793,' *RR*, lvi [1965], 35); Mélanie de Sallignac's observations (A.-T., i, 334–42). Although Diderot stated that she died in 1763 (A.-T., i, 334), his letters show that she was still alive in 1766 (Diderot, *Corr.*, vi, 109, 159, 163).

6. Diderot, *Corr.*, iv, 190–1, 193–4, 208, 219, and esp. 283. For further efforts in 1765 on Fayolle's behalf, see ibid., v, 144–5, 234–5; and in 1766 (ibid., vi, 35).

7. Diderot, *Corr.*, iv, 43 (14 July 1762).

8. Diderot, *Corr.*, iv, 198 (17 Oct. 1762).

9. Diderot, *Corr.*, iv, 169 (26 Sept. 1762).

10. Diderot, *Corr.*, iv, 165–6 (23 Sept. 1762).

11. Sartine had been one of the witnesses at the burial of D'Holbach's first wife, 27 Aug. 1754 (Naville, *Paul Thiry d'Holbach*, 445).

12. Diderot, *Corr.*, iv, 157–9 (19 Sept. 1762). Writing in 1785, Mme de Vandeul says (Mme de Vandeul, xlvii) that 'M. de Sartines eut l'honnêteté de prévenir mon père que c'était un espion de police'; this is certainly not the way Diderot reported the incident to Sophie at the time it occurred. The character of Glénat may have served in fixing Diderot's characterization of the Nephew in *Le Neveu de Rameau* (Jean Pommier, 'Etudes sur Diderot,' *RHPHGC*, Nouvelle série, No. 30 [April–June 1942], 159).

13. Diderot, *Corr.*, iv, 164 (23 Sept. 1762).

14. Diderot, *Corr.*, iv, 83 (31 July 1762). Cf. Roland Mortier, 'Diderot et la notion du "peuple",' *Europe*, Nos. 405–6 (Jan.–Feb. 1963), 78–88.

15. Diderot, *Corr.*, iv, 117 (26 Aug. 1762).

16. A.-T., i, xlvii–1. For other references to Rivière, see A.-T., iii, 539, and A.-T., viii, 384–5.

17. A.-T., xvii, 481–5; and O'Gorman, *Diderot the Satirist*, 242–51. Cf. Desné, 'Le Neveu de Rameau dans l'ombre et la lumière du XVIIIᵉ siècle,' *SVEC*, xxv, 496–7; also Desné in his ed. of Diderot, *Le Neveu de Rameau*, xix–xx. Although Diderot in *Lui et Moi* does not identify his interlocutor by name, his reference to 'cet impertinent apologue de la fourmi et du fourmilion' (A.-T., xvii, 483) would seem to be conclusive. Written about 1762: Diderot mentions in *Lui et Moi* a conte called *Les Zélindiens*. This was reviewed

in the *Corr. litt.*, v, 90 (1 June 1762). For further information about Rivière, see O'Gorman, *Diderot the Satirist*, 21–5, and for critical comment on *Lui et Moi*, ibid., 25–31.

18. Diderot, *Corr.*, iv, 291–5 (? mid-April 1764).

19. Diderot, *Corr.*, iv, 45, 46 (14 July 1762); see also ibid., 50–4, 60–4, 65–6, 74, 148.

20. Diderot, *Corr.*, iv, 54 (18 July 1762); ibid., 101–2 (12 Aug. 1762); also ibid., 75. Is this not an extremely early reference to a seeing-eye dog?

21. Grimm's absence and Diderot's writing for the *Corr. litt.* (Diderot, *Corr.*, iv, 184–5, 189, 192, 209; also Smiley, *Diderot's Relations with Grimm*, 85; Jeanne R. Monty, *La Critique littéraire de Melchior Grimm* [Geneva, 1961], 33). Diderot's review of the 'heretical almoner' (A.-T., ix, 225–34; passages cited, 225, 233).

22. Diderot, *Corr.*, iv, 57–9, 78, 120–4, 150, 150–1, 167.

23. Diderot, *Corr.*, iv, 191–2, 201–2, 207, 209, 211, 217–8, 226–7 (14, 17, 24, 31 Oct. and 11 and 21 Nov. 1762); see also ibid., v, 218. For Diderot's manuscript on 'cyclométrie,' see Dieckmann, *Inventaire*, 54–5. For expert analysis of Diderot's results, see Jean Mayer, 'Diderot et la quadrature du cercle,' *RGS*, LXII (1955), 132–8; and R. J. Gillings, 'The Mathematics of Denis Diderot (1713–1784),' *Australian Mathematics Teacher*, XI (1955), 2–4.

24. 'Diderot, *Plan d'un opéra comique*,' *Europe*, No. 111 (March 1955), 9–29; accompanied by Yves Benot's comments, 'Le Rire de Diderot,' loc. cit., 3–8; J. Robert Loy, 'Diderot's unedited *Plan d'un opéra comique*,' *RR*, XLVI (1955), 3–24. For the date of 1763, see Paul Vernière, 'Histoire littéraire et papyrologie: A propos des autographes de Diderot,' *RHLF*, LXVI (1966), 418.

25. Jacques Proust, 'A Propos d'un plan d'opéra-comique de Diderot,' *Revue d'Histoire du Théâtre*, VII (1955), 173–88, this quotation 188.

26. Diderot, *Corr.*, iv, 212–3 (7 Nov. 1762); ibid., iv, 221 (11 Nov. 1762).

27. A.-T., vi, 308; Diderot, *Corr.*, iv, 211 (31 Oct. 1762).

28. Diderot, *Corr.*, iv, 154; ibid., 144–5, 156, 160. Mme Diderot's illness first mentioned on 25 July 1762 (ibid., iv, 70).

29. Diderot, *Corr.*, iv, 184; ibid., 182, 209.

30. Diderot, *Corr.*, iv, 288.

31. Diderot, *Corr.*, iv, 203; ibid., 188, 192, 200, 202.

32. Diderot, *Corr.*, iii, 344.

33. '. . . elle lit couramant dedans lansiens testamant' (Mme Diderot to Denise Diderot, 22 Nov. 1758 [(Paris. Bibliothèque Nationale, *Diderot, 1713–1784* (Paris, 1963), item 182]). Mme de Vandeul, xlvi–xlvii. Regarding the children born previously, see Part I, 12, 44, 54–5, 83, 119, 740 n. 10.

34. Diderot, *Corr.*, iii, 299–300; ibid., iv, 86, 188.

35. Diderot, *Corr.*, iv, 154.

36. Diderot, *Corr.*, iii, 300.

37. Diderot, *Corr.*, iv, 156; ibid., 203; also ibid., 166, 184, 192.

38. Diderot, *Corr.*, iv, 74.

39. Diderot, *Corr.*, iv, 188; also ibid., 74, 86, 108–9, 171.

40. Diderot, *Corr.*, iv, 43 (14 July 1762); ibid., iii, 325–6 (2 Oct. 1761).

41. Terms of the settlement (Diderot, *Corr.*, iv, 85); see also ibid., iv, 75, 105–6.

42. Diderot, *Corr.*, iii, 212, 337; ibid., iv, 44, 76.

43. Diderot, *Corr.*, iv, 75–6, 102.

44. For various documents and references in this tangled business, see Diderot, *Corr.*, iii, 96–7 (28 Sept. 1760), 345–6 (25 Oct. 1761); ibid., iv, 85, 124, 155, 156, 237–45, 311–2; Marcel, *Le Frère de Diderot*, 11 n.

45. Diderot, *Corr.*, iv, 274 (Sept. or Oct. 1763); cf. Diderot to Caroillon La Sallette, 22 Sept. 1763 (ibid., 272–3). About 1762 Denise Diderot wrote a very cutting letter to Denis, though it is not known whether she sent it (described by J. Massiet du Biest, 'Denise, la soeur de Diderot,' *Etudes Langroises d'Art et d'Histoire*, II [1962], 11–2).

46. Diderot, *Corr.*, iv, 172 (26 Sept. 1762), 189 (7 Oct. 1762). Cf. May, 'The Influence of English Fiction on the French Mid-Eighteenth-Century Novel,' in *Aspects of the Eighteenth Century*, ed. Wasserman, 268.

47. Sterne, *Letters*, 151 (to Garrick, 31 Jan. 1762), 254, 275.
48. Sterne, *Letters*, 219, 212. Sterne's sermon, preached from a rather unfortunate and almost too appropriate text (Sterne, *Letters*, 218–9), was published in his *Sermons of Mr. Yorick* (London, 1784), III, 21–47; Diderot and D'Holbach subscribed to vols. III and IV of this edition (Sterne, *Letters*, 168 n. 2, 239 nn. 2 and 7).
49. Diderot's presence at the chapel does not rest upon solid evidence; it is reported, though with diffidence, by Wilbur L. Cross, *The Life and Times of Laurence Sterne*, 3d ed. (New Haven, 1929), 347; Willard Connely, *Laurence Sterne as Yorick* (London, [1958]), 124; Fredman, *Diderot and Sterne*, 7; Texte, *Jean-Jacques Rousseau et les origines du cosmopolitisme littéraire*, 341.
50. To Mrs. Dorothea Gibbon, 12 Feb. 1763 (Edward Gibbon, *The Letters of Edward Gibbon*, ed. J. E. Norton, 3 vols. [London, (1956)], I, 133).
51. Gibbon's journal (B.M., Add. MSS, 34874, foll. 55v, 55, 71v, 55v, respectively).
52. Diderot, *Corr.*, v, 194–7 (to Sophie Volland, 30 Nov. 1765). For Wilkes's early friendship with D'Holbach (W. H. Wickwar, *Baron d'Holbach: A Prelude to the French Revolution* [London, (1935)], 19; Naville, *Paul Thiry d'Holbach*, 17).
53. Diderot, *Corr.*, XI, 210–1 (19 Oct. 1771), 223–4 (14 Nov. 1771); F. C. Green, 'Autour de quatre lettres inédites de Diderot à John Wilkes,' *RLC*, xxv (1951), 453–4. On 10 July 1770 Wilkes wrote his daughter, 'My best respects to messieurs Diderot and Grimm, whose many great and amiable qualities I remember with pleasure' (John Wilkes, *The Correspondence of the late John Wilkes*, ed. John Almon, 5 vols. [London, 1805], IV, 68).
54. Diderot, *Corr.*, VII, 19 (26 Jan. 1767). Garrick refers to Diderot as a friend in letters of 1773 and 1776 (David Garrick, *Letters*, ed. David M. Little and George M. Kahrl, 3 vols. [Cambridge (Mass.), 1963], Letters 730, 755, 989). Background information in Frank Arthur Hedgcock, *A Cosmopolitan Actor: David Garrick and his French Friends* (New York, [1912]), 214 and *passim;* Cru, 101–4. It is regrettable but true that Garrick makes no reference to any of the *philosophes* in his *Journal of David Garrick Describing his Visit to France and Italy in 1763*, ed. George Winchester Stone, Jr. (New York, 1939).
55. David Bayne Horn, *The British Diplomatic Service, 1689–1789* (Oxford, 1961), 158; David Hume, *Letters*, ed. J. Y. T. Greig, 2 vols. [Oxford, 1932], I, 409; Diderot, *Corr.*, v, 133–4).
56. To the Rev. Hugh Blair (Hume, *Letters*, I, 419).
57. Andrew Stuart to Baron Mure, probably June 1764 (R. A. Leigh, 'An Unpublished Note from Diderot to Hume,' in Victoria University of Manchester, *Studies in Romance Philology and French Literature Presented to John Orr . . .* [Manchester, 1953], 175).
58. Diderot, *Corr.*, IX, 39 (17 March 1769); ibid., VIII, 16 (22 Feb. 1768); Rudolf Mertz [really Metz], 'Les Amitiés françaises de Hume,' *RLC*, IX (1929), 701. Cf. Ernest Campbell Mossner, 'Hume and the French Men of Letters,' *Revue Internationale de Philosophie*, VI (1952), 222–35; and Antonio Santucci, 'Hume e i "philosophes",' *Rivista di Filosofia*, LVI (1965), 150–77, esp. 167–8.
59. Sartine's replacement of Malesherbes (Diderot, *Corr.*, IV, 275; Jacques Proust, 'Pour servir à une édition critique de la *Lettre sur le commerce de la librairie*,' *DS III* [1961], 328–9). Written Sept.–Dec. 1763 (Proust, art. cit., 328; Denis Diderot, *Sur la liberté de la presse*, ed. Jacques Proust [Paris, 1964], 15). Although the manuscript copies of the *Lettre sur le commerce* in the Fonds Vandeul are dated 10 Aug. 1763 (Dieckmann, *Inventaire*, 6–8, 61, 131), this cannot be the final date because Diderot refers in the manuscript itself to Sept. 1763 (Proust, art. cit., 328; Diderot, *Sur la liberté de la presse*, ed. Proust, 51). The ingenious article by Lucien Brunel, 'Observations critiques et littéraires sur un opuscule de Diderot (Lettre sur le commerce de la librairie),' *RHLF*, x (1903), 1–24, has now been superseded by more recent information, as have also (in this one respect) David T. Pottinger, 'Protection of Literary Property in France during the Ancien Régime,' *RR*, XLII (1951), 101; and the same, *The French Book Trade in the Ancien Régime, 1500–1791* (Cambridge [Mass.], 1958), 233. Until the recent publications of Proust, cited earlier in this note, and Vernière, 'Histoire littéraire et papyrologie,' *RHLF*, LXVI, 413, 418, it had been supposed that Diderot wrote the *Lettre sur le commerce de la librairie* in 1767 (A.-T., XVIII, 5–6).

60. Diderot, *Sur la liberté de la presse*, ed. Proust, 17. This edition does not reproduce the first and last parts of the *Lettre sur le commerce de la librairie*, the former being mainly historical and derivative, the latter having mainly to do with book peddlers. For these parts, see A.-T., xviii, 3–28, 68–75. The *Lettre sur le commerce de la librairie* was first published by G. Guiffrey (Paris, 1861); it was published separately again, using the A.-T. text, by Bernard Grasset in 1937 (Denis Diderot, *Lettre adressée à un magistrat sur le commerce de la librairie* [Paris, 1937]). For a careful comparison of Diderot's original manuscript (what Proust calls the *Mémoire sur la liberté de la presse*) and the memoir submitted by the syndic to Sartine on 8 March 1764, see Proust, 'Pour servir à une édition critique . . . ,' *DS III*, 325, 334–45. The memoir of 8 March 1764 has never been published, but is accessible in B.N., MSS, Fr. 22183, foll. 1–82. Regarding this episode, see also Raymond Birn, 'The Profits of Ideas: *Privilèges en librairie* in Eighteenth-Century France,' *Eighteenth-Century Studies*, iv (1970–1), 152–3.
61. A.-T., xviii, 7, 47, 9, 21. Dialogue form of the *Lettre* (A.-T., xviii, 15, 61, 63).
62. A.-T., xviii, 7.
63. J. Proust, in Diderot, *Sur la liberté de la presse*, ed. Proust, 33. Diderot was strongly in favor of greatly extending the practice of granting *permissions tacites* (ibid., 76–90); it is interesting to discover that the number of these permissions was much greater in Sartine's administration than it had been before. See tables in Robert Estivals, *La Statistique bibliographique de la France sous la monarchie au XVIIIe siècle* (Paris, [1965]), 286–8. Regarding censorship, see Nicole Herrmann-Mascard, *La Censure des livres à Paris à la fin de l'Ancien Régime (1750–1789)* (Paris, 1968), esp. 36, 56, 86, 114–21; and Shaw, *Problems and Policies of Malesherbes as* Directeur de la Librairie *in France (1750–1763)*, passim.
64. Diderot, *Salons*, i, 195, supplemented by ibid., ii, vii-viii. Diderot speaks similarly in the *Réfutation de l'ouvrage d'Helvétius intitulé l'Homme* (A.-T., ii, 385).
65. Diderot, *Salons*, i, 248, 249, 209.
66. Dieckmann, *Cinq leçons sur Diderot*, 130; Philipp Fehl, in *College Art Journal*, xviii (1958–9), 362.
67. Diderot, *Salons*, i, 197, 125, 222.
68. Jean Seznec, 'Diderot and Historical Painting,' in *Aspects of the Eighteenth Century*, ed. Wasserman, 129–42.
69. Diderot, *Salons*, i, 214.
70. Diderot, *Salons*, i, 217. For the *Lettre sur les sourds et muets*, cf. Part I, 123.
71. Diderot, *Salons*, i, 217.
72. Diderot, *Salons*, i, 208, 221, 201, 207, 209–11, 215–6.
73. Diderot, *Salons*, i, 233; regarding Boucher (ibid., 205).
74. Diderot, *Salons*, i, 188, 245–7. A.-T., xiii, 40–7; these quotations, 42–3, 47.
75. A.-T., ii, 80–8. Date of composition, 1764 (Proust, *Diderot et* l'Encyclopédie, 315 and n. 97); however, Grimm speaks of 'Le Prosélyte répondant par lui-même' as being written in 1769 (De Booy, 'Inventaire,' 377). Naigeon's testimony as to the origin of the piece (A.-T., ii, 73–4). Copies of the 'Introduction aux grands principes ou réception d'un philosophe' (of which 'Le Prosélyte répondant par lui-même' is a part) are in the manuscript collections of the Fonds Vandeul and at Leningrad (Dieckmann, *Inventaire*, 60, 127, 145; J. Viktor Johansson, *Etudes sur Denis Diderot: Recherches sur un volume-manuscrit conservé à la Bibliothèque Publique de l'Etat à Leningrad* [Göteborg, 1927], 70–2, 150).
76. A.-T., ii, 88. Crocker argues that the 'Introduction aux grands principes' and Diderot's reply to it, 'Le Prosélyte répondant par lui-même,' simply reveal the 'moral nihilism' to which Diderot's principles lead (Lester G. Crocker, *Two Diderot Studies: Ethics and Esthetics* [Baltimore, 1952], 14 n., 28–30; the same, *Nature and Culture: Ethical Thought in the French Enlightenment* [Baltimore, 1963], 377).
77. A.-T., ii, 85 and n. This doctrine is completely consistent with Diderot's 'Lettre à Landois' of 1756 (Proust, *Diderot et* l'Encyclopédie, 315–8; cf. Part I, 249–52).
78. A.-T., ii, 85 and n.; cf. A.-T., iii, 312; and A.-T., ix, 429. See also Robert Mauzi, *L'Idée du bonheur au XVIIIe siècle* (Paris, 1960), 555–6.
79. All this is noted and hailed by writers of Marxist convictions (I. K. Luppol, *Diderot*

[Paris, 1936], 334; Lefebvre, *Diderot,* 299; József Szigeti, *Denis Diderot: Une grande figure du matérialisme militant du XVIIIe siècle* [Budapest, 1962], 52; Marcelle Barjonet, 'Une Oeuvre révolutionnaire: l'Encyclopédie,' *Cahiers du Communisme,* xxviii[2] [1951], 936–47).

80. A.-T., ii, 83, 87 and n.; cf. *Pensées philosophiques,* pensée xxvi. For the 'essentialism' of Grotius and for the influence of Grotius upon Diderot's political thought, see Leland J. Thielemann, 'Diderot's Encyclopedic Article on Justice: Its Sources and Significance,' *DS IV* (1963), 269, 276, 279.

81. Piquet (Diderot, *Corr.,* iv, 171; *CI,* i, 273). Checkers (Diderot, *Corr.,* iv, 40). Cafés (Diderot, *Corr.,* iii, 328; *CI,* i, 277).

82. *Corr. litt.,* v, 433; A.-T., xiii, 31–2.

83. 'Avis à un jeune poëte [Ɖorat] qui se proposait de faire une tragédie de Régulus' (A.-T., viii, 443–8; *Corr. litt.,* vi, 221–8 [15 March 1765]).

84. Jean Romilly to J.-J. Rousseau (mid-May 1763) (Michel Launay, 'Madame de Baugrand et Jean Romilly, horloger: Intermédiaires entre Rousseau et Diderot,' *Europe,* Nos. 405–6 [Jan.–Feb. 1963], 256; date, 250).

85. Diderot, *Corr.,* iv, 93 (5 Aug. 1762).

86. *Corr. litt.,* v, 365 (15 Aug. 1763); regarding this item, see Georges Roth, 'A propos d'une certaine "Lettre à Sophie",' *RHLF,* lviii (1958), 52–5. Cf. Diderot, *Corr.,* iii, 351: 'A Paris, ce   octobre 1761. Remplissez la date, je ne la sçais pas.' For other instances, see Diderot, *Corr.,* ii, 223, and v, 61.

87. Diderot, *Corr.,* iv, 219 (11 Nov. 1762).

88. Diderot, *Corr.,* iv, 289 (5 March 1764).

89. 'Le Péril du moment' (A.-T., ix, 65; *Corr. litt.,* vi, 68 [1 Sept. 1764]).

90. A.-T., vi, 336–8; Grimm used it in the *Corr. litt.,* v, 426–8 (1 Jan. 1764); he also inserted it in the article 'Poème lyrique,' the only article that he wrote for the *Encyclopédie* (xii, 832b–3a), but without indication of its source or that it is a translation by Diderot. Darius Milhaud used Diderot's translation for the words of his *La Mort d'un tyran* (1932).

91. *Corr. litt.,* v, 395 (1 Oct. 1763).

92. Sir James Macdonald of the Isles to Mrs. Elizabeth Montagu, Paris, 11 April 1764 (Elizabeth R. Montagu, *Mrs. Montagu, "Queen of the Blues",* ed. Reginald Blunt, 2 vols. [New York, (1924)], i, 97).

93. Voltaire to Damilaville (Besterman, Nos. 10931, 10958, 10960); see also Voltaire's expostulations to Palissot, 4 April and 26 July 1764 (Besterman, Nos. 10973 and 11179).

94. Diderot explains all this to D'Alembert, *c.* 10 May 1765 (Diderot, *Corr.,* v, 32); see also Damilaville to Voltaire, 18 April 1765 (Besterman, No. 11707).

95. Betzki to Grimm, 16 March 1765 (Diderot, *Corr.,* v, 26). Cf. Grimm to Louise-Dorothée de Saxe-Gotha, Jan. 1766 (Etienne Charavay, 'Grimm et la cour de Saxe-Gotha (1763–1767),' *Revue des Documents Historiques,* v (1878), 59.

96. Diderot to the Duc de Praslin, 27 April 1765 (Diderot, *Corr.,* v, 28).

97. Diderot to the Comte de Saint-Florentin, 27 April 1765 (Diderot, *Corr.,* v, 28). Saint-Florentin to Diderot, 1 May 1765 (ibid., 29–30); Praslin to Diderot, 7 May 1765 (ibid., 30). Cf. Albert Lortholary, *Le Mirage russe en France au XVIIIe siècle* (Paris, [1951]), 95–7. For the subsequent history of Diderot's library in Russia, see Jacques Proust, 'La Bibliothèque de Diderot,' *RScH,* No. 90 (April–June 1958), 257–73, and No. 94 (April–June 1959), 179–83; Wilson, 'Leningrad, 1957: Diderot and Voltaire Gleanings,' *FR,* xxxi, 351–6; Vladimir Sergeevich Liublinskiĭ, 'Sur la trace des livres lus par Diderot,' *Europe,* Nos. 405–6 (Jan.–Feb. 1963), 276–90.

98. D'Alembert to Catherine II, 26 October 1765 (Russkoe Istoricheskoe Obshchestvo, *Sbornik,* 148 vols. [St. Petersburg, 1867–1916], x [1872], 44 n.); Catherine II to D'Alembert, 21 Nov. 1765 (Diderot, *Corr.,* v, 187–8). She wrote to Voltaire in similar terms, 28 Nov./9 Dec. 1765 (Besterman, No. 12166). Diderot mentioned the sale of his library in a letter to D'Alembert *c.* 10 May 1765 (Diderot, *Corr.,* v, 31–3).

99. Damilaville to Voltaire, 18 April 1765 (Besterman, No. 11707); D'Holbach to Joseph Servan, 27 April 1765 (Marie-Jeanne Durry, *Autographes de Mariemont,* 2 parts in 4 vols. [Paris, 1955–9], i[2], 557–8); D'Holbach to David Garrick, 16 June 1765 (Victoria and

Albert Museum, London: Forster Bequest, Garrick Letters, vol. 31, fol. 62ᵛ); Toussaint-Pierre Lenieps to J.-J. Rousseau, 18 May 1765 (Rousseau, *Corr. gén.*, XIII, 317); Bachaumont, *Mémoires secrets*, II, 195 (14 April 1765).

100. *Année Littéraire*, vol. IV for 1765, 338–42.

101. Dorat's *Epître* was published in the *Année Littéraire*, loc. cit., 324–8; and separately, de grand luxe (Claude-Joseph Dorat, *Epître à Catherine II, impératrice de toutes les Russies* [Paris, 1765]). Cf. Bachaumont, *Mémoires secrets*, II, 233–4 (25 July 1765); also Lortholary, *Le Mirage russe en France au XVIIIᵉ siècle*, 98. Légier's *Epître à M. Diderot* was published in Pierre Légier, *Amusements poétiques* (London and Paris, 1769), 177–81); it is reprinted in Diderot, *Corr.*, IX, 10–2. Diderot said of it, 'L'Epître qu'il m'a adressée à l'occasion du bienfait que j'ai reçu de l'impératrice de Russie, est peut-être la meilleure pièce du recueil' (A.-T., VI, 371). Cf. Jérôme Vercruysse, 'Petite suite sur Diderot: La Beaumelle — Dorat — Légier,' *DS VIII* (1966), 258–63; also Mortier, 'Diderot et ses "Deux Petits Allemands",' *RLC*, XXXIII, 197.

102. Besterman, No. 11707 (18 April 1765).

CHAPTER 35

1. Diderot, *Corr.*, IV, 176 (29 Sept. 1762).
2. Nicolas-Charles-Joseph Trublet to Samuel Formey, 2 June 1760 (Werner Krauss, 'La Correspondance de Formey,' *RHLF*, LXIII [1963], 209).
3. *Année Littéraire*, vol. III for 1760, 254–5.
4. For lists of contributors, see Proust, *Diderot et l'Encyclopédie*, 511–29; Frank A. Kafker, 'A List of Contributors to Diderot's *Encyclopedia*,' *French Historical Studies*, III (1963–4), 106–22; and Takeo Kuwabara, Syunsuke Turumi, and Kiniti Higuti, 'Les Collaborateurs de l'*Encyclopédie* — Les Conditions de leur organisation,' *Zinbun*, No. 1 [1957], 1–22.
5. Regarding Diderot's authorship of articles in the *Encyclopédie*, see the authoritative lists given by Proust, *Diderot et l'Encyclopédie*, 530–8; in the excellent articles in Lough, 'Problem,' 327–90; and by Richard N. Schwab, 'The Diderot Problem, the Starred Articles and the Question of Attribution in the *Encyclopédie*,' *Eighteenth-Century Studies*, II (1969), 240–85, 370–438.
6. Diderot, *Corr.*, IV, 14; original in Houghton Library, Harvard University, Ms Fr. 189.
7. E.g., Pierre Francastel, 'L'Esthétique des Lumières,' in P. Francastel, ed., *Utopie et institutions au XVIIIᵉ siècle. Le Pragmatisme des Lumières* (Paris, 1963), 336.
8. *Encyc.*, s.v. 'Chaldéens' (A.-T., XIV, 79); *Encyc.*, s.v. 'Encyclopédie' (A.-T., XIV, 462–3).
9. Abraham Rees, ed., *The Cyclopedia; or, Universal Dictionary of Arts, Sciences, and Literature*, 1ˢᵗ American ed., 41 vols. (Philadelphia, 1810–42), XII, s.v. 'Diderot.' Burney the author of this article (Roger Lonsdale, *Dr. Charles Burney: A Literary Biography* [Oxford, 1965], 95).
10. *Corr. litt.*, IX, 207 (1 Jan. 1771).
11. Ibid., IX, 208.
12. Diderot, *Corr.*, IV, 303, 306 (12 Nov. 1764).
13. *Corr., litt.*, IX, 207–8. Le Breton's foreman was named Brullé (*Encyc.*, XIII, 503b, s.v. 'Prote': 'Cet article est de M. Brullé, prote de l'imprimerie de M. le Breton. . . .').
14. *Encyc.*, XII, 396b; 'May fairly be attributed to Diderot' (Lough, 'Problem,' 375–6).
15. Diderot, *Corr.*, IV, 304, 302, 301, 304.
16. *Corr. litt.*, IX, 208–9; Diderot, *Corr.*, IV, 301. Only Briasson and David were mentioned, the other partner, Laurent Durand, having died. His funeral occurred at St.-Séverin, 13 May 1763 (B.N., MSS, Fr. 22155, fol. 3).
17. Diderot, *Corr.*, III, 343 (19 Oct. 1761); ibid., IV, 192–3 (14 Oct. 1762); ibid., IV, 305–6, 304. For other references to the Le Bretons, see Diderot, *Corr.*, III, 322–4, 338, 340; ibid., IV, 36 (20 April 1762), 82 (31 July 1762), 189 (7 Oct. 1762). Regarding the 'slippery' nature of Le Breton's early career, see James Doolittle, 'The Four Booksellers and the *Encyclopédie*,' in Bernice Slote, ed., *Literature and Society* (Lincoln [Neb.], 1964), 23–6.
18. Diderot, *Corr.*, IV, 302; Mme de Vandeul, xlv; Diderot, *Corr.*, IX, 29 (4 March 1769). In this 1769 letter Diderot puzzlingly refers to the mutilation of a total of seven volumes,

not ten. Grimm, too, declared that the damage was very extensive (*Corr. litt.*, IX, 207–8).
19. Diderot, *Corr.*, IV, 305.
20. This precious and unique set is now owned by Douglas H. Gordon of Baltimore. Its contents were analyzed by him and Norman L. Torrey in the indispensable monograph, *The Censoring of Diderot's* Encyclopédie *and the Re-established Text* (New York, 1947). The article 'Luxure' (Gordon and Torrey, 69; 'may fairly be attributed to Diderot' [Lough, 'Problem,' 374]).
21. Gordon and Torrey, 71–4, 73; article 'Périr' attributed to Diderot (Lough, 'Problem,' 371).
22. Gordon and Torrey, 68; see their comment on this article (ibid., 42). Article 'may reasonably be attributed to Diderot' (Lough, 'Problem,' 367). Article 'Infidélité,' as published (A.-T., XV, 217–8).
23. A.-T., XVI, 471–92. Montaigne (ibid., 485–6; cf. Jean Thomas, *L'Humanisme de Diderot,* 2d ed. [Paris, 1938], 89–90; Casini, *Diderot "philosophe",* 260; Maturin Dréano, *La Renommée de Montaigne en France au XVIIIᵉ siècle, 1677–1802* [Angers, 1952], 301; Jerome Schwartz, *Diderot and Montaigne: The* Essais *and the Shaping of Diderot's Humanism* [Geneva, 1966], 75).
24. The passage on Bayle as finally published (A.-T., XVI, 486–91); the deleted passages (Gordon and Torrey, 75, 76–7). 'Playing with fire' (Gordon and Torrey, 49). For Bayle's influence on Diderot (and also the limits of that influence), see Richard H. Popkin, 'Scepticism in the Enlightenment,' *SVEC,* XXVI (1963), 1336–8.
25. Gordon and Torrey, 95; 'may fairly be attributed to Diderot' (Lough, 'Problem,' 383).
26. Passage deleted by Le Breton (Gordon and Torrey, 83). *Encyc.,* XV, 261a–5b, esp. 262b, 265; also in A.-T., XVII, 151–66, esp. 156. Diderot's paraphrase of Brucker, *Historia critica philosophiae,* I, 522–83 (Proust, *Diderot et* l'Encyclopédie, 554); the passage evidently referring to Rousseau (A.-T., XVII, 166). Diderot's self-identification with Socrates (Trousson, *Socrate devant Voltaire, Diderot et Rousseau,* 80–7; cf. Seznec, *Essais sur Diderot et l'antiquité,* 1–22).
27. Gordon and Torrey, 37; photograph of this page of proof (ibid., facing 36). Similar surcharged marginal comments on the proofs of 'Ménace' and 'Souveraineté' (ibid., 36–7, 83–4).
28. Diderot, *Corr.,* IV, 301; *Corr. litt.,* IX, 209.
29. Gordon and Torrey, 43–4, 60–1, 62, 68–107.
30. Gordon and Torrey, 40. Concerning the deletion of De Jaucourt's article 'Tolérance,' the page proof bears the notation 'd'ailleurs consenti par M. Did.' (Gordon and Torrey, 95 n.). Kuwabara, Turumi, and Higuti, art. cit., 14, argue that Le Breton has been too much criticized: 'Il faudrait lui rendre plus de justice.'
31. John Lough, 'The *Encyclopédie:* Two Unsolved Problems,' *FS,* XVII (1963), 126; he makes the same point in 'New Light on the Encyclopedia of Diderot and d'Alembert,' *History Today,* XV (1965), 173.
32. Gordon and Torrey, 38–9.
33. Diderot, *Corr.,* X, 20; Diderot, *Mémoires pour Catherine II,* ed. Paul Vernière (Paris, 1966), 262. Luneau de Boisjermain claimed that Diderot told him that Le Breton had 'carpentered' Vols. VIII–XIV (Diderot, *Corr.,* X, 21), thus suggesting that Vols. XV–XVII were not tampered with.
34. Mme de Vandeul, XLV.
35. The author of this book went to Leningrad to search for this set. For an account of his efforts, see Wilson, 'Leningrad, 1957: Diderot and Voltaire Gleanings,' *FR,* XXXI, 356, 360.
36. Gordon and Torrey, 7. Diderot possessed a set as it had been altered by Le Breton (Diderot, *Corr.,* IV, 305); he had entered many notes on the margins. This set, which would also be of great interest to Diderot scholars, has never been found either.
37. Gordon and Torrey, 39.
38. Diderot, *Oeuvres,* ed. J.-A. Naigeon, 15 vols. (Paris, 1798), I, xxvii n., cited by Lough, 'The *Encyclopédie:* Two Unsolved Problems,' *FS,* XVII, 129.
39. Diderot, *Corr.,* IV, 303, 301, 303.
40. Gordon and Torrey, 84.
41. Lenieps to J.-J. Rousseau (Rousseau, *Corr. gén.,* XIII, 284).

42. Diderot, *Corr.*, v, 46, 64; 92, 91; 119.
43. Diderot, *Corr.*, v, 94 (18 Aug. 1765); *Encyc.*, viii, i.
44. Lough, 'D'Alembert's Contribution,' in his *Essays on the* Encyclopédie *of Diderot and D'Alembert*, 244–9.
45. Naves, *Voltaire et l'Encyclopédie*, 120–1, 134, 136–8, 173–82.
46. Lough, 'D'Holbach's Contribution,' in his *Essays on the* Encyclopédie *of Diderot and D'Alembert*, 130; cf. the article, loc. cit., 111–229, esp. 125, 226. Herbert Dieckmann, 'L' "Encyclopédie" et le Fonds Vandeul,' *RHLF*, li (1951), 332.
47. Besterman, No. 8257; Marquise de Jaucourt, 'La Famille de Jaucourt,' *Bulletin de la Société de l'Histoire du Protestantisme français*, i (1853), 403–4.
48. Cambridge (Richard N. Schwab, 'Un Encyclopédiste Huguenot: Le Chevalier de Jaucourt,' *Bulletin Historique et Littéraire de la Sociéte de l'Histoire du Protestantisme Français*, cviii [1962], 51–2; the whole letter, 24 April 1727, published by Lough, *Essays on the* Encyclopédie *of Diderot and D'Alembert*, 474–6). Richard N. Schwab, 'The Extent of the Chevalier de Jaucourt's Contribution to Diderot's *Encyclopédie*,' *MLN*, lxxii (1957), 507–8. Cf. James Doolittle, 'Jaucourt's Use of Source Material in the *Encyclopédie*,' *MLN*, lxv (1950), 387–92.
49. *Encyc.*, ix, s.v. 'Louvre.' The idea had been mooted before: see James L. Connelly, Jr., 'The Movement to Create a National Gallery of Art in Eighteenth-Century France,' *Dissertation Abstracts*, xxiv (1963–4), 713–4.
50. *Encyc.*, xv, 106a, s.v. 'Sermon de J. C.'
51. *Encyc.*, x, 229a–60a.
52. *Encyc.*, xvii, s.v. 'Voorhout' (the village where Boerhaave was born). See also De Jaucourt's very competent article 'Roterdam,' also containing interesting biographical sketches (because they were born in Rotterdam) of Erasmus, Admiral Cornelius Tromp, and the Duke of Monmouth.
53. *Encyc.*, xi, esp. 951b and 956b. Regarding De Jaucourt's supplying previous omissions, see Richard N. Schwab 'The Chevalier de Jaucourt and Diderot's "Encyclopédie",' *Modern Language Forum*, xlii (1957), 48. Knowledge of De Jaucourt has been much increased by recent articles by Richard N. Schwab, loc. cit., and Lough, 'Louis, Chevalier de Jaucourt (1704–1780)' in Durham, England, University, *Essays Presented to C. M. Girdlestone*, 195–217; and John Lough, 'Louis, Chevalier de Jaucourt: Some Further Notes,' *FS*, xv (1961), 350–7.
54. Diderot, *Corr.*, iii, 248 (9 and 10 Nov. 1760), 265 (25 Nov. 1760).
55. *Encyc.*, viii, i: 'Avertissement.' De Jaucourt, together with Helvétius, was elected to the Prussian Academy on 31 Dec. 1763 (Eduard Winter, *Die Registres der Berliner Akademie der Wissenschaften, 1746–1766* [Berlin, 1957], 293; and subsequently he very nearly became President of the Academy, though in the end Frederick II failed to invite him, perhaps because the King disliked the article 'Prusse' written by De Jaucourt for the *Encyclopédie* (Jean-Henri-Samuel Formey, *Souvenirs d'un citoyen*, 2 vols. [Berlin, 1789], ii, 206; Christian-Jean-Guillaume Bartholmess, *Histoire philosophique de l'Académie de Prusse depuis Leibniz jusqu'à Schelling, particulièrement sous Frédéric-le-Grand*, 2 vols. [Paris, 1850–1], i, 220–3).
56. Proust, *Diderot et* l'Encyclopédie, 20; all of ch. i of this work ('Diderot, les Encyclopédistes et la société du XVIIIᵉ siècle,' [9–43]) is of the greatest interest; see reviews by Michèle Duchet in *Annales: Economies, Sociétés, Civilisations*, xix (1964), esp. 953–5, and by Roland Desné in *DS VI* (1964), 251–62, esp. 252–3. See also Proust, *L'Encyclopédie*, 92–103. For a most interesting study of stratification in *ancien régime* society, see Elinor G. Barber, *The Bourgeoisie in Eighteenth Century France* (Princeton, 1955). Respecting Freemasonry, see Robert Shackleton, 'The *Encyclopédie* and Freemasonry,' in *SPTB*, 223–37.
57. A.-T., xv, 52, s.v. 'Grecs.' The paragraph from which this sentence is taken is Diderot's own and not an adaptation from Brucker (Proust, *Diderot et* l'Encyclopédie, 204 n.).
58. *Encyc.*, ix, 803b–36b (signed 'M. Lucote').
59. *Encyc.*, ix, 213a–22a; 'Lorsque nous y étions . . . [at Namur]' (ibid., 213b).
60. *Encyc.*, xiv, 558a–68b, s.v. 'Salines de Franche-Comté.'

61. *Encyc.*, IX, 222a, s.v. 'Laiton.'
62. *Encyc.*, XIII, 533, s.v. 'Prusse;' A.-T., VI, 322–3.
63. *Encyc.*, XII, 105b; also in A.-T., XVI, 204.
64. *Encyc.*, XI, 34a; also in A.-T., XVI, 139. *Encyc.*, IX, 245a; Lough, 'Problem,' 367.
65. *Encyc.*, IX, 792b–93a; also in A.-T., XVI, 31.
66. *Encyc.*, XIII, 502a; also in A.-T., XVI, 440; Lough, 'Problem,' 376.
67. *Encyc.*, XV, 698b; Lough, 'Problem,' 383.
68. *Encyc.*, XIII, 859b; Lough, 'Problem,' 377.
69. 'Bramines' (*Encyc.*, II, 394a).
70. *Encyc.*, VIII, ii: 'Avertissement.'
71. Jean Mayer, 'Illusions de la philosophie expérimentale au XVIIIe siècle,' *RGS*, LXIII (1956), 354. Article 'Méthode' (*Encyc.*, X, 445a–6b; 'may fairly be attributed to Diderot' [Lough, 'Problem,' 374]; the importance of this article is emphasized by Lucien Plantefol, 'Les Sciences naturelles dans l'*Encyclopédie*,' *AUP*, 182).
72. *Encyc.*, VIII, 417a–8a. For comment on the importance of this article, see Mayer, art. cit., LXIII, 356; and Aram Vartanian, *Diderot and Descartes* (Princeton, 1953), 169–70.
73. *Encyc.*, XVI, 532b, 533a, s.v. 'Traite des Nègres.'
74. *Encyc.*, VIII, 344b–8a, this quotation 347a; Lough, 'Problem,' 344, believes it is probably by Diderot; it is asterisked. See David Brion Davis, *The Problem of Slavery in Western Culture*, I (Ithaca, [1966]), 410; and Edward D. Seeber, *Anti-Slavery Opinion in France during the Second Half of the Eighteenth Century* (Baltimore, 1937), 49, 56, 62; also Shelby T. McCloy, *The Humanitarian Movement in Eighteenth-Century France* (Lexington [Ky.], 1957), 88.
75. A.-T., XV, 314.
76. *Encyc.*, VIII, 284a; 'may fairly be attributed to Diderot' (Lough, 'Problem,' 373).
77. *Encyc.*, XIII, 907a, s.v. 'Réfugiés'; Lough, 'Problem,' 357.
78. *Encyc.*, XIII, 268a.
79. A.-T., XV, 253–4; for comment upon the importance of this article, see Proust, *Diderot et l'Encyclopédie*, 410.
80. A.-T., XV, 240; 'may reasonably be attributed to Diderot' (Lough, 'Problem,' 367).
81. Frank A. Kafker, 'The Effect of Censorship on Diderot's Encyclopedia,' *Library Chronicle* [University of Pennsylvania], XXX (1964–5), 46; cf. Lough, 'The *Encyclopédie*: Two Unsolved Problems,' *FS*, XVII, 134.
82. *Encyc.*, XI, 10; accepted as by Diderot (Lough, 'Problem,' 355). Albert Soboul, ed., *Textes choisis de l'*Encyclopédie (Paris, [1962]), 171.
83. A.-T., XV, 524.
84. Lough, *Essays on the* Encyclopédie *of Diderot and d'Alembert*, 440–62. Cf. Part I, 142–3, 154, 234, 753 n. 30.
85. 'Indépendance' (A.-T., XV, 198; attributed to Diderot with a question mark [Lough, 'Problem,' 367]). 'Souverains' (A.-T., XVII, 166–70; attributed to Diderot with a question mark [Lough, 'Problem,' 372]). 'Monarchie absolue' and 'Monarchie limitée' (*Encyc.*, X, 636b–637a, 637b); 'Loi fondamentale' and 'Liberté politique' (*Encyc.*, IX, 660b, 472a–b).
86. 'Prêtres' (*Encyc.*, XIII, 340b–1b); 'Théocratie' (A.-T., XVII, 238–42 [erroneously attributed to Diderot]; for proof of these articles being by D'Holbach, see Dieckmann, 'L' "Encyclopédie" et le Fonds Vandeul,' *RHLF*, LI, 332. 'Presse' (*Encyc.*, XIII, 320b); 'superstition and barbarism' (*Encyc.*, IX, 459a, s.v. 'Libelle'). Cf. G.-D. Zioutos, 'La Presse et l'Encyclopédie. Esquisse du développement de la presse française dans la première moitié du XVIIIe siècle,' *Etudes de Presse*, Nouvelle série, V (1953), 313–25.
87. 'Calamitous' (*Encyc.*, XIV, 928a, s.v. 'Sel, impôt sur le'); 'Impôt' (*Encyc.*, VIII, 601a–4a).
88. *Corr. litt.*, VIII, 224.
89. *Encyc.*, XVII, 874b; the whole article (ibid., 855–90).
90. *Encyc.*, X, 521a; 'may fairly be attributed to Diderot' (Lough, 'Problem,' 374).
91. *Encyc.*, XIII, 389a, s.v. 'Privilège'; attribution to Diderot (Lough, 'Problem,' 376).
92. A.-T., XVI, 253–4; 'may reasonably be attributed to Diderot' (Lough, 'Problem,' 371).

93. *Apologie de M. l'Abbé de Prades* (A.-T., I, 469). 'Obvier' (A.-T., XVI, 154; 'may reasonably be attributed to Diderot' [Lough, 'Problem,' 369]); 'Parlementaire' (*Encyc.*, XII, 69a, 'may reasonably be attributed to Diderot' [Lough, 'Problem,' 375]). See John Lough, 'The "Encyclopédie" and the Remonstrances of the Paris Parlement,' *MLR*, LVI (1961), 393–5; also Alfred Cobban, 'The *Parlements* of France in the Eighteenth Century,' *History*, XXXV (1950), 64–80.

94. *Encyc.*, VIII, 809a, s.v. 'Intendans & commissaires'; cf. Gordon and Torrey, 41, and Lough, 'Problem,' 373.

95. Owen Ruffhead, in the *Monthly Review*, XXXIX (1768), 545. For discussions of the political theory in the *Encyclopédie*, see also Arthur M. Wilson, 'Why Did the Political Theory of the Encyclopedists Not Prevail?' *French Historical Studies*, I (1959–60), 283–94; and Eberhard Weis, *Geschichtsschreibung und Staatsauffassung in der französischen Enzyklopädie* (Wiesbaden, 1956), 171–237.

96. To Sophie Volland, 26 Sept. 1762 (Diderot, *Corr.*, IV, 172).

CHAPTER 36

1. *Corr. litt.*, VI, 211 (15 Feb. 1765).
2. Diderot, *Corr.*, IV, 169–70; *Corr. litt.*, VI, 392 (15 Oct. 1765). In *L'Histoire et le secret de la peinture en cire* (1755) Diderot had referred to Montamy as 'un des bons chimistes de ce pays-ci, et un des plus honnêtes hommes du monde' (A.-T., X, 60 n.). For other references to Montamy in Diderot's correspondence, see Diderot, *Corr.*, II, 270; ibid., III, 117, 118, 335, 351, 354, 357; ibid., IV, 36, 199, 204, 215, 219, 229. Montamy died 8 Feb. 1765.
3. *Corr. litt.*, VI, 211 (15 Feb. 1765); Diderot, *Corr.*, VI, 99 (15 Feb. 1766).
4. Didier d'Arclais de Montamy, *Traité des Couleurs pour la Peinture en Email et sur la Porcelaine; précédé de l'Art de Peindre sur Email, et suivi de plusieurs Mémoires sur différents sujets intéressants, tels que le travail de la Porcelaine, l'Art du Stuccateur, la manière d'exécuter les Camées & les autres Pierres figurées, le moyen de perfectionner la composition du verre blanc & le travail des Glaces &c.* (Paris, 1765), 284: Privilège du Roi, et approbation [by the censor Belley, 20 June 1765]. Diderot's assignment of 'le présent Privilège' to the bookseller Cavelier, 13 Aug. 1765 (ibid., 287). A note from Diderot to Suard about an extract from Montamy would seem to relate to this time, *c.* 1765 (Diderot, *Corr.*, V, 79). Fréron published a favorable review of the book by Montamy (*Année littéraire*, vol. VI for 1765, 209–16).
5. See the biographical memoir by Diderot (D'Arclais de Montamy, *Traité des Couleurs*, IX–XIV [also A.-T., XIII, 48–50]). Note on cobalt (D'Arclais de Montamy, *Traité des Couleurs*, 143–50 [and in A.-T., XIII, 66–9]; cf. Proust, *Diderot et l'Encyclopédie*, 195 n.).
6. A.-T., XIII, 71, 70 (15 July 1765); also ascribed to Diderot by Vincent E. Bowen, 'Diderot's Contributions to the Stockholm Copy of the *Correspondance Littéraire*, 1760–1772,' *RR*, LV (1964), 187. However, according to De Booy, 'Inventaire,' 367, 'Grimm n'attribue pas cet article à Diderot, et il n'est sans doute pas de lui.'
7. *Corr. litt.*, VI, 290 (1 June 1765): 'Cet article est en partie de M. Diderot.' Memoir also in A.-T., VI, 473–6; passages quoted, 475. Cf. Mayer, *Diderot homme de science*, 11. Rameau died on 12 Sept. 1764.
8. 19 Sept. 1765 ('Horace Walpole's Paris Journals' [Horace Walpole, *Correspondence*, ed. Wilmarth S. Lewis, VII (New Haven, 1939), 262]).
9. André Morellet, *Memoires inédits*, 2ᵈ ed., 2 vols. (Paris, 1822), I, 133–4. *Sur Térence* was published without a title as a book review in the *Gazette Littéraire de l'Europe*, VI, 129–46 (15 July 1765) (Herbert Dieckmann, 'Diderot "Sur Térence." Le texte du manuscrit autographe,' in Anna G. Hatcher and K. L. Selig, ed., *Studia philologica et litteraria in honorem L. Spitzer* [Bern, (1958)], 149). It was republished, without attribution of authorship, by [Abbé François Arnaud and Jean-Baptiste-Antoine Suard, ed.], *Variétés littéraires, ou recueil de pièces tant originales que traduites concernant la philosophie, la littérature & les arts*, 4 vols. (Paris, 1768–9), IV, 95–114. Eight days (Naigeon, 194). For

Diderot's extensive knowledge of classical texts displayed in *Sur Térence* (Michael Riffaterre, 'Diderot et le philosophe esclave,' *DS III* [1961], 347–59); also Roger Bauer, 'Diderot, lecteur de Térence . . . et de Donat,' *Arcadia*, iv (1969), 117–37.

10. A.-T., v, 228–38, esp. 228–30, 234–5, 235–7. The most authoritative text is that edited by Dieckmann [see previous note], 149–74, who also supplies excellent critical commentary.

11. Abel-François Villemain, *Tableau de la littérature au XVIIIe siècle*, nouvelle ed., 4 vols. (Paris, 1858–9), ii, 129.

12. A.-T., v, 232, 231–2.

13. Mme de Vandeul to her husband, 7 vendémiaire An vi (Jean Massiet du Biest, *Angélique Diderot* [Paris, 1960], 52).

14. To Sophie, 5 June 1765 (Diderot, *Corr.*, v, 39); also to Damilaville (ibid., v, 41). See also Diderot to Sophie, 25 July 1765 (ibid., 61–2); still another indigestion is chronicled on 20 Oct. 1765 (ibid., 146); also 24 Sept. 1767 (Diderot, *Corr.*, vii, 141).

15. To Sophie, 25 July 1765 (Diderot, *Corr.*, v, 62).

16. To Sophie, 28 July 1765 (Diderot, *Corr.*, v, 68–70).

17. Fausto Nicolini, 'Intorno a Ferdinando Galiani a proposito d'una pubblicazione recente,' *Giornale Storico della Letteratura Italiana*, lii (1908), 29 n.; Joseph Rossi, *The Abbé Galiani in France* (New York, 1930), 12–3; Busnelli, *Diderot et l'Italie*, 23 n.

18. To Sophie, 1 Aug. 1765 (Diderot, *Corr.*, v, 73). Damilaville returned to Paris in Oct. 1765 (ibid., v, 146).

19. Helvétius arrived in London on 12 March 1764 (Ian Cumming, 'Helvetius in England,' *Etudes Anglaises*, xvi [1963], 113); cf. Diderot, *Corr.*, v, 136. For the visit to Potsdam (*Corr. litt.*, vi, 229 [15 March 1765]; Diderot, *Corr.*, v, 22).

20. Garrick's remark (Diderot, *Corr.*, v, 131). D'Holbach left for England early in August 1765 (ibid., v, 77), and had returned by 20 Sept. (ibid., v, 125). His impressions of England and of British politics (ibid., v, 125–6, 129–32, 170–3).

21. Diderot, *Corr.*, v, 129. Cf. Frances Acomb, *Anglophobia in France, 1763–1789* (Durham [N.C.], 1950), *passim*.

22. Naigeon first mentioned (Diderot, *Corr.*, v, 59 [21 July 1765]). In his *Mémoires . . . sur la vie et les ouvrages de D. Diderot*, 386, Naigeon claimed to have known Diderot the last 28 years of Diderot's life, which would date the friendship from 1756.

23. Diderot, *Corr.*, v, 63 (25 July 1765).

24. Diderot, *Corr.*, v, 94 (18 Aug. 1765); Cazes, *Grimm et les encyclopédistes*, 349. Cf. Lester G. Crocker, 'Mme. Necker's Opinion of Diderot,' *FR*, xxix (1955–6), 113–6.

25. Diderot, *Corr.*, v, 103, 101 (21 Aug. 1765). Marie-Madeleine Jodin (b. 27 June 1741) was of a violent and ungovernable temper. Not long after her father's death on 6 March 1761, both she and her mother were confined for a time in La Salpêtrière for prostitution. The Comédie-Française was officially ordered on 16 May 1765 to allow her to make a début (Diderot, *Corr.*, xvi, 73–4). Regarding her, see Diderot, *Corr.*, v, 97–100; Georges Roth, 'Diderot et sa pupille Mademoiselle Jodin,' *Lettres Nouvelles*, No. 4[44] (Dec. 1956), 699–714; Eugène Ritter, 'Jean Jodin (1713–1761) et son frère Pierre Jodin,' *Mémoires et Documents de la Société d'Histoire et d'Archéologie de Genève*, xxii (1886), 366–70; Max Fuchs, *Lexique des troupes de comédiens au XVIIIe siècle* (Paris, 1944), 121; and, above all, Paul Vernière, 'Marie Madeleine Jodin, amie de Diderot et témoin des Lumières,' *SVEC*, lviii (1967), 1765–75. Mlle Jodin was highly praised as an actress in 'Vers à Mlle Jodin' published in the *Journal de Politique et de Littérature*, 25 Nov. 1775, 394–5.

26. Diderot, *Corr.*, v, 50.

27. Diderot, *Corr.*, v, 106. Pierre-Philippe Choffard (1730–1809) was an engraver and book illustrator.

28. Diderot, *Corr.*, v, 113 (8 Sept. 1765); Horace Walpole, *Correspondence* [see note 8, supra], 267. Cf. Alastair Smart, *The Life and Art of Allan Ramsay* (London, 1952), 132.

29. *Corr. litt.*, vi, 438–46 (15 Dec. 1765); this quotation (ibid., 441 n.).

30. Diderot, *Corr.*, v, 205. Cf. ibid., v, 230.

31. A.-T., viii, 383; also Diderot to Le Monnier, 5 Dec. 1765 (Diderot, *Corr.* v, 210–2).

32. See the excellent sketch of Sedaine written by Mme de Vandeul in 1797 (*Corr. litt.*, XVI, 234–46; this quotation, 239).

33. Not an envious man (A.-T., VIII, 382 [*Paradoxe sur le comédien*]); cf. Diderot, *Corr.*, V, 206. See Robert Niklaus, 'Diderot et Rousseau: Pour et contre le théâtre,' *DS IV* (1963), 173.

34. Walpole, *Correspondence*, VII, 283. Walpole mentions meeting Diderot at D'Holbach's on six occasions: 19 Sept., 6 Oct., 17 Nov., 8 Dec. 1765, and 19 Jan. and 2 Feb. 1766 (ibid., VII, 262, 267, 272, 283, 296, 299). Diderot further discussed duelling in a book review he wrote in 1769 for the *Corr. litt.* (A.-T., VI, 390–2).

35. Diderot, *Corr.*, V, 225.

36. Diderot, *Corr.*, V, 115.

37. Diderot, *Corr.*, V, 190 (21 Nov. 1765).

38. Diderot, *Corr.*, V, 223 (20 Dec. 1765).

39. Diderot, *Corr.*, V, 225. For the Douglas Cause, see the *Dictionary of National Biography*, s.v. 'Douglas, Lady Jane (1698–1753)'; and (James Boswell), *Boswell in Search of a Wife, 1766–1769*, ed. Frank Brady and Frederick A. Pottle (New York, 1956), xiii–xiv and *passim*.

40. Jean Fabre, 'Deux frères ennemis: Diderot et Jean-Jacques,' *DS III* (1961), 155–213.

41. Julie Bondeli to J. G. Zimmermann, 21 Jan. 1763 (Eduard Bodemann, *Julie von Bondeli und ihr Freundeskreis* [Hannover, 1874], 248).

42. Diderot, *Corr.*, IV, 55 (18 July 1762); ibid., IV, 71–2 (25 July 1762).

43. Rousseau, *Corr. gén.*, IX, 341; ibid., X, 26.

44. Julie Bondeli to Sophie de La Roche, 4 Nov. 1763 (Mortier, *Diderot en Allemagne*, 198).

45. Bachaumont, *Mémoires secrets*, II, 132–3 (21 Nov. 1764); Thadd E. Hall, 'The Development of Enlightenment Interest in Eighteenth-Century Corsica,' *SVEC*, LXIV (1968), 180.

46. Launay, 'Madame de Baugrand et Jean Romilly, Horloger: . . . , *Europe*, Nos. 405–6, 248 (10 Nov. and 14 Dec. 1763).

47. Leigh, 'An Unpublished Note from Diderot to Hume,' in Victoria University of Manchester, *Studies in Romance Philology and French Literature Presented to John Orr. . . ,* 169, 173 (between 10 March and 16 April 1765); Diderot, *Corr.*, V, 23.

48. *Corr. litt.*, VI, 181–2 (15 Jan. 1765); also in A.-T., XIX, 466–7; cf. Dieckmann, *Inventaire*, 64. Read in page proof (Lenieps to Rousseau, 30 Nov. 1764 [Rousseau, *Corr. gén.*, XII, 103]).

49. François-Louis d'Escherny, *Mélanges de littérature, d'histoire, de morale et de philosophie*, 3 vols. (Paris, 1811), III, 111–2; Rousseau to D'Escherny, 6 April 1765 (Rousseau, *Corr. gén.*, XIII, 186–7). Cf. Diderot, *Corr.*, V, 23–5.

50. Diderot, *Corr.*, V, 222, 226–7. At some time, impossible to date exactly, Diderot gave to Sophie Volland the copy of *Le Devin du village* that Rousseau had inscribed and presented to him (Alan J. Freer, 'L'Exemplaire du "Devin du Village" offert par Rousseau à Diderot,' *RHLF*, LXVI [1966], 401–8).

51. D'Holbach to Garrick, 9 Feb. 1766 (in English) (Victoria and Albert Museum, Forster Bequest, Garrick Letters, vol. 21, fol. 65ʳ); published in Hedgcock, *A Cosmopolitan Actor: David Garrick and his French Friends*, 312–3; and in Max Pearson Cushing, *Baron d'Holbach: A Study of Eighteenth-Century Radicalism in France* (New York, 1914), 72–4. D'Holbach to Hume, 16 March 1766 (in English) (John Hill Burton, *Letters of Eminent Persons Addressed to David Hume* [Edinburgh, 1849], 254–5). In the letter to Garrick, D'Holbach wrote, 'I look on that man [Rousseau] as a mere philosophical quack, full of affectations, of pride, of oddities and even villainies. . . .' (Victoria and Albert Museum, loc. cit., fol. 64ᵛ).

52. Rousseau to Hume, 10 July 1766 (Rousseau, *Corr. gén.*, XV, 312).

53. See Margaret H. Peoples, 'La Querelle Rousseau-Hume,' *AJJR*, XVIII (1927–8), 1–331; Henri Roddier, 'La Querelle Rousseau-Hume,' *RLC*, XVIII (1938), 452–77; John N. Pappas, 'Rousseau and D'Alembert,' *PMLA*, LXXV (1960), 46–60; and Ronald Grimsley, 'D'Alembert and Hume,' *RLC*, XXXV (1961), 583–95. No doubt Hume would have liked to have Diderot publicly on his side; he wrote to a French lady about Rousseau, 'nor is his Conduct towards me worse than toward M. Diderot about seven years ago'

(Hume to Mme Durieu de Meinières, 25 July 1766 [Albert Schinz, 'La Querelle Rousseau-Hume. Un document inédit,' *AJJR*, xvii (1926), 40-1]).

54. Cf. D'Holbach to Servan, 14 March 1765 (Paul Vernière, 'Deux cas de prosélytisme philosophique au XVIIIᵉ siècle. A propos de deux lettres inédites du Baron d'Holbach,' *RHLF*, lv [1955], 496).

55. Diderot, *Corr.*, v, 139 (10 Oct. 1765).

56. 'Avis au Public,' Jan. 1766 (printed in *Mémoire à consulter pour les libraires associés à l'Encyclopédie*, 16); Le Gras, *Diderot et l'Encyclopédie*, 158-9. The Associated Publishers had entered into an agreement with Fauche on 26 Feb. 1762 (Charly Guyot, *Le Rayonnement de l'Encyclopédie en Suisse française* [Neuchâtel, 1955], 40 n.). Fauche, who founded his printshop in 1762, subsequently published works by Mirabeau (Charly Guyot, 'Le Rayonnement de l'Encyclopédie en Suisse,' *CAIEF*, No. 2 [1952], 51 n.).

57. Gabriel Lepointe, *L'Organisation et la politique financières du Clergé de France sous le règne de Louis XV* (Paris, 1923), 24, 33, 321; Michel Péronnet, 'Les Assemblées du Clergé de France sous le règne de Louis XVI (1775-1788),' *AHRF*, xxxiv (1962), 13; Norman Ravitch, *Sword and Mitre. Government and Episcopate in France and England in the Age of Aristocracy* (The Hague, 1966), 154-79. For the Assembly of 1765-6, see Siméon-Prosper Hardy, *'Mes Loisirs,'* ed. Maurice Tourneux and Maurice Vitrac (Paris, 1912), 16-8, 43, 48, 50-1, 52.

58. *Corr. litt.*, vi, 411 (15 Nov. 1765); cf. *Actes de l'Assemblée-générale du Clergé de France sur la religion* (Paris, 1765) [B.N., MSS, Fonds Joly de Fleury 1479, foll. 48-77]; Félix Rocquain, *L'Esprit révolutionnaire avant la Révolution, 1715-1789* (Paris, 1878), 251 n.

59. Quoted by Pierre Lanfrey, *L'Eglise et les philosophes au dix-huitième siècle* (Paris, 1857), 203. Reported also by François-Antoine de Boissy-d'Anglas, *Essai sur la vie, les écrits et les opinions de Malesherbes*, 2 vols. (Paris, 1819), i, 17, 384.

60. 12,000,000 livres (David Hume to Secretary of State Conway, 11 Sept. 1765 [David Hume, *New Letters of David Hume*, ed. Raymond Klibansky and Ernest C. Mossner (Oxford, 1954), 113-7, esp. 115]).

61. Hedgcock, *A Cosmopolitan Actor: David Garrick and his French Friends*, 313; also Grimm to Garrick, 15 Feb. 1766 (David Garrick, *The Private Correspondence of David Garrick*. . . , 2 vols. [London, 1831-2], ii, 465). A thousand sets by mid-January (*Corr. litt.*, vi, 476 [15 Jan. 1766]); cf. also Grimm to the Duchess of Saxe-Gotha, Jan. 1766 (Charavay, 'Grimm et la cour de Saxe-Gotha,' *Revue des Documents Historiques*, v, 57 [also in *Corr. litt.*, xvi, 443-4]). 'Notre ouvrage paroît . . . dans toutes les provinces de France, excepté à Paris . . .' (To Sophie, 27 Jan. 1766 [Diderot, *Corr.*, vi, 36]). Cf. Norman L. Torrey, 'L' "Encyclopédie" de Diderot: "Une grande aventure" dans le domaine de l'édition,' *RHLF*, li (1951), 315. Voltaire received his copy at Ferney by 5 April 1766 (Besterman, No. 12362).

62. Bachaumont, *Mémoires secrets*, iii, 14 (29 March 1766).

63. D'Hémery to Sartine, 23 April 1766 (B.N., MSS, Nouv. acq. fr. 1214, fol. 460ᵛ); Hardy, *'Mes Loisirs,'* 42 (23 April 1766); Bachaumont, *Mémoires secrets*, iii, 25 (24 April 1766); *Corr. litt.*, vii, 44 (15 May 1766); Frantz Funck-Brentano, *Les Lettres de cachet à Paris. Etude suivie d'une liste des prisonniers de la Bastille, 1659-1789* (Paris, 1903), 371-2. Cf. Le Gras, *Diderot et l'Encyclopédie*, 161; and Lough, 'Luneau de Boisjermain v. the Publishers of the *Encyclopédie*,' *SVEC*, xxiii, 157-8.

64. Diderot, *Corr.*, ix, 242 (28 Dec. 1769).

65. Diderot, *Corr.*, vi, 352-3 (27 Nov. 1766).

66. D'Holbach to [Joseph Servan], 4 Dec. 1766 (*Amateur d'autographes*, iii [1864], 75-7); published also in Alfred Morrison, *Catalogue of the Collection of Autograph Letters and Historical Documents formed . . . by A. Morrison*, 13 vols. (privately printed, 1883-97), ii, 299; cf. Lough, 'Luneau de Boisjermain v. the Publishers of the *Encyclopédie*,' *SVEC*, xxiii, 156-9. Galiani wrote to Tanucci, 24 Nov. 1766, that the sale of the *Encyclopédie* was still forbidden in Paris and Versailles, but that 'Questo rigore fu di mano amica, e non ostile, che prevedeva lo strepito di Parigi' (Augusto Bazzoni, 'Carteggio dell'Abate Ferdinando Galiani col Marchese Tanucci,' *Archivio Storico Italiano*, 4ᵉ série, i [1878], 450-1).

67. Diderot, *Corr.*, VI, 335. See the interesting accounts of the case in *Corr. litt.*, VII, 74–9 (15 July 1766); Gaston Marchou, 'Le Chevalier de La Barre et la Raison d'Etat,' *Revue de Paris*, July–Aug. 1965, 112–25; and Gay, *Voltaire's Politics*, 278–82. The *Grande Encyclopédie*, s.v. 'La Barre, Jean-François Le Fèvre, chevalier de,' and the Larousse *Grand Dictionnaire Universel du XIXe Siècle*, s.v. the same, are eloquent and detailed about the case.
68. *Corr. litt.*, VII, 77; Diderot, *Corr.*, VI, 334–5. Pasquier was councillor of the Parlement and of the Grand'chambre of Parlement. The *philosophes* gave him the nickname of *boeuf-tigre*: cf. Delisle de Sales to Voltaire, 26 Feb. [1776], 'Ce *boeuf-tigre* a dit en plein parlement . . . "Quoy! messieurs nous ne brûlerions donc jamais que des livres!"' (Besterman, No. 18821).
69. *Corr. litt.*, VII, 75. For the Lally case, see Hardy, '*Mes Loisirs*,' 43–7.
70. Diderot, *Corr.*, VI, 334–5 (*c.* 8 or 10 Oct. 1766); the original of this letter is in the B.M., Add. MSS 44936, foll. 25–6.
71. Cf. Diderot, *Corr.*, VI, 236–8, 249–50, 332–3, 350–1.
72. Part I, 288–9.
73. Diderot, *Corr.*, VI, 335, 334. For the reading *nasse* ('network') instead of *masse*, see Samuel S. B. Taylor, 'Voltaire's *L'Ingénu*, the Huguenots and Choiseul,' *SPTB*, 117.
74. Diderot, *Corr.*, VI, 337.

CHAPTER 37

1. 10 Nov. 1765 (Diderot, *Corr.*, V, 167).
2. Diderot, *Salons*, II, 206–25, esp. 208, 212, 214–9.
3. Diderot, *Salons*, II, 151.
4. Diderot, *Salons*, II, 108, 78, 201, 86. Cf. Raymond Trousson, 'Diderot helléniste,' *DS XII* (1969), 141–243, esp. 153–62.
5. To Sophie, 21 Nov. 1765 (Diderot, *Corr.*, V, 190).
6. Diderot, *Diderot et Falconet. Correspondance: Les six premières lettres*, ed. Herbert Dieckmann and Jean Seznec [*Analecta Romanica*, Heft 7] (Frankfurt am Main, [1959]), 44 (4 Dec. 1765). Diderot's side of the argument admirably summarized by Gay, *The Enlightenment*, II, 90–1.
7. Diderot, *Salons*, II, 214.
8. Gay, *The Enlightenment*, II, 221; Herbert Dieckmann, 'An Unpublished Notice of Diderot on Falconet,' *Journal of the Warburg and Courtauld Institutes*, XV (1952), 257. Cf. a similar characterization of Falconet in the *Salon de 1765* (Diderot, *Salons*, II, 214).
9. Diderot's apprehension lest Falconet publish the letters (Diderot, *Corr.*, VII, 133 [Sept. 1767]). In 1828 the first four of Diderot's letters were published (Jean-François Barrière, *Tableaux de genre et d'histoire* . . . [Paris, 1828], 119–200). The whole series of Diderot's letters in A.-T., XVIII, 79–336. The best critical edition, but including only the first six letters, is edited by Dieckmann and Seznec; cf. Herbert Dieckmann, 'Diderot's Letters to Falconet: Critical Observations on the Text,' *FS*, V (1951), 307–24. A very useful critical edition containing all of Falconet's letters as well as Diderot's is that of Diderot, *Le Pour et le contre. Correspondance polémique sur le respect de la postérité, Pline et les anciens*, ed. Yves Benot (Paris, [1958]).
10. Diderot, *Diderot et Falconet*, ed. Dieckmann and Seznec, 42.
11. Diderot, *Le Pour et le contre*, ed. Benot, 76, 78; same passages in A.-T., XVIII, 98, 101.
12. Diderot, *Le Pour et le contre*, ed. Benot, 100–1; A.-T., XVIII, 125. Cf. similar passages (Diderot, *Le Pour et le contre*, ed. Benot, 77, 79; A.-T., XVIII, 100, 125).
13. Falconet's irritation with men of letters (Jean Seznec, 'Falconet, Voltaire et Diderot,' *SVEC*, II [1956], 43–59). Georges Roth, in Diderot, *Corr.*, V, 9; Roland Mortier, in *Revue Belge de Philologie et d'Histoire*, XLI (1963), 1257; Paul Vernière, 'Diderot critique d'art,' *Quinzaine Littéraire*, 1–15 May 1968, 16.
14. Pliny a dotard (Diderot, *Diderot et Falconet*, ed. Dieckmann and Seznec, 60–1); 'sacristain' (A.-T., XVIII, 167). Cf. Seznec, *Essais sur Diderot et l'antiquité*, 45–51.
15. Diderot, *Diderot et Falconet*, ed. Dieckmann and Seznec, 43; Diderot, *Le Pour et le*

contre, ed. Benot, 49. Cf. remarks by the editors in Diderot, *Diderot et Falconet,* ed. Dieckmann and Seznec, 12, 14.

16. The idea of a 'model' (A.-T., v, 277 [*'Les Deux amis de Bourbonne'*]); taste (A.-T., XII, 76 [*Pensées détachées sur la peinture*]). Regarding the 'ideal model,' see David Funt, *Diderot and the Esthetics of the Enlightenment* (*DS XI* [1968]), 149–50.

17. Diderot, *Diderot et Falconet,* ed. Dieckmann and Seznec, 43.

18. 'Un long intervalle de tems' (Diderot, *Corr.,* x, 176 [1770?]). See also A.-T., IV, 95: the taste of a nation 'est toujours le produit des siècles. . . .' Cf. Giancarlo Marmori, 'Diderot e Falconet,' *Il Mondo,* 3 Feb. 1959, 9.

19. Diderot, *Le Pour et le contre,* ed. Benot, 99–100; also A.-T., XVIII, 125. The phrase 'le respect de la postérité' occurs three times in this passage. Also ibid.: 'je n'en respecterai pas moins la postérité.'

20. Diderot, *Diderot et Falconet,* ed. Dieckmann and Seznec, 55.

21. Diderot, *Le Pour et le contre,* ed. Benot, 82, 152; these passages in A.-T., XVIII, 105, 179.

22. Francastel, 'L'Esthétique des Lumières,' in Francastel, ed., *Utopie et institutions au XVIIIᵉ siècle: Le Pragmatisme des Lumières,* 340.

23. A.-T., XVIII, 81–2; Diderot, *Corr.,* VI, 180. Charles du Peloux, *Répertoire biographique et bibliographique des artistes du XVIIIᵉ siècle français* (Paris, 1930), 181.

24. Diderot's letter of 16 April 1766 is not extant. Betzki to Diderot, May 1766 (Diderot, *Corr.,* VI, 180–2).

25. *Lettre de congé* from the Marquis de Marigny authorizing Falconet to go to Russia (B.N., MSS, Nouv. acq. fr. 24983, fol. 328 [26 Aug. 1766]); Diderot, *Corr.,* VI, 235, 248, 251.

26. Published by Charles Cournault, 'Etienne-Maurice Falconet et Marie-Anne Collot,' *Gazette des Beaux-Arts,* 2ᵉ période, II (1869), 127–9; also in *Sbornik,* XVII (1876), 375–7. Cf. Louis Réau, *Etienne-Maurice Falconet,* 2 vols. (Paris, 1922), I, 86–7. 200,000 livres (Galitzin to Panin, 31 Aug. 1766 [*Sbornik,* XVII (1876), 373]; Galitzin went on to say, 'Tous les autres salaires et les frais de voyage sont de même beaucoup moindres que ce que les autres artistes m'avaient demandé' [ibid.]).

27. 8 Sept. (A.-T., XVIII, 82). Galitzin wrote Panin from Compiègne on 13 Sept., saying Falconet had left there the day before (*Sbornik,* XVII [1876], 379). Falconet sent Diderot a note from Berlin on 28 Sept. (A.-T., XVIII, 215). Arrival at Saint Petersburg (Diderot, *Corr.,* VI, 338). Regarding Mlle Collot, see Stanislas Lami, *Dictionnaire des sculpteurs de l'école française au dix-huitième siècle,* 2 vols. (Paris, 1910–1), I, 335–8.

28. See the detailed edition of this letter by W. D. Halls, 'A Letter from Diderot to General Betzky,' *FS,* XI (1957), 135–48; also Diderot, *Corr.,* VI, 277–87.

29. Diderot, *Le Pour et le contre,* ed. Benot, 168.

30. Catherine II to Mme Geoffrin, 21 Oct. 1766 (*Sbornik,* I [1867], 289; A.-T., XVIII, 82).

31. Nevertheless Diderot wrote to Sophie somewhat sympathetically about the Dauphin (20 Dec. 1765 [Diderot, *Corr.,* v, 225–6]). See the interesting article by Agnès Joly, 'Le Dauphin et les Encyclopédistes,' *Revue de l'Histoire de Versailles et de Seine-et-Oise,* LI (1954), 95–106.

32. 3 and 20 Feb. 1766 (Diderot, *Corr.,* VI, 41–5, 100–4); it was Cochin who asked Diderot (Diderot, *Salons,* III, 5). Diderot's suggestions for the monument (A.-T., XIII, 72–5; also *Corr. litt.,* VII, 21–3 [15 April 1766]); cf. Seznec, *Essais sur Diderot et l'antiquité,* 38–42. For Diderot's severe criticism of the fawning eulogy of the Dauphin written by Antoine-Léonard Thomas (A.-T., VI, 347–50; also *Corr. litt.,* VII, 16–20 [15 April 1766]).

33. Finished in July 1766 (Diderot, *Oeuvres esthétiques,* ed. Vernière, 659).

34. Mme Volland and Sophie sublet a first-floor apartment in the Hôtel d'Uzès, Rue des Filles-Saint-Thomas-du-Louvre, and moved in in Aug. 1766. Soon thereafter Mme de Blacy and her blind daughter Mélanie moved to the floor above (Diderot, *Corr.,* VI, 174, 249).

35. Marie Champion married Michel Billard sometime not later than 15 June 1741 (Archives départementales de la Haute-Marne, fonds Vandeul E 10 [Louis-François Marcel, 'Le mariage de Diderot: Etude critique,' *Nouvelle Revue de Champagne et de Brie,* VI (1928), 9 n.]). By 19 Nov. 1754 Billard was living at the Hospital for Incurables at Paris (Diderot,

Corr., I, 171) and died there on 29 Jan. 1760 (Marcel, art. cit., 10). Mme Billard lived in the parish of Saint-Etienne-du-Mont of Paris until 1766 (Diderot, *Corr.*, III, 17; *CI*, I, 152 n.; *CI*, II, 136 n.).

36. Diderot to Guéneau de Montbeillard, Jan. (?) 1767 (Diderot, *Corr.*, VII, 15). Betzki's letter to Diderot, 30 Oct. 1766 (*Corr. litt.*, VII, 201–2 [15 Jan. 1767]; Diderot, *Corr.*, VI, 354). Cf. *Corr. litt.*, VII, 345 (15 June 1767); Bachaumont, *Mémoires secrets*, III, 124 (12 Dec. 1766). Committed to live 50 years (Diderot to Betzki, 29 Nov. 1766 [Diderot, *Corr.*, VI, 360]).

37. Diderot, *Corr.*, VI, 355, 356. Diderot describes this to Falconet in almost identical words (Diderot, *Corr.*, VII, 54).

38. The verses were first published anonymously in a collection edited, also anonymously, by Jean Devaines (A.-T., V, 6), *Recueil de quelques articles tirés de différents ouvrages périodiques* (Paris, An VII [1799]), 21–4: 'Remerciment de M. Diderot à l'Impératrice de Russie.' This publication stated that 'Diderot pria un de ses amis d'exprimer sa reconnaissance, et celui-ci fit cette Epître qui fut envoyée à Catherine en 1766' (ibid., 21 n.). Georges Roth, 'Diderot et la Tsarine,' *Revue de Paris*, March 1958, 123, stated positively that the verses were by Devaines. Similarly Diderot had recently requested Sedaine to supply verses for a special occasion (Diderot, *Corr.*, V, 87–8). Regarding Devaines, see the excellent article by Paul Vernière, 'Diderot et Jean Devaines,' *Saggi e Ricerche di Letteratura Francese*, II (1961), 151–61.

39. To Sophie, 10 Dec. 1765 (Diderot, *Corr.*, V, 217).

40. Proust, *Diderot et l'Encyclopédie*, 107 n. Regarding Diderot's income, see also English Showalter, Jr., 'Money Matters and Early Novels,' *Yale French Studies*, No. 40 (1968), 121 and *passim*.

41. 1500 livres per annum (Diderot, *Corr.*, II, 198, 199). The sum of 4000 livres is arrived at as follows: 1500 from his father's estate; 1500 from the associated publishers, which had been coming in since 1761 when Diderot agreed to receive henceforth the interest on the 30,000 livres they owed him (May, 77–8); 200 'from another source,' as Diderot wrote vaguely in 1759 (Diderot, *Corr.*, II, 199); and 800 from the sale of his library (16,000 livres figured at 5%). The annuity of 1500 livres from the associated publishers was passed on to Angélique Diderot in article 6 of her wedding contract (*Cahiers Haut-Marnais*, No. 24 [1951], 19–22). However, in 1766 Diderot wrote Falconet that he had more than 4,600 livres of income through investments (29 Dec. 1766 [Diderot, *Corr.*, VI, 374; also A.-T., XVIII, 222–3]).

42. Claude Alasseur, *La Comédie française au 18e siècle: Etude économique* (Paris, 1967), 125–6, 198.

43. Beccaria to Morellet, 26 Jan. 1766 (Franco Venturi, ed., *Illuministi Italiani, III: Riformatori Lombardi, Piemontesi e Toscani* [Milan, (1958)], 202, 203–4, 206, 210).

44. Allan Ramsay to Diderot, Jan. 1766 (Diderot, *Corr.*, V, 246). On Diderot's reading Italian, see Galiani to Tanucci, 12 Nov. 1764 (Bazzoni, 'Carteggio. . . ,' *Archivio Storico Italiano*, 4e série, I (1878), 30–1); also the very interesting testimony by A. [Adert], in *Intermédiaire des Chercheurs et Curieux*, XIV, No. 318 (10 Aug. 1881), col. 504, showing that Diderot had read a ten-volume Italian edition of Goldoni in 1769.

45. A.-T., IV, 60.

46. A.-T., IV, 51. Jacques-André Naigeon's editorial note in his ed. of *Oeuvres de D. Diderot*, 15 vols. (Paris, 1798), IX, 449; quoted in A.-T., IV, 51.

47. Morellet invited Beccaria to come to Paris, 3 Jan. 1766 (Venturi, *Illuministi Italiani*, III, 11–2; Marcello T. Maestro, *Voltaire and Beccaria as Reformers of Criminal Law* [New York, 1942], 68, 69). Diderot, *Corr.*, VI, 338–9; Busnelli, *Diderot et l'Italie*, 63–4. Alessandro to Pietro Verri, 19 Oct. 1766 (Pietro and Alessandro Verri, *Carteggio di Pietro e di Alessandro Verri*, ed. Emanuele Greppi, F. Novati, and Alessandro Giulini, 6 vols. [Milan, 1910–26], I, 23–4).

48. D'Holbach to John Wilkes, 10 Nov. 1766 (Paul Vernière, 'Deux lettres inédites de d'Holbach à Wilkes,' *RLC*, XXVIII [1954], 484); also Alessandro to Pietro Verri, Paris, 13 March 1767 (Verri, *Carteggio di Pietro e di Alessandro Verri*, ed. Greppi. . . , I, 299); Venturi, *Illuministi Italiani*, III, 13.

49. Catherine II and Beccaria (Franco Venturi, 'Beccaria in Russia,' *Il Ponte*, IX [1953], 163–74; T. Cizova, 'Beccaria in Russia,' *Slavonic and East European Review*, XL [1961–2], 384–408).

50. These documents are in the Ambrosian Library at Milan. Alessandro to Pietro Verri, London, 15 Jan. 1767 (Verri, *Carteggio di Pietro e di Alessandro Verri*, ed. Greppi. . . , I, 210); Busnelli, *Diderot et l'Italie*, 69 n. Morellet to Beccaria, *c.* 15 March 1767 (Cesare Beccaria, *Dei delitti e delle pene*, ed. Franco Venturi [Turin, 1965], 410).

51. Diderot's notes probably written in 1766 before Beccaria came to Paris (Morellet to Beccaria, Sept. 1766 [Maestro, *Voltaire and Beccaria as Reformers of Criminal Law*, 70]). These notes were first published in Cesare Beccaria, *Traité des délits et des peines . . . accompagnée de notes de Diderot.* . . , (Paris, An V [1797]), 11–2, 24–5, 30–1, 46, 47–9, 54, 55, 67–8, 72–3, 76–7, 81–2, 87–8, 95, 109–10. Published in A.-T., IV, 63–9. It is possible that Marmontel is the author of these notes; see discussion by Venturi in his edition of Beccaria, *Dei delitti e delle pene*, 398.

52. A.-T., IV, 67, 61, 66, 61.

53. Diderot to Guéneau de Montbeillard, 27 Nov., 7 and 29 Dec. 1766; and Jan., 5 Feb., and 8 April 1767 (Diderot, *Corr.*, VI, 351–4, 362–5, 367–9; ibid., VII, 14–5, 29, 48–9); not all of Guéneau's letters are extant. Cf. Georges Roth, 'Un ami de Diderot: Guéneau de Montbeillard,' *Mercure de France*, CCCXXXVIII (1960), 71–91; Hubert Fabureau, 'Un Episode inconnu de la vie de Diderot,' *Mercure de France*, CCCVII (1949), 776–9; P. Brunet, 'Guéneau de Montbeillard,' *Mémoires de l'Académie des sciences, arts et belles-lettres de Dijon, 1925–1926*, 125–31. Guéneau de Montbeillard wrote the article 'Etendue' for the *Encyc.*, VI, 43b–46a. On 7 May 1766 he personally and successfully inoculated his son against smallpox (Diderot, *Corr.*, VI, 353 n.). On 6 Nov. 1769 Diderot asked Guéneau to look up the family of another Diderot servant (Diderot, *Corr.*, IX, 201–3).

54. Diderot to Falconet (A.-T., XVIII, 218, 226); cf. Lortholary, *Le Mirage russe en France au XVIIIe siècle*, 369, n. 45.

55. The diplôme (Paris. Bibliothèque Nationale, *Diderot, 1713–1784*, item 470); A.-T., XVIII, 242 (July 1767). Diderot's application (A.-T., XIX, 492–3; Diderot, *Corr.*, VII, 27–8). Cf. Jacques Proust, 'Diderot, l'Académie de Pétersbourg et le projet d'une *Encyclopédie russe*,' *DS XII* (1969), 104–5.

56. Diderot, *Corr.*, VI, 358, 374; ibid., VII, 41, 54, 89–92.

57. Cf. Part I, 18–9, 121–5, 135, 137–9.

58. Diderot, *Corr.*, VII, 89.

59. Diderot, *Corr.*, VII, 89, cf. 55; 88, 92–3.

60. See Louis-Philippe May, 'Le Mercier de la Rivière, intendant des Iles du Vent (1759–1764),' *Revue d'Histoire Economique et Sociale*, XX (1932), 44–74.

61. Adam Smith, *Wealth of Nations*, Book IV, ch. ix; on Le Mercier de La Rivière's standing as a Physiocrat, see Paul Harsin, 'La Théorie fiscale des Physiocrates,' *Revue d'Histoire Economique et Sociale*, XXXVI (1958), 12–3. Diderot, *Corr.*, VIII, 111 (6 Sept. 1768); *Corr. litt.*, VII, 444–6 (15 Oct. 1767).

62. Diderot, *Corr.*, VII, 77. Damilaville's feelings were hurt, for apparently he had been saying the same things for years without Diderot's ever paying any attention; they almost quarreled, and Diderot wrote Damilaville a letter of apology (Diderot, *Corr.*, VII, 75–80).

63. French consul general Rossignol to Choiseul, 19 March 1768 (Charles de Larivière, 'Mercier de La Rivière à Saint-Pétersbourg en 1767, d'après de nouveaux documents,' *RHLF*, IV [1897], 599).

64. Diderot, *Corr.*, VII, 93–5; ibid., VIII, 112; Abbé Guyot, French chargé d'affaires, to Choiseul, 28 Aug. 1767 (Larivière, art. cit., 598). Dates of Le Mercier de La Rivière's journeys (ibid., 599–600).

65. Lortholary, *Le Mirage russe en France au XVIIIe siècle*, 183; for a caustic account of the whole episode (ibid., 179–86).

66. Diderot, *Corr.*, VII, 196–7.

67. Rossignol to Choiseul, 19 March 1768 (Larivière, art. cit., 599–600).

68. Dieckmann, 'Diderot's Letters to Falconet,' *FS*, V, 321–3. See Grimm's very prejudicial account of La Rivière's *L'Ordre naturel*, which must have arrived in Russia at about the

same time that he himself did (*Corr. litt.*, VII, 443–50 [15 Oct. 1767]).

69. Diderot to Falconet, May 1768 (Diderot, *Corr.*, VIII, 35; similarly, same to same, 6 Sept. 1768 [ibid., 129]).

70. 12–14 June 1767 (Marie de Vichy Chamrond du Deffand, *Correspondance complète . . .*, 3 vols. [Paris, 1866], I, 116).

71. Moscow, 10 March 1767 (Etienne-Maurice Falconet, *Correspondance de Falconet avec Catherine II, 1767–1778*, ed. Louis Réau [Paris, 1921], 7). Le Mercier de La Rivière wrote Diderot, 4/15 Oct. 1767: 'Je sais qu'elle désire beaucoup de vous voir icy; elle y compte même, à ce qu'on m'a dit' (Diderot, *Corr.*, VII, 197).

72. Diderot, *Corr.*, VII, 66 (15 May 1767). Cf. ibid., VII, 87.

73. Diderot, *Corr.*, VII, 60, 67, 68–70; unsuccessful at a court, ibid., 96.

74. Dieckmann, 'Diderot's Letters to Falconet,' *FS*, V, 323. Showing the letter to Catherine (Falconet to Catherine, 30 Sept. 1767 [Falconet, *Correspondance de Falconet avec Catherine II*, ed. Réau, 22]).

CHAPTER 38

1. Diderot, *Corr.*, VII, 99 (15 Aug. 1767); cf. Diderot, *Salons*, III, 52.

2. Diderot, *Salons*, III, 4; Diderot, *Oeuvres esthétiques*, ed. Vernière, xvi.

3. Jacques Proust, 'L'Initiation artistique de Diderot,' *Gazette des Beaux-Arts*, 6ᵉ période, LV (1960), 225–32; Jacques Proust, 'Diderot et la physiognomonie,' *CAIEF*, No. 13 (June 1961), 317–29. See Michael T. Cartwright, *Diderot critique d'art et le problème de l'expression* (*DS XIII* [1969]), 36–8.

4. Cf. Part I, 124, 204–7. See the excellent article by Robert Niklaus, 'Diderot et la peinture: La critique d'art et le philosophe,' *Europe*, Nos. 405–6 (Jan.–Feb. 1963), 231–3. In Oct. 1762 (Diderot, *Corr.*, IV, 192), Diderot wrote a review of Webb for the *Corr. litt.* (op. cit., V, 200–6; also in A.-T., XIII, 33–9). Regarding the influence of Du Bos on Diderot, see A.-T., III, 486; Alfred Lombard, *L'Abbé du Bos, un initiateur de la pensée moderne (1670–1742)* (Paris, 1913), 335–6; and Władysław Folkierski, *Entre le classicisme et le romantisme: Etude sur l'esthétique et les esthéticiens du XVIIIᵉ siècle* (Paris, 1925), 175–81, esp. 181. Regarding Père André, see Diderot's remarks in A.-T., X, 17–20; also André Fontaine, *Les Doctrines d'art en France* (Paris, 1909), 196–7, 295 n. Regarding Roger de Piles, see Gita May, 'Diderot et Roger de Piles,' *PMLA*, LXXXV (1970), 444–55. See the important article by Paul O. Kristeller, 'The Modern System of the Arts: A Study in the History of Aesthetics,' *JHI*, XII (1951), 496–527, and XIII (1952), 17–46. Also for Du Bos, see Rémy G. Saisselin, *The Rule of Reason and the Ruses of the Heart* (Cleveland, 1970), 21–4, 67–70, 90–2, 98–100, 140–2, 171–5, and esp. 263–6.

5. Jean Seznec, 'Le "Musée" de Diderot,' *Gazette des Beaux-Arts*, 6ᵉ période, LV (1960), 343–56; Jean Seznec, 'Diderot and the Pictures in Edinburgh,' *Scottish Art Review*, VIII (1961–2), No. 3, 21–4, 32; ibid., VIII, No. 4, 23–5; Jean Seznec, 'Diderot et les plagiats de Monsieur Pierre,' *Revue des Arts*, V (1955), 67–74.

6. Diderot, *Salons*, III, 52.

7. Diderot, *Corr.*, VII, 57 (15 May 1767). Cf. Gita May, 'Diderot devant la magie de Rembrandt,' *PMLA*, LXXIV (1959), 387–97. Cornelius Poelenburg (1586–1660), Dutch landscapist and painter of pastoral scenes.

8. 'Le sommet de la peinture' (Diderot, *Salons*, III, 115 n.; see ibid., Plate No. 37); the original is now in the Royal Museum, Copenhagen. For references to Poussin, see A.-T., X, 166–7, 189, 266, 374, 384, 388, 470, 497, 508; A.-T., XI, 13, 14, 41, 82, 161, 171, 178, 280–1, 312, 326, 338, 340, 346, 355, 370, 436, 438, 439, 517; A.-T., XII, 61, 102, 115, 121, 131; A.-T., XIII, 46; A.-T., XVIII, 139.

9. Diderot, *Salons*, III, 53; Diderot, *Corr.*, VII, 174 (11 Oct. 1767).

10. Diderot, *Salons*, III, 67.

11. Georges May, in *FS*, XVIII (1964), 168.

12. Diderot, *Salons*, III, 56, 173, 121–6, 129–67, 95. Cf. Albert Nahon, 'Le Comique de Diderot dans les *Salons*,' *DS X* (1968), 121–32.

13. Diderot, *Salons*, III, 252–3, 254. Cf. Otis Fellows and Donal O'Gorman, 'Another Addition

to the *Salon de 1767?' DS III* (1961), 215–7; and Diderot, *Salons,* III, 358–9. Concerning Mme Therbouche, see Ulrich Thieme and Felix Becker, *Allgemeines Lexikon der bildenden Künstler,* XXIII (Leipzig, 1929), 282–3, s.v. 'Lisiewski'; also Diderot, *Salons,* III, 34. Her portrait of Diderot is lost; an engraving of it, done in 1823, reproduced in Diderot, *Salons,* III, Pl. 9. Mme Therbouche in Falconet's house (Diderot to Falconet, May and 6 Sept. 1768 [A.-T., XVIII, 254, 284]).

14. A.-T., I, 358–9. For an excellent discussion relating Diderot's *Lettre sur les sourds et muets* to his later ideas on aesthetics and expression, see Cartwright, *Diderot critique d'art et le problème de l'expression (DS XIII),* 69–98.

15. Diderot, *Salons,* III, 186, 187. Cf. Langen, 'Die Technik der Bildbeschreibung in Diderots "Salons",' *RFor,* LXI, 352–3.

16. See Rensselaer W. Lee, '*Ut pictura poesis:* The Humanistic Theory of Painting,' *Art Bulletin,* XXII (1940), 197–269; also Irving Babbitt, *The New Laokoon: An Essay on the Confusion of the Arts* (Boston, 1910), 3–57; and William G. Howard, '*Ut pictura poesis,*' *PMLA,* XXIV (1909), 40–123. See also the important and more recent comments of Rémy G. Saisselin, '*Ut pictura poesis:* DuBos to Diderot,' *JAAC,* XX (1961), 145–56; and Herbert Dieckmann, 'Die Wandlung des Nachahmungsbegriffes in der französischen Ästhetik des 18. Jahrhunderts,' in Jauss, ed., *Nachahmung und Illusion,* 54–8.

17. Diderot, *Salons,* III, 108; A.-T., I, 386. Cf. Seznec, *Essais sur Diderot et l'antiquité,* 58–78; and Part I, 122–4; also Basil Munteano, 'Le Problème de la peinture en poésie dans la critique française du XVIIIᵉ siècle,' in International Federation for Modern Languages and Literatures, *Acta,* V (Florence, 1955), 325–38.

18. Gotthold Ephraim Lessing, *Sämtliche Schriften,* 23 vols. (Stuttgart, Leipzig, Berlin, 1886–1924), IV, 413–27. See Mortier, *Diderot en Allemagne, 1750–1850,* 345–7; and Paul H. Meyer, in his critical edition of Diderot, *Lettre sur les sourds et muets* (DS VII [1965]), 24–5; cf. K. Heinrich von Stein, *Die Entstehung der neueren Aesthetik* (Stuttgart, 1886), 253 n., and Karl Ludwig Werner Leo, *Diderot als Kunstphilosoph* (Erlangen, 1918), 2, 6–13. Also Robert R. Heitner, 'Concerning Lessing's Indebtedness to Diderot,' *MLN,* LXV (1950), 82–8; and Corrado Rosso, ' "Aufklärung" e "Encyclopédie": Diderot e Lessing,' *Filosofia,* VI (1955), 554–73.

19. Diderot, *Salons,* III, 111–2, 213 [cf. Diderot, *Salons,* II, 183], 108–9, 78.

20. Diderot, *Salons,* III, 91–2, 288–90, 331; A.-T., X, 500; cf. A.-T., XIII, 94. Cf. Abbé Jean-Baptiste Du Bos, *Reflexions critiques sur la poésie et la peinture,* première partie, section 24: 'Des actions allégoriques & des personnages allégoriques par rapport à la Peinture.' Folkierski, *Entre le classicisme et le romantisme,* 181.

21. Diderot, *Salons,* III, 97, 218–20; and in his *Essais sur la Peinture* (A.-T., X, 499, 505–6).

22. Jean Locquin, 'La Lutte des critiques d'art contre les portraitistes au XVIIIᵉ siècle,' *Archives de l'Art Français,* nouvelle période, VII (1913), 309–20.

23. Diderot, *Salons,* II, 174.

24. The classic study on this is Gita May, 'Diderot and Burke: A Study in Aesthetic Affinity,' *PMLA,* LXXV (1960), 527–39; see also Dixon Wecter, 'Burke's Theory concerning Words, Images, and Emotion,' *PMLA,* LV (1940), 176, 177 n; cf. Folkierski, *Entre le classicisme et le romantisme,* 509, 510–1. For passages in Diderot showing Burke's influence, see Edmund Burke, *A Philosophical Enquiry . . . ,* ed. J. T. Boulton (London, [1958]), cxxi–cxxii.

25. Diderot, *Salons,* III, 165; cf. J.-J. Mayoux, 'Diderot and the Technique of Modern Literature,' *MLR,* XXXI (1936), 528.

26. Diderot, *Salons,* III, 165, 166.

27. Diderot, *Salons,* III, 227, 228–9, 176.

28. Diderot, *Salons,* III, 298. Diderot may have been fortified in his appreciation of sketches by the enthusiasm of Roger de Piles for them (May, 'Diderot et Roger de Piles,' *PMLA,* LXXXV, 451–2). See also Michael T. Cartwright, 'Gabriel de Saint-Aubin: An Illustrator and Interpreter of Diderot's Art Criticism,' *Gazette des Beaux-Arts,* LXXIII (1969), 219.

29. Diderot, *Salons,* III, 241, 248, 303. See the excellent article by Herbert Dieckmann, 'Esthetic Theory and Criticism in the Enlightenment: Some Examples of Modern Trends,' in Robert Mollenauer, ed., *Introduction to Modernity: A Symposium on Eighteenth-Century Thought*

(Austin [Texas], 1965), 99 and *passim*. Regarding sketches, see also Cartwright, *Diderot critique d'art et le problème de l'expression* (DS XIII), 149.

30. In *De la poésie dramatique* (1758) (A.-T., VII, 371; cf. Part I, 330).

31. Ancient and primitive peoples (A.-T., X, 506). Ossian (Diderot, *Salons*, III, 191–2; also see *supra*, ch. 32 and notes 71–2 of that chapter). 'Quelque chose de sauvage . . . et d'énorme' (*Essais sur la peinture* [A.-T., X, 499]; see also the excellent article by Herbert Dieckmann, 'Das Abscheuliche und Schreckliche in der Kunsttheorie des 18. Jahrhunderts,' in *Die Nicht Mehr Schönen Künste*, ed. Hans R. Jauss [Munich, 1968], esp. 300–5). Allan Ramsay had sent Diderot a copy of Gray's *Odes* in 1766 (Diderot, *Corr.*, V, 245; Cru, 441).

32. Watteau (A.-T., X, 499; XI, 242, 495, 521; XII, 75). A.F., ' "Cet imbécile de Diderot . . . ," Watteau et Teniers,' *Mercure de France*, CCXCIII (1939), 758–9; cf. Dieckmann, *Cinq leçons sur Diderot*, 145.

33. Errol Bedford, in *MLR*, LX (1965), 284; cf. Jean Seznec, in Diderot, *Salons*, III, viii.

34. The account of Diderot's aesthetic theory in Katharine Everett Gilbert and Helmut Kuhn, *A History of Esthetics* (Bloomington [Ind.], 1953), 280–7, though well known, is tied too exclusively to Diderot's early article on 'Beau' and therefore does not do justice to the development and complexity of Diderot's aesthetic thought. The best account is that in Gay, *The Enlightenment: An Interpretation*, II, 249–61, 274–90.

35. A.-T., X, 461–520. Completed in July 1766 (Diderot, *Oeuvres esthétiques*, ed. Vernière, 659; Diderot, *Sur l'art et les artistes*, ed. Jean Seznec [Paris, 1967], 10). The first five chapters of the *Essais sur la peinture* were circulated in the *Corr. litt.* beginning 1 Aug. 1766 (De Booy, 'Inventaire,' 368–9). At some later date Diderot added the two chapters that conclude the work (A.-T., X, 510–20), as well as the enlargement of ch. iii entitled 'Examen du clair-obscur' (A.-T., X, 480–4); see Diderot, *Oeuvres esthétiques*, ed. Vernière, 659–61. The *Essais sur la peinture* was first published in 1795.

36. Diderot, *Salons*, II, 234.

37. A point made by Gita May, 'Les "Pensées détachées sur la peinture" de Diderot et la tradition classique de la "maxime" et de la "pensée",' *RHLF*, LXX (1970), 52; see also Dieckmann, 'Esthetic Theory and Criticism in the Enlightenment,' in Mollenauer, ed., *Introduction to Modernity*, 65–105, esp. 105.

38. A.-T., X, 460–7, esp. 467; ibid., 468.

39. Impressionism, cubism (A.-T., X, 475–9; Jean Pierre, in Diderot, *Oeuvres choisis*, V: *Essais sur la peinture* [Paris, (1955)], 32). See also Jean Pierre, 'Compétence et leçons de Diderot critique d'art,' *Pensée*, No. 40 [Jan.–Feb. 1952], 81–90, esp. 89, and No. 41 [March–April 1952], 80–6; Gerhard Weber, 'Diderot, First of the Art Critics,' *Connoisseur*, CLIX [1965], 239). For passages on chiaroscuro in the *Salon de 1767*, see Diderot, *Salons*, III, 215, 337–8.

40. A.-T., X, 501–3.

41. In this connection see Cartwright, *Diderot critique d'art et le problème de l'expression* (DS XIII), 157–74, esp. 160.

42. J. Rouge, 'Goethe et *l'Essai sur la peinture* de Diderot,' *Etudes Germaniques*, IV (1949), 227–36; Mortier, *Diderot et l'Allemagne, 1750–1850*, 305–18; Herbert Dieckmann, 'Goethe und Diderot,' *Deutsche Vierteljahrsschrift für Literaturwissenschaft und Geistesgeschichte*, X (1932), 478–503, esp. 481–90; Erhard John, 'Goethes Bermerkungen zu Diderots "Versuch über die Malerei",' *Weimarer Beiträge*, VI (1960), 1029–39. For Schiller, see Edmond Eggli, 'Diderot et Schiller,' *RLC*, I (1921), 68–127, esp. 76–7, 88, 100. There was also a translation by Carl Friedrich Cramer in Denis Diderot, *Sämmtliche Werke von Dionysius Diderot* (Riga, 1797), II, 1–428; this edition has been studied in an unpublished thesis by H. Müller, *Stilistische Untersuchung zu Diderot: Essai sur la peinture an Hand der Übersetzungen von Goethe und K. F. Cramer* (Tübingen, 1954), summarized by Helmut Hatzfeld and Yves Le Hir, *Essai de bibliographie critique de stylistique française et romane (1955–1960)* (Paris, 1961), 56.

43. Diderot, *Salons*, III, 61.

44. Schlösser, *Rameaus Neffe*, 102.

45. Gilman, 'The Poet according to Diderot,' *RR*, XXXVII, 37–54, esp. 54.

46. A.-T., II, 121. This passage often quoted and emphasized by critics and biographers (Thomas, *L'Humanisme de Diderot*, 41; Hermand, *Les Idées morales de Diderot*, xiii). See Felix Vexler, *Studies in Diderot's Esthetic Naturalism* (New York, 1922), 7, 102.

47. Diderot, *Salons*, III, 60–1.

48. Diderot, *Le Neveu de Rameau*, ed. Fabre, 12–3; cf. Diderot, *Salons*, III, 61. The whole problem, before, after, and including Diderot, is studied in Heitmann, *Ethos des Künstlers und Ethos der Kunst*, *passim*, esp. 21 *et sqq.*

49. Diderot, *Corr.*, IV, 125–7 (2 Sept. 1762); *Essais sur la peinture* (A.-T., X, 519).

50. A.-T., XVIII, 139; Diderot, *Salons*, III, 238. See also Diderot's remarks on 'L'Anticomanie' in Maurice Tourneux, 'Fragments inédits de Diderot,' *RHLF*, I (1894), 173.

51. Trousson, 'Diderot helléniste,' *DS XII*, 141–326; Raymond Trousson, 'Diderot et Homère,' *DS VIII* (1966), 185–216; Raymond Trousson, 'Diderot et l'antiquité grecque,' *DS VI* (1964), 215–45; Seznec, *Diderot et l'antiquité*, *passim*, esp. 97–117.

52. A.-T., VI, 378 (1769).

53. Frederic Will, 'Two Critiques of the Elgin Marbles: William Hazlitt and Quatremère de Quincy,' *JAAC*, XIV (1955–6), 464.

54. Diderot, *Salons*, II, 206–7. See Georges Matoré, 'Les Notions d'art et d'artiste à l'époque romantique,' *RScH*, Nos. 62–3 (July 1951), 121–4; also Funt, *Diderot and the Esthetics of the Enlightenment (DS XI)*, 143–4.

55. Diderot, *Salons*, III, 60.

56. Diderot, *Salons*, III, 61.

57. Diderot, *Salons*, III, 339.

58. Diderot, *Salons*, III, 63.

59. Regarding Diderot's theory of imitation, see Crocker, *Two Diderot Studies: Ethics and Esthetics*, 70–7. For an excellent discussion of eighteenth-century theories of mimesis and imitation, see Rudolf Wittkower, 'Imitation, Eclecticism, and Genius,' in Earl R. Wasserman, ed., *Aspects of the Eighteenth Century* (Baltimore, 1965), 143–61, esp. 144–5.

60. Diderot, *Salons*, III, 64; cf. René Wellek, *A History of Modern Criticism, 1750–1950*, 2 vols. (New Haven, 1955), I, 54. For the various meanings of the word 'nature' as used by Diderot, see Arthur O. Lovejoy, ' "Nature" as Aesthetic Norm,' *MLN*, XLII (1927), 444–50.

61. Funt, *Diderot and the Esthetics of the Enlightenment (DS XI)*, 75–82.

62. Robert Niklaus, 'L'Esprit créateur de Diderot,' *CAIEF*, No. 20 (May 1968), 39–54, esp. 39–40; Ernst Cassirer, *The Philosophy of the Enlightenment* (Princeton, 1951), 312–21; Dieckmann, *Cinq leçons sur Diderot*, 116.

63. Margaret Gilman, *The Idea of Poetry in France from Houdar de La Motte to Baudelaire* (Cambridge [Mass.], 1958), 27; regarding Diderot's ideas on aesthetics, see also the very important reviews of this book by Jean Seznec in *FS*, XIII (1959), 353–5, and B. F. Bart in *Symposium*, XIV (1960), 65–9. Gilman, 'The Poet according to Diderot,' *RR*, XXXVII, 37 n.: 'The word *poète* is consistently used by Diderot, not only for the writer in verse, but far more frequently for what we should call the "creative writer" in general;' see also Margaret Gilman, 'Imagination and Creation in Diderot,' *DS II* (1952), 200–20.

64. For the Diderot quotations in this paragraph, see Diderot, *Salons*, III, 60, 59, 224, 63–4.

65. Trahard, in *Les Maîtres de la sensibilité française au XVIIIᵉ siècle* (II, 126–86), interprets the career and writings solely in terms of *sensibilité*. For more recent views, see Gay, *The Enlightenment*, II, 274–80, 286–8; Wilson, 'The Biographical Implications of Diderot's *Paradoxe sur le comédien*,' *DS III*, 369–83, esp. 375–80. Very important in this connection is the ingenious and heavily documented work by Belaval, *L'Esthétique sans paradoxe de Diderot*, which argues that the development in Diderot's aesthetic thought from *sensibilité* to self-control was consistent and without any element of being paradoxical. Regarding Diderot's theories of creativity, see Crocker, *Two Diderot Studies: Ethics and Esthetics*, 87–95.

66. Alexander Gottlieb Baumgarten, *Aesthetica*, 2 vols. (Frankfort on Oder, 1750–8); see Wellek, *A History of Modern Criticism*, I, 144.

67. A.-T., X, 519. For a discussion of Diderot's doctrine of taste, see Cassirer, *The Philosophy of the Enlightenment*, 307–12. For Diderot's dealing with the problem in earlier years,

see Part I, 205–7. See also A.-T., IV, 95: 'le goût de la nation, qui est toujours le produit des siècles. . . .'

68. Francastel, 'L'Esthétique des Lumières,' in Francastel, ed., *Utopie et institutions au XVIIIe siècle: Le Pragmatisme des Lumières*, 338, 340.

69. Diderot, *Salons*, III, 55. See Albert Dresdner, *Die Entstehung der Kunstkritik im Zusammenhang der Geschichte des europäischen Kunstlebens* (Munich, 1968), 111–4. For Diderot's dislike of 'amateurs,' see Seznec, *Essais sur Diderot et l'antiquité*, 93–6. Cf. Francis H. Taylor, *The Taste of Angels* (Boston, 1948), esp. 374–400: 'The *Curieux* and the *Philosophes*.'

70. That such was Diderot's role is a point made by the reviewer of Diderot's *Salons* in the *Times Literary Supplement*, 7 March 1968, 200: 'He [the art critic] was the creature of social mobility, of changing patterns of communication and of an age which, having lost instinctive canons of taste, had not yet acquired their rationalized equivalents. Nowhere can the nature and function of art critic be more rewardingly studied than in the works of the first great exemplar of the type, Denis Diderot.' See also the remarks of Herbert Dieckmann, as reported by Roger P. McCutcheon, 'Eighteenth-Century Aesthetics: A Search for Surviving Values,' *Harvard Library Bulletin*, x (1956), 299.

71. A.-T., x, 517.

72. A.-T., x, 519; Cassirer, *The Philosophy of the Enlightenment*, 309–12; Vexler, *Studies in Diderot's Esthetic Naturalism*, 102. For Diderot's theory of taste, see Crocker, *Two Diderot Studies: Ethics and Esthetics*, 96–8.

73. Funt, *Diderot and the Esthetics of the Enlightenment* (*DS XI*), 180. Cf. Thomas J. Durkin, 'Three Notes to Diderot's Aesthetic,' *JAAC*, xv (1956–7), 331–9.

74. L. D. Ettlinger, 'Taste and Patronage: The Role of the Artist in Society,' in Alfred Cobban, ed., *The Eighteenth Century* (New York, 1969), 252–3.

75. Diderot, *Salons*, III, 198.

76. Baudouin (Diderot, *Salons*, III, 197–9). Boucher (Diderot, *Salons*, II, 64, 75–6; A.-T., x, 501–2); but later Diderot wrote about the children painted by Boucher, 'J'ai dit trop de mal de Boucher; je me rétracte' (A.-T., XII, 122). Regarding Diderot on Boucher and Baudouin, see also James A. Leith, *The Idea of Art as Propaganda in France, 1750–1799* (Toronto, 1965), 30–2.

77. A.-T., x, 502; *Pensées détachées sur la peinture* (A.-T., XII, 84).

78. Armand Behets, *Diderot, critique d'art* (Brussels, 1944), 13–4.

79. The decline of the rococo and the rise of neo-classicism is well described by Rémy G. Saisselin, 'Neo-classicism: Virtue, Reason and Nature,' in Henry Hawley, *Neo-classicism: Style and Motif* (Cleveland, 1964), 1–8; see also Rémy G. Saisselin, 'The Rococo Muddle,' *SVEC*, XLVII (1966), 233–55. An excellent treatment of the 'rococo muddle' is to be found in Herbert Dieckmann, 'Reflections on the Use of Rococo as a Period Concept,' in *The Disciplines of Criticism: Essays in Literary Theory, Interpretation, and History*, ed. Peter Demetz and others (New Haven, 1968), 419–36, esp. 430. Important comments upon this subject are also to be found in Arnold Hauser, *The Social History of Art*, 2 vols. (New York, 1952), I, 533–4; Locquin, *La Peinture d'histoire en France de 1747 à 1785*, x, 145–7, 229–37, 264–71; Dieckmann, *Cinq leçons sur Diderot*, 144–5; Jean Seznec, 'Diderot et Phryné,' *Gazette des Beaux-Arts*, 6e période, XXXVII (1950), 325–8; Jean Seznec, 'Diderot and "The Justice of Trajan",' *JWCI*, xx (1957), 106–11; Seznec, 'Les *Salons* de Diderot,' *Harvard Library Bulletin*, v, 285.

80. A.-T., x, 502. But see the convincing defense of Diderot's moralism made by Meyer Schapiro, 'Diderot on the Artist and Society,' *DS V* (1964), 9–11; also Dresdner, *Die Entstehung der Kunstkritik*, 221–4.

81. Rémy G. Saisselin, in *JAAC*, xxv (1966–7), 338.

82. A.-T., x, 507; Diderot, *Salons*, I, 233; ibid., II, 155. 'Fricassée d'enfants' (A.-T., x, 351 n.; ibid., XI, 443 n.). For the popularity of Greuze with the eighteenth-century public, see Dresdner, *Die Entstehung der Kunstkritik*, 180–1.

83. Diderot, *Salons*, II, 145–8.

84. Seznec, 'Diderot and the Pictures in Edinburgh,' *Scottish Art Review*, VIII, No. 4 (1962), 25.

85. Diderot, *Salons*, I, 125; ibid., II, 108, 111.
86. Diderot, *Salons*, I, 125; ibid., II, 111, 121; ibid., III, 317; ibid., IV, 83, 178, 185. Cf. Rémy G. Saisselin, *Taste in Eighteenth-Century France: Critical Reflections on the Origins of Aesthetics* (Syracuse [N.Y.], 1965), 104.
87. Diderot, *Salons*, III, 129. Cf. Roger Fry, 'The Double Nature of Painting,' *Apollo*, LXXXIX (1969), 369; Errol Bedford, in *MLR*, LIII (1958), 591; Seznec, 'Les *Salons* de Diderot,' *Harvard Library Bulletin*, V, 286–7.
88. 'La largeur de faire' (Diderot, *Salons*, I, 66–7). Other references (Diderot, *Salons*, I, 195; ibid., II, 108; A.-T., X, 470, 473).
89. 'La Lumière et les reflets' (Diderot, *Salons*, I, 222; ibid., IV, 84); for other references, see Diderot, *Salons*, II, 111, 113, 114. For excellent remarks on Diderot's criticism, including his appreciation of Chardin, see Jean Starobinski, *The Invention of Liberty, 1700–1789* (Geneva, 1964), 10, 117, 127, 134–6.
90. Diderot, *Salons*, IV, 178. There are some excellent pages on Diderot's appreciation of Chardin in George R. Havens, *The Age of Ideas* (New York, 1955), 320–2; the most comprehensive analysis is to be found in the excellent article by May, 'Chardin vu par Diderot et par Proust,' *PMLA*, LXXII, 403–18.
91. Charles-Augustin Sainte-Beuve, 'Diderot,' *Causeries du lundi*, feuilleton for 20 Jan. 1851. Another very fine nineteenth-century appraisal of Diderot is the essay by G. A. Simcox, 'Diderot as an Art Critic,' *Portfolio*, III (1872), 140–4. F. J. B. Watson, in *Connoisseur*, CXLI (Jan.–June 1958), 110.
92. Ferdinand Brunetière, 'Les Salons de Diderot,' *RDM*, 3ᵉ période, XXXIX (May–June 1880), 456–69, this quotation 469; for a critique of Brunetière's attack, see Dresdner, *Die Entstehung der Kunstkritik*, 196–8. For another sharp criticism of Diderot — 'litterato, sopratutto litterato' — see Mary Pittaluga, 'Eugène Fromentin e le origini de la moderna critica d'arte,' *Arte*, XX (1917), 121–3, 126.
93. Virgil W. Topazio, 'Art Criticism in the Enlightenment,' *SVEC*, XXVII (1963), 1648. See the amplification of these views in Topazio, 'Diderot's Limitations as an Art Critic,' *FR*, XXXVII (1963–4), 3–11. The rejoinder by Gita May, 'In Defense of Diderot's Art Criticism,' ibid., 11–21, defends Diderot very ably.
94. Georges de Traz [pseud. François Fosca], *De Diderot à Valéry: Les écrivains et les arts visuels* (Paris, 1960), 168. For other examples of critical approval, see Stein, *Die Entstehung der neueren Aesthetik*, 254–7; Denys Sutton, 'Diderot as an Art Critic,' *Apollo*, LXVI (1957–8), 100–1; Jean de Cayeux, 'Diderot et l'art vivant,' *Réforme*, 23 June 1951, 7; Jean-Gabriel Lemoine, 'Les vraies idées de Diderot sur l'art,' *Art Vivant*, V (1929), 679–83; the same, 'Les idées de Diderot sur la sculpture,' *Bulletin des Musées de France*, VIII (1936), 140–2; Friedrich Bassenge, 'Diderot und die bildende Kunst,' *WZUB*, XIII (1964), 197–205; Henri Bassis, 'Diderot, théoricien du réalisme en peinture,' *Europe*, No. 82 (Oct. 1952), 70–8; Rémy G. Saisselin, 'Some Remarks on French Eighteenth-Century Writings on the Arts,' *JAAC*, XXV (1966–7), 194. See also Saisselin's comments on the articles by Topazio and Gita May ('Diderot as Art Critic,' *FR*, XXXVII [1963–4], 457–60). For judicious and comprehensive remarks on Diderot's aesthetics, see Saisselin, *The Rule of Reason and the Ruses of the Heart*, 253–63.
95. Jacques Barzun, 'Why Diderot?', in Burnshaw, ed., *Varieties of Literary Experience*, 33. For an excellent treatment of Diderot as an art critic, see Dresdner, *Die Entstehung der Kunstkritik*, 188–227. This book, first published in 1915, has been very important in enhancing the appreciation of Diderot in our century; see Herbert Dieckmann, in *RHLF*, LIX (1959), 226.

CHAPTER 39

1. 'Rätselhafte' and 'démoniaque' (Herbert Dieckmann, in *Literaturblatt für germanische und romanische Philologie*, LIII [1932], 405; *CI*, II, 280). Rue Sainte-Anne (Diderot, *Corr.*, V, 111, 176). Jean-Rodolphe Perronet (1708–94) was Vialet's superior in the Ponts et Chaussées; eventually he became First Engineer in that service; for references to him, see Diderot, *Corr.*, IV, 112; V, 49, 63, 96, 113, 126, 192, 234; VI, 24–5, 157, 159, 176. The

tutor, Jacques-Marie Digeon (Diderot, *Corr.*, VII, 109–10). Socratic dialogue about the tutor (Diderot, *Corr.*, VII, 113–4, 118–23, 128–9).

2. Diderot indirectly refers to her death in his letter to Sophie, 8 Oct. 1768 (Diderot, *Corr.*, VIII, 189). See also ibid., VIII, 105; ibid., IX, 125, 149. The tutor Digeon married Mme Le Gendre's daughter in Nov. 1769 (Diderot, *Corr.*, IX, 212). Mme Le Gendre's husband died in 1770, evidently not long before 23 Aug. (Diderot, *Corr.*, X, 113). In 1766 Diderot had tried to advise Vialet with regard to Mme Le Gendre (Diderot, *Corr.*, VI, 175–9); for his very critical estimate of her character (Diderot, *Corr.*, VII, 182–5, 189–92, 195, 200, 206). Pierre Daix, ' "La Religieuse" de Diderot, mystification, documentaire ou roman?' *Lettres Françaises*, 2–8 June 1966, 3–6, observes that in Diderot's letters there is no expression of sorrow over the death of Mme Le Gendre.

3. First mention of Vialet, 2 Sept. 1760 (Diderot, *Corr.*, III, 51); thereafter (ibid., III, 313, 333, 349; IV, 111–2, 35, 50, 55–6, 92, 142, 207; V, 36, 96, 192; VI, 108; VII, 108). Vialet was an associate member of the Academy of Châlons-sur-Marne (Henri Menu, 'La Société littéraire et l'Académie des sciences, arts et belles-lettres de Châlons-sur-Marne, 1750–1792,' Société d'Agriculture, Commerce, Sciences et Arts du Département de la Marne, *Mémoires*, [1868], 258, 272). The drawings and explanations of the slate industry in the Meuse valley were done for the *Encyc.* by Vialet (*Encyc.*, *Planches*, 5e livraison ou 6e vol., 'Exposition,' 6).

4. Diderot, *Corr.*, VII, 181–95, 200–10, 212–5; cf. Diderot to Sophie, 17 Oct. 1767 (ibid., VII, 179–80).

5. To Mme d'Epinay (Diderot, *Corr.*, VII, 154–7, 169–72, 210–1). Cf. Diderot's complaint about Grimm, Sept. 1767 (ibid., VII, 129–31, 138), and in 1768 about Grimm and D'Holbach (ibid., VIII, 213–4, 222–3).

6. Denise Diderot to Denis, beginning of June 1768 (Diderot, *Corr.*, VIII, 53–4), in reply to his letter of 29 May 1768 (ibid., 47–50). Previously Denise had acted with power of attorney for Denis Diderot on 3 Feb. 1767 in a contract the terms of which are not stated (Marcel, *Le Frère de Diderot*, 11 n.); on 17 May 1768 Denise had passed a contract allocating the house at Cahons to the Abbé Diderot, the family home at Langres to herself, and the house at Chassigny to Denis (Diderot, *Corr.*, VIII, 46). Diderot objected to this explosively, for he wanted Cahons instead of Chassigny. The ensuing letters are rather painful, full of bitter remarks about the Abbé and reiterated declarations of his own virtue; but he ended up with the house at Chassigny (Diderot, *Corr.*, VIII, 55–62, 87–91, 180–2, 193–5). Diderot sold the Chassigny property for 2000 livres, 15 Oct. 1769 (Diderot, *Corr.*, IX, 173).

7. Herbert Dieckmann, art. cit. [*supra*, n. 1], 405.

8. Jean-Nicolas Dufort, comte de Cheverny, *Mémoires*, 2e ed., 2 vols. (Paris, 1909), I, 459. Cheverny was at one time Introducteur des Ambassadeurs at Versailles. He mentions (ibid., 458–9) that for some winters he and Diderot and Sedaine and Dorat and a few others, never more than eight at a time, used to dine on Wednesdays at the Marquis de Pezay's, regarding whom see Diderot, *Corr.*, XIV, 244–5.

9. Diderot, *Corr.*, VIII, 35–7, 110–5, 118–22, 135, 137–8.

10. Mlle Jodin was for some time a member of a French troupe at Warsaw and Dresden (Ludwik Bernacki, *Teatr, Dramat i Muzyka za Stanisława Augusta*, 2 vols. [Lwow, 1925], II, 390 n.; Diderot, *Corr.*, VI, 250 and n.; ibid., VII, 215–6). Diderot's letters to her (Diderot, *Corr.*, VI, 166–8, 200–2, 239–41, 377–9; ibid., VII, 11–4, 83–4). In 1768 Diderot offered her a position in a troupe being formed to go to Russia (Diderot, *Corr.*, VIII, 14), but this fell through. See also ibid., VIII, 23–4, 65–70, 163–6, 224–7, 237–9.

11. Diderot to Gayet de Sansale, 30 July, 1 and 28 Aug. 1768 (Diderot, *Corr.*, VIII, 73–8, 82–4, 97–100). 'All my womenfolk' (ibid., VIII, 234 [22 Nov. 1768]; Mme Diderot's elder sister, Mme Billard, was now living with the Diderots).

12. To Garrick, 26 Jan. 1767 (Diderot, *Corr.*, VII, 17–9). Fenouillot was rather pertinacious: see his letters to Garrick, *c.* 25 Jan., 29 March and 18 Nov. 1767 (Diderot, *Corr.*, VII, 16–7, 45–6, 219). He also wrote to Hume, taking care to mention Diderot, 18 Nov. 1767 (J.S.T. Greig, 'Some Unpublished Letters to David Hume,' *RLC*, XII [1932], 850–1; see also Ronald Grimsley, 'A French Correspondent of David Hume: Fenouillot de Falbaire,'

MLR, LVI [1961], 561-3). Regarding Fenouillot de Falbaire and his play, *L'Honnête Criminal*, see *Corr. litt.*, VIII, 3-8 (1 Jan. 1768).

13. To Hume, 24 Nov. 1767 and 22 Feb. 1768 (Diderot, *Corr.*, VII, 220-1; ibid., VIII, 14-8); Hume to the Rev. John Gardner, 4 March 1768 (*New Letters of David Hume*, ed. Klibansky and Mossner, 181); see also ibid., 187.

14. To Sophie, 21 Sept. 1768 (Diderot, *Corr.*, VIII, 177, 178).

15. To Sophie, 24 Aug. and 10 Sept. 1768 (Diderot, *Corr.*, VIII, 95-6, 162). Mme de Vandeul, l, speaks of this incident at some length. The minister was the Comte de Saint-Florentin (Diderot, *Corr.*, VIII, 91 and n.). Some years later Diderot again asked the Comte, now become Duc de la Vrillière, to see that the woman, a widow named Panet, received admission to the Hospital for Incurables (Diderot, *Corr.*, XI, 219, 220-1).

16. Diderot, *Corr.*, VII, 140 (24 Sept. 1767); ibid., VIII, 212 (4 Nov. 1768).

17. To Hume, 22 Feb. 1768, and to Falconet, May 1768 (Diderot, *Corr.*, VIII, 15, 27). Milk diet (6 and 10 Sept. 1768 [ibid., VIII, 124, 162]).

18. 'Oui, j'ai prêté mes 70 mille francs à un fermier général . . .' (to Denise Diderot, 15 Aug. 1768 [Diderot, *Corr.*, VIII, 90; see also ibid., 194]); Diderot's criticisms of farmers-general (Diderot, *Corr.*, VIII, 183-4); his general worries about his new wealth (to Sophie, mid-Nov. 1767 [Diderot, *Corr.*, VII, 216-7]). Two documents mentioned in Diderot, *Corr.*, VIII, 20, evidently refer to this investment: a *Consentement des sieurs d'Allainville, Did, rot et autres au sieur Augeard, fermier général*, 21 March 1768; and a *Procès-verbal aux fermes*, signed by Augeard and Diderot, 27 March 1768.

19. Diderot, *Corr.*, VI, 145-6 (24 Sept. 1767), and ibid., VIII, 27-8 (May 1768). For the question of protocol involved, see Tourneux, *Diderot et Catherine II*, 80 n. The chargé d'affaires was Nicholas Khotinski, formerly Russian secretary of embassy at Madrid.

20. For information concerning Mlle Dornet, see Denis Diderot, *Quatre contes*, ed. Jacques Proust (Geneva, 1964), 135-40; and Yves Benot, *Diderot, de l'athéisme à l'anticolonialisme* (Paris, 1970), 115-8. For her visit to the Vollands (Diderot, *Corr.*, VII, 110-1 and 110 n., 115-6, 125, 145).

21. Amélie de Schmettau. They were married at Aix-la-Chapelle, 10 Aug. 1768 (Diderot, *Oeuvres esthétiques*, ed. Vernière, 368 n.).

22. For Desbrosses, see Diderot, *Quatre contes*, ed. Proust, 160-1, 166-8.

23. Diderot refers to the hoax in his letters to Sophie of 21 Sept., 1 and 26 Oct., and 15 Nov. 1768 (Diderot, *Corr.*, VIII, 179-80, 184, 205-6, 223). The man script's existence discovered by Dieckmann, *Inventaire*, 91. It was first published in 1954 (*Lettres françaises*, 4-11 Feb. 1954, 1 and 10; and ibid., 11-18 Feb. 1954, 12); also in a small book (Denis Diderot, *Mystification ou histoire des portraits*, ed. Pierre Daix, with notes by Yves Benot [Paris, 1954]; this edition in German translation, *Mystifikation oder die Porträtgeschichte* [Berlin, 1956]). There is also a German edition with supplement by Herbert Dieckmann (Denis Diderot, *Mystifikation* [Frankfort, 1966]). Regarding this dialogue, see Yves Benot, 'A propos de Diderot. Mystification, ironie romantique et recherche de la vérité,' *Pensée*, No. 82 (Nov.-Dec. 1958), 65-74; translated in *Sinn und Form*, XI (1959), 330-44. See also the excellent edition in Diderot, *Quatre contes*, ed. Proust, xi-xiv, 3-39, 156-68.

24. Diderot, *Corr.*, VIII, 28-9 (May 1768); also ibid., VIII, 72 (18 July 1768).

25. Diderot, *Corr.*, VIII, 222 (15 Nov. 1768); ibid., IX, 36 (6 March 1769); also IX, 56-7. The pictures cost Catherine II 17,535 livres (Pierre Descargues, *The Hermitage Museum, Leningrad* [New York, 1961)], 25-6).

26. ' . . . qu'il me soit permis de dire, Etre immortel, tout-puissant, éternel, qui fais les grandes destinées, & qui veilles sur elles, conserve à la Russie Catherine II.' The date of the censor's approbation of the volume was 11 June 1768; it was distributed to subscribers in September of that year (*Mémoire à consulter pour les libraires associés à l'Encyclopédie*, 12).

27. Claude-Carloman de Rulhière, *Oeuvres posthumes de Rulhière*, 4 vols. (Paris, 1819), IV, 255-373; this quotation, 368. The foreword was dated 10 Feb. 1768. For especially significant passages, see ibid., 267-9, 311, 378-9, 382-8.

28. Ségur, *Le Royaume de la rue Saint-Honoré: Madame Geoffrin et sa fille*, 223-4; Lortholary,

Le Mirage russe en France au XVIIIe siècle, 188–9. Grimm wrote in the *Corr. litt.*, VIII, 493–4 (1 April 1770) that he had heard Rulhière read his manuscript at Mme Geoffrin's. For the whole episode, see Marie-Célestine-Amélie, comtesse d'Armaillé, *La Comtesse d'Egmont, fille du Maréchal de Richelieu, 1740–1773, d'après ses lettres inédites à Gustave III* (Paris, 1890), 119–20. For Diderot and Rulhière, see also Alice Chevalier, *Claude-Carloman de Rulhière, premier historien de Pologne, sa vie et son oeuvre historique* (Paris, 1939), 106–10. Diderot describes Rulhière most interestingly in the *Satire I sur les caractères et les mots de caractère* . . . (A.-T., VI, 311–3).

29. Diderot, *Corr.*, VIII, 32–3.

30. Prince Alexander Galitzin to Khotinski, 24 June/5 July 1768 (Tourneux, *Diderot et Catherine II*, 32–3; also in Diderot, *Corr.*, VIII, 63–4). Falconet had transmitted Diderot's information to Catherine on 13/24 June 1768; she replied the next day about the orders to Khotinski (Falconet, *Correspondance de Falconet avec Catherine II, 1767–1778*, ed. Réau, 48, 49, 51).

31. Diderot, *Corr.*, VIII, 128, 137. Dr. Tronchin to his daughter, 9 April 1769 (Callatay, *Madame de Vermenoux*, 70). See Diderot's account to Princess Dashkov regarding these negotiations (Ekaterina Romanovna Dashkova, *Memoirs of the Princess Daschkaw. . . ,* ed. Mrs. W. Bradford, 2 vols. [London, 1840], I, 168–70).

32. Diderot did not have this quite right: the volume, *Perevodi iz Enziklopedǔ* (Moscow, 1767), contained a selection of articles from all the volumes. For a description of this edition, as well as of other editions of translations from the *Encyclopédie* published in Russia, see Venturi, 'Beccaria in Russia,' *Il Ponte*, IX, 167; and M. M. Strange, 'Enziklopediya Didro i ee russkie perevodchiki,' *Frantsuzskǔ Ezhegodnik, 1959*, 76–88; see also the latter's 'Diderot et la société russe de son temps,' *AHRF*, XXXV (1963), 298–300, 302–3. Also useful is P. N. Berkov, 'Histoire de l'*Encyclopédie* dans la Russie du XVIIIe siècle,' *Revue des Etudes Slaves*, XLIV (1965), 47–58.

33. Diderot, *Corr.*, VIII, 80, 130. Translated by Sergii Glebov (St. Petersburg, 1765); see Strange, 'Diderot et la société russe de son temps,' *AHRF*, XXXV, 297. A Russian translation of *Le Fils naturel* was published in 1764 (*Svodnyǐ Katalog russkoǐ knigi XVIII veka, 1725–1800* [Moscow, 1962–ㅤ], I, 290–1, item No. 1861; see also Strange, art. cit., 297); and esp. L. B. Svetlov, 'Russkie perevody proizvedenii Didro [Russian Translations of Diderot's Works],' *Frantsuzskǔ Ezhegodnik*, 1965, 213–28.

34. Diderot, *Corr.*, VIII, 123 (6 Sept. 1768). About this time Diderot complained to his sister that 'les libraires viennent de faire jeter chez moi un fardeau de cent trente planches' (Diderot, *Corr.*, VIII, 195).

35. *Corr. litt.*, VII, 296–7 (15 April, 1767).

36. Hermann Bräuning-Oktavio, 'Goethe und Diderot im Jahre 1772,' *Goethe*, XXIV (1962), 247; the same, 'Die Bibliothek der grossen Landgräfin Caroline von Hessen,' *Archiv für Geschichte des Buchwesens*, VI (1966), 692.

37. Diderot, *Corr.*, VIII, 211 (4 Nov. 1768), 229–30 (22 Nov. 1768). *Corr. litt.*, VIII, 221–2 (15 Dec. 1768).

38. *Corr. litt.*, VIII, 213–4 (15 Dec. 1768).

39. The course of his illness may be followed in Diderot, *Corr.*, VIII, 93–4, 160, 172, 179, 184, 188, 210, 223, 240.

40. D'Alembert to Voltaire, 14 Nov. 1767 (Besterman, No. 13623).

41. *Corr. litt.*, VIII, 222–4 (15 Dec. 1768), this quotation 223. See Caussy, 'Damilaville ou le gobe-mouche de la philosophie,' *Mercure de France*, CIII, 76–97.

42. Diderot, *Corr.*, VIII, 169, 20. Assiduous in visiting Damilaville (Diderot, *Corr.*, VIII, 93, 101, 172, 211, 236). Bachaumont's *Mémoires secrets*, IV, 210, mentioned Diderot's faithfulness. See also the feeling reference to Damilaville in Diderot's essay 'De la manière' (Diderot, *Salons*, III, 335).

43. See, e.g., Diderot, *Corr.*, VIII, 182, 191, 214–5.

44. To Damilaville, 30 Jan. 1767 (Besterman, No. 13002).

45. Diderot, *Corr.*, VIII, 89; *Corr. litt.*, VII, 297.

46. Diderot, *Corr.*, VIII, 45, 231–2, 103.

47. Diderot, *Corr.*, VIII, 231; Massiet du Biest, *La Fille de Diderot*, 180.

48. Massiet du Biest, *La Fille de Diderot*, 4–5. 'Un pauvre que la Providence lui a adressé' (Diderot, *Corr.*, VIII, 102). The sculptor Simon (Diderot, *Corr.*, VIII, 45–6, 63, 64, 65, 126–7, 128). The market incident occurred on 17 Dec. 1768; the police would have sent Mme Diderot's principal assailant to jail had not Mme Diderot asked that she be let off (A.N., Y 13,777; printed in Emile Campardon, *Les Prodigalités d'un fermier général* [Paris, 1882], 124–7).

49. The best edition is that edited by Jean Seznec in Diderot, *Salons*, IV, 386–91, these quotations 386, 388; published in A.-T., IV, 5–12. Grimm's account of the Czartoryski visit (*Corr. litt.*, VIII, 276). Grimm circulated the *Regrets* in the *Corr. litt.*, 15 Feb. 1769 (De Booy, 'Inventaire,' 370). The first printed edition, now very rare, was published in 1772 by F. D. Ring (Roland Mortier, 'Le "Journal de Lecture" et l'esprit "philosophique",' *RLC*, XXIX [1955], 217); a copy of this may be seen at the British Museum (T 977, No. 4). Another printing is dated 1775 (example in Kongelige Bibliotek, Copenhagen, call-number 178^{III} 126). It was also published in the unauthorized five-vol. *Collection complette des oeuvres philosophiques, littéraires et dramatiques de M. Diderot*, IV, 319–31. The first printing of it in France was in the *Journal de Lecture*, XII (1779), 2, 160–7 (Mortier, art. cit., 217). There have also been four separate editions: Basel, 1874; Paris, 1935; Paris, 1946 (*Les Cahiers d'Estienne, 1946*, No. 12); The Hague, 1959. For an analysis of Diderot's style and imagery in the *Regrets*, see Spitzer, *Linguistics and Literary History: Essays in Stylistics*, 171–2.

50. Diderot, *Corr.*, VII, 132 (Sept. 1767); ibid., VIII, 202 (26 Oct. 1768). For a complete discussion of the Vernet, the bronze and gold clock, and other possessions mentioned by Diderot, see Jean Seznec, 'A propos de la vieille robe de chambre,' in *Europäische Aufklärung: Herbert Dieckmann zum 60. Geburtstag*, ed. Hugo Friedrich and Fritz Schalk (Munich, 1967), 271–80. Diderot described his Vernet at considerable length in the *Salon de 1769* (Diderot, *Salons*, IV, 88–9). Vernet asked Diderot what he wanted and then painted the picture to Diderot's specifications (Diderot, *Corr.*, XII, 260–1).

51. For a very critical appraisal of Diderot by Mme Geoffrin, see Part I, 224. A vivid sketch of Mme Geoffrin and her salon is contained in a letter, 16 Nov. 1768, of a German author visiting Paris in the entourage of Christian VII of Denmark (Helfrich Peter Sturz, quoted in Werner Krauss, *Die französische Aufklärung im Spiegel der deutschen Literatur des 18. Jahrhunderts* [Berlin, 1963], 132–5).

52. Diderot, *Corr.*, VIII, 44–5, 186–7; cf. ibid., VII, 139, 143. Bachaumont, *Mémoires secrets*, IV, 125–6 (2 Oct. 1768).

53. D'Holbach's letter, 6 March 1769 (Edmond and Jules de Goncourt, *Portraits intimes du dix-huitième siècle*, 2 vols. [Paris, n.d.], II, 226). See the very thorough article by Manfred Naumann, 'Zur Publikationsgeschichte des "Christianisme dévoilé",' in Werner Krauss, ed., *Neue Beiträge zur Literatur der Aufklärung*, 155–83.

54. Arthur I. Bloomfield, 'The Foreign-Trade Doctrines of the Physiocrats,' *American Economic Review*, XXVIII (1938), 734, 735.

55. Ronald L. Meek, *The Economics of Physiocracy: Essays and Translations* (Cambridge [Mass.], 1962), 39; Georges Weulersse, *Les Physiocrates* (Paris, 1931), 29.

56. *Encyc.*, IX, 148a; may reasonably be attributed to Diderot (Lough, 'Problem,' 367). Printed also in A.-T., XV, 407–9. This article frequently quoted by Georges Weulersse, *Le Mouvement physiocratique en France (de 1756 à 1770)*, 2 vols. (Paris, 1910), I, 260, 263, 271, 336–7, 360, 427, 557, 561 n.; II, 471. Regarding Quesnay's articles, see Part I, 184, 253, 277. Diderot's praise of Le Mercier (Diderot, *Corr.*, VII, 76–9). For the affinities in intellectual method between the Physiocrats and the pre-1769 Diderot, see Ellen Marie Strenski, 'Diderot, For and Against the Physiocrats,' *SVEC*, LVII (1967), 1435–55.

57. 'Le marchand de mauvaise foi' (*Ephémérides du Citoyen*, vol. V for 1769, 133–4; also in *Corr. litt.*, VIII, 370–1 nn.; and in A.-T., IV, 80–1). 'Le Bal de l'Opéra' (*Ephémérides du Citoyen*, vol. XII for 1769, 99; also in *Corr. litt.*, VIII, 370–1 nn.; see Diderot, *Corr.*, IX, 61–2). For Diderot's friendliness with Dupont, see Pierre-Samuel Du Pont de Nemours, *L'Enfance et la jeunesse de Du Pont de Nemours, racontées par lui-même*, ed. H.-A. Du Pont de Nemours (Paris, 1906), 152–3. Dupont admired Diderot, but found Mme Diderot 'brusque' and 'de mauvais ton,' and Angélique 'glacée, du moins pour moi' (ibid.).

58. A.-T., IV, 82–3.
59. For references to the famine of 1764, see Galiani's first dialogue (the best edition of this work is Ferdinando Galiani, *Dialogues sur le commerce des bleds*, ed. Fausto Nicolini [Milan, (1959)], this reference 4–5, 12). On the development of Galiani's ideas, see the useful pages by Philip Koch in Ferdinando Galiani, *Dialogues entre M. Marquis de Roquemare et Mᵉ. le Chevalier Zanobi*, ed. Koch (*Analecta Romanica*, Heft 21) (Frankfort on Main, 1968), 1–23; also Philip Koch, 'The Genesis of Galiani's *Dialogues sur le commerce des blés*,' FS, xv (1961), 314–23.
60. Diderot, *Corr.*, VIII, 233 (22 Nov. 1768), also 216 (12 Nov. 1768).
61. Giuseppe Ferraioli, 'Un fallo diplomatico dell'abate Galiani,' *Archivio Storico per le Province Napoletane*, v (1880), 690–8; Krzysztof Zaboklicki, 'L'abate Ferdinando Galiani nelle carte dell'Archivio del Quai d'Orsay,' *Problemi di lingua e letteratura italiana del Settecento. Atti del IV Congresso Internazionale di Studi Italiana* (Wiesbaden, 1965), 191–5. For an excellent essay on Galiani, see Harold M. M. Acton, 'Ferdinando Galiani,' in Italian Institute, London, *Art and Ideas in Eighteenth-Century Italy* (Rome, 1960), 45–63; also Harold M. M. Acton, *The Bourbons of Naples (1734–1825)* (London, 1956), 90–2, 108–10, 159–63, 191, 199–200.
62. 25 June 1769 (Galiani, *Dialogues sur le commerce des bleds*, ed. Nicolini, xiv). 'En sanglotant' (Galiani, *Dialogues entre M. Marquis de Roquemare et Mᵉ. le Chevalier Zanobi*, ed. Koch, 45). For the history of the composition of the *Dialogues*, see the useful pages in ibid., 24–47.
63. This can be followed by comparing the printed book (e.g., the Nicolini 1959 edition) with the Galiani manuscript, now in the Houghton Library at Harvard and definitively edited by Philip Koch; see esp. Galiani, *Dialogues entre M. Marquis de Roquemare. . . ,* ed. Koch, 292–316. See also Herbert Dieckmann and Philip Koch, 'The Autograph Manuscript of Galiani's *Dialogues sur le commerce des blés*,' *Harvard Library Bulletin*, IX (1955), 110–8, esp. 115. Mme d'Epinay wrote to Galiani on 26 July 1769, 'depuis onze heures du matin jusqu'à minuit, sans relâche, nous avons lu et corrigé avec le plus grand soin' (Galiani, *Dialogues. . . ,* ed. Nicolini, 338); other references to the process of revision (Diderot, *Corr.*, IX, 130–1, 144).
64. For the financial arrangements with the publisher Merlin, see Galiani, *Dialogues. . . ,* ed. Koch, 293–4; I take the letter in Diderot, *Corr.*, IX, 172, as being addressed to Merlin rather than to Le Breton. Proof-reading (Mme d'Epinay to Galiani, 11 Dec. 1769 [Galiani, *Dialogues. . . ,* ed. Nicolini, 351]). Galiani was quite displeased with Diderot's business arrangements with Merlin and with the edition (Diderot, *Corr.*, x, 92–3).
65. Diderot, *Corr.*, IX, 144 (20 Sept. 1769); see also Mme d'Epinay to Galiani, 1 Sept. 1769 (ibid., 130–1).
66. D'Holbach to Galiani, 24 Sept. 1769 (Fausto Nicolini, 'Lettres inédites du baron et de la baronne d'Holbach à l'abbé Galiani,' *Etudes Italiennes*, XII [1931], 27; see also, 11 Aug. 1769 [ibid., 25]).
67. Censor trouble (Diderot, *Corr.*, IX, 139, 144, 151, 159, 170–1, 239). Maynon d'Invau, contrôleur général des finances, resigned on 21 Dec. 1769 and was succeeded by the Abbé Joseph-Marie Terray, who was hostile to the Physiocrats. Though the *Dialogues* were evidently published in the last days of 1769, the title page bears the date 1770. For an account of all these vicissitudes, see Louise de La Live d'Epinay, *La Signora d'Epinay e l'abate Galiani*, ed. Fausto Nicolini (Bari, 1929), 16–7, 20–1, 36–8.
68. Armand-Henri Baudoin de Guémadeuc (1737–1817); identification made in Mme d'Epinay to Galiani, 27 May 1770 (Fausto Nicolini, 'Dal Carteggio dell'ab. Galiani,' *Critica*, I [1903], 483; see also ibid., 481 n., 484 n.). Regarding the excellence of Galiani's imitation of Croismare, see Mme d'Epinay to Galiani, 9 Sept. 1769 (Galiani, *Dialogues. . . ,* ed. Nicolini, 341–2). For an enthusiastic contemporary account of Galiani in 1768, see that by Sturz, in Krauss, *Die französische Aufklärung im Spiegel. . . ,* 134–5.
69. Albert Mathiez, 'Les Doctrines politiques des Physiocrates,' *AHRF*, XIII (1936), 193–203, esp. 193; cf. Strenski, 'Diderot, For and Against the Physiocrats,' *SVEC*, LVII, 1444–5.
70. Galiani's historicism is emphasized by Claude-J. Gignoux, 'L'Abbé Galiani et la querelle des grains au XVIIIᵉ siècle,' *Revue d'Histoire Economique et Sociale*, x (1922), 26–7;

and in the excellent work by Eugène Gaudemet, *L'Abbé Galiani et la question du commerce des blés à la fin du règne de Louis XV* (Paris, 1899), 2, 12, 45. Vico's influence on Galiani's thought is discussed by Fausto Nicolini, 'Giambattista Vico e Ferdinando Galiani,' *Giornale Storico della Letteratura Italiana*, LXXI (1918), 137-207; and alluded to by Rossi, *The Abbé Galiani in France*, 50-1. Gino Arias, 'Ferdinando Galiani et les Physiocrates,' *Revue des Sciences Politiques*, XLV (1922), 346-66, usefully emphasizes Galiani's historicism, esp. 359-66.

71. Galiani, *Dialogues*. . . , ed. Nicolini, 262; Galiani, *Dialogues*. . . , ed. Koch, 262.

72. Turgot to Mlle de Lespinasse, 26 Jan. 1770 (Turgot, *Oeuvres*, ed. Daire, II, 800). See also Turgot to Morellet, 17 Jan. 1770 (ibid.).

73. Diderot, *Corr.*, X, 32-5 (10 March 1770). Diderot told Sartine that he hoped the report would be shown to Morellet (Mme d'Epinay to Galiani, 18 March 1770 [Diderot, *Corr.*, X, 39-40]).

74. For this progression, see the excellent article by Franco Venturi, 'Galiani tra enciclopedisti e fisiocrati,' *Rivista Storica Italiana*, LXXII (1960), 45-64. The impounding of Morellet's *Réfutation* (Diderot, *Oeuvres politiques*, ed. Paul Vernière [Paris, 1963], 71 n.; see also the account in Jean-Paul Belin, *Le Mouvement philosophique de 1748 à 1789* [Paris, 1913], 292-3).

75. Diderot's *Apologie de l'Abbé Galiani* was finished in Jan. 1771 (Diderot, *Oeuvres politiques*, ed. Vernière, 65). It was first published, edited by Yves Benot, in *Pensée*, No. 55 (May–June 1954), 12-35; now also available in Diderot, *Oeuvres politiques*, ed. Vernière, 59-124. For the various manuscripts of the work in the Fonds Vandeul, see Dieckmann, *Inventaire*, 62-3, 86, 90, 114. Diderot published anonymously in the *Mercure de France* for June 1771, 167-71, his very informative 'Lettre concernant M. l'Abbé Galiani.' This is reprinted in A.-T., VI, 440-3; see also Dieckmann, *Inventaire*, 128; and Diderot, *Corr.*, XI, 46-51.

76. Diderot, *Oeuvres politiques*, ed. Vernière, 118, 117, 110-1, 91, 76, 84. See also Wilson, 'The Development and Scope of Diderot's Political Thought,' *SVEC*, XXVII, 1884-6; and Georges Dulac, 'La Question des blés,' *Europe*, Nos. 405-6 (Jan.–Feb. 1963), 103-9. Diderot's knowledge of local conditions of landholding also displayed in his 'Voyage à Langres' (A.-T., XVII, 358). Regarding the class interests of the Physiocrats, see Norman J. Ware, 'The Physiocrats: A Study in Economic Rationalization,' *American Economic Review*, XXI (1931), 607-19. For Diderot's review of the book on wheat smut (*Corr. litt.*, III, 38-40 [15 June 1755]; see also the open letter of Georges Le Roy to Diderot on this subject [*Mercure de France*, vol. 1 for Oct. 1756, 155-7; reprinted in Diderot, *Corr.*, V, 14-5]).

77. Diderot, *Oeuvres politiques*, ed. Vernière, 87.

CHAPTER 40

1. De Booy, 'Inventaire,' 372. Grimm left Paris 18 May 1769 (May, *Quatres visages de Denis Diderot*, 102) and returned on 10 Oct. (Georges May, 'L'Année 1769: Voltaire, Rousseau et Diderot,' *Pensée*, No. 146 [Aug. 1969], 119; Diderot, *Corr.*, IX, 168-9).

2. Diderot, *Corr.*, IX, 50, 51, 80, 83. See also ibid., 120, 123. 'Tablier' (ibid., 123, 148, 165, 176, 188, 194). In 1767 Diderot told Naigeon that 'depuis dix à douze ans, j'avois donné à Grimm plus de mois que je ne lui demandai de quarts d'heure' (Diderot, *Corr.*, VII, 138).

3. A.-T., V, 239-59; passages quoted, 239, 240 n., 246, 240, 251. See also Hubert Gillot, *Denis Diderot, l'homme. Ses idées philosophiques, esthétiques, littéraires* (Paris, 1937), 241-4. In a letter to Mme de Maux Diderot repeated many of his judgments about *Les Saisons* (Diderot, *Corr.*, IX, 209).

4. 'Delicieux' (Diderot, *Corr.*, IX, 100, cf. ibid., 125); Diderot especially admired his own review of a poem entitled *Narcisse dans l'île de Vénus* (A.-T., VI, 355-61). Progress and J.-J. Rousseau (A.-T., XVII, 495-6). Maledictions (A.-T., VI, 373). On the theme of Enlightenment, see Roland Mortier, ' "Lumière" et "Lumières": Histoire d'une image et d'une idée au XVIIᵉ et au XVIIIᵉ siècle,' in his *Clartés et ombres du siècle des lumières*, 13-59.

5. Diderot, *Corr.*, IX, 83; cf. also ibid., 91, 166. For a picture of Diderot's life in 1769, see

May, *Quatre visages de Denis Diderot*, 100–55: 'Diderot et l'été 1769'; see also Georges May, 'L'Année de la comète,' *Dix-Huitième Siècle*, I (1969), 7–30; and May, 'L'Année 1769: Voltaire, Rousseau et Diderot,' *Pensée*, No. 146, 110–27.

6. First published in Diderot, *Mémoires, correspondance et ouvrages inédits de Diderot, publiés d'après les manuscrits confiés, en mourant, par l'auteur à Grimm,* 4 vols. (Paris, 1830–1), IV, 103–239. *Le Rêve de d'Alembert* was circulated in the *Corr. litt.* in 1782 (De Booy, 'Inventaire,' 392–3). The history of the various manuscripts of *Le Rêve* is a tangled one. Naigeon published a long paraphrase of it in 1821, which ever since has been fully as puzzling to scholars as it is informative (Naigeon, *Mémoires . . . sur la vie et les ouvrages de D. Diderot,* 207–307; see Herbert Dieckmann, 'J.-A. Naigeon's Analysis of Diderot's *Rêve de d'Alembert*,' *MLN*, LIII [1938], 479–86); also Jean Pommier, 'Le Problème Naigeon,' *RScH*, No. 53 [Jan.–March 1949], 2–11). Then the discovery of the autograph manuscript in the Fonds Vandeul (see Dieckmann, *Inventaire,* 25–6) made possible the preparation of the elaborate edition of *Le Rêve de d'Alembert,* ed. Paul Vernière (Paris, 1951); see ibid., vii–xxxiii, for a discussion of the filiation of manuscripts and other textual problems; also the review of this edition by Herbert Dieckmann, *RR*, XLIII (1952), 139–43. Further discoveries have rendered the Vernière edition out of date. See Jean Pommier, 'Du nouveau sur le "Rêve de d'Alembert",' *Progrès Médical*, LXXIX (1951), 626; reprinted in his *Dialogues avec le passé* (Paris, 1967), 52–6. Also Jean Pommier, 'La Copie Naigeon du "Rêve de d'Alembert" est retrouvée,' *RHLF*, LII (1952), 25–47. Also to be consulted is Jean Th. de Booy, 'Quelques renseignements inédits sur un manuscrit du *Rêve de d'Alembert*,' *Neophilologus*, XL (1956), 81–93. Indispensable is Jean Varloot, 'Les Copies du "Rêve de d'Alembert",' *CAIEF*, No. 13 (June 1961), 353–66; on these findings M. Varloot has based his own edition of *Le Rêve de d'Alembert* (Paris, 1962); for a comprehensive review of this edition, see Jacques Proust, in *RHLF*, LXIII (1963), 281–7.

7. Jacques Proust points out that the article 'Animal' is a kind of dialogue with Buffon (Proust, in *RHLF*, LXI [1961], 263); for a striking passage in this article prefiguring *Le Rêve de d'Alembert*, see *Encyc.*, I, 474a. See also the remarks by Jacques Proust in *CAIEF*, No. 13 (June 1961), 406–7; and in his *Diderot et l'Encyclopédie*, 288–91; also in his *L'Encyclopédie*, 135–6. Cf. Otis Fellows, 'Buffon's Place in the Enlightenment,' *SVEC*, xxv (1963), 603–29, esp. 620–4; Jacques Roger, *Les Sciences de la vie dans la pensée française du XVIIIe siècle* (Paris, 1963), 598.

8. *Pensées sur l'interprétation de la nature* (A.-T., II, 57–60). Diderot, *Corr.*, v, 141 (10 Oct. 1765).

9. *Corr. litt.*, VIII, 152–3; Diderot, *Salons*, III, 77, 111, 112, 178, 304. Cf. Diderot's review of *Les Saisons* (A.-T., v, 241); another reference, in 1769 (A.-T., XIII, 94). See the excellent article by Ian H. Smith, ' "*Le Rêve de d'Alembert*" and "*De Rerum Natura*",' *AUMLA*, No. 10 (May 1959), 128–34; see also C.-A. Fusil, 'Lucrèce et les philosophes du XVIIIe siècle,' *RHLF*, xxxv (1928), 194–210, esp. 201–2. About all that is known of La Grange can be found in the anonymous 'Eloge historique de Monsieur de la Grange,' *Le Nécrologe des Hommes Célèbres de France*, XII (1777), 185–210. Regarding his translation, see Gustav R. Hocke, *Lukrez in Frankreich von der Renaissance bis zur Revolution* (Cologne, 1935), 146–51. For the general topic, see Wolfgang Bernard Fleischmann, 'The Debt of the Enlightenment to Lucretius,' *SVEC*, xxv (1963), 631–43.

10. To Sophie, 31 Aug. 1769 (Diderot, *Corr.*, IX, 126); Diderot likewise wrote to Mme de Maux, '. . . j'y aurois trop perdu' (Diderot, *Corr.*, IX, 130). 'Democritus, Hippocrates, Leucippus' (Jean Varloot, 'Le Projet "antique" du *Rêve de d'Alembert* de Diderot,' *Beiträge zur romanischen Philologie*, II [1963], 49–61). There is some uncertainty as to the date of the letter here given as 31 Aug. 1769, a matter of importance because the letter dates the composition of *Le Rêve de d'Alembert*. See Jean Varloot, 'La Date des lettres 480 et 483 à Sophie Volland,' *RHLF*, LXI (1961), 419–22; and Philip Koch, 'Redating a Letter to Sophie Volland,' *Symposium*, XI (1957), 296–302.

11. Gabrijela Arneri, 'Diderot et le génie de dédoublement,' *Studia Romanica et Anglica Zagrebiensia*, Nos. 15–16 (July–Dec. 1963), 139 n.; on this whole subject see Aram Vartanian, 'Diderot and the Phenomenology of the Dream,' *DS VIII* (1966), 217–53.

12. Diderot, *Corr.*, IX, 126–7.

13. Errol Bedford, in *MLR*, LVII (1962), 262; for the description of the Fragonard picture, see Diderot, *Salons*, II, 188–98. Regarding dreams, see Lester G. Crocker, 'L'Analyse des rêves au XVIIIe siècle,' *SVEC*, XXIII (1963), 271–310; and Vartanian, 'Diderot and the Phenomenology of the Dream,' *DS VIII*, 220.

14. Herbert Dieckmann, *Die künstlerische Form des Rêve de D'Alembert* (Cologne and Opladen, 1966), 21; Mayer, *Diderot homme de science*, 271–2.

15. Belaval, 'Les Protagonistes du "Rêve de d'Alembert",' *DS III*, 27–53.

16. That D'Alembert was a materialist is denied by Georg Klaus, 'D'Alembert und die Materialisten. Eine Entgegnung auf die Arbeit von Hermann Ley, "Zur Bedeutung D'Alemberts",' *WZUL*, II (1952–3), 353–62; see also his 'Bemerkungen zur Erkenntnistheorie D'Alemberts,' *WZUL*, III (1953–4), 373–83. Klaus regards D'Alembert as a theist; Hermann Ley, 'D'Alembert und die Idealisten,' *WZUL*, II (1952–3), 487–97, and in his later 'Nochmals D'Alembert,' *WZUL*, V (1955–6), 269–79, argues that D'Alembert was a materialist. My own impression is that the view that D'Alembert was a deist is the more nearly correct. For D'Alembert's philosophy, see the masterly article by Paolo Casini, 'D'Alembert epistemologo,' *Rivista Critica di Storia della Filosofia*, XIX (1964), 28–53, esp. 53. See also Paolo Casini, 'Il problema d'Alembert,' *Rivista di filosofia*, LXI (1970), 26–47.

17. The article 'Crise' is printed in Jacques Proust, *L'Encyclopédisme dans le Bas-Languedoc au XVIIIe siècle* (Montpellier, 1968), 141–86. Regarding Bordeu's contributions to medicine, see Charles G. Cumston, *An Introduction to the History of Medicine* . . . (New York, 1926), 351–6; also A. P. Cawadias, 'Théophile de Bordeu: An Eighteenth Century Pioneer in Endocrinology,' in Royal Society of Medicine, London, *Proceedings*, XLIII (1950), 93–8; F. Courtès, 'L'Esthétique de Diderot et la biologie de Bordeu,' *Le Scalpel*, 114e Année, No. 8 (25 Feb. 1961), 180–5; Shelby T. McCloy, *French Inventions of the Eighteenth Century* (Lexington [Ky.], [1952]), 149–50. The word 'tissue' applied to medicine (Augustin Cabanès, *Médecins amateurs* [Paris, (1932)], 175). For an account of Bordeu's career up to 1765, see Proust, *L'Encyclopédisme dans le Bas-Languedoc au XVIIIe siècle*, 35–43; see also the important article by Herbert Dieckmann, 'Théophile Bordeu und Diderots "Rêve de d'Alembert",' *RFor*, LII (1938), 55–122; also Roger, *Les Sciences de la vie dans la pensée française du XVIIIe siècle*, 618–30. Bordeu the physician of Mme Le Gendre and Damilaville (Diderot, *Corr.*, VI, 56–7, 108–9, 131; ibid., VIII, 161). In 1770 Diderot consulted Bordeu about the health of Sophie's mother (Diderot, *Corr.*, X, 186–7). Mme Diderot's illness in 1771 and her consultation of Bordeu in 1773 (ibid., XI, 68–9, and XIII, 39).

18. Several critics, esp. Vartanian, *Diderot and Descartes*, 3 and *passim*, argue that Descartes' real convictions were materialistic.

19. Lester G. Crocker, 'John Toland et le matérialisme de Diderot,' *RHLF*, LIII (1953), 289–95; Paolo Casini, 'Toland e l'attività della materia,' *Rivista Critica di Storia della Filosofia*, XXII (1967), 24–53, esp. 53; Arnolds Grava, 'Diderot and Recent Philosophical Trends,' *DS IV* (1963), 90 n. The translation of *Letters to Serena* (Naville, *Paul Thiry d'Holbach*, 415). For a very illuminating discussion of Toland's influence on the thought of the Enlightenment, see Franco Venturi, *Utopia and Reform in the Enlightenment* (Cambridge, 1971), 49–67.

20. Paolo Casini, 'Il Concetto di "molecola organica" nella filosofia naturale del Settecento,' *Giornale Critico della Filosofia Italiana*, 3rd series, XII (1958), 359–74.

21. Grimsley, *Jean d'Alembert*, 295. Alfred Cobban, *In Search of Humanity: The Role of the Enlightenment in Modern History* (London, 1960), 143, speaks of *Le Rêve* as 'an amazing medley of wild but sometimes prophetic speculation.' Concerning Diderot's reaching out toward cellular theory, see Julien Offray La Mettrie, *La Mettrie's L'Homme machine: A Study in the Origins of an Idea*, ed. Aram Vartanian (Princeton, 1960), 118: '. . . the chief merit of the *Rêve de D'Alembert* lay in its conception of cellular structure, which was made the basis of the various special theories that Diderot elaborated to explain the formation and behavior of the organism as a whole.' 'C'était déjà la théorie cellulaire' (J. Charpentier, 'Diderot et la science de son temps,' *Revue du Mois*, XVI [1913], 548).

22. Stanley L. Miller, 'Production of Some Organic Compounds under Possible Primitive Earth Conditions,' *Journal of the American Chemical Society*, LXXVII [2] (1955), 2351–61; see also Harold C. Urey, 'On the Early Chemical History of the Earth and the Origin of Life,' *Proceedings of the National Academy of Sciences*, XXXVIII (1952), 351–63. See also A. I. Oparin, *The Origin of Life* (New York, 1938), *passim*. The Miller experiment demonstrated that by subjecting a model 'primitive atmosphere' of methane, ammonia, hydrogen, and water vapor to electric sparks, amino acids can be synthesized. This suggests that organic compounds billions of years ago were synthesized without the aid of micro-organisms.

23. Diderot, *Le Rêve de d'Alembert*, ed. Jean Varloot (Paris, [1962]), 5. The Crocker ed., 181, renders the word 'sensibilité' as 'sentience,' a translation I gladly adopt. Cf. Funt, *Diderot and the Esthetics of the Enlightenment*, DS IX, 117. Sensitivity a general property of matter (*Le Rêve de d'Alembert*, ed. Varloot, 17).

24. See Alexander, 'Philosophy of Organism and Philosophy of Consciousness in Diderot's Speculative Thought,' in Victoria University of Manchester, *Studies in Romance Philology and French Literature Presented to John Orr*, 3–4. Paul Janet, in an article otherwise more confusing than enlightening, noticed that Diderot's 'vitalisme universel' was very different from the doctrine of the classical and modern atomists (Paul Janet, 'La Philosophie de Diderot: Le dernier mot d'un matérialiste,' *Nineteenth Century*, IX [Jan.–June 1881], 699–700). 'Vitalistic monism' (Paul Sakmann, 'Diderot,' *Preussische Jahrbücher*, CLIII [1913], 307; see also Paul Sakmann, 'Diderotprobleme,' *Geisteswissenschaften*, I [1913], 142). 'Matérialisme vitaliste' (Emile Callot, *La Philosophie de la vie au XVIIIe siècle* [Paris, 1965], 284). See also Jean Ehrard's review of Roger, *Les Sciences de la vie dans la pensée française du XVIIIe siècle*, in *Annales: Economies, Sociétés, Civilisations*, XIX (1964), 947–52, esp. 951.

25. *Le Rêve de d'Alembert*, ed. Varloot, 7. In 1741 André-François Boureau-Deslandes published *Pigmalion, ou la Statue animée*, but it is not known whether Diderot was aware of the existence of this pamphlet. See Rolf Geissler, *Boureau-Deslandes: Ein Materialist der Frühaufklärung* (Berlin, 1967), 19, 91–5, 181–3, 193. In the *Lettre sur les sourds et muets* (1751) Diderot developed the idea of a statue endowed successively with the five senses, and Condillac set forth a very similar idea in his *Traité des sensations* (see Part I, 252, 759 n. 8). See John L. Carr, 'Pygmalion and the *Philosophes*: The Animated Statue in Eighteenth-Century France,' *JWCI*, XXIII (1960), 239–55.

26. These 'molecules' are genes, according to the interpretation of Jean Rostand, 'La Molécule et le philosophe,' *Nouvelles Littéraires*, 19 Dec. 1963, 7.

27. *Le Rêve de d'Alembert*, ed. Varloot, 7–9; the translation is from Diderot, *Rameau's Nephew and Other Works*, ed. Bowen, 95–7, by kind permission of the translator.

28. Henri Roddier, 'Diderot et la littérature expérimentale,' in International Federation for Modern Languages and Literatures, *Acta*, VI: *Literature and Science* (Oxford, 1955), 194.

29. *Le Rêve de d'Alembert*, ed. Varloot, 26–9. In the *Georgics*, IV, vv. 557–8, which Diderot had recently read, there is a description of bees swarming (May, *Quatre Visages de Denis Diderot*, 141). Cf. Théophile Bordeu, *Oeuvres*, I, 187: 'Nous comparons le corps vivant, pour bien sentir l'action particulière de chaque partie, à un essaim d'abeilles . . .' (quoted by Dieckmann, 'Théophile Bordeu und Diderots "Rêve de d'Alembert",' *RFor*, LII, 87). Vartanian, 'Diderot and the Phenomenology of the Dream,' *DS VIII*, 245.

30. *Encyc.*, XV, 38–52; written by Henri Foucquet, regarding whom see Proust, *L'Encyclopédisme dans le Bas-Languedoc au XVIIIe siècle*, 51–3. The article 'Sensibilité' (ibid., 187–222; this quotation 206). For the influence of the Montpellier school upon Diderot, see Roger, *Les Sciences de la vie dans la pensée française du XVIIIe siècle*, 630–41; Courtès, 'L'Esthétique de Diderot et la biologie de Bordeu,' *Le Scalpel*, 114e Année, No. 8, 184–5.

31. *Le Rêve de d'Alembert*, ed. Varloot, 10; cf. Gerd Buchdahl, *The Image of Newton and Locke in the Age of Reason* (London, 1961), 19–20. 'Peut-être est-ce par la notion du temps, du devenir, que Diderot innove le plus' (Roland Desné, 'Sur le matérialisme de Diderot,' *Pensée*, No. 108 [March–April 1963], 105).

32. *Le Rêve de d'Alembert*, ed. Varloot, 35. *Rerum novus nascitur ordo* (probably suggested by the verse in Virgil, *Eclogues*, IV, 5: *Magnus ab integro saeclorum nascitur ordo*).

33. *Le Rêve de d'Alembert*, ed. Varloot, 100. See the excellent essay by Robert Niklaus, 'Diderot,' in John Cruickshank, ed., *French Literature and its Background: The Eighteenth Century* (London, 1968), 100–16, esp. 105. Regarding Diderot's interest in 'monsters' Part I, 98; G. Norman Laidlaw, 'Diderot's Teratology,' *DS IV* [1963], 105–29; Cabanès, *Médecins amateurs*, 185). Emita Hill, 'Materialism and Monsters in *Le Rêve de d'Alembert*,' *DS X* (1968), 67–93, argues that Diderot was appalled by, and recoiled from, his own doctrine of 'monsters' (esp. 87–93). This is a very controversial interpretation.

34. The chicken and the egg (*Le Rêve de d'Alembert*, ed. Varloot, 9–10). Diderot's transformism (Part I, 193–5). The best treatment of this subject is the admirable article by Lester G. Crocker, 'Diderot and Eighteenth Century French Transformism,' in Hiram Bentley Glass and others, ed., *Forerunners of Darwin: 1745–1859* (Baltimore, [1959]), 114–43.

35. Quoted by Arthur O. Lovejoy, *The Great Chain of Being: A Study of the History of an Idea* (Cambridge [Mass.], 1936), 144–5. See also ibid., 57, 229–30.

36. For Diderot's article on 'Leibnitzianisme' in the *Encyclopédie*, see *supra*, ch. 28, note 35. For Leibniz' influence upon Diderot, which is pervasive but hard to identify positively, see Belaval, 'Note sur Diderot et Leibniz,' *RScH*, No. 112, 435–51; also Alexander, 'Philosophy of Organism and Philosophy of Consciousness in Diderot's Speculative Thought,' in Victoria University of Manchester, *Studies in Romance Philology . . . Presented to John Orr*, 3–4, 13. Crocker, 'Diderot and Eighteenth Century French Transformism,' loc. cit., 117–8, 122, 132, 134, 142, has some judicious pages on the subject. The well-known work by Barber, *Leibniz in France. . . , 1670–1760*, 174, is too brief on Diderot, but it intentionally confines itself to a period before *Le Rêve de d'Alembert;* see the critique of this work, in respect to Diderot, by Richard A. Brooks, in *RR*, XLVII (1956), 66–7. There are some illuminating pages on Diderot and Leibniz in Luppol, *Diderot*, 228–32; and in Richard A. Brooks, *Voltaire and Leibniz* (Geneva, 1964), 43–6; see also Jacques Proust, in *RHLF*, LXIII (1963), 286–7; and Francis C. Haber, 'Fossils and the Idea of a Process of Time in Natural History,' in Glass *et al.*, ed., *Forerunners of Darwin: 1745–1859*, 237. For sensible remarks by older authorities, see Fernand Papillon, 'La Philosophie de Leibniz et la science contemporaine,' *RDM*, XCII (March–April 1871), 327–48, esp. 338; and Harald Höffding, *A History of Modern Philosophy*, 2 vols. (London, 1900), I, 475–8.

37. *Le Rêve de d'Alembert*, ed. Varloot, 12. See Alexander, art. cit., I, 10, 16; Grava, 'Diderot and Recent Philosophical Trends,' *DS IV*, 77, 91–101; Jean A. Perkins, 'Diderot and La Mettrie,' *SVEC*, x (1959), 62–3.

38. *Le Rêve de d'Alembert*, ed. Varloot, 12–20, esp. 14. For an excellent study of the doctrine of 'resonances' in Diderot's writings, see Jacques Proust, 'Variations sur un thème de l' "Entretien avec d'Alembert",' *RScH*, No. 112 (Oct.–Dec. 1963), 453–70; and the useful discussion in Dieckmann, *Die künstlerische Form des Rêve de D'Alembert*, 30–1. In reviewing Saint-Lambert's *Les Saisons*, Diderot spoke of this analogy of animal tissue and resonant strings (A.-T., v, 254).

39. *Le Rêve de d'Alembert*, ed. Varloot, 12.

40. *Le Rêve de d'Alembert*, ed. Varloot, 46–7. Perkins, 'Diderot and La Mettrie,' *SVEC*, x, 63–4, 80–1. For the pantheistic implications of this analogy of the spider and the web, see Hassan El Nouty, 'Le Panthéisme dans les lettres françaises au dix-huitième siècle: Aperçus sur la fortune du mot et de la notion,' *RScH*, No. 100 (Oct.–Dec. 1960), 448.

41. *Le Rêve de d'Alembert*, ed. Varloot, 60–4. See Crocker, 'Diderot and Eighteenth Century Transformism,' art. cit., 138; Crocker, 'L'Analyse des rêves au XVIIIe siècle,' *SVEC*, XXIII, 277, 285–6, 290.

42. *Le Rêve de d'Alembert*, ed. Varloot, 15–7, 50–1. See Jean Rostand, 'Esquisse d'une histoire de l'atomisme en biologie,' *RHS*, II (1949), 247–8; also Jean Rostand, 'Diderot, philosophe de la Biologie,' in his *Biologie et humanisme* (Paris, 1964), 222. Grava, 'Diderot and Recent Philosophical Trends,' *DS IV*, 82.

43. *Le Rêve de d'Alembert*, ed. Varloot, 50–1; the translation quoted here is from Diderot, *Rameau's Nephew and Other Works*, ed. Bowen, 129–30, by kind permission of the translator. Aram Vartanian, 'The Problem of Generation and the French Enlightenment,'

DS VI (1964), 348–50; also Vartanian, *Diderot and Descartes*, 264–6; see also Maurice Mandelbaum, 'The Scientific Background of Evolutionary Theory in Biology,' *JHI*, XVIII (1957), 358. Diderot also observed and commented upon the phenomenon of atavism (*Le Rêve de d'Alembert*, ed. Varloot, 56–7; see Grava, 'Diderot and Recent Philosophical Trends,' *DS IV*, 83).

44. *Le Rêve de d'Alembert*, ed. Varloot, 42. Rostand, *Biologie et humanisme*, 231–2. Vartanian, *Diderot and Descartes*, 282–6, esp. 284. Marcel Landrieu, 'Lamarck et ses précurseurs,' *Revue Anthropologique*, XVI (1906), 157–60, esp. 159. Charles Coulston Gillispie, 'Lamarck and Darwin in the History of Science,' in Glass *et al.*, ed., *Forerunners of Darwin: 1745–1859*, 270; for some trenchant criticism of Diderot's ideas in *Le Rêve de d'Alembert*, see Gillispie, ibid., 279–82.

45. *Le Rêve de d'Alembert*, ed. Varloot, 93–104. Roland Mortier, 'Note sur un passage du *Rêve de d'Alembert*: Réaumur et le problème de l'hybridation,' *RHS*, XIII (1960), 309–16.

46. *Le Rêve de d'Alembert*, ed. Varloot, 85–8. Robert Mauzi, 'Les Rapports du bonheur et de la vertu dans l'oeuvre de Diderot,' *CAIEF*, No. 13 (June 1961), 264. See also Roger, *Les Sciences de la vie dans la pensée française du XVIIIᵉ siècle*, 614–5, 676.

47. A.-T., XIV, 453; Part I, 245.

48. See Charles Frankel, *The Faith of Reason: The Idea of Progress in the French Enlightenment* (New York, 1948), 97. The dissolution of the animal-human antinomy (*Le Rêve de d'Alembert*, ed. Varloot, 16; cf. Diderot, *Corr.*, IX, 101; May, *Quatre visages de Denis Diderot*, 126; Cru, 216–7).

49. HOBBES: See *Le Rêve de d'Alembert*, ed. Varloot, 84–8, which follows the order and argument of the *Leviathan*, Part I, chs. ii–iii, and esp. ch. vi, where Hobbes defines the will as 'the last appetite in deliberating' (cf. *Le Rêve de d'Alembert*, ed. Varloot, 85: 'la dernière impulsion du désir et de l'aversion'). Cf. Belaval, 'Le "Philosophe" Diderot,' *Critique*, VIII, 241 n.

TREMBLEY: See Aram Vartanian, 'Trembley's Polyp, La Mettrie, and Eighteenth-Century French Materialism,' *JHI*, XI (1950), 270, 274; Crocker, 'Diderot and Eighteenth Century French Transformism,' in Glass *et al.*, ed., *Forerunners of Darwin: 1745–1859*, 116; Part I, 751 n. 26.

ROBINET: Diderot was probably substantially influenced by J.-B.-R. Robinet's *De la nature* (1761–6): see J. Mayer, 'Robinet, philosophe de la nature,' *RScH*, No. 75 (July–Sept. 1954), 295–309; Corrado Rosso, 'Il "paradosso" di Robinet,' *Filosofia*, V (1954), 37–62; and Crocker, art. cit., 134–6; and also Roger, *Les Sciences de la vie dans la pensée française du XVIIIᵉ siècle*, 642–51.

Charles BONNET's *Contemplation de la nature*, 2 vols. (Amsterdam, 1764), was greatly interested in generation, in the chain of being, and in animal sociology; see the praise of Bonnet in *Corr. litt.*, VI, 198 (1 Feb. 1765). Regarding him, see Bentley Glass, 'Heredity and Variation in the Eighteenth Century Concept of the Species,' in Glass *et al.*, ed., *Forerunners of Darwin: 1745–1859*, 164–70.

NEEDHAM, John Turberville (1713–81): see Roger, *Les Sciences de la vie dans la pensée française du XVIIIᵉ siècle*, 494–520.

LA METTRIE: Perkins, 'Diderot and La Mettrie,' *SVEC*, X, 49–100; La Mettrie, *La Mettrie's L'Homme machine*, ed. Vartanian, 117–20 and *passim*.

Regarding Albrecht von HALLER, whose *Elementa physiologiae corporis humani* was published from 1757 to 1766, see Joseph Needham, *A History of Embryology* (Cambridge, 1934), 170–8, 202; Roger, *Les Sciences de la vie dans la pensée française du XVIIIᵉ siècle*, 705–12. 'Il [Diderot] avait lu deux fois, et la plume à la main, sa [Haller's] grande *Physiologie*' (Naigeon, *Mémoires . . . sur la vie et les ouvrages de D. Diderot*, 222 n.).

MAUPERTUIS: see Crocker, art. cit., in Glass *et al.*, ed., *Forerunners of Darwin: 1745–1859*, 125–7, 132–3; Bentley Glass, 'Maupertuis, Pioneer of Genetics and Evolution,' in ibid., 51–83; Needham, *A History of Embryology*, 195–7.

'C'est que tout tient dans la nature . . .' (*Le Rêve de d'Alembert*, ed. Varloot, 11). For a summary of the philosophy of *Le Rêve de d'Alembert*, see Jean Varloot, 'Diderots Philosophie im "Rêve de d'Alembert",' *Sinn und Form*, XIV (1962), 704–28; and the excellent *analyse* by Casini, *Diderot 'philosophe,'* 262–95. See also the admirable introduction by Varloot in *Le Rêve de d'Alembert,* vii-cxxxv. *Le Rêve de d'Alembert* summarized in Frankel, *The Faith of Reason,* 94–100.

50. Dieckmann, *Die künstlerische Form des 'Rêve de D'Alembert,'* 23; see also Konrad Bieber's review of Dieckmann, in *FR,* XL (1966–7), 841.

51. Robert Niklaus, 'The Mind of Diderot,' *Filosofia,* XIV (1963), 933; Robert Niklaus, 'Présence de Diderot,' *DS VI* (1964), 21.

52. Georges May, 'Diderot, artiste et philosophe du décousu,' in *Europäische Aufklärung: Herbert Dieckmann zum 60. Geburtstag,* ed. Friedrich and Schalk, 187. For an extended analysis of the literary complexity of *Le Rêve de d'Alembert,* see Georges Daniel, 'Autour du *Rêve de d'Alembert:* Réflexions sur l'esthétique de Diderot,' *DS XII* (1969), 13–73.

53. *Le Rêve de d'Alembert,* ed. Varloot, 35–6. Aram Vartanian, 'Erotisme et philosophie chez Diderot,' *CAIEF,* No. 13 (June 1961), 367–90, esp. 367, 383–9.

54. Raymond Jean, 'Le Sadisme de Diderot,' *Critique,* XIX (1963), 33, 50.

55. Tourneux, *Diderot et Catherine II,* 63 n. The date of this letter is unknown.

56. Naigeon, *Mémoires . . . sur la vie et les ouvrages de D. Diderot,* 409.

57. A.-T., IX, 251–2. It is not known to whom the *'Lettre d'envoi,'* which is undated, is addressed. M. Roth (Diderot, *Corr.,* IX, 156–8) thought it was to D'Alembert, but this seems quite unlikely. Moreover, a later volume (Diderot, *Corr.,* XIV, 164–6) tentatively suggests that it was addressed to Grimm and Mme d'Epinay, especially the latter.

58. 'The *Lettre d'envoi,* if carefully examined, appears a rather unreliable document. I am inclined to find in the story of the destruction many features of a mystification' (Herbert Dieckmann, in *RR,* XLIII [1952], 140; see also Dieckmann, *Cinq leçons sur Diderot,* 19). Jacques Proust speaks (*RHLF,* LXIII, 283) of 'la légende de l'incinération de l'original autographe du *Rêve. . . .'* On this point see also *Le Rêve de d'Alembert,* ed. Varloot, liii–lv, lxxiv–lxxv.

59. B.N., MSS, Nouv. acq. fr. 13727 (Dieckmann, *Inventaire,* 13–4; see also ibid., 26).

60. De Booy, 'Inventaire,' 392–3.

61. Diderot revised *Le Rêve de d'Alembert* and added to it in Oct. and Nov. 1769, using Grimm's copyist Hénault (Diderot, *Corr.,* IX, 170, 190, 207, 217, 219). It is therefore possible that Grimm secreted a copy without Diderot's authorization or knowledge. It certainly is true that Diderot made D'Alembert feel that he was sacrificing the manuscript for D'Alembert's sake. The crucial question is, 'Mais croyait-il son acte irréparable?' (Pommier, 'La Copie Naigeon du "Rêve de d'Alembert" est retrouvée,' *RHLF,* LII, 47 n.). See also Michel Butor, 'Diderot le fataliste et ses maîtres,' *Critique,* XXII (1966), 395.

62. Lionel Gossman, 'Voltaire's Heavenly City,' *Eighteenth-Century Studies,* III (1969–70), 79–80.

63. 'Misticismo materialistico' (Casini, *Diderot 'philosophe,'* 292); see also Cassirer, *The Philosophy of the Enlightenment,* 92. It has not infrequently been noticed that a twentieth-century counterpart of Diderot in views about the cosmos is Teilhard de Chardin (Rostand, 'La Molécule et le philosophe,' *Nouvelles Littéraires,* 19 Dec. 1963, 7; *Le Rêve de d'Alembert,* ed. Varloot, xcv; Jacques Proust, in *RHLF,* LXIII [1963], 287 n.).

CHAPTER 41

1. An early instance of addressing them as 'bonnes amies' (Diderot, *Corr.,* VII, 179 [17 Oct. 1767]). '. . . cette négligence me surprend moins qu'elle ne m'afflige' (Diderot, *Corr.,* IX, 70 [30 June 1769]). Not answering in 1768 (Diderot, *Corr.,* VIII, 182, 191, 214–5).

2. A.-T., IV, 85; Diderot, *Corr.,* IX, 166.

3. First published by André Babelon, *SV,* III, 263–96. These fragments are in Naigeon's handwriting (Dieckmann, *Inventaire,* 147). Jean Pommier was the first to suggest that these are fragments of letters to Mme de Maux (Pommier, 'Etudes sur Diderot,' *RHPHGC,* Nouvelle série, No. 30 [1942], 176–8; reprinted in his *Dialogues avec le passé: Etudes et portraits littéraires* [Paris, 1967], 260–4, with the argument reviewed and reinforced, ibid., 264–6).

4. Diderot, *Corr.,* IX, 89–90. Regarding Mme de Maux, see J. Lortel, 'Une Rectification: Un

Amour inconnu de Diderot,' *RHLF*, XXIII (1916), 501–3; May, *Quatre Visages de Denis Diderot*, 116–7; and esp. May, 'L'Année 1769: Voltaire, Rousseau et Diderot,' *Pensée*, No. 146, 115–6. Lydia-Claude Hartman, 'A propos de Sophie Volland,' *DS XII* (1969), 75–102, argues that Diderot never wavered or cooled in his affection for Sophie.

5. Brother of Mlle Collot (Diderot, *Corr.*, IX, 74–5, 97). Damilaville's nephew, 14 March 1769 (ibid., IX, 38). Mlle Jodin (ibid., IX, 23–5, 42, 47–9, 77–8, 87, 180–4). M. Chabert (ibid., IX, 121–2). Joseph-Ignace Magnan Chabert, *ancien directeur et garde-magasin des marbres du Roi*, was imprisoned in the Bastille from 4 Jan. to 19 April 1768 and then exiled 50 leagues from Paris for dishonesty and insubordination. Sartine wrote Saint-Florentin that Diderot had offered to accept responsibility for Chabert's getting employment; his recall from exile was authorized on 4 Sept. 1769 (*Archives de la Bastille*, ed. François Ravaisson-Mollien, 19 vols. [Paris, 1866–1904], XIX, 377, 383). Diderot mentioned Chabert in his *Mystification* (Diderot, *Quatre contes*, ed. Proust, 28).

6. Nathan G. Goodman, *Benjamin Rush, Physician and Citizen, 1746–1813* (Philadelphia, 1934), 17–9. Benjamin Rush, *A Memorial containing Travels through Life or Sundry Incidents in the Life of Dr. Benjamin Rush*, ed. Louis Alexander Biddle (Philadelphia, 1905), 42. Rush showed Diderot his M.D. thesis, *Dissertatio physica inauguralis, de coctione ciborum in ventriculo* (Edinburgh, 1768); his research consisted in experimenting upon himself (by emetics and chemical analysis) to prove that acetous fermentation of food occurs invariably and naturally in the human stomach. Diderot wrote to Hume, '. . . ce jeune homme a fait des expériences dangereuses sur lui même' (Diderot, *Corr.*, IX, 40).

7. I. Bernard Cohen, 'A Note Concerning Diderot and Franklin,' *Isis*, XLVI (1955), 268–72.

8. Rush, *A Memorial. . .*, ed. Biddle, 43; Diderot, *Corr.*, IX, 39–40 (17 March 1769).

9. This point is discussed in detail by Mortier, *Diderot en Allemagne*, 24–7; more briefly, but to the same effect, in Robert T. Clark, Jr., *Herder: His Life and Thought* (Berkeley, 1955), 107. While in Paris Herder attended a performance of *Le Père de famille* at the Comédie-Française (Mortier, *Diderot en Allemagne*, 103). For a comparison of the intellectual interests of Diderot and Herder, see Johann Hankiss, 'Diderot und Herder,' *ASNSL*, CXL (1920), 59–74, esp. 60, 74 n.

10. See the editorial remarks in Dom Deschamps, *Le Vrai système, ou le mot de l'énigme métaphysique et morale*, ed. Jean Thomas and Franco Venturi (Paris, 1939), 18–9, 64. In this same year (1769) Diderot reviewed savagely (A.-T., VI, 368–70) an intolerant work entitled *Lettres sur l'esprit du siècle*. According to a note in Diderot's hand in the Bibliothèque du Louvre, now destroyed, Diderot attributed this work to Dom Deschamps (Emile-Jacques-Armand Beaussire, *Antécédents de l'hégélianisme dans la philosophie française. Dom Deschamps, son système et son école d'après un manuscrit et des correspondances inédites du XVIIIe siècle* [Paris, 1865], vii). Regarding the materialism of Dom Deschamps, see Roland Desné, *Les Matérialistes français de 1750 à 1800* (Paris, 1965), 41–4, 61, 123–7, 135–8, 274–9. See also Jean Wahl, 'Dom Deschamps et Diderot,' *Revue de Métaphysique et de Morale*, LXXV (1970), 47–9; also the comprehensive *analyse* in Charles Rihs, *Les Philosophes utopistes* (Paris, 1970), 206–37.

11. Dom Deschamps to the Marquis de Voyer, 13 Aug. 1769 (Beaussire, op. cit., 173–4; Deschamps, *Le Vrai système*, ed. Thomas and Venturi, 21). See also the same to the same, 14 Sept. 1769 (Beaussire, op. cit., 175; Deschamps, *Le Vrai système*, 21).

12. Diderot, *Corr.*, IX, 128, 245. Deschamps' opinion of Diderot (Beaussire, op. cit., 173–5; Deschamps, *Le Vrai système*, ed. Thomas and Venturi, 21).

13. Beaussire, op. cit., 175. Regarding Morelly and the *Code de la nature*, see R. N. C. Coe, 'A la recherche de Morelly: Etude bibliographique et biographique,' *RHLF*, LVII (1957), 321–34, 515–23; the same, 'The Fortunes of the *Code de la Nature* between 1755 and 1848,' *FS*, XI (1957), 117–26; also Richard N. Coe, *Morelly. Ein Rationalist auf dem Wege zum Sozialismus* (Berlin, 1961), 296, 297. Diderot wrote to his brother, 24 May 1770, 'Ce *Code de la nature* que vous m'avez donné . . . est un ouvrage que je n'ai pas même lu' (Diderot, *Corr.*, X, 61). Voltaire wrote on the title page of his set of this unauthorized *Oeuvres philosophiques de M^r D ****, 6 vols. (Amsterdam, 1772), which contained the *Code de la nature* in vol. I, 'Ce code n'est pas de M. Diderot qui s'est plaint de le voir joint à ses ouvrages' (Wilson, 'Leningrad, 1957: Diderot and Voltaire

Gleanings,' *FR*, xxxi, 361). For novel conjectures concerning Diderot's relations with Dom Deschamps, see B. F. Poršnev, 'Meslier, Morelly, Deschamps,' in *Au Siècle des Lumières* (Paris-Moscow, 1970), 236–7.

14. *Mercure de France*, Sept. 1769, 171; the whole passage (ibid., 171–3) is of considerable critical interest. There were performances on 9, 12, 16, 19, 23, 26, and 30 Aug.; 2, 6, and 9 Sept.; and 13 and 16 Dec. 1769. In 1770 there were performances on 24 and 28 March; 3, 6, and 21 Oct.; and 23 Dec. In 1771 there were performances on 13 and 15 April (Lancaster, *The Comédie Française, 1701–1774. . .*, 825–7, 829–30). 'Le *Père de famille* was given on several occasions every year between its revival in 1769 and 1789 (108 times in all) and . . . was given there as late as 1839' (Lough, *Paris Theatre Audiences in the Seventeenth & Eighteenth Centuries*, 251). *L'Année Littéraire*, vol. viii for 1769, 315, did not share the *Mercure de France*'s esteem for *Le Père de famille*; but Bachaumont reported that 'one counted as many handkerchiefs as there were spectators: some of the ladies were overcome' (Bachaumont, *Mémoires secrets*, iv, 321 [10 Aug. 1769]; v, 35 [17 Dec. 1769]). See also ibid., xix, 103, 110, 115. The husband of one of these ladies so afflicted called on Diderot to thank him (Diderot, *Corr.*, ix, 146–8); this was J.-B. Mercier-Dupaty, avocat général au Parlement de Bordeaux. Diderot wrote enthusiastically about one of his pleadings (A.-T., vi, 388–9).

15. Diderot, *Corr.*, ix, 103, 118–9, 120, 136–7; cf. ibid., 132–3. Of interest are Antoine-Léonard Thomas' remarks to Nicolas-Thomas Barthe about *Le Père de famille*, 19 Aug. 1769 (Henriet, 'Correspondance inédite entre Thomas et Barthe,' *RHLF*, xxvii [1920], 598–600); also Barthe's reply (ibid., 601). Horace Walpole noted in his journal for 23 Aug. 1769, 'To the *Père de famille* with Mme du Deffand and Mrs. Cholmondeley' (Walpole, *Correspondence*, vii, 325).

16. Belle's house, a comfortable and commodious one, is now an Armenian private secondary school, the Collège Arménien Moorat, 26, Rue Troyon, Sèvres. It was damaged in the air raid on the nearby Renault workshops in April 1943, but has been restored. Mme Diderot and Angélique at Sèvres (Diderot, *Corr.*, ix, 79–80, 170, 194). Diderot vouched for Belle's honesty and good reputation in a letter to Sartine, 13 Oct. 1761 (Diderot, *Corr.*, iii, 339–40).

17. Diderot, *Corr.*, ix, 85; Diderot, *Salons*, iv, 71; also ibid., iv, 66. The complete *Salon de 1769* was sent to Grimm's subscribers in the number of 15 Dec. 1769 (De Booy, 'Inventaire,' 372).

18. Angélique's illness (Diderot, *Salons*, iv, 102, 105; see also Diderot, *Corr.*, ix, 206, 229). Many years later Mme de Vandeul wrote, 'A l'age de seize ans, mon estomac se dérangea' (Massiet du Biest, *La Fille de Diderot*, 218). Suicide of Desbrosses (Diderot, *Salons*, iv, 91–2, 95; see also Diderot, *Corr.*, ix, 219, 229; for Grimm's footnote on the suicide [Diderot, *Salons*, iv, 96]). 'O la sotte condition des hommes!' (Diderot, *Salons*, iv, 102).

19. Diderot, *Salons*, iv, 77, 79, 84–6, 105, 107, 88. See Jean Seznec, 'Diderot et l'affaire Greuze,' *Gazette des Beaux-Arts*, 6e période, lxvii (1966), 339–56. See also Diderot, *Corr.*, ix, 132, 166.

20. Diderot, *Corr.*, ix, 88, 89–90, 207, 214, 218; ibid., x, 19, 24.

21. Diderot, *Corr.*, ix, 61. The fragments of letters believed to be addressed to Mme de Maux are in ibid., ix, 46, 61–2, 94–6, 112–6, 129–30, 154–5, 160–1, 179–80, 185–6, 196–200, 203–5, 208–10.

22. 20 Sept. 1769 (Jean Fabre, 'Sagesse et morale dans *Jacques le fataliste*,' *SPTB*, 173 n.). Diderot, *Corr.*, ix, 167, 154–5. See Philip Stewart, 'Comètes et Lumières,' *RScH*, No. 140 (Oct.–Dec. 1970), 503–20. The identification of Mlle Olympe is propounded by Hartman, 'A propos de Sophie Volland,' *DS XII*, 101–2; cf. Diderot, *Corr.*, v, 87–8.

23. Diderot, *Corr.*, ix, 185–6, 207.

24. Diderot, *Corr.*, ix, 229–30 (25 Nov. 1769). Diderot's volunteering (ibid., ix, 191). Grimm returned to Paris in Oct., probably 10 Oct. (ibid., ix, 168).

25. Diderot's complaint (Tourneux, 'Fragments inédits de Diderot,' *RHLF*, i, 169; intended for *Corr. litt.*, [ibid., 164]). *L'Esprit de l'Encyclopédie*, which was compiled by the Abbé Joseph de La Porte and went through several editions, claimed to be published at Geneva, but the title page announced that it was procurable at Le Breton's and at Briasson's in Paris; there-

fore this must have been a venture of the publishers themselves. The *Histoire générale des dogmes et opinions philosophiques* purported to be published in London but was really published at Bouillon (Fernand Clément, 'Pierre Rousseau et l'édition des suppléments de l'*Encyclopédie*,' *RScH*, No. 86 [April–June 1957], 137; Raymond F. Birn, *Pierre Rousseau and the* philosophes *of Bouillon* [*SVEC*, xxix (1964)], 82). For these two collections, with a list of their contents. see Lough, *Essays on the* Encyclopédie *of Diderot and d'Alembert*, 43–8.

26. Jaucourt to Reybaz (Bibliothèque Publique et Universitaire de Genève, Archives Tronchin 198, fol. 41). 980 livres (Lough, *Essays on the* Encyclopédie *of Diderot and d'Alembert*, 38, 44, 62 n.). By 1770 all the 4250 sets had been sold, and for over two years the *Encyclopédie* had been selling at a premium of about 300 livres (Charles-Georges Fenouillot de Falbaire de Quingey, *Avis aux gens de lettres* [Liège, 1770], 44). Out of print, Aug. 1768 (George B. Watts, 'The Swiss Edition of the *Encyclopédie*,' *Harvard Library Bulletin*, ix [1955], 214). Rarity of first seven volumes (*Journal Encyclopédique*, Sept. 1769, 461–2). A prospectus for a new edition (B.N., MSS., Fr. 22069, fol. 170v) stated that 'le prix actuel de cette première Edition est de 13 à 14 cens livres, quand on peut la trouver; car les sept premiers Volumes sur-tout sont devenus très rares.'

27. Abbé Fromageot to Le Breton, 9 Feb. 1768, and Le Breton's reply, 2 March 1768 ('Extra Volume,' foll. 55–7, 59–70; cf. Gordon and Torrey, 109–10).

28. George B. Watts, 'Charles Joseph Panckoucke, "l'Atlas de la librairie française",' *SVEC*, lxviii (1969), 67–205, esp. 111–4. Rumors of this new edition (Bachaumont, *Mémoires secrets*, iv, 215 [19 Jan. 1769]).

29. Diderot, *Corr.*, ix, 123–4. For further information on re-editions of the *Encyclopédie*, see esp. Lough, *Essays on the* Encyclopédie *of Diderot and d'Alembert*, 15–51, 52–110; and George B. Watts, 'Forgotten Folio Editions of the *Encyclopédie*,' *FR*, xxvii (1953–4), 22–9; George B. Watts, 'The Geneva Folio Reprinting of the *Encyclopédie*,' *Proceedings of the American Philosophical Society*, cv (1961), 361–7; George B. Watts, 'Thomas Jefferson, the "Encyclopédie," and the "Encyclopédie méthodique",' *FR*, xxxviii (1964–5), 318–25. D'Alembert mentioned to Voltaire on 9 Nov. 1769 that he had refused to be editor (Besterman, No. 15003).

30. Seizure of the Racine edition, 21 Aug. 1768 (Fenouillot de Falbaire, *Avis aux gens de lettres*, 14; J. Pierre, 'Luneau de Boisjermain,' *Bulletin de la Société académique du Centre* [Châteauroux], iv [1898], 105). On 30 Jan. 1770 Sartine ordered restitution of the confiscated books, forbade further seizures of the sort, and fined the guild 300 livres plus costs and interest. He also fined Luneau 50 livres for injurious statements (*Jugement rendu par M. de Sartine . . .* [n.p., 1770], 6–7, bound as Pièce 2 of *Recueil des mémoires composés par P. J. Fr. Luneau de Boisjermain, sur le procès auquel l'Encyclopédie a donné lieu* [B.N., Imprimés, 4° Fm. 34420]); see also Bachaumont, *Mémoires secrets*, v, 95–6. Diderot's acquaintance with Luneau (Diderot, *Corr.*, ix, 240–1); 'A mâcher des feuilles de laurier' (ibid., ix, 171 [13 Oct. 1769]). Luneau presented Diderot, 2 Dec. 1769, a set of this edition of Racine as well as his *Cours d'histoire* (*Lettre de M. Luneau de Boisjermain à M. Diderot, et Reponses à la lettre adressée aux Srs Briasson & Le Breton par M. Diderot* [Paris, 1771], 4 n. [B.N., 4° Fm. 34420 (12)]).

31. Diderot's letter of self-justification (Diderot, *Corr.*, ix, 239–44 [28 Dec. 1769]).

32. *Recueil philosophique ou Mélange de Pieces sur la Religion & la Morale*, ed. Naigeon, i, 105–28; ii, 113–24. See also Part I, 60.

33. The historian of this rift is Pappas, 'Voltaire et la guerre civile philosophique,' *RHLF*, lxi, 525–49. For a comprehensive synopsis and critique of the *Système de la nature*, see Naville, *Paul Thiry d'Holbach*, 223–311; see also Virgil W. Topazio, *D'Holbach's Moral Philosophy: Its Background and Development* (Geneva, 1956), *passim*. The *Système de la nature* was first mentioned by Bachaumont on 19 Feb. 1770 (Bachaumont, *Mémoires secrets*, v, 80).

34. '. . . man glaubt, Hr. Diderot hat es geschrieben' (Jacob Jonas Björnståhl, *Briefe auf seinen ausländischen Reisen. . .* , 6 vols. [Leipzig, 1777–83], i, 161 [Geneva, 10 Oct. 1770]). Bachaumont, *Mémoires secrets*, xxvi, 191 (24 Aug. 1784); J. H. Meister's testimony (*Corr. litt.*, xv, 417; but see Virgil W. Topazio, 'Diderot's Supposed Contribution

to D'Holbach's Works,' *PMLA*, LXIX [1954], 173–88; cf. John Lough, in *FS*, XI (1957), 64. For distinctions between D'Holbach's philosophy and Diderot's, see Manfred Naumann, 'Diderot und das "Système de la Nature",' *WZUB*, XIII (1964), 145–55.

35. First published (1792) by Naigeon in the *Encyclopédie méthodique*, in the vols. edited by him on 'Philosophie ancienne et moderne,' II, 192–5; published in A.-T., II, 64–70, and in Diderot, *Oeuvres philosophiques*, ed. Vernière, 389–400. Inspired by the *Système de la nature* (Henry Guerlac, 'Three Eighteenth-Century Social Philosophers: Scientific Influences on their Thought,' *Daedalus*, LXXXVII [1958], 24; see also Virgil W. Topazio, 'D'Holbach's Conception of Nature,' *MLN*, LXIX [1954], 412–6, esp. 415).

36. Anti-Cartesian (Vartanian, *Diderot and Descartes*, 106; Abraham Lerel, *Diderots Natur-philosophie* [Vienna, 1950], 24, 27, 98–9). According to Frankel, *The Faith of Reason*, 86, the *Principes philosophiques* 'exhibits an acute awareness of the limits of the Cartesian view of matter.' Influence of Toland (Crocker, art. cit., *RHLF*, LIII, 289–95; Casini, 'Toland e l'attività della materia,' *Rivista Critica di Storia della Filosofia*, XXII, 53 n.; Roger, *Les Sciences de la vie dans la pensée française du XVIIIe siècle*, 653 n.). Unlike Toland, Diderot strongly emphasizes the heterogeneity of matter (A.-T., II, 67, 68–9); see *Le Rêve de d'Alembert*, ed. Varloot, lxii–lxiii.

37. A.-T., II, 65, 69. See Desné, 'Sur le matérialisme de Diderot,' *Pensée*, No. 108, 101.

38. Rouelle died 3 Aug. 1770; Diderot's essay about him (A.-T., VI, 405–10). Galiani called it 'un chef-oeuvre. . . . Je crois qu'on a connu Rouelle, quand on a lu ce portrait' (Diderot, *Corr.*, XI, 157). Regarding Rouelle, see Douglas McKie, 'Guillaume-François Rouelle (1703–1770),' *Endeavour*, XII (1953), 130–3; also Rhoda Rappaport, 'G.-F. Rouelle: An Eighteenth-Century Chemist and Teacher,' *Chymia*, VI (1960), 68–101; and Pierre Lemay, 'Les Cours de Guillaume-François Rouelle,' *Revue d'Histoire de la Pharmacie*, XIII (March 1949), 434–42. 'Our sublunar world' (Yvon Belaval, 'Sur le matérialisme de Diderot,' in *Europäische Aufklärung: Herbert Dieckmann zum 60. Geburtstag*, ed. Friedrich and Schalk, 20).

39. Conservation of energy and electronic theory of matter (Luc, *Diderot*, 118; Diderot, *Oeuvres philosophiques*, ed. Vernière, 393 n.). 'Moi, qui suis physicien et chimiste' (A.-T., II, 66; this striking passage quoted by Maurice Crosland, 'The Development of Chemistry in the Eighteenth Century,' *SVEC*, XXIV [1963], 428; for his comments on Diderot, see ibid., 428–30). Roger, *Les Sciences de la vie dans la pensée française du XVIIIe siècle*, 614; see also Lefebvre, *Diderot*, 162. For an excellent analysis of the *Principes philoso-phiques sur la matière et le mouvement*, see Marx W. Wartofsky, 'Diderot and the Development of Materialist Monism,' *DS II* (1952), 298–304; Wartofsky calls Diderot's remarks 'sketchy but brilliant' (ibid., 298).

40. Diderot, *Corr.*, X, 72–5 (June 1770); *Corr. litt.*, IX, 50–5.

41. 17 April 1770 (*Corr. litt.*, IX, 14–7 [1 May 1770]). Diderot's soliciting subscriptions (Diderot, *Corr.*, X, 54–5, 90–1). Neither D'Holbach nor Naigeon subscribed to this project (Pappas, 'Voltaire et la guerre civile philosophique,' *RHLF*, LXI, 547), and Mme Geoffrin was extremely scornful of it (see her letter to King Stanislas Poniatowski, 3 Feb. 1771 [Gustave Lanson, *Choix de lettres du XVIIIe siècle* (Paris, [1909]), 419–20]). Oppo-sition of 'les ennemis des lettres et de la philosophie' (Morellet, *Mémoires inédits*, I, 198; Falconet, *Correspondance de Falconet avec Catherine II*, ed. Réau, 126). Diderot's influ-ence on Pigalle (Morellet, op. cit., I, 200). An accurate and lengthy account of the episode is in Gustave Le Brisoys Desnoiresterres, *Voltaire et la société au XVIIIe siècle*, 8 vols. (Paris, 1871–6), VII, 312–50, who says (VII, 346) that the subscription raised 18,774 livres. The statue is now in the collections of the Louvre.

42. Diderot, *Corr.*, IX, 200, 206.

43. Diderot to his sister, 5 and 23 March, 4 May, June (?), 1770 (Diderot, *Corr.*, X, 29–31, 40–3, 48–51, 81–2); to his brother, 24 May 1770 (ibid., X, 58–64).

44. Diderot, *Corr.*, X, 48, 51, 58–64, 106–8, 111. Mme de Vandeul, LIX. For Gabriel Gauchat, see Diderot, *Corr.*, X, 106 n.; also ibid., X, 133 (4 Oct. 1770). The Abbé's refusal to see the *philosophe* (Diderot, *Corr.*, XII, 103, 106).

45. A.-T., V, 281–308; the best editions are now Diderot, *Contes*, ed. Dieckmann, 83–118, and

Diderot, *Oeuvres philosophiques,* ed. Vernière, 403–43. See Maurice Roelens, 'L'Art de la digression dans L'Entretien d'un père avec ses enfants,' *Europe,* Nos. 405–6 (Jan.–Feb. 1963), 172–82; also Aimé Dupuy, 'Diderot et Langres,' *Europe,* Nos. 405–6 (Jan.–Feb. 1963), 24–5, 29; also Peter France, 'Public Theatre and Private Theatre in the Writings of Diderot,' *MLR,* LXIV (1969), 522–8. The *Entretien* appeared in the *Corr. litt.* for 1 and 15 March 1771 (De Booy, 'Inventaire,' 374).

46. To Sophie, 23 Aug. 1770 (Diderot, *Corr.,* x, 108–9); to Grimm, 8 Sept. 1770 (ibid., x, 123). Diderot and Grimm left Paris on 2 Aug., arriving at Langres the next day. Grimm went on to Bourbonne the day after that (4 Aug.) and Diderot joined him there on 10 Aug., staying on until 17 Aug. Grimm meanwhile departed on 12 Aug. and returned to Paris. Diderot returned to Langres for the period 17–28 Aug., was then in Bourbonne for a second visit from 29 Aug. until 5 Sept., when he returned to Langres. He and his future son-in-law left Langres on 12 Sept.; stayed at Isle (at the Vollands') from 14–21 Sept.; at Châlons-sur-Marne (21–24 Sept.) at the house of Damilaville's other former mistress, Mme Duclos; and arrived at Paris on 26 Sept. (Diderot, *Corr.,* x, 109, 111 n., 116, 123–4, 136–7; also A.-T., XVII, 333).

47. Diderot, *Corr.,* x, 110; A.-T., XVII, 345, 346.

48. Diderot, *Corr.,* x, 110, 114–5; A.-T., XVII, 333. Dr. Auguste Roux (1726–76) was a member of the D'Holbach circle; Horace Walpole mentioned meeting him there, 17 Nov. 1765 (Walpole, *Correspondence,* VII, 272).

49. A.-T., XVII, 338. Geological changes (ibid., 347–8); cf. a similar passage in Diderot's *Lettre sur Boulanger* (A.-T., VI, 343). The *Voyage à Bourbonne* (A.-T., XVII, 333–54) was first published in 1831. It was reprinted in Dr. Emile Bougard, *Bibliotheca borvoniensis* . . . (Chaumont and Paris, 1865), 428–56. Diderot also wrote for Grimm a *Voyage à Langres* (A.-T., XVII, 355–61), mostly a historical account of the city, and a rather dry and dull one. Dieckmann, *Inventaire,* 71.

50. Origin of the tale (Diderot to Grimm, 8 Sept. 1770 [Diderot, *Corr.,* x, 124–5]). The original edition of *Les Deux amis, conte iroquois,* privately printed, is very rare; there is a copy in the Newberry Library, Chicago. It was republished in the *Oeuvres philosophiques de Saint Lambert,* 5 vols. (Paris, An IX [1801]), V, 287–336. A long letter from Mme de Prunevaux to Naigeon, 5 Sept. 1770, incorporating the first version of the tale (A.-T., XVII, 330–2), may be completely by Diderot; on stylistic grounds I am inclined to think it is. The *Deux Amis de Bourbonne* appeared in the *Corr. litt.,* 15 Dec. 1770 (De Booy, 'Inventaire,' 373; see also Grimm's introductory remarks, not completely accurate, in *Corr. litt.,* IX, 185–6). Diderot's revising the tale (Diderot, *Corr.,* x, 146, 154, 219–20, 238; see esp. Edward J. Geary, 'The Composition and Publication of *Les Deux Amis de Bourbonne,*' *DS* I [1949], 27–45). A later addition (A.-T., V, 267) has been studied by Friedrich Bassenge, 'The Testalunga-Romano Episode in the Later Editions of *Les Deux Amis de Bourbonne,*' *DS* X (1968), 13–22; and the same, 'Diderots Testalunga-Romano-Episode,' *RFor,* LXXXII (1970), 589–96. The best editions of *Les Deux Amis de Bourbonne* are Diderot, *Contes,* ed. Dieckmann, 63–82, and Diderot, *Quatre contes,* ed. Proust, 41–68.

51. A.-T., V, 267. A type absolutely new (Diderot, *Quatre contes,* ed. Proust, lxxvii). Goethe (Dieckmann, 'Goethe und Diderot,' *Deutsche Vierteljahrsschrift für Literaturwissenschaft und Geistesgeschichte,* x, 479. Schiller read *Les Deux Amis de Bourbonne* and traces of it can be observed in his *Die Räuber* as well as in other of his works (Eggli, 'Diderot et Schiller,' *RLC,* I, 83–6; Friedrich Schiller, *Die Räuber,* ed. L. A. Willoughby [London, 1922], 25–6; also Fausto Nicolini, in *Etudes Italiennes,* XIII [1932], 96).

52. Ducros, *Diderot,* 340–2; James Doolittle, in *FR,* XXIV (1950–1), 67; James Doolittle, 'Criticism as Creation in the Work of Diderot,' *Yale French Studies,* No. 3 (1949), 22–3.

53. A.-T., V, 276–7. See the excellent article by Herbert Dieckmann, 'The Presentation of Reality in Diderot's Tales,' *DS* III (1961), 101–28; also May, *Quatre visages de Denis Diderot,* 156–209.

54. Diderot, *Corr.,* x, 137. Duclos was director of the vingtième for the province of Champagne; his wife had been Damilaville's mistress, a position that she came to share quite

amicably with Mme de Maux. References to M. and Mme Duclos (Diderot, *Corr.*, III, 23, 83, 154, 344). Diderot had expected to visit them in 1765, but was unable to (Diderot, *Corr.*, V, 138–42).

55. Praise of Foissy (Diderot, *Corr.*, X, 136, 125 n.). Pre-arrangement to meet at Châlons-sur-Marne (ibid., X, 123). Diderot's letters to Grimm discussing his love affair are of 15 and 21 Oct. and 2 and 10 Nov. 1770 (Diderot, *Corr.*, X, 141–3, 143–7, 151–6, 162–3); see esp. 141, 144, 143.

56. Diderot, *Corr.*, X, 144, 145, 151, 155. 'Mistress' (ibid., X, 154).

57. Diderot, *Corr.*, X, 164 (10 Nov. 1770). Subsequent references to Mme de Maux (Diderot, *Corr.*, X, 170, 173, 179; ibid., XI, 32–3; ibid., XII, 43, 65, 69, 181; ibid., XIII, 237; ibid., XIV, 213).

58. Diderot, *Corr.*, X, 188 (28 Nov. 1770).

59. See esp. the convincing pages by Herbert Dieckmann in Denis Diderot, *Supplément au Voyage de Bougainville,* ed. Dieckmann (Geneva, 1955), cxvii–cxxvii; also, Jacques Proust, in Diderot, *Quatre contes,* ed. Proust, viii, xix.

60. A.-T., V, 311–32; passage quoted, 321; see a very similar remark about *femmes fatales* in a review Diderot wrote in 1764 (A.-T., VIII, 451). The best texts are now Diderot, *Contes,* ed. Dieckmann, 119–45; and Diderot, *Quatre contes,* ed. Proust, 69–100. *Ceci n'est pas un conte* appeared in the *Corr. litt.* in April 1773 (De Booy, 'Inventaire,' 383). The reader as interlocutor (Dieckmann, 'The Presentation of Reality in Diderot's Tales,' *DS III,* 112; also Dieckmann, *Cinq leçons sur Diderot,* 36–7; also Dorothy M. McGhee, *The Cult of the 'Conte Moral': The Moral Tale in France — Its Emergence and Progress* [Menasha (Wis.), 1960], 29). For important critical remarks, see also the introductory notes by Werner Krauss, 'Zu einer Prosa Diderots,' *Sinn und Form,* XIV (1962), 161–5, to his translation of Diderot, *Das ist gar keine Erzählung,* ibid., XIV, 166–86; also Charles Ferguson, 'Fiction versus Fact in the Age of Reason: Diderot's *Ceci n'est pas un conte,*' *Symposium,* XXI (1967), 231–40. The anonymous editor of *Ceci n'est pas un conte* in *Oeuvres Libres,* Nouvelle série, No. 133 (1957), 283–306, remarked (283) that 'c'est peut-être dans les dialogues contemporains de l'Hemingway de *Mort dans l'après-midi* que l'on retrouve le ton le plus proche de celui-ci.' Regarding Mlle de La Chaux, see T. V. Benn, 'Les "Political discourses" de David Hume et un conte de Diderot,' in *Currents of Thought in French Literature: Essays in Memory of G. T. Clapton* (Oxford, [1965]), 253–76.

61. 'Bizarre' (A.-T., V, 354); the whole tale (ibid., 333–57). The best editions are now Diderot, *Contes,* ed. Dieckmann, 147–76; and Diderot, *Quatre contes,* ed. Proust, 101–34. The opening and closing passages of *Madame de La Carlière* are a transcription, broken up into dialogue, of the *Encyclopédie* article 'Evaporation,' which then is continued into the opening passage of the *Supplément au Voyage de Bougainville,* thus proving the close connection in Diderot's consciousness of these two pieces (Jacques Proust, 'Quelques aspects de la création littéraire chez Diderot,' in Jean Pommier, ed., *Collège de France: Chaire d'histoire des créations littéraires en France: Six conférences* [Nogent-le-Rotrou, 1964], 49). Regarding Diderot's technique in these tales, see Robert Niklaus, 'Diderot's Moral Tales,' *DS VIII* (1966), 309–18; Robert Niklaus, 'Diderot et le conte philosophique,' *CAIEF,* No. 13 (June 1961), 299–315; Yvon Belaval, 'Le Conte philosophique,' in *SPTB,* 309; Erich Loos, 'Die Gattung des *Conte* und das Publikum in 18. Jahrhundert,' *RFor,* LXXI (1959), 113–37. See also Armin Volkmar Wernsing, 'Ferne, Schauspiel, Wirklichkeit. Diderots "Sur l'inconséquence du jugement public",' *Germanisch-Romanische Monatsschrift,* XVII (1967), 249–53. *Madame de La Carlière,* entitled simply 'Second Conte,' appeared in the *Corr. litt.* in May 1773 (De Booy, 'Inventaire,' 384).

62. Diderot's 'preview' (A.-T., II, 199–206); passages quoted, 206, 203. For a reliable and readily accessible edition of Bougainville's *Voyage autour du monde,* see the one edited by Michel Hérubel (Paris, 1966). The definitive monograph on Bougainville is by Jean-Etienne Martin-Allanic, *Bougainville navigateur et les découvertes de son temps,* 2 vols. (Paris, 1964); see ibid., 1380–4 for his discussion of Diderot's *Supplément.* The literary relationships between Diderot's work for Raynal and his *Supplément au Voyage de Bougainville* are complex: see Michèle Duchet, 'Le "Supplément au Voyage de Bougainville" et la collaboration de Diderot à "L'Histoire des Deux Indes",' *CAIEF,* No. 13

(June 1961), 173–87; Michèle Duchet, 'Bougainville, Raynal, Diderot et les sauvages du Canada: Une source ignorée de l' "Histoire des Deux Indes",' *RHLF*, LXIII (1963), 228–36; Michèle Duchet, 'Le Primitivisme de Diderot,' *Europe*, Nos. 405–6 (Jan.–Feb. 1963), 126–37. See also Michèle Duchet, *Anthropologie et Histoire au siècle des lumières* (Paris, 1971), 438–44, 452–9, and *passim*.

63. The best editions of the *Supplément au Voyage de Bougainville* are those edited by Gilbert Chinard (Paris, 1935), the introduction of which emphasizes the influences of travel literature and primitivism on Diderot; and by Herbert Dieckmann, the introduction of which stresses structural and literary features. The *Supplément au Voyage de Bougainville* appeared in the *Corr. litt.* for Sept. and Oct. 1773 and March and April 1774 (De Booy, 'Inventaire,' 384–5). It was first published in 1796 (Simon-Jérôme Bourlet de Vauxcelles, ed., *Opuscules philosophiques et littéraires, la plupart posthumes ou inédites* [Paris, 1796], 187–270); in A.-T., II, 207–50. Diderot's 'Les Adieux du vieillard' and 'L'Entretien de l'aumonier et d'Orou' were probably greatly influenced by his knowledge of the writings of Lahontan (Louis-Armand de Lahontan, *Dialogues curieux entre l'auteur et un sauvage de bon sens qui a voyagé. . .* , ed. Gilbert Chinard [Baltimore, 1931], 72, 68). Territorial imperative; continental drift (A.-T., II, 211, 209).

64. A.-T., II, 219–39; passages quoted or paraphrased, 220, 224. Alfred de Musset's *Souvenir* (1841) has several stanzas thought to be inspired by this passage in the *Supplément*. Diderot expresses similar ideas in *Jacques le fataliste* (A.-T., VI, 117); see also *Le Père de famille* (A.-T., VII, 224); and the *Salon de 1767* (Diderot, *Salons*, III, 228–9).

65. Passages quoted (A.-T., II, 233, 225). The quotation from Bentham is the first words of *An Introduction to the Principles of Morals and Legislation*. For the development of utilitarianism in Enlightenment thought, see Kingsley Martin, *French Liberal Thought in the Eighteenth Century*, ed. J. P. Mayer (New York, 1954), 177–83. Useful here is Charles Tilquin, 'Diderot et la théorie de la nature de la morale d'après le supplément au voyage de Bougainville,' *Cahiers Haut-Marnais*, No. 75 (4ᵉ trimestre 1963), 178–94.

66. Eugenics (A.-T., II, 237–8). Diderot includes in the *Supplément au Voyage de Bougainville* the story of Miss Polly Baker, haled before a Connecticut court for having become pregnant out of wedlock for the fifth time. Miss Baker stoutly defended herself, declaring that she deserved well of the state (Diderot, *Supplément au Voyage de Bougainville*, ed. Chinard, 154–9; ibid., ed. Dieckmann, 36–8; Diderot, *Rameau's Nephew and Other Works*, ed. Bowen, 214–6; not included in A.-T.). The Polly Baker story appears only in the Leningrad MS of the *Supplément au Voyage de Bougainville* (Johansson, *Etudes sur Denis Diderot*, 161–92). This literary episode, a hoax invented by Benjamin Franklin, has been exhaustively and most interestingly studied by Max Hall, *Benjamin Franklin & Polly Baker: The History of a Literary Deception* (Chapel Hill [N.C.], [1960]), esp. 66–73; see also Alfred Owen Aldridge, *Franklin and his French Contemporaries* (New York, 1957), 100–4. Diderot probably added the Polly Baker story to his manuscript about 1780 (Hall, op. cit., 72).

67. A.-T., II, 232, 235.

68. A.-T., II, 240. 'Insoluble questions' (Diderot, *Supplément au Voyage de Bougainville*, ed. Dieckmann, cix n.). 'Alternative moral positions' (Gay, *The Enlightenment*, II, 96).

69. A.-T., II, 240–1. Diderot used these same terms in a letter previously written to Falconet, 6 Sept. 1768 (Diderot, *Corr.*, VIII, 117).

70. A.-T., II, 240. References to incest (A.-T., II, 233, 234–5, 246); cf. Diderot, *Supplement au Voyage de Bougainville*, ed. Dieckmann, xl; also Barry Ivker, 'Towards a Definition of Libertinism in 18ᵗʰ-Century French Fiction,' *SVEC*, LXXIII (1970), 226.

71. A.-T., II, 249. Freud (Henry L. Brugmans, 'Les Paradoxes du philosophe [i.e., Diderot],' *Neophilologus*, XLI [1957], 174).

72. Peter Gay, *The Party of Humanity* (New York, 1964), 161.

73. A.-T., II, 249, 241.

74. A.-T., II, 249. Conformism (Hans Hinterhäuser, *Utopie und Wirklichkeit bei Diderot: Studien zum "Supplément au voyage de Bougainville"* (Heidelberg, [1957]), 95 n., 117–25). But cf. Emile Henriot, 'Diderot relu,' *Le Monde*, 14 Aug. 1957, 7: 'Le "jusqu'à ce qu'on les réforme" de Diderot implique de sa part la certitude que la réforme se fera, et

donc qu'un progrès est possible.' Cf. Diderot, *Supplément au Voyage de Bougainville*, ed. Chinard, 198 n.

CHAPTER 42

1. Diderot, *Corr.*, x, 198; to Caroillon de Vandeul (ibid., 200–1). At Château-Thierry they had taken the road to Soissons instead of the one to Paris; it is probably to this that Diderot refers (ibid., x, 137).
2. Both letters (*CI*, ii, 77). Diderot's letter to Denise at the same time (*CI*, ii, 77–8). Denise Diderot did indeed come to visit them in May 1771 (Diderot, *Corr.*, xi, 32, 39).
3. See Diderot, *Corr.*, ix, 84, 101, 127, 130.
4. Diderot, *Corr.*, xi, 211 (19 Oct. 1771). In March 1771 Angélique was invited to Mlle Biheron's for dinner and for a lesson in anatomy afterwards (Diderot to Grimm [Diderot, *Corr.*, x, 245]). The principal source of information regarding Mlle Biheron is P. Dorveaux, 'Notes sur Mademoiselle Biheron,' *La Médecine Anecdotique, Historique, Littéraire* (1900–1), 165–71. The 1759 report of the Académie des Sciences declared that 'on a trouvé qu'elle étoit parvenue à copier et imiter la Nature dans cette partie avec une précision et une vérité dont jamais personne n'avoit encore approché' (ibid., 167). See also Pierre Huard, 'L'Enseignement médico-chirurgical,' in René Taton, ed., *Enseignement et diffusion des sciences en France au XVIIIᵉ siècle* (Paris, 1964), 182; 'Notice sur Mademoiselle Basseporte, peintre du Roi,' in *Le Nécrologe des hommes célèbres de France*, xvi (Paris, 1781), 179–81; McCloy, *French Inventions of the Eighteenth Century*, 163; and Diderot, *Corr.*, viii, 211 n. In April 1761 Mlle Biheron published a four-page leaflet advertising the exhibition of her models (*Anatomie artificielle* [B.N., Ta⁶⁴.47]). For an enthusiastic first-hand report of Mlle Biheron's exhibits, see Björnståhl, *Briefe aus seinen ausländischen Reisen*, i, 68–9 (3 Feb. 1770). Diderot warmly recommended Mlle Biheron to teach in the School for Noble Girls founded by Catherine II (Diderot to Betzki, 15 June 1774 [Diderot, *Corr.*, xiv, 44–7; also Diderot, *Mémoires pour Catherine II*, ed. Vernière, 193–4]). She did not go to Russia, however.
5. Diderot, *Corr.*, x, 199.
6. Diderot to Sophie, 2 Nov. 1770 (Diderot, *Corr.*, x, 158). For allusions to Angélique's musical development in letters to Grimm, see ibid., ix, 189–90, 200, 206, 213; x, 46, 78–9, 85, 155, 243–4, 244–6. When Philidor went to England in 1771 he carried with him a letter of introduction to Dr. Charles Burney from Diderot (Diderot, *Corr.*, xi, 37–9) and a plan of the book that Diderot had written for Philidor's new English edition of his manual on chess (Frances Burney d'Arblay, *The Early Diary of Frances Burney, 1768–1778*, ed. Annie Raine Ellis, 2 vols. [London, 1889], i, 116–7).
7. 14 Dec. 1770 (Charles Burney, *The Present State of Music in France and Italy*, 2ⁿᵈ ed. [London, 1773], 405). In his private journal Dr. Burney did say of Mlle Diderot, however, ' — has a good Finger, but is not quite correct in Time — ' (Ralph A. Leigh, 'Les Amitiés françaises du Dʳ Burney: Quelques documents inédits,' *RLC*, xxv [1951], 171). Visit on 14 Dec. (ibid., 170).
8. Diderot, *Corr.*, viii, 93. Johann Gottfried Eckhardt (*c.* 1735–1809) was a well-known harpsichordist. For another example of the profound effect of music upon Diderot, see Diderot, *Corr.*, v, 175, 177–8. 'Fou de musique' (Diderot, *Corr.*, ix, 206).
9. Diderot, *Corr.*, x, 157. Diderot was much interested in the marriage of the musician Marie-Emmanuelle Baillon to Victor Louis (Diderot, *Corr.*, x, 79–80) and may have arranged it (Massiet du Biest, *La Fille de Diderot*, 161). He was accustomed to referring to her as an angel (Diderot, *Corr.*, x, 87–8). Regarding Cohault, see *Grove's Dictionary of Music and Musicians*, s.v. 'Kohault.'
10. Diderot, *Corr.*, ix, 213. For the circumstances of their meeting, see Diderot's account of it in A.-T., xii, 525–6; also Diderot, *Le Neveu de Rameau*, ed. Fabre, 91–2; D'Escherny, *Mélanges de littérature, d'histoire, de morale et de philosophie*, iii, 132–3.
11. A.-T., xii, 530.
12. A.-T., xii, 526; this quotation is from the review Diderot wrote for the *Corr. litt.*, 1 Sept. 1771 (De Booy, 'Inventaire,' 378). Romain Rolland called the *Leçons de Clavecin et*

Principes d'Harmonie 'charming' (*Revue d'Art Dramatique et Musical au XXe siècle*, III [1903], 447).

13. *Leçons de Clavecin et Principes d'Harmonie. Par Mr Bemetzrieder* (Paris, 1771). On 24 Aug. 1770 Diderot had written Grimm, 'L'ouvrage de Bemetz tire à sa fin' (Diderot, *Corr.*, x, 115); on 2 Nov. 1770 he wrote Grimm, 'J'ai mis au net pour la seconde fois le *Traité d'harmonie* du petit maître de ma fille' (ibid., 159). The work was approved by the censor on 10 Dec. 1770 (Leigh, 'Les Amitiés françaises du Dr Burney,' *RLC*, xxv, 177 n.); the license to publish was issued on 17 Jan. 1771 (Diderot, *Corr.*, xi, 37 n). Publication was, however, much delayed, for Diderot wrote to Dr. Burney on 15 May 1771 that 'Le traité d'harmonie que je fais imprimer touche à sa fin' (Diderot, *Corr.*, xi, 38).

For the text of the *Leçons de clavecin*, see A.-T., XII, 171–524. It was reviewed very favorably in the *Mercure de France*, vol. II for Oct. 1771, 135–47. There were two editions of the English translation: *Music Made Easy to Every Capacity, in a Series of Dialogues . . . by Monsieur Bemetzrieder, Musick Master to the Queen of France . . . (with a Preface) by the Celebrated Monsieur Diderot* (London, 1778); 2nd ed. (London, 1785). There was published in Spain a pirated translation, closely modeled on the structure and sequence of Bemetzrieder's book but without mentioning his name and with very little of the dialogue form in it: Benito Bails, *Lecciones de Clave, y Principios de Harmonia* (Madrid, 1775).

14. A.-T., XII, 176–7. For authorities who ascribe the *Leçons de clavecin* to Diderot as practically an original work, see esp. the excellent article by Paul Henry Lang, 'Diderot as Musician,' *DS X* (1968), 95–6; also Maurice Tourneux, in A.-T., XII, 173–4; and José Bruyr, 'Diderot et la musique,' *Europe*, Nos. 405–6 (Jan.–Feb. 1963), 227–9. Trahard, championing Diderot's originality, refers to him as the 'pseudo-Bemetzrieder' (Trahard, *Les Maîtres de la sensibilité française au XVIIIe siècle*, II, 246; see his whole chapter, 'La Sensibilité musicale,' ibid., 243–70). For a stimulating discussion of the technical aspects of the *Leçons de clavecin*, together with Diderot's aesthetic and philosophical ideas revealed therein, see Robert Niklaus, 'Diderot and the *Leçons de clavecin et principes d'harmonie* par Bemetzrieder (1771),' in *Modern Miscellany Presented to Eugène Vinaver*, ed. T. E. Lawrenson, F. E. Sutcliffe, and G. F. A. Gadoffre (Manchester, 1969), 180–94; also useful is Felix Vexler, 'Diderot and the "Leçons de clavecin",' in *Todd Memorial Volumes*, ed. John D. Fitz-Gerald and Pauline Taylor, 2 vols. (New York, 1930), II, 231–49. Diderot is thought to have been the author of the article 'Clavecin' in the *Encyclopédie*: see Frank Hubbard, 'The *Encyclopédie* and the French Harpsichord,' *Galpin Society Journal*, IX (1956), 37–50; and the same, *Three Centuries of Harpsichord Making* (Cambridge [Mass.], 1965), 84, 192, 224. Regarding Diderot's over-all musicianship, see also Raymond Leslie Evans, *Les Romantiques français et la musique* (Paris, 1934), 2; Alfred Richard Oliver, *The Encyclopedists as Critics of Music* (New York, 1947), 71–3, 114–20, 157–8.

15. Quotation (Lang, art. cit., *DS X*, 96). For an example of his plodding, see Anton Bemetzrieder, *Le Tolérantisme musical* (Paris, 1779), 32 pp. Jean Thomas, 'Diderot et la musique,' *Livres de France*, xv, No. 8 (Oct. 1964), 10–1. For a comprehensive philosophical and aesthetic analysis of Diderot's ideas about music, see Enrico Fubini, 'Diderot e la musica,' *Atti della Accademia delle Scienze di Torino*, CII (1967–8), 89–142; for the *Leçons de clavecin et principes d'harmonie* (ibid., 136–40).

16. Burney, *The Present State of Music in France and Italy*, 405–6. See also Burney to D'Holbach about Diderot's knowledge of music, 23 May 1771 (Leigh, 'Les Amitiés françaises du Dr Burney,' *RLC*, xxv, 190). Diderot protested to Burney over being praised so highly (Diderot, *Corr.*, xi, 96–7 [18 Aug. 1771]). Nevertheless, Burney republished this passage in his second edition. Burney first met Diderot 13 Dec. 1770 (Leigh, art. cit., 166–7); the manuscripts Diderot gave him were on 'ancient Music, Accents, poetry, &c.' (ibid., 170). In this same year Diderot had written an article 'Sur les systèmes de musique des anciens peuples' (A.-T., IX, 443–50). Burney seems to have made no use of the Diderot manuscripts, although they were still in his possession in 1802 (Lonsdale, *Dr. Charles Burney: A Literary Biography*, 95).

17. D'Arblay, *The Early Diary of Frances Burney*, I, 138; see also Burney to Diderot, 10 Oct.

1771 (Diderot, *Corr.*, XI, 207). An undated draft (prob. March 1771) of a letter from Burney to Diderot stated that Burney planned to translate Bemetzrieder (James M. Osborn Collection, Beinecke Library, Yale University; this draft letter also mentioned by Lonsdale, *Dr. Charles Burney*, 100).

18. Diderot, *Corr.*, XI, 37–9, 97, 196–7. Johann-Christian Bach appears to have visited Paris in 1762 on his way from Milan to his new post in England; but if so, it seems to be unknown to his biographers. The principal one of them, Charles Sanford Terry, *John Christian Bach* (London, 1929) does not mention it. The pianoforte was still quite new at Paris when Diderot ordered one; it was first heard at the Concerts Spirituels in 1768 (Leigh, art. cit., 167 n.; regarding the Concerts Spirituels, see Jacques-Antoine Dulaure, *Nouvelle Description des Curiosités de Paris*, 2 vols. [Paris, 1786], I, 175–6). Diderot's piano was made by Johannes Zumpf at London (Diderot, *Corr.*, XI, 213).

19. 'Sur la Princesse Dashkoff' (A.-T., XVII, 487–94, quotations, 487, 492); cf. Dieckmann, *Inventaire*, 86.

20. Dashkova, *Memoirs of the princess Daschkaw*, I, 168; cf. A.-T., XVII, 492.

21. A.-T., XVII, 491–2. This was Robert Walpole, son of Horatio Walpole, thus a nephew of Sir Robert Walpole and a first cousin of Horace Walpole (David Bayne Horn, *British Diplomatic Representatives, 1689–1789* (Edited for the Royal Historical Society, Camden Third Series, XLVI) [London, 1932], 23). He had been secretary of embassy in 1768–9, but at the time of Diderot's encounter with him he was Minister Plenipotentiary (1769–71). Dr. Burney wrote of him, 'He is of a very cold and grave appearance . . .' (Charles Burney, *Dr. Burney's Musical Tours in Europe*, ed. Percy A. Scholes, 2 vols. [London, 1959], I, 23).

22. Diaz, *Filosofia e Politica nel Settecento Francese*, 440–9: Robert R. Palmer, *The Age of the Democratic Revolution*, 2 vols. (Princeton, 1959–64), I, 93–9. For a well-edited collection of documents, see John Rothney, *The Brittany Affair and the Crisis of the Ancien Régime* (New York, 1969). Louis-René Caradeuc de La Chalotais was already a well-known public figure because of his authorship of the *Essai d'éducation nationale, ou plan d'études pour la jeunesse* (n.p., 1763); see *Corr. litt.*, VI, 58. The best treatment of his career is by B.-A. Pocquet du Haut-Jussé, 'La Chalotais. Essai de biographie psychologique,' *Annales de Bretagne*, LXXII (1965), 263–98.

23. A.-T., VI, 391.

24. Diderot to François Tronchin, June (?) 1769 (Diderot, *Corr.*, IX, 62). The Diderot review is in A.-T., VI, 402–4, but a better text is supplied by Diderot, *Corr.*, IX, 63–6, passage quoted 66. Regarding the *Histoire du Parlement de Paris*, see Gay, *Voltaire's Politics*, 317–9; Nuci Kotta, 'Voltaire's *Histoire du parlement de Paris*,' *SVEC*, XLI (1966), 219–30.

25. Diderot, *Corr.*, XI, 20. See the excellent article by William Doyle, 'The Parlements of France and the Breakdown of the Old Régime, 1771–1788,' *French Historical Studies*, VI (1969–70), 435, 452.

26. Maupeou was inaugurated Chancellor of France on 24 Nov. 1768. The standard biography of him, though now needing to be brought up to date, is Jules Flammermont, *Le Chancelier Maupeou et les Parlements* (Paris, 1883); highly to be recommended is David C. Hudson, *Maupeou and the Parlements: A Study in Propaganda and Politics* (manuscript Ph.D. thesis, Columbia University Library, 1967). Restoration of the Jesuits (Hudson, op. cit., 231). Heavier censorship under Maupeou (Hudson, op. cit., 231, 320). For Malesherbes, see Jean Egret, 'Malesherbes, premier président de la Cour des Aides (1750–1775),' *Revue d'Histoire Moderne et Contemporaine*, III (1956), 97–119; his remonstrance on lettres de cachet (ibid., 112; Grosclaude, *Malesherbes, témoin et interprète de son temps*, 230–4). The rivalry between the families of Maupeou and Malesherbes was of long standing (Hudson, op. cit., 83).

27. Diderot to Princess Dashkov, 3 April 1771 (Diderot, *Corr.*, XI, 20); Anne-Robert-Jacques Turgot, *Oeuvres*, ed. Gustave Schelle, 5 vols. (Paris, 1913–23), III, 475 (28 Feb. 1771). Regarding the Maupeou reforms, see also J. H. Shennan, *The Parlement of Paris* (Ithaca [N.Y.], 1968), 316–9.

28. Bergier to Jacques-Joseph Trouillet, 15 April 1771 (Léonce Pingaud, 'Lettres inédites de Bergier,' *Académie des Sciences, Belles-Lettres & Arts de Besançon, Année 1891* [Besançon,

1892], 251). Of Bergier Diderot wrote, 'Je vis d'amitié avec lui' (Diderot, *Corr.*, x, 62). Anecdote of Diderot's 'wearing mourning' (Bachaumont, *Mémoires secrets*, vi, 81–2 [5 Jan. 1772]).

29. A.-T., iv, 86–9; quotations 88, 89. Diderot, *Corr.*, xi, 20.

30. A.-T., ix, 9–19; the best text is that edited by Jean Varloot, in *Europe*, Nos. 405–6 (Jan.–Feb. 1963), 211–9. For excellent critical and textual notes, see Varloot, 'Le poète Diderot: Vers inconnus ou méconnus,' ibid., 203–10.

31. See Diderot's important introduction to *Les Eleuthéromanes* (A.-T., ix, 9–11); to be compared with his reflections on the nature of the ode as a poetical genre (A.-T., vi, 412–3 [written in 1770]); see also the same ideas expressed by Diderot in *Corr. litt.*, ix, 463–4 (1 March 1772). See the very thoughtful remarks on Diderot as a poet in Edouard Guitton, 'Les Tentatives de libération du vers français dans la poésie de 1760 à la Révolution,' *CAIEF*, No. 21 (May 1969), 21–35.

32. 'Le Code Denis' (A.-T., ix, 3–4; first published in 1781 in the *Journal de Monsieur*, vi, 388–91, and then in the *Almanach des Muses, 1782*, 49–50; also in the *Année Littéraire*, vol. 1 for 1782, 53–5). 'Complainte en Rondeau' (A.-T., ix, 5–6; first published in the *Almanach des Muses, 1782*, 251–2, and then in the *Année Littéraire*, vol. 1 for 1782, 131–3). 'Vers après avoir été deux fois roi de la fève' (A.-T., ix, 7–8). Other poems by Diderot published about this time are (1) 'Charade à Madame de Prunevaux' (A.-T., ix, 50–2; it appeared in the *Corr. litt.* for 1 May 1770 [De Booy, 'Inventaire,' 373]); (2) 'Vers aux femmes' (A.-T., ix, 58–9; first published in the *Almanach des Muses, 1772*, 31–2); (3) 'Vers pour mad. la comtesse de ***' (*Almanach des Muses, 1773*, 162 [attributed to Diderot, ibid., 192]; (4) a very beautiful and touching 'Envoi' (A.-T., ix, 35; first published in the *Almanach des Muses, 1773*, 56 [attributed to Diderot, ibid., 192]). For these attributions in the *Almanach des Muses*, see also Frédéric Lachèvre, *Bibliographie sommaire de l'Almanach des Muses (1765–1883)* (Paris, 1928), 195.

33. Herbert Dieckmann, 'Three Diderot Letters, and *Les Eleuthéromanes*,' *Harvard Library Bulletin*, vi (1952), 80. See also Jean Meslier, *Oeuvres complètes*, ed. Roland Desné (Paris, 1970–   ), i, lxi, 514–5.

34. Herbert Dieckmann, 'The Abbé Jean Meslier and Diderot's *Eleuthéromanes*,' *Harvard Library Bulletin*, vii (1953), 231–5. *Les Eleuthéromanes* was first published in *La Décade philosophique, littéraire et politique*, x, No. 87 (30 Fructidor An iv [16 Sept. 1796]), 553–8. A more accurate text, plus Diderot's preliminary remarks (as later published in A.-T., ix, 9–11), appeared in the *Journal d'économie publique, de morale, et de politique*, i, No. viii (20 Brumaire An v), 360–7.

35. Diderot, *Pages inédites contre un tyran*, ed. Franco Venturi (Paris, 1937). The manuscript from which this is taken (B.N., MSS, Nouv. acq. fr. 6203, foll. 35–44) is entitled merely 'Lettre de M. Denis Diderot sur l'examen de l'Essai sur les préjugés.' The text is now more readily accessible in Diderot, *Oeuvres politiques*, ed. Vernière, 129–48.

36. Frederick to D'Alembert, 17 May 1770 (Diderot, *Oeuvres politiques*, ed. Vernière, 130); and to Voltaire, 24 May 1770 (Besterman, No. 15353). Passages quoted, see Diderot, *Oeuvres politiques*, ed. Vernière, 145, 148. Regarding Diderot's views on war and peace, see Elizabeth V. Souleyman, *The Vision of World Peace in Seventeenth and Eighteenth Century France* (New York, 1941), 125–6. The philosophical importance of Diderot's views expressed in the *Pages inédites contre un tyran* is emphasized by Lester G. Crocker, 'The Problem of Truth and Falsehood in the Age of the Enlightenment,' *JHI*, xiv (1953), 594–5; and by Roland Mortier, 'Esotérisme et lumières: Un dilemme de la pensée du XVIIIe siècle,' in his *Clartés et ombres du siècle des lumières*, 91–2.

37. *Times Literary Supplement*, 7 March 1968, 220. The collection came on the market following the death of Baron Thiers on 15 Dec. 1770. On 31 Dec. 1770 François Tronchin of Geneva remarked in a letter to his brother Jean-Robert, a farmer-general at Paris, on the beauty of the collection. Jean-Robert Tronchin then spoke to Diderot about it on 9 Jan. 1771. It seems to have been on this occasion that Diderot got the idea of suggesting to Catherine II that she buy it. 'Comme sa tête est un volcan,' wrote Jean-Robert Tronchin to François on 15 Jan. 1771, Diderot suggested right there that François Tronchin should be the appraiser (Diderot, *Corr.*, x, 213–4, 218–9; for this and subsequent negotiations,

see Henry Tronchin, *Le Conseiller François Tronchin et ses amis.* . . , [Paris, 1895],
308–9, 310–2, 316–7, and *passim*. See also the important article by Jean-Daniel Candaux,
'Le Manuscrit 180 des Archives Tronchin: Inventaire critique et compléments à la correspondance de Diderot,' *Dix-Huitième Siècle*, II (1970), 13–32; also the documents
published in Diderot, *Corr.*, XVI, 74–81.

38. Keeping in touch with Galitzin (Diderot, *Corr.*, XI, 204). Diderot retained a Parisian
appraiser named Ménageot (Diderot, *Corr.*, X, 236; ibid., XI, 90, 205), but to preclude
collusion he also insisted upon having Tronchin. The negotiations may be followed in
Diderot, *Corr.*, X, 213–4, 218–9, 236; ibid., XI, 26 (erroneously duplicated, 66–7), 82–3,
89–92, 124–5, 193–4, 200–1, 204–5, 251–2; ibid., XII, 22–4, 30–1. The contract, drawn
up by Diderot's notary, Pot d'Auteuil, was signed on 4 Jan. 1772 (Paris. Bibliothèque
Nationale, *Diderot et l'Encyclopédie*, item 100). The collection included 8 Rembrandts, 5
Raphaels, a Leonardo, 7 Van Dycks, 3 Correggios, 10 Titians, 2 Dürers, 12 Rubens, 6
Poussins, 3 Claude Lorrains, etc. The price was 460,000 livres (B.N., MSS, Nouv. acq. fr.
24941, foll. 40–1 [18 Jan. 1772]). See also Diderot, *Corr.*, XII, 11–2 and Diderot to
Falconet, 17 April 1772 (Diderot, *Corr.*, XII, 48–50). Eleven pictures from the Crozat
collection are reproduced in color in *Leningrad, Ermitazh: Dutch and Flemish Masters*,
ed. V. F. Levinson-Lessing and the staff of the State Hermitage (London, [1964]), Pl.
8–9, 10–1, 12–3, 16, 17, 45, 52, 69, 73–5, 76, 79–80. In 1770 Diderot acquired a Van
Dyck for Catherine II from the La Live de Jully auction (ibid., viii and Pl. 15).

39. The two Poussins (Diderot, *Corr.*, XII, 89–91). In the Choiseul sale Diderot purchased
for Catherine II a Wouwermans, 2 Murillos, a Rembrandt, a Van Dyck, 2 Teniers, a Jan
Steen, and others (Diderot, *Corr.*, XII, 88–9). For interesting information about all these
purchases, see Descargues, *The Hermitage Museum, Leningrad*, 33–7; see also Maurice
Tourneux, 'Diderot et le musée de l'Ermitage,' *Gazette des Beaux-Arts*, 3ᵉ période, XIX
(1898), 333–43; also Tourneux, *Diderot et Catherine II*, 44–58. 'Je jouis de la haine
publique la mieux décidée' (Diderot to Falconet, 20 March 1771 [Diderot, *Corr.*, X, 250]).

40. Grimm in England (De Booy, 'Inventaire,' 378–9). He was back in Paris for a fortnight
in Nov., then accompanied the Prince to Germany and returned finally to Paris on 23
Jan. 1772 (Diderot, *Corr.*, XI, 227; ibid., XII, 25 n.). Diderot in charge from Sept. 1771
(*Corr. litt.*, IX, 366).

41. *Salon de 1771* (Diderot, *Salons*, IV, 165–229). Regarding this *Salon*, see ibid., IV, ix–xv;
also Jean Seznec, 'Les Derniers *Salons* de Diderot,' *FS*, XIX (1965), 111–24. For the
hypothesis that the *Salon de 1771* was the result of Diderot's collaboration with an
anonymous friend, see Else Marie Bukdahl, *Diderot est-il l'auteur du "Salon" de 1771?* in
Historisk-filosofiske Meddelelser udgivet af det Kongelige Danske Videnskabernes Selskab,
XLI, No. 2 (Copenhagen, 1966), *passim* and esp. 146, 148–9. See Jean Seznec's review of
this monograph in *RHLF*, LXVIII (1968), 660.

42. Diderot's review of this pamphlet (A.-T., XVII, 500–1). For his unacknowledged paraphrasing from it (Diderot, *Salons*, IV, x–xiv). Diderot reviewed three other pamphlets on
the Salon of 1771; published in *Corr. litt.*, IX, 375–7. Attribution to Diderot (De Booy,
'Inventaire,' 380).

43. The authenticity of the *Salon de 1771* was put in question by Langen, 'Die Technik der
Bildbeschreibung in Diderots "Salons",' *RFor*, LXI, 384; and by Dresdner, *Die Entstehung
der Kunstkritik*, 278–80. I follow Seznec in believing it authentic but unfinished. It is
noteworthy that the *Salon de 1771* was not circulated in the *Corr. litt.*

44. Diderot, *Salons*, IV, 226. About the bust by Houdon, see ibid., IV, 159. For details, see
Louis Réau, *Houdon, sa vie et son oeuvre*, 2 vols. (Paris, 1964), I, 78, 352–4; ibid., II,
30. Also worth consulting, though decried by Réau, is Georges Giacometti, *Le Statuaire
Jean-Antoine Houdon et son époque (1741–1828)*, 3 vols. (Paris, 1918–9), II, 115–41.
For a contemporary critique, see Bachaumont, *Mémoires secrets*, XIII, 101 (13 Sept. 1771).

45. Undated (Diderot, *Corr.*, XI, 70–2, this quotation 71–2). Petit's reply, 22 July 1771 (ibid.,
XI, 74–7); see also ibid., XI, 77–81, for another doctor's reply, identity unknown. All these
documents also in A.-T., IX, 239–49. At some time Diderot had studied anatomy 'chez
Verdier' (Diderot, *Corr.*, XI, 72). César Verdier (1685–1759) was a member of the
Montpellier school of doctors.

46. Diderot, *Salons*, II, 115–7; see also Diderot to Falconet, 2 May 1773 (Diderot, *Corr.*, XII, 246). The chapter 'Hercule et Antinoüs' in Seznec, *Essais sur Diderot et l'antiquité*, 25–42, is an excellent and comprehensive treatment of this subject; see also J. T. A. Burke, 'A Classical Aspect of Hogarth's Theory of Art,' *JWCI*, VI (1943), 151–3. Hogarth develops his theory of Antinoüs and Hercules in *The Analysis of Beauty*, ch. I, X, and esp. XI. In the edition edited by Joseph Burke (Oxford, 1955) the editor refers to Diderot as a 'plagiarist' and calls the episode 'discreditable' (lix).

47. Regarding Chappe d'Auteroche, see Harry Woolf, *The Transits of Venus: A Study of Eighteenth-Century Science* (Princeton, 1959), 115–26.

48. To Grimm, 4 March 1771 (Diderot, *Corr.*, X, 236–7). Chappe 'un sot' (To Sophie, Nov. 1760 [Diderot, *Corr.*, III, 242]). The *Antidote* was published in French in 1770 and in English at London in 1772. As might be expected, Grimm was very sarcastic and crushing about Chappe d'Auteroche's *Voyage en Sibérie* (*Corr. litt.*, VIII, 298–304 [1 March 1769]); but it has been severely criticized also by a twentieth-century historian (Dmitri S. von Mohrenschildt, *Russia in the Intellectual Life of Eighteenth-Century France* [New York, 1936], 114, 212). See Lortholary, *Le Mirage russe en France au XVIIIᵉ siècle*, 191–7, 363–5.

49. Diderot to Falconet, 20 March 1771 (Diderot, *Corr.*, X, 249); Falconet to Catherine II, 29 May 1771 (ibid., XI, 43).

50. In the *Corr. litt.*, IX, 414–5 (1 Jan. 1772) the *Antidote* was attributed to Princess Dashkov or to Falconet. Diderot probably wrote this, Grimm not yet having returned. 'Il y a dans cet *Antidote* trop d'injures . . .' (ibid., 415).

51. 21 Aug. 1771 (Diderot, *Corr.*, XI, 128). Diderot wrote letters of introduction to Falconet for Romilly, 15 March 1770 (Diderot, *Corr.*, X, 36–7); and for a bookseller named Weinacht, 20 March and 21 Aug. 1771 (Diderot, *Corr.*, X, 248–9; ibid., XI, 128–9).

52. Etienne-Maurice Falconet, *Observations sur la statue de Marc-Aurèle . . .* (Amsterdam: chez Marc-Michel Rey, 1771), 1–153; later republished, with some changes, in Etienne Falconet, *Oeuvres. . .*, 6 vols. (Lausanne, 1781), I, 157–348. Falconet states (ibid., I, 177 n.) that the *Observations* were written in April 1770. They were reviewed, rather blandly, in the *Année Littéraire*, vol. V for 1771, 194–206; and very caustically by Grimm in the *Corr. litt.*, IX, 344–5 (1 July 1771). (For the attribution to Grimm, see the important remarks in De Booy, 'Inventaire,' 375–6). See also Anne Betty Weinshenker, *Falconet: His Writings and his Friend Diderot* (Geneva, 1966), 55, 87, 93.

53. The best editing of this letter is by Herbert Dieckmann and Jean Seznec, 'The Horse of Marcus Aurelius. A Controversy between Diderot and Falconet,' *JWCI*, XV (1952), 198–228; see also Dieckmann, *Inventaire*, 104–5. Published also in Diderot, *Le Pour et le contre*, ed. Benot, 369–82; and Diderot, *Corr.*, XII, 235–63. It is possible that Diderot took the letter of 2 May 1773 with him to Saint Petersburg and delivered it by hand (Dieckmann and Seznec, art. cit., 200).

54. Previously produced in Vienna in Feb. 1771 (Diderot, *Le Fils naturel . . . représenté par les comédiens françois du théâtre impérial au mois de Février 1771* (Vienna: Jean-Thomas de Trattnern, [1771]). In Jan. 1771 Maria-Theresa was present at a production of *Le Père de famille*. The Lessing translation was used (Mortier, *Diderot en Allemagne*, 108).

55. Mme d'Epinay (*Corr. litt.*, IX, 378 [1 Nov. 1771]). Molé (Collé, *Journal et Mémoires*, III, 325–6).

56. Rehearsal in July (Leif Nedergaard, 'Quelques témoignages du XVIIIᵉ siècle sur Diderot et Langres,' *Cahiers Haut-Marnais*, No. 30 [3ᵉ trimestre 1952], 149). 1051 spectators (Lancaster, *The Comédie Française, 1701–1774. . .*, 832). Bachaumont, *Mémoires secrets*, V, 371–2 (30 Sept. 1771); a manuscript news letter written by one Marin, a censor of the *Gazette de France*, for Count Ossolinski, reported on 30 Sept. 1771 that 'le public l'a très mal accueilli' (Bibliothèque historique de la Ville de Paris, MS 628, fol. 191ᵛ); see also, for another account, Nedergaard, art. cit., 149. The notice in the *Mercure de France*, vol. II for Oct. 1771, 165–6, was mercifully brief.

57. *Corr. litt.*, IX, 378–81; Collé, *Journal et Mémoires*, III, 325–6.

58. Diderot, *Un Factum inconnu de Diderot*, ed. Maurice Tourneux (Paris, 1901), 17; first published in the *Bulletin du Bibliophile et du Bibliothécaire*, Nos. 8–9 for 1901, 349–85.

59. See the convenient and complete list of these in Lough, 'Luneau de Boisjermain v. the Publishers of the *Encyclopédie*,' *SVEC*, xxiii, 174–7. 174 livres 8 sols (*Mémoire à consulter pour les libraires associés à l'Encyclopédie*, 17). Brewing since early 1770 (Bachaumont, *Mémoires secrets*, v, 93–5 [13 March 1770]); for further developments, see ibid., 337, 342.

60. Sarcasms (Hardy, '*Mes Loisirs*,' 280, 284; Bachaumont, *Mémoires secrets*, v, 346–7 [27 Aug. 1771]). 'Depuis longtems on n'avoit vu au palais une affluence de monde aussi prodigieuse' (ibid., v, 350 [31 Aug. 1771]).

61. Diderot, *Corr.*, xi, 145–53; first published in *Mémoire pour les libraires associés à l'Encyclopédie contre le sieur Luneau de Boisjermain* (Paris, 1771), 68–74. Grimm to Nesselrode, 7 Feb. 1774 (Vasiliĭ Alekseevich Bil'basov, *Didro v Peterburge* [St. Petersburg, 1884], 174).

62. Bachaumont, *Mémoires secrets*, v, 372 (30 Sept. 1771); see also ibid., v, 352–4 (6 Sept. 1771), 364 (21 Sept. 1771).

63. Diderot, *Corr.*, xi, 130; the letter is dated by Gerbier's mentioning that 'Luneau a débuté hier,' i.e., 21 Aug. 1771.

64. Diderot, *Corr.*, x, 20.

65. 'Enlevée dans un jour' (*Lettre de M. Luneau de Boisjermain à M. Diderot, et Réponses à la lettre adressée aux Srs Briasson & Le Breton par M. Diderot* [Paris, 1771], 31). This *Lettre* is dated 1 Dec. 1771; it is also published in Diderot, *Corr.*, xi, 228–48, this quotation 248. Luneau's first reply to Diderot was dated 1 Sept. 1771; it is the *Précis pour le sieur Luneau de Boisjermain, servant de réponse au Mémoire distribué contre lui sous le nom des libraires associés à l'Encyclopédie et aux pièces y jointes* (Paris, 1771), 10–28, passages quoted 12, 25–6; also published in Diderot, *Corr.*, xi, 158–78, first quotation not included, second quotation 174.

66. This amplification was the *Lettre de M. Luneau de Boisjermain. . . ,* cited above, passages cited, 7–8, 2–3; in Diderot, *Corr.*, xi, 233, 229–31.

67. Gerbier's letters to Diderot (Diderot, *Corr.*, xi, 155, 190–1, 191–2, 253–4); cf. Dieckmann, *Inventaire*, 59. 'Superb force and logic' (Lough, 'Luneau de Boisjermain v. the Publishers of the *Encyclopédie*,' *SVEC*, xxiii, 116). The intensity of Diderot's desire to publish his *Au public et aux magistrats* is reflected in his emotionally charged letters to Grimm, 3, 15, and 26 May 1772 (Diderot, *Corr.*, xii, 58, 64–5, 69). 'Infallible oracle of literature' (*Année Littéraire*, vol. vi for 1772, 6; the whole article, ibid., 3–28).

68. Each vol. of engravings carries the censor's approval: for vol. viii, 24 Oct. 1771; ix, 5 Nov. 1771; x and xi, 14 Feb. 1772. Daubenton (Diderot, *Corr.*, xvi, 35–8 [2 March 1769]; ibid., ix, 28–35 [4 March 1769]); Diderot also alluded to these circumstances in his *Au public et aux magistrats* (Diderot, *Un Factum inconnu*, ed. Tourneux, 31–2; also in Diderot, *Corr.*, xi, 113–5). See also Lough, 'Luneau de Boisjermain v. the Publishers of the *Encyclopédie*,' *SVEC*, xxiii, 145–7. In his 'Avis aux souscripteurs' in the forepage of the Cinquième Livraison ou Sixième Volume of the *Planches* (Paris, 1768), Diderot explained why the volume cost extra. In a long account of the history of the *Encyclopédie*, Grimm mentioned Le Breton's depredations, but of course this information was highly confidential (*Corr. litt.*, ix, 203–17 [1 Jan. 1771]).

69. Le Tourneur (Diderot, *Corr.*, x, 55–7). The Dutch acquaintance, Willem van Hogendorp, to Diderot, 1771 (Diderot, *Corr.*, xi, 58–62); Diderot to Hogendorp, 26 June 1771 (ibid., 62–5). Hogendorp replied very sarcastically and maliciously, 30 June 1772 (ibid., xii, 80–2); he also tried to get Marmontel to say that he was right and Diderot was wrong (ibid., xii, 93–6). To Grimm about grammar (Diderot, *Corr.*, xi, 33). La Harpe (Diderot, *Corr.*, xi, 181, 184; *Corr. litt.*, ix, 387 [1 Nov. 1771]).

70. André-Ernest-Modeste Grétry, *Réflexions d'un solitaire*, 4 vols. (Brussels, 1919–22), iii, 254–5; A.-E.-M. Grétry, *Mémoires, ou Essais sur la musique*, 3 vols. (Paris, An v [1796]), i, 225; cf. ibid., iii, 377–8. This fitting of words to music always interested Diderot: see his discussion at this time with Burney (Diderot, *Corr.*, xi, 205–7, 214–6); A.-T., viii, 506–10.

71. Examples are (1) *Lettre de Mons. le Comte de Lauraguais à M. Diderot* (n.p., 1766), about porcelain making, a critique of the book by Montamy. (Benjamin Franklin's pre-

sentation copy is owned by the Historical Society of Pennsylvania); (2) [Alexandre-Frédéric-Jacques Masson de Pezay], *Lettre d'Ovide à Julie, précédée d'une lettre en prose à M. Diderot* (n.p., 1767); (3) dedication to Diderot, 8 Aug. 1766, by Arthur Masson, *Nouveau recueil de pièces choisies des meilleurs auteurs français, . . . à l'usage des écoles* (John Lough, 'The "Encyclopédie" in Eighteenth-Century Scotland,' *MLR*, XXXVIII [1943], 38–40); (4) *Lettre de Valcour à son père, pour servir de suite et de fin au roman de Zéila. Précédée d'une apologie de l'Héroïde, en réponse à la lettre d'un anonyme à M. Diderot* (Paris, 1767); (5) Pascal Boyer, *Lettre à M. Diderot, sur le projet de l'unité de clef dans la musique et la réforme des mesures . . .* (Paris, 1767). Regarding this last item, see Diderot, *Corr.*, XVI, 86.

72. Really written by Mme Marie-Geneviève-Charlotte Thiroux d'Arconville (J.-M. Quérard, *Les Supercheries littéraires dévoilées*, 2ᵉ ed., 3 vols. [Paris, 1869–70], I, 937. Cf. Mortier, *Diderot en Allemagne*, 352–4). There was also a German edition, *Des Herrn Diderot Moralische Werke*, 2 vols. (Frankfort, 1770).

73. These four editions are (1) *Oeuvres philosophiques et dramatiques de M. Diderot*, 6 vol. in-12 (Amsterdam, 1772). This edition contains no works wrongly attributed to Diderot; it is conceivable that he may have had some connection with it (R. A. Leigh, 'A Neglected Eighteenth-Century Edition of Diderot's Works,' *FS*, VI [1952], 148–52; also Johansson, *Etudes sur Denis Diderot*, 193–4).

(2) *Oeuvres philosophiques de M. Diderot*, 3 vols. in-12 (Amsterdam, 1772). A set of this is available in the Jefferson Collection of the Library of Congress. This edition likewise contains no works wrongly attributed to Diderot.

(3) *Oeuvres philosophiques de Mr. D ****, 6 vols. in-8 (Amsterdam: M.-M. Rey, 1772). The only works falsely attributed to Diderot in this edition are in vol. I: *Code de la nature* [by Morelly] (1755), and *Mémoire pour Abraham Chaumeix, contre les prétendus Philosophes Diderot et d'Alembert* (1759), concerning which see Part I, 338.

(4) *Collection complette des oeuvres philosophiques, littéraires et dramatiques de M. Diderot*, 5 vols. (London [Bouillon], 1773). See Proust, *Diderot et l'Encyclopédie*, 539 n.; Clément, 'Pierre Rousseau et l'édition des suppléments de l'*Encyclopédie*,' *RScH*, No. 86, 137. This is the edition that contains most of the false attributions (see next note).

74. About the *Code de la nature* (Diderot to his brother, 24 May 1770 [Diderot, *Corr.*, X, 61]). The *Code de la nature* was printed in vol. I of the 6-vol. 1772 edition and in the 5-vol. 1773 edition, II, 319–466. Babeuf often referred to the *Code de la nature* during his trial in 1797 and always ascribed it to Diderot. This false attribution long plagued Diderot's reputation (F. Génin, 'Diderot, La Harpe et Naigeon. D'où vient à Diderot sa réputation d'athéisme; — Mensonge de La Harpe; — Falsifications de Naigeon,' *Revue Indépendante*, 2ᵉ série, VI [1846], 65–74). Other false attributions were (1) Etienne Beaumont, *Principes de philosophie morale* (1754), printed in the 5-vol. 1773 ed., II, 279–318; (2) Gabriel-François Coyer, *Lettre au R. P. Berthier, sur le matérialisme* (1759), printed in the 5-vol. 1773 ed., IV, 283–318; (3) Charles-Antoine-Joseph Leclerc de Montlinot, *Justification de plusieurs articles du Dictionnaire encyclopédique, ou Préjugés légitimes contre Abraham-Joseph de Chaumeix* (1760), printed in the 5-vol. 1773 ed., IV, 333–424; (4) *L'Humanité, ou le tableau de l'indigence, triste drame par un aveugle Tartare* (The Hague, 1761), printed in the 5-vol. 1773 ed., V, 333–401. Concerning this heavy-handed parody, see Fred O. Nolte, 'The Authorship of a Curious Eighteenth Century "Drame",' *PMLA*, XLV (1930), 1023–34.

75. 22 Feb. 1768 (Diderot, *Corr.*, VIII, 18). See also Diderot's very harsh estimate of Rousseau's character, and very flattering estimate of his own, in a letter to Falconet, 6 Sept. 1768 (Diderot, *Corr.*, VIII, 107–8); this passage written 'avec un pharisaïsme assez révoltant . . .' (Mauzi, *L'Idée du bonheur au XVIIIᵉ siècle*, 618).

76. Pierre Manuel, *La Police de Paris dévoilée*, 2 vols. (Paris, An II [1794]), I, 97–8; cf. Scherer, *Melchior Grimm*, 423–4; also *Les Pseudo-Mémoires de Madame d'Epinay*, ed. Roth, I, xxii n.

77. Begun in the mid-fifties (Epinay, *Les Pseudo-Mémoires de Madame d'Epinay*, ed. Roth, I, xvii–xviii). In mid-Nov. 1770 Diderot refers in a letter to Grimm to a Mme d'Epinay manuscript evidently large enough to require some time to read; this is thought to be

her *Mémoires de Madame de Montbrillant* (Diderot, *Corr.*, x, 174; cf. *Les Pseudo-Mémoires de Madame d'Epinay*, ed. Roth, I, xiv; and Fabre, 'Deux frères ennemis: Diderot et Jean-Jacques,' *DS III*, 199 n.).

78. Mme d'Epinay's will, 1782 (*Les Pseudo-Mémoires de Madame d'Epinay*, ed. Roth, I, xix). Epinay, *Mémoires et correspondance de Mme d'Epinay, où elle donne des détails sur ses liaisons avec Duclos, J.-J. Rousseau, Grimm, Diderot, le baron d'Holbach, Saint-Lambert, Mme d'Houdetot, et autres personnages du dix-huitième siècle*, 2ᵈ ed.; 3 vols. (Paris, 1818). *Mémoires de Madame d'Epinay*, ed. Paul Boiteau, 2 vols. (Paris, 1863).

79. 'Ebauche d'un long roman' (*Corr. litt.*, xiii, 398). Diderot's annoyance with Mme d'Epinay (Diderot, *Corr.*, ix, 229).

80. *Les Pseudo-Mémoires de Madame d'Epinay*, ed. Roth, I, xiii–xv; for 'Les sept scélératesses du citoyen Rousseau,' see ibid., iii, 585–8; also, and most importantly, John Pappas and Georges Roth, 'Les "Tablettes" de Diderot,' *DS III* (1961), 309–20; and in Leigh, v, 281–5. Also in *Corr. litt.*, xvi, 218–22.

81. Frederika Macdonald, *Jean Jacques Rousseau: A New Criticism*, 2 vols. (London and New York, 1906), *passim.*

82. This letter, dated simply 'Le 5 au soir,' Garnier to Volx, appears in *Les Pseudo-Mémoires de Madame d'Epinay*, ed. Roth, iii, 257–8; for important editorial comment, see ibid., 258 n. Printed as authentic in A.-T., xix, 446–7, but as of 'authenticité douteuse' in Diderot, *Corr.*, I, 258–61. See the trenchant remarks by R. A. Leigh in *Historical Journal*, xii (1969), 550, as well as in Leigh, v, 284, n. 'k.'

83. For the text of these remarks, see Denis Diderot, *Essai sur Sénèque*, ed. Hisayasu Nakagawa, 2 vols. (Tokyo, 1966), I, 83–93; the corresponding pages in A.-T., iii, 90–100.

84. To Lecourt de Villière, Grimm's secretary and former factotum of Mme d'Epinay (*Les Pseudo-Mémoires de Madame d'Epinay*, ed. Roth, I, ix).

85. Grimm in Paris, 1791–2 (*Les Pseudo-Mémoires de Madame d'Epinay*, ed. Roth, I, ix). The *Mémoires de Madame Montbrillant* also presented a very unfavorable view of the character of Duclos; this is best analyzed in Paul Meister, *Charles Duclos (1704–1772)* (Geneva, 1956), 79–88; see also F. C. Green's review of this book, in *MLR*, lii (1957), 439–42. Scholars now universally accept the fact that Mme d'Epinay's 'memoirs' are not a reliable source, with the result that the character of Jean-Jacques Rousseau has greatly improved in the past half-century. The pros and cons of the extent of Diderot's moral guilt are well set forth by Fabre, 'Deux frères ennemis: Diderot et Jean-Jacques,' *DS III*, 194–203; see also the review of this article by Paul H. Meyer, in *Modern Philology*, lxi (1963), 60. Some scholars, like Yvon Belaval, in *Critique*, viii (1952), 649–53, think that Diderot's guilt may have been exaggerated and besides was no worse than what any of us might do.

86. Diderot, *Corr.*, x, 219, 223–4, 241–2.

87. Paul Vernière, 'Une Anecdote inédite de Diderot: Diderot et M. de Bignicourt,' *RHLF*, lv (1955), 339–41.

88. 16 Aug. 1771 (A.-T., ix, 456–71).

89. Le Monnier was a friend of the Vollands and Diderot may first have met him there; for earlier letters of Diderot to him, see Diderot, *Corr.*, v, 186–7; ibid., ix, 91–3; ibid., x, 85–7, 88, 95; and A.-T., xix, 368, 369. For an example of Diderot's meticulously polishing Le Monnier's verse, see A.-T., xix, 361–4). Diderot sometimes saw Le Monnier in company with Sedaine (A.-T., xix, 370); all three were friends. In the Salon of 1771 there was a portrait of Le Monnier by Mme Roslin; see Diderot's comments on it (Diderot, *Salons*, iv, 203). References to the Persius edition (Diderot, *Corr.*, xi, 26–7, 54); one of the copies of the Le Monnier translation owned by the Bibliothèque Nationale bears a manuscript notation that the proofs were corrected by Diderot (*Catalogue général des livres imprimés de la Bibliothèque Nationale*, cxxxiv [1935], 359, item 234). Previously Diderot had solicited subscriptions for Le Monnier's translation of Terence (1771) (Diderot to Grimm, 19 Feb. 1770 [Diderot, *Corr.*, x, 26]). In 1773 Le Monnier published his *Fables, Contes et Epîtres*. Fable xxix (98–9) was entitled 'Le Philosophe et sa femme,' an incident from the lives of the Diderots; and 'L'Enfant bien corrigé' (136–43) is about a small boy who plucked all the feathers off a live bird and then was made to

feel sorry for what he had done. According to *Le Déjeuner*, No. 99, 9 April 1797 (20 Germinal An v), the juvenile bird plucker was Diderot (Jean Th. de Booy, 'Diderot, Voltaire et les "Souvenirs de Madame de Caylus",' *RScH*, No. 109 [Jan.–March 1963], 32–3).

90. Gustave Charlier and Léon Herrmann, 'Diderot, annotateur de Perse,' *RHLF*, xxxv (1928), 39–63, this quotation 61. This article is a study of MS. II 2321 of the Bibliothèque Royale de Belgique. In the *Salon de 1767* there is a 'Satire contre le luxe, à la manière de Perse' (Diderot, *Salons*, III, 121–6).

91. On 31 Jan. 1772 Galitzin inquired eagerly though sceptically of François Tronchin about this experiment (Candaux, 'Le Manuscrit 180 des Archives Tronchin,' *Dix-Huitième Siècle*, II, 22). Apparently the subject was a model of the tomb for the Maréchal de Saxe (Yves Benot, 'La Vieillesse de Diderot,' *Europe*, Nos. 382–3 [Feb.–March 1961], 240). For Diderot's description to Falconet of this experiment, 2 May 1773, see Dieckmann and Seznec, 'The Horse of Marcus Aurelius,' *JWCI*, xv, 217–8.

92. Diderot's proposal (J. H. Meister to Gessner [Johann Jakob Hottinger, *Solomon Gessner* (Zurich, 1796), 246]); proposal dated May 1771 (Diderot, *Corr.*, xi, 34). Satyrs among nymphs (A.-T., v, 264). Diderot's words to Huber (A.-T., vi, 401); a similar passage reported to Gessner by Meister (Hottinger, *Salomon Gessner*, 243). Michael Huber (1727–1804) was a Bavarian and a friend of the engraver Wille; he taught Turgot German and in 1760 translated (with Turgot as a silent partner) Gessner's *La Mort d'Abel*, which Diderot reviewed for the *Corr. litt.* on 15 Feb. 1760 (A.-T., vi, 324–31; De Booy, 'Inventaire,' 361–2). Huber also translated Gessner's *Idylles et poëmes champêtres* (Lyon. 1762). Regarding Huber, who went to Leipzig in 1766 as professor of French literature, see *Corr. litt.*, vii, 55 (1 June 1766); and Hanns Heiss, 'Studien über einige Beziehungen zwischen der deutschen und der französischen Literatur im 18. Jahrhundert. I. Der Übersetzer und Vermittler Michael Huber (1727–1804),' *RFor*, xxv (1908), 720–800.

93. Meister to Gessner, c. 1770 (Hottinger, *Salomon Gessner*, 242). Meister (1744–1826) had been ordained at the age of 19, but was banished from Zurich in 1769 for having written *De l'origine des principes religieux* (1768). Diderot reviewed the book very favorably and regarded the case as a particularly flagrant example of religious intolerance (Tourneux, 'Fragments inédits de Diderot,' *RHLF*, i, 169–71). From 1769 on, Meister lived in Paris; regarding him, see Paul Usteri and Eugène Ritter, 'Henri Meister,' *RDM*, 5ᵉ période, xii (1902), 148–71; and Paul Otto Bessire, *Jacob-Henri Meister (1744–1826). Sa vie et ses oeuvres* (Delémont, 1912). Particularly informative is the article by H. Breitinger, 'Heinrich Meister, der Mitarbeiter Melchior Grimm's,' *ZFSL*, Supplement Heft iii (1885), 53–77.

94. Meister to Gessner, end of April or early May 1771 (Johann Jakob Hottinger, *Salomon Gessner*, tr. J. H. Meister [Zurich, 1797], 262; date suggested by Louis Wittmer, 'Au temps des bergerades: Gessner et Watelet,' *RLC*, II [1922], 564 n.); see also Geary, 'The Composition and Publication of *Les Deux Amis de Bourbonne*,' *DS I*, 34. Gessner to Meister, 16 May 1771 (Paul Usteri, 'Briefwechsel Salomon Gessners mit Heinrich Meister, 1770–1779,' *ASNSL*, cxx [1908], 345–6). Meister to Gessner, 20 Aug. 1771 (ibid., 347–8).

95. Diderot's procrastination greatly inconvenienced Gessner (Gessner to Meister, 2 Oct. 1771 and 14 Feb. 1772 [Usteri, art. cit., 349–51]). Huber translated Gessner into French and Gessner Diderot into German (ibid., 350), but Huber's translation needed to be touched up. Meister, urged by Diderot, reluctantly did it himself (Meister to Gessner, 9 Feb. 1772 [ibid., 352–3]). The editions were *Moralische Erzählungen und Idyllen von Diderot und S. Gessner* (Zurich, 1772); and *Contes moraux et nouvelles idylles de D . . . et Salomon Gessner* (Zurich, 1773). Regarding the German edition, see Daniel Muller, 'La véritable édition originale de deux contes de Diderot,' *Bulletin du Bibliophile et du Bibliothécaire*, 1928, 261–8; also Bräuning-Oktavio, 'Goethe und Diderot im Jahre 1772,' *Goethe*, xxiv, 239–41; and esp. Mortier, *Diderot en Allemagne*, 184–97.

96. Meister to Gessner, 26 July [1773] (Usteri, art. cit., 366).

97. Geary, 'The Composition and Publication of *Les Deux Amis de Bourbonne*,' *DS I*, 38–9. *Jacques le fataliste* in 1771 (father of Heinrich Jakob Meister to Bodmer, 12 Sept. 1771 [Jack Undank, 'A New Date for *Jacques le fataliste*,' *MLN*, LXXIV (1959), 436]). Turgot wrote to a friend on 9 June 1773 that 'Les *Contes* de Diderot n'ont pas eu grand succès'

(Turgot, *Oeuvres*, ed. Schelle, III, 650); Gessner wrote to Van Goens from Zurich, 9 Feb. 1774, about Diderot's two tales, that 'Frankreich selbst war am unbilligsten gegen ihm' (Koninklijke Bibliotheek, The Hague, MS 130 D 14, Folder L). The *Journal Encyclopédique*, vol. III for 1773, Partie I, 479–81, reviewed 'ces deux contes d'un anonyme' very harshly.

98. Diderot to Vandeul, 7 Jan. 1771 (Diderot, *Corr.*, x, 209–11); to Grimm, Aug. 1771 (ibid., XI, 85). François Tronchin expressed his sympathy to Diderot about the marriage (ibid., XII, 98). Regarding Vandeul's character, see Jean Massiet du Biest, *Monsieur de Vandeul, gendre de Diderot, capitaine d'industrie (1746–1813)* (Langres, 1967), *passim* and esp. 13, 149.

99. Diderot to Denise, 27 Aug. 1771 (Diderot, *Corr.*, XI, 137–44). For the text of the marriage contract, see *Cahiers Haut-Marnais*, No. 24 (1er trimestre 1951), 19–22, supplemented by Diderot, *Corr.*, XII, 119–21.

100. To Denise, 25 Sept. 1772 (ibid., XII, 141); Diderot to Mme Caroillon, 11 March 1771 (Diderot, *Corr.*, x, 242). Regarding Vandeul's promises to remain in Paris, see Massiet du Biest, *La Fille de Diderot*, 16, 34.

101. 'A tous mes protecteurs' (Diderot to Mme Caroillon, Aug. 1772 [Diderot, *Corr.*, XII, 109]). Necker and Trudaine (Diderot to Denise, 27 Aug. 1771 [ibid., XI, 137]). Jean-Charles-Philibert Trudaine de Montigny (1733–77) was intendant général des finances since 1769. 'Mr et made de Trudaine, qui ont vraiment pris de l'amitié pour moi' (Diderot to Sophie Volland, 11 Sept. 1769 [Diderot, *Corr.*, IX, 142; see also ibid., 149]).

102. D'Aiguillon (Diderot to Grimm, 29 April 1772 [?] [Diderot, *Corr.*, XII, 57]). Devaines (Diderot, *Corr.*, XI, 137); regarding him, see Vernière, 'Diderot et Jean Devaines,' *Saggi e richerche di letteratura francese*, II, 151–61; also J. F. Bosher, 'The *Premiers Commis des Finances* in the Reign of Louis XVI,' *French Historical Studies*, III (1963–4), 477, 493. Diderot assisting Devaines in job-hunting (Diderot, *Corr.*, x, 181–6 [internal evidence suggests the date of 19 Nov. 1770]); see Diderot's letter of recommendation of Devaines to Turgot, 26 Feb. 1771 (ibid., x, 225–6); also Diderot to Devaines, 30 May 1771 (ibid., XVI, 41–3).

103. Petitions and applications (Diderot, *Corr.*, XI, 199–200 [27 Sept. 1771]). Diderot to Denise, 27 Aug. 1771 (ibid., XI, 137). Diderot to Mme Caroillon, 11 March and 29 Dec. 1771, 25 Sept. 1772 (ibid., x, 242; XI, 257; XII, 137). See also ibid., XII, 148, 154.

104. Diderot, *Corr.*, XII, 66, 101–2, 113–5. Diderot to Mme Necker (Diderot, *Corr.*, XI, 67–8); this letter is difficult to date, so that Roth inadvertently published it twice (ibid., x, 52–3). It is probably either 1770 or 1771. See also Diderot to Mme Necker (ibid., x, 147–9). Lester G. Crocker, 'Mme. Necker's Opinion of Diderot,' *FR*, XXIX (1955–6), 113–6. Regarding Mme Necker's efforts to use her salon to advance her husband's political career, see Herbert Luethy, *La Banque protestante en France*. Vol. II: *De la Banque aux Finances (1730–1794)* (Paris, 1961), 369–76, 398 n.

105. Diderot, *Corr.*, XII, 78, 128. The *Supplément au Voyage de Bougainville* was still being revised on 7 Oct. 1772 (ibid., XII, 144). 'Et surtout être honnête et sincère jusqu'au scrupule' (A.-T., II, 249).

106. *Sur les femmes* (A.-T., II, 251–62; passages quoted, 251, 252, 260, 257, 258). It appeared in the *Corr. litt.* for 1 July 1772 (De Booy, 'Inventaire,' 382); Diderot mentioned to Grimm, 26 May 1772, that he was working on it (Diderot, *Corr.*, XII, 68). Temptation to re-do a book (A.-T., IV, 94). Klopstock (Mortier, *Diderot en Allemagne*, 21 and n.; Peter Sturz wrote, 'Ich kenne den einzigen Diderot nur, der sich Gesänge aus dem Messias mühsam dolmetschen lässt . . .' [Max Koch, *Helferich Peter Sturz* (Munich, 1879), 176]). Medical insights (F. Helme, 'Diderot médecin,' *Médecine Moderne*, XI, 49–52 [24 Jan. 1900]; Mayer, *Diderot homme de science*, 343–5). See Paul Lecoq, 'Sur les femmes,' *Europe*, Nos. 405–6 (Jan.–Feb. 1963), 118–26. Peter Gay speaks of *Sur les femmes* as 'a sensible essay' (Gay, *The Enlightenment*, II, 34). See also Georges Ascoli, 'Essai sur l'histoire des idées féministes en France du XVIe siècle à la Révolution,' *Revue de Synthèse Historique*, XIII (1906), 25–57, 161–84, esp. 182–3; also J. Lortel, 'Le Féminisme de Diderot,' *Revue Mondiale*, CXLVI (Jan.–Feb. 1922), 426–36. In the *Réfutation d'Helvétius* (A.-T., II, 294), Diderot says of women, 'leur servitude n'est déjà que trop grande.'

107. Angélique to the Abbé Diderot, 21 Aug. 1772 (Diderot, *Corr.*, XII, 105–7). The bishop alluded to may have been Ignace-Charles Massalski, Bishop of Vilna; Diderot mentions dining with him on 6 Oct. 1772 (Diderot, *Corr.*, XII, 144). Denis Diderot to the Abbé Diderot (21 Aug. 1772 [ibid., XII, 103–5]). Abbé Diderot to Angélique, 27 Aug. 1772 (ibid., XII, 112–3); his interpretation of the advances being made to him (ibid., XII, 160–2). Diderot was acutely aware that the Abbé was a childless man with a good deal of property inherited from Angélique's grandfather (Diderot, *Corr.*, XI, 140).

108. Aunt Denise' intentions (art. xi of the marriage contract [*Cahiers Haut-Marnais*, No. 24 (1er trimestre 1951), 20]). Attendants and witnesses at the wedding (Diderot, *Corr.*, XII, 122). Diderot's apology to Grimm for being unable to invite him to the wedding (ibid., XII, 121–2).

109. Diderot, *Corr.*, XII, 139; see also ibid., XII, 127–8. Mme Diderot (ibid., XII, 136–7, 140, 144–5). Diderot to his brother, 25 Sept. 1772 (ibid., XII, 132–5) and 13 Nov. 1772 (ibid., XII, 158–76). Abbé Diderot to Denis Diderot (ibid., XII, 177, 183–9). The Abbé's last letter, 14 Dec. 1772, was returned by the *philosophe* unopened (ibid., XII, 189–90). Diderot to his daughter (ibid., XII, 123–7).

110. 'Dans mon bec la plume ou le brin de paille' (Diderot, *Corr.*, XII, 137, 140, 150). Eckardt (ibid., XII, 147, 180). 'Partons, partons vite' (Diderot to Grimm, 9 Dec. 1772 [ibid., XII, 178–81, this quotation 180]). Angélique's and Vandeul's illness (Diderot, *Corr.*, XII, 149, 149–51, 153–5, 155; also described in an undated and unpublished letter from Diderot to Mme Necker [Houghton Library, Harvard University]).

111. Writing for Raynal (Diderot to Grimm, 26 and 28 May 1772 [Diderot, *Corr.*, XII, 68–9, 70]). Regarding these pieces, see Herbert Dieckmann, 'Les Contributions de Diderot à la "Correspondance littéraire" et à l' "Histoire des Deux Indes",' *RHLF*, LI (1951), 417–40. Reflecting on the art of the actor: see Diderot's review (A.-T., VIII, 339–59) of *Garrick ou les acteurs anglais*. Diderot spoke of this in a letter to Grimm, 14 Nov. 1769 (Diderot, *Corr.*, IX, 213); it appeared in the *Corr. litt.* on 15 Oct. and 1 Nov. 1770 (De Booy, 'Inventaire,' 373). *Lettre à Monsieur l'abbé Galiani sur la sixième ode du troisième livre d'Horace*, 25 May 1773 (A.-T., VI, 289–302; Diderot, *Corr.*, XII, 212–27). It appeared in the *Corr. litt.* for July 1773 (De Booy, 'Inventaire,' 384). Regarding it, see Ernst Howald, 'Diderot und Horaz,' in *Westöstliche Abhandlungen: Rudolf Tschudi zum siebzigsten Geburtstag überreicht von Freunden und Schülern*, ed. Fritz Meyer (Wiesbaden, 1954), 54–62.

CHAPTER 43

1. Decision in 1772 (because Falconet received word of it in St. Petersburg 21 Jan./1 Feb. 1773 [Diderot, *Corr.*, XII, 196]). Rumors of his going (A.-L. Thomas to N.-T. Barthe, 23 Jan. and 4 March 1773 [Henriet, 'Correspondance inédite entre Thomas et Barthe,' *RHLF*, XXXIV, 128, and XXXIV, 405], Falconet to Catherine II, 2/13 March 1773 [Falconet, *Correspondance de Falconet avec Catherine II*, ed. Réau, 194]; Mme d'Epinay to Galiani, 24 April and 25 May 1773 [Louise de La Live d'Epinay, *Gli ultimi anni della Signora d'Epinay. Lettere inedite all'Abate Galiani (1773–1782)*, ed. Fausto Nicolini (Bari, 1933), 30, 36]; J.-B. Suard to the Margrave of Bayreuth, 30 May 1773 [Gabriel Bonno, *Correspondance littéraire de Suard avec le Margrave de Bayreuth (University of California Publications in Modern Philology, XVIII)* (Berkeley, 1934), 160]). On 24 May 1773 Mlle de Lespinasse wrote to Guibert that Diderot intended to leave on 6 June (Julie de Lespinasse, *Correspondance entre Mademoiselle de Lespinasse et le Comte de Guibert*, ed. Comte de Villeneuve-Guibert [Paris, 1906), 6).

2. 11 June 1773 (Mme d'Epinay to Galiani, 13 June 1773 [Epinay, *Gli ultimi anni*, ed. Nicolini, 37]); this date accepted by Jean Varloot (Diderot, *Corr.*, XIII, 12), correcting the date of 10 June given by Roth (ibid., XII, 233). Mme de Vandeul gave 10 May 1773 as the date of departure (Mme de Vandeul, lii), but Diderot's own correspondence shows this to be erroneous (A.-T., I, lxv–lxvi nn.; Diderot, *Corr.*, XII, 227 n.; ibid., XIII, 15).

3. 'Pour ce voyage d'Italie si souvent projeté, il ne se fera jamais' (Diderot, *Salons*, III, 52); also, 'cette Italie après laquelle j'ai si longtems soupiré' (Diderot to his wife [1773] [Diderot, *Corr.*, XIII, 72]).

4. Diderot, *Corr.*, XIII, 15.

5. To Sophie Volland, 12 Oct. 1760 (Diderot, *Corr.*, III, 131). The same sentiments in the *Salon de 1767* (Diderot, *Salons*, III, 221).

6. Paris. Bibliothèque Nationale, *Diderot, 1713–1784*, item 480.

7. Diderot, *Corr.*, XIII, 11; cf. ibid., XII, 196–7. In the month before leaving Paris, Diderot signed contracts on behalf of Catherine II with Pierre-Charles Levesque (7 May 1773) and with Antoine-Nicolas Imbert (13 May 1773) to be governors of the School of Cadets at St. Petersburg (contracts published in *Cahiers Haut-Marnais*, No. 24 [1er trimestre 1951], 13–4, 14–5). Diderot highly recommended Levesque to Falconet and Mlle Collot, 30 May 1773 (Diderot, *Corr.*, XII, 227–30); for Levesque's later career, see Diderot, *Corr.*, XII, 229 n., and esp. André Mazon, 'Pierre-Charles Levesque, humaniste, historien et moraliste,' *Revue des Etudes Slaves*, XLII (1963), 7–66. Also before leaving Paris, Diderot made Naigeon his literary executor by a document dated 3 June 1773 (A.-T., I, lxv–lxvi nn.; for a facsimile, see *Isographie des hommes célèbres*, 4 vols. arranged alphabetically [Paris, 1828–30], s.v. 'Diderot'; also Diderot, *Corr.*, XII, 231).

8. Charles Brifaut, *Souvenirs d'un académicien sur la Révolution, le Premier Empire et la Restauration*, 2 vols. (Paris, 1921), I, 33–5, this quotation 34.

9. Epinay, *Gli ultimi anni*, ed. Nicolini, 37–8.

10. Diderot, *Corr.*, XIII, 15 (18 June 1773); A.-T., XVII, 443. A. W. de Vink, 'De Huizen aan den Kneuterdijk No. 22,' *Die Haghe Jaarboek 1921–1922* ('s-Gravenhage, 1921), 120–92, esp. 186.

11. Diderot, *Corr.*, XIII, 31, 34, 38, 47.

12. Diderot, *Corr.*, XIII, 32, 35–6.

13. A.-T., XVII, 443, 449; Diderot, *Corr.*, XIII, 31, 32, 33, 36.

14. Diderot asked Jean-Nicolas-Sébastien Allamand, a professor at Leyden, to find a publisher for him (Allamand to M.-M. Rey, 17 June 1773 [Dieckmann, *Cinq leçons sur Diderot*, 20]); on that date Rey received a letter from François-Michel Leuchsenring, also saying that Diderot desired to publish his works. Allamand sent a second letter on 26 June and Leuchsenring a second one on 2 August: 'Il m'a dit . . . que vous vouliez ses manuscrits pour rien' (ibid.).

15. A.-T., XVII, 450–7; Diderot, *Corr.*, XIII, 15. Galitzin wrote Mme Geoffrin that Diderot became acquainted with all the professors at Leyden and that Galitzin 'ne le peut tirer d'auprès d'eux . . .' (Mme d'Epinay to Galiani, 26 June 1773 [Epinay, *Gli ultimi anni*, ed. Nicolini, 39]).

16. The Bentincks (Diderot, *Corr.*, XIII, 32–3, 36–7; see also Rousseau, *Corr., gén.*, X, 277 n.). For Diderot's relations with Rijkloff Michael van Goens, see the excellent article by Brugmans, 'Autour de Diderot en Hollande,' *DS III*, 55–71. Diderot, *Corr.*, XIII, 22, would seem to indicate that they first met in 1773, but Brugmans believes 1774 to be correct.

Regarding Diderot's relations with François Hemsterhuis (1720–90), see Diderot, *Corr.*, XIII, 24–7, and especially Henri L. Brugmans, 'Diderot, Le Voyage de Hollande,' in *Connaissance de l'étranger: Mélanges offerts à la mémoire de Jean-Marie Carré* (Paris, 1964), 154–8.

Isaac de Pinto, a Portuguese Sephardic Jew, died at The Hague in 1787. In 1768 he published in London *On Card Playing. In a Letter from Monsieur de Pinto to Monsieur Diderot*, republished under the title of *Lettre de l'auteur à Mr. D. sur le jeu des cartes* in his *Traité de la circulation et du crédit* (Amsterdam, 1771), 345–52. Regarding him, see Freer, 'Isaac de Pinto e la sua *Lettre à Mr. D[iderot] sur le jeu des cartes*,' *Annali della Scuola Normale Superiore di Pisa*, série II, XXXIII, 93–117; and the same, 'Ancora su Isaac de Pinto e Diderot,' ibid., XXXV (1966), 1–7; see also Arthur Hertzberg, *The French Enlightenment and the Jews* (New York, 1968), 61, 74–5, 142–53, 154–5, 179–83). Diderot mentions him to Mme d'Epinay, 22 July 1773 (Diderot, *Corr.*, XIII, 34–5), and in his *Voyage de Hollande* (A.-T., XVII, 405), and may have had him in mind when revising *Le Neveu de Rameau* (ed. Fabre, 100–2, 234).

At the Galitzins' Diderot met two persons unmentioned in his correspondence or writings: (1) Mme van Hogendorp, the wife of the man who appealed to Diderot about French prosody (see Diderot, *Corr.*, XI, 58–65; ibid., XII, 80–2). See her interesting letter to her husband, 19 July 1773 (Diderot, *Corr.*, xiii, 30–1); (2) Isabella Agneta van Tuyll de Charrière (1740–1805), who wrote in her *Eclaircissements relatifs à la publication des Confessions de Rousseau* (quoted by Jacques Voisine in his ed. of Rousseau, *Les Confessions* [Paris: Garnier Frères, 1964], 980) that she saw Diderot several times at the Galitzins' in 1773: 'Il ne pleurait pas quand je le questionnais sur Rousseau; mais il prenait un air de Tartufe, parlait de mauvais coeur, d'ingratitude, d'amis indignement trahis, et se taisait du reste, par discrétion, par humanité! . . .'

17. Voltaire to D'Alembert, 16 and 26 June and 14 July, 1773 (Besterman, Nos. 17342, 17353, 17382). The French ambassador at The Hague, Noailles, wrote to the Duc d'Aiguillon, 14 Sept. 1773, that he suspected Diderot of being the author of the preface (Diderot, *Corr.*, xiii, 56). Diderot's reading *De l'Homme* at The Hague (Diderot, *Corr.*, xiii, 37, 46).

18. To Mme d'Epinay, 18 Aug. 1773 (Diderot, *Corr.*, xiii, 46). The best text of the *Satire première*, with copious notes, is in O'Gorman, *Diderot the Satirist*, 223–41; see also ibid., 3–17. There is also a reliable text, handsomely illustrated, in Diderot, *Le Neveu de Rameau*, ed. Desné, 153–84. It is also published in A.-T., vi, 303–16. Dieckmann, *Inventaire*, 71–2. See also Dieckmann, 'The Relationship between Diderot's *Satire I* and *Satire II*,' *RR*, xliii, 12–26; and Marlou Switten, 'Diderot's Theory of Language as the Medium of Literature,' *RR*, xliv (1953), 185–96, esp. 191. Lester G. Crocker, *La Correspondance de Diderot* [by L. G. Krakeur] (New York, 1939), 104, suggested the possibility that 'la petite satyre' might perhaps be the fragment on Colbert published by Gabriel Bonno, 'Un Article inédit de Diderot sur Colbert,' *PMLA*, xlix (1934), 1101–6. 'Authenticité très douteuse' (Proust, *Diderot et l'Encyclopédie*, 583, s.v. 'Bonno').

19. 'C'est un beau paradoxe,' (Diderot to Grimm, 14 Nov. 1769 [Diderot, *Corr.*, ix, 213). Diderot's review appeared in the *Corr. litt.* for 15 Oct. and 1 Nov. 1770 (De Booy, 'Inventaire,' 373). Regarding the intricate filiation of the books that may have influenced Diderot in writing the *Paradoxe*, see Toby Cole and Helen Krich Chinoy, ed., *Actors on Acting* (New York, [1949]), 123; also Jacques Chouillet, 'Une Source anglaise du "Paradoxe sur le Comédien",' *Dix-Huitième Siècle*, ii (1970), 209–26. Marie-Rose de Labriolle, *Le Pour et contre et son temps* (*SVEC*, xxxiv–xxxv [1965]), xxxiv, 259.

20. A.-T., viii, 365, 370.

21. *Hamlet*, Act II, Scene ii. Though Diderot knew Shakespeare fairly well, there is no evidence that he was familiar with these particular lines. See Roland Desné, 'Diderot et Shakespeare,' *RLC*, xli (1967), 532–69.

22. A.-T., viii, 369, 370.

23. Alan J. Freer, 'Talma and Diderot's Paradox on Acting,' *DS VIII* (1966), 23–76. Coquelin thoroughly agreed with Diderot (Constant Coquelin, *L'Art et le comédien* [Paris, 1880]; and in English tr., *The Art and the Actor* [New York, 1915], esp. 56–7). Coquelin's opinion involved him in a dispute with Henry Irving over the merits of Diderot's doctrine; see Columbia University, Dramatic Museum, *Papers on Acting*, ii, *The Art of Acting* (1926), 5–82. Copeau was very little impressed by Diderot's views (Jacques Copeau, 'Réflexions d'un comédien sur le "Paradoxe" de Diderot,' *Revue Universelle*, xxxiii (1928), 641–50, esp. 644, an article that served as introduction to Copeau's edition of Diderot, *Paradoxe sur le comédien* (Paris, 1929). Mme Béatrix Dussane, who was opposed to Diderot's doctrine, discusses it in the title essay of her *Le Comédien sans paradoxe* (Paris, [1933]), 3–23. Louis Jouvet, *Le Comédien désincarné* (Paris, 1954), 12 and *passim*.

24. Denis Diderot, *Paradoxe sur le comédien, avec, recueillies et présentées par Marc Blanquet, les opinions de* [21 well-known French actors and actresses] (Paris, [1949]); see also Jean Nepveu-Degas, 'Le Paradoxe sur le comédien,' *Revue de l'Histoire du Théâtre*, ii (1950), 203–8. Thirteen young actors and actresses were interviewed by Germaine Lot, 'Ils répondent à Diderot,' *Nouvelles Littéraires*, 28 Feb. 1963, 10. The replies were various; some of them give the impression that their authors really agree with Diderot while supposing they do not. A recent doctoral dissertation available in microfilm brings out the 'unrecognized affinities' between modern French actors and Diderot (Janine Lea Bruneau, 'Le "Paradoxe" de Diderot et les comédiens modernes en France,' *Dissertation Abstracts*, xxvi [1965–6], 6018–9). For further bibliographical information, see Freer, art. cit., *DS VIII*, 74–5.

25. William Archer, *Masks or Faces? A Study in the Psychology of Acting* (London, 1888), *passim*, esp. 26, 35, 39, 52, 70, 86, 165, 212. The quotation is from the introductory essay by Lee Strasberg in Archer, *Masks or Faces?*, ed. Eric Bentley (New York, 1957), xii. See also Roger Vailland, 'Expérience du drame,' *Pensée*, Nos. 48–9 (1953), 184–98, esp. 186, 192.

26. Diderot, *Corr.*, vi, 168.

27. A.-T., viii, 381–2. See also Diderot's comments on Garrick in 1765, on seeing Le Moyne's bust of Garrick (Diderot, *Salons*, ii, 213); Garrick quoted in the *Salon de 1767* (Diderot, *Salons*, iii, 63–4).

28. 21 Aug. 1765 (Diderot, *Corr.*, v, 102).

29. Suard to Garrick, 28 Feb. 1776 (Hedgcock, *A Cosmopolitan Actor: David Garrick and his French Friends*, 336–7, 406; Diderot, *Corr.*, xiv, 185). Wilson, 'The Biographical Implications of Diderot's *Paradoxe sur le comédien*,' *DS III*, 378–9. Garrick promised Suard, 7 March 1776, that he would write his remarks upon the Diderot 'essay you left in my hands' (Garrick, *Letters*, ed. Little and Kahrl, Letter 989), but it is not known whether he did.

30. A.-T., viii, 366. Gibbon's 'My own Life' (B.M., Add. MSS. 34,874, fol. 55 v). For an excellent essay on Mlle Clairon, see J. Christopher Herold, *Love in Five Temperaments* (New York, 1961), 261–327.

31. Garrick, *Letters*, ed. Little and Kahrl, Letter 528.

32. Claude Bernard, the French physiologist, thought that Diderot was right (Helen Trudgian, 'Claude Bernard and the "Groupe de Médan",' in International Federation for Modern Languages and Literatures, *Acta*, vi, *Literature and Science* [Oxford, 1955], 274). On the other hand, Alfred Binet, the experimental psychologist, thought Diderot wrong, although Binet's observations, without his seeming to notice it, confirm Diderot's statements (A. Binet, 'Réflexions sur le paradoxe de Diderot,' *Année Psychologique*, iii [1897], 279–95). More recently, André Bonnichon, *La Psychologie du comédien* (Paris, 1942), while praising Diderot, points out that he raises many general problems of the structure of consciousness and of epistemology, besides simply those of the actor's art (op. cit., 30, 56, 89). See also Henri Delacroix, *Psychologie de l'Art* (Paris, 1927), 33, 36 n. That Diderot's views can still make people apoplectic may be seen in the case of Auréliu Weiss, 'Diderot et l'art du comédien,' *L'Esprit Créateur*, viii (1968), 53–7. For a judicious estimate of the *Paradoxe sur le comédien*, see Robert Niklaus, *Diderot and Drama* (Exeter [Devon], 1953), 14.

33. Charlotte Hogsett, 'Jean Baptiste Dubos on Art as Illusion,' *SVEC*, lxxiii (1970), 161.

34. First published in *Mémoires, correspondance et ouvrages inédits de Diderot. . .* , 4 vols. (Paris, 1830–1), iv, 1–101. In 1902 the hypothesis was set forth that it was Naigeon, not Diderot, who was the author of the *Paradoxe* (Diderot, *Paradoxe sur le comédien*, ed. Ernest Dupuy [Paris, 1902]). Several articles examined this contention (René Doumic, 'Les Manuscrits de Diderot,' *RDM*, 5ᵉ période, xi [Sept.–Oct. 1902], 924–35; Georges Grappe, 'A propos du "Paradoxe sur le comédien",' *Revue Latine*, i [1902], 601–9; Emile Faguet, 'Diderot et Naigeon,' *Revue Latine*, i [1902], 705–54; Alphonse Aulard, 'La Question de l'authenticité du Paradoxe sur le comédien de Diderot,' *Révolution Française*, xliv [1903], 5–12). The coup de grâce was administered to this hypothesis by Joseph Bédier, 'Le "Paradoxe sur le comédien" est-il de Diderot?' *Revue Latine*, ii (1903), 65–85. For an account of this episode, see André Morize, *Problems and Methods of Literary History* (Boston, 1922), 158–66.

35. A.-T., viii, 367. When posing this same question in his earlier book review Diderot had included the sculptor and omitted the poet (ibid., 347).

36. A.-T., viii, 368. See Earl R. Wasserman, 'The Sympathetic Imagination in Eighteenth-Century Theories of Acting,' *Journal of English and Germanic Philology*, xlvi (1947), 264–72.

37. 'Mes Salons' (A.-T., viii, 391). Regarding Diderot's theory of imitation, which in fact, he says, requires in the theater an exaggeration of nature, see A.-T., viii, 375, 404; Gaetano Capone Braga, 'Il Significato del "Paradoxe sur le Comédien" di Diderot,' Cagliari. Università. Facoltà di lettere e filosofià, *Annali*, xviii (1951), 15–56.

38. Herbert Dieckmann, 'Le Thème de l'acteur dans la pensée de Diderot,' *CAIEF*, No. 13 (June 1961), 157–72; see also his lecture to the Berlin Academy of Sciences, 'Das Thema des Schauspielers bei Diderot,' *Sinn und Form*, XIII (1961), 438–56.

39. Quotation from *Dorval et Moi* [1757] (A.-T., VII, 108). Diderot speaks of a 'modèle idéale' in *De la Poésie dramatique* [1758] (A.-T., VII, 393). Quotation from 1769 (Diderot, *Le Rêve de d'Alembert*, ed. Varloot, 80–1). In a stimulating and noteworthy book it has been argued that Diderot's aesthetic development was always consistent and evolutionary and thus neither inconsistent nor paradoxical (Belaval, *L'Esthétique sans paradoxe de Diderot*, *passim*; regarding his analysis of the *Paradoxe sur le comédien*, see André Villiers, 'A propos du *Paradoxe* de Diderot,' *Revue d'Histoire du Théâtre*, IV [1952], 379–81).

40. These references are, respectively, A.-T., VIII, 391, 395–6, 373, 382, 398, 382–3, 383, 384–5, 383–4, 391, 401, 414, 412, 409. Regarding the *Père de famille* at Naples, see also ibid., VII, 177 and VIII, 409, as well as Diderot, *Corr.*, XII, 194, 195.

41. A.-T., VIII, 396, 368, 393. For an interesting analysis of *sensibilité* from the point of view of characterology, see Pierre Mesnard, 'Le Caractère de Diderot,' *Revue de la Méditerranée*, VII (1949), 268–98, 664–95, esp. 682–3. See also Pierre Mesnard, *Le Cas Diderot. Etude de caractérologie littéraire* (Paris, 1952), esp. 93–113.

42. A.-T., VIII, 408. See the corresponding passage in his review, written in 1769 (ibid., 356).

43. Henri Peyre, *Literature and Sincerity* (New Haven, 1963), 75; Dieckmann, 'Le Thème de l'acteur dans la pensée de Diderot,' *CAIEF*, No. 13, 170, 172. See also Niklaus, *Diderot and Drama*, 15.

44. François Hemsterhuis, *Lettre sur l'homme et ses rapports, avec le commentaire inédit de Diderot*, ed. Georges May (New Haven, 1964), 331, 333. I am grateful to my friend Ramon Guthrie for the translation of this passage.

45. This was the burden of my essay on 'The Biographical Implications of Diderot's *Paradoxe sur le comédien*,' *DS III*, 381–3, published just before the *Commentaire* on Hemsterhuis appeared. In consequence of the new evidence that I quote here, I have now abandoned the speculation in that essay regarding Diderot's possible insincerity in private life.

46. Paris (Mlle de Lespinasse to Guibert, 24 June 1773 [Lespinasse, *Correspondance*, ed. Villeneuve-Guibert, 25]; Mme d'Epinay to Galiani, 26 June and 2 and 23 Aug. 1773 [Epinay, *Gli ultimi anni*, ed. Nicolini, 39, 46, 52]). St. Petersburg (Catherine II to Falconet, 13 June 1773 [Falconet, *Correspondance de Falconet avec Catherine II*, ed. Réau, 206]; Falconet to Catherine II, 1 and 6 July [ibid., 206–7]; Catherine II to Falconet, 8 and 13 July 1773 [ibid., 208–9]).

47. See Diderot to Sophie Volland, 13 Aug. 1773 (Diderot, *Corr.*, XIII, 41–3); to Devaines, 13 Aug. (ibid., 44–5). Diderot wrote Mme d'Epinay on 18 Aug., 'le sort en est jeté, et il est trop tard pour regarder en arrière' (ibid., 45–8, this quotation 48).

48. Diderot, *Corr.*, XII, 230; see also Diderot to Sophie Volland, 13 Aug. 1773 (Diderot, *Corr.*, XIII, 41); and Diderot to Mme d'Epinay, 18 Aug. 1773 (ibid., XIII, 45). Falconet wrote Catherine II, probably in Sept. 1773, that 'C'est M. de Narychkine qui l'amène, ainsi que cela étoit convenu entre eux et le prince de Galitzine' (Diderot, *Corr.*, XIII, 50). For a letter from Narishkin to Beccaria, Aix-la-Chapelle, 2 May 1773, see Beccaria, *Dei delitti e delle pene*, ed. Venturi (1965), 648–50. The best source of information I have found regarding Narishkin is Anne Basanoff, 'La Bibliothèque russe de Diderot,' Association des Bibliothécaires français, *Bulletin d'Informations*, No. 29 (June 1959), 72.

CHAPTER 44

1. Diderot, *Corr.*, XIII, 46, 49; Grimm to Nesselrode, 11 and 25 Sept. 1773 (*Sbornik*, XVII [1876], 282–3).

2. Grimm to Nesselrode, 28 Dec. 1773 (Bil'basov, *Didro v Peterburgě*, 165; *Sbornik*, XVII, 283–4).

3. As Diderot himself realized (Diderot, *Corr.*, XIII, 64).

4. Grimm to Nesselrode, 5 Oct. 1773 (*Sbornik*, XVII, 283). Billy, *Diderot*, 552. At Duisburg Diderot was treated by the well-known Dr. Leidenfrost, a member of the Prussian Academy (Tourneux, *Diderot et Catherine II*, 72). For Diderot's description of this illness, see

Diderot, *Corr.*, XIII, 64–5. Diderot's own notes of his itinerary, giving distances but not the exact dates, are in Dieckmann, *Inventaire*, 267–8.

5. Diderot was Jacobi's guest at his estate, Pempelfort, near Düsseldorf (Mortier, *Diderot en Allemagne*, 32); regarding Pempelfort, see Herbert Dieckmann, in *MLN*, LXXXIV (1969), 679. Jacobi wrote Christoph Martin Wieland on 5 Oct. 1773 that posterity would suppose that Hippias in Wieland's novel *Agathon* was intended as a satire of Diderot's behavior. This was something less than high praise, and such was Jacobi's intention (Friedrich Heinrich Jacobi, *Friedrich Heinrich Jacobi's auserlesener Briefwechsel. . . ,* 2 vols. [Leipzig, 1825–7], I, 145–6); see also ibid., I, 142; and Mortier, *Diderot en Allemagne*, 33.

6. Hagedorn (Paul Vernière, 'Diderot et C. L. de Hagedorn: Une étude d'influence,' *RLC*, XXX [1956], 254). In 1764 Hagedorn had become director of the Académie des Beaux-Arts of Saxony (Jacques Koscziusko, 'Diderot et Hagedorn,' *RLC*, XVI [1936], 664). Regarding Diderot and Hagedorn, see also May, 'Les "Pensées détachées sur la peinture" de Diderot et la tradition classique de la "maxime" et de la "pensée",' *RHLF*, LXX, 55–6. The Spanish ambassador at Dresden was Don Joseph Onis (Diderot, *Mémoires pour Catherine II*, ed. Vernière, 166–7, 302).

7. Georg Joachim Zollikofer to Christian Garve, Leipzig, 18 Sept. 1773 (Daniel Jacoby, 'Diderot in Leipzig,' *Euphorion*, VI [1899], 646, 647); the whole letter (ibid., 645–9) is of great interest. The second source of information, though perhaps not an eyewitness, was Karl Lessing, who wrote to his elder brother Gotthold Ephraim on 21 Oct. 1773, 'Rathe, was er da gethan hat! Oeffentlich vor dem Thore, im Kreise einer Menge Professoren und Kaufleute, den Atheismus gepredigt' (Lessing, *Sämtliche Schriften*, XX, 287–8).

8. 'The Servant Girl' (Dieckmann, *Inventaire*, 280; the recently discovered holograph of this is in the Koninklijke Bibliotheek at The Hague, MS 130 D 5, fol. 62). For a list of the poems, see Brugmans, 'Autour de Diderot en Hollande,' *DS III*, 68, who publishes Nos. 7 and 8, previously *inédites* (ibid., 68–71); for Nos. 3, 4, 5, and 6, see Dieckmann, *Inventaire*, 279–82; For Nos. 1 and 2 (A.-T., IX, 20–7, 36–41). It is possible that Diderot wrote some of these in 1774, during his journey from Russia back to The Hague.

9. To his wife, 9 Oct. 1773 (Diderot, *Corr.*, XIII, 63–5).

10. Diderot, *Corr.*, XIII, 65–7. Diderot to Falconet, 20 May 1773 (A.-T., XVIII, 329). Falconet's house and atelier were in the Millionaya, a street parallel to the Neva and very close to the Hermitage; see Diderot, *Mémoires pour Catherine II*, ed. Vernière, i.

11. Mme de Vandeul, lii–liii; Diderot, *Corr.*, XIII, 145. Young Falconet's arrival, 19 Aug. 1773 (Falconet père to Catherine II, 20 Aug. 1773 [Falconet, *Correspondance de Falconet avec Catherine II*, ed. Réau, 212–3]). Pierre-Etienne Falconet was born in 1741; he married the sculptress Marie-Anne Collot in 1777.

12. To his wife, 9 Oct. 1773 (Diderot, *Corr.*, XIII, 64, 68). Gunning to Suffolk, 1/12 Oct. 1773 (P.R.O., State Papers Foreign 91 (Russia), vol. 94, fol. 84).

13. Gunning to Suffolk, 8/19 Oct. 1773 (P.R.O., loc. cit., fol. 93).

14. D'Alembert to Catherine II, 30 Oct. 1772 (Jean Le Rond d'Alembert, *Oeuvres et correspondances inédites de d'Alembert*, ed. Charles Henry [Paris, 1887], 250–5); her reply, 20 Nov. 1772 (ibid., 255–6); his reiterated request, 31 Dec. 1772 (ibid., 256–60); her final refusal (ibid., 260–1). This exchange also in *Sbornik*, XIII (1874), 279–84, 288–92. For this incident, see Lortholary, *Le Mirage russe en France au XVIIIe siècle*, 199–204, 366–8.

15. Diderot, *Corr.*, XIII, 82 (Oct. 1773).

16. Mme Geoffrin left Paris for Warsaw via Vienna on 21 May 1766, and left Warsaw for her return on 13 Sept., arriving in Paris on 10 Nov. 1766 (Ségur, *Le Royaume de la rue Saint-Honoré*, 251; Stanislas II, *Correspondance inédite du roi Stanislas-Auguste Poniatowski et de Madame Geoffrin (1764–1777)*, ed. Charles de Mouÿ [Paris, 1875], 241 n.). 'L'accueil le plus distingué' (Grimm to Mme Geoffrin, 10 Nov. 1773 [Stanislas II, *Correspondance inédite du roi Stanislas. . . ,* ed. Mouÿ, 464 n.]). Vernière, in Diderot, *Mémoires pour Catherine II*, ed. Vernière, iv.

17. Diderot, *Corr.*, XIII, 76–7, 79, 81–2; Falconet, *Correspondance de Falconet avec Catherine II*, ed. Réau, 223–4.

18. Grimm to Mme Necker, 13 Nov. 1773 (Gabriel-Paul-Othenin de Cléron, comte d'Hausson-

ville, *La Salon de Mme. Necker, d'après des documents tirés des archives de Coppet*, 2 vols. [Paris, 1882]; quotation from the London ed. [1882], I, 143). 'L'Impératrice en est vraiment enchantée' (Grimm to Nesselrode, 2 Nov. 1773 [Bil'basov, *Didro v Peterburgě*, 158]). 'Ce Denis a auprès de S. M. le succès le plus brillant et le plus complet' (same to the same, 19 Nov. 1773 [ibid., 160]). Diderot 'comblé de bontés par l'Impératrice' (Grimm to J. H. Meister, 8 Nov. 1773 [Clara Adèle Luce Herpin (pseud. Lucien Perey) and Gaston Maugras, *Une Femme du monde au XVIIIe siècle. Dernières années de Madame d'Epinay*, 2e ed. (Paris, 1883), 480]). Grimm's arrival in mid-September (Catherine II to Voltaire, 11/22 Sept. 1773 [Besterman, No. 17467]).

19. Grimm to Nesselrode, 2 Nov. 1773 (Bil'basov, *Didro v Peterburgě*, 158).
20. The source for this widely known and frequently quoted anecdote is Escherny, *Mélanges de littérature, d'histoire. . .*, III, 131. D'Escherny introduced his recollection of the Catherine II letter by saying, 'En voici le teneur' (ibid.).
21. L. H. Nicolay to (?) Ring, 11/22 Oct. 1773 (Jacques Donvez, 'Diderot, Aiguillon et Vergennes,' *RScH*, No. 87 [July–Sept. 1957], 288–9). A similar apprehension of the courtiers' shallowness in regard to Diderot was expressed by a German named Bauer writing to Nesselrode from St. Petersburg on 14 Oct. 1773 (*Sbornik*, XVII, 282). Diderot attended the masked ball held as part of the wedding festivities, a few days after 9 Oct. (Grimm to Mme Geoffrin, 10 Nov. 1773 [Stanislas II, *Corr. inédite du roi Stanislas. . .*, ed. Mouÿ, 464 n.]).
22. *Procès-verbaux des séances de l'Académie impériale des Sciences depuis sa fondation jusqu'à 1803*, ed. K. S. Veselovskiĭ, 3 vols. (1897–1900), III, 104.
23. Diderot to the Academy, 27 Oct./7 Nov. 1773 (photograph published by Inna Liubimenko, ed., *Uchenaia Korrespondentsia Akademii Nauk XVIII Vieka, 1766–1782* [*Trudy Arkhiva*, No. 2, 1937], 439; text printed, ibid., 441); published in Russian by M. V. Krutikova and A. M. Chernikov, 'Didro v Akademii Nauk,' *Akademii Nauk SSSR, Vestnik*, No. 6 for 1947, 69–73. Perhaps Diderot's cryptic remark about 'l'Académie de Paris' referred to his nomination, in competition with Vaucanson, in 1757 (see *supra*, ch. 27, n. 22); cf. also Part I, 308–9.

    Jean-Albert Euler, Perpetual Secretary of the Academy, wrote Diderot of his election the day it occurred, 23 Oct./3 Nov. 1773 (Liubimenko, ed., *Uchenaia Korrespondentsia*, Letter No. 1141, 240); Diderot replied to Euler 25 Oct./5 Nov. (facsimile in Denis Diderot, *Le Neveu de Rameau*, ed. Gustave Isambert [Paris, 1883], facing 94; also in Diderot, *Corr.*, XIII, 85; and Tourneux, *Diderot et Catherine II*, 74). A previous letter of acceptance, addressed by mistake to Academician Staehlin, has never been found (Diderot, *Corr.*, XIII, 85).

    Voltaire had been a member of the Academy since 1746 and D'Alembert since 1764 (Liubimenko, ed., *Uchenaia Korrespondentsia*, 442 n.); foreign honorary members received a pension of 200 rubles a year (ibid., 39).
24. *Procès-verbaux des séances de l'Académie impériale des Sciences. . . jusqu'à 1803*, III, 105. Diderot's letter of acceptance was read to the Academy at its séance of 28 Oct. (ibid., 104).
25. This questionnaire and the answer, prepared by a Professor Erik Laxmann, are published by Proust, 'Diderot, l'Académie de Pétersbourg et le projet d'une *Encyclopédie russe*,' *DS* XII, 113–7, 118–25. Regarding Laxmann, see ibid., 117–8, 128.
26. *Procès-verbaux des séances de l'Académie impériale des Sciences . . . jusqu'à 1803*, III, 105, 109.
27. Ibid., III, 105–18 and *passim*.
28. Diderot, *Mémoires pour Catherine II*, ed. Vernière, 1–36, esp. 34.
29. Ibid., 242–3, 253–4, 97–104, 45–7.
30. *Mélanges philosophiques, historiques, etc. . . . dont on trouvera la table page suivante. Année 1773 depuis le 15 oct. jusqu'au 3 décemb. Même année.* The manuscript is now No. 728 in the Department of Manuscripts of the Library of the Winter Palace, which is now housed at the Central Historical Archives in Moscow (Diderot, *Mémoires pour Catherine II*, ed. Vernière, vii–viii).
31. First published by Tourneux, *Diderot et Catherine II*, 91–457. The deficiencies of this edi-

tion were made known by S. Kuz'min, 'Zabytaia rukopis Didro' ['A Forgotten Manuscript of Diderot'], *Literaturnoe Nasledstvo*, LVIII (1952), 927–48. See also Paul Vernière, 'Les Mémoires à l'Impératrice: Autour d'un manuscrit de Diderot perdu et retrouvé,' *AUP*, XXXVI (1966), 34–42. Diderot, *Corr.*, XV, 266–7 (25 Aug. 1781). Diderot, *Mémoires pour Catherine II*, ed. Vernière, viii.

32. Yves Benot, 'Le Philosophe et l'Impératrice ou le malentendu,' *Europe*, No. 450 (Oct. 1966), 229–34.

33. Voltaire to D'Alembert, 26 June 1773 (Besterman, No. 17353). 'Ma rêverie à moi Denis le philosophe' (Diderot, *Mémoires pour Catherine II*, ed. Vernière, 37–44).

34. Diderot, *Corr.*, XIII, 82. Diderot, *Mémoires pour Catherine II*, ed. Vernière, 48–9, 50–1, 59–60, 129–44, 145–60, 92–4, 204–5, 250–1, 269–70.

35. Durand to D'Aiguillon, 9 Nov. 1773 (*Sbornik*, XVII, 288–9).

36. 'The soul of Brutus with the charms of Cleopatra' (Diderot to Princess Dashkov, 24 Dec. 1773 [Diderot, *Corr.*, XIII, 135–6]). Praise to her face (Diderot, *Mémoires pour Catherine II*, ed. Vernière, 42–4); to Falconet about her, 6 Dec. 1773 (Diderot, *Corr.*, XIII, 121); to his wife and daughter, 30 Dec. 1773 (ibid., XIII, 142–4). A quatrain by Diderot appeared in the Stockholm copy of the *Corr. litt.* for Jan. 1774 (Bowen, 'Two Unpublished Poems by Diderot,' *MLN*, LXXIII, 191):

> Ah! qu'ils sont vastes ces palais!
> Ils le seraient bien davantage
> S'il fallait y placer l'image
> De tous les heureux qu'elle a faits.

37. Diderot, *Mémoires pour Catherine II*, ed. Vernière, 39–40. For much sharper comment by Diderot on the Partition of Poland, see A.-T., III, 264.

38. Diderot, *Mémoires pour Catherine II*, ed. Vernière, 117–8. Cf. Wilson, 'The Development and Scope of Diderot's Political Thought,' *SVEC*, XXVII, 1890–1.

39. Versailles, 2 Dec. 1773 (Diderot, *Corr.*, XIII, 101–2). Permission to go to Russia (Bachaumont, *Mémoires secrets*, XIII, 145 n. [21 Sept. 1773]).

40. Durand de Distroff to the Duc d'Aiguillon, 6 Nov. 1773 (Tourneux, *Diderot et Catherine II*, 78–9). D'Aiguillon replied, 2 Dec. 1773, 'L'exhortation que vous avez faite à M. Diderot est très bien placée' (ibid., 246).

41. Tourneux, *Diderot et Catherine II*, 245.

42. Sir Robert Gunning to the Earl of Suffolk, 12/23 Nov. 1773 (P.R.O., State Papers Foreign 91 (Russia), vol. 94, fol. 136). I have modernized capitalization and punctuation.

43. Durand to D'Aiguillon (*Sbornik*, XVII, 289). D'Aiguillon replied, 29 Jan. 1774, 'On ne peut que savoir gré à M. Diderot de travailler à détruire l'ascendant du Roi de Prusse sur Catherine' (ibid., 290).

44. Grimm to Nesselrode (Bil'basov, *Didro v Peterburge*, 163). On *das Heimweh*, see the interesting article by Jean Starobinski, 'La Nostalgie: Théories médicales et expression littéraire,' *SVEC*, XXVII (1963), 1505–18.

45. Diderot, *Corr.*, XIII, 78, 80. The child was christened Marie-Anne. Mme Diderot's moving the furniture (Vandeul to his mother, 5 July 1773 [Paris. Bibliothèque Nationale, *Diderot et l'Encyclopédie: Exposition commémorative*, item 95]; Diderot, *Corr.*, XIII, 73).

46. Colic in Nov. and Dec. (Diderot to Alexander Galitzin, 25 Nov. 1773 [Diderot, *Corr.*, XIII, 114]; Grimm to Nesselrode, 6 Dec. 1773 [Bil'basov, *Didro v Peterburge*, 164]). Mme de Vandeul, LIII. The 'Neva distemper' (Diderot to his wife and daughter, 30 Dec. 1773 [Diderot, *Corr.*, XIII, 141–2, 143]; and to Sophie Volland, [ibid., XIII, 141]); 'J'ai eu deux fois la *néva* à Pétersbourg' (9 April 1774 [Diderot, *Corr.*, XIII, 227]). Illness in Jan. and Feb. (Besterman, No. 17664; Baron de Nolcken to J. F. Beylon, 3 March 1774 [Tourneux, *Diderot et Catherine II*, 467–9]; Grimm to Nesselrode, 1 March 1774 [Bil'basov, *Didro v Peterburge*, 177]).

47. Diderot, *Corr.*, XIII, 144–5, (30 Dec. 1773). In April 1774 Diderot wrote that he had worked 'infiniment' at St. Petersburg (Diderot, *Corr.*, XIII, 228).

48. Regarding Levitskii (1735–1822), see Denis Roche, 'Un portraitiste petit-russien au temps de Catherine II: Dmitri-Grigoriévitch Lévitski,' *Gazette des Beaux-Arts*, 3e période, XXIX (1903), 494–507; also Louis Réau, *L'Art russe de Pierre le Grand à nos jours* (Paris, 1922), 125–8. This portrait now hangs in the Musée d'Art et d'Histoire in Geneva.

49. Jacques Proust, 'La Grammaire russe de Diderot,' *RHLF*, LIV (1954), 329–31; Jacques Proust, 'Diderot et le XVIIIᵉ siècle français en U.R.S.S.,' *RHLF*, LIV (1954), 324; V. I. Tchoutchmariev, 'Ob izuchenii Deni Didro russkogo îazyka,' *Voprosy filosofii*, No. 4 for 1953, 192–206; this article was also published in translation, 'Diderot et l'étude de la langue russe,' *Pensée*, No. 53 (Jan.–Feb. 1954), 67–74.

50. Diderot, *Corr.*, XIII, 116–7; see also Diderot's comments in Dieckmann, *Inventaire*, 230–1. The boulder was got into its present location by Sept. 1770; see the account of moving it in Edmund Hildebrandt, *Leben, Werke und Schriften des Bildhauers E.-M. Falconet, 1716–1791* (Strasbourg, 1908), 46–7.

51. Visits of the Swedish ambassador (Tourneux, *Diderot et Catherine II*, 465, 468). Nicolay, *L. H. Nicolay*, ed. Heier, 83. Grimm to Nesselrode, 30 Dec. 1773 (Bil'basov, *Didro v Peterburge*, 167).

52. A.-T., XVIII, 282; Mortier, 'Diderot et ses "Deux Petits Allemands",' *RLC*, XXXIII, 194.

53. Nicolay, *L. H. Nicolay*, ed. Heier, 83. Sir Robert Gunning reported to the Earl of Suffolk on 22 Nov./3 Dec. 1773 (in code) that 'His [Diderot's] Flattery to the Great Duke was full as gross, but, to this Young Prince's Honour, He has shown as much contempt for it as Abhorrence of this boasted Philosopher's pernicious principles' (P.R.O., State Papers Foreign 91 (Russia), vol. 94, fol. 183); similarly, same to the same, 7/18 Jan. 1774, in clear (ibid., 95, foll. 67 v-68). Gunning's source of information was probably Panin.

54. Diderot, *Mémoires pour Catherine II*, ed. Vernière, xii–xiii. Diderot sent greetings to these various persons when he wrote to Clerc from The Hague, 8 April 1774 (Diderot, *Corr.*, XIII, 213–7).

55. Diderot, *Mémoires pour Catherine II*, ed. Vernière, 52–3, 258; cf. Diderot's 'Projet d'une pièce de théâtre,' modeled after Molière's *Les Femmes savantes* (ibid., 95–6).

56. To Catherine II, 6 Dec. 1775 (Diderot, *Corr.*, XIV, 175).

57. Paris. Bibliothèque Nationale, *Diderot, 1713–1784*, item 493. A photograph of this undated document (Georges Dulac, 'Diderot dans le monde,' *Le Français dans le monde*, No. 35 [Sept. 1965], 31). Signatories beside Betzki were Alexei Dournow, Andreyan Lapouhin (?), Nicolai Saltikoff, Alexandr Pavloff, Bogdan Oumskoÿ, Prince Michel Dolgarouky, and Petr Naschokin.

58. To Princess Dashkov, 24 Dec. 1773 (Diderot, *Corr.*, XIII, 138). Letter to Münich, 31 Jan. 1774 (A.-T., XX, 45–6; also in Tourneux, *Diderot et Catherine II*, 558–9). The questionnaire (A.-T., XX, 46–8; Tourneux, *Diderot et Catherine II*, 559–61). Diderot wrote to Clerc, 8 April 1774: 'Ne me laissez pas oublier de Mʳ. le comte de Münich. Toutes les fois que je voudrai me faire une juste image de la sagesse, de la modération, de la raison, je penserai de lui' (Diderot, *Corr.*, XIII, 215).

59. Tourneux, *Diderot et Catherine II*, 532–56; reprinted in Diderot, *Corr.*, XIII, 162–91. Catherine's remark about the worker loving his land (Tourneux, *Diderot et Catherine II*, 541; Diderot, *Corr.*, XIII, 170).

60. 7/18 Jan. 1774 (Besterman, No. 17664); 19/30 Jan. 1774 (Besterman, No. 17683); 15/26 March 1774 (Besterman, No. 17770).

61. Durand to D'Aiguillon, 31 Dec. 1773 (Diderot, *Corr.*, XIII, 146).

62. For a discussion of this question, see Diderot, *Mémoires pour Catherine II*, ed. Vernière, xxiii–xxiv.

63. Diderot, *Corr.*, XIII, 142; also to Princess Dashkov, 24 Dec. 1773 (ibid., 136).

64. Louis-Philippe Ségur, *Memoirs and Recollections*, 3 vols. (London, 1825–7), III, 34–5.

65. Sir Robert Gunning to the Earl of Suffolk, 22 Oct./2 Nov. 1773 (P.R.O., State Papers Foreign 91 (Russia), vol. 94, fol. 106 v).

66. Richard Oakes to William Fraser, 5/16 Nov. 1773 (P.R.O., loc. cit., 94, fol. 126); Gunning to Suffolk, 28 Jan./8 Feb. 1774 (P.R.O., loc. cit., 95, fol. 98). For other reports regarding the attempt to keep secrecy (P.R.O., loc. cit., 94, foll. 118, 193).

67. Diderot, *Corr.*, XIV, 108 (20 Nov. 1774).

68. Sir Robert Gunning's reports of worsening conditions (P.R.O., loc. cit., 94, foll. 199 v, 204, 208, 212). D'Alembert to Voltaire, 26 Feb. 1774 (Besterman, No. 17722).

69. Gunning to Suffolk, 24 Jan./4 Feb. 1774, and same to same, 14/25 Feb. 1774 (Private and most confidential) (P.R.O., loc. cit., 95, foll. 96, 114). Pugachev was handed over

to the authorities on 15 September 1774 and was executed on 10 Jan. 1775. Two excellent studies on the Pugachev revolt have recently appeared: John T. Alexander, *Autocratic Politics in a National Crisis: The Imperial Russian Government and Pugachev's Revolt/ 1773–1775* (Bloomington [Ind.], 1969); and Marc Raeff, 'Pugachev's Rebellion,' in *Preconditions of Revolution in Early Modern Europe,* ed. Robert Forster and Jack P. Greene (Baltimore, [1970]), 161–202.

70. The book review (Tourneux, *Diderot et Catherine II,* 523–31). Inspired by Frederick II or written by him (ibid., 76–7; Diderot, *Corr.,* XIII, 133; Adrienne D. Hytier, 'Le Philosophe et le despote: Histoire d'une inimitié, Diderot et Frédéric II,' *DS VI* [1964], 74–5). Written by Formey (Grimm to Nesselrode, 7 Feb. 1774 [Bil'basov, *Didro v Peterburgê,* 174]; Guy Turbet-Delof, 'A propos d' "Emile et Sophie",' *RHLF,* LXIV [1964], 54). Within three weeks, and circulated by the Prussian ambassador (Count von Solms) (Grimm to Nesselrode, 14 Jan. 1774 [Bil'basov, *Didro v Peterburgê,* 171]). Diderot felt injured by this attack, which he referred to quite openly (Durand to D'Aiguillon, 29 Jan. 1774 [*Sbornik,* XVII, 289–90]).

71. Grimm to Nesselrode, 28 and 30 Dec. 1773 and 14 Jan. 1774 (Bil'basov, *Didro v Peterburgê,* 165, 167, 171; cf. Hytier, art. cit., 74–9); Durand to D'Aiguillon, 29 Jan. 1774 (*Sbornik,* XVII, 289). Diderot led Goertz to believe that he might go by way of Berlin after all (Grimm to Nesselrode, 1 and 11 March 1774 [Bil'basov, *Didro v Peterburgê,* 177, 179]).

72. Frederick to D'Alembert (Mortier, *Diderot en Allemagne,* 39).

73. 7 Jan. 1774 (Diderot, *Corr.,* XIII, 147). In reply, 14 Feb. 1774, D'Alembert courteously and tactfully defended Diderot (D'Alembert, *Oeuvres,* v, 346–7); see also same to same, 25 April and 1 July 1774 (ibid., v, 348–9, 351).

74. Dieudonné Thiébault, *Mes Souvenirs de vingt ans de séjour à Berlin,* 3ᵈ ed., 4 vols. (Paris, 1813), II, 305–6. Cf. Part I, 90–1. For another example of a rumor about Diderot originating in Berlin, see Grimm to Nesselrode, 1 March 1774 (Bil'basov, *Didro v Peterburgê,* 177–8).

75. February departure (Catherine II to Voltaire, 7/18 Jan. 1774 [Besterman, No. 17664]; also Diderot to Sophie Volland, 29 Dec. 1773 [Diderot, *Corr.,* XIII, 141]). On 6 Dec. 1773 Grimm had asked Nesselrode whether Diderot would be welcome at Berlin (Bil'basov, *Didro v Peterburgê,* 164).

76. Grimm to Nesselrode, 28 and 30 Dec. 1773 (Bil'basov, *Didro v Peterburgê,* 165, 167). Mme Geoffrin's letters to Stanislas Poniatowski, 8 May and 27 June 1774, prove that he had hoped that Diderot would visit him at Warsaw (Stanislas II, *Correspondance inédite du roi Stanislas-Auguste Poniatowski et de Madame Geoffrin (1764–1777),* ed. Mouÿ, 465, 470). In April 1774 Grimm did visit Warsaw on his way to Berlin (Jean Fabre, *Stanislas-Auguste Poniatowski et l'Europe des lumières* [Paris, 1952], 348).

77. Grimm to Nesselrode, 17 Jan. 1774 (Bil'basov, *Didro v Peterburgê,* 172).

78. The Hague, 9 April 1774 (Diderot, *Corr.,* XIII, 238). On the journey to The Hague Diderot composed 60 lines of verse (Diderot, *Corr.,* XIII, 220) satirizing Frederick II (Morris Wachs, 'Diderot's "Parallèle de César et de Frédéric",' *DS XIV* [1971], 259–65).

79. To Princess Dashkov, 25 Jan. 1774 (Diderot, *Corr.,* XIII, 152–5); regarding Crillon, see Tourneux, *Diderot et Catherine II,* 466 n. To Jean-Albert Euler, Secretary of the Academy of Sciences, 22 Feb. [O.S. (?)] 1774 (Diderot, *Corr.,* XIII, 196–7; first published by Henri Tronchon, 'Une Lettre inédite de Diderot,' *Monde Nouveau,* XI [1929–30], 814–5). To Catherine II, 11/22 Feb. 1774 (Diderot, *Corr.,* XIII, 198–201).

80. 'Viro doctissimo atque honoratissimo Dno Dideroto hunc sacrum librum dono mittit Plato Archiepiscopus Twerensis et Caszinensis. Petropoli 1774. Jannuarii 28 die' (B.N., Rés. A 461). Sale to the Bibliothèque du Roi (Jean Porcher, 'Russkie knigi Diderota v Parizhe,' *Vremennik Obshchestva Druzei Russkoi Knigi,* III [1932], 128–33; Basanoff, art. cit., 86).

81. 25 Jan. 1774 (Tourneux, *Diderot et Catherine II,* 466).

82. Part I, 90–1.

83. 14 Jan. 1774 (Bil'basov, *Didro v Peterburgê,* 171). General-Quartermaster Fedor Vilimovich Bayer [Bauer] to Nesselrode, 10 and 24 Jan. and 27 Feb. 1774 (*Sbornik,* XVII, 282).

Nolcken to Beylon, 29 Nov./10 Dec. 1773 and 20 Feb./3 March 1774 (Tourneux, *Diderot et Catherine II*, 464–5, 468–9).

84. Bala (Grimm to Nesselrode, 7 Feb. 1774 [Bil'basov, *Didro v Peterburgě*, 173]; 'homme de mérite' (Nolcken to Beylon, 20 Feb./3 March 1774 [Tourneux, *Diderot et Catherine II*, 468]; for particulars regarding Bala, see Bil'basov, *Didro v Peterburgě*, 322–3). Diderot's esteem for him (Diderot, *Corr.*, xiii, 218–20). For the Conference of Foksiany, see the *New Cambridge Modern History*, viii: *The American and French Revolutions* (Cambridge, 1965), 263.

85. First mention of return via The Hague (Grimm to J. H. Meister, 29 Jan. 1774 [Herpin (Perey) and Maugras, *Dernières années de Madame d'Epinay*, 480–1]). 5 March 1774 (Diderot, *Corr.*, xiii, 226). Diderot had allowed Count Goertz to believe that he might after all decide to go by way of Berlin, never intending to do so (Grimm to Nesselrode, 30 Dec. 1773 and 1 March 1774 [Bil'basov, *Didro v Peterburgě*, 167, 177]).

86. Grimm to Nesselrode, 19 Nov. 1773 (Bil'basov, *Didro v Peterburgě*, 161); Diderot to his family, 30 Dec. 1773 (Diderot, *Corr.*, xiii, 143); Nolcken to Beylon, 20 Feb./3 March 1774 (Tourneux, *Diderot et Catherine II*, 468).

87. 3,000 rubles (Diderot, *Corr.*, xiii, 229–30). Cup and saucer (ibid., xiii, 233). Cameo (Grimm to Nesselrode, 1 and 11 March 1774 [Bil'basov, *Didro v Peterburgě*, 177, 180]). Gunning reported to Suffolk, 28 Feb./11 March 1774, that Catherine gave Diderot 22,000 rubles (P.R.O., State Papers Foreign 91 (Russia), vol. 95, fol. 149).

88. Grimm's approval (Diderot, *Corr.*, xiii, 235). The farewell letter (ibid., xiii, 198–201). Warmed over for Sophie Volland (ibid., xiii, 209). Catherine II to Voltaire, 15/26 March 1774 (Besterman, No. 17770).

89. To Mme Necker, 6 Sept. 1774 (Diderot, *Corr.*, xiv, 72). 'Cinq ans avant que Diderot y vînt, des 3.699 maisons de Pétersbourg 573 étaient en pierre . . .' (Henri Tronchon, *Romantisme et préromantisme* [Paris, 1930], 262).

90. Gustave Lanson, in *RHLF*, vi (1899), 639; he was reviewing Tourneux, *Diderot et Catherine II*, where the relevant passages are 176–7 (also in Diderot, *Mémoires pour Catherine II*, ed. Vernière, 66–7). Private tutor to the Czarevitch (Pierre Leguay, *Universitaires d'aujourd'hui* [Paris, 1912], 70).

91. Dieckmann, *Inventaire*, 70.

92. Diderot, *Corr.*, xiv, 72–3.

CHAPTER 45

1. Diderot, *Corr.*, xiii, 209, 233.

2. Diderot, *Corr.*, xiii, 218. For Diderot's notes on his itinerary, listing distances and indicating where they changed carriages, see Dieckmann, *Inventaire*, 274–8. To one correspondent Diderot wrote that they had broken 'deux ou trois voitures' (Diderot, *Corr.*, xiii, 214), but to two others he wrote that they had smashed up four (ibid., 223, 227).

3. A.-T., ix, 28–31. Diderot wrote at least the first two stanzas by 8 April, for he quotes them to Catherine II (Diderot, *Corr.*, xiii, 218–9). Regarding his fright, see ibid., xiv, 47.

4. Morris Wachs, 'Diderot's Letters to Carl Philipp Emanuel Bach,' *RFor*, lxxvii (1965), 359–62; Diderot, *Corr.*, xiii, 211–2, supplemented importantly by Jacques Proust's review in *RHLF*, lxviii (1968), 580; see Diderot, *Corr.*, xvi, 49–51. As for the robe de chambre, Grimm wrote Stanislas Poniatowski, 15 April 1774, 'Pour être sûr de ne faire aucune visite, chemin faisant, il [Diderot] est parti en robe de chambre' (Fabre, *Stanislas-Auguste Poniatowski et l'Europe des lumières*, 642, n. 256).

5. 5 April (Dieckmann, *Inventaire*, 278). See his letters to the Vollands, Mme Diderot, M. *** [Suard?], Mme d'Epinay (Diderot, *Corr.*, xiii, 207–11, 222–5, 229–36, 225–8, 237–40). 'Il n'y a sortes d'affabilités que je n'aie trouvées chez les grands' (ibid., xiii, 210, also 226). Brutus and Cleopatra (Diderot, *Corr.*, xiii, 209; cf. also ibid., xiv, 12–3).

6. *Les Plans et les Statuts, des différents établissements ordonnés par Sa Majesté Impériale Catherine II. pour l'éducation de la jeunesse, et l'utilité générale de Son Empire, écrits en langue russe par Mr. Betzky & traduits en langue françoise, d'après les originaux, par Mr. Clerc.* There were two editions published simultaneously by M.-M. Rey at Amsterdam, a

quarto *de luxe* printed at The Hague (Diderot, *Corr.*, xiv, 36, 43, 56), and a duodecimo printed by Rey at Amsterdam. For passages written by Diderot (*Les Plans et les Statuts* [quarto edition], i, 10–1 [reprinted in A.-T., iii, 545–6]; ibid., ii, 157 [A.-T., iii, 413–4; and see *Corr. litt.*, xi, 103). Diderot's opinion of Dutch printers and publishers (Diderot, *Corr.*, xiv, 64). For references to his work on *Les Statuts*, see Diderot, *Corr.*, xiii, 207, 214, 220–1, 223, 228, 229, 239, 241; ibid., xiv, 13.

7. See his interesting account of his association with the *Encyclopédie* (Diderot, *Mémoires pour Catherine II*, ed. Vernière, 262–8, this quotation 266).

8. Farewell letter to Catherine II, 11/22 Feb. 1774 (Diderot, *Corr.*, xiii, 198–201). The five months of negotiation with Betzki (ibid., 200). Diderot refers to Clerc's letter in his reply to Clerc, 8 April 1774 (Diderot, *Corr.*, xiii, 213–5); see also Diderot to Catherine II, 8 or 9 April 1774 (ibid., 221). Diderot to his wife, 9 April 1774 (ibid., 230–1). Regarding Clerc, see the excellent pages in Hans Rogger, *National Consciousness in Eighteenth-Century Russia* (Cambridge [Mass.], 1960), 227–34.

9. Diderot's own works (Diderot, *Corr.*, xiv, 42). Betzki wrote Diderot on 9 May (ibid., 83–4), to which Diderot replied on 15 June 1774 (ibid., 44–50). Diderot to Catherine II, 13 Sept. 1774 (ibid., 83–4). For this whole episode, see Proust, 'Diderot, l'Académie de Pétersbourg et le projet d'une *Encyclopédie russe*,' *DS XII*, 103–40.

10. Hemsterhuis, *Lettre sur l'homme et ses rapports, avec le commentaire inédit de Diderot*, ed. May, 46, 44. For speculation as to when Hemsterhuis first met Diderot and asked for his comments, see ibid., 6–9, 19. It is significant that in refuting Hemsterhuis Diderot refers to the *Système de la nature* (ibid., 443). See Roland Desné, 'Un inédit de Diderot retrouvé en Amérique ou les objections d'un matérialiste à une théorie idéaliste de l'homme,' *Pensée*, No. 118 (Nov.–Dec. 1964), 93–110, esp. 96–7.

11. See the comments by Paolo Alatri, 'Un'opera inedita di Diderot,' *Studi Storici*, vi (1965), 99–113; and by Alan J. Freer, 'A proposito di un inedito di Diderot,' *Critica Storica*, iv (1965), 800–17, esp. 804; also by Robert Niklaus, in *MLR*, lxi (1966), 131–2, and by Roland Mortier, in *Revue Belge de Philologie et d'Histoire*, xliv (1966), 606–9.

12. Hemsterhuis, *Lettre sur l'homme et ses rapports*, ed. May, 513.

13. Ibid., 41.

14. Diderot, *Corr.*, xiii, 228; ibid., xiv, 13, 15, 34.

15. A.-T., ii, 461–502; the best edition is now that in Diderot, *Oeuvres politiques*, ed. Vernière, 159–207. For a description of the various manuscripts of this text, see ibid., 151–6, and Dieckmann, *Inventaire*, 60–1; also Johansson, *Etudes sur Denis Diderot*, 77–83, 146–9. On 13 Sept. 1774 Diderot wrote Catherine II, 'Tandis qu'on y imprimoit vos statuts, je m'occupois de la lecture de Tacite; et il en est résulté un pamphlet intitulé: *Notes marginales d'un souverain sur l'histoire des empereurs*' (Diderot, *Corr.*, xiv, 84). The *Principes de politique des souverains* was circulated in the *Corr. litt.* in Aug. and Sept. of 1775 (De Booy, 'Inventaire,' 386). For Diderot's familiarity with Tacitus, see Jürgen von Stackelberg, *Tacitus in der Romania. Studien zur literarischen Rezeption des Tacitus in Italien und Frankreich* (Tübingen, 1960), 228–33, 256, esp. 232.

16. Aimed at Frederick II (Diderot, *Oeuvres politiques*, ed. Vernière, 206; Hytier, 'Le Philosophe et le despote,' *DS VI*, 80–1). For a convincing argument that Diderot also had Catherine II in mind, see Szigeti, *Denis Diderot: Une grande figure du matérialisme militant du XVIIIᵉ siècle*, 81–2.

17. A.-T., ii, 473; Diderot, *Oeuvres politiques*, ed. Vernière, 173. In the *Observations sur le Nakaz*, Diderot wrote, 'Modelez-vous sur les Suisses et vous serez libres comme eux' (ibid., 443). Regarding the difficulty of interpreting the *Principes de politique*, see Daniel, 'Autour du *Rêve de d'Alembert*: Réflexions sur l'esthétique de Diderot,' *DS XII*, 24–5.

18. The best text is in Diderot, *Oeuvres politiques*, ed. Vernière, 343–458; for information about the several manuscripts of the *Observations sur le Nakaz*, see ibid., 336–40. See also the useful edition edited by Yves Benot: Diderot, *Textes politiques* (Paris, [1960]), 61–177.

19. Diderot, *Mémoires pour Catherine II*, ed. Vernière, 59–60, 80–1. See also Diderot to Catherine II, 17 Dec. 1774 (Diderot, *Corr.*, xiv, 122).

20. Diderot, *Corr.*, xiv, 85. The 1768 English translation of the *Nakaz* is available in

W. F. Reddaway, ed., *Documents of Catherine the Great* (Cambridge, 1931), 215–309.

21. Diderot, *Corr.*, xiv, 122. Catherine II to Grimm, 22 Nov. 1785 (Tourneux, *Diderot et Catherine II*, 519–20).

22. Russia a European state (*Nakaz*, § 6). For Catherine's distortion of Montesquieu, see the excellent articles by Georg Sacke, 'Zur Charakteristik der gesetzgebenden Kommission Katharinas II. von Russland,' *Archiv für Kulturgeschichte*, xxi (1931), 166–91, esp. 175–6, 188; and the same, 'Katharina II. im Kampf um Thron und Selbstherrschaft,' ibid., xxiii (1933), 191–216, esp. 203.

23. Diderot, *Oeuvres politiques*, ed. Vernière, 345, 361, 457.

24. See the excellent article by Sergio Cotta, 'L'Illuminisme et la science politique: Montesquieu, Diderot, et Catherine II,' *Revue Internationale d'Histoire Politique et Constitutionnelle*, iv (1954), 237–87, esp. 285.

25. Diderot, *Oeuvres politiques*, ed. Vernière, 343, 354, 357.

26. Ibid., 377, 362, 343.

27. Serfdom (ibid., 386; cf. also 406–8). 'Si en lisant ce que je viens d'écrire . . .' (ibid., 345).

28. A.-T., xvii, 363–471. Influence of Linnaeus (Sergio Moravia, 'Philosophie et géographie à la fin du XVIIIe siècle,' *SVEC*, lvii [1967], 968–9); Diderot mentioned on 18 Aug. 1773 that he was taking notes on the Dutch (Diderot, *Corr.*, xiii, 46). Begun in 1773 (A.-T., xvii, 388). The two previously published handbooks were (1) François-Michel Janiçon, *Etat présent de la République des Provinces-Unies et des Païs qui en dépendent*, 2 vols. (The Hague, 1729–30), and (2) François-Alexandre Aubert de La Chesnaye des Bois, *Lettres hollandoises, ou les moeurs, les usages et les coutumes des Hollandois, comparés avec ceux de leurs voisins*, 2 vols. (Amsterdam, 1750). Regarding Diderot's extensive and unacknowledged borrowings, see Gustave Charlier, 'Diderot et la Hollande,' *RLC*, xxi (1947), 193–227.

29. A.-T., xvii, 430, 429, 398, 455, 432, 415 (and for other observations on Dutch women, ibid., 378, 455–6). Workmen, etc. (ibid., 413, 449, 420–1, 379). Haarlem (ibid., 450). Dutch colonial practices (ibid., 398). Regarding the MS of the *Voyage de Hollande* in the Fonds Vandeul, see Dieckmann, *Inventaire*, 70.

30. A.-T., xvii, 378. 'Mes adieux au pays de la liberté' (ibid., 458).

31. A.-T., ii, 503–28; the best text is now that in Diderot, *Oeuvres philosophiques*, ed. Vernière, 519–53. '. . . j'ai ébauché un petit dialogue entre la maréchale de *** et moi' (Diderot to Catherine II, 13 Sept. 1774 [Diderot, *Corr.*, xiv, 85]); on 26 Aug. 1774, the French chargé d'affaires at The Hague reported to Vergennes that Diderot had tried unsuccessfully to sell his manuscript of a *Dialogue entre ce philosophe et une maréchale* to a Dutch publisher (Donvez, 'Diderot, Aiguillon et Vergennes,' *RScH*, No. 87, 291).

32. Benot, *Diderot, de l'athéisme à l'anticolonialisme*, 48. Diderot had the *Entretien* translated into Italian and then published it under the name of Tomasso Crudeli (1703–1745): see Naigeon, *Mémoires . . . sur la vie et les ouvrages de D. Diderot*, 378. This edition is *Pensées philosophiques, en français et en italien, auxquelles on a ajouté un Entretien d'un Philosophe avec M^{de} la Duchesse de ****. Ouvrage posthume de Thomas Crudeli, en italien et en français . . .* (London [Amsterdam], 1777): B.N., R. 13211. Diderot at some time translated one of Crudeli's sonnets (A.-T., ix, 70), but it is very difficult to know just when (De Booy, 'Inventaire,' 366–7). For Crudeli and Diderot, see Busnelli, *Diderot et l'Italie*, 172–9. For the 1777 edition, see also Jean Th. de Booy, 'Diderot et l'édition originale de l' "Entretien avec la Maréchale",' *RHLF*, lx (1960), 215–9.

33. A.-T., ii, 515–6, 508–10, 519, 520–1, 518. Regarding the existence of God, Diderot tells a parable of a young Mexican on a raft (ibid., 524–6). This story appears in Diderot's writings as early as the *Essai sur le mérite et la vertu* (A.-T., i, 27 n.) and the fact that it appears also in *Qu'en pensez-vous* (A.-T., iv, 444–8) suggests that though Diderot may not have written the tale he strongly influenced it (see *supra*, ch. 33, n. 24). The man on the raft reappears in *Les Pseudo-Mémoires de Madame d'Epinay*, ed. Roth, ii, 426–30; and see Masson, 'Mme d'Epinay, Jean-Jacques . . . et Diderot chez Mlle Quinault,' *AJJR*, ix, 1–28.

34. Tourneux, *Diderot et Catherine II*, 484; Denis Diderot, *Le Neveu de Rameau*, ed. Herbert Dieckmann (Paris, 1957), xlvii.

35. Diderot, *Corr.*, xiv, 15–6. Desnoyers to Vergennes, 26 Aug. 1774 (Donvez, 'Diderot, Aiguillon et Vergennes,' *RScH*, No. 87, 291). This is confirmed by a letter from N. Hennert to the younger Euler, Utrecht, 14 June 1775: 'Mr Diderot n'a pas fait grand éclat à la Haië. Peu de gens l'ont vu. . . . Il m'a beaucoup parlé de M^r votre père' (Archives of the Akademia Nauk USSR [Leningrad], Φ. 1, oII. 3, No. 62, fol. 125v.).

36. Björnståhl, *Briefe auf seinen ausländischen Reisen*, iii, part ii, 233 (31 Oct. 1774). Hemsterhuis to Princess Galitzin, 20 Dec. 1784 and 23 April 1780 (Jean Th. de Booy, 'A propos de l' "Encyclopédie" en Espagne: Diderot, Miguel Gijón et Pablo de Olavide,' *RLC*, xxxv [1961], 598 and n.). Diderot, *Corr.*, xiv, 87.

37. *De Denker*, xii, 177–84 (6 June 1774). 'Een voornaam *Fransch Deist* komt in ons Land' (ibid., xii, summary of contents, s.v. 'No. 597'). Brugmans, 'Diderot, Le Voyage de Hollande,' in *Connaissance de l'étranger: Mélanges . . . Jean-Marie Carré*, 155.

38. A.-T., xvii, 428.

39. Early in 1774 the rumor had run in Paris that at St. Petersburg 'il est vrai que le surplus de sa cour goûte peu ce Philosophe' (Bachaumont, *Mémoires secrets*, xxvii, 236 [8 April 1774]). Princess Galitzin recalled in 1782 that Diderot 'me répugnait à cause de ses principes' (De Booy, 'Quelques renseignements inédits sur un manuscrit du *Rêve de d'Alembert*,' *Neophilologus*, xl, 92 n.). For Princess Galitzin, see also Pierre Brachin, *Le Cercle de Münster (1779–1806) et la pensée religieuse de F. L. Stolberg* (Lyon and Paris, [1951]), 15–7, 416.

40. Diderot, *Corr.*, xiv, 28–33 (21 May 1774); Diderot to Dmitri Galitzin, 10 May 1774 (Diderot, *Corr.*, xiv, 20–5).

41. Journey with Gleichen (A.-T., xvii, 451, 455; see also incidental information about the trip, Diderot to Van Goens, n.d., [Koninklijke Bibliotheek te s'Gravenhage, MS 130 D 14, Folder M, fol. 2]); Brugmans, 'Autour de Diderot en Hollande,' *DS III*, 60–1. Dr. J. Wille, *De Literator R. M. van Goens en Zijn Kring* (Zutphen, 1937), 446–8 (British Museum call number 11869. K. 11).

42. Lalande (Hélène Monod-Cassidy, 'Un Astronome-philosophe, Jérôme de Lalande,' *SVEC*, lvi [1967], 917, 925; also Brugmans, 'Diderot, Le Voyage de Hollande,' in *Connaissance de l'étranger: Mélanges . . . Jean-Marie Carré*, 154 n.). Dr. Robert and Gordon (A.-T., xvii, 444–7). Camper (ibid., 447). On 13 Sept. 1774 Diderot wrote in the album of Laurent Van Santen some lines from Horace (Jean Th. de Booy, 'Note sur la publication de l' "Entretien avec la Maréchale" (1777): Diderot et Laurent Van Santen,' *Studi Francesi*, viii [1964], 282–3). He also wrote in Björnståhl's album, 20 Sept. 1774 (Diderot, *Corr.*, xiv, 88–9), first published by Wilson, 'Leningrad, 1957: Diderot and Voltaire Gleanings,' *FR*, xxxi, 358; cf. Diderot, *Corr.*, xiv, 107.

43. Jean Th. de Booy, 'Sur une lettre de Diderot à Pierre Camper,' *RHLF*, lvii (1957), 411–5; also in Diderot, *Corr.*, xiv, 96–8. Joseph Daoust, 'Diderot et la petite vérole,' *BSHAL*, No. 156 (May 1953), 154–60; see also Tourneux, *Diderot et Catherine II*, 574–8.

44. Diderot, *Corr.*, xiv, 67, 64.

45. Jean Massiet du Biest, 'Lettres inédites de Naigeon à M^r et Mme de Vandeul (1786–1787) . . .' *BSHAL*, 1 Jan. 1948, 5. Cf. Diderot, *Corr.*, xiv, 65–6.

46. Grimm to Princess Galitzin, 28 April 1775 (Diderot, *Corr.*, xiv, 137; for the whole letter, see *Corr. litt.*, xvi, 497–500. Diderot to Galitzin, 9 Oct. 1780 (Diderot, *Corr.*, xv, 191–5).

47. Emmanuel Croÿ, duc de, *Journal inédit*, ed. Vte de Grouchy and Paul Cottin, 4 vols. (Paris, 1906–7), iii, 153.

48. 13 Sept. 1774 (Diderot, *Corr.*, xiv, 82). Referring to the death of Louis xv, Diderot had written to the Vollands, 'Il est arrivé sur votre horizon un grand événement' (Diderot, *Corr.*, xiv, 34).

49. Mme Necker (Diderot, *Corr.*, xiv, 91–2). Diderot to Turgot, 9 Aug. 1772 (Georges Dulac, 'Une Lettre de Diderot à Turgot,' *Studi Francesi*, xii [1968], 454–8; Diderot, *Corr.*, xvi, 44–7). Diderot, *Corr.*, xiv, 56.

50. Diderot, *Corr.*, xiv, 62. Arthur M. Wilson, 'An Unpublished Letter of Diderot to Du Pont de Nemours (9 December 1775),' *MLR*, lviii (1963), 222–5; also in Diderot, *Corr.*, xiv, 180–1.

51. Diderot, *Corr.*, XII, 27, 43–4, 201; ibid., XIV, 69.
52. 3 Sept. 1774 (Diderot, *Corr.*, XIV, 68). Rue Montmartre (ibid., 67 n., 69).
53. Grimm had arrived at The Hague by the time that Isaac de Pinto wrote to Van Goens on 6 Oct. 1774 (Wille, *De Literator R. M. van Goens en zijn Kring*, 447). The Counts Rumiantzev matriculated at the University of Leyden (*Corr. litt.*, XVI, 499). Mme d'Epinay to Galiani, 24 Oct. 1774 (Epinay, *Gli ultimi anni*, ed. Nicolini, 125). Arrival in Paris on 21 Oct. (ibid., 125).
54. Senlis (A.-T., XVII, 471). Mme de Vandeul, liv.
55. *Année Littéraire*, vol. VII for 1774, 115–22, esp. 117–8, 121. Not all sets of the *Année Littéraire* contain this article (e.g., the Slatkine reprint); that belonging to the B.N. does (Z. 40652). Because of this article, the *Année Littéraire* was suspended, by arrêt of 2 April 1775 (Bachaumont, *Mémoires secrets*, VIII, 5 [10 April 1775]; see also Ernest Bersot, *Etudes sur le XVIIIᵉ siècle, Etude générale* (Paris, 1855), 112; and Diderot, *Corr.*, XIV, 136).
56. See the news letter of Suard to the Margrave of Bayreuth, 20 Nov. 1774 (Bibliothèque Historique de la Ville de Paris, cote provisoire 3861, fol. 84v; Diderot, *Corr.*, XIV, 109).
57. Jean-François de La Harpe, *Correspondance littéraire, adressée à Son Altesse Impériale Mᵍʳ le Grand-duc. . . , depuis 1774 jusqu'à 1789*, 6 vols. (Paris, 1801–7), I, 33 (1 Dec. 1774). Suard, loc. cit., fol. 84; also Diderot, *Corr.*, XIV, 107.
58. Diderot, *Corr.*, XIV, 75.
59. Lespinasse, *Correspondance*, ed. Villeneuve-Guibert, 229. D'Angiviller and Darcet (Mme de Vandeul, liv; Diderot, *Corr.*, XIV, 102 nn. 2, 3). On 24 Dec. 1773 Diderot had asked Princess Dashkov to request Prince Paul G. Demidov, the principal entrepreneur of the mines and ironworks in the Urals, to have assembled for Diderot's taking to France a natural history collection, including minerals (Diderot, *Corr.*, XIII, 137–9).
60. Mme de Vandeul, liv, liii. 'Notre russe . . . commence à se dérussiser . . .' (Diderot, *Corr.*, XIV, 117 [12 Dec. 1774]).
61. *Corr. litt.*, XI, 65. Caroillon des Tillières to his mother, 28 Dec. 1774 (Massiet du Biest, *La Fille de Diderot*, 23; also in Diderot, *Corr.*, XIV, 123–4).
62. Diderot, *Mémoires pour Catherine II*, ed. Vernière, 258, 316. These are probably the *Premières Notions sur les Mathématiques à l'usage des enfants*, in the Fonds Vandeul (B.N., MSS, Nouv. acq. fr. 13752; see Dieckmann, *Inventaire*, 54).
63. Regarding Diderot's efforts to square the circle, see Mayer, 'Diderot et la quadrature du cercle,' *RGS*, LXII, 132–8; also Krakeur and Krueger, 'The Mathematical Writings of Diderot,' *Isis*, XXXIII, 223–4. For Naigeon's later comments about this effort, including Condorcet's critique of it, see Mayer, art. cit., 136–8; also Diderot, *Corr.*, XIV, 128–30. 'Un excellent somnifère' (ibid., 131). Hemsterhuis to Princess Galitzin, 12 Feb. 1784 (Brugmans, 'Diderot, Le Voyage de Hollande,' in *Connaissance de l'étranger: Mélanges . . . Jean-Marie Carré*, 157 n.). See Diderot's pages on squaring the circle in his *Réfutation . . . d'Helvétius* (A.-T., II, 399–400).
64. *Corr. litt.*, XI, 65. Regarding Diderot's project for publishing these memoranda, see Diderot, *Corr.*, XIV, 127–8, as well as the comments in Dieckmann, *Inventaire*, 54–5. This undated fragment of a letter is very difficult to date: Jacques Proust, 'A propos d'un fragment de lettre de Diderot,' *Studi Francesi*, No. 7 (1959), 88–91, dates it as 'probablement de la fin de 1769,' and this date was accepted by M. Roth (Diderot, *Corr.*, IX, 198–9). M. Varloot, however, thinks it is *c.* Feb. 1775 (ibid., XIV, 126 n.), and so do I.
65. Diderot's receipt for 900 livres, dated 2 May 1775 and with a partial list of the books in his own hand (B.N., Estampes, Cote N 2 Sup.; see also Diderot, *Corr.*, XIV, 138 n.). Both receipt and list printed in Porcher, 'Russkie knigi Diderota v Parizhe,' *Vremennik Obshchestva Druzei Russkoi Knigi*, III, 123–5, 126; for a full bibliographical description of these books, see ibid., 128–33, and esp. Basanoff, 'La Bibliothèque russe de Diderot,' Association des Bibliothécaires français, *Bulletin d'Informations*, No. 29, 76–86. There is some information on Diderot's collection in V. I. Tchoutchmariev, 'Frantsuzckie entsiklopedisty XVIII veka ob uspekhakh razvitiia russkoĭ kul'tury,' *Voprosy Filosofii*, No. 6 for 1951, 179–93; this article has been translated under the title of 'Diderot et les

Encyclopédistes devant les progrès de la culture russe,' *Pensée*, No. 41 (March–April 1952), 87–96. For special information regarding four of these books, see Paris, Bibliothèque Nationale, *Diderot, 1713–1784*, items 494, 510, 511, 512.

CHAPTER 46

1. A.-T., vi, 315 (*Satire I sur les caractères et les mots de caractère, de professions, etc.*). Arthur M. Wilson, 'The Concept of *Moeurs* in Diderot's Social and Political Thought,' *SPTB*, 188–99.
2. Diderot, *Le Rêve de d'Alembert*, ed. Varloot, 23.
3. A.-T., vi, 439. Concerning this passage, see Robert Mauzi, 'Diderot et le bonheur,' *DS III* (1961), 264–71; also Mauzi, 'Les Rapports du bonheur et de la vertu dans l'oeuvre de Diderot,' *CAIEF*, No. 13, 255–7.
4. A.-T., ii, 322.
5. A.-T., ii, 270 (*Réflexions sur le livre De l'Esprit*).
6. For the 'Lettre à Landois,' see Diderot, *Corr.*, i, 209–17; Part I, 249–52.
7. Art. 'Modification, Modifier, Modificatif, Modifiable' (A.-T., xvi, 120); art. 'Malfaisant' (ibid., 57). Both attributed to Diderot by Naigeon (Lough, 'Problem,' 355). The importance of this passage, and its similarity to the 'Lettre à Landois,' is noted by Hermand, *Les Idées morales de Diderot*, 86–7; cf. Dieckmann, *Cinq leçons sur Diderot*, 60.
8. A.-T., ii, 275–456. Portions of the *Réfutation d'Helvétius* are published in Diderot, *Oeuvres philosophiques*, ed. Vernière, 563–620, and Diderot, *Oeuvres politiques*, ed. Vernière, 463–76. For a list of corrections of the A.-T. text, see Roland Desné, 'Les Leçons inédites de *La Réfutation de l'Homme* d'après le manuscrit autographe de Diderot,' *DS X* (1968), 35–46. Diderot's comment that *De l'Homme* would have caused Helvétius trouble (A.-T., ii, 358) is borne out by the fact that the Parlement of Paris on 10 Jan. 1774 condemned the book to be burnt by the public executioner (B.N., MSS, Fr. 22179, foll., 425–8).
9. Diderot to Mme d'Epinay, 22 July 1773 (Diderot, *Corr.*, xiii, 37). A reference to England and 'l'extravagance de la guerre actuelle contre les colonies' proves that he was still adding touches after 1776 (A.-T., ii, 422). No intention of publishing (A.-T., ii, 444).
10. 'En réalité, *La Réfutation* est un dialogue brillant, énergique, nerveux, . . .' (Dieckmann, *Cinq leçons sur Diderot*, 34); see also Sergio C. Landucci, 'Diderot "philosophe",' *Belfagor*, xviii (1963), 330.
11. A.-T., ii, 330, 340, 379. Helvétius' 'sagacity' (ibid., 312, 317, 363).
12. Hermann Ley, 'Diderots Réfutation des Helvétius,' *WZUB*, xiii (1964), 120.
13. Diderot, *Salons*, iii, 148.
14. A.-T., ii, 397, 300–1, 300; see also the important pages (ibid., 302–3). The importance of these passages emphasized by Crocker, *Two Diderot Studies: Ethics and Esthetics*, 43; and in Lester G. Crocker, *Nature and Culture: Ethical Thought in the French Enlightenment* (Baltimore, [1963]), 132–3; Lester G. Crocker, *An Age of Crisis: Man and World in Eighteenth Century French Thought* (Baltimore, 1959), 359.
15. Newton and Leibniz (A.-T., ii, 368). Regarding Helvétius' oversimplified psychology, see Vartanian, *La Mettrie's L'Homme machine*, 121. Cf. J. A. Passmore, 'The Malleability of Man in Eighteenth-Century Thought,' in *Aspects of the Eighteenth Century*, ed. Wasserman, 21–46.
16. A.-T., ii, 303.
17. A.-T., ii, 336; on this passage, see Crocker, *An Age of Crisis*, 123–4. Mention of the brain (A.-T., ii, 296, 323, 361, 367). See the excellent article by Douglas G. Creighton, 'Man and Mind in Diderot and Helvétius,' *PMLA*, lxxi (1956), 705–24, esp. 709, 720.
18. A.-T., ii, 365–6. This subject has been touched upon by Nedd Willard, *Le Génie et la folie au dix-huitième siècle* (Paris, 1963), but still invites further study.
19. A.-T., ii, 338; Diderot uses the same words in the *Eléments de physiologie* (Diderot, *Eléments de physiologie*, ed. Jean Mayer [Paris, 1964], 138). See Jean Rostand, 'La Conception de l'homme selon Helvétius et selon Diderot,' in *RHS, L' "Encyclopédie" et le progrès des sciences et des techniques*, ed. Delorme and Taton, 16 and n.

20. A.-T., II, 331; cf. Rostand, art. cit., 15. O'Gorman, *Diderot the Satirist*, 47. For a noteworthy analysis of Diderot's materialistic humanism, see Gillot, *Denis Diderot*, 54–63.

21. A.-T., II, 277. Mediocrity (ibid., 340–1). An even more elaborate analogy from the breeds of dogs (ibid., 406–7; cf. Rostand, art. cit., 14, 19). Misfits in society (A.-T., II, 312). Purpose of education (ibid., 374–5).

22. A.-T., II, 340, 280, 279.

23. Diderot an 'idealist' in this work (Georgĭ V. Plekhanov, *Essays in the History of Materialism* [London, 1934], 255–6). That *De l'Homme* made Diderot even more of a materialist is a point made by Desné, 'Un Inédit de Diderot retrouvé en Amérique. . . ,' *Pensée*, No. 118, 95; and by Vernière in Diderot, *Oeuvres philosophiques*, ed. Vernière, 558–9. On this point see also the excellent pages in Casini, *Diderot 'philosophe,'* 358–68. 'Réagissant contre les excès d'Helvétius, Diderot dessine une conception plus souple et plus concrète du matérialisme' (Guy Besse, 'Observations sur la *Réfutation d'Helvétius* par Diderot,' *DS VI* [1964], 29; see also his 'Observations sur la "Réfutation" d'Helvétius par Diderot,' *WZUB*, XIII [1964], 137–43).

24. A.-T., II, 314–5. For a summary of the contrasting positions taken by Helvétius and Diderot, see C. Kiernan, 'Helvétius and a Science of Ethics,' *SVEC*, LX (1968), 241–3.

25. A.-T., II, 310.

26. A.-T., II, 312, 315.

27. A.-T., II, 315.

28. John Stuart Mill, *Utilitarianism* (various eds.), ch. ii. Diderot and Socrates (Seznec, *Essais sur Diderot et l'antiquité*, 1–22; Trousson, *Socrate devant Voltaire, Diderot et Rousseau*, 80–7).

29. A.-T., II, 345. Carl L. Becker, *The Heavenly City of the Eighteenth-Century Philosophers* (New Haven, 1932), 80: 'from all of Diderot's writings there emerges an anxious concern for morality.'

30. To Johann Jakob Bodmer (Undank, 'A New Date for *Jacques le fataliste,*' *MLN*, LXXIV, 436. Breitinger, 'Heinrich Meister, der Mitarbeiter Melchior Grimm's,' *ZFSL*, Supplement Heft III (1885), 66. 'En fait, c'est le conte qui a pris la place du traité' (Jean Fabre, 'Allégorie et symbolisme dans *Jacques le Fataliste,*' in *Europäische Aufklärung: Herbert Dieckmann zum 60. Geburtstag*, ed. Friedrich and Schalk, 74; see also Jean Fabre, '*Jacques le fataliste*: Problèmes et recherches,' *SVEC*, LVI [1967], 489).

31. Mortier, *Diderot en Allemagne*, 222–4. *Jacques le fataliste* appeared in the *Corr. litt.* from Nov. 1778 to June 1780 (De Booy, 'Inventaire,' 388–9).

32. Ian H. Smith, 'Diderot's *Jacques le Fataliste*: Art and Necessity,' *AUMLA*, No. 8 (1958), 20; Jean-Louis Leutrat, *Diderot* (Paris, 1968), 61, 74, 75–7; Hans Mølbjerg, *Aspects de l'esthétique de Diderot* (Copenhagen, 1964), 194–205. Regarding publication in 1796, see Jean Th. de Booy and Alan J. Freer, Jacques le fataliste *et la* Religieuse *devant la critique révolutionnaire (1796–1800)*, (*SVEC*, XXXIII [1965]), *passim*. The first publication was *Jakob und sein Herr, Aus Diderots ungedruckten Nachlasse*, tr. W. C. S. Mylius, 2 vols. (Berlin, 1792) (B.M. call-number 12512.b.13). For interesting information on the various manuscripts and stages of composition of *Jacques le fataliste*, see Jean Varloot, ' "Jacques le Fataliste" et la "Correspondance Littéraire",' *RHLF*, LXV (1965), 629–36.

33. For an analysis of this technique, see Robert Mauzi, 'La Parodie romanesque dans "Jacques le Fataliste",' *DS VI* (1964), 118–26. Yvon Belaval (Diderot, *Jacques le fataliste et son maître*, ed. Belaval [Paris, (1953)], separate pagination, 17), speaks of this technique as adding a new dimension to the novel.

34. Herbert Dieckmann, 'Diderot et son lecteur,' *Mercure de France*, CCCXXIX (April 1957), 645–8. For an example of an older and unfavorable view, see the usually sympathetic Ducros, *Diderot*, 204–9, and A. Collignon, *Diderot* (Paris, 1895), 131, 138–40.

35. For parallel passages, see J. Robert Loy, *Diderot's Determined Fatalist* (New York, 1950), 32–9. Other excellent works on the Sterne-Diderot nexus are Fredman, *Diderot and Sterne*, *passim* and esp. 3–4, 130–1; and Rainer Warning, *Illusion und Wirklichkeit in Tristram Shandy und Jacques le Fataliste* (Munich, 1965); the latter contrasts Sterne's use of 'oddity' and the 'hobby-horse' with Diderot's concept of the 'bizarre,' judging the latter

to be a deeper and more successful way of probing human nature (ibid., 10–1, 95–111). See also the excellent pages on *Jacques le fataliste* by Charles Sears Baldwin, 'The Literary Influence of Sterne in France,' *PMLA*, XVII (1902), 226–9; Henri Fluchère, *Laurence Sterne: De l'homme à l'oeuvre* (Paris, 1961), 386, 473. A greatly exaggerated picture of Sterne's influence upon *Jacques le fataliste* was given in the now outmoded monograph by Francis Brown Barton, *Etude sur l'influence de Laurence Sterne en France au dix-huitième siècle* (Paris, 1911), esp. 112, 118.

36. Eight days (Loy, *Diderot's Determined Fatalist*, 60–7). Don Quixote (Karl Rosenkranz, *Diderot's Leben und Werke*, 2 vols. [Leipzig, 1866], II, 318).

37. Clifton Cherpack, '*Jacques le fataliste* and *Le Compère Mathieu*,' *SVEC*, LXXIII (1970), 167; see also Clifton Cherpack, 'The Literary Periodization of Eighteenth-Century France,' *PMLA*, LXXXIV (1969), 326. Emily Zants, 'Dialogue, Diderot, and the New Novel in France,' *Eighteenth-Century Studies*, II (1968–9), 175. See also Roger Laufer, 'La Structure et la signification de "Jacques le Fataliste",' *RScH*, No. 112 (Oct.–Dec. 1963), 517–35; and the same, *Style rococo, style des 'lumières'* (Paris, 1963), 135.

38. Francis Pruner, *Clés pour le Père Hudson: Lumières et ombres sur une "digression"* de Jacques le Fataliste (*Archives des Lettres Modernes*, No. 68) (Paris, 1966); Paul Vernière, 'Diderot et l'invention littéraire: A propos de "Jacques le fataliste",' *RHLF*, LIX (1959), 161–4.

39. Ian H. Smith, 'The Mme de la Pommeraye Tale and its Commentaries,' *AUMLA*, No. 17 (1962), 18–30; see also the comment of a man who has himself written a fine novel on *The Horrors of Love* (Jean Dutourd, *Le Fond et la forme* [Paris, 1958], 269–71). J. Robert Loy, 'Love/Vengeance in the Late Eighteenth-Century French Novel,' *L'Esprit Créateur*, III (1963), 165. *Mme de La Pommeraye* was first published in a review edited by Schiller: 'Merkwürdiges Beispiel einer weiblichen Rache,' *Thalia*, I (1785), 27–94; and this was retranslated into French by J.-P. Doray-Longrais: *Exemple singulier de la vengeance d'une femme* (Paris, 1793). The story was made into a three-scene play, *Madame de la Pommeraye*, by Paul Degouy and produced at the Odéon in 1901 (Emile Faguet, *Propos de théâtre*, 2ᵉ série [Paris, 1905], 212–24). It was dramatized also by Carl Sternheim, *Die Marquise von Arcis* (Leipzig, 1919); English tr., *The Mask of Virtue* (London, 1935). Croce writes of Diderot's novella approvingly, but in general has a low opinion of Diderot's literary work (Benedetto Croce, 'Diderot,' *Critica*, XXXVIII [1940], 257–62).

40. The film is *Les Dames du Bois de Boulogne* (1942), directed by Robert Bresson and with a script adapted by Jean Cocteau. For an excellent comparison of Diderot's novella and the Cocteau script, see Victor Bol, 'De "Madame de la Pommeraye" aux "Dames du Bois de Boulogne",' in Kinshasa, Congo, Université Lovanium, *Publications*, XXII (1968), 35–68. Montage (Robert Niklaus, '*Tableaux mouvants* as a Technical Innovation in Diderot's Experimental Novel, *Jacques le Fataliste*,' in *Eighteenth Century French Studies. Literature and the Arts*, ed. E. T. Dubois, E. Ratcliff, and P. J. Yarrow [Newcastle upon Tyne, (1969)], 79; also ibid., 81).

41. A.-T., VI, 45, 11, 222–3. Regarding what would now be called power-struggles, see ibid., 72–3; Lester G. Crocker, '*Jacques le Fataliste*, an "expérience morale",' *DS III* (1961), 90.

42. A.-T., VI, 59. Cf. Cherpack, art. cit., *SVEC*, LXXIII, 171–2. Diderot and Gide (Kevin O'Neill, in *MLR*, LX [1965], 456).

43. Albert Chesneau, 'La Structure temporelle de *Jacques le fataliste:* Jacques et son maître à la recherche du temps perdu,' *RScH*, No. 131 (July–Sept. 1968), 401–13. See the excellent and moving essay on Diderot by Georges Poulet, *Etudes sur le temps humain*, 2 vols. (Paris, 1950–2), I, 194–217. Douglas A. Bonneville, 'Two Examples of Time-Technique in *Jacques le fataliste*,' *Romance Notes*, VIII (1966–7), 217–20.

44. Jacques Smietanski, *Le Réalisme dans* Jacques le fataliste (Paris, 1965), *passim*. For Diderot's novelistic techniques, see Alice G. Green, 'Diderot's Fictional Worlds,' *DS I* (1949), 1–26.

45. Vernière, 'Diderot et l'invention littéraire: . . . ,' *RHLF*, LIX, 153–67.

46. Venturi, *Jeunesse de Diderot*, 14–5, 337–8; Dieckmann, *Inventaire*, XLI.

47. A.-T., VI, 259.

48. Hans Mayer, 'Diderot und sein Roman "Jacques le Fataliste",' in *Grundpositionen der französischen Aufklärung,* ed. Krauss, 80; this article published separately in Hans Mayer, *Deutsche Literatur und Weltliteratur* (Berlin, [1957]), 317–49. Fabre, 'Allégorie et symbolisme dans *Jacques le fataliste,*' in *Europäische Aufklärung: Herbert Dieckmann zum 60. Geburtstag,* ed. Friedrich and Schalk, 70.

49. Stendhal (Alan Freer, 'Diderot et Stendhal,' Toulouse. Université, Faculté des Lettres, *Annales: littéraires,* XI [1962], 63–79). Balzac (Stephen J. Gendzier, 'L'Interprétation de la figure humaine chez Diderot et chez Balzac,' *Année Balzacienne,* III [1962], 181–93; Stephen J. Gendzier, 'Art Criticism and the Novel: Diderot and Balzac,' *FR,* XXXV [1961–2], 302–10; Stephen J. Gendzier, 'Balzac's Changing Attitudes toward Diderot,' *FS,* XIX [1965], 125–43; Stephen J. Gendzier, 'Diderot's Impact on the Generation of 1830,' *SVEC,* XXIII [1963], 93–103; Jean Seznec, 'Diderot et Sarrasine,' *DS IV* [1963], 237–45; Margaret Gilman, 'Balzac and Diderot: *Le Chef-d'oeuvre inconnu,*' *PMLA,* LXV [1950], 644–48). Warning, *Illusion und Wirklichkeit in Tristram Shandy und Jacques le fataliste,* 123; Jauss, 'Diderots Paradox über das Schauspiel (*Entretiens sur le 'Fils Naturel'*),' *Germanisch-Romanische Monatsschrift,* Neue Folge, XI, 410.

50. Fabre, 'Allégorie et symbolisme dans *Jacques le fataliste,*' op. cit., 69, 75. The article by Erich Köhler, ' "Est-ce que l'on sait où l'on va?" — Zur strukturellen Einheit von Diderots *Jacques le Fataliste et son Maître,*' *Romanistisches Jahrbuch,* XVI (1965), 126–48, is particularly illuminating. Also excellent is Jean Ehrard, 'Lumières et roman, ou les paradoxes de Denis le Fataliste,' in *Au Siècle des Lumières,* Ecole Pratique des Hautes Etudes — Sorbonne et L'Académie des Sciences de l'U.R.S.S. (Paris and Moscow, 1970), 137–55, esp. 150–1, 154–5.

51. Otis Fellows and Alice G. Green, 'Diderot and the Abbé Dulaurens,' *DS I* (1949), 78; Grimsley, 'L'Ambiguïté dans l'oeuvre romanesque de Diderot,' *CAIEF,* No. 13, 227. The most authoritative treatment of Spinoza's influence on Diderot is that by Paul Vernière, *Spinoza et la pensée française avant la Révolution* (Paris, 1954), 555–611; see also the useful review of this work by Roger Mercier, in *RHLF,* LVII (1957), 252–4; and by Roland Mortier, in *RLC,* XXXII (1958), 122–8. Also excellent is Loy, *Diderot's Determined Fatalist,* 150–5; see too its review by Paul Vernière, in *RHLF,* LI (1951), 391–2. See also Francis Pruner, *L'Unité secrète de* Jacques le fataliste (Paris, 1970), 13, 64, 124, 154, 167, 200, 202, 205, 283, 285–6, 291–3, 297.

52. Guy Robert, 'Le Destin et les lois dans Jacques le Fataliste,' *Information Littéraire,* III (1951), 128. In the *Réfutation d'Helvétius* Diderot spoke of the difficulty of dealing with this problem when all the concepts have to be expressed in language that presupposes freedom of the will. 'On est devenu philosophe dans ses systèmes et l'on reste peuple dans son propos' (A.-T., II, 373). 'Ces deux phrases forment le meilleur commentaire qu'on ait jamais écrit sur *Jacques le Fataliste*' (Jacques Proust, 'Diderot et les problèmes de langage,' *RFor,* LXXIX [1967], 26 n.).

53. Otis Fellows, '*Jacques le fataliste* Revisited,' *L'Esprit Créateur,* VIII (1968), 47; Ronald Grimsley, 'Morality and Imagination in *Jacques le Fataliste,*' *MLQ,* XIX (1958), 284. The pioneer major work in the recent crescendo of interest in *Jacques le fataliste* is Loy's excellent *Diderot's Determined Fatalist;* on Diderot's treatment of fatalism, see ibid., 128–60. Loy's book was the inspiration for an ecstatic and somewhat outré appreciation of *Jacques le fataliste* by Wilhelm Lunen, 'Appeal for an English Edition of Diderot's "Jack the Fatalist",' *Contemporary Issues,* IV (1952–3), 149–201; the same, 'Diderots "Jacques der Fatalist und sein Herr." (Gelegentlich des Fehlens einer englischen Ausgabe),' *Dinge der Zeit,* Folge 5, Heft 19 (July–Aug. 1955), 170–236. The interpretation of Jacques as being endowed with 'a degree of self-awareness which enables him to partake in the general creative process of life itself in a conscious way' is very well made by Jean A. Perkins, *The Concept of the Self in the French Enlightenment* (Geneva, 1969), 135–6.

54. A.-T., VI, 180–1; cf. also ibid., 168. Diderot used this same argument (that humanity is moral because it is illogical) in the *Entretien d'un philosophe avec la Maréchale de **** (A.-T., II, 510).

55. Cassirer, *The Philosophy of the Enlightenment,* 71–2. See also Per Nykrog, 'Les Etapes des amours de Jacques,' in *Etudes romanes dédiées à Andreas Blinkenberg à l'occasion de*

son 70ᵉ anniversaire (Copenhagen, 1963), 113–26, esp. 126. See also Per Nykrog, 'Un Diderot plus enthousiaste que nature,' *Orbis Litterarum*, XIX (1964), 227–8.

56. 'Diderot in search of an ethic' (Nola M. Leov, *'Jacques le fataliste*, poème parabolique,' *AUMLA*, No. 23 [1965], 24–48, esp. 30).

57. Hemsterhuis, *Lettre sur l'homme et ses rapports*, ed. May, 207; review of *Dieu et l'homme* (1771) par M. de Valmire (A.-T., IV, 93). See the penetrating comments by Jean Fabre, 'Actualité de Diderot,' *DS IV* (1963), 17–39, esp. 34–5.

58. See the excellent article by Georges May, 'Le Maître, la chaîne et le chien dans *Jacques le fataliste*,' *CAIEF*, No. 13 (June 1961), 269–82, esp. 280–1.

59. Cromwell (A.-T., VI, 274–5; Köhler, ' "Est-ce que l'on sait où l'on va?",' *Romanistisches Jahrbuch*, XVI, 139–40).

60. Jean Dutourd, 'Le Prolétaire errant,' *Nouvelle Nouvelle Revue Française* (Oct. 1958), 684–9, esp. 686. I have found especially valuable the brilliant essay by Jean Fabre, 'Sagesse et Morale dans *Jacques le Fataliste*,' *SPTB*, 171–87.

CHAPTER 47

1. Catherine II to Grimm, 10 March 1775 (Diderot, *Corr.*, XIV, 134–5).

2. Feeling complimented (Diderot to Catherine II, 6 Dec. 1775 [Diderot, *Corr.*, XIV, 172]). Quotation is from A.-T., III, 433. The preliminary 'Essai sur les études en Russie,' which especially recommends German and Protestant models (A.-T., III, 415–28), is now thought to be the work of Grimm; see Pierre C. Oustinoff, 'Notes on Diderot's Fortunes in Russia,' *DS I* (1949), 131–7.

3. 'Une affection de poitrine' (Diderot to Sartine, 12 July 1775 [Diderot, *Corr.*, XIV, 150]). Finished about late July (ibid., 172). Catherine II to Grimm, 10 Dec. 1775 and 31 Jan. 1776 (ibid., 181, 184).

4. A.-T., III, 429, 433. Gay, *The Enlightenment*, II, 520.

5. A.-T., III, 433, 530, 510–1.

6. A.-T., III, 436, 522, 524. Voltaire (ibid., 444).

7. A.-T., III, 435–6, 469–73. For Diderot's interesting but somewhat irrelevant discussion of a great range of classical authors (A.-T., III, 477–88).

8. Diderot's omission of modern languages (E. Merle, 'Diderot et son programme d'éducation (D'après le "Plan pour une université"),' *Technique — Art — Science: Revue de l'Enseignement Technique*, Nouvelle Série, No. 114 [Jan. 1958], 43–52, and No. 115 [Feb. 1958], 39–45, this reference No. 115, 45). Inspections, etc. (A.-T., III, 508, 531). Virtuous and enlightened men (A.-T., III, 439; see Hermand, *Les Idées morales de Diderot*, 49).

9. A.-T., III, 499, 503. Anatomy in Russia (ibid., 500). A bad doctor an epidemic (ibid., 498). Cf. A. Bigot, 'Diderot et la médicine,' *Cahiers Haut-Marnais*, No. 24 (1ᵉʳ trimestre 1951), 37–47.

10. To Catherine II, 6 Dec. 1775 (Diderot, *Corr.*, XIV, 173–4); A.-T., III, 532–3. Regarding the *Plan d'une Université*, see Denise-Jacqueline Chevalier, 'Diderot et l'éducation,' *Pensée*, No. 146 (Aug. 1969), 128–41; Avédik Mesrobian, *Les Conceptions pédagogiques de Diderot* (Paris, [1913]), *passim* and esp. 79–80; and Mortier, 'The "Philosophes" and Public Education,' *Yale French Studies*, No. 40, 72–3. Finishing the *Plan* hastily (Diderot to Grimm, 13 Dec. 1776 [Diderot, *Corr.*, XV, 27]). Also Diderot to Grimm, 9 June 1777 (ibid., 61–2).

11. A.-T., III, 540–4; in Diderot, *Corr.*, XII, 36–42, where it is dated as being *c.* 1772. It is also in Johansson, *Etudes sur Denis Diderot*, 94–108; see ibid., 110–4, which may possibly be the essay written by the Comtesse de Forbach. Dieckmann, *Inventaire*, 83.

12. Diderot to Grimm, ? May and 28 June 1770 (Diderot, *Corr.*, X, 56, 78). Marie-Anne, née Camasse, married Christian IV of Zweibrücken on 3 Sept. 1757 (ibid., XII, 35–6).

13. The Countess de Forbach introduced to the Diderot family a young Strasburg painter and architect named Mannlich. Many years later, probably between 1813 and 1818, Mannlich wrote his memoirs, which were first published in 1910 (Eugen Stollreither, *Ein deutscher Maler und Hofmann. Lebenserinnerungen des Johann Christian von Mannlich, 1741–1822, nach der französischen Originalhandschrift herausgegeben* [Berlin, 1910],

ix–x, 3). Mannlich's memoirs, which he boasted he wrote from memory and without benefit of notes (Stollreither, op. cit., x), contain some sensational pages on the Diderots (ibid., 212–5, 217–9, 222, 234–8, 281). The Countess, says Mannlich (ibid., 243), wanted him to marry Angélique Diderot. In February 1774 (ibid., 250) Mannlich says that he was in Paris and visited Diderot at that time, who told him that Angélique had eloped! Inasmuch as Diderot at this time was in Russia and Angélique had been married to Vandeul since 1772, these anachronisms throw a heavy cloud over the veridicality of Mannlich's recollections. Mannlich's vindictiveness, it has been conjectured, was caused by his being an unsuccessful suitor for Angélique's hand; see the convincing article by Hubert Gautier, 'A propos de Madame Diderot et du mariage de sa fille,' *Bulletin de la Société d'Emulation du Bourbonnais*, xxxvi (1933), 253–64. A notorious Diderot-hater, Ernest Seillière, gave publicity to Mannlich's recollections (Ernest Seillière, 'Quelques documents nouveaux sur Diderot,' *Séances et Travaux de l'Académie des Sciences Morales et Politiques*, clxxviii [1912], 568–75; the same, 'Un Témoin de la vie parisienne au temps de Louis XV. Les "Mémoires" du peintre J.-C. de Mannlich,' *RDM*, ccxxxii [1 July 1912], 199–228). It is noticeable that serious researchers have ignored Mannlich's testimony.

14. Diderot to Catherine II, 6 Dec. 1775 (Diderot, *Corr.*, xiv, 174–5); Diderot, *Mémoires pour Catherine II*, ed. Vernière, 81. For some crumbs of information on Diderot and the army, see Emile-G. Léonard, *L'Armée et ses problèmes au XVIIIᵉ siècle* (Paris, [1958]), 260–3. The diplomat was Marie-Daniel Bourrée, Baron de Corberon, *Un Diplomate français à la cour de Catherine II, 1775–1780*, ed. L.-H. Labande, 2 vols. (Paris, 1901), I, 19 [sometime between 17 Feb. and 12 April 1775]. Corberon later wrote that Diderot had not responded to a list of questions he had given him (ibid., I, 216).

15. Diderot, *Corr.*, xiv, 157–8.

16. See his defense of Turgot's abolition of the guilds (Diderot to Galiani via Mme d'Epinay [Diderot, *Corr.*, xiv, 190–2]; also A.-T., ii, 393 [*Réfutation d'Helvétius*]).

17. George Rudé, *The Crowd in History: A Study of Popular Disturbances in France and England, 1730–1848* (New York, 1964), 22–30; with an excellent map, p. 25. Cf. Vladimir Sergeevich Liublinskiĭ, 'Voltaire et la guerre des farines,' *AHRF*, xxxi (1959), 127–45.

18. Diderot, *Corr.*, xiv, 142–7.

19. Charles Nauroy, *Le Curieux*, 2 vols. (Paris, 1883–8), I, 11 (15 Oct. 1883); Diderot, *Corr.*, xiv, 148. 'Grandpérisé' (Diderot, *Corr.*, xiv, 151). Diderot to Denise, 8 Dec. 1775 (ibid., xiv, 179).

20. 12 July 1775 (Diderot, *Corr.*, xiv, 151, 152).

21. D'Angiviller to Diderot, 17 Oct. 1775 (Diderot, *Corr.*, xiv, 167–9). Charles-Claude de La Billarderie, Comte d'Angiviller, *Mémoires*, ed. Louis Bobé (Copenhagen, 1933), 44–6. D'Angiviller, who was a believer and once got into an argument with Diderot at the Neckers' about the existence of God, declared Diderot to be a 'cynique impudent et hypocrite à la fois' (ibid., 40, 29; also 36, 39, 42, 58, 60). D'Angiviller had known Angélique Diderot since 1772 at least (Diderot, *Corr.*, xii, 115). Regarding him, see Leith, *The Idea of Art as Propaganda in France*, 77–80.

22. Diderot, *Salons*, iv, xv–xvii; for the text of the *Salon de 1775*, see ibid., 274–92.

23. Text in Diderot, *Oeuvres esthétiques*, ed. Vernière, 743–840; also in A.-T., xii, 75–133. Written in 1775–6 (May, 'Les "Pensées détachées sur la peinture" de Diderot. . . ,' *RHLF*, lxx, 57). Possibility of later revision (Diderot, *Oeuvres esthétiques*, ed. Vernière, 746; Robert Niklaus, in *MLR*, lxiv [1969], 172).

24. Quotation (Diderot, *Oeuvres esthétiques*, ed. Vernière, 826). Other references (ibid., 772, 801, 802, 807, 810, 826, 827). As an appendix to his MS of the *Pensées détachées*, Diderot added a list of *Noms des peintres et leur genre* (Dieckmann, *Inventaire*, 48–9). Part of this was published by Franco Venturi from the Diderot MSS in Leningrad; it mentions paintings seen at Düsseldorf, Dresden, and The Hague (Denis Diderot, 'Fragments inédits d'un projet de Dictionnaire des Peintres,' *Hippocrate*, vi [1938], 321–7). Regarding one of the entries in Diderot's list, see Gita May, 'Diderot et la *Présentation au Temple* de Giotto,' *MLN*, lxxv (1960), 229–33.

25. Diderot's single reference to Hagedorn (Diderot, *Oeuvres esthétiques*, ed. Vernière, 835). For parallel passages in Hagedorn and Diderot, see Vernière, 'Diderot et C. L. de Hagedorn: Une étude d'influence,' *RLC*, xxx, 242–51; and Friedrich Bassenge, 'Diderots Pensées Détachées sur la Peinture und Hagedorns Betrachtungen über die Malerei,' *Germanisch-romanische Monatsschrift*, Neue Folge, xvii (1967), 260–3. Quotation (Vernière, art. cit., 254). For a severe but not intemperate judgment of the *Pensées détachées*, see Cartwright, *Diderot critique d'art et le problème de l'expression* (*DS XIII*), 209–18.
26. Diderot, *Oeuvres esthétiques*, ed. Vernière, 767, 769. For an excellent general essay on this transformation, see Rémy G. Saisselin, 'The Transformation of Art into Culture: From Pascal to Diderot,' *SVEC*, lxx (1970), esp. 214–7.
27. May, 'Les "Pensées détachées sur la peinture" de Diderot. . . ,' *RHLF*, lxx, 54; Koscziusko, 'Diderot et Hagedorn,' *RLC*, xvi, 668.
28. Diderot, *Oeuvres esthétiques*, ed. Vernière, 825, 824. The *Pensées détachées* was circulated in the *Corr. litt.* in 1777 (De Booy, 'Inventory,' 386). It is possible that Schiller had access to it and that Diderot's conception of the naïve influenced Schiller's essay contrasting naïve with sentimental poetry (cf. Jean-Jacques Mayoux, 'Les Doctrines littéraires de Diderot et l' "Encyclopédie",' *AUP*, 122). Regarding Diderot's doctrine of the naïve as the opposite of the hypocritical, the mannered, or the vicious, see David Funt, 'On the Conception of the "Vicieux" in Diderot,' *DS X* (1968), 58, 62–3.
29. Diderot, *Oeuvres esthétiques*, ed. Vernière, 812–3, 825.
30. 'Etrennes du philosophe à sa vieille amie' (*Corr. litt.*, xi, 405–6 [Jan. 1777]). For a detailed and authoritative appreciation of the *Pensées détachées*, see May, 'Les "Pensées détachées sur la peinture" de Diderot. . . ,' *RHLF*, lxx, 45–63; see also Saisselin, 'Some Remarks on French Eighteenth-Century Writings on the Arts,' *JAAC*, xxv, 194–5.
31. At Sèvres (Diderot, *Corr.*, xiv, 205; xv, 15, 30). At Grandval (ibid., xiv, 239). Quotation (ibid., xv, 15).
32. Diderot to Voltaire, 19 June 1776 (Diderot, *Corr.*, xiv, 202–3); to Dr. Burney, first fortnight in June 1776 (ibid., 196–7); to John Wilkes, first fortnight in June 1776 (ibid., 198–200). Wilkes noted that he had received this letter 25 June 1776. For Voltaire's reply about the Marquis de Limon (Diderot, *Corr.*, xiv, 208–9).
33. First quotation (Diderot, *Corr.*, xiv, 218); second quotation (ibid., xv, 24 [13 Dec. 1776]). Grimm in Saint Petersburg (*Corr. litt.*, i, 21). Dr. Roux (Diderot, *Corr.*, xiv, 204). Mlle de Lespinasse (ibid., 193; *Corr. litt.*, xi, 262–5 [May 1776]). Mme Geoffrin (Diderot, *Corr.*, xiv, 213).
34. To Denise, 7 Oct. 1776 (Diderot, *Corr.*, xiv, 230); to Grimm, 13 or 14 Oct. 1776 (ibid., xiv, 238–9). The relevant sentence is (239): '. . . je n'en porte [pas] moins en l'air le lituus augural.' Nicolas de Chamfort wrote in his *Caractères et anecdotes* (Paris, 1924), 101, item cclxxi: 'Diderot, âgé de soixante-deux ans, et amoureux de toutes les femmes, disait à un de ses amis: "Je me dis souvent à moi-même: vieux fou, vieux gueux, quand cessaras-tu donc de t'exposer à l'affront d'un refus ou d'un ridicule?" ' This well-known anecdote does not seem to me to be very characteristic of Diderot; it implies a degree of would-be promiscuity that is not confirmed or reinforced by other sources.
35. Galiani (Diderot, *Corr.*, xiv, 190–2). Intercepted letters (Diderot to M.-M. Rey, 14 April 1777 [Diderot, *Corr.*, xv, 49–52; see also ibid., 53]). Diderot to Grimm, 17 Nov. 1776 (ibid., xv, 17).
36. Diderot, *Corr.*, xiv, 212. For a contemporaneous discussion of these events, see *Corr. litt.*, xi, 214–21, 299, 379–83.
37. Desné, 'Diderot et Shakespeare,' *RLC*, xli, 565, 571. Diderot, *Corr.*, xv, 37–9 (18 Dec. 1776). Diderot also compared Shakespeare to the St. Christopher in the *Paradoxe sur le comédien* (A.-T., viii, 384). Tronchin, *Le Conseiller François Tronchin et ses amis. . . ,* 221. Diderot's ébauche of *Térentia* (A.-T., viii, 287–336).
38. Diderot to Denise, 18 Dec. 1776 (Diderot, *Corr.*, xv, 33); for a detailed account of the growth of Vandeul's fortune, see ibid., 31–2; see also Massiet du Biest, *Monsieur de Vandeul*, 73–6. Diderot to Necker, 3 April 1777 (ibid., 45–7); also Diderot to Grimm, 9 June 1777 (ibid., 60).
39. Caroillon de la Charmotte [Vandeul's brother] to their mother, 11 April 1777 (Diderot, *Corr.*, xv, 48).

40. Mme de Vandeul, LIV.

41. Diderot's contributions can be studied best of all in the parallel columns set up by Hans Wolpe, *Raynal et sa machine de guerre: L'*Histoire des deux Indes *et ses perfectionnements* (Stanford [Cal.], 1957), Appendice II: 'Diderot et l'*Histoire des deux Indes,*' 190–203, 210–37. Although Naigeon wrote that 'M. Diderot n'a rien mis du sien dans la 2e édition de l'Abbé Raynal' (Massiet du Biest, 'Lettres inédites de Naigeon à M^r et Mme de Vandeul (1786–1787). . . ,' *BSHAL*, 1 Jan. 1948, 4), the Wolpe analysis (see esp. Wolpe, op. cit., 250) proves Naigeon's statement erroneous. Virgil W. Topazio, 'Diderot's Supposed Contributions to Raynal's Work,' *Symposium*, XII (1958), 103–16, argues that Diderot's total contribution was sparse and relatively insignificant.

42. Michèle Duchet, 'Diderot collaborateur de Raynal: A propos des "Fragments imprimés" du Fonds Vandeul,' *RHLF*, LX (1960), 543 and n.; Duchet, *Anthropologie et Histoire au siècle des lumières*, 410–3, 469–75.

43. Mme de Vandeul, LIV. Regarding the continuing intellectual growth of Diderot in these years, see the remarks by Herbert Dieckmann, 'Les Contributions de Diderot à la "Correspondance littéraire" et à l' "Histoire des Deux Indes",' *RHLF*, LI (1951), 435; also Duchet, art. cit., 545, 546.

44. Diderot to Grimm, 25 March 1781 (Dieckmann, *Inventaire*, 252; also in Diderot, *Corr.*, XV, 225–6). Meister reports a similar conversation in his *Aux Mânes de Diderot* (A.-T., I, xvii n.).

45. A.-T., I, xvii n.

46. Dieckmann, art. cit., *RHLF*, LI, 418–9. According to an author hostile to the *philosophes,* Jacques Mallet du Pan, *Mémoires et correspondance de Mallet du Pan pour servir à l'histoire de la Révolution française*, ed. Pierre-André Sayous, 2 vols. (Paris, 1851), I, 46 n., Diderot received 10,000 livres. Mallet du Pan claimed he had seen the contract.

47. The best summary of the present state of researches is in Duchet, art. cit., 531–2. The most important studies on this subject are those by Dieckmann, *Inventaire,* 93–4, 123–6, 136–41, 151–5; and in his 'Les Contributions de Diderot. . . ,' *RHLF*, LI, 417–40. Also Wolpe, op. cit., *passim*, and Duchet, art. cit., 532–56. Also important is Benot, *Diderot, de l'athéisme à l'anticolonialisme*, 162–259. These studies confirm the earlier hypotheses of Anatole Feugère, 'Raynal, Diderot et quelques autres "historiens des deux Indes",' *RHLF*, XX (1913), 343–78; see also Anatole Feugère, *Un Précurseur de la Révolution: L'Abbé Raynal (1713–1796)* (Angoulême, 1922), ch. v.

48. 'Un troupeau de bêtes' (A.-T., VI, 448). For the passage in which Diderot speaks of 'volonté générale' and 'lèse-société,' see the text in Dieckmann, 'Les Contributions de Diderot à la "Correspondance Littéraire" et à l'"Histoire des Deux Indes",' *RHLF*, LI, 437–8. Regarding Diderot's authorship of this and similar passages, see Dieckmann, ibid., 419. 'Peuples, . . . votre volonté générale' (A.-T., VI, 448).

49. Diderot, *Corr.,* XV, 50–1, 54; see the plausible conjectures in ibid., 106–7.

50. Diderot, *Corr.,* XV, 40, 50, 57 n., 60, 64, 71.

51. Diderot, *Corr.,* XV, 60, 34; cf. ibid., 30.

52. To Beaumarchais, 5 Aug. 1777 (Diderot, *Corr.,* XV, 71–2). To Sébastien Mercier, June–July 1777 (?) (ibid., 64–6); I follow Jean Varloot in concluding that the Mercier letter is of this time and is somehow tied to the Beaumarchais project.

53. *Corr. litt.,* XI, 474.

54. François Tronchin to Diderot, 6 July 1777 (Diderot, *Corr.,* XV, 67–9); Diderot to Tronchin, 23 Dec. 1777 (ibid., 80–3). Incised on the base of the bust is: 'Diderot, par Pigalle, son compère, tous deux agés de 63 ans.' This bust is barely mentioned, and then only vaguely, by P. Tarbé, *La Vie et les oeuvres de Jean-Baptiste Pigalle, sculpteur* (Paris, 1859), 94.

55. Diderot to Grimm, 9 June 1777 (Diderot, *Corr.,* XV, 61). *La Pièce et le prologue* is edited best in Diderot, *Est-il bon? Est-il méchant?,* ed. Undank (*SVEC*, XVI), 148–397; it is also published in A.-T., VIII, 69–133. It appeared in the *Corr. litt.* for July and August 1777 (De Booy, 'Inventaire,' 386–7). For a discussion of the chronology of the various stages of evolution of the play, see Diderot, *Est-il bon? Est-il méchant?,* ed. Undank, 31–6.

56. Diderot, *Est-il bon? Est-il méchant?,* ed. Undank, 141–7; A.-T., VIII, 61–8. It appeared in the *Corr. litt.* for Nov. 1775 (De Booy, 'Inventaire,' 386).

57. For an analysis of the complicated history of the successive stages, see the Undank ed., 13–30; also Dieckmann, *Inventaire*, 4–5, 33–4. The play was first published in the *Revue Rétrospective*, première série, III (1834), 161–261. The best edition now is that by Undank; in the A.-T. edition it is VIII, 145–244. *Est-il bon? Est-il méchant?* was produced in a revised and abridged version by Antoine, at the Odéon in 1913 (Paul Degouy, 'Diderot: "Est-il bon? Est-il méchant?",' *Grande Revue*, LXXXI [1913], 326 n.). The première at the Comédie-Française was 22 Nov. 1955; it received a total of 35 performances. Among the reviews, Diderot's language was especially praised by Jean Gandrey-Rety, in *Lettres Françaises*, 1–7 Dec. 1955, 9; and Jacques Lemarchand, 'Diderot,' *Nouvelle Nouvelle Revue Française*, IV (1956), 128–31; also Jean de Beer, 'Diderot et la Comédie-Française,' *Europe*, Nos. 405–6 (Jan.–Feb. 1963), 225–6.

58. Act III, scene iii. Worth remembering is the article by Louis Ganderax, 'A propos du centénaire de Diderot,' *RDM*, 15 July 1884, 454, 463.

59. Rue Taranne (Act I, scene viii); Sedaine (Yves Benot, 'A propos de la création d' "Est-il bon? Est-il méchant?" à la Comédie Française. Sedaine "nègre" de Diderot,' *Lettres Françaises*, 24–30 Nov. 1955, 1, 8). Dubucq (Diderot, *Corr.*, V, 142–3, 144–5 [20 Oct. 1765], 235; ibid., VI, 35; ibid., XV, 161 [9 Oct. 1779]). See also A.-T., VI, 417–8). Rodier (Diderot, *Corr.*, III, 164; ibid., IV, 318; also Jacques Proust, in *RHLF*, LXIII, 318 n.).

60. Diderot, *Corr.*, VIII, 201–2 [26 Oct. 1768], 209. For the biographical and autobiographical sources of the play, see Diderot, *Est-il bon? Est-il méchant?*, ed. Undank, 40–6, 63–5, 401–6, 94–135. See also Beverly S. Ridgely, 'Additional Sources for Diderot's *Est-il bon? Est-il méchant?*,' *MLN*, LXVII (1952), 443–6.

61. *Paradoxe sur le comédien* (A.-T., VIII, 382), in a revision written not later than 29 June 1777 (Diderot, *Est-il bon? Est-il méchant?*, ed. Undank, 399–401).

62. Comment by the Abbé Arnaud (Joseph Reinach, *Diderot* [Paris, 1894], 146).

63. Fritz Schalk, 'Zur französischen Komödie der Aufklärung,' in *Europäische Aufklärung: Herbert Dieckmann zum 60. Geburtstag*, ed. Friedrich and Schalk, 258–9. A very perceptive article by Roberto F. Giusti, 'Diderot,' *Cursos y Conferencias* (Revista del Colegio Libre de Estudios Superiores, Buenos Aires), XXXIX (1951), 223–45, speaks of Hardouin's relation to the other personages in the play as being like that of Pirandello's *Six Characters in Search of an Author* (223, 227).

64. Diderot, *Est-il bon? Est-il méchant?*, ed. Undank, 132–3; Jacques Proust, reviewing the Undank edition, in *RHLF*, LXIII (1963), 319; Lefebvre, *Diderot*, 245; Lecercle, 'Diderot et le réalisme bourgeois dans la littérature du XVIIIe siècle,' *Pensée*, No. 38, 66.

65. See the Undank edition, 94–114: 'Hardouin et Diderot'; Ronald Grimsley, in *MLR*, LVII (1962), 613.

66. Voltaire to Diderot, 8 Dec. 1776 (Diderot, *Corr.*, XV, 18; Besterman, No. 19311). Diderot eloquently defended Voltaire to Naigeon, and at a time, too, when Voltaire was favoring Maupeou and was also being critical of the *Système de la nature* (Diderot, *Corr.*, XII, 53–5).

67. François Métra, *Correspondance secrète, politique et littéraire*, 18 vols. (London, 1787–90), VI, 292 (13 June 1778). Regarding the identity of Métra, see J. Viktor Johansson, *Sur la Correspondance littéraire secrète et son éditeur* (Paris and Gothenburg, [1960]), esp. 93–7.

68. Métra, *Correspondance secrète, politique et littéraire*, VI, 424–6 (8 Sept. 1778). Marie-Jean Hérault de Séchelles, *Voyage à Montbar, contenant des détails très-intéressans sur le caractère, la personne et les écrits de Buffon* (Paris, An IX [1803]), 133.

69. A.-T., III, 394.

70. Diderot, *Corr.*, XV, 87 n.

71. It is just possible that Voltaire went to Sèvres to see Diderot; this would explain why there were no eye-witnesses (Jean Fabre, 'Deux définitions du philosophe: Voltaire et Diderot,' *Table Ronde*, No. 122 [Feb. 1958], 138–40). However, M. Fabre remarks (ibid., 140 n.) that Ira O. Wade 'a bien voulu me confirmer qu'il ne croyait pas plus que moi-même à l'historicité de la rencontre entre Voltaire et Diderot.' Neither does Paul Vernière (Diderot, *Oeuvres esthétiques*, ed. Vernière, 332 n.). Desnoiresterres, *Voltaire et la société au XVIIIe siècle*, VIII, 127, asserts that the interview took place and that it occurred at the hôtel of Voltaire's niece, Mme de Villette, but he adduces no evidence.

72. The *première* of Barthe's *L'Homme personnel* took place on 21 Feb. 1778; for Diderot's assistance, see *Corr. litt.*, XII, 61. The verses are 'Mon Portrait et mon horoscope' (A.-T.,

IX, 56–7), and 'Le Marchand de Loto' (A.-T., IX, 66–7); see Diderot, *Corr.*, XV, 84. Diderot to Mme Necker [1777] (Diderot, *Corr.*, XV, 76–9), in behalf of a Mme Pillain de Val du Fresne. Diderot to Münich, winter of 1777–8 (Diderot, *Corr.*, XV, 94–6), in behalf of a Mme Testart.

73. 25 Nov. 1778 (Diderot, *Corr.*, XV, 126). The Diderots had previously helped a Diderot cousin named Humblot, who was in the hospital, and had paid for the keep of a little girl in a convent, 'pour sauver son innocence exposée, même à cet âge [elle avait dix ans], dans la maison paternelle.' Diderot sent word to his brother the Abbé that he would gladly receive help from the Abbé for these charities (Diderot, *Corr.*, XIV, 231–2 [7 Oct. 1776]; ibid., XV, 34 [18 Dec. 1776]). The Abbé had sometime not long previously received Mme de Vandeul on one of her visits to Langres (Diderot, *Corr.*, XV, 133), and it may be that the tension in family relations was now somewhat relaxed. Now and again, in 1778 and 1779, Diderot talked of visiting Langres himself (Diderot, *Corr.*, XV, 127 and n., 137, 152).

74. Adriaan-Gilles Camper, *Notice de la vie et des écrits de Pierre Camper* (Paris, An XI [1803]), xli. Francis Decrue de Stoutz, *L'Ami de Rousseau et des Necker, Paul Moultou, à Paris en 1778* (Paris, 1926), 127. Diderot to Desessarts, 28 Oct. 1778 (Diderot, *Corr.*, XV, 109–10).

75. Diderot, *Corr.*, XV, 65; see also ibid., 68. Decrue, op. cit., 127. Approbation (Diderot, *Corr.*, XV, 125). Publication (A.-T., III, 4).

76. La Grange died 18 Oct. 1775 (*Le Nécrologe des hommes célèbres de France*, XII, 207; *Corr. litt.*, XI, 144–5). Diderot, *Corr.*, XV, 111, 114; Diderot, *Essai sur Sénèque*, ed. Nakagawa, I, 5, 8. Mme de Vandeul, liv.

77. A.-T., I, 118 n. His recanting (Diderot, *Essai sur Sénèque*, ed. Nakagawa, I, 164–7). 'La difficulté & la dignité de son rôle' (ibid., I, 7).

78. Diderot, *Essai sur Sénèque*, ed. Nakagawa, II, 78.

79. The Rev. Dr. Warner to George Selwyn, Paris, 28 Dec. [1778] (John Heneage Jesse, *George Selwyn and his Contemporaries*, 4 vols. [London, 1882], III, 378).

80. *Corr. litt.*, XII, 194, 196.

81. *Année Littéraire*, vol. 1 for 1779, 36–70, 104–36; quotations, ibid., 64, 107, 106. Fréron died on 10 March 1776 (*Journal de Politique et de Littérature*, 15 March 1776, 337).

82. Rousseau's request (Pierre Chevallier, 'Les Philosophes et le Lieutenant de Police (1775–1785),' *FS*, XVII [1963], 110). Bachaumont, *Mémoires secrets*, XII, 46.

83. Diderot, *Essai sur Sénèque*, ed. Nakagawa, I, 83–4; A.-T., III, 90–1. *Corr. litt.*, XII, 197. A comprehensive criticism appearing in the Abbé Grosier's *Journal de Littérature, des Sciences et des Arts*, vol. 1 for 1779, 177–206, 343–72, called the attack upon Rousseau 'a cowardly insult' (371). For Diderot's reply (which omitted any reference to Rousseau), see *Corr. litt.*, XII, 297–302 (Sept. 1779). Likewise very critical was the long review in the *Journal de Paris*, 25 Jan. 1779, 97–9: 'L'Auteur de l'*Essai sur la vie de Sénèque* a voulu qu'il ne manquât à son livre aucune espèce de bizarrerie' (99).

84. Noteworthy is Fritz Schalk, *Diderots Essai über Claudius und Nero* (Cologne, 1956), esp. 13; reprinted in his *Studien zur französischen Aufklärung* (Munich, 1964), 148–70. Also J. Robert Loy, 'L'Essai sur les règnes de Claude et de Néron,' *CAIEF*, No. 13 (June 1961), 239–54. A very thoughtful comparison of the two editions is made by Douglas A. Bonneville, *Diderot's* Vie de Sénèque: *A Swan Song Revised* (Gainesville [Fla.], 1966), *passim*.

85. The autobiographical nature of the *Essai* is mentioned by Schalk, op. cit., 24, 27; Loy, art. cit., 248; Bonneville, op. cit., 6; and most especially by Casini, *Diderot 'philosophe,'* 386–8.

86. '. . . Diderot était le législateur sans efficacité d'un autre tyran' (Jean Fabre, in *CAIEF*, No. 13 [June 1961], 396). References to Catherine II (Diderot, *Essai sur Sénèque*, ed. Nakagawa, I, 96; II, 24, 205; in A.-T., III, 103, 219, 400).

CHAPTER 48

1. Diderot was in touch with Leuchsenring as early as 1773 (Diderot, *Corr.*, XIII, 14, 40). Regarding him, see Mortier, *Diderot en Allemagne*, 41–3; and Mortier, 'Le "Journal de

Lecture" de F.-M. Leuchsenring (1775–1779) et l'esprit "philosophique",' *RLC*, xxix, 205–22. In 1775 Leuchsenring proposed to Lavater that Diderot collaborate in a revision and translation of Lavater's *Physiognomische Fragmente*, but nothing came of this suggestion (ibid., 209; Diderot, *Corr.*, xiv, 182). That Diderot was much interested in physiognomy is proved by Proust, 'Diderot et la physiognomonie,' *CAIEF*, No. 13 (June 1961), 317–29. In 1778 Leuchsenring published the *Lettre à Madame la Comtesse de Forbach sur l'éducation des enfants* (*Journal de Lecture*, xi [1778], 217–28), and in 1779 the *Regrets sur ma vieille robe de chambre* (ibid., xii [1779], 160–7); an itemized list of these publications in Mortier, art. cit., 217–8.

2. Dominique-Joseph Garat, 'Lettre aux auteurs du Journal de Paris, sur la notice qu'ils ont donnée de la Vie de Sénèque,' *Mercure de France*, 15 Feb. 1779, 172–4. The whole 'Lettre' is 172–90; also in Diderot, *Corr.*, xv, 130–1.

3. Diderot, *Essai sur Sénèque*, ed. Nakagawa, ii, 196–7; A.-T., iii, 392. See the interesting article by Roland Mortier, 'L' "Original" selon Diderot,' *Saggi e Richerche di Letteratura Francese*, iv (1963), 141–57.

4. 10 Feb. 1774 (Elme Caro, *La Fin du dix-huitième siècle: Etudes et portraits*, 2nd ed., 2 vols. [Paris, 1881], i, 326 n.).

5. Jean-François de La Harpe, *Cours de littérature*, 14 vols. (Paris, 1829), i, ix–x. La Harpe, who was born in 1739, says this interview occurred when he was seventeen.

6. Luneau de Boisjermain (A.-T., xx, 134 n. 3). Björnståhl, *Briefe aus seinen ausländischen Reisen*, iii, 222 (31 Oct. 1774).

7. *Journal Encyclopédique*, vol. iii for 1786, partie I, 51–60, esp. 59–60 (1 April 1786). A.-T., xx, 135 n. 1. Sometimes Diderot describes to his correspondents his pantomime: cf. Diderot, *Corr.*, v, 75 (1 Aug. 1765); or visualizes what his demeanor would have been in a given situation (*Corr. litt.*, iii, 26 [15 May 1755]).

8. '. . . de cette grâce, de cette onction qu'il donne à ce qu'il dit' (Suard to the Margrave de Bayreuth, 20 Nov. 1774 [Diderot, *Corr.*, xiv, 107]).

9. Mlle de Lespinasse to Guibert, 25 Oct. 1774 and 24 June 1773 (Lespinasse, *Correspondance*, ed. Villeneuve-Guibert, 229, 25).

10. 'Il est comme un enfant . . .' (Grimm to Nesselrode, 25 Nov. 1773 [*Sbornik*, xvii, 283]); '. . . il faut le traiter comme un enfant . . .' (same to the same, 7 Feb. 1774 [ibid., 284]).

11. Mlle de Lespinasse to Guibert, 30 Oct. 1774 (Lespinasse, *Correspondance*, ed. Villeneuve-Guibert, 237); Suard to the Margrave of Bayreuth, 20 Nov. 1774 (Diderot, *Corr.*, xiv, 108).

12. Hemsterhuis to Princess Galitzin, 28 July 1777 (Brugmans, 'Diderot, Le Voyage de Hollande,' in *Connaissance de l'étranger: Mélanges . . . Jean-Marie Carré*, 158); cf. same to same, 12 Feb. 1784 (ibid., 157 n.).

13. Diderot, *Corr.*, xv, 146, 146–7; cf. ibid., 143.

14. For all this correspondence, see Diderot, *Corr.*, xv, 155–8, 159–63, 164–5. The letter to the Abbé Le Monnier, 9 Oct. 1779 (ibid., 159–63) is Diderot at his best. Michèle Duchet, 'Un Ami de Diderot en Guyane: Vallet de Fayolle,' *DS VIII* (1966), 15–21. Concern for Vallet de Fayolle is frequently expressed in Diderot's letters to Sophie; cf. Diderot, *Corr.*, v, 234–5 (30 Dec. 1765); ibid., vii, 123–4 (13 Sept. 1767), 218 (Nov. 1767).

15. Diderot to Catherine II, 29 June 1779 (Diderot, *Corr.*, xv, 149–50; cf. also ibid., xv, 143, 145, 153). Previously, Diderot had asked Catherine II some favor in behalf of his son-in-law, to judge from a cryptic fragment of her letter to Grimm, 18 Feb. 1778 (Tourneux, *Diderot et Catherine II*, 506; *Sbornik*, xxiii, 82).

16. De Booy, 'A propos de l' "Encyclopédie" en Espagne: Diderot, Miguel Gijón et Pablo de Olavide,' *RLC*, xxxv, 596–616, esp. 598–9 and 602.

17. 'Don Pablo Olavidès. Précis historique rédigé sur des mémoires fournis à M. Diderot par un Espagnol' (A.-T., vi, 467–72, passage quoted 472; also published [in the text from the Fonds Vandeul] in Marcelin Defourneaux, *Pablo de Olavide ou l'Afrancesado (1725–1803)* [Paris, 1959], 471–5). Published in the *Corr. litt.* for Feb. 1780 (De Booy, 'Inventaire,' 389). Olavide came to reside in Paris in May 1781; M. de Booy has conclusively shown that he and Diderot became well acquainted (De Booy, art. cit., 611–4).

18. A.-T., vi, 458–66. Published in the *Corr. litt.* for April 1780 (De Booy, 'Inventaire,' 389). Cf. Defourneaux, *Pablo de Olavide*, 471.

19. Procès-verbal de la délibération du Conseil municipal de Langres, 29 Aug. 1780 (Diderot, *Corr.*, xv, 183–4); Rivot, maire de Langres, to Diderot, 2 Sept. 1780 (ibid., 185–6); same to the same, 11 Sept. 1780 (ibid., 187–9); same to the same, 8 April 1781 (ibid., 228–31); procès-verbal de la municipalité de Langres, 30 April 1781 (ibid., 233–5); mayor and aldermen of Langres to Diderot, 1 May 1781 (ibid., 235–6). The 'frugal repast' took place on 30 April 1781 (ibid., 234); its menu is to be found in Marcel, *Le Frère de Diderot*, 112–3 and n., and in Billy, *Diderot*, 595–6. Mme de Vandeul, lix–lx; Diderot, *Corr.*, xv, 246.

20. Diderot to Galitzin, 9 Oct. 1780 (Diderot, *Corr.*, xv, 191–5); the Swiss publisher, J.-P. Heubach of Lausanne, also wrote to Diderot, 27 Jan. 1781, regarding the publication of these letters (ibid., 202–5).

21. Haller's work appeared from 1757 to 1766. The best edition of Diderot's *Eléments de physiologie* is that by Jean Mayer (Paris, 1964). It is based upon a comparison of the text in the Fonds Vandeul with that in Leningrad, and completely supersedes the text in A.-T., ix, 253–429.

22. Casini, *Diderot 'philosophe,'* 263 n.; Dieckmann, 'J.-A. Naigeon's Analysis of Diderot's *Rêve de d'Alembert,'* *MLN*, liii, 485.

23. Diderot to François Tronchin, 29 Aug. 1780 (Diderot, *Corr.*, xv, 181–3). Diderot's dependence on Haller is emphasized by Y. and T. François, 'Quelques remarques sur les "Eléments de Physiologie" de Diderot,' *RHS*, v (1952), 77–82.

24. 'Sur l'*Histoire de la Chirurgie*, par M. Peyrilhe' (A.-T., ix, 470–6, this quotation 472; regarding the dating of this piece, see Diderot's letter to an unidentified publisher [Diderot, *Corr.*, xv, 198–9]).

25. For an excellent analysis of the textual and chronological problems presented by the *Eléments de physiologie*, see Aram Vartanian, 'The Enigma of Diderot's *Eléments de physiologie,'* *DS X* (1968), 285–301, this quotation 287. See also Jean Pommier, 'Lueurs nouvelles sur les manuscrits de Diderot,' *Bulletin du Bibliophile et du Bibliothécaire, 1954,* 201–17. Also valuable is Roger, *Les Sciences de la vie dans la pensée française du XVIIIe siècle*, 672–8. For useful information on the manuscript of the *Eléments* in the Fonds Vandeul, see Dieckmann, *Inventaire*, 19–20, 76–8. It is probable that the 'Mélanges' published in A.-T., ix, 430–40, as well as 'Les Parents et l'éducation,' first published in Dieckmann, *Inventaire*, 192–235, were part of Diderot's notes for his 'histoire naturelle et expérimentale de l'homme' (Dieckmann, *Inventaire*, 187).

26. B.N., MSS, Nouv. acq. fr. 24932, foll. 138–9; published, with useful comments, in Mayer, *Diderot homme de science*, 275–6, 51–2. Naigeon, *Mémoires . . . sur la vie et les ouvrages de D. Diderot*, 291.

27. Vartanian, art. cit., *DS X*, 298–301. Georges Barral, 'Diderot et la médecine — Un ouvrage projeté par Claude Bernard,' *Chronique Médicale*, vii (1900), 126–8; Jean Rostand, 'Diderot et la biologie,' *RHS*, v (1952), 5–17.

28. E.g., Diderot, *Eléments de physiologie*, ed. Mayer, 78–86, 106–36. Lefebvre, *Diderot*, 189. See esp. Callot, *La Philosophie de la vie au XVIIIe siècle*, 289–91; and Walter Hofmann, 'Diderots Auffassungen vom allgemeinen Empfindungsvermögen, von der Entstehung und Einheit des Bewusstseins,' *WZUB*, xiii (1964), 175–80. For the view that neither Diderot nor anyone else in the eighteenth century made much progress in brain research, see François Laplassotte, 'Quelques étapes de la physiologie du cerveau du XVIIe au XIXe siècle,' *Annales: Economies, Sociétés, Civilisations*, xxv (1970), 601, 609.

29. Diderot, *Eléments de physiologie*, ed. Mayer, 241–9. Mayer, *Diderot homme de science*, 333–4; May, 'Chardin vu par Diderot et par Proust,' *PMLA*, lxxii, 407 n. Funt, *Diderot and the Esthetics of the Enlightenment (DS XI)*, 158–60.

30. Diderot, *Eléments de physiologie*, ed. Mayer, 266. For a brief discussion of this subject, see Jean Mayer, 'Der Glücksgedanke bei Diderot,' *WZUB*, xiii (1964), 169–73.

31. 'Ce que nous conaissons le moins, c'est nous' (A.-T., ix, 346; a slight variant in the corresponding passage in Diderot, *Eléments de physiologie*, ed. Mayer, 240). Forms, virtue (ibid., 307–8). Roger, *Les Sciences de la vie dans la pensée française du XVIIIe siècle*, 678.

32. Diderot, *Corr.*, xv, 202. *Corr. litt.*, xii, 498–500 (April 1781). Regarding the edition of

1780, see C. P. Courtney, 'Burke, Franklin et Raynal: A propos de deux lettres inédites,' *RHLF*, LXII (1962), 78–9.

33. First published by Dieckmann, *Inventaire*, 238–53; now also in Diderot, *Corr.*, XV, 208–27, quotations 211, 221. Callatay, *Madame de Vermenoux*, 47.

34. Diderot, *Corr.*, XV, 213–4; the reading 'des plus dangereux' is supplied by Diderot, *Oeuvres philosophiques*, ed. Vernière, 630.

35. Apostrophe to Louis XVI (Guillaume Raynal, *Histoire des deux Indes*, 3ᵈ ed., Book IV, ch. xviii). Eliza Draper (op. cit., Book III, ch. xv); see A. Bigot, 'Eliza Draper et son éloge,' *Cahiers Haut-Marnais*, No. 75 (4ᵉ trimestre 1963), 195–226. Diderot, *Corr.*, XV, 222. 'On sait particulièrement que l'éloge d'Elisa est de lui [Diderot]' ([Anon.], *G. T. Raynal démasqué, ou Lettres sur la vie et les ouvrages de cet écrivain* [n. p., 1791], 7).

36. Diderot, *Corr.*, XV, 227.

37. Diderot, *Corr.*, XV, 223. Regarding the 'radicalization' of Diderot's political thought, see Yves Benot, 'Diderot, Pechmeja, Raynal et l'anticolonialisme,' *Europe*, Nos. 405–6 (Jan.–Feb. 1963), 137–53; and Benot, *Diderot, de l'athéisme à l'anticolonialisme, passim* and esp. 180–92.

38. Diderot, *Corr.*, XV, 227. Bachaumont, *Mémoires secrets*, XVII, 196–7, 212, 216–8, 219–20 (18, 27, 29, and 30 May 1781). Regarding the condemnation, see Belin, *Le Mouvement philosophique de 1748 à 1789*, 306–12.

39. Naigeon to Diderot, 27 July 1780, and Diderot to Naigeon, 28 July 1790 (Diderot, *Corr.*, XV, 175–6, 177–9).

40. Diderot, *Salons*, IV, 377; the whole *Salon* (ibid., 352–83). For a fascinating analysis of the changes then occurring in French art (ibid., 298–302). Diderot's *Salon de 1781* appeared in the *Corr. litt.* in Oct., Nov., and Dec. 1781 (De Booy, 'Inventaire,' 391).

41. Denis Diderot, *Lettre sur les aveugles*, ed. Robert Niklaus, 2ᵉ ed. (Geneva, 1963), 71–85; Diderot, *Oeuvres philosophiques*, ed. Vernière, 151–64. The 'Additions' appeared in the *Corr. litt.* for May 1782 (De Booy, 'Inventaire,' 392). Mme de Blacy's assistance (ed. Niklaus, 75; ed. Vernière, 155).

42. *Corr. litt.*, XIII, 376 (Oct. 1783). Philidor's consulting with Diderot (Giuseppe Baretti, 'The Introduction to the "Carmen Seculare",' *Prefazioni e polemiche* [Bari, 1911], 310). For mention of Philidor's success, see Bachaumont, *Mémoires secrets*, XV, 25–7, 28–30 (19 and 23 Jan. 1780). Diderot wrote Philidor, 10 April 1782, imploring him to renounce chess for music (Diderot, *Corr.*, XV, 293–5).

43. Joseph Joubert, *Les Carnets de Joseph Joubert*, ed. André Beaunier, 2 vols. (Paris, [1938]), I, 12–3. Cf. Charles-Augustin Sainte-Beuve, 'M. Joubert,' *Causeries du lundi*, I, 159–78, esp. 161; Paul J. Sturm, 'Joubert and Voltaire: A Study in Reaction,' *Yale Romanic Studies*, XVIII (1941), 190–1. For Joubert's unfavorable literary judgments of Diderot, see *Les Carnets de Joseph Joubert*, 345, 676, 706. Cf. André Beaunier, *La Jeunesse de Joseph Joubert* (Paris, 1918), 58–116; and Margaret Gilman, 'Joubert on Imagination and Poetry,' *RR*, XL (1949), 251. Regarding Chabrit (Diderot, *Corr.*, XV, 266–8 [25 Aug. 1781]; see *Corr. litt.*, XIV, 196–7 [Aug. 1785], for an obituary notice of Chabrit). Sometime in the 1780's Diderot became acquainted with Friedrich Wilhelm Basilius von Ramdohr, a young German acquaintance of Grimm (Mortier, *Diderot en Allemagne*, 43–5).

44. Diderot to Panckoucke, 5 April 1781 (Diderot, *Corr.*, XV, 228).

45. These documents first published by Herbert Dieckmann, 'Diderot, membre honoraire de la Société d'Antiquaires d'Ecosse,' *Cahiers Haut-Marnais*, No. 24 (1ᵉʳ trimestre 1951), 23–6. Now in Diderot, *Corr.*, XV, 258–9, 270–3, this quotation 272–3.

46. Diderot, *Corr.*, XV, 273. To his copyist Roland Girbal (ibid., XV, 277–8 [Oct. 1781?]; also in A.-T., XX, 107). See the important comments by M. Varloot on 'La grande entreprise de copie' (Diderot, *Corr.*, XV, 273–6). Four copyists (ibid., XV, 279). Letter to Sedaine, 11 Oct. 1781 (ibid., XV, 279–80). For important comments upon Diderot's effort, see also Herbert Dieckmann, 'Observations sur les manuscrits de Diderot conservés en Russie,' *DS IV* (1963), 53–71; Jean Th. de Booy, 'Diderot et son copiste Roland Girbal,' *FS*, XVI (1962), 324–33; and Paul Vernière, *Diderot: Ses manuscrits et ses copistes* (Paris, 1967), 25–40.

47. Sèvres (Diderot, *Corr.*, xv, 255). Possible visit to Langres (Louis-François Marcel, *La Soeur de Diderot: Denise Diderot* (*27 janvier 1715–26 mars 1797*) [Langres, 1925], 23; Diderot, *Corr.*, xv, 152 n., 281–2).
48. Prince Grigor Orlov (Grimm to Catherine II, 1/12 Jan. 1781 [*Sbornik*, xLIV, 130]). [Ekaterina Romanovna Dashkova], *Mémoires de la Princesse Daschkoff*, ed. Pascal Pontremoli (Paris, 1966), 136, 138, 139–40. Diderot to François Tronchin, 25 March 1781 (Diderot, *Corr.*, xv, 208), and Tronchin to Diderot, 4 May 1781 (ibid., 237–8). A. J. Lexell to Jean-Albert Euler, Paris, 1 Dec. 1780 (Akademiya Nauk U.S.S.R., Leningrad, Archiv, Fond 1, oII. 3, vol. 65, fol. 124 v). Same to the same, Paris, 15 Jan. 1781 (loc. cit., vol. 65, fol. 157).
49. Nicolay, *L. H. Nicolay*, ed. Heier, 84; *Corr. litt.*, xiii, 147 (June 1782). The Grand Duke and Duchess arrived at Paris on 28 May 1782 (Nicolay, op. cit., 45).
50. John Quincy Adams (*Memoirs of John Quincy Adams*, ed. Charles Francis Adams, 12 vols. [Philadelphia, 1874–7], ii, 69 [17 Nov. 1809]). Diderot's words: 'Ouvrez la veste; vous verrez le poil.' Diderot and the Grand Duchess (Nicolay, *L. H. Nicolay*, ed. Heier, 84).
51. Samuel Romilly, *Memoirs of the Life of Sir Samuel Romilly, Written by Himself*, 3 vols. (London, 1840), i, 63. See also Romilly to the Rev. John Roget, 10 and 16 Nov. 1781 (ibid., i, 174–6, 179–80). Another Romilly, Jean Romilly of Geneva, knew Diderot for many years, but wrote to J.-J. Rousseau on 3 Nov. 1767, 'Je crois que je ne verrai plus guère ce dernier [i.e., Diderot]. Il devient trop repoussant' (Launay, 'Madame de Baugrand et Jean Romilly, Horloger: . . . ,' *Europe*, Nos. 405–6, 259).
52. Implied in Diderot's letter to Suard [10 June 1781] (Diderot, *Corr.*, xv, 243; Arthur M. Wilson, 'An Unpublished Letter from Diderot to Suard,' *Studi Francesi*, viii [1964], 67–8).
53. Chevallier, 'Les Philosophes et le Lieutenant de Police (1775–1785),' *FS*, xvii, 111. For Le Noir's authorizing the copies to be sent to him, see Benot, *Diderot, de l'athéisme à l'anticolonialisme*, 38 n. On 1 Jan. 1782 Diderot called on Pierre Rousseau, the editor of the *Journal Encyclopédique* and one of the syndicate of publishers at Bouillon, to urge him to hasten the printing of the edition (Gustave Charlier and Roland Mortier, *Le Journal Encyclopédique* (*1756–1793*) [Paris, (1952)], 27). By March 1782 the *Essai sur les règnes de Claude et de Néron* was reviewed in the *Corr. litt.*, xiii, 103–5.
54. Chevallier, art. cit., 111–3. Some critics have raised the question as to whether Diderot showed cowardice in his confrontation with the authorities in 1749 (Henri Guillemin, *A vrai dire* [Paris, 1956], 7; Benot, *Diderot, de l'athéisme à l'anticolonialisme*, 32–4).
55. The relevant passages are in Diderot, *Essai sur Sénèque*, ed. Nakagawa, i, 83–93; ii, 187. La Harpe, *Correspondance littéraire*, iii, 348. Bachaumont, *Mémoires secrets*, xx, 253 (15 May 1782).
56. Wade, *The 'Philosophe' in the French Drama of the Eighteenth Century*, 48. In this production the name Dortidius was changed to Marphurius (ibid., 53). La Harpe, *Correspondance littéraire*, iii, 383–5; Bachaumont, *Mémoires secrets*, xx, 306–7, 309–10. Rumor that the revival was by order of high authority (*Année Littéraire*, vol. vii for 1782, 219).
57. 'Dix-sept ans de suite' (Diderot, *Essai sur Sénèque*, ed. Nakagawa, i, 171). Mme Latour de Franqueville, *Jean-Jacques Rousseau vangé par son amie* (n.p., 1779), 45. Cf. Wallace Katz, 'Le Rousseauisme avant la Révolution,' *Dix-Huitième Siècle*, iii (1971), 206–8.
58. *Corr., litt.*, xiii, 104 (March 1782). For high praise of Diderot's translation of Tacitus, see Jürgen von Stackelberg, 'Rousseau, D'Alembert et Diderot traducteurs de Tacite,' *Studi Francesi*, ii (1958), 395–407, esp. 404, 405, 406, 407. The *Essai sur les règnes de Claude et de Néron* was harshly and scornfully reviewed in the *Journal de Monsieur*, vol. i for 1782, 52–96, and vol. v for 1782, 193–215. An astonishingly high estimate of the literary value of Diderot's *Essai sur les règnes de Claude et de Néron* was made by George E. A. Saintsbury, *A History of Criticism and Literary Taste in Europe*, 3 vols. (New York, 1904), iii, 94–5.
59. Diderot, *Essai sur Sénèque*, ed. Nakagawa, i, 6, 236–7; ii, 143, 206.
60. Ibid., ii, 179, 17–8.
61. For examples of previous scorn or criticism, see A.-T., iv, 76 (this appeared in the *Corr.*

litt., 15 Dec. 1769 [De Booy, 'Inventaire,' 371–2]); A.-T., VIII, 376 (Paradoxe sur le comédien); A.-T., XII, 105 (Pensées détachées sur la peinture). Quotations (Dieckmann, Inventaire, 257; Diderot, Essai sur Sénèque, ed. Nakagawa, II, 34).

62. Diderot, Essai sur Sénèque, ed. Nakagawa, II, 57–8, 134. Turgot, Malesherbes, and Necker (ibid., I, 146–7; another favorable mention of Turgot, in both editions [ibid., II, 134]). 'Le moderne Tacite' (Bachaumont, Mémoires secrets, XX, 253 [15 May 1782]; for other allusions to this, see Corr. litt., XIII, 104–5 [March 1782]; Année Littéraire, vol. VII for 1782, 219). 'La foiblesse . . .' (Diderot, Essai sur Sénèque, ed. Nakagawa, I, 30); for other references transparently aimed at Louis XV (ibid., I, 47, 64). The existence in the Essai of numerous covert allusions to current conditions in France is emphasized by Schalk, Diderots Essai über Claudius und Nero, 18–9.

63. Diderot, Corr., III, 130 (12 Oct. 1760). Cf. Wilson, 'The Concept of Moeurs in Diderot's Social and Political Thought,' SPTB, 188–99, esp. 192–3. For a good comparison of Diderot's political attitudes in 1778 and 1782, see Bonneville, Diderot's Vie de Sénèque, 20–30.

64. See esp. the important fragment 'Le Peuple' (Dieckmann, Inventaire, 232–3). For the numerous semantic distinctions in Diderot's use of the word 'peuple,' see Mortier, 'Diderot et la notion du "peuple",' Europe, Nos. 405–6, 78–88.

65. Diderot, Essai sur Sénèque, ed. Nakagawa, II, 135.

66. A.-T., II, 276 (Réfutation d'Helvétius). Diderot wrote the same formula to John Wilkes, 14 Nov. 1771 (Diderot, Corr., XI, 223). Cf. Raynal, Histoire des deux Indes, ed. 1780, III, 103: 'C'est l'image du vieil Aeson, à qui Médée ne rendit la jeunesse qu'en le dépeçant et en le faisant bouillir.'

67. Diderot, Essai sur Sénèque, ed. Nakagawa, II, 22–3. Crocker, Two Diderot Studies: Ethics and Esthetics, 45.

68. Proust, Diderot et l'Encyclopédie, 328. For La Mettrie's philosophy, see Aram Vartanian, 'Le Philosophe selon La Mettrie,' Dix-Huitième Siècle, I (1969), 161–78, as well as his introduction to La Mettrie's L'Homme-Machine, ed. Vartanian, esp. 116–9. See also Perkins, 'Diderot and La Mettrie,' SVEC, X, 49–100, esp. 68–9, 90; and Loy, 'L'Essai sur les règnes de Claude et de Néron,' CAIEF, No. 13, 245–6; Crocker, Nature and Culture, 386–7; the comments in Lefebvre, Diderot, 74–7, are especially useful. Some years earlier, Diderot had commented bitterly about La Mettrie's ethical doctrines (Hemsterhuis, Lettre sur l'homme et ses rapports, ed. May, 45).

69. See the very illuminating discussion of Diderot's ethical theory in Proust, Diderot et l'Encyclopédie, 325–38; and, reviewing that volume, by Otis Fellows, RR, LVI (1965), 273–4. 'A parler rigoureusement, il n'y a qu'un devoir: c'est d'être heureux; il n'y a qu'une vertu: c'est la justice' (Diderot, Essai sur Sénèque, ed. Nakagawa, II, 123). Very similar passages in A.-T., II, 85 (Introduction aux grands principes); and Diderot, Eléments de physiologie, ed. Mayer, 308.

70. Mauzi, L'Idée du bonheur au XVIIIᵉ siècle, 627–31; Mauzi, 'Les Rapports du bonheur et de la vertu dans l'oeuvre de Diderot,' CAIEF, No. 13, 264; O'Gorman, Diderot the Satirist, 45.

71. Jean A. Perkins, 'Diderot's Concept of Virtue,' SVEC, XXIII (1963), 81. This whole essay (77–91) is very useful.

72. Diderot, Essai sur Sénèque, ed. Nakagawa, II, 24. Casini, Diderot 'philosophe,' 388.

73. Grimm to Catherine II, 12 March 1783 (Diderot, Corr., XV, 311–2).

74. Corr. litt., XIII, 363–4. Slight improvement during the summer (Diderot, Corr., XV, 313–4).

75. Diderot, Corr., XV, 315, 318, 321. See De Booy, 'Diderot et son copiste Roland Girbal,' FS, XVI, 324–33.

76. Mme de Vandeul, LVI. Grimm to François Tronchin, 14 Nov. 1783 (Diderot, Corr., XV, 316); see also his letters to the same, 15 Dec. 1783 and 18 Jan. 1784 (ibid., 317, 319). Continued trouble with dropsy (Vandeul to Denise Diderot, 24 April 1784 [Diderot, Corr., XV, 330–1]).

77. Emphysema (Diderot, Corr., XV, 316, 317, 319, 329). Willingness to move to a ground floor (ibid., 320).

78. Mme de Vandeul, LV–LVI. Dr. Henry Ronot, 'La Maladie et la mort de Diderot,' Cahiers

Haut-Marnais, No. 24 (1ᵉʳ trimestre 1951), 47–51; Dr. Henry Ronot, 'La Maladie et la mort de Diderot,' *Médecine de France,* No. 123 (1961), 9–12.

79. Diderot, *Corr.,* xv, 325, 328, 331.

80. Charlemagne (Diderot, *Corr.,* xv, 148). Family letters alluding to Marie-Anne's death (ibid., xv, 326–8). For the only known letter written by Marie-Anne de Vandeul, see Diderot, *Corr.,* xv, 310.

81. For the exchange of letters between Grimm and Catherine II during Diderot's illness, see Diderot, *Corr.,* xv, 311, 313 n., 316, 328, 334. Grimm wrote to Galiani, 6 Sept. 1785, that he rented for Diderot 'un superbe rez-de-chaussée' (Galiani, *Dialogues sur le commerce des bleds,* ed. Nicolini, 410). Regarding the Hôtel de Bezons, rented for Diderot, see Jacques Hillairet, *Dictionnaire historique des rues de Paris,* 2 vols. (Paris, 1963), ii, 342; also Jacques Hillairet, *La Rue de Richelieu* (Paris, [1966]), 43. Mme de Vandeul, lvii. Negotiations concerning occupancy (Diderot, *Corr.,* xv, 335, 337).

82. Bachaumont, *Mémoires secrets,* xxiii, 226 (28 Oct. 1783), 243 (6 Nov. 1783).

83. Ibid., xxiii, 241 (5 Nov. 1783).

84. Mme de Vandeul, lvi–lvii.

85. Mme de Vandeul, lvii. Pensée xxxi (Diderot, *Pensées philosophiques*).

86. Mme de Vandeul, lvii–lviii. She correctly stated that he died on a Saturday, but mistakenly gave the date as 30 instead of 31 July. Mme Diderot wrote in her *livre de raison,* 'Ce 31 juliet 1784 deni Diderot est desédée' (Paris. Bibliothèque Nationale. *Diderot et l'Encyclopédie,* item 105). The Jansenist *Nouvelles Ecclésiastiques,* sourly hostile to both Diderot and the Abbé Marduel, *curé* of Saint-Roch, published a long account alleging that Diderot had died in the country and that the cadaver was brought into Paris (op. cit., 26 Nov. 1784, 192). This story went all over Catholic Christendom. See, for example, Don Joseph Domenichini, *El Éxito de la muerte correspondiente à la vida de los tres supuestos heroes del siglo XVIII, Voltaire, D'Alambert* [sic], *y Diderot* (Madrid, 1792), 286–91 (Biblioteca Nacional de España, call-number 3/11243). The same story appears in the well-known work by the Abbé Augustin Barruel, *Mémoires pour servir à l'histoire du jacobinisme,* 4 vols. (London, 1797–8), i, 384–7. These stories are disproved by Canon Louis Marcel, 'La Mort de Diderot, d'après des documents inédits,' *Revue d'Histoire de l'Eglise de France,* xi (1925), 41–2.

87. Performed by Drs. Bacher, Dupuy, and Lesne (Herbert Dieckmann, 'The Autopsy Report on Diderot,' *Isis,* xli [1950], 289–90). Mme de Vandeul, lviii. Cf. Vandeul to his brother, De Melleville, beginning of Aug. 1784 (Marcel, 'La Mort de Diderot,' loc. cit., 224 n.).

88. Mme de Vandeul, lviii. '1,500 à 1,800 livres' (*Corr. litt.,* xiv, 18 [Aug. 1784]). Grimm was not in Paris when Diderot died; he had visited briefly in Langres in mid-July (Mme de Caroillon to her son, De Melleville, 17 July 1784 [Diderot, *Corr.,* xv, 337–8]), on a trip to meet Prince Henry of Prussia, and thereafter he visited Lyon to buy silks for Catherine II (Cazes, *Grimm et les encyclopédistes,* 178; Marcel, 'La Mort de Diderot,' loc. cit., 223 n.).

89. B.N. MSS, Nouv. acq. fr. 24941, foll. 88, 89, 92. The *faire-part de décès* is reproduced in *Cahiers Haut-Marnais,* No. 24 (1ᵉʳ trimestre 1951), 'Supplément illustré'; there is also a specimen in B.N., MSS, Nouv. acq. fr. 24941, fol. 86. There were 350 printed, 'grand format,' according to the bill presented to Vandeul on 3 Aug. (ibid., fol. 92). The *faire-part* described Diderot as being a member of the Swedish Academy of Sciences, but I have been assured by letter from the Secretary of the Academy that Diderot's name does not appear on their rolls. Similarly, the *faire-part* described Diderot as being a member of the Académie de Châlons-sur-Marne, but this has not been verified by subsequent research. For example, Diderot's name does not appear in the list of members studied by Daniel Roche, 'La Diffusion des lumières. Un exemple: L'Académie de Châlons-sur-Marne,' *Annales: Economies-Sociétés - Civilisations,* xix (1964), 887–922.

90. A.-T., xiii, 5–6, 7.

91. For the entry in the parish register of Saint-Roch regarding Diderot's burial, see *Cahiers Haut-Marnais,* No. 24 (1ᵉʳ trimestre 1951), 47. Also printed in Paris. Bibliothèque Nationale, *Diderot et l'Encyclopédie,* item 104. For a slightly fuller quotation of the

registre (B.N., MSS, Nouv. acq. fr. 3617, fiche No. 2729). A photograph of this entry (*Cahiers Haut-Marnais*, No. 38 [3ᵉ trimestre 1954], 137). For a contemporary account of Diderot's death and burial, though not a very circumstantial one, see Bachaumont, *Mémoires secrets*, XXVI, 151, 153, 159 (2, 3, and 6 Aug. 1784).

When an air duct was built in the vault of the Chapelle de la Vierge in 1879, no trace was found of Diderot's remains. Many coffins in Saint-Roch were desecrated during the Revolution in order to obtain lead. For this and other interesting information, see the valuable report by Charles Sellier, 'Rapport présenté par M. Charles Sellier, au nom de la 2ᵉ Sous-commission, sur les fouiles exécutées à l'église Saint-Roch pour la recherche des restes de Duguay-Trouin,' Paris, *Bulletin de la Commission du Vieux Paris*, 10 March 1906, 52–5.

92. Sellier, art. cit., 54.

EPILOGUE

1. A.-T., II, 370 (*Réfutation d'Helvétius*).
2. Diderot, *Essai sur Sénèque*, ed. Nakagawa, I, 63; A.-T., III, 70.
3. Diderot, *Corr.*, v, 206 (3 Dec. 1765).
4. A.-T., XIV, 494.
5. A.-T., XVIII, 16 (*Lettre sur le commerce de la librairie*); Proust, *Diderot et* l'Encyclopédie, 83.
6. *Encyc.*, x, 860a, s.v. 'Multitude'; attributed to Diderot by Naigeon (Lough, 'Problem,' 355). Cf. Diderot to Falconet, 15 Feb. 1766 (Diderot, *Corr.*, VI, 84): 'Le peuple, mon ami, n'est à la longue que l'écho de quelques hommes de goût; et la postérité, que l'écho du présent rectifié par l'expérience.'
7. A.-T., xv, 183–4 (attributed to Diderot by Naigeon [Lough, 'Problem,' 355]). For a similar passage in the *Voyage à Bourbonne*, see A.-T., XVII, 342.
8. A.-T., I, 183–4.
9. Diderot, *Essai sur Sénèque*, ed. Nakagawa, II, 24; A.-T., III, 219.
10. Hemsterhuis, *Lettre sur l'homme et ses rapports*, ed. May, 513.
11. *Eloge de Richardson* (A.-T., v, 226).
12. J. H. Smith, in *MLR*, LVII (1962), 613.
13. Diderot, *Essai sur Sénèque*, ed. Nakagawa, II, 185.

Bibliography

I. ARCHIVAL AND MANUSCRIPT MATERIAL, ETC.

BALTIMORE–Mr. Douglas H. Gordon's Extra Volume. For a description of the contents of this volume, see Douglas H. Gordon and Norman L. Torrey, *The Censoring of Diderot's Encyclopédie and the Re-established Text* (New York, 1947), 109–12.

CAMBRIDGE (Mass.)–Houghton Library, Harvard University: MS. Fr. 189: Diderot to Le Breton (?), *c.* 1751. Diderot to Mme Necker, undated, *c.* 1773.

CHAUMONT–Archives Départementales de la Haute-Marne, Série E (Fonds Vandeul). A manuscript catalogue of these family papers has been compiled by M. Jean Massiet du Biest and is available in the Archives at Chaumont (Jean Massiet du Biest, *La Fille de Diderot* [Tours, 1949], vii).

GENEVA–Bibliothèque Publique et Universitaire:
Collection Rilliet: Letter from Diderot to Vernes (?), 9 Jan. 1759.
Tronchin Archives, vols. 167, 180, 198, 296.

LANGRES–Archives Municipales, Hôtel de Ville.
Bibliothèque Municipale, Hôtel de Ville:
  MS 94: *La Pièce et le prologue.*
       94: Diderot to (?), 28 Dec. 1769 (see Arthur M. Wilson, 'An Unpublished Letter of Diderot, December 28, 1769,' *MLN,* LXVII [1952], 439–43; and in Diderot, *Corr., IX,* 239–44).

LENINGRAD–Archives of the Akademia Nauk USSR:
Ф. 1, oII 3, vol. 62, fol. 125: N. Hennert to Jean-Albert Euler, 14 June 1775; ibid., vol. 65, foll. 124, 157: A. J. Lexell to Jean-Albert Euler, 1 Dec. 1780 and 15 Jan. 1781.
Saltykov-Shchedrin Public Library: Department of Manuscripts. Regarding the Diderot manuscripts, see Arthur M. Wilson, 'Leningrad, 1957: Diderot and Voltaire Gleanings,' *FR,* XXXI (1957–8), 356–60; and Herbert Dieckmann, 'Observations sur les manuscrits de Diderot conservés en Russie,' *DS IV* (1963), 53–71.

LONDON–British Museum:
Additional Manuscripts 30867, foll. 14, 18–9, 20–1: Early letters from D'Holbach to Wilkes; ibid., 30869, foll. 39–40, 81–2, 173–4, same to same, 22 May, no year given; 10 Nov. 1766 and 10 Dec. 1767, respectively; ibid., 30870, foll. 59–60, D'Holbach to Wilkes, 17 July 1768.
Add. MSS 30877, fol. 85: Diderot to John Wilkes, 10 July 1772.
Add. MSS 34874: Edward Gibbon, 'My own Life.'
Add. MSS 44936, foll. 25–6: Diderot to Voltaire, 8 or 10 Oct. 1766.
Egerton Manuscripts, vol. 19, fol. 46: Diderot to Le Bret, 29 Nov. 1757.
Public Record Office: State Papers Foreign 91 (Russia), vols. 94–5.
Victoria and Albert Museum: Garrick Papers, Miscellaneous, 1766–1788: Foreign MS 30, foll. 1–8, 37–8, 66–9, 77, 92–7, 119–26; Foreign MS 31, foll. 7–8, 62–5.

NEW HAVEN (Conn.)–Beinecke Library, Yale University:
James Marshall and Marie-Louise Osborn Collection: Dr. Charles Burney to Diderot (draft), prob. March 1771; and Diderot to Burney, 15 May and 26 Sept. 1771 and 12 April 1777.

NEW YORK–The Pierpont Morgan Library:

Diderot to Le Breton, undated (1751?).

PARIS–Archives de l'Académie des Sciences, Registers for 1757, 1758, 1759.

Archives de la Comédie-Française.

Archives Départementales de la Seine, 417868x: copy of the birth certificate of Sophie Volland.

Archives Nationales: o¹*, 407 fol. 161, No. 450, Saint-Florentin to Diderot, 1 May 1765; Y 77, fol. 167; Y 12594, Y 13777, AD VIII 8 (Année 1745), pièce 67, T 319⁵, U 1051.

Bibliothèque de l'Arsenal: MS 4978 ('Préface-Annexe de La Religieuse'); Cartons 10300–303, 10305, 11671.

Bibliothèque Historique de la Ville de Paris: MS 627–9, newsletter of M. Marin to Count Ossolinski, 1767–74; MS cote provisoire 3861, newsletter of Suard to the Margrave of Bayreuth, 1774.

Bibliothèque Nationale:

Archives Administratives, vol. 56.

Département des Estampes, série N2; Ma mat. 1 (a collection of engravings that Diderot may have used as models for the *planches* in the *Encyclopédie*).

Département des Imprimés: Prêt 5 (notation of books borrowed by Diderot).

Département des Manuscrits:

Fonds Français: vols. 12303–4, 12763, 12768, 14307, 15230, 21813, 21928, 21958–60, 21997, 22068–9, 22086, 22092, 22094, 22112, 22120, 22137–40, 22155–65, 22176–7, 22179, 22183, 22191. Volumes 22061–193 of this *fonds* are inventoried by Ernest Coyecque, *Inventaire de la Collection Anisson sur l'histoire de l'imprimerie et de la librairie, principalement à Paris,* 2 vols. (Paris, 1900).

Fonds Joly de Fleury: vols. 292, 1479–80, 1687, 1708. This collection has been inventoried by A. Molinier, *Inventaire sommaire de la Collection Joly de Fleury* (Paris, 1881).

Fonds Latin, vol. 9158.

Fonds Nouvelles Acquisitions Françaises, vols. 31, 558, 717, 1182–3, 1185–6, 1214, 1311, 2777, 3344–8, 3531, 3617, 4200, 4411, 4719, 5184, 6203, 9197, 9216, 10165, 10781–3, 12961, 13004, 13720–4, 13727–9, 13735, 13737, 13752, 13781, 21196, 24340, 24930–2, 24941, 24983.

The Fonds Vandeul is now accessioned in the Département des Manuscrits, Fonds Nouvelles Acquisitions Françaises 13720–83 and 24930–41. For a detailed inventory of this collection, see Herbert Dieckmann, *Inventaire du Fonds Vandeul et Inédits de Diderot* (Geneva, 1951).

PHILADELPHIA–The Historical Society of Pennsylvania:

Dreer Collection of Autographs: Diderot to Voltaire, 11 June 1749 (Arthur M. Wilson, 'Une Partie inédite de la lettre de Diderot à Voltaire, le 11 juin 1749,' *RHLF,* LI [1951], 257–60; see Diderot, *Corr.,* I, 75–82).

Simon Gratz Collection of Autographs, Case 11, Box 22: Diderot to the Abbé Le Monnier, 9 Oct. 1779.

STOCKHOLM–Kungliga Biblioteket, MSS, Vu. 29: 1–16. Grimm's *Correspondance littéraire,* 1760–74.

THE HAGUE–Koninklijke Bibliotheek, MSS, 128 F 14, 130 D 5, 130 D 14 (S. Gessner to Van Goens about the reception of Diderot's *Les Deux amis de Bourbonne,* 9 Feb. 1774). MS 130 D 14, dossier M, contains an undated note from Diderot to Van Goens, sealed with a very clear impression of the head of Socrates in red wax.

–Koninklijk Huis Archief, G 16-A 67, A 68, A 69.

TONNERRE–Bibliothèque Municipale, Dossier J: Le Chevalier d'Eon de Beaumont, Correspondance 1769–1771, fol. 96: Mlle Jodin to the Chevalier d'Eon, 3 July 1770 (now available in Diderot, *Corr.,* x, 83–4).

VIENNA–Österreichische Nationalbibliothek, Autographe V, 25: foll. 273–83, holograph manuscript of Diderot, *Sur Térence.* This document has now been carefully studied and edited by Herbert Dieckmann.

WASHINGTON, D.C.–The Library of Congress, John Boyd Thacher Collection, dossier 56: Diderot to Suard, undated (Arthur M. Wilson, 'An Unpublished Letter from Diderot to Suard,' *Studi Francesi*, VIII [1964], 67–8). Also in dossier 56: receipt by Diderot for an engraving for the *Encyclopédie*, undated.

WILMINGTON (Del.)–Eleutherian Mills Historical Library:
Turgot to Du Pont, 21 Sept. 1774; Du Pont to Turgot, 29 Oct. 1774; Diderot to Du Pont, 9 Dec. 1775 (Arthur M. Wilson, 'An Unpublished Letter of Diderot to Du Pont de Nemours (9 December 1775),' *MLR*, LVIII [1963], 222–5).

II. REMARKS CONCERNING THE EDITIONS OF DIDEROT

All students of Diderot are looking forward eagerly to the forthcoming critical edition of the *Oeuvres complètes de Diderot*, the Publication Committee of which is composed of Herbert Dieckmann, Jean Fabre, and Jacques Proust, with Jean Varloot as its Secretary General. The most nearly complete edition up to this time has been the *Oeuvres complètes*, ed. Jules Assézat and Maurice Tourneux, 20 vols. (Paris, 1875–7). This edition, however, has become badly out-of-date and grievously incomplete, not only because a century has elapsed but also because the availability of the Diderot manuscripts in the Fonds Vandeul at the Bibliothèque Nationale, together with the possibility for Western scholars of studying and comparing the Diderot manuscripts in Russia, have revolutionized the opportunities and potentialities of Diderot studies.

The result has been that during this past quarter-century numerous scholars have produced excellent critical editions of single works by Diderot. I honor here the names of these scholars, among them Herbert Dieckmann, Jean Seznec, Jean Fabre, Jacques Proust, Jean Varloot, Paul Vernière, Gilbert Chinard, Robert Niklaus, Georges May, Jean Mayer, Paul Meyer, Jack Undank, Roland Desné, Jean Parrish, Yvon Belaval, J. Robert Loy, Hisayasu Nakagawa, and Yves Benot. I have used their editions in the foregoing pages, with full bibliographical references in the notes. I shall not therefore repeat this bibliographical information here, especially as the forthcoming critical edition of the *Oeuvres complètes de Diderot* will be incorporating most of them.

Especially meritorious has been the invaluable and indispensable edition of Diderot's *Correspondance*, 16 vols. (Paris, 1955–70), edited by Georges Roth, with Jean Varloot in collaboration for vols. XIV–XVI.

For inexpensive editions of Diderot's writings that are also well edited and comprehensive, the reader is referred to the volumes in the Classiques Garnier: Diderot, *Oeuvres philosophiques*, ed. Paul Vernière; Diderot, *Oeuvres esthétiques*, ed. Vernière; Diderot, *Oeuvres romanesques*, ed. Henri Bénac; and Diderot, *Oeuvres politiques*, ed. Vernière.

When translations into English of Diderot's works are available, I have indicated the edition at the bottom of the page of my book where the information is relevant. Mention should also be made of *Diderot's Early Philosophical Works*, tr. and ed. Margaret Jourdain (Chicago, 1916); *Diderot, Interpreter of Nature: Selected Writings*, tr. Jean Stewart and Jonathan Kemp (New York, 1938; reprinted, 1963); and *Dramatic Essays of the Neoclassic Age*, ed. Henry Hitch Adams and Baxter Hathaway (New York, 1950), 349–60: Diderot's 'Essay on Dramatic Poetry,' tr. John Gaywood Linn [an abridgement]; and esp. *Diderot's Selected Writings*, ed. Lester G. Crocker (New York, 1966).

III. BIBLIOGRAPHICAL GUIDES FOR THE STUDY OF DIDEROT

The following works include such comprehensive bibliographies regarding Diderot that the reiterated itemization here of the individual works utilized in this biography is unnecessary, especially as each such item has already received a full entry at the relevant point in the notes.

1. David C. Cabeen, gen. ed., *A Critical Bibliography of French Literature*, IV: *The Eighteenth Century*, ed. George R. Havens and Donald F. Bond (Syracuse, 1951). The excellent sections on 'Diderot' (items 2203–343) and '*Encyclopédie*' (items 1288–1322) were done by Herbert Dieckmann and Norman L. Torrey, and by Lester G. Crocker, respectively.

Also to be consulted is the *Supplement*, ed. Richard A. Brooks (Syracuse, 1968). In the Volume IV, *Supplement* the sections on 'Diderot' (items 4986–5362) and *'Encyclopédie'* (items 4299–4347) have been contributed by Mary T. and Arthur M. Wilson, and by Jean A. Perkins, respectively. All entries in both these volumes are fully and critically described.

2. Alexandre Cioranescu, *Bibliographie de la Littérature Française du Dix-huitième Siècle*, 3 vols. (Paris: Centre National de la Recherche Scientifique, 1969).

3. *Bibliographie der französischen Literaturwissenschaft*, ed. Otto Klapp (Frankfort on Main, 1960–   ).

4. *The Year's Work in Modern Language Studies*, The Modern Humanities Research Association (London, 1931–   ).

5. René Rancoeur, *Bibliographie de la littérature française du moyen âge à nos jours* (Paris, 1955–   ). A yearbook.

6. Modern Language Association of America, *MLA International Bibliography of Books and Articles on the Modern Languages and Literatures* (New York, 1965–   ).

7. An excellent bibliography, published some years ago, is that by Herbert Dieckmann, 'Bibliographical Data on Diderot,' *Studies in Honor of Frederick W. Shipley* ('Washington University Studies — New Series: Language and Literature — No. 14' [St. Louis, 1942]), 181–220.

Special mention should be made of a bibliographical essay that traces the historiography of Diderot from the eighteenth century to the present. This essay is by Paolo Casini, 'Studi su Diderot,' *Rassegna di Filosofia*, VII (1958), 5–26, 150–73, 234–54. Also excellent is Yvon Belaval, 'Le "Philosophe" Diderot,' *Critique*, No. 58 (March 1952), 230–53; and the same, 'Nouvelles recherches sur Diderot,' *Critique*, No. 100–1 (Sept.–Oct. 1955), 793–9, No. 107 (April 1956), 291–318, No. 108 (May 1956), 400–22, No. 109 (June 1956), 534–53. Two other essays, older but still valuable, are by Jean Thomas, *L'Humanisme de Diderot*, 2nd ed. (Paris, 1938), 161–82: 'Etat présent des travaux sur Diderot'; and Herbert Dieckmann, *Stand und Probleme der Diderot-Forschung* (Bonn, 1931).

The existence and success of a well-edited serial publication devoted exclusively to Diderot studies has been a great boon to researchers in this field. This publication is *Diderot Studies*, founded and edited by Otis Fellows. Norman L. Torrey was his co-editor for Vols. I and II, and Gita May for Vol. III. Diana Guiragossian has been co-editor for Vol. VIII and thereafter. For an *analyse*, see J. Robert Loy, *'Diderot Studies:* A Profile,' *Modern Philology*, LXVI (1968–9), 265–72.

IV. Some General Biographical Books and Articles

a. in english:

Carlyle, Thomas: 'Diderot,' in *Critical and Miscellaneous Essays.* Crusty old Carlyle made up in insight for what he lacked, inevitably, in information.

Crocker, Lester Gilbert: *The Embattled Philosopher: A Biography of Denis Diderot* (East Lansing [Mich.], 1954); revised, and reprinted under the title of *Diderot: The Embattled Philosopher* (New York, 1966).

Ellis, Havelock: 'Diderot,' in *The New Spirit*, 4th ed. (New York, [1926]), 34–68.

Laski, Harold: 'Diderot,' in *Studies in Law and Politics* (New Haven, 1932), 48–65.

Morley, John: *Diderot and the Encyclopaedists*, 2 vols. (London, 1878).

Wade, Ira O.: 'The Rediscovery of Diderot,' *Symposium*, VI (1952), 197–208.

b. in german:

Kassner, Rudolf: *Denis Diderot* (Berlin, [1906]).

Kesten, Hermann: 'Denis Diderot: Ein Revolutionär in Frankreich,' in his *Lauter Literaten; Porträts, Erinnerungen* (Vienna, Munich, and Basel, 1963), 84–214.

Lücke, Theodor: *Denis Diderot; Skizze eines enzyklopädischen Lebens* (Berlin, 1949).

Rosenkranz, Karl: *Diderot's Leben und Werke*, 2 vols. (Leipzig, 1866).

c. in italian:

Alatri, Paolo: 'Diderot,' in his *Voltaire, Diderot e il "Partito Filosofico"* (Messina and Florence, 1965), 255–338.

Casini, Paolo: *Diderot "philosophe"* (Bari, 1962).

d. IN RUSSIAN:

Akimova, Alisa Akimovna: *Didro* (Moscow, 1963).

e. IN DANISH:

Nedergaard, Leif: *Diderot: Filosoffens Liv og Virke* (Copenhagen, 1953).

f. IN FRENCH:

The essays by Sainte-Beuve, 'Diderot,' *Premiers lundis,* 1, 372–93, and 'Diderot,' *Portraits littéraires,* 1, 239–64, are still of great verve and literary merit. Other nineteenth-century biographies of Diderot have tended to fade:

Collignon, A.: *Diderot: sa vie, ses oeuvres, sa correspondance* (Paris, 1895).

Ducros, Louis: *Diderot: l'homme et l'écrivain* (Paris, 1894).

Reinach, Joseph: *Diderot* (Paris, 1884).

Scherer, Edmond: *Diderot* (Paris, 1880).

Among twentieth-century biographies, the following are especially worthy of note:

Billy, André: *Diderot* (Paris, 1932); revised and enlarged edition (Paris, 1943). Well-informed and comprehensive, but unfortunately not provided with documentation.

Garcin, Philippe: 'Diderot et la philosophie du style,' *Critique,* No. 142 (March 1959), 195–213.

Gillot, Hubert: *Denis Diderot: l'homme, ses idées philosophiques, esthétiques, littéraires* (Paris, 1937).

Lefebvre, Henri: *Diderot* (Paris, 1949).

Luppol, I. K.: *Diderot* (Paris, 1936). Translated from the Russian.

Mornet, Daniel: *Diderot: l'homme et l'oeuvre* (Paris, [1941]).

Also to be noted:

Cresson, André: *Diderot: sa vie, son oeuvre* (Paris, 1949).

Meyer, E.: *Diderot* (Paris, [1923]).

Seillière, Ernest: *Diderot* (Paris, 1944).

Two biographical sketches of unusual merit are:

Leutrat, Jean-Louis: *Diderot* (Paris, 1968).

Pomeau, René: *Diderot, sa vie, son oeuvre avec un exposé de sa philosophie* (Paris, 1967).

A Survey of Publications Since 1957 on Diderot's Early Years

The picture of Diderot and the *Encyclopédie* has been made more detailed by the monumental contribution of Jacques Proust, *Diderot et* l'Encyclopédie (Paris, 1962; revised ed., 1967). This brilliant and fruitful work reveals how much Diderot's labors on the *Encyclopédie* contributed to his development as an ethical and political thinker, and how they facilitated his command of the technology, science, and philosophy of his time. This masterly work also traces in greater depth than has been done before the mechanics of the financing and production of the *Encyclopédie*.

The early years of this great publishing venture have been the subject of articles by John Lough, 'Le Breton, Mills et Sellius,' *Dix-Huitième Siècle*, 1 (1969), 267–87; and James Doolittle, 'From Hack to Editor — Diderot and the Booksellers,' *MLN*, LXXV (1960), 133–9. Nor should it be overlooked that Franco Venturi has published a second and revised edition of his very valuable *Le Origini dell'Enciclopedia* (Turin, 1963). The vicissitudes of the *Encyclopédie* during its middle years has been studied by John Lough, 'Contemporary Books and Pamphlets on the *Encyclopédie*,' and 'Contemporary French Periodicals and the *Encyclopédie*,' in his *Essays on the* Encyclopédie *of Diderot and d'Alembert* (London, 1968), 252–338, 339–423; and by Raymond Birn, 'The French-language Press and the *Encyclopédie*, 1750–1759,' *SVEC*, LV (1967), 263–86. There is now available an admirably edited English translation of D'Alembert's *Preliminary Discourse to the Encyclopedia of Diderot*, ed. Richard N. Schwab (Library of Liberal Arts [Bobbs-Merrill], 1963).

The abiding influence of Lord Shaftesbury upon the young Diderot — and upon the mature Diderot as well — has been a point of interest held in common by Dorothy B. Schlegel, 'Diderot as the Transmitter of Shaftesbury's Romanticism,' *SVEC*, XXVII (1963), 1457–78; by Władysław Folkierski, 'Comment Lord Shaftesbury a-t-il conquis Diderot?,' in *Studi in onore di Carlo Pelligrini* (Turin, [1964]), 319–46; and by Paolo Casini, in a brilliant and definitive analysis, 'Diderot e Shaftesbury,' *Giornale Critico della Filosofia Italiana*, XXXIX (1960), 253–73.

The development of Diderot's thought, especially his transition from deism to atheism, continues to fascinate scholars. This is the theme of Jacques Roger, 'Le Déisme du jeune Diderot,' in *Europäische Aufklärung: Herbert Dieckmann zum 60. Geburtstag*, ed. Hugo Frederick and Fritz Schalk (Munich, 1967), 237–45; see also his 'Diderot et Buffon en 1749,' *DS IV* (1963), 221–36. Continuing interest in the *Pensées philosophiques* is proved by the publication of the second (1957) and third (1965) editions edited by Robert Niklaus, and no less by the publication of the persuasive article by Andrée M. F. Kail, 'Un Argument des "Pensées philosophiques": Scolastique et siècle des lumières,' *FR*, XXXI (1957–8), 517–23; and the magisterial one by René Etiemble, 'Structure et sens des *Pensées philosophiques*,' *RFor*, LXXIV (1962), 1–10.

Scholars have also been interested in Diderot's other early writings. His translation of Temple Stanyan has been studied by Roland Desné, 'Das erste Werk Diderots. (Die Übersetzung der Histoire de Grèce von Temple Stanyan),' *WZUB*, XIII (1964), 157–61; see also Roland Desné's 'L'Apparition du mot "philosophe" dans l'oeuvre de Diderot,' *AHRF*, XXXV (1963), 287–94. The influence of Dr. Robert James's *A Medicinal Dictionary* in moulding the encyclopedist Diderot is suggested by James Doolittle, 'Robert James, Diderot, and the *Encyclopédie*,' *MLN*, LXXI (1956), 431–4.

Les Bijoux indiscrets, after having been too long scorned or, if appreciated, appreciated for the wrong reasons, is decidedly coming into its own. Otis Fellows, 'Metaphysics and the *Bijoux indiscrets*: Diderot's debt to Prior,' *SVEC*, LVI (1967), 509–40, is a pleasing contribution to comparative literature as well as to knowledge about Diderot. Also valuable are Robert J. Ellrich, 'The Structure of Diderot's *Les Bijoux indiscrets*,' *RR*, LII (1961), 279–89, and Nola M. Leov, 'Literary Techniques in "Les bijoux indiscrets",' *AUMLA*, No. 19 (1963), 93–106. The principal points of the novel are summarized in Kirsten Lassen, 'Un Roman de Diderot: *Les Bijoux indiscrets*,' *Revue Romane*, II (1967), 38–47. There has even been an article — and a good one — on *L'Oiseau blanc*: Vivienne Mylne and Janet Osborne, 'Diderot's Early Fiction: *Les Bijoux indiscrets* and *L'Oiseau blanc*,' *DS XIV* (1971), 143–66.

Important research has been published on *La Promenade du sceptique*. The history of the work is the subject of an admirable monograph by J. Th. de Booy, *Histoire d'un manuscrit de Diderot: "La Promenade du Sceptique"* (Analecta Romanica, Heft 14) (Frankfort on Main, 1964). The literary character of *La Promenade* is emphasized in a masterly paper by Herbert Dieckmann, 'Diderot's *Promenade du sceptique*: A Study in the Relationship of Thought and Form,' *SVEC*, LV (1967), 417–38. Also thought-provoking is Jacques Chouillet, 'Le Personnage du sceptique dans les premières oeuvres de Diderot (1745–1747),' *Dix-Huitième Siècle*, I (1969), 195–211.

Since the publication of *The Testing Years*, Diderot's *Lettre sur les sourds et muets* has been edited with admirable competence and loving care by Paul H. Meyer, in *DS VII* (1965). Georges May provided a sparkling introduction to this edition, 'A l'usage de ceux qui lisent la *Lettre sur les sourds et muets*,' *DS VII*, xiii–xxvi. A review essay by Norman Rudich, '*Lettre sur les sourds et muets*, Critical Edition by Paul Meyer,' *DS X* (1968), 265–83, admirably draws out the philosophical importance of this early work. A useful article by Paul H. Meyer, not superseded by his own later edition, is 'The "Lettre sur les sourds et muets" and Diderot's Emerging Concept of the Critic,' *DS VI* (1964), 133–55.

The response in Germany to Diderot's early writings continues to be studied by Roland Mortier, 'La Réaction allemande aux premières oeuvres philosophiques de Diderot,' *DS IV* (1963), 131–51; and it should be recorded here that his well-known monograph on *Diderot en Allemagne* has been translated, in a revised edition, *Diderot in Deutschland, 1750–1850* (Stuttgart, 1967). Also to be noted is Werner Krauss, 'Die früheste Reaktion auf Diderots Jugendwerke in Deutschland,' *RFor*, LXXI (1959), 103–12.

There has been a number of publications throwing light on some of Diderot's early friends and on his relations with them in the period before 1759. Regarding Toussaint, see T. J. Barling, 'Toussaint's *Les Moeurs*,' *FS*, XII (1958), 14–20. A very useful study of Condillac's thought has been published by Isabel F. Knight, *The Geometric Spirit: The Abbé de Condillac and the French Enlightenment* (New Haven, 1968). Concerning D'Holbach, there has been a revised edition of Pierre Naville's *Paul Thiry d'Holbach et la philosophie scientifique au XVIIIᵉ siècle* (Paris, 1967). On the Abbé de Prades Professor J. S. Spink has recently published two authoritative articles, 'The Abbé de Prades and the Encyclopaedists: Was There a Plot?,' *FS*, XXIV (1970), 225–36, and 'Un Abbé Philosophe: L'Affaire de J.-M. de Prades,' *Dix-Huitième Siècle*, III (1971), 145–80.

Since the publication of *The Testing Years*, two splendid books on D'Alembert have appeared. One is Ronald Grimsley's *Jean d'Alembert, 1717–83* (Oxford, 1963); the other is Thomas L. Hankins, *Jean D'Alembert: Science and the Enlightenment* (New York, 1970). Also excelling in this rapidly extending area of scholarly interest are John N. Pappas, 'Diderot, d'Alembert et l'Encyclopédie,' *DS IV* (1963), 191–208; Paolo Casini, 'D'Alembert epistemologo,' *Rivista Critica di Storia della Filosofia*, XIX (1964), 28–53; and the same, 'Il problema d'Alembert,' *Rivista di Filosofia*, LXI (1970), 26–47. There have also appeared some excellent studies of Helvétius and the publication of *De l'Esprit*. Especially to be noted are D. W. Smith, 'The Publication of Helvétius's *De l'Esprit* (1758–9),' *FS*, XVIII (1964), 332–44; the same, *Helvétius: A Study in Persecution* (Oxford, 1965); Didier Ozanam, 'La Disgrâce d'un premier commis: Tercier et l'affaire de l'*Esprit* (1758–1759),' *Bibliothèque de l'Ecole des Chartes*, CXIII (1955), 140–70; and Ian Cumming, *Helvétius: His Life and Place in the History of Educational Thought* (London, [1955]).

Of all Diderot's early friends, Rousseau is the one whose relationship with Diderot of course continues to excite the most interest. The *querelle des bouffons* is discussed again by Servando Sacaluga, 'Diderot, Rousseau, et la Querelle Musicale de 1752. Nouvelle Mise au Point,' *DS X* (1968), 133–73. George R. Havens, 'Diderot, Rousseau, and the *Discours sur l'Inégalité*,' *DS III* (1961), 219–62, sifts all the evidence of the relationship of the two men in the early 1750's. Guy Turbet-Delof, 'A propos d' "Emile et Sophie",' *RHLF*, LXIV (1964), 44–59, presents evidence for a very persuasive theory regarding the source of Rousseau's anger with Diderot over *Le Fils naturel*. The contrasting views of Diderot and Rousseau regarding 'natural' and 'social' man are analyzed by Robert Niklaus, 'Diderot et Rousseau: Pour et contre le théâtre,' *DS IV* (1963), 153–89. The tangled circumstances of their quarrel have been meticulously analyzed and judiciously weighed by Lester G. Crocker in the chapter 'Storm and Separation' of his *Jean-Jacques Rousseau: The Quest (1712–1758)* (New York, 1968). The text of Diderot's 'tablettes,' summarizing the reasons for the break as he saw them, has been edited by John Pappas and Georges Roth, 'Les "Tablettes" de Diderot,' *DS III* (1961), 309–20; see also Leigh, v (1967), 281–5.

Continuing (and increasing) interest in *Le Fils naturel* is evidenced in the article by Herbert Dieckmann, 'Currents and Crosscurrents in *Le Fils naturel*,' in *Linguistic and Literary Studies in Honor of Helmut A. Hatzfeld*, ed. Alessandro S. Crisafulli (Washington, 1964), 107–16; as well as articles by Aimé Guedj, 'Les Drames de Diderot,' *DS XIV* (1971), 15–95, and Blandine McLaughlin, 'A New Look at Diderot's *Fils naturel*,' *DS X* (1968), 109–19. Especially valuable are Jacques Proust, 'Le Paradoxe du *Fils naturel*,' *DS IV* (1963), 209–20, and Hans Robert Jauss, 'Diderots Paradox über das Schauspiel (Entretiens sur le 'Fils naturel'),' *Germanisch-Romanische Monatsschrift*, xi (1961), 380–413. A possible though unacknowledged influence upon *Le Fils naturel* is discussed by English Showalter, Jr., 'Diderot and Madame de Graffigny's *Cénie*,' *FR*, xxxix (1965–6), 394–7.

On Diderot's dramatic theory in general, see Francis Pruner, 'Diderot et le théâtre,' *Cahiers Haut-Marnais*, No. 75 (4ᵉ trimestre 1963), 150–61. Roger Lewinter pursues a familiar theme in 'L'Exaltation de la vertu dans le théâtre de Diderot,' *DS VIII* (1966), 119–69. Two books of unusual interest recently published are Raymond Joly, *Deux études sur le préhistoire du réalisme* (Quebec, 1969), and Herbert Josephs, *Diderot's Dialogue of Language and Gesture* (Columbus [O.], 1969).

Aspects of Diderot's political theory in these early years have recently been studied in the following articles: Lester G. Crocker, 'Diderot et la loi naturelle,' *Europe*, Nos. 405–6 (Jan.–Feb. 1963), 57–65; Ronald Grimsley, 'Quelques aspects de la théorie du droit naturel au Siècle des lumières,' *SVEC*, xxv (1963), 721–40; Jacques Proust, 'La Contribution de Diderot à l'*Encyclopedie* et les théories du droit naturel,' *AHRF*, xxxv (1963), 257–86; John S. Spink, 'La Vertu politique selon Diderot ou le paradoxe du bon citoyen,' *RScH*, No. 112 (Oct.–Dec. 1963), 471–83; and Arthur M. Wilson, 'The Development and Scope of Diderot's Political Thought,' *SVEC*, xxvii (1963), 1871–1900. An important re-examination of Diderot's article 'Autorité politique' in the first volume of the *Encyclopédie* has been made by John Lough, 'The Article AUTORITÉ POLITIQUE,' in his *Essays on the Encyclopédie of Diderot and d'Alembert*, 424–62.

Emendations to *The Testing Years*

Page 8: The comparison of Diderot with Plato or Aristotle was not made by Rousseau, but was attributed to him by Cousin d'Avalon in 1810 (T. C. Walker, 'The Authorship of Rousseau's *Jugement sur Diderot,*' FS, xii [1958], 21–9).

P. 102: It was Frederick II, not Voltaire, who suggested placing Mme du Châtelet's child among her miscellaneous works.

Pp. 125–6: Respecting the authorship of Diderot's two letters to Père Berthier, it has been discovered that D'Alembert claimed to have written them. The Abbé Goujet (1697–1767) noted in the catalogue of his library that 'M^r D'Alembert m'a dit que c'étoit lui-même qui avoit fait ces deux lettres sous le nom de Mr *Diderot,* son associé à l'Encyclopédie' (B.N., MSS, Nouv. acq. fr. 1012, fol. 257). I owe this reference to the kindness of A. W. Fairbairn of the University of Newcastle-upon-Tyne, who discovered it.

The standard work regarding Père Berthier's editorship of the *Journal de Trévoux* is by John N. Pappas, *Berthier's Journal de Trévoux and the philosophes* (*SVEC,* iii [1957]).

Pp. 135–6: Although I ascribed the article *'Aristotélisme'* to Diderot, in reality it was written by the Abbé Yvon (Lough, *Essays on the* Encyclopédie *of Diderot and d'Alembert,* 426).

Pp. 209–10: The article 'Christianisme' is now thought not to be by Diderot (Lough, *Essays on the* Encyclopédie *of Diderot and d'Alembert,* 392, 426).

P. 277: The *'Avis Utile'* about the Cacouacs was written by the Abbé de Saint-Cyr and not by Jacob-Nicolas Moreau (Voltaire, *Correspondence,* ed. Besterman, xxxiii, App. 94).

Index

Abbeville (Somme), 504
Abélard, Peter, 66
Académie Française, 94, 97, 214, 221, 232, 244, 264, 265, 291, 309, 392, 393, 400, 432, 681, 686, 711
Académie Goncourt, 230
Academy of Beaux-Arts (St. Petersburg), 516
Academy of Sciences (Paris), 68, 78, 241-3, 309, 431, 432, 594; nominates Diderot for membership (1757), 362, 633, 775-6 n. 22; and the *Descriptions des Arts et Métiers*, 360-4, 440
Adams, Henry, 134
Adams, John Quincy, 704
Addition aux Pensées philosophiques (Diderot), 444-5, 579
'Additions à la Lettre sur les aveugles' (Diderot), 449, 702
Aelius Lampridius, 465
Aeneid, 124
Aeschylus, 217
Aesculapius, 93, 155
Aguesseau, Henri-François d', chancellor of France, 76-7, 84, 120, 161, 165; authorizes expansion of the *Encyclopédie*, 81; designates Diderot as chief editor, 82
Aigues-Mortes (Gard), 441
Aiguillon, Emmanuel-Armand, duc d', 597, 614, 635
Aine, Suzanne d', mother-in-law of D'Holbach, 176, 375-6, 409
Aix-la-Chapelle, 300, 628; treaty of, 94
Alainville, Henri-Louis d', 384, 407, 788 n. 30
Alembert, Jean Le Rond d', 47-8, 68, 89, 90, 117-8, 158, 164, 179-80, 185, 193, 201, 217, 220-1, 263, 304, 312, 318, 364, 373, 379, 380, 396, 411, 441, 458, 467, 480, 502, 515, 519, 574, 576, 581, 600, 643, 675, 686, 741 n. 52, 766 n. 53, 771 n. 30; and the *Encyclopédie*, 54, 78-80, 107, 115, 154, 158, 165-8, 351; and

the 'Preliminary Discourse,' 100, 131-4, 135, 150, 152, 157, 166, 170, 191, 199, 201, 221, 238, 344, 380; and the article 'Genève,' 280-90, 299, 308; other *Encyclopédie* articles by, 199, 207-8, 210-1, 214, 235, 277, 480; retirement from the *Encyclopédie*, 287-90, 307-9, 326, 332, 351, 469; relations with Diderot, 66, 111, 113, 166-8, 220-1, 289, 291, 302, 335, 337, 338, 356, 430-2, 560, 563, 569-70; and Catherine II, 443, 631, 641; and Frederick II, 642-3; and Voltaire, 253-4, 276, 280, 287-90, 393, 397, 400; and the Jesuits, 125, 152, 157, 211-2; membership in academies of, 68, 127, 129, 221, 232, 264, 265, 275; illnesses of, 494-5, 709; death and burial of, 711
Alsted, Johann Heinrich, 73, 240
Amsterdam, 169, 447, 619, 652, 685
Anacreon, 18, 326
Analysis of Beauty (Hogarth), 602
André, Yves-Marie, père, 522
'Anecdotes sur la révolution de Russie en l'année 1762' (Rulhière), 546-7
Angel, Brother, 29-30, 38, 41
Angiviller, Charles-Claude de Flahaut de la Billarderie d', comte, 657, 677-8, 873 n. 21
Annals (Tacitus), 649-50, 695
Année Littéraire (Fréron), 196-7, 221, 281, 285, 360, 363; quoted, 197, 262-3, 377, 398, 399, 412, 415, 430-1, 606, 656-7, 691
Annonces, Affiches, et Avis Divers, 396, 398, 411, 412
Antidote (Catherine II), 603
Anti-Sénèque (La Mettrie), 708
Antin, Louis de Pardaillan de Gondrin, duc d', 75
Apologie de l'Abbé Galiani (Diderot), 555-6, 683

895